# CONCORDIA
## THE LUTHERAN CONFESSIONS

# CONCORDIA

## THE LUTHERAN CONFESSIONS
### A READER'S EDITION OF THE BOOK OF CONCORD

Based on the translation by
William Hermann Theodore Dau
Gerhard Friedrich Bente

Revised, Updated, and Annotated by
Paul Timothy McCain
Robert Cleveland Baker
Gene Edward Veith
Edward Andrew Engelbrecht

CONCORDIA PUBLISHING HOUSE · SAINT LOUIS

# TABLE OF CONTENTS

# PREFACE

With fervent prayer we offer this edition of the Lutheran Confessions, as contained in the Book of Concord of 1580. May God use it to encourage, equip, strengthen, and preserve Christians in the one, true faith as revealed in His holy Word, the Sacred Scriptures of the Old and New Testaments. God grant it for the sake of our Lord Jesus Christ, to whose glory this volume is dedicated. The text of this edition is based on the English translation in the *Concordia Triglotta* by William H. T. Dau and Gerhard F. Bente.

This edition of the Book of Concord is a "reader's edition" because it is designed to serve the needs of those who may not be familiar with the Lutheran Confessions. It is intended for use in homes, congregations, classrooms, parish halls, and any place that people gather to reflect on God's Word and how that Word is correctly believed, taught, and confessed. We trust that the various resources and features we have included will help the reader understand the persons, places, events, and teachings discussed in these documents.

We have included a number of original commentaries and essays on the important ideas and guiding principles necessary for a proper understanding of the Lutheran Confessions. Before each individual document is a specific introduction providing its historical setting and purpose, along with an overview of the specific Confessions in this book. The reader will also find a historical timeline and pictures of the chief authors of the Lutheran Confessions. Finally, within each document, the various chapters and articles are briefly explained.

This work is a collaboration of the undersigned. With gratitude to God for the opportunity He provided to work together on this edition of the Book of Concord, we acknowledge the individual contributions made. Rev. Paul T. McCain conceived of this edition and is responsible for the Augsburg Confession, all general introductions, the specific introductions to each document, as well as various notes and helps. Rev. Robert C. Baker worked on the Apology to the Augsburg Confession and the charts. Dr. Gene Edward Veith is responsible for the Smalcald Articles and the Treatise on the Power and Primacy of the Pope. Along with various notes, Rev. Edward Engelbrecht is responsible for the planning and formatting of this edition. He worked on the Small Catechism, Large Catechism, and the Formula of Concord (both the Epitome and the Solid Declaration).

May God the Holy Trinity—the Father, Son, and Holy Spirit—bless all who use this reader's edition of the Book of Concord, strengthening and preserving them in the true faith, unto life everlasting. To God alone be the glory!

The Editors:
Paul Timothy McCain
Robert Cleveland Baker
Gene Edward Veith
Edward Andrew Engelbrecht

June 25, 2005
The 475th Anniversary of the Augsburg Confession
The 425th Anniversary of the Book of Concord

# WITH INTREPID HEARTS
# WE BELIEVE, TEACH, AND CONFESS
## A General Introduction to the Book of Concord

*This declaration . . . is our faith, doctrine, and confession.
By God's grace, with intrepid hearts, we are willing to appear before
the judgment seat of Christ with this confession.*

—Formula of Concord, Solid Declaration, XII 40

Intrepid hearts indeed! What could possibly be so important that you would stake eternity on it? What gives a person such courage and conviction? Only one thing—the truth. This is what this book is all about, the truth of God's Word.

God's people have always spoken this way. For example, the psalmist wrote, "I will speak of Your testimonies before kings and shall not be put to shame" (Psalm 119:46). Peter confessed his faith when Jesus asked him what he believed, "You are the Christ, the Son of the living God" (Matthew 16:16). Paul wrote, "Since we have the same spirit of faith according to what has been written, 'I believed, and so I spoke,' we also believe, and so we also speak" (2 Corinthians 4:13).

Lutherans have used the Confessions of faith contained in this book for nearly five hundred years as their public witness and testimony of what the Bible teaches. These Confessions give clear, unambiguous, and certain witness to the Christian faith. They unite all those who bear the name Lutheran and wish to be—and remain—genuinely Lutheran. That is why this book uses the word *Concordia* as a title.

### The Meaning of Concordia

*Concordia* comes from two Latin words meaning "with" and "heart." It describes a commitment to the truth so strong and so deep, it is as if those who share it have a single heart beat. To many twenty-first-century minds, the claim that there is objective truth is regarded with deep suspicion. To suggest that there is one, and only one, absolute truth about God is regarded by many today as absurd, foolish, ridiculous, or the sign of an intolerant and weak mind. Sadly, even many modern Christians now view claims of truth and certainty with a good deal of suspicion.

But truth and falsehood are real. It is possible to know truth and it is necessary to reject all errors that contradict the truth. God reveals absolute truth in His Word, which is precisely what the documents in the Book of Concord assert, with complete and total conviction.

The Bible is the rock-solid foundation for the documents in the Book of Concord. Christians who embrace the documents in this book as their teaching, their belief, and their confession also believe that it is possible for people to know and be certain about truth. They are convinced. They are certain. They are sure. Why? Because of the One who has called them to this conviction: the Lord Jesus Christ. He said, "If you abide in My word, you are truly My disciples, and you will know the truth, and the truth will set you free" (John 8:31–32).

### Genuine, Historic Lutheranism

To embrace the freedom of truth means rejecting the slavery of error. That is why this book uses two phrases to capture the essence of biblical confession: "we believe, teach, and confess" and "we reject and condemn." One cannot believe, teach, and confess the truth without also rejecting and condemning everything that endangers or contradicts the truth. This spirit of "confessional Lutheranism" is what continues to animate people today who hold to this collection of affirmations, professions, and confessions of faith.

Not all churches that go by the name "Lutheran" still regard the Book of Concord as highly as they once did. Some prominent Lutheran Church bodies in the United States and around the world regard these statements of faith as "historically conditioned." They say that the older confessions are not necessarily correct in what they teach about God's Word. These churches have embraced various ecumenical agreements with non-Lutheran churches that contradict what Lutheranism has taught historically.

Confessional Lutheran churches regard these compromises not only as a compromise of historic Lutheranism, but also as an actual denial of the truth of God's Word. (A most serious matter indeed!) It is important to keep in mind this distinction among churches that use the name "Lutheran." This is all the more reason to make sure that these Confessions are not merely historical documents in congregations that are genuinely Lutheran. They must be well known by laypeople and church workers alike.

Historic, genuine Lutheranism holds that the Bible is actually the Word of the Living God. We believe that it is both incapable of error and free from error. We hold strongly to the Lutheran Confessions because we are absolutely convinced that these confessions of faith are a pure exposition and explanation of God's Word. Lutherans agree with the apostle Peter, who said, "We cannot but speak of what we have seen and heard" (Acts 4:20).

When God the Holy Spirit gives the gift of trust in Jesus Christ as the Savior, this gift of faith creates a desire to confess, to bear witness, to testify, to proclaim, and to speak this faith. That is what the documents in this book are all about. They are not musty, old relics from history. They are the living confession of God's people, who have clung to the truths in these documents for nearly five hundred years. Today, we who hold to these Confessions make the Book of Concord our confession, our witness, our public testimony of what the Bible teaches. With Martin Luther, we say, "Here we stand. We cannot do otherwise. God help us. Amen."

### A Story of Personal Sacrifice for the Truth

The historical introductions in this book will help you understand the personal sacrifice made to achieve this "Concordia," this harmony in the teaching of God's Word. During the years when these Confessions were written and defended, faithful men and women of God, both laypeople and clergy, sacrificed all they had—in some cases their very lives—to defend and extend the truths of God's holy Word as confessed by the Lutheran Church. Men died in battle fighting to defend the right to teach Lutheran precepts in classrooms and preach the Lutheran faith in pulpits. They died defending their cities and towns—and most important, their convictions—from armies of political and church leaders trying to stamp out Lutheranism forever.

For example, during the Thirty Years' War (1618–48) Roman Catholic rulers attacked the Protestant regions of Germany with the hope of stamping out the Reformation. The battles that followed forced tens of thousands of people out of their homes. Disease and famine deepened the misery, causing a level of suffering similar to what we see today in parts of Africa. Finally, the Swedish king, Gustavus Adolfus II (1594–1632), led his armies to defend the Protestants. His army's victory at the battle of Lutzen ensured the survival of the Reformation. But Gustavus himself died in the fighting. Every Lutheran who values his or her Confession of faith should remember this "Lion of the North" and thank God for his sacrifice.

The courage of the first Lutherans is awe-inspiring for us today. It is difficult for us to imagine sacrificing everything for the sake of what we believe. It is hard for us today to even imagine a situation similar to what happened to Lutherans in the sixteenth and seventeenth centuries. Today, the attitude toward truth is very much one of compromise at all costs, rather than confession at all costs. There is within many churches today a "go along to get along" attitude. This attitude was around at the time of the writing of the Lutheran Confessions as well, but was eventually resoundingly rejected.

### A Book for All People

Rev. Dr. C. F. W. Walther explained how important the Book of Concord is for all Lutherans.

> The Book of Concord should be in every Lutheran home. For that reason [our Church] should provide a good, inexpensive copy, and pastors should see to it that every home has one. . . . If a person isn't familiar with this book, he'll think, "That old book is just for pastors. I don't have to preach. After [working] all day, I can't sit down and study in the evening. If I read my morning and evening devotions, that's enough." No, that is not enough! The Lord doesn't want us to remain children, who are blown to and fro by every wind of doctrine; instead of that, He wants us to grow in knowledge so that we can teach

others. (*Essays for the Church*, vol. 2 [St. Louis: Concordia Publishing House, 1992], 51)

This is not just a book for pastors and church "professionals" or "academics." In fact, it is important to realize that the people most directly responsible for the Lutheran Confessions were laymen, not pastors and theologians. At tremendous personal risk to their own lives, their property, and their profession, laymen boldly stepped before the emperor and the pope's representatives. They asserted that these Confessions were their own. They did not back down or compromise. For this reason, it is unfortunate that down through the years the Book of Concord has come to be regarded more as a book for pastors and professional theologians.

Tucked into the middle of this book is the most widely used of all the Lutheran Confessions: Martin Luther's Small Catechism. Luther wrote this document not simply as a resource for the church and school, but, first and foremost, for the head of the household. Luther intended this little book to be used by laypeople, daily, to help them remain anchored to the solid teachings of God's holy Word, the Bible. So keep this important fact in mind: The Book of Concord exists because of the faith and conviction of laypeople, who risked their very lives in order to have these Confessions produced, published, and distributed. The Book of Concord is a book for all Christians, church workers and laypeople alike.

Christians who want to be true and faithful to the teachings of the Bible return, again and again, to this book. In these confessions of faith they find agreement, unity, and harmony in the truths of God's Word. These documents never take the place of the Bible. They distinguish between what the Bible teaches and the false teachings of others, which undermine the use of God's Word. They give Christians a common voice to confess their faith to the world.

Reaching out boldly with the Gospel of Jesus Christ is the goal of the Lutheran Confessions. They are not to be treated like museum pieces, kept under glass as interesting curiosities. Neither are they holiday decorations taken out once a year and admired, soon to be put away and forgotten. Nor are the Lutheran Confessions clubs used to bash people or shields to prevent contact with others or trophies set on a shelf. The Lutheran Confessions are resources for extending and defending vigorously the Gospel of Jesus Christ. They are powerful tools for everyone to use, in all circumstances, for preaching, teaching, and proclaiming the Gospel of Jesus Christ and all the truths of God's Word in the church, school, home, workplace, community, and throughout the world.

Lutherans particularly enjoy "Concordia" through these confessions. United in common conviction about God's Word, they live together with a common heartbeat, declaring to the world and to one another, "This is what we believe, teach, and confess."

# AN OVERVIEW OF THE BOOK OF CONCORD

The Book of Concord contains documents Christians have used since the fourth century to explain what they believe and teach on the basis of the Holy Scriptures. First, it includes the three creeds that originated in the Ancient Church: the Apostles' Creed, the Nicene Creed, and the Athanasian Creed. Second, it contains the Reformation writings known as the Augsburg Confession, the Apology of the Augsburg Confession, the Smalcald Articles, the Treatise on the Power and Primacy of the Pope, Luther's Small and Large Catechisms, and the Formula of Concord.

The Catechisms and the Smalcald Articles came from the pen of Martin Luther; the Augsburg Confession, its Apology, and the Treatise were written by Luther's co-worker, the scholarly Phillip Melanchthon; the Formula of Concord was given its final form chiefly by Jacob Andreae, Martin Chemnitz, and Nicholas Selnecker.

## I. The Creeds

The Apostles' Creed was not composed by the apostles but is a faithful Confession of apostolic doctrine; it is a "daughter" of the creed used by early Christians in Rome. The wording of the creed, as we confess it today, can be traced to southern Gaul (France).

The Nicene Creed is spoken today in many Lutheran congregations during Communion services or festive occasions. It was formulated by the Council of Nicaea (AD 325) and revised by the Council of Constantinople (AD 381). (This popular history has been challenged. Another theory is that the creed had its roots in the creed of Jerusalem adopted by Epiphanius of Cyprus.) One addition to the original formula—that the Holy Spirit proceeds from the Father "and the Son"—is Western in origin and appears as early as the Synod of Toledo (AD 589).

The Athanasian Creed is the longest of the three. Though included in Lutheran hymnals, many congregations use it only on Trinity Sunday (the First Sunday after Pentecost). It is named after Athanasius, the great fourth-century champion of orthodoxy against heretics who denied the deity of Christ. The creed originated in southern Gaul, probably about the middle of the sixth century.

The inclusion of the three ancient creeds in the Book of Concord shows that Lutherans are not a sect but that they embrace and confess the ancient and orthodox faith.

## II. *The Lutheran Confessions*

Among the particular Lutheran Confessions, the two catechisms of Dr. Martin Luther are the earliest. Luther published them in the spring of 1529 to help pastors, teachers, and parents give instruction in the chief parts of Christian doctrine.

The Augsburg Confession was written by Melanchthon in 1530. Emperor Charles V had invited the Lutheran princes and theologians to attend a meeting of government leaders at Augsburg. He wanted to discuss how the religious controversy in his

| NAME | DATE | AUTHOR |
|---|---|---|
| Apostles' Creed | Second Century | Unknown |
| *Baptismal Creed used in Rome.* | | |
| Nicene Creed | 325, 381 | Assembled church leaders at the Council of Nicaea (325) and the Council of Constantinople |
| *This Creed intends to clearly state on the basis of Scripture that Jesus Christ is true God, equal with the Father, and that the Holy Spirit is also true God, equal with the Father and the Son.* | | |
| Athanasian Creed | Sixth–Eighth Centuries | Unknown; named after the great Church Father Athanasius, who was instrumental in the drafting of the Nicene Creed |
| *Confesses the teaching of the Trinity and the person and work of Jesus Christ.* | | |
| Small Catechism | 1529 | Martin Luther |
| *A short work that was to educate the laity in the basics of the Christian faith.* | | |
| Large Catechism | 1529 | Martin Luther |
| *Though covering the same chief parts of Christian doctrine as the Small Catechism, the Large Catechism is really a series of re-edited sermons that Luther preached.* | | |
| Augsburg Confession | June 25, 1530 | Philip Melanchthon |
| *Often viewed as the chief Lutheran Confession; it was presented by the Lutherans to Emperor Charles V at the Imperial Diet of Augsburg as a statement of the chief articles of the Christian faith as understood by Lutherans; also contains a listing of abuses that the Lutherans had corrected.* | | |

Empire could be settled, so that German Lutheran princes would join the Imperial forces to keep the Turks out of Europe. The Augsburg Confession is composed from several documents that already existed but which were combined by Melanchthon to give a clear but conciliatory summary of the teachings and practices of the Lutheran pastors and congregations. To this day it is the basic Lutheran Confession.

The Apology (or defense) of the Augsburg Confession was published in 1531. After the Augsburg Confession had been read to the emperor, a committee of

| NAME | DATE | AUTHOR |
| --- | --- | --- |
| Apology of the Augsburg Confession | 1531 | Philip Melanchthon |

*After the Roman theologians had condemned many of the teachings of the Augsburg Confession, Melanchthon authored this lengthy defense. Rightly considered a Christian classic.*

| Smalcald Articles | 1536 | Martin Luther |
| --- | --- | --- |

*Articles of faith intended by Luther to be an ecumenical platform for an upcoming ecumenical council. Stated what the Lutherans could not compromise and why.*

| Treatise on the Power and Primacy of the Pope | 1537 | Philip Melanchthon |
| --- | --- | --- |

*Was intended to serve as a supplement to the Augsburg Confession, giving the Lutheran position on the pope.*

| Formula of Concord | 1577 | Jacob Andreae, Martin Chemnitz, Nicholas Selnecker |
| --- | --- | --- |

*A restatement of some teachings in the Augsburg Confession over which Lutherans had become divided. The Solid Declaration is the unabridged version. The Epitome is an abridged version intended for congregations to study. Over 8,100 pastors and theologians signed it, as well as over 50 government leaders.*

Romanist theologians prepared a reply called the Confutation. The Apology defends the Augsburg Confession against the accusations of the Confutation.

The Smalcald Articles were written by Luther in late 1536. On June 4, 1536, Pope Paul III announced that a council would be held in Mantua beginning May 8, 1537, to deal with the concerns of the Protestants. The elector (or prince) of Saxony requested Luther to prepare some articles for discussion at the council. Luther indicated on which points Lutherans would stand fast and on which points a compromise might be possible. These articles were never used for their intended purpose, but Lutherans at once recognized their value as a statement of pure evangelical doctrine, and they were therefore included in the Book of Concord.

The Treatise on the Power and Primacy of the Pope was prepared by Melanchthon at the meeting at Smalcald in 1537. Luther's Smalcald Articles were to be discussed at the meeting; but, partly because Luther became ill, they were never publicly presented to the assembly. Instead, Melanchthon was requested to prepare a treatise, which is actually an appendix to the Augsburg Confession.

The Formula of Concord was written a generation after Luther's death. Serious controversies had arisen among theologians of the Augsburg Confession; these threatened the very life of the Reformation. The Formula of Concord deals with these dissensions and presents the sound biblical doctrine on the disputed issues.

No doubt much will—and should—be made of the Book of Concord as we observe its anniversary. But the most worthy and God-pleasing way for Lutherans of the twenty-first century to commemorate the publication of the Book of Concord would be to engage in earnest study of the precious Confessions it contains and to commit themselves anew to the glorious truths of God's Word that they teach.

A number of years ago, Professor William Arndt eloquently described the significance of the confessional writings. In the *Concordia Theological Monthly* (now the *Concordia Journal*), he wrote:

> The Confessions are the brightest jewel in the crown of the Lutheran Church. In speaking of our Confessions we dwell on facts that should make the heart of every Lutheran swell with joy and thanksgiving. We look here on one of the brightest pages of our history as a Church. It is true, I admit, that the laurels of our fathers must not become the soft bed of the children on which they repose in sweet indolence, and it may be that there is somebody who speaks about the achievements of his ancestors to such an extent that he entirely forgets about the plowing, harvesting, and threshing which he himself ought to do. But my plea is that we do not become so occupied with our daily tasks in the churches that we forget the magnificent treasures which are furnished us in our Confessions. To study them, to read them frequently, to ponder their content, is like traveling in a mountain country, where the air is pure, the brooks sparkle, the birds sing their most beautiful songs, and the clatter of the noisy streets cannot disturb and intrude.

# HOW TO USE THIS BOOK

For 425 years, the Book of Concord has united and guided Lutheran congregations, schools, pastors, and teachers. Yet today, many Lutherans are virtually unaware of its existence and use. As a result, when someone mentions the Book of Concord, one often hears, "Aren't we just supposed to follow the Bible?" as though Christians do not use other publications based on the Bible (e.g., creeds, hymnals, catechisms, devotionals). One may even hear the Book of Concord compared to documents like the Book of Mormon, as though Lutherans were trying to add new texts to the Bible.

To overcome these misunderstandings, please read "With Intrepid Hearts We Believe, Teach, and Confess" and "An Overview of the Book of Concord." Take note that the Book of Concord functions very much like the Apostles' and Nicene Creeds, summarizing or clarifying what the Bible teaches on controversial topics. In particular, it thoroughly teaches God's love and forgiveness for all people based on Jesus' life, death, and resurrection—reminding us that this is the chief teaching of the Christian faith.

Here are some suggested uses for this book:

Laypeople. Every Lutheran layperson should read and understand several key documents in the Book of Concord: (1) the ecumenical creeds, (2) the Small Catechism, (3) the Large Catechism, and (4) the Augsburg Confession. These documents were written for laypeople. After reading these documents, many will want to deepen their understanding of what it means to be Lutheran. They can do this best by thoroughly reading the Book of Concord (see reading guide, pp. 19–22).

Confirmation Teachers. All Lutheran congregations should use Luther's Small Catechism for the instruction of both youth and adults. Confirmation teachers should supplement and explain the Small Catechism with the Large Catechism. This is what Luther himself described in his preface to the Small Catechism (p. 339–41).

Leaders of Congregations and Schools. Pastors and teachers take their vows of service based on the Book of Concord. Therefore, those who work with them must also be familiar with this book, such as laypeople involved in the call process and serving on various boards. For example, elders' or board meetings could begin with a brief discussion of a particular article or passage. In this way, understanding of Lutheran doctrine and practice would continually grow among the people, with the Book of Concord becoming a resource for guiding the congregation or school.

Pastors, Teachers, and Other Church Professionals. When pastors and other church workers are ordained or commissioned for service in a Lutheran congregation or school, they vow that they will teach the Bible in conformity with the Book of Concord. In view of this vow, they should read and study the entire Book of Concord in college or seminary. During their ministry, they should continually refresh themselves through its teaching and application (see the reading guide, pp. 19–22). Circuit conferences, District conferences, and other gatherings are excellent opportunities for church professionals to study and reflect on the Book of Concord together. This continued study will foster unity and understanding, benefits this book has provided since the sixteenth century.

Pastors and other church professionals should also note that we have greatly enlarged the Bible reference section provided in the original Triglotta edition. The Bible references now include hundreds of biblical allusions. These references will help church professionals discover how the Reformers interpreted and applied God's Word. Preachers will be able to look up their sermon texts. They should also note the Illustrations Index, which shows how to find sermon-style illustrations used by the Reformers to teach the Christian faith.

# A Book of Concord Reading Guide

T.    14–27

F.    28–42

**WEEK 27. APOLOGY (PP. 241–52)**

M.    43–58

T.    59–71

W.    XXIV 1–12

T.    13–24

F.    25–32

**WEEK 28. APOLOGY (PP. 252–61)**

M.    33–43

T.    44–57

W.    58–70

T.    71–83

F.    84–92

**WEEK 29. APOLOGY (PP. 261–70)**

M.    93–99

T.    XXVII 1–12

W.    13–23

T.    24–33

F.    34–44

**WEEK 30. APOLOGY (PP. 270–77)–SMALCALD ARTICLES (PP. 285–88)**

M.    45–57

T.    58–69

W.    XVIII 1–11

T.    12–27

SMALCALD ARTICLES

F.    Preface 1–15

**WEEK 31. SMALCALD ARTICLES (PP. 288–98)**

M.    Part I–Part II 1 5

T.    II 1–15

W.    16 – III 2

T.    IV 1–16

F.    Part III I–II 5

**WEEK 32. SMALCALD ARTICLES (PP. 298–307)**

M.    III 1–14

T.    15–26

W.    27–40

T.    41–VI 5

F.    VII 1–VIII 13

**WEEK 33. SMALCALD ARTICLES–THE POWER AND PRIMACY OF THE POPE (PP. 307–28)**

M.    Article IX–XV 5

THE POWER AND PRIMACY OF THE POPE

T.    1–11

W.    12–24

T.    25–38

F.    39–53

**WEEK 34. THE POWER AND PRIMACY OF THE POPE (PP. 328–31)–PREFACE TO THE BOOK OF CONCORD (PP. 29–35)**

M.    54–71

T.    72–82

PREFACE TO THE BOOK OF CONCORD

W.    1–7

T.    8–16

F.    17–20

**WEEK 35. PREFACE TO THE BOOK OF CONCORD (PP. 36–38)–EPITOME (PP. 491–99)**

M.    21–25

FORMULA OF CONCORD: EPITOME

T.    Summary, 1–I 10

W.    11–25

T.    II 1–15

F.    16–III 11

**WEEK 36. EPITOME (PP. 499–509)**

M.    12–IV 15

T.    16–V 11

W.    VI 1–VII 5

T.    6–20

F.    21–42

**WEEK 37. EPITOME (PP. 509–17)**

M.    VIII 1–15

T.    16–32

W.    33–X 2

T.    3–XI 3

F.    4–15

**WEEK 38. EPITOME (PP. 517–20)–SOLID DECLARATION (PP. 535–39)**

M.    16–XII 11

T.    12–31

FORMULA OF CONCORD: SOLID DECLARATION

W.    Introduction 1–10

T.    Summary 1–7

F.    8–13

**WEEK 39. SOLID DECLARATION (PP. 539–45)**

M.    14–20

T.    I 1–6

W.    7–15

T.    16–25

F.    26–32

# A REFORMATION TIMELINE

The world was changing. New scientific discoveries had opened pathways for understanding more about our complex universe. The ocean, once feared for its danger and depth, was tamed for travel and trade. Peasants and workers, laboring under harsh and relentless conditions, sought revolution. The bubonic plague had claimed the lives of about 75 million people from 1347 to 1351. It continued to reappear and panic European cities. Political alliances, long forged between pope and prince, fractured as power centers shifted. Gutenberg's press (1455), the first to use moveable type, transported ideas from one person to the next with swiftness and ease. As the medieval era collapsed into the modern, changes seemed everywhere and limitless.

Yet even during these changing times one thing remained constant: our God, who grants forgiveness and grace to His people through Jesus Christ. Despite advances and transformations in science and society, politics and publication, God was working. He gave hope and life by His Spirit through Word and Sacraments. He bestowed comfort and joy in trying and often perilous situations. In changing times, His promises through His Son did not change, nor will they ever. They will never be altered, nor revoked. His Word pronounces us righteous through faith in His Son, Jesus Christ. He alone is our Life and our Peace.

The following Reformation Timeline has been provided to aid you in reading *Concordia: The Lutheran Confessions*. Significant people and events in the "Old World" as well as the "New" have been included for the years 1475 to 1600. Additional references include scientific discoveries, substantive works of art, and the arrivals of European explorers to the Americas.

This timeline confirms what we know by experience: change will take place. But in changing times God's Word reminds us that He is always faithful to His people. With hearty confidence and trust we can say with King David, "My times are in Your hands" (Psalm 31:15).

1564   Shakespeare born
       Galileo born

## —1575—

1572   St. Bartholomew's Day Massacre of
       Protestant Huguenots in France

1574   Crypto-Calvinists fully exposed in
       Wittenberg; Lutheranism restored by
       Augustus I

1576   Torgau Conference

       *Formula of Concord's "Epitome"*
       completed

1577   *Formula of Concord's "Solid Declara-
       tion"* completed

       Francis Drake begins circumnavigat-
       ing globe

1580   *Book of Concord* **published on the
       50th anniversary of presentation of**
       *Augsburg Confession,* **June 25**

1582   Gregorian calendar implemented by
       Pope Gregory XIII

1584   Leipzig edition of *Book of Concord*
       published (revised Latin)

1588   English defeat Spanish Armada

1595   Zacharias Janssen develops com-
       pound microscope

1598   **Formula of Concord subscribed in
       Strasbourg**

# CONCORDIA

## THE PIOUS CONFESSION OF FAITH AND DOCTRINE

Repeated by Unanimous Consent of the Electors, Princes, and Estates of the
Empire, and of Their Theologians, who Embrace the Augsburg Confession.

In addition there has been added from Holy Scripture,
that Only Norm and Rule of Doctrine,

A Thorough Explanation of Certain Articles, which after Dr. Martin Luther's
blessed departure from this life were the subject of controversy.

Published by the joint resolution and order of the said Electors, Princes,
and Estates of the Empire for the Instruction and Admonition
of their Subjects, Churches, and Schools
as a MEMORIAL TO POSTERITY.

Published at Dresden, 1580. Issued for the second time at Leipzig, 1584.
With the gracious privilege of the Elector of Saxony.

*Verbum Domini Manet in Aeternum*

The Word of the Lord Endures Forever

---

*Verbum Domini Manet in Aeternum* is the motto of the Lutheran Reformation, a confident expression of the enduring power and authority of God's Word. The motto is based on 1 Peter 1:24–25. It first appeared in the court of Frederick the Wise in 1522. He had it sewn onto the right sleeve of the court's official clothing, which was worn by prince and servant alike. It was used by Frederick's successors, his brother John the Steadfast, and his nephew John Frederick the Magnanimous. It became the official motto of the Smalcaldic League and was used on flags, banners, swords, and uniforms as a symbol of the unity of the Lutheran laity who struggled to defend their beliefs, communities, families, and lives against those who were intent on destroying them.

# PREFACE TO THE CHRISTIAN BOOK OF CONCORD

This preface is written in the formal court style of its day. Readers who are new to the Lutheran Confessions should consult the Reading Guide (p. 19–22).

1    To the readers, one and all, of these our writings: we are the electors, princes, and deputies of the Holy Roman Empire in Germany, supporters of the Augsburg Confession, who subscribed our names to that document. We announce and declare—according to the dignity and rank of each person—our devotion, friendship, and greeting, combined with willing service.

## The Issues

2    In these Last Times and in this old age of the world (Acts 2:17), what a remarkable favor of Almighty God has arisen after the darkness of papal superstitions! According to His unspeakable love, patience, and mercy, He willed that the light of His Gospel (2 Corinthians 4:4) and Word—through which alone we receive true salvation—should arise and shine clearly and purely in Germany, our most beloved fatherland. Therefore, a brief and succinct Confession was prepared from God's Word—the most holy writings of the prophets and apostles (2 Peter 3:2). At the Diet of Augsburg, in the year 1530, this Confession was offered in the German and Latin languages by our most godly ancestors, to the Emperor Charles V, of excellent memory. It was laid before the deputies of the Empire. Finally, it was circulated publicly in the entire world among all people professing Christian doctrine. So it was spread everywhere and began to be found in the mouths and speech of all.

3    Later, many churches and schools embraced and defended this Confession as a current symbol for the chief articles of faith. This was done especially by those involved in controversy with the Romanists and various corruptions of the heavenly doctrine. With lasting agreement they appealed to the Augsburg Confession without any controversy and doubt. They knew that the doctrine included in it was both supported by firm testimonies of Scripture and approved by the ancient and accepted symbols [creeds]. They have also constantly judged this Confession to be the only and lasting consensus of the true, believing Church. In the past this consensus was defended against many heresies and errors—now it is repeated.

4    No one can be ignorant of this fact: immediately after Dr. Martin Luther (that most distinguished hero, endowed with most eminent piety) was removed from human affairs, Germany, our dear fatherland, experienced most perilous times and most severe disturbances. In these difficulties, and in the sad division of a government that was earlier flourishing and well regulated, the enemy of mortals [Satan] cunningly labored. He scattered the seeds of false doctrine and dissensions in the churches and schools (Matthew 13:24–30). He also labored to stir up divisions (Romans 16:17) combined with offense. By these arts of his, he labored to corrupt the purity of the heavenly doctrine, to sever the bond of Christian love and godly agreement (Ephesians 4:3), and to hinder and delay to a greater degree the spread of the most holy Gospel. It is also known to all

how the enemies of the heavenly doctrine seized this opportunity to speak against our churches and schools, to disguise their errors, and to draw alarmed and erring consciences away from the purity of Gospel teaching. They did this to make people more willing to bear and tolerate the yoke of papal slavery, and also to embrace other corruptions conflicting with God's Word.

5    We conclude that nothing more agreeable could happen or should be sought more eagerly and prayerfully from almighty God than the following: (a) both our churches and our schools should persevere in the pure doctrine of God's Word and in that longed-for and godly oneness of mind (1 Corinthians 1:10), and, (b) as was the case while Luther was still alive, they should be regulated by the divine Word, which was handed down to posterity in a godly and excellent way. However, we notice something else happening. (This happened in apostolic times, in those churches where the apostles themselves had planted the Gospel of Christ [1 Corinthians 3:6].) Corruptions were introduced by false brethren (Galatians 2:4). So, because of our sins and the looseness of these times, this trouble has been allowed by an angry God against our churches (Hebrews 10:30–31).

6    Therefore, mindful of our duty (we know this has been divinely commanded to us) we think that we should apply ourselves diligently to the work of attacking the false teachings that have been spread in our provinces and realms. Such teachings are gradually gaining favor for themselves in the manner and familiarity of the people. We should see to it that the subjects in our government may persevere in the straight way of godliness (Hebrews 12:13) and in the truth of the heavenly doctrine. This has been acknowledged, retained, and defended so far. The people should not be allowed to be led away from it. In this matter, indeed, partly our most worthy predecessors, partly we ourselves, were eagerly at work. Then, in the year of Christ 1558, the Diet was held by the electors at Frankfurt on the Main. A resolution was adopted by a unanimous vote that a special, general assembly should be held. In a thorough but friendly manner, there would be a conference among us about the things that are hatefully charged by our adversaries against our churches and schools.

# The Naumburg Conference (1561)

After the deliberations at Frankfurt, our    7 predecessors (of godly and excellent memory) gathered with some of us at Naumburg in Thuringia. We took in hand the Augsburg Confession that was offered to the Emperor Charles V in the great assembly of the Empire at Augsburg in the year 1530 (mentioned by us several times previously). We all subscribed with one mind to that godly Confession, built upon solid testimonies of the truth expressed in God's Word, which cannot be shaken (Hebrews 12:27–28). In this way, of course, we meant to provide for the interests of future generation, and to enable and encourage them (as far as we could) to avoid false doctrines conflicting with God's Word. We also did this so that, both for his Imperial Majesty (our most clement Lord) and also universally for all, there might be this permanent testimony: it has never been our intention to defend or spread any new and strange teaching. Rather, we desired (God aiding us) to constantly support and retain the truth that we professed at Augsburg in 1530. We were also led to hold a certain hope that in this way those who oppose the pure, evangelical doctrine would stop making false charges and accusations. We hoped that other good and well-intentioned people would be attracted by our renewed and repeated Confession. With greater zeal and care, we hoped that they would seek and investigate the truth about the heavenly doctrine, which alone is our guide to salvation. And, for the soul's salvation and their eternal happiness, we hoped they would agree with our Confession, all further controversies and disputations being rejected.

## The Naumburg Conference Failed

8 But, not without disappointment, we were informed that our declaration and that repetition of a godly Confession had too little importance among our adversaries. So neither we, nor our churches, were delivered from the most painful slanders arising from their prejudice. Our adversaries had circulated these things against us among the people. Also, the adversaries of true religion have taken the things we have done (with the best intention and purpose) to mean that we were uncertain about our religion and had so often altered it from one formula to another that it was no longer clear to us or our theologians what Confession was offered to the emperor at Augsburg. These fictions of the adversaries have deterred and alienated many good people from our churches, schools, doctrine, faith, and Confession. To these disadvantages there is also added this: (a) teaching conflicting with the institution of the Holy Supper of the body and blood of Christ and (b) other corruptions introduced here and there into the churches and schools by people claiming to follow the Augsburg Confession.

9 Some godly men, lovers of peace and harmony, and also learned theologians, noticed all these things. They decided that these slanders and religious disagreements, which were constantly increasing more and more, could not be addressed better than if the controversial articles would be thoroughly and accurately set forth and explained from God's Word. The false teachings would be rejected and condemned. On the other hand, the divinely delivered truth would be clearly and lucidly presented. These godly men were convinced that, by this method, silence could be imposed upon the adversaries. Also, the more simple and godly would be shown a sure way and plan for how they should act in these disagreements. Aided by divine grace, they could also avoid corruptions of doctrine in the future.

10 In the beginning, the theologians wrote to one another certain documents on this subject. These writings were comprehensive enough, and were taken from God's Word. They showed clearly and skillfully how these controversies, which were not without offense to the churches, could be put to rest and removed from sight without any loss to the truth of the Gospel (Galatians 2:5). The result would be that the opportunities and claims sought for slander would be cut off and removed from the adversaries. Finally, in the fear of God, the theologians took up and accurately pondered and explained the controversial articles. In a special writing they stated completely in what way and by what method the dissensions that had arisen could be settled in a right and godly manner.

11 Having been informed about the theologians' godly purpose, we have not only approved it, but have also decided that it should be promoted by us with great earnestness and zeal. We do so in view of the office and duty divinely committed to us.

## The Torgau Conference (1576)

12 And so, by the counsel of some other electors and princes agreeing with us in reli-

gion, we, by God's grace, the Duke of Saxony, the Elector, and so forth, summoned certain well-known and least-suspected theologians to Torgau in 1576. These men were also experienced and endowed with the best learning. Their purpose was to promote the godly goal of harmony among the Church's teachers. When they had gathered, they devoutly met with one another over the controversial articles and the peace document, which we have just mentioned. After prayers had first been offered to Almighty God, and to His praise and glory, they put together a very good and suitable document with extraordinary care and diligence—the Spirit of the Lord aiding them by His grace. It included all those things that seemed to apply to, and to be required for, this deliberation. Afterward this book was sent to some chief supporters of the Augsburg Confession—electors, princes, and deputies. It was asked that they themselves (calling to their aid the most well-known and most learned theologians) should read this book with anxious care and godly zeal. They were asked to examine it diligently and to write down their opinion and criticism of it. Finally, they were asked to express their judgment and the reasons for them about the whole book and each part.

13    When we had received these criticisms, we found many godly and useful suggestions in them. We saw how the declaration of the pure Christian doctrine we sent could be fortified and strengthened by the testimonies of Holy Scripture against corruptions and perversions. Then, in time, godless doctrines would not be concealed under its name. Instead, a completely unvarnished declaration of the pure truth might be passed on to future generations (Psalm 145:4). Therefore, the book of godly concord was written from the suggestions that had been considered best when they came to us.

It was completed in the form in which it will be submitted.

For certain reasons (which stood in our   14
way) not all of us, nor some others as well, were able to review the book at that time. Some of our rank have caused this book to be recited clearly, article by article to the theologians and the ministers of the church and of the schools (collectively and individually). They have caused them to be encouraged for a diligent and accurate consideration of those parts of the doctrine that are contained in it.

After they saw that the explanation of the   16
controversial articles agreed especially with God's Word and also with the Augsburg Confession, they then received this Book of Concord with a very ready mind and expressed their gratitude toward God. For the book expresses the godly and genuine meaning of the Augsburg Confession. Having freely, and indeed accurately, pondered and considered this, they approved this book, subscribed to it, and publicly bore witness about it with heart, mouth, and hand. Therefore, that godly agreement is called, and forever will be called the harmonious and concordant Confession of not just some of our theologians, but, in general, of the ministers of our churches and rectors of schools, jointly and separately, in our provinces and realms.

# The Role
# of the Augsburg Confession

Now, our conferences and those of our illustrious predecessors were held with a godly and sincere intention. First they were held at Frankfurt on the Main, and afterward at Naumburg, and were recorded in writing. These conferences did not accomplish the goal and peaceful settlement that was desired. Instead, a defense for errors and false doctrines was even sought by some at the conferences. But it never entered our mind, by our writing, either to introduce, furnish a cover for, or establish any false doctrine. Nor in the least did we ever intend to withdraw from the Confession presented in 1530 at Augsburg. But rather, all of us who participated in the work at Naumburg wholly reserved that work for ourselves. We promised besides that if, in the course of time, any [explanation] would be desired for the Augsburg Confession, or as often as necessity would seem to demand it, we would further declare all things thoroughly and at length. And that is the reason why we explained in this Book of Concord (with great and godly agreement) a declaration of our constant and perpetual, wish, and a repetition of our Christian faith and Confession.

So, no one may permit himself to be disturbed by the charges of our adversaries, spun out of their own mind. They boast that not even we are sure which confession is the true and genuine Augsburg Confession. But those who are still living and also future generations may be clearly and firmly taught and informed about what that godly Confession is. For both we and the churches and schools of our realms always professed and embraced it. We emphatically testify that after the pure and unchangeable truth of God's Word, we want to embrace the first Augsburg Confession alone. It was presented to the Emperor Charles V, in the year 1530, at the famous Diet of Augsburg. (This Confession alone, we say, and no other.) Copies of that Confession were deposited in the archives of our predecessors (of excellent memory), who presented it in the Diet to Charles V himself. We caused the copies to be compared by men worthy of confidence with the copy that was presented to the emperor himself and is preserved in the archives of the Holy Roman Empire. (We did this lest we should be found lacking in most accurate regard for diligence.) We are sure that our copies, both the Latin and the German, correspond to the original in all things, with like meaning. For this reason also we wanted to insert the Confession presented at Augsburg in our explanation. This will be submitted here or in the Book of Concord. Then all may understand that we have resolved to tolerate no other doctrine in our realms, churches, and schools than what was approved at Augsburg in 1530, in a solemn Confession, by the above-mentioned electors, princes, and deputies of the Empire. By God's help, we will retain this Confession to our last breath, when we shall go forth from this life to the heavenly fatherland, to appear with a joyful, undaunted mind and a pure conscience before the court of our Lord Jesus Christ (2 Corinthians 5:9–10). Therefore, we hope that our adversaries will spare both us and the ministers of our churches. We hope they will not use these customary and most grievous accusations: (a) we cannot decide with certainty among ourselves about our faith, and (b) we are forging new confessions almost every year, yes, even every month.

## The Second Edition of the Augsburg Confession

Furthermore, we write about the second 17 edition of the Augsburg Confession. We note that mention is made about this in the transcripts at Naumburg. What is also known to all is that, by appealing to the wording of this latter edition, some have wanted to cover and conceal corruptions regarding the Lord's Supper and other errors. They have attempted to thrust their errors upon an ignorant populace by means of published writings. They have not been motivated by the distinct words of the Augsburg Confession—which was presented first. These errors are openly rejected by the first Augsburg Confession and a far different meaning than these people want can be shown in that document. Therefore, we have decided in this writing to testify publicly about this and to inform all: we wanted neither then nor now in any way to defend, excuse, or approve false and godless doctrines and opinions. Such things may lie concealed under certain coverings of words, as though they agreed with the Gospel doctrine. Indeed, we never understood the second edition in a different sense in any part from the first edition that was presented. Neither do we think that other useful writings of Dr. Philip Melanchthon, or of Brentz, Urban Rhegius, Pomeranus, or others, should be rejected and condemned. As long as, in all things, those writings agree with the standard that has been set forth in the Book of Concord.

18     Now, some theologians (and Luther himself among them), when they wrote about the Lord's Supper, were drawn, against their will, by their adversaries to disputes about the personal union of the two natures in Christ. Yet our theologians in the Book of Concord, and by its standard of sound doctrine, testify what is our constant and never-ending opinion and that of this book: for the Lord's Supper, godly people should be led to no other foundations than the words of institution in the testament of our Lord Jesus Christ. For He is both almighty and true. So it is easy for Him to do those things that He has both instituted and promised in His Word. When this foundation is not attacked by their adversaries, our theologians will not fight back in this kind of argument about other methods of proof. But, in true simplicity of faith, they will firmly insist upon Christ's very plain words. (That is the safest method, and it is best suited for the instruction of uneducated people. For they do not understand those things that have been discussed with greater exactness.) Indeed, it is our assertion that the simple meaning of the words of Christ's testament are attacked by the adversaries. The adversaries' attacks are rejected as godless and conflicting with the nature of true faith. Finally, we say they are contrary to the Apostles' Creed. (Especially to the statements about the incarnation of God's Son, His ascension into heaven, and His sitting at the right hand of the almighty power and majesty of God [Hebrews 1:3].) Therefore, their attacks are false. So it must be shown by a true and thorough interpretation of these articles that our opinion differs neither from Christ's words nor from these articles.

## The Book of Concord

Now, about the phrases and forms of expression that are used in this Book of Concord. We speak of the majesty of the human nature in the person of Christ, elevated and placed at God's right hand. We do this in order to remove all subtle suspicions and causes of offense that might arise from the different uses of the word *abstract* (as both the schools and the fathers have used this term up to now). In distinct and clear words, our theologians want to testify that this majesty is in no way to be ascribed to Christ's human nature outside of the personal union. Neither are we to grant that Christ's human nature possesses this majesty as its own or by itself (even in the personal union) essentially, formally, habitually, subjectively. (The schools like these terms, although they are not good Latin.) For if we would adopt this method of speaking and teaching, the divine and human natures, with their properties, would be confused. And the human, with its essence and properties, would be made equal to the divine. Indeed, the human nature would be completely denied. Therefore, the theologians conclude that we should believe that this union happens according to the method and order of the personal union. Learned antiquity has spoken cautiously about this subject—it is a mystery so great that it exceeds all the powers of our natural ability and understanding.

20    Now, about the condemnations, censures, and rejections of godless doctrines, and especially about what has arisen concerning the Lord's Supper. These had to be clearly set forth in this, our declaration, thorough explanation, and decision about controversial articles. This was done not only so that all may guard against these condemned doctrines, but also for certain other reasons that could in no way be ignored. So it is not at all our plan and purpose to condemn people who err because of a certain simplicity of mind, but are not blasphemers against the truth of the heavenly doctrine. Much less, indeed, do we intend to condemn entire churches that are either under the Roman Empire of the German nation or elsewhere. Rather, it has been our intention and desire in this way to openly criticize and condemn only the fanatical opinions and their stubborn and blasphemous teachers. (We judge that they should in no way be tolerated in our dominions, churches, and schools.) For these errors conflict with God's clear Word. They do so in such a way that they cannot be reconciled with the Word. We have written condemnations also for this reason: that all godly persons might be diligently warned to avoid these errors. For we have no doubt whatsoever that—even in those churches that have not agreed with us in all things— many godly and by no means wicked people are found. They follow their own simplicity and do not correctly understand the matter

itself. But in no way do they approve the blasphemies that are cast forth against the Holy Supper as it is administered in our churches, according to Christ's institution. With the unanimous approval of all good people, the Lord's Supper is taught according to the words of Christ's testament itself (Matthew 26:28). We are also in great hope that, if these simple people would be taught correctly about all these things—the Spirit of the Lord aiding them—they would agree with us, and with our churches and schools, to the infallible truth of God's Word (John 17:17). And certainly, a duty is laid especially upon all the Church's theologians and ministers. With such fitting moderation (Philippians 4:5), they should also teach from God's Word those who have erred from the truth (2 Timothy 2:18), either from a certain simplicity or ignorance. They should teach about the peril of their salvation. They should fortify them against corruptions lest all may perish while the blind are leaders of the blind (Matthew 15:14). Therefore, by our writing, we testify in the sight of almighty God and before the entire Church that it has never been our purpose, by means of this godly formula for union, to create trouble or danger to the godly who are suffering persecution today. We have already entered into the fellowship of grief (Romans 12:15) with them, moved by Christian love, so that we are shocked at the persecution and most painful tyranny that is used against these poor people with such severity. We sincerely detest it. In no way do we agree to the shedding of that innocent blood (Proverbs 6:17), which undoubtedly will be required with great severity from the persecutors at the Lord's awful judgment and before Christ's court (Romans 14:10). They will then certainly render a most strict account (1 Peter 4:5) and suffer fearful punishment.

21    In these matters (as we have mentioned earlier), this has always been our purpose: in our lands, dominions, schools, and churches no other doctrine should be proclaimed and accurately set forth except that which is founded upon God's Word and contained in the Augsburg Confession and the Apology (when properly understood in its genuine sense). Opinions conflicting with these are not allowed. Indeed, this formula of agreement was begun and completed with this purpose. So, before God and all mortals, we once more declare and testify that in the declaration of the controversial articles (of which mention has already been made several times) we are not introducing a new Confession. Nor are we introducing one different from that which was presented in 1530 to Charles V, of happy memory. But we wished indeed to lead our churches and schools, first of all, to the fountains of Holy Scripture, and to the Creeds, and then to the Augsburg Confession (which we have mentioned before). We most earnestly encourage that the young men be instructed in this faithfully and diligently, especially those who are being educated for the holy ministry of the churches and schools. Then the pure doctrine and profession of our faith may, by the Holy Spirit's help, be preserved and spread also to our future generations, until the glorious advent of Jesus Christ (Titus 2:13), our only Redeemer and Savior.

22    This is the case: being instructed from the prophetic and apostolic Scriptures, we are sure about our doctrine and Confession. By the grace of the Holy Spirit, our minds and consciences have been confirmed to a greater degree. Therefore, we have thought that this Book of Concord should be published. For it seemed very necessary that, amid so many errors that had arisen in our times, as well as causes of offense, variances, and these long-continued disagreements, there should exist a godly explanation and agreement about all these controversies. It should be derived from God's Word, according to the terms by which the pure doctrine might be distinguished and separated from the false. Besides, this matter is important also for another reason. There are troublesome and contentious people who do not allow themselves to be bound to any formula of the pure doctrine. They may not have the freedom to stir up controversies, according to their good pleasure, that cause grounds for offense, or to publish and fight for extreme opinions. For eventually the result of these things is that the pure doctrine is hidden and lost. Then nothing is passed on to future generations except academic opinions and delays of judgment. Another consideration was also added to these that agreed with the office committed to us by God. We understand that we owe our subjects this service: we should diligently care for the things that apply to this life and the life to come. We should take pains, with the greatest earnestness and our utmost ability, to attend to those matters that promote (a) the extension of God's name and glory; (b) the spread of His Word (from which alone we hope for salvation); (c) the peace and tranquility of churches and schools; and (d) the instruction and consolation of disturbed consciences. We must do this. For it is certainly a settled fact that this healthy work of Christian concord has already been longed for and expected with anxious prayers and the greatest desire by many good and sincere people both of the highest and the lowest rank. We have not held the following opinion from the beginning of this work of peaceful settlement, neither do we hold it even now: this work of concord (so healthy and most necessary) should be removed from the people's eyes

and completely concealed; the light of heavenly truth should be placed under a bushel or table (Matthew 5:15). Therefore, we should in no way delay its publication. Nor do we doubt that all the godly (who are lovers of the heavenly truth and of concord pleasing to God) will approve of this healthy, useful, godly, and very necessary undertaking with us. We believe they will act so that nothing may be lacking in them, even to the greatest effort, by which God's glory and the common welfare may be promoted in both temporal and eternal things.

## Conclusion

23    We repeat in conclusion what we mentioned several times earlier. In this work of concord, we have not at all wished to create something new or to depart from the truth of the heavenly doctrine, which our ancestors (renowned for their piety) as well as we ourselves, have acknowledged and professed. We mean the doctrine that, having been taken from the prophetic and apostolic Scriptures, is contained (a) in the three ancient Creeds; (b) in the Augsburg Confession, presented in the year 1530 to the Emperor Charles V (of excellent memory); (c) in the Apology, which was added to this; (d) in the Smalcald Articles; and lastly (e) in both the Catechisms of that excellent man, Dr. Luther. Therefore, we also determined not to depart even a finger's breadth either from the subjects themselves, or from the phrases that are found in them. But, the Spirit of the Lord aiding us, we intend to persevere constantly, with the greatest harmony, in this godly agreement. And we intend to examine all controversies according to this true norm and declaration of the pure doctrine. Then—with the rest of the electors, princes, and deputies of the Holy Roman Empire and other kings, princes, and magnates of the Christian state, in accordance with the constitution of the Holy Empire and the agreements that we have with them—we determined and desired to cultivate peace and harmony. We determined to render to each one, according to his rank, all duties belonging to us, together with the services of friendship.

24    Besides, having made known our goals, we will also earnestly apply ourselves with great strictness and the most ardent zeal to the defense of this work of concord. We will do this by diligently visiting the churches and schools in our realms, overseeing printing offices, and other helpful means, according to opportunities and circumstances that may be offered to us and others. We will also take pains—if controversies already mentioned should be renewed, or new controversies about religion should arise—to remove and settle them speedily. We will work to avoid offense, without long and dangerous delays.

25    As a clear testimony of this, we have with great consent subscribed our names, and attached also our seals:
*Louis*, Count Palatine on the Rhine, Elector. *Augustus*, Duke of Saxony, Elector. *John George*, Margrave of Brandenburg, Elector. *Joachim Frederick*, Margrave of Brandenburg, Administrator of the Archbishopric of Magdeburg. *John*, Bishop of Meissen. *Eberhard*, Bishop of Lübeck, Administrator of the Episcopate of Werden. *Philip Louis*, Count Palatine on the Rhine. The guardians of *Frederick William* and *John*, Dukes of Saxony. The guardians of *John Casimir* and *John Ernest*, Dukes of Saxony. *George Frederick*, Margrave of Brandenburg. *Julius*, Duke of Brunswick and Lüneburg. *Otho*, Duke of Brunswick and Lüneburg. *Henry the Younger*, Duke of Brunswick and Lüneburg. *William the Younger*, Duke of Brunswick and Lüneburg. *Wolfgang*, Duke of Brunswick and

Lüneburg. *Ulrich*, Duke of Mecklenburg. The guardians of *John* and *Sigismund Augustus*, Dukes of Mecklenburg. *Louis*, Duke of Württemberg. The guardians of *Ernest* and *Jacob*, Margraves of Baden. *George Ernest*, Count and Lord of Henneburg. *Frederick*, Count of Württemberg and Mömpelgard. *John Gunther*, Count of Schwartzburg. *William*, Count of Schwartzburg. *Albert*, Count of Schwartzburg. *Emich*, Count of Leiningen. *Philip*, Count of Hanau. *Gottfried*, Count of Öttingen. *George*, Count and Lord in Castel. *Henry*, Count and Lord in Castel. *Otho*, Count of Hoya and Burgkhausen. *John*, Count of Oldenburg and Delmenhorst. *John Hoier*, Count of Mansfeld. *Bruno*, Count of Mansfeld. *Hoier Christopher*, Count of Mansfeld. *Peter Ernest Jr.*, Count of Mansfeld. *Christopher*, Count of Mansfeld. *Albert George*, Count of Stolberg. *Wolfgang Ernest*, Count of Stolberg. *Louis*, Count of Gleichen. *Charles*, Count of Gleichen. *Ernest*, Count of Reinstein. *Boto*, Count of Reinstein. *Louis*, Count of Lewenstein. *Henry*, Baron of Limburg, Semperfrei. *George*, Baron of Schönburg. *Wolfgang*, Baron of Schönburg. *Anarc Frederick*, Baron of Wildenfels. Mayor and Council of the City of *Lübeck*. Mayor and Council of the City of *Lüneburg*. Mayor and Council of the City of *Hamburg*. Council of the City of *Brunswick*. Mayor and Council of the City of *Landau*. Mayor and Council of the City of *Münster* in the Gregorian Valley. Council of the City of *Goslar*. Mayor and Council of the City of *Ulm*. Mayor and Council of the City of *Esslingen*. Council of the City of *Reutlingen*. Mayor and Council of the City of *Nördlingen*. Mayor and Council of *Rothenburg* on the Tauber. Mayor and Council of the City of *Hall* in Swabia. Mayor and Council of the City of *Heilbronn*. Mayor and Council of the City of *Memmingen*. Mayor and Council of the City of *Lindau*. Mayor and Council of the City of *Schweinfurt*. Council of the City of *Donauwoerth*. Chamberlain and Council of the City of *Regensburg*. Mayor and Council of the City of *Wimpffen*. Mayor and Council of the City of *Giengen*. Mayor and Council of *Bopfingen*. Mayor and Council of the City of *Aalen*. Mayor and Council of the City of *Kaufbeuren*. Mayor and Council of the City of *Isna*. Mayor and Council of the City of *Kempten*. Council of the City of *Göttingen*. Mayor and Council of the City of *Leutkirch*. The entire Government of the City of *Hildesheim*. Mayor and Council of the City of *Hamelin*. Mayor and Councilmen of the City of *Hanover*. Council of *Mühlhausen*. Council of *Erfurt*. Council of the City of *Einbeck*. Council of the City of *Nordheim*.

# THE THREE UNIVERSAL
# OR
# ECUMENICAL CREEDS

The Holy Trinity

Albrecht Dürer achieved the highest woodcut artistry with his picture of the Holy Trinity. God the Father receives God the Son as the sacrifice for the world's sins, while God the Holy Spirit, in the form of a dove, hovers over them. Angels hold the various instruments of our Lord's torture and execution. Left: The cross, crown of thorns, and whip. Right: Hyssop branch with the sponge and the post where Christ was beaten. Dürer deeply admired Martin Luther and was won over for the Lutheran Reformation.

# Introduction to the Ecumenical Creeds

Lutheranism is not a new faith, but a continuation of the historic, Christian faith of all times and places. In this sense Lutheranism is *catholic*, a word that comes from two Greek words, meaning "according to the whole." With Christians of all times, and in all places, we confess what God's Word teaches—nothing more, and nothing less.

For this reason, it was important for the Lutheran laymen at Augsburg to make it clear to the emperor that they fully accepted the ancient creeds of the Church. The Augsburg Confession refers to "the Fathers," a reference to formative teachers in the history of the Church, most notably the Early Church Fathers who lived and worked between the first and fifth centuries. Lutheranism embraces this history as its own—but with discernment. Lutheranism does not regard the traditions and teachings of the Fathers of the Church as equal to Scripture, but always subject to evaluation in light of Scripture.

Neither Martin Luther nor any of his colleagues ever claimed to be starting a new church. Such a thought was the farthest thing from their minds. They regarded those on the sectarian side of the Reformation as radicals and revolutionaries. They continually condemned almost everything these radicals stood for. Lutheranism is not about revolution, but reformation. It is not about throwing away the past, but about retaining and preserving the best, while filtering out whatever covers and contradicts God's Word.

The Lutherans never wanted to reject and rebel against the Roman Church. They were, however, held captive by the force of the clear truth of God's Word. They refused to compromise that truth. They denied the claim by Rome that it was in fact the "true Church." They regarded Romanism to be a deep corruption of the genuine Church catholic (universal) of the New Testament and of the Early Fathers of the Church. The claim of "catholicity" was reserved by the Lutherans only for that which was biblically true, not what was merely a long-honored tradition within the Roman Church. Many years after being forced out of fellowship with Rome, Martin Luther finally let his name be associated with his teachings by speaking of "Lutheranism."

The most ancient of all Confessions of faith in the Western Church are the Apostles' Creed, the Nicene Creed, and the Athanasian Creed.

# THE THREE UNIVERSAL OR ECUMENICAL CREEDS

## The Apostles' Creed

I believe in God, the Father Almighty, maker of heaven and earth.

And in Jesus Christ, His only Son, our Lord, who was conceived by the Holy Spirit, born of the virgin Mary, suffered under Pontius Pilate, was crucified, died and was buried. He descended into hell. The third day He rose again from the dead. He ascended into heaven and sits at the right hand of God the Father Almighty. From thence He will come to judge the living and the dead.

I believe in the Holy Spirit, the holy Christian Church, the communion of saints, the forgiveness of sins, the resurrection of the body, and the life everlasting. Amen.

## The Nicene Creed

I believe in one God, the Father Almighty, maker of heaven and earth and of all things visible and invisible.

And in one Lord Jesus Christ, the only-begotten Son of God, begotten of His Father before all worlds, God of God, Light of Light, very God of very God, begotten, not made, being of one substance with the Father, by whom all things were made; who for us men and for our salvation came down from heaven and was incarnate by the Holy Spirit of the virgin Mary and was made man; and was crucified also for us under Pontius Pilate. He suffered and was buried. And the third day He rose again according to the Scriptures and ascended into heaven and sits at the right hand of the Father. And He will come again with glory to judge both the living and the dead, whose kingdom will have no end.

And I believe in the Holy Spirit, the Lord and Giver of Life, who proceeds from the Father and the Son, who with the Father and the Son together is worshiped and glorified, who spoke by the prophets. And I believe in one holy Christian and apostolic Church, I acknowledge one Baptism for the remission of sins, and I look for the resurrection of the dead and the life of the world to come. Amen.

# The Creed of Athanasius

Written against the Arians.

Whoever desires to be saved must, above all, hold the catholic faith.

Whoever does not keep it whole and undefiled will without doubt perish eternally.

And the catholic faith is this,

that we worship one God in trinity and Trinity in unity, neither confusing the persons nor dividing the substance.

For the Father is one person, the Son is another, and the Holy Spirit is another.

But the Godhead of the Father and of the Son and of the Holy Spirit is one: the glory equal, the majesty coeternal.

Such as the Father is, such is the Son, and such is the Holy Spirit:

the Father uncreated, the Son uncreated, the Holy Spirit uncreated;

the Father infinite, the Son infinite, the Holy Spirit infinite;

the Father eternal, the Son eternal, the Holy Spirit eternal.

And yet there are not three Eternals, but one Eternal,

just as there are not three Uncreated or three Infinites, but one Uncreated and one Infinite.

In the same way, the Father is almighty, the Son almighty, the Holy Spirit almighty;

and yet there are not three Almighties but one Almighty.

So the Father is God, the Son is God, the Holy Spirit is God;

and yet there are not three Gods, but one God.

So the Father is Lord, the Son is Lord, the Holy Spirit is Lord;

and yet there are not three Lords, but one Lord.

Just as we are compelled by the Christian truth to acknowledge each distinct person as God and Lord,

so also are we prohibited by the catholic religion to say that there are three Gods or Lords.

The Father is not made nor created nor begotten by anyone. The Son is neither made nor created, but begotten of the Father alone.

The Holy Spirit is of the Father and of the Son, neither made nor created nor begotten but proceeding.

Thus, there is one Father, not three Fathers; one Son, not three Sons; one Holy Spirit, not three Holy Spirits.

And in this Trinity none is before or after another; none is greater or less than another;

but the whole three persons are coeternal with each other and coequal so that in all things, as has been stated above, the Trinity in Unity and Unity in Trinity is to be worshiped.

Therefore, whoever desires to be saved must think thus about the Trinity.

But it is also necessary for everlasting salvation that one faithfully believe the incarnation of our Lord Jesus Christ.

Therefore, it is the right faith that we believe and confess that our Lord Jesus Christ, the Son of God, is at the same time both God and man.

He is God, begotten from the substance of the Father before all ages; and He is man, born from the substance of His mother in this age:

perfect God and perfect man, composed of a rational soul and human flesh;

equal to the Father with respect to His divinity, less than the Father with respect to His humanity.

Although He is God and man, He is not two, but one Christ:

one, however, not by the conversion of the divinity into flesh but by the assumption of the humanity into God;

one altogether, not by confusion of substance, but by unity of person.

For as the rational soul and flesh is one man, so God and man is one Christ,

who suffered for our salvation, descended into hell, rose again on the third day from the dead,

ascended into heaven, and is seated at the right hand of the Father, from whence He will come to judge the living and the dead.

At His coming all people will rise again with their bodies and give an account concerning their own deeds.

And those who have done good will enter into eternal life, and those who have done evil into eternal fire.

This is the catholic faith; whoever does not believe it faithfully and firmly cannot be saved.

# THE CONFESSION OF FAITH

## THE AUGSBURG CONFESSION

which was submitted to
His Imperial Majesty Charles V at the
Imperial Meeting of Augsburg
in the Year 1530
by certain princes and cities

*I will also speak of Your testimonies before kings
and shall not be put to shame.*

Psalm 119:46

The Wise Men Adore Christ

During the Imperial Meeting [Diet] of Augsburg, Lutheran princes confessed their faith boldly before the most powerful leaders of Europe. The powerful and mighty are always most wise when they bow in humble adoration before Christ.

# Introduction to the Augsburg Confession

Against the gates of hell, with the grace and help of God.

—Layman Gregory Brück

On Saturday, June 25, 1530, at three o'clock in the afternoon, Dr. Christian Beyer stood, walked toward the Emperor of the Holy Roman Empire, Charles V, and began reading the Augsburg Confession in a loud and distinct voice. Through the open windows a hushed crowd outside in the courtyard hung on his every word, as did the two hundred or so people gathered in the hall. Beside Dr. Beyer stood Dr. Gregory Brück, holding a copy of the Augsburg Confession in Latin. The German princes around them stood up to indicate their support for the Confession. The emperor motioned for them to sit down.

When Dr. Beyer finished reading, Dr. Brück took the German copy of the Confession from him, handed both copies to the emperor, and said, "Most gracious Emperor, this is a Confession that will even prevail against the gates of hell, with the grace and help of God." Thus was the Augsburg Confession presented as a unique Confession of the truth of God's holy Word, distinct from Romanism on the one hand, and Reformed, Anabaptists, and radicals on the other. June 25, 1530, is a date every bit as important for Lutherans as is the more familiar date of October 31, 1517— the day on which Luther posted his Ninety-five Theses.

## Events Leading to Augsburg

The presentation of the Augsburg Confession was a decisive moment, one long in coming. It is important to understand the history leading up to the Imperial Meeting at Augsburg. Nine years earlier, on April 18, 1521, at the Imperial Meeting in Worms, Charles had listened as Martin Luther refused to recant his teachings, saying, "I cannot and will not recant. I cannot do otherwise. Here I stand. God help me. Amen." Now Charles was watching as the most important rulers in his German territories confessed their faith openly and courageously in spite of the threats to their lives from both the government and the Church.

Martin Luther had been declared a criminal and a heretic; he was excommunicated and sentenced to death in April of 1521. By 1526, the Reformation had spread to the point that during an Imperial Meeting at Speyer, the Lutheran princes forced through a resolution that gave each of them the right to arrange religious matters in their respective territories—in any way he felt was best—until the emperor was able to have the pope call a General Council of the Church. So from 1526 to 1529, little changed in the Holy Roman Empire. As a result, most of Northern Germany became Lutheran, along with many cities in Southern Germany. At the second Imperial Meeting in Speyer (1529) the princes loyal to Rome reversed the decision made three years earlier. The princes loyal to the Lutheran Reformation and other reforming movements fiercely protested this decision. Thus the Lutherans, along with other reformers, were labeled *Protestants*. The name has stuck ever since.

Charles ordered all rulers within the Empire to go to Augsburg to attend the Imperial Meeting (also known as a *Reichstag* or a *Diet*). He wanted to settle, once and for all, the controversies in the churches throughout his Germany. The armies of the Turkish Empire were literally at the eastern gates of Charles's Empire. He wanted unity so that the Turkish threat could be met. He hoped that a combination of kindness, cajoling, and finally, threats, would stop the Lutheran movement and restore Romanism throughout the Empire. But things did not go as Charles had hoped.

## The Schwabach, Marburg, and Torgau Articles

Lutheranism was only tolerated where it could not be eliminated by military force. Lutherans had no protection in German territories that were loyal to Rome. After the 1529 Diet of Speyer, Philip of Hesse sought to create a political federation for the mutual defense of those who had protested the autocratic action of Charles V. Philip of Hesse and Jacob Sturm united Saxony and Hesse with certain Southern German evangelical cities (with Ulm, Strasbourg, and Nürnberg as the nucleus). The coalition was created on April 22, 1529, in a secret agreement at Speyer. To clear the way for possible inclusion of the Swiss in the federation, Philip of Hesse planned to settle the dispute between Luther and Ulrich Zwingli at a meeting at Philip's castle in Marburg.

The Lutherans were concerned by Philip of Hesse's desire to put political unity ahead of doctrinal unity. After the Diet of Speyer, Philip Melanchthon (who had kept silent regarding differences between the German Lutherans and the Swiss) had a change of heart and tried to thwart the federation. Luther also opposed a federation without confessional unity. The Schwabach Articles were prepared by Luther and others sometime between July 25 and September 14 of that year.

The Marburg Colloquy took place October 2–4, 1529. Ulrich Zwingli and Martin Luther faced each other across a table for most of the meeting. The two groups identified much that they agreed about, yet the talks broke down. The disagreement had to do with the Lord's Supper. Zwingli was willing to settle for an "agreement to disagree" approach, but Luther insisted that Jesus' words "This is My body" mean "This *is* My body." In fact, he took a piece of chalk and wrote the words "This is My body" on the table itself (*Hoc est Corpus Meum*). Whenever Zwingli or the other Swiss Reformers tried to disagree with Luther about the reality of those words, Luther would lift the tablecloth and point to the words. The Marburg Articles therefore indicate "We are not agreed as to whether the true body and blood of Christ are bodily present in the bread and wine."

The Marburg Articles, along with the Schwabach Articles, provided a firm foundation for the writing of the Augsburg Confession. The seventeen Schwabach Articles were first presented on October 16, 1529. They insisted on unity in doctrine as a prerequisite for any cooperation among the various Protestant groups in Germany.

Charles V persisted with his efforts to eliminate the religious controversies in his territories. He was facing pressure from the threat of a Turkish invasion from the East. He was also mindful that the pope might, at any time, strike an alliance with the ruler of France and attack his Empire from the West. The Empire was a coalition of relatively independent territories and free cities. The key rulers of the Empire were known as "electors," for they actually elected the emperor. (See chart, p. 313.) Charles depended on them both militarily and politically. He could not afford to alienate them. Charles was very devout and felt strongly that it was his duty to protect the Roman Church from the threat posed by the Lutherans and other Protestant reformers. He hoped that the meeting at Augsburg would settle all disputes.

The elector of Saxony, John the Steadfast, at first refused to attend the meeting in Augsburg. But Charles urged him to do so. Since Charles invited everyone attending to share their "opinions, thoughts, and notions," Elector John asked the Wittenberg theologians, led by Martin Luther, to prepare a statement of confession. Martin Luther, Philip Melanchthon, Justas Jonas, and John Bugenhagen met in Torgau and went to work immediately. Their document was given to Elector John at the Torgau Castle in March of 1530, and is therefore known as the Torgau Articles.

### Philip Melanchthon (1497–1560)

Philip Melanchthon was asked by the Elector to write a comprehensive statement of faith. He did so without close consultation with Luther, but he relied heavily on the Schwabach, Marburg, and Torgau Articles—each of which were very much a product of Martin Luther. Luther indicated he approved of Melanchthon's work, though he pointed out that he would never have been able "to tread as lightly" as Melanchthon did.

# The Gathering at Augsburg

On April 4, Elector John left Torgau with Martin Luther, Philip Melanchthon, Justas Jonas, and Veit Dietrich (a secretary to Luther). Ten days later, on Good Friday, they arrived at Coburg Castle. Luther and the Elector remained at Coburg while the others traveled on to Augsburg. There, Philip Melanchthon was given the responsibility of leading the Lutheran theologians. (However, the Elector had set up a special courier service to make sure letters between Luther and his colleagues would be sent and received quickly.) Elector John arrived in Augsburg on May 2.

The meeting began with a clear signal that the courageous Lutheran laymen were not about to concede to the emperor's demands, nor compromise their convictions. As Charles's royal procession approached Augsburg, it was met by a large delegation

Emperor Charles V (1500–58)

Charles V became Holy Roman Emperor on June 28, 1519. Four months later, Martin Luther posted the Ninety-five Theses. For forty years Charles struggled against Lutheranism. This woodcut depicts him in Erlangen in 1532, two years after the Diet of Augsburg. In 1547 he captured Wittenberg. His knights wanted to desecrate Luther's grave. Charles explained that he made war against the living, not the dead. He relinquished his throne in 1558, having failed to exterminate Lutheranism in his lands. He died in a monastery in Spain, a lonely, broken man who had suffed emotionally, physically, and spiritually.

from the city, including the Lutheran princes. The pope's ambassador stood to give the whole assembly a special blessing from the pope. When the crowd knelt, Elector John and his fellow Lutheran princes refused to kneel. Charles and those with him made their way into the city and arrived at the cathedral, where a special Mass was held. The crowd noticed that again Elector John and Philip of Hesse refused to kneel and remained standing, with their heads covered, during the blessing.

Later that evening, Charles and his brother Ferdinand, the King of Austria, met privately with the Lutheran princes. They ordered them to forbid any Lutheran preaching in Augsburg during the meeting. They commanded them to attend the Corpus Christi festival the next day with the emperor. George, Margrave of Brandenburg, spoke boldly for the Lutherans. He refused to concede to Charles's demands, saying, "Before I let anyone take from me the Word of God and ask me to deny my God, I will kneel and let them strike off my head." The emperor, clearly taken aback by George's boldness, sputtered in broken German, "Not cut off head, dear prince. Not cut off head."

## Writing the Augsburg Confession

The plan to present the Torgau Articles had to be scrapped when it was found out that a lengthy, slanderous attack on Luther had been prepared by John Eck—Luther's old nemesis. At Leipzig in 1519, it was Eck who had tried to brand Luther as a heretic. Now, he had secretly written a lengthy attack on Luther and his followers in a book titled *Four Hundred and Four Articles for the Diet in Augsburg*. It included quotations from Martin Luther's writings, as well as from other Protestant reformers.

The book was highly inaccurate and tried to equate the Lutherans with the teachings of Ulrich Zwingli and the most radical of all the reformers, known as the Anabaptists. Eck's goal was to identify Lutheranism with the most extreme reformers, some of whom denied the most basic doctrines of historic Christianity. In light of this development, the Lutherans were forced to prepare a new statement of faith and specifically distance themselves from Zwinglians, Anabaptists, and others.

The Augsburg Confession was intentionally crafted to present a gentle and peaceful response to the emperor. It was intended only to speak for Saxony. However, as various German leaders read it they indicated that they, too, wanted to sign their names and make it their Confession.

So on June 25, 1530, courageous Lutheran laymen confessed their faith and told the emperor and the Roman Church what they believed, taught, and confessed. They relied on the promise of God's Word, as contained in Psalm 119:46, "I will also speak of Your testimonies before kings and shall not be put to shame." The Augsburg Confession was presented as a statement of biblical truth and a proposal for true unity in the Christian faith. It has never been withdrawn.

| TIMELINE | OUTLINE |
|---|---|
| | Preface to Emperor Charles V |
| 1521 Luther excommunicated by papal bull *Decet Romanum Pontificem*; appears before Diet of Worms; refuses to recant | I. God |
| | II. Original Sin |
| Anabaptist Thomas Münzer begins preaching against infant Baptism | III. The Son of God |
| | IV. Justification |
| 1524 Peasants' War begins, lead in part by Thomas Münzer | V. The Ministry |
| | VI. New Obedience |
| 1525 George Blaurock is rebaptized by Conrad Grebel; marks formal beginning of Anabaptist movement | VII. The Church |
| | VIII. What the Church Is |
| Luther marries Katharina von Bora, June 13 | IX. Baptism |
| | X. The Lord's Supper |
| 1526 Diet of Speyer grants German princes right to establish religion in their territory | XI. Confession |
| | XII. Repentance |
| 1529 Luther publishes *Small Catechism* and *Large Catechism* | XIII. The Use of the Sacraments |
| | XIV. Order in the Church |
| Following Second Diet of Speyer, term *Protestant* used to refer to those who agree with Luther | XV. Church Ceremonies |
| | XVI. Civil Government |
| Schwabach Articles drafted, July–September | XVII. Christ's Return for Judgment |
| | XVIII. Free Will |
| Luther, Melanchthon, and Zwingli meet for Marburg Colloquy; unable to agree on Lord's Supper; Marburg Articles drafted | XIX. The Cause of Sin |
| | XX. Good Works |
| Turks unsuccessfully lay siege to Vienna | XXI. Worship of the Saints |
| |     A Summary of the Conflict |
| 1530 Torgau Articles drafted, March |     A Review of the Various Abuses That Have Been Corrected |
| *Augsburg Confession* presented to Charles V at Diet of Augsburg, June 25 | XXII. Both Kinds in the Sacrament |
| | XXIII. The Marriage of Priests |
| 1531 *Augsburg Confession* and *Apology* published, April–May; *Apology's* second edition published, September | XXIV. The Mass |
| | XXV. Confession |
| | XXVI. The Distinction of Meats |
| Ulrich Zwingli dies on Swiss battlefield at Kappel am Albis | XXVII. Monastic Vows |
| | XXVIII. Church Authority |
| | Conclusion |

# THE AUGSBURG CONFESSION

## Preface

### To Emperor Charles V

1 Most invincible Emperor, Caesar Augustus, most clement Lord: Your Imperial Majesty has summoned a meeting of the Empire here at Augsburg to consider taking action against the Turk, discussing how best to stand effectively against his fury and attacks by means of military force. The Turk is the most atrocious and ancient hereditary enemy of the Christian name and religion. 2 This meeting is also to consider disagreements in our holy religion, the Christian faith, by hearing everyone's opinions and judgments in each other's presence. They are to be considered and evaluated among ourselves in mutual charity, mercy, and kindness. 3 After the removal and correction of things that either side has understood differently, these matters may be settled and brought back to one simple truth and Christian concord. 4 Then we may embrace and maintain the future of one pure and true religion under one Christ, doing battle under Him (Psalm 24:8), living in unity and concord in the one Christian Church.

5 We, the undersigned elector and princes, have been called to this gathering along with other electors, princes, and estates in obedient compliance with the Imperial mandate. Therefore, we have promptly come to Augsburg. We do not mean to boast when we say this, but we were among the first to be here.

6 At the very beginning of the meeting in Augsburg, Your Imperial Majesty made a proposal to the electors, princes, and other estates of the Empire. Among other things, you asked that the several estates of the Empire—on the strength of the Imperial edict—should submit their explanations, opinions, and judgments in German and Latin. On the 7 following Wednesday, we informed Your Imperial Majesty that after due deliberation we would present the articles of our Confession in one week. Therefore, concerning this religious matter, we offer this Confession. It is 8 ours and our preachers'. It shows, from the Holy Scriptures and God's pure Word, what has been up to this time presented in our lands, dukedoms, dominions, and cities, and taught in our churches.

In keeping with your edict, the other 9 electors, princes, and estates of the Empire may present similar writings, in Latin and German, giving their opinions in this religious matter. We, and those princes previously mentioned, are prepared to discuss, in 10 a friendly manner, all possible ways and means by which we may come together. We will do this in the presence of your Imperial Majesty, our most clement Lord. In this way, dissensions may be put away without offensive conflict. This can be done honorably, with God's help, so that we may be brought back to agreement and concord. As your 11 edict shows, we are all under one Christ and do battle under Him (Exodus 15:3). We ought to confess the one Christ and do everything according to God's truth. With the most fervent prayers, this is what we ask of God.

However, regarding the rest of the elec- 12 tors, princes, and estates, who form the other side: no progress may be made, nor any result achieved by this treatment of religious matters, as Your Imperial Majesty has wisely determined that it should be dealt with and treated, by mutual presentation of writings and calm conferring together among our-

13 selves. We will at least leave with you a clear testimony. We are not holding back from anything that could bring about Christian concord, such as could be effected with

14 God and a good conscience. Your Imperial Majesty—and the other electors and estates of the Empire, and all moved by sincere love and zeal for religion, who will give an impartial hearing to this matter—please graciously offer to take notice of this and to understand this from our Confession.

15 Your Imperial Majesty, has—not once but often—graciously pointed something out to the electors, princes, and estates of the Empire. At the meeting of Speyer (1526), according to the form of Your Imperial instruction and commission, this point was given and prescribed. Your Imperial Majesty caused it to be stated and publicly pro-

16 claimed that Your Majesty—in dealing with this religious matter, for certain reasons that were alleged in Your Majesty's name—was not willing to decide and could not determine anything. But that Your Majesty would diligently use Your Majesty's office with the Roman Pontiff for the convening of a Gener-

17 al Council. The same matter was publicly set forth at greater length a year ago at the last meeting of the Empire, at Speyer. There Your

18 Imperial Majesty (through His Highness Ferdinand, King of Bohemia and Hungary, our friend and clement Lord, as well as through the Orator and Imperial Commissioners) caused the following to be submitted among other things: concerning the calling of a council, Your Imperial Majesty had taken notice of and has pondered, the resolution of (a) Your Majesty's Representative in the Em-

pire, and of (b) the President and Imperial Counselors, and (c) the Legates from other Estates convened at Ratisbon. Your Imperial

19 Majesty also judged that it was helpful to convene a Council. Your Imperial Majesty did not doubt that the Roman pontiff could be persuaded to hold a General Council. For the matters between Your Imperial Majesty and the Roman pontiff were nearing agreement and Christian reconciliation. Your Im-

20 perial Majesty himself pointed out that he would work to secure the said chief pontiff's consent for convening a General Council, together with your Imperial Majesty, to be announced as soon as possible by letters that were to be sent out.

21 Therefore, if the outcome should be that the differences between us and the other parties in this religious matter should not be settled with friendliness and charity, then here, before Your Imperial Majesty, we obediently offer, in addition to what we have already done, to appear and defend our cause in such a general, free Christian Council. There has always been harmonious action and agreement among the electors, princes, and other estates to hold a Council, in all the Imperial Meetings held during Your

22 Majesty's reign. Even before this time, we have appealed this great and grave matter, to the assembly of this General Council, and to your Imperial Majesty, in an appropriate

23 manner. We still stand by this appeal, both to your Imperial Majesty and to a Council. We have no intention to abandon our appeal, with this or any other document. This would not be possible, unless the matter between us and the other side is settled with friendliness and charity, resolved and brought to Christian harmony, according to

24 the latest Imperial Citation. In regard to this appeal we solemnly and publicly testify here.

John the Steadfast of Saxony (1468–1532)

John the Steadfast, brother of Frederick the Wise and father of John Frederick the Magnanimous, was the leader of the Lutheran princes and cities who gathered for the Diet of Augsburg. He well deserved to be called "Steadfast." He boldly confessed the truth of God's Word and risked everything rather than compromise and lose the Gospel of Jesus Christ.

Gregory Brück (1485–1557)

Courageous Lutheran layman, counselor and aid to Frederick the Wise.
He wrote the preface and the conclusion of the Augsburg Confession.
He stood with Christian Beyer as he publicly read the Augsburg Confession (June 25, 1530). Then Brück handed the German and Latin copies
to the Emperor.

# CHIEF ARTICLES OF FAITH

## ARTICLE I

# God

Martin Luther never intended to start a new church, but rather to purify the one, holy, catholic, and apostolic Church. The Augsburg Confession strongly affirms the doctrine of the Trinity confessed at the Council of Nicaea (325), and later affirmed by the Council of Constantinople (381). God is one divine essence in three distinct persons—Father, Son, and Holy Spirit. The Scriptures reveal this great mystery, confessed by all Christians.

During the Reformation, radical groups espoused various forms of earlier heresies. The Augsburg Confession condemns the ancient heresies concerning God. Article I proves that Lutheranism is deeply anchored in the historic doctrine of biblical Christianity. It embraces the faith of the Church through the ages and rejects all the errors the Church has rejected. (See also Ap I; SA I.)

---

1    Our churches teach with common consent that the decree of the Council of Nicaea about the unity of the divine essence and the

2  three persons is true. It is to be believed without any doubt. God is one divine essence who is eternal, without a body, without parts, of infinite power, wisdom, and goodness. He is the maker and preserver of all things, visible and invisible (Nehemiah 9:6).

3  Yet there are three persons, the Father, the Son, and the Holy Spirit (Matthew 28:19). These three persons are of the same essence

4  and power. Our churches use the term *person* as the Fathers have used it. We use it to signify, not a part or quality in another, but that which subsists of itself.

Our churches condemn all heresies 5 (Titus 3:10–11) that arose against this article, such as the Manichaeans, who assumed that there are two "principles," one Good and the other Evil. They also condemn the Valentinians, Arians, Eunomians, Muslims, and all heresies such as these. Our churches also 6 condemn the Samosatenes, old and new, who contend that God is but one person. Through sophistry they impiously argue that the Word and the Holy Spirit are not distinct persons. They say that *Word* signifies a spoken word, and *Spirit* signifies motion created in things.

## ARTICLE II

# Original Sin

Sin is much more than thinking, saying, and doing things that are wrong. It is a terminal disease. We are all conceived and born in sin; we inherit it from our first parents, Adam and Eve. The disease of sin can be overcome, but only by one medicine: the cleansing, healing, and forgiving blood of God's own Son. By rejecting Pelagian errors in Article II, the Augsburg Confession subtly refers to the Roman view of sin. The Roman Church taught and still teaches that concupiscence (the inborn inclination to sin) is not actually sin. By misdiagnosing our fatal illness, Rome leads people to believe they are able to cooperate with God's grace for salvation. Lutheranism rejects all teachings that imply we are responsible for or contribute to our salvation. (See also Ap II; SA III, I; FC Ep I and SD I.)

---

Our churches teach that since the fall of 1 Adam (Romans 5:12), all who are naturally born are born with sin (Psalm 51:5), that is, without the fear of God, without trust in God, and with the inclination to sin, called

2   concupiscence. Concupiscence is a disease and original vice that is truly sin. It damns and brings eternal death on those who are not born anew through Baptism and the Holy Spirit (John 3:5).

3   Our churches condemn the Pelagians and others who deny that original depravity is sin, thus obscuring the glory of Christ's merit and benefits. Pelagians argue that a person can be justified before God by his own strength and reason.

## ARTICLE III

# The Son of God

The Augsburg Confession teaches the historic, biblical doctrine of Christ. Many early controversies about Christ's human and divine natures were resolved through careful study of God's Word, and are reflected in the Nicene Creed. Article III echoes that creed—our Lord Jesus Christ is one person having two natures: truly God and truly man. This is another mystery of the Christian faith that we receive with thanks, bowing before Christ in humble adoration. His incarnation in the womb of His virgin mother, Mary, was for our salvation. He is, and remains, for all eternity the God-man, the One who appeased, or propitiated, God's wrath against our sin and won for us eternal life. Even now He is present with us through His appointed means of grace—the Gospel and the Sacraments. He comes to strengthen, sustain, and support us, and to bring us safely to our heavenly home. (See also Ap III; SA II I; FC Ep VIII and SD VIII.)

1   Our churches teach that the Word, that is, the Son of God (John 1:14), assumed the human nature in the womb of the Blessed

2   Virgin Mary. So there are two natures—the divine and the human—inseparably joined in one person. There is one Christ, true God and true man, who was born of the Virgin Mary, truly suffered, was crucified, died, and was buried. He did this to reconcile the Fa-   3 ther to us and to be a sacrifice, not only for original guilt, but also for all actual sins of mankind (John 1:29).

He also descended into hell, and truly   4 rose again on the third day. Afterward, He ascended into heaven to sit at the right hand of the Father. There He forever reigns and has dominion over all creatures. He sanctifies   5 those who believe in Him, by sending the Holy Spirit into their hearts to rule, comfort, and make them alive. He defends them against the devil and the power of sin.

The same Christ will openly come again   6 to judge the living and the dead, and so forth, according to the Apostles' Creed.

## ARTICLE IV

# Justification

There is a historic saying in Lutheranism that the Church stands or falls on the article of justification. To *justify* means "to declare righteous." God's sure and certain declaration that we are righteous in His eyes is possible only because of our Savior, Jesus Christ. Through His life, Jesus satisfied God's demand for perfect obedience. Through His sacrificial death, Jesus took God's wrath and atoned for the sins of the world. The Holy Spirit, through the means of grace, works in us saving faith, which personally apprehends what Christ has done for us. Our justification before God, therefore, is brought about by the One who lived, suffered, and died for our salvation. We cannot merit God's favor through our obedience; we cannot offer sacrifices to pay for our sins. But what we cannot do for ourselves, Christ has done for us. He is the solid Rock on which God builds His Church. On Him, and Him alone, we stand forgiven. (See also Ap IV; SA III XIII; FC Ep III and SD III.)

---

1  Our churches teach that people cannot be justified before God by their own
2  strength, merits, or works. People are freely justified for Christ's sake, through faith, when they believe that they are received into favor and that their sins are forgiven for Christ's sake. By His death, Christ made sat-
3  isfaction for our sins. God counts this faith for righteousness in His sight (Romans 3:21–26; 4:5).

## ARTICLE V
# The Ministry

How can what Christ did for us two thousand years ago—through His life, death, and resurrection—become effective in our lives today? God has given us sure, certain, and objective means by which He distributes the blessings of Christ's salvation. These means are the Gospel proclaimed and taught, and the Sacraments administered according to Christ's institution. Through these means the Holy Spirit creates and sustains our trust in Jesus' merits. And through these means of grace the objective reality of Christ's work is applied to us personally.

God established the Office of the Holy Ministry precisely to distribute Christ's good gifts. He sends shepherds, whom the Holy Spirit appoints as overseers, to care for His flock. The German version of the Augsburg Confession uses a very concrete expression to describe this office of pastoral ministry: "preaching office" (*Predigtamt*). During the Reformation, and even today, some imagine they can experience the Holy Spirit through their own reflections, by enjoying nature, or by ecstatic religious experiences. The Holy Spirit does not operate that way. Rather, He works through the powerful, external, objective Gospel in Word and Sacrament. (See also SA III VII and X; Treatise.)

---

1  So that we may obtain this faith, the ministry of teaching the Gospel and administer-
2  ing the Sacraments was instituted. Through the Word and Sacraments, as through instruments, the Holy Spirit is given (John 20:22). He works faith, when and where it pleases God (John 3:8), in those who hear the good
3  news that God justifies those who believe that they are received into grace for Christ's sake. This happens not through our own merits, but for Christ's sake.

4  Our churches condemn the Anabaptists and others who think that through their own preparations and works the Holy Spirit comes to them without the external Word.

## ARTICLE VI
# New Obedience

Lutherans are sometimes accused of denying that Christians should do good works. The article on new obedience follows on the heels of the articles on justification and the ministry, and clearly states that Lutherans do insist on good works. The faith given by the Holy Spirit is a living and active power in our lives, bearing the fruit of good works. We must do good works. God commands them. However, they do not save us. They are always the result of saving faith. This article refers to an Early Church Father as proof that this teaching is anchored in the Church's historic teaching and practice. (See also Ap V.)

---

1  Our churches teach that this faith is bound to bring forth good fruit (Galatians 5:22–23). It is necessary to do good works commanded by God (Ephesians 2:10), because of God's will. We should not rely on

those works to merit justification before
2 God. The forgiveness of sins and justification is received through faith. The voice of Christ testifies, "So you also, when you have done all that you were commanded, say, 'We are unworthy servants; we have only done
3 what was our duty'" (Luke 17:10). The Fathers teach the same thing. Ambrose says, "It is ordained of God that he who believes in Christ is saved, freely receiving forgiveness of sins, without works, through faith alone."

## ARTICLE VII

# The Church

Article VII has been rightly called the evangelical Magna Carta of the Lutheran Church. It cuts through the clutter of man-made ceremonies that had accumulated by the sixteenth century, focuses on the very heart of the matter, and defines *church* with eloquent simplicity. Outward unity in the Church is shaped, defined, and normed by biblical truth (teaching), not the other way around. Church fellowship is common participation in the saving treasures of the Church: Christ's gifts, His Gospel, and His Sacraments. Not any "Gospel" will do, but only that Gospel which is *purely* taught alongside *correctly* administered Sacraments (as noted in the German version). (See also Ap VII and VIII; SA III XII.)

----

1 Our churches teach that one holy Church is to remain forever. The Church is the congregation of saints (Psalm 149:1) in which the Gospel is purely taught and the Sacra-
2 ments are correctly administered. For the true unity of the Church it is enough to agree about the doctrine of the Gospel and the ad-
3 ministration of the Sacraments. It is not necessary that human traditions, that is, rites or ceremonies instituted by men, should be the

same everywhere. As Paul says, "One Lord, 4 one faith, one baptism, one God and Father of all" (Ephesians 4:5–6).

## ARTICLE VIII

# What the Church Is

This article elaborates on Article VII and makes it clear that the Church consists only of believers in Christ, those made holy by His mercy. Hypocrites are not in this sense any part of the Church. One may think of the term *church* in a broad and narrow sense. The Church, broadly speaking, is all those who assemble around Word and Sacrament. Narrowly speaking, the Church encompasses only believers. There are not two churches, one "visible," and one "invisible." Rather, we understand that here on the earth the Church is hidden because faith, or spiritual life, is "hidden with Christ in God" (Colossians 3:3). This hidden Church has public, visible marks, by which it is recognized with absolute certainty: Christ's Gospel and Sacraments, purely preached and administered. (See also Ap VII and VIII; SA III XII.)

----

Strictly speaking, the Church is the congre- 1 gation of saints and true believers. However, because many hypocrites and evil persons are mingled within them in this life (Matthew 13:24–30), it is lawful to use Sacraments administered by evil men, according to the saying of Christ, "The scribes and the Pharisees sit on Moses' seat" (Matthew 23:2). Both the Sacra- 2 ments and Word are effective because of Christ's institution and command, even if they are administered by evil men.

Our churches condemn the Donatists, 3 and others like them, who deny that it is lawful to use the ministry of evil men in the Church, and who think that the ministry of evil men is not useful and is ineffective.

## ARTICLE IX

# Baptism

The Bible teaches that Baptism is a gift of God's grace by which He applies the benefits of Christ's life, death, and resurrection to us personally. Because all people are conceived and born in sin, we all need salvation. Because Baptism is God's way of bringing us salvation, infants should also be baptized. During the Reformation, as now, some Christian groups turned Baptism from God's saving activity into an act of Christian obedience. This view of Baptism arises from the denial of original sin and a semi-Pelagian view of salvation, whereby faith becomes the good work we contribute. This article concentrates on what God gives in this Sacrament. (See also Ap IX; SA III V; LC IV.)

1    Concerning Baptism, our churches teach that Baptism is necessary for salvation (Mark
2  16:16) and that God's grace is offered through Baptism (Titus 3:4–7). They teach that children are to be baptized (Acts 2:38–39). Being offered to God through Baptism, they are received into God's grace.
3    Our churches condemn the Anabaptists, who reject the Baptism of children, and say that children are saved without Baptism.

## ARTICLE X

# The Lord's Supper

By the time the Augsburg Confession was written, deep divisions had arisen among the various reformers concerning the Lord's Supper. The Lutherans were very careful to distance themselves from those who reject that the body and blood of Christ are in fact truly present in His Supper and distributed to all those who eat and drink. Transubstantiation, consubstantiation, or any other human spec-ulation asks the wrong question: *how* is Christ present? Lutheranism has no theory or philosophical explanation of how Christ is present. Rather, Lutherans insist on answering the *what* of the Lord's Supper. We believe, teach, and confess that of the bread, Christ said, "This is My body," and of the wine, "This is My blood." These are given and shed "for the forgiveness of sins" (Matthew 26:26–28). We reject any teaching that is contrary to our Lord's Word. (See also Ap X; SA III VI; LC V; FC Ep VII and SD VII.)

Our churches teach that the body and  1
blood of Christ are truly present and distributed to those who eat the Lord's Supper (1 Corinthians 10:16). They reject those who  2
teach otherwise.

## ARTICLE XI

# Confession

By the time of the Reformation, the practice of confessing sins privately and confidentially to a pastor had been a well-accepted church practice for over a thousand years. Private Confession and Absolution was never something Lutherans wanted to get rid of. As time went on, the practice fell into disuse, but clearly Article XI assumes that private Confession and Absolution will take place in the Lutheran Church. The problem addressed by this article is that the Roman Church demanded every sin be recalled and confessed. Clearly, this is humanly impossible and makes our forgiveness dependent on our work. Such teaching is certainly dangerous to repentant consciences, which need firm assurance that Christ forgives all sin. (See also Ap XI; SA III VIII; LC V, An Exhortation to Confession.)

Our churches teach that private Absolu-  1
tion should be retained in the churches, al-

**IOANNES OECOLAMPADIVS**
Basiliensis Ecclesiæ Pastor.

John Oecolampadius (1482–1531)

Ally of Zwingli who opposed Luther at the Marburg Colloquy (1529). Condemned in Article X of the Augsburg Confession.

ANNO AETATIS EIVS XLVIIL.

Ulrich Zwingli (1484–1531)

Leader of the "Sacramentarians." The Romanists tried to lump all Protestants together. The Augsburg Confession was clear that Lutherans rejected the teachings of Zwingli and others like him. After Zwingli died in battle, John Calvin continued Zwingli's work, creating the Reformed churches.

though listing all sins is not necessary for Confession. For, according to the Psalm, it is impossible. "Who can discern his errors?" (Psalm 19:12).

2

## ARTICLE XII

# Repentance

The Roman teaching about repentance was the spark that ignited the Lutheran Reformation. When Luther learned his congregational members were buying indulgences, hoping to avert God's punishment for sins by paying money, he was incensed. Repentance is not about "paying off" God or making some satisfaction for our sin. Repentance is recognizing the reality of our sin and turning to God in faith for His mercy. God reveals our sin through His Law; He forgives our sin and restores us to a right relationship with Him through His Gospel. While we affirm there is fruit of repentance, the focus of the Gospel must be clear: our sins are forgiven only because of Christ. Our lives in Christ are lives of repentance, returning again and again to the fount and source of all mercy, our Savior. Notice that this article rejects any teaching that implies our works of satisfaction are part of true repentance. Article XII strikes a fatal blow at the very heart of the Roman sacramental system. (See also Ap XII; SA III III; LC V, An Exhortation to Confession.)

### Selling Indulgences

The Pope (center) hands a commission to sell indulgences to a monk. Right: The purchase of an indulgence, with people being directed where to put their money. Left: A lame man asks for help, while others purchase their indulgences. Their names are being written on the indulgence receipt.

1 Our churches teach that there is forgiveness of sins for those who have fallen after
2 Baptism whenever they are converted. The Church ought to impart Absolution to those who return to repentance (Jeremiah 3:12).
3 Now, strictly speaking, repentance consists of
4 two parts. One part is contrition, that is, terrors striking the conscience through the
5 knowledge of sin. The other part is faith, which is born of the Gospel (Romans 10:17) or the Absolution and believes that for Christ's sake, sins are forgiven. It comforts the conscience and delivers it from terror.
6 Then good works are bound to follow, which are the fruit of repentance (Galatians 5:22–23).
7 Our churches condemn the Anabaptists, who deny that those who have once been jus-
8 tified can lose the Holy Spirit. They also condemn those who argue that some may reach such a state of perfection in this life that they cannot sin.
9 The Novatians also are condemned, who would not absolve those who had fallen after Baptism, though they returned to repentance.
10 Our churches also reject those who do not teach that that forgiveness of sins comes through faith, but command us to merit grace through satisfactions of our own.

They also reject those who teach that it is necessary to perform works of satisfaction, commanded by Church law, in order to remit eternal punishment or the punishment of purgatory.

## ARTICLE XIII

# The Use of the Sacraments

God gives the Sacraments to His people for their forgiveness, life, and salvation, and this happens as they call forth trust and confidence in Christ, the Savior. By the sixteenth century, the Roman Church had developed a complicated sacramental system that had transformed the Sacraments into meritorious works performed by priests. This was especially evident in the Mass, where priests "sacrificed" Christ again and again on behalf of the living and the dead. The Bible, however, reveals the key to the Sacraments: the promises of God. God attaches His Word of promise to the element of the Sacrament— water, wine, or bread—and gives and strengthens the faith of those receiving them. (See also Ap XIII.)

1 Our churches teach that the Sacraments were ordained, not only to be marks of profession among men, but even more, to be signs and testimonies of God's will toward us. They were instituted to awaken and con-
2 firm faith in those who use them. Therefore, we must use the Sacraments in such a way that faith, which believes the promises offered and set forth through the Sacraments, is increased (2 Thessalonians 1:3).
3 Therefore, they condemn those who teach that the Sacraments justify simply by the act of doing them. They condemn those who do not teach that faith, which believes that sins are forgiven, is required in the use of the Sacraments.

## ARTICLE XIV

# Order in the Church

When this article speaks of a rightly ordered call, it refers to the Church's historic practice of placing personally and theologically qualified men into the office of preaching and teaching the Gospel and administering the Sacraments. This is done by means of a formal, public, and official call from the Church to do so. When this article was presented, it was understood that a call into the preaching office would be confirmed and formally recognized by means of the apostolic rite of ordination (with prayer and the laying on of hands). (See also Ap XIV; SA III X.)

---

Our churches teach that no one should publicly teach in the Church, or administer the Sacraments, without a rightly ordered call.

## ARTICLE XV

# Church Ceremonies

Lutheranism embraces the good historic traditions of the Church, especially those of the Western Church. These include such things as following the pattern of the Church year, lectionary readings from the Bible, a liturgical order of worship, various festival days, vestments worn by clergy, and the use of candles, crucifixes, and other objects. As this article makes very clear, in the Lutheran Church, rites, decorations, or traditions are never used or followed to appease God's wrath or to earn the forgiveness of sins. Lutheranism removed from the Church useless and harmful traditions such as monastic vows and insisting on certain foods on certain days. (See also Ap XV; SA III XV; FC Ep X and SD X.)

---

1    Our churches teach that ceremonies ought to be observed that may be observed without sin. Also, ceremonies and other practices that are profitable for tranquility and good order in the Church (in particular, holy days, festivals, and the like) ought to be observed.

2    Yet, the people are taught that consciences are not to be burdened as though observing such things was necessary for salvation (Colossians 2:16–17). They are also
3  taught that human traditions instituted to

make atonement with God, to merit grace, and to make satisfaction for sins are opposed to the Gospel and the doctrine of faith. So  4 vows and traditions concerning meats and days, and so forth, instituted to merit grace and to make satisfaction for sins, are useless and contrary to the Gospel.

## ARTICLE XVI

# Civil Government

It was important for Lutherans to make clear they did not share the beliefs of the radical reformers of the sixteenth century. Some of these radicals rejected all forms of order and authority, in both Church and State, even rejecting their homes and families in order to be "super spiritual." This article points to the biblical doctrine of the two kingdoms, a way of speaking about God's care for us spiritually though the Church and temporally through the various orders in society; chiefly, home and government. Christians live out their various callings in life in service to God and their fellow humans, doing so in the stations, or situations, to which God has called them. (See also Ap XVI.)

---

Our churches teach that lawful civil regu-  1
lations are good works of God. They teach  2
that it is right for Christians to hold political office, to serve as judges, to judge matters by Imperial laws and other existing laws, to impose just punishments, to engage in just wars, to serve as soldiers, to make legal contracts, to hold property, to take oaths when required by the magistrates, for a man to marry a wife, or a woman to be given in marriage (Romans 13; 1 Corinthians 7:2).

Our churches condemn the Anabaptists  3
who forbid these political offices to Christians. They also condemn those who do not  4
locate evangelical perfection in the fear of

5 God and in faith, but place it in forsaking political offices. For the Gospel teaches an eternal righteousness of the heart (Romans 10:10). At the same time, it does not require the destruction of the civil state or the family. The Gospel very much requires that they be preserved as God's ordinances and that love be practiced in such ordinances. There-
6 fore, it is necessary for Christians to be obe-
7 dient to their rulers and laws. The only exception is when they are commanded to sin. Then they ought to obey God rather than men (Acts 5:29).

## ARTICLE XVII

# Christ's Return for Judgment

This article affirms the biblical view of the end times. It pointedly rejects any speculation or opinion about believers ruling the world before the final resurrection of the dead. It also rejects all theories about a "millennial" earthly rule of Christ as contrary to God's Word. (See also Ap XVII.)

———————

1 Our churches teach that at the end of the world Christ will appear for judgment and will raise all the dead (1 Thessalonians
2 4:13–5:2). He will give the godly and elect
3 eternal life and everlasting joys, but He will condemn ungodly people and the devils to be tormented without end (Matthew 25:31–46).
4 Our churches condemn the Anabaptists, who think that there will be an end to the punishments of condemned men and devils.
5 Our churches also condemn those who are spreading certain Jewish opinions, that before the resurrection of the dead the godly shall take possession of the kingdom of the world, the ungodly being everywhere suppressed.

## ARTICLE XVIII

# Free Will

By the time of the Reformation, the Roman Church had fully developed a false and potentially damning doctrine, one that stated that a person is able, to some degree, to strive for and receive God's mercy. Article XVIII asserts Scripture's teaching that people, apart from God's grace, are wholly incapable of perceiving spiritual things. The longest quote from a Church Father in the Augsburg Confession occurs here. It demonstrates Lutheranism's continuity with the Church catholic —in contrast to Roman error on this doctrine. Augustine echoes the Bible's teaching that while we humans can perform acts of civil righteousness, which may be called "good," spiritually we are evil and enemies of God. However, in Christ, our loving God breaks down the wall of hostility separating us from Him. By His Spirit, through His Word, He gives us Christ's perfect righteousness as a gift. In external, worldly matters we do have the freedom to make decisions according to human reason, but this does not mean, apart from God's grace, that we have similar powers in matters of eternal life. (See also Ap XVIII; FC Ep II and SD II.)

———————

1 Our churches teach that a person's will has some freedom to choose civil righteousness and to do things subject to reason.
2 It has no power, without the Holy Spirit, to work the righteousness of God, that is, spiritual righteousness. For "the natural person does not accept the things of the Spirit of
3 God" (1 Corinthians 2:14). This righteousness is worked in the heart when the Holy Spirit is received through the Word (Galatians 3:2–6).
4 This is what Augustine says in his *Hypog-*

*nosticon*, Book III:

We grant that all people have a free will. It is free as far as it has the judgment of reason. This does not mean that it is able, without God, either to begin, or at least to complete, anything that has to do with God. It is free only in works of this life, whether
5  good or evil. *Good* I call those works that spring from the good in nature, such as willing to labor in the field, to eat and drink, to have a friend, to clothe oneself, to build a house, to marry a wife, to raise cattle, to learn various useful arts, or whatsoever
6  good applies to this life. For all of these things depend on the providence of God. They are from Him
7  and exist through Him. Works that are willing to worship an idol, to commit murder, and so forth, I call *evil.*

8  Our churches condemn the Pelagians and others who teach that without the Holy Spirit, by natural power alone, we are able to love God above all things and do God's
9  commandments according to the letter. Although nature is able in a certain way to do the outward work (for it is able to keep the hands from theft and murder), yet it cannot produce the inward motions, such as the fear of God, trust in God, chastity, patience, and so on.

## ARTICLE XIX
# The Cause of Sin

The blame for sin rests solely with the devil and with us, not with God. Apart from God's mercy in Christ, there is no hope for the wicked. Years after the Augsburg Confession was written, in order to accentuate the depth of mankind's sinful condition, some Lutherans would imply that sin is of the very

essence of people. (See pp. 530–31.) The result of this faulty teaching is that God becomes responsible for, indeed the Creator of, sin. Sin is a deep corruption of that which God created, and is entirely mankind's fault. (See also Ap XIX; SA III I.)

---

Our churches teach that although God creates and preserves nature, the cause of sin is located in the will of the wicked, that is, the devil and ungodly people. Without God's help, this will turns itself away from God, as Christ says, "When he lies, he speaks out of his own character" (John 8:44).

## ARTICLE XX
# Good Works

This is another key article in the Augsburg Confession. Article XX offers more details about faith and works than what was previously written. Lutherans insist on the biblical truth that our good works do not save us. So they are sometimes accused of opposing good works. This article sets forth the Bible's clear teaching that good works are the fruit of faith, not the cause of our salvation. The Lutheran hymn "Salvation unto Us Has Come" offers a short, powerful summary of these essential Gospel truths:

Faith clings to Jesus' cross alone
And rests in Him unceasing;
And by its fruits true faith is known,
with love and hope increasing.
For faith alone can justify;
Works serve our neighbor and supply
The proof that faith is living.

> (Paul Speratus, 1484–1531; tr.
> *The Lutheran Hymnal*, 1941, alt.)

Rome continues to insist that people are saved by God's grace, but not through faith alone. This teaching dangerously encourages people to believe they are able, even in some small way, to contribute toward their salvation. This diverts their focus from Christ and His merits to their own works. It also leads to despair, doubt, and uncertainty when people come to realize the enormity of their sin and wonder if in fact they have done "enough" to merit or deserve God's favor. After setting forth the proper biblical distinction between faith and good works, the Augsburg Confession asserts very clearly that our good works are necessary, not to merit grace, but because this is God's will for our lives. God's gift of saving faith enables us to do good works. (See also Ap XX; SA III XIII; FC Ep IV and SD IV.)

---

1   Our teachers are falsely accused of for-
2   bidding good works. Their published writings on the Ten Commandments, and other similar writings, bear witness that they have usefully taught about all estates and duties of life. They have taught well what is pleasing to God in every station and vocation in life.
3   Before now, preachers taught very little about these things. They encouraged only childish and needless works, such as particular holy days, particular fasts, brotherhoods, pilgrimages, services in honor of the saints, the use of rosaries, monasticism, and such things.
4   Since our adversaries have been admonished about these things, they are now unlearning them. They do not preach these unhelpful
5   works as much as they used to. In the past, there was only stunning silence about faith, but now they are beginning to mention it.
6   They do not teach that we are justified only by works. They join faith and works together, and say that we are justified by faith and
7   works. This teaching is more tolerable than the former one. It can offer more consolation than their old teaching.

The doctrine about faith, which ought to   8
be the chief doctrine in the Church, has remained unknown for so long. Everyone has to admit that there was the deepest silence in their sermons concerning the righteousness of faith. They only taught about works in the churches. This is why our teachers teach the churches about faith in this way.

First, they teach that our works cannot   9
reconcile God to us or merit forgiveness of sins, grace, and justification. We obtain reconciliation only by faith when we believe that we are received into favor for Christ's sake. He alone has been set forth as the Mediator and Atoning Sacrifice (1 Timothy 2:5), in order that the Father may be reconciled through Him. Therefore, whoever believes   10
that he merits grace by works despises the merit and grace of Christ (Galatians 5:4). In so doing, he is seeking a way to God without Christ, by human strength, although Christ Himself said, "I am the way, and the truth, and the life" (John 14:6).

This doctrine about faith is presented   11
everywhere by Paul, "By grace you have been saved through faith. And this is not your own doing; it is the gift of God" (Ephesians 2:8).

If anyone wants to be tricky and say that   12
we have invented a new interpretation of Paul, this entire matter is supported by the testimony of the Fathers. Augustine defends   13
grace and the righteousness of faith in many volumes against the merits of works. Am-   14
brose, in his book *The Calling of the Gentiles*, and elsewhere, teaches the same thing. In *The Calling of the Gentiles* he says,

Redemption by Christ's blood would be worth very little, and God's mercy would not surpass man's works, if justification, which is accomplished through grace, were due to prior merits. So justification would not be the free gift from a donor, but the reward due the laborer.

15 Spiritually inexperienced people despise this teaching. However, God-fearing and anxious consciences find by experience that it brings the greatest consolation. Consciences cannot be set at rest through any works, but only by faith, when they take the sure ground that for Christ's sake they have a

16 gracious God. As Paul teaches, "since we have been justified by faith, we have peace with

17 God" (Romans 5:1). This whole doctrine must be related to the conflict of the terrified conscience. It cannot be understood apart

18 from that conflict. Therefore, inexperienced and irreverent people have poor judgment in this matter because they dream that Christian righteousness is nothing but civil and philosophical righteousness.

19 Until now consciences were plagued with the doctrine of works. They did not

20 hear consolation from the Gospel. Some people were driven by conscience into the desert and into monasteries, hoping to

21 merit grace by a monastic life. Some people came up with other works to merit grace

22 and make satisfaction for sins. That is why the need was so great for teaching and renewing the doctrine of faith in Christ, so that anxious consciences would not be without consolation but would know that grace, forgiveness of sins, and justification are received by faith in Christ.

23 People are also warned that the term *faith* does not mean simply a knowledge of a history, such as the ungodly and devil have (James 2:19). Rather, it means a faith that believes, not merely the history, but also the effect of the history. In other words, it believes this article: the forgiveness of sins. We have grace, righteousness, and forgiveness of sins through Christ.

The person who knows that he has a Fa- 24 ther who is gracious to him through Christ truly knows God (John 14:7). He also knows that God cares for him (1 Peter 5:7), and he calls upon God (Romans 10:13). In a word, he is not without God, as are the heathen. For 25 devils and the ungodly are not able to believe this article: the forgiveness of sins. Hence, they hate God as an enemy (Romans 8:7) and do not call Him (Romans 3:11–12) and expect no good from Him. Augustine also 26 warns his readers about the word *faith* and teaches that the term is used in the Scriptures, not for the knowledge that is in the ungodly, but for the confidence that consoles and encourages the terrified mind.

Furthermore, we teach that it is necessary 27 to do good works. This does not mean that we merit grace by doing good works, but because it is God's will (Ephesians 2:10). It is 28 only by faith, and nothing else, that forgiveness of sins is apprehended. The Holy Spirit 29 is received through faith, hearts are renewed and given new affections, and then they are able to bring forth good works. Ambrose 30 says: "Faith is the mother of a good will and doing what is right." Without the Holy Spirit 31 people are full of ungodly desires. They are too weak to do works that are good in God's sight (John 15:5). Besides, they are in the 32 power of the devil, who pushes human beings into various sins, ungodly opinions, and open crimes. We see this in the philosophers, 33 who, although they tried to live an honest life could not succeed, but were defiled with many open crimes. Such is human weakness, 34 without faith and without the Holy Spirit, when governed only by human strength.

Therefore, it is easy to see that this doc- 35 trine is not to be accused of banning good works. Instead, it is to be commended all the more because it shows how we are enabled

36  to do good works. For without faith, human nature cannot, in any way, do the works of the First or Second Commandment (1 Corinthians 2:14).

37  Without faith, human nature does not call upon God, nor expect anything from Him, nor bear the cross (Matthew 16:24). Instead, human nature seeks and

38  trusts in human help. So when there is no faith and trust in God, all kinds of lusts and human intentions rule in the heart (Genesis

39  6:5). This is why Christ says, "Apart from Me you can do nothing" (John 15:5). That is

40  why the Church sings: "Lacking Your divine favor, there is nothing in man. Nothing in him is harmless."

## ARTICLE XXI

# Worship of the Saints

The Early Church had developed an appreciation for those who confessed, and sometimes died for, their faith. However, deep corruption had developed within the Church regarding the honor given to the saints, resulting in what could only be described as idolatrous worship. Those who have gone before us in the faith are to be honored, remembered, and imitated according to our various stations and callings in life. That is clear. However, it is clearly contrary to Scripture to teach that the saints are to be prayed to and invoked for aid. There is simply no command, no example, and no promise in Scripture indicating that we should pray to our departed brothers and sisters in Christ. (See also Ap XXI; SA II II.)

1    Our churches teach that the history of saints may be set before us so that we may follow the example of their faith and good works, according to our calling. For example, the emperor may follow the example of David (2 Samuel) in making war to drive away the Turk from his country. For both are

2    kings. But the Scriptures do not teach that we are to call on the saints or to ask the saints for help. Scripture sets before us the one Christ as the Mediator, Atoning Sacrifice, High Priest, and Intercessor (1 Timothy 2:5–6).

3    He is to be prayed to. He has promised that He will hear our prayer (John 14:13). This is the worship that He approves above all other worship, that He be called upon in all afflictions. "If anyone does sin, we have an advo-

4    cate with the Father" (1 John 2:1).

## A Summary of the Conflict

1    This then is nearly a complete summary of our teaching. As can be seen, there is nothing that varies from the Scriptures, or from the Church universal, or from the Church of Rome, as known from its writers. Since this is the case, those who insist that our teachers are to be regarded as heretics are judging harshly. There is, how-

2    ever, disagreement on certain abuses that have crept into the Church without rightful authority. Even here, if there are some differences, the bishops should bear with us patiently because of the Confession we have just reviewed. Even the Church's canon law is not so severe that it demands the same rites everywhere. Nor, for that

3    matter, have the rites of all churches ever been the same. Although, in large part, the

4    ancient rites are diligently observed among us. It is a false and hate-filled charge that our churches have abolished all the ceremonies instituted in ancient times. But the

5    abuses connected with the ordinary rites have been a common source of complaint. They have been corrected to some extent since they could not be approved with a good conscience.

## A Review of the Various Abuses That Have Been Corrected

1 Our churches do not dissent from any article of the faith held by the Church catholic. They only omit some of the newer abuses. They have been erroneously accepted through the corruption of the times, contrary to the intent of canon law. Therefore, we pray that Your Imperial Majesty will graciously hear what has been changed and why the people are not compelled to observe those things that are abuses against their

2 conscience. Your Imperial Majesty should not believe those who have tried to stir up hatred against us by spreading strange lies

3 among the people. They have given rise to this controversy by stirring up the minds of good people. Now they are trying to increase the controversy using the same methods.

4 Your Imperial Majesty will undoubtedly find that the form of doctrine and ceremonies among us are not as intolerable as these un-

5 godly and ill-intentioned men claim. Besides, the truth cannot be gathered from common

6 rumors or the attacks of enemies. It can easily be judged that if the churches observed ceremonies correctly, their dignity would be maintained and reverence and piety would increase among the people.

## ARTICLE XXII

# Both Kinds in the Sacrament

Prior to the Reformation, the practice had developed of withholding the consecrated wine from the laity during the Lord's Supper. Only the consecrated bread was distributed to them. However, priests who celebrated Mass drank from the cup. Theories developed within the Church to help support this practice. One stated that the bread alone was enough for the laity, since Christ's body must also contain His blood. The practice of withhold-

ing the cup from the congregation was clearly contrary to Scripture and was an insult to God's royal priests—all those who trust in Christ for the forgiveness of sins. The Early Church Fathers spoke about *all* of God's people receiving both "kinds," or elements, of this Holy Meal. (See also Ap XXII; SA III VI; FC Ep VII and SD VII.)

---

1 The laity are given both kinds in the Sacrament of the Lord's Supper because this practice has the Lord's command, "Drink of it, all of you" (Matthew 26:27). Christ has

2 clearly commanded that all should drink from the cup.

3 And lest anyone misleadingly say that this refers only to priests, in 1 Corinthians 11:27 Paul cites an example. From this it appears that the whole congregation used both kinds.

4 This practice has remained in the Church for a long time. It is not known when, or by whom, or by whose authority, it was changed. Cardinal Cusanus mentions the time when it

5 was approved. Cyprian in some places testifies that the blood was given to the people.

6 Jerome testifies to the same thing when he says, "The priests administer the Eucharist and distribute the blood of Christ to the people." Indeed, Pope Gelasius commands that

7 the Sacrament not be divided (dist. II., *De Consecratione, cap. Comperimus*). Only a re-

8 cent custom has changed this.

9 It is clear that any custom introduced against God's commandments is not to be allowed, as Church law bears witness (dist. III., *cap. Veritate*, and the following chapters).

10 This custom has been received, not only against the Scripture, but also against old canon law and the example of the Church.

11 Therefore, if anyone preferred to use both kinds in the Sacrament, they should not have been compelled to do otherwise, as an of-

12 fense against their conscience. Because the

division of the Sacrament does not agree with the ordinance of Christ, it is our custom to omit the procession [with the host], which has been used before.

## ARTICLE XXIII

# The Marriage of Priests

Underlying the issue of forced priestly celibacy, as with other abuses arising in the Church, is the authority of the Church to command and forbid something not mentioned in Scripture. The Lutherans maintained that the Church has no authority from God to command what He has not commanded, nor to forbid what He has not forbidden. The Bible clearly teaches that the Apostle Peter had a wife. This example should have served as convincing proof that priestly marriages were God pleasing. That there are men who are given the gift of chastity is affirmed, but the view that the Church can, and should, forbid all who wish to be priests from marrying is resoundingly rejected. Marriage is a gift from God to be received with thanksgiving both by laypeople and clergy. To suggest otherwise is to introduce a teaching of the evil one into the Church. (See also Ap XXIII; SA III XI.)

1 Complaints about unchaste priests are 2 common. Platina writes that it is for this reason that Pope Pius is reported to have said that although there are reasons why marriage was taken away from priests, there are far more important reasons why it should be 3 given back. Since our priests wanted to avoid these open scandals, they married wives and taught that it was lawful for them to enter 4 into marriage. First, because Paul says, "Because of the temptation to sexual immorality, each man should have his own wife" and "It is better to marry than to be aflame with passion" (1 Corinthians 7:2, 9b).

Second, Christ says, "Not everyone can 5 receive this saying" (Matthew 19:11), where He teaches that not everyone is able to lead a single life. God created human beings for procreation (Genesis 1:28). It is not within a 6 person's power, without God giving a unique gift, to change this creation. (For it is clear, as many have confessed, that no good, honest, chaste life, no Christian, sincere, upright conduct has resulted from the attempt to lead a single life. Instead, a horrible, fearful unrest and torment of conscience has been felt by many until the end.) Therefore, those who 7 are not able to lead a single life ought to marry. No human law, no vow, can destroy 8 God's commandment and ordinance. For 9 these reasons the priests teach that it is lawful for them to marry wives.

It is clear that in the Ancient Church 10 priests were married men. For Paul says, "An 11 overseer must be the husband of one wife" (1 Timothy 3:2). Four hundred years ago in 12 Germany, for the first time, priests were violently forced to lead a single life. They offered such resistance that when the Archbishop of Mainz was about to publish the pope's decree about celibacy, he was almost killed in a riot by enraged priests. This matter was handled 13 so harshly that not only was marriage forbidden in the future, but existing marriages were torn apart, contrary to all laws, both divine and human. This was even contrary to canon law itself, as made by not only popes, but also by the most celebrated synods.

Seeing that man's nature is gradually 14 growing weaker as the world grows older, it is good to be on guard to make sure no more vices work their way into Germany.

Furthermore, God ordained marriage to 15 be a help against human weakness. Canon 16 law itself says that the old rigor ought to be relaxed now and then, in these latter times, because of human weakness. We wish this

17 would also be done in this matter. We expect that at some point churches will lack pastors if marriage continues to be forbidden.

18 While God's commandment is in force, and the custom of the Church is well known, impure celibacy will cause many scandals, adulteries, and other crimes that deserve punishment from just rulers. In light of all this, it is incredibly cruel that the marriage of

19 priests is forbidden. God has commanded

20 that marriage be honored. Marriage is most highly honored in the laws of all well-ordered commonwealths, even among the hea-

21 then. But now men, even priests, are cruelly put to death, contrary to the intent of canon law, for no other reason than that they are

22 married. Paul, in 1 Timothy 4, says that a doctrine of demons forbids marriage (vv.

23 1–3). This is clearly seen by how laws against marriage are enforced with such penalties.

24 Since no human law can destroy God's command, neither can it be done by any vow.

25 So Cyprian advises women who do not keep the promise they made to remain chaste, that they should marry. He says (Book I, Epistle XI), "If they are unwilling or unable to persevere, it is better for them to marry than to fall into the fire by their lusts. They should certainly give no offense to their brothers and

26 sisters." And even canon law shows some leniency toward those who have taken vows before the proper age, as has been the case up to this point.

## ARTICLE XXIV

# The Mass

This article clearly demonstrates Lutheranism's desire to continue—not to reject—the wholesome, beneficial, and historic worship practices of the Church. Lutheranism retained the traditional form of the Mass, that is, the service of Holy Communion. In many respects, the ceremonies and liturgy of the Lutheran Church were very similar to those of the Roman Church. The difference lay in Lutheranism's rejection of false teaching concerning the Mass: that somehow, and without faith, simply by attending and observing the spectacle of the Mass, people could merit the forgiveness of sins. Worst of all was Rome's teaching that a priest saying Mass is actually offering Christ in an unbloody manner to appease God and secure His favor. Masses became a source of considerable revenue for the Church, since people were encouraged to "sponsor" the saying of a Mass for their living—and dead—friends and relatives. All this is entirely contrary to Christ's institution of the Lord's Supper. He gave the Church this Sacrament as a gift and blessing, to be used in faith by the people of God. See chart, p. 245. (See also Ap XXIV; SA III II; FC Ep X and SD X.)

———————

Our churches are falsely accused of abolishing the Mass. The Mass is held among us 1 and celebrated with the highest reverence. Nearly all the usual ceremonies are also pre- 2 served, except that the parts sung in Latin are interspersed here and there with German hymns. These have been added to teach the people. For ceremonies are needed for this 3 reason alone, that the uneducated be taught what they need to know about Christ. Not 4 only has Paul commanded that a language understood by the people be used in church (1 Corinthians 14:2, 9), but human law has also commanded it. All those able to do so 5 partake of the Sacrament together. This also increases the reverence and devotion of public worship. No one is admitted to the Sacra- 6 ment without first being examined. The peo- 7 ple are also advised about the dignity and use of the Sacrament, about how it brings great consolation to anxious consciences, so that they too may learn to believe God and to ex-

8 pect and ask from Him all that is good. This worship pleases God (Colossians 1:9–10). Such use of the Sacrament nourishes true

9 devotion toward God. Therefore, it does not appear that the Mass is more devoutly celebrated among our adversaries than among us.

10 It is clear that for a long time the most public and serious complaint among all good people is that the Mass has been made base and profane by using it to gain filthy wealth

11 (1 Timothy 3:3). Everyone knows how great this abuse is in all the churches. They know what sort of men say Masses for a fee or an income, and how many celebrate these Mass-

12 es contrary to canon law. Paul severely threatens those who use the Eucharist in an unworthy manner, "Whoever eats the bread or drinks the cup of the Lord in an unworthy manner will be guilty of profaning the body and blood of the Lord (1 Corinthians 11:27).

13 Therefore, when our priests were warned about this sin, private Masses were discontin-ued among us, since hardly any private Mass-es were celebrated except for the sake of filthy gain.

14 The bishops were not ignorant of these abuses. If they had corrected them in time,

15 there would now be less discord. But until now they have been responsible for many

16 corruptions seeping into the Church. Now, when it is too late, they begin to complain about the Church's troubles. This distur-bance has been caused simply by those abuses that were so open that they could no

17 longer be tolerated. There have been great disagreements about the Mass, that is, the

18 Sacrament. Perhaps the world is being pun-ished for profaning the Mass for such a long time and for tolerating this in the churches for so many centuries by the very

men who were both able and duty-bound to correct this situation. It is written in the 19 Ten Commandments, "The LORD will not hold him guiltless who takes His name in vain" (Exodus 20:7). But since the world 20 began, nothing that God ever ordained seems to have been so abused for filthy wealth as the Mass.

An opinion was added that infinitely in- 21 creased private Masses. It states that Christ, by His passion, made satisfaction for origi-nal sin and instituted the Mass as an offering for daily sins, both venial and mortal. From 22 this opinion has arisen the common belief that the Mass takes away the sins of the liv-ing and the dead simply by performing the outward act. Then they began to argue 23 about whether one Mass said for many is worth as much as special Masses for individ-uals. This resulted in an infinite number of Masses. With this work, people wanted to obtain from God all that they needed, and in the meantime, trust in Christ and true wor-ship were forgotten.

Our teachers have warned that these 24 opinions depart from the Holy Scripture and diminish the glory of the passion of Christ. For Christ's passion was an offering and sat- 25 isfaction, not only for original guilt, but also for all other sins, as it is written, "We have 26 been sanctified through the offering of the body of Jesus Christ once for all" (Hebrews 10:10). Also, "By a single offering He has 27 perfected for all time those who are being sanctified" (Hebrews 10:14). (It is an un-heard-of innovation in the Church to teach that by His death Christ has made satisfac-tion only for original sin and not for all other sin. So it is hoped that everybody will under-stand that this error has been rebuked for good reason.)

Scripture teaches that we are justified 28 before God, through faith in Christ, when

29 we believe that our sins are forgiven for Christ's sake. Now if the Mass takes away the sins of the living and the dead simply by performing it, justification comes by doing Masses, and not of faith. Scripture does not allow this.

30 But Christ commands us, "Do this in remembrance of Me" (Luke 22:19). Therefore, the Mass was instituted so that those who use the Sacrament should remember, in faith, the benefits they receive through Christ and how their anxious consciences

31 are cheered and comforted. To remember Christ is to remember His benefits. It means to realize that they are truly offered to us.

32 It is not enough only to remember history. (The Jewish people and the ungodly also re-

33 member this.) Therefore, the Mass is to be used for administering the Sacrament to those that need consolation. Ambrose says, "Because I always sin, I always need to take the medicine."

34 Because the Mass is for the purpose of giving the Sacrament, we have Communion every holy day, and if anyone desires the Sacrament, we also offer it on other days, when it is given to all who ask for it. This cus-

35 tom is not new in the Church. The Fathers before Gregory make no mention of any private Mass, but they speak a lot about the

36 common Mass, or Communion. Chrysostom says "that the priest stands daily at the altar, inviting some to the Communion and keep-

37 ing back others." It appears from the ancient council decisions that one person celebrated the Mass from whom all the other presbyters and deacons received the body of the Lord.

38 The records of the decisions of the Council of Nicaea state, "Let the deacons, according to their order, receive the Holy Communion after the presbyters, from the bishop or from

39 a presbyter." Paul, in 1 Corinthians 11:33, has this command in regard to Communion:

"wait for one another" so that there may be a common participation.

40 Therefore, since the Mass among us follows the example of the Church, taken from the Scripture and the Fathers, we are confident that it cannot be disapproved. This is especially so because we keep the public ceremonies, which are for the most part similar to those previously in use. Only the number of Masses differs. Without a doubt, these might be reduced in a helpful way, because of very great and clear abuses. For in older

41 times, even in churches attended the most often, the Mass was not celebrated every day, as the *Tripartite History* (Book 9, chap. 33) testifies, "In Alexandria, every Wednesday and Friday the Scriptures are read, and the doctors expound them, and all things are done, except the solemn rite of Communion."

## ARTICLE XXV

# Confession

The practice of private Confession and Absolution with one's pastor has fallen out of use in many Lutheran congregations. This was never Luther's intention. Neither was private Confession and Absolution abandoned during the first two centuries of Lutheran history. What the Lutheran Reformation corrected were the false teachings about Confession. Problems arose in the Church when teachings about Confession made "satisfactions" such a prominent part of it. When people were told to do certain activities (e.g., repeating the Hail Mary or doing acts of contrition) to "make up" for their sins, Christ's Gospel was overshadowed, if not completely hidden. Lutheranism, therefore, did away with the anti-biblical teaching about satisfaction for sins and the requirement that people try to remember and confess each sin committed.

(See also SA III VIII; LC V, An Exhortation to Confession.)

––––––––––

1   Confession in the churches is not abolished among us. The body of the Lord is not usually given to those who have not been examined (1 Corinthians 11:27–28) and absolved.
2   The people are very carefully taught about faith in the Absolution. Before, there was profound silence about faith.
3   Our people are taught that they should highly prize the Absolution as being God's voice and pronounced by God's command.
4   The Power of the Keys (Matthew 16:19) is set forth in its beauty. They are reminded what great consolation it brings to anxious consciences and that God requires faith to believe such Absolution as a voice sounding from heaven (e.g., John 12:28–30). They are taught that such faith in Christ truly obtains and receives the forgiveness of sins.
5   Before, satisfactions were praised without restraint, but little was said about faith, Christ's merit, and the righteousness of faith. Therefore, on this point, our churches are by no means to be blamed.
6   Even our adversaries have to concede the point that our teachers have diligently taught the doctrine of repentance and laid it open.
7   Our churches teach that naming every sin is not necessary and that consciences should not be burdened with worry about naming every sin. It is impossible to recount all sins, as Psalm 19:12 testifies: "Who can discern his errors?"
8   Also Jeremiah 17:9, "The heart is deceitful above all things, and desperately sick; who can understand it?"
9   If only sins that can be named are forgiven, consciences could never find peace. For many sins cannot be seen or remembered.
10   The ancient writers also testify that a listing of sins is not necessary.
11   For in the Decrees, Chrysostom is quoted. He says,

I do not say that you should make your sins known in public, nor that you should accuse yourself before others, but I would have you obey the prophet who says, 'Make known your ways before God' [Psalm 37:5]. Therefore, confess your sins before God, the true Judge, with prayer. Tell your errors, not with the tongue, but with the memory of your conscience, and so forth.

12   And the Gloss (*Of Repentance*, Distinct. V, *Cap. Consideret*) admits that Confession is of human right only.
13   Nevertheless, because of the great benefit of Absolution, and because it is otherwise useful to the conscience, Confession is retained among us.

## ARTICLE XXVI

# The Distinction of Meats

Choosing not to eat particular foods, or any food at all, at particular times or on particular occasions is entirely a matter of Christian freedom. By the time of the Reformation, however, the Church had devised complex regulations commanding abstinence from certain foods on certain days. Church teaching misled people into believing that by following such regulations they merited God's grace and favor. Such a theory is entirely contrary to the Gospel, overturns the all-sufficient merit of Jesus Christ, and replaces Him with human works. Contrived laws such as these placed enormous burdens on the common people, who frequently considered themselves less spiritual than the monks and nuns who adhered to these dietary regulations very closely. Bodily discipline and working to curb one's sinful desires is entirely appropriate and necessary, but never is it to be suggested that such activities earn God's grace. In highlighting the issue of dietary restrictions, the Augsburg Confession once more repeats that Lutherans do not do away with good traditions and practices, such as the order of Bible readings in the Communion Service, but only such things as take away from the Gospel. (See also SA III XV.)

---

1    Not only the people, but also those teaching in the churches, have generally been persuaded to believe in making distinctions between meats, and similar human traditions. They believe these are useful works for meriting grace and are able to make satisfaction
2 for sins. From this there developed the view that new ceremonies, new orders, new holy days, and new fastings were instituted daily. Teachers in the Church required these works as a necessary service to merit grace. They greatly terrified people's consciences when
3 they left any of these things out. Because of this viewpoint, the Church has suffered great damage.
4    First, the chief part of the Gospel—the doctrine of grace and of the righteousness of faith—has been obscured by this view. The Gospel should stand out as the most prominent teaching in the Church, in order that Christ's merit may be well known and faith, which believes that sins are forgiven for Christ's sake, be exalted far above works.
5 Therefore, Paul also lays the greatest stress on this article, putting aside the Law and human traditions, in order to show that Christian righteousness is something other than such works (Romans 14:17). Christian righteousness is the faith that believes that sins
6 are freely forgiven for Christ's sake. But this doctrine of Paul has been almost completely smothered by traditions, which have produced the opinion that we must merit grace and righteousness by making distinctions in
7 meats and similar services. When repentance

was taught, there was no mention made of faith. Only works of satisfaction were set forth. And so repentance seemed to stand entirely on these works.

Second, these traditions have hindered  8 God's commandments, because traditions were placed far above God's commandments. Christianity was thought to stand wholly on the observance of certain holy days, rites, fasts, and vestments. These ob-  9 servances won the exalted title of the "spiritual life" and the "perfect life." Meanwhile,  10 God's commandments, according to each one's vocation, or calling, were without honor. These works include a father raising his children, a mother bearing children, a prince governing the commonwealth—these were considered to be worldly and thus imperfect works, far below the glittering observances of the Church. This error greatly tor-  11 mented people with devout consciences. They grieved that they were held in an imperfect state of life, as in marriage, in the office of ruler, or in other civil services. They admired the monks and others like them. They falsely thought that these people's observances were more acceptable to God.

Third, traditions brought great danger to  12 consciences. It was impossible to keep all traditions, and yet people considered these observances to be necessary acts of worship. Gerson writes that many fell into despair,  13 and that some even took their own lives, because they felt that they were not able to satisfy the traditions. All the while, they had never heard about the consoling righteousness of faith and grace. We see that the  14 academics and theologians gather the traditions and seek ways to relieve and ease consciences. They do not free consciences enough, but sometimes entangle them even more! The schools and sermons have been  15 so occupied with gathering these "traditions" that they do not even have enough leisure time to touch on Scripture. They do not pursue the far more useful doctrine of faith, the cross, hope, the dignity of secular affairs, and consolation for severely tested

16 consciences. Therefore, Gerson and some other theologians have complained sadly that because of all this striving after traditions, they were prevented from giving atten-

17 tion to a better kind of doctrine. Augustine forbids that people's consciences should be burdened. He prudently advises Januarius that he must know that they are to be observed as things neither commanded by God nor forbidden, for such are his words.

18    Therefore, our teachers must not be regarded as having taken up this matter rashly or from hatred of the bishops, as some false-

19 ly suspect. There was a great need to warn the churches of these errors that arose from mis-

20 understanding the traditions. The Gospel compels us to insist on the doctrine of grace and the righteousness of faith in the churches. This cannot be understood if people think that they merit grace by observances of their own choice.

21    So our churches have taught that we cannot merit grace or be justified by observing human traditions. We must not think that such observances are necessary

22 acts of worship. Here we add testimonies of Scripture. Christ defends the Apostles who had not observed the usual tradition (Matthew 15:3). This had to do with a matter that was not unlawful, but rather, neither commanded or forbidden. It was similar to the purifications of the Law. He said in Matthew 15:9, "In vain do they worship Me, teaching as doctrines the commandments of

23 men." Therefore, He does not require a useless human service. Shortly after, He adds, "It is not what goes into the mouth that defiles a person, but what comes out of the

mouth; this defiles a person" (Matthew 15:11). So also Paul, in Romans 14:17, "The 24 kingdom of God is not a matter of eating and drinking but of righteousness and peace and joy in the Holy Spirit," and in Colossians 2:16, "Let no one pass judgment 25 on you in questions of food and drink, or with regard to . . . a Sabbath." And again, "If 26 with Christ you died to the elemental spirits of the world, why, as if you were still alive in the world, do you submit to regulations— 'Do not handle, Do not taste, Do not touch'" (Colossians 2:20–21). Peter says, 27 "Why are you putting God to the test by placing a yoke on the neck of the disciples that neither our fathers nor we have been able to bear? But we believe that we will be saved through the grace of the Lord Jesus, just as they will" (Acts 15:10–11). Here 28 Peter forbids burdening consciences with many rites, either from Moses or others. In 29 1 Timothy 4:1–3 Paul calls the prohibition of meats a teaching of demons. It is contrary to the Gospel to institute or do such works thinking that we merit grace through them, or as though Christianity could not exist without such service of God.

Our adversaries object by accusing our 30 teachers of being against discipline and the subduing of the flesh. Just the opposite is true, as can be learned from our teachers' writings. They have always taught that 31 Christians are to bear the cross (Matthew 16:24) by enduring afflictions. This is gen- 32 uine and sincere subduing of the flesh (1 Peter 2:11), to be crucified with Christ through various afflictions. Furthermore, 33 they teach that every Christian ought to train and subdue himself with bodily restraints, or bodily exercises and labors. Then neither over-indulgence nor laziness may tempt him to sin. But they do not teach that we may merit grace or make sat-

34 isfaction for sins by such exercises. Such outward discipline ought to be taught at all
35 times, not only on a few set days. Christ commands, "Watch yourselves lest your hearts be weighed down with dissipation
36 and drunkenness" (Luke 21:34). Also in Matthew 17:21, "This kind never comes out
37 except by prayer and fasting." Paul also says, "I discipline my body and keep it
38 under control" (1 Corinthians 9:27). Here he clearly shows that he was keeping his body under control, not to merit forgiveness of sins by that discipline, but to keep his body in subjection and prepared for spiritual things, for carrying out the duties
39 of his calling. Therefore, we do not condemn fasting in itself (Isaiah 58:3–7), but the traditions that require certain days and certain meats, with peril of conscience, as though such works were a necessary service.
40     Nevertheless, we keep many traditions that are leading to good order (1 Corinthians 14:40) in the Church, such as the order of Scripture lessons in the Mass and
41 the chief holy days. At the same time, we warn people that such observances do not justify us before God, and that it is not sinful if we omit such things, without causing
42 offense. The Fathers knew of such freedom
43 in human ceremonies. In the East they kept Easter at another time than at Rome. When the Romans accused the Eastern Church of schism, they were told by others that such practices do not need to be the
44 same everywhere. Irenaeus says, "Diversity concerning fasting does not destroy the harmony of faith." Pope Gregory says, in Dist. XII, that such diversity does not violate the
45 unity of the Church. In the *Tripartite History*, Book 9, many examples of different rites are gathered, and the following statement is made:

It was not the mind of the apostles to enact rules concerning holy days, but to preach godliness and a holy life.

## ARTICLE XXVII

# Monastic Vows

This article has in view Martin Luther's experience in the monastery, along with what other former monks had to say about life in the cloister. The idea that a person should hide himself behind the walls of a monastery, and perform spiritual works to make himself more worthy of God's favor, has no biblical justification at all. During the Middle Ages, many common people believed that only priests, monks, or nuns were truly performing spiritual work. But such a view contradicts God's Word, which teaches how all of life is an opportunity to serve God—giving Him glory by serving our neighbor. Even today, it is assumed that activities at church are somehow of greater value than the common, everyday duties life requires of us. This article extols such biblical duties as being a faithful husband, wife, son, or daughter, and takes great care to reject monasticism and explain how harmful and dangerous it is for those who are entrapped in it. Forcing chastity on those who have not been given this gift is particularly harmful, since many are led to believe they merit God's grace by means of their sacrifice, not the sacrifice of Christ. (See also Ap XXVII; SA III XIV.)

It will be easier to understand what we 1 teach about monastic vows by considering the state of the monasteries and how many things were done every day contrary to canon law. In Augustine's time they were 2 free associations. Later, when discipline was corrupted, vows were added for the purpose of restoring discipline, as in a carefully

3 planned prison. Gradually, many other reg-
4 ulations were added besides vows. These binding rules were laid upon many before the lawful age, contrary to canon law.

5    Many entered monastic life through ignorance. They were not able to judge their own strength, though they were old enough.
6 They were trapped and compelled to remain, even though some could have been freed by
7 the kind provision of canon law. This was more the case in convents of women than of monks, although more consideration should have been shown the weaker sex (1 Peter 3:7).
8 This rigor displeased many good people before this time, who saw that young men and women were thrown into convents for a living. They saw what unfortunate results came of this procedure, how it created scandals, and what snares were cast upon consciences!
9 They were sad that the authority of canon law in so great a matter was utterly set aside
10 and despised. In addition to all these evil things, a view of vows was added that displeased even the more considerate monks. They taught that monastic vows were equal
11 to Baptism. They taught that a monastic life merited forgiveness of sins and justification
12 before God. Yes, they even added that the monastic life not only merited righteousness before God, but even greater merit, since it was said that the monastic life not only kept God's basic law, but also the so-called "evangelical counsels."
13    So they made people believe that the profession of monasticism was far better than Baptism, and that the monastic life was more meritorious than that of rulers, pastors, and others, who serve in their calling according to God's commands, without any man-
14 made services. None of these things can be denied. This is all found in their own books about monasticism.

How did all this come about in monas- 15
teries? At one time they were schools of theology and other branches of learning, producing pastors and bishops for the benefit of the Church. Now it is another thing. It is needless to go over what everyone knows. Before, they came together for the sake of 16 learning, now they claim that monasticism is a lifestyle instituted to merit grace and righteousness. They even preach that it is a state of perfection! They put monasticism far above all other kinds of life ordained by God. We have mentioned all these things without 17 hateful exaggeration so that our teachers' doctrine on monasticism may be better understood.

First, concerning monks who marry, our 18 teachers say that it is lawful for anyone who is not suited for the single life to enter into marriage. Monastic vows cannot destroy what God has commanded and ordained. God's commandment is this, "Because of the 19 temptation to sexual immorality, each man should have his own wife" (1 Corinthians 7:2). It is not just a command given by God. 20 God has created and ordained marriage for those who are not given an exception to natural order by God's special work. This is what is taught according to the text in Genesis 2:18, "It is not good that the man should be alone." Therefore, those who obey this com- 21 mand and ordinance of God do not sin.

What objection can be raised to this? Let 22 people praise the obligation of a monastic vow as much as they want, but they will never be able to destroy God's commandment by means of a monastic vow. Canon 23 law teaches that superiors can make exceptions to monastic vows; how much less are such monastic vows in force that are contrary to God's commandments!

If, in fact, an obligation to a monastic 24 vow could never be changed for any reason,

George, Margrave of Brandenburg (1484–1543)

A courageous ally of John the Steadfast. Stood up to the emperor at the Diet of Augsburg, telling Charles he would sooner have his head cut off than deny Christ and His Word. Also called George the Pious.

the Roman popes could never have granted exceptions to the vows. For it is not lawful for someone to make an exception to what is

25 truly from God. The Roman pontiffs have wisely judged that mercy is to be observed in these monastic obligations. That is why we read that many times they have made special arrangements and exceptions with monastic

26 vows. The case of the King of Aragon, who was called back from the monastery, is well known, and there are also examples in our own times.

27    In the second place, why do our adversaries exaggerate the obligation or effect of a vow when, at the same time, they do not have anything to say about the nature of the

28 vow itself? A vow should be something that is possible; it should be a decision that is made freely and after careful deliberation. We all know how possible perpetual chasti-

29 ty actually is in reality, and just how few people actually do take this vow freely and deliberately! Young women and men, before they are able to make their own decision about this, are persuaded, and sometimes even forced, to take the vow of chastity.

30 Therefore, it is not fair to insist so rigorously on the obligation. Everyone knows that taking a vow that is not made freely and deliberately is against the very nature of a true vow.

31    Most canonical laws overturn vows made before the age of fifteen. Before that age a person does not seem able to make a wise judgment and to decide to make a lifelong com-

32 mitment like this. There is another canon law that adds even more years to this limit, showing that the vow of chastity should not be made before the age of eighteen. So which of

33 these two canon laws should we follow? Most people leaving the monastery have a valid excuse, since they took their vows before they were fifteen or eighteen.

34    Finally, even though it might be possible

to condemn a person who breaks a vow, it does not follow that it is right to dissolve such a person's marriage. Augustine denies 35 that they ought to be dissolved (XXVII. Quaest. I, Cap. *Nuptiarum*). Augustine's authority should not be taken lightly, even though some wish to do so today.

Although it appears that God's com- 36 mand about marriage delivers many from their vows, our teachers introduce another argument about vows to show that they are void. Every service of God, established and chosen by people to merit justification and grace, without God's commandment, is wicked. For Christ says in Matthew 15:9, "In vain do they worship Me, teaching as doctrines the commandments of men." Paul 37 teaches everywhere that righteousness is not to be sought in self-chosen practices and acts of worship, devised by people. Righteousness comes by faith to those who believe that they are received by God into grace for Christ's sake.

It is clear for all to see that the monks 38 have taught that services made up by people make satisfaction for sins and merit grace and justification. What else is this than detracting from Christ's glory and hiding and denying the righteousness that comes through faith? Therefore, it follows that 39 monastic vows, which have been widely taken, are wicked services of God and, consequently, are void. For a wicked vow, taken 40 against God's commandment, is not valid; for (as the Canon says) no vow ought to bind people to wickedness.

Paul says, "You are severed from Christ, 41 you who would be justified by the law; you have fallen away from grace" (Galatians 5:4). Therefore, anyone wanting to be justified by 42 his vows makes Christ useless and falls from grace. Anyone who tries to connect justifica- 43 tion to monastic vows bases his justification on his own works, which properly belongs to Christ's glory.

44 It cannot be denied that the monks have taught that they were justified and merited forgiveness of sins by means of their vows and observances. Indeed, they even invented greater absurdities, saying that they could 45 give others a share in their works. If anyone wanted to make more of this point, to make our opponents look even worse, even more things could be mentioned, things that even 46 the monks are ashamed of now. And on top of all this, the monks persuaded people that the services that they invented were a state of 47 Christian perfection. What else is this other 48 than assigning our justification to works? It is no light offense in the Church to set before the people a service invented by people, without God's commandment, and then to teach them that such service justifies. For the righteousness of faith, which ought to be the highest teaching in the Church, is hidden when these "wonderful" and "angelic" forms of worship, with their show of poverty, humility, and celibacy, are put in front of people.

49 God's precepts, and God's true service, are hidden when people hear that only monks are in a state of perfection. True Christian perfection is to fear God from the heart, to have great faith, and to trust that for Christ's sake we have a God who has been reconciled (2 Corinthians 5:18–19). It means to ask for and expect from God His help in all things with confident assurance that we are to live according to our calling in life, being diligent in outward good works, serv-50 ing in our calling. This is where true perfection and true service of God is to be found. It does not consist in celibacy or in begging or 51 in degrading clothes. The people come up with all sorts of harmful opinions based on 52 the false praise of monastic life. They hear celibacy praised without measure and feel guilty about living in marriage. They hear 53 that only beggars are perfect, and so they keep their possessions and do business with guilty consciences. They hear that it is an 54 even higher work, a Gospel-counsel, not to seek revenge. So some in private life are not afraid to take revenge, for they hear that it is but a counsel and not a commandment. Others come to the conclusion that a Chris-55 tian cannot rightly hold a civil office or be a ruler.

There are on record examples of men 56 who hid themselves in monasteries because they wanted to forsake marriage and participation in society. They called this fleeing 57 from the world, and said they were seeking a kind of life that would be more pleasing to God. They did not realize that God ought to be served according to the commandments that He Himself has given, not in commandments made up by people. Only a life that 58 has God's commandment is good and perfect. It is necessary to teach the people about 59 these things.

Before our times, Gerson rebukes the 60 monks' error about perfection. He testifies that in his day it was a new saying that the monastic life is a state of perfection. So 61 many wicked opinions are inherent in monastic vows—that they justify, that they cause Christian perfection, that they make it possible to keep the counsels and commandments, that they are works over and above God's commandments. All these things are 62 false and empty. They make monastic vows null and void.

## ARTICLE XXVIII

# Church Authority

Article XXVIII expands on Articles V and XIV. What authority, or power, do bishops have in the Church? Over the course of centuries, bishops had become not merely Church leaders, but political figures as well, claiming the right to govern both Church and State and to make and enforce laws in both realms. By returning to a biblical understanding of *church,* the Augsburg Confession clarifies that the true authority, or power, of bishops is the preaching of the Gospel, the forgiving and withholding of forgiveness of sins, and the administering of the Sacraments. The Church is not to interfere in the government, but is to keep its focus on the Gospel. This article is the foundation for the Lutheran understanding of the two kingdoms: God's work and rule in the world by means of the Church (the kingdom or regiment of the right hand) and the State (the kingdom or regiment of the left hand). Bishops, or pastors, have authority in the Church only to forgive sins in the name of Christ, to reject false doctrine and reprove those who uphold it, and to exclude persons who refuse to repent of open and manifest sin. This article, like the others, places the focus on the chief teaching of the Gospel: we are justified by God's grace through faith in Christ alone. (See also Ap XXVIII; SC Table of Duties.)

---

1   There has been great controversy about the power of the bishops, in which some have terribly confused the power of the Church
2   with the power of the State. This confusion has produced great war and riot. All the while the popes, claiming the Power of the Keys, have instituted new services and burdened consciences with Church discipline and excommunication. But they have also tried to transfer the kingdoms of this world to the Church by taking the Empire away
3   from the emperor. Learned and godly people have condemned these errors in the Church for a long time. Therefore, our
4   teachers, in order to comfort people's consciences, were constrained to show the difference between the authority of the Church and the authority of the State. They taught that both of them are to be held in reverence and honor, as God's chief blessings on earth, because they have God's command.

5   Our teachers' position is this: the authority of the Keys (Matthew 16:19), or the authority of the bishops—according to the Gospel—is a power or commandment of God, to preach the Gospel, to forgive and retain sins, and to administer Sacraments.
6   Christ sends out His apostles with this command, "As the Father has sent Me, even so I am sending you . . . Receive the Holy Spirit. If you forgive the sins of anyone, they are forgiven; if you withhold forgiveness from anyone, it is withheld" (John 20:21–22). And in
7   Mark 16:15, Christ says, "Go . . . proclaim the Gospel to the whole creation."

8   This authority is exercised only by teaching or preaching the Gospel and administering the Sacraments, either to many or to individuals, according to their calling. In this way are given not only bodily, but also eternal things: eternal righteousness, the Holy Spirit, and eternal life. These things cannot
9   reach us except by the ministry of the Word and the Sacraments, as Paul says, "The Gospel . . . is the power of God for salvation to everyone that believes" (Romans 1:16). Therefore, the Church has the authority to
10   grant eternal things and exercises this authority only by the ministry of the Word. So it does not interfere with civil government anymore than the art of singing interferes with civil government. For civil government
11   deals with other things than the Gospel does. Civil rulers do not defend minds, but bodies and bodily things against obvious injuries. They restrain people with the sword and

physical punishment in order to preserve civil justice and peace (Romans 13:1–7).

12 Therefore, the Church's authority and the State's authority must not be confused. The Church's authority has its own commission to teach the Gospel and to administer the

13 Sacraments (Matthew 28:19–20). Let it not break into the office of another. Let it not transfer the kingdoms of this world to itself. Let it not abolish the laws of civil rulers. Let it not abolish lawful obedience. Let it not interfere with judgments about civil ordinances or contracts. Let it not dictate laws to civil

14 authorities about the form of society. As Christ says, "My kingdom is not of this

15 world" (John 18:36). Also, "Who made Me a judge or arbitrator over you?" (Luke 12:14).

16 Paul also says, "Our citizenship is in heaven"

17 (Philippians 3:20). And, "The weapons of our warfare are not of the flesh but have divine power to destroy strongholds" (2 Corinthians 10:4).

18 This is how our teachers distinguish between the duties of these two authorities. They command that both be honored and acknowledged as God's gifts and blessings.

19 If bishops have any authority of the State, this is not because they are bishops. In other words, it is not by the Gospel's commission. It is an authority they have received from kings and emperors for the purpose of administering the civil affairs of what belongs to them in society. This is another office, not the ministry of the Gospel.

20 Therefore, when a question arises about the bishops' jurisdiction, civil authority must be distinguished from the Church's jurisdic-

21 tion. Again, the only authority that belongs to the bishops is what they have according to the Gospel, or by divine right, as they say. For they have been given the ministry of the Word and Sacraments. They have no other authority according to the Gospel than the authority to forgive sins, to judge doctrine, to reject doctrines contrary to the Gospel, and to exclude from the communion of the Church wicked people, whose wickedness is known. They cannot exclude people with human force, but simply by the Word. Ac-

22 cording to this Gospel authority, as a matter of necessity, by divine right, congregations must obey them, for Luke 10:16 says, "The one who hears you hears Me." But when

23 they teach or establish anything against the Gospel, then the congregations are forbidden by God's command to obey them.

> Beware of false prophets. (Matthew 7:15)

> But even if we or an angel from heav-  24
> en should preach to you a Gospel
> contrary to the one we preached to
> you, let him be accursed. (Galatians
> 1:8)

> For we cannot do anything against  25
> the truth, but only for the truth . . .
> the authority that the Lord has given  26
> me for building up, and not for tear-
> ing down. (2 Corinthians 13:8–10)

The Canonical Laws also command this  27
(II. Q. VII. Cap., *Sacerdotes*, and Cap. *Oves*)
And Augustine writes:  28

> Neither must we submit to catholic
> bishops if they chance to err, or hold
> anything contrary to the canonical
> Scriptures of God. (*Contra Petiliani
> Epistolam*)

If the bishops have any other authority or  29
jurisdiction, in hearing and judging certain cases, as of matrimony or of tithes, they have this authority only by human right. If the bishops do not carry out their duties in these areas, the princes are bound, even if they do not want to, to dispense justice to their subjects in order to maintain peace.

There is also a dispute about whether or  30

not bishops, or pastors, have the right to introduce ceremonies in the Church, and to make laws about meats, holy days, and grades, that is, orders of ministers, and so on. 31 Those who say that the bishops do have this right refer to this testimony of Christ in John 16:12–13, "I still have many things to say to you, but you cannot bear them now. When the Spirit of truth comes, He will guide you 32 into all the truth." They also refer to the example of the apostles, who commanded that Christians abstain from blood and from 33 things strangled (Acts 15:29). They refer to the Sabbath day as having been changed into the Lord's Day, contrary to the Decalog, as they understand it. In fact, they make more of the supposed change of the Sabbath day than any other example they can think of. They say that the Church's authority is so great, it has even done away with one of the Ten Commandments.

34   But on this question, for our part (as we have shown earlier) we teach that bishops have no authority to decree anything against the Gospel. The Canonical Laws 35 teach the same thing (Dist. IX). It is against Scripture to establish or require the observance of any traditions for the purpose of making satisfaction for sins, or to merit 36 grace and righteousness. When we try to merit justification by observing such things, we cause great harm to the glory of Christ's 37 merit. It is quite clear that by such beliefs, traditions have almost multiplied to an infinite degree in the Church, while at the same time, the doctrine about faith and the righteousness through faith has been suppressed. Gradually more holy days were made, fasts appointed, new ceremonies and services in honor of saints instituted. Those responsible for such things thought that by 38 these works they were meriting grace. So the Penitential Canons increased. We still see some traces of this in the satisfactions.

Those who establish such traditions are 39 acting contrary to God's command when they locate sin in foods, days, and similar things. They burden the Church with bondage to the Law, as if there needs to be something similar to the services commanded in Leviticus (chapters 1–7) in order to merit justification. They say that Christ has committed the arrangement of such services to the apostles and bishops. They have written about the 40 Law of Moses in such a way that the popes have been mislead to some degree. This is 41 how they have burdened the Church, by making it a mortal sin—even if nobody else is offended—to do manual labor on holy days, or to skip the canonical hours, or that certain foods dirty the conscience, or that fasting is a work that appeases God. Or they say that, in a reserved case, sin can only be forgiven by the person who reserved the case, even though canon law speaks only of reserving the ecclesiastical penalty, not the guilt.

Who has given the bishops the right to 42 lay these traditions on the Church, by which they snare consciences? In Acts 15:10, Peter forbids us from putting a yoke on the neck of the disciples, and Paul says in 2 Corinthians 13:10 that the authority given to him was for edification, not for destruction. Why do the adversaries increase sins with their traditions?

There are clear testimonies that forbid 43 creating traditions in such a way as to suggest that they merit grace or are necessary to salvation. Paul says in Colossians 2:16, "There- 44 fore let no one pass judgment on you in questions of food and drink, or with regard to a festival or a new moon or a Sabbath." And later: 45

If with Christ you died to the elemental spirits of the world, why, as if you were still alive in the world, do you submit to regulations—'Do not handle, Do not taste, Do not touch' (referring to things that all perish as they are used)—according to human precepts and teachings? These have indeed an appearance of wisdom. (Colossians 2:20–23)

46  Also in Titus 1:14 he openly forbids traditions with these words: "not devoting themselves to Jewish myths and the commands of people who turn away from the truth."

47  In Matthew 15:14, Christ says of those who require traditions, "Let them alone; they 48  are blind guides." In verse 13 He rejects such services: "Every plant that My heavenly Father has not planted will be rooted up."

49  If bishops have the right to burden churches with infinite traditions, and to snare consciences, why does Scripture so often forbid making and listening to traditions? Why does it call them "teachings of demons" (1 Timothy 4:1)? Did the Holy Spirit warn of these things in vain?

50  Therefore, ordinances instituted as though they are necessary, or with the view that they merit grace, are contrary to the Gospel. Therefore, it follows that it is not lawful for any bishop to institute and require 51  such services. It is necessary that the doctrine of Christian freedom be preserved in the churches. In other words, the bondage of the Law is not necessary in order to be justified, as it is written in the Epistle to the Galatians, "do not submit again to a yoke of slav- 52  ery" (5:1). It is necessary for the chief article of the Gospel to be preserved, namely that we obtain grace freely by faith in Christ, and not by certain observances or acts of worship devised by people.

53  What, then, are we to think of the Sunday rites, and similar things, in God's house? We answer that it is lawful for bishops, or pas-

tors, to make ordinances so that things will be done orderly in the Church, but not to teach that we merit grace or make satisfaction for sins. Consciences are not bound to regard them as necessary services and to think that it is a sin to break them without offense to others. So in 1 Corinthians 11:5, Paul concludes 54  that women should cover their heads in the congregation and in 1 Corinthians 14:30, that interpreters be heard in order in the church, and so on.

55  It is proper that the churches keep such ordinances for the sake of love and tranquility, to avoid giving offense to another, so that all things be done in the churches in order, and without confusion (1 Corinthians 14:40; comp. Philippians 2:14). It is 56  proper to keep such ordinances just so long as consciences are not burdened to think that they are necessary to salvation, or to regard it as sin if they are changed without offending others. For instance, no one will say that a woman sins who goes out in public with her head uncovered, as long as no offense is given.

57  This kind of ordinance in the Church is observing the Lord's Day, Easter, Pentecost, and similar holy days and rites. It is a great 58  error for anyone to think that it is by the authority of the Church that we observe the Lord's Day as something necessary, instead of the Sabbath Day. Scripture itself has abol- 59  ished the Sabbath Day (Colossians 2:16–17). It teaches that since the Gospel has been revealed, all the ceremonies of Moses can be omitted. Yet, because it was necessary to ap- 60  point a certain day for the people to know when they ought to come together, it appears that the Church designated the Lord's Day (Revelation 1:10) for this purpose. This day seems to have been chosen all the more for this additional reason: so people might have an example of Christian freedom and might

know that keeping neither the Sabbath nor any other day is necessary.

61 There are monstrous debates about changing the law, ceremonies of the new law, and changing the Sabbath Day. They have all sprung from the false belief that in the Church there must be something similar to the services set forth in Leviticus (1–7), and that Christ had commissioned the apostles and bishops to come up with new

62 ceremonies necessary to salvation. These errors crept into the Church when the righteousness that comes through faith was

63 not taught clearly enough. Some debate whether or not keeping the Lord's Day is not a divine right, but similar to it. They prescribe the extent to which is it is lawful

64 to work on holy days. What else are such disputes except traps for the conscience? Even when they try to modify the traditions, nobody will understand the modifications as long as the opinion remains that these traditions are necessary and must remain. There the righ- teousness of faith and Christian freedom is not known.

65 In Acts 15:20, the apostles commanded to abstain from blood. Who observes this now? Those who choose to eat blood do not sin, for not even the apostles themselves wanted to burden consciences with bondage to traditions. They forbid the eating of the blood to

66 avoid giving offense. For in this decree we must always keep in mind what the aim of the Gospel is.

67 Scarcely any canon laws are kept with exactness. From day to day many go out of use, even among those who are the most zealous

68 advocates of traditions. In order to treat the conscience properly, we must realize that canon laws are to be kept without regarding them as necessary. No harm is done to the conscience even though traditions may go out of use.

69 The bishops might easily retain the legitimate obedience of the people if they would not insist upon the observance of traditions that cannot be kept with a good conscience. Instead, they command celibacy and accept

70 no preachers—unless they swear that they will not teach the Gospel's pure doctrine.

71 The churches are not asking the bishops to restore concord at the expense of their honor, even though it would be proper for good pastors to do this. They ask only that

72 the bishops release unjust burdens that are new and have been received contrary to the custom of the universal Church. It may be

73 that in the beginning there were plausible reasons for some of these ordinances, but they are not adapted to later times. It is also

74 clear that some were adopted through erroneous ideas. Therefore, it would be in keeping with the popes' mercy to change them now. Such a modification does not shake the Church's unity. Many human traditions have been changed over time, as the canons themselves show. But if it is impossible for the ad-

75 versaries to change those traditions, which they say is sinful to change, we must follow the apostolic rule, which commands us to "obey God rather than men" (Acts 5:29).

76 In 1 Peter 5:3, Peter forbids bishops to be

77 lords and rule over the churches. It is not our intention to take oversight away from the bishops. We ask only this one thing, that they allow the Gospel to be taught purely, and that they relax a few observances that they claim it is sinful to change. If they will not give

78 anything up, it is for them to decide how they will give an account to God for causing schism by their stubbornness.

## Conclusion

1 These are the chief articles that seem to be in controversy. We could have mentioned more abuses. But here we have set forth only

the chief points in order to avoid making this Confession too long. From these chief points 2 the rest may be easily judged. There have been, for example, great complaints about indulgences, pilgrimages, and the abuse of excommunication. Our parishes have been troubled in many ways by dealers in indulgences. There were endless arguments between the pastors and the monks about who has the right in parishes to hear confessions, do funerals, give sermons on extraordinary 3 occasions, and innumerable other things. We have passed over such issues so that the chief points in this matter, briefly set forth, might 4 be more easily understood. Nothing has been said or brought up for the rebuke of 5 anyone. We have mentioned only those things we thought it was necessary to talk about so that it would be understood that in doctrine and ceremonies we have received nothing contrary to Scripture or the Church universal. It is clear that we have been very careful to make sure no new ungodly doctrine creeps into our churches.

6 We present these articles in accordance with Your Imperial Majesty's edict, in order to show our Confession and let people see a summary of our teachers' doctrine. 7 If there is anything that anyone might desire in this Confession, we are ready, God willing, to present more thorough information according to the Scriptures.

| | |
|---|---|
| Your Imperial Majesty's faithful subjects: | 8 |
| John, Duke of Saxony, Elector. | 9 |
| George, Margrave of Brandenburg. | 10 |
| Ernest, Duke of Lüneberg. | 11 |
| Philip, Landgrave of Hesse. | 12 |
| John Frederick, Duke of Saxony. | 13 |
| Francis, Duke of Lüneberg. | 14 |
| Wolfgang, Prince of Anhalt. | 15 |
| Senate and Magistracy of Nürnberg. | 16 |
| Senate of Reutlingen. | 17 |

ᏬᎷᏮᎶ

# UNDERSTANDING INDULGENCES

The following is a translation of an actual indulgence administered in 1515 by Albert, the Archbishop of Mainz and Magdeburg. It was designed to raise money for the completion of St. Peter's Cathedral in Rome. It guarantees forgiveness and provides for the reception of Communion, even when a person's territory was under a Communion ban (interdict) by the pope. For example,

> Simply visit the church or churches of your choice on a day in Lent or another holiday . . . you will obtain as many indulgences and forgiveness of sins as if you had visited the church or churches in Rome on that same day.

During an interdict, a bishop or pope would not permit Masses to be said or any other Sacraments to be administered in any churches of a given territory. Often interdicts were issued whenever the monarch of a country defied Church authority. It was an effective weapon used by the Medieval Church to keep monarchs in line. The common people, in fear of dying outside of a state of grace, would frequently pressure their king to yield to the Church's demands.

---

# We Grant Indulgence

Albert, by the grace of God and of the Apostolic See: Archbishop of Mainz and Magdeburg, Administrator of the churches of Halberstadt, Primate of Germany, Arch-Chancellor and Elector-Prince of the Holy Roman Empire, Duke of Mark Brandenburg, Stettin, Pomerania, the Cashubians, and Slavs, Burggrave of Nürnberg, Prince of Rugia. Greetings in the Lord to those dear to us in Christ.

You have agreed to undertake an act of sincere and fervent devotion for the Church of Rome. You have given to the building of the Basilica of St. Peter, an immense undertaking requiring skillful production. Your contribution will not only benefit that city, but it also shows that you are obedient to our commands.

Since you have given generously to our cause, you encourage and persuade us to agree to [fulfill] your requests. You have long and fervently asked us that you might have an altar stone on which Mass can be said. You have been looking for an altar where Mass can be said without the meddling of foreign laws; we hereby grant your request.

If you should happen to enter into regions placed under ecclesiastical interdict by the authority of an ordinary bishop, nonetheless, you will not find yourself standing outside the doors of the church, excommunicated as it were. Instead, as long as you live, you will be able to celebrate Mass by yourself, if you are a priest. If you are a layperson, you may have Mass celebrated for you. You may use your own priest or any other priest. It does not matter whether the priest is a diocesan priest or a member of a religious order. This permission extends especially to the Easter Mass, even the mass at sunrise. Of course, you may do this only if you yourself have not committed the sin that caused the land to be placed under the interdict.

You also may get as many indulgences and pardons for sin by visiting a church of your choice as if you had made a pilgrimage to Rome. Simply visit the church or churches of your choice on a day in Lent or another holiday when pilgrims visit the various churches around Rome. By taking a trip to a local church or churches, you will obtain as many indulgences and forgiveness of sins as if you had visited the church or churches in Rome on that same day.

You can also be given full Christian burial, even if you happen to die when your country is under an interdict. Of course, to receive this benefit you must not have committed the sin for which the land has been put under the interdict.

We issue this decree by the apostolic authority given to us by the letter "We Grant Indulgence," written by our Most Holy Lord Leo X, Pope by the grace of God. Nonetheless, please do not use a dispensation of this kind until the day you celebrate Mass or have it celebrated on your behalf. For when our Lord Jesus Christ (who is the radiance of eternal light) is being sacrificed in the liturgy of the altar, it is fitting that it not be done in the darkness of night but in the light. We order that the individual be communed into whose trust the present letter has been given and the seal has been affixed.

Date: In the year of our Lord 1515, on the _____ day of the month of _____, during the pontificate of our aforementioned lord, the Pope.

# THE APOLOGY
# OF THE
# AUGSBURG CONFESSION

Sacrifice of Isaac
From Luther's translation of the Pentateuch, 1523

Article IV of the Apology is the longest and most extensive explanation of the Christian faith's chief article: the doctrine of justification by grace through faith in Christ alone. This doctrine is the heartbeat of the entire Book of Concord. The offering of Isaac, and the ram sacrificed in his place, powerfully foreshadow the sacrifice of Jesus Christ.

# Introduction to the Apology
## of the Augsburg Confession

> Emperor Charles is an excellent man; he hopes to restore unity and peace.
> I don't know whether he will be able to do this, besieged as he is by so many
> demonic monsters.
>
> —Martin Luther to Nicholaus Hausmann
> September 23, 1530 (LW 49:422)

After the public reading and presentation of the Augsburg Confession on June 25, 1530, the Lutherans waited to receive the emperor's reply, which came on August 3. It was read to the Lutherans and soon became known as the *Pontifical Confutation of the Augsburg Confession*. They heard the reply, but were not given a copy of it. Couched in careful diplomatic language, the emperor's message was clear: Back down or else. Further meetings were called for between the Lutherans and the emperor's theologians.

Two series of meeting were held, the first, August 13–21, and the second, August 24. During these meetings, Philip Melanchthon was willing to compromise the Lutheran Confession. However, the Lutheran laymen prevailed and remained firm. In private, Emperor Charles tried everything he could think of to pressure the Lutheran princes to back down. He threatened to exile them from their territories and to seize by force all their property and possessions. Martin Luther, writing from the Coburg castle, encouraged them to stand strong. On September 22, Charles officially declared the Imperial Meeting to be in recess. He stated that the Pontifical Confutation had sufficiently answered the Lutheran Confession and gave the Lutherans until April 15, 1531, to concede to his demands. They refused.

The Lutherans were never given a copy of the Pontifical Confutation, but were ordered to do the following: accept all the conditions it imposed, accept the Confutation's conclusions, make no reply to it, and not allow it to be published. Such outrageous demands were wholly unacceptable to the Lutherans. Fortunately, while the Confutation was being read, professional stenographers were writing the Confutation down, word for word, so they had an accurate transcript of its contents. The Lutheran princes asked Chancellor Brück and Philip Melanchthon to work on a reply. By September 22, a first draft was ready. They tried to give Charles a copy, but he refused to accept it. Then the Lutheran party left Augsburg. Melanchthon began working on a thorough revision of what was called the "Apology of the Augsburg Confession." (The word *apology* in the Greek language, which Melanchthon taught at the university in Wittenberg, means "defense.") Not until 1573 did the Roman Church officially publish the *Confutation of the Augsburg Confession*. This was long after the Council of Trent (1546–63) had formally adopted the Confutation's conclusions.

Melanchthon worked on a thorough revision of the Apology of the Augsburg Confession from the end of September 1530 until April 15, 1531. Melanchthon was firm and confident as he replied to the Roman Church. He had taken courage from the example of the Lutheran laymen at Augsburg and was bolstered by Martin Luther personally, who continued to encourage him to remain strong.

The Apology of the Augsburg Confession is the longest and most detailed confession in the Book of Concord. It carefully works through the Roman response to the Augsburg Confession, refuting errors and setting forth the truth. The driving force in the Apology is the repeated insistence that the Bible's most important and comforting teaching is justification by grace alone, through faith alone, on account of Christ alone. Again and again, Melanchthon returns to this teaching.

The Apology of the Augsburg Confession was first released as Melanchthon's personal opinion, since it was not formally adopted by the Lutheran princes in Augsburg. It soon became popular throughout Lutheran Germany. Justas Jonas, colleague and friend of both Luther and Melanchthon, prepared the German translation of the Apology. In 1531, the Smalcaldic League, an organization of German territories and cities, was formed. A requirement of membership was acceptance of both the Augsburg Confession and the Apology of the Augsburg Confession. In 1533, in a letter to Christians in Leipzig, Luther urged them to "adhere to our [Augsburg] Confession *and apology*." In 1577, the Apology was included in the Formula of Concord's list of doctrinal statements.

Please note that in the longer articles of the Apology some subheads are added for the convenience of the reader.

Justas Jonas (1493–1555)

Justas Jonas was a close friend and ally of Martin Luther. He came to Wittenberg in 1521 to lead the Foundation of All Saints at the Castle Church and helped Luther end this last bastion of Romanism in Wittenberg. With Luther, Bugenhagen, and Melanchthon, Jonas produced the Torgau Articles, a predecessor of the Augsburg Confession. He was at Luther's side when he died in 1546. Jonas translated the Apology into German. (Melanchthon affirmed his work.) He translated many of Luther's Latin writings into German.

## TIMELINE

1530   *Torgau Articles* drafted, March

Augsburg Confession presented to Charles V at Diet of Augsburg, June 25

Meetings concerning *Augsburg Confession*, August

Augsburg Diet ends, September; Lutherans asked to concede by April 15, 1531

1531   *Augsburg Confession* and *Apology* published, April–May; *Apology's* second edition published, September

Smalcaldic League formed, requires acceptance of *Augsburg Confession* and *Apology*

Ulrich Zwingli dies on Swiss battlefield at Kappel am Albis

1532   In exchange for religious tolerance, Protestant princes agree to assist Charles V in war against the Turks until religious issues can be resolved by church council and imperial court

Luther publishes *An Admonition to Prayer against the Turks*, September

1533   English King Henry VIII excommunicated

Luther urges Christians in Leipzig to adhere to *Augsburg Confession* and *Apology*

1534   Luther publishes complete German Bible

Ignatius of Loyola founds Society of Jesus (Jesuits)

1536   Luther, Melanchthon, and Englishmen Edward Fox and Robert Barnes agree to *Wittenberg Articles*; rejected by Zwinglians

John Calvin publishes *Institutes of the Christian Religion*

1538   Luther's *Smalcald Articles* published

## OUTLINE

The outline for the Apology, or "defense," of the Augsburg Confession has two sets of numbers. Neither set is fully in order because of the way Melanchthon responded to the issues presented by the Pontifical Confutation (see introduction above).

The numbers on the left generally correspond with the articles of the Augsburg Confession. However, note that there is no Article VI, XXV, or XXVI in the Apology, since similar articles were treated together. (The article on "New Obedience" was treated with the article on "Justification"; the article on "Confession" was treated with the article on "Repentance"; and the article on "The Distinction of Meats" was treated with the article on the "The Mass.")

The numbers on the right, in parentheses, show which articles were disputed by the Pontifical Confutation. The section on "Confession and Satisfaction" is marked in some editions as Article VI. Note that this second numbering system does not include an Article IX.

Greeting

I. God

II. Original Sin (I)

III. Christ

IV. Justification (II)

  What Is Justifying Faith

  Faith in Christ Justifies

  We Obtain Forgiveness of Sins by Faith Alone in Christ

  Scripture Affirms This Teaching

  The Church Fathers Affirm This Teaching

  The Adversaries Reject This Teaching

V. Love and Fulfilling the Law (III)

  No One Can Keep the Law Perfectly

# THE APOLOGY OF THE AUGSBURG CONFESSION

## Philip Melanchthon Presents His Greeting to the Reader

1    After our princes' Confession was read publicly, certain theologians and monks prepared a "Confutation." His Imperial Majesty had it read in the assembly of the princes. Then he demanded that the princes agree with it.

2    Our princes heard that many articles were not approved, which they could not abandon without offense to conscience. Therefore, they asked for a copy of the Confutation so they could see what the adversaries condemned and refute their arguments.

In such an important matter of religion and the instruction of consciences, they thought that the adversaries would share their writing without any hesitation. But our princes could only get a copy under the most dangerous conditions, which were impossible for them to accept.

3    Negotiations for peace were begun. It was clear that our princes avoided no burden, however grievous, that could be borne without offense to conscience. But the adversaries 4 stubbornly demanded that we approve certain clear abuses and errors. Since we could not do this, His Imperial Majesty again demanded that our princes agree with the Confutation. Our princes refused to do so.

For in a matter of religion, how could our princes agree with a writing they had not seen, especially since they had heard some articles condemned? It was impossible for them, without grievous sin, to approve the adversaries' opinions.

5    They commanded me and some others to prepare an *Apology of the Confession*. This would be set forth for His Imperial Majesty the reasons why we could not receive the Confutation. The adversaries' objections would also be refuted. During the reading 6 [of the Confutation] some of us had taken down the chief points of the topics and arguments. The princes offered this Defense 7 to His Imperial Majesty when they left Augsburg, so that he would know that we were hindered from approving the Confutation by the greatest and most important reasons. But His Imperial Majesty did not receive the offered writing.

Afterward, a decree was published in 8 which the adversaries boast that they have refuted our Confession from the Scriptures.

Reader, you now have our Apology. 9 From it you will understand not only what the adversaries said about our Confession (for we have reported in good faith), but also that—contrary to the clear Scripture of the Holy Spirit—they condemned several articles. That is how far they are from overthrowing our statements by means of the Scriptures.

Originally we drew up the Apology after 10 consulting with others. Yet, as it passed through the press, I made some additions. That is why I give my name, so that no one can complain that the book has been published anonymously.

In these controversies, as far as I was able 11 at all, it has always been my custom to keep the traditional form of doctrine. I did this so that at some time unity could be reached more readily. I am not departing far from this custom now, even though I could justly lead people today even farther away from the opinions of the adversaries.

12   The adversaries are dealing with these issues in a way that shows they are seeking neither truth nor concord, but to drain our blood.

13   I have written with the greatest moderation possible. If any expression appears too severe, I must say that I am arguing with the theologians and monks who wrote the Confutation, not with the emperor or the

14   princes, whom I hold in due esteem. I recently saw the Confutation and noticed how cunningly and slanderously it was written, so that on some points it could deceive even the cautious.

15   Yet I did not discuss all their sophistries, for it would be an endless task. Instead I deal with the chief arguments, so that all nations will have a clear testimony from us that we hold the Gospel of Christ correctly and pi-

16   ously. Disagreement does not delight us, neither are we indifferent to our danger. We readily understand the extent of it when we see how inflamed our adversaries are by bitterness and hatred. Yet we cannot abandon truth that is clear and necessary for the Church.

That is why we believe that troubles and dangers for Christ's glory and the Church's good should be endured. We are confident that God approves our faithfulness to duty. We hope that the judgment of future generations about us will be more just.

17   It is undeniable that many topics of Christian doctrine, whose place in the Church is most important, have been brought to view and explained by our theologians. We are not inclined to repeat here under what sort of opinions, and how dangerously, these topics used to lay buried in the writings of the monks, canonists, and sophistic theologians.

18   We have the public testimony of many good men, who give thanks to God for this great blessing: our Confession teaches many necessary things better than any of our adversaries' books.

19   We will commend our cause to Christ, who will someday judge these controversies. We beg Him to look upon the afflicted and scattered churches and to bring them back to godly and continuous harmony.

# Apology of the Augsburg Confession

## ARTICLE I
## God

Lutherans clearly identify themselves with the historic Church of all times and places by confessing the biblical doctrine of the Holy Trinity and by rejecting the teachings of all those who deny the one, true God: Father, Son, and Holy Spirit. (See the Apostles', Nicene, and Athanasian Creeds; AC I; SA I; SC II; LC II.)

---

1   Our adversaries approve Article I of our Confession, in which we declare that we believe and teach that there is one divine, undivided essence. Yet, there are three distinct persons, of the same divine essence, and co-

2   eternal: Father, Son, and Holy Spirit. We have always taught and defended this article. We believe that it has sure and firm testimonies in Holy Scripture that cannot be overthrown. We constantly affirm that those thinking otherwise are outside of Christ's Church, are idolaters, and insult God.

God Creates the World

The Fall

## ARTICLE II

# Original Sin

By the sixteenth century, Roman theologians had come to view original sin merely as a weakness in human nature. The Scriptures, however, teach that original sin is the absence of original righteousness and the root cause of all sinful thoughts, words, and deeds. Original sin damns a person to hell, the Bible asserts, so clear definitions were needed. Rome sought some way to preserve mankind's ability to choose God's grace and cooperate with it. So it regarded *concupiscence*, the powerfully strong tendency in us to sin, not as sin, but as mere tinder (Latin: fomes), which could ignite into sinful behavior. The Bible, as the Lutherans were concerned to prove, also names as sin our inborn tendency to sin.

Article II of the Apology is essential for understanding what follows in Articles III and IV. Melanchthon points out the key comforting truth of God's Word: In Christ, God removes the condemnation of all sin, including concupiscence. He does so by forgiving us our sins through Christ's blood and by applying to us Christ's righteousness, holiness, and innocence. So, while in this life sin remains, the Holy Spirit continually brings it under check, beats it down and kills it, and works within us to increase and strengthen our faith in God and love for our neighbor. (See AC II; SA III I; FC Ep I and SD I.)

1    The adversaries approve Article II, "Original Sin," But they define original sin in such a way that they actually condemn our definition, which we gave in passing. Here, right at the outset, Your Majesty will discover that the Confutation's writers were lacking not only judgment, but also honesty. We simply wanted to mention the things that original sin includes. But these men, by creating a misleading interpretation, cleverly twist a statement that in itself contains nothing wrong. So they say, "To lack fear of God and to lack faith is actual guilt." Therefore, they deny it is original sin.

Clearly, these sorts of subtleties start in 2 the schools, not in the emperor's council. Even though such sophistry can be easily refuted, we ask that the Augsburg Confession in German be examined, so that all good people will understand that we do not teach anything absurd in this matter. This will free us from the suspicion of teaching something new. For there it is written:

It is further taught that since Adam's fall all human beings, who are naturally conceived, are born in sin. From their mother's womb they are all filled with evil desire and the inclination toward evil. By nature, they have no true fear of God and no true faith in God.

As this passage demonstrates, we teach 3 that those who are born according to the fleshly nature have concupiscence. This means people not only lack fear and trust in God, but also do not even have the power or gifts to produce fear and trust in God. What fault can be found with this point? Indeed, we think that we have explained and defended ourselves well enough to good men. For in this sense the Latin description denies to nature the ability, gifts, and energy to produce fear and trust in God. In adults, we deny the ability actually to do anything truly good. So, when we mention concupiscence, we understand not only the acts or fruit, but also the constant inclination of the nature.

Now we will show more fully that our de- 4 scription agrees with the usual and ancient definition. First, we must show why we prefer to use these words in this place. In their schools, the adversaries confess that "the material" (as they call it) "of original sin is concupiscence." We should not have passed by this fact in framing our definition, precisely because some are offering philosophical speculations in a way that is not appropriate for teachers of religion.

5    Some of them claim that original sin is not a depravity or corruption in human nature, but is just a condition imposed on us as a result of our own mortality. They say that it is not inherent in our nature, but is rather a burden put on us as a result of Adam's sin, not that we have any such depravity of our own. Besides, they add that no one is condemned to eternal death on account of original sin, just as a child born of a slave woman becomes a slave not as a result of any personal fault, but as a result of his mother's condition. 6 To show that this impious opinion is displeasing to us, we used the word *concupiscence*. With the best intention, we have explained this term as "diseases" and said that "the nature of human beings is born corrupt and full of faults."

7    We have not only used the word *concupiscence*, but we have also said that "the fear of God and faith are lacking." We added this comment because the scholastic teachers do not understand the definition of original sin well enough. They take what they received from the Fathers and extend the definition of original sin. They argue that the evil inclination (*fomes*) is a quality (like a blemish) on the body. With their usual folly, they ask whether this quality is caused from the contagiousness of the apple or from the breath of the serpent, and whether medicines can cure the condition. They suppress the main point with such questions. 8 So, when they talk about original sin, they do not mention the more serious faults of human nature, such as

ignorance of God, contempt for God, total lack of fear of God and confidence in God, hatred of God's judgment, fleeing from God when He judges us, despairing of God's grace, putting trust in things of this world, and so forth. The Scholastics do not notice all these diseases that are totally contrary to God's Law. They even say that human nature is entirely capable of loving God above all things and fulfilling God's commandments "according to the substance of the act." These diseases are totally contrary to God's Law, but the Scholastics do not notice them. They do not even realize that they are contradicting themselves. For what else is being able, by 9 one's own strength, to love God above all things and fulfill His commandments except original righteousness? If human nature is so 10 strong that it is able, on its own, to love God above all things, as the Scholastics confidently affirm, what then is original sin? Why do we need Christ's grace if we can be justified as a result of our own righteousness? Why do we need the Holy Spirit if we are strong enough on our own to love God above all things and fulfill God's commandments? Is 11 there anyone who does not realize that our adversaries' ideas are absurd? They recognize the less serious diseases in human nature, but the more serious they do not even acknowledge. Scripture everywhere warns us, as the Prophets constantly complain, about putting our confidence in our human abilities, contempt for God, hating God, and similar faults with which we are born. (See Psalm 13 and other passages, such as Psalm 14:1–3; 140:3; 36:1.) After the Scholastics mixed philosoph- 12 ical speculations about the perfection of nature (the light of reason) with Christian doctrine, they credited more than was possible to the ability of free will. They taught that people are justified before God by philosophical or civic righteousness. We, too, confess that such things are subject to reason, and so to some degree are within our power. However, as a result of their speculations they could not see the inner uncleanness of human na-

13 ture. This can only be evaluated and understood on the basis of God's Word, which the Scholastics do not use very often in their discussions.

14 All of these things are the reason why we made mention of concupiscence in our description of original sin, and why we deny to human nature the ability to fear and trust in God. We wanted to show that original sin contains these diseases: ignorance of God, contempt for God, not having fear and trust in God, the inability to love God. These are the chief faults of human nature because they conflict with the First Table of the Ten Commandments (Exodus 20:3–11).

15 We have not said anything new. The ancient definition of original sin, understood correctly, says precisely the same thing. "Original sin is the absence of original righteousness." But what is righteousness? Here the Scholastics wrangle over philosophical questions. They do not explain what original

16 righteousness is. In the Scriptures, righteousness consists not only in obeying the Second Table of the Ten Commandments (which are about good works in serving our fellowman), but also the First Table, which teaches about fearing God, faith, and loving

17 God. Therefore, original righteousness includes not only physical health in all ways, as they contend (such as pure blood and unimpaired physical ability), but also these gifts: a sure and certain knowledge of God, fear of God, confidence in God, and the desire and

18 ability to give God these things. Scripture testifies this when it says in Genesis 1:27 that man was made in the image and likeness of God. What else was this image and likeness other than that man was created with wis-

dom and righteousness so that he could apprehend God and reflect God? Mankind was given the gift of knowing God, fearing God, and being confident in God. This is how Ire- 19 naeus and Ambrose interpret the likeness of God. Ambrose not only says many things to this effect, but especially declares, "That soul is not, therefore, in the image of God, in which God is not [dwelling] at all times." Paul shows in Ephesians 5:9 and Colossians 20 3:10 that the image of God is the knowledge of God, righteousness, and truth. Lombard is 21 not afraid to say that original righteousness "is the very likeness to God which God implanted in man." We recount the opinions of 22 the ancients, which in no way interfere with Augustine's interpretation of the image.

The ancient definition of original sin is 23 that it is a lack of righteousness. This definition not only denies that mankind is capable of obedience in his body, but also denies that mankind is capable of knowing God, placing confidence in God, fearing and loving God, and certainly also the ability to produce such things. For even the theologians themselves teach in their schools that these are not produced without certain gifts and the aid of grace. In order that the matter may be understood, we say that these gifts are precisely the knowledge of God and fear and confidence in God. From these facts it appears that the ancient definition says precisely the same thing that we say, denying fear and confidence toward God. It denies not only the actions, but also the gifts and ability to produce these acts.

Of equal importance is the definition of 24 original sin found in the writings of Augustine. He is used to defining original sin as concupiscence (wicked desire). He means that when righteousness had been lost, concupiscence came in its place. Since diseased nature cannot fear and love God and believe

God, it seeks and loves carnal things. By nature, when we are secure, we hold God's judgment in contempt. When we are terrified, we hate God's judgment. This is why Augustine includes both the defect and the vicious habit that has come in its place in his

25 definition of original sin. Concupiscence is not only a corruption of physical qualities, but also, in the higher powers, a vicious turning to fleshly things. These people do not realize the contradiction in what they are saying. At the same time, they attribute to mankind a concupiscence that is not entirely destroyed by the Holy Spirit and also the ability to love God above all things.

26 We are right in our description of original sin when we say that it is not being able to believe God and not being able to fear and love God. We are right when we say that it includes concupiscence, which seeks fleshly things contrary to God's Word. This means when it seeks not only the pleasure of the body, but also fleshly wisdom and righteousness. Therefore, it holds God in con-

27 tempt when it trusts in these as good things. It is not only the ancient teachers, but even the more recent teachers (at least the wiser ones among them), who teach that original sin is both the defects I have mentioned and concupiscence. Thomas Aquinas says:

> Original sin includes the loss of original righteousness, and with this a disorderly arrangement of the parts of the soul; therefore, it is not pure loss, but a corrupt habit.

28 Bonaventure says:

> When the question is asked, "What is original sin?" the correct answer is that it is immoderate concupiscence. The correct answer is, also, that it is a lack of the righteousness that is due. And in one of these replies the other is included.

This is also Hugo's opinion when he says 29 that "original sin is ignorance in the mind and concupiscence in the flesh." He is saying that when we are born, we bring with us ignorance of God, unbelief, distrust, contempt, and hatred of God. When he men- 30 tions ignorance, he includes these other things. These opinions also agree with Scripture. Paul sometimes clearly calls it a defect, as in 1 Corinthians 2:14, "The natural person does not accept the things of the Spirit of God." In another place, he calls it concupiscence, "at work in our members to bear fruit for death" (Romans 7:5). We could cite 31 more passages relating to both parts, but when a fact is so clear there is no need of further testimonies. The intelligent reader realizes easily that to be without the fear of God and without faith are more than passive "actual guilt." They are actively abiding defects in our unregenerate nature.

When it comes to original sin, we hold 32 nothing different from either Scripture or the Church catholic. Rather, we cleanse from corruptions and restore to light the most important declarations of Scripture and the Fathers, which have been covered over by the sophistry and controversies of the theologians of our day. It is more than clear that modern theologians do not notice what the Fathers mean when they speak about a "defect." The knowledge of original sin is ab- 33 solutely necessary. The magnitude of Christ's grace cannot be understood unless our diseases are recognized. (Christ says in Matthew 9:12 and Mark 2:17, "Those who are well have no need of a physician.") The entire notion that a person is righteous is mere hypocrisy before God. We must acknowledge that our heart is, by nature, destitute of fear, love, and confidence in God. For this reason 34 the prophet Jeremiah says, "After I was instructed, I slapped my thigh; I was ashamed, and I was confounded" (31:19). Likewise, "I said in my alarm, 'All mankind are liars' " (Psalm 116:11). That is, they do not think correctly about God.

35 Here our adversaries attack Martin Luther because he wrote that "original sin remains after Baptism." They add that this point was justly condemned by Leo X. But His Imperial Majesty will discover a clear slander on this point. Our adversaries know in what sense Luther intended this remark that original sin remains after Baptism. Luther always writes that Baptism removes the guilt of original sin. However, the *material*, as they call it, of the sin (concupiscence) remains. He also adds that the Holy Spirit, given through Baptism, begins to put to death the concupiscence and begins to create

36 new movements within a person. Augustine speaks in the same way when he says, "Sin is forgiven in Baptism, not in such a way that it no longer exists, but so that it is not charged." Here he confesses openly that sin exists. It remains, although it is not counted against us any longer. Augustine's judgment on this point was so agreeable to those who came after him that it is often quoted in the decrees of Church councils. In *Against Julian*, Augustine says:

> The Law, which is in the members, has been overturned by spiritual regeneration and remains in the mortal flesh. It has been overturned because the guilt has been forgiven in the Sacrament, by which believers are born again; but it remains, because it produces desires, against which believers struggle.

37 Our adversaries know that Luther believes and teaches this, and since they cannot deny this, they instead try to pervert his words in an effort to crush an innocent man.

38 They argue that concupiscence is a penalty, but not a sin. Luther maintains that it is a sin. It has been said above that Augustine defines original sin as concupiscence. If they don't like this, then let them argue with Augustine. Besides, Paul says in Romans 7:7, "I 39 would not have known what it is to covet [concupiscence] if the law had not said, 'You shall not covet.' " Likewise, "I see in my members another law waging war against the law of my mind and making me captive to the law of sin that dwells in my members" (Romans 7:23). No amount of sophistry can 40 overthrow these points. They clearly call concupiscence sin, which is not charged against those who are in Christ (Romans 8:1), although by nature it is deserving of death (Romans 6:23) where it is not forgiven. All 41 controversies aside, this is what the Fathers believe. Augustine, in a long discussion, refutes the opinion of those who think that concupiscence in a person is not a fault, but merely an incidental and inconsequential matter just as color of the body or ill health is said to be an adiaphoron, like saying that having a black or white body is neither good nor evil.

But when our adversaries argue that the 42 evil inclination (*fomes*) is an adiaphoron, not only many passages of Scripture, but simply the entire Church, contradict them. Who has ever dared to say that the following things are indifferent matters: doubt about God's wrath, His grace, God's Word, anger at the judgments of God, being provoked because God does not at once deliver one from afflictions, murmuring because the wicked enjoy a better fortune than the good, to be urged on by wrath, lust, the desire for glory, wealth, and so on? Godly people acknowl- 43 edge these things in themselves, as appears in the Psalms and the Prophets. But in the scholastic academies they took from philosophy entirely different ideas: desires and inclinations are neither good nor evil, neither praiseworthy nor worthy of blame. Likewise, that sin is only sin if it is a voluntary action. Philosophers were expressing such ideas about civil righteousness, not about God's judgment. They unwisely add other ideas as well, saying that nature is not evil. Properly understood, we do not reject this idea, but it is not right to take this understanding of what God creates as good and apply it to original sin. This is precisely what we read in the works of the Scholastics, who wrongly mingle philosophy and civil teachings about

44  ethics with the Gospel. These matters were not only disputed in the schools, but as is usually the case, were carried from the schools to the people. That is why these teachings prevailed and nourished confidence in human strength and suppressed the

45  knowledge of Christ's grace. Therefore, Luther wanted to make clear how great the consequences of original sin are and how weak human beings are as a result. So he taught that these remnants of original sin (after Baptism) are not, by nature, unimportant, but that we need Christ's grace so that they are not counted against us as sin. And, to put them to death [mortify them], we need the Holy Spirit (Romans 8:13).

46  The Scholastics minimize sin and punishment when they teach that people can fulfill God's commandments under their own power. But in Genesis, the punishment imposed because of original sin is described differently. For there human nature is subjected not only to death and other bodily evils, but also to the devil's kingdom. In Genesis 3:15, there is this fearful sentence that proclaims, "I will put enmity between you and the woman, and between your offspring and her

47  offspring." Defects and concupiscence are both sin and punishment. Death and other bodily evils, and the dominion of the devil, are properly understood to be punishments. Human nature has been delivered into slavery and is held captive by the devil (Colossians 1:13). He fills human nature with a passionate desire for wicked opinions and errors and pushes it to sins of every kind. Just as the devil  48 cannot be conquered except by Christ's help, so we cannot free ourselves from this slavery by our own strength. World history shows  49 how great and powerful the devil's kingdom is. The world is full of blasphemies against God and wicked opinions. The devil keeps all tied up many hypocrites who appear holy and who are wise and righteous in the world's eyes. Even greater vices are seen in other peo-  50 ple. Since Christ was given to us to remove both these sins and these punishments and to destroy the devil's kingdom, sin, and death (1 John 3:8), we will never be able to recognize Christ's benefits unless we understand our evils. For this reason our preachers have diligently taught all about these things. They have not delivered anything that is new, but have set forth Holy Scripture and the judgment of the Holy Fathers.

We think this will satisfy His Imperial  51 Majesty about the childish and trivial sophistry the adversaries use to pervert our article on original sin. We know that we believe correctly, in harmony with the Church catholic of Christ. If the adversaries renew this controversy, there will be more than enough of us to reply and to defend the truth. In this case our adversaries, to a great extent, do not understand what they are saying. They often speak in a contradictory way and do not explain, either correctly or logically, what is the essence of original sin and what they call a "defect." We are unwilling here to examine their arguments in any further subtle detail. We think it is worthwhile just to recite, in customary and well-known words, the belief of the Holy Fathers, which we also follow.

## ARTICLE III

# Christ

It was very important for the Lutherans to affirm the historic biblical confession of the Church: Christ is fully God and fully man. In his *Confession concerning Christ's Supper* of 1528, Luther wrote,

> Here you must take your stand and say that wherever Christ is according to His divinity, He is there as a natural divine person and He is also naturally and personally there, as His conception in His mother's womb proves conclusively. For if He was the Son of God, He had to be in His mother's womb naturally and personally, and become Man. . . . He is not two separate persons but a single person. Wherever this person is, it is the single, indivisible person, and if you can say, "Here is God," then you must also say, "Christ the Man is present too."

The article on justification is rooted in this article on Christ. (See the Apostles', Nicene, and Athanasian Creeds; AC III; SA II I; SC II; LC II; FC Ep VIII and SD VIII.)

---

52    The adversaries approve Article III, in which we confess that there are two natures in Christ. The human nature is assumed by the Word into the unity of His person (John 1:14). Christ suffered and died to reconcile the Father to us and was raised again to reign, to justify, and to sanctify believers according to the Apostles' Creed and the Nicene Creed.

## ARTICLE IV (II)

# Justification

Article IV of the Apology is the most complex article in the entire Book of Concord. Because it deals with our salvation, that is, how God has forgiven our sins and has reconciled us to Himself in Christ, it is also the most important. This article is the very heart of the Gospel and the most important teaching in the Holy Scriptures; therefore, the Apology goes into great detail about the doctrine of justification. All Scripture leads us to, from, and back to the truth of Christ's work of atonement. God applies Christ's work to individuals freely by grace, through faith, without works. The article on Christ (AC III) proclaims how God atones for sins. The article on the Church's ministry of the means of grace (AC V) confesses how God applies to individuals the merits won by Christ. What brings these two articles together is the article on justification (AC IV), which describes how we are justified, that is, declared righteous by God. (See AC IV; SA III XIII; FC Ep III and SD III.)

---

In Articles V, VI, and XX, they condemn us for teaching that "people obtain forgiveness of sins not because of their own merits, but freely for Christ's sake, through faith in Christ." They condemn us both for denying that people obtain forgiveness of sins because of their own merits and for affirming that—through faith—people obtain forgiveness of sins and are justified through faith in Christ. But in this controversy, the chief topic of Christian doctrine is treated. When it is understood correctly, it illumines and amplifies Christ's honor. It brings necessary and most abundant consolation to devout consciences. Therefore, we ask His Imperial Majesty to hear us with patience in matters 1

2

3  of such importance. For the adversaries do not understand what the forgiveness of sins or faith or grace or righteousness is. Therefore, they sadly corrupt this topic, hide Christ's glory and benefits, and rob devout consciences of the consolation offered in

4  Christ. In order that we may strengthen the position of our Confession, and also remove the charges that the adversaries advance against us, certain points are to be set forth in the beginning. Then the sources of both kinds of doctrine (that of our adversaries and our own) may be known.

5     All Scripture ought to be distributed into these two principal topics: the Law and the promises. For in some places Scripture presents the Law, and in others the promises about Christ. In other words, in the Old Testament, Scripture promises that Christ will come, and it offers, for His sake, the forgiveness of sins, justification, and life eternal. Or in the Gospel, in the New Testament, Christ Himself (since He has appeared) promises the forgiveness of sins, justification, and life

6  eternal. Furthermore, in this discussion, by *Law* we mean the Ten Commandments, wherever they are read in the Scriptures. We say nothing at present about the ceremonies and judicial laws of Moses.

7     Of these two parts of Scripture the adversaries choose the Law, because in some way human reason naturally understands the Law (for it has the same judgment divinely written in the mind). By the Law they seek

8  the forgiveness of sins and justification. The Ten Commandments require outward civil works, which reason can in some way produce. But they also require other things placed far above reason: truly to fear God, truly to love God, truly to call upon God, truly to be convinced that God hears us, and to expect God's aid in death and in all afflictions. Finally, it requires obedience to God, in

death and all afflictions, so that we may not run from these commandments or refuse them when God lays them upon us.

Here the Scholastics have followed the  9
philosophers. They teach only a righteousness of reason. That is, they teach civil works. Besides that, they pretend reason can love God above all things without the Holy Spirit. For, as long as the human mind is at ease, and does not feel God's wrath or judgment, it can pretend that it wants to love God, that it wants to do good for God's sake. In this way, they teach that people merit forgiveness of sins by doing what is in them, namely, when reason produces an act of love toward God by grieving over sin or when reason is active in doing what is good for God's sake. Because  10
this notion naturally flatters people, it has brought forth and multiplied in the Church many services, monastic vows, and abuses of the Mass. In the course of time with this opinion, someone has come up with one act of worship and observances, and someone else, others. To nourish and increase confi-  11
dence in such works, the Scholastics have asserted that God must give grace to a person who does such works, not that He is forced to, but that God will not change.

In this opinion there are many great and  12
deadly errors, which would be too boring to list. Let the careful reader think only about this: If this is Christian righteousness, what difference is there between philosophy and Christ's teaching? If we merit forgiveness of sins by these acts, of what benefit is Christ? If we can be justified by reason and the works of reason, what need is there of Christ or regeneration (1 Peter 1:18–21)? From these  13
opinions the matter has now reached the point that many ridicule us because we teach that a righteousness different from philosophic righteousness must be sought. We  14
have heard that some preachers, after setting

aside the Gospel, have explained Aristotle's ethics instead of a sermon. Not that such men err if those things the adversaries defend are true. For Aristotle wrote about civil morals in such a learned way that nothing further about the topic needs to be de-

15 manded. We see books published in which certain sayings of Christ are compared with the sayings of Socrates, Zeno, and others. It's as though Christ had come to deliver certain laws through which we might merit forgiveness of sins, as though we did not receive this

16 freely because of His merits. Therefore, if we here accept the teaching of the adversaries—that by the works of reason we merit forgiveness of sins and justification—there will be no difference between righteousness of philosophers (or certainly of Pharisees) and of Christians.

17 Yet the adversaries do not give up on Christ completely. They require a knowledge of the history about Christ. They credit Him by writing that from His merit a way of life is given to us or, as they say, "first grace" (*prima gratia*). They understand this as a *habit*, inclining us to love God more readily. Yet, what they credit to this habit is of little importance. For they imagine that the human will's acts are the same before and after this habit. They imagine that the will can love God; but, nevertheless, this habit stimulates it to love more cheerfully. They tell us, "First, merit this habit by your earlier merits." Then they tell us we should merit an increase of this habit and life eternal by the works of the

18 Law. In this way they bury Christ, so that people may not benefit from Him as a Mediator and believe that they freely receive forgiveness of sins and reconciliation for His sake. They let people dream that by their own fulfillment of the Law, they merit forgiveness of sins, that by their own fulfillment of the Law, they are counted righteous be-

fore God. However, the Law is never satisfied since reason does nothing except certain civil works. In the meantime, a person neither fears God nor truly believes that God cares. Although they speak about this habit, God's love cannot exist in a person without the righteousness of faith, nor can His love be understood.

19 They make up a distinction between due merit and true, complete merit (*meritum congrui* and *meritum condigni*). This is only a tactic, so that they do not appear to agree openly with the Pelagians. If God must give grace for the due merit, it is no longer due merit, but a true duty and complete merit. They do not know what they are saying. After this habit of love is in a person, they imagine that such a person can gain merit in a wholly deserving way (*de condigno*). Yet they tell us to doubt whether there is a habit present. Therefore, how do they know whether they gain merit in a merely agreeable way or a wholly deserving way (*de congruo* or *de*

20 *condigno*)? This whole matter was made up by idle men. They did not know how forgiveness of sins happens and how, by God's judgment and the terrors of conscience, trust in works is driven out of us. Secure hypocrites always judge that they gain merit in a wholly deserving way, whether the habit is present or is not present, because people naturally trust in their own righteousness. But terrified consciences waver and hesitate. Then they seek and heap up other works in order to find peace. Such consciences never think that they gain merit in a wholly deserving way, and they rush into despair unless they hear—in addition to the teaching of the Law—the Gospel about free forgiveness of sins and righteousness of faith.

21 So the adversaries teach nothing but righteousness of reason, or certainly about the Law. They see the Law just like the Jewish people see

The Bronze Snake in the Wilderness

The Sacrifice of Isaac

Moses' veiled face. In self-secure hypocrites, who think that they fulfill the Law, they stir up assumptions and empty confidence in works and cause them to have contempt for the grace of Christ. On the other hand, they also drive timid consciences to despair. The timid labor with doubt. They can never experience what faith is and how effective it is. So at last they completely despair.

22   We think about the righteousness of reason like this: God requires it. Because of God's commandment, the honorable works commanded by the Ten Commandments must be done, according to Galatians 3:24, "The law was our guardian." Likewise, 1 Timothy 1:9 says, "The law is not laid down for the just but for the lawless." For God wants wild sinners to be restrained by civil discipline. To maintain discipline, He has given laws, letters, doctrine, rulers, and penalties.

23   To a certain extent reason can, by its own strength, perform this civil righteousness. Yet it is often overcome by natural weakness and by the devil pushing it to do obvious crimes.

24   We cheerfully credit this righteousness of reason with the praises that are due it. (This corrupt nature has no greater good.) Aristotle rightly says, "Neither the evening star nor the morning star is more beautiful than righteousness," and God also honors it with bodily rewards. However, it ought not to be praised by dishonoring Christ.

25   So it is false that we merit forgiveness of sins by our works.

26   It is false that people are counted righteous before God because of the righteousness of reason.

27   It is false that reason, by its own strength, is able to love God above all things and to fulfill God's Law. In other words, reason cannot truly fear God, be truly confident that God hears prayer, be willing to obey God in death and other divine matters, not covet what belongs to others, and so on. Yet reason can do civil works.

28   The following is also false and dishonoring to Christ: people do not sin who, without grace, do God's commandments.

29   We have testimonies in favor of our belief not only from the Scriptures, but also from the Fathers. For in opposition to the Pelagians, Augustine argues at great length that grace is not given because of our merits. In *On Nature and Grace,* he says:

> If natural ability, through the free will, is enough for learning how one ought to live and for living aright, then Christ has died in vain. Then the offense of the cross is made void. Why may I not also cry out about this? Yes, I will cry out! And, with Christian grief, I will rebuke them: "You are severed from Christ, you who would be justified by the law; you have fallen away from grace" (Galatians 5:4; cf. 2:21). For they, being ignorant of God's righteousness, and going about to establish their own righteousness, have not submitted themselves unto God's righteousness. "For Christ is the end of the law for righteousness to everyone who believes" (Romans 10:4).

30

31   John 8:36 says, "If the Son sets you free, you will be free indeed." Therefore, by reason we cannot be freed from sins and merit forgiveness of sins. In John 3:5, it is written, "Unless one is born of water and the Spirit, he cannot enter the kingdom of God." But if it is necessary to be born again of the Holy Spirit, the righteousness of reason does not justify us before God and does not fulfill the Law. Ro-

32   mans 3:23 says, "All have sinned and fall short of the glory of God." They totally lack the wisdom and righteousness of God, which acknowledges and glorifies God. Likewise,

Romans 8:7–8 says, "For the mind that is set on the flesh is hostile to God, for it does not submit to God's law; indeed, it cannot. Those who are in the flesh cannot please God."

33 These testimonies are so clear that, to use Augustine's words in this case, they do not need a keen understanding, but only an attentive hearer. If the carnal mind is hostile against God, the flesh certainly does not love God. If it cannot be subject to God's Law, it cannot love God. If the carnal mind is hostile against God, the flesh sins, even when we do outward civil works. If it cannot be subject to God's Law, it certainly sins even when it has deeds that are excellent and praiseworthy according to human judgment. The adversaries consid-

34 er only the teachings of the Second Table, which contain civil righteousness that reason understands. Content with this, they think that they fulfill God's Law. In the meantime, they do not see the First Table, which commands that we love God, that we declare God is certainly angry with sin, that we truly fear God, that we declare God certainly hears prayer. But the human heart without the Holy Spirit either feels secure and despises God's judgment, or in punishment flees from

35 God and hates Him when He judges. Therefore, it does not obey the First Table. So, contempt for God, doubt about God's Word, and doubt about the threats and promises dwell in human nature. People truly sin, even when—without the Holy Spirit—they do virtuous works. This is because they act with a wicked heart according to Romans 14:23: "Whatever does not proceed from faith is sin." For such people do their works with contempt for God, just as Epicurus does not believe that God cares for him or that he is regarded or heard by God. This contempt ruins works that seem virtuous because God judges the heart.

36 Lastly, it was very foolish for the adver-

saries to write that people who are under eternal wrath merit forgiveness of sins by an act of love, which springs from their mind. For it is impossible to love God unless forgiveness of sins is received first by faith. The heart, truly feeling that God is angry, cannot love God unless He is shown to have been reconciled. As long as He terrifies us and seems to cast us into eternal death, human nature is not able to take courage. It cannot love a wrathful, judging, and punishing God.

37 It is easy for idle men to invent such dreams about love, such as a person guilty of mortal sin can love God above all things, because they do not feel what God's wrath or judgment is. But in agony of conscience and in conflicts (with Satan), conscience experiences the emptiness of these philosophical

38 speculations. Paul says in Romans 4:15, "The law brings wrath." He does not say that by the Law people merit forgiveness of sins. For the Law always accuses and terrifies consciences. Therefore, it does not justify, because a conscience terrified by the Law runs from God's judgment. They err who assume that by the Law—by their own works—they merit for-

39 giveness of sins. It is enough for us to have said these things about the righteousness of reason or of the Law, which the adversaries teach. Later, when we will declare our belief about the righteousness of faith, the subject itself will drive us to present more testimonies. These also will be of service in overthrowing the adversaries' errors that we have reviewed so far.

40 By their own strength, people cannot fulfill God's Law. They are all under sin, subject to eternal wrath and death. Because of this, we cannot be freed by the Law from sin and be justified. But the promise of forgiveness of sins and of justification has been given us for Christ's sake, who was given for us in order that He might make satisfaction for the sins

41 of the world. He has been appointed as the Mediator and Atoning Sacrifice. This promise does not depend on our merits, but freely offers forgiveness of sins and justification, as Paul says in Romans 11:6, "But if it is by grace, it is no longer on the basis of works; otherwise grace would no longer be grace." And in another place, Romans 3:21, "The righteousness of God has been manifested apart from the law." In other words, forgiveness of sins is freely offered. Nor does recon-

42 ciliation depend on our merits. Because if forgiveness of sins were to depend on our merits, and reconciliation were from the Law, it would be useless. Since we do not fulfill the Law, it would also follow that we would never gain the promise of reconciliation. Paul reasons this way in Romans 4:14, "For if it is the adherents of the law who are to be the heirs, faith is null and the promise is void." If the promise would depend on our merits and the Law, which we never fulfill, it would follow that the promise would be useless.

43 Since justification is gained through the free promise, it follows that we cannot justify ourselves. Otherwise, why would there be a need to promise? Since the promise can only be received by faith, the Gospel (which is properly the promise of forgiveness of sins and of justification for Christ's sake) proclaims the righteousness of faith in Christ. The Law does not teach this, nor is this the

44 righteousness of the Law. For the Law demands our works and our perfection. But, for Christ's sake, the Gospel freely offers reconciliation to us, who have been vanquished by sin and death. This is received not by works, but by faith alone. This faith does not bring to God confidence in one's own merits, but only confidence in the promise, or the

45 mercy promised in Christ. This special faith (by which an individual believes that for Christ's sake his sins are forgiven him, and

that for Christ's sake God is reconciled and sees us favorably) gains forgiveness of sins and justifies us. In repentance, namely, in terrors, this faith comforts and encourages hearts. It regenerates us and brings the Holy Spirit so that we may be able to fulfill God's Law: to love God, truly fear God, truly be confident that God hears prayer, and obey God in all afflictions. This faith puts to death concupiscence and the like. So faith freely re- 46 ceives forgiveness of sins. It sets Christ, the Mediator and Atoning Sacrifice, against God's wrath. It does not present our merits or our love. This faith is the true knowledge of Christ and helps itself to the benefits of Christ. This faith regenerates hearts and comes before the fulfilling of the Law. Not a 47 syllable exists about this faith in the teaching of our adversaries. Therefore, we find equal fault with the adversaries because (a) they teach only the righteousness of the Law, and (b) they do not teach the righteousness of the Gospel, which proclaims the righteousness of faith in Christ.

## What Is Justifying Faith?

No other article in the Book of Concord so thoroughly presents how the Roman Church errs when it comes to the central teaching of Scripture. The Pontifical Confutation stated adamantly that justification is "not by faith alone, which some incorrectly teach, but faith which works through love." This view was affirmed by the Council of Trent and remains the doctrine of the Roman Catholic Church to this day. The Council of Trent condemns the Bible's teaching that man is saved apart from any works, by grace alone, through faith alone. This condemnation is still clearly evident in the most recent edition of the Catholic Catechism.

---

The adversaries pretend that faith is only 48

a knowledge of the history of Christ. Therefore, they teach that it can coexist with mortal sin. They say nothing about faith, by which Paul so frequently says that people are justified. For those who are counted as righteous before God do not live in mortal sin. But *the faith that justifies* is not merely a knowledge of history. It is to believe in God's promise. In the promise, for Christ's sake, forgiveness of sins and justification are freely offered. And so that no one may suppose that this is mere knowledge, we will add further: it is to want and to receive the offered promise of forgiveness of sins and of justification.

49 The difference between this faith and the righteousness of the Law can be easily discerned. Faith is the divine service (*latreia*) that receives the benefits offered by God. The righteousness of the Law is the divine service (*latreia*) that offers to God our merits. God wants to be worshiped through faith so that we receive from Him those things He promises and offers.

50 Faith means not only a knowledge of the history, but the kind of faith that believes in the promise. Paul plainly testifies about this when he says in Romans 4:16, "That is why it depends on faith, in order that the promise may rest on grace and be guaranteed." He judges that the promise cannot be received unless it comes through faith. Therefore, he puts them together as things that belong to one another. He connects the promise and 51 faith. It will be easy to decide what faith is if we consider the Creed, where this article certainly stands: the forgiveness of sins. It is not enough to believe that Christ was born, suffered, was raised again, unless we add also this article, which is the purpose of the history: *the forgiveness of sins.* To this article the rest must be referred. I mean that because of Christ, and not because of our merits, for- 52 giveness of sins is given to us. For what need

was there that Christ was given for our sins if our merits can make satisfaction for our sins?

53 Whenever we speak of justifying faith, we must keep in mind that these three objects belong together: the *promise, grace,* and *Christ's merits as the price and atonement.* The promise is received through faith. Grace excludes our merits and means that the benefit is offered only through mercy. Christ's merits are the price, because there must be a certain atonement for our sins. Scripture fre- 54 quently cries out for mercy; the Holy Fathers often say that we are saved by mercy. There- 55 fore, whenever mercy is mentioned, we must keep in mind that faith, which receives the promise of mercy, is required there. Again, whenever we speak about faith, we want an object of faith to be understood, namely, the promised mercy. For faith justifies and saves, 56 not because it is a worthy work in itself, but only because it receives the promised mercy.

57 Throughout the Prophets and the Psalms this worship (this *latreia*) is highly praised, even though the Law does not teach the free forgiveness of sins. The Old Testament Fathers knew the promise about Christ, that God for Christ's sake wanted to forgive sins. They understood that Christ would be the price for our sins. They knew that our works are not a price for so great a matter. So they received free mercy and forgiveness of sins by faith, just as the saints in the New Testament. To this point belong those frequent repeti- 58 tions about mercy and faith that appear in the Psalms and the Prophets. For example, Psalm 130:3 says, "If You, O LORD, should mark iniquities, O Lord, who could stand?" Here David confesses his sins and does not list his merits. He adds, "But with You there is forgiveness" (v. 4). Here he comforts himself by his trust in God's mercy, and he refers to the promise, "I wait for the LORD, my soul waits, and in His word I hope" (v. 5). This

means, "Because You have promised the forgiveness of sins, I am sustained by Your promise." Therefore, the Fathers also were justified, not by the Law, but by the promise and faith. It is amazing that the adversaries diminish faith to such a degree, even though they see that it is everywhere praised as a great service. For example, Psalm 50:15 says, "Call upon Me in the day of trouble; I will deliver you." God wants Himself to be known, He wants Himself to be worshiped, so that we receive benefits from Him and receive them because of His mercy, not because of our merits. This is the richest consolation in all afflictions. The adversaries ban such consolation when they diminish and disparage faith and teach only that by means of works and merits people interact with God.

## Faith in Christ Justifies

While the Roman Church does not bypass Christ or God's grace, it does base its doctrine of justification on our cooperation with God's grace rather than on Christ's work alone. Inclination toward goodness is increased by participation in the Church's sacramental system, whereby we receive grace from the merits of Christ and the saints. Through our cooperation with this grace, we earn eternal life. This teaching is subtly and deceptively nuanced, and must be exposed as false and potentially damning (Galatians 3:10–14). It diverts our eyes from Christ and His full, complete, and perfect satisfaction for sins. Through careful analysis of religious terms and their use, Melanchthon shows that the Roman Catholic teaching on justification is contrary to the Holy Scriptures, that it confuses grace and works, and that it obscures the merit and glory of Jesus Christ.

In the first place, lest anyone think that we speak about an idle knowledge of history, we must state how faith is obtained. Afterward, we will show both that faith justifies and how this ought to be understood. We will also explain the objections of the adversaries. Christ, in the last chapter of Luke, commands "that repentance and forgiveness of sins should be proclaimed in His name" (24:47). The Gospel convicts all people that they are under sin, that they are subject to eternal wrath and death. It offers, for Christ's sake, forgiveness of sin and justification, which is received through faith. The preaching of repentance (which accuses us) terrifies consciences with true and grave terrors. In these matters, hearts ought to receive consolation again. This happens if they believe Christ's promise, that for His sake we have forgiveness of sins. *This faith, encouraging and consoling in these fears, receives forgiveness of sins, justifies, and gives life.* For this consolation is a new birth and spiritual life. These things are plain and clear and can be understood by the pious. They also have testimonies of the Church. The adversaries cannot say how the Holy Spirit is given. They imagine that the Sacraments give the Holy Spirit by the outward act (*ex opere operato*), without a good emotion in the one receiving them, as though, indeed, the gift of the Holy Spirit were a useless matter.

We speak of the kind of faith that is not an idle thought, but that liberates from death and produces a new life in hearts. This is the work of the Holy Spirit. This does not coexist with mortal sin. As long as faith is present, it produces good fruits, as we will explain later. About the conversion of the wicked, or about the way of regeneration, what can be said that is simpler and clearer? Let the Scholastics, from so great a host of writers, produce a single commentary upon

66 the *Sentences* that speaks about the way of regeneration. When they speak of the habit of love, they imagine that people merit it through works. They do not teach that it is received through the Word. They teach just 67 like the Anabaptists teach at this time. But God cannot be interacted with, God cannot be grasped, except through the Word. So justification happens through the Word, just as Paul says in Romans 1:16, "[The Gospel] is the power of God for salvation to everyone who believes." Likewise, he says in 10:17, "Faith comes from hearing." Proof can be derived even from this: faith justifies because, if justification happens only through the Word, and the Word is understood only by faith, it follows that faith jus-68 tifies. There are other and more important reasons. We have said these things so far in order that we might show the way of regeneration and that the nature of faith (what faith is or is not), about which we speak, might be understood.

69 Now we will show that *faith justifies.* Here, in the first place, readers must be taught about this point: Just as it is necessary to keep this statement—Christ is Mediator— so is it necessary to defend that faith justifies. For how will Christ be Mediator if we do not use Him as Mediator in justification, if we do not hold that we are counted righteous for His sake? To believe is to trust in Christ's merits, that for His sake God certainly wish-70 es to be reconciled with us. Here is a similar point: Just as we should defend that the promise of Christ is necessary apart from the Law, so also we should defend that faith justifies. For the Law cannot be performed unless the Holy Spirit is received first. It is, therefore, necessary to defend that the promise of Christ is necessary. But this cannot be received except through faith. Therefore, those who deny that faith justifies teach nothing but the Law, both Christ and the Gospel being set aside.

When it is said that faith justifies, some 71 perhaps understand it to mean that faith is the beginning of justification or the preparation for justification. Then it is not faith through which we are accepted by God, but the works that follow. So they dream that faith is highly praised because it is the beginning. For great is the importance of the beginning, as they commonly say, "The beginning is half of everything." They speak as if one would say that grammar makes the teachers of all arts, because it prepares for other arts. (In fact, it is one's own art that makes everyone an artist.) We do not believe like this about faith, but we hold—properly and truly—we are for Christ's sake counted righteous, or are acceptable to God through faith itself. "To be justified" means that just 72 people are made out of unjust men, or born again. It also means that they are pronounced, or counted, as just. For Scripture speaks in both ways. So we wish to show this first: *Faith alone makes a just person out of an unjust person;* in other words, that person receives forgiveness of sins.

The term *alone* offends some people, even 73 though Paul says in Romans 3:28, "For we hold that one is justified by faith apart from works of the law." He says in Ephesians 2:8–9, "It is the gift of God, not a result of works, so that no one may boast." He says in Romans 3:24, "justified by His grace as a gift." If the exclusive term *alone* displeases, let them remove from Paul also the exclusives *freely, not of works, it is the gift,* and so on. For these also are exclusives. *It is, however, the notion of merit that we exclude.* We do not exclude the Word or Sacraments, as the adversaries falsely charge against us. We have said that faith is conceived from the Word. We honor the ministry of the Word in the highest degree.

74 Love and works must also follow faith. Therefore, they are not excluded so that they do not follow faith, but *confidence in the merit of love or of works is excluded in justification.* We will clearly show this.

## We Obtain Forgiveness of Sins through Faith Alone in Christ

The Bible teaches that mankind stands entirely damned before God. He demands that we be righteous and holy in His sight, without exception. Certainly we are able to perform works that are considered worthy in the eyes of the world (Ap IV 23), but these are insufficient for God's requirements and cannot atone for our sins. There is nothing within us that merits His grace and mercy. As sinners, how can we stand before a holy, righteous, and just God? We can, but only by His grace. God restores us to a right relationship with Himself through Christ Jesus. By grace, God justifies us through faith in His Son.

The biblical definition of grace is God's unmerited favor in Christ, His love active in the salvation brought about by Christ (Titus 2:11). Saving, or justifying, grace, is the undeserved kindness that God gives sinful people because of what Christ has done (John 3:16; Titus 3:4–5). Grace stands in stark contrast to the works that human beings do. The Bible clearly teaches that since our salvation is purely by grace, all human works are entirely excluded from justification (Romans 11:6; Ephesians 2:8–9). This biblical definition of grace is important. If we relied on ourselves for justification before God, one of three things would happen: we could despair of our efforts to earn God's favor, we could become self-righteous hypocrites, or we could completely reject our Savior.

In the Roman Church, both then and now, "grace" is more of a quality or power that God infuses into man's natural goodness, allowing him to reach a point where he pleases God. The Catechism of the Catholic Church carefully states that man is involved in the process of his own justification. Through grace, God begins the process, but it is up to man to complete his justification before God. Man's good works, begun by God's grace, merit for him a right relationship with God. True, it is claimed that these merits are ultimately derived from the operation of the Holy Spirit. But in the end, man contributes to his own justification. This is a dangerous mixture of grace and works. In this system, how can we be sure of a right standing with God? How can we know if we are justified?

---

We think even the adversaries acknowledge that the forgiveness of sins is necessary first in justification. We are all under sin. Therefore, we reason as follows: 75

To receive the forgiveness of sins is to be justified, according to Psalm 32:1, "Blessed is the one whose transgression is forgiven." 76

*By faith alone in Christ*—not through love, not because of love or works—we receive the forgiveness of sins, although love follows faith. *Therefore, by faith alone we are justified.* We understand justification as the making of a righteous person out of an unrighteous one, or that a person is regenerated. 77 78

It will become easy to state the minor premise (that we receive forgiveness of sin by faith, not by love) if we know how forgiveness of sins happens. With great indifference the adversaries dispute whether forgiveness of sins and infusion of grace are the same change. Being useless men, they did not know how to answer this question. In the forgiveness of sins, the terrors of sin and of eternal death must be overcome in the heart. 79

The Crucifixion

Paul testifies about this in 1 Corinthians 15:56–57, "The sting of death is sin, and the power of sin is the law. But thanks be to God, who gives us the victory through our Lord Jesus Christ." In other words, sin terrifies consciences. This happens through the Law, which shows God's wrath against sin. But we gain the victory through Christ. How? Through faith, when we comfort ourselves by confidence in the mercy promised for

80 Christ's sake. Therefore, we prove the minor premise. God's wrath cannot be appeased if we set our own works against it. For Christ has been set forth as an Atoning Sacrifice so, that for His sake, the Father may be reconciled to us. But Christ is not received as a Mediator except by faith. Therefore, *by faith alone we receive forgiveness of sins* when we comfort our hearts with confidence in the

81 mercy promised for Christ's sake. Likewise, Paul says in Romans 5:2, "Through Him we have also obtained access" and adds, "by faith." Therefore, we are reconciled to the Father and receive forgiveness of sins when we are comforted with confidence in the mercy promised for Christ's sake. The adversaries regard Christ as Mediator and Atoning Sacrifice for this reason: He has merited the habit of love. They do not encourage us to use Him now as Mediator. They act as though Christ were certainly in the grave. They imagine that we have access to God through our own works. They think they merit this habit through these, and afterward, by this love, come to God. Is this not to bury Christ altogether and to take away the entire teaching of faith? Paul, on the contrary, teaches that we have access to God (that is, reconciliation) through Christ. To show how this happens, he adds that we have access *by faith. By faith, for Christ's sake, we receive forgiveness of sins.* We cannot set up our own love and our own works against God's wrath.

*Second*. It is certain that sins are forgiven 82 for the sake of Christ as our Atoning Sacrifice, "whom God put forward as a propitiation" (Romans 3:25). Furthermore, Paul adds, "by faith." Therefore, this atonement benefits us in this way: We receive the mercy promised in Him by faith and set it against God's wrath and judgment. To the same effect, it is written in Hebrews 4:14, 16, "Since then we have a great high priest . . . let us then with confidence draw near." The apostle tells us to come to God, not with confidence in our own merits, but with confidence in Christ as the High Priest. The apostle requires faith.

*Third*. Peter says in Acts 10:43, "To Him all 83 the prophets bear witness that everyone who believes in Him receives forgiveness of sins through His name." How could this be said more clearly? Peter says we receive forgiveness of sins through Christ's name, that is, for His sake. It is not for the sake of our merits, not for the sake of our contrition, attrition, love, worship, or works. He adds: *When we believe in Him.* Peter requires faith. For we cannot receive Christ's name except by faith. Besides, he refers to the agreement of all the prophets. This is truly to cite the authority of the Church. We will speak again later on this topic, when describing "repentance."

*Fourth*. Forgiveness of sins is something 84 promised for Christ's sake. It cannot be received except through faith alone. For a promise cannot be received except by faith alone. Romans 4:16 says, "That is why it depends on faith, in order that the promise may rest on grace and be guaranteed." It is as though he says, "If the matter were to depend on our merits, the promise would be uncertain and useless. For we never could determine when we would have enough merit." Experienced consciences can easily understand this. So Paul says in Galatians 3:22,

"But the Scripture imprisoned everything under sin, so that the promise by faith in Jesus Christ might be given to those who believe." He takes merit away from us because he says that all are guilty and included under sin. Then he adds that the promise (namely, forgiveness of sins and justification) is given, and he shows how the promise can be received—by faith. This reasoning, derived from the nature of a promise, is the chief reasoning in Paul and is often repeated. Nor can anything be devised or imagined by which Paul's argument can be overthrown. Therefore, let not good minds allow themselves to be forced from the conviction that we receive forgiveness of sins for Christ's sake, through faith alone. In this they have sure and firm consolation against the terrors of sin, against eternal death, and against all the gates of hell.

85

### Scripture Affirms This Teaching

The Bible teaches that "to justify" is to declare righteous. In the Gospel of Christ, God declares that we are forgiven, righteous, and holy in His sight. Melanchthon elaborates on this point in Article IV. St. Paul teaches that justification is only by grace, through faith, apart from any works of righteousness on man's part (Romans 3:28). Lutherans insist that justification is not a process through which God brings us up to a certain level of holiness, which then qualifies us to receive more grace. Rather, it is God's declaration that the dead are alive, the condemned are not guilty, and the sinful are forgiven because of Jesus.

In contrast to biblical justification, the Roman Church teaches that God's grace is a power infused to begin good works, and that justification is the entire process by which this occurs. This confuses justification (whereby God declares us righteous because of Christ) and sanctification (whereby He begins to conform us to Christ). Such a teaching causes grave doubts in the heart of the believer, who may never be sure whether he is truly justified. The Scriptures provide hope, comfort, peace, and joy in knowing that Christ has accomplished all for us through His life, death, and resurrection. The Roman Church's teaching leads to doubt and despair.

We are justified through faith. Melanchthon explains at length what the Bible teaches about faith. Christ's perfect obedience to His Father's will (Galatians 4:4–5) and His sacrificial death on the cross (Colossians 1:22) won forgiveness of sins for the whole world (1 John 2:2). How do we personally receive Christ's universal righteousness and atonement? We receive these gifts through faith and faith alone. God gives us faith as a gift, through which Christ's righteousness is credited to us (Ephesians 2:8–9) and our sins are forgiven (Romans 3:22–24). Melanchthon carefully states that by no means do the Lutherans consider faith to be mere intellectual assent to historic truths; the devil and ungodly people have this sort of "faith." Justifying faith is God-instilled trust that believes the life, death, and resurrection of Christ is "for me." It is firm acceptance of God's offer promising forgiveness of sins and justification. Faith is always personal and individual. No one can have faith for another.

---

Since we receive forgiveness of sins and the Holy Spirit through faith alone, *faith alone justifies.* For those reconciled are counted as righteous and as God's children. This is not because of their own purity, but through mercy for Christ's sake, provided only that they receive this mercy through faith. So Scripture testifies that *by faith we are accounted righteous* (Romans 3:26). We will add 86 testimonies that clearly declare that faith is that very righteousness through which we are accounted righteous before God. This is not because faith is a work that is worthy in itself. It is because faith receives the promise by which God has declared that, for Christ's sake, He wishes to show favor to those believing in Him, or because God knows that Christ Jesus was "made our wisdom and our righteousness and sanctification and redemption" (1 Corinthians 1:30).

87 In the Epistle to the Romans, Paul discusses this topic specifically. He declares that when we believe God (for Christ's sake) is reconciled to us, we are justified freely through faith. This point, which contains the statement of the entire discussion, Paul sets forth in the third chapter: "For we hold that one is justified by faith apart from works of the law" (Romans 3:28). The adversaries conclude that this passage refers to Levitical ceremonies. But Paul speaks not only of the ceremonies, but of the whole Law. For he quotes afterward (7:7) from the Ten Commandments: "You shall not covet." If moral works would merit the forgiveness of sins and justification, there would also be no need for Christ and the promise. All that Paul says about the promise would be overthrown. He would also have been wrong in writing to the Ephesians, "For by grace you have been saved through faith. And this is not your own doing; it is the gift of God, not a result of works" (2:8–9). Paul, likewise, refers to Abraham and David in Romans 4:1, 6. But they had God's command for circumcision. Therefore, if any works justified, these works must also have justified at the time that they had a command. But Augustine teaches correctly that Paul speaks of the entire Law, as he discusses at length in his book *On the Spirit and the Letter*, where he finally says:

These matters, having been considered and treated, according to the ability that the Lord has thought worthy to give us, we conclude that a person is not justified by the precepts of a good life, but by faith in Jesus Christ.

88 Lest we may decide that "faith justifies" came from Paul without consideration, he fortifies and confirms this teaching by a long discussion in Romans 4. Afterward, he repeats it in all his letters. So he says in Romans 89 4:4–5:

Now to the one who works, his wages are not counted as a gift but as his due. And to the one who does not work but trusts Him who justifies the ungodly, his faith is counted as righteousness.

Here he clearly says that faith itself is credited for righteousness. Faith is that thing God declares to be righteousness. Paul adds that righteousness is credited freely. He says that it could not be credited freely if it were due because of works. Therefore, he excludes also the merit of moral works. For if justification before God were due to these moral works, faith would not be credited for righteousness without works. Afterward, in Romans 4:9, 90 "We say that faith was counted to Abraham as righteousness." Romans 5:1 says, "Since we 91 have been justified by faith, we have peace with God." This means we have consciences that are peaceful and joyful before God. Romans 10:10 says, "With the heart one be- 92 lieves and is justified." Here he declares that faith is the righteousness of the heart.

We also have believed in Christ Jesus, 93 in order to be justified by faith in Christ and not by works of the law. (Galatians 2:16)

For by grace you have been saved through faith. And this is not your

Preaching Justification

own doing; it is the gift of God, not a result of works, so that no one may boast. (Ephesians 2:8–9)

94 But to all who did receive Him, who believed in His name, He gave the right to become children of God, who were born, not of blood nor of the will of the flesh nor of the will of man, but of God. (John 1:12–13)

95 And as Moses lifted up the serpent in the wilderness, so must the Son of Man be lifted up, that whoever believes in Him may have eternal life. (John 3:14–15)

96 For God did not send His Son into the world to condemn the world, but in order that the world might be saved through Him. Whoever believes in Him is not condemned. (John 3:17–18)

97 Let it be known to you therefore, brothers, that through this man forgiveness of sins is proclaimed to you, and by Him everyone who believes is freed from everything from which you could not be freed by the law of Moses. (Acts 13:38–39)

How could the office of Christ and justification be declared more clearly? Paul says that the Law does not justify. Therefore, Christ was given, that we may believe that for His sake we are justified. He plainly denies justification by the Law. So for Christ's sake we are accounted righteous when we believe that God, for His sake, has been reconciled to us.

98 This Jesus is the stone that was rejected by you, the builders, which has become the cornerstone. And there is salvation in no one else, for there is no other name under heaven given among men by which we must be saved. (Acts 4:11–12)

Christ's name is received only by faith. Therefore, we are saved by confidence in Christ's name, and not by confidence in our works. For "the name" here means the cause that is mentioned, because of which salvation is gained. To call upon Christ's name is to trust in His name as the cause, or price, because of which we are saved. Acts 15:9 says, 99 "cleansed their hearts by faith." Therefore, the faith that the apostles speak about is not useless knowledge, but a reality. It receives the Holy Spirit and justifies us.

Habakkuk 2:4 says, "The righteous shall 100 live by his faith." Here he says, first, that people are just by faith. By faith they believe that God is favorable, and he adds that the same faith gives life because this faith produces peace and joy in the heart and eternal life.

Isaiah 53:11 says, "By His knowledge shall 101 the righteous one, My servant, make many to be accounted righteous." What is Christ's knowledge unless it means to know Christ's benefits, the promises He has scattered throughout the world by the Gospel? To know these benefits is properly and truly to believe in Christ, to believe that He will certainly fulfill what God has promised for Christ's sake.

Scripture is full of such testimonies. For 102 in some places it presents the Law, and in others it presents the promises about Christ, forgiveness of sins, and free acceptance of the sinner for Christ's sake.

## The Church Fathers Affirm This Teaching

In the Apology, Melanchthon strongly refutes the Roman Church's understanding of faith, drawing on examples from Scripture and the Church Fathers. The Roman Church teaches that grace is infused into the human soul. Man cooperates with this infused grace to produce certain virtues, faith being among them. By freely assenting to the doctrines of the Roman Church, one demonstrates "faith." This view of faith reduces God's gracious, supernatural gift to a mere initiating power. It also diminishes personal faith in Christ to simple agreement with the teachings of the Church. Instead of heartfelt trust in our gracious God and Savior, faith becomes mere intellectual assent to the history of Jesus.

In the Roman Church's theology, justification is given only partially in this life. The Scriptures and Article IV of the Apology, however, clearly teach and confess that justification is complete and total because of the sufficient, atoning, once for all sacrifice of Christ on the cross.

---

103     Here and there among the Fathers similar testimonies exist. For Ambrose says in his letter to a certain Irenaeus:

> Furthermore, the world was subject to God by the Law because, according to the command of the Law, all are indicted. And yet, by the works of the Law, no one is justified. For, by the Law, sin is perceived, but guilt is not taken away. The Law, which declared all people sinners, seemed to have done harm. But when the Lord Jesus Christ came, He forgave to all people the sin, which no one could avoid. And, by the shedding of His own blood, He blotted out the handwriting that was against us. This is what he says in Romans 5:20, "The law came in to increase the trespass, but where sin increased, grace abounded all the more." Because after the whole world became subject, Christ took away the sin of the whole world, as John testified, saying in John 1:29, "Behold, the Lamb of God, who takes away the sin of the world!" And for this reason let

no one boast about works, because no one is justified by his deeds. But he who is righteous has righteousness given to him because he was justified from the washing of Baptism. Faith, therefore, is that which frees through the blood of Christ, because he is blessed "whose transgression is forgiven, whose sin is covered" (Psalm 32:1).

These are the words of Ambrose, which 104 clearly favor our doctrine. He denies justification to works and teaches that faith sets us 105 free through the blood of Christ. Let all the commentators on the *Sentences*, who are adorned with magnificent titles, be collected into one heap. For some are called "angelic," others "subtle," and others "unanswerable" (that is, doctors who cannot err). When all these have been read and reread, they will not be worth half as much for understanding Paul as is this one passage of Ambrose.

    In the same way, Augustine writes many 106 things against the Pelagians. In *On the Spirit and the Letter,* he says:

> The righteousness of the Law—that he who has fulfilled the Law shall live in it—is set forth for this reason: when anyone has recognized his weakness he may attain and do the Law and live in it, reconciling the Justifier not by his own strength nor by the letter of the Law itself (which cannot be done), but by faith. In a justified person, there is no right work by which he who does that work may live. But justification is received by faith.

Here Augustine clearly says that the Justifier is reconciled by faith and that justification is received by faith. A little after:

> By the Law we fear God; by faith we hope in God. But to those fearing

punishment grace is hidden. And the soul laboring under this fear resorts by faith to God's mercy, in order that He may give what He commands.

Here he teaches that hearts are terrified by the Law, but they receive consolation by faith. He also teaches us to receive mercy by faith, before we try to fulfill the Law. We will quote certain other passages shortly.

### The Adversaries Reject This Teaching

107 Truly, it is amazing that the adversaries are in no way moved by so many passages of Scripture, which clearly credit justification to faith. Indeed, Scripture denies this ability to 108 works. Do they think that the same point is repeated so often for no purpose? Do they think that these words fell thoughtlessly from 109 the Holy Spirit? But they have also come up with sophisticated tricks by which they escape these passages. They say that these passages of Scripture (that speak of faith) ought to be received as referring to faith that has been formed (*fides formata*). This means they do not credit justification to faith except on account of love. Yes, they do not credit justification to faith in any way, but only to love, because they dream that faith can coexist 110 with mortal sin. Where does this go? They again abolish the promise and return to the Law. If faith receives forgiveness of sins because of love, forgiveness of sins will always be uncertain, because we never love as much as we ought to. Indeed, we do not love unless our hearts are firmly convinced that forgiveness of sins has been granted to us. So the adversaries, in forgiveness of sins and justification, require confidence in one's own love. In this way, they completely abolish the Gospel about the free forgiveness of sins; although, at the same time, they do not offer this love or understand it, unless they believe that forgiveness of sins is freely received.

We also say that love ought to follow 111 faith, as Paul also says in Galatians 5:6: "For in Christ Jesus neither circumcision nor uncircumcision counts for anything, but only faith working through love."

Yet, we must not think that by confidence 112 in this love, or because of this love, we receive forgiveness of sins and reconciliation, just as we do not receive forgiveness of sins because of other works that follow. But forgiveness of sins is received by faith alone. Indeed, this is properly called faith because the promise cannot be received except by faith. Faith, 113 properly called, is what believes this promise. Scripture speaks of this faith. Because faith 114 receives forgiveness of sins and reconciles us to God, we are (like Abraham) counted as righteous for Christ's sake before we love and before we do the works of the Law, although love necessarily follows.

Nor, indeed, is this faith an idle knowl- 115 edge, neither can it coexist with mortal sin. It is a work of the Holy Spirit, by which we are freed from death and terrified minds are encouraged and brought to life. Because this 116 faith alone receives forgiveness of sins, makes us acceptable to God, and brings the Holy Spirit, it could be more correctly called "grace making one pleasing to God" (*gratia gratum faciens*). It could not be called an effect following faith (i.e., love).

In order that the subject might be made 117 quite clear, we have shown well enough so far, both from testimonies of Scripture and arguments derived from Scripture, that we receive forgiveness of sins for Christ's sake through faith alone. We have shown that through faith alone we are justified, that is, unrighteous people are made righteous, or regenerated. How necessary the knowledge 118 of this faith is can be easily judged. Because Christ's office is recognized in this alone, we receive Christ's benefits by this alone. Only

The Risen Christ

this teaching brings sure and firm consolation to pious minds. In the Church there must be the teaching by which the pious may receive the sure hope of salvation. For the adversaries give people bad advice when they tell them to doubt whether they receive forgiveness of sins. How will such persons sustain themselves in death who have heard nothing of this faith and think that they ought to doubt whether they receive forgiveness of sins? Besides, it is necessary that the Gospel be kept in Christ's Church, namely, the promise that sins are freely forgiven for Christ's sake. Those who teach nothing of this faith we speak about, completely abolish the Gospel. But the Scholastics mention not even a word about this faith. Our adversaries follow them and reject this faith. Nor do they see that by rejecting this faith they abolish the entire promise about the free forgiveness of sins and the righteousness of Christ.

## ARTICLE V (III)

# Love and Fulfilling the Law

Good works do not cause justification; rather, they are the result of justification. Melanchthon carefully distinguishes between the effect of the Law before a person is justified and the effect of the Law after a person is justified. Rome had garbled these critical biblical distinctions with disastrous consequences. Melanchthon returns to them constantly, writing the longest article in the Apology. Lutherans believe that Christians improve at keeping the Law, and they require good works. However, good works are not necessary for salvation, but are the necessary fruit of salvation.

Justification is not merely an initial grace, but the entire reconciliation we receive from God for Christ's sake. While the Law always accuses us, any beginnings we make at keeping

God's Law pleases Him only because of faith, which holds on to Christ. This important discussion of faith and works proceeds with absolute clarity. Melanchthon goes right to the heart of the matter by stating that we can never pit our works against the wrath and judgment of God. Only Christ, our Mediator, can stand for us in our place, take God's wrath and punishment (which we deserve), and win for us eternal life, joy, and peace. (See AC VI; SA III XIII; FC Ep IV, V, and VI; FC SD IV, V, and VI.)

———————

On this topic the adversaries quote 1 against us, "If you would enter life, keep the commandments" (Matthew 19:17); likewise, "It is the doers of the law who will be justified" (Romans 2:13), and many other things about the Law and works. Before we reply to this, we must first declare *what we believe about love and the fulfilling of the Law.*

I will put My law within them, and I 2 will write it on their hearts. (Jeremiah 31:33)

Do we then overthrow the law by this faith? By no means! On the contrary, we uphold the law. (Romans 3:31)

If you would enter life, keep the commandments. (Matthew 19:17)

But [if I] have not love, I gain nothing. (1 Corinthians 13:3)

These and similar sentences testify that we 3 are to keep the Law when we have been justified by faith, and so grow in fulfilling the Law more and more (by the Spirit). Furthermore, we are not talking about ceremonies, but about the Law that addresses the movements of the heart, namely, the Ten Commandments. Faith brings the Holy Spirit and pro- 4 duces a new life in hearts. It must also produce spiritual movements in hearts. The prophet Jeremiah shows what these movements are when he says, "I will put My law within them, and I will write it on their hearts" (31:33). Therefore, when we have been justified by faith and regenerated, we begin to fear and love God, to pray to Him, to expect aid from Him, to give thanks and praise Him, and to obey Him in times of suffering. We also begin to love our neighbors, because our hearts have spiritual and holy movements.

5   These things cannot happen until we have been justified through faith and regenerated (we receive the Holy Spirit). That's because the Law cannot be kept without Christ; likewise, the Law cannot be kept without the

6   Holy Spirit. But the Holy Spirit is received through faith, as Paul declares in Galatians 3:14, "that we might receive the promised

7   Spirit through faith." Also remember, how can the human heart love God while it knows that He is terribly angry and is oppressing us with earthly and endless distress? The Law always accuses us. It always shows that God is

8   angry. God is not loved until we receive mercy through faith. Not until then does He become someone we can love.

9   Civil works (i.e., the outward works of the Law) can be done in some measure, without Christ and without the Holy Spirit. Nevertheless, from what we have said, it seems that what belongs only to the divine Law (i.e., the heart's affections toward God), which are commanded in the First Table,

10   cannot be done without the Holy Spirit. But our adversaries are fine theologians. They focus on the Second Table and political works. They don't care about the First Table. They act as though the First Table were of no matter. They certainly require only outward fulfillment of the Law. They in no way consider the Law that is eternal and placed far above the sense and intellect of all creatures.

Deuteronomy 6:5 says, "You shall love the LORD your God with all your heart."

11   Christ was given for this purpose, that forgiveness of sins might be bestowed on us for His sake. He was also given so that the Holy Spirit might bring forth in us new and eternal life and eternal righteousness. Therefore, the Law cannot truly be kept unless the Holy Spirit is received through faith. So Paul says that *the Law is established through faith, and not made useless,* because the Law can only be kept when the Holy Spirit is given.

12   Paul teaches, *The veil that covered the face of Moses cannot be removed except by faith in Christ, by which the Holy Spirit is received.* (See 2 Corinthians 3:14–18.) For he says, "Yes, to this day whenever Moses is read a veil lies over their hearts. But when one turns to the Lord, the veil is removed. Now the Lord is the Spirit, and where the Spirit of the Lord is, there is freedom" (2 Corinthians 3:15–17).

13   Paul understands by the "veil" the human opinion about the entire Law, the Ten Commandments and the ceremonies. In other words, hypocrites think that outward and civil works satisfy God's Law, and that sacrifices and observances justify a person before God by the outward act (*ex opere operato*).

14   But then this veil is removed from us (i.e., we are freed from this error) when God shows to our hearts our uncleanness and the hatefulness of sin. Then, for the first time, we see that we are far from fulfilling the Law. We learn to know how flesh is self-secure and doesn't care. It does not fear God and is not completely certain that we are cared for by God. It imagines that people are born and die by chance. Then we experience that we do not believe that God forgives and hears us. But when we hear about the Gospel and the forgiveness of sins, we are consoled through faith, we receive the Holy Spirit so that now we are able to think correctly about God, to

Agricola (1494?–1566)

John Agricola taught that God's Law plays no part in the life of a person who has been converted by the Gospel. Luther opposed Agricola's antinomian (anti-law) views. Years later a similar controversy over good works surfaced and was resolved by Article VI of the Formula of Concord.

fear and believe God, and so on. From these facts it is clear that the Law cannot be kept without Christ and the Holy Spirit.

15    We profess that the work of the Law must be begun in us, and that it must be kept continually more and more. At the same time we also speak about both spiritual movements and outward good works. *Therefore, the adversaries falsely charge that our theologians do not teach good works. They not only require good works, but they also show how* 16    *they can be done.* The result convicts the hypocrites, who by their own powers try to fulfill the Law. For they cannot do the things 17    they attempt. Human nature is far too weak to resist the devil by its own powers. He holds as captive everyone who has not been 18    freed through faith. There is need for Christ's power against the devil. For we know that for Christ's sake we are heard and have the promise. We may pray for the governance and defense of the Holy Spirit, that we may neither be deceived and err, nor be pushed to do anything against God's will. Psalm 68:18 teaches this very thing: "You ascended on high, leading a host of captives in Your train and receiving gifts among men." Christ has overcome the devil, and has given to us the promise and the Holy Spirit, in order that—by divine aid—we ourselves may also overcome. So 1 John 3:8 says, "The reason the Son of God appeared was to destroy the works of the devil." Again, we teach 19    not only how the Law can be kept, but also how God is pleased if anything is done. This is not because we satisfy the Law, but because we are in Christ, as we shall explain shortly. Therefore, it is clear that we require 20    good works. In fact, we also say this: Our love for God, even though it is small, cannot possibly be separated from faith. For we come to the Father through Christ. When forgiveness of sins has been received, then

we are truly certain that we *have a God* (Exodus 20:3), that is, that God cares for us. We call upon Him, we give Him thanks, we fear Him, we love Him as 1 John 4:19 teaches, "We love because He first loved us." In other words, we love Him because He gave His Son for us and forgave us our sins. In this way John shows that faith comes first and love follows. Likewise, the faith of which we 21 speak exists in repentance. I mean that faith is conceived in the terrors of conscience, which feels God's wrath against our sins and seeks forgiveness of sins, seeks to be freed from sin. In such terrors and other troubles, this faith ought to grow and be strengthened. Therefore, it cannot exist in people 22 who live by the flesh, who are delighted by their own lusts and obey them. So, Paul says in Romans 8:1, "There is therefore now no condemnation for those who are in Christ Jesus." So, too, "We are debtors, not to the flesh, to live according to the flesh. For if you live according to the flesh you will die, but if by the Spirit you put to death the deeds of the body, you will live" (8:12–13). Paul is 23 writing about faith that receives forgiveness of sins in a terrified heart and flees from sin. Such faith does not remain in those who obey their desires, neither does it dwell with mortal sin.

From these effects of faith the adversaries 24 select one, namely, love, and teach that love justifies. It is clear that they only teach the Law. They do not teach that forgiveness of sins is first received through faith. They do not teach about Christ as Mediator, that we have a gracious God for Christ's sake, but for the sake of our love. Yet, they do not say what the nature of this love is, neither can they say. They proclaim that they fulfill the 25 Law, although this glory belongs to Christ alone. They set up confidence in their own works against God's judgment. For they say that they merit according to righteousness (*de condigno*) grace and eternal life. This confidence is absolutely ungodly and useless. For in this life we cannot satisfy the Law, because the sinful nature does not stop bringing forth evil inclination and desire, even though the Spirit in us resists them.

26 But someone may say, "Since we also confess that love is a work of the Holy Spirit, and since it is righteousness, because it is the fulfilling of the Law, why do we not teach that love justifies?" To this we must reply: In the first place, it is certain that we do not receive forgiveness of sins through our love or for the sake of our love, but only for Christ's 27 sake, by faith. Faith alone looks upon the promise. It knows that because of the promise, it is absolutely certain that God forgives, because Christ has not died in vain. Such faith overcomes the terrors of sin and death.

28 If anyone doubts whether sins are forgiven him, he dishonors Christ. For he judges that his sin is greater or more effective than Christ's death and promise, even though Paul says, "Where sin increased, grace abounded all the more" (Romans 5:20). This means that 29 mercy is more comprehensive than sin. If anyone thinks that he receives forgiveness of sins because he loves, he dishonors Christ and will discover in God's judgment that this confidence in his own righteousness is wicked and useless. Therefore, it is necessary 30 that faith alone reconciles and justifies. We do not receive forgiveness of sins through other powers of the Law, or because of these: patience, chastity, obedience toward magistrates, and so on. (Nevertheless, these virtues ought to follow faith.) Therefore, we do not receive forgiveness of sins because of love for 31 God, even though this must follow. Besides, this way of speaking is well known. At times we use a word for something and we use the same word for the cause and effects of that

thing *(synecdoche)*. For example, in Luke 7:47, Christ says, "Her sins, which are many, are forgiven—for she loved much." Christ Himself interprets this when He adds, "Your faith has saved you" (7:50). Christ did not mean that the woman had merited forgiveness of sins by that work of love. That is why 32 He adds, "Your faith has saved you." But faith is that which freely obtains God's mercy because of God's Word. If anyone denies that this is faith, he does not understand at all what faith is. The story in this passage shows 33 what Christ calls "love." The woman came with the opinion that forgiveness of sins should be sought in Christ. This worship is the highest worship of Christ. She could think nothing greater about Christ. To seek forgiveness of sins from Him was truly to acknowledge the Messiah. To think of Christ this way, to worship Him this way, to embrace Him this way, is truly to believe. Furthermore, Christ used the word *love* not toward the woman, but against the Pharisee. He contrasted the entire worship of the Pharisee with the entire worship offered by the woman. He rebuked the Pharisee because he did not acknowledge that He was the Messiah, even though he performed the outward duties that a guest and a great and holy man deserved. Christ points to the woman and praises her worship, ointment, tears, and so forth. These were all signs of faith and a confession—with Christ she sought forgiveness of sins. It is indeed a great example. Not without reason, this moved Christ to rebuke the Pharisee, who was a wise and honorable man, but not a believer. He charges him with lack of holiness and admonishes him by the example of the woman. In this way, Christ shows that it is disgraceful for the Pharisee. While an unlearned woman believes God, he, a doctor of the Law, does not believe. He does not acknowledge the Messiah and does not seek from Him forgiveness of sins and salvation.

34 So Christ praises her entire worship. This often happens in the Scriptures, that by one word we embrace many things. Below we shall speak at greater length about similar passages such as Luke 11:41, "But give as alms those things that are within, and behold, everything is clean for you." He requires not only alms, but also the righteousness of faith. He says here, "Her sins, which are many, are forgiven—for she loved much" (Luke 7:47). This means she has truly worshiped Me with faith and faith's exercises and signs. He means the entire worship. Meanwhile, He teaches this: Forgiveness of sins is properly received by faith, even though love, confession, and other good fruit ought to follow. He does not mean that these fruit are the price, or are the atonement that reconciles us to God, because of which the forgiveness of sins is

35 given. We are disputing about a great subject, about Christ's honor, and where good minds may seek for sure and firm consolation. We are disputing whether confidence

36 is to be placed in Christ or in our works. If it is to be placed in our works, the honor of Mediator and Atoning Sacrifice will be withdrawn from Christ. Yet we shall find, in God's judgment, that this confidence is useless. From this confidence, consciences rush directly into despair. If forgiveness of sins and reconciliation do not happen freely for Christ's sake, but for the sake of our love, no one will have forgiveness of sins. He would only have it when he had fulfilled the entire Law, because the Law does not justify as long as it can accuse us. Therefore, it is clear

37 that we are justified through faith, since justification is reconciliation for Christ's sake. For it is very certain that forgiveness of sins is received through faith alone.

## No One Can Keep the Law Perfectly

Now let us reply to the objection stated 38 above: The adversaries are right in thinking that love is the fulfilling of the Law and that obedience to the Law is certainly righteousness. But they make a mistake in this matter. They think that we are justified by the Law. Since we are not justified by the Law, we receive forgiveness of sins and reconciliation through faith for Christ's sake. This is not because of love or the fulfilling of the Law; it follows necessarily that we are justified through faith in Christ.

In the second place, this fulfilling of the 39 Law, or obedience toward the Law, is indeed righteousness, when it is complete. But it is small and impure in us. So our righteousness is not pleasing for its own sake and is not accepted for its own sake. From what 40 has been said above, it is clear that *justification* means not the beginning of the renewal, but the reconciliation by which we are accepted afterward. It can now be seen much more clearly that starting to fulfill the Law does not justify, because such fulfillment is only accepted on account of faith. Nor must we trust that we are accounted righteous before God by our own perfection and fulfilling of the Law, but rather for Christ's sake.

In the third place, Christ does not stop 41 being our Mediator after we have been renewed. They err who imagine that He has merited only a *first grace*, and that, afterward, we please God and merit eternal life by our fulfilling of the Law. Christ remains Me- 42 diator, and we should always be confident that for His sake we have a reconciled God, even though we are unworthy. Paul clearly teaches this when he says, "I am not aware of anything against myself, but I am not thereby acquitted" (1 Corinthians 4:4). Paul knows that through faith he is counted righteous for Christ's sake, according to the passage "Blessed is the one whose transgression is forgiven" (Psalm 32:1; see also Romans 4:7). But this forgiveness is always received through faith. Likewise, the credit for the righteousness of the Gospel comes from the promise. Therefore, it is always received through faith. It must always be regarded as certain that we are counted righteous

43 through faith for Christ's sake. If the regenerate afterward think that they will be accepted because of the fulfilling of the Law, when would a conscience be certain that it

44 pleased God? We never satisfy the Law! So we must always run back to the promise. Our infirmity must be recognized in this matter. We must regard it as certain that we are counted righteous for the sake of Christ, "who is at the right hand of God, who indeed is interceding for us" (Romans 8:34). If anyone thinks that he is righteous and accepted because of his own fulfillment of the Law, and not because of Christ's promise, he dishonors this High Priest. This cannot be understood. How could someone imagine that a person is righteous before God when Christ is excluded as the Atoning Sacrifice and Mediator?

45     In the fourth place, what need is there of a long discussion? All Scripture, all the Church cries out that the Law cannot be satisfied. Therefore, starting to fulfill the Law does not please on its own account, but on

46 account of faith in Christ. Otherwise, the Law always accuses us. For who loves or fears God enough? Who has enough patience to bear the troubles brought by God? Who does not frequently doubt whether human affairs are ruled by God's counsel or by chance? Who does not frequently doubt whether he is heard by God? Who is not frequently enraged because the wicked enjoy a better life than the righteous, because the righteous are oppressed by the wicked? Who fulfills his own calling? Who loves his neighbor as himself? Who is not tempted by lust? Paul says,

47 "For I do not do the good I want, but the evil I do not want is what I keep on doing" (Romans 7:19). Likewise, "I myself serve the law of God with my mind, but with my flesh I serve the law of sin" (7:25). Here he openly declares that he serves the law of sin. David says in Psalm 143:2, "Enter not into judgment with Your servant, for no one living is righteous before You." Here even God's servant prays for the removal of judgment. Likewise, "Blessed is the man against whom the LORD counts no iniquity" (Psalm 32:2). Therefore, in our weakness sin is always present, which could be charged against us. A little while after he says, "Therefore let everyone who is godly offer prayer to You" (32:6). Here he shows that even saints ought to seek forgiveness of sins. They are more than blind

48 who do not realize that wicked desires in the flesh are sins, of which Paul says, "For the desires of the flesh are against the Spirit, and the desires of the Spirit are against the flesh" (Galatians 5:17). The flesh distrusts God,

49 trusts in present things, seeks human aid in trouble, even contrary to God's will. It flees from suffering, which it ought to bear because of God's commands. It doubts God's mercy and so on. The Holy Spirit in our hearts fights against such tendencies in order to suppress and kill them and to produce new spiritual motives. We will collect more

50 testimonies below about this topic, although they are clearly everywhere not only in the Scriptures, but also in the Holy Fathers.

## Church Fathers and St. Paul Affirm Justification through Faith

Augustine well says, "All God's com-

51 mandments are fulfilled when whatever is not done, is forgiven." Therefore, he requires

faith even in good works. He says this to show that we may believe we please God for Christ's sake, and even our works are not worthy and pleasing of themselves. Jerome, against the Pelagians, says:

> Then we are righteous when we confess that we are sinners, and that our righteousness stands not in our own merit, but in God's mercy.

53 Therefore, when starting to fulfill the Law, faith ought to be present, which certainly believes that we have a reconciled God for Christ's sake. For mercy cannot be received except through faith, as has been repeatedly said above. Paul says in Romans 3:31, "Do we then overthrow the law by this faith? By no means! On the contrary, we uphold the law." Here's what we ought to understand: People regenerated through faith not only receive the Holy Spirit, and have motives that agree with God's Law, but we ought also to realize that they are far distant from the Law's perfection. This point has the greatest importance by far, and we must add it to the argument also. We cannot conclude that we are counted righteous before God because of our fulfilling of the Law. Justification must be sought elsewhere in order that the conscience may become peaceful. For we are not righteous before God as long as we flee from God's judgment and are angry with God. Therefore, we must conclude that we are counted righteous for Christ's sake being reconciled through faith. This is not because of the Law or our works. Because of faith, beginning to fulfill the Law pleases God. Because of faith, there is no charge that we fulfill the Law imperfectly, even though the sight of our impurity terrifies us. If justification is to be sought elsewhere, our love and works do not justify.

57 Christ's death and satisfaction ought to be placed far above our purity, far above the Law

itself. This truth ought to be set before us so that we can be sure of this: We have a gracious God because of Christ's satisfaction and not because of our fulfilling the Law.

58 Paul teaches this in Galatians 3:13, when he says, "Christ redeemed us from the curse of the law by becoming a curse for us." This means that the Law condemns all people. But Christ—without sin—has borne the punishment of sin. He has been made a victim for us and has removed that right of the Law to accuse and condemn those who believe in Him. He Himself is the Atonement for them. For His sake they are now counted righteous. Since they are counted righteous, the Law cannot accuse or condemn them, even though they have not actually satisfied the Law. Paul writes the same way to the Colossians, "You have been filled in Him" (2:10). This is like saying, "Although you are still far from the perfection of the Law, the remnants of sin do not condemn you. For Christ's sake we have a sure and firm reconciliation, if you believe, even though sin dwells in your flesh."

59 The promise should always be in sight. Because of His promise, God wishes to be gracious and to justify for Christ's sake, not because of the Law or our works. In this promise timid consciences should seek reconciliation and justification. By this promise they should sustain themselves and be confident that they have a gracious God for Christ's sake, because of His promise. So works can never make a conscience peaceful. Only the promise can. If justification and peace of conscience must be sought in something other than love and works, then love and works do not justify. This is true even though they are virtues and belong to the righteousness of the Law, insofar as they are a fulfilling of the Law. Obedience to the Law justifies by the righteousness of the Law—if a

person fulfills it. But imperfect righteousness of the Law is not accepted by God unless it is accepted because of faith. So legal righteousness does not justify, that is, it neither reconciles nor regenerates nor by itself makes us acceptable before God.

61    From this it is clear that *we are justified before God through faith alone.* Through faith alone we receive forgiveness of sins and reconciliation, because reconciliation or justification is a matter promised for Christ's sake, not for the Law's sake. Therefore, it is received through faith alone, although, when the Holy Spirit is given, the fulfilling of the Law follows.

## Reply to the Adversaries' Arguments

62    Now, when the grounds of this case have been understood (the distinction between the Law and the promises, or the Gospel), it will be easy to resolve the adversaries' objections. For they quote passages about the Law and works and leave out passages about the

63    promises. But a final reply can be made to all opinions about the Law. I mean that the Law cannot be kept without Christ, and that if civil works are done without Christ, they do not please God. Therefore, when works are commended, it is necessary to add that faith is required. They are commended because of faith. They are the fruit and testimonies of

64    faith. Ambiguous and dangerous cases produce many and various solutions. For the judgment of the ancient poet is true:

An unjust cause, being in itself sick, requires skillfully applied remedies.

In just and sure cases, one or two explanations derived from the sources correct all things that seem to offend. This happens also in our case here. For the rule I have just quoted explains all the passages that are quoted

65    about the Law and works. We acknowledge that Scripture teaches the Law in some places

and the Gospel in other places (i.e., the free promise of forgiveness of sins for Christ's sake). But our adversaries absolutely abolish the free promise when they deny that faith justifies and when they teach that we receive forgiveness of sins and reconciliation because of love and our works. If forgiveness of  66 sins depends on our works, it is completely uncertain. The promise will be abolished. Therefore, we tell godly minds to consider  67 the promises, and we teach about free forgiveness of sins and about reconciliation, which happens through faith in Christ. Afterward, we add also the teaching of the Law. It is necessary to distinguish these things aright, as Paul says in 2 Timothy 2:15. We must see what Scripture says about the Law and what it says about the promises. For it praises works in such a way that it does not remove the free promise.

Good works are to be done because of  68 God's command and for the exercise of faith—confessing the faith and giving thanks. Good works must be done for these reasons. They are done in the flesh, which is not as yet entirely renewed. The flesh hinders the Holy Spirit's motives and adds some of its uncleanness to the works. Yet, because of Christ, they are holy, divine works, sacrifices, and acts belonging to the rule of Christ, who in this way displays His kingdom before this world. For in these works He sanctifies hearts and represses the devil. In order to retain the Gospel among people, He openly sets the confession of saints against the kingdom of the devil and, in our weakness, declares His power. Consider the dangers, labors, and ser-  69 mons of the apostle Paul, of Athanasius, Augustine, and the rest who taught the churches. These deeds are holy works and true sacrifices acceptable to God. They are Christ's battles (Colossians 2:15) through which He repressed the devil and drove him

Christ Confronts Saul on the Road to Damascus

70 away from those who believed. David's labors, in waging wars and in his home government, are holy works, true sacrifices, and battles fought by God. They defend the people who had God's Word against the devil, in order that the knowledge of God might not

71 be entirely extinguished on earth. We think this way also about every good work in the humblest callings and in private affairs. Through these works Christ celebrates His victory over the devil, just as the distribution of alms by the Corinthians (1 Corinthians 16:1) was a holy work, a sacrifice and battle of Christ against the devil, who labors so that

72 nothing may be done to praise God. To demean such works (the confession of doctrine, sufferings, works of love, suppression of the flesh) would be to demean the outward rule of Christ's kingdom among peo-

73 ple. Here also we add something about rewards and merits. We teach that rewards have been offered and promised for the works of believers. We teach that good works have merit, not for forgiveness of sins, for grace, or for justification (for these we receive only through faith), but for other rewards, bodily and spiritual, in this life and after this life. For Paul says in 1 Corinthians 3:8, "Each will re-

74 ceive his wages according to his labor. There will be different rewards according to different labors. But forgiveness of sins is given alike and equal to all people, just as Christ is one, and is offered freely to all who believe that for His sake their sins are forgiven. Therefore, forgiveness of sins and justification are received only through faith, not because of any works. This is clear because of the terrors of conscience, because none of our works can turn away God's wrath, as Paul clearly says in Romans 5:1, "Therefore, since we have been justified by faith, we have peace with God through our Lord Jesus Christ. Through Him we have also obtained

access by faith." Because faith makes sons of 75 God, it also makes coheirs with Christ. Because by our works we do not merit justification, through which we are made sons of God, and coheirs with Christ. We do not merit eternal life by our works. Faith receives it because faith justifies us and has a reconciled God. But eternal life is due to the justified, according to the passage in Romans 8:30, "Those whom He justified He also glorified." Paul (Ephesians 6:2) tells us the com- 76 mandment about honoring parents, by mentioning the reward added to that commandment. He does not mean that obedience to parents justifies us before God. But when obedience happens in those who have been justified, it merits other great rewards. God puts His saints to work in various ways 77 and often holds back the rewards of works-righteousness. He does this so that they may learn not to trust in their own righteousness and may learn to seek God's will rather than the rewards. This can be seen with Job, Christ, and other saints. And many psalms teach us about this. They console us against the happiness of the wicked, as Psalm 37:1 says, "Be not envious." Christ says in Matthew 5:10, "Blessed are those who are persecuted for righteousness' sake, for theirs is the kingdom of heaven." By these praises of 78 good works, believers are undoubtedly moved to do good works. Meanwhile, the 79 teaching of repentance is also proclaimed against the godless, whose works are wicked. God's wrath, which He has threatened against all who do not repent, is displayed. Therefore, we praise and require good 80 works and show many reasons why they ought to be done.

Paul also teaches this about works when he says in Romans 4:9–25 that Abraham received circumcision. He did not seek to be justified by this work, for he had already attained justification through faith. He was counted righteous. But circumcision was added so that (a) Abraham might have a written sign in his body, (b) admonished by this, he might exercise faith, and (c) by this work he might also confess his faith before others and, by his testimony, invite others to

81 believe. "By faith Abel offered to God a more acceptable sacrifice" (Hebrews 11:4). Because he was just by faith, the sacrifice that he made was pleasing to God. It is not that he merited forgiveness of sins and grace by this work, but he exercised his faith and showed it to others, in order to invite them to believe.

82 In this way good works ought to follow faith. Yet people who cannot believe and be sure that they are freely forgiven for Christ's sake, and that freely they have a reconciled God for Christ's sake, use works in a far different way. When they see the works of saints, they judge in a human way that saints have merited forgiveness of sins and grace through these works. So they imitate them, thinking that through similar works they merit forgiveness of sins and grace. They think that through these works they appease God's wrath and are counted righ-

83 teous for the sake of these works. We condemn this godless opinion about works. In the first place, it hides Christ's glory when people offer to God these works as a price and atonement. This honor, due to Christ alone, is credited to our works. Second, they do not find peace of conscience in these works. In true terrors, heaping up works upon works, they eventually despair because they find no work important and precious enough. The Law always accuses and produces wrath. Third, such persons never attain the knowledge of God. For in anger they run from God, who judges and afflicts them. They never believe that they are

84 heard. But faith shows God's presence, since it is certain that God freely forgives and hears us.

85 Furthermore, this godless opinion about works always has existed in the world. The heathen had sacrifices, derived from the fathers. They imitated their works. They did not maintain their faith, but thought that the works were an atonement and price by which God would be reconciled to them.

86 The people in the Law (the Israelites) imitated sacrifices with the opinion that they would appease God *by means of these works*, so to say, *ex opere operato*. We see here how seriously the prophets rebuke the people: Psalm 50:8, "Not for your sacrifices do I rebuke you," and Jeremiah 7:22, "I did not speak to your fathers or command them concerning burnt offerings and sacrifices." Such passages do not condemn works, which God certainly had commanded as outward exercises in this government. They condemn the godless opinion that people thought, that by their works they appeased God's wrath, and

87 so cast away faith. Because no works ease the conscience, new works, in addition to God's commands, were made up from time to time. The people of Israel had seen the prophets sacrificing on high places (e.g., 1 Samuel 9:10–14, 19). Besides, the examples of the saints very greatly move the minds of people who hope to obtain grace by similar works just as these saints received it. Therefore, the people began, with remarkable zeal, to imitate their work, in order that by such a work they might merit forgiveness of sins, grace, and righteousness. But the prophets had been sacrificing on high places, not so that they might merit forgiveness of sins and grace by these works, but because they taught on these places. So they presented a testimo-

88 ny of their faith there. The people had heard that Abraham had sacrificed his son (Genesis 22). Therefore, they also, in order to appease

God by a most cruel and difficult work, put their sons to death (e.g., 2 Kings 16:3). But Abraham did not sacrifice his son with the opinion that this work was a price and atoning work by which he was counted righteous.

89 In a similar way, the Lord's Supper was instituted in the Church. So by remembering Christ's promises (about which we are taught in this Sacrament), faith would be strengthened in us, and we would publicly confess our faith and proclaim Christ's benefits, as Paul says in 1 Corinthians 11:26, "For as often as you eat this bread and drink the cup, you proclaim the Lord's death until He comes." But our adversaries contend that the Mass is a work that justifies us by the outward work (*ex opere operato*) and removes the guilt and liability to punishment in those for whom it is celebrated. That's what Gabriel Biel writes.

90 Anthony, Bernard, Dominic, Francis, and other Holy Fathers selected a certain kind of life either for the sake of study or other useful exercises. In the meantime, they believed that by faith they were counted righteous for Christ's sake and that God was gracious to them, not because of their own exercises. But the multitude since then has imitated not the faith of the Fathers, but their example without faith. By such works the multitude thought they might merit forgiveness of sins, grace, and righteousness. They did not believe that they received these freely on account of Christ as the Atoning

91 Sacrifice. The world judges that all works are an atonement by which God is appeased. They are a price by which we are counted righteous. It does not believe that Christ is the Atonement. It does not believe that through faith we are freely counted righteous for Christ's sake. Since works cannot ease the conscience, other works are continually chosen, new rites are performed, new

vows are made, and new orders of monks are formed beyond God's command, in order that some great work may be sought that may be set against God's wrath and judgment. Contrary to Scripture, the adver- 92 saries uphold these godless opinions about works. They say these things about our works: they are an atonement, they merit forgiveness of sins and grace, and we are counted righteous before God by them (and not through faith, for Christ's sake as the Atonement). What is this other than to deny Christ the honor of Mediator and Atoning Sacrifice? We believe and teach that good 93 works must be done (*fulfilling of the Law ought to follow faith*). Nevertheless, we give Christ His own honor. We believe and teach that through faith, for Christ's sake, we are counted righteous before God. We are not counted righteous because of works without Christ as Mediator. We do not merit forgiveness of sins, grace, and righteousness by works. We cannot set our works against God's wrath and justice. Works cannot overcome the terrors of sin. But the terrors of sin are overcome through faith alone. Only Christ the Mediator is to be presented by faith against God's wrath and judgment. If 94 anyone thinks differently, he does not give Christ due honor. Christ has been set forth so that He might be an Atonement, that through Him we might have access to the Father. We are speaking now about the righ- 95 teousness through which we approach God (not humans) but by which we receive grace and peace of conscience. Conscience, how- 96 ever, cannot be eased before God, unless through faith alone. Faith is certain that God for Christ's sake is reconciled to us, according to Romans 5:1, "Therefore, since we have been justified by faith, we have peace." This is because justification is only a matter freely promised for Christ's sake. Therefore, it is always received before God through faith alone.

## Passages the Adversaries Misuse

97 Now we will reply to those passages that the adversaries quote in order to prove that we are justified by love and works. From 1 Corinthians 13:2, they quote, "If I have all faith . . . but have not love, I am nothing." Here they triumph greatly. Paul testifies to the entire Church (they say) that faith alone 98 does not justify. But a reply is easy after we have shown above what we teach about love and works. This passage of Paul requires love. We also require this. For we have said above that renewal and beginning to fulfill the Law must exist in us, according to Jeremiah 31:33, "I will put My law within them, and I will write it on their hearts." If anyone should cast away love, even though he has great faith, he does not keep his faith. For he 99 does not keep the Holy Spirit. Nor indeed does Paul in this passage talk about the way of justification. Instead, he writes to those who, after they had been justified, should be urged to bring forth good fruit lest they lose 100 the Holy Spirit. Furthermore, the adversaries treat the matter in a ridiculous way. They quote this one passage, in which Paul teaches about fruit. Yet they leave out many other passages in which he discusses the way of justification in a regular order. Besides, they always add a correction to the other passages that speak of faith, namely, that the passages ought to be understood as applying to "faith formed by love." They add no correction that there is also need for faith, which believes we are counted righteous for Christ's sake as the Atonement. So the adversaries exclude Christ from justification and teach only a righ-101 teousness of the Law. But let us return to Paul. No one can conclude anything more from this text than this: love is necessary. We confess this. It is also necessary not to steal. But the reasoning will not be correct if someone would put the argument like this: "Not to commit theft is necessary. Therefore, not to commit theft justifies." Justification is not the approval of a particular work, but of the entire person. Therefore, this passage from Paul does not harm us. Only, the adversaries must not add to it whatever they please by imagination. Paul does not say that love justifies. He says, "I am nothing" (1 Corinthians 13:2). In other words, faith—however great it may have been—is extinguished. He does not say that love overcomes the terrors of sin and of death, that we can set our love against God's wrath and judgment, or that our love satisfies God's Law. He does not say that we have access to God by our love without Christ as the Atoning Sacrifice, that we receive the promised forgiveness of sins by our love. Paul says nothing about this. He does not, therefore, think that love justifies, because we are justified only when we receive Christ as the Atoning Sacrifice and believe that for Christ's sake God is reconciled to us. Neither is justification even to be dreamed of without Christ as the Atonement. If there is no need of Christ, if we can overcome death by our love, if we have access to God by our love without Christ as the Atonement, then 102 let our adversaries remove the promise about 103 Christ. Let them abolish the Gospel. The adversaries corrupt very many passages, because they bring to them their own opinions and do not derive the meaning from the passages themselves. For what difficulty is there in this passage if we remove the interpretation that the adversaries attach to it out of their own mind? They do not understand what justification is or how it occurs. The Corinthians, being justified before, had received many excellent gifts. In the beginning, they glowed with zeal, just as is generally the

case. Then dissensions began to arise among them, as Paul points out. They began to dislike good teachers. So Paul rebuked them, calling them back to offices of love. These are necessary. Yet it would be foolish to imagine that works of the Second Table (through which we interact with humans and not properly with God) justify us. But in justification we interact with God. His wrath must be appeased and conscience must be eased about God. None of these happen through the works of the Second Table.

104 But they object that love is preferred to faith and hope. For Paul says in 1 Corinthians 13:13, "The greatest of these is love." Now, it is reasonable that the greatest and chief virtue should justify. Yet Paul, in this passage, properly speaks about love toward one's neighbor and indicates that love is the greatest, because it has the most fruit. Faith and hope have to do only with God. But love has infinite offices outwardly toward humanity. Indeed, let us grant to the adversaries that love toward God and our neighbor is the greatest virtue, because the chief commandment is this: "You shall love the Lord your God" (Matthew 22:37). But how will they conclude from this that love justifies? They say, "The greatest virtue justifies." By no means! For just as the greatest, or first, Law does not justify, so also the Law's greatest virtue does not justify. But the virtue that justifies receives Christ, which brings to us Christ's merits, by which we receive grace and peace from God. This virtue is faith. As it has often been said, faith is not just knowledge. But it is willing to receive or take hold of those things that are offered in the promise about Christ. Furthermore, this obedience toward God (i.e., to want to receive the offered promise) is no less a divine service (*latreia*) than is love. God wants us to believe Him and to receive from Him blessings. He declares this to be true divine service.

105

106

107

108 The adversaries base justification on love because they everywhere teach and require the righteousness of the Law. We cannot deny that love is the Law's highest work. Human wisdom gazes at the Law and seeks justification in it. So the scholastic doctors, great and talented men, proclaim love as the Law's highest work and base justification on this work. Deceived by human wisdom, they did not look upon the uncovered, but upon the veiled face of Moses, just like the Pharisees, philosophers, and followers of Muhammad. But we preach the foolishness of the Gospel, in which another righteousness is revealed: for Christ's sake as the Atonement, we are counted righteous when we believe that God has been reconciled to us for Christ's sake. Neither are we ignorant about how far distant this teaching is from the judgment of reason and the Law. Nor are we ignorant that the Law's teaching about love makes a much greater show. For it is wisdom. But we are not ashamed of the Gospel's foolishness. We defend this truth for the sake of Christ's glory and ask Christ, by His Holy Spirit, to help us so that we may be able to make this clear and obvious.

109

110 The adversaries, in the Confutation, have also quoted Colossians 3:14 against us, "love, which binds everything together in perfect harmony." From this they conclude that love justifies because it makes people perfect. Although a reply about perfection could be made here in many ways, we will simply recite Paul's meaning. It is certain that Paul spoke about love toward one's neighbor. We must not think that Paul would credit either justification or perfection to the works of the Second Table, rather than to the works of the First. If love makes people perfect, there will then be no need of Christ as the Atonement (for faith receives Christ as the only Atonement). This is far distant from Paul's mean-

111 ing, who never allows Christ to be excluded as the Atonement. Therefore, he speaks not about personal perfection, but about the integrity common to the Church. For this reason, he says that love is a bond or connection to show that he speaks about the binding and joining together of the many members of the Church. In all families and in all states unity should be nourished by mutual offices, and peace cannot be maintained unless people overlook and forgive certain mistakes among themselves. In a similar way, Paul commands that there should be love in the Church in order that it may preserve unity, bear with the harsher manners of brethren as there is need, and overlook certain less serious mistakes. This must happen or else the Church will fly apart into various schisms, and hostilities and factions and heresies will arise from the schisms.

112 Unity cannot last (is necessarily dissolved) whenever the bishops impose heavier burdens upon the people, or when they have no respect for weakness in the people. Dissensions arise when the people judge too severely the conduct of teachers or despise the teachers because of certain less serious faults. For then, another kind of teaching and other 113 teachers are sought after. On the other hand, perfection (i.e., the Church's integrity) is preserved when the strong bear with the weak, when the people put up with some faults in the conduct of their teachers, and when the bishops make some allowances for the peo- 114 ple's weakness. The books of all the wise are full of these teachings about fairness, namely, that in everyday life we should make many allowances mutually for the sake of common peace. Paul teaches about this frequently both here and elsewhere. Therefore, the adversaries do not argue carefully from the term *perfection* that love justifies. For Paul speaks of common integrity and peace. Am-

brose interprets this passage in this way, "Just as a building is said to be perfect or entire when all its parts are fitly joined together with one another." Furthermore, it is dis- 115 graceful for the adversaries to preach so much about love while they don't show it anywhere. What are they doing now? They are tearing apart churches. They are writing laws in blood and asking the most merciful prince, the emperor, to enforce them. They are killing priests and other good men if any one of them has slightly indicated that he does not entirely approve of their clear abuses. What they are doing is not consistent with their claims of love, which if the adversaries would follow, the churches would be peaceful and the state would have peace. This turmoil would be lessened if the adversaries would stop being so bitter about certain traditions. These traditions are useless for godliness and are hardly observed by those very persons who most earnestly defend them. The adversaries easily forgive themselves, but do not likewise forgive others according to the passage in the poet, " 'I forgive myself,' Maevius said." But what they do is very far 116 from those praises of love that they recite here from Paul. They do not understand the word any more than the walls of a building that echo it back. They cite also this sentence 117 from Peter, "Love covers a multitude of sins" (1 Peter 4:8). Peter also speaks of love toward one's neighbor because he joins this passage to the rule that commands love for one another. No apostle would have imagined (a) our love overcomes sin and death, (b) love satisfies God's wrath and reconciles us to God, while excluding Christ as Mediator, and (c) love in and of itself is righteousness before God without Christ as Mediator. For this love, if such a thing could exist, would be a righteousness of the Law, not of the Gospel. The Gospel promises reconciliation and righteousness to us if we believe that, for the sake of Christ as Reconciler, the Father has been reconciled, and that Christ's merits are 118 given to us. Peter urges us, a little before, to come to Christ that we may be built upon Him. He adds in 1 Peter 2:6, "Whoever believes in Him will not be put to shame." When God judges and convicts us, our love does not free us from confusion. But faith in Christ frees us from these fears because we know that for Christ's sake we are forgiven.

119 Besides, this sentence about love is taken from Proverbs 10:12, where the complete opposite clearly shows how love ought to be understood, "Hatred stirs up strife, but love 120 covers all offenses." This verse teaches precisely the same thing as Paul does in Colossians: if any dissensions would occur, they should be moderated and settled by our fair and patient conduct. Dissensions, it says, increase by means of hatred. We often see that tragedies arise from the most trifling offenses. Certain petty offenses occurred between Gaius Caesar and Pompey. If one had yielded a very little to the other, civil war would not have arisen. But while each gave in to his own hatred, the greatest commotions arose 121 from a matter of no importance. Many heresies have also arisen in the Church only from the hatred of the teachers. Therefore, this verse does not refer to a person's own faults, but to the faults of others. When it says that "love covers a multitude of sins," it means those of others. Even though these offenses occur, love overlooks, forgives, and yields to them, not carrying all things to the extremity of justice. Peter, therefore, does not mean that love merits the forgiveness of sins in God's sight or that it is an atoning sacrifice excluding Christ as Mediator. He also does not mean that such love regenerates and justifies, but that it is not gloomy, harsh, and uncooperative toward people. It overlooks

the mistakes of its friends, while it deplores the harsher manners of others. A well-known saying puts it this way: *Know, but do not hate, the manners of a friend.* Nor did the 122 apostle thoughtlessly teach so often about this office what the philosophers call leniency (*epieikeia*). For this virtue is necessary for keeping public harmony (in the Church and the civil government). Harmony in the Church cannot last unless pastors and churches mutually overlook and pardon many things.

From James 2:24, they cite, "You see that a 123 person is justified by works and not by faith alone." No other passage is supposed to be more contrary to our belief. But the reply is easy and plain. If the adversaries do not attach their own opinions about the merits of works, the words of James have in them nothing that is unhelpful to us. But wherever there is mention of works, the adversaries add their own false, godless opinions. They say we merit the forgiveness of sins by means of good works, that good works are a satisfaction and price on account of which God is reconciled to us, and that good works overcome the terrors of sin and of death. They also say that good works are accepted in God's sight on account of their goodness, and that they do not need mercy and Christ as Reconciler. None of these things came into James's mind. Yet, the adversaries defend such teachings like this passage of James as an excuse.

First, we must consider that the passage is 124 more against the adversaries than against us. For the adversaries teach that a person is justified by love and works. They say nothing about faith, by which we receive Christ as Reconciler. In fact, they condemn this faith, not only in sentences and writings, but also by the sword and capital punishment. They endeavor to exterminate it in the Church.

James teaches much better. He does not leave out faith, or present love in preference to faith, but retains faith, so that in justification Christ may not be excluded as Reconciler! When Paul forms a summary of the Christian life, he also includes faith and love in 1 Timothy 1:5, "The aim of our charge is love that issues from a pure heart and a good conscience and a sincere faith."

125 Second, the subject matter itself shows that the works spoken of here follow faith and that such faith is not dead, but living and effective in the heart. James did not believe that we earn the forgiveness of sins and grace by good works. After all, he is talking about the works of those who have been justified, who have already been reconciled and accepted, and who have received forgiveness of sins. Therefore, the adversaries err when they conclude that James teaches that we merit forgiveness of sins and grace by good works and that we have access to God by our works, apart from Christ as Reconciler.

126 Third, James said a little earlier that regeneration happens through the Gospel. For he says in James 1:18, "Of His own will He brought us forth by the word of truth, that we should be a kind of firstfruits of His creatures." When James says that we have been reborn by the Gospel, he teaches that we have been born again and justified through faith. For the promise about Christ is grasped only through faith when we set it against the terrors of sin and of death. James does not, therefore, think that we are born again through our works.

127 From these things it is clear that James does not contradict us. He criticized lazy and secure minds that imagine they have faith, although they do not have it. He made a distinction between dead and living faith. He

128 says that faith that does not bring forth good works is dead. He also says that a living faith brings forth good works. Furthermore, we have shown already several times what we mean by faith. For we do not mean passive knowledge, such as devils have. Instead, we mean faith that resists the terrors of conscience and encourages and comforts terrified hearts. Such faith is not an easy matter,

129 as the adversaries dream. Neither is it a human power, but it is a divine power. Through faith we are reborn and overcome the devil and death. Paul says to the Colossians that faith is powerful through the power of God and overcomes death, "In which you were also raised with Him through faith in the powerful working of God" (2:12). Since this faith is a new life, it necessarily produces new movements and works. So James is right in denying that we are justified by such a faith that is without works. But when he says that we are justified

130 by faith and works, he certainly does not say that we are born again by works. Neither does he say that Christ is our Reconciler only partly, and our works are our atoning sacrifice in part. Nor does he describe the way of justification, but only the nature of the just, after they have already been justified and regenerated. Here "to be justified" does not

131 mean that a righteous person is made from a wicked person. It means to be pronounced righteous in a judicial sense, as in Romans 2:13, "For it is not the hearers of the law who are righteous before God, but the doers of the law who will be justified." These words "doers of the law who will be justified" contain nothing contrary to our doctrine. We, too, believe about James's words, "A person is justified by works and not by faith alone" (2:24) because people are certainly pronounced righteous having faith and good works. As we have said, the saints' good works are righteous and please God because

of faith. For James praises only works produced by faith, as he testifies when he says of Abraham, "Faith was completed by his works" (2:22). "Doers of the law who will be justified," namely, those who believe God from the heart are pronounced righteous. Afterward, they have good fruit, which please Him because of faith. So they are the fulfill-

132 ment of the Law. These things, simply put, contain nothing incorrect. However, they are distorted by the adversaries, who attach to them godless opinions made in their mind. For it does not follow that (a) works earn the forgiveness of sins, (b) works regenerate hearts, (c) works are an atoning sacrifice, (d) works please without Christ as the Atoning Sacrifice, and (e) works do not need Christ as the Atoning Sacrifice. James says nothing about these things. Yet, the adversaries shamelessly conclude such things from James's words.

133 Certain other passages about works are also cited against us.

> Forgive, and you will be forgiven. (Luke 6:37)

> Is it not to share your bread with the hungry? . . . Then you shall call, and the LORD will answer. (Isaiah 58:7, 9)

> Break off your sins . . . by showing mercy to the oppressed. (Daniel 4:27)

> Blessed are the poor in spirit, for theirs is the kingdom of heaven. (Matthew 5:3)

134 Blessed are the merciful, for they shall receive mercy. (Matthew 5:7)

Even these passages would contain nothing contrary to us if the adversaries would not falsely attach something to them. For they contain two things. One is a preaching either of the Law or of repentance. This preaching not only convicts those doing wrong, but also commands them to do what is right. The other is a promise that is added. But it is not said that sins are forgiven without faith, or that works themselves are an atoning sacrifice. Furthermore, these two things should always be understood in the preaching of the Law. First, the Law cannot be obeyed unless we have been reborn through faith in Christ, just as Christ says in John 15:5, "Apart from Me you can do nothing." Second, some outward works can certainly be done. But this general judgment, which interprets the whole Law, must be retained. "Without faith it is impossible to please [God]" (Hebrews 11:6). The Gospel must also be retained, that through Christ we have access to the Father. (See Hebrews 10:19; Romans 5:2.) For it is clear that we are not justified by the Law. Otherwise, why would we need Christ or the Gospel, if the preaching of the Law alone would be enough? So, in the preaching of repentance, it is not enough to preach the Law, or the Word that convicts of sin. The Law works wrath and only accuses. The Law terrifies consciences, because consciences never are at rest unless they hear God's voice clearly promising the forgiveness of sins. So the Gospel must be added, that for Christ's sake sins are forgiven and that we obtain the forgiveness of sins by faith in Christ. If the adversaries exclude Christ's Gospel from the preaching of repentance, they are rightly judged blasphemers against Christ.

Isaiah preaches repentance as follows: 137

> Cease to do evil, learn to do good; seek justice, correct oppression; bring justice to the fatherless, plead the widow's cause. "Come now, let us reason together, says the Lord: though your sins are like scarlet, they shall be as white as snow." (Isaiah 1:16–18)

So the prophet both urges repentance and adds the promise. But in such a sentence it would be foolish to consider only the words "correct oppression; bring justice to the fatherless." For he says in the beginning, "Cease to do evil," where he criticizes impiety of heart and requires faith. Also, the prophet does not say that through the works "correct oppression; bring justice to the fatherless," they can merit the forgiveness of sins by the outward act (*ex opere operato*), but he insists that such works are necessary in the new life. At the same time, he means that the forgiveness of sins is received through faith. So the

138 promise is added. We must understand all similar passages in this way. Christ preaches repentance when He says, "Forgive," and He adds the promise, "and you will be forgiven" (Luke 6:37). He does not say that when we forgive we merit the forgiveness of sins by our outward act (*ex opere operato*) as they term it. But He requires a new life, which certainly is necessary. At the same time, He means that forgiveness of sins is received through faith. So when Isaiah says, "Share your bread with the hungry" (58:7), he requires a new life. Nor does the prophet speak of this work alone, but, as the text shows, of the entire repentance. At the same time, he means that the forgiveness of sins is received

139 through faith. For the following is sure, and none of the gates of hell can overthrow it: the preaching of the Law is not enough in the preaching of repentance. This is true because the Law works wrath and always accuses. But the preaching of the Gospel should be added so that forgiveness of sins is granted us. Our sins are forgiven if we believe that our sins are forgiven for Christ's sake. Otherwise, why would we need the Gospel? Why would we need Christ? This belief should always be in view so that it may oppose those who cast Christ and the Gospel aside and wickedly distort the Scriptures to human opinions, such as the idea that we purchase the forgiveness of sins by our works.

140 Faith is required also in the sermon of Daniel (4:24–27). For Daniel did not mean that the king should only give alms. He includes repentance when he says, "Break off your . . . iniquities by showing mercy to the oppressed" (4:27). This means, break off your sins by a change of heart and works. Here also, faith is required. Daniel proclaims to him many things about the worship of the only God, the God of Israel. He converts the king not only to give alms, but much more, to have faith. For we have the excellent confession of the king about the God of Israel, "There is no other god who is able to rescue in this way" (Daniel 3:29). Therefore, in Daniel's sermon there are two parts. One part gives a commandment about the new life and the works of the new life. In the other part, Daniel promises the forgiveness of sins to the king. This promise of the forgiveness of sins is not a preaching of the Law, but a truly prophetic and evangelical voice. Daniel certainly meant that the promise should be

141 received in faith. For Daniel knew that the forgiveness of sins in Christ was promised not only to the Israelites, but also to all nations. Otherwise, he could not have promised to the king the forgiveness of sins. For without God's sure Word about His will, a person has no power to claim, especially when terrified by sin, that God ceases to be angry. In his own language, Daniel speaks clearly about repentance and even more clearly brings out the promise, "Break off your sins by practicing righteousness, and your iniquities by showing mercy to the oppressed" (4:27). These words teach about all of repentance. They direct the king to become righteous, then to do good works, to defend the miserable against injustice, as was the king's duty.

142 Righteousness is faith in the heart. Furthermore, sins are redeemed by repentance. In other words, the obligation or guilt is re-

moved because God forgives those who repent, as it is written in Ezekiel 18:21–22. Nor are we to conclude from this that He forgives on account of works that follow, on account of alms. Rather, He forgives only those who take hold of it on account of His promise. Only those who truly believe take hold of this promise, and through faith overcome sin and death. These, being reborn, should produce fruit worthy of repentance, just as John the Baptist says. (See Matthew 3:8.) The promise, therefore, was added, "There may perhaps be a lengthening of your prosperity" (Daniel 143 4:27). Jerome expresses some doubt here, which is beside the matter. In his commentaries he argues much more unwisely that the forgiveness of sins is uncertain. But let us remember that the Gospel gives a sure promise of the forgiveness of sins. To deny that there must be a sure promise of the forgiveness of sins would completely abolish the Gospel. Let us dismiss Jerome concerning this passage. The promise is displayed even in the words "Break off," for it shows that the forgiveness of sins is possible, that sins can be redeemed, that is, that their obligation or guilt can be removed or God's anger can be appeased. But our adversaries, overlooking the promises everywhere, consider only the laws. They falsely attach the human opinion that forgiveness happens on account of works. The text does not say this, but instead requires faith. For wherever a promise is, there faith is required. For a promise cannot be received unless through faith.

144  Works are recognizable among human beings. Human reason naturally admires works. Reason sees only works and does not understand or consider faith. Therefore, it dreams that these works merit forgiveness of sins and justify. This opinion of the Law naturally sticks in people's minds. It cannot be driven out, unless we are divinely taught.

The mind must be recalled from such earthly opinions to God's Word. We see that the Gospel and the promise about Christ have been laid before us. When, therefore, the Law is preached, when works are commanded, we should not reject the promise about Christ. But the promise must first be grasped, in order that we may be able to produce good works pleasing to God, as Christ says, "Apart from Me you can do nothing" (John 15:5). Therefore, if Daniel would have used words like these, "Redeem your sins by repentance," the adversaries would not have noticed this passage. Since Daniel has actually expressed this thought in other words, the adversaries distort his words to the harm of the doctrine of grace and faith. However, Daniel meant his words most especially to include faith. Therefore, we respond to the words of Daniel 146 as follows: Since he is preaching repentance, he is teaching not only about works, but also about faith, as the story itself testifies in the context. Second, because Daniel clearly presents the promise, he necessarily requires faith, which believes that sins are freely forgiven by God. In repentance he mentions works. Yet he does not say that we merit the forgiveness of sins by these works. Daniel speaks not only about the forgiveness of the punishment, for forgiveness of the punishment is sought in vain unless the heart first receives the forgiveness of guilt. Besides, if 147 the adversaries understand Daniel as speaking only about the forgiveness of punishment, this passage will prove nothing against us. It will then become necessary for them also to confess that the forgiveness of sin and free justification come before good works. Afterward, even we concede that the punishments by which we are chastised are soothed. This happens by our prayers, by our good works, and finally by our entire repentance, according to 1 Corinthians 11:31, "But if we judged ourselves truly, we would not be judged."

> If you return, I will restore you. (Jeremiah 15:19)

> Return to Me, says the LORD of hosts, and I will return to you, says the LORD of hosts. (Zechariah 1:3)

> Call upon Me in the day of trouble. (Psalm 50:15)

148    Therefore, in all our praising of works and in the preaching of the Law, let us keep this rule: the Law is not kept without Christ. As He Himself has said, "Apart from Me you can do nothing" (John 15:5). Likewise, "Without faith it is impossible to please [God]" (Hebrews 11:6). For it is very certain that the doctrine of the Law is not intended to remove the Gospel and to remove Christ as the Atoning Sacrifice. Let the Pharisees, our adversaries, be cursed. They interpret the Law to assign Christ's glory to works. (In other words, they say works are an atoning sacrifice, that they merit the forgiveness of sins.) Works are always rightly praised in this way: they are pleasing because of faith. For works do not please without Christ as the Atoning Sacrifice. "Through Him we have also obtained access [to God]" (Romans 5:2), not by works with-

149    out Christ as Mediator. Therefore, when it is said in Matthew 19:17, "If you would enter life, keep the commandments," we must believe that without Christ the commandments are not kept and cannot please. So in the Decalogue itself, in the First Commandment, the most liberal promise of the Law is added, "But showing steadfast love to thousands of those who love Me and keep My commandments" (Exodus 20:6). But this Law is not kept without Christ. For it always accuses the conscience that does not satisfy the Law. Therefore, the conscience flies in terror from the Law's judgment and punishment. For the

Law works anger (Romans 4:15). A person keeps the Law when he hears that for Christ's sake God is reconciled to us, even though we cannot satisfy the Law. When Christ is apprehended as Mediator through this faith, the heart finds rest and begins to love God and to keep the Law. It knows that now, because of Christ as Mediator, it is pleasing to God, even

150    though the inborn fulfilling of the Law is far from perfection and is very impure. We must conclude this about the preaching of repentance. For although the Scholastics have said nothing at all about faith in the doctrine of repentance, yet we think that none of our adversaries is so mad as to deny that Absolution is a voice of the Gospel. And Absolution ought to be received through faith, in order that it may comfort the terrified conscience.

151    The doctrine of repentance—because it not only commands new works, but also promises the forgiveness of sins—necessarily requires faith. The forgiveness of sins is not received unless through faith. Therefore, in those passages that refer to repentance, we should always understand that not only works, but also faith is required. For example, Matthew 6:14 says, "For if you forgive others their trespasses, your heavenly Father will also forgive you." Here a work is required, and the promise of the forgiveness of sins is added. This does not happen because of the work,

152    but through faith, because of Christ. Just as Scripture testifies in many passages:

> To Him all the prophets bear witness that everyone who believes in Him receives forgiveness of sins through His name. (Acts 10:43)

> Your sins are forgiven for His name's sake. (1 John 2:12)

> We have redemption through His blood, the forgiveness of our trespasses. (Ephesians 1:7)

153     What need is there to recite testimonies? This is the very voice unique to the Gospel, namely, that for Christ's sake, and not for the sake of our works, we obtain the forgiveness of sins through faith. Our adversaries work to suppress this voice of the Gospel by means of distorted passages, which contain the doctrine of the Law or of works. It is true that in the doctrine of repentance works are required, because certainly a new life is required. But here the adversaries wrongly add that by such works we merit the forgiveness of sins, or justification.

154     Christ often connects the promise of the forgiveness of sins to good works, yet not because He means that good works are an atoning sacrifice (for they follow reconciliation). Christ makes this connection for two reasons. One is because good fruit must necessarily follow. He reminds us that if good fruit do not follow, the repentance is hypocritical and fake. The other reason is that we have need of outward signs of so great a promise. A conscience full of fear

155     has need of much consolation. Baptism and the Lord's Supper are signs that continually remind, cheer, and encourage despairing minds to believe more firmly that their sins are forgiven. So the same promise is written and portrayed in good works, in order that these works may remind us to believe more firmly. Those who produce no good works do not encourage themselves to believe, but despise these promises. On the other hand, the godly embrace them and rejoice that they have the signs and testimonies of so great a promise. So they exercise themselves in these signs and testimonies. Therefore, just as the Lord's Supper does not justify us by the outward act (*ex opere operato*) without faith, so alms do not justify us by the outward act (*ex opere operato*) without faith.

156     The address of Tobit 4:11 ought to be received this way also, "Alms free from every sin and from death." We will not say that this is an exaggeration, although we should see it that way so that we do not detract from the praise of Christ, whose right it is to free from sin and death. But we must come back to the rule that without Christ, the doctrine of the Law is of no profit. Therefore, those alms 157 please God that follow reconciliation or justification, and not those that come before. They do not free from sin and death by the outward act (*ex opere operato*). As we have said above about repentance, we ought to embrace faith and its fruit. So here we must say about alms that this entire newness of life saves. Alms also are the exercises of faith, which receives the forgiveness of sins and overcomes death, while it exercises itself more and more, and in these exercises receives strength. We grant also this, that alms merit many favors from God, lessen punishments, and merit our defense in the dangers of sins and of death, as we have said a little before about the entire repentance. Tobit's 158 address, regarded as a whole, shows that faith is required before alms, "Be mindful of the Lord, your God, all your days" (4:5). Afterward, "Bless the Lord, your God, always, and desire of Him that your ways be directed by Him" (4:19). This, however, belongs properly to that faith, which believes that God is reconciled to it because of His mercy, and which wishes to be justified, sanctified, and governed by God. But our adversaries, 159 charming men, pick out mutilated sentences in order to deceive those who are unskilled. Afterward, they attach something from their own opinions. Therefore, entire passages are to be required. According to the common rule it is inappropriate, before the entire Law is thoroughly examined, to judge or reply when any single clause of it is presented. When produced in their entirety, passages very frequently bring the interpretation with them.

The Golden Calf

160    Luke 11:41 is also cited in a mutilated form, namely, "But give as alms those things that are within, and behold, everything is clean for you." The adversaries are very stupid. Time and again we have said that the Gospel about Christ should be added to the preaching of the Law. Because of Christ, good works are pleasing. But our adversaries teach everywhere that, Christ being excluded, justification is merited by the works of the

161    Law. When this passage is produced unmutilated, it will show that faith is required. Christ rebukes the Pharisees, who think that they are cleansed before God (that is, that they are justified) by frequent bathings. This is just as some pope or other who says that holy water "sanctifies and cleanses the people," and the gloss says that it cleanses "from venial" sins. Such also were the opinions of the Pharisees that Christ rebuked. Against this phony cleansing He sets up a double cleanness: one inward, the other outward. He bids them be cleansed inwardly and adds concerning the outward cleanness: "But give as alms those things that are within, and be-

162    hold, everything is clean for you." The adversaries do not rightly apply the phrase "everything," for Christ adds this conclusion to both parts: "All things will be clean unto you, if you will be clean within, and will outwardly give alms." He shows that outward cleanness is to be connected to works commanded by God, and not to human traditions. These traditions were the bathings held at that time, like the daily sprinkling of water. (The clothing of monks, the distinctions of food, and similar pompous acts appear this way to us now.) But the adversaries distort the meaning by transferring the universal phrase

163    to only one part like Sophists. Yet Peter says in Acts 15:9, "having cleansed their hearts by faith." When this entire passage is examined, it presents a meaning harmonizing with the rest of Scripture. If the hearts are cleansed and then outwardly alms are added (i.e., all the works of love), they are entirely clean (i.e., not only within, but also without). Why is not Christ's entire speech added to it? There are many parts of the rebuke, some of which give commandments about faith and others about works. It is not the place of an honest reader to pick out the commands about works, while the passages about faith are skipped.

Last, readers are to be reminded of this: 164 the adversaries give the worst advice to godly consciences when they teach that the forgiveness of sins is earned by works. Conscience, in seeking forgiveness through works, cannot be confident that the work will satisfy God. It is always tormented, and continually invents other works and other acts of worship, until it completely despairs. This course is described by Paul in Romans 4:5. There he proves that the promise of righteousness is not obtained because of our works. We could never affirm that we had a reconciled God, for the Law always accuses. So the promise would be in vain and uncertain. He concludes that this promise of the forgiveness of sins and of righteousness is received through faith, not because of works. This is Paul's true, simple, and genuine meaning. In it the greatest consolation is offered to godly consciences, and Christ's glory is shown forth. He certainly was given to us for this purpose, namely, that through Him we might have grace, righteousness, and peace.

So far we have reviewed the chief passages 165 that the adversaries cite against us. They point to these passages to try to show that faith does not justify, and that we merit the forgiveness of sins and grace by our works. But we hope that we have shown clearly enough to godly consciences that (a) these passages are not opposed to our doctrine; (b) the adversaries wickedly distort the Scripture to their opinions; (c) most of the passages that they cite have been garbled; (d) while leaving out the clearest passages about faith, they only select from the Scripture passages about works, and even these they distort; (e) everywhere they add certain human opinions to what the words of Scripture say; (f) they teach the Law in such a way as to suppress the Gospel about Christ. The entire doctrine of the adversaries is, in part, derived from human reason. In part, it is a doctrine of the Law, not of the Gospel. For they teach two ways of justification: one derived from reason, and the other derived from the Law, not from the Gospel, or the promise about Christ.

## The Adversaries' Teaching Based on Reason and the Law

167    The former way of justification they teach is that people merit grace by good works both in a merely agreeable way (*de congruo*) and in a wholly deserving way (*de condigno*). This way is a doctrine of reason. For reason, not seeing the uncleanness of the heart, thinks that it pleases God if it performs good works. Therefore, other works and other acts of worship are constantly invented by people in great peril, to defend against the terrors of conscience. The pagans and the Israelites slew human victims and undertook many other most painful works in order to appease God's anger. Afterward, orders of monks were invented, and these challenged each other in the severity of their observances against the terrors of conscience and God's anger. This way of justification (because it is according to reason and is completely occupied with outward works) can be understood and be done to a certain extent. To this end the canon lawyers have distorted the misunderstood Church ordinances, which were en-

acted by the Fathers for a far different purpose. The Fathers did not intend that we follow the ordinances in order to seek after righteousness, but they were given for the sake of mutual peace among people, so there might be a certain order in the Church. In this way, the canon lawyers also distorted the Sacraments, and most especially the Mass. Through them they seek righteousness, grace, and salvation by the outward act.

168    Another way of justification is handed down by the scholastic theologians when they teach that we are righteous through a habit infused by God, which is love. They say that, aided by this habit, we keep God's Law outwardly and inwardly, and that this fulfilling of the Law is worthy of grace and of eternal life. This doctrine is plainly the doctrine of the Law. For what the Law says is true, "You shall love the LORD your God" (Deuteronomy 6:5). Also, "You shall love your neighbor" (Leviticus 19:18). Love is, therefore, the fulfilling of the Law.

169    But it is easy for a Christian to judge about both of these ways [of justification] because both exclude Christ. They are, therefore, to be rejected. In the former, which teaches that our works are an atoning sacrifice for sin, the impiety is clear. The latter way contains much that is harmful. It does not teach that, when we are born again, we make use of Christ. It does not teach that justification is the forgiveness of sins. It does not teach that we attain the forgiveness of sins before we love, but falsely represents that we rouse in ourselves the act of love, through which we merit the forgiveness of sins. Nor does it teach that we overcome the terrors of sin and death through faith in Christ. It falsely claims that, by their own fulfilling of the Law, without Christ as the Atoning Sacrifice, people come to God. Finally, it claims that this very fulfilling of the Law, without Christ

as the Atoning Sacrifice, is righteousness worthy of grace and eternal life. Nevertheless, scarcely a weak and feeble fulfilling of the Law happens even in saints.

170 Truly, if anyone will think about it, he will most easily understand that the Gospel has not been given in vain to the world, and that Christ has not been promised and set forth, has not been born, has not suffered, has not risen again in vain. He will most easily understand that we are justified not by reason or by the Law. Therefore, in regard to justification, we are compelled to disagree with the adversaries. For the Gospel shows another way. The Gospel compels us to make use of Christ in justification. The Gospel teaches that through Christ we have access to God through faith. It teaches that we ought to set Him as Mediator and Atoning Sacrifice against God's anger. The Gospel teaches that through faith in Christ the forgiveness of sins and reconciliation are received, and the ter-171 rors of sin and of death are overcome. Paul also says that righteousness is not of the Law, but of the promise. The Father has promised that He wants to forgive, that for Christ's sake He wants to be reconciled. This promise, however, is received through faith alone, as Paul testifies in Romans 4:13. This faith alone receives the forgiveness of sins, justifies, and regenerates. Then love and other good fruit follow. Therefore, we teach that a person is justified (as we have said above) when conscience, terrified by the preaching of repentance, is cheered and believes that for Christ's sake it has a reconciled God. "Faith is counted as righteousness [before God]" (Romans 172 4:3, 5). When the heart is cheered and quickened through faith in this way, it receives the Holy Spirit. He renews us, so that we are able to keep the Law, to love God and God's Word, to be submissive to God in afflictions, to be chaste, to love our neighbor, and so on.

Even though these works are far from the perfection of the Law, on account of faith they please God. Through faith we are accounted righteous, because we believe that for Christ's sake we have a reconciled God. These things are plain and in harmony with the Gospel and can be understood by persons of sound mind. From this foundation it 173 can easily be decided why we attribute justification to faith, and not to love. Love follows faith, because love is the fulfilling of the Law (Romans 13:10). But Paul teaches that we are justified not from the Law, but from the promise, which is received only through faith. We neither come to God without Christ as Mediator, nor receive the forgiveness of sins for the sake of our love, but for the sake of Christ. Likewise, we are not able 174 to love God while He is angry, and the Law always accuses us, always presents an angry God to us. Therefore, we must first take the promise through faith that for Christ's sake the Father is reconciled and forgives. After- 175 ward, we begin to keep the Law. Our eyes are to be cast—far away from human reason, far away from Moses—upon Christ. We are to believe that Christ is given to us, in order that for His sake we may be counted righteous. In the flesh we never satisfy the Law. Therefore, 176 we are counted righteous, not because of the Law, but because of Christ. His merits are granted us, if we believe on Him. We are not justified by the Law, because human nature cannot keep God's Law and cannot love God. We are justified from the promise, in which, for Christ's sake, reconciliation, righteousness, and eternal life have been promised. If anyone, therefore, has considered these foundations, he will easily understand that justification must necessarily be attributed to faith. It is not in vain that Christ has been promised and set forth, that He has been born and has suffered and been raised again. The promise of grace in Christ is not in vain. It was made immediately from the beginning of the world, apart from and beyond the Law. The promise should be received through faith, as 1 John 5:10–12 says:

> Whoever does not believe God has made Him a liar, because he has not believed in the testimony that God has borne concerning His Son. And this is the testimony, that God gave us eternal life, and this life is in His Son. Whoever has the Son has life; whoever does not have the Son of God does not have life.

Christ says, "So if the Son sets you free, you will be free indeed" (John 8:36). Paul says in Romans 5:2, "Through Him we have also obtained access by faith into this grace in which we stand." By faith in Christ, therefore, the promise of the forgiveness of sins and of righteousness is received. Neither are we justified before God by reason or by the Law.

177 These things are so plain and so clear we wonder how the insanity of the adversaries is so great that it calls them into doubt. The proof is clear. Since we are justified before God not from the Law, but from the promise, it is necessary to attribute justification to faith. What can be opposed to this proof, unless someone wishes to abolish the entire

178 Gospel and the entire Christ? Christ's glory becomes more brilliant when we teach that we make the most of Him as our Mediator and Atoning Sacrifice. Godly consciences see that the most abundant consolation is offered to them in this doctrine. They see that they ought to believe and most firmly assert that they have a reconciled Father for Christ's sake, and not for the sake of our righteousness. Yet, they also see that Christ aids

179 us, so that we are able to keep the Law as well. The adversaries deprive the Church of such great blessings as these when they condemn,

and work to wipe out, the doctrine about the righteousness of faith. Therefore, let all good minds beware of consenting to the godless counsels of the adversaries. In the adversaries' teaching about justification, no mention is made of Christ and how we ought to set Him against God's anger, as though we were able to overcome His anger by love, or

180 to love an angry God. In regard to these things, consciences are left in uncertainty. For if they think that they have a reconciled God because they love and keep the Law, they will always doubt whether they have a reconciled God. This is so because they either do not feel this love, as the adversaries acknowledge, or they certainly feel that it is very small. Much more often they feel that they are angry at God's judgment. They feel He oppresses human nature with many terrible evils, with troubles of this life, the terrors of eternal anger, and so on. When, therefore, will conscience be at rest? When will it be quieted? When, in this doubt and in these terrors, will it love God? What else is the doctrine of the Law than a doctrine of despair?

181 Let any one of our adversaries come forward to teach us about this love, how he himself loves God. They do not at all understand what they say. They only echo, just like the walls of a house, the little word *love* without understanding it. Their teaching is confused and shadowy. It not only transfers Christ's glory to human works, but also leads con-

182 sciences either to arrogance or to despair. But our teaching, we hope, is readily understood by pious minds and brings godly and wholesome consolation to terrified consciences. For as the adversaries mock that "also many wicked people and devils believe" (cf. James 2:19), we have frequently said already that we speak of faith in Christ, namely, of faith in the forgiveness of sins, of faith that truly and heartily assents to the promise of grace. This

is not brought about without a great struggle in human hearts. People of sound mind can easily judge the faith that believes we are cared for by God, that we are forgiven and heard by Him. It is something that surpasses nature. For by itself the human mind makes no such decision about God (1 Corinthians 2:14–16). Therefore, this faith of which we speak is neither in the wicked nor in devils.

183 Furthermore, if any learned person objects that righteousness is in the will and, therefore, it cannot be attributed to faith, which is in the intellect, the reply is easy. In the schools even such persons acknowledge that the will commands the intellect to agree with God's Word. We say also quite clearly, "Just as the terrors of sin and death are not only thoughts of the intellect, but also horrible movements of the will fleeing God's judgment, so faith is not only knowledge in the intellect, but also confidence in the will. In other words, it is to want and to receive that which is offered in the promise, namely, reconciliation and the forgiveness of sins."

184 Scripture uses the term *faith* this way, as the following sentence of Paul testifies in Romans 5:1, "Therefore, since we have been justified by faith, we have peace with God through our Lord Jesus Christ." Furthermore, in this passage, to justify means (according to court language) to acquit a guilty person and declare him righteous. But this happens because of the righteousness of another, namely, of Christ. This righteousness

185 is communicated to us through faith. Therefore, since our righteousness in this passage is the credit of the righteousness of another, we must here speak about righteousness in a way different than in philosophy or in a civil court. (There we seek after the righteousness of one's own work, which certainly is in the will.) So Paul says in 1 Corinthians 1:30, "He is the source of your life in Christ Jesus, whom God made our wisdom and our righteousness and sanctification and redemption." And in 2 Corinthians 5:21, "For our sake He made Him to be sin who knew no sin, so that in Him we might become the righteousness of God." But because Christ's 186 righteousness is given to us through faith, faith is righteousness credited to us. In other words, it is that by which we are made acceptable to God on account of the credit and ordinance of God, as Paul says, "Faith is counted as righteousness" (Romans 4:3, 5). Although, because of certain hard-to-please 187 people, we must say technically: Faith is truly righteousness, because it is obedience to the Gospel. For it is clear that obedience to the command of a superior is truly a kind of distributive justice. This obedience to the Gospel is credited for righteousness. So, only because of this—because we grasp Christ as the Atoning Sacrifice—are good works, or obedience to the Law, pleasing. We do not satisfy the Law, but for Christ's sake this is forgiven us, as Paul says, "There is therefore now no condemnation for those who are in Christ Jesus" (Romans 8:1). This faith gives 188 God the honor, gives God that which is His own. By receiving the promises, it obeys Him. Just as Paul also says, "No distrust made him waver concerning the promise of God, but he grew strong in his faith as he gave glory to God" (Romans 4:20). So the worship 189 and divine service of the Gospel is to receive gifts from God. On the contrary, the worship of the Law is to offer and present our gifts to God. However, we can offer nothing to God unless we have first been reconciled and born again. This passage, too, brings the greatest comfort, as the chief worship of the Gospel is to desire to receive the forgiveness of sins, grace, and righteousness. Christ says of this worship, "For this is the will of My Father, that everyone who looks on the Son and be-

lieves in Him should have eternal life, and I will raise him up on the last day" (John 6:40). And the Father says, "This is My beloved Son, with whom I am well pleased; listen to Him"

190 (Matthew 17:5). The adversaries speak of obedience to the Law, but they do not speak of obedience to the Gospel. We cannot obey the Law, unless we have been born again through the Gospel. We cannot love God, unless we have received the forgiveness of

191 sins. For as long as we feel that He is angry with us, our human nature runs away from His anger and judgment. If anyone should object that this view of faith (which desires those things offered by the promise) becomes confused with hope, we answer as follows. Hope expects promised things, and hope and faith cannot be separated in reality. Such needless debate takes place in the schools. The Epistle to the Hebrews defines faith as "the assurance (*exspectatio*) of things hoped for" (Hebrews 11:1). Yet if anyone wants a distinction between faith and hope, we say that the object of hope is properly a future event, but that faith is concerned with future and present things. Faith receives the forgiveness of sins offered in the promise in the present.

192 From these statements we hope that it is clear both what faith is and that we are justified, reconciled, and regenerated through faith. We are compelled to hold on to these teachings because we want to teach the righteousness of the Gospel, not the righteousness of the Law. For those who teach that we are justified by love teach the righteousness of the Law. They do not teach us in justification to trust in Christ as Mediator.

193 These things are also clear. We overcome the terrors of sin and death not through love, but through faith. For we cannot set up our love and fulfilling of the Law against God's wrath, because Paul says, "Through [Christ] we have also obtained access [to God] by faith" (Romans 5:2). We often emphasize this sentence so that we are understood. The sentence shows most clearly our whole argument and, when carefully considered, can teach abundantly about the whole matter. It can console good minds. So, it is helpful to have it at hand and in sight, that we may be able to set it against the doctrine of our adversaries. They teach that we come to God not through faith, but through love and merits, without Christ as Mediator. This sentence also helps us when we fear, so that we

194 may cheer ourselves and exercise faith. This is also clear. We cannot keep the Law without Christ's aid. He Himself says, "Apart from Me you can do nothing" (John 15:5). So, before we keep the Law, our hearts must be born again through faith.

## Results of the Adversaries' Teaching

195 It is clear why we find fault with the adversaries' doctrine about good works rewarded because of God's generosity (*meritum condigni*). The decision is very easy.

*First.* The adversaries do not even mention faith, that we please God through faith for Christ's sake. Rather, they imagine that good works, worked by the aid of the habit of love, make a righteousness worthy to please God by itself, and also worthy of eternal life. So they have no need of Christ as Mediator.

196 What else is this than to transfer Christ's glory to our works? It means we would please God because of our works, not because of Christ. But this robs Christ of the glory of being the Mediator. He is the Mediator forever, and not merely in the beginning of justification. Paul also says that if one justified in Christ seeks righteousness elsewhere, he affirms that Christ is a minister of sin (Galatians 2:17), that is, that He does not fully jus-

197 tify. What the adversaries teach is most silly.

They teach that good works merit grace because of God's mercy (*de condigno*). They mean that after the beginning of justification, if conscience is terrified (which happens), grace must be sought through a good work, and not through faith in Christ.

198 *Second.* The doctrine of the adversaries leaves consciences in doubt, so that they never can be quieted. This is so because the Law always accuses us, even in good works. For always "the desires of the flesh are against the Spirit" (Galatians 5:17). How will an unbelieving conscience have peace if it believes that for the sake of one's own work, it ought now to please God and not for Christ's sake? What work will it find, what will it trust as worthy of eternal life if, indeed, hope begins from merits? Against these doubts Paul says, "Therefore, since we have been justified by faith, we have peace with God" (Romans 5:1). We should be firmly convinced that we are granted righteousness and eternal life for Christ's sake. He says about Abraham, "In hope he believed against hope" (Romans 4:18).

200 *Third.* How will a conscience know when a work was done by the inclination of this habit of love so that it is possible to conclude that the work merits grace in a wholly deserving way (*de condigno*)? This very distinction has been created to dodge the Scriptures. It teaches that people merit grace at one time in a merely agreeable way (*de congruo*) and at another time in a wholly deserving way (*de condigno*). As we have said above, the intention of the one who works does not matter. Hypocrites, in their security, simply think their works are worthy and that they are regarded righteous. On the other hand, terrified consciences have doubts about all works, and for this reason continually seek other works. For this is what it means to merit "in a merely agreeable way" (*de con-*

*gruo*). It means to doubt and, without faith, to work, until despair takes place. In short, all that the adversaries teach about this matter is full of errors and dangers.

201 *Fourth.* The entire Church confesses that eternal life is attained through mercy. Augustine speaks this way in *On Grace and Free Will.* There he speaks about the works of the saints completed after justification, "God leads us to eternal life not by our merits, but according to His mercy." He says in his Confessions, Book IX: "Woe to the life of man, however much it may be worthy of praise, if it be judged with mercy removed." And Cyprian, in his treatise on the Lord's Prayer, says this:

> Lest anyone should flatter himself that he is innocent, and by exalting himself, should perish the more deeply, he is instructed and taught that he sins daily, in that he is told to ask forgiveness daily for his sins.

202 But the subject is well known and has very many and very clear testimonies in Scripture and in the Church Fathers. They all declare with one mouth that, even though we have good works, yet in these very works we need 203 mercy. Faith, looking upon this mercy, cheers and consoles us. The adversaries teach wrongly when they praise merits and add nothing about this faith that takes hold of mercy. For, as we have said before, the promise and faith mutually agree with each other. The promise is grasped only through faith. So we say that the promised mercy agrees with the requirement of faith and cannot be taken hold of without faith. So we justly find fault with the doctrine about wholly deserving merit (*meritum condigni*), since it teaches nothing of justifying faith. It also hides 204 Christ's glory and office as Mediator. We should not be regarded as teaching anything

new in this matter. The Church Fathers have clearly handed down the doctrine that we need mercy even in good works.

205    Scripture also often teaches the same. "Enter not into judgment with Your servant, for no one living is righteous before You" (Psalm 143:2). This passage denies absolutely—even to all saints and servants of God—the glory of righteousness, if God does not forgive, but judges and convicts their hearts. For when David boasts in other places about his righteousness, he speaks about his own cause against the persecutors of God's Word. He does not speak of his personal purity. He asks that God's cause and glory be defended, "Judge me, O LORD, according to my righteousness and according to the integrity that is in me" (Psalm 7:8) Likewise, in Psalm 130:3, he says that no one can endure God's judgment, if God were to mark our sins:

> "If You, O LORD, should mark iniquities, O Lord, who could stand?"

206    I become afraid of all my suffering. (Job 9:28) [Vulgate: *opera*, works]

> If I wash myself with snow and cleanse my hands with lye, yet You will plunge me into a pit. (Job 9:30–31)

> Who can say, "I have made my heart pure; I am clean from my sin"? (Proverbs 20:9)

207    If we say we have no sin, we deceive ourselves, and the truth is not in us. (1 John 1:8)

208    In the Lord's Prayer the saints ask for the forgiveness of sins. Therefore, even the saints have sins. The innocent shall not be innocent (Numbers 14:18; cf. Exodus 34:7).

> For the LORD your God is a consuming fire, a jealous God. (Deuteronomy 4:24)

> Be silent, all flesh, before the LORD. (Zechariah 2:13)

> All flesh is grass, and all its beauty is like the flower of the field. The grass withers, the flower fades when the breath of the Lord blows on it. (Isaiah 40:6–7)

Namely, flesh and righteousness of the flesh cannot endure God's judgment. Jonah 2:8   209 also says, "Those who pay regard to vain idols forsake their hope of steadfast love," that is, all confidence is empty, except confidence in mercy. Mercy delivers us; our own merits, our own efforts, do not. So Daniel also prays:   210

> For we do not present our pleas before You because of our righteousness, but because of Your great mercy. O Lord, hear; O Lord, forgive. O Lord, pay attention and act. Delay not, for Your own sake, O my God, because Your city and Your people are called by Your name. (Daniel 9:18–19)

So Daniel teaches us in praying to seize mercy, that is, to trust in God's mercy and not to trust in our own merits before God. We also wonder what our adversaries do in   211 prayer, if the ungodly people ever ask anything of God. If they declare that they are worthy because they have love and good works and ask for grace as a debt, they pray precisely like the Pharisee who says, "I am not like other men" (Luke 18:11). He who prays for grace in this way does not rely upon God's mercy and treats Christ with disrespect. After all, He is our High Priest, who intercedes for us. So prayer relies upon God's   212 mercy, when we believe that we are heard for Christ's sake. He is our High Priest, as He Himself says, "Whatever you ask in My name, this I will do, that the Father may be glorified in the Son. If you ask Me anything in My name, I will do it" (John 14:13–14).

Without this High Priest we cannot approach the Father.

### Salvation Is by God's Mercy

213　Here Christ's declaration also applies, "So you also, when you have done all that you were commanded, say, 'We are unworthy servants; we have only done what was our duty'" (Luke 17:10). These words clearly declare that God saves by mercy and because of His promise, not that it is due because of the 214　value of our works. But at this point the adversaries play wonderfully with Christ's words. In the first place, they turn His words around and then turn them against us. Even more, they claim it can be said: "If we have believed all things, say, we are unprofitable servants." Then they add that works do not 215　profit God, but works do profit us. See how the childish study of slick logic delights the adversaries? Although these foolish things do not deserve a response, we will still reply to

them in a few words. Their reversal of words is defective. In the first place, the adversaries 216 are deceived regarding the term *faith*. If faith would signify historical knowledge that the wicked and the devils also possess, the adversaries would correctly argue that faith is unprofitable when they say: "When we have believed all things, say, 'We are unprofitable servants.'" But we are not speaking of historical knowledge, but of confidence in God's promise and mercy. This confidence in the promise confesses that we are unprofitable servants. Yes, this confession that our works are unworthy is the very voice of faith, as appears in this example of Daniel 9:18, which we cited, "We do not present our pleas before You because of our righteousness." Faith 217 saves because it takes hold of mercy, or the promise of grace, even though our works are unworthy. Understood this way, namely, that our works are unworthy, the word reversal does not injure us: "When you shall have be-

Jesus, the Good Shepherd

lieved all things, say, 'We are unprofitable servants.'" We teach the same as the entire Church when we teach that we are saved by

218 mercy. But if they mean to argue from these similar statements: "When you have done all things, do not trust in your works," also, "When you have believed all things, do not trust in the divine promise," there is no connection. These statements are not alike. The causes and objects of confidence in the former statement are very different from those of the latter. In the former, confidence lies in our own works. In the latter, confidence lies in the divine promise. Christ, however, condemns confidence in our works; He does not condemn confidence in His promise. He does not wish us to lose hope of God's grace and mercy. He attacks our works as unworthy, but does not attack the promise that

219 freely offers mercy. Here Ambrose says well, "Grace is to be acknowledged; but nature

220 must not be disregarded." We must trust in the promise of grace and not in our own nature. The adversaries act predictably and distort, against faith, the judgments that have been given on behalf of faith. We leave, how-

221 ever, these thorny points to the schools. The slick logic is plainly childish when they interpret "unprofitable servant" to mean that works are unprofitable to God, but are profitable to us. Christ does speak about that profit that makes God a debtor of grace to us, although it is out of place to discuss here about what is profitable or unprofitable. For "unprofitable servants" means "insufficient," because no one fears God as much, loves God as much, and believes God as much as he

222 should. Let us overlook these cold jokes of the adversaries. If they are ever brought to the light, levelheaded people will easily decide what they should conclude. The adversaries have found a flaw in words that are very plain and clear. But everyone sees that

confidence in our own works is condemned in this passage.

Let us hold on to this confession of the   223 Church: we are saved by mercy. Let no one think, "Hope will be uncertain if we are to be saved by mercy. It will be unsure without something coming out first that distinguishes those who obtain salvation from those who do not." We must give such a person a satisfactory answer. For the Scholastics, moved by this reason, seem to have invented the doctrine of wholly deserving merit (*meritum condigni*). Thinking about such a thing   224 can greatly exercise the human mind. We will, therefore, reply briefly. It is essential to believe that we are saved by mercy so that hope may be sure, so that there may be a resulting distinction between those who obtain salvation and those who do not. When this is expressed in this way without explanation, it seems foolish. For in civil courts and in human judgment, issues about rights or debts are certain, and mercy is uncertain. But the matter is different in God's judgment. Here mercy has a clear and certain promise and command from God. The Gospel is properly the command that directs us to believe that God is reconciled to us for Christ's sake. "For God did not send His Son into the world to condemn the world, but in order that the world might be saved through Him" (John 3:17). Whenever mercy is spoken of,   225 faith in the promise must be added. This faith produces sure hope, because it relies upon God's Word and command. If hope would rely upon works, then it would be uncertain, because works cannot quiet the conscience, as has been said before. Faith makes   226 a distinction between those who obtain salvation and those who do not obtain it. Faith makes the distinction between the worthy and the unworthy, because eternal life has been promised to the justified. Faith justifies.

227 Here again the adversaries will cry out that there is no need of good works if they do not merit eternal life. These lies we have refuted above. Of course, it is necessary to do good works. We say that eternal life has been promised to the justified. But those who walk according to the flesh (Galatians 5:19–21) retain neither faith nor righteousness. For this very reason we are justified: being righteous, we may begin to do good works and to obey

228 God's Law. We are regenerated and receive the Holy Spirit for the very reason that the new life may produce new works, new dispositions, the fear and love of God, hatred of lustful desires (concupiscence), and so on.

229 This faith arises in repentance and should be established and grow amid good works, temptations, and dangers. This is so that we may continually be more firmly persuaded that God cares for us, forgives us, and hears us for Christ's sake. This is not learned without many and great struggles. How often is conscience aroused, how often does it awaken even to despair when it shows either old or new sins, or the impurity of our nature! This handwriting is not blotted out without a great struggle (Colossians 2:14). Experience

230 testifies what a difficult matter faith is. While we are encouraged in the midst of the terrors and receive comfort, other spiritual movements grow at the same time: knowledge of God, fear of God, hope and love of God. We are "renewed," as Paul says, "in knowledge after the image of its creator" (Colossians 3:10) and, "Beholding the glory of the Lord, [we] are being transformed into the same image" (2 Corinthians 3:18). In other words, we receive the true knowledge of God, so that we truly fear Him, we truly trust that we are cared for by Him, and that we are heard by

231 Him. This regeneration is the beginning of eternal life as Paul says, "If Christ is in you, although the body is dead because of sin, the Spirit is life because of righteousness" (Romans 8:10). And, "Longing to put on our

232 heavenly dwelling, if indeed by putting it on we may not be found naked" (2 Corinthians 5:2–3). The honest reader can judge from these statements that we certainly require good works, since we teach that faith arises in repentance and is bound to increase in repentance. We place Christian and spiritual perfection in these matters, if repentance and faith grow together in repentance. The godly can understand this better than the adversaries' teaching about contemplation or per-

233 fection. However, just as justification applies to faith, so also eternal life applies to faith. Peter says, "Obtaining the outcome [or fruit] of your faith, the salvation of your souls" (1 Peter 1:9). For the adversaries confess that the justified are children of God and coheirs

234 of Christ. Afterward, because works please God on account of faith, they earn other bodily and spiritual rewards. For there will be distinctions in the glory of the saints.

235 Here the adversaries reply that eternal life is called a reward and that, therefore, it is merited in a wholly deserving way (de condigno) by good works. We reply briefly and plainly. Paul calls eternal life a "gift" (Romans 6:23), because by the righteousness presented for Christ's sake, we are made at the same time sons of God and coheirs of Christ. As John says, "Whoever believes in the Son has eternal life" (John 3:36). Augustine says, as also do very many others who follow him, "God crowns His gifts in us." Elsewhere it is written, "Your reward is great in heaven" (Luke 6:23). If these passages seem to conflict for the adversaries, they themselves may explain them. But the adversaries are not fair

236 judges. They leave out the word *gift*. They also leave out the primary teachings of the entire matter. Further, they select the word *reward* and twist its meaning not only against

Scripture, but also against the common use of language. In this way, they conclude that because our works are called a reward, there should be a price paid for eternal life. They assume they are worthy of grace and life eternal and do not stand in need of mercy or of Christ as Mediator or of faith. This logic is altogether new. We hear the term *reward* and are supposed to conclude that there is no need of Christ as Mediator, or of faith having access to God for Christ's sake, not for the sake of our works! Who does not see that these are unrelated sentences wrongly joined together? We do not argue about the term *reward*. We argue whether good works are of themselves worthy of grace and of eternal life, or whether they please only on account of faith, which takes hold of Christ as Mediator. Our adversaries not only attribute this to works, namely, that they are worthy of grace and of eternal life, but they also state falsely that works have surplus merits. The adversaries maintain that these merits can be granted to other people to justify them, as when monks sell to others the merits of their orders. They heap up these freakish ideas in the manner of Chrysippus, especially about this one word *reward*.

> It is called a reward; therefore, works are the price paid for it. So works please by themselves, and not for the sake of Christ as Mediator. And since one has more merits than another, some have surplus merits. Those who have earned them can sell them to others.

Stop, dear reader! You don't have the whole chain of arguments. For certain "sacraments" of this purchase must be added: the hood is placed upon the dead. The blessings brought to us in Christ, and the righteousness of faith, have been hidden by such additions.

We are not trying to start a needless word battle about the term *reward*. But this is a great, exalted, and very important matter about where Christian hearts can find true and certain comfort. It is about whether our works can give consciences rest and peace, whether we are to believe that our works are worthy of eternal life, or whether that is given to us for Christ's sake. These are the real questions regarding these matters. If consciences are not rightly taught about these, they can have no certain comfort. However, we have stated clearly enough that good works do not fulfill the Law, that we need God's mercy, that through faith we are accepted by God, that good works—be they ever so precious, even if they were the works of St. Paul himself—cannot bring rest to the conscience. It makes sense that we are to believe that we receive eternal life through Christ by faith, not because of our works or of the Law. But what do we say of the reward that Scripture mentions? If the adversaries will admit that we are regarded righteous through faith because of Christ, and that good works please God because of faith, we will not afterward argue much about the term *reward*. We confess that eternal life is a reward; it is something due because of the promise, not because of our merits. For the justification has been promised, which we have previously shown to be properly God's gift. To this gift the promise of eternal life has been added, according to Romans 8:30, "Those whom He justified He also glorified." Here belongs what Paul says, "There is laid up for me the crown of righteousness, which the Lord, the righteous judge, will award to me" (2 Timothy 4:8). The justified are due the crown because of the promise. Saints should know this promise, not that they may labor for their own profit, for they ought to labor for God's glory. But saints should know it so they may not despair in troubles. They should know God's will: He desires to aid, to deliver, and to protect them. Although the perfect hear the mention of penalties and rewards in one way, the weak hear it in another way. The weak labor for the sake of their own advantage. Yet the 244 preaching of rewards and punishments is necessary. God's wrath is set forth in the preaching of punishments. This applies to the preaching of repentance. Grace is set forth in the preaching of rewards. Just as Scripture, in the mention of good works, often embraces faith—for it wishes righteousness of the heart to be included with the fruit—so sometimes it offers grace together with other rewards. We find this in Isaiah 58:8–14, and frequently in other 245 places in the Prophets. We also affirm what we have often said, that although justification and eternal life go along with faith, nevertheless, good works merit other bodily and spiritual rewards and degrees of reward. According to 1 Corinthians 3:8, "Each will receive his wages according to his labor." The righteousness of the Gospel, which has to do with the promise of grace, freely receives justification and new life. But the fulfilling of the Law, which follows faith, has to do with the Law. In it a reward is offered and is due, not freely, but according to our works. Those who earn this are justified before they do the Law. As Paul says, "He has . . . transferred us to the kingdom of His beloved Son," and we are "fellow heirs with Christ" (Colossians 246 1:13; Romans 8:17). But whenever merit is mentioned, the adversaries immediately transfer the matter from other rewards to justification. Yet the Gospel freely offers justification because of Christ's merits and not of our own. His merits are delivered to us through faith. Works and troubles do not merit justification, but other payments, as the reward is offered for the works in these

passages: "Whoever sows sparingly will also reap sparingly, and whoever sows bountifully will also reap bountifully" (2 Corinthians 9:6). Here clearly the measure of the reward is connected with the measure of the work. "Honor your father and your mother, that your days may be long in the land" (Exodus 20:12). Also here the Law offers a reward to a certain work. The fulfilling of the Law earns 247 a reward, for a reward properly relates to the Law. Yet we should be mindful of the Gospel, which freely offers justification for Christ's sake. We neither obey the Law, nor can obey it, before we have been reconciled to God, justified, and reborn. Nor would fulfilling the Law please God, unless we were accepted because of faith. People are accepted because of faith. For this very reason the initial fulfilling of the Law pleases and has a reward in this life and in the next. Regarding the term 248 *reward*, many other remarks, derived from the nature of the Law, might be made here. Since they are too long, they must be explained in another connection.

### The Adversaries' Other Arguments

The adversaries insist that good works 249 have the right to merit eternal life, because Paul says:

He will render to each one according to his works. (Romans 2:6)

Glory and honor and peace for everyone who does good. (Romans 2:10)

Those who have done good to the resurrection of life. (John 5:29)

I was hungry and you gave Me food, I was thirsty and you gave Me drink, I was a stranger and you welcomed Me. (Matthew 25:35)

In these and all similar passages in which 250 works are praised in the Scriptures, it is necessary to understand not only outward works, but also the faith of the heart. Scrip-

The Last Judgment Depicted as a Harvest

251 ture does not speak of hypocrisy, but of the righteousness of the heart with its fruit. Furthermore, whenever the Law and works are mentioned, we must know that Christ cannot be excluded as Mediator. He is the end of the Law, and He Himself says, "Apart from Me you can do nothing" (John 15:5). We have said above that all passages about works can be judged according to this rule. When eternal life is granted to works, it is granted to those who have been justified. Only justified people, who are led by the Spirit of Christ, can do good works. Without faith and Christ as Mediator, good works do not please, according to Hebrews 11:6: "Without faith it is impossible to please [God]." When

252 Paul says, "He will render to each one according to his works," not only the outward work ought to be understood, but all righteousness or unrighteousness. So, "Glory and honor and peace for everyone who does good," namely, to the righteous. "You gave Me food" (Matthew 25:35) is cited as the fruit and witness of the righteousness of the heart and of faith and, therefore, eternal life is given to

253 righteousness. In this way Scripture, at the same time with the fruit, embraces the righteousness of the heart. Scripture often names the fruit, so that the inexperienced understand better. It also names them to show that a new life and rebirth are required, and not hypocrisy. But rebirth happens through faith, in repentance.

254 No sane person can judge otherwise. Neither do we needlessly attempt to make a fine distinction, trying to separate the fruit from the righteousness of the heart. If only the adversaries would have conceded that the fruit pleases because of faith, and because of Christ as Mediator, and that by themselves they are not worthy of grace and of eternal

255 life. We condemn this failure in the doctrine of the adversaries. In some passages of Scripture, understood either in a philosophical or a Jewish manner, they abolish the righteousness of faith and exclude Christ as Mediator. From these passages they conclude that works merit grace, sometimes in a merely agreeable way (*de congruo*), and at other times in a wholly deserving way (*de condigno*), namely, when love is added. They maintain that works justify, and because they are righteousness they are worthy of eternal life. This error clearly abolishes the righteousness of faith, which believes that we have access to God for Christ's sake, not for the sake of our works. It also contradicts the truth that through Christ, as Priest and Mediator, we are led to the Father and have a reconciled Father, as has been said well

256 enough before. This teaching about the righteousness of faith is not to be neglected in Christ's Church, because without it we cannot consider Christ's office. Then the doctrine of justification that is left is only a doctrine of the Law. We should keep the Gospel and the doctrine about the promise, granted for Christ's sake.

### Conclusion

257 We are not arguing with the adversaries about a small matter. We are not trying to make a fine distinction when we find fault with them for teaching that we merit eternal life by works, while faith that takes hold of Christ as Mediator is left out. For there is not

258 a syllable in the Scholastics about this faith that believes the Father is reconciled to us for Christ's sake. Everywhere they hold that we are accepted and righteous because of our works, completed either from reason, or certainly worked by the inclination of that love

259 they speak about. Yet they have certain sayings, proverbs, as it were, of the old writers. They distort these in interpretation. In the

260 schools it is boasted that good works please

because of grace and that confidence must be put in God's grace. Here they understand grace as a habit by which we love God. It is as though the ancients meant that we should trust in our love, even though from experience we know how small and how impure it is. It is strange how they ask us to trust in love, since they teach us that we are not able to know whether it is present. Why do they not present the grace, the mercy of God toward us? While they are at it, they should add faith. For the promise of God's mercy, reconciliation, and love toward us is not grasped unless by faith. With this view they would rightly say that we should trust in grace, that good works please because of grace, when 261 faith takes hold of grace. In the schools it is bragged that our good works work by virtue of Christ's passion. Well said! But why add nothing about faith? For Christ is an Atoning Sacrifice, as Paul says, "by faith" (Romans 3:25). When fearful consciences are comforted by faith, and are convinced that our sins have been blotted out by Christ's death, and that God has been reconciled to us because of Christ's suffering, then, indeed, Christ's suffering profits us. If the teaching about faith is left out, saying that works are useful by virtue of Christ's passion is of no use at all.

262    They corrupt very many other passages in the schools because they do not teach the righteousness of faith and because they understand faith as merely a knowledge of the history or of dogmas. They do not understand faith to be a virtue, which takes hold of the promise of grace and of righteousness, and which enlivens hearts in the terrors of 263 sin and of death. When Paul says, "With the heart one believes and is justified, and with the mouth one confesses and is saved" (Romans 10:10), we think that the adversaries admit that confession justifies or saves, not by the outward act, but only because of the faith of the heart. Paul says that confession saves in order to show what sort of faith receives eternal life, namely, that which is firm and active. That faith, however, that does not 264 present itself in confession is not firm. So other good works please because of faith, just as the prayers of the Church ask that all things may be accepted for Christ's sake (John 14:13–14). They likewise ask all things for Christ's sake. For it is clear that this clause is always added at the close of prayers: "Through Christ, our Lord." So we conclude 265 that we are justified before God, are reconciled to God and reborn through faith. In repentance this faith lays hold of the promise of grace and truly enlivens the terrified mind. It is convinced that for Christ's sake God is reconciled and favorable toward us. "Through" this faith, 1 Peter 1:5 says, "[We] are being guarded . . . for a salvation ready to be revealed." The knowledge of this faith is 266 necessary to Christians, brings the most abundant comfort in all troubles, and shows us Christ's office. Those who deny that people are justified through faith and that Christ is Mediator and the Atoning Sacrifice, deny the promise of grace and the Gospel. When it comes to justification, they teach only the doctrine either of reason or of the Law. We 267 have shown how this came to be, so far as can be done here. We have also explained the objections of the adversaries. Good people will easily judge these things if they will think in this way whenever a passage about love or works is quoted. It is certain that the Law cannot be kept without Christ and that we cannot be justified from the Law, but from the Gospel, that is, from the grace promised in Christ. We hope that this discussion, al- 268 though brief, will be helpful to good people for strengthening faith and teaching and comforting the conscience. For we know that what we have said is in harmony with the

prophetic and apostolic Scriptures, with the Holy Fathers, Ambrose, Augustine, and very many others, and with Christ's whole Church, which certainly confesses that Christ is the Atoning Sacrifice and Justifier.

269    Nor do we immediately conclude that the Roman Church agrees with everything that the pope or cardinals or bishops or some of the theologians or monks approve. For it is clear that most pontiffs consider their own authority of greater concern than Christ's Gospel. It has been determined that most of them are openly mere searchers for pleasure. Clearly theologians have mingled more of philosophy with Christian doctrine than was

270    necessary. Their influence should not appear so great that it will be unlawful to disagree with their arguments, because at the same time many clear errors are found among them. One of these maintains that, from purely natural powers, we are able to love God above all things. This preaching, although it is clearly false, has produced many

271    other errors. For the Scriptures, the Holy Fathers, and the judgments of all the godly everywhere respond. Therefore, popes, or some theologians, and monks in the Church have taught us to seek the forgiveness of sins, grace, and righteousness through our own works and to invent new forms of worship, which have clouded over Christ's office and have made out of Christ not the Atoning Sacrifice and Justifier, but only a Legislator. Yet, the knowledge of Christ has always remained

272    with some godly persons. Scripture, furthermore, has predicted that the righteousness of faith would be clouded over by human traditions and the teaching of works in this way. Paul often complains about this. (See Galatians 4:9; 5:7; Colossians 2:8, 16–19; 1 Timothy 4:2–5; etc.) There were even during his time those who—instead of the righteousness of faith—taught that people were reconciled to God and justified by their own works and own acts of worship, and not through faith for Christ's sake. People judge by nature that God should be appeased by works. Nor does 273 reason see a righteousness other than the righteousness of the Law, understood in a civil sense. So there have always been some who have taught this earthly righteousness alone to the exclusion of the righteousness of faith. Such teachers will always exist. The 274 same thing happened among the people of Israel. The majority of the people thought that they merited the forgiveness of sins by their works. Therefore, they piled up sacrifices and acts of worship. On the contrary, the prophets, in condemnation of this opinion, taught the righteousness of faith. What happened among the people of Israel are illustrations of those things that were to happen in the Church (1 Corinthians 10:11). Therefore, let the multitude of the adver- 275 saries, who condemn our doctrine, not disturb godly minds. For the adversaries' spirit can easily be judged, because in some articles they have condemned truth that is so clear and apparent that their godlessness appears openly. The bull of Leo X condemned a very 276 necessary article, which all Christians should hold and believe. It stated that we should trust that we have been forgiven not because of our sorrow, but because of Christ's word "Whatever you bind . . ." (Matthew 16:19). And now, in this assembly, the authors of the 277 Confutation have clearly condemned the following: (a) faith is a part of repentance, (b) we obtain forgiveness of sins by faith, (c) and by faith we overcome the terrors of sin, so the conscience is soothed. Who does not see that this article—that by faith we obtain the forgiveness of sins—is most true, most certain, and especially necessary to all Christians? Who to all posterity, hearing that such a doctrine has been condemned, will judge that

the authors of it had any knowledge of Christ?

278    It is possible to make a guess about their spirit based on that inexpressible cruelty, which it is agreed they exercised among many good people up to this point. We received ⌐news⌐ in this gathering about a certain reverend father of the imperial senate. When opinions were stated about our confession, he saw nothing more useful to say to the council than "to write back with blood" to what we wrote in ink. Could Phalaris say anything more cruel? Some princes also have judged this expression unworthy to be spoken in such a meeting. Even though the adversaries claim the name of the Church for themselves, we know that Christ's Church is with those who teach Christ's Gospel, not with those who defend wicked opinions contrary to the Gospel. As the Lord says, "My sheep hear My voice" (John 10:27). And Augustine says:

279

> The question is, "Where is the Church?" What, therefore, are we to do? Are we to seek it in our own words or in the words of its Head, our Lord Jesus Christ? I think that we ought to seek it in the words of Him who is Truth, and who knows His own body best.

In this way the judgments of our adversaries will not disturb us, since they defend human opinions contrary to the Gospel, contrary to the authority of the Holy Fathers who have written in the Church, and contrary to the testimonies of godly minds.

## ARTICLES VII AND VIII (IV)

# The Church

Defining "Church" was naturally one of the more controversial topics during the Reformation. The Medieval Church had developed a massive organizational structure for operating the Church. The foundation of this structure was the papacy. According to Rome, Jesus Christ established the office of the pope, who is Christ's visible representative, or vicar, on earth. All churchly authority resides with the pope, who delegates it to others, primarily the bishops. Obedience to the pope is to be absolute in all matters of faith and morals. Those who deny the pope's authority and teachings as Christ's representative cannot be saved.

The Lutherans insisted that the Church cannot be defined by its outward organization. Rather, as the Augsburg Confession had defined earlier, the Church is primarily the gathering of God's people around Christ's Word and Sacraments. Rome accused the Lutherans of saying that even unbelievers were truly part of this Church. The Lutherans were careful not to say this. In Articles VII and VIII of the Apology, Melanchthon speaks of the Church in a wide sense, including all who are seen to gather around Word and Sacraments, and in a narrow sense, that is, all who genuinely have faith in Christ, an aspect of Church that cannot be seen. Fellowship around, in, and through the Word and Sacraments defines unity in the faith. (See also AC VII/VIII; SA III XII; LC II, The Third Article.)

---

1    They have condemned Article VII of our Confession, in which we said that the Church is the congregation of saints. The adversaries have added a long essay stating that the wicked are not to be separated from the Church, since John the Baptist has compared the Church to a threshing floor on which wheat and chaff are heaped together (Matthew 3:12), and Christ has compared it to a net in which there are both good and bad fish (Matthew 13:47). This is a true saying: 2

"There is no remedy against the attacks of the slanderer." Nothing can be spoken with such care that it can escape ridicule. For this reason we have added Article VIII. Let no one think that we separate the wicked and hypocrites from the outward fellowship of the Church, or that we deny power to Sacraments administered by hypocrites or wicked men. There is no need here of a long defense against this slander. Article VIII is enough to acquit us. For we grant that in this life hypocrites and wicked people have been mingled with the Church, and that they are members of the Church according to the outward fellowship of the signs of the Church, that is, of Word, profession, and Sacraments (especially if they have not been excommunicated). Neither are the Sacraments powerless because they are administered by wicked men. Yes, we can even be right in using the Sacraments administered by wicked men. For Paul also predicts, "[The antichrist] takes his seat in the temple of God" (2 Thessalonians 2:4). In other words, he will rule and bear office in the Church.

But the Church is not only the fellowship of outward objects and rites, as other governments, but at its core, it is a fellowship of faith and of the Holy Spirit in hearts. Yet this fellowship has outward marks so that it can be recognized. These marks are the pure doctrine of the Gospel and the administration of the Sacraments in accordance with the Gospel of Christ. This Church alone is called Christ's body, which Christ renews, sanctifies, and governs by His Spirit. Paul testifies about this when he says, "And gave Him as head over all things to the Church, which is His body, the fullness of Him who fills all in all" (Ephesians 1:22–23). Those in whom Christ does not act are not the members of Christ. The adversaries admit this too. The wicked are "dead" members of the Church. We wonder why the adversaries have found fault with our description that speaks of living members. Neither have we said anything new. Paul has defined the Church precisely in the same way, that it should be cleansed in order to be *holy*. He adds the outward marks, *the Word and Sacraments*. For he says:

> Christ loved the Church and gave Himself up for her, that He might sanctify her, having cleansed her by the washing of water with the word, so that He might present the Church to Himself in splendor, without spot or wrinkle or any such thing, that she might be holy and without blemish. (Ephesians 5:25–27)

In the Confession, we have presented this sentence almost word for word. The Church is defined by the Third Article of the Creed, which teaches us to believe that there is a *holy Catholic Church*. The wicked indeed are not a holy Church. The words that follow, namely, "the communion of saints," seems to be added in order to explain what the Church signifies: the congregation of saints, who have with each other the fellowship of the same Gospel or doctrine and the same Holy Spirit, who renews, sanctifies, and governs their hearts.

This article has been presented for a necessary reason. We see the infinite dangers that threaten the destruction of the Church. In the Church itself, the number of the wicked who oppress it is too high to count. Therefore, this article in the Creed shows us these consolations in order that we may not despair, but may know that the Church will remain (until the end of the world). No matter how great the multitude of the wicked is, we may know that the Church still exists and Christ provides those gifts He has promised to the Church—to forgive sins, to hear

10    prayer, to give the Holy Spirit. It says *Church catholic*, in order that we may not understand the Church to be an outward government of certain nations. Rather, the Church is people scattered throughout the whole world. They agree about the Gospel and have the same Christ, the same Holy Spirit, and the same Sacraments, whether they have the same or

11    different human traditions. The explanation appearing in the *Decrees* says, "The Church in its wide sense embraces good and evil." Likewise, it says that the wicked are in the Church only in name, not in fact. The good are in the Church both in fact and in name. To this effect there are many passages in the Fathers. For Jerome says, "The sinner, therefore, who has been soiled with any blotch cannot be called a member of Christ's Church, neither can he be said to be subject to Christ."

12    Hypocrites and wicked people are members of this true Church according to outward rites (titles and offices). Yet, when the Church is defined, it is necessary to define what is the living body of Christ and what is, in name and in fact, the Church. There are

13    many reasons for this. We should understand what chiefly makes us members—living members—of the Church. If we will define the Church only as an outward political order of the good and wicked, people will not understand that Christ's kingdom is righteousness of heart and the gift of the Holy Spirit (Romans 14:17). People will conclude that the Church is only the outward observance of certain forms of worship and rites.

14    Likewise, what difference will there be between the people of the Law and the Church if the Church is only an outward political order? But Paul distinguishes the Church from the people of the Law [Israel] in this way: The Church is a spiritual people. It has not been distinguished from the pagans by civil rites (its polity and civil affairs). Instead, it is God's true people, reborn by the Holy Spirit. Among the people of the Law [Israel], apart from Christ's promise, even the earthly seed had promises about bodily things such as government. Even though the wicked among them were called God's people (because God had separated this earthly seed from other nations by certain outward ordinances and promises), the wicked did not please God (Deuteronomy 7:6–11). But the    15 Gospel brings not merely the shadow of eternal things, but the eternal things themselves: the Holy Spirit and righteousness. By the Gospel we are righteous before God.

Only those people who receive this promise of the Spirit receive it according to the    16 Gospel. Besides, the Church is Christ's kingdom, distinguished from the devil's kingdom. It is certain, however, that the wicked are in the devil's power and members of his kingdom. Paul teaches this when he says that the devil "is now at work in the sons of disobedience" (Ephesians 2:2). Christ says to the Pharisees, who certainly had outward fellowship with the Church, that is, with the saints among the people of the Law (as officeholders, sacrificers, and teachers), "You are of your father the devil" (John 8:44). Therefore, the Church, which is truly Christ's kingdom, is properly the congregation of saints. For the wicked are ruled by the devil and are captives of the devil. They are not ruled by the Spirit of Christ.

Why say more when the matter is clear? If    17 the Church, which is truly Christ's kingdom, is distinguished from the devil's kingdom, it follows necessarily that the wicked are not the Church, since they are in the devil's kingdom. It is true that, because Christ's kingdom has not yet been revealed, the wicked are mixed in with the Church and hold offices. But the wicked are not Christ's kingdom,    18 even though that revelation has not yet been made. For Christ enlivens His true kingdom by His Spirit, whether it is revealed or is covered by the cross, just as the glorified Christ is the same Christ who was afflicted (John 17:1). Christ's parables clearly agree with this. He says, "The good seed is the children of the kingdom. The weeds are the sons of the evil one" (Matthew 13:38). "The field," He says, "is the world," *not the Church*. John the Baptist speaks about the entire Jewish people and says that eventually the true Church will be separated from that people. Therefore, this passage is more against the adversaries than in favor of them, because it shows that the true and spiritual people are to be separated from the earthly people. Christ also speaks of the outward appearance of the Church when He says, "The kingdom of heaven is like a net" (Matthew 13:47), likewise, "ten virgins" (Matthew 25:1). He teaches that the Church has been covered by a lot of evils, so that this stumbling block may not offend the pious, and so that we may know that the Word and Sacraments are powerful even when administered by the wicked. Meanwhile, He teaches that these godless people, although they have fellowship in outward signs, are not Christ's true kingdom and members. They are members of the devil's kingdom. We are not dreaming of a Platonic state, as some wickedly charge. But we do say that this Church exists: truly believing and righteous people scattered throughout the whole world. We add the marks: the pure teaching of the Gospel and the Sacraments. This Church is properly the pillar of the truth (1 Timothy 3:15). For it keeps the pure Gospel as Paul says in 1 Corinthians 3:11. The "foundation" is the true knowledge of Christ and faith. There are also many weak persons, who build upon the foundation stubble that will perish (v. 12), holding

certain harmful opinions. Nevertheless, because the weak do not overthrow the foundation, they are both forgiven and corrected. The writings of the Holy Fathers declare that sometimes even they built stubble upon the foundation, but that this did not overthrow their faith. But most of those errors do overthrow faith. Our adversaries defend these errors. Among them is their condemnation of the article about the forgiveness of sins, in which we say that the forgiveness of sins is received through faith. Likewise, it is a clear and deadly error when the adversaries teach that people merit the forgiveness of sins by loving God, before grace. This is an example of removing "the foundation," Christ. Likewise, why do we need faith if the Sacraments justify by the outward act, without a good motive on the part of the one using them? Just as the Church has the promise that it will always have the Holy Spirit, so it also has warnings that there will be wicked teachers and wolves (Acts 20:29). Yet, the Church in the proper sense has the Holy Spirit. Although wolves and wicked teachers become violent in the Church, they are not properly Christ's kingdom. Just as Lyra also testifies when he says:

> The Church does not consist of people in power or ecclesiastical or secular dignity, because many princes and archbishops and others of lower rank have been found to have apostatized from the faith. Therefore, the Church consists of those persons in whom there is a true knowledge and confession of faith and truth.

We have said nothing more in our Confession than what Lyra says here.

The adversaries perhaps require that the Church be defined in the following way. To them, the Church is the supreme outward monarchy of the whole world. In this Church

Pentecost

the Roman pontiff's power is unquestioned. No one is allowed to argue against it or criticize it. He sets up articles of faith or abolishes them and abolishes the Scriptures according to his pleasure. He approves worship ceremonies and sacrifices to frame whatever laws he may wish. He dispenses and exempts from whatever laws (divine, canonical, or civil) he may wish. From him, the emperor and all kings receive the power and right to hold their kingdoms according to Christ's command. It must be understood that this right was transferred from Christ (since the Father subjected all things to Him) to the pope. Therefore, the pope must necessarily be lord of the whole world, of all the kingdoms of the world, of all things private and public. He must have absolute power in earthly and spiritual things and both swords, the spiritual and temporal. Besides, this definition (not of Christ's Church, but of the papal kingdom) has as its authors not only the canon lawyers, but also Daniel 11:36–39.

24

25 Now, if we would define the Church in this way, we would perhaps have fairer judges. For there exist many excessive and wicked writings about the pope of Rome's power, for which no one has ever been charged. We alone are blamed, because we proclaim Christ's graciousness, that by faith in Christ we obtain forgiveness of sins, and not by worship ceremonies created by the pope. Furthermore, Christ, the prophets, and the apostles define Christ's Church very different than the papal kingdom. Neither must we transfer to the popes what belongs to the true Church (as though the popes are pillars of the truth who do not err). How many of the popes care for the Gospel or judge that it is worth being read? Many in Italy and elsewhere even publicly ridicule all religions. Or, if they approve anything, they approve only things that are in harmony with human rea-

26

27

son. They regard the rest like fables and like the tragedies of the poets. According to the Scriptures, we hold that the Church, properly called, is the congregation of saints who truly believe Christ's Gospel and have the Holy Spirit. We confess that in this life many hypocrites and wicked people are mixed in with these. They have the fellowship in outward signs, are members of the Church according to this fellowship in outward signs, and so hold offices in the Church (preach, administer the Sacraments, and bear the title and name of Christians). However, the fact that the Sacraments are administered by the unworthy does not detract from the Sacraments' power. Because of the call of the Church, the unworthy still represent the person of Christ and do not represent their own persons, as Christ testifies, "The one who hears you hears Me" (Luke 10:16). (Even Judas was sent to preach.) When they offer God's Word, when they offer the Sacraments, they offer them in the stead and place of Christ. Those words of Christ teach us not to be offended by the unworthiness of the ministers.

28

In the Confession, we said clearly enough that we condemn the Donatists and Wycliffites. They thought that people sinned when they received the Sacraments from the unworthy in the Church. These points seem, for the present, to be enough for the defense of our description of the Church. Neither do we see how, when the Church, properly called, is named *the body of Christ*, it should be described differently than we have described it. For it is clear that the wicked belong to the devil's kingdom and body. He drives them on and holds them captive. Such things are clearer than the light of noonday. However, if the adversaries continue to pervert them, we will not hesitate to reply at greater length.

29

30 The adversaries also condemn the part of Article VII in which we said that "for the true unity of the Church it is enough to agree about the doctrine of the Gospel and the administration of the Sacraments. It is not necessary that human traditions, that is, rites or ceremonies instituted by men, should be the same everywhere." Here they distinguish between *universal* and *particular* rites. They approve our article if it is understood concerning particular rites; they do not approve it 31 concerning universal rites. We do not completely understand what the adversaries mean. We are speaking of true, spiritual unity. Without faith in the heart, or righteousness of heart before God, such unity cannot exist. Similarity of human ceremonies, whether universal or particular, is not necessary. The righteousness of faith is not a righteousness bound to certain traditions. The righteousness of the Law was bound to the Mosaic ceremonies. But righteousness of the heart is a matter that enlivens the heart. Human traditions, whether they are universal or particular, contribute nothing to this new life. Neither are traditions effects of the Holy Spirit, as are self-control, patience, the fear of God, love for one's neighbor, and the works of love.

32 The reasons why we presented this article were not small. Clearly many foolish opinions about traditions had crept into the Church. Some thought that human traditions were necessary services for earning justification. Afterward, they argued how God came to be worshiped with such variety, as though these observances were acts of worship and not outward and political ordinances. Such ordinances have no connection with the righteousness of heart or the worship of God. These ordinances vary, according to the circumstances, for certain probable reasons, sometimes in one way, and at other times in another. Likewise, some churches have excommunicated others because of such traditions as the observance of Easter, icons, and the like. So the ignorant have imagined that faith (or the righteousness of the heart before God) cannot exist without these ceremonies. Many foolish writings of the Summists and of others exist on this matter.

33 We believe that the true unity of the Church is not injured by dissimilar ceremonies instituted by humans, just as the dissimilar length of day and night does not injure the unity of the Church. However, it is pleasing to us that, for the sake of peace, universal ceremonies are kept. We also willingly keep the order of the Mass in the churches, the Lord's Day, and other more famous festival days. With a very grateful mind we include the beneficial and ancient ordinances, especially since they contain a discipline. This discipline is beneficial for educating and training the people and those who are ignorant (the young people). We 34 are not discussing now whether it is helpful to keep them because of peace or bodily profit. We speak of something else. The question at hand is whether the observances of human traditions are acts of worship necessary for righteousness before God. This is the point to be judged in this controversy. When this is decided, it can be judged later whether it is necessary that human traditions should everywhere be the same for the true unity of the Church. For if human traditions are not acts of worship necessary for righteousness before God, it follows that those not having the traditions received elsewhere can be righteous and the sons of God as well. For example, if the style of German clothing is not worship of God and necessary for righteousness before God, it follows that people can be righteous and God's sons, and Christ's Church, even

though they use a costume that is not German, but French.

35 Paul clearly teaches this to the Colossians:

> Therefore let no one pass judgment on you in questions of food and drink, or with regard to a festival or a new moon or a Sabbath. These are a shadow of the things to come, but the substance belongs to Christ. (2:16–17)

Likewise:

> If with Christ you died to the elemental spirits of the world, why, as if you were still alive in the world, do you submit to regulations—"Do not handle, Do not taste, Do not touch" (referring to things that all perish as they are used)—according to human precepts and teachings? These have indeed an appearance of wisdom in promoting self-made religion and asceticism. (2:20–23)

36 The meaning is this: Righteousness of the heart is a spiritual matter, a matter of enlivening hearts. Clearly human traditions do not enliven hearts and are not effects of the Holy Spirit. Such efforts are love for one's neighbor, self-control, and so on. They are not tools through which God moves hearts to believe, as are the divinely given Word and Sacraments. Rather, traditions are customs that have no connection to the heart. They perish with the using, and we must not believe that they are necessary for righteousness before God. To the same effect Paul says, "For the kingdom of God is not a matter of eating and drinking but of righteousness and peace and joy in the Holy Spirit" (Romans 14:17).

37 But there is no need to cite many testimonies. For they are everywhere clear in the Scriptures, and we have gathered many of them in the latter articles of our Confession. In this controversy the point to be decided must be repeated, namely, whether human traditions are acts of worship necessary for righteousness before God. In due course we will discuss this matter more fully.

38 The adversaries say that universal traditions should be observed because they were supposedly handed down by the apostles. What religious men they are! They wish that the ceremonies received from the apostles be kept. Yet, they do not wish the apostles' doctrine to be kept. 39 They should judge these rites just as the apostles themselves judge them in their writings. For the apostles did not want us to believe that we are justified through such ceremonies, or that such ceremonies are necessary for righteousness before God. The apostles did not want to put such a burden upon consciences. They did not want to place righteousness and sin in the observance of days, food, and the like. 40 Yes, Paul calls such opinions "teachings of demons" (1 Timothy 4:1). Therefore, the apostles' will and advice should be taken from their writings. It is not enough to mention their example. The apostles observed certain days, not because this observance was necessary for justification, but in order that the people might know at what time they should gather. They observed also certain other ceremonies and orders of lessons whenever they gathered. The people kept the customs of the Fathers (from their Jewish festivals and ceremonies). As is commonly the case, the apostles adapted to the history of the Gospel certain things, although somewhat changed. Among these things were the Passover and Pentecost. The apostles did this so that not only by teaching, but also through these examples, they might hand down to posterity the memory of the most important subjects. But if these things 41 were handed down as necessary for justification, why, afterward, did the bishops change many things in these very matters? If they

42 were matters of divine right, it was not lawful to change them by human authority. Before the Synod of Nicaea, some observed Easter at one time and others observed it at another time. Neither did this lack of uniformity harm faith. Afterward, the plan was adopted by which our Passover (Easter) did not fall at the same time as that of the Jewish Passover. The apostles had commanded the churches to observe the Passover with the brethren who had been converted from Judaism. Therefore, after the Synod of Nicaea, certain nations held firmly to the custom of observing the Jewish time. The apostles, by this decree, did not wish to put a demand upon the churches, as the words of the decree testify. For it asks no one to be troubled, even though his brothers and sisters, in observing Easter, do not change the time correctly. The words of the decree are found in Epiphanius:

> Do not calculate, but celebrate it whenever your brethren of the circumcision do; celebrate it at the same time with them, and even though they may have erred, let not this be a care to you.

Epiphanius writes that these are the words presented in a decree about Easter. The wise reader can easily conclude from the decree that the apostles wished to free the people from the foolish opinion of a fixed time, to help them from being troubled, if a mistake 43 should be made in setting the date. However, some in the East, who followed the teaching of Audians, argued that because of this decree of the apostles, the Passover should be observed with the Jews. In refuting them, Epiphanius praises the decree and says that it contains nothing that departs from the faith or rule of the Church. He blames the Audians because they do not correctly understand the expression. Epiphanius interprets it in the sense in which we interpret it, because the apostles thought it unimportant what time the Passover should be observed. Nevertheless, for harmony's sake and because prominent brothers and sisters had been converted from the Jews, who observed their custom, the adversaries wished the rest to follow their example. They wisely warned the reader nei- 44 ther to remove the freedom of the Gospel, nor to burden consciences. The apostles thought that consciences should not be troubled, even though there should be an error in setting the date.

Many things like this can be collected 45 from the historical accounts. In them it appears that a lack of uniformity in human observances does not harm the unity of faith. What need is there of discussion? The adversaries do not at all understand what the righteousness of faith is, what Christ's kingdom is. That is clear when they judge that uniformity of observances in food, days, clothing, and the like (which do not have God's command) is necessary. Look at these religious 46 men, our adversaries. They require uniform human observances for the unity of the Church. They do this even though they themselves have changed Christ's ordinance in the use of the Supper, which certainly was a universal ordinance before. If universal ordinances are so necessary, why do they themselves change the ordinance of Christ's Supper, which is not human, but divine? We will have to speak about this entire controversy a little later.

Article VII has been approved entirely, in 47 which we confess that hypocrites and wicked persons have been mixed in with the Church and that the Sacraments are powerful even though given by wicked ministers. Ministers act in Christ's place and do not represent their own persons, according to Luke, "The one who hears you hears Me" (10:16).

48  Ungodly teachers are to be deserted because they no longer act in Christ's place, but are antichrists. Christ says, "Beware of false prophets" (Matthew 7:15). Paul says, "If anyone is preaching to you a gospel contrary to the one you received, let him be accursed" (Galatians 1:9).

49     Furthermore, Christ has warned us concerning the Church in His parables. When offended by the private sins of priests or people, we should not stir up divisions, as the

50  Donatists have wickedly done. However, concerning those who have stirred up division because they denied that priests are permitted to hold possessions and property, we hold that they are completely rebellious. To hold property is a civil ordinance. It is lawful, however, for Christians to use civil ordinances, just as they use the air, the light, food, and drink. For as this order of the world and fixed movements of the heavenly bodies are truly God's ordinances and are preserved by God, so lawful governments are truly God's ordinances, preserved and defended by God against the devil.

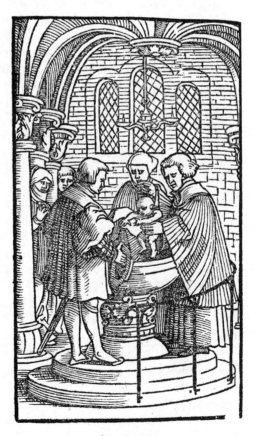

Infant Baptism

## ARTICLE IX

# Baptism

The Pontifical Confutation accepted the Augsburg Confession's teaching on Baptism. Here again, Melanchthon repeats the Lutheran rejection of Anabaptist errors concerning Baptism in general and the Baptism of infants in particular. Baptism is treated more extensively elsewhere in the Book of Concord, most notably in Martin Luther's Large Catechism. (See also AC IX; SA III V; SC IV; LC IV.)

51      Article IX has been approved, in which we confess that "Baptism is necessary for salvation," that "children are to be baptized," and that the "Baptism of children is not in vain, but is necessary and effective for salvation."
52  Since the Gospel is taught among us purely and diligently, by God's favor we receive also this fruit from it: In our churches no Anabaptists have arisen. This is because the people have been strengthened by God's Word against the wicked and rebellious faction of these robbers. This is also among the distinct errors of the Anabaptists we condemn. They argue that the Baptism of little children is useless. For it is very certain that the promise of salvation also applies to little children. It does not, however, apply to those who are outside of Christ's Church, where there is neither Word nor Sacraments. Christ's kingdom exists only with the Word and Sacraments. Therefore, it is necessary to baptize little children, that the promise of salvation may be applied to them, according to Christ's command to baptize all nations (Matthew 28:19). Just as in this passage salvation is offered to all, so Baptism is offered to all, to men, women, children, infants. It clearly follows, therefore, that infants are to be baptized, because salvation is
53  offered with Baptism. Second, it is clear that

God approves of the Baptism of little children. Therefore, the Anabaptists, who condemn the Baptism of little children, believe wickedly. God's approval of the Baptism of little children is shown by this: He gives the Holy Spirit to those baptized (Acts 2:38–39). For if this Baptism would be empty, the Holy Spirit would be given to no one. No one would be saved. And finally, there would be no Church. This reason, even by itself, can well enough establish good and godly minds against the godless and fanatical opinions of the Anabaptists.

## ARTICLE X

# The Holy Supper

The Pontifical Confutation approved the Augsburg Confession's statement on the Lord's Supper. The Lutherans clearly rejected the Zwinglian view of the Supper. In a more refined manner, Calvin and Reformed theology would later defend Zwingli's views. Lutheranism maintains the biblical and historic Church doctrine that in the Lord's Supper the body and blood of Jesus Christ are truly present under the bread and wine, distributed, and given into the mouths of all who commune, both worthy and unworthy. This is effected by the institution of Christ who, working through His Word, continues giving what He promises: His body and blood for our forgiveness, life, and salvation, as Luther describes it in his Small Catechism. (See also AC X; SA III VI; SC VI; LC V; FC Ep VII and SD VII.)

Article X has been approved, in which we   54 confess the following: We believe that in the Lord's Supper Christ's body and blood are truly and substantially present and are truly administered with those things that are seen (bread and wine) to those who receive the

The Last Supper

Signatures
on the Marburg Articles

The controversy over the Lord's Supper
led to the decisive Marburg Colloquy
(1529). Martin Luther, Justas Jonas, and
Philip Melanchthon met with represen-
tatives of Southern German cities. Here
are their signatures (Latin) affixed to the
Marburg Articles: Martinus Lutherus,
Justus Jonas, Phillippus Melanchthon,
Andreas Osiander, Stephanus Agricola,
Joannes Brentius, Joannes Oecolampa-
dius, Huldrychus Zuinglius, Martinus
Bucerus, Caspar Hedio.

Sacrament. We constantly defend this belief, as the subject has been carefully examined and considered. Since Paul says, "The bread that we break, is it not a participation in the body of Christ?" (1 Corinthians 10:16), it would follow that if the Lord's body were not truly present, the bread is not a communion

55  of the body, but only of Christ's spirit. We have determined that not only the Roman Church affirms Christ's bodily presence. The Greek Church also now believes, and formerly believed, the same. Their canon of the Mass testifies to this. In the canon the priest clearly prays that the bread may be changed and become Christ's very body. Vulgarius, who does not seem to be an unimportant writer to us, says clearly that "bread is not a mere figure, but is truly changed into flesh."

56  There is a long commentary by Cyril on John 15, in which he teaches that Christ is bodily offered to us in the Supper. For he says:

> Nevertheless, we do not deny that we are joined spiritually to Christ by true faith and sincere love. But that we have no way of connection with Him, according to the flesh, this indeed we entirely deny. We say this idea is completely foreign to the divine Scriptures. For who has doubted that Christ is in this manner a vine, and we the branches, deriving life for ourselves from this? Hear Paul saying, "For you are all one in Christ Jesus; so we, though many, are one body in Christ; for we all partake of the one bread" (Galatians 3:28; Romans 12:5; 1 Corinthians 10:17). Does he perhaps think that the virtue of the mystical benediction is unknown to us? Since this is in us, does it not also, by the communication of Christ's flesh, cause Christ to dwell in us bodily? And a little after: Therefore, we must

consider that Christ is in us not only according to the habit, which we call love, but also by natural participation.

57  We have cited these testimonies, not to undertake a discussion here about this subject, for His Imperial Majesty does not disapprove of this article. But we cite them so that all who read them may more clearly discern that we defend the doctrine received in the entire Church. In the Lord's Supper, Christ's body and blood are truly and actually present. They are truly administered with those things that are seen, bread and wine. And we speak of the presence of the living Christ, for we know that "death no longer has dominion over Him" (Romans 6:9).

## ARTICLE XI

# Confession

The Pontifical Confutation accepted the Augsburg Confession's statement about Confession, but insisted that the Church could order people to confess before a priest at least once a year. Melanchthon explains how in Lutheran churches the Sacraments are received often, but no laws are made about how often. Of particular concern is the Roman insistence on the recalling of all sins, or at least the effort to name them all. At no point did the Lutheran Church ever reject private Confession and Absolution. Rather, the Lutherans commended it as a very beneficial practice. (See also AC XI; SA III VIII; SC V; LC V, An Exhortation to Confession.)

---

58  Article XI, "Confession," is approved. But they add a correction in reference to Confession. They say that the regulation headed *Omnis utriusque* be observed and annual confession be made. They also say that, although all sins cannot be named, they should

be recalled with diligence. Those that can be recalled should be specified. We will speak at greater length about this entire article after a while, when we will explain our entire opin-

59 ion about repentance. It is well known that we have made clear and praised the benefit of Absolution and the Power of the Keys. Many troubled consciences have derived comfort from our teaching. They have been comforted after they heard that it is God's command, no, rather the very voice of the Gospel, that we should believe the Absolution and regard it as certain that the forgiveness of sins is freely granted to us for Christ's sake. We should believe that through this faith we are truly reconciled to God. This belief has encouraged many godly minds and, in the beginning, brought Luther the highest praise from all good people. This belief shows consciences sure and firm comfort. Previously, the entire power of Absolution had been kept under wraps by teachings about works. For the learned persons and monks taught nothing about faith and free forgiveness.

60 Concerning the *time*, certainly most people in our churches frequently use the Sacraments (Absolution and the Lord's Supper) during the year. Those who teach about the worth and fruit of the Sacraments speak in a way that invites the people to use the Sacraments frequently. There are many writings by our theologians about this subject that the adversaries, if they are good men, will un-

61 doubtedly approve and praise. Excommunication is also pronounced against the openly wicked and the haters of the Sacraments. These things are done both according to the

62 Gospel and according to the old canons. A fixed time for Confession is not prescribed because all are not ready in the same way at the same time. Yes, if all were to come at the same time, they could not be heard and instructed in order. The old canons and Fathers

do not appoint a fixed time. The canon speaks only in this way:

> If any enter the Church and be found never to commune, let them be taught that, if they do not commune, they come to repentance. If they commune (if they wish to be regarded as Christians), let them not be thrown out; if they fail to do so, let them be excommunicated.

Christ [Paul] says that those who eat unworthily eat judgment to themselves (1 Corinthians 11:29). So the pastors do not force those who are not qualified to use the Sacraments.

Concerning the *enumeration of sins in* 63 *Confession*, people are taught in such a way as not to trap their consciences. It is helpful to familiarize inexperienced people, to name some things, in order that they may be more readily taught. We are now discussing what is necessary according to divine Law. Therefore, the adversaries should not quote for us the regulation *Omnis utriusque*, which we already know, but they should show from the divine Law that complete naming of sins is necessary for obtaining their forgiveness. The entire Church, throughout all Europe, 64 knows what sort of snares this point of the regulation has cast upon consciences by commanding that all sins be confessed. The matter was only made worse by the Summists, who collected the circumstances of the sins and added their own ideas. What mazes there were! How great a torture for the best minds! The immoral and ungodly were in no way moved by these instruments of terror. Afterward, what tragedies did the questions 65 about one's own priest stir up among the pastors and brethren, who then were by no means brethren when they were warring about jurisdiction of confessions! We believe that, according to divine Law, a complete listing of sins is not necessary. This is also pleasing to Panormitanus and very many other learned legal scholars. Nor do we want to burden the consciences of our people by the regulation *Omnis utriusque*. We judge it to be like any other human tradition. They are not acts of worship necessary for justification. This regulation commands that we do something impossible—that we should confess all sins. However, it is clear that most sins we neither remember nor understand, according to Psalm 19:12, "Who can discern his errors?"

66    If the pastors are good men, they will know to what extent they should examine inexperienced persons. But we do not want to sanction the torture of the Summists. It would have been more tolerable if they had added one word about faith, which comforts and encourages consciences. About this faith, which obtains the forgiveness of sins, there is not a syllable in so great a mass of regulations, commentaries, summaries, or books of confession. Christ is nowhere read there. Only the lists of sins are read. The greater part is occupied with sins against human traditions. This is most useless. This doctrine 67 has forced many to despair. Godly minds were not able to find rest because they believed that by divine Law listing was necessary. Yet they experienced that it was impossible. Other faults of no less importance cling to the doctrine of the adversaries about repentance, which we will now recount.

Confession and Absolution

## ARTICLE XII (V)

# Repentance

The Pontifical Confutation rejected the Lutheran teaching that penance, or repentance, consists only of contrition and faith. God's Law brings about contrition, which is a profound realization of one's sins. The Gospel creates faith, which trusts that God forgives our sins for the sake of Christ. By teaching that repentance consists of three things—contrition, confession, and satisfaction—Rome attributes our forgiveness to human works and denies itself the comforting Gospel.

According to the Roman Church, the eternal penalty of sin is forgiven by Absolution. But in order to escape temporal punishment, one must make satisfaction for sin, either here on earth or later in purgatory. Roman Catholicism still teaches a system of indulgences, which is traditionally associated with the Roman practice of confession. The sale and corresponding abuses of indulgences caused Luther to post his Ninety-five Theses in 1517. Melanchthon carefully demolishes this horrendous error concerning how we are forgiven: "Scripture often teaches that the forgiveness of sins arises freely for Christ's sake, that Christ is the Victor over sin and death (1 Corinthians 15:57). The merit of satisfaction is not to be patched over this" (Ap XII [VI] 60). (See also AC XII; SA III III; SC V; LC V, An Exhortation to Confession.)

---

1    In Article XII, the adversaries approve of the first part, in which we present this: those who have fallen after Baptism may obtain the forgiveness of sins whenever and as often as they are converted. They condemn the second part, in which we say that the parts of repentance are *contrition and faith*. They deny that faith is the second part of repentance. O Charles, most invincible Emperor, 2 what should we do? This is the very voice of the Gospel: through faith we obtain the forgiveness of sins. These writers of the Confutation condemn this voice of the Gospel. Therefore, we can in no way agree to the Confutation. We cannot condemn the voice of the Gospel; it is beneficial and full of comfort. What else is the denial that we obtain the forgiveness of sins by faith than contempt for Christ's blood and death? We beg you, O 3 Charles, most unconquerable Emperor. Patiently and diligently hear and examine this most important subject. It contains the chief topic of the Gospel, the true knowledge of Christ, and the true worship of God. For all good people will determine that especially on this subject we have taught things that are true, godly, beneficial, and necessary for Christ's whole Church. All good people will determine from the writings of our theologians that very much light has been added to the Gospel and many deadly errors have been corrected. By these errors, through the opinions of the Scholastics and canonists, the doctrine of repentance was previously covered up.

Before we defend our position, we must 4 first say this: All good people of all situations, even the theological profession, undoubtedly confess that the teaching of repentance was very much confused before Luther's writings appeared. Theologians were never able to ex- 5 plain satisfactorily the numberless questions found in the books of the commentaries on the *Sentences*. The people could not grasp the big picture, nor could they see what things were necessary for repentance, in which peace of conscience could be found. Let any 6 one of the adversaries come forth and tell us when the forgiveness of sins takes place. O good God, there is such darkness! The adversaries do not know whether the forgiveness of sins happens in attrition or contrition. If forgiveness happens because of contrition, why do we need Absolution? What does the Power of the Keys bring about, if sins have been forgiven already? Here they work even harder and wickedly divert from the Power of 7 the Keys. Some imagine that guilt is not forgiven by the Power of the Keys, but that eternal punishments are changed into temporal ones. So the most beneficial power would be the service, not of life and the Spirit, but only of God's anger and punishments. The more cautious imagine that sins are forgiven before the Church, and not before God, by the Power of the Keys. This also is a deadly error. For if the Power of the Keys does not comfort us before God, what will quiet the con-8 science? What follows is even more involved. The adversaries teach that we merit grace by contrition. In reference to this, if anyone should ask why Saul, Judas, and similar persons (who were dreadfully contrite) did not receive grace, here is the answer: We take it from faith and according to the Gospel, that Judas did not believe. He did not support himself by the Gospel and Christ's promise. For faith shows the distinction between the contrition of Judas (Matthew 27:3–5) and of Peter (Matthew 26:75). But the adversaries take their answer from the Law, that Judas did not love God, but feared the punish-9 ments. When will a terrified conscience be able to decide whether it fears God for His own sake or is fleeing from eternal punishments? The Psalms and the Prophets describe those serious, true, and great terrors, which the truly converted experience. Such great emotions can be distinguished in letters and terms, but they are not separated in fact, 10 as these dear philosophers imagine. Here we appeal to the judgments of all good and wise people. Undoubtedly, they will confess that these discussions in the writings of the ad-

versaries are very confused and intricate. Still, the most important subject is at stake, the chief topic of the Gospel, the forgiveness of sins. In the writings of the adversaries, this entire doctrine about these questions is full of errors and hypocrisy and clouds over Christ's benefit, the Power of the Keys, and the righteousness of faith.

These things happen in the first act of this 11 play. What about *Confession*? What a work there is in the endless listing of sins. Nevertheless, this is in great part devoted to sins against human traditions! So that good minds may be more tortured by this, the adversaries falsely assert that this listing is of divine right. They demand this listing under 12 the claim of divine right. In the meantime, they speak coldly about Absolution, which is truly of divine right. They falsely assert that the Sacrament itself bestows grace by the mere performance of one act (*ex opere operato*) without a good disposition on the part of the one using it. They do not mention faith grasping the Absolution and comforting the conscience. This is truly what is generally called departing before the mysteries.

The third act of this play, *concerning satis-* 13 *factions,* remains. It contains the most confused discussions. The adversaries imagine that eternal punishments are switched to the punishments of purgatory and teach that a part of them is forgiven by the Power of the Keys and that a part is to be redeemed by means of satisfactions. Further, they add that 14 satisfactions should be extraordinary works (supererogation). They make these consist of most foolish observances, such as pilgrimages, rosaries, or similar observances that do not have God's command. Then, just as they 15 redeem purgatory by means of satisfactions, so a scheme was created for redeeming satisfactions, which was most abundant in revenue. They sell indulgences, which they in-

Allegorical Woodcut of Luther Posting the Ninety-five Theses

This woodcut, produced shortly after Luther posted the Ninety-five Theses, is based on a legendary dream that Frederick the Wise had in Schweinitz, the night before Luther posted the Ninety-five Theses. According to the legend, Frederick dreamt that God sent him a monk. The saints came with him to say the monk would do God's will. Right background: Frederick listens as the saints point to Christ. Luther receives a revelation from heaven. On left: Saints ask Frederick to allow Luther to write something on the church door. The words "Concerning Absolution" are large enough for the Elector to read them from Schweinitz. Luther's pen reaches Rome, pierces a lion's ears, and knocks off the pope's threefold crown. Cardinals and princes try to prevent the crown from falling. (Frederick said that he saw himself and his brother, John, reaching out to steady the crown as well.) The lion roars mightily so that Rome and all territories of the Holy Roman Emperor run to see what is wrong. The harder Rome tries to break Luther's pen, the stronger it becomes. Other pens pop out of Luther's pen. Lower right: Books burn, with a goose in the middle of the flames. The goose symbolizes John Hus. Top left: The pope, bishops, and cardinals put up a barrier to keep people from Luther. Top center: A monk promotes indulgences. This woodcut shows how printing was used effectively to spread news of the Reformation.

terpret as the pardon of satisfactions. This revenue is not only from the living, but is much more plentiful from the dead. Nor do they redeem the satisfactions of the dead only by indulgences, but also by the sacrifice

16 of the Mass. In a word, the topic of satisfactions is infinite. The doctrine of the righteousness of faith in Christ and the benefit of Christ lies buried among these scandals (for we cannot list everything) and doctrines of devils. Therefore, all good people understand that the doctrine of the learned persons and canon lawyers about repentance has been criticized for a useful and godly purpose. For the following teachings are clearly false and foreign, not only to Holy Scripture, but also to the Church Fathers:

17     1. Through good works, apart from grace, we merit grace from the divine covenant.

18     2. We merit grace by attrition.

19     3. Merely hating the crime is enough for the blotting out of sin.

20     4. We obtain forgiveness of sins because of contrition, and not by faith in Christ.

21     5. The Power of the Keys provides the forgiveness of sins before the Church, but not before God.

22     6. Sins are not forgiven before God by the Power of the Keys; rather, the Power of the Keys has been set up to transfer eternal punishments to temporal, to put certain satisfactions upon consciences, to set up new acts of worship, and to put consciences in debt to such satisfactions and acts of worship.

23     7. The listing of offenses in Confession, as taught by the adversaries, is necessary according to divine right.

24     8. Canonical satisfactions are necessary for redeeming the punishment of purgatory, or they benefit as a compensation for blotting out guilt. This is how uninformed persons understand it.

25     9. Without a good disposition on the part

of the one using it, that is, without faith in Christ, the reception of the Sacrament of repentance by the outward act (*ex opere operato*) obtains grace.

10. Our souls are freed from purgatory   26
through indulgences by the Power of the Keys.

11. In the reservation of cases, not only   27
canonical punishment, but also the guilt, should be reserved for one who is truly converted.

### The Two Parts of Repentance

To deliver godly consciences from these   28
mazes of the learned persons, we have attributed these two parts to repentance: contrition and faith. If anyone desires to add a third—fruit worthy of repentance, that is, a change of the entire life and character for the better—we will not oppose it. We separate   29
from contrition those useless and endless discussions regarding grief from loving God and from fearing punishment. We say that contrition is the true terror of conscience, which feels that God is angry with sin and grieves that it has sinned. This contrition takes place when sins are condemned by God's Word. The sum of the preaching of the Gospel is this: to convict of sin; to offer for Christ's sake the forgiveness of sins and righteousness, the Holy Spirit, and eternal life; and that as reborn people we should do good works. So Christ includes the sum of the   30
Gospel when He says, "Repentance and forgiveness of sins should be proclaimed in His name to all nations" (Luke 24:47). Scripture   31
speaks about these terrors:

> For my iniquities have gone over my head; like a heavy burden, they are too heavy for me. I am feeble and crushed; I groan because of the tumult of my heart. (Psalm 38:4, 8)

> Be gracious to me, O LORD, for I am

languishing; heal me, O LORD, for my bones are troubled. My soul also is greatly troubled. But You, O Lord—how long? (Psalm 6:2–3)

I said, In the middle of my days I must depart; I am consigned to the gates of Sheol for the rest of my years. I calmed myself until morning; like a lion he breaks all my bones. (Isaiah 38:10, 13)

32 In these terrors, conscience feels God's wrath against sin. This is unknown to secure people living according to the flesh. The conscience sees the corruption of sin and seriously grieves that it has sinned. Meanwhile, it also runs away from God's dreadful anger. Human nature, unless sustained by God's 33 Word, cannot endure His anger. So Paul says, "For through the law I died to the law" (Gala-34 tians 2:19). For the Law only accuses and terrifies consciences. In these terrors our adversaries say nothing about faith. They present only the Word that convicts of sin. When this is taught alone, it is the doctrine of the Law, not of the Gospel. By these griefs and terrors, they say, people merit grace, as long as they love God. But how will people love God in true terrors when they feel God's horrible wrath, which is beyond words? What besides despair do those people teach who, during these terrors, show forth only the Law?

35 As the second part of repentance we add *faith in Christ*. The Gospel, in which the forgiveness of sins is freely promised concerning Christ, should be presented to consciences in these terrors. They should believe that, for Christ's sake, their sins are freely forgiven. 36 This faith cheers, sustains, and enlivens the contrite, according to Romans 5:1, "Since we have been justified by faith, we have peace with God." This faith obtains the forgiveness of sins. It justifies before God, as the same

passage testifies, "since we have been justified by faith." This faith shows the distinction between the contrition of Judas and Peter, of Saul and David. The contrition of Judas or Saul (Matthew 27:3–5; 1 Samuel 31:4–6) is useless because faith is not added. Faith grasps the forgiveness of sins, given as a gift for Christ's sake. So the contrition of David or Peter (2 Samuel 12:13; Matthew 26:75) helps because faith, which takes hold of the forgiveness of sins granted for Christ's sake, is added to it. Love is not present before rec- 37 onciliation has been made through faith. For without Christ, the Law is not performed, according to Romans 5:2, "Through [Christ] we have also obtained access [to God]." This faith grows gradually and throughout the entire life, struggles with sin, in order to overcome sin and death. Love follows faith, as we have said above. So childlike fear can be 38 clearly defined as anxiety that has been connected with faith, that is, where faith comforts and sustains the anxious heart. It is slavish fear when faith does not sustain the anxious heart.

Furthermore, the Power of the Keys ad- 39 ministers and presents the Gospel through Absolution, which is the true voice of the Gospel. We also include Absolution when we speak of faith, because "faith comes from hearing," as Paul says in Romans 10:17. When the Gospel is heard and the Absolution is heard, the conscience is encouraged and receives comfort. Because God truly 40 brings a person to life through the Word, the Keys truly forgive sins before God. According to Luke 10:16, "The one who hears you hears Me." Therefore, the voice of the one absolving must be believed no differently than we would believe a voice from heaven. Absolu- 41 tion can properly be called a Sacrament of repentance, as even the more learned scholastic theologians say. Meanwhile, in 42 temptations this faith is nourished in a variety of ways: through the declarations of the Gospel and the use of the Sacraments. For these are signs of the New Testament, that is, signs of the forgiveness of sins. They offer the forgiveness of sins as the words of the Lord's Supper clearly testify, "This is My body, which is given for you. This is the cup of the New Testament," and so on. (See Matthew 26:26, 28.) So faith is conceived and strengthened through Absolution, through the hearing of the Gospel, through the use of the Sacraments, so that it may not give in to the terrors of sin and death while it struggles. 43 This method of repentance is plain and clear. It increases the worth of the Power of the Keys and of the Sacraments. It illumines Christ's benefit and teaches us to make use of Christ as Mediator and the Atoning Sacrifice.

## Scriptural Proofs

44     Because the Confutation condemns us for having assigned these two parts to repentance, we must show that Scripture expresses these as the chief parts in repentance or conversion. Christ says, "Come to Me, all who labor and are heavy laden, and I will give you rest" (Matthew 11:28). Here there are two parts. The "labor" and the burden signify the contrition, anxiety, and terrors of sin and death. To "come to" Christ is to believe that sins are forgiven for Christ's sake. When we believe, our hearts are brought to life by the 45 Holy Spirit through Christ's Word. Here, therefore, are these two chief parts: contrition and faith. In Mark 1:15, Christ says, "Repent and believe in the gospel." In the first clause He convicts of sins, and in the second He comforts us and shows the forgiveness of sins. Believing the Gospel is not the general faith that devils also have, but in the proper sense it is believing that the forgiveness of sins has been granted for Christ's sake. This is

revealed in the Gospel. You see also here that the two parts are joined: contrition when sins are rebuked; and faith when it is said, "Believe in the gospel." If anyone should say here that Christ also includes the fruit of repentance or the entire new life, we shall not disagree. For this satisfies us, that contrition and faith are named as the chief parts.

46     When Paul describes conversion or renewal, he almost everywhere designates these two parts, *making dead and making alive*, as in Colossians 2:11, "In Him also you were circumcised with a circumcision made without hands," namely, "by putting off the body of the flesh." And afterward, "in which you were also raised with Him through faith in the powerful working of God" (2:12). Here are the two parts. One is putting off the body of sins, the other is the rising again through faith. Neither should these terms "making dead," "making alive," "putting off the body of sins," "rising again" be understood in a Platonic way, about a fake change. Rather, "making dead" means true terrors, such as those of the dying, which nature could not sustain unless it were supported by faith. Paul calls that "the putting off the body of sins," which we ordinarily call contrition. In these griefs the natural, lustful desire is purged away. The "making alive" should not be understood as a Platonic fancy, but as comfort that truly sustains life that flickers in contrition. Here, therefore, are two parts: 47 contrition and faith. For conscience cannot be quieted except through faith. Therefore, faith alone makes alive, according to this declaration: "The righteous shall live by his faith" (Habakkuk 2:4; Romans 1:17).

48     Colossians 2:14 says, "[Christ canceled] the record of debt that stood against us with its legal demands." Here also there are two parts, the handwriting and the blotting out of the handwriting. The handwriting, how-

ever, is conscience, convicting and condemning us. The Law, furthermore, is the Word that rebukes and condemns sins. Therefore, this voice that says, "I have sinned against the LORD," as David says (2 Samuel 12:13), is the handwriting. Wicked and secure people do not seriously give forth this voice, for they do not see. They do not read the sentence of the Law written in the heart. This sentence is perceived in true griefs and terrors. Therefore, the handwriting that condemns us is contrition itself. To blot out the handwriting is to chisel away the sentence by which we declare that we shall be condemned and to engrave the sentence by which we know that we have been freed from this condemnation. Faith is the new sentence. It reverses the former sentence and gives peace and life to the heart.

49    What need is there to cite many testimonies since they are everywhere clear in the Scriptures?

> The LORD has disciplined me severely, but He has not given me over to death. (Psalm 118:18)

> My soul melts away for sorrow; strengthen me according to Your word! (Psalm 119:28)

Here, contrition is contained in the first clause, and how we are revived in contrition is clearly described in the second. We are revived by God's Word, which offers grace.
50    This sustains and enlivens hearts.

> The LORD kills and brings to life; He brings down to Sheol and raises up. (1 Samuel 2:6)

Contrition is meant by one of these; faith is meant by the other.

51    [The LORD] will be roused; to do His deed—strange is His deed! and to work His work—alien is His work! (Isaiah 28:21)

He calls it the "strange" work of the Lord when He terrifies, because to make alive and comfort is God's own proper work. But He terrifies, Isaiah says, for this reason—that there may be a place for comfort and making alive. For hearts that are secure and do not feel God's wrath hate consolation. In this 52 manner Scripture is accustomed to join these two, the terrors and the consolation. It does this to teach that there are these chief parts in repentance: contrition and faith that comforts and justifies. Neither do we see how the nature of repentance can be presented more clearly and simply.

God's two chief works among people are 53 these: to terrify; to justify and make alive those who have been terrified. Into these two works all Scripture has been distributed. The one part is the *Law*, which shows, reproves, and condemns sins. The other part is the *Gospel*, that is, the promise of grace bestowed in Christ. This promise is constantly repeated in the whole of Scripture, first having been delivered to Adam ("I will put enmity" in Genesis 3:15), afterward, to the patriarchs. Then, it was still more clearly proclaimed by the prophets. Lastly, it was preached and set forth among the Jewish people by Christ and then spread out over the entire world by the apostles. All the saints were justified through 54 faith in this promise, and not by their own attrition or contrition.

The examples also show these two parts. 55 After his sin, Adam is rebuked and becomes terrified; this was contrition. Then, God promises grace and speaks of a future seed (the blessed seed, that is, Christ) by which the devil's kingdom, death, and sin will be destroyed (Genesis 3:15). There He offers the forgiveness of sins. These are the chief things. For although the punishment is added afterward, it does not merit the forgiveness of sin.

We will speak about this kind of punishment a little later.

56 David is rebuked by Nathan in this way. Terrified, he says, "I have sinned against the LORD" (2 Samuel 12:13). This is contrition. Afterward, he hears the Absolution, "The LORD also has put away your sin; you shall not die." This voice encourages David, and through faith it sustains, justifies, and enlivens him. A punishment is also added, but this punishment does not merit the forgiveness of sins. Nor are special punishments always added. In repentance these two things ought always to exist, namely, contrition and faith, as in Luke 7. The woman, who was a sinner, came to Christ weeping. By these tears the contrition is recognized. Afterward, she hears the Absolution, "Your sins are forgiven. Your faith has saved you; go in peace" (vv. 48, 50). This is the second part of repentance, namely, faith that encourages and comforts her. From all these it is clear to godly readers that we assign to repentance those parts that properly belong to it in conversion, or the new birth, and the forgiveness of sin. Worthy fruit and punishments follow rebirth and the forgiveness of sin. For this reason we have mentioned these two parts so that the faith required in repentance might be seen better, and so that faith, which the Gospel proclaims, can be better understood when it is contrasted with contrition and making dead.

57

58

### Forgiveness of Sins Received by Faith

59 Since the adversaries clearly condemn our statement that people obtain the forgiveness of sins by faith, we shall add a few proofs. From these it will be understood that the forgiveness of sins is received not by the outward deed (*ex opere operato*) because of contrition, but by that special faith by which an individual believes that sins are pardoned for him. For this is the chief article that we are debating with our adversaries and the knowledge we regard is necessary to all Christians. However, we have said enough already about the same subject and will be brief. For the doctrine of repentance and justification are very closely related.

When the adversaries speak of faith, saying that it comes before repentance, they understand faith this way: not that faith justifies, but that, in a general way, it believes that God exists, that punishments have been threatened to the wicked, and so on. In addition to this faith, we require that each one believe that his sins are pardoned. We are arguing about this specific faith, and we contrast it to the opinion that asks us to trust not in Christ's promise, but in the outward act (*opus operatum*) of contrition, confession, satisfactions, and so on. This faith follows terrors in such a way as to overcome them and make the conscience peaceful. We attribute justification and regeneration to this faith, since it frees from terrors and produces not only peace and joy, but also a new life in the heart. With God's help, we shall defend to eternity and against all the gates of hell that this faith is truly necessary for the forgiveness of sins, and so place it among the parts of repentance. Nor does Christ's Church believe otherwise, although our adversaries contradict us.

60

Furthermore, we ask the adversaries whether or not Absolution is a part of repentance. If they separate it from Confession (they are clever in making the distinction), we do not see what benefit Confession has without Absolution. If, however, they do not separate Absolution from Confession, it is necessary for them to hold that faith is a part of repentance, because Absolution is not received except through faith. However, that Absolution is received only through faith is proven from Paul, who teaches that the

61

promise cannot be received *except by faith* (Romans 4:16). Absolution is the promise of the forgiveness of sins. Therefore, it necessar-

62    ily requires faith. Neither do we see how the person who does not yield to Absolution may be said to receive Absolution. What else is the refusal to yield to Absolution but charging God with falsehood? If the heart doubts, it regards those things that God promises as uncertain and of no account. So, it is written, "Whoever does not believe God has made Him a liar, because he has not believed in the testimony that God has borne concerning His Son" (1 John 5:10).

63    Second, we think that the adversaries recognize that the forgiveness of sins is either a part of repentance or its end (the *terminus ad quem*). Therefore, whatever receives the forgiveness of sins is correctly added to the parts of repentance. However, it is very certain that even though all the gates of hell contradict us, the forgiveness of sins cannot be received except by faith alone. This faith believes that sins are pardoned for Christ's sake, according to Romans 3:25, "whom God put forward as a propitiation by His blood, to be received by faith." Likewise, "Through Him we have also obtained access by faith into this grace" (Romans 5:2). For a terrified conscience cannot

64    set our works or our love against God's wrath. It is eventually quieted when it takes hold of Christ as Mediator and believes the promises given for His sake. For those who imagine that hearts become quieted without

The Good Shepherd and False Shepherds

65 faith in Christ do not understand what the forgiveness of sins is or how it came to us. So 1 Peter 2:6 cites from Isaiah 49:23 and 28:16, "Whoever believes in Him will not be put to shame." It is necessary, therefore, that hypocrites be puzzled. They are confident that they receive the forgiveness of sins because of their own works, and not because of Christ. Peter also says, "To Him all the prophets bear witness that everyone who believes in Him receives forgiveness of sins" (Acts 10:43). What he says, through His name, could not be expressed more clearly. He adds, "everyone who believes in Him." So we receive the forgiveness of sins only through Christ's name, that is, for Christ's sake, and not for the sake of any merits and works of our own. This happens when we believe that our sins are forgiven for Christ's sake.

66 Our adversaries cry out that they are the Church, that they are following the general agreement of the Church. But Peter also cites here in our issue the consensus of the Church, "To Him all the prophets bear witness that everyone who believes in Him receives forgiveness of sins" (Acts 10:43). The general agreement of the prophets is certainly to be judged as the general agreement of the Church universal. We admit neither to the pope nor to the Church the power to make decrees against this general agreement 67 of the prophets. But the bull of Leo openly condemns this article, "Repentance," and the adversaries condemn it in the Confutation. It is clear what sort of a Church we must judge these men to be. By their decrees they not only condemn the doctrine that we obtain the forgiveness of sins through faith (not on account of our works, but because of Christ), but they also give the command to abolish it by force and the sword and by every kind of cruelty to put to death good people who believe this way.

68 They have famous authors, Scotus, Gabriel Biel, and the like, and passages of the Fathers that are quoted in a butchered form in the decrees. Certainly, if the quotations are to be counted, they win. For there is a very great crowd of most silly writers on the *Sentences*. As though they had worked together, they defend these fables about the merit of attrition and of works and other things that we have mentioned previously. But let no 69 one be moved by the multitude of citations. There is no great weight in the testimonies of the later writers. They did not create their own writings, but only, by compiling from the writers before them, transferred these opinions from some books into others. They have exercised no judgment. Just like petty judges they have silently approved the errors of their superiors, which they have not understood. Therefore, let us not hesitate to use 70 this saying of Peter, which summarizes the Prophets and opposes ever so many legions of the commentators on the *Sentences*. The 71 Holy Spirit's testimony is added to this statement of Peter. For the text speaks in this way, "While Peter was still saying these things, the Holy Spirit fell on all who heard the word" (Acts 10:44). Therefore, let godly consciences 72 know that God's command is this: They are to believe that they are freely forgiven for Christ's sake, and not for the sake of our works. Let them sustain themselves against despair and against the terrors of sin and of death by this command of God. Let them 73 know that this belief has existed among saints from the beginning of the world. For Peter clearly cites the general agreement of the Prophets, and the writings of the apostles confirm that they believe the same thing. Nor are testimonies of the Fathers lacking. For Bernard says the same thing in words that are in no way hidden:

It is necessary first of all to believe that you cannot have forgiveness of sins except by the indulgence of God, but add yet that you believe also this, namely, that through Him sins are forgiven to you. This is the testimony that the Holy Spirit asserts in your heart, saying: "Your sins are forgiven you." For so the apostle concludes that a person is justified freely through faith.

74 These words of Bernard shed a wonderful light upon our cause, because he not only requires that we believe in a general way that sins are pardoned through mercy, but he also asks us to add special faith, by which we believe that our sins are forgiven. He teaches how we can be sure about the forgiveness of sins, namely, when our hearts are encouraged through faith and become peaceful through the Holy Spirit. What more do the adversaries require? Do they still dare deny that we receive the forgiveness of sins through faith or that faith is a part of repentance?

75 Third, the adversaries say that sin is pardoned because an attrite or contrite person brings forth an act of love to God, and by this act deserves the forgiveness of sins. This is nothing but teaching the Law, the Gospel being blotted out, and the promise about Christ being abolished. For they require only the Law and our works because the Law demands love. Besides, they teach us to be confident that we obtain forgiveness of sins because of contrition and love. What else is this than to put confidence in our works, not in God's Word and promise about Christ? But if the Law is enough for receiving the forgiveness of sins, what need is there of the Gospel? What need is there of Christ if we receive forgiveness of sins because of our own work?

76 We, on the other hand, call consciences away from the Law to the Gospel, and from confidence in their own works to confidence in the promise and Christ. We do so because the Gospel presents Christ to us and freely promises the forgiveness of sins for Christ's sake. In this promise it asks us to trust, namely, that we are reconciled to the Father for Christ's sake, not for the sake of our own contrition or love. For there is no other Mediator or Atoning Sacrifice than Christ. Neither can we do the works of the Law unless we have first been reconciled through Christ. If we would do anything, we must believe that for Christ's sake, as Mediator and Atoning Sacrifice, we receive the forgiveness of sins, and not for the sake of these works.

77 Yes, it is a disgrace to Christ and a repeal of the Gospel to believe that we receive the forgiveness of sins because of the Law, or any way other than through faith in Christ. We discussed this before in the article on justification. There we declared why we confess that people are justified through faith, not through love. The doctrine of the adversaries 78 is merely the doctrine of the Law, when they teach that by their own contrition and love people receive the forgiveness of sins and trust in this contrition and love. Even so, it is not understood (they do not understand the kind of love toward God it demands), just as the Jewish people looked upon Moses' veiled face (2 Corinthians 3:15). Let us imagine that love is present, and let us imagine that works are present. Yet neither love nor works can be an atoning sacrifice for sin. The adversaries cannot even be opposed to God's wrath and judgment, according to Psalm 143:2, "Enter not into judgment with Your servant, for no one living is righteous before You." Neither should Christ's honor be transferred to our works.

79 For these reasons Paul argues that we are not justified by the Law. He contrasts the Law to the promise of the forgiveness of sins,

which we freely receive and which is granted for Christ's sake. Paul calls us away from the Law to this promise. Upon this he asks us to look. The promise certainly will be void if we are justified by the Law before we are justified through the promise, or if we receive the forgiveness of sins because of our own righ- 80 teousness. Clearly the promise was given to us and Christ was offered to us because we cannot do the works of the Law. Therefore, it is necessary that we are reconciled by the promise before we do the works of the Law. The promise, however, is received only through faith. It is necessary for contrite persons to take hold of the promise of the forgiveness of sins granted for Christ's sake through faith and to be confident that they have a reconciled Father freely for Christ's 81 sake. This is Paul's meaning when he says, "That is why it depends on faith, in order that the promise may rest on grace and be guaranteed" (Romans 4:16). And, "The Scripture imprisoned everything under sin, so that the promise by faith in Jesus Christ might be given to those who believe" (Galatians 3:22). This means that all are under sin, neither can they be freed except by grasping the promise of the forgiveness of sins 82 through faith. Therefore, we must accept the forgiveness of sins through faith before we do the works of the Law. Although, as has been said before, love follows faith because the reborn person receives the Holy Spirit and so begins to do the works of the Law.

83    We would cite more testimonies if they were not clear in the Scriptures to every godly reader. We do not wish to be too wordy, so that we may bring this case to a 84 conclusion. Neither is there any doubt that we are defending Paul's meaning. He teaches that through faith we receive the forgiveness of sins for Christ's sake, and that through faith we should set Christ as Mediator against God's wrath, and not our works. Nor should godly minds be disturbed when the adversaries find fault with Paul's judgments. Nothing is said so simply that it cannot be distorted by objecting. We know that we have mentioned Paul's true and genuine meaning. We know that our belief brings sure comfort to godly consciences, without which no one can stand in God's judgment.

Let these legalistic opinions of the adver- 85 saries be rejected. Among these are that we do not receive the forgiveness of sins by faith, but that it should be merited by our love and works. Another opinion is that we should set our love and our works against God's wrath. This doctrine is not of the Gospel, but of the Law. It wrongly teaches that a person is justified by the Law before he has been reconciled through Christ to God. Christ says, "Apart from Me you can do nothing"; likewise, "I am the vine; you are the branches" (John 15:5). But the adversaries wrongly teach that we are 86 branches not of Christ, but of Moses. For they want to be justified by the Law and to offer their love and works to God before they are reconciled to God through Christ, before they are branches of Christ. On the other hand, Paul argues that the Law cannot be obeyed without Christ. We must receive the promise first so that through faith we may be reconciled to God on account of Christ. Then we can do the works of the Law. Those who truly feel and have experienced sin and anguish of conscience must cling to the promise of grace. We think that these things are clear 87 enough to godly consciences. In this way they will understand why we have declared before that people are justified through faith, not through love. We must set against God's anger not our love or works (or trust in our love or works), but Christ as Mediator. We must grasp the promise of the forgiveness of sins before we do the works of the Law.

88    Finally, when will conscience be quieted if we receive forgiveness of sins on the ground that we love, or that we do the works of the Law? The Law will always accuse us, because we never satisfy God's Law. Just as Paul says, "The law brings wrath" (Romans 4:15). Chrysostom asks about repentance, "Where are we made sure that our sins are forgiven?" The adversaries also, in their *Sentences,* ask about the same subject. This cannot be explained; consciences cannot be made at peace unless they know it is God's command and the very Gospel that they should be firmly confident that sins are forgiven freely for Christ's sake, and that they should not doubt this. If anyone doubts, he charges the divine promise with falsehood, as 1 John 5:10 says. We teach that the Gospel requires this certainty of faith. The adversaries leave consciences uncertain and wavering. Con-

89    sciences, however, do nothing by faith when they constantly doubt whether they have forgiveness. In this doubt how can they call upon God? How can they be confident that they are heard? So the entire life would be without God and without the true worship of God. This is what Paul says, "Whatever does not proceed from faith is sin" (Romans 14:23). Because they are constantly occupied with this doubt, they never experience what faith is. So finally they rush at last into despair. Such is the doctrine of the adversaries, the doctrine of the Law, the setting aside of

90    the Gospel, the doctrine of despair. We are glad to refer judgment about this subject of repentance (for it is clear) to all good people. They can decide whether we or the adversaries have taught those things that are more godly and healthful to consciences. Indeed, these disagreements in the Church do not delight us. If we did not have great and necessary reasons for disagreeing with the adversaries we would, with the greatest pleasure, be silent. But since they condemn the clear truth, it is not right for us to abandon what is not our own cause, but the cause of Christ and the Church.

### Faith and Repentance

91    We have declared why we assigned these two parts, *contrition and faith,* to repentance. We have done this willingly. Many writings about repentance are published that cite the Fathers in a butchered way. The adversaries have distorted these to put faith out of sight. Among these are, "Repentance is to lament past evils, and not to commit again deeds that ought to be lamented." Again, "Repentance is a kind of vengeance of him who grieves, thus punishing in himself what he is sorry for having committed." In these passages, no mention is made of faith. Not even in the schools, when they interpret them, is anything added about faith.

92    Therefore, in order that the doctrine of faith might be clearer, we have named it among the parts of repentance. For experience shows that those passages are dangerous that require contrition or good works, and make no mention of justifying faith.

93    Caution can justly be desired in those who have collected these centos of the *Sentences* and decrees. Since the Fathers speak in some places about one part of repentance, and in other places about another part, it would have been good to select and combine their judgments not only about one part but about both, that is, about contrition and faith.

94    Tertullian speaks very well about faith, discussing the oath in the prophet Ezekiel, "As I live, declares the Lord GOD, I have no pleasure in the death of the wicked, but that the wicked turn from his way and live" (33:11). As God swears that He does not want the death of a sinner, He shows that

faith is required, in order that we may believe the one swearing and be firmly confident that He forgives us. In our estimation, the authority of the divine promises should be great by itself. But this promise has also been confirmed by an oath. Therefore, if anyone is not confident that he is forgiven, he denies that God has sworn what is true. A more horrible blasphemy cannot be imagined. For Tertullian says this:

> He invites by reward to salvation, even swearing. Saying, "I live," He desires that He be believed. Oh, blessed we, for whose sake God swears! Oh, most miserable if we believe not the Lord even when He swears!

95 Here we must know that this faith should be confident that God freely forgives us for Christ's sake, for the sake of His own promise, not for the sake of our works, contrition, confession, or satisfactions. For if faith relies upon these works, it immediately becomes uncertain, because the terrified conscience
96 sees that these works are unworthy. So Ambrose speaks well about repentance:

> Therefore, it is proper for us to believe both that we are to repent, and that we are to be pardoned, but in such a way as to expect pardon from faith, which obtains pardon as from a handwriting.

Again,

> It is faith that covers our sins.

97 Therefore, there are sentences written by the Fathers not only about contrition and works, but also about faith. But the adversaries, since they understand neither the nature of repentance nor the language of the Fathers, select passages about a part of repentance, namely, about works. They overlook the declarations made elsewhere about faith, since they do not understand them.

# Confession and Satisfaction (VI)

The Roman Church transformed the great blessing of Confession and Absolution into a legalistic burden on the back of every Christian. In addition to requiring every sin to be confessed, Rome demanded satisfaction, or meritorious works, in order to "make up" for confessed sins. Absolution, the sweet announcement of forgiveness of sins through Christ, became tangled in the web of indulgences, satisfactions, and other human works that Rome required from her faithful. Melanchthon makes it clear that Lutherans cherish private Absolution, which is God's forgiveness in Christ applied personally to the believer burdened with guilt and sorrow over sin. He writes that those who despise Absolution understand neither forgiveness nor the Office of the Keys.

When death confronts a human being, he must face it with Christ alone, not with human works and satisfactions. We receive God's forgiveness freely because Christ Jesus is the Victor over sin, death, and Satan. Melanchthon discusses this extensively, because the teaching pointed to Luther's evangelical breakthrough in recovering the centrality of Christ and the Gospel in the Church. Lutherans never denied that good works follow the gift of faith and the blessings of the Gospel. But these gifts are not earned, merited, or deserved. By teaching that our participation with God's grace is what brings about eternal life, Roman theology horribly distorted and obscured the Gospel and robbed Christ of His place as our only Mediator, who makes satisfaction for our sin. (See AC XI and XXV; SA III VIII; SC V; LC V, An Exhortation to Confession.)

1    Good people can easily conclude that it is very important that the true doctrine be preserved about the above-mentioned parts: contrition and faith. Therefore, we have always been busier with making these topics clear and have argued nothing as yet about 2 *confession and satisfaction*. We also keep Confession, especially because of the Absolution. Absolution is God's Word which, by divine authority, the Power of the Keys pronounces 3 upon individuals. Therefore, it would be wicked to remove private Absolution from 4 the Church. If anyone despises private Absolution, he does not understand what the forgiveness of sins or the Power of the Keys is. 5 Regarding the complete listing of offenses in Confession, we have said above that we hold 6 that it is not necessary by divine right. Some object to this, saying that a judge should investigate a case before he rules on it, which has nothing to do with this subject. The ministry of Absolution is favor or grace; it is not 7 a legal process or law. Ministers in the Church have the command to forgive sin. They do not have the command to investi- 8 gate secret sins. Indeed, they absolve us from those sins that we do not remember. For that reason Absolution, which is the voice of the Gospel forgiving sins and comforting consciences, does not require judicial examination.

9    It is ridiculous to apply to this discussion the saying of Solomon, "Know well the condition of your flocks" (Proverbs 27:23). For Solomon says nothing about Confession. He gives to the father of a family a domestic precept, that he should use what is his own and refrain from what is another's. Solomon commands the father to take good care of his own property. Yet he should do so in such a way that, with his mind occupied with the increase of his resources, he should not cast away the fear of God or faith or care in God's Word. But our adversaries, by a wonderful change, transform Scripture passages to whatever meaning they please. Here to "know" means to them hearing confessions, "the condition," not the outward life, but the secrets of conscience. And "your flocks" mean people. The interpretation is truly neat and is worthy of these haters of pursuing eloquence. If anyone desires to transfer by analogy a precept from a father of a family to a pastor of a Church, he should certainly interpret "the condition" as applying to the outward life. This comparison will be more consistent.

10    Let us skip such matters as these. Confession is mentioned at different times in the Psalms. "'I will confess my transgressions to the LORD,' and You forgave the iniquity of my sin" (32:5). Such confession of sin, which is made to God, is contrition itself. When confession is made to God, it must be made with the heart, not only with the voice, like actors on the stage. Confession is contrition in which, feeling God's anger, we confess that God is justly angry and that He cannot be reconciled by our works. Yet, we seek for mercy because of God's promise. Such is the 11 following confession, "Against You, You only, have I sinned . . . so that You may be justified in Your words and blameless in Your judgment" (Psalm 51:4). This means, "I confess that I am a sinner and have merited eternal wrath. Nor can I set my righteousnesses, my merits, against Your wrath. So I declare that You are just when You condemn and punish us. I declare that You are clear when hypocrites judge You to be unjust in punishing them or in condemning the well-deserving. Yes, our merits cannot satisfy Your judgment. But we will be justified in this way, namely, if You justify us, if through Your mercy You count us righteous." Perhaps someone may 12 also cite James 5:16, "Confess your sins to

one another." But here the reference is not to confession made to priests, but is the reconciliation of brothers to each other. Confession should be mutual.

13    Our adversaries will condemn many well-respected teachers if they will agree that in Confession a listing of offenses is necessary according to divine Law. We approve of Confession, and conclude that some examination is helpful, so that people may be instructed better. Yet, Confession must be done in such a way that consciences are not entrapped. They never will be quieted if they think that they cannot receive the forgiveness of sins 14 unless this precise listing is made. What the adversaries have expressed in the Confutation is certainly most false: A full confession is necessary for salvation. This is impossible. What traps they lay for the conscience when they require a full confession! When will a conscience be sure that the confession is 15 complete? Church writers mention Confession. However, they do not speak about this listing of secret offenses, but about the rite of public repentance. The fallen or notorious sinners were not received [into fellowship] without fixed satisfactions. They confessed to the presbyters, so that satisfactions might be prescribed to them according to the degree of their guilt. This type of confession has nothing similar to the listing about which we are arguing. This kind of confession was made, not because the forgiveness of sins before God could not happen without it, but because satisfactions could not be prescribed unless the kinds of offense were first known. Different offenses had different rules.

## The Church Fathers on Satisfaction

16    The word *satisfaction* has been left from this rite of public repentance. The Holy Fathers were unwilling to welcome back the fallen or the notorious sinners unless, as far as it was possible, their repentance had been first examined and shown publicly. There seem to have been many causes for this. To discipline those who had fallen served as an example, as the gloss upon the decrees reminds us. Also, it was improper to admit notorious people immediately to Communion. These customs have long since grown obsolete. It is not necessary to restore them, because they are not necessary for the forgiveness of sins before God. The Fathers did not 17 maintain that people merit the forgiveness of sins through such customs or works. These spectacles (outward ceremonies) usually lead astray the ignorant, who thought that they merited the forgiveness of sins before God by these works. If anyone believes this, he has the faith of a Jewish person and a pagan. For even the pagans had certain remedies for offenses through which they imagined they were reconciled to God. Now, even though 18 the custom has been cast aside, the word *satisfaction* still remains. A small part of the custom also remains of prescribing in confession certain satisfactions, which they define as works that are not required. We call them *canonical satisfactions*. Like the complete list- 19 ing of sins, we hold that canonical satisfactions are not necessary by divine Law for the forgiveness of sins. Neither were those ancient displays of satisfactions in public repentance necessary by divine Law for the forgiveness of sins. The teaching about faith must be kept, that we receive the forgiveness of sins for Christ's sake through faith, not for the sake of our works that precede or follow. This is why we have discussed especially the question of satisfactions—the righteousness of faith should not be clouded over in submitting to them. Nor should people think that they receive the forgiveness of sins for the sake of these works. Many current say- 20 ings in the schools aid the error. Among these

are those that give the definition of satisfaction, namely, that it is done to reconcile divine displeasure.

21 Nevertheless, the adversaries admit that satisfactions do not help in the pardon of guilt. They imagine that satisfactions help in delivering one from punishment, whether of purgatory or other punishments. They teach that God pardons guilt in the forgiveness of sins. Yet, because divine justice requires sin to be punished, He transfers eternal punishment into temporal punishment. Further, they add that a part of this temporal punishment is pardoned by the Power of the Keys, but that the rest is delivered by means of satisfactions. It cannot be understood which punishments the Power of the Keys partially forgive, unless the adversaries say that a part of the punishments of purgatory is forgiven. That would mean that satisfactions are only punishments delivering from purgatory. They say satisfactions benefit, even though they are presented by those who have fallen again into mortal sin, as though indeed the divine displeasure could be appeased by

22 those who are in mortal sin. This entire matter is fake and recently made up without Scriptural authority and the old writers of the Church. Not even Lombard speaks of sat-

23 isfactions in this way. The Scholastics saw that there were satisfactions in the Church. They did not notice that these displays had been set up both for the purpose of example and for testing those who desired to be welcomed back by the Church. In a word, they did not see that it was a discipline and entirely a secular matter. So they superstitiously imagined that these [displays] benefit not for discipline before the Church, but for reconciling God. In other places, they frequently, with great incompetence, have confused spiritual and civil matters. The same happens

24 also regarding satisfactions. But at various places the explanation of the canons confirms that these observances were set up for the sake of Church discipline.

## Misuses of Scripture

25 In the Confutation, the adversaries had the nerve to impose on His Imperial Majesty. Let us see how they prove these fables of theirs. They cite many passages from the Scriptures to impress the inexperienced. They do this as though this subject—unknown even in the time of Lombard—had authority from the Scriptures. They promote such passages as these: "Bear fruit in keeping with repentance" (Matthew 3:8; see also Mark 1:15). "Present your members as slaves to righteousness" (Romans 6:19). Christ preaches repentance, "Repent" (Matthew 4:17). Again, Christ commands the apostles to preach repentance (Luke 24:47), and Peter preaches repentance (Acts 2:38). Afterward, the adversaries quote certain passages of the Fathers and the canons, and conclude that satisfactions in the Church are not to be set aside. This is contrary to the plain Gospel and the decrees of the councils and Fathers. They even claim that those who have been absolved by the priest should finish the repentance that has been directed. They base this on Paul's declaration, "Who gave Himself for us to redeem us from all lawlessness and to purify for Himself a people for His own possession who are zealous for good works" (Titus 2:14).

26 May God confuse these godless philosophers. They wickedly distort God's Word to their own most empty dreams! What good person is not moved by such insult? "Christ says, 'Repent,' the apostles preach repentance; therefore, eternal punishments are relieved by the punishments of purgatory; therefore, the Keys have the power to pardon part of the punishments of purgatory; therefore, sat-

isfactions deliver from the punishments of purgatory!" Who has taught these asses such logic? Yet this is neither logic nor slick thinking, but deceitful trickery. They appeal to the expression "repent" in such a way that, when the inexperienced hear such a passage cited against us, they may come to the opinion that we deny repentance in its entirety. By these moves they try hard to turn away minds and to stir up hatred. They do this so that the inexperienced may cry out against us, that the deadly heretics that disapprove of repentance should be removed from their midst.

27 We hope that these lies may make little headway among good people. We also hope that God will not put up with such rudeness and wickedness much longer. The pope of Rome has not become any more dignified using such patrons, because he has entrusted a very important matter of the greatest importance to the judgment of these philosophers. Since we include almost all of the Christian doctrine in the Confession, judges should have been appointed to declare about important and various matters. Their learning and faith would have been more acceptable than the learning of these philosophers 28 who have written this Confutation. It was very fitting of you, O Campegius, according to your wisdom, to have made sure that they should write nothing about important matters that, either now or later, might appear to lower respect for the Roman See. If the Roman See determines that all nations should recognize her as mistress of the faith, she should try very hard to have educated and godly people investigate religious matters. What will the world conclude if at any time the adversaries' writing is brought to light? What will future generations think about these disgraceful judicial investiga-29 tions? You see, O Campegius, that these are the last days. Christ predicted that the great-

est danger to religion would happen in them (Matthew 24:9–28). You, who should sit on the watchtower (Hosea 9:8) and control religious matters, should in these times also use unusual wisdom and diligence. Unless you heed them, there are many signs that threaten a change to the Roman state. And you 30 make a mistake if you think that churches should be kept only by force and arms. The people are asking to be taught about religion. How many do you suppose there are, not only in Germany, but also in England, in Spain, in France, in Italy, and finally even in the city of Rome? Since controversies have come up about subjects of the greatest importance, they are beginning to doubt here and there, to be silently insulted that you refuse to investigate and rightly judge such weighty subjects. They doubt and are insulted that you do not help wavering consciences, that you only ask us to be overthrown and destroyed by arms. To many 31 good people this doubt is more bitter than death. You do not think enough about how great a subject religion is, if you think that good people are in anguish for little reason when they doubt any teaching. This doubt can have no other effect than to produce the greatest bitterness of hatred against those who hinder the explanation of the subject when they should heal consciences. We are 32 not saying here that you should fear God's judgment. The religious leaders think that they can easily ensure against this since they hold the Keys. Of course, they can open heaven for themselves whenever they want. We are speaking of the judgments of people and the silent desires of all nations. At this time they require that these matters be investigated and decided so that good minds may be healed and freed from doubt. For, according to your wisdom, you can easily decide what will happen if at any time this hatred should break out against you. By this favor you will be able to bind all nations to yourself. All sane people regard it as the highest and most important matter if you heal 33 doubting consciences. We have said these things not because we doubt our Confession. For we know that it is true, godly, and useful to godly consciences. It is likely that there are many in many places who waver about matters of no small importance. Yet they do not hear teachers that are able to heal their consciences.

34 Let us return to the main point. The Scriptures cited by the adversaries do not speak of canonical satisfactions and of the opinions of the Scholastics, since it is clear that the latter were born only recently. Therefore, it is pure slander when they distort Scripture to their own opinions. We say that good fruit, good works in every kind of life, should follow repentance, that is, conversion or regeneration. Neither can there be true conversion or true contrition where the putting to death of the flesh and bearing good fruit do not follow. True terrors, true griefs of mind, do not allow the body to satisfy itself in sensual pleasures, and true faith is not ungrateful to God. Neither does true faith hate God's commandments. In a word, there is no inner repentance unless it also produces the 35 outward putting to death of the flesh. We say that this is John's meaning when he says, "Bear fruit in keeping with repentance" (Matthew 3:8). Likewise of Paul when he says, "Present your members as slaves to righteousness" (Romans 6:19); just as he likewise says elsewhere, "Present your bodies as a living sacrifice" (Romans 12:1), and so forth. When Christ says, "Repent" (Matthew 4:17), He certainly speaks of repentance in its entirety, of the entire newness of life and its fruit. He does not speak of those hypocritical satisfactions that the Scholastics imagine

benefit by delivering from the punishment of purgatory or other punishments when they are made by those in mortal sin.

36 Many arguments, likewise, can be brought together to show that these Scripture passages have nothing to do with scholastic satisfactions. [First,] these men imagine that satisfactions are works that are not due. However, Scripture, in these passages, requires works that are due. For this word of Christ, "Repent," is the word of a commandment. Likewise, the adversaries 37 write that if anyone who goes to Confession should refuse to undertake satisfactions, he does not sin, but will pay these penalties in purgatory. Now the following passages are, without controversy, rules having to do with this life: "repent," "bear fruit in keeping with repentance," "present your members as slaves to righteousness." Therefore, they cannot be twisted to the satisfactions that are permitted to be refused. Refusing God's commandments is not permitted. Third, indulgences 38 pardon these satisfactions, as is taught in the article "Repentance" (beginning *Quum ex eo*), and so on. But indulgences do not free us from these commandments: "repent," "bear fruit in keeping with repentance." Clearly these Scripture passages have been wickedly twisted to apply to canonical satisfactions. See further what follows. If the punishments 39 of purgatory are satisfactions, or "satispassions," or if satisfactions are a pardoning of the punishments of purgatory, do the passages also command that souls be punished in purgatory? Since this must follow from the opinions of the adversaries, these passages should be interpreted in a new way: "bear fruit in keeping with repentance," "repent," that is, suffer the punishments of purgatory after this life. But we do not care to respond 40 any further to the silly points of the adversaries. Clearly, Scripture speaks of works that

are required, of the entire newness of life, and not of these observances of works that are not required, of which the adversaries speak. Yet, by these fables they defend orders of monks, the sale of Masses, and endless observances, calling them works that, if they do not make satisfaction for guilt, can still make satisfaction for punishment.

41    The Scripture passages cited do not say that eternal punishments are to be paid by works that are not required. So the adversaries are rash to assert that these satisfactions are paid by canonical satisfactions. The Keys do not have the command to transfer some punishments and, likewise, to pardon a part of the punishments. For where are such things read in the Scriptures? Christ speaks of the forgiveness of sins when He says, "Whatever you loose . . ." (Matthew 18:18). He means sin being forgiven, eternal death taken away, and eternal life bestowed. "Whatever you bind" does not speak of requiring punishments, but of retaining the sins of those 42    who are not converted. Furthermore, the declaration of Lombard about pardoning a part of the punishments has been taken from the canonical punishments; the pastors forgave a part of these. We hold that repentance should produce good fruit for the sake of God's glory and command. Good fruit, true fastings, true prayers, true alms, and so forth, have God's commands. Yet in the Holy Scriptures we find nowhere that eternal punishments are only pardoned because of the punishment of purgatory or canonical satisfactions, that is, because of certain works not required, or that the Power of the Keys has the command to transfer their punishments or to forgive a portion. The adversaries were going to prove these things.

43    Besides, Christ's death is a satisfaction not only for guilt, but also for eternal death, according to Hosea 13:14, "O Death, where are your plagues?" It is freakish to say that the satisfaction of Christ redeemed from the guilt, but our punishments redeem from eternal death. The expression "I will be your death" does not get understood about Christ, but about our works and, indeed, not about the works commanded by God, but about some dull observances created by men! These are said to abolish death, even when they are completed in mortal sin. It is with 44    incredible grief we recite these foolish points of the adversaries. They only cause one who considers them to be enraged against such demonic teachings. The devil has spread these teachings in the Church to hinder the knowledge of the Law and Gospel, of repentance and being made alive, and of Christ's benefits. For of the Law they speak this way: 45

> God, deferring to our weakness, has given to people a measure of those things that necessarily binds them. This is obeying laws, so that from what is left, that is, from works of supererogation, he can present satisfaction with reference to offenses that have been committed.

Here people imagine that they can keep God's Law in such a way that they do even more than the Law requires (Romans 3:10–20). But Scripture shouts everywhere that we are far away from the perfection that the Law requires. Still these people imagine that God's Law affects only outward and civil righteousness. They do not see that it requires true love for God "with all your heart" (Deuteronomy 6:4) and that it condemns all lustful desires in human nature. Therefore, no one does as much as the Law requires. Their imagination that we can do more is ridiculous. We *can* perform outward works not commanded by God's Law. Yet confidence that satisfaction has accomplished God's Law is empty and wicked. True prayers, true alms, 46 and true fastings have God's command. Where they have God's command, they cannot be left out without sin. But because these other works have not been commanded by God's Law, but have a fixed form derived from human rule, they are works of human traditions. Christ says about such works, "In vain do they worship Me, teaching as doctrines the commandments of men" (Matthew 15:9). Such works include certain fasts appointed not for restraining the flesh, but so that honor may be given to God, as Scotus says, and so that eternal death be made up for. Likewise, such works include a fixed number of prayers, a fixed measure of alms when they are offered in worship by the outward act (*ex opere operato*), giving honor to God, and making up for eternal death. For they assign satisfaction to these works by the outward act because they teach that they benefit even

47   those who are in mortal sin. There are works that depart still farther from God's commands, such as pilgrimages. There is a great variety of these. One makes a journey (to St. Jacob) clothed in metal armor, and another with bare feet. Christ calls these "vain acts of worship." They do not serve to reconcile God's displeasure, contrary to what the adversaries say. Yet they decorate these works with magnificent titles. They call them works of supererogation. To these works the honor is assigned of being a price paid instead of

48   eternal death. They are preferred over the works of God's commandments. So God's Law is clouded over in two ways. One, because satisfaction is thought to be rendered to God's Law by means of outward and civil works. The other, because human traditions are added, whose works are preferred over the works of the divine Law.

49   In the second place, repentance and grace are clouded over. Eternal death is not atoned for by this payment of works because it is idle

and does not taste of death in the present life. Something else must be set up against death when it tests us. For just as God's anger is overcome through faith in Christ, so death is overcome through faith in Christ. Just as Paul says, "But thanks be to God, who gives us the victory through our Lord Jesus Christ" (1 Corinthians 15:57). He does not say, "Who gives us the victory if we set up our satisfactions against death." The adversaries foster   50 needless debates about the pardon of guilt. They do not see how, in the pardon of guilt, the heart is freed through faith in Christ from God's anger and eternal death. Christ's death is a satisfaction for eternal death. The adversaries themselves confess that these works of satisfactions are works that are not required, but are works of human traditions, of which Christ says that they are vain acts of worship (Matthew 15:9). Therefore, we can safely affirm that canonical satisfactions are not necessary by divine Law for the pardon of guilt or eternal punishment or the punishment of purgatory.

## Additional False Teachings

The adversaries object that revenge or   51 punishment is necessary for repentance, because Augustine says that "repentance is revenge punishing" and so on. We grant that revenge or punishment is necessary in repentance. Yet it is not necessary as merit or price, as the adversaries imagine that satisfactions are necessary. But revenge is in repentance formally, that is, because rebirth itself happens by a continuous putting to death of the oldness of life. The saying of Scotus may indeed be very beautiful, that penitence (*poenitentia*) is so called because it is "holding to punishment" (*poenae tenentia*). But what punishment, what revenge, does Augustine speak about? Certainly true punishment, true revenge, namely, contrition, true terrors. Nor do we exclude here the outward putting to death (mortification) of the body, which follows true grief of mind. The adversaries

52 make a great mistake if they imagine that canonical satisfactions are more truly punishments than are true terrors in the heart. It is most foolish to twist the name of punishment to these dull satisfactions, and not to refer people to those horrible terrors of conscience of which David says, "The cords of death encompassed me" (Psalm 18:4; see also 2 Samuel 22:5). Who would not rather, clad in metal armor and equipped, seek the Church of James, the basilica of Peter, and so on, than bear that violence of grief that is beyond words and exists even in persons of ordinary lives, if there be true repentance?

53 They say that it belongs to God's justice to punish sin. He certainly punishes it in contrition, when in these terrors He shows His wrath. Just as David shows when he prays, "O LORD, rebuke me not in Your anger" (Psalm 6:1). And Jeremiah, "Correct me, O LORD, but in justice; not in Your anger, lest You bring me to nothing" (10:24). Here, indeed, the most bitter punishments are spoken of. The adversaries admit that contrition can be so great that satisfaction is not required. Contrition is, therefore, more truly a punishment

54 than is satisfaction. Besides, saints are subject to death and all general afflictions, as 1 Peter 4:17 says, "For it is time for judgment to begin at the household of God; and if it begins with us, what will be the outcome for those who do not obey the gospel of God?" Although these afflictions are for the most part the punishments of sin, yet in the godly they have a better end, namely, to exercise them, that they may learn amid trials to seek God's aid, to acknowledge the distrust of their own hearts, and so forth. As Paul says of himself, "Indeed, we felt that we had received the sentence of death. But that was to make us

rely not on ourselves but on God who raises the dead" (2 Corinthians 1:9). Isaiah says, "They poured out a whispered prayer when Your discipline was upon them" (26:16), that is, afflictions are a discipline by which God exercises the saints. Likewise, afflictions are 55 inflicted because of present sin, since in the saints they put to death and extinguish lustful desires, so that they may be renewed by the Spirit, as Paul says, "The body is dead because of sin" (Romans 8:10). The body is put to death (mortified) because of present sin that is still left in the flesh. Death itself serves this 56 purpose, namely, to abolish this flesh of sin, that we may rise absolutely new (1 Corinthians 15:42). Since by faith the believer has overcome death's terrors, there is no longer in the believer's death that sting and sense of anger of which Paul says, "The sting of death is sin, and the power of sin is the law" (1 Corinthians 15:56). This strength of sin, this sense of wrath, is truly a punishment as long as it is present. Without this sense of wrath, death is not properly a punishment. Furthermore, canonical satisfactions do not 57 belong to these punishments. The adversaries wrongly say that by the Power of the Keys a part of the punishments is forgiven. Likewise, according to these very men, the Keys pardon the satisfactions and the punishments because of which the satisfactions are made. But it is clear that common troubles are not removed by the Power of the Keys. If the adversaries wish to be understood regarding these punishments, why do they add that satisfaction is to be accomplished in purgatory?

They object to Adam's example, and also 58 to David's, who was punished for his adultery. From these examples they get the universal rule that peculiar temporal punishments in the forgiveness of sins correspond to individual sins. It has been said before that 59 saints suffer punishments, which are God's

Life in the Sixteenth Century

Job's Misfortune

works. They suffer contrition or terrors; they also suffer other common troubles. So, for example, some suffer punishments of their own that have been applied by God. These punishments have nothing to do with the Keys, because the Keys can neither apply nor pardon them. But God, without the ministry of the Keys, applies and pardons them.

Neither does their universal rule follow. A peculiar punishment was put upon David (2 Samuel 12:11–14). Therefore, in addition to common troubles, [they say] there is another punishment of purgatory, in which 60 each degree corresponds to each sin. Where does Scripture teach that we cannot be freed from eternal death except by the payment of certain punishments in addition to common troubles? On the other hand, Scripture often teaches that the forgiveness of sins arises freely for Christ's sake, that Christ is the Victor over sin and death (1 Corinthians 15:57). The merit of satisfaction is not to be patched over this. Although troubles still remain, Scripture interprets these as the putting to death of present sin, and not as the payments of eternal death or as prices for eternal death.

61 Job is excused though he was not troubled by past evil deeds (Job 2:3–10). Therefore, troubles are not always punishments or signs of wrath. Indeed, terrified consciences should be taught that there are more important purposes for afflictions (2 Corinthians 12:9), so that they do not think God is rejecting them when they see nothing but God's punishment and anger in troubles. The other more important purposes are to be considered, that is, that God is doing His strange work so that He may be able to do His own work, as Isaiah 28 teaches in a long speech. 62 When the disciples asked about the blind man who sinned, Christ replies that the cause of his blindness is not sin, but that "the works of God might be displayed in him" (John

9:2–3). In Jeremiah it is said, "If those who did not deserve to drink the cup must drink it . . ." (49:12). So the prophets, John the Baptist, and other saints were killed (Matthew 5:11). Therefore, troubles are not always 63 punishments for certain past deeds, but they are God's works, intended for our benefit, and that God's power might be made more apparent in our weakness.

So Paul says God's strength "is made perfect in weakness" (2 Corinthians 12:9). Because of God's will, our bodies should be sacrifices, to declare our obedience, and not to pay for eternal death. God has another price for that: the death of His own Son. Gregory 64 interprets David's punishment in this sense, when he says:

> If God had threatened that David would be humbled this way by his son because of that sin, why did He fulfill that which He had threatened against him when the sin was forgiven? The reply is that this forgiveness was made so that man might not be hindered from receiving eternal life. The example of the threatening followed, in order that the piety of humanity might be exercised and tested even in this humility. So because of sin, God inflicted upon humanity the death of the body. After the forgiveness of sins, He did not remove the affliction for the sake of exercising justice, namely, so that the righteousness of those who are sanctified might be exercised and tested.

Nor are common disasters, properly speak- 65 ing, removed by these works of canonical satisfactions, that is, by these works of human traditions. The adversaries say that these satisfactions benefit by the outward work (*ex opere operato*) in such a way that, even though they are done in mortal sin, they still deliver from the punishments. When the pas- 66 sage of Paul is cited against us, "But if we judged ourselves truly, we would not be judged [by the Lord]" (1 Corinthians 11:31), "to judge" should be understood to include all of repentance and required fruit, not works that are not required. Our adversaries pay the penalty for hating grammar when they understand "to judge" to equal making a pilgrimage dressed in armor to the Church of St. James, or similar works. "To judge" means all of repentance; it means to condemn sins.

67 This condemnation truly happens in contrition and the change of life. All of repentance—contrition, faith, and good fruit—receives the reduction of public and private punishments and disasters, as Isaiah 1:16–19 teaches, "Cease to do evil, learn to do good. . . . Though your sins are like scarlet, they shall be as white as snow. . . . If you are willing and obedient, you shall eat the good of

68 the land." Neither should a most important and beneficial meaning be transferred from all of repentance, and from works required or commanded by God, to the satisfactions and works of human traditions. It is beneficial to teach the following: common evils are reduced by our repentance and by the true fruit of repentance, by good works completed from faith, not, as these men imagine,

69 completed in mortal sin. Here belongs the example of the Ninevites (Jonah 3:10), who by their repentance (all of repentance) were reconciled to God and received the favor that their city was not destroyed.

70    Furthermore, the mentioning of satisfaction by the Fathers, and the framing of canons by the councils, was a matter of Church discipline set up as an example, as we have said before. Nor did the councils hold that this discipline is necessary for the pardon either of the guilt or of the punishment. If some of them mention purgatory, they interpret it neither as payment for eternal pun-

ishment nor as satisfaction, but as purification of imperfect souls. Just as Augustine says that "venial offenses are consumed," that is, distrust toward God and other similar tendencies are destroyed. Now and then the 71 writers transfer the term *satisfaction* from the rite itself or spectacle, to illustrate true putting to death (mortification). So Augustine says:

> True satisfaction is to cut off the causes of sin, that is, to put the flesh to death, likewise to hold the flesh in check, not in order that eternal punishments may be paid for, but so that the flesh may not be drawn to sin.

About repayment, Gregory says that repen-    72 tance is false "if it does not satisfy those whose property we have taken." For the person who still steals does not truly grieve that he has stolen or robbed. He is a thief or robber as long as he is the unjust possessor of the property of another. This civil satisfaction is necessary, because it is written, "Let the thief no longer steal" (Ephesians 4:28). Likewise,    73 Chrysostom says, "In the heart, contrition; in the mouth, confession; in the work, entire humility." This amounts to nothing against us. Good works should follow repentance. It should be repentance (not a show), a change of the entire life for the better.

Likewise, the Fathers wrote that it is    74 enough if once in life this public or ceremonial penitence happens, for which the canons about satisfactions have been made. Clearly, they held that these canons are not necessary for the forgiveness of sins. In addition to this ceremonial penitence, they frequently want penitence to be done another way, in which canons of satisfactions were not required.

The composers of the Confutation write    75 that the setting aside of satisfactions (which are contrary to the plain Gospel), is not to be tolerated. So far we have shown that these canonical satisfactions, that is, unrequired works performed to pay for punishment, do not have the command of the Gospel. The subject itself shows this. If works of satisfaction are works that are not required, why do they cite the plain Gospel? For if the Gospel would command that punishments be paid for by such works, the works would already be required. But they speak in this way in order to burden the inexperienced, and they cite testimonies that speak of required works, although they themselves in their own satisfactions prescribe works that are not required. Indeed, in their schools they themselves admit that satisfactions can be refused without sin. Therefore, they write here falsely that we are compelled by the plain Gospel to undertake these canonical satisfactions.

## True Repentance Produces Good Works

We have already frequently testified that repentance should produce good fruit. These good fruit are what the commandments teach: prayer, thanksgiving, the confession of the Gospel, teaching the Gospel, obeying parents and rulers, and being faithful to one's calling. We should not kill, not hold on to hatred, but we should be forgiving and give to the needy, so far as we can according to our means. We should not commit sexual sins or adultery, but should hold in check, bridle, and chastise the flesh, not for a repayment of eternal punishment, but so as not to obey the devil or offend the Holy Spirit. Likewise, we should speak the truth. These fruit have God's command and should be produced for the sake of God's glory and command. They have their rewards also. But Scripture does not teach that eternal punishments are only pardoned through the payment offered by certain traditions or by purgatory. Indulgences used to be pardon for these public observances, so that people should not be burdened excessively. But if, by human authority, satisfactions and punishments can be pardoned, this payment is not necessary by divine Law. A divine Law is not set aside by human authority. Further, since the custom is no longer used and the bishops ignore it in silence, these pardons are not necessary. Yet the word *indulgences* remained. Satisfactions were understood not referring to outward discipline, but referring to the payment of punishment. So indulgences were incorrectly understood to free souls from purgatory. But the Keys have the power of binding and loosing only upon earth [not in purgatory], according to Matthew 16:19, "Whatever you bind on earth shall be bound in heaven, and whatever you loose on earth shall be loosed in heaven." As we have said before, the Keys do not have the power to impose penalties or to institute rites of worship, but only the command to forgive sins (John 20:23) to those who are converted and to convict and excommunicate (1 Corinthians 5) those who are unwilling to be converted. For just as to *loose* means to forgive sins, so to *bind* means not to forgive sins. Christ speaks of a spiritual kingdom, and God's command is that ministers of the Gospel should absolve those who are converted, according to 2 Corinthians 10:8, "our authority, which the Lord gave for building you up." Therefore, the reservation of cases is a secular affair. It is a reservation of canonical punishment. It is not a reservation of guilt before God in those who are truly converted. The adversaries judge rightly when they confess that in the matter of death the reservation of cases should not hinder Absolution.

We have presented all of our doctrine about repentance. We certainly know it is godly and beneficial to good minds. If good people will compare our doctrine with the very confused discussions of our adversaries, they will see that the adversaries have left out the doctrine about faith justifying and comforting godly hearts. They will also see that the adversaries invent many things about the merits of attrition, about the endless listing of offenses, and about satisfactions. They say things that agree neither with human law nor divine Law, and which not even they themselves can explain clearly enough.

ARTICLE XIII (VII)

# The Number and Use of the Sacraments

The Pontifical Confutation demanded that Lutherans teach that there are exactly seven Sacraments. Melanchthon's approach was to emphasize that the word *sacrament* is somewhat fluid in its meaning. The term is not strictly biblical (though it does appear in the Latin Vulgate as a translation for the Greek term *mysterion*; e.g., 1 Corinthians 4:1). As such, the term is capable of different uses in the Church. If the Church chooses to consider the Sacraments rites that God has commanded, to which the promise of grace is added, then there would be three: Baptism, the Lord's Supper, and Absolution or Repentance. Martin Luther generally spoke of Holy Baptism and the Sacrament of the Altar as Sacraments and regarded Confession and Absolution to be an extension of Baptism. Quibbling over the number of the Sacraments is unproductive and is to be avoided. It is better to focus on the gifts of God given in and through the Sacraments. Melanchthon is even willing in this article to regard ordination to the Church's ministry as a Sacrament, but only in relation to the ministry of the Word. Melanchthon makes the number of Sacraments an issue only because Rome did. He

was forced to respond in more detail. What is important is receiving God's gracious gifts through faith, making sure that we never regard Sacraments as works to appease God or to merit His favor. (See AC XIII.)

———————

In Article XIII, the adversaries approve 1 our statement that the Sacraments are not just marks of profession among people, as some imagine. Rather, they are signs and testimonies of God's will toward us. Through them God moves hearts to believe. But here they ask us to count seven Sacra- 2 ments. We hold that the matters and ceremonies instituted in the Scriptures, whatever the number, should not be neglected. Neither do we believe it to be of any consequence. However, for teaching purposes, different people do count differently, provided they still rightly keep the matters handed down in Scripture. The ancients also did not count in the same way.

If we call Sacraments "rites that have the 3 command of God, and to which the promise of grace has been added," it is easy to decide what are true Sacraments. For rites instituted by human beings will not be called true Sacraments. For human authority cannot promise grace. Therefore, signs set up without God's command are not sure signs of grace, even though signs perhaps instruct the unlearned or admonish about something. Therefore, *Baptism*, the *Lord's Supper*, and 4 *Absolution* (which is the Sacrament of Repentance) are truly Sacraments. For these rites have God's command and the promise of grace, which is peculiar to the New Testament. When we are baptized, when we eat the Lord's body, when we are absolved, our hearts must be firmly assured that God truly forgives us for Christ's sake. At the same 5 time, by the Word and by the rite, God moves hearts to believe and conceive faith, just as Paul says, "Faith comes from hearing" (Romans 10:17). But just as the Word enters the ear in order to strike our heart, so the rite itself strikes the eye, in order to move the heart. The effect of the Word and of the rite is the same. It has been well said by Augustine that a Sacrament is *a visible Word*, because the rite is received by the eyes and is, as it were, a picture of the Word, illustrating the same thing as the Word. The result of both is the same.

6    *Confirmation* and *extreme unction* are rites received from the Fathers that not even the Church requires as necessary to salvation, because they do not have God's command. Therefore, it is useful to distinguish these rites from the former, which have God's direct command and a clear promise of grace.

7    The adversaries understand *priesthood* not about the ministry of the Word, and giving out the Sacraments to others, but as referring to sacrifice. This is as though there should be a priesthood like the Levitical one (Leviticus 8–9) to sacrifice for the people and merit the forgiveness of sins for others in the New Testament. We teach that the sacrifice of

8    Christ dying on the cross has been enough for the sins of the whole world. There is no need for other sacrifices, as though Christ's sacrifice were not enough for our sins. So people are justified not because of any other sacrifices, but because of this one sacrifice of Christ, if they believe that they have been redeemed by this sacrifice. So they are called

9    priests, not in order to make any sacrifices for the people as in the Law, that by these they may merit forgiveness of sins for the people. Rather, they are called to teach the Gospel and administer the Sacraments to the people.

10    Nor do we have another priesthood like the Levitical, as the Epistle to the Hebrews

11    teaches well enough (Hebrews 8). But if or-

dination is understood as carrying out the ministry of the Word, we are willing to call ordination a Sacrament. For the ministry of the Word has God's command and has glorious promises, "The gospel . . . is the power of God for salvation to everyone who believes" (Romans 1:16). Likewise, "So shall My word be that goes out from My mouth; it shall not return to Me empty, but it shall accomplish that which I purpose" (Isaiah 55:11). If ordi-    12 nation is understood in this way, neither will we refuse to call the laying on of hands a Sacrament. For the Church has the command to appoint ministers, which should be most pleasing to us, because we know that God approves this ministry and is present in the ministry. It is helpful, so far as can be    13 done, to honor the ministry of the Word with every kind of praise against fanatical people. These fanatics imagine that the Holy Spirit is given not through the Word, but through certain preparations of their own. For example, they imagine He is given if they sit unoccupied and silent in far-off places, waiting for illumination, as the Enthusiasts formerly taught and the Anabaptists now teach.

*Marriage* was not first instituted in the    14 New Testament, but in the beginning, immediately after the creation of the human race (Genesis 1:28). Furthermore, it has God's command. It has also promises, not truly having to do with the New Testament, but rather having to do with bodily life. Therefore, if anyone wishes to call it a Sacrament, he or she should still distinguish it from those preceding ones. They are truly signs of the New Testament and testimonies of grace and the forgiveness of sins. But if marriage has the name    15 "Sacrament" because it has God's command, other states or offices also, which have God's command, may be called Sacraments, as, for example, the government.

Finally, if among the Sacraments every-    16

thing should be numbered that has God's command, and to which promises have been added, why do we not add prayer, which most truly can be called a Sacrament? For it has both God's command and very many promises. If numbered among the Sacraments, although in a more prominent place,

17 it would encourage people to pray. Alms could also be counted here and, likewise, troubles. These are themselves signs to which God has added promises. But let us leave out these things. For no levelheaded person will labor greatly about the number or the term, if only those things are still kept that have God's command and promises.

18 It is more important to understand *how the Sacraments are to be used.* Here we condemn the whole crowd of scholastic doctors, who teach that the Sacraments give grace by the outward act (*ex opere operato*), without a good frame of mind on the part of the one using them, provided he does not place a hindrance in the way. This is absolutely a Jewish opinion, to hold that we are justified by a ceremony, without a good tendency of the heart, that is, without faith. Yet this ungodly and deadly opinion is taught with great authority throughout the entire realm of the

19 pope. Paul contradicts this, and denies (Romans 4:9) that Abraham was justified by circumcision. He asserts that circumcision was an illustration presented for exercising faith. So we teach that in the use of the Sacraments, *faith* should be added. Faith should believe these promises and receive the promised

20 things offered in the Sacrament. The reason is plain and thoroughly grounded. The promise is useless unless it is received by faith. The Sacraments are the signs of the promises. Therefore, faith should be added in the use of the Sacraments. If anyone uses the Lord's Supper, he should use it by faith. This is a Sacrament of the New Testament, as

Christ clearly says (Luke 22:20). For this very reason he should be confident that the free forgiveness of sins promised in the New Testament is offered. Let him receive this by faith, let him comfort his alarmed conscience and know that these testimonies are not false. They are as sure as though (and still surer than if) God by a new miracle would declare from heaven that it was His will to grant forgiveness. What advantage would these mira-

21 cles and promises be to an unbeliever? Here we speak of *special faith* that believes the present promise that the forgiveness of sins is offered. This use of the Sacrament consoles

22 godly and alarmed minds. We are not speaking of a faith that only in general believes that God exists.

23 It is beyond words what abuses the fanatical opinion about outward works (*opus operatum*) has produced in the Church (without a good disposition on the part of the one using the Sacraments). From it has come the endless profanation of the Masses. We shall speak about this later. A single letter cannot be produced from the old writers that supports the Scholastics in this matter. On the contrary, Augustine says the faith that uses the Sacrament, and not the Sacrament, justifies. And the declaration of Paul is well-known, "With the heart one believes and is justified" (Romans 10:10).

## ARTICLE XIV

# Order in the Church

Here Melanchthon affirms Lutheranism's desire to maintain whatever best contributes to good order, peace, and harmony in the Church. Therefore, Lutherans have insisted on a rightly ordered call and ordination for those who will serve the Church as ministers of Word and Sacrament. For the sake of human order, Lutherans are willing for bishops to continue serving in the Church. However, bishops are nowhere given authority to impose nonbiblical teachings on the Church. After Luther's death, Lutherans in Germany established local clergy groups called consistories, with one of the pastors named as superintendent. These groups usually included learned laymen. In other Lutheran countries such as Sweden, the office of bishop was continued. The external order of the Church was left free. Lutheranism has never insisted on one form of Church government over another, like the Roman Catholic or Reformed Churches. Melanchthon makes clear that the important thing is the Word of God being purely taught and the Sacraments being properly given to the people. (See AC XIV; SA III X.)

---

24    In Article XIV, we say that no one should administer the Word and Sacraments *unless he is rightly called.* The adversaries accept the article, but on the condition that we use canonical ordination. About this subject we have often testified in this assembly that it is our greatest desire to keep Church orders and ranks, even though they have been made by human authority. We know that Church discipline in the manner laid down in the ancient canons was set up by the Fathers for a 25  good and useful purpose. But the bishops either urge our priests to reject and condemn the doctrine we have confessed or, by a new and unheard-of cruelty, they put the poor innocent men to death. These causes hinder our priests from recognizing such bishops. The cruelty of the bishops is the reason why the canonical government, which we greatly desired to keep, is dissolved in some places. Let them see how they will answer to God for 26  tearing apart the Church. In this matter our consciences are not in danger. Since we know that our Confession is true, godly, and

catholic, we should not approve the cruelty of those who persecute this doctrine. We  27 know that the Church is among those who teach God's Word rightly and administer the Sacraments rightly. The Church it is not with those who try hard to wipe out God's Word by their orders and also put to death those who teach what is right and true. Toward them even the very canons are gentler, even though they do something contrary to the canons. Furthermore, we want to declare  28 again that we will gladly keep Church and canonical government, so long as the bishops stop attacking our churches. Our request will acquit us, both before God and among all nations forever, from the charge that we have undermined the authority of the bishops. People will acquit us when they read and hear that, although protesting against the unrighteous cruelty of the bishops, we could not obtain justice.

## ARTICLE XV (VIII)

# Human Traditions in the Church

The Pontifical Confutation accepted Article XV of the Augsburg Confession, in which the Lutherans affirmed that traditions contributing to peace and order should be observed. But the Confutation opposed the Augsburg Confession's statement that any traditions created to appease God, merit His grace, and earn forgiveness be rejected. Melanchthon expresses surprise that Rome would demand anything contrary to this. Once more he returns to the constant refrain throughout the Apology: Anything that obscures the Gospel is to be rejected. This article provides more reasons why suggesting, implying, or teaching that human traditions merit God's grace is contrary to the Gospel of free and full forgiveness of sins in Christ alone. In this article

Melanchthon states that the "chief service of God is to preach the Gospel." Preaching enables hearers to receive good things from God (Ap V 189). This turns on its ear the Roman notion that worship is primarily what we do to please or placate God. Worship is most essentially gathering to receive, through faith, God's gifts in Christ, by means of His Gospel and Sacraments. Our praise and thanksgiving for God's gifts is a response to His grace, not a condition for receiving it. (See also AC XV; SA III XV; FC Ep X and SD X.)

---

1    In Article XV, the adversaries accept the first part, in which we say that *ecclesiastical rites* are to be kept that can be observed without sin and are beneficial in the Church for peace and good order. They completely condemn the second part, in which we say that human traditions (set up to reconcile God, to merit grace, and make satisfactions for sins) 2 are contrary to the Gospel. In the Confession itself, we spoke long enough about traditions such as the distinction of meats. Yet certain things should be briefly reviewed here.

3    We supposed that the adversaries would defend human traditions on other grounds. Yet we did not think that this would happen, that they would condemn this article: We do not merit the forgiveness of sins or grace by celebrating human traditions. Since this article has been condemned, we have an easy and 4 straightforward case. The adversaries are now openly Judaizing (Acts 15:1); they are openly hindering the Gospel by the doctrines of demons (1 Timothy 4:1). For Scripture calls traditions *doctrines of demons* when it is taught that religious rites serve to merit the forgiveness of sins and grace. For they are then clouding over the Gospel, Christ's ben- 5 efit, and the righteousness of faith. The Gospel teaches that through faith we receive

freely, for Christ's sake, the forgiveness of sins and are reconciled to God. The adversaries, on the other hand, appoint another mediator: these traditions. By these they want to gain forgiveness of sins; by these they want to reconcile God's anger. But Christ clearly says, "In vain do they worship Me, teaching as doctrines the commandments of men" (Matthew 15:9).

We have already discussed at length that 6 people are justified through faith when they believe that they have a reconciled God, not because of our works, but freely, for Christ's sake. It is certain that this is the doctrine of the Gospel because Paul clearly teaches, "By grace you have been saved through faith. And this is not your own doing; it is the gift of God, not a result of works" (Ephesians 2:8–9). Now these men say that people merit 7 the forgiveness of sins by these human celebrations. What else is this than to appoint another justifier, a mediator other than Christ? Paul says to the Galatians, "You are 8 severed from Christ, you who would be justified by the law" (5:4). This means, if you hold that by obeying the Law you merit righteousness before God, Christ will benefit you nothing. Why do they need Christ who hold that they are righteous by their obeying the Law? God has presented Christ with the 9 promise that, because of this Mediator, and not because of our righteousness, He wishes to be gracious to us. But these men hold that God is reconciled and gracious because of the traditions, not because of Christ. Therefore, they take the honor of Mediator away from Christ. So far as this matter is con- 10 cerned, there is not any difference between our traditions and Moses' ceremonies. Paul condemns Moses' ceremonies (Galatians 3:10–12), just as he condemns traditions, because they were regarded as works that merit righteousness before God. So the office of

## George, Duke of Saxony
### (1471–1539) c. 1533

Duke George was Luther's most bitter opponent among the rulers of Germany. He ruled
Ducal Saxony, northeast of Electoral Saxony.
Around George's neck hangs a symbol of the
Order of the Golden Fleece, established to support the Roman Church and to honor the
knightly virtues of courage, honor, loyalty, and
kindness to others; virtues not extended by
George to his Lutheran opponents. George persecuted all Lutherans in his territory and refused Christian burial to them. He reimbursed
people who turned over Luther's books for
burning. His efforts to stamp out Lutheranism
did not succeed. His son-in-law Philip of Hesse
became one of the most energetic Lutheran
princes.

## Albert, Archbishop of Mainz
### (1490–1545)

Pope Leo X permitted Albert to publish an indulgence (1514) to help pay for the construction
of St. Peter's Cathedral, Rome. Albert became a
leading bishop in Germany by paying the papacy to waive the canon law preventing one person from holding more than one office. Albert
ardently supported the new Jesuit order, which
was established to exterminate Lutheranism and
other "heresies" threatening the Roman Church.

Christ and the righteousness of faith were clouded over. With the Law and traditions removed, he argues that the forgiveness of sins has been promised not because of our works, but freely, because of Christ, if only we receive it through faith. For the promise is

11 not received except through faith. Since we receive the forgiveness of sins through faith, since we have a merciful God for Christ's sake by faith, it is an error and sin to declare that we merit the forgiveness of sins because of

12 these observances. If anyone should say that we do not merit the forgiveness of sins, but that those who have already been justified by these traditions merit grace, Paul again replies, "Christ [is] then a servant of sin" (Galatians 2:17). The same would be true if we were to hold that, after justification, we were not counted righteous for Christ's sake, but we should first, by other observances, merit that we are counted righteous. Likewise, "Even with a man-made covenant, no one annuls it or adds to it once it has been ratified" (Galatians 3:15). We should not add to God's covenant, for God promises that He will be merciful to us for Christ's sake. Nor should we add that we must first get such merit in order to be regarded as accepted and righteous through these observances.

13 Why do we need a long discussion? No tradition was set up by the Holy Fathers for the purpose of meriting the forgiveness of sins, or righteousness. Rather, they were in-stituted for the sake of good order in the

14 Church and for the sake of peace. When any-one wants to set up certain works to merit the forgiveness of sins, or righteousness, how will he know that these works please God since there is no testimony of God's Word? How, without God's command and Word, will he make people certain of God's will? Doesn't God forbid people everywhere in the Prophets from setting up peculiar rites of

worship without His commandment? In Ezekiel it is written, "Do not walk in the statutes of your fathers, nor keep their rules, nor defile yourselves with their idols. I am the LORD your God; walk in My statutes, and be careful to obey My rules" (20:18–19). If 15 people are allowed to set up religious rites, and through these rites merit grace, the reli-gious rites of all the pagans will have to be approved. The rites instituted by Jeroboam (1 Kings 12:26–33) and by others, apart from the Law, will have to be approved. What dif-ference does it make? If we have been al-lowed to institute religious rites that help merit grace, or righteousness, why were the pagans and the Israelites not allowed the same? The religious rites of the pagans and 16 the Israelites were rejected for the very rea-son that they believed they merited forgive-ness of sins and righteousness by these rites. Yet they did not know the righteousness of faith. Finally, where are we made certain that 17 rites instituted by men justify without God's command, since nothing can be affirmed of God's will without His Word? What if God does not approve these services? How, there-fore, do the adversaries affirm that they jus-tify? Without God's Word and testimony, this cannot be affirmed. Paul says, "Whatev-er does not proceed from faith is sin" (Ro-mans 14:23). Since these services have no testimony of God's Word, conscience must doubt if they please God.

Why do we need words on a subject so 18 clear? If the adversaries defend these human services as meriting justification, grace, and the forgiveness of sins, they simply set up the kingdom of Antichrist. The kingdom of An-tichrist is a new service of God, devised by human authority rejecting Christ (2 Thessa-lonians 2:3–4), just as the kingdom of Muhammad has services and works through which it wishes to be justified before God. It does not hold that people are freely justified before God through faith, for Christ's sake. So the papacy will also be a part of the kingdom of Antichrist if it defends human services as justifying in this way. For honor is taken away from Christ when they teach that we are not justified freely through faith, for Christ's sake, but by such services. This is especially true when they teach that such services are not only useful for justification, but are also necessary, as they maintain in Article VII. There they condemn us for saying that for true unity of the Church it is not necessary that rites instituted by human beings

19 should be alike everywhere. Daniel 11:38 indicates that new human services will be the very form and basic principle of the kingdom of Antichrist. He says this, "He shall honor the god of fortresses instead of these. A god whom his fathers did not know he shall honor with gold and silver, with precious stones." Here Daniel describes new services, because he says that the fathers were ignorant

20 of the god that shall be worshiped. Although the Holy Fathers themselves had both rites and traditions, they did not maintain that these are useful or necessary for justification. They did not cloud over Christ's glory and office, but taught that we are justified by faith for Christ's sake, and not for the sake of these human services. The Fathers celebrated human rites for the body's benefit. For example, by such rites the people would know what time they should gather so that, for the sake of example, all things might be done in order and properly in the churches (1 Corinthians 14:40) and that the common people might receive a sort of training. Distinctions of times and the variety of rites

21 help in reminding the common people. The Fathers maintained the rites for these reasons. We also conclude it is proper for these reasons to keep traditions. We are greatly surprised that the adversaries argue for another design of traditions, that they may merit the forgiveness of sins, grace, or justification. What else is this than to honor God *with gold and silver, with precious stones* (as Daniel 11:38 says), that is, to hold that God becomes reconciled by a variety in clothing, ornaments, and by similar rites, which are countless in human traditions?

22 Paul writes to the Colossians that traditions have "an appearance of wisdom" (2:23). Indeed, they have. Good order is very fitting in the Church, and is for this reason necessary. Human reason, because it does not understand the righteousness of faith, naturally imagines that such works justify

23 people because they reconcile God. Among the Israelites the common people thought this, and by this opinion increased such ceremonies. Among us ceremonies have grown in the monasteries. Human reason also

24 thinks this about bodily exercises, such as fasts. Although the purpose of these bodily exercises is to hold the flesh in check, reason falsely adds that they are services that justify. As Thomas writes, "Fasting avails for the extinguishing and the prevention of guilt." These are Thomas's words. The look of wisdom and righteousness in such works tricks people. The examples of the saints are added. When people want to imitate these, they imitate, for the most part, the outward exercises. They do not imitate their faith.

25 After this look of wisdom and righteousness has deceived people, then countless evils follow. The Gospel about the righteousness of faith in Christ is clouded over, and empty confidence in such works succeeds. Then God's commandments are clouded over. These human works assume the title of a perfect and spiritual life. They are preferred more than the works of God's commandments (works of one's own calling,

26 the administration of the state, the management of a family, married life, and the bringing up of children). Compared with those ceremonies, the latter are judged to be ungodly, so that they are exercised by many with doubting consciences. For it is known that many have left the administration of the state and married life to welcome these human ceremonies as better and holier.

27 Nor is this enough. When the belief has possessed minds that such ceremonies are necessary for justification, consciences are in miserable anxiety because they cannot exactly perform all ceremonies. How many are there who could list all these ceremonies? There are immense books, indeed, whole libraries, containing not a syllable about Christ, about faith in Christ, about the good works of one's own calling. They only collect the traditions and interpretations by which they are sometimes made quite strict and sometimes relaxed. How that most excellent

28 man Gerson is tortured while he searches for the steps and extent of the rules! Yet, he is not able to fix mitigation (*epieikeian*) in a definite grade. Meanwhile, he deeply regrets the dangers to godly consciences that this strict interpretation of the traditions produces.

29 Against this look of wisdom and righteousness in human rites, which tricks people, let us strengthen ourselves by God's Word. Let us know, first of all, that these rights neither merit the forgiveness of sins or justification before God, nor are they neces-

30 sary for justification. We have mentioned some testimonies above. Paul is full of them. To the Colossians he clearly says:

> Therefore let no one pass judgment on you in questions of food and drink, or with regard to a festival or a new moon or a Sabbath. These are a shadow of the things to come, but the substance belongs to Christ. (2:16–17)

Here he welcomes both Moses' Law and human traditions at the same time, so that the adversaries may not dodge these testimonies, according to their custom, on the ground that Paul speaks only about Moses' Law. He clearly testifies here that he is speaking of human traditions. However, the adversaries do not see what they are saying. If the Gospel says that Moses' ceremonies—which were divinely instituted—do not justify, how much less do human traditions justify!

31 Neither do the bishops have the power to institute services, as though they justified, or were necessary for justification. Yes, the apostles say, "Why are you putting God to the test by placing a yoke" (Acts 15:10), and so forth, where Peter declares this effort to burden the Church a great sin. Paul forbids the Gala-

32 tians, "Do not submit again to a yoke of slavery" (5:1). Therefore, it is the will of the apostles that this freedom remain in the Church, that no services of the Law or of traditions be considered necessary (just as ceremonies were necessary for a time in the Law), lest the righteousness of faith be clouded over. This would be the case if people judged that these services merited justification or are necessary

33 for justification. Many seek various mitigations (*epieikeias*) in traditions to heal consciences. Yet they do not find any sure steps by which to free consciences from these

34 chains. Just as Alexander solved the Gordian knot once for all by cutting it with his sword when he could not disentangle it, so the apostles free consciences from traditions once for all, especially if they are taught to merit justification. The apostles drive us to oppose this doctrine by teaching and examples. They drive us to teach that traditions do not justify, that they are not necessary for justification, and that no one should invent or receive traditions with the opinion that

35 they merit justification. Then, even if anyone

36 should celebrate them, let them be celebrated as civil customs without superstition, just as soldiers are clothed in one way and scholars in another without superstition. The apostles violate traditions and are excused by Christ. The example was shown to the Pharisees that

37 these services do not benefit. If our people neglect some traditions that are of little help, they are now excused well enough, when these are required as though they merit justification. For such an opinion regarding traditions is ungodly.

38 We cheerfully hold the old traditions made in the Church for the sake of usefulness and peace. We interpret them in a more moderate way and reject the opinion that

39 holds they justify. Our enemies falsely accuse us of setting aside good ordinances and Church discipline. We can truly declare that the public form of the churches is more fitting with us than with the adversaries. If anyone will consider it in the right way, we conform to the canons more closely than the

40 adversaries. Among the adversaries, unwilling celebrants, and those hired for pay, and very frequently only for pay, celebrate the Masses. They sing psalms, not that they may learn or pray, but for the sake of the service (as though this work were a service) or, at least, for the sake of reward. Among us many use the Lord's Supper every Lord's Day. They do so after they have been first instructed, examined, and absolved. The children sing psalms in order that they may learn. The people also sing so that they may either learn

41 or pray. Among the adversaries there is no catechizing of the children whatever, about which even the canons give commands. Among us the pastors and ministers of the churches are encouraged publicly to instruct and hear the youth. This ceremony produces

42 the best fruit. Among the adversaries, in many regions, no sermons are delivered during the entire year, except during Lent. Yet the chief service of God is to preach the Gospel. When the adversaries do preach, they speak of human traditions, of the worship of saints and similar trifles, which the people justly hate. Therefore, they are immediately deserted in the beginning, after the reading of the Gospel text. A few better ones begin now to speak of good works; but about the righteousness of faith, faith in Christ, and the comfort of consciences, they say nothing. Indeed, this most wholesome part of the Gospel they rail at with their re-

43 proaches. On the contrary, in our churches all the sermons are filled with such topics as these: repentance; the fear of God; faith in Christ, the righteousness of faith, the comfort of consciences by faith; the exercises of faith; prayer, what its nature should be, and that we should be fully confident that it is powerful, that it is heard; the cross; the authority of officials and all civil ordinances; the distinction between the kingdom of Christ, or the spiritual kingdom, and political affairs; marriage; the education and instruction of children; chastity; all the offices

44 of love. From this condition of the churches it may be determined that we earnestly keep Church discipline, godly ceremonies, and good Church customs.

45 We teach this about the putting to death of the flesh and discipline of the body. Just as the Confession states, a true and not a false putting to death [mortification] happens through the cross and troubles, by which God exercises us. In them we must obey God's will, as Paul says, "Present your bodies as a living sacrifice" (Romans 12:1). They are the spiri-

46 tual exercises of fear and faith. In addition to this putting to death, which happens through the cross, there is also a necessary, voluntary exercise. Christ says, "But watch yourselves lest your hearts be weighed down with dis-

sipation" (Luke 21:34). And Paul says, "I discipline my body and keep it under control"

47 (1 Corinthians 9:27), and so on. These exercises are to be accepted not because they are services that justify, but because they are assumed to control the flesh, should overindulgence overpower us, and make us secure and unconcerned. This results in people indulging and obeying the tendencies of the flesh. This effort [at mortification] should be constant because it has God's permanent command.

48 The required order of certain meats and times does nothing toward controlling the flesh. For it is more overflowing and costly than other feasts. Not even the adversaries obey the order given in the canons.

49 This topic about traditions contains many and difficult controversial questions. We have actually experienced that traditions are truly traps of consciences. When traditions are required as necessary, they torture in terrible ways the conscience, leaving out any ceremony. The repeal of ceremonies has

50 its own evils and its own questions. But we have an easy and plain case because the adversaries condemn us for teaching that human traditions do not merit the forgiveness of sins. Likewise, the adversaries require universal traditions, as they call them, as necessary for justification. Here we have Paul as a constant champion, who argues everywhere that these ceremonies neither justify nor are they necessary additions to

51 the righteousness of faith. Still, we teach that freedom should be so controlled that the inexperienced may not be offended and, because of freedom's abuse (Romans 14: 13–23), may not become more opposed to the true doctrine of the Gospel. Nothing in customary rites should be changed without a reasonable cause. So to nurture unity, old customs that can be kept without sin or

52 great inconvenience should be kept. In this very assembly we have shown well enough that for love's sake we do not refuse to keep adiaphora with others, even though they may be burdensome. We have judged that such public unity, which could indeed be produced without offending consciences, should be preferred. We shall speak about this entire subject later, when we present on vows and Church authority.

## ARTICLE XVI

# Political Order

To clearly move away from the Anabaptists and other radical reformers, the Augsburg Confession states very plainly that Lutherans support the role of government. Christians have the freedom and the duty to participate in proper political order. The Lutheran understanding of God's work in the Church and in the world has come to be known as the doctrine of the two kingdoms. Here Melanchthon articulates the distinction between the kingdom of Christ, which is spiritual and a matter of faith and the righteousness of Christ, and the kingdom of the world. Lutheranism confesses firmly that Christ came to set up no particular external government. God has, can, and will work through a variety of political organizations and forms to enact His will in the world. The Church, as Church, is not to interfere, as Rome clearly and often did, with the rule of the state. Today the Roman Catholic Church no longer makes grand claims of possessing all authority in both the realms of the Church and secular authority. (See also AC XVI.)

----

53 The adversaries accept Article XVI without exception. In it we have confessed that it is lawful for the Christian to hold public office, sit in judgment, determine matters by the imperial laws and other laws currently in

force, set just punishments, engage in just wars, act as a soldier, make legal contracts, hold property, take an oath (when public officials require it), and contract marriage. Finally, we have confessed that legitimate public ordinances are good creations of God and divine ordinances, which a Christian can

54 safely use. This entire topic *about the distinction between the spiritual kingdom of Christ and a political kingdom* has been explained in the literature of our writers. Christ's kingdom is spiritual (John 18:36). This means that the knowledge of God, the fear of God and faith, eternal righteousness, and eternal life begin in the heart. Meanwhile, Christ's kingdom allows us outwardly to use legitimate political ordinances of every nation in which we live, just as it allows us to use medicine or the art of building, or food, drink,

55 and air. Neither does the Gospel offer new laws about the public state, but commands that we obey present laws, whether they have been framed by heathens or by others. It commands that in this obedience we should exercise love. Carlstadt was crazy to impose

56 on us Moses' judicial laws. Our theologians have written more fully about these subjects. They have done so because the monks spread many deadly opinions in the Church. They called holding property in common the governance of the Gospel. They said that not holding property, or not acquitting oneself at law, were evangelical counsels. These opinions greatly cloud over the Gospel and the spiritual kingdom and are dangerous to the

57 commonwealth. For the Gospel does not destroy the state or the family, but rather approves them and asks us to obey them as a divine ordinance, not only because of punishment, but also because of conscience.

58   Julian the Apostate, Celsus, and very many others objected to Christians that the Gospel would tear states apart because it forbade legal remedy and taught certain other things ill-suited to political association. Origen, Nazianzus, and others wonderfully worked on these questions. However, they can be easily explained if we keep this in mind: The Gospel does not introduce laws about the public state, but is the forgiveness of sins and the beginning of a new life in the hearts of believers. Besides, the Gospel not only approves outward governments, but also subjects us to them (Romans 13:1). In a similar way we have been necessarily placed under the laws of seasons, the changes of winter and summer, as divine ordinances. The Gospel forbids private 59 remedy. Christ instills this often so that the apostles do not think they should seize the governments from those who held otherwise, just as the Jewish people dreamed about the kingdom of the Messiah. Christ did this so that the apostles might know they should teach that the spiritual kingdom does not change the public state. Therefore, private remedy is prohibited not by advice, but by a command (Matthew 5:39; Romans 12:19). Public remedy, made through the office of the public official, is not condemned, but is commanded and is God's work, according to Paul (Romans 13). Now the different kinds of public remedy are legal decisions, capital punishment, wars, and military service. Clearly, many writers have thought wrongly 60 about these matters. They were in the error that the Gospel is an outward, new, and monastic form of government. Also, they did not see that the Gospel brings eternal righteousness to hearts, while it outwardly approves the public state.

It is also a most empty myth that Christian perfection consists in not holding property. For Christian perfection does not consist in contempt for public ordinances, but in the inclinations of the heart, in great fear of God, and in great faith. Abraham, David, and

Wise King Solomon

Daniel, even in great wealth and while exercising public power, were no less perfect than any hermits. But the monks have spread this outward hypocrisy before the eyes of the people. They have done this so that the things in which true perfection exists could not be seen. How they have praised holding property in common, as though it were evangelical! But these praises are very dangerous, especially since they are very different than the Scriptures. Scripture does not command that we hold property in common. The Law of the Ten Commandments, when it says, "You shall not steal" (Exodus 20:15), distinguishes rights of ownership and commands each one to hold what is his own. Clearly Wycliffe was speaking madness when he said that priests were not allowed to hold property. There are countless discussions about contracts. Good consciences can never be satisfied about them unless they know the rule that it is lawful for a Christian to make use of public ordinances and laws. This rule protects consciences. It teaches that contracts are lawful before God just to the extent that the public officials or laws approve them.

This entire topic about public affairs has been clearly set forth by our theologians. Very many good people working in the state and in business have declared that they have been greatly benefited by it. Before, troubled by the opinion of the monks, they doubted whether the Gospel allowed these public offices and business. As a result, we have repeated these things so that outsiders may also understand that the doctrine we follow does not wreck the authority of magistrates and the dignity of all public ordinances. Rather, they are strengthened even more. Previously the importance of these matters was greatly clouded over by those silly monastic opinions. They preferred the hypocrisy of poverty and humility to the state and the family. The latter have God's command, while this Platonic community (monasticism) does not.

## ARTICLE XVII
# Christ's Return for Judgment

During the Reformation, radical groups made numerous predictions about the end of the world. Such foolishness still plagues the Church today. The vast majority of Christians agree on the basics of this important article of faith. These are also beautifully summarized in the Apostles' Creed. (See AC XVII.)

---

66     The adversaries accept Article XVII without qualification. In it we confess that Christ will appear at the consummation of the world. He will raise up all the dead and will give eternal life and eternal joys to the godly (2 Timothy 4:8), but He will condemn the ungodly to endless punishment with the devil (Matthew 25:46).

## ARTICLE XVIII
# Free Will

A key discussion in the Apology is found here. Melanchthon exposes Rome's Pelagian attitudes about a person's ability, under his own powers, to bring himself to love God. This remains Rome's view of free will. The 1994 Catholic Catechism teaches that we co-operate with the power and action of the Holy Spirit for our justification. In other words, since we have been given free will, that is, the ability to choose good and evil, we seek to do what is good.

Melanchthon explains that we have free will in earthly matters, but not in spiritual matters (in that which is beneath us, not in what is above us, as Luther explained in *The Bondage of the Will*). We are able to apply ourselves to temporal concerns, but not matters of divine revelation. Rome is now careful to speak of God's grace as being responsible for initiating the relationship between God and man, but also still maintains that man's response to grace is, in fact, what causes justification. Lutherans still maintain that mankind has no free will in spiritual matters, having lost it in the fall into sin. (See also AC XVIII; FC Ep II and SD II.)

---

The adversaries accept Article XVIII, 67 "Free Will," although they add some references having nothing to do with this case. They also add a speech that neither should the free will be granted too much, like the Pelagians, nor should all freedom be denied it, like the Manichaeans. Very well, but what 68 difference is there between the Pelagians and our adversaries, since both hold that people can love God and perform His commandments with respect to the substance of the acts and can merit grace and justification by works that reason performs by itself, without the Holy Spirit? How many foolish 69 things follow from these Pelagian opinions, which are taught with great authority in the schools! Augustine, following Paul, disapproves of these with great emphasis. We have repeated his opinion in the article "Justification." (See 119, 1 and 153, 106.) We do not 70 deny freedom to the human will. The human will has freedom in the choice of works and things that reason understands by itself. To a certain extent reason can display public righteousness or the righteousness of works. It can speak of God, offer to God a certain service by an outward work, and obey public officials and parents. In choosing an outward work, it can hold back the hand from murder, adultery, and theft. Because human nature has been left with reason and judgment about objects subjected to the senses, choice between these things, the liberty and power to produce public righteousness, are also left. Scripture calls this the righteousness of the flesh, which the carnal nature (that is, reason) produces by 71 itself, without the Holy Spirit. However, the power of lustful desire is such that people more often obey evil inclinations than sound judgment. The devil, who is powerful in the godless, does not cease to stir up this weak nature to various offenses, as Paul says in Ephesians 2:2. For these reasons even public righteousness is rare among people. Not even the philosophers, who seem to have hoped for this righteousness, achieved 72 it. But it is false to say whoever performs the works of the commandments without grace does not sin. The adversaries add further that such works also merit the forgiveness of sins and justification in merely an agreeable way (*de congruo*). For without the Holy Spirit, human hearts lack the fear of God. Without trust toward God, they do not believe that they are heard, forgiven, helped, and preserved by God. Therefore, they are godless. For "a diseased tree [cannot] bear good fruit" (Matthew 7:18). And "without faith it is impossible to please [God]" (Hebrews 11:6).

73 Although we admit that free will has the freedom and power to perform the extreme works of the Law, we do not assign spiritual matters to free will. These are to truly fear God, believe God, be confident and hold that He cares for us, hears us, and forgives us. These are the true works of the First Table, which the heart cannot produce without the Holy Spirit, as Paul says, "The natural person [namely, a person using only natural strength] does not accept the things of the Spirit of God" (1 Corinthians 2:14).

74 People can determine this if they consider what their hearts believe about God's will, whether they are truly confident God cares for and hears them. Even the saints find keeping this faith difficult (which is not possible in unbelievers). But, as we have said before, it begins when terrified hearts hear the Gospel and receive comfort.

75 Their distinction is helpful. Civil righteousness is assigned to free will, and spiritual righteousness is assigned to the governing of the Holy Spirit in the reborn. In this way, outward discipline is kept, because all people should know that God requires this civil righteousness and that, to some extent, we can achieve it. And yet a distinction is shown between human and spiritual righteousness, between philosophical teaching and the teaching of the Holy Spirit. It can be understood why the Holy Spirit is needed. 76 We did not invent this distinction; Scripture clearly teaches it. Augustine also presents it, and recently William of Paris has presented it very well. But those who dream that people can obey God's Law without the Holy Spirit, and that the Holy Spirit is given so that obeying the Law may be considered meritorious, have wickedly hindered the distinction.

## ARTICLE XIX

# The Cause of Sin

(See also AC XIX; SA III I.)

77 The adversaries accept Article XIX. In it we confess that only God and He alone has created all nature and preserves all things that exist. Yet the cause of sin is the will of the devil and people turning away from God, according to the saying of Christ about the devil, "When he lies, he speaks out of his own character" (John 8:44).

## ARTICLE XX

# Good Works

The Confutation rejected the Lutheran insistence that we do not merit the forgiveness of sins by good works. On this point, more so perhaps than on any other, Roman Catholic doctrine is revealed to be, at its essence, deeply anti-Gospel. Melanchthon puts it this way: "What is more certain in the Church than that the forgiveness of sins happens freely for Christ's sake, that Christ, and not our works, is the Atoning Sacrifice for sins?" Melanchthon makes it plain that the writers of the Confutation are blaspheming Christ by suggesting otherwise. Rome has considerably toned down its teaching on the merit of human good works. Now it carefully asserts that God's grace is responsible for man's response, but still attributes merit to that response, thus contradicting and obscuring the full and sufficient grace of God. (See also AC XX; SA III XIII; FC Ep IV and SD IV.)

78 In Article XX, they clearly state that they reject and condemn our statement that people do not merit the forgiveness of sins by good works. Mark this well! They clearly declare that they reject and condemn this article. What more can be said on a subject so 79 clear? Here the framers of the Confutation display what spirit leads them. What is more certain in the Church than that the forgiveness of sins happens freely for Christ's sake, that Christ, and not our works, is the Atoning Sacrifice for sins, as Peter says, "To Him all the prophets bear witness that everyone who believes in Him receives forgiveness of sins" (Acts 10:43)? We would rather give agreement to this Church of the prophets than to these godless writers of the Confutation, who 80 so rudely blaspheme Christ. There were writers who held that after the forgiveness of sins, people are righteous before God, not by faith, but by works themselves. Yet, they did not hold that the forgiveness of sins happens because of our works, not freely for Christ's sake.

The blasphemy of assigning Christ's 81 honor to our works cannot be tolerated. These theologians are now entirely shameless if they dare to bring such an opinion into the Church. Nor do we doubt that His Most Excellent Imperial Majesty and many of the princes would not have allowed this passage to remain in the Confutation had they been advised about it. Here we could cite count- 82 less passages from Scripture and from the Fathers. But we have said enough about this subject before. One who knows why Christ has been given to us, and who knows that Christ is the Atoning Sacrifice for our sins, needs no further proof. Isaiah says, "The LORD has laid on Him the iniquity of us all" (53:6). The adversaries, on the other hand, teach that God does not lay our offenses on Christ, but on our works. Neither are we inclined to mention here the sort of works that they teach. We see that a horrible decree has 83 been prepared against us, which would terrify us still more if we were arguing about doubtful or silly subjects. Our consciences understand that the adversaries condemn the clear truth, whose defense is necessary for the Church and increases Christ's glory. Therefore, we easily look down on the terrors of the world, and we will bear with a strong spirit all suffering for Christ's glory and the Church's benefits. Who would not 84 joyfully die in the confession of these articles, that we receive the forgiveness of sins through faith freely for Christ's sake, and that we do not merit the forgiveness of sins by our works? The consciences of the pious 85 will not have sure enough comfort against

Faith Leads to Love and Good Works (Fruit)

the terrors of sin and of death, and against the devil tempting with despair, if they do not know that their confidence lies in the forgiveness of sins freely for Christ's sake. This faith sustains and enlivens hearts in that most violent conflict with despair.

86 The cause is so worthy that we should refuse no danger. To every one of you who has agreed to our Confession, "Do not yield to the wicked, but, on the contrary, go forward the more boldly." Do not yield when the adversaries, by means of terrors and tortures and punishments, try hard to drive away from you that comfort presented to the en-

87 tire Church in our article. Those seeking Scripture passages to settle their minds will find them. As the saying goes, at the top of his voice, Paul cries out that sins are freely forgiven for Christ's sake. "It depends on faith," he says, "in order that the promise may rest on grace and be guaranteed" (Romans 4:16; see also Romans 3:24–25). If the promise were to depend upon our works, it would not be sure. If forgiveness of sins were to be given because of our works, when would we know that we had received it? When would a terrified conscience find a work that it would consider enough to reconcile God's anger?

88 We spoke fully about this entire matter before. The reader can get the references there. The unworthy presentation of the subject has forced us not to discuss, but complain. They have clearly gone on record as disapproving of our article, that we receive forgiveness of sins not because of our works, but through faith and freely because of Christ.

89 The adversaries also add references to their own condemnation, and it is worthwhile to provide several of them. They quote from 2 Peter 1:10, "Be all the more diligent to make your calling and election sure." Now you see, reader, that our adversaries have not wasted any effort in learning logic, but have

the art of concluding whatever pleases them from the Scriptures. For they conclude, "Make your calling sure by good works." Therefore, they think that works merit the forgiveness of sins. This is a very nice way of thinking, if one would argue this way about a person whose death sentence had been pardoned: "The judge commands that from now on you stop stealing from others. Therefore, you have earned the pardon from the punishment, because you no longer steal from others." To argue in this way makes a cause 90 out of no cause. Peter speaks of works following the forgiveness of sins and teaches why they should be done. They should be done so that the calling may be sure, that is, should they fall from their calling if they sin again. Do good works in order that you may persevere in your calling, in order that you do not lose the gifts of your calling. They were given to you before, and not because of works that follow, and which now are kept through faith. Faith does not remain in those who lose the Holy Spirit and reject repentance. As we have said before (Article XII 1), faith exists in repentance.

They add other references that make no 91 more sense. Finally, they say that this opinion was condemned a thousand years before, in Augustine's time. This also is quite false. For Christ's Church always held that the forgiveness of sins is received freely. Indeed, the Pelagians were condemned. They argued that grace is given because of our works. Besides, 92 we have shown above well enough that we hold that good works should follow faith. "Do we then overthrow the law?" asks Paul. "On the contrary, we uphold the law" (Romans 3:31), because when we have received the Holy Spirit through faith, the fulfilling of the Law necessarily follows. Patience, chastity, and other fruit of the Spirit gradually grow by this love.

## ARTICLE XXI (IX)

# The Invocation of Saints

Melanchthon says that after numerous protests all the Confutation has done is prove that the saints should be honored and that living saints may pray for others, which is all the Lutherans said to begin with. In Roman Catholicism, then and still today, the saints take on a non-biblical role. The saints are said to have a storehouse of merits that they use to intercede for us. Melanchthon provides a careful discussion of what a propitiator (atonement maker) is and is not. Only Christ may be called a propitiator. Only the merit of Christ is counted as meritorious for us in God's eyes. This Lutheran assertion, then as well as now, stands in stark contrast to what Rome teaches about these things. Melanchthon rightly points out how, in popular devotion and practice, Mary has completely replaced Christ in the minds of many. This is still very much a problem in Roman Catholicism today. (See also AC XXI; SA II II.)

1   They absolutely condemn Article XXI because we do not require the invocation of saints. On no other topic do they speak more smoothly or wordily. Yet they are not able to prove anything other than that the saints should be honored, or that living saints pray for others, as though invoking dead saints 2 were necessary for that reason. They cite Cyprian because he asked Cornelius, while he was still alive, to pray for his brothers after his death. By this example they prove the invocation of the dead. They quote also Jerome against Vigilantius. "On this field," they say, "eleven hundred years ago, Jerome overcame Vigilantius." So the adversaries triumph, as though the war had already ended. Nor do those asses see that in Jerome, against Vigi-

lantius, there is not a syllable about invocation. He speaks about honors for the saints, not about invocation. Before Gregory, none 3 of the other ancient writers mentioned invocation. Certainly this kind of invocation, and the opinions that the adversaries now teach about the application of merits, are not confirmed by the ancient writers.

Our Confession approves honoring the 4 saints in three ways. The first is thanksgiving. We should thank God because He has shown examples of mercy, because He wishes to save people, and because He has given teachers and other gifts to the Church. These gifts, since they are the greatest, should be amplified. The saints themselves, who have faithfully used these gifts, should be praised just as Christ praises faithful businessmen (Matthew 25:21, 23). The second service is 5 the strengthening of our faith. When we see Peter's denial forgiven, we also are encouraged to believe all the more that grace truly superabounds over sin (Romans 5:20). The 6 third honor is the imitation, first of faith, then of the other virtues. Everyone should imitate the saints according to his calling. The adversaries do not require these true 7 honors. They argue only about invocation, which, even if it were not dangerous, still is not necessary.

Besides, we also grant that the angels pray 8 for us. For there is a passage in Zechariah 1:12, where an angel prays, "O LORD of hosts, how long will You have no mercy on Jerusalem?" We admit that, just as the saints 9 (when alive) pray for the Church universal in general, so in heaven they pray for the Church in general. However, no passage about the praying of the dead exists in the Scriptures, except the dream taken from the Second Book of Maccabees (15:14).

Furthermore, even if the saints do pray 10 for the Church, that does not mean they should be invoked. Our Confession affirms only this: Scripture does not teach the invocation of the saints, or that we are to ask the saints for aid. Since neither a command nor a promise nor an example can be produced from the Scriptures about the invocation of saints, it makes sense that conscience remains uncertain about this invocation. Since prayer should be made from faith, how do we know that God approves this invocation? Without the testimony of Scripture, how do we know that the saints know about the prayers of

11   each one? Some plainly ascribe divinity to the saints, namely, that they discern the silent thoughts of our minds. They argue about morning and evening knowledge, perhaps because they doubt whether the saints hear us in the morning or the evening. They invent these things, not to honor the saints, but

12   to defend profitable services. The adversaries cannot produce anything against this argument. Since the invocation of saints does not have a testimony from God's Word, it cannot be affirmed that the saints understand our invocation or, even if they understand it, that

13   God approves it. Therefore, the adversaries should not force us into an uncertain matter, because a prayer without faith is not prayer. For when they cite the Church's example, it is clear that this is a new custom in the Church. Although the old prayers mention the saints, they do not invoke the saints. This new invocation in the Church is unlike the invocation of individuals.

14       Further, the adversaries not only require invocation in worshiping the saints, but also apply the merits of the saints to others. They make the saints not only intercessors, but also people who make atonement. This cannot be tolerated. Here honor that belongs to Christ alone is completely transferred to the saints. The adversaries make them mediators and atonement makers. Although they dis-

tinguish between mediators of *intercession* and mediators (the Mediator) of *redemption*, they plainly make the saints mediators of redemption. Without the testimony of Scrip-   15 ture, they declare that the saints are mediators of intercession. This, be it said ever so reverently, still clouds over Christ's office and transfers to the saints the confidence of mercy belonging to Christ. People imagine that Christ is stricter and the saints more easily appeased. They trust the saints' mercy rather than Christ's mercy. They flee from Christ and seek the saints. So they actually make the saints mediators of redemption.

Therefore, we will show that the adver-   16 saries truly make the saints not just intercessors, but atonement makers, that is, mediators of redemption. Here we will not describe the abuses of the common people. We are still speaking about the opinions of the doctors. Regarding the rest, even the inexperienced can judge.

In a person who makes atonement, two   17 things are required. First, there should be a Word of God from which we certainly know that God wants to pity, and listen to, those calling upon Him through this atonement maker. There is such a promise about Christ, "Whatever you ask of the Father in My name, He will give it to you" (John 16:23). There is no such promise about the saints. Therefore, consciences cannot be completely confident that we are heard by the invocation of saints. This invocation, therefore, does not spring from faith. We also have the command to call   18 upon Christ:

"Come to Me, all who labor.
(Matthew 11:28)

In that day the root of Jesse, who shall stand as a signal for the peoples—of Him shall the nations inquire. (Isaiah 11:10)

The people of Tyre will seek Your favor with gifts, the richest of the people. (Psalm 45:12)

May all kings fall down before Him. (Psalm 72:11)

May prayer be made for Him continually. (Psalm 72:15)

That all may honor the Son, just as they honor the Father. (John 5:23)

Now may our Lord Jesus Christ Himself, and God our Father . . . comfort your hearts and establish them. (2 Thessalonians 2:16–17)

19 What commandment, what example, can the adversaries produce from the Scriptures about the invocation of saints? The second requirement for an atonement maker is that his merits are shown to make satisfaction for other people. They are divinely given to others, so that through them, just as by their own merits, other people may be regarded righteous. For example, when any friend pays a debt for a friend, the debtor is freed by the merit of another, as though it were by his own. So Christ's merits are given to us so that, when we believe in Him, we may be regarded righteous by our confidence in Christ's merits as though we had merits of our own.

20 From both of these—the promise and the giving of merits—arises confidence in mercy. Such confidence in the divine promise, and likewise in Christ's merits, should be promoted when we pray. For we should be truly confident, both that for Christ's sake we are heard and that by His merits we have a reconciled Father.

21 Here the adversaries ask us first to invoke the saints, although they have neither God's

The Rich Man and Lazarus

promise nor a command nor an example from Scripture. Yet they incite greater confidence in the saints' mercy than in Christ's mercy, although Christ asked us to come to 22 Him and not to the saints. Second, they apply the saints' merits, just as Christ's merits, to others. They ask us to trust in the saints' merits as though we were regarded righteous because of their merits, just as we are regarded righteous by Christ's merits. We are making 23 none of this up. In indulgences, the adversaries say that they apply the saints' merits. And Gabriel Biel, the interpreter of the canon of the Mass, confidently declares, "According to the order instituted by God, we should betake ourselves to the aid of the saints, in order that we may be saved by their merits and vows." These are Gabriel's words. Nevertheless, still more silly things are read here and there in the adversaries' books and sermons. What is this other than creating people who make atonement? If we must trust that we are saved by their merits, they are made completely equal to Christ.

24   Where has this arrangement, to which Gabriel refers when he says that we should resort to the aid of the saints, been instituted by God? Let him produce an example or command from the Scriptures. Perhaps they get this arrangement from the courts of kings, where friends must be used as intercessors. But if a king has appointed a certain intercessor, he will not want cases brought to him through others. So, since Christ has been appointed Intercessor and High Priest, why do we seek others?

25   Here and there this form of Absolution is used:

The passion of our Lord Jesus Christ, the merits of the most blessed Virgin Mary and of all the saints, be to you for the forgiveness of sins.

Here the Absolution is pronounced on the theory that we are reconciled and regarded righteous not only by Christ's merits, but also by the merits of the other saints. Some of 26 us have seen a doctor of theology dying. A certain theologian, a monk, was enlisted to comfort him. He pressed on the dying man nothing but this prayer, "Mother of grace, protect us from the enemy; receive us in the hour of death."

Granted, the blessed Mary prays for the 27 Church. Does she receive souls in death? Does she conquer death? Does she make alive? What does Christ do if the blessed Mary does these things? Although she is most worthy of the most plentiful honors, yet she does not want to be made equal to Christ. Instead she wants us to consider and follow her example. The very subject reveals 28 that in public opinion the blessed Virgin has taken over Christ's place. People have invoked her, have trusted in her mercy, and through her have wished to appease Christ, as though He were not an Atoning Sacrifice, but only a dreadful judge and avenger. We 29 believe, however, we must not trust that the saints' merits are applied to us, that because of these God is reconciled to us, regards us just, or saves us. For we receive forgiveness of sins only by Christ's merits when we believe in Him. Of the other saints it has been said, "Each will receive his wages according to his labor" (1 Corinthians 3:8), that is, they cannot mutually give their own merits, one to the other, as the monks sell the merits of their orders. Even Hilary says of the foolish 30 virgins (cf. Matthew 25:1–13):

As the foolish virgins could not go forth with their lamps extinguished, they sought those who were prudent to lend them oil; to whom they replied that they could not give the oil because there might not be enough for all. In other words, no one can be aided by the works and merits of another, because it is necessary for every one to buy oil for his own lamp.

31 The adversaries teach us to place confidence in the invocation of saints, although they have neither God's Word nor the example of Scripture. They apply the saints' merits on behalf of others in the same way they apply Christ's merits, and they transfer to the saints the honor belonging only to Christ. Therefore, we cannot accept their opinions about the worship of the saints, nor the practice of invocation. For we know that confidence is to be placed in Christ's intercession, because this alone has God's promise. We know that Christ's merits alone atone for us. Because of His merits we are regarded righteous when we believe in Him, as the text says, "Whoever believes in Him will not be put to shame" (1 Peter 2:6; see also Romans 9:33; Isaiah 28:16). Neither are we to trust that we are regarded righteous by the merits of the blessed Virgin or of the other saints.

32 The following error persists also among the educated. Each saint has been given a particular duty: Anna gives riches, Sebastian wards off disease, Valentine heals epilepsy, George protects horsemen. These opinions have clearly sprung from pagan examples. Among the Romans, Juno was thought to give wealth, Febris to ward off fever, Castor and Pollux to protect horsemen, and so on. If the

33 invocation of saints were taught with the greatest caution, even such speculation is dangerous. Why defend it when it has no command or testimony from God's Word? Indeed, it does not even have the testimony of

34 the ancient writers. First, as I have said before, when other mediators are sought in addition to Christ, and confidence is put in others, the entire knowledge of Christ is hindered. The subject shows this. In the beginning, mention

of the saints seems to have been permitted. It was viewed as tolerable, as in the ancient prayers. Afterward, invocation followed, and abuses that are unnatural and more than pagan followed invocation. From invocation the next step was to images. These also were worshiped. A force was supposed to exist in them, just as magicians imagine that a force exists in images of the heavenly bodies carved at a particular time. In a certain monastery we have seen a statue of the blessed Virgin. It moved automatically by a trick, seeming to turn away (from those who did not make a large offering) or to nod to those making a request.

35 The incredible stories about the saints, which are taught with great authority in public, go beyond the marvelous tales of the statues and pictures. While being tormented, Barbara asks for the reward that no one invoking her should die without the Eucharist. Standing on one foot, another recited the whole Psalter daily. Some wise man painted Christopher. He did so to illustrate that there should be great strength of mind in those who bear Christ, that is, those who teach or confess the Gospel. It is necessary for them to undergo the greatest dangers. Then the foolish monks taught the people that they should invoke Christopher, as though such a Polyphemus had once existed. The saints per-

36 formed very great deeds, either useful to the state or providing private examples. Remembering these acts would go far toward strengthening faith and following their example in the administration of affairs. However, no one has searched for these from true stories. Indeed, it is helpful to hear how holy men ruled governments, what disasters and dangers they underwent, how holy men helped kings in great dangers, how they taught the Gospel, what encounters they had with heretics. Examples of mercy help as well,

such as when we see Peter forgiven his denial (Mark 16:7), when we see Cyprian forgiven for having been a magician, when we see Augustine, having experienced faith's power in sickness, steadily affirming that God truly hears believers' prayers. It was beneficial that these examples, which contain reminders for either faith or fear or the rule of the state, be 37 repeated. But certain silly persons, having knowledge neither of faith nor for governing states, have invented stories sounding like poems. They contain superstitious models for certain prayers, fastings, and additional works for bringing in gain. These are the miracles that have been invented about rosaries and similar ceremonies. There is no need to recite further examples here. For the legends, as they call them, the mirrors of examples, and the rosaries, in which there are very many things not unlike the true stories of Lucian, are still in existence.

38    The bishops, theologians, and monks praise these freakish and wicked stories because they help them get their daily bread. They do not put up with us. So that Christ's honor and office may be more evident, we do not require the invocation of saints, and we condemn the abuses in the worship of saints. 39 All good people everywhere greatly wanted the bishops' authority or the preachers' diligence to help correct these abuses. Yet in the Confutation our adversaries completely overlook other apparent sins. They do so as though they wish, by receiving the Confutation, to push us to accept even the most scandalous abuses.

40    The Confutation has been written untruthfully, not only on this topic, but almost everywhere. There is no passage in the Confutation in which they distinguish between apparent abuses and their teachings. Nevertheless, if any of them can think, they confess that many false opinions are con-tained in the teaching of the Scholastics and canon lawyers. Besides, they keep many abuses that crept into the Church due to the pastors' ignorance and negligence. For Luther 41 was not the first to complain about public abuses. Long before these times, many educated and excellent men greatly regretted the abuses of the Mass, confidence in monastic observances, services to the saints intended to gain a profit, and the confusion of the doctrine about repentance. The latter should be as clear and plain in the Church as possible. We ourselves have heard that excellent theologians desire moderation in the scholastic teaching. It contains much more for philosophical quarrels than for piety. Nevertheless, the older theologians are generally closer to Scripture than are the recent theologians. Their theology has worsened more and more. Many good men, who at the beginning were friendly to Luther, saw that he was freeing people's minds from these mazes of most confused and countless discussions held by the scholastic theologians and canon lawyers. They saw that Luther was teaching things beneficial for godliness.

When they wanted us to agree to the 42 Confutation, the adversaries were not honest in overlooking the abuses. If they wanted to help the Church, they should encourage our most excellent emperor to take measures to correct abuses. We see plainly enough that the emperor wants the healing and well establishing of the Church. But the adversaries do not act to help the emperor's most honorable and most holy will, but they act in every way to crush us. Many signs show that they 43 have little anxiety about the state of the Church. They make no effort to see that the people have a summary of the Church's teachings. They defend clear abuses by new and unusual cruelty. They continue every day to shed innocent blood. They do not allow suitable teachers in the churches. Good people can easily decide if these things help. In this way they care neither for their own authority nor for the Church. After the good teachers have been killed and sound teaching hindered, fanatical spirits will rise up. The adversaries will not be able to restrain them. They will disturb the Church with godless teachings and will overthrow the entire Church government. We wish very much to keep this government.

44    Most excellent Emperor Charles, for the sake of Christ's glory, which doubtlessly you wish to praise and magnify, we beg you not to agree to the violent advice of our adversaries. Rather, we beg you to seek other honorable ways of establishing harmony so that godly consciences are not burdened, that no cruelty is exercised against innocent people (as we have seen before) and that sound teaching is not hindered in the Church. To God above all you owe the duty to preserve sound teaching and hand it down to future generations, to defend those who teach what is right. For God demands this when He honors kings with His own name, calling them gods, saying, "I said, 'You are gods' " (Psalm 82:6). They should work toward the preservation and growth of divine things, that is, the Gospel of Christ on the earth (Acts 12:24). As God's representatives, they should defend the life and safety of the innocent.

## ARTICLE XXII (X)

# Both Kinds in the Lord's Supper

The Pontifical Confutation rejected the Lutheran request that the laity receive both the consecrated bread and wine in the Lord's Supper. It said that insistence on such a thing "is an abuse and disobedience," and that the layperson should be content receiving the Lord's Supper under one kind, since Christ is completely present in both the bread and the wine. This remains the view of Rome, though today it is stated more gently, and in some parishes communicants may receive both bread and wine. Melanchthon chides the Roman theologians in the Apology and again insists that there is no legitimate biblical reason to withhold the consecrated wine, the blood of Christ, from the laity. (See also AC XXII; SA III VI; FC Ep VII and SD VII.)

———————

There is no doubt that using both parts in 1 the Lord's Supper is godly and in agreement with Christ's institution and Paul's words. For Christ instituted both parts, not for a portion of the Church, but for the whole Church. Not only the presbyters, but the entire Church uses the Sacrament by Christ's authority, and not by human authority. We suppose the adversaries recognize this. If 2 Christ has instituted the Supper for the entire Church, why is one kind denied to a part of the Church? Why is the use of the other kind prohibited? Why is Christ's ordinance changed, especially when He Himself calls it His testament? If it is unlawful to set aside a man's testament, it is more unlawful to set aside Christ's testament. Paul says, "For I re- 3 ceived from the Lord what I also delivered to you" (1 Corinthians 11:23). He had delivered the use of both kinds, as the text, 1 Corinthians 11, clearly shows. He says, "Do this" (11:24), first *about His body*; afterward, Paul repeats the same words *about the cup* (Christ's blood). And then, "Let a person examine himself, then, and so eat of the bread and drink of the cup" (11:28). These are the words of Him who has instituted the Sacrament. Indeed, He says before that those who will use the Lord's Supper should use both.

4   It is clear, therefore, that the Sacrament was instituted for the whole Church. The custom still remains in the Greek churches, and was once also observed in the Latin churches, as Cyprian and Jerome testify. For Jerome says on Zephaniah: "The priests who administer the Eucharist, and distribute the Lord's blood to the people," and so on. The Council of Toledo gives the same testimony. Nor would it be difficult to gather a great multitude of 5 references. We are not exaggerating. We will allow the levelheaded reader to determine what should be held about the divine ordinance.

6       In the Confutation, the adversaries do not try hard to relieve the Church, to which one part of the Sacrament has been denied. This would have been fitting to good and religious men. A strong reason for relieving the Church should have been sought, and consciences, which would have received only a part of the Sacrament, should have been instructed. Now these very men maintain that it is right to ban the other part of the Sacra- 7 ment and forbid the use of both parts. First, they imagine at the Church's beginning, it was customary at some places to give out only one part of the Sacrament. However, they are not able to produce any ancient example for this. They quote the passages mentioning bread, as Luke 24:35, where it is written that the disciples recognized Christ in the breaking of bread. They quote also other passages (Acts 2:42, 46; 20:7) about the breaking of bread. Although we do not object if some interpret these passages as referring to the Sacrament, it does not make sense that only one part of the Sacrament was given. According to the ordinary usage of language, nam- 8 ing one part also means the other. They also refer to lay Communion, which was not the use of only one kind, but of both. Whenever priests are commanded to use lay Commu-

nion, it is meant that they have been removed from the ministry of consecration. The adversaries are not ignorant of this, but they abuse the ignorance of the uneducated. When the uneducated hear of lay Communion, they imagine the custom of our time, by which only a part of the Sacrament is given to laypeople.

     Consider the adversaries' rudeness. 9 Gabriel Biel recalls among other reasons why both parts are not given: to distinguish between laymen and presbyters. It is credible that the chief reason why one part is prohibited is this: the clerical order may be more dignified by a religious rite. To say nothing more extreme, this is a human design. It can easily be judged whether this helps. In the 10 Confutation they also mention Eli's sons. After the loss of the high priesthood, they were to seek the one part applying to the priests. (See 1 Samuel 2:36.) Here they say that the use of one kind was meant. They add: "So, our laypeople should also be content with one kind, with only the priests receiving the other." The adversaries are clearly being silly when they transfer the history of Eli's descendants to the Sacrament. Eli's punishment is described there. Will they also say that, as a punishment, laypeople have been separated from the other part? The Sacrament was instituted to comfort terrified minds. This happens when they believe that Christ's flesh is given as food for the life of the world (John 6:51) and when they believe that, being joined to Christ, they are made alive. But the adversaries argue that laypeople are separated from the other part as a punishment. "They should," they say, "be content." This is enough for a dictator. Why 11 should they withhold both parts of the Sacrament? "The reason must not be asked, but let whatever the theologians say be law." This is Eck's doing. We recognize those proud words. If we wanted to criticize, there would be no lack of words. You see how great the rudeness is. He commands, as a tyrant in the tragedies: "Whether they will or not, they must be content." Will the reasons that he cites excuse, in God's judgment, those who ban a part of the Sacrament and attack people using an entire Sacrament? If they make the prohibition in order that there may be a distinguishing mark between priests and laity, this very reason should move us not to agree with the adversaries, even though we could go along with their custom, but for other reasons. There are marks that distinguish the order of priests from the people, but it is clear why they defend this distinction so earnestly. We do not want to ridicule the value of the order, so we will not say more about the adversaries' real intent.

They also bring up the danger of spilling (the wine) and certain similar things. These are not serious enough to change Christ's ordinance. Certainly, if we assume that we are free to use either one part of the Sacrament or both, how can prohibiting the use of both kinds be defended? The Church does not allow itself to change Christ's ordinances into unimportant matters. We certainly excuse the Church that has suffered since it could not receive both parts. But we do not excuse the writers who maintain that using the entire Sacrament is justly banned and who now not only ban, but even excommunicate and violently persecute, those using the entire Sacrament. Let them figure out how they will answer God for their decisions. It should not be immediately judged that the Church decides or approves whatever the pontiffs decide, especially since Scripture prophesies about the bishops and pastors in this regard, as Ezekiel 7:26 says, "The law perishes from the priest."

## ARTICLE XXIII (XI)

# The Marriage of Priests

In this article, Melanchthon rebuts the Confutation's argument that priests should not marry. He anchors his argument in the institution of marriage at creation. Marriage is a divine ordinance that the Church cannot contradict. Melanchthon is not saying that a minister who chooses to remain celibate should be married; rather, he insists that the Church cannot command people to be celibate who want to be ministers in the Church, when clearly the gift of celibacy is reserved only for a very few. Nowhere in the Bible is forced celibacy, or forced marriage, tied to ministry. The apostles were both married and single. Priestly celibacy is yet another example of antiscriptural traditions in the Roman Church. (See also AC XXIII; SA III XI.)

In spite of the great scandal about their filthy celibacy, the adversaries arrogantly defend pontifical law under the wicked and false excuse of the divine name. They even encourage the emperor and princes, to the disgrace and scandal of the Roman Empire, to not allow the marriage of priests. This is how they speak.

Where in any history can one read of greater rudeness than this of the adversaries? We will review their arguments later. Now let the wise reader consider how shameful these good-for-nothing men are. They claim that marriages produce scandal and disgrace to the government, as though this public scandal of criminal and unnatural lusts glowing among these very Holy Fathers were a great ornament to the Church, while they pretend that they are Curii and live like bacchanals! Most things done with the greatest license by these men cannot even be named without a

3  breach of modesty. These are their lusts, which they ask you to defend with your chaste right hand, Emperor Charles. Certain ancient predictions name you as the king of modest face, for the saying appears about you, "One modest in face shall reign everywhere." Contrary to divine Law, the law of nations, and the canons of the councils, they ask you to break apart marriages, to punish innocent men horribly merely for the sake of marriage, to put priests to death, whom even barbarians reverently spare, to exile banished women and fatherless children. They bring such laws to you, most excellent and most chaste Emperor, to which no barbarity, however monstrous and cruel, could lend its ear.

4  But because disgrace or cruelty does not stain your character, we hope that you will deal with us mildly in this matter, especially when you have learned that we have the weightiest reasons for our belief, taken from God's Word, which the adversaries reject with the most silly and vain opinions.

5  Nevertheless, they do not seriously defend celibacy. They are not ignorant of how few there are who practice chastity. They create a counterfeit religion for their domain, which they think that celibacy helps. So we understand that Peter was right to advise that "there will be false teachers among you, who will secretly bring in destructive heresies" (2 Peter 2:1). The adversaries say, write, or do nothing truly, frankly, and candidly in this entire case. They actually argue only about the domain they falsely think is in danger, and which they try hard to support with a wicked excuse of godliness.

6  We cannot approve this law about celibacy that the adversaries defend, because it conflicts with divine and natural law and disagrees with the very canons of the councils. It is clearly superstitious and dangerous. It produces countless scandals, sins, and corruption of public morals. Our other disagreements need some discussion by the doctors. But in this matter the subject is so clear to both parties that it requires no discussion. It only requires as judge a man who is honest and fears God. Although we defend the clear truth, the adversaries still have created certain reproaches for mocking our arguments.

## Arguments for the Marriage of Priests

First, Genesis 1:28 teaches that people 7 were created to be fruitful, and that one sex should desire the other in a proper way. We are not speaking about lustful desire, which is sin, but about that appetite that was in nature in its perfection. They call this physical love. This love of one sex for the other is truly a divine ordinance. But since this ordinance of God cannot be removed without an extraordinary work of God, it makes sense that statutes or vows cannot remove the right to contract marriage.

The adversaries object to these arguments. 8 They say that in the beginning, the commandment was given to populate the earth. Now that the earth has been populated, marriage is not commanded. See how wisely they judge! Human nature is so formed by God's Word that it is fruitful not only in the beginning of creation, but as long as this nature of our bodies exists. Humanity is fruitful just as the earth becomes fruitful by the Word, "Let the earth sprout vegetation, plants yielding seed" (Genesis 1:11). Because of this ordinance, the earth not only started to produce plants in the beginning, but as long as this natural order exists, the fields are covered every year. Therefore, just as human laws cannot change the nature of the earth, so, without God's special work, neither vows nor a human law can change a human being's nature.

9 Second, because this creation, or divine ordinance, in humanity is a natural right, jurists have said wisely and correctly that the union of male and female belongs to natural right. Natural right is unchangeable. Therefore, the right to contract marriage must always remain where nature does not change, that ordinance which God gave nature does not change. It cannot be removed

10 by human laws. Therefore, it is ridiculous for the adversaries to babble that marriage was commanded in the beginning, but is not now. This is the same as if they would say, "Formerly, when people were born, they were born with gender; now they are not. Formerly, when they were born, they brought with them natural right; now they do not." No craftsman (*Faber*) could produce anything more crafty than these foolish things. They were created to dodge a

11 natural right. Therefore, let this point remain, that both Scripture teaches and the jurist says wisely: the union of male and fe-

12 male belongs to natural right. Furthermore, a natural right is truly a divine right because it is an ordinance divinely imprinted on nature. Because this right cannot be changed without an extraordinary work of God, the right to contract marriage remains, the natural desire of one sex for the other sex is an ordinance of God in nature, and for this reason is a right. Otherwise, why would

13 both sexes have been created? As it has been said before, we are not speaking of lustful desires, which is sin, but of that desire called physical love. Lustful desire has not removed this physical love from nature, but inflames it, so that now physical love has greater need of a cure. Marriage is necessary not only for the sake of procreation, but also as a cure. These things are clear and so well established that they cannot be disputed.

14 Third, Paul says, "Because of the tempta-

tion to sexual immorality, each man should have his own wife" (1 Corinthians 7:2). This is a clear command having to do with everyone unfit for celibacy. The adversaries ask to 15 be shown a commandment that commands priests to marry, as though priests are not men! We certainly judge that the things we hold about human nature in general also have to do with priests. Does not Paul in this 16 passage command marriage for those who do not have the gift of chastity? Paul interprets himself a little later when he says, "It is better to marry than to be aflame with passion" (7:9). And Christ has clearly said, "Not everyone can receive this saying, but only those to whom it is given" (Matthew 19:11). Since Adam's fall into sin, these two things agree: natural appetite and lustful desire. Lustful desire inflames the natural appetite, so that now there is more need of marriage than in nature in its perfection. So Paul speaks of marriage as a cure, and because of these flames he commands marriage. Neither can any human authority, law, or vows remove this declaration, "It is better to marry than to be aflame with passion," because they do not remove the nature or lustful desire. Therefore, all who burn keep the 17 right to marry. By this commandment of Paul, "Because of the temptation to sexual immorality, each man should have his own wife" (1 Corinthians 7:2), all are held bound who do not truly keep themselves chaste. The decision about chastity is one of individual conscience.

Here the adversaries command seeking 18 chastity from God, weakening the body through labor and hunger. Why do they not proclaim these magnificent commandments to themselves? As we have said before, the adversaries are only playing; they are doing nothing seriously. If chastity were possible to 19 all, it would not require a peculiar gift. But

Christ shows that it needs a peculiar gift. Therefore, not everyone has it. God wishes the rest to use the common law of nature, which He has instituted. He does not wish His ordinances, His creations, to be hated. He wishes people to be chaste in this way, that they use the remedy divinely presented, just as He wishes that we use food and drink 20 so that our life is nourished. Gerson also testifies that there have been many good men who tried very hard to subdue the body, and yet made little progress. So, Ambrose is right in saying, "Virginity is only a thing that can be recommended, but not commanded; it is 21 a matter of vow rather than of precept." If anyone here would object that Christ praises those "who have made themselves eunuchs for the sake of the kingdom of heaven" (Matthew 19:12), let him also consider that He praises those having the gift of chastity. Because of this He adds, "Let the 22 one who is able to receive this receive it." For an impure chastity does not please Christ. We also praise true chastity. But now we are arguing about the law, and about those who do not have the gift of chastity. The matter should be left free, and traps should not be cast upon the weak through this law.

23    Fourth, the pontifical law differs also from the canons of the councils. The ancient canons do not ban marriage. Neither do they dissolve marriages that have been contracted, even though they remove from clerical office those who contracted marriage during their ministry. At those times this dismissal was an act of kindness. The new canons, which have not been framed in the synods, but have been made according to the private judgment of the popes, both ban the contraction of marriages and dissolve them when contracted. This is to be done openly, contrary to Christ's command, "What therefore God has joined together, let not man separate" (Matthew 19:6). In the Confutation the adversaries exclaim that the councils command celibacy. We do not find fault with the councils' decrees. Under a certain condition they allow marriage. However, we do find fault with the laws enacted since the ancient synods, which the popes of Rome have created contrary to the authority of the synods. The popes hate the authority of the synods, just as much as they want that authority to appear holy to others. Therefore, this law about permanent 25 celibacy is peculiar to this new pontifical tyranny. Nor is it without a reason. For Daniel 11:37 attributes this mark to the kingdom of Antichrist: hatred for women.

Fifth, the adversaries do not defend the 26 law because of superstition. For they see that it is not generally obeyed. Yet, they spread superstitious opinions, while giving an appearance of religion. They claim that they require celibacy because it is purity, as though marriage were impure and a sin, or as though celibacy merited justification more than marriage! To this end they cite the cere- 27 monies of the Mosaic Law, because under the Law at the time of ministering, the priests were separated from their wives. The priest in the New Testament, because he should always pray, should always practice chastity. This silly comparison is presented as a proof that should urge priests to permanent celibacy, although in this very comparison marriage is allowed. Only during the time of ministry was its use prohibited. It is one thing to pray; it is another to minister. The saints prayed even when they did not exercise the public ministry. Conjugal intercourse did not hinder them from praying.

We will reply to these daydreams in an or- 28 derly way. In the first place, the adversaries should acknowledge that in believers, marriage is pure because it has been sanctified by God's Word. That is to say, it is a matter that

29 is permitted and approved by God's Word, as Scripture testifies abundantly. Christ calls marriage a divine union when He says, "What therefore God has joined together"

30 (Matthew 19:6). And Paul says of marriage, of meats and similar things, "It is made holy by the word of God and prayer" (1 Timothy 4:5), that is, "by the Word," by which consciences become certain that God approves, and "by prayer," that is, by faith, which uses it with thanksgiving as God's gift.

31 Likewise, "The unbelieving husband is made holy because of his wife" (1 Corinthians 7:14), that is, the use of marriage is permitted and holy because of faith in Christ, just as it

32 is permitted to use meat, and so on. Likewise, "She will be saved through childbearing," and so on (1 Timothy 2:15). If the adversaries could produce such a passage about celibacy, then certainly they would celebrate a wonderful triumph. Paul says that woman is saved by childbearing. What more honorable thing could be said against the hypocrisy of celibacy than that woman is saved by the conjugal works themselves, by conjugal intercourse, by bearing children and the other duties? But what does St. Paul mean? Let the reader observe that faith is added, and that domestic duties without faith are not praised. "If they continue," he says, "in faith." For he speaks of the whole class of mothers. Therefore, he requires especially faith, through which a woman receives the forgiveness of sins and justification. Then he adds a particular work of the calling, just as in every person a good work of a particular calling should follow faith. This work pleases God because of faith. So the duties of the woman please God because of faith, and the believing woman is saved who devoutly serves her calling in such duties.

33 These references teach that marriage is a lawful thing. Therefore, if purity illustrates that which is allowed and approved before God, marriages are pure, because they have been approved by God's Word. Paul says

34 about lawful things, "To the pure, all things are pure" (Titus 1:15), to those who believe in Christ and are righteous by faith. Therefore, as virginity is impure in the godless, so in the godly, marriage is pure because of God's Word and faith.

35 Again, if purity is properly opposed to lustful desires, it illustrates purity of heart, that is, lustful desires put to death [mortified]. For the Law does not prohibit marriage, but lustful desires, adultery, fornication. Therefore, celibacy is not purity. There may be greater purity of heart in a married man, as in Abraham or Jacob, than in most of those who are even truly chaste.

36 Finally, if they understand that celibacy is pure in the sense that it merits justification more than marriage does, we most forcefully deny it. We are justified neither because of virginity nor because of marriage, but freely for Christ's sake, when we believe that for His

37 sake God is merciful to us. Here perhaps they will cry out that, like Jovinian, marriage is made equal to virginity. But, because of such racket, we will not reject the truth about the righteousness of faith, which we explained

38 before. Yet, we do not make virginity and marriage equal. For just as one gift excels another, as prophecy excels power of speech, the science of military affairs excels agriculture, and power of speech excels architecture, so virginity is a more excellent gift than mar-

39 riage. Just as a public speaker is not more righteous before God because of his ability to speak than an architect because of his skill in architecture, so a virgin does not merit justification by virginity any more than a married person merits it by conjugal duties. Each person should faithfully serve in his own gift and believe that for Christ's sake he receives

the forgiveness of sins and through faith is regarded righteous before God.

40    Neither Christ nor Paul praise virginity because it justifies, but because it is freer and less distracted by domestic occupations in praying, teaching, and serving. For this reason Paul says, "The unmarried man is anxious about the things of the Lord" (1 Corinthians 7:32). Virginity, therefore, is praised because of meditation and study. So Christ does not simply praise those "who have made themselves eunuchs," but adds, "for the sake of the kingdom of heaven," that is, they may have freedom to learn or teach the Gospel. He does not say that virginity merits the forgiveness of sins or salvation.

41    To the examples of the Levitical priests we have replied that they do not establish the duty of demanding permanent celibacy from the priests. Furthermore, the Levitical impurities are not to be transferred to us. Then intercourse contrary to the Law was an impurity. Now it is not an impurity because Paul says, "To the pure, all things are pure" (Titus 1:15). The Gospel frees us from these Levitical impurities. If anyone defends the law of
42    celibacy with the intent to burden consciences by these Levitical commands, we must labor against this, just as the apostles in Acts 15:10 labored against those who required circumcision and tried to force Moses' Law upon Christians.

43    In the meantime, good people will know how to control the use of marriage, especially when they occupy public offices. These often give good people so much labor that all domestic thoughts are expelled from their minds. Good people know this also, that Paul commands everyone "to control his own body in holiness" (1 Thessalonians 4:4). They also know that they must rest sometimes, so that there may be freedom

for prayer. Paul does not wish this to be per-   44
manent (1 Corinthians 7:5). Such chastity is easy to those who are well occupied. But the great crowd of unemployed priests in the fraternities cannot afford, in this sensuality, even this Levitical chastity, as the facts show. The lines are well known, "The boy used to pursuing a lazy life hates those who are busy."

Many heretics misunderstand the Law of   45
Moses and have treated marriage with contempt. Yet they admire celibacy very much. Epiphanius complains that, especially by this approval, the Encratites captured the minds of the gullible. They refrained from wine even in the Lord's Supper. They refrained from eating the flesh of all animals, in which they excelled the Dominican brethren, who live upon fish. They refrained also from marriage, and this in particular gained the chief admiration. They thought that these works and services merited grace more than the use of wine, flesh, and marriage. To them those things appeared to be profane and unclean and could scarcely please God, even though they were not condemned.

In Colossians 2:18, Paul greatly disap-   46
proves these angelic forms of worship. For when people believe that they are pure and righteous because of such hypocrisy, they hinder the knowledge of Christ and the knowledge of God's gifts and commandments. God wishes us to use His gifts in a godly way. We might mention examples   47
where certain godly consciences were greatly disturbed because of the lawful use of marriage. This evil was taken from the opinions of monks superstitiously praising celibacy. Yet, we do not find fault with self-control or   48
chastity. We have said before that spiritual exercises and putting the flesh to death are necessary. Certainly we deny that confidence should be placed in certain ceremonies, as

49 though they made one righteous. Epiphanius has said elegantly that these ceremonies should be praised "for restraining the body or because of public morals," just as certain rites were set up for instructing the ignorant, and not as services that justify.

50 Our adversaries do not require celibacy through superstition. They know that chastity is not ordinarily practiced. The adversaries fake superstitious opinions to fool the ignorant. They should be hated more than the Encratites, who seem to have erred by a show of religion. These Sardanapali (Epicureans) willingly misuse the appearance of religion.

51 Sixth, we have many reasons for disapproving the law of permanent celibacy. Besides these, there are also dangers to souls and public scandals. Even if the law were just, these should discourage good people from approving such a burden that has destroyed countless souls.

52 For a long time, good people have complained about this burden, either for themselves or for others whom they saw to be in danger. But the popes do not listen to these complaints. It is beyond doubt that this law is injurious to public morals, and has produced vices and shameful lusts. The Roman comedic plays still exist. Rome still recognizes and reads its own morals in them.

53 So God punishes the hatred of His own gift and ordinance in those who ban marriage. For other laws the custom was that if a benefit could clearly be shown, they were changed. Why isn't the same done with this law? There are weighty reasons to support such a change, especially now. Nature is growing old and is gradually becoming weaker. Vices are increasing. Therefore, the

54 divine cures should be used. We see what vice God condemned before the flood and before the burning of the five cities. Similar vices

have come before the destruction of many other cities, such as Sybaris and Rome. These illustrate what it will be like in the end times. So now, marriage should be strongly defended 55 by the strictest laws and warning examples. People should be encouraged to marry. This duty belongs to public officials, who should maintain public discipline. Meanwhile, the teachers of the Gospel should do both of these things: encourage unchaste people to marry; encourage others not to hate the gift of chastity.

The popes daily enact and change other 56 excellent laws. However, when it comes to the law of celibacy, they are as hard and cold as iron, even though it is clear that this is simply a human right. They are now mak- 57 ing this law more burdensome in many ways. The canon asks them to suspend priests. These rather unfriendly interpreters suspend them not from office, but from trees. They cruelly kill many men for nothing but marriage. These very murders of 58 close relatives show that this law is a doctrine of demons (1 Timothy 4:1). Since the devil is a murderer (John 8:44), he defends his law by these murders.

We know that there is some offense re- 59 garding schism. We seem to have separated from those who are considered regular bishops. But our consciences are very secure. We know that, though we earnestly desire to establish harmony, we cannot please the adversaries unless we cast away clear truth and then willingly agree with these very men to defend this unjust law, to dissolve marriages that have been contracted, to put priests to death if they do not obey, and to drive poor women and fatherless children into exile. But since these conditions clearly displease God, we cannot feel sorry that we are not allied with the multitude of murderers among the adversaries.

## Conclusion

60    We have explained why we cannot with a good conscience agree with the adversaries when they defend the pontifical law about permanent celibacy. It conflicts with divine and natural law, and it varies from the canons themselves. It is superstitious and full of danger. Finally, the whole affair is insincere. For the law is enacted not for the sake of religion. It was enacted for the sake of control, and this is wickedly given the appearance of religion. No sane person can produce anything against these most firmly estab-

61    lished reasons. The Gospel allows marriage for those to whom it is necessary. Nevertheless, it does not compel marriage for those who can be chaste, provided they are truly chaste. We hold that the priests should be allowed this freedom also. We do not wish to compel anyone to be celibate by force, nor do we want to break up marriages that have been contracted.

62    We have also shown on the side how the adversaries object to several of our arguments while we presented them. We have explained away these false accusations. As briefly as possible, we will now relate what important reasons they claim to have for de-

63    fending the law. First, they say that it has been revealed by God. You see the extreme rudeness of these sorry fellows. They dare to affirm that the law of permanent celibacy has been divinely revealed, although it is contrary to clear Scripture passages. These passages command that "because of the temptation to sexual immorality, each man should have his own wife" (1 Corinthians 7:2). Likewise, they forbid breaking up marriages that have been contracted. (See Matthew 5:32; 19:6; 1 Corinthians 7:27.) Paul reminds us what kind of author such a law has when he calls it "teachings of demons" (1 Timothy

4:1). Fruit show their author; many monstrous lusts and murders are now committed under the appearance of that law.

The second argument of the adversaries is    64
that the priests should be pure, according to Isaiah 52:11, "Purify yourselves, you who bear the vessels of the LORD." And they cite many things to this effect. We have dealt with this particularly false reason before. We have said that virginity without faith is not purity before God, and marriage is pure because of faith, according to Titus 1:15, "To the pure, all things are pure." We have also said that outward purity and the ceremonies of the Law are not to be demanded today, because the Gospel requires purity of heart. A husband's heart, as in the case of polygamists Abraham or Jacob, may be purer and burn less with lusts than that of many virgins who are truly chaste. What Isaiah says, "Purify yourselves, you who bear the vessels of the LORD," should be understood as referring to the cleanness of heart and to the whole of repentance. Besides, in the exercise of marriage    65
the saints will know to what extent it is beneficial to restrain its use, and as Paul says, "to control his own body in holiness" (1 Thessalonians 4:4). Finally, since marriage is pure,    66
those who are not chaste in celibacy are rightly told that they should marry wives to be pure. So the same law, "Purify yourselves, you who bear the vessels of the LORD," commands that impure celibates become pure husbands.

The third argument is horrible: the mar-    67
riage of priests is the heresy of Jovinian. Fine-sounding words! This is a new crime, that marriage is a heresy! In the time of Jovinian the world did not as yet know the law about permanent celibacy. Therefore, it is a rude lie that the marriage of priests is the heresy of Jovinian, or that such marriage was then condemned by the Church. In such passages    68

we can see what plan the adversaries had in writing the Confutation. They determined that the ignorant would be the most easily excited if they would hear frequently the charge of heresy, and if they pretend that our cause had been condemned and executed by many previous decisions of the Church. So they frequently cite falsely the Church's judgment. Because they knew about this, they were unwilling to show us a copy of their Apology, lest this lie and these charges be ex-

69 posed. We have already expressed our opinion, however, regarding Jovinian, which concerns the comparison of virginity and marriage. We do not make marriage and virginity equal, although neither virginity nor marriage merits justification.

70 The adversaries defend a law that is godless and destructive to good morals by such false arguments. By such reasons they set the minds of princes firmly against God's judgment. God will call them to explain why they have broken apart marriages and why they have tortured and killed priests. For do not doubt that, as the blood of dead Abel cried out (Genesis 4:10), so the blood of many good men, whom they have unjustly attacked, will also cry out. God will punish this cruelty. There you will discover how worthless are these reasons of the adversaries. You will discern that in God's judgment no lies against God's Word remain standing, as Isaiah says, "All flesh is grass, and all its beauty is like the flower of the field" (40:6).

71 Whatever may happen, our princes will be able to comfort themselves with the consciousness of right counsels. Even if the priests had done wrong in contracting marriages, this disruption of marriages, these prohibitions, and this cruelty are clearly contrary to God's will and Word. Neither novelty nor dissent delights our princes. Especially in an undoubted matter more regard had to be paid to God's Word than to anything else.

## The Divine Service

Unlike other reformers, Luther's revisions to the medieval Roman Mass were quite conservative. Calvin and Zwingli threw out all traditional services; enthusiasts substituted spiritualism for Word and Sacrament. But for Luther, true reform did not equal total rejection. He restored the Gospel to its proper place in the life of the Church and purged the liturgy of false teaching and practice. Below, compare the medieval Mass with Luther's Divine Service for the Church at Wittenberg. Other than the unscriptural Canon of the Mass, the two services are strikingly similar.

| *Luther's Form of the Mass, 1523* | *Medieval Roman Mass* |
|---|---|
| 1. Introit | 1. Introit |
| 2. Kyrie, *"Lord have mercy upon us."* | 2. Kyrie |
| 3. Gloria, *"Glory be . . ."* (may be omitted) | 3. Gloria (may be omitted) |
| 4. Collect (only one permitted) | 4. Collects |
| 5. Epistle | 5. Epistle |
| 6. Gradual/Alleluia | 6. Gradual/Alleluia |
| 7. Sequences (only one of three permitted) | 7. Sequences (all but four later rejected by Council of Trent) |
| 8. Gospel (candles and incense optional) | 8. Gospel/Sermon |
| 9. Nicene Creed (may be sung) | 9. Nicene Creed |
| 10. Sermon | 10. Offertory and Secret (inaudible prayer; only conclusion heard) |
| 11. Order for Holy Communion | 11. Order for Holy Communion |
|   a. Sursum Corda, *"The Lord be with you . . ."* and Preface |   a. Sursum Corda and Preface |
|   b. Words of Institution (preferably sung) |   b. Sanctus and Benedictus |
|   c. Sanctus, *"Holy, Holy, Holy . . ."* and Benedictus, *"Blessed is He who comes . . ."* (with elevation of body and blood) |   c. Canon of the Mass (numerous prayers referencing the Mass as a sacrifice for the living and dead; commemoration of angels and saints; numerous genuflections and sign of the cross; includes Words of Institution) |
|   d. Lord's Prayer |   d. Lord's Prayer |
|   e. Pax, *"The peace of the Lord . . ."* |   e. Pax |
|   f. Agnus Dei, *"Lamb of God . . ."* (sung by choir during administration) |   f. Agnus Dei |
|   g. Communion (antiphonal Psalm, during which priest communes first, then people) |   g. Communion |
|   h. Benedicamus, *"Let us bless the Lord"* (optional Alleluia in place of "Ite missa est," *"Go; it is the dismissal"*) |   h. Post-Communion prayer (and Benedicamus when Gloria is omitted at beginning of service) |
|   i. Aaronic Benediction, *"The Lord bless you and keep you . . ."* |   i. Deacon: "Ite missa est." Response: *"Thanks be to God."* |

## ARTICLE XXIV (XII)

# The Mass

Melanchthon asserts that Lutherans keep all the traditional forms of worship that do not conflict with the Gospel. The Zwinglian and Calvinistic branches of the Reformation tended toward "iconoclasm," that is, the rejection of pictures and statues of Christ and the saints, traditional clerical vestments, and other liturgical items. This same attitude prevailed when it came to the historic liturgy, whereby even what is perfectly biblical was stripped away. Unlike Zwinglianism and Calvinism, Lutheranism retained the historic aesthetic and liturgical forms of the Western Church, which had developed through pious use over the centuries.

In the Western Church, many abuses had become associated with the primary worship service, the Mass. Melanchthon rejects these abuses and explains how the Bible clearly declares that Christ's sacrifice on the cross was once-for-all-time. The Mass is a "sacrifice," Melanchthon maintains, but in the sense that we offer to God prayer, praise, and thanksgiving for what He has already done for us in Christ. While we do receive Christ's true body and blood in the Sacrament, the priest does not re-sacrifice Christ in the Mass. This is one of the most important articles in the Apology because it so clearly explains the two kinds of sacrifice and since many of Rome's false teachings and quite lucrative religious practices were connected with the Mass. (See also AC XXIV; SA II II; FC Ep X and SD X.)

------

1     At the outset, we must again make this preliminary statement: we do not abolish the Mass, but religiously keep and defend it. Masses are celebrated among us every Lord's Day and on the other festivals. The Sacrament is offered to those who wish to use it, after they have been examined and absolved. And the usual public ceremonies are observed, the series of lessons, of prayers, vestments, and other such things.

2     The adversaries have a long speech about the use of the Latin language in the Mass. In this speech, they joke about how it benefits an unlearned hearer to hear, in the faith of the Church, a Mass that he does not understand (cf. 1 Corinthians 14:9–12). They clearly imagine that the mere work of hearing is a service, that it benefits without being understood. 3 We are unwilling to rebelliously pursue these things, but we leave them to the judgment of the reader. We mention them only for the purpose of stating, in passing, that we keep also the Latin lessons and prayers.

However, ceremonies should be celebrated to teach people Scripture, that those admonished by the Word may conceive faith and godly fear, and may also pray. (This is the intent of ceremonies.) So, we keep the Latin language to aid those who are learning and understand Latin. We mix with it German hymns so that the people also may have something to learn, and by which faith and godly fear may be produced. 4 This custom has always existed in the churches. Some more frequently, and others more rarely, introduced German hymns into the service. Yet almost everywhere the people sang something in their own tongue. 5 However, it has never been written or presented that people benefit from hearing lessons they cannot understand or that ceremonies benefit, not because they teach or admonish, but by the outward act (*ex opere operato*) because they are performed that way or are looked upon. Away with such pharisaic opinions!

6     The fact that we hold only public or com-

mon Mass is no offense against the Church catholic. For even today private Masses are not held in the Greek churches. There is only a public Mass, and that on the Lord's Day and festivals. In the monasteries daily Mass is held, but this is only public. These are the traces of former customs. Before Gregory no 7 ancient writer mentions private Masses. We no longer recognize how they got started. Clearly after the begging monks came to power, mostly from false opinions and because of financial gain, private Masses increased to the point that for a long time all good people desired to set some limit on private Masses. St. Francis wished to correct this matter, so he decided that each fraternity should be content with a single, daily, common Mass. Later this was changed, either by superstition or for the sake of financial gain. 8 So, where it is advantageous to them, they themselves change the institutions of the Fathers. Later they cite the Fathers' authority against us. Epiphanius writes that in Asia Communion was celebrated three times a week, and that there were no daily Masses. Indeed, he says that this custom was handed down from the apostles. For he says, "Assemblies for Communion were set up by the apostles to be held on the fourth day, on the evening of the Sabbath, and on the Lord's Day."

9 The adversaries compile many references on this topic to prove that the Mass is a sacrifice. Yet this great war of words will be quieted when the single reply is put forward that this line of authorities, reasons, and references, however long, does not prove that the Mass bestows grace by the outward act (*ex opere operato*) or that, when applied on behalf of others, it merits the forgiveness of venial and mortal sins, of guilt and punishment for them. This one reply overthrows all objections of the adversaries, not only in this

Confutation, but in all writings about the Mass that they have published.

This is the issue our readers are to be re- 10 minded about. Aeschines reminded the judges that, just as boxers struggle with one another for their position, so they should labor with their adversaries about the disputed point and not permit him to wander beyond the discussion. In the same way our adversaries should be compelled to speak on the subject as presented. When the disputed point has been thoroughly understood, a decision about the arguments on both sides will be very easy.

We showed in our Confession our belief 11 that the Lord's Supper does not give grace by the outward act (*ex opere operato*) and that, when applied on behalf of others, alive or dead, it does not merit for them the forgiveness of sins, guilt, or punishment by the outward act. This position is supported by a 12 clear and firm proof. It is impossible to receive the forgiveness of our sins because of our own work by the outward act. The terrors of sin and death must be overcome through faith when we comfort our hearts with the knowledge of Christ and believe that for His sake we are forgiven and that His merits and righteousness are granted to us, "since we have been justified by faith, we have peace" (Romans 5:1). These things are so sure and so firm that they can stand against all the gates of hell (Matthew 16:18).

If we are to say only as much as is neces- 13 sary, the main point has already been stated. No sane person can accept that pharisaic and pagan opinion about the outward act (*opus operatum*). Yet, this opinion still exists among the people and has increased countlessly the number of Masses. For Masses are purchased to reconcile God's anger, and by this work they want to receive the forgiveness of guilt and of punishment. They want to obtain whatever is necessary in every kind of life. They even want to free the dead. Monks and philosophers have taught this pharisaic opinion in the Church.

14 Although our main point has already been stated, because the adversaries foolishly pervert many Scripture passages to defend their errors, we will add a few things on this topic. In the Confutation, they said many things about "sacrifice," although we purposely avoided this term in our Confession because of its ambiguity. We have presented what those persons (whose abuses we now condemn) understand by "sacrifice." To explain the Scripture passages that have been wickedly perverted, we must first present

15 what a sacrifice is. For ten years the adversaries have published many volumes about sacrifice, and yet not one of them so far has defined sacrifice. They only grab the word *sacrifices* either from the Scriptures or the Fathers. Afterward, they add their own thoughts, as though a sacrifice means whatever they please.

## What Is a Sacrifice, The Kinds of Sacrifice

16 In the *Phaedrus* of Plato, Socrates says that he is especially fond of distinctions, because without these nothing in speech can either be explained or understood. If he discovers anyone skilful in making distinctions, he says that he pays attention and follows his footsteps as those of a god. (He instructs the one to separate the parts of speech in their very joints. So like an inept cook, he breaks some part of speech to pieces.) But the adversaries truly hate these basic rules and, according to Plato, are truly poor butchers. For they break the parts of "sacrifice." This can be understood when we have listed the kinds of

17 sacrifice. Theologians are rightly familiar with distinguishing between a Sacrament

and a sacrifice. Therefore, let them be subdivided into either a ceremony or a sacred work. A Sacrament is a ceremony or work in 18 which God presents to us what the promise of the ceremony offers. Baptism is not a work that we offer to God. It is a work in which God baptizes us. In other words, a minister baptizes us on God's behalf. God here offers and presents the forgiveness of sins, and so forth, according to the promise "Whoever believes and is baptized will be saved" (Mark 16:16). A sacrifice, on the contrary, is a ceremony or work that we give to God in order to provide Him honor.

Furthermore, there are two kinds of sac- 19 rifice and no more. One is the *atoning sacrifice*, that is, a work that makes satisfaction for guilt and punishment. It reconciles God, or reconciles His wrath and merits the forgiveness of sins for others. The other kind is the *eucharistic sacrifice*, which does not merit the forgiveness of sins or reconciliation. It is practiced by those who have been reconciled, so that we may give thanks or return gratitude for the forgiveness of sins that has been received, or for other benefits received.

In this controversy, as well as in many 20 other discussions, we should especially have these two kinds of sacrifice in view and present them. Special care must be taken lest they should be confused. (If the limits of this book would permit it, we would add the reasons for this distinction. It has many references in the Epistle to the Hebrews and elsewhere.) All Levitical sacrifices can be referred 21 to either of these two distinctions. In the Law certain sacrifices were named *atoning* because of their meaning or by comparison. They were not called sacrifice because they merited the forgiveness of sins before God, but because they merited the forgiveness of sins according to the righteousness of the Law, so that those for whom they were made

The Last Supper

might not be excluded from that commonwealth (from the people of Israel). Therefore, for a trespass, the sacrifices were called sin offerings and burnt offerings. But the eucharistic sacrifices were the grain offering, the drink offering, thank offerings, firstfruits, tithes (Leviticus 1–7).

22    In fact there has been only one atoning sacrifice in the world, namely, Christ's death, as the Epistle to the Hebrews teaches, "It is impossible for the blood of bulls and goats to take away sins" (10:4). A little later, of the will of Christ, "By that will we have been sanctified through the offering of the body" (10:10). Isaiah interprets the Law, so that we

23    may know Christ's death is truly a satisfaction for our sins, or remedy, and that the ceremonies of the Law are not. He says, "When his soul makes an offering for sin, he shall see his offspring," and so on (Isaiah 53:10). The word used here means a victim for transgression (asham). In the Law this illustrated that a certain Victim was to come to make satisfaction for our sins and reconcile God. This was so that people might know that God wishes to be reconciled to us, not because of our own righteousnesses, but because of another's merits: Christ. Paul interprets the same word (asham) as sin, "For sin, he condemned sin" (Romans 8:3), that is, He punished sin for sin, that is, by a Victim for sin. The meaning of the word is more easily understood from pagan customs. These were adopted from their misunderstanding of statements by the Fathers. The Latins called a victim a piaculum, which was offered to reconcile God's anger in great calamities, where He seemed to be especially enraged. Sometimes they sacrificed human victims, perhaps because they had heard that a human victim would reconcile God for the entire human race. The Greeks sometimes called them cleansing (katharmata) and sometimes wiping away (peripsemata). Isaiah and Paul, therefore, mean that Christ became a victim, that is, a remedy, that by His merits, and not by our own, God might be reconciled. Let

24    this remain the case: Christ's death alone is truly an atoning sacrifice. For the Levitical atoning sacrifices were so called only to illustrate a future remedy. Because of a certain resemblance they were satisfactions delivering the righteousness of the Law and preventing those persons who sinned from being excluded from the commonwealth. But after the revelation of the Gospel, those sacrifices had to end. Since they had to end in the revelation of the Gospel, they were not true atoning sacrifices, for the Gospel was promised specifically to present an atoning sacrifice.

Now the rest are eucharistic sacrifices, 25 which are called sacrifices of praise (Leviticus 3; 7:11–18; Psalm 56:12). These are the preaching of the Gospel, faith, prayer, thanksgiving, confession, the troubles of saints, yes, all good works of saints. These sacrifices are not satisfactions for those making them, nor can they be applied to others to merit the forgiveness of sins or reconciliation by the outward act (ex opere operato). They are made by those who have been reconciled. These are the sacrifices of the New Testa-    26 ment, as Peter teaches, "a holy priesthood, to offer spiritual sacrifices" (1 Peter 2:5). Spiritual sacrifices, however, are contrasted not only with those of cattle, but even with human works offered by the outward act, because spiritual refers to the movements of the Holy Spirit in us. Paul teaches the same thing, "Present your bodies as a living sacrifice, holy and acceptable to God, which is your spiritual worship" (Romans 12:1). "Spiritual worship" means, however, a service in which God is known and is grasped by the mind. This happens in the movements of fear and trust toward God. Therefore, it contrasts not only with the Levitical service, in which cattle are slain, but also with a service in which a work is imagined to be offered by the outward act. The Epistle to the Hebrews teaches the same thing, "Through Him then let us continually offer up a sacrifice of praise to God" (13:15). He adds the interpretation, that is, the fruit of our lips, giving thanks to His name. He asks us to offer praises, that is, prayer, thanksgiving, confession, and the like. These benefit not by the outward act, but because of faith. This is taught by the clause "Through Him then let us continually offer," that is, by faith in Christ.

27    In short, the worship of the New Testament is spiritual. It is the righteousness of faith in the heart and the fruit of faith. New Testament worship sets aside Levitical services. Christ says, "True worshipers will worship the Father in spirit and truth, for the Father is seeking such people to worship Him. God is spirit, and those who worship Him must worship in spirit and truth" (John 4:23–24). This passage clearly condemns opinions about sacrifices that, as the adversaries imagine, benefit by the outward act (ex opere operato). In contrast, it teaches that people should worship in spirit, that is, with the in-

28    clinations of the heart and by faith. So, even in the Old Testament, the prophets condemn the opinion of the people about the outward act (opus operatum) and teach the righteousness and sacrifices of the Spirit. "I did not speak to your fathers or command them concerning burnt offerings and sacrifices. But this command I gave them: 'Obey My voice, and I will be your God,'" and so on (Jeremiah 7:22–23). How do we suppose that the Jews received this charge, which seems to conflict openly with Moses? God clearly gave the fathers commands about burnt offerings and victims. But Jeremiah condemns the

opinion about sacrifices that God had not delivered, namely, that these services please Him by the outward act. Concerning faith, he adds that God had commanded this: "Hear Me," that is, "believe Me that I am your God, and that I wish to be known when I care for you and help you. I do not need your sacrificial victims. Believe that I want to be God the Justifier and Savior, not because of works, but because of My Word and promise. Truly seek and expect help from Me from the heart."

29    Psalm 50:13–15, which rejects sacrificial victims and requires prayer, also condemns the opinion about the outward act (opus operatum): "Do I eat the flesh of bulls . . .?" "Call upon Me in the day of trouble; I will deliver you, and you shall glorify Me." The psalmist testifies that this is true service and true honor if we call upon Him from the heart.

Likewise, "Sacrifice and offering You have not desired, but You have given me an open ear" (Psalm 40:6), that is, "You have offered me Your Word that I may hear it, and You do require that I believe Your Word and Your promises. You truly desire to care for me and to help," and so on. Likewise, "You will not be pleased with a burnt offering. The sacrifices of God are a broken spirit; a broken and contrite heart, O God, You will not despise" (Psalm 51:16–17). "Offer right sacrifices, and put your trust in the LORD" (Psalm 4:5). He asks us to hope, and says that this is a righteous sacrifice, meaning that other sacrifices are not true and righteous sacrifices. And, "I will offer to You the sacrifice of thanksgiving and call on the name of the LORD" (Psalm 116:17).

30    Scripture is full of such references that teach that sacrifices by the outward act (ex opere operato) do not reconcile God. Since Levitical services have been repealed, the

New Testament teaches that new and pure sacrifices will be made: faith, prayer, thanksgiving, confession, the preaching of the Gospel, troubles on account of the Gospel, and the like.

31    Malachi speaks about these sacrifices, "For from the rising of the sun to its setting My name will be great among the nations, and in every place incense will be offered to My name, and a pure offering" (1:11). The adversaries perversely apply this passage to the Mass and quote the authority of the Fathers. A reply, however, is easy. Even if this passage spoke most particularly about the Mass, it would not make sense that the Mass justifies by the outward act (*ex opere operato*) or that, when applied to others, it merits the forgiveness of sins. The prophet says nothing about those things that the monks and

32   philosophers rudely make up. Besides, the very words of the prophet express his meaning. First, his words say this: the name of the Lord will be great. This is accomplished by the preaching of the Gospel. Through this preaching, Christ's name is made known and the Father's mercy, promised in Christ, is recognized. The preaching of the Gospel produces faith in those who receive the Gospel (Romans 10:17). They call upon God, give thanks to God, bear troubles for their confession, and produce good works for Christ's glory. So the name of the Lord becomes great among the Gentiles (Malachi 1:11). Therefore, *incense* and a *pure offering* means not a ceremony by the outward act, but all those sacrifices through which the name of the Lord becomes great: faith, invocation, the preaching of the Gospel, confession, and so

33   on. If anyone would have this term include the ceremony (of the Mass), we readily concede it, provided he neither understands the ceremony alone nor teaches that the ceremony benefits by the outward act. We include

the preaching of the Word among the sacrifices of praise, that is, among the praises of God. So the reception itself of the Lord's Supper can be praise or thanksgiving. But it does not justify by the outward act, neither is it to be applied to others to merit the forgiveness of sins for them. Later we will explain how even a ceremony is a sacrifice. Malachi speaks about all the services of the New Testament, and not only about the Lord's Supper. Likewise, since he does not favor the pharisaic opinion of the outward act (*opus operatum*), he is not against us, but rather helps us. He requires services of the heart, through which the name of the Lord becomes truly great.

Another passage also is cited from   34
Malachi, "He will purify the sons of Levi and refine them like gold and silver, and they will bring offerings in righteousness" (3:3). This passage clearly requires the sacrifices of the righteous, and so does not favor the opinion about the outward act (*opus operatum*). But the sacrifices of the sons of Levi, that is, of those teaching in the New Testament, are the preaching of the Gospel and the good fruit of preaching. About this Paul says, "To be a minister of Christ Jesus to the Gentiles in the priestly service of the gospel of God, so that the offering of the Gentiles may be acceptable, sanctified by the Holy Spirit" (Romans 15:16). He means that the Gentiles may be offerings acceptable to God through faith. In the Law the slaying of victims illustrated both Christ's death and the preaching of the Gospel, by which this old flesh should be put to death and new and eternal life be begun in us.

But everywhere the adversaries wrongly apply the name *sacrifice* to the ceremony alone. They leave out the preaching of the Gospel, faith, prayer, and similar things, although the ceremony has been established because of these. The New Testament should have sacrifices of the heart, not ceremonies for sin that are to be performed like the Levitical priesthood.

35 They cite also the *daily sacrifice*. (See Exodus 29:38–39; Daniel 8:11; 12:11.) Just as there was a daily sacrifice in the Law, so the Mass should be a daily sacrifice of the New Testament. The adversaries have made out well if we allow ourselves to be overcome by allegories. Clearly allegories do not produce firm proofs. We readily allow the Mass to be understood as a daily sacrifice, as long as that includes the entire Mass: the ceremony with the preaching of the Gospel, faith, invocation, and thanksgiving. Joined together, these are a daily sacrifice of the New Testament because the ceremony of the Mass, or the Lord's Supper, was set up because of these things. The Mass is not to be separated from them. So Paul says, "For as often as you eat this bread and drink the cup, you proclaim the Lord's death until He comes" (1 Corinthians 11:26). But it cannot be shown from this Levitical type that a ceremony justifying by the outward work (*ex opere operato*) is necessary, or should be applied on behalf of others, that it may merit the forgiveness of sins for them.

36 The type represents appropriately not only the ceremony, but also the preaching of the Gospel. In Numbers 28:4–8, three parts of that daily sacrifice are represented: the burning of the lamb, the drink offering, and the offering of wheat flour. The Law had pictures or shadows of future things (Colossians 2:17). So Christ and the entire worship of the New Testament are shown in this picture. The burning of the lamb illustrates Christ's death. The drink offering illustrates that everywhere in the entire world, by the preaching of the Gospel, believers are sprinkled with the blood of that Lamb, that is,

sanctified. Peter says, "In the sanctification of the Spirit, for obedience to Jesus Christ and for sprinkling with His blood" (1 Peter 1:2). The offering of wheat flour means faith, prayer, and thanksgiving in hearts. There- 37 fore, in the Old Testament, the shadow is discerned. In the New, the thing illustrated should be sought, and not another type, as sufficient for a sacrifice.

Although a ceremony is a memorial of 38 Christ's death, it alone is not the daily sacrifice. The memory itself is the daily sacrifice, that is, preaching and faith. Faith truly believes that, by Christ's death, God has been reconciled. A drink offering is required, that is, the effect of preaching, in order that, being sprinkled by the Gospel with the blood of Christ, we may be sanctified, as those put to death and made alive. Offerings also are required, that is, thanksgiving, confessions, and troubles.

The pharisaic opinion of the outward act 39 (*opus operatum*) being cast aside, let us understand that spiritual worship and a daily sacrifice of the heart are meant, because in the New Testament the substance of good things should be sought for. This means the Holy Spirit, putting the flesh to death, and new life. These things should make it clear 40 that the type of the daily sacrifice declares nothing against us, but rather for us, because we look for all the parts illustrated by the daily sacrifice. The adversaries falsely imagine that the ceremony alone is meant, and not also the preaching of the Gospel, putting the flesh to death, and enlivening of heart, and so forth.

Now, good people, it can easily be deter- 41 mined that the complaint against us—that we abolish the daily sacrifice—is entirely false. Experience shows what sort of Antiochi they are who hold power in the Church. Under the appearance of religion, they assume to themselves the kingdom of the world. They rule without concern for religion and the teaching of the Gospel. They wage war like kings of the world, and they set 42 up new services in the Church. The adversaries keep only the ceremony in the Mass and publicly apply this to sacrilegious gain. Afterward, they misrepresent that this work, as applied for others, merits grace and all 43 good things for them. They do not teach the Gospel in their sermons, they do not comfort consciences, they do not show that sins are freely forgiven for Christ's sake. Rather, they present the worship of saints, human satisfactions, and human traditions, and they affirm that people are justified before God by these. Although some of these traditions are clearly godless, they still defend them by violence. If any preacher wants to be regarded as more learned, he presents philosophical questions, which neither the people nor even those who propose them understand. Lastly, those who are more tolerable teach the Law and say nothing about the righteousness of faith.

44 In the Confutation, the adversaries fuss over the desertion of churches. Altars stand unadorned, lacking candles and images. They regard these trifles as ornaments to 45 churches. It is a far different desertion that Daniel means (11:31; 12:11), namely, ignorance of the Gospel. Overwhelmed by the multitude and variety of traditions and opinions, the people were in no way able to wel-46 come the sum of Christian doctrine. Among the people, who ever understood the doctrine of repentance as presented by the adversaries? Yet this is the chief topic of Christian doctrine.

Consciences were tormented by the listing of offenses and by satisfactions. The adversaries never mention faith, by which we freely receive the forgiveness of sins. All the

books and all the sermons of the adversaries were silent about the exercises of faith, struggling with despair, and the free forgiveness of sins for Christ's sake. To these, 47 the horrible profanation of the Masses and many other godless services in the churches were added. This is the desertion described by Daniel.

On the contrary, by God's favor, our 48 priests attend to the ministry of the Word, teach the Gospel about Christ's blessings, and show that the forgiveness of sins happens freely for Christ's sake. This doctrine brings sure comfort to consciences. The doctrine of good works that God commands is also added. The worth and use of the Sacraments are declared.

If the daily sacrifice was the proper use of 49 the Sacrament, we would keep the sacrifice. The adversaries would not. For their priests use the Sacrament to make money. There is a more frequent and more conscientious use. The people use it after having first been instructed and examined. People are taught about the true use of the Sacrament. It was set up to be a seal and testimony of the free forgiveness of sins, and so that it should remind alarmed consciences to be truly confident and believe that their sins are freely forgiven. Since we keep both the preaching of the Gospel and the lawful use of the Sacrament, the daily sacrifice remains with us.

If we must speak of outward appearances, 50 Church attendance among us is better than among the adversaries. The audiences are held by useful and clear sermons. (Neither the people nor the teachers have ever understood the doctrine of the adversaries.) The 51 true adornment of the churches is godly, useful, and clear doctrine, the devout use of the Sacraments, fervent prayer, and the like. Candles and similar adornments are fitting, but they are not the proper adornment belonging to the Church. If the adversaries make these things the focus of worship, and not the preaching of the Gospel, in faith (and the struggles of faith) they are to be numbered among those whom Daniel describes as worshiping their god with gold and silver (Daniel 11:38).

52 They quote also from the Epistle to the Hebrews, "For every high priest chosen from among men is appointed to act on behalf of men in relation to God, to offer gifts and sacrifices for sins" (5:1). They conclude that, since there are high priests and priests in the New Testament, that means there is also a sacrifice for sins. This passage particularly impresses the unlearned, especially when the showiness of the priesthood and the sacrifices of the Old Testament are spread before the eyes. This resemblance deceives the ignorant, so that they decide that a ceremonial sacrifice should also exist among us in the same way, which should be applied for the sins of others, like in the Old Testament. The service of the Mass and the rest of the polity of the pope is nothing more than false zeal for the misunderstood Levitical order.

53 The main proofs for our belief are in the Epistle to the Hebrews. Yet, the adversaries twist mutilated passages from this Epistle against us, as in this very passage, where it is said that every high priest is ordained to offer sacrifices for sins. Scripture immediately adds that Christ is the High Priest (Hebrews 5:5–6, 10). The preceding words speak about the Levitical priesthood and show that the Levitical priesthood was an image of Christ's priesthood. The Levitical sacrifices for sins did not merit the forgiveness of sins before God. They were only an image of Christ's sacrifice, which was to be the one atoning 54 sacrifice, as we said before. To a great extent the Epistle speaks about how the ancient priesthood and the ancient sacrifices were set

up not to merit the forgiveness of sins before God or reconciliation, but only to illustrate the future sacrifice of Christ alone. In the Old 55 Testament, saints had to be justified by faith, which receives the promise of the forgiveness of sins granted for Christ's sake, just as saints are also justified in the New Testament. From the beginning of the world all saints had to believe that Christ would be the promised offering and satisfaction for sins, as Isaiah 53:10 teaches, "when His soul makes an offering for sin."

In the Old Testament, sacrifices did not 56 merit reconciliation, except as a picture (for they merited civil reconciliation), but they illustrated the coming sacrifice. This means that Christ is the only sacrifice applied on behalf of the sins of others. Therefore, in the New Testament, no sacrifice is left to be applied for the sins of others, except the one sacrifice of Christ upon the cross.

Those who imagine that Levitical sacri- 57 fices merited the forgiveness of sins before God, and by this example require sacrifices in the New Testament that are to be applied on behalf of others in addition to Christ's death, are completely mistaken. This imagination absolutely destroys the merit of Christ's passion and the righteousness of faith, and it corrupts the doctrine of the Old and New Testaments. Instead of Christ, it makes for us other mediators and atonement makers out of the priests and sacrificers, who daily sell their work in the churches.

If anyone argues that in the New Testa- 58 ment a priest is needed to make offering for sins, this can only be said about Christ. The entire Epistle to the Hebrews confirms this explanation. In addition to Christ's death, if we were to look for any other satisfaction that applies to the sins of others and so to reconcile God, this would be nothing more than to make other mediators in addition to Christ.

59 The priesthood of the New Testament is the Spirit's ministry, as Paul teaches (2 Corinthians 3:6). So it has only Christ's one sacrifice, which is enough and applies to the sins of others. Besides, this priesthood has no sacrifices like the Levitical order, which could be applied by the outward act (*ex opere operato*) to others. Rather, it offers the Gospel and the Sacraments to others, so that they may conceive faith and the Holy Spirit through them and be brought from death to life. So the Spirit's ministry conflicts with the application of an outward act (*opus operatum*). The Spirit's ministry is that through which the Holy Spirit is powerful in hearts. Therefore, this ministry is beneficial to others when it is powerful in them and regenerates and enlivens them. This does not happen by applying someone's work to another.

60 We have shown why the Mass does not justify by the outward act (*ex opere operato*) and why, when applied to others, it does not merit forgiveness. This is because both conflict with the righteousness of faith. For it is impossible that sins should be forgiven and the terrors of death and sin be overcome by anything other than faith in Christ, according to Romans 5:1, "Since we have been justified by faith, we have peace."

61 Also, we have shown that the Scriptures, which are quoted against us, do not approve the godless opinion of the adversaries about the outward act (*opus operatum*). Every person everywhere can determine this. There-

62 fore, Thomas's error is to be rejected. He wrote:

> That the body of the Lord, once offered on the cross for original debt, is continually offered for daily offenses on the altar, in order that, in this, the Church might have a service by which to reconcile God to herself.

63 The other common errors are also to be rejected, such as that the Mass by the outward act (*ex opere operato*) gives grace to the one using it. Or, that when the Mass is applied for others (even wicked persons, provided they do not introduce an obstacle), it merits the forgiveness of sins, guilt, and punishment for them. All these things are false and godless and are recently invented by unlearned monks. They cloud over the glory of Christ's passion and the righteousness of faith.

64 From these errors sprang countless others, such as Masses benefit when applied for many, just as much as when applied individually. The philosophers have particular degrees of merit, just as moneychangers have varying weights for gold or silver. Besides, they sell the Mass as the cost for receiving what each one seeks. Merchants pay so that business may be prosperous, hunters so that hunting may be successful, and countless other things. Finally, they also apply it to the dead. By applying the Sacrament, they free souls from the pains of purgatory, even though the Mass does not even help the living without faith. The adversaries are unable

65 to produce even one syllable from the Scriptures to defend these fables, which they teach with great authority in the Church. They do not have the testimonies of the ancient Church or of the Fathers.

### What the Fathers Thought about Sacrifice

66 Since we have explained the Scripture passages that are quoted against us, we must also reply about the Fathers. We know well that the Fathers call the Mass a sacrifice. Yet, they do not mean that the Mass gives grace by the outward act (*ex opere operato*) and that, when applied to others, it merits the forgiveness of sins, guilt, and punishment for

them. Where can such freakish stories be found in the Fathers? The adversaries openly declare that they speak about thanksgiving. 67 So they call it a *eucharist*. However, we have said before that a eucharistic sacrifice does not merit reconciliation, but is made by those who have been reconciled, just as troubles do not merit reconciliation, but are eucharistic sacrifices when those who have been reconciled tolerate them.

In general, this reply to the sayings of the Fathers defends us well enough against the adversaries. Certainly these daydreams about the merit of the outward act (*opus operatum*) cannot be found in the Fathers. But so that the whole matter may be better understood, we will also state those things that actually agree with the Fathers and Scripture about the use of the Sacrament.

### The Use of the Sacrament: The Sacrifice

68    Some clever men imagine that the Lord's Supper was set up for two reasons. First, that it might be a mark and reference of profession, just as a particular shape of a hood is the sign of a particular monastic profession. Second, they think that such a mark was especially pleasing to Christ, namely, a feast to illustrate mutual union and friendship among Christians, because banquets are signs of covenant and friendship. But this is a secular view. It does not show the chief use of the things delivered by God. It speaks only about the exercise of love, which people, however profane and worldly, understand. It does not speak of faith, the nature of which few understand.

69    The Sacraments are signs of God's will toward us and not merely signs of people among one another. Those who define Sacraments in the New Testament as signs of grace are correct. There are two things in a Sacrament: a sign and the Word. In the New Testa-

ment, the Word is the promise of grace added. The promise of the New Testament is the promise of the forgiveness of sins, "This is My body, which is given for you. This [cup] is My blood of the new testament, which is shed for you for the forgiveness of sins." (See Matthew 26:26–28; Mark 14:22–24; Luke 22:19–20; 1 Corinthians 11:24–25.) So the 70 Word offers the forgiveness of sins. A ceremony is a sort of picture, or seal, as Paul (Romans 4:11) calls it, the Word making known the promise. Therefore, just as the promise is useless unless it is received through faith, so a ceremony is useless unless faith, which is truly confident that the forgiveness of sins is here offered, is added. This faith encourages penitent minds. Just as the Word has been given to excite this faith, so the Sacrament has been set up so that what meets the eyes might move the heart to believe. The Holy Spirit works through these: Word and Sacrament.

Such a use of the Sacrament, in which 71 faith enlivens terrified hearts, is a service of the New Testament. That is because the New Testament requires spiritual inclinations, making dead and alive. Christ instituted the Sacrament for this use, since He commanded the disciples to do this in remembrance of Him. Remembering Christ is not the useless 72 celebration of a show. It is not something set up for the sake of example, as the memory of Hercules or Ulysses is celebrated in tragedies. Rather, it is remembering Christ's benefits and receiving them through faith, to be enlivened by them. So Psalm 111:4–5 says, "He has caused His wondrous works to be remembered; the LORD is gracious and merciful. He provides food for those who fear Him." The Sacrament illustrates that God's will and mercy should be discerned in the ceremony. Faith that grasps mercy enlivens. 73 This is the chief use of the Sacrament. It is clear who are fit for the Sacrament (namely, terrified consciences) and how they should use it.

74　　The sacrifice also is added. For there are several reasons with one purpose. After a conscience encouraged through faith has determined from what terrors it is freed, it fervently gives thanks for Christ's benefit and passion. It also uses the ceremony itself to God's praise, to show its gratitude by this obedience. It declares that it holds God's gifts in high esteem. So the ceremony becomes a sacrifice of praise.

75　　The Fathers certainly speak of a twofold effect: the comfort of consciences and thanksgiving, or praise. The former of these effects has to do with the nature of the Sacrament; the latter has to do with the sacrifice. Ambrose says about comfort:

> Go to Him and be absolved, because He is the forgiveness of sins. Do you ask who He is? Hear Him when He says, "I am the bread of life; whoever comes to Me shall not hunger, and whoever believes in Me shall never thirst" (John 6:35).

This passage declares that the forgiveness of sins is offered in the Sacrament. It also declares that this should be received through faith. Countless references with this meaning are found in the Fathers, all of which the adversaries pervert to the outward act (*opus operatum*) and to a work applied to others. Yet the Fathers clearly require faith and speak of the comfort belonging to everyone, and not of the application.

76　　Besides these, expressions are also found about thanksgiving. One beautiful expression by Cyprian is about those communing in a godly way. "Piety, in thanking the Bestower of such abundant blessing, makes a distinction between what has been given and what has been forgiven." This means piety regards both what has been given and what has been forgiven, that is, it compares the greatness of God's blessings and the greatness of our evils, sin and death, with each other, and gives thanks, and so on. In this way the term *eucharist* arose in the Church. Certainly the 77 ceremony itself—the giving of thanks by the outward act (*ex opere operato*)—does not apply to others. It does not merit the forgiveness of sins for others and free souls of the dead. These opinions conflict with the righteousness of faith. Without faith, a ceremony cannot benefit either the one performing it or others.

### The Term *Mass*

The adversaries also refer us to linguistics. 78 They get arguments from the names of the Mass, which do not require a long discussion. For even though the Mass is called a sacrifice, it does not make sense that it must give grace by the outward act (*ex opere operato*) or, when applied to others, merits the forgiveness of sins for them. *Leitourgia*, they say, 79 means a sacrifice, and the Greeks call the Mass *liturgy*. (Why do they leave out here the old name *synaxis*, which shows that the Mass used to be the communion of many?) Let us discuss the word *liturgy*. This word 80 does not properly mean a sacrifice, but rather the public ministry. Liturgy agrees well with our belief that one minister offers the body and blood of the Lord to the rest of the people, just as one minister who preaches offers the Gospel to the people. As Paul says, "This is how one should regard us, as servants of Christ and stewards of the mysteries of God" (1 Corinthians 4:1), that is, of the Gospel and the Sacraments. And, "We are ambassadors for Christ, God making His appeal through us. We implore you on behalf of Christ, be reconciled to God" (2 Corinthians 5:20).

81 So the term *leitourgia* agrees well with the ministry. For it is an old word, ordinarily used in public civil administrations. To the Greeks it meant public burdens, such as tribute, the expense of equipping a fleet, or similar things. *For Leptines,* the oration of Demosthenes, speaks about such things, discussing at length public duties and exemptions: "He will say that some unworthy men, having found an exemption, have withdrawn from public burdens." And so they spoke in the time of the Romans, as the reply of Pertinax, *On the Law of Exemption,* shows: "Even though the number of children does not liberate parents from all public burdens." And the Commentary on Demosthenes states that *leitourgia* is a kind of tribute, the expense of the games, the expense of equipping vessels, of attending to the gymnasia and similar

82 public offices. In 2 Corinthians 9:12, Paul uses it for a collection. Taking a collection not only supplies those things that the saints lack, but also causes them to give more thanks abundantly to God. In Philippians 2:25, he calls Epaphroditus a "minister to my need," where certainly a sacrificer cannot be

83 understood. Further references are not needed, since examples are understandable for those reading the Greek writers, in whom *leitourgia* is used for public civil burdens or ministries. Because of the pair of vowels, grammarians do not get this term from *lite*, which means prayers, but from public goods, which they call leita, so that *leitourgeo* means "I pay attention to," or "I administer public goods."

84 Their conclusion that, since the Holy Scriptures mention an altar, the Mass must be a sacrifice is ridiculous. Paul refers to the

85 figure of an altar only by comparison. They invent the idea that the Mass was named from an altar (*midzbeah*). Why do they need such far-fetched sources for words unless

they want to show their knowledge of the Hebrew language? Why seek the sources for words from a distance when the term *Mass* is found in Deuteronomy 16:10, where it means the collections or gifts of the people, not the offering of the priest? Individuals coming to the celebration of the Passover were obliged to bring some gift as a contribution. Early Christians also kept this cus-  86 tom. Coming together, they brought bread, wine, and other things, as the canons of the apostles declare. From there a portion was taken to be consecrated; the rest was given out to the poor. With this custom they also kept *Mass* as the name of the contributions. Because of such contributions, it appears also that in other places the Mass was called *agape,* unless one would prefer that it was so called because of the common feast. Let us  87 leave out these silly things. It is ridiculous that the adversaries should produce such trifling guesses about such an important matter. Although the Mass is called an offering, how does the term favor the dreams about the outward act (*opus operatum*), and their application, which merits the forgiveness of sins for others? Can it be called an offering because prayers, thanksgivings, and the entire worship are offered there, as it is also called a eucharist? Neither ceremonies nor prayers benefit by the outward act (*ex opere operato*) without faith. We are not arguing here about prayers, but particularly about the Lord's Supper.

The Greek canon also says many things  88 about the offering, but it plainly shows that it is not speaking properly of the body and blood of the Lord, but of the whole service, of prayers and thanksgivings. For it says this, "Make us worthy to bring to You prayers and requests and bloodless sacrifices on behalf of all people." When this is rightly understood, it is not offensive. It prays that we be made worthy to *offer prayers* and supplications and bloodless sacrifices for the people. He calls even prayers "bloodless sacrifices." Just as also a little afterward, "We offer," he says, "this reasonable and bloodless service." Those who would rather interpret this as a reasonable sacrifice, and transfer it to Christ's very body, do so inappropriately. The canon speaks of the entire worship, and in opposition to the outward act (*opus operatum*) Paul has spoken of reasonable service (*logike latreia*; Romans 12:1), namely, of the worship of the mind, of fear, of faith, of prayer, of thanksgiving, and so on.

### The Mass for the Dead

89    Our adversaries have no references and no command from Scripture for defending the use of the ceremony for freeing the souls of the dead. Yet they receive unlimited revenue from this. Certainly it is no light sin to establish such services in the Church without God's command and without the example of Scripture and to apply the Lord's Supper to the dead. (It was set up for commemoration and preaching among the living.) This violates the Second Commandment by abusing God's name.

First, it dishonors the Gospel to hold that a ceremony by the outward act (*ex opere operato*), without faith, is a sacrifice reconciling God and making satisfaction for sins. It is a horrible saying to assign as much importance to the work of a priest as to Christ's death. Again, sin and death cannot be overcome except by faith in Christ, as Paul teaches, "Since we have been justified by faith, we have peace with God" (Romans 5:1). Therefore, the punishment of purgatory cannot be overcome by applying to one person the work of another.

90    Now we will leave out the sort of references about purgatory that the adversaries have, what kinds of punishments they think there are in purgatory, what grounds the doctrine of satisfactions has, which we have shown above to be most empty. We will only present the following in opposition. Certainly the Lord's Supper was set up because of the pardon of guilt. It offers the forgiveness of sins, where it is necessary that guilt be truly understood. Yet, it does not make satisfaction for guilt; otherwise, the Mass would be equal to Christ's death. The pardon of guilt can be received only through faith. Therefore, the Mass is not a satisfaction, but a promise and Sacrament that require faith.

91    Certainly all godly persons should be seized with the bitterest grief if they consider that the greater portion of the Mass has been transferred to the dead and to satisfactions for punishments. This banishes the daily sacrifice from the Church. This is the kingdom of Antiochus, who transferred the most beneficial promises about the pardon of guilt and about faith to the emptiest opinions about satisfactions. This pollutes the Gospel and corrupts the use of the Sacraments. Paul said that these persons are "guilty of profaning the body and blood of the Lord" (1 Corinthians 11:27). They have hindered the doctrine about faith and the forgiveness of sins and, under the appearance of satisfactions, have devoted the Lord's body and blood to sacrilegious profit. At some time they will pay the penalty for this sacrilege. Therefore, we and all godly consciences should guard against approving the abuses of the adversaries.

92    Let us return to the matter. The Mass is not a satisfaction, either for punishment or for guilt, without faith (*ex opere operato*). Therefore, applying it to the dead is useless. There is no need here of a longer discussion. Clearly these applications for the dead have no references from the Scriptures. Neither is

it safe, without the authority of Scripture, to set up forms of worship in the Church. If it is ever necessary, we will speak at greater length about this entire subject. Why should we now argue with adversaries who misunderstand sacrifice, Sacrament, the forgiveness of sins, and faith?

93    The Greek canon does not apply the offering as a satisfaction for the dead because it applies it equally for all the blessed patriarchs, prophets, and apostles. Apparently the Greeks make an offering as thanksgiving and do not apply it as satisfaction for punishments. Furthermore, they do not speak of offering solely the Lord's body and blood, but of the other parts of the Mass, namely, prayers and thanksgiving. After the consecra-tion they pray that it may benefit those who partake of it; they do not speak of others. Then they add:

> Yet we offer to you this reasonable service for those having departed in faith, forefathers, fathers, patriarchs, prophets, apostles.

"Reasonable service" (Romans 12:1), however, does not mean the offering itself, but prayers and all things that are preferred there. Regarding the adversaries' quoting the 94 Fathers about the offering for the dead, we know that the ancients speak of prayer for the dead, which we do not ban. We disapprove of applying the Lord's Supper for the dead by the outward act (*ex opere operato*).

Elijah versus the Prophets of Baal

The ancients do not favor the adversaries regarding the outward act (*opus operatum*). Even though they have the references especially of Gregory or the moderns, we hold up to them the most clear and certain Scrip-

95 tures. There is a great diversity among the Fathers. They were men and could err and be deceived. If they were alive now and would see their sayings assigned as falsehood for the scandalous lies that the adversaries teach about the outward act (*opus operatum*), they would interpret themselves far differently.

96    The adversaries also falsely quote against us the condemnation of Aerius, who, they say, was condemned for denying that an offering is made for the living and the dead in the Mass. They often use this clever turn: quote the ancient heresies and falsely compare our cause with them to crush us by this comparison. Epiphanius declares that Aerius maintained prayers for the dead are useless. He finds fault with this. We do not favor Aerius either, but we do argue with you because you defend a heresy that clearly conflicts with the prophets, apostles, and Holy Fathers. This heresy is that the Mass justifies by the outward act (*ex opere operato*), that when applied it merits the pardon of guilt and punishment even for the unjust if they do not present an obstacle. We object to these deadly errors, which divert people from the glory of Christ's passion and entirely overthrow the doctrine about the

97 righteousness of faith. In the Law, the godless had a similar belief. That is, they believed they merited the forgiveness of sins, not freely through faith, but through sacrifices by the outward act. Therefore, they increased these services and sacrifices, set up the worship of Baal in Israel, and even sacrificed in the groves in Judah. Therefore, the prophets condemn this belief and war

against not only the worshipers of Baal, but also other priests who made sacrifices ordained by God with this godless belief (cf. 1 Kings 18:1–40). This belief, that such services and sacrifices atone, remains and always will remain in the world. Carnal people cannot tolerate that the honor of an atoning sacrifice belongs solely to Christ's sacrifice because they do not understand the righteousness of faith. Rather, they assign equal honor to the rest of the services and sacrifices. The godless priests in Judah 98 held a false belief about such sacrifices; Baal worship even continued in Israel. Nevertheless, a Church of God was there that objected to these godless services (1 Kings 19:18). Baal worship remains in the realm of the pope: the abuse of the Mass. By it they think they can merit the pardon of guilt and punishment for the unrighteous. It seems that this Baal worship will persist as long as the reign of the pope. It will continue until Christ comes to judge and by the glory of His return destroy the reign of the Antichrist (2 Thessalonians 2:1–8). Meanwhile, all who truly believe the Gospel should condemn these wicked services. Against God's command, they were created to cloud over Christ's glory and the righteousness of faith.

We have briefly said these things about 99 the Mass for the following reasons. First, we hope that all good people everywhere understand that we keep the dignity of the Mass and show its true use with the greatest zeal. Second, our reasons for disagreeing with the adversaries are most just. Further, we would encourage all good people not to help the adversaries in the profanation of the Mass, burdening themselves with other people's sin. This is an important cause and an important subject, no less important than the work of the prophet Elijah, who condemned the worship of Baal. We have presented this important discussion with the greatest restraint and now reply without using abusive words. But if the adversaries push us to collect all kinds of abuses of the Mass, we will not present the discussion with such toleration.

## ARTICLE XXVII (XIII)

# Monastic Vows

The Pontifical Confutation, as one would have expected, rejects the Augsburg Confession's position on monasticism. Melanchthon's additional comments explain the biblical reasons why Lutheranism does not, and cannot, condone or support the view that monasticism is a "higher calling" than other vocations. The key point again is the Roman assertion that monasticism and the practices, promises, and customs associated with it are means by which people can merit God's grace and forgiveness. Lutheranism restored to the Church a proper regard for how men and women should, can, and do serve God in all the various callings and stations in life. (See also AC XXV and XXVII; SA III VIII and XIV; SC Table of Duties.)

1    To our knowledge there was a monk named John Hilten in the Thuringian town of Eisenach. Thirty years ago, he was thrown into prison by his religious order because he had condemned certain scandalous abuses. We have seen his writings, which clearly explain the nature of his doctrine. Those who knew him declare that he was mild in his old 2 age and serious indeed, but not gloomy. He predicted many things, some of which have already happened. Others still seem close at hand, but we do not want to repeat them, lest it may be inferred that they are told either from hatred toward one or from preference toward another. Finally, either because of his age or the foulness of the prison, he became ill. He sent for the guard to tell him of his sickness. Inflamed with pharisaic hatred, the guard began to rebuke the man harshly because of his kind of doctrine, which seemed to interfere with the work of the kitchen. Without mentioning his sickness, Hilten said with a sigh that he was patiently bearing these injuries for Christ's sake, since he had neither written nor taught anything that could undermine the monastic life, but had only criticized some well-known abuses. "Another one," he said, "will come in AD 3 1516. He will destroy you, and you will be unable to resist him." Later, his friends found this very prediction about the declining influence of the monastic orders and the very date written in his surviving commentaries dealing with certain passages of Daniel. The 4 outcome will show how much emphasis should be given to this declaration, yet there are other signs that threaten a change in the monks' power, no less certain than oracles. It is clear how much hypocrisy, ambition, and greed there are in the monasteries, how much ignorance and cruelty exists among all the unlearned, what pride there is in their sermons, and how they continually create new ways of making money. There are other faults, which we do not care to mention. Monasteries were schools for Christian in- 5 struction; now they have deteriorated, as though from a golden to an iron age (or as Plato says, the cube deteriorates into bad harmonies bringing destruction). All the most wealthy monasteries support only a lazy crowd, which gorges itself upon the public alms of the Church. Christ, however, teaches 6 that the salt that has lost its savor should be cast out and be trodden underfoot (Matthew 5:13). By such morals the monks are singing their own fate (a requiem, and it will soon be over with them). Now another sign is added, 7

Martin Luther, 1520

Lucas Cranach the Elder portrays Luther as he appeared in 1520, with Augustinian monk's hood (cowl) and haircut (tonsure). Luther dressed as a monk until October 9, 1524, when he first appeared in public in Wittenberg wearing secular clothing. A week later he discarded his cowl permanently. He had continued to dress and live as a monk for the sake of the weak, but realized that old believers interpreted his behavior as uncertainty about his teachings. His friend James Propst, former Augustinian monk, challenged him to practice his teachings. After 1524 Luther dressed as a doctor of theology [see color plate 9] and appeared that way until his death (1546).

because in many places, they are the instigators of the death of good men. No doubt, God

8 will soon avenge these murders. Certainly we do not accuse every one of them, for here and there some good men in the monasteries decide fairly about human and "factitious" services, as some writers call them, and do not approve the cruelty exercised by the hypocrites among them.

9 Now we are discussing the kind of teaching that the writers of the Confutation defend, not the question of whether vows should be kept. We hold that legitimate vows should be kept. However, we are discussing different questions: Can these services merit the forgiveness of sins and justification? Are they satisfactions for sins? Are they equal to Baptism? Are they the obedience to basic rules and counsels? Are they evangelical perfection? Do they have the merits of superabundance? Do these merits, when applied to others, save them? Are vows made with these beliefs legitimate? Are vows legitimate that are made under the appearance of religion, merely for the sake of the belly and laziness? Are those true vows that have been forced either from the unwilling or from those who because of age were not able to understand this kind of life, whom parents or friends thrust into the monasteries so that they might be supported at public expense, without the loss of their private inheritance? Are vows legitimate that openly come to a bad end, either because they are not kept due to weakness, or because those in the monastic orders are pushed to approve and help the abuses of the Mass, the godless worship of saints, and the counsels attacking good peo-

10 ple? We have said many things in the Confession about such vows that even the canons of the popes condemn. Yet, the adversaries command that everything we have produced must be rejected. They have used these words.

It is worthwhile to hear how they distort our reasoning and what they mention to support their own case. So we will briefly review a few of our arguments. In passing, we will explain away the adversaries' slick logic in reference to them. However, this entire case has been carefully and fully discussed by Luther in his book *On the Vows of the Monks*. We wish to be seen as repeating that case here.

11 First, it is very clear that a vow is illegitimate if the person who makes the vow thinks that the forgiveness of sins before God is merited by it or satisfaction is made before God for sins. This opinion clearly insults the Gospel, which teaches that the forgiveness of sins is freely granted to us for Christ's sake, as has been said at some length before. Therefore, we have quoted correctly Paul's declaration to the Galatians, "You are severed from Christ, you who would be justified by the law; you have fallen away from grace" (5:4). Those who seek the forgiveness of sins, not through faith in Christ, but through monastic works, divert people from Christ's honor and crucify Christ again. Listen, listen how the writers of the Confutation look for a way

12 out! They explain this passage of Paul only in relation to Moses' Law, and they add that the monks obey all things for Christ's sake. They try hard to live nearer to the Gospel in order to merit eternal life. They add a horrible conclusion in these words, "Therefore, those things are wicked that are here alleged

13 against monasticism." O Christ, how long will You bear these accusations with which our enemies present Your Gospel? In the Confession we said that the forgiveness of sins is received freely for Christ's sake, through faith. O Christ, who is in the bosom of the Father, You revealed the Gospel to the world. If our teaching is not the very voice of the Gospel, if it is not the eternal Father's judgment, we are rightly blamed. But Your

death is a witness, Your resurrection is a witness, the Holy Spirit is a witness, Your entire Church is a witness of this: the true meaning of the Gospel is that we receive forgiveness of sins, not because of our merits, but because of You, through faith.

14   When Paul denies that by Moses' Law people merit the forgiveness of sins, he withdraws this praise much more from human traditions. He clearly presents this in Colossians 2:16. If Moses' Law, which was divinely revealed, did not merit the forgiveness of sins, how much less do these silly observances, hostile to the civil custom of life, merit the forgiveness of sins!

15   The adversaries wrongly claim that Paul abolishes Moses' Law and that Christ follows in such a way that He does not freely grant the forgiveness of sins, but forgives because of the works of other laws, if any are now created. By this godless and fanatical imagination they bury Christ's benefit. Then they wrongly claim that among those who obey this "Law of Christ," the monks obey it better than others, because of their hypocritical poverty, obedience, and chastity, since indeed all these things are full of sham. They brag about poverty most of all. No class of men has greater license than the monks; they boast of obedience. We do not like to speak about celibacy. Gerson indicates how pure this is in most of those who desire to be sexually pure. How many of them do desire to be chaste?

16

17   Of course, in this sham life the monks live more closely according to the Gospel! Christ does not follow Moses in such a way as to forgive sins because of our works, but to set His own merits and His own atoning sacrifice against God's wrath for us, so that we may be freely forgiven. Now, apart from Christ's atoning sacrifice, whoever applies his own merits to God's wrath and tries to receive the forgiveness of sins because of his own merits (whether the works of Moses' Law or of the Ten Commandments or of the rule of Benedict or of the rule of Augustine or of other rules) *does away with Christ's promise, has cast away Christ, and has fallen from grace.* This is Paul's verdict (Galatians 5:4).

18   Look, most merciful Emperor Charles. Look, you princes. Look, all you ranks, how great is the rudeness of the adversaries! Although we have quoted Paul's declaration to this effect, they have written, "Wicked are those things that are here cited against monasticism." What is more certain than that men receive the forgiveness of sins through faith for Christ's sake? And these wretches dare to call this a wicked belief! We do not doubt that if you had been advised about this passage, you would have taken care that such blasphemy be removed from the Confutation.

19

20   It has been fully shown above that this belief is wicked: We receive the forgiveness of sins because of our works. Therefore, we shall be briefer here. For the levelheaded reader will easily determine that we do not merit the forgiveness of sins by monastic works. Therefore, this blasphemy, which appears in Thomas, also cannot be tolerated, "The monastic profession is equal to Baptism." It is insane to make human tradition, which has neither God's command nor promise, equal to Christ's ordinance. Baptism has both God's command and promise, which contains the covenant of grace and of eternal life.

21   Second, religious exercises, obedience, poverty, and celibacy—provided the latter is not impure—are adiaphora. Therefore, the saints can use them without impiety, just as Bernard, Francis, and other holy men used them. They used them to restrain the body,

so that they might have more freedom to teach and to perform other godly offices, not that these works themselves are, by themselves, works that justify or merit eternal life. Finally, these exercises are of the type that Paul says, "Bodily training is of some value" (1 Timothy 4:8). It is believable that in some places there are also currently good men, engaged in the ministry of the Word, who use these exercises without wicked opinions. But to hold that these exercises are [justifying] services because they are counted just before God, and through which they merit eternal life, conflicts with the Gospel about the righteousness of faith. This Gospel teaches that for Christ's sake righteousness and eternal life are granted to us. It conflicts also with Christ's saying, "In vain do they worship Me, teaching as doctrines the commandments of men" (Matthew 15:9). It conflicts also with this statement, "Whatever does not proceed from faith is sin" (Romans 14:23). But how can the adversaries affirm that God approves these services as righteousness before Him when they have no testimony of God's Word?

See how rude the adversaries are! Not only do they teach that these exercises are justifying services, but they add that these services are more perfect, that is, meriting more the forgiveness of sins and justification than do other kinds of life. Here many false and deadly beliefs agree. The adversaries imagine that they observe basic rules and counsels. Afterward, these generous men, dreaming that they have the merits of superabundance, sell these to others. These things are full of pharisaic pride. It is the height of ungodliness to hold that these merits satisfy the Ten Commandments in such a way that merits remain, while such basic rules as these accuse all the saints, "You shall love the LORD your God with all your heart" (Deuteronomy 6:5). Likewise, "You shall not

covet" (Romans 7:7). The prophet says, "All mankind are liars" (Psalm 116:11), that is, not thinking rightly about God, not fearing God enough, not believing Him enough. Therefore, the monks falsely brag that the commandments are fulfilled in the obedience of a monastic life, and more is done than what is commanded.

This is also false: monastic observances are works of the counsels of the Gospel. The Gospel does not advise about distinguishing clothing and meats and the giving up of property. These are human traditions, about which it has been said, "Food will not commend us to God" (1 Corinthians 8:8). Therefore, they are neither justifying services nor perfection. Indeed, when they are presented covered with these titles, they are mere "teachings of demons" (1 Timothy 4:1).

Virginity is recommended, but to those who have the gift, as has been said before. However, it is a most deadly error to hold that evangelical perfection lies in human traditions. In this way even the monks of the Muslims could brag that they have evangelical perfection. Neither is virginity part of the things called adiaphora. Because God's kingdom is *righteousness and life in hearts* (Romans 14:17), perfection is growth in the fear of God, growth in confidence in the mercy promised in Christ, and growth in devotion to one's calling. Paul also describes perfection this way, "[We] are being transformed into the same image from one degree of glory to another. For this comes from the Lord who is the Spirit" (2 Corinthians 3:18). He does not say, "We are continually receiving another hood or other sandals or other girdles." It is regrettable that such pharisaic, indeed, Muslim, expressions should be read and heard in the Church. For they say the perfection of the Gospel and Christ's kingdom (which is eternal life) should be wed along with these foolish observances about vestments and similar trifles.

28  Now hear our Areopagites (excellent teachers) on what an unworthy declaration they have recorded in the Confutation. They say:

> It has been clearly declared in the Holy Scriptures that the monastic life merits eternal life if maintained by a due observance, which by the grace of God any monk can maintain. And, indeed, Christ has promised this much more abundant to those who have left home or brothers, and so on (Matthew 19:29).

29  These are the words of the adversaries, in which it is first said most rudely that the Holy Scriptures say that a monastic life merits eternal life. Where do the Holy Scriptures speak of a monastic life? The adversaries plead their case this way, so men of no account quote the Scriptures. Although no one is ignorant that the monastic life is a recent creation, yet they quote the authority of Scripture and say, too, that their decree has been clearly declared in the Scriptures.

30  Besides, they dishonor Christ when they say that men merit eternal life by monasticism. Not even to His Law has God assigned the honor that it should merit eternal life, as He clearly says in Ezekiel, "I gave them statutes that were not good and rules by 31 which they could not have life" (20:25). First, it is certain that a monastic life does not merit the forgiveness of sins, but we receive this freely through faith, as has been said before. 32 Second, for Christ's sake, through mercy, eternal life is granted to those who through faith receive forgiveness and do not apply their own merits against God's judgment, as Bernard also says with very great force:

> It is necessary first of all to believe that you cannot have the forgiveness of sins except by God's good will. Second, you cannot have any good work, unless He has given it. Finally, you cannot merit eternal life by works, unless this also is freely given.

We have quoted above the rest of the passage, which speaks in the same way. Furthermore, Bernard adds at the end, "Let no one deceive himself, because if he will reflect well, he will undoubtedly find that with ten thousand he cannot meet Him (namely, God) who comes against him with twenty thousand." We do 33 not merit the forgiveness of sins or eternal life by the works of the divine Law, but it is necessary to seek the mercy promised in Christ. The honor of meriting the forgiveness of sins or eternal life cannot be assigned to monastic observances, since they are mere human traditions.

Those who teach that the monastic life 34 merits the forgiveness of sins or eternal life, and transfer the confidence owed Christ to these foolish observances, completely suppress the Gospel about the free forgiveness of sins and the promised mercy in Christ, which is to be grasped. Instead of Christ they worship their own hoods and their own filth. But since even they need mercy, they act wickedly by inventing works of supererogation and selling them to others.

We speak more briefly here about these 35 subjects, because from what we have said before about justification, repentance, and human traditions, it is clear that monastic vows are not rewarded with the forgiveness of sins and eternal life. Since Christ calls traditions useless services, they are in no way evangelical perfection.

The adversaries deceitfully wish to appear 36 as if they modify the common opinion about perfection. They say that a monastic life is not perfection, but that it is a state in which one acquires perfection. What a pretty phrase! We remember that this change is found in Gerson. Clearly levelheaded people, although they did not risk removing monastic life from being praised as perfection, were offended by its excessive praise. So they made the change that monasticism is a state 37 in which one acquires perfection. If we follow this logic, monasticism will be no more a state of perfection than the life of a farmer or mechanic. For these are also states in which one acquires perfection. All people, in every vocation, should seek perfection, that is, grow in the fear of God, in faith, in love toward one's neighbor, and similar spiritual virtues.

38   In the accounts of the hermits there are stories of Anthony and others that make the various stations in life equal. It is written that when Anthony asked God to show him how he was progressing in this kind of life, he was shown in a dream a certain shoemaker in the city of Alexandria for comparison. The next day Anthony came into the city and went to the shoemaker to determine his exercises and gifts, and he spoke with the man. He heard nothing except that early in the morning the shoemaker prayed a few words for the entire state and then worked his trade. Here Anthony learned that justification is not to be assigned to the kind of life that he had entered.

Although the adversaries now lessen their 39 praises about perfection, they actually think otherwise. They sell and apply merits to others under the appearance that they are obeying basic rules and counsels. So they actually maintain that they possess surplus merits. What is this other than assuming perfection to oneself? The Confutation states that the monks try hard to live more closely in line with the Gospel. So it assigns perfection to human traditions if they are living more clearly in line with the Gospel by not having property, being unmarried, and obeying the monastic rule regarding clothing, meats, and similar silly things.

The Confutation also says that the monks 40 merit eternal life more abundantly and quotes Scripture, "everyone who has left houses," and so on (Matthew 19:29). So here it claims perfection also for man-made religious rites. But this Scripture passage in no way favors monastic life. Christ does not mean that leaving parents, wife, and siblings is a work that must be done because it merits the forgiveness of sins and eternal life. Indeed, such leaving is cursed. Anyone who leaves parents or wife to merit the forgiveness of sins or eternal life by this work dishonors Christ.

There are two kinds of leaving. One hap- 41 pens without a call, without God's com-

An Augustinian Monk
(Luther was an Augustinian)

mand, which Christ does not approve (Matthew 15:9). The works we choose are useless services. When Christ speaks about leaving wife and children, it becomes clear that He does not approve this kind of leaving. We know that God's commandment forbids leaving wife and children. God's command to leave is different, that is, when power or tyranny pushes us either to leave or to deny the Gospel. Here we are commanded to bear injury and should rather allow not only wealth, wife, and children, but life to be taken from us. Christ approves of this kind of leaving, and so He adds for the Gospel's "sake" (Mark 10:29). He does so to illustrate that He is speaking not of those who injure wife and children, but who bear injury be-

42 cause of the confession of the Gospel. For the Gospel's sake we should even leave our body. Here it would be ridiculous to hold that it would serve God to kill oneself and to leave the body without God's command. So, too, it is ridiculous to hold that it is a service to God without His command to leave possessions, friends, wife, and children.

43   Clearly, they wickedly twist Christ's word into a monastic life. Unless perhaps the declaration that they "receive a hundredfold in this life" is in place here. Many become monks not because of the Gospel, but because of extravagant living and laziness. They find the most plentiful riches instead of slen-

44 der inheritances. Because the entire subject of monasticism is full of shams, they deceptively quote Scripture passages. So they sin doubly. They trick people and that, too, under the appearance of the divine name.

45   They also quote another passage about perfection, "If you would be perfect, go, sell what you possess and give to the poor, and you will have treasure in heaven; and come, follow Me" (Matthew 19:21). This passage has stirred up many who have imagined that casting away possessions and the control of property is perfection. Let us allow the 46 philosophers to praise Aristippus, who cast a great weight of gold into the sea. Such stories have nothing to do with Christian perfection. The division, control, and possession of property are civil ordinances, approved by God's Word in the commandment "You shall not steal" (Exodus 20:15). The abandonment of property has no command or advice in the Scriptures. Evangelical poverty does not come from the abandonment of property, but from not being greedy, from not trusting in wealth, just as David was poor in a most wealthy kingdom.

Since the abandonment of property is 47 merely a human tradition, it is a useless service. The praises in the *Extravagant* are also excessive. This papal bull says that abandoning ownership of all things for God's sake gains merit, is holy, and is a way of perfection. It is very dangerous to praise so excessively a matter that conflicts with political order. But they say Christ speaks about per- 48 fection here. Indeed, those who quote the text in a butchered way violate it. Perfection is found in what Christ adds, "Follow Me" (Matthew 19:21). Here He presents an ex- 49 ample of obedience to one's calling. Because not all callings are the same, this calling does not belong to everyone, but only to that person with whom Christ speaks. In the same way we are not to imitate the call of David to the kingdom (1 Samuel 16) or of Abraham to slay his son (Genesis 22). Callings are personal, just as business matters themselves vary with times and persons. However, the example of obedience is general. Perfection would have belonged to 50 that young man if he had believed and obeyed this vocation. So with us perfection is that everyone with true faith should obey his own calling.

51    Third, chastity is promised in monastic vows. We have said above, however, about the marriage of priests, that the law of nature in human beings cannot be removed by vows or enactments. Because not everyone has the gift of chastity (Matthew 19:12), many are not successful at it because of weakness. Neither, indeed, can any vows or any enactments set aside the Holy Spirit's command: "Because of the temptation to sexual immorality, each man should have his own wife" (1 Corinthians 7:2). Therefore, this vow is illegitimate in those who do not have the gift of chastity, but who are polluted because of 52 weakness. We have already said enough about this topic. Regarding this, it certainly is strange that the adversaries still defend their traditions contrary to God's clear command, since the dangers and scandals are clearly visible to all. Not even Christ's voice moves them. He scolded the Pharisees (Matthew 23:13–36), who had made traditions contrary to God's command.

53    Fourth, those who live in monasteries are released from their vows by godless ceremonies such as these: the Mass applied to the dead for profit and the worship of saints. In the latter, there are two faults. First, the saints are put in Christ's place, and they are wickedly worshiped, just as the Dominicans invented the rosary of the Blessed Virgin, which is mere babbling, as foolish as it is wicked, and nourishes the most empty arrogance. Then, too, these very impieties are applied only for 54 profit. Likewise, they neither hear nor teach the Gospel about the free forgiveness of sins for Christ's sake, the righteousness of faith, true repentance, or works having God's command. They are occupied with philosophic discussions or preserving ceremonies that conceal Christ.

55    We will not discuss here the entire service of ceremonies, the lessons, singing, and similar things. They could be tolerated if they were regarded simply as exercises, such as school lectures. Their purpose is to teach the hearers and, while teaching, to move some to fear or faith. But now the adversaries wrongly describe these ceremonies as services of God that merit the forgiveness of sins for themselves and for others. Because of this they increase the number of these ceremonies. However, if they would use them to teach and encourage the hearers, brief and pointed lessons would be more profitable than these limitless babblings. So, the entire 56 monastic life is full of hypocrisy and false beliefs. Further, there is this danger: some in these monastic communities are driven to yield to those persecuting the truth. Therefore, there are many important and compelling reasons that free good people from the obligation to this kind of life.

Finally, the canons themselves release 57 many who either without discretion made vows when seduced by the tricks of monks or when compelled by friends. Not even the canons declare such vows to be legitimate. Consider all these things. Clearly there are many reasons showing that monastic vows made in the past are illegitimate. Because of this, a life full of hypocrisy and false beliefs can be safely abandoned.

The adversaries object to this and present 58 an argument taken from the Law of the Nazirites (Numbers 6:2–21). However, the Nazirites did not make their vows with the same opinion of the monks, which we condemn. The rite of the Nazirites was an exercise or a declaration of faith before the people. It did not merit the forgiveness of sins before God and did not justify before God. Further, just as circumcision or slaying victims would not be a service of God now, so the rite of the Nazirites should not be presented now as a service. It should be regarded simply as an adiaphoron. It is not right to compare (a) monasticism, created without God's Word, as a service that should merit the forgiveness of sins and justification with (b) the rite of the Nazirites, which had God's Word and was not taught for the purpose of meriting the forgiveness of sins. The rite of the Nazirites was an outward exercise, just as other ceremonies of the Law. The same can be said about other ceremonies required in the Law.

59    The Rechabites are also quoted. They did not have any possessions and did not drink wine, as Jeremiah 35:6–10 says. Indeed, the example of the Rechabites agrees beautifully with our monks, whose monasteries excel the palaces of kings and who live most extravagantly! Yet the Rechabites, in their poverty of all things, were married. Our monks, although overflowing with self-indulgence, profess celibacy.

60    Besides, examples should be interpreted according to the rule, that is, according to certain and clear Scripture passages, not contrary to the rule, that is, contrary to the
61    Scriptures. Certainly our observances do not merit the forgiveness of sins or justification. Therefore, when the Rechabites are praised, it is necessary [to point out] that they have observed their custom, not because they believed (a) they merited forgiveness of sins by it or (b) that the work was itself a justifying service or (c) that it was a service by which they obtained eternal life instead of by God's mercy, for the sake of the promised Seed (Genesis 3:15; Galatians 3:16). Their obedience is praised because they had their parents' command. One of God's commandments relates to this, "Honor your father and your mother" (Exodus 20:12).

62    The custom also had a particular purpose. Because they were foreigners, not Israelites, it is clear that their father wanted to distinguish them from their fellow citizens by certain marks so that they might not relapse into the impiety of their countrymen. By these marks he wanted to encourage them in the doctrine of faith and immortality. That is a legitimate reason. Far different reasons are given for monasticism. They pretend that monastic works are a [justifying] service; they pretend that they merit the forgiveness of sins and justification. The    63
Rechabites' example is, therefore, different from monasticism. (We leave out the other evils in monasticism, which still continue.)

The    adversaries    also    quote    from    64
1 Timothy 5 about widows. As widows served the Church, they were supported at public expense, where it is said, "They desire to marry and so incur condemnation for having abandoned their former faith" (5:11–12). First, let us suppose that the apostle speaks    65
here of vows. Still, this passage will not support monastic vows, which are made for godless services and with the opinion that they merit the forgiveness of sins and justification. With ringing voice, Paul condemns all services, all laws, all works if they are obeyed to merit the forgiveness of sins. Or he condemns the idea that because of them, instead of through Christ's mercy, we receive forgiveness of sins. Therefore, the vows of widows, if there were any, must have been different from monastic vows.

Besides, if the adversaries do not stop    66
misapplying the passage to vows, the prohibition "Let a widow be enrolled if she is not less than sixty years of age" (1 Timothy 5:9) must be misapplied in the same way. So vows    67
made before this age will be of no account. The Church did not know this kind of vows. So Paul condemns widows, not because they marry, for he commands the younger to marry. But he condemns because, when supported at the public expense, they became unchaste, thus casting off faith. He calls this

"former faith," clearly not in a monastic vow, but in Christianity. In this sense he understands faith in the same chapter, "But if anyone does not provide for his relatives, and especially for members of his household, he has denied the faith and is worse than an un-

68 believer" (5:8). Paul speaks of faith differently than the philosophers. He does not assign faith to those who have mortal sin. So he says that people cast off faith who do not care for their relatives. In the same way he also says that unchaste women cast off faith.

69 We have repeated some of our reasons and, in passing, have dismissed the adversaries' objections. We have collected these matters, not simply because of the adversaries, but much more because of godly minds, that they may see the reasons why they should condemn hypocritical and fictitious monastic services. All such things certainly are done away with by this one saying of Christ, "In vain do they worship Me, teaching as doctrines the commandments of men" (Matthew 15:9). Therefore, the vows themselves and the observances of meats, lessons, chants, vestments, sandals, girdles are useless services in God's sight. All godly minds should certainly know that the following opinions are simply pharisaic and condemned: (a) these observances merit the forgiveness of sins, (b) we are regarded righteous because of them, (c) we receive eternal life because of them, and not through mercy because of Christ. The holy people who have lived this kind of life must have learned— having rejected confidence in such observances—that they had the forgiveness of sins freely. They must have learned that for Christ's sake through mercy they would receive eternal life, and not for the sake of these services. God only approves services set up by His Word, which are of benefit when used in faith.

## ARTICLE XXVIII (XIV)

# Church Authority

This topic would be covered in more detail six years later in Melanchthon's *Treatise on the Power and Primacy of the Pope* for the Smalcaldic League. The issue in this article is whether the Church, through its bishops, has the authority to command man-made regulations and impose them on people. Whether the Church has the duty to assign certain persons to carry out supervisory responsibilities is not at issue. All who are called and ordained to the office of preaching and administering the Sacraments share the same biblical authority or "power." This power is the Gospel ministry of Word and Sacrament in the Church and the authority to excommunicate persons and withhold the Sacrament of the Altar from them. The Church's ministers are not tyrants who can act and do whatever they want. Regulations must be in place to provide order and peace, but they must never suggest that anyone receives forgiveness from God by following them. (See also AC XXVIII; SA II IV; The Power and Primacy of the Pope; SC, Table of Duties.)

---

The adversaries cry out violently here 1 about the privileges and immunities of the Church estate, and they add these condoning remarks, "All things are vain which are stated in the present article against the immunity of the churches and priests." This is a sheer lie, 2 for we have argued about other things in this article. Besides, we have testified frequently that we do not find fault with political ordinances and the gifts and privileges granted by princes.

If only the adversaries would hear, on the 3 other hand, the complaints of the churches and of godly minds! The adversaries coura-

Preaching the Word and Administering the Sacraments

geously guard their own dignities and wealth. Meanwhile, they neglect the condition of the churches. They do not care that the churches are rightly taught and that the Sacraments are duly administered. They let all kinds of men into the priesthood without proper selection. Afterward, they impose intolerable burdens, as though they delighted in the destruction of their fellows. They demand that their traditions be observed far

4　more accurately than the Gospel. In the most important and difficult controversies, in which people urgently desire instruction, so that they can with certainty follow something, the adversaries do not relieve minds tortured with doubt. Rather, they only call people to arms. Besides, in matters against clear truth they present decrees written in blood, which threaten horrible punishments against people unless they clearly act against

5　God's command. On the other hand, you should see the tears of the poor and hear the pitiful complaints of many good people. God undoubtedly considers and regards them, and one day you will give an account of your stewardship.

6　Although we have in this article embraced various topics in the Confession, the adversaries do not reply, except to say that the bishops have the power of rule and forceful correction to direct their subjects to the goal of eternal blessedness, and that the power of ruling requires the power to judge, to define, to distinguish, and to fix those things that are serviceable or lead to the results just mentioned. These are the Confutation's words, by which the adversaries teach us that the bishops are authorized to enact laws useful for receiving eternal life. The controversy is about this article.

7　We must keep in the Church the doctrine that we receive the forgiveness of sins freely for Christ's sake, through faith. We must also keep the doctrine that human traditions are useless services and, therefore, neither sin nor righteousness should be placed in meat, drink, clothing, and like things. Christ wished the use of such things to be left free, since He says, "It is not what goes into the mouth that defiles a person" (Matthew 15:11); and Paul says, "The kingdom of God is not a matter of eating and drinking" (Romans 14:17). Therefore, the bishops have no 　8 right to enact traditions in addition to the Gospel, so that people must merit the forgiveness of sins, or that they think are services that God approves as righteousness. They must not burden consciences (as though it were a sin to leave such observances undone). All this is taught by that one passage in Acts 15:9, where the apostles (Peter) say that hearts are cleansed through faith. Then they prohibit the imposing of a yoke and show how great a danger this is, and multiply the sin of those who burden the Church. "Why do you tempt God?" they say. Our adversaries are not terrified even by this thunderbolt. They defend traditions and godless opinions with violence.

The adversaries also condemned Article 　9 XV, in which we stated that traditions do not merit the forgiveness of sins. They here say that traditions lead to eternal life. Do they merit the forgiveness of sins? Are they services that God approves as righteousness? Do they enliven hearts? Writing to the Colos-　10 sians (2:20–23), Paul says that traditions do not help with respect to eternal righteousness and eternal life, because food, drink, clothing, and the like are things that perish through use. Eternal life is worked in the heart by eternal things, that is, by God's Word and the Holy Spirit. Therefore, let the adversaries explain how traditions lead to eternal life.

The Gospel clearly testifies that traditions 　11

should not be imposed upon the Church to merit the forgiveness of sins, to be services that God approves as righteousness, to burden consciences, so that leaving them out is regarded as sin. The adversaries will never be able to show that the bishops have the power to set up such services.

12 Besides, we have declared in the Confession what kind of power the Gospel assigns to bishops. Those who are now bishops do not perform the duties of bishops according to the Gospel. Indeed, they may be bishops according to canonical polity, which we do not condemn. But we are speaking of a bishop 13 according to the Gospel. We are pleased with the ancient division of power into (a) power of the order and (b) power of *jurisdiction*. Therefore, the bishop has the power of the order, that is, the ministry of the Word and Sacraments. He also has the power of jurisdiction. This means the authority to excommunicate those guilty of open crimes and again to absolve them if they are converted 14 and seek absolution (John 20:23). But their power is not to be tyrannical, without a fixed law. Nor is it to be regal, above the law. Rather, they have a fixed command and a fixed Word of God, according to which they should teach and exercise their jurisdiction. Even though they should have some temporal jurisdiction, it does not mean that they are able to set up new services. Spiritual services have nothing to do with temporal jurisdiction. They have the Word, the command, and how far they should exercise jurisdiction, if anyone did anything contrary to that Word they have received from Christ.

15 In the Confession we also have discussed to what extent they may legitimately enact traditions, not as necessary services, but only for the sake of order in the Church and for peace. These traditions should not entrap consciences, as though to require necessary services. Paul teaches when he says, "Stand firm therefore, and do not submit again to a yoke of slavery" (Galatians 5:1). The use of 16 such ordinances should be left free, so long as offenses are avoided and they are not determined to be necessary services. In the same way the apostles themselves ordained many things that have been changed with time. Neither did they hand them down in such a way that they never could be changed. They did not depart from their own writings, in which they greatly labored should the Church be burdened with the opinion that human rites are necessary services.

This is the simple way of interpreting tra- 17 ditions: they are services that are not necessary. Yet, for the sake of avoiding offense, we should observe them in the proper place. Many learned and great people in the 18 Church have understood it this way. Nor do we see what can be said against this. Clearly, the expression "the one who hears you hears Me" (Luke 10:16) is not speaking about traditions, but is directed primarily against traditions. It is not a bestowal of unlimited authority (*a mandatum cum libera*), as they call it, but it is a caution about something prescribed (*a cautio de rato*). Regarding the special command (Luke 10:16), that is, the testimony given to the apostles that we believe them with respect to the word of another, not their own. Christ wishes to assure us, as was necessary, that we should know that the Word delivered by human beings is powerful, and that no other Word should be sought from heaven. "The one who hears you hears 19 Me" cannot be understood of traditions. Christ requires that they teach in such a way that He Himself is heard because He says, "The one . . . hears Me." Therefore, He wishes His own voice, His own Word, to be heard, not human traditions. So a saying that clearly supports us and contains the most important comfort and doctrine is distorted by these stupid men into the most silly matters: the distinctions of food, vestments, and the like.

20 The adversaries also quote Hebrews 13:17, "Obey your leaders." This passage requires obedience to the Gospel. It does not establish a dominion for the bishops apart from the Gospel. Neither should the bishops enact traditions contrary to the Gospel or interpret their traditions contrary to the Gospel. When they do this, obedience is prohibited, according to Galatians 1:9, "If anyone is preaching to you a gospel contrary to the one you received, let him be accursed."

21 We make the same reply to Matthew 23:3, "So practice and observe whatever they tell you," because clearly a universal command is not given that we should receive all things, since elsewhere Scripture asks us to "obey God rather than men" (Acts 5:29). Therefore, they teach wicked things; they should not be heard. These are wicked things: human traditions are services of God, they are necessary services, and they merit the forgiveness of sins and eternal life.

22 The adversaries object, arguing that public offenses and turmoil have arisen under the appearance of our doctrine. We briefly 23 reply to these. If all the scandals were combined, still the one article about the forgiveness of sins—that for Christ's sake through faith we freely receive the forgiveness of sins—brings so much good it hides all evils. In the beginning, this gained for Luther not 24 only our approval, but also that of many who are now fighting against us. "Former favor ceases, and mortals are forgetful," says Pindar. Yet, we neither desire to desert truth necessary for the Church, nor can we agree with the adversaries in condemning it. For 25 "we must obey God rather than men" (Acts 5:29). Those who earlier condemned clear truth, and are now persecuting it with the greatest cruelty, will give an account for the schism that has arisen (Matthew 12:36). Are there no scandals among the adversaries? How much evil is there in the sacrilegious 26 profanation of the Mass performed for profit! What a disgrace is celibacy! But let us leave out comparisons. For now, this is our response to the Confutation. Now we leave it 27 to the discernment of all the godly whether the adversaries are right in bragging that they have actually, from the Scriptures, refuted our Confession.

~

# THE SMALCALD ARTICLES

## ARTICLES OF CHRISTIAN DOCTRINE

that we would have presented to the council, if one had been
convened at Mantua or elsewhere, pointing out what we could
give up and what we could not.

Written by
*Dr. Martin Luther*
in the Year 1537.

The Luther Rose

The Luther Rose is the most well-known symbol of Lutheranism.
Here is how Martin Luther explained it:

First, there is a black cross in a heart that remains its natural color. This is to remind me that it is faith in the Crucified One that saves us. Anyone who believes from the heart will be justified (Romans 10:10). It is a black cross, which mortifies and causes pain, but it leaves the heart its natural color. It doesn't destroy nature, that is to say, it does not kill us but keeps us alive, for the just shall live by faith in the Crucified One (Romans 1:17). The heart should stand in the middle of a white rose. This is to show that faith gives joy, comfort, and peace—it puts the believer into a white, joyous rose. Faith does not give peace and joy like the world gives (John 14:27). This is why the rose must be white, not red. White is the color of the spirits and angels (cf. Matthew 28:3; John 20:12). This rose should stand in a sky-blue field, symbolizing that a joyful spirit and faith is a beginning of heavenly, future joy, which begins now, but is grasped in hope, not yet fully revealed. Around the field of blue is a golden ring to symbolize that blessedness in heaven lasts forever and has no end. Heavenly blessedness is exquisite, beyond all joy and better than any possessions, just as gold is the most valuable and precious metal. (Letter to Lazarus Spengler, July 8, 1530 [WA Br 5:445]; tr. P. T. McCain)

# Introduction to the Smalcald Articles

*We cannot yield without becoming guilty of treason against God,*
*even though property and life, peace or war, are at stake.*

—Elector John Frederick, "The Magnanimous"

Since the start of the Reformation the Lutherans had been asking the Church to convene a general council. For example, in his *Letter to the Christian Nobility of the German Nation* (1520), Luther called for an open and free council. The Holy Roman Emperor, Charles V, assured the reformers that he supported their call for a general council. They were hopeful that such a gathering would give their concerns a fairer hearing than was possible if they had to deal only with the pope and his representatives. Finally, on June 4, 1536, Paul III, who had only recently been installed as pope, issued a formal decree for a general council to be held in Mantua, Italy, beginning on May 23, 1537.

The Lutheran rulers debated whether they should attend the council. Martin Luther encouraged them to attend because he considered it to be a great opportunity to speak the truth and perhaps persuade some people. Luther's own prince, Elector John Frederick, nephew of Luther's first protector, Frederick the Wise, did not want to attend. His reason was that by the very act of attending, the Lutherans would be, in effect, acknowledging the pope as head of the Church. His concerns grew all the more when on September 23, 1536, the pope made clear that the purpose of the council would be "the utter extirpation of the poisonous, pestilential Lutheran heresy" ("Bull concerning the Reforms of the Roman Court," LW 16:1914). So much for a free, open council.

John Frederick was finally persuaded to attend, but ordered that the Lutherans from his territory attend only with adequate preparation. Just as the Lutheran princes came to the Imperial Meeting at Augsburg (1530) with a Confession in hand, so also they should attend Mantua firmly united in what they believed, taught, confessed, and practiced in their respective territories. This time their Confession must be more clear, direct, and firm than the Augsburg Confession.

## Writing the Articles

On December 1, 1536, John Frederick commissioned Martin Luther to prepare a statement of faith in the form of confessional articles for presentation to a meeting of Lutheran theologians and lay leaders on February 7, 1537, in Smalcald, Germany. He said, "It will nevertheless be very necessary for Doctor Martin to prepare his foundation and opinion from the Holy Scriptures, namely, the articles as hitherto taught, preached, and written by him, and which he is determined to adhere to and abide by at the council, as well as upon his departure from this world and before the judgment of Almighty God, and in which we cannot yield without becoming guilty of treason against God, even though property and life, peace or war, are at stake" (Bente, 120). This was serious business indeed.

Luther began working on the document. But on December 18 he became seriously ill, experiencing what may have been a heart attack. He was convinced that death was near. It is important to keep this in mind as one considers just how seriously Luther regarded the Smalcald Articles. He thought this would be his only chance to prepare something for a general council. What is more, Luther believed that the document he was working on would be the last chance he had to confess his faith. As it turned out, Luther lived almost ten more years. At the time, though, he was convinced he was at death's door. The Smalcald Articles, therefore, truly are to be regarded as Luther's "last will and testament."

Luther's document was to be presented and discussed at the meeting of the Smalcaldic League, an association of Lutheran territories and cities formed in 1531 in Smalcald, Germany, as a defense against any who would try to eliminate Lutheranism by force. Public agreement (subscription) to the Augsburg Confession was required for membership. Just how seriously the Smalcaldic League took such subscription is seen by the fact that King Henry VIII of England was not permitted to join when he refused to agree with the Augsburg Confession.

## The Meeting at Smalcald

On December 28, 1536, theologians from Wittenberg reviewed Luther's first draft of the document. They had a few minor changes to suggest. Luther accepted these changes, and together they signed his document and sent it on to Elector John Frederick. John then presented Luther's document to the meeting of the Smalcaldic League on February 8, 1537. The elector was sure that the articles would be acceptable and adopted by everyone there. Things did not turn out as he had planned.

Some of the members of the League were concerned that Luther's statement of faith was too strong. Instead, they wanted simply to present the Augsburg Confession, along with the Apology to the Augsburg Confession. Philip Melanchthon signed Luther's document, but added a caveat that if the pope were to allow the Gospel, his authority could be accepted for the sake of order in the Church—only by human right, not by divine institution.

Unfortunately, Luther was not able to be present personally as the Lutherans met in Smalcald. He lay sick in a house nearby. As a result, Philip Melanchthon persuaded the gathering to set aside Luther's document.

It should be mentioned that by this time Melanchthon had become more favorably inclined toward the representatives of cities in Southern Germany who had been influenced by Ulrich Zwingli and so did not want to upset them by endorsing a document that clearly rejected their view of the Lord's Supper. Philip's tendency to compromise, even at the cost of watering down essential doctrinal truths, would cause great problems after Luther's death.

Although Luther's articles were not formally adopted by the Smalcaldic League, forty-four of the Lutherans present did sign them. Five delegates from cities in southern Germany, who were inclined toward the Zwinglian view of the Lord's Supper, did not sign the articles. By the time the Formula of Concord was completed and adopted in 1577, Luther's articles were highly regarded and adopted as part of the Lutheran Church's formal confession of faith. It should be noted as well that by 1577 the compromising doctrinal position of Philip Melanchthon and his followers had been thoroughly exposed and rejected.

## The Content and Use of the Articles

The Smalcald Articles very clearly establish the differences between Romanism and Lutheranism. This very sharply worded document leaves little to the imagination. When clear confession is necessary, it is wrong to speak in ways that can be interpreted to fit everyone's opinion. Faithfulness and clarity demand a precise twofold presentation that (a) rejects error and (b) affirms truth.

Luther left Smalcald disappointed that his articles had not been formally adopted. He revised them a bit more, and in 1538 he had the document published as a last will and testament, as he says, "In case I should die before there would be a council (as I fully expect and hope). For those scoundrels who run away from the light and avoid the day are taking pains to delay and prevent the council. If I do die, those who are alive and those who come after me will have my testimony and confession (in addition to the one I have issued previously). I have remained in this confession up to now, and by God's grace, I will remain in it" (SA, Preface 3).

Ironically, Luther's words proved true. The Council of Mantua never took place. Delay after delay prevented it. The council was postponed until finally it did meet, in the city of Trent, Italy, beginning in 1545, right before Luther's death. It met in various sessions until 1563. At the end of the process, the Council of Trent's decisions set in stone the doctrinal position of the Roman Catholic Church as it is known today. The published decisions from Trent, *The Canons and Decrees of the Council of Trent*, became for Rome what the Book of Concord is for Lutherans. A second Lutheran named Martin prepared the definitive Lutheran response to Trent. Martin Chemnitz wrote *The Examination of the Council of Trent*. To this day Chemnitz's work is the best biblical analysis and refutation of the errors of Roman Catholicism.

The Smalcald Articles were held in high esteem by Lutheran laypeople and rulers. Elector John Frederick cherished them. As his own death drew near in 1554, he ordered them to be printed as part of his last will and testament. By 1577, the Formula of Concord said that the Smalcald Articles had "everywhere been regarded as the common, unanimously accepted meaning of our churches" (FC SD Rule and Norm 11). This is why it was included in the Book of Concord of 1580.

## TIMELINE

## OUTLINE

# SMALCALD ARTICLES

## Preface of Dr. Martin Luther

1    Pope Paul III called a council last year that was supposed to assemble at Mantua around Pentecost. Later, he moved it from Mantua. Now, no one knows where he will or can hold it. On our side, we expected either to be summoned to the council or to just be condemned without being summoned. I was told to set forth and pull together the articles of our doctrine. In the deliberations at the council, we could then be clear about what we would be willing and able to concede to the papists, and what points we intended to persist with and stand for to the end.

2    So I have compiled these articles and presented them to our side, which has unanimously accepted and confessed them. We have resolved to present these publicly to set forth the confession of our faith. (Perhaps the pope with his supporters would be so bold as to hold a truly free Christian council, seriously and in good faith, as is his duty, without lying and cheating.)

3    The Roman court, though, is terribly afraid of a free Christian council. They are ashamed to be exposed to the light. The Roman court has dashed the hope, even of those who are on their side, that they will ever permit a free council—much less hold one themselves. Many on the pope's side are greatly offended and rightly troubled at this negligence. For they realize that the pope would rather see all Christendom perish and all souls damned than allow either himself or his followers to be reformed even a little or to have their tyranny be limited. Yet I have decided to publish these articles in plain print in case I should die before there would be a council (as I fully expect and hope). For those scoundrels who run away from the light and avoid the day are taking pains to delay and prevent the council. If I do die, those who are alive and those who come after me will have my testimony and confession (in addition to the one I have issued previously). I have remained in this confession up to now, and by God's grace, I will remain in it.

4    What should I say? Why should I complain? I am still alive—writing, preaching, and lecturing daily. Yet poisonous people—not only adversaries, but also false brothers who profess to be on our side—dare to cite my writings and doctrine directly against me. They let me look on and listen, even though they know very well that I teach differently from what they say. They want to dress up their poison with my labor. Under my name, they want to mislead the poor people. What will happen, dear God, when I am dead?

5    I should reply to everything while I am still alive. Then again, how can I stop all the mouths of the devil by myself? Especially of those so poisoned that they will not listen or pay attention to what we write. Instead, with all diligence, they only busy themselves with how they can most shamefully twist and pervert every letter of our words. These I let the devil answer, or, ultimately, God's wrath, as they deserve. I often think of the good Gerson, who doubts whether anything good should be written for the public and published. If it is not published, many souls are neglected who could be freed. But if it is published, the devil is there with malignant, de-

Duke John Frederick of Saxony (The Magnanimous; 1503–54)
c. 1533, Gotha

Portrait of John Frederick, shortly after he became Elector in 1532. He was educated by Luther's lifelong friend Spalatin and considered Martin Luther his spiritual father. John Frederick defended and spread the Reformation. He was the leading force behind the formation of the Smalcaldic League and asked Luther to prepare a statement of faith for the League (the Smalcald Articles). He cherished the Smalcald Articles and made them part of his last will and testament.

7  ceitful tongues without number that poison and pervert everything, so that the usefulness of the writing is prevented. Yet what they gain by doing this is obvious. Even though they have lied so shamefully against us and by their lies tried to get the people on their side, God has constantly advanced His work. He has been making their following ever smaller and ours greater. He has caused them to be shamed with their lies and still causes this.

8  I have to tell a story. A doctor was sent here to Wittenberg from France, who openly told us that his king was convinced that we have no Church, no government, no marriage, but that we all live promiscuously like

9  cattle and do as we please. Imagine those whose writings have instilled such crude lies into the king and other countries, presenting them as the pure truth. How will they face us when we are brought before the judgment seat of Christ (2 Corinthians 5:10)? Christ, the Lord and Judge of us all, knows well that they lie and have lied. They, in turn, must hear His sentence. I know that certainly. May God convert to repentance those who can be converted! To the rest will be said, "Woe and alas!" for eternity.

10  And so I return to the subject. I really would like to see a truly Christian council, so that many people and issues might be helped. Not that we need help. Our churches are now, through God's grace, enlightened and equipped with the pure Word and right use of the Sacraments, with knowledge of the various callings and right works. So, on our part, we ask for no council. On such points, we have nothing better to hope or expect from a council. But we see throughout the bishops' jurisdictions so many parishes vacant and desolate that it breaks our heart. Still, neither the bishops nor the Church officials care how the poor people live or die. Christ has died for them, and yet they are not allowed to hear

Him speak as the true Shepherd with His sheep (John 10:11–18).This makes me shud- 11 der and fear that someday He might send a council of angels upon Germany who will utterly destroy us like Sodom and Gomorrah (Genesis 19:1–25) for wickedly mocking Him with the pretext of a council.

Besides such necessary Church affairs, 12 many important matters in the political realm could also be improved. The princes and the estates disagree. Interest rates and greed have burst in like a flood and are defended under the law. Also, disrespect, lust, extravagance in dress, gluttony, gambling, pomp, and all kinds of bad habits and evil. Subjects, servants, and workers in every trade are insubordinate. The demands on the peasants are unfair. Prices are exorbitant. (Who can list everything?) These things have increased so much that they cannot be corrected by ten councils and twenty commissions. The council would have their hands full if 13 such important issues of the spiritual and earthly realms that are contrary to God would be considered. The childish absurdity of long official gowns, large tonsures, broad sashes, bishops' or cardinals' hats, maces, and other vanities would be forgotten. If we had first followed God's command and ordering in the spiritual and secular realms, we could then find enough time to reform food, clothing, tonsures, and surplices. As long as we want to swallow camels and strain at gnats (Matthew 23:24), ignore the logs and judge the specks (Matthew 7:3), we might be satisfied with the council.

That is why I have presented just a few arti- 14 cles. We already have so many commands of God to observe in the Church, the state, and the family that we can never fulfill them. So what good are decrees and statutes from a council, especially when the important matters commanded by God are ignored? As if He had to honor our vanities as a reward for our treading His solemn commandments under foot. But our sins weigh upon us and cause God not to be gracious to us. For we do not repent and instead want to defend every abomination.

15 O Lord Jesus Christ, may You Yourself hold a council! Deliver Your servants by Your glorious return (Titus 2:13)! The pope and his followers are done for. They will have none of You. Help us who are poor and needy, who sigh to You, and who pray to You earnestly (Romans 8:23, 26), according to the grace You have given us through Your Holy Spirit (Romans 12:3, 6), who lives and reigns with You and the Father, blessed forever. Amen.

# THE FIRST PART

## The Awe-Inspiring Articles on the Divine Majesty

Luther repeats the historic creedal formulas that confess God the Holy Trinity and the two natures in Christ. He concludes by indicating how these articles are the historic Confession of the Christian Church. When Luther uses the word *catechism* he is not referring to his Small Catechism but to the historic teaching of the faith in the Western Church: the Ten Commandments, the Lord's Prayer, and the Apostles' Creed. The Romanists and Lutherans agreed on these points of biblical, orthodox Christianity, so there was no need for Luther to elaborate on them. (See the Apostles', Nicene, and Athanasian Creeds; AC I; SC II; LC II.)

---

1. The Father, Son, and Holy Spirit, three distinct persons in one divine essence and nature (Matthew 28:19), are one God, who has created heaven and earth (1 Corinthians 8:6).

2. The Father is begotten of no one; the Son is begotten of the Father (John 1:14); the Holy Spirit proceeds from the Father and the Son (John 15:26).

3. Neither the Father nor the Holy Spirit, but the Son became man (John 1:14).

4. The Son became man in this manner: He was conceived, without the cooperation of man, by the Holy Spirit (Luke 1:34–35), and was born of the pure, holy Virgin Mary. Afterward, He suffered, died, was buried, descended to hell, rose from the dead (1 Corinthians 15:3–4), ascended to heaven (Acts 1:9–11), sits at the right hand of God (Acts 2:33), will come to judge the quick and the dead, and so on, as the Apostles' and Athanasian Creeds and our children's catechism teach.

Concerning these articles, there is no argument or dispute. Both sides confess them. Therefore, it is not necessary now to discuss them further.

# THE SECOND PART

## The Articles That Refer to the Office and Work of Jesus Christ; That Is, Our Redemption

### ARTICLE I

## The Chief Article

Agreeing on the content of the historic Christian Creed is one thing. Agreeing on what it means is quite another. Luther launches immediately into the "chief article" of the Christian faith: Christ's saving work can never be given up, or compromised, for the sake of peace and unity in the Church. This teaching is the very heart of the Gospel itself; therefore, it must be kept pure and free from error and proclaimed boldly and thoroughly. Luther returns to this chief article over and over again throughout the rest of the Smalcald Articles, demonstrating how the various errors and abuses in the Church of his day originate from false teaching about justification by grace through faith. (See the Apostles',

Nicene, and Athanasian Creeds; AC III; SC II; LC II; FC Ep VIII and SD VIII.)

---

The first and chief article is this:

1    Jesus Christ, our God and Lord, died for our sins and was raised again for our justification (Romans 4:24–25).

2    He alone is the Lamb of God who takes away the sins of the world (John 1:29), and God has laid upon Him the iniquities of us all (Isaiah 53:6).

3    All have sinned and are justified freely, without their own works or merits, by His grace, through the redemption that is in Christ Jesus, in His blood (Romans 3:23–25).

4    This is necessary to believe. This cannot be otherwise acquired or grasped by any work, law, or merit. Therefore, it is clear and certain that this faith alone justifies us. As St. Paul says:

For we hold that one is justified by faith apart from works of the law. (Romans 3:28)

That He might be just and the justifier of the one who has faith in Jesus. (Romans 3:26)

Nothing of this article can be yielded or surrendered, even though heaven and earth and everything else falls (Mark 13:31).    5

For there is no other name under heaven given among men by which we must be saved. (Acts 4:12)

And with His stripes we are healed. (Isaiah 53:5)

Upon this article everything that we teach and practice depends, in opposition to the pope, the devil, and the whole world. Therefore, we must be certain and not doubt this doctrine. Otherwise, all is lost, and the pope, the devil, and all adversaries win the victory and the right over us.

### The Seven-Headed Luther

An example of the savage attacks launched against Luther by his opponents; in this case, it is by John Cochlaeus. This woodcut portrays Luther as a seven-headed monster. Heads from left to right: Luther as (1) Doctor of theology, (2) Martin, (3) Luther, (4) Churchman, (5) Schwärmer (enthusiast), (6) Visitator, and (7) Barabbas, a revolutionary. Luther's reaction? He said the picture would have looked better if the heads had necks.

## ARTICLE II

# The Mass

Nowhere was Rome's corruption of the doctrine of justification more clearly seen than in the abuses and errors associated with the celebration of Holy Communion (the Mass; see article, p. 245). Luther forcefully calls the Roman Mass a "horrible abomination" because it thoroughly contradicts the chief article of the faith, justification. Notice how, over and over again, Luther takes his stand against the corruptions of the Mass by showing that God did not command the Church to perform these corrupt ceremonies. (See AC XXI and XXIV; FC Ep X and SD X.)

1   The Mass in the papacy has to be the greatest and most horrible abomination, since it directly and powerfully conflicts with this chief article. Above and before all other popish idolatries the Mass has been the chief and most false. For this sacrifice or work of the Mass is thought to free people from sins, both in this life and also in purgatory. It does so even when offered by a wicked scoundrel. Yet only the Lamb of God can and will do this (John 1:29), as said above. Nothing of this article is to be surrendered or conceded, because the first article does not allow it.

2   If there were reasonable papists, we might speak moderately and in a friendly way, like this: First, why do they so rigidly uphold the Mass? It is just a purely human invention and has not been commanded by God. Every human invention we may safely discard, as Christ declares, "In vain do they worship Me, teaching as doctrines the commandments of men" (Matthew 15:9).

3   Second, the Mass is unnecessary and can be omitted without sin and danger.

4   Third, the Sacrament can be received in a better and more blessed way (indeed, the only blessed way): according to Christ's institution (Matthew 26:26–28). Why, then, do they drive the world to woe and misery for something fictitious and unnecessary when it can be had in a different, more blessed way?

5   One should publicly preach the following to the people: (a) the Mass, as a human invention, can be left out without sin; (b) no one will be condemned who does not observe it; (c) they can be saved in a better way without the Mass. I wager that the Mass will then collapse of itself, not only among the crude common people, but also among all pious, Christian, reasonable, God-fearing hearts. This would happen all the more, when people hear that the Mass is dangerous, fabricated, and invented without God's will and Word.

6   Fourth, the Mass should be abandoned because so many unspeakable abuses have arisen in the whole world from the buying and selling of Masses. Even if the Mass in itself had something advantageous and good, it should be abolished for no other reason than to prevent abuses. How much more should we abandon it since it is also completely unnecessary, useless, and dangerous; and since we can have everything by a more necessary, profitable, and certain way without the Mass?

7   Fifth, the Mass is and can be nothing more than a human work (as Church law and all the books declare, even when it is performed by wicked scoundrels). The attempt is to reconcile oneself and others to God (see 2 Corinthians 5:18–20), and to merit and deserve the forgiveness of sins and grace by the Mass. (This is how the Mass is held at its very best. Otherwise, what purpose would it serve?) This is why it must and should be condemned and rejected. For the Mass directly conflicts with the chief article, which says that it is not someone paid to perform

the Mass (whether wicked or godly) who takes away our sins with his work, but the Lamb of God, the Son of God.

8 If anyone says that he wants to administer the Sacrament to himself as an act of devotion, he cannot be serious. If he sincerely wishes to commune, the surest and best way for him is in the Sacrament administered according to Christ's institution. To administer Communion to oneself is a human notion. It is uncertain, unnecessary, even prohibited. He does not know what he is doing, because without God's Word he follows a false human

9 opinion and invention. It is not right (even if otherwise done properly) to use the Sacrament that belongs to the community of the Church for one's own private devotion. It is wrong to toy with the Sacrament without God's Word and apart from the community of the Church.

10 This article about the Mass would completely preoccupy the council. Even if they could concede all the other articles, they could not concede this. Cardinal Campeggius said at Augsburg that he would rather be torn to pieces than give up the Mass. So, by God's help, I, too, would rather be burned to ashes than allow someone paid to perform a Mass—whether he is good or bad—to be made equal to Christ Jesus, my Lord and Savior, or to be exalted above Him. In this, we remain eternally separated and opposed to one another. They know well that when the Mass falls, the papacy lies in ruins. Before they will let this happen, they will, if they can, put us all to death.

11 In addition to all this, this dragon's tail (Revelation 12:3–4)—that is, the Mass—has begotten many vermin and a multitude of idolatries.

12 First, purgatory. They carried their trade into purgatory by selling Masses for the souls of the dead. They started vigils; weekly, monthly, and yearly celebrations of funeral anniversaries; special services for the Common Week and All Souls' Day; and soul baths. So the Mass is used almost solely for the dead, although Christ has instituted the Sacrament solely for the living. Therefore, purgatory, along with every service, rite, and commerce connected with it, should be regarded as nothing more than the devil's ghost. For it conflicts with the chief article: only Christ, and not human works, can set souls free (Galatians 5:1). Besides, God has commanded or assigned us nothing about the dead. Therefore, all this may be safely left out, even if it were not error and idolatry.

13 The papists quote Augustine and some of the Church Fathers who are said to have written about purgatory. They think we do not understand why they spoke as they did. St. Augustine does not write that there is a purgatory. Nor does he have evidence from Scripture as a basis. Rather, he leaves it in doubt whether purgatory exists. He does say that his mother asked to be remembered at the altar or Sacrament. This is nothing but human devotion, indeed of individuals, and does not establish an article of faith, which is God's privilege alone.

14 Our papists, though, cite such human opinions so people will believe in their horrible, blasphemous, and cursed traffic in Masses for souls in purgatory. But they will never prove these things from Augustine. Once they have abolished the traffic in Masses for purgatory, which Augustine never dreamed of, then we can discuss whether to accept what Augustine said beyond Scripture and whether the dead should be remembered at the Eucharist. It will not do to frame articles 15 of faith from the works or words of the holy Fathers. Otherwise, their kind of food, clothing, houses, and such, would have to become an article of faith, as was done with relics.

The true rule is this: God's Word shall establish articles of faith, and no one else, not even an angel can do so (Galatians 1:8).

16    Second: Following these things, evil spirits have produced many wicked tricks by appearing as the souls of the departed (1 Samuel 28), and with unspeakable lies and tricks demanded Masses, vigils, pilgrimages,

17  and other alms.  All of this we were expected to receive as articles of faith and to live accordingly. The pope confirmed these things, as he did the Mass and all other abominations. Here, too, there must be no yielding or surrendering.

18    Third, pilgrimages. Here, too, the forgiveness of sins and God's grace were sought, for the Mass controlled everything. Pilgrimages, without God's Word, have not been commanded. Nor are they necessary, since the soul can be cared for in a better way. These pilgrimages can be abandoned without any sin and danger. So why do they leave behind their own callings, their parishes, their pastors, God's Word, their wives, their children, and such? These *are* ordained and commanded. Instead, they run after these unnecessary, uncertain, dangerous illusions of the

19  devil.  Perhaps the devil had been riding the pope, causing him to praise and establish these practices. By them, the people again and again revolted from Christ to their own works, and, worst of all, became idolaters. Furthermore, pilgrimages are neither necessary nor commanded, but are senseless, doubtful, and harmful. On this, too, there

20  can be no yielding or surrendering.  Let it be preached that pilgrimages are not necessary, but dangerous, and then see what will happen to them.

21    Fourth, monastic societies. Monasteries, foundations, and representatives have assigned and transferred (by a legal contract and sale) all Masses, good works, and such, both for the living and the dead. This is nothing but a human trick, without God's Word and entirely unnecessary and not commanded. It is also contrary to the chief article on redemption. Therefore, it cannot in any way be tolerated.

22    Fifth, relics. So many falsehoods and such foolishness are found in the bones of dogs and horses that even the devil has laughed at such swindles. Relics should have been condemned long ago, even if there were some good in them, and all the more because they are without God's Word. Since they are neither commanded nor counseled, relics are entirely unnecessary and useless. Worst of

23  all, these relics have been imagined to cause indulgence and the forgiveness of sins. People have revered them as a good work and service of God, like the Mass and other such practices.

24    Sixth: Here belong the precious indulgences granted—but only for money—both to the living and the dead. By indulgences, the miserable Judas, or pope, has sold Christ's merit, along with the extra merits of all saints, of the entire Church, and such things. Every single one of these things is unbearable. They are not only without God's Word, are unnecessary and not commanded, but are against the chief article. For Christ's merit is obtained not by our works or pennies, but from grace through faith, without money and merit (Ephesians 2:8–9). It is offered not through the pope's power, but through the preaching of God's Word (1 Corinthians 1:21).

## The Invocation of Saints

25  The invocation of saints is also one of the Antichrist's abuses that conflicts with the chief article and destroys the knowledge of Christ (Philippians 3:8). It is neither commanded nor counseled, nor has it any

warrant in Scripture. Even if it were a precious thing—which it is not—we have everything a thousand times better in Christ.

26    The angels in heaven pray for us, as does Christ Himself (Romans 8:34). So do the saints on earth and perhaps also in heaven (Revelation 6:9–10). It does not follow, though, that we should invoke and adore the angels and saints (Revelation 22:8–9). Nor should we fast, hold festivals, celebrate Mass, make offerings, and establish churches, altars, and divine worship in their honor. Nor should we serve them in other ways or regard them as helpers in times of need. Nor should we divide different kinds of help among them, ascribing to each one a particular form of assistance, as the papists teach and do. This is idolatry. Such honor belongs

27    to God alone. As a Christian and saint upon earth, you can pray for me in many necessities. But this does not mean that I have to adore and call upon you. I do not need to celebrate festivals, fast, make sacrifices, or hold Masses for your honor. I do not have to put my faith in you for my salvation. I can honor, love, and thank you in

28    Christ in other ways. If such idolatrous honor were withdrawn from angels and departed saints, the remaining honor would be harmless and quickly forgotten. When advantage and assistance (both bodily and spiritual) are no longer expected, the saints will not be troubled, neither in their graves nor in heaven. No one will much remember or esteem or honor them without a reward or just out of pure love.

29    In short, we cannot tolerate the Mass or anything that proceeds from it or is attached to it. We have to condemn the Mass in order to keep the holy Sacrament pure and certain, according to Christ's institution, used and received through faith.

## ARTICLE III

# Chapters and Cloisters

Reflecting on his own experiences as a monk, Luther rejects the Roman system of monastic life. By making monasticism meritorious for eternal life, Rome contradicted the chief article of the Christian faith. Monasteries were originally founded as institutions of education. Luther advocates returning them to that noble purpose; otherwise they should be destroyed.

1    Monastic colleges and communities were formerly founded with the good intention of educating learned men and virtuous women. They should be used for that again. They could produce pastors, preachers, and other ministers for the churches. They could also produce essential personnel for the secular government in cities and countries, as well as well-educated young women for mothers, housekeepers, and such.

2    If these institutions will not serve this purpose, it is better to abandon them or tear them down than have their blasphemous, humanly invented services regarded as something better than the ordinary Christian life and the offices and callings ordained by God. This too is contrary to the chief article on the redemption through Jesus Christ. Like all other human inventions, these religious institutions have not been commanded. They are needless and useless. They are also occasions for dangerous annoyances and empty works (Isaiah 29:20), what the Hebrew prophets call *Aven* (i.e., pain and labor).

## ARTICLE IV

# The Papacy

This article contains the most vigorous rejection of the papacy in the Book of Concord.

Luther flatly asserts that the pope is truly the Antichrist, a statement that may sound outrageous to most modern ears. The Bishop of Rome is no more than a pastor of God's people in Rome and of all those who voluntarily attach themselves to him—he is nothing more than this. The institution of the papacy developed on the basis of false claims to an authority that Christ had never bestowed. Luther points out how the papacy, as it existed in his time, did not exist for nearly five hundred years in the West and never was received by the Eastern Church (the "Greek" Church).

Luther's harsh words about the papacy are motivated by his passion for the chief article of the Christian faith: salvation by God's grace alone, through faith alone, on account of Christ alone. The Roman papacy in Luther's day was engaged not only in spiritual warfare against the truth of the Scripture regarding Christ, but it also took up arms to kill and destroy those who adhered faithfully to the article of justification. Today the papacy continues to insist that salvation is not by grace alone, through faith alone, and thus continues to set itself against the central teaching of the Christian faith. Melanchthon has much more to say about this point in the Treatise on the Power and Primacy of the Pope (pp. 315–32). (See also AC XXVIII; SC Table of Duties.)

1    The pope is not, according to divine law or God's Word, the head of all Christendom. This name belongs to One only, whose name is Jesus Christ (Colossians 1:18). The pope is only the bishop and pastor of the Church at Rome and of those who have attached themselves to him voluntarily or through a human agency (such as a political ruler). Christians are not under him as a lord. They are with him as brethren, colleagues, and companions, as the ancient councils and the age of St. Cyprian show.

2    Today, though, none of the bishops dare to address the pope as "brother" as was done in the time of Cyprian. Even kings or emperors have to call him "most gracious lord." We will not, cannot, and must not approve this arrogance with a good conscience. Whoever wants to, can do it without us.

3    It follows that all the pope has done and undertaken from such false, mischievous, blasphemous, and arrogant power are devilish affairs and transactions. (With the exception of what relates to the secular government, where God often allows much good to be done for a people, even through a tyrant and scoundrel.) The pope does this all for the ruin of the entire holy Christian Church (so far as it is in his power) and for the destruction of the chief article about the redemption made through Jesus Christ.

4    For there stand all the pope's bulls and books. He roars like a lion in them (as the angel in Revelation 12 depicts him), crying out that no Christian can be saved without obeying him and being subject to him in all that he wishes, says, and does. All of this amounts to nothing less than this: Although you believe in Christ and have in Him alone everything you need for salvation, yet it is nothing and all in vain unless you regard me as your god, and be subject and obedient to me. It is clear that the holy Church has been without the pope for over five hundred years at least. To this day, the churches of the Greeks and of many other languages neither have been nor are presently under the pope. Besides, as is often remarked, the papacy is a human invention that is not commanded and is not necessary but useless. The holy Christian Church can exist very well without such a head. It would certainly have re-

6 mained purer if such a head had not been raised up by the devil. The papacy is also of no use in the Church, because it exercises no Christian office. Therefore, it is necessary for the Church to continue and to exist without the pope.

7 Suppose that the pope would yield this point. He would not to be supreme by divine right or from God's command, but just because we need a head, to whom all the rest cling in order to preserve the unity of Christians against sects and heretics. Suppose that such a head were chosen, and that people had the choice and the power to change or remove this head. (The Council of Constance nearly adopted this course with reference to the popes, deposing three and electing a fourth.) Suppose, I say, that the pope and See at Rome would yield and accept this (though this is impossible, for then he would have to let his entire realm and estate be overthrown and destroyed, with all his rights and books, which, to put it briefly, he cannot do). Nevertheless, even if this were done, Christianity would not be helped, but many more sects would arise than before.

8 People would have to be subject to this head, not from God's command, but from their personal good pleasure. Such a head would easily and in a short time be despised, and finally not have any members. The head would not have to be forever confined to Rome or any other place. It might be wherever and in whatever church God would grant a man fit for the office. Oh, how complicated and confused that would be!

9 The Church can never be better governed and preserved than if we all live under one head, Christ. All the bishops should be equal in office (although they may be unequal in gifts). They should be diligently joined in unity of doctrine, faith, sacraments, prayer, works of love, and such. According to St. Jerome, this is how the priests at Alexandria governed the churches, together and in common. So did the apostles and, afterward, all bishops throughout all Christendom, until the pope raised his head above all.

10 This teaching shows forcefully that the pope is the true Endchrist or Antichrist (1 John 2:18). He has exalted himself above and opposed himself against Christ. For he will not permit Christians to be saved without his power, which, nevertheless, is nothing, and is neither ordained nor commanded by God. This is, properly speaking, how he

11 "exalts himself against every so-called god" as Paul says (2 Thessalonians 2:4). Even the Turks or the Tartars, great enemies of Christians as they are, do not do this. They take bodily tribute and obedience from Christians, but they allow whoever wishes to believe in Christ.

12 The pope, however, bans this faith. He says that to be saved a person must obey him. This we are unwilling to do, even though we must die in God's name because of this. This

13 all proceeds from the pope wishing to be called the supreme head of the Christian Church by divine right. So he had to make himself equal and superior to Christ. He had to have himself proclaimed the head and then the lord of the Church, and finally of the whole world. This makes him simply God on earth, to the point that he has dared to issue commands even to the angels in heaven.

14 When we distinguish the pope's teaching from, or compare it to, Holy Scripture, it is clear that the pope's teaching at its best has been taken from the imperial and heathen law. It deals with political matters and decisions or rights, as the decretals show. His law also teaches ceremonies about churches, garments, food, persons, and childish, theatrical, and comical things without measure. But in all of this, nothing at all is taught about

Christ, faith, and God's commandments. Finally, the papacy is nothing else than the devil himself, because above and against God the pope pushes his falsehoods about Masses, purgatory, the monastic life, one's own works, and false worship. (This, in fact, is the papacy.) He also condemns, murders, and tortures all Christians who do not exalt and honor his abominations above all things. Therefore, just as we cannot worship the devil himself as Lord and God, so we cannot endure his apostle—the pope or Antichrist—in his rule as head or lord. For what his papal government really consists of (as I have very clearly shown in many books) is to lie and kill and destroy body and soul eternally.

15 They will have enough to condemn in the council in these four articles. For they cannot and will not concede to us even the least point in one of these articles. Of this we can be certain. We must be sure and consider the hope that Christ, our Lord, has attacked His adversary. He will press and attack him both by His Spirit and His coming. Amen.

16 In the council we will not stand before the emperor or the political ruler, as at Augsburg (where the emperor published a most gracious edict, and caused matters to be heard kindly). Instead, we will appear before the pope and devil himself, who intends to listen to nothing, but will just condemn, murder, and force us to idolatry. Therefore, we should not here kiss his feet, or say, "you are my gracious lord." Rather, we should say as the angel [of the LORD] in Zechariah 3:2 said to the devil, "The LORD rebuke you, O Satan!"

## THE THIRD PART

We may be able to discuss the following articles with learned and reasonable people, or among ourselves. The pope and his government do not care much about these. With them conscience is nothing, but money, honors, and power are everything.

## ARTICLE I

# Sin

The major point of this article is to make sure that original sin is clearly seen as the root cause of all sin. Roman doctrine denied that even the very inclination to sin (concupiscence) is itself sin. By teaching that within a person there remains an ability to grasp and respond to grace, Rome effectively denies the absolute necessity and total sufficiency of Christ's sacrificial death to merit our salvation. They, of course, vigorously deny this, but by making a person's response to grace part of salvation, a denial of Christ's sufficiency is precisely the result. (See AC II and XIX; FC Ep I and SD I.)

1 Here we must confess, as Paul says in Romans 5:12, that sin originated from one man, Adam. By his disobedience, all people were made sinners and became subject to death and the devil. This is called original or the chief sin.

2 The fruit of this sin are the evil deeds that are forbidden in the Ten Commandments (Galatians 5:19–21). These include unbelief, false faith, idolatry, being without the fear of God, pride, despair, utter blindness, and, in short, not knowing or regarding God. Also lying, abusing God's name, not praying, not calling on God, not regarding God's Word, being disobedient to parents, murdering, being unchaste, stealing, deceiving, and such.

3 This hereditary sin is such a deep corruption of nature that no reason can understand it. Rather, it must be believed from the revelation of Scripture. (See Psalm 51:5; Romans 6:12–13; Exodus 33:3; Genesis 3:7–19.) Therefore, it is nothing but error and blind-

ness that the scholastic doctors have taught in regard to this article:

4 Since Adam's fall the natural powers of human beings have remained whole and uncorrupted, and by nature people have a right reason and a good will, as the philosophers teach.

5 A person has a free will to do good and not to do evil, and, on the other hand, to not do good and do evil.

6 By natural human powers a person can observe and keep all God's commands.

7 By natural human powers, a person can love God above all things and love his neighbors as himself.

8 If a person does as much as is in him, God certainly grants him His grace.

9 If a person wishes to go to the Sacrament, there is no need of a good intention to do good. It is enough if a person does not have a wicked purpose to commit sin, so entirely good is human nature and so effective is the Sacrament.

10 Scripture does not teach that the Holy Spirit with His grace is necessary for a good work.

11 These and many similar ideas have arisen from lack of understanding and ignorance, both about sin and about Christ, our Savior. They are truly heathen teachings that we cannot endure. For if such teaching were true, then Christ has died in vain. A human being would have no defect or sin for which He would have died. Or He would have died only for the body, not for the soul, since the soul is sound, and only the body is subject to death.

## ARTICLE II

# The Law

The Lutheran Reformation restored the proper biblical understanding of the chief purpose of the Law: to reveal mankind's total corruption because of sin, driving people to seek salvation only in Christ. While the Law does hold outward sin (that is, gross outbursts of sin) in check, its chief purpose is to lead mankind to realize the damning consequences of original sin. The Roman Church had leaned far too heavily on pagan philosophy in developing its doctrine about sin. It had accepted the unscriptural notion that a person could truly keep the Law by means of his or her own abilities. This article also summarizes well the three different reactions of sinners to the Law.

---

Here we hold that the Law was given by 1 God, first, to restrain sin by threats and the dread of punishment and by the promise and offer of grace and benefit. All this failed because of the evil that sin has worked in humanity. For by the Law some people were 2 made worse sinners, those who are hostile to the Law because it forbids what they like to do and commands what they do not like to do (Romans 3:20; 7:7–9). Wherever they can escape punishment, they do more against the Law than they did before. Those are the unrestrained and wicked, who do evil wherever they have the opportunity.

The rest become blind and arrogant. As 3 has been said above about the scholastic theologians, they conceive the opinion that they are able to keep the Law by their own powers. From this come the hypocrites and false saints.

But the chief office or force of the Law is 4 to reveal original sin with all its fruit. It shows us how very low our nature has fallen, how we have become utterly corrupted. The Law must tell us that we have no God, that we do not care for God, and that we worship other gods (Romans 3:10–18)—something we would not have believed before and without the Law. In this way, we become terrified, humbled, depressed. We despair and anxiously want help, but see no escape (Romans 7:21–24). We begin to be an enemy of God and to complain, and so on (Romans 5:10). 5 This is what Paul says, "The law brings wrath" (Romans 4:15). Sin is increased by the Law, "The law came in to increase the trespass" (Romans 5:20).

## ARTICLE III

# Repentance

Luther puts forward the proper biblical teaching about repentance, which is the interplay between the Law and the Gospel. The Law reveals sin and drives us to cling to Christ alone. The Gospel, imparted by means of Word and Sacrament, comforts and soothes consciences. This interplay of the Law revealing sin and the Gospel forgiving and restoring is what true repentance is all about.

Luther condemns Rome's false teaching about repentance, which assumes that original sin has not totally corrupted all human spiritual abilities. Roman theologians held that God bestows His grace on those who do as much as they can on the basis of their own free will. Rome's entire penitential and sacramental system—in fact, the entire papal system—is based on this false view of human abilities in spiritual matters. They turn repentance into something other than what it is according to God's Word; namely, repenting of sin and being turned again to Christ alone. In the Roman system of "penance" or repentance, not only must sorrow be present, but also satisfaction must be made for sin. This robs Christ of His place as full and complete satisfaction for all sins.

In this article Luther also rejects more radical reformers who were teaching that once a person is saved, he or she is never in danger of falling. He points to David as an example of a person who did truly fall away and was again restored through the prophet's preaching of Law and Gospel to him. (See AC XII; SC V; LC V, An Exhortation to Confession.)

---

The New Testament keeps and urges this 1 office of the Law, as St. Paul does when he says, "The wrath of God is revealed from heaven against all ungodliness and unrighteousness of men" (Romans 1:18). Also, "the whole world may be accountable to God. . . . No human being will be justified in His sight" (Romans 3:19–20). And, Christ says, the Holy Spirit will convict the world of sin (John 16:8).

This is God's thunderbolt. By the Law He 2 strikes down both obvious sinners and false saints. He declares no one to be in the right, but drives them all together to terror and despair. This is the hammer. As Jeremiah says, "Is not My word like . . . a hammer that breaks the rock in pieces?" (23:29). This is not active contrition or manufactured repentance. It is passive contrition, true sorrow of heart, suffering, and the sensation of death.

This is what true repentance means. Here 3 a person needs to hear something like this, "You are all of no account, whether you are obvious sinners or saints (in your own opinions). You have to become different from what you are now. You have to act differently than you are now acting, whether you are as great, wise, powerful, and holy as you can be. Here no one is godly."

But to this office of the Law, the New Testament immediately adds the consoling 4 promise of grace through the Gospel. This must be believed. As Christ declares, "Repent and believe in the gospel" (Mark 1:15). That is, become different, act differently, and believe My promise. John the Baptist (preced- 5 ing Christ) is called a preacher of repentance, but this is for the forgiveness of sins. That is, John was to accuse all and convict them of being sinners. This is so they can know what they are before God and acknowledge that they are lost. So they can be prepared for the Lord (Mark 1:3) to receive grace and to expect and accept from Him the forgiveness of

6 sins. This is what Christ Himself says, "Repentance and forgiveness of sins should be proclaimed in [My] name to all nations" (Luke 24:47).

7 Whenever the Law alone exercises its office, without the Gospel being added, there is nothing but death and hell, and one must despair, as Saul and Judas did (1 Samuel 31; Matthew 27:5). St. Paul says, through sin the

8 Law kills. (See Romans 7:10.) On the other hand, the Gospel brings consolation and forgiveness. It does so not just in one way, but through the Word and the Sacraments and the like, as we will discuss later. As Psalm 130:7 says against the dreadful captivity of sin, "with the LORD is . . . plentiful redemption."

9 However, we now have to contrast the false repentance of the sophists with true repentance, in order that both may be understood better.

## The False Repentance of the Papists

10 It was impossible for them to teach correctly about repentance, since they did not know what sin really is. As has been shown above, they do not believe correctly about original sin. Rather, they say that the natural powers of human beings have remained unimpaired and uncorrupted. They believe that reason can teach correctly, so that the will can do what is right, and God certainly bestows His grace when a person does as much as he can, according to his free will.

11 According to that dogma, they need to do penance only for actual sins. Those would include only the evil thoughts that a person yields to. Or evil words and evil deeds that free will could easily have prevented. (According to these people, wicked emotions, lust, and improper attitudes are not sins.)

12 They divide repentance into three parts: contrition, confession, and satisfaction. They add this consolation and promise: If a person truly confesses, and renders satisfaction, he *merits* forgiveness. He has paid for his sins before God. So even in repentance, they taught people to put confidence in their own works. This is where the expres-

13 sion comes from that was used in the pulpit when Public Absolution was announced to the people: "Prolong O God, my life, until I can make satisfaction for my sins and amend my life."

14 There was here no mention of Christ and faith. People hoped to overcome and blot out sins before God by their own works. With this intention, we became priests and monks, so we could protect ourselves against sin.

15 As for contrition, this is how it was done. No one could remember all his sins (especially those committed over an entire year), so they inserted this provision: If an unknown sin is remembered later, it too has to be repented of and confessed, and so on. Until then, the person was commended to God's grace.

16 Furthermore, since no one could know how great the contrition ought to be in order to be enough before God, they gave this consolation: He who could not have contrition at least ought to have "attrition." I call that half a contrition, or the beginning of contrition. The fact is, they themselves do not understand either of these terms, anymore than I do. But such attrition was counted as contrition when a person went to Confession.

17 If anyone said that he could not have contrition or lament his sins (as might be the case with illicit love or the desire for revenge, etc.), they asked whether he wished or desired to have contrition. When one would reply "yes"—for who, save the devil himself, would say "no"?—they accepted this as contrition. They forgave him his sins on account of this good work of his. Here they cited the example of St. Bernard and others.

18 Here one sees how blind reason gropes around in matters belonging to God (1 Corinthians 2:14). According to its own imagination, reason seeks consolation in its own works and cannot remember Christ and faith. Viewed in the light, this contrition is a manufactured and fictitious thought. It comes from our own powers, without faith and without the knowledge of Christ. When he reflected on his own lust and desire for revenge, the poor sinner might have laughed rather than wept—unless he had either been truly struck by the lightning of the Law (Psalm 77:18) or had been tormented by the devil with a sorrowful spirit (1 Samuel 16:14). With everyone else, such contrition was certainly mere hypocrisy and did not put to death the lust for sins. They had to grieve, but if they were free, they would rather have kept on sinning.

19 As for Confession, the procedure was this: Everyone had to list all his sins (which is impossible). This was a great torment. If anyone had forgotten some sins, he would be absolved on the condition that, if they would occur to him, he must still confess them. So he could never know whether he had made a sufficiently pure confession or if confessing would ever come to an end. Yet he was pointed to his own works. He was comforted like this: The more fully you confess, and the more you humiliate yourself and debase yourself before the priest, the sooner and better you render satisfaction for your sins. Such humility would certainly earn grace before God.

20 Here, too, there was neither faith nor Christ. The power of the Absolution was not declared to him. Rather, his consolation depended upon his listing of sins and his self-abasement. What torture, fraud, and idolatry this kind of confession has produced is more than can be said.

21 As for satisfaction, this is by far the most complex part of all. For no one can know how much to render for a single sin, let alone how much for all. They resorted to the device of imposing a small satisfaction, which could indeed be rendered, as five "Our Fathers," a day's fast, or such. Then, for the rest of their repentance, they were directed to purgatory.

22 Here, too, there was nothing but anguish and extreme misery. Some thought they would never get out of purgatory. According to the old Church laws, seven years' penance in purgatory is required for a single mortal sin. Yet, confidence was placed in our work 23 of satisfaction. If the satisfaction could be perfect, confidence would be placed in it entirely. Neither faith nor Christ would be necessary. But such confidence was impossible. For even though someone had done penance that way for a hundred years, he would still not know whether he had finished his penance. That meant doing penance forever and never coming to repentance.

24 Then the Holy See at Rome, coming to the aid of the poor Church, invented indulgences. With these, it forgave and remitted satisfaction. First, for a single sin, an indulgence could cancel seven years in purgatory. Or an indulgence could cancel a hundred years. They distributed them among the cardinals and bishops, so that one could grant indulgence for a hundred years and another for a hundred days. But the pope re-

served to himself alone the power to cancel the entire satisfaction.

25    Since indulgences began to yield money and as the traffic in bulls became profitable, the pope devised the golden jubilee year (compare to Leviticus 25)—a truly *gold-bearing year*—and established it at Rome. He said this would give the cancellation of all punishment and guilt. The people came running, because everyone would gladly be freed from this grievous, unbearable burden. This was meant to find and raise the treasures of the earth. Immediately, the pope pressed still further and multiplied the golden years one after another. The more he devoured money, the bigger his appetite grew.

Later, by his representatives to the countries, the pope issued his golden years everywhere, until all churches and houses were full

26    of the golden year. Ultimately, he made an inroad into purgatory, among the dead. First, he founded Masses and vigils, and, afterward, indulgences and the golden year. Finally, souls became so cheap that he released one for a penny.

27    But all this, too, did nothing. Even though the pope taught people to depend on and trust these indulgences for salvation, he made the matter uncertain again. In his bulls he declares that whoever wants to share in the indulgences or a golden year has to be contrite and have confessed and pay money. We have already seen how, with the papacy, contrition and confession are uncertain and hypocritical. Besides, no one knew what soul was in purgatory. If some souls were in purgatory, no one knew who had properly repented and confessed. So the pope took the precious money, comforting people with his power and indulgence. But then he directed them again to their uncertain works.

28    Now some did not believe themselves guilty of actual sins in thought, word, and deeds. I, and people like me in monasteries and religious communities, wanted to be monks and priests. We fought against evil thoughts by doing such things as fasting, staying awake, praying, saying Mass, wearing coarse garments, and sleeping on hard beds. In total sincerity and with great effort, we wanted to be holy. Yet the hereditary, inborn evil sometimes came out in sleep, as happens (St. Augustine and St. Jerome, among others, also confess this). Still, each one held the other in high esteem. According to our teaching, some monks were regarded as holy, without sin, and full of good works. Also, since we had more good works than we needed to get to heaven, we could communicate and sell our good works to others. This is actually true. Seals, letters, and examples are at hand to prove that this happened.

29    These holy ones did not need repentance. What would they repent of, since they had not indulged their wicked thoughts? What would they confess about words they never said? What should they render satisfaction for, since they were so guiltless that they could even sell their extra righteousness to poor sinners? In the time of Christ, the Pharisees and scribes were these kinds of saints (Matthew 23).

30    But here comes the fiery angel of St. John (Revelation 10), the true preacher of repentance. With one bolt of lightning, he hurls together both those selling and those buying works. He says: "Repent!"( Matthew 3:2).

31    Now one group imagines, "Why, we have repented!" The other says, "We need no repentance."

32    John says, "Repent, both of you. You false penitents and false saints, both of you need the forgiveness of sins. Neither of you know what sin really is. Much less your duty to repent of it and shun it. For no one of you is good. You are full of unbelief, stupidity, and

ignorance of God and God's will. But He is present here, of whose 'fullness we have all received, grace upon grace'" (John 1:16). Without Him, no one can be righteous before God. Therefore, if you want to repent, repent rightly. Your works of penance will accomplish nothing. As for you hypocrites, who do not need repentance, you serpents' brood, who has assured you that you will escape the wrath to come and other judgments?" (Matthew 3:7; Luke 3:7).

33   In the same way Paul also preaches, "None is righteous, no, not one; no one understands; no one seeks for God. All have turned aside; together they have become worthless; no one does good, not even one"

34   (Romans 3:10–12). And God now "commands all people everywhere to repent" (Acts 17:30). "All people," He says. No one is an ex-

35   ception who is a human being. This repentance teaches us to discern sin: We are completely lost; there is nothing good in us from head to foot; and we must become absolutely new and different people.

36   Such repentance is not partial and fragmentary, like that which does penance for actual sins. Nor, like that, is it uncertain. For it does not debate what is or is not sin. Rather, it hurls everything together and says: Everything in us is nothing but sin (there is nothing in us that is not sin and guilt [Romans 7:18]). What is the use of always investigating, dividing, or distinguishing? This contrition is certain. For we cannot think of any good thing to pay for sin. There is nothing left. There is only a sure despairing about all that we are, think, speak, do, and so on.

37   Confession, too, cannot be false, uncertain, or fragmentary. A person who confesses that everything in him is nothing but sin includes all sins, excludes none, forgets none.

38   Neither can the satisfaction be uncertain, be-

cause it is not our uncertain, sinful work. Rather, it is the suffering and blood of the innocent Lamb of God, who takes away the sin of the world (John 1:29).

39   This is the repentance John the Baptist preaches (Matthew 3:1–12). And afterward, Christ does this in the Gospel (Mark 1:15), and so do we. By this preaching of repentance, we dash to the ground the pope and everything built upon our good works. For all of that is built upon a rotten and vain foundation, which is called a good work or law. And yet, this foundation has no good works but only wicked works. No one keeps the Law (as Christ says) but all transgress it (John 7:19). Therefore, the building that is raised upon that rotten foundation is nothing but falsehood and hypocrisy, even where it seems most holy and beautiful.

40   In Christians, this repentance continues until death. For through one's entire life, repentance contends with the sin remaining in the flesh. Paul testifies that he wars with the law in his members (Romans 7:14–25) not by his own powers, but by the gift of the Holy Spirit that follows the forgiveness of sins (Romans 8:1–17). This gift daily cleanses and sweeps out the remaining sins and works to make a person truly pure and holy.

41   The pope, the theologians, the Church lawyers, and the rest know nothing about this. But it is a doctrine from heaven (revealed through the Gospel), and the godless saints must call it heresy.

42   On the other hand, certain sects may arise; some may already exist. During the peasant rebellion, I encountered some who held that those who had once received the Spirit or the forgiveness of sins or had become believers—even if they later sin— would still remain in the faith. Such sin, they think, would not harm them. They say, "Do whatever you please. If you believe, it

Title page for first complete "Luther Bible" (Wittenberg, 1534). Top: The motto of the Saxony rulers and many faithful Lutheran lay leaders: "God's Word remains forever," the German version of *Verbum Domini Manet in Aeternum* ("The Word of the Lord endures forever"). Left: Coat of arms of the Marshall of the Empire, an honorary title historically given to the rulers of Saxony. Right: Coat of Arms of Saxony. The center text says, "Bible: that is, the entire Holy Scripture in German. Martin Luther, Wittenberg. Specially Gifted with a Saxon Electoral License. Printed by Hans Lufft, 1534." Lufft was given the right to print the first copies of the Luther Bible, an event he celebrated every year with his associates.

all amounts to nothing. Faith blots out all sins," and such. They also say that if anyone sins after he has received faith and the Spirit, he never truly had the Spirit and faith. I have seen and heard many such madmen. I fear that such a devil is still in some of them.

43    So it is necessary to know and to teach this: When holy people—still having and feeling original sin and daily repenting and striving against it—happen to fall into manifest sins (as David did into adultery, murder, and blasphemy [2 Samuel 11]), then faith and the

44    Holy Spirit have left them. The Holy Spirit does not permit sin to have dominion, to gain the upper hand so it can be carried out, but represses and restrains it from doing what it wants (Psalm 51:11; Romans 6:14). If sin does what it wants, the Holy Spirit and faith are

45    not present. For St. John says, "No one born of God makes a practice of sinning . . . and he cannot keep on sinning" (1 John 3:9). And yet it is also true when St. John says, "If we say we have no sin, we deceive ourselves, and the truth is not in us" (1:8).

## ARTICLE IV
# The Gospel

Luther details how the Gospel comes to us: through the preached Word of forgiveness. God lavishly and generously gives His gifts, providing the Gospel in other forms as well, including Holy Baptism, the Lord's Supper, and the Gospel shared among Christians who console and comfort one another with the Word of Christ. Through each of these means God grants us forgiveness, life, and salvation.

———————

We will now return to the Gospel, which does not give us counsel and aid against sin in only one way. God is superabundantly generous in His grace: First, through the spoken Word, by which the forgiveness of sins is preached in the whole world (Luke 24:45–47). This is the particular office of the Gospel. Second, through Baptism. Third, through the holy Sacrament of the Altar. Fourth, through the Power of the Keys. Also through the mutual conversation and consolation of brethren, "Where two or three are gathered" (Matthew 18:20) and other such verses (especially Romans 1:12).

## ARTICLE V
# Baptism

Echoing the language he uses in his Small Catechism, Luther emphasizes that the power and promise of Holy Baptism are located entirely in the life-giving Word of mercy and grace. Therefore, he rejects any notion that the water by itself or the actions in the ritual have any spiritual power. Rather, God's Word is the key to Baptism's strength and blessing. Certainly infants and children should be baptized, for they are just as much a part of Christ's redeeming work and God's kingdom as anyone else. (See AC IX; SC IV; LC IV.)

———————

Baptism is nothing other than God's    1
Word in the water, commanded by His institution. As Paul says, it is a "washing . . . with the word" (Ephesians 5:26). As Augustine says, "When the Word is joined to the element or natural substance, it becomes a Sacrament." This is why we do not agree    2
with Thomas Aquinas and the monastic preachers who forget the Word (God's institution). They say that God has imparted to the water a spiritual power, which through the water washes away sin. Nor do we agree    3
with Scotus and the Barefooted Monks, who teach that Baptism washes away sins by the

assistance of the divine will. They believe this washing occurs only through God's will, and not at all through the Word or water.

4    Of the Baptism of children, we hold that children should be baptized, for they belong to the promised redemption made through Christ (Acts 2:39). Therefore, the Church should administer Baptism to them.

## ARTICLE VI

# The Sacrament of the Altar

In the most vivid and realistic language about the Lord's Supper found in the Book of Concord, Luther asserts that the bread and wine are the body and blood of Christ. They are present, distributed, and received by all who commune. Both bread and wine are to be given to communicants. The theory of transubstantiation is rejected as deceptive reasoning. The plain sense of Scripture is all that matters here, because is it the word and promise of Christ. (See AC X and XXII; SC VI; LC V; FC Ep VII; SD VII.)

1    Of the Sacrament of the Altar, we hold that the bread and wine in the Supper are Christ's true body and blood. These are given and received not only by the godly but also by wicked Christians (1 Corinthians 11:29–30).

2    We do not hold that only one kind of the Sacrament is to be given (e.g., the bread alone). We do not need that "high reasoning" that teaches there is as much under the one kind as under both, as the sophists and the

3    Council of Constance teach. Even if that were true, giving the one kind only is not the entire ordinance and institution commanded

4    by Christ (Galatians 1:9). We especially condemn and in God's name curse those who

not only refuse to give both kinds but also quite tyrannically prohibit, condemn, and blaspheme giving both kinds as heresy. In doing so, they exalt themselves against and above Christ, our Lord and God.

5    As for transubstantiation, we care nothing about the sophistic cunning by which they teach that bread and wine leave or lose their own natural substance so that only the appearance and color of bread remain, and not true bread. For it is in perfect agreement with Holy Scriptures that there is, and remains, bread, as Paul himself calls it, "The bread that we break" (1 Corinthians 10:16) and "Let a person . . . so eat of the bread" (1 Corinthians 11:28).

## ARTICLE VII

# The Keys

The authority to bind sins and not forgive them, or to loose sins by forgiving them, is an office and power entrusted by Christ to His Church, not just to the pope and the papal hierarchy.

1    The Keys are an office and power given by Christ to the Church for binding and loosing sin (Matthew 16:19). This applies not only to gross and well-known sins, but also the subtle, hidden sins that are known only to God. As it is written, "Who can discern his errors?" (Psalm 19:12). And St. Paul himself complains that "with my flesh I serve the law of sin" (Romans 7:25). It is

2    not in our power to judge which, how great, and how many the sins are. This belongs to God alone. As it is written, "Enter not into judgment with your servant, for no one living is righteous before you" (Psalm 143:2).

3    Paul says, "I am not aware of anything against myself, but I am not thereby acquitted" (1 Corinthians 4:4).

## ARTICLE VIII

# Confession

Luther never intended to abolish private Confession and Absolution, only to do away with the errors and abuses that had come to be associated with it. A particularly great abuse was the requirement for a complete enumeration of sins. Luther insists on the biblical view of God's mercy and grace, which comes by the external, objective, and outward Word.

Radical reformers taught that people should seek God outside of His Word, looking instead to their inner feelings, thoughts, and other so-called spiritual experiences. (Luther calls them *enthusiasts* or *Schwärmer*, a German word for the buzzing of bees.) Many make the same claims today! This error is rooted deeply in all people as a result of the Fall. It must be battled constantly. It is also the root source of papal errors. Luther makes this key point, "God does not wish to deal with us in any other way than through the spoken Word and the Sacraments." He speaks; we listen. At His speaking, it is done. (See AC XI and XXV; SC V; LC V, An Exhortation to Confession.)

---

1   Absolution, or the Power of the Keys, is an aid against sin and a consolation for a bad conscience; it is ordained by Christ in the Gospel (Matthew 16:19). Therefore, Confession and Absolution should by no means be abolished in the Church. This is especially for the sake of timid consciences and untrained young people, so they may be examined and instructed in Christian doctrine.

2   But the listing of sins should be free to everyone, as to what a person wishes to list or not to list. For as long as we are in the flesh, we will not lie when we say, "I acknowledge that I am a miserable sinner, full of sin." "I see in my members another law," and such (Romans 7:23). Since private Absolution originates in the Office of the Keys, it should not be despised, but greatly and highly esteemed, along with all other offices of the Christian Church.

3   In issues relating to the spoken, outward Word, we must firmly hold that God grants His Spirit or grace to no one except through or with the preceding outward Word (Galatians 3:2, 5). This protects us from the enthusiasts (i.e., souls who boast that they have the Spirit without and before the Word). They judge Scripture or the spoken Word and explain and stretch it at their pleasure, as Münzer did. Many still do this today, wanting to be sharp judges between the Spirit and the letter, and yet they do not know what they are saying (2 Corinthians 3:6). Actually, the papacy too is nothing but 4 sheer enthusiasm. The pope boasts that all rights exist in the shrine of his heart. Whatever he decides and commands within his church is from the Spirit and is right, even though it is above and contrary to Scripture and the spoken Word.

5   All this is the old devil and old serpent (Revelation 12:9), who also turned Adam and Eve into enthusiasts. He led them away from God's outward Word to spiritualizing and self-pride (Genesis 3:2–5). And yet, he did this through other outward words. In 6 the same way, our enthusiasts today condemn the outward Word. Yet they themselves are not silent. They fill the world with their babbling and writings, as if the Spirit could not come through the apostles' writings and spoken Word, but has to come through their writings and words. Why don't they leave out their own sermons and writings and let the Spirit Himself come to people without their writings before them, as they boast that He has come into them

without the preaching of the Scriptures? We do not have time now to argue about this in more detail. We have treated this well enough elsewhere.

7    For even those who believe before being baptized, or become believing in Baptism, believe through the outward Word, which came first. For example, adults who have come to reason must first have heard "Whoever believes and is baptized will be saved" (Mark 16:16), even though they are at first unbelieving and receive the Spirit and Baptism ten years afterward. Cornelius, living among the Jews, had heard long before about the coming Messiah, through whom he was righteous before God (Acts 10:1–2). In such faith, his prayers and alms were acceptable to God (since Luke calls him devout and God-fearing). Without the Word coming first and without hearing it, he could not have believed or been righteous (Romans 10:17). St. Peter, though, had to reveal to him that the Messiah (in whom he had previously believed as one who would come in the future) now had come, lest his faith in the coming Messiah hold him captive among the Jewish people, who were hardened and unbelieving. He must now know that he is saved by the present Messiah and must not, with the Jewish people, deny or persecute Him.

9    In a word, enthusiasm dwells in Adam and his children from the beginning to the end of the world. Its venom has been implanted and infused into them by the old serpent. It is the origin, power, and strength of all heresy, especially of that of the papacy and Muhammad.

10   Therefore, we must constantly maintain this point: God does not want to deal with us in any other way than through the spoken Word and the Sacraments. Whatever is praised as from the Spirit—without the Word and Sacraments—is the devil himself. God wanted to appear even to Moses through the burning

11   bush and spoken Word (Exodus 3:2–15). No prophet, neither Elijah nor Elisha, received the Spirit without the Ten Commandments or the spoken Word. John the Baptist was not conceived without the word of Gabriel coming first, nor did he leap in his mother's womb without Mary's voice (Luke 1:11–20, 41). Peter says, "For no prophecy was ever produced by the will of man, but men spoke from God as they were carried along by the Holy Spirit" (2 Peter 1:21). Without the outward Word, however, they were not holy. Much less would the Holy Spirit have moved them to speak when they were still unholy. They were holy, says he, since the Holy Spirit spoke through them.

## ARTICLE IX

# Excommunication

Luther's remarks here are especially interesting since he had been placed under the pope's ban and had lived under it since 1521. Luther rejects any suggestion that the pope can ban people from both Church and society. Ministers have no authority to mix civil penalties with excommunication from the Church. However, Luther clearly does acknowledge biblical excommunication, that is, preventing openly unrepentant sinners from receiving Holy Communion and other fellowship in the Church until they repent and turn from their sin.

---

The greater excommunication, as the pope calls it, we regard only as a civil penalty, and it does not concern us ministers of the Church. But the lesser, truly Christian excommunication, is this: Open and hard-hearted sinners are not admitted to the Sacrament and other communion of the Church until they amend their lives and avoid sin (1 Corinthians 5). Ministers should not mingle secular punishments with this punishment from the Church, or excommunication.

## ARTICLE X
# Ordination and the Call

Luther is willing to permit the role of bishops if they would do the work the Bible prescribes for them; namely, serve the Church for the sake of the Gospel. He rejects any notion that ordination from a bishop is necessary for a pastor to have a valid and legitimate call to ministry. He points out how the bishops of his day had fallen terribly far from the biblical understanding of episcopal oversight. Luther insists that the authority and right to ordain is to be used within the Church, with or without the bishops' consent. Only men who have been judged capable of discharging the ministerial office should be ordained. Even the practice of the early Church demonstrates that pastors can, and should, ordain other men to be pastors, without bishops. (See AC XIV; SA III X.)

1    If the bishops would be true bishops and would devote themselves to the Church and the Gospel, we might grant them to ordain and confirm us and our preachers. This would be for the sake of love and unity, but not because it was necessary. However, they would have to give up all comedies and spectacular display of unchristian parade and

2    pomp. But they do not even want to be true bishops, but worldly lords and princes, who will neither preach, nor teach, nor baptize, nor administer the Lord's Supper, nor perform any work or office of the Church. Furthermore, they persecute and condemn those who do discharge these functions, having been called to do so. So the Church should not be deprived of ministers because of the bishops.

3    Therefore, as the ancient examples of the Church and the fathers teach us, we ourselves should ordain suitable persons to this office. Even according to their own laws, they do not have the right to forbid or prevent us. For their laws say that those ordained even by heretics are truly ordained and stay ordained. As St. Jerome writes of the Church at Alexandria, at first it was governed in common by priests and preachers, without bishops.

## ARTICLE XI
# The Marriage of Priests

The fact that priests were denied marriage under the pope is a clear indication of the anti-Christian nature of the papacy. Just as we cannot make a man a woman, or a woman a man, so the Church cannot forbid what God has created and ordained: marriage. It is a doctrine of demons to teach otherwise. (See AC XXIII.)

1    They have neither the authority nor the right to ban marriage and to burden the divine order of priests with perpetual celibacy. They have acted like anti-Christian, tyrannical, desperate scoundrels, and by this have caused all kinds of horrible, outrageous, innumerable sins of unchastity, in which they themselves still wallow. Now, neither we nor

2    they have been given the power to make a woman out of a man or a man out of a woman, or to nullify either sex. So they have had no authority to separate such creatures of God, or to forbid them from living honestly in marriage with one another. There-

3    fore, we are unwilling to agree to their outrageous celibacy, nor will we tolerate it. We want to have marriage free as God has instituted it, and we want neither to repeal nor hinder His work. For Paul says that this ban on marriage is the "teachings of demons" (1 Timothy 4:1–3).

## ARTICLE XII

# The Church

In his writings, Luther would often refer to a young child as capable of understanding doctrine better than theologians. Here Luther presents a seven-year-old child as knowing very simply and clearly that the Church consists of those who hear and follow the voice of the Good Shepherd. The Church's holiness is not found in man-made rituals and decorations, but only in the Word of God, which creates and calls forth true faith in Christ. (See AC VII/VIII; LC II, The Third Article.)

1    We do not agree with them that they are the Church. They are not the Church. Nor will we listen to those things that, under the name of Church, they command or forbid.
2    Thank God, today a seven-year-old child knows what the Church is, namely, the holy believers and lambs who hear the voice of
3    their Shepherd (John 10:11–16). For the children pray, "I believe in one holy Christian Church." This holiness does not come from albs, tonsures, long gowns, and other ceremonies they made up without Holy Scripture, but from God's Word and true faith.

## ARTICLE XIII

# How One Is Justified before God and Does Good Works

As Luther approaches the end of his Confession, he asserts once more, very plainly, the doctrine of justification. This teaching cannot be changed in the least. Saving faith and renewal produces in us a harvest of good works. The entire person is declared righteous. All is covered over in the mercy of Christ, including our sinful and flawed "good works." It follows, then, that a person in whom there are no good works does not in fact have true faith. Works do not save; they are the fruit of salvation, not its cause. (See AC IV, VI, XX; FC Ep III–VI and SD III–VI.)

1    I do not know how to change in the least what I have previously and constantly taught about justification. Namely, that through faith, as St. Peter says, we have a new and clean heart (Acts 15:9–11), and God will and does account us entirely righteous and holy for the sake of Christ, our Mediator (1 Timothy 2:5). Although sin in the flesh has not yet been completely removed or become dead (Romans 7:18), yet He will not punish or remember it.
2    Such faith, renewal, and forgiveness of sins are followed by good works (Ephesians 2:8–9). What is still sinful or imperfect in them will not be counted as sin or defect, for Christ's sake (Psalm 32:1–2; Romans 4:7–8). The entire individual, both his person and his works, is declared to be righteous and holy from pure grace and mercy, shed upon us and spread over us in Christ. Therefore, we can-
3    not boast of many merits and works, if they are viewed apart from grace and mercy. As it is written, "Let the one who boasts, boast in the Lord" (1 Corinthians 1:31); namely, that he has a gracious God. For with that, all is well. We say, besides, that if good works do
4    not follow, the faith is false and not true.

## ARTICLE XIV

# Monastic Vows

As in the article on marriage, Luther is speaking here autobiographically, as a former monk. He asserts very plainly that monastic vows are, in fact, blasphemy against God.

1    Since monastic vows directly conflict with the first chief article, they must be absolutely abolished. It is about them that Christ says,

"Many will come in my name, saying, 'I am the Christ,' and they will lead many astray" (Matthew 24:5, 23–24). He who makes a 2 vow to live as a monk believes that he will enter upon a way of life holier than ordinary Christians lead. He wants to earn heaven by his own works, not only for himself, but also 3 for others. This is to deny Christ. They also boast from their St. Thomas Aquinas that a monastic vow is equal to Baptism. This is blasphemy.

## ARTICLE XV

# Human Traditions

Luther concludes his confession by rejecting any suggestion that human traditions produce the forgiveness of sins. He also asserts how strongly he feels about these articles of faith. For Luther, none of these teachings could be compromised. In one final condemnation of a whole host of superstitious Roman practices, he indicates we should have nothing to do with them. (See AC XV; FC Ep X and SD X.)

———————

1    The declaration of the papists that human traditions serve for the forgiveness of sins or merit salvation is unchristian and condemned. As Christ says, "In vain do they worship Me, teaching as doctrines the commandments of men" (Matthew 15:9). Again, "the commands of people who turn away 2 from the truth" (Titus 1:14). When they declare that it is a mortal sin if someone breaks these ordinances, this, too, is not right.

3    These are the articles on which I must stand, and, God willing, shall stand, even to my death. I do not know how to change or yield anything in them. If anyone wants to yield anything, let him do it at the peril of his conscience.

4    Finally, there still remains the pope's bag of tricks about foolish and childish articles, such as the dedication of churches, the baptism of bells, the baptism of the altar stone, and the inviting of sponsors to these rites who would make donations towards them. Such baptizing is a mockery and scorning of Holy Baptism, and so should not be tolerated. Furthermore, concerning the consecra- 5 tion of wax candles, palm branches, cakes, oats, spices, and such, these cannot be called consecrations, but are sheer mockery and fraud. Such tricks are without number. We commend them for adoration to their god and to themselves, until they weary of it. We will have nothing to do with them.

Doctor Martin Luther subscribed.    1

Doctor Justus Jonas, Rector, subscribed with his 2 own hand.

Doctor John Bugenhagen, Pomeranus, sub- 3 scribed.

Doctor Caspar Creutziger subscribed.    4

Nicholas Amsdorf of Magdeburg subscribed.    5

George Spalatin of Altenburg subscribed.    6

I, Philip Melanchthon, also approve the above 7 articles as right and Christian. But regarding the pope, I hold that, if he would allow the Gospel, we could agree to his superiority over the bishops, which he has otherwise by human right. This would be for the sake of peace and the general unity of those Christians who are also under him and may be under him hereafter.

John Agricola of Eisleben subscribed.    8

Gabriel Didymus [Zwilling] subscribed.    9

I, Doctor Urban Rhegius, Superintendent of the 10 churches in the Duchy of Lüneburg, subscribe in my own name and in the name of my brothers, and of the Church of Hanover.

I, Stephen Agricola, Minister at Hof, subscribe.    11

Also I, John Draconites, Professor and Minister 12 at Marburg, subscribe.

13 I, Conrad Figenbotz, for the glory of God, subscribe that I have thus believed, and am still preaching and firmly believing.

14 I, Andreas Osiander of Nürnberg, subscribe.

15 I, Magister Veit Dietrich, Minister at Nürnberg, subscribe.

16 I, Erhard Schnepf, Preacher at Stuttgart, subscribe.

17 Conrad Ötinger, Preacher of Duke Ulrich at Pforzheim.

18 Simon Schneeweiss, Pastor of the Church at Crailsheim.

19 I, John Schlaginhaufen, Pastor of the Church at Köthen, subscribe.

20 The Reverend Magister George Helt of Forchheim.

21 The Reverend Magister Adam [Krafft] of Fulda, Preacher in Hesse.

22 The Reverend Magister Anthony Corvinus, Preacher in Hesse.

23 I, Doctor John Bugenhagen, Pomeranus, again subscribe in the name of Schoolmaster John Brentz, as on departing from Smalcald he directed me orally and by a letter, which I have shown to those brothers who have subscribed.

24 I, Dionysius Melander, subscribe to the Confession, the Apology, and the Concordia on the subject of the Eucharist.

25 Paul Rhodius, Superintendent of Stettin.

26 Gerhard Öniken, Superintendent of the Church at Minden.

27 I, Brixius Northanus, Minister of the Church of Christ which is at Söst, subscribe to the Articles of the Reverend Father Martin Luther, and confess that up till now I have believed and taught this way, and by the Spirit of Christ I will continue thus to believe and teach.

28 Michael Cölius, Preacher at Mansfeld, subscribed.

29 The Reverend Magister Peter Geltner, Preacher at Frankfort, subscribed.

30 Wendel Faber, Pastor of Seeburg in Mansfeld.

31 I, John Aepinus, subscribe.

32 Likewise, I, John [Tieman from] Amsterdam of Bremen.

33 I, Frederick Myconius, Pastor of the Church at Gotha in Thuringia, subscribe in my own name and in that of Justus Menius of Eisenach.

34 I, Doctor John Lang, Preacher of the Church at Erfurt, subscribe with my own hand in my own name, and in that of my other co-workers in the Gospel, namely:

35 The Reverend Licentiate Ludwig Platz of Melsungen.

36 The Reverend Schoolmaster Sigismund Kirchner.

37 The Reverend Wolfgang Kiswetter.

38 The Reverend Melchior Weitmann.

39 The Reverend John Tall.

40 The Reverend John Kilian.

41 The Reverend Nicholas Faber.

42 The Reverend Andrew Menser.

43 And I, Egidius Melcher, have subscribed with my own hand.

# Temporal and Spiritual Leadership in the Holy Roman Empire (The Two Kingdoms)

The early Christians distinguished temporal leadership (the temporal estate) from spiritual leadership (the spiritual estate). Religious leadership in the Christian West was under the direction of the bishop of Rome (the pope) and his princes, the cardinals and bishops of the Church. Over time their power and control within the temporal estate grew as strong as their claims for obedience within the spiritual estate, creating competition and confusion between the two estates.

Luther rejected this competition and confusion between the two estates as unbiblical. By virtue of Baptism, he argued, all Christians were priests in the spiritual estate and shared equally in the blessings God gives through His means of grace. The spiritual estate (however ordered) proclaims God's Word and administers the Sacraments. The temporal estate (however ordered) enforces the Law and punishes those who disobey. Both are God's estates, and He rules within them in different ways.

The Reformation started among the peers of the spiritual estate when Luther spoke against the abuses caused by indulgences. The laity of Germany quickly agreed with Luther for both spiritual and temporal reasons. As members of the spiritual estate, they craved relief from the fear and guilt imposed by Medieval Church doctrine and practice (e.g., indulgences, purgatory, complete enumeration of sins during confession, bans from the Sacrament, pilgrimages, extreme forms of penance). As members of the temporal estate, they felt the financial strain and political pressure the pope wielded through indulgences and other practices. Luther soon received strong support from many princes and peers of the temporal estate. Their support rescued Luther from certain death and allowed the Reformation to take root among the laity through catechesis. In these ways, Luther's understanding of the two estates came to pass. The temporal and spiritual estates supported each other.

Today, Lutherans continue to support the temporal estate by teaching obedience to temporal authority (beginning with parents), love for one's neighbor (moral behavior and compassion), and productive labor. They expect the temporal estate to support the spiritual estate by providing security and justice, so that churches may freely spread the Gospel and administer the Sacraments.

## TEMPORAL ESTATE

### Primacy

Holy Roman Emperor

Kings of various nations or territories

### Princes

Electors (i.e., those who elect the Holy Roman Emperor): Archbishops of Mainz, Trier, and Cologne; the king of Bohemia; the count palatine of the Rhine; the duke of Saxony; the margrave of Brandenburg (established by the "Golden Bull," published by Charles IV at the Diet of Nürnberg in 1356)

Grand dukes, dukes, and princes

### Peers

Margraves, landgraves, counts of Palatine, other counts

### Public

Citizens of free cities, certain civil servants, employed professionals, merchants, guilded craftsmen

### Peons and Peasants

Landless agricultural, industrial, and other workers; indentured servants

## SPIRITUAL ESTATE

### Primacy

The Roman pontiff (bishop of Rome, called pope)

### Princes

College of Cardinals (elect the pope)

Patriarchs, archbishops, and bishops

Prelates, abbots, superiors of religious orders

### Peers

Priests, subordinate clergy, monks and nuns of religious orders

### Public

Laity

# THE POWER AND PRIMACY OF THE POPE

## A TREATISE COMPILED
## BY THE THEOLOGIANS ASSEMBLED
## AT SMALCALD IN THE YEAR 1537.

Christ breaks down the gates of hell

One of the most significant errors of Rome is the belief that Christ builds His Church on Peter and his successors in the papacy. The rock on which the Church is built is not Peter, or any person, but the confession of Christ, who has stormed Satan's kingdom to rescue us from sin, death, and the power of the devil.

# Introduction to the Treatise on the Power and Primacy of the Pope

We will show from the Gospel that the Roman bishop is not above other
bishops and pastors by divine right.

—Philip Melanchthon, Tr 7

How do Christians receive pastors? How is the Church organized, structured, and governed? The Roman Catholic answer is that everything depends on the pope, the "vicar of Christ," the one who is said to be the immediate successor to the Apostle Peter. Through the pope, so it is thought, flows Christ's authority to His Church on earth. This is not the Bible's answer. In this document Philip Melanchthon provides the Lutheran view of authority in the Church and the basis on which the Church is founded and continued.

This Treatise on the Power and Primacy of the Pope is often considered an appendix to the Smalcald Articles. In reality, it is not. It was regarded as a follow-up to Augsburg Confession and the Apology. When Lutheran leaders in Smalcald gathered in February 1537 to consider Luther's articles, most of them signed them, but they were not formally adopted by the Smalcaldic League. Instead, it was this Treatise that was adopted. The Smalcaldic League wanted some document that would provide their position on the papacy for the general council scheduled for Mantua. And so, at the end of their meeting, they adopted Melanchthon's Treatise.

In the Treatise, Melanchthon presents the position Luther took in the Smalcald Articles on the Papacy (SA IV). He said to a friend later, "I wrote this Treatise somewhat more sharply than I wanted" (*Corpus Reformatorum*, 3:271, 292). No doubt, Elector John Frederick insisted that Melanchthon write something clear and to the point, something that would not be misunderstood later.

The Treatise has two basic parts. The first (pars. 1–59) analyzes the claims made by the Medieval Church about the papacy down through the years. Rome claimed that the pope is the supreme head of the Church by divine right and, therefore, the pope has final and ultimate authority in both the Church and the world. Rome asserted that it is necessary for salvation to believe these things about papal authority because the pope is the vicar (representative) of Christ on earth. The assertion that the pope is the Antichrist strikes modern ears as radical, perhaps even offensive. The point simply is that the "marks of Antichrist plainly agree with the kingdom of the pope and his followers" (Tr 39). The reasons for this claim are provided in detail by Melanchthon.

The foundation of all Roman Catholic arguments for the authority of the pope rests on the interpretation of Matthew 16:18 and John 21:15–17. Rome claims that Matthew 16:18 is the "proof text" for papal authority. The argument goes like this:

The Lord chose St. Peter to be the head of the apostles, and as such, Christ promises to build His Church on Peter, the Rock. A careful study of the actual words of this text reveals that in fact Christ is playing off Peter's name, "Petros," to speak about the "Petra," the rock-solid truth that Peter is expressing, namely, the truth about Christ. On the rock of Peter's confession—not Peter himself—Christ says He is building His Church.

## Church Authority Today

The Treatise is also very helpful for the proper understanding of the role of bishops and pastors in the Church today. Lutheranism rejects any suggestion that differences in the way clergy are ordered in the Church is a divine mandate. Orders and ranks in the clergy are a matter of human arrangement, in Christian freedom, for the sake of good order in the Church. However, every pastor is equal in office when it comes to the essence of the ministry: proclaiming the Gospel, administering the Sacraments, and other duties. As the Gospel is one, so the ministry of the Gospel is one.

Placing men into the pastoral office through ordination is something the church can always do through its pastors. The Gospel is what is at stake in these issues. The Gospel does not depend on anything but Christ for its validity and efficacy. So Melanchthon quotes Augustine favorably to explain that Christians can, and even should, administer Baptism to one another when a pastor is not available (e.g., an emergency Baptism).

Today, people still wonder whether Rome continues to insist on papal authority. The best way to answer that question is to look at the *Catechism of the Catholic Church*, the most definitive presentation of Roman Catholic doctrine since the Council of Trent in the sixteenth century. Just read paragraphs 880–87 and you will realize that the claims made by the Roman Catholic Church about papal authority, though clearly presented in gentler tones and also clearly more evangelical in nature, are still every bit as absolute. Therefore, the Treatise on the Power and Primacy of the Pope is as true and necessary today as it was in the sixteenth century.

## TIMELINE

1531 Smalcaldic League meets, February 8

1536 English Reformer William Tyndale strangled, then burned at stake for heresy

Pope Paul III issues decree for general council to be held in Mantua, Italy, on May 23, 1537

John Frederick commissions Luther to prepare statement of faith, December

1538 Luther's *Smalcald Articles* published

Reforms of John Calvin and William Farel lead to banishment from Geneva

1539 Frankfurt Truce enacted between Protestant and Catholic territories

1540 Melanchthon's *Treatise on the Power and Primacy of the Pope* published

Melanchthon publishes his revised *Augsburg Confession,* the *Variata*

1541 John Calvin returns to Geneva and establishes theocratic government

John Knox leads Reformation in Scotland

1543 Copernicus publishes *On the Revolution of Heavenly Bodies,* describing a sun-centered universe

1545 Council of Trent's first session

1546 Luther dies at Eisleben, February 18

1549 Francis Xavier introduces Christianity in Japan

1552 Luther's wife, Katharina von Bora, dies, December 20

1555 Peace of Augsburg allows territorial rulers to decide religion for their subjects

1560 Philip Melanchthon dies, April 19

1563 Council of Trent ends, settling Roman doctrine and establishing the Roman Catholic Church

## OUTLINE

Introduction

Testimony of Scripture

Testimony of History

Refutation of Roman Arguments

A Contrast between Christ and the Pope

The Marks of the Antichrist

The Power and Jurisdiction of Bishops

Doctors and Preachers Who Subscribed

# The Power and Primacy of the Pope

Melanchthon presents three major objections to the papacy: (1) The pope claims the right to set himself above all other bishops and pastors in the Church; (2) the pope claims to possess authority in the realms of both Church and state; (3) the pope demands people acknowledge his authority in the Church as a requirement for salvation. These positions have changed and moderated over the years, but the claim of papal supremacy above all other Christian pastors is still very much part of Roman Catholic doctrine.

---

1 The Roman pontiff claims for himself that he is supreme above all bishops and pastors by divine right.

2 Second, he adds that by divine right he has both swords, that is, the authority also to enthrone and depose kings, regulate secular dominions, and such.

3 Third, he says that to believe this is necessary for salvation. For these reasons, the Roman bishop calls himself the vicar of Christ on earth.

4 These three articles we hold to be false, godless, tyrannical, and destructive to the Church.

5 So that our proof may be better understood, we will first define what they call being above everyone by "divine right." They mean that the pope is universal, or, as they say, he is the ecumenical bishop, from whom all bishops and pastors throughout the entire world should seek ordination. He is to have the right of electing, ordaining, confirming, and
6 deposing all bishops. Besides this, he claims for himself the authority to make laws about acts of worship, about changing the Sacraments, and about doctrine. He wants his articles, his decrees, and his laws to be considered equal to the divine laws. In other words, he holds that people's consciences are so bound by the papal laws that those who neglect them, even without public offense, sin mortally. What he adds is even more horrible; namely, that it is necessary to believe all these things in order to be saved.

## Testimony of Scripture

Melanchthon presents basic biblical texts refuting papal claims—chiefly Christ's words forbidding lordship among the apostles, His sending them out as equals, Paul's explicit denial that he received authority from any of the other apostles, and Paul's comments placing all pastors on equal footing in the Church. The authority of the ministry comes not from Peter but from the Word of God.

---

In the first place, therefore, we will show from the Gospel that the Roman bishop is not above other bishops and pastors by divine right. 7

I. Luke 22:24–27. Christ clearly bans lordship among the apostles. This was the very question: When Christ spoke of His passion, the apostles were disputing over who should be the head of the others, and, as it were, the vicar of the absent Christ. Christ rebukes this error of the apostles and teaches that there shall not be lordship or superiority among them. Instead, the apostles would be sent forth as equals to the common ministry of the Gospel. So, He says, "The kings of the Gentiles exercise lordship over them, and those in authority over them are called bene- 8 factors. But not so with you. Rather, let the greatest among you become as the youngest, and the leader as one who serves" (22:25–26). The contrast here shows that lordship [among the apostles] is not approved.

II. Matthew 18:2. When Christ, in the same dispute about the Kingdom, places a little child in their midst, He is teaching the same thing by parable. Just as a child neither takes nor seeks sovereignty for himself, so this shows that there is not to be sovereignty among ministers.

9    III. John 20:21. Christ sends forth His disciples in equality, without any distinction. He says, "As the Father has sent Me, even so I am sending you." He says that He sends them individually in the same way He Himself was sent (John 12:44–50). Therefore, He grants no one a privilege or lordship above the rest.

10    IV. Galatians 2:7–10. St. Paul clearly affirms that he was neither ordained nor confirmed by Peter. Nor does he acknowledge Peter to be one from whom confirmation should be sought. He plainly maintains on this point that his call does not depend upon Peter's authority. If Peter were superior by divine right, he should have acknowledged Peter as a superior. Paul says that he had preached the Gospel without consulting Peter (Galatians 1:10–12). Also, "from those who seemed to be influential (what they were makes no difference to me; God shows no partiality)." And, "Those, I say, who seemed influential added nothing to me" (2:6). Paul clearly testifies that he did not even wish to seek the confirmation of Peter to preach, even when Paul had come to him. He teaches that the authority of the ministry depends upon God's Word, and that Peter was not superior to the other apostles. Ordination or confirmation was not to be sought from this one individual, Peter.

V. In 1 Corinthians 3, Paul makes ministers equal. He also teaches that the Church is more than the ministers. Superiority or lordship over the Church or the rest of the ministers is not attributed to Peter. For he says, "All things are yours, whether Paul or Apollos or Cephas" (3:21–22). That is, do not let the other ministers or Peter assume for themselves lordship or superiority over the Church. Do not let them burden the Church with traditions. Do not let the authority of anyone prevail more than God's Word. Do not let the authority of Cephas be opposed to the authority of the other apostles, as they reasoned at that time, "Cephas, who is an apostle of higher rank, observes this. Therefore, both Paul and the rest ought to observe this." Paul removes this claim from Peter and denies that his authority is to be preferred to the rest or to the Church.    11

## Testimony of History

History also shows that the claims of the Roman bishop lack foundation in the Church's practice through the ages. In the fourth century it was understood that the Bishop of Alexandria would administer the churches in the East and the Roman bishop would serve the same function in the West. The Roman bishop's position derived from human decisions made at a council for the sake of order in the Church, not out of some special institution by Christ. Bishops were historically chosen by their own congregations, not by the Roman bishop. There were, and continue to be, many churches throughout the world that do not depend on Roman authority to exist. Many of the Church's historic councils were held without the Roman bishop's presiding over them. Various Church Fathers are cited as speaking of equality among the bishops. Even Gregory the Great, who Rome says is a pope, rejected the title of universal bishop and rejected notions of primacy.

-------

12    VI. The Council of Nicaea resolved that the bishop of Alexandria should administer the churches in the East and the Roman bishop the *suburban* churches, that is, those in the Roman provinces in the West. From this start by a human law (i.e., the resolution of the council), the authority of the Roman bishop first arose. If the Roman bishop already had the superiority by divine law, it would not have been lawful for the council to take away any right from him and transfer it to the bishop of Alexandria. No, all the bishops of the East should always have sought ordination and confirmation from the bishop of Rome.

13    VII. The Council of Nicaea also determined that bishops should be elected by their own churches, in the presence of one or more

14    neighboring bishops. This was observed also in the West in the Latin churches, as Cyprian and Augustine testify. For Cyprian says in his fourth letter to Cornelius:

> So as for the divine observance and apostolic practice, you must carefully keep and practice what is also observed among us and in almost all the provinces. To celebrate ordination properly, whatever bishops of the same province live near by should come together with the people for whom a pastor is being appointed. The bishop should be chosen in the presence of the people, who most fully know the life of each candidate. We have seen this done among us at the ordination of our colleague Sabinus. By the vote of the entire brotherhood and by the judgment of the bishops who had assembled in their presence, the bishop's office was conferred and hands were laid on him.

Cyprian calls this custom "a divine tradition and an apostolic observance." He affirms that it is observed in almost all the provinces.    15

In the greater part of the world, in the Latin and Greek Churches, neither ordination nor confirmation was sought from a bishop of Rome. Therefore, it is clear enough that the churches did not then grant superiority and domination to the bishop of Rome.

Such superiority is impossible. It is just    16 not possible for one bishop to be the overseer of the churches of the whole world. Churches in the most distant lands cannot seek ordination from only one person. It is clear that Christ's kingdom is scattered throughout the whole world. Today there are many churches in the East that do not seek ordination or confirmation from the Roman bishop. Since the superiority the pope claims for himself is impossible and has not been acknowledged by churches in the greater part of the world, it is clear enough that it was not instituted.

VIII. Many ancient councils have been    17 proclaimed and held in which the bishop of Rome did not preside, such as that of Nicaea and most others. This, too, testifies that the Church did not then acknowledge the primacy or superiority of the bishop of Rome.

IX. Jerome says:    18

> If there is a question about authority, the world is greater than the city. Wherever there has been a bishop, whether at Rome, or Eugubium, or Constantinople, or Rhegium, or Alexandria, he has the same dignity and priesthood.

X. Pope Gregory, writing to the patriarch    19 at Alexandria, forbids that he be called universal bishop. In the records he says that in the Council of Chalcedon the primacy was offered to the bishop of Rome, but it was not accepted.

20    XI. Last, how can the pope be over the entire Church by divine right when the Church elects him? And what of the custom that gradually prevailed of bishops of Rome
21  being confirmed by the emperors? When for a long time there had been conflicts over the primacy between the bishops of Rome and Constantinople, the Emperor Phocas finally determined that the primacy should be assigned to the bishop of Rome. But if the ancient Church had acknowledged the primacy of the Roman pontiff, this conflict could not have occurred. Nor would the emperor have needed to make the decree.

# Refutation of Roman Arguments

Melanchthon deals clearly with the Bible verse most commonly used by the Roman Church to establish papal superiority: Matthew 16:18, the famous "you are Peter" passage. Peter is representative of the apostolic band, and so what is said to him is spoken to them all. The Keys are given not just to Peter but to all the apostles, to be used in service for the Church. They belong to the whole Church, not just the Church's ministers. Further, the ministry of the Word is founded not on a man, Peter, but upon his confession. "On this rock" refers not to Peter but to the New Testament ministry of confessing Christ. On the rock of what Peter confessed the Church is built. Christ nowhere gave His followers anything but spiritual authority. Even if the bishop of Rome did have divine authority, faithless popes teaching and advancing false doctrine should be rejected and opposed; for nobody, not even an angel, can teach anything contrary to the revealed Gospel in the Scriptures (Galatians 1:8).

They cite against us certain passages, 22 namely, Matthew 16:18–19, "You are Peter, and on this rock I will build My church." Also, "I will give you the keys." Also, John 21:15, "Feed My lambs," and some others. Since this entire controversy has been fully and accurately treated elsewhere in the books of our theologians and everything cannot be reviewed here, we refer to those writings and wish them to be considered repeated here. Yet we will briefly reply about the interpretation of the passages above.

In all these passages, Peter is the represen- 23 tative of the entire assembly of apostles, as appears from the text itself. Christ does not ask Peter alone, when He says, "Who do you say that I am?" (Matthew 16:15). What is said here to Peter alone in the singular number, "I will give you [singular] the keys; and whatever you [singular] bind" (16:19), is elsewhere expressed in the plural (e.g., Matthew 18:18, "Whatever you [plural] bind"; John 20:23, "If you [plural] forgive the sins of anyone"). These words show that the Keys are given to all the apostles alike and that all the apostles are sent forth alike.

In addition, it must be recognized that 24 the Keys belong not to the person of one particular man, but to the Church. Many most clear and firm arguments show this. For Christ, speaking about the Keys, adds, for example, "If two of you agree on earth" (Matthew 18:19). Therefore, He grants the Keys first and directly to the Church. This is why it is first the Church that has the right of calling.

Therefore, these passages demonstrate that Peter is the representative of the entire assembly of the apostles. They do not grant Peter any privilege or superiority or lordship.

As for the declaration "on this rock I 25 will build My church" (Matthew 16:18), certainly the Church has not been built upon the authority of a man. Rather, it has been built upon the ministry of the confession Peter made, in which he proclaims that Jesus is the Christ, the Son of God (Matthew 16:16). Therefore, Christ addresses Peter as a minister, "On this rock," that is, this ministry.

26    Furthermore, the ministry of the New Testament is not bound to places and persons like the Levitical [Old Testament] ministry was. Rather, it is spread throughout the whole world. That is where God gives His gifts, apostles, prophets, pastors, and teachers (Ephesians 4:11). Nor does this ministry work because of the authority of any person, but because of the Word given by Christ (Romans 10:17). Most of the holy Church

27    Fathers, such as Origen, Cyprian, Augustine, Hilary, and Bede, interpret the passage "on this rock" in this way, as not referring to the

28    person of Peter. Chrysostom says this:

> "Upon this rock," not upon Peter. For He built His Church not upon man, but upon the faith of Peter. But what was his faith? "You are the Christ, the Son of the living God."

29    Hilary says:

> The Father revealed to Peter that he should say, "You are the Son of the living God" (Matthew 16:17). Therefore, the building of the Church is upon this rock of confession. This faith is the foundation of the Church.

30    As for what is said in John 21:15–19, "Feed My lambs," and "Do you love Me more than these?" it does not follow from this passage that a peculiar superiority was given Peter. Christ tells him "feed" (i.e., teach the Word, or rule the Church with the Word), which task Peter has in common with the other apostles.

31    The second article is even clearer. Christ gave the apostles only spiritual power (i.e., the command to teach the Gospel, to announce the forgiveness of sins, to administer the Sacraments, to excommunicate the godless without bodily force). He did not give them the power of the sword (the right to establish, occupy, or bestow kingdoms of the world; Romans 13:4). For Christ says, "Go . . . teaching them to observe all that I have commanded you" (Matthew 28:19–20). Also, "As the Father has sent Me, even so I am sending you" (John 20:21).

It is clear that Christ was not sent to bear the sword or possess a worldly kingdom, as He Himself says, "My kingdom is not of this world" (John 18:36). And Paul says, "Not that we lord it over your faith" (2 Corinthians 1:24); and "The weapons of our warfare are not of the flesh" (2 Corinthians 10:4), and so forth.

## A Contrast between Christ and the Pope

32    Christ in His passion is crowned with thorns and led forth to be ridiculed in royal purple (John 19:2). This symbolizes that in the future, after His spiritual kingdom was despised (i.e., the Gospel was suppressed), another kingdom of a worldly kind would be set up with the appearance of churchly

33    power. (So the Constitution of Boniface VIII and the chapter *Omnes*, Distinction 22, and similar opinions are false and godless, for they argue that the pope is by divine right the ruler of the kingdoms of the world.) From

34    this notion, horrible darkness has been brought into the Church and, after that, great commotions have arisen in Europe. The ministry of the Gospel was neglected (Acts 6:1–4; 1 Timothy 4:13–14) and the knowledge of faith and the spiritual kingdom became extinct. Christian righteousness was assumed to be the outward government the pope had established.

Woodcuts from the September and December printing
of Luther's translation of the New Testament, 1522

Sixteenth-century polemics were harsh. Some felt that Luther's polemics got carried away, others thought he didn't go far enough. Left: The original version of a woodcut that appeared in the first printing of Martin Luther's New Testament translation (September, 1522). The beast from hell wears the Pope's threefold crown. Right: A simple, less offensive crown was used later (December, 1522).

35   Next, the popes began to seize kingdoms for themselves. They transferred kingdoms. They harassed with unjust excommunications and wars the kings of almost all nations in Europe, but especially the German emperors. Sometimes they did this for the purpose of occupying cities of Italy. Other times they wanted to conquer the bishops of Germany and wrest away from the emperors the right to appoint bishops. In fact, it is even written in the Clementines, "When the empire is vacant, the pope is the legitimate successor."

The pope has not only seized dominion,   36 which is contrary to Christ's command. He has also exalted himself above all kings like a tyrant. The following should not be condemned as much as detested: (a) He makes his claim on the authority of Christ. (b) He transfers the Keys to a worldly government. And (c) then he binds salvation to these godless and criminal opinions when he insists that, believing this dominion belongs to him by divine right, is necessary for salvation.

Since these great errors cloud over faith   37

and Christ's kingdom, they are in no way to be ignored. Their consequences show that they have been great plagues to the Church.

38    In the third place, this must be added: Even if the bishop of Rome did have the primacy and superiority by divine right, nevertheless, obedience would not be due those pontiffs who defend godless services, idolatry, and doctrine conflicting with the Gospel. No, such pontiffs and such a government should be held accursed, as Paul clearly teaches, "If we or an angel from heaven should preach to you a gospel contrary to the one we preached to you, let him be accursed" (Galatians 1:8). And, "We must obey God rather than men" (Acts 5:29). Likewise, the church laws also clearly teach that "a heretical pope is not to be obeyed."

The Levitical high priest was the chief priest by divine right (Leviticus 8), and yet godless high priests were not to be obeyed. As Jeremiah and other prophets dissented from the high priests (Jeremiah 26:1–11), so the apostles dissented from Caiaphas and did not have to obey him (Acts 4:19–20; 5:29).

## The Marks of the Antichrist

The establishment and defense of godless doctrine by Roman popes clearly fulfills St. Paul's warnings in 2 Thessalonians 2. There he prophesies that a leader will take a seat in God's Church, insisting on false teachings and practices. The Lutheran Confessions call this person the "Antichrist" (based on 1 John 2:18). Because Scripture warns of his coming within the Church, the Confessions call the Roman pope Antichrist. Melanchthon identifies three clear signs that the papacy is Antichrist. First, the pope claims the right to change and establish doctrine. (Most notably this power was exercised in the nineteenth and twentieth centuries with declarations concerning "papal infallibility" and the "immaculate conception" of Mary and her "bodily assumption" to heaven.) Second, the pope claims the authority to act as judge over souls, even after death. Third, the pope is unwilling to be subject to the judgment of Church councils. For these reasons, Melanchthon insists that all Christians should abandon the pope and his followers as the kingdom of Antichrist.

---

It is clear that the Roman pontiffs, with    39 their followers, defend godless doctrines and godless services. And the marks of Antichrist plainly agree with the kingdom of the pope and his followers. For Paul, in describing Antichrist to the Thessalonians, calls him an enemy of Christ, "Who opposes and exalts himself against every so-called god or object of worship, so that he takes his seat in the temple of God" (2 Thessalonians 2:4). He is not speaking about heathen kings, but about someone ruling in the Church. He calls him the enemy of Christ, because he will invent doctrine conflicting with the Gospel and will claim for himself divine authority.

Furthermore, it is clear, in the first place,    40 that the pope rules in the Church and has established this kingdom for himself by the claim of churchly authority and of the ministry. He gives these words as a basis, "I will give you the keys" (Matthew 16:19). Second, the doctrine of the pope conflicts in many ways with the Gospel. Third, the pope claims for himself divine authority in a threefold manner: (a) He takes for himself the right to change Christ's doctrine and services instituted by God, and wants his own doctrine and his own services to be observed as divine. (b) He takes to himself the power not only of binding and loosing in this life, but also jurisdiction over souls after this life. (c) He does not want to be judged by the Church or by anyone and puts his own authority ahead of the decision of councils and the entire

Church. To be unwilling to be judged by the Church or by anyone else is to make oneself God. Finally, he defends these horrible errors and this impiety with the greatest cruelty and puts to death those who disagree.

41    This being the case, all Christians should beware of participating in the godless doctrine, blasphemies, and unjust cruelty of the pope. They should desert and condemn the pope with his followers as the kingdom of Antichrist, just as Christ has commanded, "Beware of false prophets" (Matthew 7:15). Paul commands that godless teachers should be avoided and condemned as cursed (Galatians 1:8; Titus 3:10). And he says, "Do not be unequally yoked with unbelievers. . . . What fellowship has light with darkness?" (2 Corinthians 6:14).

42    To dissent from the agreement of so many nations and to be called schismatics is a serious matter. But divine authority commands everyone not to be allies and defenders of impiety and unjust cruelty.

In this, our consciences are excused well enough, for the errors of the kingdom of the pope are clear. Scripture with its entire voice cries out that these errors are a *teaching of demons* (1 Timothy 4:1–3) and of Antichrist.

43    The idolatry in the abuse of the Masses is clear. The Masses are used for the most

44    shameful moneymaking. The doctrine of repentance has been utterly corrupted by the pope and his followers. They teach that sins are forgiven because of the value of our works. Then they tell us to doubt whether the forgiveness takes place. They nowhere teach that sins are forgiven freely for Christ's sake, and that by this faith we obtain forgiveness of sins (Ephesians 2:8–9).

So they hide Christ's glory and rob consciences of firm consolation. They abolish true divine services (i.e., the exercises of faith struggling with despair).

They have clouded over the doctrine   45 about sin. They have invented a tradition about the listing of offenses, producing many errors and despair.

In addition, they have invented satisfactions, with which they have also hidden Christ's benefit.

From these, indulgences have been born.   46 These are pure lies, fabricated for the sake of making money.

How many abuses and what horrible   47 idolatry the invocation of saints has produced!

What shameful acts have arisen from the   48 tradition of celibacy!

What darkness the doctrine of vows has spread over the Gospel! They pretend that vows are righteousness before God and merit the forgiveness of sins. So they have transferred the benefit of Christ to human traditions and have completely snuffed out the doctrine about faith. They have pretended that the most silly traditions are services of God and perfection. They have preferred these to the works of the callings that God requires and has ordained. These errors should not be treated lightly. They detract from Christ's glory and bring destruction to souls. They cannot be passed by unnoticed.

To these errors, two great sins are added:   49 (a) The pope defends these errors by unjust cruelty and the death penalty. (b) He grabs the decision away from the Church and does not permit religious controversies to be judged in the right way. Indeed, he argues that he is above the council and can rescind the decrees of councils. Church law sometimes shamelessly says this. But the evidence shows that the popes act even more shamelessly:

Question 9, canon 3, [of Gratian's Second   50 Decretal] says:

No one shall judge the main [the pope's] throne. For the judge is judged neither by the emperor, nor by all the clergy, nor by the kings, nor by the people.

51    The pope exercises a twofold tyranny: (a) He defends his errors by force and by murders, and (b) he forbids judicial examination. The latter does even more harm than any executions. When the true judgment of the Church is removed, godless dogmas and godless services cannot be removed. They destroy countless souls for many ages.

52    Therefore, let the godly consider the great errors of the kingdom of the pope and his tyranny. Let them ponder, (a) that the errors must be rejected and the true doctrine embraced, for the glory of God and the salvation of souls. Then (b) let them ponder also how

53    great a crime it is to aid unjust cruelty in killing saints, whose blood God will undoubtedly avenge (Revelation 6:10).

54    The chief members of the Church, the kings and princes, should especially guard the interests of the Church. They should see to it that errors are removed and consciences are healed. God specifically warns kings, "Now therefore, O kings, be wise; be warned, O rulers of the earth" (Psalm 2:10). It should be the first care of kings to advance God's glory. It would be very shameful for them to use their influence and power to confirm idolatry (e.g., 1 Kings 14:14–16) and endless other crimes and to slaughter saints.

55    Even if the pope holds councils, how can the Church be healed if he allows nothing to be decreed against his will? Or if he allows no one to express an opinion except his followers, whom he has bound by dreadful oaths and curses to defend his tyranny and impiety without leaving any place for God's Word?

56    The decisions of councils are the decisions of the Church, and not of the popes. So it is especially dependent upon kings to restrain the excesses of the popes. Kings must

act so that the power of judging and decreeing from God's Word is not snatched away from the Church. As the rest of the Christians must condemn all other errors of the pope, so they must also rebuke the pope when he avoids and hinders the true investigation and true decision of the Church.

57    Therefore, even if the bishop of Rome did have the primacy by divine right, since he defends godless services and doctrine conflicting with the Gospel, obedience is not due him. Indeed, it is necessary to resist him as Antichrist. The pope's errors are clear, and they are not small.

58    The cruelty he exercises is also clear. God clearly commands us to flee idolatry (1 Corinthians 10:14), godless doctrine (1 Timothy 6:3–4), and unjust cruelty (Proverbs 11:17). On this account, all the godly have great, compelling, and clear reasons for not obeying the pope. These compelling reasons comfort the godly against all of the reproaches usually cast against them about causing offenses, schism, and discord.

59    Those who agree with the pope and defend his doctrine and services defile themselves with idolatry and blasphemous opinions. They become guilty of the blood of the godly, whom the pope persecutes (see Acts 9:1, 4–5; 1 Corinthians 11:27). They detract from God's glory and hinder the Church's welfare because they confirm errors and crimes through all generations.

## The Power and Jurisdiction of Bishops

This portion of the Treatise is one of the most important commentaries in the Book of Concord on the office and duties of pastors. Melanchthon expands on what he had written earlier in "The Confession"—the Augsburg Confession—and the Apology. In the Church the power or authority of the ministry consists in preaching the Gospel, forgiving sins, administering the Sacraments, and excommunicating persons guilty of public sins. This is the only authority or "right" the Church's ministers have. Melanchthon indicates how the early Church understood that this was for both bishops and presbyters, or pastors. All distinctions in grades of bishops and pastors are merely by human ordering, not by divine institution or command. Ordination was normally performed by bishops, but it is valid by divine right when a pastor performs it in his own congregation. The right to call and ordain pastors belongs to the entire Church, and bishops can never deprive congregations of the Office of the Ministry. The Church, not bishops, has the authority, duty, and right from God to provide ministers for herself. She can, therefore, ordain men into the Office of the Ministry through her pastors. Melanchthon concludes this section with a stern warning against bishops who follow the pope and defend false doctrine and error in the Church; these bishops are no bishops at all.

---

60 The Gospel assigns those who preside over Churches the command to teach the Gospel (Matthew 28:19), to forgive sins (John 20:23), to administer the Sacraments, and also to exercise jurisdiction (i.e., the command to excommunicate those whose crimes are known and to absolve those who repent).

61 Everyone confesses, even our adversaries, that this power is common to all who preside over churches by divine right, whether they are 62 called pastors, elders, or bishops. So Jerome explicitly teaches in the apostolic letters that all who preside over churches are both bishops and elders. He cites from Titus 1:5–6, "This is why I left you in Crete, so that you might . . . appoint elders in every town." Then [the Letter to] Titus adds that a bishop must be "the husband of one wife." Likewise, Peter and John call themselves elders (1 Peter 5:1; 2 John 1). Then Jerome adds:

> But afterward, one was chosen to be placed over the rest. This was done as a remedy for schism, lest each one by attracting a congregation to himself might tear apart the Church of Christ. For at Alexandria, from Mark the evangelist to the bishops Heracles and Dionysius, the elders always elected one from among themselves and placed him in a higher station, calling him bishop, just as an army would make a commander for itself. The deacons, moreover, may elect from among themselves one whom they know to be active and name him archdeacon. For with the exception of ordination, what does the bishop have that the elder does not?

63 Jerome, therefore, teaches that it is by human authority that the grades of bishop and elder or pastor are distinct. The content itself says this, because the power is the same, as he has said above. Later, only one thing 64 made a distinction between bishops and pastors, namely, ordination. For it was arranged that one bishop would ordain ministers in a number of churches.

65 Since the grades of bishop and pastor are not different by divine authority, it is clear that ordination administered by a pastor in his own church is valid by divine law.

66 Therefore, when the regular bishops become enemies of the Church or are unwilling to administer ordination, the churches retain their own right [to ordain their own ministers].

67 Wherever the Church is, there is the authority to administer the Gospel. Therefore, it is necessary for the Church to retain the authority to call, elect, and ordain ministers. This authority is a gift that in reality is given

to the Church. No human power can take this gift away from the Church. As Paul testifies to the Ephesians, when "He ascended . . . He gave gifts to men" (Ephesians 4:8). He lists among the gifts specifically belonging to the Church "pastors and teachers" (4:11), and adds that they are given for the ministry, "for building up the body of Christ" (4:12). So wherever there is a True Church, the right to elect and ordain ministers necessarily exists. In the same way, in a case of necessity even a layman absolves and becomes the minister and pastor of another. Augustine tells the story of two Christians in a ship, one of whom baptized the catechumen, who after Baptism then absolved the baptizer.

68    Here belong the statements of Christ that testify that the Keys have been given to the Church, and not merely to certain persons, "Where two or three are gathered in My name . . ." (Matthew 18:20).

69    Finally, Peter's statement also confirms this, "You are . . . a royal priesthood" (1 Peter 2:9). These words apply to the True Church, which certainly has the right to elect and ordain ministers, since it alone has the priesthood.

70    A most common custom of the Church also testifies to this. Formerly, the people elected pastors and bishops (Acts 14:23). Then came a bishop, either of that church or a neighboring one, who confirmed the one elected by the laying on of hands (1 Timothy 4:14). Ordination was nothing else than

71    such a ratification. Afterward, new ceremonies were added, many of which Dionysius describes. But he is a recent and fictitious author, whoever he may be, just as the writings of Clement also are spurious. Then more modern writers added, "I give you the power to sacrifice for the living and the dead." This is not even in Dionysius.

72    From all of this, it is clear that the Church retains the right to elect and ordain ministers. Therefore, when the bishops are heretics or refuse to administer ordination, the churches are by divine right compelled to ordain pastors and ministers for themselves by having their pastors do it. The impiety and tyranny of bishops cause schism and discord. Therefore, Paul commands that bishops who teach and defend a godless doctrine and godless services should be considered accursed (Galatians 1:7–9).

73    We have spoken of ordination, which alone, as Jerome says, distinguished bishops from other elders. There is no need to discuss the other duties of bishops. It is not necessary to speak about confirmation or the consecration of bells, which are almost the only things they have kept. Something, though, must be said about jurisdiction.

74    Certainly, the common jurisdiction of excommunicating those guilty of clear crimes belongs to all pastors (1 Corinthians 5). The bishops have tyrannically transferred this to themselves alone and have used it for their own gain. It is certain that the officials, as they are called, used an intolerable license. Either because of greed or because of other immoral desires, they tormented people and excommunicated them without any due process of law.

75    What tyranny it is for the officials in the states to have arbitrary power to do this! In what kinds of issues did they abuse this power? Not in punishing true offenses, but in punishing violations of fasts or festivals, or such silly things! They sometimes did punish adulteries, but in this they often harass innocent and honorable people. Besides, since adultery is a most grievous offense, certainly no one should be condemned without due process of law.

76    Since bishops have tyrannically transferred this jurisdiction to themselves alone and have basely abused it, there is no need to

obey bishops. Since there are just reasons why we do not obey, it is also right to restore this jurisdiction to godly pastors and to make sure that it is legitimately exercised for the reformation of morals and the glory of God.

77 There remains the jurisdiction, according to Church law, in cases that relate to the Church court, as they call it, and especially in cases of marriage. This, too, the bishops have only by human right, which is not a very old one. According to the *Codex* and *Novellae* of Justinian, decisions about marriage at that time belonged to the rulers. By divine right, earthly rulers must make these decisions if the bishops are negligent. Church law also concedes this. So for this jurisdiction also, it

78 is not necessary to obey bishops. Since the bishops have framed unjust laws about marriages and observe them in their courts, there is a need to establish other courts. The traditions [banning the marriage] of those who have a spiritual relationship are unjust. Also unjust is the tradition forbidding an innocent person to marry after divorce (Matthew 5:32). Also unjust is the law that in general approves all secret and deceitful engagements in violation of parental rights. Also unjust is the law requiring the celibacy of priests. There are also other snares of conscience in their laws. There is no need to recite them all. It is enough to say that there are many unjust laws of the pope regarding marriage. Because of these, the rulers should establish other courts.

79 So the bishops who are devoted to the pope defend godless doctrine and godless services. They do not ordain godly teachers, and they aid the cruelty of the pope. Besides, they have wrestled away the jurisdiction from pastors and exercise it tyrannically for their own profit. Finally, in marriage cases they observe many unjust laws. So there are enough and necessary reasons why the churches should not recognize these men as bishops.

80 They themselves should remember that riches have been given to bishops as alms for the administration and advantage of the churches. As the rule says, "The benefit is given because of the office." Therefore, they cannot with a good conscience possess these alms and defraud the Church. The Church has need of this money to support ministers, aid education, care for the poor, and establish

81 courts, especially for marriage. So great is the variety and extent of marriage controversies that there is need for a special court, for which the endowments of the Church are

82 needed. Peter predicted that there would be godless bishops who would abuse the alms of the Church for luxury and neglect the ministry (2 Peter 2:13). Therefore, let those who defraud the Church know that they will pay God the penalty for this crime.

# Doctors and Preachers Who Subscribed to the Augsburg Confession and Apology,
## A.D. 1537

According to the command of the most illustrious princes and of the orders and states professing the doctrine of the Gospel, we have reread the articles of the Confession presented to the Emperor in the Assembly at Augsburg. By God's favor, all the preachers who have been present in this Assembly at Smalcald harmoniously declare that they believe and teach in their churches according to the articles of the Confession and Apology. They also declare that they approve the article about the primacy of the pope and his power, and the power and jurisdiction of bishops, which was presented to the princes in this assembly at Smalcald. So they subscribe their names.

1  I, Doctor John Bugenhagen, Pomeranus, subscribe the Articles of the Augsburg Confession, the Apology, and the Article presented to the princes at Smalcald concerning the Papacy.

2  I also, Doctor Urban Rhegius, Superintendent of the Churches in the Duchy of Lüneburg, subscribe.

3  Nicholas Amsdorf of Magdeburg subscribed.

4  George Spalatin of Altenburg subscribed.

5  I, Andreas Osiander, subscribe.

6  Magister Veit Dietrich of Nürnberg subscribed.

7  Stephen Agricola, Minister at Hof, subscribed with his own hand.

8  John Draconites of Marburg subscribed.

9  Conrad Figenbotz subscribed to all throughout.

10  Martin Bucer.

11  I, Erhard Schnepf, subscribe.

12  Paul Rhodius, Preacher in Stettin.

13  Gerhard Öniken, Minister of the Church at Minden.

14  Brixius Northanus, Minister at Söst.

15  Simon Schneeweiss, Pastor of Crailsheim.

16  I, Pomeranus, again subscribe in the name of Schoolmaster John Brentz, as he ordered me.

17  Philip Melanchthon subscribes with his own hand.

18  Anthony Corvinus subscribes with his own hand, as well as in the name of Adam [Krafft] of Fulda.

19  John Schlaginhaufen subscribes with his own hand.

20  Schoolmaster George Helt of Forchheim.

21  Michael Cölius, Preacher at Mansfeld.

22  Peter Geltner, Preacher of the church of Frankfort.

23  Dionysius Melander subscribed.

24  Paul Fagius of Strasbourg.

25  Wendel Faber, Pastor of Seeburg in Mansfeld.

26  Conrad Ötinger of Pforzheim, Preacher of Ulrich, Duke of Württemberg.

27  Boniface Wolfart, Minister of the Word of the Church at Augsburg.

28  John Aepinus, Superintendent of Hamburg, subscribed with his own hand.

29  John [Tieman] of Amsterdam of Bremen does the same.

30  John Fontanus, Superintendent of Lower Hesse, subscribed.

31  Frederick Myconius subscribed for himself and Justus Menius.

32  Ambrose Blaurer.

I have read, and again and again reread, the Confession and Apology presented at Augsburg by the Most Illustrious Prince, the Elector of Saxony, and by the other princes and estates of the Roman Empire, to his Imperial Majesty. I have also read the Formula of Concord concerning the Sacrament, made at Wittenberg with Dr. Bucer and others. I have also read the articles written at the Assembly at Smalcald in the German language by Dr. Martin Luther, our most revered teacher, and the tract concerning the Papacy and the Power and Jurisdiction of Bishops. In my humble opinion I judge that all these agree with Holy Scripture and with the belief of the true and genuine catholic Church. But although I am in so great a number of most learned men who have now assembled at Smalcald, I acknowledge that I am the least of all. Yet, as I am not permitted to await the end of the assembly, I ask you, most renowned man, Dr. John Bugenhagen, most revered Father in Christ, that your courtesy may add my name, if it be necessary, to all that I have above mentioned. For I testify in this my own handwriting that I thus hold, confess, and constantly will teach, through Jesus Christ, our Lord.

John Brentz, Minister of Hall.
Done at Smalcald,
February 23, 1537.

# ENCHIRIDION
# THE SMALL CATECHISM

of Dr. Martin Luther
for Ordinary Pastors and Preachers

The Canaanite Woman

Luther's Small Catechism provides clear, direct, memorable summaries of the Bible. Like the Canaanite woman, we are grateful even for crumbs that fall from the Master's table. Our gracious Lord invites us to the banquet of life and salvation He provides through Word and Sacrament.

# INTRODUCTION TO THE CATECHISMS

God Himself is not ashamed to teach these things daily. He knows nothing better to teach. . . . Can we finish learning in one hour what God Himself cannot finish teaching?

—Martin Luther (LC Preface 16)

## Echoing the Truth: What Does *Catechesis* Mean?

The term *catechism* comes from the Greek word *katecho*, which literally means to "sound back and forth." (The word *echo* also comes from this Greek word.) Thus the "catechetical" method of teaching is rooted in classical Greek and Roman educational methods and was used throughout the Middle Ages down to Luther's time: The teacher asks a question; the student responds with a fixed and set answer, and so it goes, echoing back and forth. Repetition and recitation of the material is used to instill in the student the words, phrases, and concepts being taught. An explanation is also added, according to the student's level of understanding. In this way, the Christian Church taught, or *catechized*, the faith. The students learning the faith are known as *catechumens*, and they receive careful and thorough *catechesis* (instruction) in the Christian faith.

## The Catechism in the Middle Ages

In Luther's day there were any number of catechisms and catechetical materials. They were often extremely extensive and required the young people to memorize not only the Ten Commandments, the Lord's Prayer, and the Creed, but also a list of seven spiritual gifts, seven cardinal virtues, the seven Sacraments, seven words of mercy, the eight beatitudes of God, and on and on and on. Luther cleared away the medieval clutter and retained the core texts of the catechisms: The Ten Commandments, the Creed, and the Lord's Prayer. He then added explanations to Baptism, Absolution, and the Sacrament of the Altar. Instead of prayers to Mary and the saints, Luther provided prayers for the beginning and end of the day, and also prayers before and after meals. Luther's goal with his Small Catechism was to provide something that was much shorter, easier to teach and to learn, memorable, and to the point. The Large Catechism was designed by Luther to provide more information and further material both for teachers and learners. Luther's hope was that students who had mastered the Small Catechism would move on to the Large Catechism.

## The Origin of the Catechisms

Martin Luther was first and foremost a Bible professor at the University of Wittenberg, but he was also a parish preacher who served at both the city and castle churches in Wittenberg. In 1516 Luther preached a thorough sermon series on the

Ten Commandments. In 1517 he preached a sermon series on the Lord's Prayer and wrote a short explanation of the Ten Commandments to help the members of the parish confess their sins. In 1518 Luther published his exposition of the Ten Commandments. In the next two years he published other short tracts based on his catechetical sermons. In 1520 he gathered these resources together and had them published under the title *A Short Form of the Ten Commandments, the Creed, and the Lord's Prayer.*

Luther wanted this book to serve the laypeople. While Luther built on catechetical customs, his work stood out as a clear departure from much of medieval catechesis. There were three key reasons for this: First, Luther removed a lot of the additional materials that had accumulated throughout the Middle Ages and focused primarily on the Ten Commandments, the Creed, and the Lord's Prayer, urging that if these three things were learned well, the most important truths of Christianity would be known. Second, Luther very intentionally arranged the catechism so that the Commandments would be first, then the Creed, then the Lord's Prayer. Third, Luther divided the Apostles' Creed into only three parts, not the traditional twelve parts. Luther wanted to focus clearly on the three persons of the Holy Trinity and their respective saving work. Luther's little 1520 book was the foundation for his later catechetical work.

In 1525 Luther formally commissioned what he called the "children's catechism" (*catechismus pueroum*), using the term *catechism* for the first time. He directed his colleagues Justus Jonas and John Agricola to do this work. Luther felt he was too busy to do it himself, but as it turned out, Jonas and Agricola also did not do the job to Luther's satisfaction.

Luther continued preaching each year on the basic parts of the catechism and added sermons equally clear and simple on the Sacraments: Baptism, Absolution, and the Lord's Supper. In 1528 he again took over catechism instruction in the parish church in Wittenberg and preached three series of sermons that year—in May, September, and December—each containing about ten sermons. These thirty sermons would serve Luther well a year later, in 1529, when he finally wrote the catechisms.

What ignited Luther's passion to put the catechisms in writing was a visit he had made to Saxony at the urging of its Elector. Luther was horrified to see how bad things were in the Saxon churches. He realized how essential it was for him to get to work on his catechisms. Here is what he said:

> The deplorable, miserable condition which I discovered lately when I, too, was a visitor, has forced and urged me to prepare this Catechism, or Christian doctrine, in this small, plain, simple form. Mercy! Good God! what manifold misery I beheld! The common people . . . have no knowledge whatever of Christian doctrine, and, alas! many pastors are altogether incapable, and incompetent to teach. Nevertheless, all maintain that they are Christians. . . . Yet they cannot recite either the Lord's Prayer, or the Creed, or the Ten Commandments, they live like dumb brutes and irrational swine. (Bente, 156–57)

Luther finished the Large Catechism in March 1529, and in mid-April the first copies were in print. The title was simply *German Catechism, Martin Luther*. He finished the Small Catechism in May 1529. Its title was *The Small Catechism for Ordinary Pastors and Preachers. Martin Luther. Wittenberg*. It was an instant best-seller, printed and reprinted many times in Wittenberg and other cities throughout Germany. In early 1529 Luther also had large posters printed containing the chief parts of the catechism. These posters were hung up on walls in churches, schools, and homes for the people to recite together.

In the years following, Luther added a few things himself to the catechisms and approved when others did the same, such as a short form for Confession and orders for baptismal and wedding services. The main portions of the Small Catechism, first produced in 1529, were never essentially changed.

## TIMELINE

| | |
|---|---|
| 1516 | Luther preaches sermon series on Ten Commandments |
| 1517 | Luther preaches sermon series on Lord's Prayer; posts Ninety-five Theses |
| 1521 | Luther excommunicated by papal bull *Decet Romanum Pontificem;* appears before Diet of Worms; refuses to recant, stating "Here I stand" |
| 1524 | Peasants' War begins, led in part by Thomas Münzer |
| 1525 | Luther asks Justus Jonas and John Agricola to produce a "catechism" |
| | Luther marries Katharina von Bora, June 13 |
| 1526 | Diet of Speyer grants German princes right to establish religion in their territory |
| | Church visitation begins to assess needs of congregations |
| 1527 | Visitation articles prepared |
| | Plague strikes Wittenberg; Luther and Katharina turn their home into a hospital |
| 1528 | Luther teaches catechism instruction at the parish church; preaches three sermon series on parts of catechism |
| 1529 | Luther publishes the *Large Catechism* in April and the *Small Catechism* in May |
| 1530 | *Augsburg Confession* presented to Charles V at Diet of Augsburg, June 25 |

## OUTLINE

Preface

I. The Ten Commandments

II. The Creed

III. The Lord's Prayer

IV. The Sacrament of Holy Baptism

V. How the Unlearned Should Be Taught to Confess

VI. The Sacrament of the Altar

Daily Prayers

Table of Duties

# ENCHIRIDION
# THE SMALL CATECHISM
## Preface of Dr. Martin Luther

*Martin Luther* to all faithful and godly pastors and preachers: grace, mercy, and peace in Jesus Christ, our Lord.

1   The deplorable, miserable condition that I discovered recently when I, too, was a visitor, has forced and urged me to prepare this catechism, or Christian doctrine, in
2   this small, plain, simple form. Mercy! Dear God, what great misery I beheld! The common person, especially in the villages, has no knowledge whatever of Christian doctrine. And unfortunately, many pastors are completely unable and unqualified to
3   teach. This is so much so, that one is ashamed to speak of it. Yet, everyone says that they are Christians, have been baptized, and receive the holy Sacraments, even though they cannot even recite the Lord's Prayer or the Creed or the Ten Commandments. They live like dumb brutes and irrational hogs. Now that the Gospel has come, they have nicely learned to abuse all freedom like experts.

4   O bishops! What answer will you ever give to Christ for having so shamefully neglected the people and never for a moment fulfilled your office (James 3:1)? May
5   all misfortune run from you! (I do not wish at this place to call down evil on your heads.) You command the Sacrament in one form and insist on your human laws, and yet at the same time you do not care at all whether the people know the Lord's Prayer, the Creed, the Ten Commandments, or any part of God's Word. Woe, woe to you forever! (See Matthew 23.)

6   Therefore, I beg you all for God's sake, my dear sirs and brethren, who are pastors or preachers, to devote yourselves heartily to your office (1 Timothy 4:13). Have pity on the people who are entrusted to you (Acts 20:28) and help us teach the catechism to the people, and especially to the young. And let those of you who cannot do better take these tables and forms and impress them, word for word, on the people (Deuteronomy 6:7), as follows:

7   In the first place, let the preacher above all be careful to avoid many versions or various texts and forms of the Ten Commandments, the Lord's Prayer, the Creed, the Sacraments, and such. He should choose one form to which he holds and teaches all the time, year after year. For young and simple people must be taught by uniform, settled texts and forms. Otherwise they become confused easily when the teacher today teaches them one way, and in a year some other way, as if he wished to make improvements. For then all effort and labor that has been spent in teaching is lost.

8   Our blessed fathers understood this well also. They all used the same form of the Lord's Prayer, the Creed, and the Ten Commandments. Therefore, we, too, should be at pains to teach the young and simple people these parts in such a way that we do not change a syllable or set them forth and repeat them one year differently than in another.

Therefore, choose whatever form you please, and hold to it forever. But when you preach in the presence of learned and intelligent people, you may show your skill. You may present these parts in varied and intricate ways and give them as masterly turns as you are able. But with the young people stick to one fixed, permanent form and manner. Teach them, first of all, these parts: the Ten Commandments, the Creed, 10 the Lord's Prayer, and so on, according to the text, word for word, so that they, too, can repeat it in the same way after you and commit it to memory.

But those who are unwilling to learn the catechism should be told that they deny 11 Christ and are not Christians. They should not be admitted to the Sacrament, accepted as sponsors at Baptism, or practice any part of Christian freedom. They should simply be turned back to the pope and his officials, indeed, to the devil himself (1 Corinthians 5:5). Furthermore, their parents and employers should refuse 12 them food and drink, and notify them that the prince will drive such rude people from the country.

Although we cannot and should not force anyone to believe, we should insist and 13 encourage the people. That way they will know what is right and wrong for those among whom they dwell and wish to make their living. For whoever desires to live in a town must know and observe the town laws, because he wishes to enjoy the protection offered by the laws whether he is a believer or at heart and in private a rascal or rogue.

In the second place, after they have learned the text well, teach them the meaning 14 also, so that they know what it means. Again, choose the form of these tables or some other brief uniform method, whichever you like, and hold to it. Do not change a sin- 15 gle syllable, as was just said about the text. Take your time in doing this. For it is not 16 necessary for you to explain all the parts at once, but one after the other. After they understand the First Commandment well, then explain the Second, and so on. Otherwise they will be overwhelmed, so that they will not be able to remember anything well.

In the third place, after you have taught them this short catechism, then take up 17 the Large Catechism and give them also a richer and fuller knowledge. Here enlarge upon every commandment, article, petition, and part with its various works, uses, benefits, dangers, and injuries, as you find these abundantly stated in many books written about these matters. In particular, urge the commandment or part that most 18 suffers the greatest neglect among your people. For example, the Seventh Commandment, about stealing, must be strongly urged among mechanics and merchants, and even farmers and servants. For among these people many kinds of dishonesty and stealing prevail. So, too, you must drive home the Fourth Commandment among the children and the common people, so that they may be quiet and faithful, obedient and peaceable. You must always offer many examples from the Scriptures to show how God has punished or blessed such persons (Deuteronomy 28).

In this matter you should especially urge magistrates and parents to rule well and 19 to send their children to school. Show them why it is their duty to do this and what a damnable sin they are committing if they do not do it. For by such neglect they

20 overthrow and destroy both God's kingdom and that of the world. They act as the worst enemies both of God and of people. Make it very plain to them what an awful harm they are doing if they will not help to train children to be pastors, preachers, clerks, and to fill other offices that we cannot do without in this life. God will punish them terribly for this failure. There is great need to preach this. In this matter parents and rulers are now sinning in unspeakable ways. The devil, too, hopes to accomplish something cruel because of these things.

21 Last, since the tyranny of the pope has been abolished, people are no longer willing to go to the Sacrament, and thus they despise it. Here again encouragement is necessary, yet with this understanding: We are to force no one to believe or to receive

22 the Sacrament. Nor should we set up any law, time, or place for it. Instead, preach in such a way that by their own will, without our law, they will urge themselves and, as it were, compel us pastors to administer the Sacrament. This is done by telling them, "When someone does not seek or desire the Sacrament at least four times a year, it is to be feared that he despises the Sacrament and is not a Christian, just as a person is not a Christian who does not believe or hear the Gospel." For Christ did not say, "Leave this out, or, despise this," but, "Do this, as often as you drink it" (1 Corinthians 11:25), and other such words. Truly, He wants it done, and not entirely neglected and despised. "Do this," He says.

23 Now, whoever does not highly value the Sacrament shows that he has no sin, no flesh, no devil, no world, no death, no danger, no hell. In other words, he does not believe any such things, although he is in them up over his head and his ears and is doubly the devil's own. On the other hand, he needs no grace, no life, no paradise, no heaven, no Christ, no God, nor anything good. For if he believed that he had so much evil around him, and needed so much that is good, he would not neglect the Sacrament, by which such evil is remedied and so much good is bestowed. Nor would it be necessary to force him to go to the Sacrament by any law. He would come running and racing of his own will, would force himself, and beg that you must give him the Sacrament.

24 Therefore, you must not make any law about this, as the pope does. Only set forth clearly the benefit and harm, the need and use, the danger and the blessing, connected with this Sacrament. Then the people will come on their own without you forcing them. But if they do not come, let them go their way and tell them that such people belong to the devil who do not regard nor feel their great need and

25 God's gracious help. But if you do not urge this, or make a law or make it bitter, it is your fault if they despise the Sacrament. What else could they be than lazy if you

26 sleep and are silent? Therefore, look to it, pastors and preachers. Our office has now become a different thing from what it was under the pope. It has now become a serious and saving office. So it now involves much more trouble and labor, dan-

27 ger and trials. In addition, it gains little reward and thanks in the world. But Christ Himself will be our reward if we labor faithfully (see Genesis 15:1). To this end may the Father of all grace help us, to whom be praise and thanks forever through Christ, our Lord! Amen.

# I. THE TEN COMMANDMENTS

GIVING OF THE COMMANDMENTS
(EXODUS 19)

As the Head of the Family Should Teach Them
in a Simple Way to His Household

# The First Commandment

WORSHIP OF THE GOLDEN CALF
(EXODUS 32)

You shall have no other gods.

*What does this mean?*

Answer: We should fear, love, and trust in God above all things.

## THE SECOND COMMANDMENT

THE SON OF SHELOMITH IS STONED FOR
BLASPHEMY (LEVITICUS 24)

You shall not take the name of the Lord, your God, in vain.

*What does this mean?*

Answer: We should fear and love God so that we may not curse,
swear, use witchcraft, lie, or deceive by His name, but call upon it in
every trouble, pray, praise, and give thanks.

# THE THIRD COMMANDMENT

HEARING AND DESPISING PREACHING
AND HIS WORD (NUMBER 15)

You shall sanctify the holy day.

*What does this mean?*

Answer: We should fear and love God so that we may not
despise preaching and His Word, but hold it sacred, and
gladly hear and learn it.

## THE FOURTH COMMANDMENT

HAM DISHONORS HIS FATHER, NOAH
(GENESIS 9)

You shall honor your father and your mother that it may be well with you and you may live long upon the earth.

*What does this mean?*

Answer: We should fear and love God so that we may not despise or anger our parents and masters, but give them honor, serve them, obey them, and hold them in love and esteem.

## THE FIFTH COMMANDMENT

CAIN KILLS ABEL
(GENESIS 4)

You shall not murder.

*What does this mean?*

Answer: We should fear and love God so that we may not hurt or harm
our neighbor in his body, but help and befriend him in every bodily
need [in every need and danger of life and body].

## THE SIXTH COMMANDMENT

DAVID AND BATHSHEBA
(2 SAMUEL 11)

You shall not commit adultery.

*What does this mean?*

Answer: We should fear and love God so that we may lead a pure and
decent life in words and deeds, and each love and honor his spouse.

# THE SEVENTH COMMANDMENT

### ACHAN THE THIEF
### (JOSHUA 7)

You shall not steal.

*What does this mean?*

Answer: We should fear and love God so that we may not take our
neighbor's money or property, nor get them with bad products or
deals, but help him to improve and protect his property and business.

## THE EIGHTH COMMANDMENT

BEARING FALSE WITNESS
AGAINST SUSANNA (SUSANNA 34–41)

You shall not bear false witness against your neighbor.

*What does this mean?*

Answer: We should fear and love God so that we may not deceitfully belie, betray, slander, or defame our neighbor, but defend him, think and speak well of him, and put the best construction on everything.

# THE NINTH COMMANDMENT

JACOB COVETS LABAN'S FLOCK
(GENESIS 30)

You shall not covet your neighbor's house.

*What does this mean?*

Answer: We should fear and love God so that we may not craftily seek to get our neighbor's inheritance or house, or obtain it by a show of justice and right, or any other means, but help and be of service to him in keeping it.

# THE TENTH COMMANDMENT

JOSEPH FLEES POTIPHAR'S WIFE
(GENESIS 39)

You shall not covet your neighbor's wife, or his manservant, or his maidservant, or his cattle, or anything that is his.

*What does this mean?*

Answer: We should fear and love God so that we may not turn, force, or entice away our neighbor's wife, servants, or cattle, but urge them to stay and carefully do their duty.

# WHAT DOES GOD SAY ABOUT ALL THESE COMMANDMENTS?

Answer: He says:

I the LORD your God am a jealous God, visiting the iniquity of
the fathers on the children to the third and the fourth generation of those who hate Me, but showing steadfast love to thousands of those who love Me and keep My commandments.
(Exodus 20:5–6)

*What does this mean?*

Answer: God threatens to punish all who sin against these commandments. Therefore, we should fear His wrath and not act contrary
to these commandments. But He promises grace and every blessing to
all who keep these commandments. Therefore, we should also love
and trust in Him and gladly do what He commands.

# II. THE CREED

As the Head of the Family Should Teach It in the Simplest Way to His Household

### THE FIRST ARTICLE

*Creation*

I believe in God, the Father Almighty, maker of heaven and earth.

*What does this mean?*

Answer: I believe that God has made me and all creatures. He has given me my body and soul, eyes, ears, and all my limbs, my reason, and all my senses, and still preserves them. In addition, He has given me clothing and shoes, meat and drink, house and home, wife and children, fields, cattle, and all my goods. He provides me richly and daily with all that I need to support this body and life. He protects me from all danger and guards me and preserves me from all evil. He does all this out of pure, fatherly, divine goodness and mercy, without any merit or worthiness in me. For all this I ought to thank Him, praise Him, serve Him, and obey Him. This is most certainly true.

THE CREATION
(GENESIS 1)

# THE SECOND ARTICLE

CHRIST CRUCIFIED
(JOHN 19)

*Redemption*

And in Jesus Christ, His only Son, our Lord, who was conceived by the Holy Spirit, born of the virgin Mary, suffered under Pontius Pilate, was crucified, died and was buried. He descended into hell. The third day He rose again from the dead. He ascended into heaven and sits at the right hand of God the Father Almighty. From thence He will come to judge the living and the dead.

*What does this mean?*

Answer: I believe that Jesus Christ, true God, begotten of the Father from eternity, and also true man, born of the Virgin Mary, is my Lord. He has redeemed me, a lost and condemned creature, purchased and won me from all sins, from death, and from the power of the devil. He did this not with gold or silver, but with His holy, precious blood and with His innocent suffering and death, so that I may be His own, live under Him in His kingdom, and serve Him in everlasting righteousness, innocence, and blessedness, just as He is risen from the dead, lives and reigns to all eternity. This is most certainly true.

# THE THIRD ARTICLE

## *Sanctification*

I believe in the Holy Spirit, the holy Christian Church, the communion of saints, the forgiveness of sins, the resurrection of the body, and the life everlasting. Amen.

### *What does this mean?*

Answer: I believe that I cannot by my own reason or strength believe in Jesus Christ, my Lord, or come to Him. But the Holy Spirit has called me by the Gospel, enlightened me with His gifts, sanctified and kept me in the true faith. In the same way He calls, gathers, enlightens, and sanctifies the whole Christian Church on earth and keeps it with Jesus Christ in the one true faith. In this Christian Church He daily and richly forgives all my sins and the sins of all believers. On the Last Day He will raise up me and all the dead and will give eternal life to me and to all believers in Christ. This is most certainly true.

PENTECOST
(ACTS 2)

# III. THE LORD'S PRAYER

As the Head of the Family Should Teach It in the Simplest Way to His Household

JESUS TEACHES THE DISCIPLES
TO PRAY (LUKE 11)

Our Father who art in heaven.

*What does this mean?*

Answer: By these words God would tenderly encourage us to believe that He is our true Father and that we are His true children, so that we may ask Him confidently with all assurance, as dear children ask their dear father.

# THE FIRST PETITION

Hallowed be Thy name.

*What does this mean?*

Answer: God's name is indeed holy in it-self. But we pray in this petition that it may become holy among us also.

*How is this done?*

Answer: When the Word of God is taught in its truth and purity and we as the children of God also lead holy lives in accordance with it. To this end help us, dear Father in heaven. But anyone who teaches and lives other than by what God's Word teaches profanes the name of God among us. From this preserve us, heavenly Father.

CHRIST TEACHING
(MATTHEW 5)

## THE SECOND PETITION

THE KINGDOM COMES
(LUKE 11)

Thy kingdom come.

*What does this mean?*

Answer: The kingdom of God comes indeed without our prayer, of itself. But we pray in this petition that it may come to us also.

*How is this done?*

Answer: When our heavenly Father gives us His Holy Spirit, so that by His grace we believe His holy Word and lead a godly life here in time and there in eternity.

## THE THIRD PETITION

Thy will be done on earth as it is in heaven.

*What does this mean?*

Answer: The good and gracious will of God is done indeed without our prayer. But we pray in this petition that it may be done among us also

*How is this done?*

Answer: When God breaks and hinders every evil counsel and will that would not let us hallow the name of God nor let His kingdom come, such as the will of the devil, the world, and our flesh. Instead, He strengthens and keeps us steadfast in His Word and in faith until we die. This is His gracious and good will.

CHRIST DOING THE WILL OF THE FATHER (MATTHEW 27)

## THE FOURTH PETITION

FEEDING THE FIVE THOUSAND
(JOHN 6)

Give us this day our daily bread.

*What does this mean?*

Answer: God gives daily bread, even without our prayer, to all wicked people; but we pray in this petition that He would lead us to realize this and to receive our daily bread with thanksgiving.

*What is meant by daily bread?*

Answer: Everything that belongs to the support and needs of the body, such as food, drink, clothing, shoes, house, home, field, cattle, money, goods, a pious spouse, pious children, pious servants, pious and faithful rulers, good government, good weather, peace, health, discipline, honor, good friends, faithful neighbors, and the like.

## THE FIFTH PETITION

And forgive us our trespasses as we forgive those who trespass against us.

*What does this mean?*

Answer: We pray in this petition that our Father in heaven would not look upon our sins nor deny such petitions on account of them. We are not worthy of any of the things for which we pray, neither have we deserved them. But we pray that He would grant them all to us by grace. For we daily sin much and indeed deserve nothing but punishment. So will we truly, on our part, also heartily forgive and readily do good to those who sin against us.

THE UNMERCIFUL SERVANT
(MATTHEW 18)

## THE SIXTH PETITION

THE TEMPTATION OF CHRIST
(MATTHEW 4)

And lead us not into temptation.

*What does this mean?*

Answer: God indeed tempts no one. But we pray in this petition that God would guard and keep us, so that the devil, the world, and our flesh may not deceive us nor seduce us into false belief, despair, and other great shame and vice. Though we are attacked by these things, we pray that still we may finally overcome them and gain the victory.

## THE SEVENTH PETITION

But deliver us from evil.

*What does this mean?*

Answer: We pray in this petition, as in a summary, that our Father in heaven would deliver us from all kinds of evil, of body and soul, property and honor. And finally, when our last hour shall come, we pray that He would grant us a blessed end and graciously take us from this vale of tears to Himself into heaven.

Amen.

*What does this mean?*

Answer: I should be certain that these petitions are acceptable to our Father in heaven and are heard by Him. For He Himself has commanded us to pray this way and has promised that He will hear us. Amen, Amen; that is, "Yes, yes, it shall be so."

CHRIST HEALS THE CANAANITE
WOMAN'S DAUGHTER
(MATTHEW 15)

# IV. THE SACRAMENT OF HOLY BAPTISM

As the Head of the Family Should Teach It in a Simple Way to His Household

THE BAPTISM OF CHRIST
(MATTHEW 3)

## FIRST

*What is Baptism?*

Answer: Baptism is not simple water only, but it is the water included in God's command and connected with God's Word.

*Which is that Word of God?*

Answer: Christ, our Lord, says in the last chapter of Matthew, "Go therefore and make disciples of all nations, baptizing them in the name of the Father and of the Son and of the Holy Spirit" (Matthew 28:19).

## SECOND

*What does Baptism give or profit?*

Answer: It works forgiveness of sins, delivers from death and the devil, and gives eternal salvation to all who believe this, as the words and promises of God declare.

*Which are these words and promises of God?*

Answer: Christ, our Lord, says in the last chapter of Mark, "Whoever believes and is baptized will be saved, but whoever does not believe will be condemned" (Mark 16:16).

### THIRD

*How can water do such great things?*

Answer: It is not the water indeed that does them, but the Word of God, which is in and with the water, and faith, which trusts this Word of God in the water. For without the Word of God the water is simple water and no Baptism. But with the Word of God it is a Baptism, that is, a gracious water of life and a washing of regeneration in the Holy Spirit. As St. Paul says in Titus chapter three, "He saved us . . . by the washing of regeneration and renewal of the Holy Spirit, whom He poured out on us richly through Jesus Christ our Savior, so that being justified by His grace we might become heirs according to the hope of eternal life. The saying is trustworthy" (vv. 5–8).

### FOURTH

*What does such baptizing with water signify?*

Answer: It signifies that the old Adam in us should, by daily contrition and repentance, be drowned and die with all sins and evil lusts. And also it shows that a new man should daily come forth and arise, who shall live before God in righteousness and purity forever.

*Where is this written?*

Answer: St. Paul says in Romans chapter 6, "We were buried therefore with Him by baptism into death, in order that, just as Christ was raised from the dead by the glory of the Father, we too might walk in newness of life" (v. 4).

CHRIST WITH THE LITTLE CHILDREN
(LUKE 18)

# V. HOW THE UNLEARNED
# SHOULD BE TAUGHT TO CONFESS

CONFESSION AND ABSOLUTION
(JOHN 21)

*What is Confession?*

Answer: Confession has two parts: the one is that we confess our sins; the other is that we receive Absolution, or forgiveness, from the confessor, as from God Himself, and in no way doubt, but firmly believe that our sins are forgiven before God in heaven by this.

*What sins should we confess?*

Answer: Before God we should plead guilty of all sins, even of those that we do not know, as we do in the Lord's Prayer. But before the confessor we should confess only those sins that we know and feel in our hearts.

*Which are these?*

Answer: Here consider your calling according to the Ten Commandments, whether you are a father, mother, son, daughter, master, mistress, a manservant or maidservant. Consider whether you have been disobedient, unfaithful, or slothful. Consider whether you have grieved anyone by words or deeds, whether you have stolen, neglected, wasted, or done other harm.

## PLEASE GIVE TO ME A BRIEF
## FORM OF CONFESSION

Answer: You should speak to the confessor like this, "Reverend and dear sir, I ask you to hear my confession, and to pronounce forgiveness to me for God's sake."

*Proceed!*

I, a poor sinner, confess myself guilty of all sins before God. I especially confess before you that I am a manservant (a maidservant, etc.). But, unfortunately, I serve my master unfaithfully. For in this and in that I have not done what has been commanded me. I have provoked him and caused him to curse. I have been negligent in many things and permitted damage to be done. I have also been immodest in words and deeds. I have argued with my equals, grumbled, and sworn at my mistress, and so forth. For all this I am sorry, and I pray for grace. I want to do better.

*A master or mistress may say this:*

In particular I confess before you that I have not faithfully trained my children, domestic servants, and wife (family) for God's glory. I have cursed, set a bad example by rude words and deeds. I have done my neighbor harm and spoken evil of him. I have overcharged, sold inferior products, and have given people less than they paid for.

And whatever else he has done against God's command and his calling, and such.

But if anyone does not find himself burdened with these sins or greater sins, he should not trouble himself or search for or invent other sins, and thereby make confession a torture. He should mention one or two sins that he knows. Say, "In particular I confess that I once cursed. Further, I once used improper words. I have once neglected this or that, and so on." Let this be enough.

But if you don't know of any sins at all (which, however, is hardly possible), then mention none in particular, but receive the forgiveness upon your general confession that you make before God to the confessor.

*Then the confessor shall say:*

God be merciful to you and strengthen your faith! Amen.

*Furthermore:*

Do you believe that my forgiveness is God's forgiveness?
Answer: Yes, dear sir.

*Then let him say:*

As you believe, so let it be done for you. And by the command of our Lord Jesus Christ I forgive you your sins, in the name of the Father and of the Son and of the Holy Spirit. Amen. Depart in peace.

But for those who have great burdens on their consciences, or are distressed and tempted, the confessor will know how to comfort and to encourage them to believe with more passages of Scripture. This is supposed to serve as a general form of confession for the unlearned.

# VI. THE SACRAMENT OF THE ALTAR

As the Head of a Family Should Teach It in a Simple Way to His Household

---

*What is the Sacrament of the Altar?*

Answer: It is the true body and blood of our Lord Jesus Christ, under the bread and wine, for us Christians to eat and to drink, instituted by Christ Himself.

*Where is this written?*

Answer: The holy Evangelists, Matthew, Mark, Luke, and St. Paul, write:

Our Lord Jesus Christ, on the night He was betrayed, took bread, and when He had given thanks, He broke it and gave it to the disciples and said: "Take, eat; this is My body, which is given for you. This do in remembrance of Me."

In the same way also, He took the cup after supper, and when He had given thanks, He gave it to them, saying: "Drink of it, all of you; this is My blood of the new testament, which is shed for you for the forgiveness of sins. This do, as often as you drink it, in remembrance of Me."

*What is the benefit of such eating and drinking?*

Answer: That is shown us in these words, "Given for you" and "shed for you for the forgiveness of sins." This means that in the Sacrament forgiveness of sins, life, and salvation are given us through these words. For where there is forgiveness of sins, there is also life and salvation.

*How can bodily eating and drinking do such great things?*

Answer: It is not the eating and drinking, indeed, that does them, but the words, which are given here, "Given . . . and shed for you, for the forgiveness of sins." These words are, beside the bodily eating and drinking, the chief thing in the Sacrament. The person who believes these words has what they say and express, namely, the forgiveness of sins.

*Who, then, receives such Sacrament worthily?*

Answer: Fasting and bodily preparation is, indeed, a fine outward training. But a person is truly worthy and well prepared who has faith in these words, "Given . . . and shed for you for the forgiveness of sins."

But anyone who does not believe these words, or doubts, is unworthy and unfit. For the words "for you" require hearts that truly believe.

# HOW THE HEAD OF THE FAMILY

Should Teach His Household to Bless Themselves in the Morning and in the Evening

## MORNING PRAYER

*In the morning, when you rise, you shall bless yourself with the holy cross and say,*
In the name of God the Father, Son, and Holy Spirit. Amen.

*Then, kneeling or standing, repeat the Creed and the Lord's Prayer. If you choose, you may, in addition, say this little prayer:*

I thank You, my heavenly Father, through Jesus Christ, Your dear Son, that You have kept me this night from all harm and danger. And I pray that You would keep me this day also from sin and all evil, so that all my doings and life may please You. For into Your hands I commend myself, my body and soul, and all things. Let Your holy angel be with me, so that the wicked foe may have no power over me. Amen.

*Then go to your work with joy, singing a hymn, like one on the Ten Commandments, or what your devotion may suggest.*

## EVENING PRAYER

*In the evening, when you go to bed, you shall bless yourself with the holy cross and say:*
In the name of God the Father, Son, and Holy Spirit. Amen.

*Then, kneeling or standing, repeat the Creed and the Lord's Prayer. If you choose, you may, in addition, say this little prayer:*

I thank You, my Heavenly Father, through Jesus Christ, Your dear Son, that You have graciously kept me this day. And I pray, forgive me all my sins, where I have done wrong, and graciously keep me this night. For into Your hands I commend myself, my body and soul, and all things. Let Your holy angel be with me, so that the wicked foe may have no power over me. Amen.

*Then go to sleep immediately and cheerfully.*

# HOW THE HEAD OF THE FAMILY
Should Teach His Household to Ask a Blessing and Return Thanks

## ASKING A BLESSING
*The children and servants shall go to the table with folded hands, reverently, and say:*

The eyes of all look to You, and You give them their food in due season. You open Your hand; You satisfy the desire of every living thing. [Psalm 145:15–16]

(Note: "To satisfy the desire" means that all animals receive so much to eat that they are made joyful and of good cheer. For worry and greed hinder such satisfaction.)

*Then say the Lord's Prayer and the following prayer:*

Lord God, Heavenly Father, bless us and these Your gifts, which we receive from Your bountiful goodness, through Jesus Christ, our Lord. Amen.

## RETURNING THANKS
*Likewise after the meal they shall reverently and with folded hands say:*

Give thanks to the LORD, for He is good, for His steadfast love endures forever.

He gives to the beasts their food, and to the young ravens that cry. His delight is not in the strength of the horse, nor His pleasure in the legs of a man, but the LORD takes pleasure in those who fear Him, in those who hope in His steadfast love. [Psalm 136:1; 147:9–11]

*Then say the Lord's Prayer and the following prayer:*

We thank You, Lord God, Father, through Jesus Christ, our Lord, for all Your benefits, who lives and reigns forever and ever. Amen.

# TABLE OF DUTIES

Certain Passages of Scripture for Various Holy Orders and Positions, by Which These people Are to Be Admonished, as a Special Lesson, about Their Office and Service

### FOR BISHOPS, PASTORS, AND PREACHERS

Therefore, an overseer [pastor] must be above reproach, the husband of one wife, sober-minded, self-controlled, respectable, hospitable, able to teach, not a drunkard, not violent but gentle, not quarrelsome, not a lover of money. He must manage his own household well, with all dignity keeping his children submissive. He must not be a recent convert, or he may become puffed up with conceit and fall into the condemnation of the devil. He must hold firm to the trustworthy word as taught, so that he may be able to give instruction in sound doctrine and also to rebuke those who contradict it. (1 Timothy 3:2–4, 6; Titus 1:9)

### WHAT THE HEARERS OWE TO THEIR PASTORS

In the same way, the Lord commanded that those who proclaim the gospel should get their living by the gospel. (1 Corinthians 9:14)

One who is taught the word must share all good things with the one who teaches. (Galatians 6:6)

Let the elders who rule well be considered worthy of double honor, especially those who labor in preaching and teaching. For the Scripture says, "You shall not muzzle an ox when it treads out the grain," and, "The laborer deserves his wages." (1 Timothy 5:17–18)

Obey your leaders and submit to them, for they are keeping watch over your souls, as those who will have to give an account. Let them do this with joy and not with groaning, for that would be of no advantage to you. (Hebrews 13:17)

### CONCERNING CIVIL GOVERNMENT

Let every person be subject to the governing authorities. For there is no authority except from God, and those that exist have been instituted by God. Therefore whoever resists the authorities resists what God has appointed, and those who resist will incur judgment. For rulers are not a terror to good conduct, but to bad. Would you have no fear of the one who is in authority? Then do what is good, and you will receive his approval, for he is God's servant for your good. But if you do wrong, be afraid, for he does not bear the sword in vain. For he is the servant of God, an avenger who carries out God's wrath on the wrongdoer. (Romans 13:1–4)

## WHAT SUBJECTS OWE TO THE RULERS

Therefore render to Caesar the things that are Caesar's, and to God the things that are God's. (Matthew 22:21)

Let every person be subject to the governing authorities. . . . Therefore one must be in subjection, not only to avoid God's wrath but also for the sake of conscience. For the same reason you also pay taxes, for the authorities are ministers of God, attending to this very thing. Pay to all what is owed to them: taxes to whom taxes are owed, revenue to whom revenue is owed, respect to whom respect is owed, honor to whom honor is owed. (Romans 13:1, 5–7)

First of all, then, I urge that supplications, prayers, intercessions, and thanksgivings be made for all people, for kings and all who are in high positions, that we may lead a peaceful and quiet life, godly and dignified in every way. (1 Timothy 2:1–2)

Remind them to be submissive to rulers and authorities, to be obedient, to be ready for every good work. (Titus 3:1)

Be subject for the Lord's sake to every human institution, whether it be to the emperor as supreme, or to governors as sent by him to punish those who do evil and to praise those who do good. (1 Peter 2:13–14)

## FOR HUSBANDS

Likewise, husbands, live with your wives in an understanding way, showing honor to the woman as the weaker vessel, since they are heirs with you of the grace of life, so that your prayers may not be hindered. (1 Peter 3:7)

Husbands, love your wives, and do not be harsh with them. (Colossians 3:19)

## FOR WIVES

Wives, submit to your own husbands, as to the Lord.

For this is how the holy women who hoped in God used to adorn themselves, by submitting to their husbands, as Sarah obeyed Abraham, calling him lord. And you are her children, if you do good and do not fear anything that is frightening. (Ephesians 5:22; 1 Peter 3:5–6)

## FOR PARENTS

Fathers, do not provoke your children to anger, but bring them up in the discipline and instruction of the Lord. (Ephesians 6:4)

## FOR CHILDREN

Children, obey your parents in the Lord, for this is right. "Honor your father and mother" (this is the first commandment with a promise), "that it may go well with you and that you may live long in the land." (Ephesians 6:1–3)

## FOR MALE AND FEMALE SERVANTS, HIRED MEN, AND LABORERS

Slaves, obey your earthly masters with fear and trembling, with a sincere heart, as you would Christ, not by the way of eye-service, as people-pleasers, but as servants of Christ, doing the will of God from the heart, rendering service with a good will as to the Lord and not to man, knowing that whatever good anyone does, this he will receive back from the Lord, whether he is a slave or free. (Ephesians 6:5–8; see also Colossians 3:22)

## FOR MASTERS AND MISTRESSES

Masters, do the same to them, and stop your threatening, knowing that he who is both their Master and yours is in heaven, and that there is no partiality with Him. (Ephesians 6:9; see also Colossians 4:1)

## FOR YOUNG PERSONS IN GENERAL

Likewise, you who are younger, be subject to the elders. Clothe yourselves, all of you, with humility toward one another, for "God opposes the proud but gives grace to the humble." Humble yourselves, therefore, under the mighty hand of God so that at the proper time he may exalt you. (1 Peter 5:5–6)

## FOR WIDOWS

She who is truly a widow, left all alone, has set her hope on God and continues in supplications and prayers night and day, but she who is self-indulgent is dead even while she lives. (1 Timothy 5:5–6)

## FOR ALL IN COMMON

The commandments . . . are summed up in this word: "You shall love your neighbor as yourself." (Romans 13:9) "First of all, then, I urge that supplications, prayers, intercessions, and thanksgivings be made for all people." (1 Timothy 2:1)

Let each his lesson learn with care, and all the household well shall fare.

# THE LARGE CATECHISM

## DR. MARTIN LUTHER

| TIMELINE | OUTLINE |
|---|---|
| | |

**TIMELINE**

1516   Luther preaches sermon series on Ten Commandments

1517   Luther preaches sermon series on Lord's Prayer; posts Ninety-five Theses

1521   Luther excommunicated by papal bull *Decet Romanum Pontificem;* appears before Diet of Worms; refuses to recant, stating "Here I stand"

1524   Peasants' War begins, led in part by Thomas Münzer

1525   Luther asks Justus Jonas and John Agricola to produce a "catechism"

Luther marries Katharina von Bora, June 13

1526   Diet of Speyer grants German princes right to establish religion in their territory

Church visitation begins to assess needs of congregations

1527   Visitation articles prepared

Plague strikes Wittenberg; Luther and Katharina turn their home into a hospital

1528   Luther teaches catechism instruction at the parish church; preaches three sermon series on parts of catechism

1529   Luther publishes the *Large Catechism* in April and the *Small Catechism* in May

1530   *Augsburg Confession* presented to Charles V at Diet of Augsburg, June 25

**OUTLINE**

Preface

Shorter Preface

Part 1: The Ten Commandments

Part 2: The Apostles' Creed

Part 3: Prayer

Part 4: Baptism

Part 5: The Sacrament of the Altar

An Exhortation to Confession

# THE LARGE CATECHISM

For a detailed introduction to the catechisms, see pp. 335–37.

In his preface to the Small Catechism, Luther vents his frustration over laypeople's abusing the freedom of the Gospel. However, in this preface he also focuses on the clergy's faults and failings. He chastises and rebukes lazy pastors who do as little as possible when it comes to preaching and teaching, and who are lax in their own personal prayer and meditation on God's Word. As usual, Luther doesn't tread lightly when expressing his concerns. He laments that people regard learning the Ten Commandments, the Creed, and the Lord's Prayer as childish. He explains how he daily recites these texts and studies them. Luther takes pastors to the woodshed for neglecting to teach their congregations carefully. He provides many reasons for continued and careful reading and studying of the Bible.

## Preface

A Christian, profitable, and necessary preface, and faithful, serious encouragement from Dr. Martin Luther to all Christians, but especially to all pastors and preachers. They should daily exercise themselves in the catechism, which is a short summary and epitome of the entire Holy Scriptures. They should always teach the catechism.

1   We have no small reasons for constantly preaching the catechism and for both desiring and begging others to teach it. For sadly we see that many pastors and preachers are very negligent in this matter and slight both their office and this teaching. Some neglect the catechism because of great and high art (giving their mind, as they imagine, to much "higher" matters). But others neglect it from sheer laziness and care for their bellies. They take no other stand in this business than to act as pastors and preachers for their bellies' sake. They have nothing to do but to spend and consume their wages as long as they live, just as they used to do under the papacy.

2   They now have everything they are to preach and teach placed before them abundantly, clearly, and easily, in so many helpful books. These truly are "Sermons That Preach Themselves," "Sleep Soundly," "Be Prepared," and "Thesaurus," as they used to be called. Yet these preachers are not even godly and honest enough to buy these books or, even when they have them, to look at them or read them. Oh, they are completely shameful gluttons and servants of their own bellies. They are more fit to be swineherds and dog tenders than caretakers of souls and pastors.

3   These pastors are now released from the useless and burdensome babbling of the seven canonical hours of prayer. I wish that, instead of these, they would read each morning, noon, and evening only a page or two in the catechism, the prayer book, the New Testament, or something else in the Bible. They should pray the Lord's Prayer for themselves and their parishioners. Then they might respond with honor and thanks to the Gospel, by which they have been delivered from obvious burdens and troubles, and might feel a little shame. For like pigs and dogs, they take nothing more from the Gospel than this lazy, deadly, shameful, worldly freedom! The com-   4
mon people also respect the Gospel altogether too lightly, and we accomplish nothing

The Creation; woodcut from the first illustrated edition
of the Large Catechism, 1530, Wittenberg

special, even though we work diligently. What, then, would be achieved if we were as negligent and lazy as we were under the papacy?

5    To this laziness such preachers add the shameful vice and secret infection of security and contentment. In other words, many see the catechism as a poor, common teaching, which they can read through once and immediately understand. They can throw the book into a corner and be ashamed to read it again.

6    Yes, even among the nobility one may find some clowns and penny pinchers, who say (a) there is no longer any need for either pastors or preachers, (b) we have everything in books, and (c) everyone can easily learn it by himself. So they are happy to let the parishes rot and become empty. They let pastors and preachers worry and go hungry, just as crazy Germans are accustomed to do. For we Germans have such disgraceful people and must put up with them.

7    But for myself I say this: I am also a doctor and preacher; yes, as learned and experienced as all the people who have such assumptions and contentment. Yet I act as a child who is being taught the catechism. Every morning—and whenever I have time—I read and say, word for word, the Ten Commandments, the Creed, the Lord's Prayer, the Psalms, and such. I must still read and study them daily. Yet I cannot master the catechism as I wish. But I must remain a

8    child and pupil of the catechism, and am glad to remain so. Yet these delicate, refined fellows would in one reading promptly become doctors above all doctors, know everything, and need nothing. Well, this, too, is a sure sign that they despise both their office and the souls of the people. Indeed, they even despise God and His Word. They do not have to fall. They have already fallen all too horribly. They need to become children and begin to

learn their alphabet, which they imagine they have long outgrown (Mark 10:15).

9    Therefore, for God's sake I beg such lazy bellies or arrogant saints to be persuaded and believe that they are truly, truly not so learned or such great doctors as they imagine! They should never assume that they have finished learning the parts of the catechism or know it well enough in all points, even though they think that they know it ever so well. For even if they know and understand the catechism perfectly (which, however, is impossible in this life), there are still many benefits and fruits to be gained, if it is daily read and practiced in thought and speech. For example, the Holy Spirit is present in such reading, repetition, and meditation. He bestows ever new and more light and devoutness. In this way the catechism is daily loved and appreciated better, as Christ promises in Matthew 18:20, "For where two or three are gathered in My name, there am I among them."

10    Besides, catechism study is a most effective help against the devil, the world, the flesh, and all evil thoughts. It helps to be occupied with God's Word, to speak it, and meditate on it, just as the first Psalm declares people blessed who meditate on God's Law day and night (Psalm 1:2). Certainly you will not release a stronger incense or other repellant against the devil than to be engaged by God's commandments and words, and speak, sing, or think them (Colossians 3:16). For this is indeed the true "holy water" and "holy sign" from which the devil runs and by which he may be driven away (James 4:7).

11    Now, for this reason alone you ought gladly to read, speak, think, and use these things, even if you had no other profit and fruit from them than driving away the devil and evil thoughts by doing so. For he cannot hear or endure God's Word. God's Word is not like some other silly babbling, like the

story about Dietrich of Berne, for example. But as St. Paul says in Romans 1:16, it is "the power of God." Yes indeed, it is the power of God that gives the devil burning pain and strengthens, comforts, and helps us beyond measure.

12    And what need is there for more words? If I were to list all the profit and fruit God's Word produces, where would I get enough paper and time? The devil is called the master of a thousand arts. But what shall we call God's Word, which drives away and brings to nothing this master of a thousand arts with all his arts and power? The Word must indeed be the master of more than a hundred thousand arts.

13    And shall we easily despise such power, profit, strength, and fruit—we, especially, who claim to be pastors and preachers? If so, not only should we have nothing given us to eat, but we should also be driven out, baited with dogs, and pelted with dung. We not only need all this every day just as we need our daily bread, but we must also daily use it against the daily and unending attacks and lurking of the devil (1 Peter 5:8), the master of a thousand arts.

14    If these reasons were not enough to move us to read the catechism daily, we should feel bound well enough by God's command alone. He solemnly commands in Deuteronomy 6:6–8 that we should always meditate on His precepts, sitting, walking, standing, lying down, and rising. We should have them before our eyes and in our hands as a constant mark and sign. Clearly He did not solemnly require and command this without a purpose. For He knows our danger and need, as well as the constant and furious assaults and temptations of devils. He wants to warn, equip, and preserve us against them, as with a good armor against their fiery darts (Ephesians 6:10–17) and with good medicine against their evil infection and temptation.

Oh, what mad, senseless fools are we! 15 While we must ever live and dwell among such mighty enemies as the devils, we still despise our weapons and defense (2 Corinthians 10:4), and we are too lazy to look at or think of them!

What else are such proud, arrogant saints 16 doing who are unwilling to read and study the catechism daily? They think they are much more learned than God Himself with all His saints, angels, prophets, apostles, and all Christians. God Himself is not ashamed to teach these things daily. He knows nothing better to teach. He always keeps teaching the same thing and does not take up anything new or different. All the saints know nothing better or different to learn and cannot finish learning this. Are we not the finest of all fellows to imagine that if we have once read or heard the catechism, we know it all and have no further need to read and learn? Can we finish learning in one hour what God Himself cannot finish teaching? He is engaged in teaching this from the beginning to the end of the world. All prophets, together with all saints, have been busy learning it, have ever remained students, and must continue to be students.

It must be true that whoever knows the 17 Ten Commandments perfectly must know all the Scriptures (Matthew 7:12). So, in all matters and cases, he can advise, help, comfort, judge, and decide both spiritual and temporal matters. Such a person must be qualified to sit in judgment over all doctrines, estates, spirits, laws, and whatever else is in the world (1 Corinthians 6:2–3). And what, indeed, is 18 the entire Book of Psalms but thoughts and exercises upon the First Commandment? Now I truly know that such lazy "bellies" and arrogant spirits do not understand a single psalm, much less the entire Holy Scriptures. Yet they pretend to know and despise the cat-

God Gives the Commandments;
from 1530 Large Catechism

echism, which is a short and brief summary of all the Holy Scriptures.

19 Therefore, I again beg all Christians—especially pastors and preachers—not to think of themselves as doctors too soon and imagine that they know everything. (For imagination, like unshrunk cloth, will fall far short of the measure.) Instead, they should daily exercise themselves well in these studies and constantly use them. Furthermore, they should guard with all care and diligence against the poisonous infection of contentment and vain imagination, but steadily keep on reading, teaching, learning, pondering, and meditating on the catechism. And they should not stop until they have tested and are sure that they have taught the devil to death, and have become more learned than God Himself and all His saints.

20 If they show such diligence, then I will promise them—and they shall also see—what fruit they will receive, and what excellent people God will make of them. So in due time they themselves will admit that the longer and the more they study the catechism, the less they know of it and the more they will find to learn. Only then, as hungry and thirsty men, will they truly relish what now they cannot stand because of great abundance and contentment. To this end may God grant His grace! Amen.

# Short Preface
# of Dr. Martin Luther

Note that Luther never intended the Small and Large Catechisms to be only "church books," but rather "house books"—to be used in laypeople's homes. In fact, Luther suggests that those who do not know the Ten Commandments, the Creed, and the Lord's Prayer by heart should not receive the Lord's Supper. He provides these texts as the most necessary parts of Christian doctrine, which should be learned until they can be repeated, word for word, by heart, from memory. Luther was always concerned that, in their preaching and teaching, pastors should speak and teach in a very clear, simple, easily understood way so that people would remember what was preached or taught.

---

This sermon is designed and undertaken 1 to be an instruction for children and the simple folk. Therefore, in ancient times it was called in Greek *catechism* (i.e., instruction for children). It teaches what every Christian 2 must know. So a person who does not know this catechism could not be counted as a Christian or be admitted to any Sacrament, just as a mechanic who does not understand the rules and customs of his trade is expelled and considered incapable. Therefore, we 3 must have the young learn well and fluently the parts of the catechism or instruction for children, diligently exercise themselves in them, and keep them busy with these parts.

Therefore, it is the duty of every father of a 4 family to question and examine his children and servants at least once a week and see what they know or are learning from the catechism. And if they do not know the catechism, he should keep them learning it faithfully. For I 5 well remember the time—indeed, even now it happens daily—that one finds rude, old persons who knew nothing and still know nothing about these things. Yet they go to Baptism and the Lord's Supper and use everything belonging to Christians, even though people who come to the Lord's Supper ought to know more and have a fuller understanding of all Christian doctrine than children and new scholars. However, for the common people 6 we are satisfied if they know the three "parts." These have remained in Christendom from of old, though little of them has been taught and used correctly until both young and old (who are called Christians and wish to be so) are well trained in them and familiar with them. These parts are the following:

# FIRST

## GOD'S TEN COMMANDMENTS

1    1. You shall have no other gods.

2    2. You shall not take the name of the Lord, your God, in vain.

3    3. You shall sanctify the holy day.

4    4. You shall honor your father and mother that it may be well with you and you may live long upon the earth.

5    5. You shall not murder.

6    6. You shall not commit adultery.

7    7. You shall not steal.

8    8. You shall not bear false witness against your neighbor.

9    9. You shall not covet your neighbor's house.

10    10. You shall not covet your neighbor's wife, or his manservant, or his maidservant, or his cattle, or anything that is his.

# SECOND

## THE CHIEF ARTICLES OF OUR FAITH

11    1. I believe in God, the Father Almighty, maker of heaven and earth.

12    2. And in Jesus Christ, His only Son, our Lord, who was conceived by the Holy Spirit, born of the virgin Mary, suffered under Pontius Pilate, was crucified, died and was buried. He descended into hell. The third day He rose again from the dead. He ascended into heaven and sits at the right hand of God the Father Almighty. From thence He will come to judge the living and the dead.

3. I believe in the Holy Spirit, the holy Christian Church, the communion of saints, the forgiveness of sins, the resurrection of the body, and the life everlasting. Amen.    13

# THIRD    14

## THE PRAYER, OR "OUR FATHER," WHICH CHRIST TAUGHT

Our Father who art in heaven.

1. Hallowed be Thy name.

2. Thy kingdom come.

3. Thy will be done on earth as it is in heaven.

4. Give us this day our daily bread.

5. And forgive us our trespasses as we forgive those who trespass against us.

6. And lead us not into temptation.

7. But deliver us from evil. [For Thine is the kingdom and the power and the glory forever and ever.] Amen.

These are the most necessary parts of Christian teaching that one should first learn to repeat word for word. And our children should be used to reciting them daily when they rise in the morning, when they sit down to their meals, and when they go to bed at night. And until they repeat them, they should not be given food or drink. Likewise, every head of a household is bound to do the same with his household, manservants, and maidservants. He should not keep them in his house if they do not know these things or are unwilling to learn them. A person who is so rude and unruly as to be unwilling to learn these things is not to be tolerated. For in these    15 16 17 18

19 three parts, everything that we have in the Scriptures is included in short, plain, and simple terms. For the holy fathers or apostles (whoever first taught these things) have summarized the doctrine, life, wisdom, and art of Christians this way. These parts speak, teach, and are focused on them.

20 Now, when these three parts are understood, a person must also know what to say about our Sacraments, which Christ Himself instituted: Baptism and the holy body and blood of Christ. They should know the texts that Matthew (28:19–20) and Mark (16:15–16) record at the close of their Gospels, when Christ said farewell to His disciples and sent them forth.

## BAPTISM

21

> Go therefore and make disciples of all nations, baptizing them in the name of the Father and of the Son and of the Holy Spirit. (Matthew 28:19)

> Whoever believes and is baptized will be saved, but whoever does not believe will be condemned. (Mark 16:16)

22 This is enough for a simple person to know from the Scriptures about Baptism. In like manner, in short, simple words, they should also know the text of St. Paul (1 Corinthians 11:23–26) about the other Sacrament.

## THE SACRAMENT

23

> Our Lord Jesus Christ, on the night He was betrayed, took bread, and when He had given thanks, He broke it and gave it to the disciples and said: "Take, eat; this is My body, which is given for you. This do in remembrance of Me."

> In the same way also, He took the cup after supper, and when He had given thanks, He gave it to them, saying: "Drink of it, all of you; this is My blood of the new testament, which is shed for you for the forgiveness of sins. This do, as often as you drink it, in remembrance of Me."

24 Then we would have all together five whole parts of Christian doctrine. These should be taught constantly and be required learning for children. You should hear them recited word for word. For you must not rely on the idea that the young people will learn and retain these things from the sermon alone. When these parts have been well learned, you may supplement and strengthen them by also setting before them some psalms or hymns, which have been composed on these parts of the catechism. Lead the young into the Scriptures this way, and make progress in them daily.

26 However, it is not enough for them to understand and recite these parts according to the words alone. The young people should also be made to attend the preaching, especially during the time that is devoted to the catechism. Then they may hear it explained and may learn to understand what every part contains, so that they can recite it the way they have heard it. Then, when asked, they may give a correct answer, so that preaching may not be useless and fruitless. For the reason we exercise such diligence in preaching the catechism often is so that it may be taught to our youth, not in a high and clever way, but briefly and with the greatest simplicity. In this way it will enter the mind easily and be fixed in the memory.

28 Therefore, we shall now take up the above-mentioned articles one by one, and in the plainest manner possible say as much as is necessary about them.

# PART 1

## THE FIRST COMMANDMENT

Luther spends more time on the First Commandment than on any other portion of the Catechism, explaining how essential it is to know, trust, and believe in the true God and to let nothing take His place. He was convinced that where this commandment was being kept, all other commandments would follow. A right relationship with God produces right relationships with fellow human beings.

———————

You shall have no other gods.

1    What this means: You shall have Me alone as your God. What is the meaning of this, and how is it to be understood? What does it mean to have a god? Or, what is God?

2    Answer: A god means that from which we are to expect all good and in which we are to take refuge in all distress. So, to have a God is nothing other than trusting and believing Him with the heart. I have often said that the confidence and faith of the heart alone make

3    both God and an idol. If your faith and trust is right, then your god is also true. On the other hand, if your trust is false and wrong, then you do not have the true God. For these two belong together, faith and God (Hebrews 11:6). Now, I say that whatever you set your heart on and put your trust in is truly your god.

4    The purpose of this commandment is to require true faith and trust of the heart, which settles upon the only true God and clings to Him alone. It is like saying, "See to it that you let Me alone be your God, and never seek another." In other words, "Whatever you lack of good things, expect it from Me. Look to Me for it. And whenever you suffer misfortune and distress, crawl and cling to Me. I,

yes, I, will give you enough and help you out of every need. Only do not let your heart cleave to or rest on any other."

This point I must unfold more clearly. It    5 may be understood and seen through ordinary, counterexamples. Many a person thinks that he has God and everything in abundance when he has money and possessions. He trusts in them and boasts about them with such firmness and assurance as to care for no one. Such a person has a god by the name of    6 "Mammon" (i.e., money and possessions; Matthew 6:24), on which he sets all his heart. This is the most common idol on earth. He    7 who has money and possessions feels secure (Luke 12:16–21) and is joyful and undismayed as though he were sitting in the midst of Paradise. On the other hand, he who has    8 no money doubts and is despondent, as though he knew of no God. For very few people can be found who are of good cheer and    9 who neither mourn nor complain if they lack Mammon. This care and desire for money sticks and clings to our nature, right up to the grave.

So, too, whoever trusts and boasts that he    10 has great skill, prudence, power, favor, friendship, and honor also has a god. But it is not the true and only God. This truth reappears when you notice how arrogant, secure, and proud people are because of such possessions, and how despondent they are when the possessions no longer exist or are withdrawn. Therefore, I repeat that the chief explanation of this point is that to "have a god" is to have something in which the heart entirely trusts.

Besides, consider our blindness, which we    11 have been practicing and doing under the papacy up until now. If anyone had a toothache, he fasted and honored St. Apollonia. If he was afraid of fire, he chose St. Lawrence as his helper. If he dreaded bubonic plague, he made a vow to St. Sebastian or Rochio. There were a countless number of such abominations, where everyone chose his own saint, worshiped him, and called to him 12 for help in distress. Here belong such people as sorcerers and magicians, whose idolatry is most great (Deuteronomy 18:9–12). They make a deal with the devil, in order that he may give them plenty of money or help them in love affairs, preserve their cattle, restore to them lost possessions, and so forth. For all such people place their heart and trust elsewhere than in the true God. They look to Him for nothing good, nor do they seek good from Him.

13   So you can easily understand what and how much this commandment requires. A person's entire heart and all his confidence must be placed in God alone and in no one else. For to "have" God, you can easily see, is not to take hold of Him with our hands or to put Him in a bag like money or to lock Him 14 in a chest like silver vessels. Instead, to "have" Him means that the heart takes hold of Him 15 and clings to Him. To cling to Him with the heart is nothing else than to trust in Him entirely. For this reason God wishes to turn us away from everything else that exists outside of Him and to draw us to Himself (John 6:44). For He is the only eternal good (Matthew 19:17). It is as though He would say, "Whatever you have previously sought from the saints, or for whatever things you have trusted in money or anything else, expect it all from Me. Think of Me as the one who will help you and pour out upon you richly all good things."

16   See, here you have the meaning of the true honor and worship of God, which pleases God, and which He commands under penalty of eternal wrath. The heart knows no other comfort or confidence than in Him. It must not allow itself to be torn from Him.

But, for Him, it must risk and disregard everything upon earth. On the other hand, 17 you can easily see and sense how the world practices only false worship and idolatry. For no people have ever been so corrupt that they did not begin and continue some divine worship. Everyone has set up as his special god whatever he looked to for blessings, help, and comfort.

For example, the heathen who put their 18 trust in power and dominion elevated Jupiter as the supreme god. Others, who were bent on riches, happiness, or pleasure, and a life of ease, elevated Hercules, Mercury, Venus, or other gods. Pregnant women elevated Diana or Lucina, and so on. So everyone made his god that interest to which his heart was inclined. So even in the mind of the heathen to have a god means to trust and believe. But their error is this: their trust 19 is false and wrong. For their trust is not placed in the only God, beside whom there is truly no God in heaven or upon earth (Isaiah 44:6). Therefore, the heathen really make 20 their self-invented notions and dreams of God an idol. Ultimately, they put their trust in that which is nothing. So it is with all idol- 21 atry. For it happens not merely by erecting an image and worshiping it, but rather it happens in the heart. For the heart stands gaping at something else. It seeks help and consolation from creatures, saints, or devils. It neither cares for God, nor looks to Him for anything better than to believe that He is willing to help. The heart does not believe that whatever good it experiences comes from God (James 1:17).

Beside this, there is also a false worship 22 and extreme idolatry, which we have practiced up to now. This is also still common in the world. All churchly orders are founded on it. It concerns the conscience alone, which seeks help, consolation, and salvation in its own works. This conscience imagines it can wrestle heaven away from God and thinks about how many requests it has made, how often it has fasted, celebrated Mass, and so on. Upon such things it depends and boasts, as though unwilling to receive anything from God as a gift. For it wants to earn or merit heaven with abundant works. The conscience acts as though God must serve us and is our debtor, and we are His liege lords. What is 23 this but reducing God to an idol—indeed, an apple-god—and elevating and regarding ourselves as God? But this point is a little too clever and is not for young pupils.

24    Let the following point be made to the simple; then they may well note and remember the meaning of this commandment: We are to trust in God alone and look to Him and expect from Him nothing but good, as from one who gives us body, life, food, drink, nourishment, health, protection, peace, and all necessaries of both temporal and eternal things. He also preserves us from misfortune. And if any evil befall us, He delivers and rescues us. So it is God alone (as has been said well enough) from whom we receive all good and by whom we are delivered from all evil.

25    So, I think, we Germans from ancient times name *God* (more elegantly and appropriately than any other language) from the word *Good*. It is as though He were an eternal fountain that gushes forth abundantly nothing but what is good. And from that fountain flows forth all that is and is called good.

26    Even though we experience much good from other people, whatever we receive by God's command or arrangement is all received from God. For our parents and all rulers and everyone else, with respect to his neighbor, have received from God the command that they should do us all kinds of good. So we receive these blessings not from them, but through them, from God. For crea-

tures are only the hands, channels, and means by which God gives all things. So He gives to the mother breasts and milk to offer to her child, and He gives corn and all kinds of produce from the earth for nourishment (Psalm 104:27–28; 147:8–9). None of these blessings could be produced by any creature of itself.

So no one should expect to take or give 27 anything except what God has commanded. Then it may be acknowledged as God's gift, and thanks may be rendered to Him for it, as this commandment requires. For this reason also, the ways we receive good gifts through creatures are not to be rejected. Nor should we arrogantly seek other ways and means than what God has commanded. For that would not be receiving from God, but seeking for ourselves.

Let everyone, then, see to it that he values 28 this commandment great and high above all things. Do not regard it as a joke! Ask and examine your heart diligently (2 Corinthians 13:5), and you will find out whether it clings to God alone or not. If you have a heart that can expect of Him nothing but what is good—especially in need and distress—and a heart that also renounces and forsakes everything that is not God, then you have the only true God. If, on the contrary, your heart clings to anything else from which it expects more good and help than from God, and if your heart does not take refuge in Him but flees from Him when in trouble, then you have an idol, another god.

God will not have this commandment 29 thrown to the winds. He will most strictly enforce it. In order that this may be known He has added (a) a terrible threat and (b) a beautiful, comforting promise. This promise is also to be taught and impressed upon young people (Deuteronomy 6:7), that they may take it to heart and hold it.

*Explanation of the Appendix to the First Commandment*

30    I the LORD your God am a jealous God, visiting the iniquity of the fathers on the children to the third and the fourth generation of those who hate Me, but showing steadfast love to thousands of those who love Me and keep My commandments. (Exodus 20:5–6)

31    These words relate to all the commandments (as we shall learn later). But they are joined to this chief commandment because it is most important that people get their thinking straight first. For where the head is right, the whole life must be right, and vice

32    versa. Learn, therefore, from these words how angry God is with those who trust in anything but Him. And again, learn how good and gracious He is to those who trust and believe in Him alone with their whole heart (Deuteronomy 6:5). His anger does not stop until the fourth generation of those who hate

33    Him. He says this so you will not live in such security and commit yourself to chance, like people with brute hearts who think that it makes no great difference how they live. On the other hand, His blessing and goodness

34    reach many thousands. He is a God who will not overlook that people turn from Him. He will not stop being angry until the fourth generation, even until they are utterly exterminated. Therefore, He is to be feared and not to be despised (Deuteronomy 10:20).

35    He has also made this known in all history, as the Scriptures abundantly show and daily experience still teaches. For from the beginning He has utterly uprooted all idolatry. Because of idolatry, He has uprooted both heathen people and Jewish people. To this day He overthrows all false worship, so that all who remain therein must finally per-

ish (2 Chronicles 7:19–20). Proud, powerful,   36
and rich men of the world (Sardanapalians and Phalarides, who surpass even the Persians in wealth) are still to be found. They boast defiantly of their Mammon. They utterly disregard whether God is angry at them or smiles on them. They dare to withstand His wrath, yet they shall not succeed. Before they are aware of it, they shall be wrecked, with all in which they trusted. All others have perished like this who have thought themselves more secure or powerful.

Such hard heads imagine that God over-   37
looks and allows them to rest in security, or that He is entirely ignorant or cares nothing about such matters. Therefore, God must deal a smashing blow and punish them, so that He cannot forget their sin unto their children's children. In that way, everyone may take note and see that this is no joke to Him. These are the people He means when He   38
says, "those who hate Me" (Exodus 20:5; i.e., those who persist in their defiance and pride). Whatever is preached or said to them, they will not listen. When they are rebuked, in order that they may learn to know themselves and make amends before the punishment begins, they become mad and foolish. They rightly deserve wrath, as we see daily in bishops and princes now.

But as terrible as these threatenings are, so   39
much more powerful is the consolation in the promise. For those who cling to God alone should be sure that He will show them mercy. In other words, He will show them pure goodness and blessing, not only for themselves, but also to their children and their children's children, even to the thousandth generation and beyond that. This   40
ought certainly to move and impel us to risk our hearts in all confidence with God (Hebrews 4:16; 10:19–23), if we wish all temporal and eternal good. For the supreme Majesty

makes such outstanding offers and presents such heartfelt encouragements and such rich promises.

41 Therefore, let everyone seriously take this passage to heart, lest it be regarded as though a man had spoken it. For you it is a question of eternal blessing, happiness, and salvation, or of eternal wrath, misery, and woe. What more would you have or desire than God so kindly promising to be yours with every blessing and to protect and help you in all need?

42 But unfortunately, here is the failure: the world believes none of this, nor regards it as God's Word. For the world sees that those who trust in God and not in Mammon suffer care and want, and that the devil opposes and resists them. They don't have money or favor or honor, and besides, can scarcely support life. On the other hand, those who serve Mammon have power, favor, honor, possessions, and every comfort in the eyes of the world. For this reason, these words must be understood to speak against the appearance of such things. And we must consider that they do not lie or deceive, but must come true.

43 Reflect for yourself or investigate and tell me: Those who have used all their care and diligence to gather great possessions and wealth, what have they finally gained? You will find that they have wasted their toil and labor, or even though they have amassed great treasures, they have been dispersed and scattered (Luke 12:16–21). So they themselves have never found happiness in their wealth, and afterward, it never reached the third generation.

44 You will find plenty of examples in all histories, also in the memory of aged and experienced people. Just watch and ponder them.

45 Saul was a great king, chosen by God, and a godly man. But when he was established on his throne, he let his heart wander from God and put his trust in his crown and power (1 Samuel 9–13). Then he had to perish with all he had, so that not even his children remained (1 Samuel 31).

46 David, on the other hand, was a poor, despised man, hunted down and chased, so that he did not feel his life was secure anywhere (1 Samuel 19–29). Yet, he had to survive in spite of Saul, and become king (2 Samuel 2). For these words of the promise had to abide and come true, since God cannot lie or deceive (Titus 1:2). Just let not the devil and the world deceive you with their show, which indeed remains for a time, but finally is nothing.

47 Let us, then, learn well the First Commandment, that we may see how God will tolerate no overconfidence nor any trust in any other object. We will see how He requires nothing greater from us than confidence from the heart for everything good. Then we may live right and straightforward and use all the blessings that God gives, just as a shoemaker uses his needle, awl, and thread for work and then lays them aside. Or we may behave like a traveler using an inn, food, and bed only to meet his present need. Each person may do this in his calling, according to God's order, and without allowing any of these things to be his lord or idol. This is 48 enough about the First Commandment, which we have had to explain at length, since it is of chief importance. For, as said earlier, where the heart is rightly set toward God (Deuteronomy 32:46) and this commandment is observed, all the other commandments follow.

## THE SECOND COMMANDMENT

The First Commandment instructs our heart toward God. This commandment guides our lips. Using God's name to cover up lies or spread falsehood is a great evil and sin, and it happens in many ways in life. There is no greater sin against the Second Commandment than using God's name to preach, teach, and spread false doctrine. Luther explains how to use God's name properly and how to take an oath without sin. By faith our hearts and our mouths honor God by confessing Him and His Word purely. Notice how Luther recommends beginning and ending each day, and each meal, by making the sign of the cross and commending ourselves to God. Making the sign of the cross is not a "Roman Catholic" practice, but has its roots in the earliest years of the Church. It is a visible way to remind ourselves whose we are and how we have been redeemed by the cross of Jesus Christ.

————————

49    You shall not take the name of the Lord, your God, in vain.

50    The First Commandment has instructed the heart and taught the faith. This commandment now leads us forward and directs the mouth and tongue to God. For the first things that spring from the heart and show themselves are words (Matthew 12:34). I have taught above how to answer the question "What does it mean to have a god?" Now you must simply learn to understand the meaning of this commandment and all the commandments, and to apply it to yourself.

51    If someone now asks, "How do you understand the Second Commandment?" or "What is meant by taking God's name in vain, or misusing God's name?" answer briefly in this way: "It means misusing God's name when we call upon the Lord God—no matter how—in order to deceive or do wrong of any kind." Therefore, this commandment makes this point: God's name must not be appealed to falsely, or taken upon the lips, while the heart knows well enough—or should know—that the truth of the matter is

different. This is what happens with people who take oaths in court, where one side lies against the other. For God's name cannot be 52 misused worse than for the support of falsehood and deceit. Let this remain the exact German and simplest meaning of this commandment.

From this everyone can easily see when 53 and in how many ways God's name is misused, although it is impossible to list all its misuses. But, to explain this in a few words, all misuse of the divine name happens first in worldly business and in matters that concern money, possessions, and honor. This applies publicly in court, in the market, or wherever else people make false oaths in God's name or pledge their souls in any matter. This is especially common in marriage affairs, where two go and secretly get engaged to one another, and afterward, break their engagement.

But the greatest abuse occurs in spiritual 54 matters. These have to do with the conscience, when false preachers rise up and offer their lying vanities as God's Word (Jonah 2:8).

Look, all this is dressing up one's self with 55 God's name, or making a pretty show, or claiming to be right. This is true whether it happens in common, worldly business or in higher, refined matters of faith and doctrine. Blasphemers also belong with the liars. I mean not just the most ordinary blasphemers, well known to everyone, who disgrace God's name without fear. (These are not for us to discipline, but for the hangman.) I also mean those who publicly disgrace the truth and God's Word and hand it over to the devil. There is now no need to speak about this further.

Here, then, let us learn and take to heart 56 the great importance of this commandment. Then, with all diligence, we may guard against and dread every misuse of the holy name as the greatest sin that can be committed outwardly. For to lie and to deceive is in itself a great sin. But such a sin gets even worse when we try to justify our lie and seek to confirm it by calling on God's name and using His name as a cloak for shame (1 Peter 2:16), so that from a single lie a double lie results—no, many lies.

57  For this reason, too, God has added a solemn threat to this commandment, "For the Lord will not hold him guiltless who takes His name in vain" (Exodus 20:7). This means that this sin shall not be pardoned for anyone or go unpunished. For just as He will not fail to avenge if anyone turns his heart from Him, so He will also not let His name 58  be used to dress up a lie. Now unfortunately, this sin is a common plague in all the world. There are so few people who do not use God's name for purposes of lying and all wickedness in contrast to those who trust in God alone with their heart.

59  By nature we all have within us this beautiful virtue, that whoever has committed a wrong would like to cover up and adorn his disgrace, so that no one may see it or know it. No one is so bold as to boast to all the world of the wickedness he has done. All wish to act by stealth and without anyone being aware of what they do. So, if anyone is caught sinning, God's name is dragged into the affair and must make the wickedness look like godli-60  ness, and the shame like honor. This is the common way of the world, which has covered all lands like a great flood. So we get what we seek and deserve as our reward: epidemics, wars, famines, raging fires, floods, wayward wives, children, servants, and all sorts of filth. Where else should so much misery come from? It is still a great mercy that the earth bears and supports us (Numbers 16:28–50).

61  Therefore, above all things, our young people should have this Second Commandment earnestly pressed upon them (Deuteronomy 6:7). They should be trained to hold this and the First Commandment in high regard. And whenever they sin, we must at once be after them with the rod (Proverbs 13:24). We must hold the commandment before them, and constantly teach it, so that we bring them up not only with punishment, but also in reverence and fear of God (Ephesians 6:4).

62  Now you understand what it means to take God's name in vain. In sum it means (a) to use His name simply for purposes of falsehood, (b) to assert in God's name something that is not true, or (c) to curse, swear, summon the devil, and, in short, to practice whatever wickedness one may.

63  Besides this you must also know how to use God's name rightly. For when He says, "You shall not take the name of the Lord, your God, in vain," He wants us to understand at the same time that His name is to be used properly. For His name has been revealed and given to us so that it may be of constant use and profit. So it is natural to 64  conclude that since this commandment forbids using the holy name for falsehood or wickedness, we are, on the other hand, commanded to use His name for truth and for all good, like when someone takes an oath truthfully when it is needed and it is demanded (Numbers 30:2). This commandment also applies to right teaching and to calling on His name in trouble or praising and thanking Him in prosperity, and so on. All of this is summed up and commanded in Psalm 50:15, "Call upon Me in the day of trouble; I will deliver you, and you shall glorify Me." For all this is bringing God's name into the service of truth and using it in a blessed way. In this way His name is hallowed, as we pray in the Lord's Prayer (Matthew 6:9).

65    Now you have the sum of the entire commandment explained. With this understanding, the question that has troubled many teachers has been easily solved: "Why is swearing prohibited in the Gospel, and yet Christ, St. Paul, and other saints often swore?" (Matthew 5:33–37; 26:29; Acts 21:20–26).

66    The explanation is briefly this: We are not to swear in support of evil, that is, to support falsehood, or to swear when there is no need or use. But we should swear for the support of good and the advantage of our neighbor. For such swearing is truly a good work, by which God is praised, truth and right are established, falsehood is refuted, peace is made among men, obedience is rendered, and quarrels are settled. For in this way God Himself intervenes and separates right and wrong, good and evil.

67    If one party swears falsely, he lives under this judgment: he shall not escape punishment. Even if this judgment is delayed a long time, he shall not succeed. So everything he may gain from his falsehood will slip out of his hands, and he will never enjoy it.

68    I have seen this in the case of many who perjured themselves in their wedding vows. They have never had a happy hour or a healthful day, and so perished miserably in body, soul, and possessions.

69    Therefore, I advise and exhort as before that with warning and threatening, restraint and punishment, the children should be trained early to shun falsehood. They should especially avoid the use of God's name to support falsehood. For where children are allowed to do as they please, no good will result. This is clear even now. The world is worse than it has ever been, and there is no government, no obedience, no loyalty, no faith, but only daring, unbridled people. No teaching or reproof helps them. All this is God's wrath and punishment for such lewd contempt of this commandment.

70    On the other hand, children should be constantly urged and moved to honor God's name and to have it always upon their lips for everything that may happen to them or come to their notice (Psalm 8:2; 34:1; Matthew 21:16; Hebrews 13:15). For that is the true honor of His name, to look to it and call upon it for all consolation (Psalm 66:2; 105:1). Then—as we have heard in the First Commandment—the heart by faith gives God the honor due Him first. Afterward, the lips give Him honor by confession.

71    This is also a blessed and useful habit and very effective against the devil. He is ever around us and lies in wait to bring us into sin and shame, disaster and trouble (2 Timothy 2:26). But he hates to hear God's name and cannot remain long where it is spoken and called upon from the heart. Indeed, many

72    terrible and shocking disasters would fall upon us if God did not preserve us by our calling upon His name. I have tried it myself. I learned by experience that often sudden great suffering was immediately averted and removed by calling on God. To confuse the devil, I say, we should always have this holy name in our mouth, so that the devil may not be able to injure us as he wishes.

73    It is also useful that we form the habit of daily commending ourselves to God (Psalm 31:5), with soul and body, wife, children, servants, and all that we have, against every need that may arise. So also the blessing and thanksgiving at meals (Mark 8:6) and other prayers, morning and evening, have begun and remained in use (Exodus 29:38–43).

74    Likewise, children should continue to cross themselves when anything monstrous or terrible is seen or heard. They can shout, "Lord God, protect us!" "Help, dear Lord Jesus!" and such. Also, if anyone meets with unexpected good fortune, however trivial, he says, "God be praised and thanked!" or "God has

bestowed this on me!" and so on, just as the children used to learn to fast and pray to St. Nicholas and other saints before. This would be more pleasing and acceptable to God than all monasticism and Carthusian acts of holiness.

75    Look, we could train our youth this way (Proverbs 22:6), in a childlike way and playfully in the fear and honor of God. Then the First and Second Commandments might be well kept and in constant practice. Then some good might take root, spring up, and bear fruit. People would grow up whom an entire land might relish and enjoy. In addition, this would be the true way to bring up children well as long as they could be trained with kindness and delight. For children who must be forced with rods and blows will not develop into a good generation. At best they will remain godly under such treatment only as long as the rod is upon their backs (Proverbs 10:13).

76

77    But teaching the commandments in a childlike and playful way spreads its roots in the heart so that children fear God more than rods and clubs. This I say with such simplicity for the sake of the young, that it may penetrate their minds. For we are preaching to children, so we must also talk like them. In this way we would prevent the abuse of the divine name and teach the right use. This should happen not only in words, but also in practice and life. Then we may know God is well pleased with this and will as richly reward good use of His name as He will terribly punish the abuse.

## THE THIRD COMMANDMENT

Luther begins by defining "holy day" and by explaining how by Christ's time the true understanding of the Sabbath had been corrupted. Because the Third Commandment describes Jewish practice in the Old Testament, Luther plainly states that the external form of this law does not apply to Christians. It is an error to say that Sunday is the New Testament Sabbath. Christians should regularly devote themselves to a day when they can hear and learn God's Word, so that they do not despise it. For this reason Luther commends worship on Sunday for the sake of good order. In this sense, every day for the Christian should be a "holy day" consecrated by God's Word. Luther presents a clever play on words when he suggests there is only one "holy thing." The German word for "holy things" (*Heiligtum*) was often used to refer to relics, items believed to have belonged to the apostles and other saints. Yet Luther says the only true "holy thing" is God's Word, which consecrates all things and apart from which nothing we do or say is holy.

---

You shall sanctify the holy day.    78

The word *holiday* is used for the Hebrew    79
word *sabbath*, which properly means "to rest," that is, to cease from labor. Therefore, we usually say, "to stop working." Or "Sanctify the Sabbath." Now, in the Old Testament,    80
God set apart the seventh day and appointed it for rest (Genesis 2:3). He commanded that it should be regarded as holy above all other days. This commandment was given only to the Jewish people for this outward obedience, that they should stop toilsome work and rest. In that way both man and beast might recover and not be weakened by endless labor (Exodus 20:8–11). Later, the Jewish    81
people restricted the Sabbath too closely and greatly abused it. They defamed Christ and could not endure in Him the same works that they themselves would do on that day, as we read in the Gospel (Matthew 12:11). They acted as though the commandment were fulfilled by doing no manual work whatsoever.

This, however, was not the meaning. But, as we shall hear, they were supposed to sanctify the holy day or day of rest.

82      This commandment, therefore, in its literal sense, does not apply to us Christians. It is entirely an outward matter, like other ordinances of the Old Testament. The ordinances were attached to particular customs, persons, times, and places, but now they have been made matters of freedom through Christ (Colossians 2:16–17).

83      The simpleminded need to grasp a Christian meaning about what God requires in this commandment. Note that we don't keep holy days for the sake of intelligent and learned Christians. (They have no need of holy days.) We keep them first of all for bodily causes and necessities, which nature teaches and requires. We keep them for the common people, manservants and maidservants, who have been attending to their work and trade the whole week. In this way they may withdraw in order to rest for a day and be refreshed.

84      Second, and most especially, on this day of rest (since we can get no other chance), we have the freedom and time to attend divine service. We come together to hear and use God's Word, and then to praise God, to sing and to pray (Colossians 3:16).

85      However, this keeping of the Sabbath, I point out, is not restricted to a certain time, as with the Jewish people. It does not have to be just on this or that day. For in itself no one day is better than another (Romans 14:5–6). Instead, this should be done daily. However, since the masses of people cannot attend every day, there must be at least one day in the week set apart. From ancient times Sunday (the Lord's Day) has been appointed for this purpose. So we also should continue to do the same, in order that everything may be done in an orderly way (1 Corinthians 14:40) and no one may create disorder by starting unnecessary practices.

86      This is the simple meaning of the commandment: People must have holidays. Therefore, such observances should be devoted to hearing God's Word so that the special function of this day of rest should be the ministry of the Word for the young and the mass of poor people (Nehemiah 8:2–3, 8). Yet the resting should not be strictly understood to forbid any work that comes up, which cannot be avoided.

87      So when someone asks you, "What is meant by the commandment: You shall sanctify the holy day?" Answer like this, "To sanctify the holy day is the same as to keep it holy." "But what is meant by keeping it holy?" "Nothing else than to be occupied with holy words, works, and life." For the day needs no sanctification for itself. It has been created holy in itself. But God desires the day to be holy to you. Therefore, it becomes holy or unholy because of you, whether you are occupied on that day with things that are holy or unholy.

88      How, then, does such sanctification take place? Not like this: sitting behind the stove and doing no rough work, or adorning ourselves with a wreath and putting on our best clothes. But as said above, we occupy ourselves with God's Word and exercise ourselves in the Word.

89      Indeed, we Christians ought always to keep such a holy day and be occupied with nothing but holy things. This means we should daily be engaged with God's Word and carry it in our hearts and upon our lips (Psalm 119:11–13). But as said above, since we do not always have free time, we must devote several hours a week for the sake of the young, or at least a day for the sake of the entire multitude, to being concerned about this alone. We must especially teach the use of the

Ten Commandments, the Creed, and the Lord's Prayer, and so direct our whole life 90 and being according to God's Word. At whatever time, then, this is being observed and practiced, there a true *holy day* is being kept. Other things shall not be called a Christians' *holy day*. For, indeed, non-Christians can also stop working and be idle, just as the entire swarm of our Church workers do. They stand daily in the churches, singing and ringing bells, but they do not keep a holy day in true holiness, because they do not preach or use God's Word but teach and live contrary to it.

91    God's Word is the sanctuary above all sanctuaries. Yes, it is the only one we Christians know and have. Though we had the bones of all the saints or all holy and consecrated garments upon a heap, still that would not help us at all. All that stuff is a dead thing that can sanctify no one. But God's Word is the treasure that sanctifies everything (1 Timothy 4:5). By the Word even all the saints themselves were sanctified (1 Corinthi-92 ans 6:11). Whenever God's Word is taught, preached, heard, read, or meditated upon, then the person, day, and work are sanctified. This is not because of the outward work, but because of the Word, which makes saints of us all. Therefore, I constantly say that all our life and work must be guided by God's Word, if it is to be God-pleasing or holy. Where this is done, this commandment is in force and being fulfilled.

93    On the contrary, any observance or work that is practiced without God's Word is unholy before God. This is true no matter how brilliantly a work may shine, even though it is covered with relics, such as the fictitious spiritual orders, which know nothing about God's Word and seek holiness in their own works.

94    Note, therefore, that the force and power of this commandment lies not in the resting, but in the sanctifying, so that a special *holy exercise* belongs to this day. For other works and occupations are not properly called holy exercises, unless the person is holy first. But here a work is to be done by which a person is himself made holy. This is done (as we have heard) only through God's Word. For this reason, particular places, times, persons, and the entire outward order of worship have been created and appointed, so that there may be order in public practice (1 Corinthians 14:40).

So much depends upon God's Word. 95 Without it, no holy day can be sanctified. Therefore, we must know that God insists upon a strict observance of this commandment and will punish all who despise His Word and are not willing to hear and learn it, especially at the time appointed for the purpose.

It is not only the people who greatly mis-96 use and desecrate the holy day who sin against this commandment (those who neglect to hear God's Word because of their greed or frivolity or lie in taverns and are dead drunk like swine). But even that other crowd sins. They listen to God's Word like it was any other trifle and only come to preaching because of custom. They go away again, and at the end of the year they know as little of God's Word as at the beginning. Up to this 97 point the opinion prevailed that you had properly hallowed Sunday when you had heard a Mass or the Gospel read. But no one cared for God's Word, and no one taught it. Now that we have God's Word, we fail to correct the abuse. We allow ourselves to be preached to and admonished, but we do not listen seriously and carefully.

Know, therefore, that you must be con-98 cerned not only about hearing, but also about learning and retaining God's Word in memory. Do not think that this is optional for you or of no great importance. Think that it is God's commandment, who will require an account from you (Romans 14:12) about how you have heard, learned, and honored His Word.

99 Likewise, those fussy spirits are to be rebuked who, after they have heard a sermon or two, find hearing more sermons to be tedious and dull. They think that they know all that well enough and need no more instruction. For that is exactly the sin that was previously counted among mortal sins and is called *akadia* (i.e., apathy or satisfaction). This is a malignant, dangerous plague with which the devil bewitches and deceives the hearts of many so that he may surprise us and secretly take God's Word from us (Matthew 13:19).

100 Let me tell you this, even though you know God's Word perfectly and are already a master in all things: you are daily in the devil's kingdom (Colossians 1:13–14). He ceases neither day nor night to sneak up on you and to kindle in your heart unbelief and wicked thoughts against these three commandments and all the commandments. Therefore, you must always have God's Word in your heart, upon your lips, and in your ears. But where the heart is idle and the Word does not make a sound, the devil breaks in and has done the damage before we are aware

101 (Matthew 13:24–30). On the other hand, the Word is so effective that whenever it is seriously contemplated, heard, and used, it is bound never to be without fruit (Isaiah 55:11; Mark 4:20). It always awakens new understanding, pleasure, and devoutness and produces a pure heart and pure thoughts (Philippians 4:8). For these words are not lazy or dead, but are creative, living words (Hebrews 4:12). And even though no other

102 interest or necessity moves us, this truth ought to urge everyone to the Word, because

thereby the devil is put to flight and driven away (James 4:7). Besides, this commandment is fulfilled and this exercise in the Word is more pleasing to God than any work of hypocrisy, however brilliant.

## THE FOURTH COMMANDMENT

Commandments four through ten describe relationships with our fellow humans. Here Luther's understanding of "vocation" is apparent. *Vocation* comes from the Latin *vocare,* meaning "to call." God calls everyone to certain roles, or stations, in life. In this commandment, Luther describes our duty before God to honor father and mother, that is, to respect authority. God instituted all forms of authority as an extension of parental authority, for our good. There are various parental authorities, or "fathers," in our lives, including pastors, teachers, and government officials. Another insight by Luther is about the life of good works to which Christians are called. We should not regard "Church work" as more holy than the other things in life that we routinely do. Rather, all callings and stations in life serve God and are opportunities for us to obey God's commandments and to serve our neighbor. The key observation Luther offers is this: faith is what makes a person holy. Faith alone. Good works serve God by serving other people.

———

So far we have learned the first three commandments, which relate to God: (a) With our whole heart we trust in Him and fear and love Him throughout all our lives. (b) We do not misuse His holy name in support of falsehood or any bad work, but use it to praise God and for the profit and salvation of our neighbor and ourselves. (c) On holidays and when at rest we diligently use and encourage the use of God's Word, so that all our actions and our entire life is guided by it. 103

Now follow the other seven commandments, which relate to our neighbor. Among them is the first and greatest:

104    You shall honor your father and your mother that it may be well with you and you may live long upon the earth.

105    To the position of fatherhood and motherhood God has given special distinction above all positions that are beneath it: He does not simply command us to love our parents, but to honor them. Regarding our brothers, sisters, and neighbors in general, He commands nothing more than that we love them (Matthew 22:39; 1 John 3:14). In this way He separates and distinguishes father and mother from all other persons upon 106    earth and places them at His side. For it is a far higher thing to honor someone than to love someone, because honor includes not only love, but also modesty, humility, and submission to a majesty hidden in them. 107    Honor requires not only that parents be addressed kindly and with reverence, but also that, both in the heart and with the body, we demonstrate that we value them very highly, and that, next to God, we regard them as the very highest. For someone we honor from the heart we must also truly regard as high and great.

108    We must, therefore, impress this truth upon the young (Deuteronomy 6:7) that they should think of their parents as standing in God's place. They should remember that however lowly, poor, frail, and strange their parents may be, nevertheless, they are the father and the mother given to them by God. Parents are not to be deprived of their honor because of their conduct or their failings. Therefore, we are not to consider who they are or how they may be, but the will of God, who has created and ordained parenthood. In other respects people are, indeed, all equal in God's eyes. But among humans there must necessarily be this inequality and ordered difference. Therefore, God commands this order to be kept, that you obey me as your father (Matthew 5:48), and that I have the supremacy.

109    Learn, therefore, what is the honor towards parents that this commandment requires. (a) They must be held in distinction and esteem above all things, as the most precious treasure on earth. (b) In our words we 110    must speak modestly toward them (Proverbs 15:1). Do not address them roughly, haughtily, and defiantly. But yield to them and be silent, even though they go too far. (c) We 111    must show them such honor also by works, that is, with our body and possessions. We must serve them, help them, and provide for them when they are old, sick, infirm, or poor. We must do all this not only gladly, but with humility and reverence, as doing it before God (Ephesians 6:6–7). For the child who knows how to regard parents in his heart will not allow them to do without or hunger, but will place them above him and at his side and will share with them whatever he has and possesses.

112    Second, notice how great, good, and holy a work is assigned to children here. Unfortunately, this is utterly neglected and disregarded (Mark 7:10–13). No one notices that God has commanded it or that it is a holy, divine Word and doctrine. For if it had been regarded as holy, everyone could have concluded that those who live according to these words must be holy people. There would have been no need to invent monasticism or spiritual orders. Every child would have abided by this commandment and could have directed his conscience to God and said, "If I am to do good and holy works, I know of none better than to give all honor and obedience to my parents, because God has Himself com-

113 manded it. For what God commands must be much better and far nobler than everything that we may come up with ourselves. Since there is no higher or better teacher to be found than God, there can certainly be no better teaching than what He provides. Now, He teaches fully what we should do if we wish to perform truly good works. By commanding such works, He shows that they please Him. If, then, it is God who commands this and does not know how to appoint anything better, I will never improve upon it."

114 Behold, in this way we would have had a godly child properly taught, reared in true blessedness, and kept at home in obedience to his parents and in their service. People would have had blessing and joy by seeing this. However, God's commandment was not permitted to be commended with such care and diligence. It had to be neglected and trampled under foot (Matthew 7:6), so that a child could not take it to heart. Meanwhile, the child would gape like a panting wolf at the things we set up, without once consulting or giving reverence to God.

115 For God's sake, let us learn this at last: placing all other things out of sight, let our youths look first to this commandment if they wish to serve God with truly good works. Then they may do what is pleasing to their fathers and mothers, or to those to whom they may be subject instead of parents. For every child that knows and does this has, in the first place, this great consolation in his heart. He can joyfully say and boast (in spite of and against all who are occupied with works of their own choice): "Behold, this work is well pleasing to my God in heaven, that I know for certain." Let them all come

116 together with their many great, distressing, and difficult works and make their boast. We will see whether they can show one work that

is greater and nobler than obedience to father and mother. For to parents God has appointed and commanded obedience next to His own majesty. For if God's Word and will are in force and being accomplished, nothing shall be valued higher than the will and word of parents, as long as that, too, is subordinated to obedience toward God and is not opposed to the preceding commandments.

117 Therefore, you should be heartily glad and thank God that He has chosen you and made you worthy to do a work so precious and pleasing to Him. Only note this: although this work is regarded as the most humble and despised, consider it great and precious. Do this not because of the worthiness of parents, but because this work is included in, and controlled by, the jewel and sanctuary, namely, the Word and commandment of God. Oh, what a high price all

118 Carthusians, monks, and nuns would pay if in all their religious activities they could bring into God's presence a single work done by virtue of His commandment, and if they were able to say with joyful heart before His face, "Now I know that this work is well pleasing to You!" Where will these poor wretched persons hide when, in the sight of God and all the world, they shall blush with shame before a young child who has lived according to this commandment (Matthew 18:1–4)? Will they not have to confess that with their whole life that they are not worthy to give that child a drink of water (Mark 9:41)? It serves them right. Because of their

119 devilish perversion in treading God's commandment under foot, they must vainly torment themselves with works of their own making and, in addition, have scorn and loss for their reward.

120 Should not the heart, then, leap and melt for joy when going to work and doing what is commanded, saying: Look! This is better

than all the holiness of the Carthusians, even though they kill themselves fasting and praying upon their knees without ceasing! For here you have a sure text and a divine testimony that God has commanded this. But concerning the holiness of Carthusians He did not command a word. This is the plight and miserable blindness of the world (2 Corinthians 4:4). No one believes these things. The devil has deceived us to such an extent with false holiness and the glamour of our own works.

121 I would be very glad—I say it again—if people would open their eyes and ears and take this to heart, lest someday we should again be led astray from God's pure Word (Psalm 12:16) to the devil's lying vanities (Psalm 31:6). If people would take this to heart, all would be well. For parents would have more joy, love, friendship, and unity in their houses. The children could captivate 122 their parents' hearts. On the other hand, when children are stubborn and will not do what they ought until a rod is laid upon their back (Proverbs 22:15; 26:3), they anger both God and their parents. In this way they deprive themselves of this treasure and joy of conscience, and they lay up for themselves 123 only misfortune. As everyone complains, the course of the world now is such that both young and old completely lack restraint and are beyond control. They have no reverence or sense of honor. They do nothing unless they are driven to it by blows, and they do what wrong and slander they can behind each other's back. Therefore, God also punishes them, so that they sink into all kinds of 124 filth and misery. As a rule, the parents, too, are themselves stupid and ignorant. One fool trains another. As the foolish parents have lived, so live their children after them.

125 This, now, I say should be the first and most important consideration that urges us to keep this commandment. Because of this, even if we had no father and mother, we should wish that God would set up wood and stone before us, so that we might call them father and mother. Since He has given us living parents, how much more should we rejoice to show them honor and obedience? For we know it is so highly pleasing to the Divine Majesty and to all angels, and it harasses all devils. Besides, this is the highest work we can do, after the grand divine worship included in the previous commandments. Giv- 126 ing to the poor and every other good work toward our neighbor is not equal to this. For God has assigned parenthood the highest place. Yes, He has set it up in His own place upon the earth. God's will and pleasure ought to be enough reason and incentive for us to do what we can with good will and pleasure.

Besides this, it is our duty before the 127 world to be grateful for benefits and every good that we have from our parents. But here 128 again the devil rules in the world (Ephesians 6:12), so that the children forget their parents. We all forget God, and no one considers how God nourishes, protects, and defends us, and how He bestows so much good on body and soul (Psalm 23). This is especially true when an evil time comes. We grow angry and grumble with impatience, and all the good that we have received throughout our life is wiped out of our memory (Psalm 78:17–31). We act the same way toward our parents, and there is no child that understands and considers what the parents have endured while nourishing and fostering him, unless the Holy Spirit grants him this grace.

God knows very well this perverseness of 129 the world; therefore, He admonishes and urges by commandments that everyone consider what his parents have done for him. Each child will discover that he has from them a body and life. He has been fed and reared when otherwise he would have perished a hundred times in his own filth.

130   Therefore, this is a true and good saying of old and wise people: "To God, to parents, and to teachers we can never offer enough thanks and compensation." The person who thinks about and considers this will give all honor to his parents without force and bear them up on his hands as those through whom God has done him all good (Psalm 91:12).

131   Over and above all this, another great reason that should move us more to obey this commandment is that God attaches to it a temporal promise: "That your days may be long in the land that the LORD your God is giving you" (Exodus 20:12).

132   From this you can see for yourself how serious God is about this commandment. He not only declares that it is well pleasing to Him and that He has joy and delight in it, but He also declares that it shall prosper us and promote our highest good, so that we may have a pleasant and agreeable life, furnished

133   with every good thing. Therefore, St. Paul also greatly emphasizes the same promise and rejoices in it when he says that this is the first commandment with a promise, "that it may go well with you and that you may live long in the land" (Ephesians 6:2–3). Although the rest of the commandments have promises in them, none is so plainly and clearly stated.

134   Here, then, you have learned the fruit and the reward, that whoever keeps this commandment shall have happy days, fortune, and prosperity. On the other hand, you also have learned the punishment, that whoever is disobedient shall perish sooner and never enjoy life. For to have long life in the sense of the Scriptures is not only to become old, but to have everything that belongs to long life: health, wife, children, livelihood, peace, good

government, and so on. Without these things this life can neither be enjoyed in cheerfulness nor long endure. If, therefore, you will 135 not obey father and mother and submit to their discipline, then obey the hangman. If you will not obey him, then submit to the skeleton man (i.e., death). For God will insist 136 on this in sum: if you obey Him, offering love and service, He will reward you abundantly with all good. If you offend Him, He will send upon you both death and the hangman.

Where do so many rogues come from that 137 must daily be hanged, beheaded, and broken upon the wheel? Don't they come from disobedience to parents, because they will not submit to discipline in kindness? By God's punishment, they cause us to behold their misfortune and grief. For it seldom happens that such perverse people die a natural or timely death.

But the godly and obedient have this blessing: they live long in pleasant quietness and see their children's children (as said above) to the third and fourth generation (Psalm 128).

Experience teaches that where there are 138 honorable, old families who do well and have many children, they certainly owe their origin to the fact that some of them were brought up well and were full of regard for their parents. On the other hand, it is written of the wicked, "May his posterity be cut off; may his name be blotted out in the second generation!" (Psalm 109:13). Therefore, note 139 well how great a thing in God's sight obedience is. He values it so highly, is so highly pleased with it, and rewards it richly. He also enforces punishment rigorously on those who act against it.

All this I say that it may be well impressed 140 upon the young (Deuteronomy 6:7). No one believes how necessary this commandment is, although it has not been valued and taught under the papacy up to this point. These are simple and easy words, and everybody thought he knew them before. Therefore, people pass by them lightly, crave other things, and do not see and believe that God is so greatly offended if these words are disregarded. They don't see that a person does a work so well pleasing and precious if he follows them.

141 In this commandment belongs a further statement about all kinds of obedience to persons in authority who have to command and to govern. For all authority flows and is born from the authority of parents. Where a father is unable alone to educate his rebellious and irritable child, he uses a schoolmaster to teach the child. If he is too weak, he gets the help of his friends and neighbors. If he departs this life, he delegates and confers his authority and government upon others who

142 are appointed for the purpose. Likewise, a father must have domestic manservants and maidservants under himself for the management of the household. So all whom we call "masters" are in the place of parents and must get their power and authority to govern from them. So also men are all called fathers in the Scriptures, who in their government perform the functions of a father, and have a paternal heart toward their subordinates. From antiquity the Romans and other nations called the masters and mistresses of the household "housefathers" and "housemothers." They called their national rulers and overlords "fathers of the entire country." This is a great shame to us who would be Christians because we do not give them the same title or, at least, do not value and honor them as fathers.

143 Now, the honor a child owes to a father and mother is owed by all who are included in the household. Therefore, manservants and maidservants should be careful to be obedient to their masters and mistresses. They should also honor them as their own fathers and mothers and do everything they know is expected of them, not forced and unwillingly, but with pleasure and joy because of what I just mentioned—it is God's command and is pleasing to Him above all other

144 works. They ought to pay for the privilege and be glad they may get masters and mistresses so that they may have such joyful consciences and know how they may do truly golden works. This is a matter that has been neglected and despised till now. Instead, everybody ran—in the devil's name—into convents or to pilgrimages and indulgences, with loss of time and money and with an evil conscience.

145 If this truth, then, could be impressed upon the poor people, a servant girl would leap and praise and thank God. With her tidy work, for which she receives support and wages, she would gain such a treasure of good works. It would be unlike all those gained by people regarded by saints. Is it not an excellent boast to know and say that if you perform your daily domestic task, this is bet-

146 ter than all the sanctity and ascetic life of monks? You have the promise, in addition, that you shall prosper in all good and fare well. How can you lead a more blessed or holier life as far as your works are concerned?

147 In God's sight faith is what really makes a person holy and serves Him alone (Romans 4:3–5), but the works are for the service of

148 people. There you have everything good: protection and defense in the Lord, a joyful conscience, and a gracious God besides. He will reward you a hundredfold (Matthew 19:27–29), so that you are like a nobleman if you are only pious and obedient. But if you are not, you have, in the first place, nothing but God's wrath and displeasure, no peace of heart, and afterward, all kinds of plagues and misfortunes.

149    Whoever will not be moved by this and lean toward godliness we hand over to the hangman and to the skeleton man. Therefore, let everyone who allows himself to be advised remember that God is not joking. Know that it is God who speaks with you and demands obedience. If you obey Him, you are His dear child (John 14:23). But if you despise obedience, then take shame, misery, and grief for your reward.

150    The same should also be said about obedience to civil government. This (as we have said) is all included in the place of fatherhood and extends farthest of all relations. Here "father" is not one person from a single family, but it means the many people the father has as tenants, citizens, or subjects. Through them, as through our parents, God gives to us food, house and home, protection, and security. They bear such name and title with all honor as their highest dignity that it is our duty to honor them and to value them greatly as the dearest treasure and the most precious jewel upon earth.

151    The person who is obedient in this is willing and ready to serve. He cheerfully does all that deals with honor. He knows that he is pleasing God and that he will receive joy and happiness for his reward. If he will not do this in love, but despises and resists authority or rebels, let him also know that he shall have no favor or blessing. Where he thinks he will gain a florin, he will lose ten times as much elsewhere. Or he will become a victim to the hangman, perish by war, pestilence, or famine. He will experience no good in his children and be obliged to suffer injury, injustice, and violence at the hands of his servants, neighbors, or strangers and tyrants. For what we seek and deserve is paid back and comes home to us (Galatians 6:7).

152    If we would ever allow ourselves to be persuaded that such works are pleasing to God and have so rich a reward, we would be completely established in abundant possessions and have what our heart desires (Psalm 37:4). But because God's Word and command are so lightly esteemed, as though some babbler had spoken it, let us see whether you are the person to oppose Him. How difficult, do you think, it will be for God to pay you back! You would certainly live 153 much better with divine favor, peace, and happiness than with His displeasure and misfortune. Why do you think the world is now 154 so full of unfaithfulness, disgrace, calamity, and murder? It is because everyone desires to be his own master and free from the emperor, to care nothing for anyone, and to do what pleases him. Therefore, God punishes one knave by another, so that, when you defraud and despise your master, another comes and deals in the same way with you. Yes, in your household you must suffer ten times more from wife, children, or servants.

We feel our misfortune, we murmur and 155 complain of unfaithfulness, violence, and injustice. But we refuse to see that we ourselves are knaves who have fully deserved this punishment. And even by this we are not reformed. We will have no favor and happiness. Therefore, it is only fair that we have nothing but misfortune without mercy. There must 156 still be somewhere upon earth some godly people, because God continues to grant us so much good! On our own account, we should not have a farthing in the house nor a straw in the field. All this I have been obliged to 157 urge with so many words, in the hope that someone may take it to heart. Then we may be relieved of the blindness and misery in which we are stuck so deeply. Then we may truly understand God's Word and will, and seriously accept it. We would learn how we could have joy, happiness, and salvation enough, both now and eternally.

158 So we have two kinds of fathers presented in this commandment: fathers in blood and fathers in office. Or, those who have the care of the family and those who have the care of the country. Besides these there are still spiritual fathers. They are not like those in the papacy, who have had themselves called fathers but have performed no function of the fatherly office (Matthew 23:9). For the only ones called spiritual fathers are those who
159 govern and guide us by God's Word. In this sense, St. Paul boasts his fatherhood in 1 Corinthians 4:15, where he says, "I became your father in Christ Jesus through the gospel."
160 Now, since they are fathers, they are entitled to their honor, even above all others. But to spiritual fathers the least amount of honor is bestowed. The way the world knows for honoring them is to drive them out of the country and to begrudge them a piece of bread. In short, spiritual fathers must be (as says St. Paul, 1 Corinthians 4:13) like the filth of the world and everybody's refuse and footrag.
161 Yet there is need that this truth about spiritual fatherhood also be taught to the people. For those who want to be Christians are obliged in God's sight to think them worthy of double honor who minister to their souls (1 Timothy 5:17–18). They are obligated to deal well with them and provide for them. For that reason, God is willing to bless
162 you enough and will not let you run out. But in this matter everyone refuses to be generous and resists. All are afraid that they will perish from bodily needs and cannot now support one respectable preacher, where for-
163 merly they filled ten potbellies. Because of this, we also deserve for God to deprive us of His Word and blessing and to allow preachers of lies to arise again and lead us to the devil. In addition, they will drain our sweat and blood.

164 But those who keep God's will and commandment in sight have this promise: everything they give to temporal and spiritual fathers, and whatever they do to honor them, shall be richly repaid to them. They will not have bread, clothing, and money for a year or two, but will have long life, support, and peace. They shall be eternally rich and blessed. So just do what is your duty. Let God
165 manage how He will support you and provide enough for you. Since He has promised it and has never lied yet, He will not be found lying to you (Titus 1:2).
166 This ought to encourage us and give us hearts that would melt in pleasure and love for those to whom we owe honor. We ought to raise our hands (1 Timothy 2:8) and joyfully thank God, who has given us such promises. For such promises we ought to run to the ends of the world, to the remotest parts of India. For although the whole world should work together, it could not add an hour to our life (Matthew 6:27) or give us a single grain from the earth. But God wishes to give you everything exceedingly and abundantly according to your heart's desire (Psalm 37:4). He who despises and casts this promise to the winds is not worthy ever to hear a word about God. More than enough has now been stated for all who belong under this commandment.
167 In addition, it would be well to preach to the parents also, and to those who bear their office. Tell them how they should behave toward those who are given to them for their governance. This is not stated in the Ten Commandments. But it is still abundantly commanded in many places in the Scripture. God wants to have this included in this commandment when He speaks of father and mother. He does not wish to have rogues and
168 tyrants in this office and government. He does not assign this honor to them, that is,

power and authority to govern, so they can have themselves worshiped. But they should consider that they are obligated to obey God. First of all, they should seriously and faithfully fulfill their office, not only to support and provide for the bodily necessities of their children, servants, subjects, and so on, but, most of all, they should train them to honor

169 and praise God (Proverbs 22:6). Therefore, do not think that this matter is left to your pleasure and arbitrary will. This is God's strict command and order, to whom also you must give account for it (1 Peter 4:5).

170 Here again the sad plight arises that no one sees or hears this truth. All live on as though God gave us children for our pleasure or amusement and servants so that we could use them like a cow or an ass, only for work. Or they live as though we were only to gratify our lewd behavior with our subjects, ignoring them, as though we have no concern

171 for what they learn or how they live. No one is willing to see that this is the command of the Supreme Majesty, who will most strictly call us to account and punish us for it. Nor does anyone see that there is so much need to

172 be seriously concerned about the young. For if we wish to have excellent and able persons both for civil and Church leadership, we must spare no diligence, time, or cost in teaching and educating our children, so that

173 they may serve God and the world. We must not think only about how we may amass money and possessions for them. God can indeed support and make them rich without us, as He daily does. But for this purpose He has given us children and issued this command: we should train and govern them according to His will. Otherwise, He would have no purpose for a father and a mother.

174 Therefore, let everyone know that it is his duty, on peril of losing the divine favor, to bring up his children in the fear and knowl-

edge of God above all things (Proverbs 1:7). And if the children are talented, have them learn and study something. Then they may be hired for whatever need there is.

If that were done, God would also richly 175 bless us and give us grace to train men by whom land and people might be improved. He would also bless us with well-educated citizens, chaste and domestic wives, who, afterward, would raise godly children and servants. Here consider now what deadly harm 176 you are doing if you are negligent and fail on your part to bring up your children to usefulness and piety. Consider how you bring upon yourself all sin and wrath, earning hell by your own children, even though you are otherwise pious and holy. Because this mat- 177 ter is disregarded, God so fearfully punishes the world that there is no discipline, government, or peace. We all complain about this but do not see that it is our fault. The way we train children and subjects spoils them and makes them disobedient. Let this be enough 178 encouragement. To draw this out further belongs to another time.

## THE FIFTH COMMANDMENT

Luther distinguishes between spiritual and civil government and authority, which we commonly refer to as the doctrine of the two kingdoms. God takes care of us in the Church through the ministry of Word and Sacraments, the means of grace. In our homes He cares for us through our parents. In the world, he cares for us by means of civil government. God gives to the civil government the authority to punish criminals and, when necessary, to execute them. The spiritual meaning of this commandment is that we are not to "kill" our neighbor in our hearts, with our thoughts, with our words, or with our hands. No one has the right, on his or her own authority, to murder another person. Only God may take a human life, and He entrusts this authority to civil rulers. So Christians can in good conscience wage war and punish and execute criminals under rightful government authority. Luther goes on to explain that we break the Fifth Commandment not only by acting against it, but also when we fail to protect our neighbor. To explain this commandment, Luther relies on the Sermon on the Mount, particularly Matthew 5:46–47.

---

79   You shall not murder.

80   We have now finished teaching about both the spiritual and the temporal government, that is, the divine and the parental authority and obedience. But now we go forth from our house among our neighbors to learn how we should live with one another, everyone himself toward his neighbor.

81   Therefore, God and government are not included in this commandment. Nor is the power to kill taken away, which God and government have. To punish evildoers, God has delegated His authority to the government, not parents. In earlier times, as we read in Moses, parents were required to bring their own children to judgment and even to sentence them to death (Deuteronomy 21:18–21). Therefore, what is forbidden in this commandment is forbidden to the individual in his relationship with anyone else, but not to the government.

82   Now, this commandment is easy enough and has often been presented, because we hear it each year in the Gospel of St. Matthew 5:20–26, where Christ Himself explains and sums it up. He says that we must not kill, neither with hand, heart, mouth, signs, gestures, help, nor counsel. Therefore, this commandment forbids everyone to be angry, except those (as we said) who are in the place of God, that is, parents and the government. For

it is proper for God and for everyone who is in a divine estate to be angry, to rebuke, and to punish because of those very persons who transgress this and the other commandments (Romans 13:4).

183   The cause and need of this commandment is that God well knows that the world is evil (Galatians 1:4), and that this life has much unhappiness. Therefore, He has set up this and the other commandments between the good people and the evil. Now, just as there are many attacks on all commandments, so the same happens also with this commandment. We must live among many people who do us harm, and we have a reason to be hostile to them.

184   For example, when your neighbor sees that you have a better house and home, a larger family and more fertile fields, greater possessions and fortune from God than he does, he gets in a bad mood, envies you, and speaks no good of you.

So by the devil's encouragement you will get many enemies who cannot bear to see you have any good, either bodily or spiritual. When we see such people, our hearts also would like to rage and bleed and take vengeance. Then there arise cursing and blows. From them misery and murder finally come. In this commandment God—like a   185 kind father—steps in ahead of us, intervenes, and wishes to have the quarrel settled, so that no misfortune comes from it and no one destroys another person. And briefly, He would in this way protect, set free, and keep in peace everyone against the crime and violence of everyone else. He would have this commandment placed as a wall, fortress, and refuge around our neighbor so that we do not hurt or harm him in his body.

186   The commandment has this goal, that no one would offend his neighbor because of any evil deed, even though he has fully de-

served it. For where murder is forbidden, all cause from which murder may spring is also forbidden. For many people, although they do not kill, curse and utter a wish that would stop a person from running far if it were to strike him on the neck. Now, this urge dwells in everyone by nature. It is common practice that no one is willing to suffer at the hands of another person. Therefore, God wants to remove the root and source by which the heart is embittered against our neighbor. He wants to make us used to keeping this commandment ever in view, always to contemplate ourselves in it as in a mirror (James 1:23–25), to regard the will of God, and to turn over to Him the wrong that we suffer with hearty confidence and by calling on His name. In this way we shall let our enemies rage and be angry, doing what they can. We learn to calm our wrath and to have a patient, gentle heart, especially toward those who give us cause to be angry (i.e., our enemies).

188    Therefore, the entire sum of what it means *not to murder* is to be impressed most clearly upon the simpleminded (Deuteronomy 6:7). In the first place, we must harm no one, either with our hand or by deed. We must not use our tongue to instigate or counsel harm. We must neither use nor agree to use any means or methods by which another person may be injured. Finally, the heart must not be ill disposed toward anyone or wish another person ill in anger and hatred. Then body and soul may be innocent toward everyone, but especially toward those who wish you evil or inflict such things upon you. For to do evil to someone who wishes you good and does you good is not human, but devilish.

189    Second, a person who does evil to his neighbor is not the only one guilty under this commandment. It also applies to anyone who can do his neighbor good, prevent or resist evil, defend, and save his neighbor so that no bodily harm or hurt happen to him—yet does not do this (James 2:15–16). If, therefore, you send away someone who is naked when you could clothe him, you have caused him to freeze to death. If you see someone suffer hunger and do not give him food, you have caused him to starve. So also, if you see anyone innocently sentenced to death or in similar distress, and do not save him, although you know ways and means to do so, you have killed him. It will not work for you to make the excuse that you did not provide any help, counsel, or aid to harm him. For you have withheld your love from him and deprived him of the benefit by which his life would have been saved.

God also rightly calls all people murderers who do not provide counsel and help in distress and danger of body and life. He will pass a most terrible sentence upon them in the Last Day, as Christ Himself has announced that He will say, "I was hungry and you gave Me no food, I was thirsty and you gave Me no drink, I was a stranger and you did not welcome Me, naked and you did not clothe Me, sick and in prison and you did not visit Me" (Matthew 25:42–43). This means: You would have allowed Me and Mine to die of hunger, thirst, and cold. You would have allowed the wild beasts to tear us to pieces, or left us to rot in prison or perish in distress. What else is that but to rebuke them as murderers and bloodhounds? For although you have not actually done all this to someone, you have still, so far as you were concerned, let him wither and perish in misfortune.

It is just as if I saw someone navigating and laboring in deep water, or one fallen into fire, and could extend to him the hand to pull him out and save him, and yet refused to do it. How would I look, even in the eyes of the world? Just like a murderer and a criminal.

93 Therefore, it is God's ultimate purpose that we let harm come to no one, but show 94 him all good and love. As we have said, this commandment is especially directed toward those who are our enemies. For to do good to our friends is an ordinary heathen virtue, as Christ says in Matthew 5:46.

95 Here again we have God's Word, by which He would encourage and teach us to do true, noble, and grand works such as gentleness, patience, and, in short, love and kindness to our enemies (Galatians 5:22–23). He would ever remind us to reflect upon the First Commandment—He is our God, which means He will help, assist, and protect us in order that He may quench the desire of revenge in us.

96 We ought to practice and teach this; then we would have our hands full by doing good 97 works. But this would not be preaching for monks. It would greatly undermine from the religious calling and interfere with the sanctity of Carthusians. It would even be regarded as forbidding good works and clearing the convents. For the ordinary state of Christians would be considered just as worthy—and even worthier than monastic life. Everybody would see how the Carthusians mock and delude the world with a false, hypocritical show of holiness (Matthew 23:27), because they have cast this and other commandments to the winds. They have considered them unnecessary, as though they were not commandments, but mere counseling. At the same time, they have shamelessly proclaimed and boasted about their hypocritical calling and works as the most perfect life. They do this so that they might lead a pleasant, easy life, without the cross and without patience. For this reason also, they have created the cloisters, so that they might not be obliged to suffer any wrong from anyone or to do that 98 person any good. But know now that the works of this commandment are the true, holy, and godly works. God rejoices in them with all the angels. In comparison with these works all human holiness is just stench and filth (Isaiah 64:6). And besides, human holiness deserves nothing but wrath and damnation.

## THE SIXTH COMMANDMENT

Luther had been married for almost four years when he wrote the Large Catechism. His former life as a monk makes his comments on the Sixth Commandment all the more interesting and powerful. Luther keenly discerns that chastity is not a matter of vowing to live a celibate life, but of honoring God and one's spouse with one's whole being: thoughts, words, and actions. Marriage should be cherished and honored as a divine estate. God created this institution before all others and blessed it above all the rest; and since He brings children into the world through it, He provides all other estates for its support and benefit. Luther condemns forced celibacy within the Roman Church, but recognizes that God does exempt some from married life, either because they are unsuited to it or because they possess the supernatural gift of chastity. The Sixth Commandment releases those who have taken a vow of chastity but who have not been given this supernatural gift. For Luther, God intended marriage not only to prevent sin, but also as a means by which husbands and wives love and cherish each other. Marriage is a precious good work far superior to the contrived spiritual estates of monks and nuns.

---

You shall not commit adultery. 199

The following commandments are easily 200 understood from the explanation of the preceding commandments. For they are all to show that we must avoid doing any kind of harm to our neighbor. But they are arranged in fine order. In the first place, they talk about our neighbor personally. Then they proceed to talk about the person nearest him, or the closest possession next after his body, namely, his wife. She is one flesh and blood with him (Genesis 2:23–24), so that we cannot inflict a higher injury upon him in any good that is his. Therefore, it is clearly forbidden here to bring any disgrace upon our neighbor

201 regarding his wife. The commandment really takes aim at adultery, because among the Jewish people it was ordained and commanded that everyone must be married. The young were engaged to be married early, and the virgin state was held in small esteem. Yet neither were public prostitution and lewdness tolerated (as now). Therefore, adultery was the most common form of unchastity among them.

202 But among us there is such a shameful mess and the very dregs of all vice and lewdness. Therefore, this commandment is directed against all kinds of unchastity, whatever it

203 may be called. Not only is the outward act of adultery forbidden, but also every kind of cause, motive, and means of adultery. Then the heart, the lips, and the whole body may be chaste and offer no opportunity, help, or

204 persuasion toward inchastity. Not only this, but we must also resist temptation, offer protection, and rescue honor wherever there is danger and need. We must give help and counsel, so as to maintain our neighbor's honor. For whenever you abandon this effort when you could resist unchastity, or whenever you overlook it as if it did not concern you, you are as truly guilty of adultery as the one

205 doing the deed. To speak in the briefest way, this much is required of you: everyone must live chastely himself and help his neighbor do the same. So by this commandment God wishes to build a hedge round about (Job

1:10) and protect every spouse so that no one trespasses against him or her.

But this commandment is aimed directly 20 at the state of marriage and gives us an opportunity to speak about it. First, understand and mark well how gloriously God honors and praises this estate. For by His commandment He both approves and guards it. He has approved it above in the Fourth Commandment, "Honor your father and your mother." But here He has (as we said) hedged it about and protected it. Therefore, He also wishes us 20 to honor it (Hebrews 13:4) and to maintain and govern it as a divine and blessed estate because, in the first place, He has instituted it before all others. He created man and woman separately, as is clear (Genesis 1:27). This was not for lewdness, but so that they might live together in marriage, be fruitful, bear children, and nourish and train them to honor God (Genesis 1:28; Psalm 128; Proverbs 22:6; Ephesians 6:4).

Therefore, God has also most richly 20 blessed this estate above all others. In addition, He has bestowed on it and wrapped up in it everything in the world, so that this estate might be well and richly provided for. Married life is, therefore, no joke or presumption. It is an excellent thing and a matter of divine seriousness. For marriage has the highest importance to God so that people are raised up who may serve the world and promote the knowledge of God, godly living, and all virtues, to fight against wickedness and the devil.

I have always taught that this estate 20 should not be despised nor held in disrepute, as is done by the blind world and our false Church leaders. Marriage should be regarded as it is in God's Word, where it is adorned and sanctified. It is not only placed on an equality with other estates, but it comes first and surpasses them all—emperor, princes, bishops, or whoever they please. For both Church and civil estates must humble themselves and all be found in this estate, as we shall hear. Therefore, it is not a peculiar estate, but the most common and noblest estate that runs through all Christendom. Yes, it extends through all the world.

In the second place, you must know also that marriage is not only an honorable but also a necessary state. In general and in all conditions it is solemnly commanded by God that men and women, who were created for marriage, shall be found in this estate. Yet there are some exceptions (although few) whom God has especially set apart. They are not fit for the married estate. Or there are individuals whom He has released by a high, supernatural gift so that they can maintain chastity without this estate (Matthew 19:11–12). For where nature has its course—since it is given by God—it is not possible to remain chaste without marriage (1 Corinthians 7). For flesh and blood remain flesh and blood. The natural desire and excitement have their course without delay or hindrance, as everybody sees and feels. In order, therefore, that it may be easier in some degree to avoid inchastity, God has commanded the estate of marriage. In this way everyone may have his proper portion and be satisfied with it. Yet God's grace is also required in order that the heart may be pure.

From this you see how this popish rabble—priests, monks, and nuns—resist God's order and commandment. For they despise and forbid matrimony, and they dare and vow to maintain perpetual chastity. Besides this, they deceive the simpleminded with lying words and appearances. For no one has so little love and desire for chastity as these very people. Because of great sanctity, they avoid marriage and either indulge in open and shameless prosti-tution or secretly do even worse, so that one dare not speak of it. Unfortunately this has been learned too fully. In short, even though they abstain from the act, their hearts are so full of unchaste thoughts and evil lusts that there is a continual burning and secret suffering, which can be avoided in the married life (1 Corinthians 7:9). Therefore, all vows of chastity outside of the married state are condemned by this commandment. Free permission to marry is granted. Indeed, even the command is given to all poor ensnared consciences that have been deceived by their monastic vows: abandon the unchaste state and enter the married life. They must consider that even if the monastic life were godly, it would still not be in their power to maintain chastity. And if they remain in their monastic vows, they must only sin more and more against this commandment.

Now, I speak of this in order that the young may be guided so that they desire the married estate and know that it is a blessed estate and pleases God. For in this way, over time we might cause married life to be restored to honor. There might be less of the filthy, loose, disorderly ends that now run riot the world over in open prostitution and other shameful vices arising from disregard for married life. Therefore, it is the duty of parents and the government to see to it that our youth are brought up with discipline and respectability. When they have become mature, parents and government should provide for them to marry in the fear of God and honorably. God would not fail to add His blessing and grace, so that people would have joy and happiness from marriage.

Let me now say in conclusion what this commandment demands: Everyone should live chaste in thought, word, and deed in his condition—that is, especially in the estate of marriage. But also everyone should love and value the spouse God gave to him (Ephesians 5:33). For where marital chastity is to be maintained, man and wife must by all means live together in love and harmony. Then one may cherish the other from the heart and with complete faithfulness. For harmony is one of the principal points that enkindles love and desire for chastity, so that, where this is found, chastity will follow without any

220 command. Therefore, St. Paul diligently encourages husband and wife to love and honor

221 one another. Here you have again precious, indeed, many and great good works. You can joyfully boast about them, against all churchly estates chosen without God's Word and commandment.

## THE SEVENTH COMMANDMENT

Stealing is not only physically robbing another's possessions, but it is also taking advantage of other people. Luther was very concerned about unjust business practices. His comments particularly challenge us today, since we live in a culture built on a free-market economy and generally agree that any price charged to people is morally acceptable. On the other hand, Luther points out how working people also steal from their employers by not giving a full day's work for a full day's pay. Though written over 475 years ago, Luther's comments on the Seventh Commandment are amazingly relevant and timely, and they point out the biblical distinction between the two kingdoms. For example, toward the end of this discussion, Luther wisely notes that the duty of the Church is to reprove sin and teach the Word of God. It is the duty of governing authorities to restrain lawlessness. The Church, as a spiritual institution, does not order society or enact societal laws; this is solely the duty of the government.

You shall not steal. 222

After the commandment about you per- 223 sonally and your spouse, next comes the commandment about temporal property. God also wants property protected. He has commanded that no one shall take away from, or diminish, his neighbor's possessions. For to steal is nothing else than to get 224 possession of another's property wrongfully. Briefly, this includes all kinds of advantage in all sorts of trade to the disadvantage of our neighbor. Now, this is indeed quite a widespread and common vice. But it is so little considered and noticed that it surpasses all measure. So if all thieves who did not want to be known as thieves were to be hanged on gallows, the world would soon be devastated. There would be a lack both of executioners and gallows. For, as we have just said, to "steal" means not only emptying our neighbor's money box and pockets. It also means grasping property in the market, in all stores, booths, wine and beer cellars, workshops, and, in short, wherever there is trading or taking and giving of money for merchandise or labor.

Let me explain this somewhat plainly for 225 the common people, that it may be seen how godly we are. For example, consider a manservant or maidservant who does not serve faithfully in the house, does damage, or allows damage to be done when it could be prevented. He ruins and neglects the goods entrusted to him, by laziness, idleness, or hate, to the spite and sorrow of master and mistress. In whatever way this can be done purposely (I'm not talking about what happens by mistake and against one's will), you can in a year steal thirty or forty florins. If another servant had taken that much money secretly or carried it away, he would be hanged with the rope. But here you (while conscious of such a great theft) may even express defiance and become rude, and no one dare call you a thief.

226 I say the same also about mechanics, workmen, and day laborers. They all follow their evil thoughts and never know enough ways to overcharge people, while they are lazy and unfaithful in their work. All these are far worse than burglars, whom we can guard against with locks and bolts and, if caught, can be treated in such a way that they will not commit the crime again. But against unfaithful workers no one can guard. No one even dares to give them an angry look or accuse them of theft. One would rather lose ten times as much money from his purse. For here are my neighbors, good friends, my own servants, from whom I expect every faithful and diligent service, yet they cheat me most of all.

227 Furthermore, in the market and in common trade also, this practice is in full swing and force to the greatest extent. There one openly cheats another with bad merchandise; false measures, weights, and coins; and by nimbleness and strange finances (Proverbs 20:10). Or he takes advantage of him with clever tricks. Likewise, one overcharges another in a trade and greedily drives a hard bargain, skins and distresses him. Who can 228 repeat or think of all these acts? To sum up, this is the most common trade and the largest union on earth. If we consider the world through all conditions of life, it is nothing but a vast, wide sales booth, full of great thieves.

229 Therefore, some are also called swivel-chair robbers, land and highway robbers, not picklocks and burglars. For they snatch away easy money, but they sit on a chair at home and are styled great noblemen and honorable, pious citizens. They rob and steal in a way assumed to be good.

230 Yes, here we might be silent about the petty individual thieves if we were to attack the great, powerful archthieves with whom lords and princes keep company. These thieves daily plunder not only a city or two, but all of Germany. Indeed, where should we place the head and supreme protector of all thieves—the Holy Chair at Rome with all its train of attendants—which has grabbed by theft the wealth of all the world, and holds it to this day?

231 This is, in short, the way of the world: whoever can steal and rob openly goes free and secure, unmolested by anyone, and even demands that he be honored. Meanwhile, the little burglars, who have once trespassed, must bear the shame and punishment to make the former thieves appear godly and honorable. But let such open thieves know that in God's sight they are the greatest thieves. He will punish them as they are worthy and deserve.

232 Now, since this commandment is so far-reaching, as just indicated, it is necessary to teach it well and to explain it to the common people. Do not let them go on in their greed and security. But always place before their eyes God's wrath, and instill the same. For we must preach this not to Christians, but chiefly to hoods and scoundrels. It would be more fitting for judges, jailers, or Master Hans (the executioner) to preach to them. Therefore, let everyone know his duty, at the 233 risk of God's displeasure: he must do no harm to his neighbor nor deprive him of profit nor commit any act of unfaithfulness or hatred in any bargain or trade. But he must also faithfully preserve his property for him, secure and promote his advantage. This is especially true when one accepts money, wages, and one's livelihood for such service.

234 Now the person who greedily despises this commandment may indeed pass by and

escape the hangman. But he shall not escape God's wrath and punishment (Galatians 6:7–8; 1 Thessalonians 5:3). When he has long practiced his defiance and arrogance, he shall still remain a tramp and beggar. In addition, he will have all plagues and mis-

235 fortune. Now you are going your own way, though you ought to preserve the property of your master and mistress. For your service you fill your throat and stomach, take your wages like a thief, and have people treat you like a nobleman. For there are many that are even rude towards their masters and mistresses and are unwilling to do them a favor or service by which to protect them from loss.

236 But consider what you will gain. When you have come into your own property and are set up in your home (to which God will help with all misfortunes), your earlier misdeeds will bob up again and come home to you. You will find that where you have cheated or done injury at the value of one mite, you will have to pay thirty again.

237 This will also be the result for mechanics and day laborers. We are now obliged to hear and suffer such intolerable hatred from them, as though they were noblemen in another's possessions and everyone is obliged to

238 give them what they demand. Just let them continue making their demands as long as they can. God will not forget His commandment. He will reward them just as they have served. He will hang them, not upon a green gallows, but upon a dry one. So all their life they shall neither prosper nor gather any-

239 thing. Indeed, if there were a well-ordered government in the land, such greediness might soon be checked and prevented. That was the custom in ancient times among the Romans. There such characters were promptly seized by the head in a way that caused others to take warning.

240 No more shall all the rest prosper who change the open, free market into a flesh pit of extortion and a den of robbery (Luke 19:46), where the poor are daily overcharged, and where new burdens and high prices are imposed. Everyone there uses the market according to his whim. He is even defiant and brags as though it were his fair privilege and right to sell his goods for as high a price as he pleases, and no one had a right to say a word

241 against it. We will indeed look on and let

242 these people skin, pinch, and hoard. But we will trust in God, who will do the following: after you have been skinning and scraping for a long time, He will pronounce such a blessing on your gains that your grain in the silo, your beer in the cellar, and your cattle in the stalls shall perish (Luke 12:16–21). Yes, where you have cheated and overcharged anyone for even a florin, your entire pile of wealth shall be consumed with rust, so that you shall never enjoy it (Matthew 6:19; James 5:1–3).

243 Indeed, we see and experience this being fulfilled daily before our eyes. No stolen or dishonestly acquired possession thrives. How many there are who rake and scrape day and night, and yet grow not a farthing richer! Though they gather much, they must suffer so many plagues and misfortunes that they cannot enjoy it with cheerfulness nor leave it to their children. But since no one cares, and

244 we go on as though it did not concern us, God must visit us in a different way and teach us manners by imposing one taxation after another. Or He must billet a troop of soldiers upon us. In one hour they empty our moneyboxes and purses and do not quit as long as we have a farthing left. In addition, by way of thanks, they burn and devastate house and home, and they outrage and kill wife and children.

245 In short, if you steal much, you can expect that much will be stolen from you. He who

robs and gets by violence and wrong will submit to one who shall act the same way toward him. For God is master of this art. Since everyone robs and steals from one another, God punishes one thief by means of another. Or else where would we find enough gallows and ropes?

246 Now, whoever is willing to be instructed, let him know that this is God's commandment. It must not be treated as a joke. For although you despise, defraud, steal, and rob us, we will indeed manage to endure your arrogance, suffer, and—according to the Lord's Prayer—forgive and show pity (Matthew 6:12). For we know that the godly shall nevertheless have enough (Psalm 37:25). But you injure yourself more than another.

247 Beware of this: The poor man will come to you (there are so many now). He must buy things with the penny of his daily wages and live upon it. When you are harsh to him, as though everyone lived by your favor, and you skin and scrape him to the bone, and when you turn him away with pride and arrogance to whom you ought to give things without payment, he will go away wretched and sorrowful. Since he can complain to no one else, he will cry and call to heaven (Psalm 20:6; 146:8–9). Then beware (I say again) as of the devil himself. For such groaning and calling will be no joke. It will have a weight that will prove too heavy for you and all the world. For it will reach Him who takes care of the poor, sorrowful hearts. He will not allow them to go unavenged (Isaiah 61:1–3). But if you despise this and become defiant, see the One you have brought upon you. If you succeed and prosper, before all the world you may call God and me a liar.

248 We have exhorted, warned, and protested enough. He who will not listen to or believe this commandment may go on until he learns this by experience. Yet it must be impressed upon the young (Deuteronomy 6:7) so that they may be careful not to follow the old lawless crowd, but keep their eyes fixed upon God's commandment, lest His wrath and punishment come upon them too. It is 249 necessary for us to do no more than to teach and to warn with God's Word. But to check such open greediness there is need for the princes and government. They themselves should take note and have the courage to establish and maintain order in all kinds of trade and commerce. They must do this lest the poor be burdened and oppressed and the leaders themselves be burdened with other people's sins.

250 This is enough of an explanation of what stealing is. Let the commandment not be understood too narrowly. But let it apply to everything that has to do with our neighbors. Briefly, in summary (as in the former commandments) this is what is forbidden: (a) To do our neighbor any injury or wrong (in any conceivable manner, by impeding, hindering, and withholding his possessions and property), or even to consent or allow such injury. Instead, we should interfere and prevent it. 251 (b) It is commanded that we advance and improve his possessions. When they suffer lack, we should help, share, and lend both to friends and foes (Matthew 5:42).

252 Whoever now seeks and desires good works will find here more than enough to do that are heartily acceptable and pleasing to God. In addition, they are favored and crowned with excellent blessings. So we are to be richly compensated for all that we do for our neighbor's good and from friendship. King Solomon also teaches this in Proverbs 19:17, "Whoever is generous to the poor lends to the LORD, and He will repay him for his deed." Here, then, you have a rich Lord. 253 He is certainly enough for you. He will not allow you to come up short in anything or to

lack (Psalm 37:25). So you can with a joyful conscience enjoy a hundred times more than you could scrape together with unfaithfulness and wrong. Now, whoever does not desire this blessing will find enough wrath and misfortune.

## THE EIGHTH COMMANDMENT

This commandment was given to protect one's name and reputation. Communicating in ways that do not uphold our neighbor's name and reputation break this commandment. The greatest violators are false preachers who, by their false doctrine, speak ill of God and His name. If we are aware of something negative about our neighbor, but have no authority to act, we should remain silent and not speak of it. However, when the proper authorities call upon us to speak to the matter, we will do so honestly. Also, if we are aware of something that requires the attention of public authorities, we will share it with them. Luther clearly states that civil magistrates, pastors, and parents must act upon hearing of something requiring their attention. Luther carefully distinguishes between secret sins and open, public sins. Secret sins should not be made public. However, when the error is open we have every right, even the duty, to speak publicly about it and to testify against the person involved. Speaking publicly about another person's public error or sin is not bearing false witness, nor is it a violation of Matthew 18. Luther concludes that putting "the best construction on everything" is a fine and noble virtue.

---

254    You shall not bear false witness against your neighbor.

255    Over and above our own body, spouse, and temporal possessions, we still have another treasure—honor and good reputa-

tion (Proverbs 22:1). We cannot do without these. For it is intolerable to live among people in open shame and general contempt. Therefore, God does not want the reputation, 256 good name, and upright character of our neighbor to be taken away or diminished, just as with his money and possessions. He wants everyone to stand in his integrity before wife, children, servants, and neighbors. In the first place, we must consider the 257 plainest meaning of this commandment, according to the words "You shall not bear false witness." This applies to the public courts of justice, where a poor, innocent man is accused and oppressed by false witnesses in order to be punished in his body, property, or honor.

Now, this commandment appears as 258 though it were of little concern to us at present. But with the Jewish people it was a quite common and ordinary matter. For the people were organized under an excellent and regular government. Where there is still such a government, instances of this sin will not be lacking. The cause of it is that where judges, mayors, princes, or others in authority sit in judgment, things never fail to go according to the way of the world. In other words, people do not like to offend anybody. They flatter and speak to gain favor, money, prospects, or friendship (Proverbs 26:28). As a result, a poor man and his cause must be oppressed, denounced as wrong, and suffer punishment. It is a common disaster in the world that in courts of justice godly men seldom preside.

To be a judge requires above all things a 259 godly man, and not only a godly man, but also a wise, modest, indeed, a brave and bold man. Likewise, to be a witness requires a fearless and especially godly man. For a person who is to judge all matters rightly and carry them through with his decision will often offend good friends, relatives, neighbors, and the rich and powerful, who may greatly serve or injure him. Therefore, he must be quite blind, have his eyes and ears closed, neither see nor hear, but go straight forward in everything that comes before him and decide accordingly.

260　Therefore, this commandment is given in the first place so that everyone shall help his neighbor to secure his rights and not allow them to be hindered or twisted. But everyone shall promote and strictly maintain these rights, no matter whether he is a judge or a witness, and let it apply to whatsoever it will.

261　A particular goal is set up here for our jurists that they be careful to deal truly and uprightly with every case, allowing right to remain right. On the other hand, they must not pervert anything by their tricks and technical points, turning black into white and making wrong out to be right (Isaiah 5:20). They must not gloss over a matter or keep silent about it, regardless of a person's money, possession, honor, or power. This is one part and the plainest sense of this commandment about all that takes place in court.

262　Next, this commandment extends very much further, if we are to apply it to spiritual jurisdiction or administration. Here it is a common occurrence that everyone bears false witness against his neighbor. For wherever there are godly preachers and Christians, they must bear the sentence before the world that calls them heretics, apostates, and indeed, instigators and desperately wicked unbelievers. Besides, God's Word must suffer in the most shameful and hateful manner, being persecuted, blasphemed, contradicted, perverted, and falsely quoted and interpreted. But let this go. For this is the way of the blind world, which condemns and persecutes the truth and God's children, and yet considers it no sin.

263　In the third place, which concerns us all, this commandment forbids all sins of the tongue (James 3), by which we may injure or confront our neighbor. To bear false witness is nothing else than a work of the tongue. Now, God prohibits whatever is done with the tongue against a fellow man. This applies to false preachers with their doctrine and blasphemy, false judges and witnesses with their verdict, or outside of court by lying and speaking evil. Here belongs particularly the 264 detestable, shameful vice of speaking behind a person's back and slandering, to which the devil spurs us on, and of which much could be said. For it is a common evil plague that everyone prefers hearing evil more than hearing good about his neighbor. We ourselves are so bad that we cannot allow anyone to say anything bad about us. Everyone would much prefer that all the world should speak of him in glowing terms. Yet we cannot bear that the best is spoken about others.

To avoid this vice we should note that no 265 one is allowed publicly to judge and reprove his neighbor—even though he may see him sin—unless he has a command to judge and to reprove. There is a great difference between 266 these two things: judging sin and knowing about sin. You may indeed know about it, but you are not to judge it (Matthew 7:1–5). I can indeed see and hear that my neighbor sins. But I have no command to report it to others. Now, if I rush in, judging and passing sentence, I fall into a sin that is greater than his. But if you know about it, do nothing other than turn your ears into a grave and cover it, until you are appointed to be judge and to punish by virtue of your office.

People are called slanderers who are not 267 content with knowing a thing, but go on to assume jurisdiction. When they know about a slight offense committed by another person, they carry it into every corner. They are delighted and tickled that they can stir up another's displeasure, just as swine delight to roll themselves in the dirt and root in it with the snout. This is nothing other than meddling with God's judgment and office and pronouncing sentence and punishment with the most severe verdict. For no judge can punish to a higher degree nor go farther than to say, "That person is a thief, a murderer, a traitor," and so on. Therefore, whoever presumes to say the same things about his neighbor goes just as far as the emperor and all governments. For although you do not wield the sword, you use your poisonous tongue to shame and hurt your neighbor (Psalm 140:3).

269 God, therefore, would have such behavior banned, that anyone should speak evil of another person even though that person is guilty, and the latter knows it well, much less if anyone does not know it and has the story only from hearsay.

270 But you say, "Shall I not say something if it is the truth?"

Answer: "Why do you not make your accusation to regular judges?"

"Ah, I cannot prove it publicly, and so I might be silenced and turned away in a harsh manner."

"Ah, indeed, do you smell the roast?"

If you do not trust yourself to stand before the proper authorities and to answer well, then hold your tongue. But if you know about it, know it for yourself and not for another. For if you tell the matter to others—although it is true—you will look like a liar, because you cannot prove it. Besides, you are acting like a rascal. We should never deprive anyone of his honor or good name unless it is first taken away from him publicly.

271
272 "False witness," then, is everything that cannot be properly proved. No one shall make public or declare for truth what is not obvious by sufficient evidence. In short, whatever is secret should be allowed to remain secret (1 Peter 4:8), or, at any rate, should be secretly rebuked, as we shall hear. Therefore, if you meet an idle tongue that betrays and slanders someone, contradict such a person promptly to his face (Proverbs 10:31), so he may blush. Then many a person will hold his tongue who otherwise would bring some poor man into bad repute, from which he would not easily free himself. For honor and a good name are easily taken away, but not easily restored (Proverbs 22:1).

273

So you see that it is directly forbidden to speak any evil of our neighbor. However, the civil government, preachers, father, and mother are not forbidden to speak out. This is based on the understanding that this commandment does not allow evil to go unpunished. Now, in the Fifth Commandment no one is to be injured in body, and yet Master Hans (the executioner) is excluded from this rule. By virtue of his office he does his neighbor no good, but only evil and harm. Nevertheless he does not sin against God's commandment. God has instituted that office on His own account. God has reserved punishment for His own good pleasure, as He threatens in the First Commandment. In the same way, although no one has a personal right to judge and condemn anybody, yet if those who serve in offices of judgment fail to judge, they sin just as surely as a person who would act on his own accord without such an office. For in matters of justice necessity requires one to speak of the evil, to prefer charges, to investigate, and to testify. This is no different from the case of a doctor who is sometimes compelled to examine and handle the private parts of the patient whom he is to cure. In the same way governments, father and mother, brothers and sisters, and other good friends are under obligation to one another to rebuke evil wherever it is needful and profitable (Luke 17:3).

274

275

276 The true way in this matter would be to keep the order in the Gospel. In Matthew 18:15, Christ says, "If your brother sins against you, go and tell him his fault, between you and him alone." Here you have a precious and excellent teaching for governing well the tongue, which is to be carefully kept against this detestable misuse. Let this, then, be your rule, that you do not too quickly spread evil about your neighbor and slander him to others. Instead, admonish him privately that he may amend his life. Likewise, if someone reports to you what this or that person has done, teach him, too, to go and admonish that person personally, if he has seen the deed himself. But if he has not seen it, then let him hold his tongue.

277 You can learn the same thing also from the daily government of the household. When the master of the house sees that the servant does not do what he ought, he admonishes him personally. But if he were so foolish as to let the servant sit at home and went on the streets to complain about him to his neighbors, he would no doubt be told,

278 "You fool, how does that concern us? Why don't you tell it to the servant?" Look, that would be acting quite brotherly, so that the evil would be stopped, and your neighbor would retain his honor. As Christ also says in the same place, "If he listens to you, you have gained your brother" (Matthew 18:15). Then you have done a great and excellent work. For do you think it is a small matter to gain a brother? Let all monks and holy orders step forth, with all their works melted together into one mass, and see if they can boast that they have gained a brother.

279 Further, Christ teaches, "But if he does not listen, take one or two others along with you, that every charge may be established by the evidence of two or three witnesses" (Matthew 18:16). So the person concerned in this matter must always be dealt with personally, and must not be spoken of without his knowledge. But if that does not work, then

280 bring it publicly before the community, whether before the civil or the Church court. For then you do not stand alone, but you have those witnesses with you by whom you can convict the guilty one. Relying on their testimony the judge can pronounce sentence and punish. This is the right and regular course for checking and reforming a wicked

281 person. But if we gossip about another in all corners, and stir the filth, no one will be reformed. Later, when we are to stand up and

282 bear witness, we deny having said so. Therefore, it would serve such tongues right if their itch for slander were severely punished, as a

283 warning to others. If you were acting for your neighbor's reformation or from love of the truth, you would not sneak about secretly nor shun the day and the light (John 3:19–20).

284 All this has been said about secret sins. But where the sin is quite public, so that the judge and everybody know about it, you can without any sin shun the offender and let him go his own way, because he has brought himself into disgrace. You may also publicly testify about him. For when a matter is public in the daylight, there can be no slandering or false judging or testifying. It is like when we now rebuke the pope with his doctrine, which is publicly set forth in books and proclaimed in all the world. Where the sin is public, the rebuke also must be public, that everyone may learn to guard against it.

285 Now we have the sum and general understanding of this commandment: Let no one do any harm to his neighbor with the tongue, whether friend or foe. Do not speak evil of him, no matter whether it is true or false, unless it is done by commandment or for his reformation. Let everyone use his tongue and

make it serve for the best of everyone else, to cover up his neighbor's sins and infirmities (1 Peter 4:8), excuse them, conceal and gar-

286   nish them with his own reputation. The chief reason for this should be the one that Christ declares in the Gospel, where He includes all commandments about our neighbor, "whatever you wish that others would do to you, do also to them" (Matthew 7:12).

287   Even nature teaches the same thing in our own bodies, as St. Paul says, "On the contrary, the parts of the body that seem to be weaker are indispensable, and on those parts of the body that we think less honorable we bestow the greater honor, and our unpresentable parts are treated with greater modesty" (1 Corinthians 12:22–23). No one covers his face, eyes, nose, and mouth, for they, being in themselves the most honorable parts that we have, do not require it. But the most weak parts, of which we are ashamed, we cover with all diligence. Hands, eyes, and the whole body must help to cover and conceal

288   them. So also among ourselves should we clothe whatever blemishes and infirmities we find in our neighbor and serve and help him to promote his honor to the best of our ability. On the other hand, we should prevent

289   whatever may be disgraceful to him. It is especially an excellent and noble virtue for someone always to explain things for his neighbor's advantage and to put the best construction on all he may hear about his neighbor (if it is not notoriously evil). Or, at any rate, forgive the matter over and against the poisonous tongues that are busy wherever they can to pry out and discover something to blame in a neighbor (Psalm 140:3). They explain and pervert the matter in the worst way, as is done now especially with God's precious Word and its preachers.

290   There are included, therefore, in this commandment quite a multitude of good works. These please God most highly and bring abundant good and blessing, if only the blind world and the false saints would recog-

291   nize them. For there is nothing on or in a person that can do both greater and more extensive good or harm in spiritual and in temporal matters than the tongue. This is true even though it is the least and weakest part of a person (James 3:5).

## THE NINTH AND TENTH COMMANDMENTS

Luther says that God gave these two commandment to ensure His people knew that stealing is not only the physical act of taking unjustly from another, but is also the desiring of something that is not ours, such as our neighbor's wife, servants, or any property belonging to our neighbor. These commandments are not broken with the hand or the mouth but with the heart. They remind people who consider themselves virtuous that they too, by nature, sin. Toward the end of his explanation, Luther offers a powerful and critical theological insight. All the commandments constantly accuse us of sin and reveal to us where we stand under the Law in God's eyes: guilty! This is the chief purpose of the Law, to show us our sin.

---

292   You shall not covet your neighbor's house.

You shall not covet your neighbor's wife, or his manservant, or his maidservant, or his cattle, or anything that is his.

293   These two commandments are given quite exclusively to the Jewish people. Nevertheless, in part they also apply to us. For they do not interpret them as referring to unchastity or theft. These are forbidden well enough above. They also thought that they

had kept all those commands when they had done or not done the external act. Therefore, God has added these two commandments in order that it be considered sinful and forbidden to desire or in any way to aim at getting our neighbor's wife or possessions. He added them especially because under the Jewish government manservants and maidservants were not free as now to serve for wages as long as they pleased. Jewish servants were their master's property with their body and all they had, as were cattle and other possessions (Deuteronomy 15:12–18). Further, every man had power over his wife to put her away publicly by giving her a bill of divorce and to take another (Deuteronomy 24:1–4). Therefore, they were in constant danger among each other. If one took a fancy to another's wife, he might declare any reason both to dismiss his own wife and to estrange his neighbor's wife from him, so that he might get her in a way that appeared right. That was not considered a sin or a disgrace among them, just as it is hardly considered a sin now with hired help, when an owner dismisses his manservant or maidservant or takes another's servants from him in any way.

In this way they interpreted these commandments, and that rightly (although the scope of the commandment reaches somewhat farther and higher). No one should consider or intend to get what belongs to another, such as his wife, servants, house and estate, land, meadows, cattle. He should not take them even with a show of right, by a trick, or to his neighbor's harm. For above, in the Seventh Commandment, the vice is forbidden where one takes for himself the possessions of others or withholds them from his neighbor. A person cannot rightly do these things. But here it is also forbidden for you to alienate anything from your neighbor, even though you could do so with honor in the eyes of the world, so that no one could accuse or blame you as though you had gotten it wrongfully.

For our natural instinct is that no one wants to see someone else have as much as himself. Each one acquires as much as he can. The other may do as best he can. Yet we pretend to be godly, know how to dress ourselves up most finely, and conceal our base character. We resort to and invent tricky ways and deceitful works (like those that are now daily and most ingeniously invented). We act as though these ways were derived from the legal codes. In fact, we even dare properly to refer to the law and boast about it. We will not have this called trickery, but shrewdness and caution. Lawyers and jurists assist in this who twist and stretch the law to suit it to their cause. They stress words and use them for a trick, despite fairness or their neighbor's need. In short, whoever is the most expert and cunning in these affairs finds the most help in the law, as they themselves say, "The laws favor the watchful."

This last commandment, therefore, is given not for cheaters in the eyes of the world. It is for the most pious, who want to be praised and to be called honest and upright people. For they have not offended against the former commandments, as especially the Jewish people claimed to live, and are even now many great noblemen, gentlemen, and princes. For the other common masses belong yet further down, under the Seventh Commandment, as people who are hardly concerned about whether they gain their possessions with honor and right.

Now, this happens most often in cases that are brought into court, where it is the purpose to get something from our neighbor and to force him from his property. For example, when people quarrel and wrangle about a large inheritance, real estate, or such, they help themselves and resort to whatever appears right. They dress and adorn everything so that the law must favor their side. They keep the property with such title that

302 no one can complain or lay claim to it. In the same way, if anyone wants to have a castle, city, duchy, or any other great thing, he makes many financial deals through relationships, by any means he can, so that the owner is legally deprived of the property (1 Kings 21). It is awarded to the other person and confirmed with deed and seal and declared to have been acquired by princely title and honesty.

303 In common trade, one carefully slips something out of another's hand, so that the latter must watch out. Or one person surprises and cheats another in a matter where he sees advantage and benefit for himself. Then the person who was cheated, perhaps on account of distress or debt, cannot regain or redeem the property without damage. The other person gains the half or even more. Yet this property must not be considered as taken by fraud or stolen, but honestly bought. Here they say, "First come, first served," and "Everyone must look to his own

304 interest, let another get what he can." Who can be so smart to come up with all these ways in which one can get many things into his possession by such believable arguments? The world does not consider this wrong and will not notice that the neighbor is placed at a disadvantage by this, by sacrificing what he cannot spare without harm. Yet no one wishes for someone to do this to himself. From this we can easily see that such devices and arguments are false.

305 The same was done in former times also with respect to wives. They knew such tricks, that if one were pleased with another woman, he personally or through others (as there were many ways and means to be in-

vented) caused her husband to become displeased with her. Or he had her resist her husband and act in such a way that he was obliged to dismiss her and let her go to the other man. That sort of thing undoubtedly prevailed much under the Law, as we also read in the Gospel about King Herod. He took his brother's wife while he was still living. Yet Herod wanted to be thought of as an honorable, pious man, as St. Mark also testi-

fies about him (Mark 6:17–20). But such an 306 example, I trust, will not happen among us. For in the New Testament those who are married are forbidden to get divorced (Mark 10:9). (Except there is the case where one man shrewdly by some trick takes away a rich bride from another man.) But it is not a rare thing with us that one estranges or alienates another's manservant or maidservant or lures them away with flattering words.

In whatever way such things happen, we 307 must know that God does not want you to deprive your neighbor of anything that belongs to him, so that he suffer the loss and you gratify your greed with it. This is true even if you could keep it honorably before the world. For it is a secret and sly trick done "under the hat," as we say, so it may not be noticed. Although you go your way as if you had done no one any wrong, you have still injured your neighbor. If it is not called stealing and cheating, it is still called coveting your neighbor's property, that is, aiming at possession of it, luring it away from him without his consent, and being unwilling to see him enjoy what God has granted him.

Even though the judge and everyone must 308 let you keep it, God will not let you keep it. For He sees the deceitful heart and world's malice, which is sure to take an extra long measure wherever you yield to her a finger's breadth. Eventually public wrong and violence follow.

309    Therefore, we allow these commandments to remain in their ordinary meaning. It is commanded, first, that we do not desire our neighbor's harm, nor even assist, nor give opportunity for it. But we must gladly wish and leave him what he has. Also, we must advance and preserve for him what may be for his profit and service, just as we wish to be 310 treated (Matthew 7:12). So these commandments are especially directed against envy and miserable greed. God wants to remove all causes and sources from which arises everything by which we harm our neighbor. Therefore, He expresses it in plain words, "You shall not covet," and so on. For He especially wants us to have a pure heart (Matthew 5:8), although we will never attain to that as long as we live here. So this commandment will remain, like all the rest, one that will constantly accuse us and show how godly we are in God's sight!

## CONCLUSION OF THE TEN COMMANDMENTS

The Ten Commandments always accuse. That is their chief use. They also serve as a rough curb against gross outbreaks of sin. But they also function as the "true fountain" from which all good works must spring. We never have to try to invent or create works to do that are pleasing to God or go beyond what He has given us. In these Ten Commandments we have the guide we need to understand what truly pleases to God. Some of Luther's most powerful remarks about the difference between God's Ten Commandments and man-made Church rules are found here. Luther thunders against the pomposity and false teaching that certain "Church works" are better in God's eyes than the simple, humble, lowly works of common life, such as a young girl taking care of a little child. He provides a brief summary of the commandments and again shows how the First Commandment is the fountain for all the rest. God has given us a great treasure by giving us the Ten Commandments.

---

Now we have the Ten Commandments, a 311 summary of divine teaching about what we are to do in order that our whole life may be pleasing to God. Everything that is to be a good work must arise and flow from and in this true fountain and channel. So apart from the Ten Commandments no work or thing can be good or pleasing to God, no matter how great or precious it is in the world's eyes. Let us see now what our great saints can 312 boast of their spiritual orders and their great and mighty works. They have invented and set these things up, while they let these commandments go, as though they were far too insignificant or had long ago been perfectly fulfilled.

I am of the opinion, indeed, that here one 313 will find his hands full and will have enough to do to keep these commandments: meekness, patience, love towards enemies, chastity, kindness, and other such virtues and their implications (Galatians 5:22–23). But such works are not of value and make no display in the world's eyes. For these are not peculiar and proud works. They are not restricted to particular times, places, rites, and customs. They are common, everyday, household works that one neighbor can do for another. Therefore, they are not highly regarded.

But the other works cause people to open 314 their eyes and ears wide. Men aid this effect by the great display, expense, and magnificent buildings with which they adorn such works, so that everything shines and glitters. There they waft incense, they sing and ring bells, they light tapers and candles, so that nothing else can be seen or heard. For when a priest stands there in a surplice garment embroidered with gold thread, or a layman continues all day upon his knees in Church, that is regarded as a most precious work, which no one can praise enough. But when a poor girl tends a little child and faithfully does what she is told, that is considered nothing. For what else should monks and nuns seek in their cloisters?

315 Look, is not this a cursed overconfidence of those desperate saints who dare to invent a higher and better life and estate than the Ten Commandments teach? To pretend (as we have said) that this is an ordinary life for the common man, but theirs is for saints and perfect ones? The miserable blind people do not see that no person can go far enough to keep one of the Ten Commandments as it should be kept. Both the Apostles' Creed and the Lord's Prayer must come to our aid (as we shall hear). By them power and strength to keep the commandments is sought and prayed for and received continually. Therefore, all their boasting amounts to as much as if I boasted and said, "To be sure, I don't have a penny to make payment with, but I confidently will try to pay ten florins."

317 All this I say and teach so that people might get rid of the sad misuse that has taken such deep root and still clings to everybody. In all estates upon earth they must get used to looking at these commandments only and to be concerned about these matters. For it will be a long time before they will produce a teaching or estate equal to the Ten Commandments, because they are so high that no one can reach them by human power. Whoever does reach them is a heavenly, angelic person, far above all holiness of the world. Just occupy yourself with them. Try your best. Apply all power and ability. You will find so much to do that

316

318

you will neither seek nor value any other work or holiness.

319 Let this be enough about the first part of the common Christian doctrine, both for teaching and urging what is necessary. In conclusion, however, we must repeat the text which belongs here. We have presented this already in the First Commandment, in order that we may learn what pains God requires so that we may learn to teach and do the Ten Commandments:

320 For I the LORD your God am a jealous God, visiting the iniquity of the fathers on the children to the third and the fourth generation of those who hate Me, but showing steadfast love to thousands of those who love Me and keep My commandments. (Exodus 20:5–6)

321 As we have heard above, this appendix was primarily attached to the First Commandment. Yet it was laid down for the sake of all the commandments, since all of them are to be referred and directed to it. Therefore, I have said that this also should be presented to and taught to the young. Then they may learn and remember it, and we may see what must move and compel us to keep these Ten Commandments. This part is to be regarded as though it were specially added to each command, so that it dwells in, and runs through, them all.

322 Now, there is included in these words (as said before) both an angry, threatening word and a friendly promise. These are to terrify and warn us. They are also to lead and encourage us to receive and highly value His Word as a matter of divine sincerity. For God Himself declares how much He is concerned about it and how rigidly He will enforce it: He will horribly and terribly punish all who despise and transgress His commandments. Also, He declares how richly He will reward, 323

bless, and do all good to those who hold them in high value and gladly do and live according to them. So God demands that all our works proceed from a heart that fears and regards God alone. From such fear the heart avoids everything that is contrary to His will, lest it should move Him to wrath. And, on the other hand, the heart also trusts in Him alone and from love for Him does all He wants. For He speaks to us as friendly as a father and offers us all grace and every good.

324    This is exactly the meaning and true interpretation of the first and chief commandment, from which all the others must flow and proceed. So this word, "You shall have no other gods before Me" (Exodus 20:3), in its simplest meaning states nothing other than this demand: You shall fear, love, and trust in Me as your only true God. For where there is a heart set in this way before God, that heart has fulfilled this commandment and all the other commandments. On the other hand, whoever fears and loves anything else in heaven and upon earth will keep neither this

325    nor any of the commandments. So then all the Scriptures have everywhere preached and taught this commandment, aiming always at these two things: fear of God and trust in Him. The prophet David especially does this throughout the Psalms, as when he says "the LORD takes pleasure in those who fear Him, in those who hope in His steadfast love" (Psalm 147:11). He writes as if the entire commandment were explained by one verse, as if to say, "The Lord takes pleasure in those who have no other gods."

326    So the First Commandment is to shine and give its splendor to all the others. Therefore, you must let this declaration run through all the commandments. It is like a hoop in a wreath, joining the end to the beginning and holding them all together. Let it be continually repeated and not forgotten, as

the Second Commandment says, so that we fear God and do not take His name in vain for cursing, lying, deceiving, and other ways of leading men astray, or trickery. But we make proper and good use of His name by calling upon Him in prayer, praise, and thanksgiving, derived from love and trust according to the First Commandment. In the same way such fear, love, and trust is to drive and force us not to despise His Word, but gladly to learn it, hear it, value it holy, and honor it.

So this teaching continues through all the    327 following commandments toward our neighbor. Everything is to flow from the First Commandment's power. We honor father and mother, masters, and all in authority, and are subject and obedient to them, not for their own sake, but for God's sake. You are not to regard or fear father or mother, nor should you do or skip anything because you love them. But note what God would have you do, what He will quite surely demand of you. If you skip that, you have an angry Judge. But if you do the work, you have a gracious Father.

Again, do your neighbor no harm, injury,    328 or violence, nor in any way oppress him with regard to his body, wife, property, honor, or rights. All these things are commanded in their order, even though you may have a chance and cause to do wrong and no person would rebuke you. But do good to all men (Galatians 6:10). Help them and promote their interest—in every way and wherever you can—purely out of love for God and to please Him. Do this in the confidence that He will abundantly reward you for everything. Now you see how the First Commandment is    329 the chief source and fountainhead that flows into all the rest. Note again, all return to that First Commandment and depend upon it. So beginning and end are fastened and bound to each other.

330     This is always profitable and necessary to teach to the young people. Admonish them and remind them of it, so that they may be brought up not only with blows and compulsion, like cattle, but in the fear and reverence of God. Let this be considered and laid to heart that these things are not human games, but are the commandments of the Divine Majesty. He insists on them with great seriousness. He is angry with and punishes those who despise them. On the other hand, He abundantly rewards those who keep them. In this way there will be a spontaneous drive

331 and a desire gladly to do God's will. Therefore, it is not meaningless that it is commanded in the Old Testament that we should write the Ten Commandments on all walls and corners, yes, even on our garments (Deuteronomy 6:8–9). This is not for the sake of merely having them written in these places and making a show of them. The Jewish people did that. But it is so we might have our eyes constantly fixed on them. We should have them always in our memory. Then we might do them in all our actions and ways.

332 Then everyone may make them his daily exercise in all cases, in every business and transaction, as though they were written in every place wherever he would look, indeed, wherever he walks or stands. Then there would be enough opportunity—both at home in our own house and abroad with our neighbors—to do the Ten Commandments, so that no one would need to run far to find them.

333     From this it again appears how highly these Ten Commandments are to be exalted and extolled above all estates, commandments, and works that are taught and done apart from them. For here we can boast and say, "Let all the wise people and saints step forth and produce, if they can, a single work like these commandments. God insists on these with such seriousness. He commands them with His greatest wrath and punishment. Besides, He adds such glorious promises to them that He will pour out upon us all good things and blessings. Therefore, they should be taught above all others and be valued precious and dear, as the highest treasure given by God."

---

# PART 2
## THE APOSTLES' CREED

The Ten Commandments show us what we are and are not to do, but the Creed shows us the One who creates, redeems, and sanctifies us. Luther broke with longstanding Church tradition by dividing the Creed into three main portions. Prior to Luther's time the Creed had been divided into twelve parts. This division was based on the legend that each apostle had contributed one part of the Creed. Luther does away with such foolish speculation and focuses properly on each person of the Holy Trinity: Father, Son, and Holy Spirit. (See the Nicene and Athanasian Creeds; AC I and III; SA I; SA II I; SC II; FC Ep VIII and SD VIII.)

---

1     So far we have heard the first part of Christian doctrine. We have seen all that God wants us to do or not to do. Now there properly follows the Creed, which sets forth to us everything that we must expect and receive from God. To state it quite briefly, the Creed teaches us to know Him fully (Ephesians 3:19). This is intended to help us do what 2 we ought to do according to the Ten Commandments. For (as said above) the Ten Commandments are set so high that all human ability is far too feeble and weak to keep them. Therefore, it is just as necessary to learn this part of Christian doctrine as to learn the for-

mer. Then we may know how to attain what they command, both where and how to re-
3 ceive such power. For if we could by our own powers keep the Ten Commandments as they should be kept, we would need nothing further, neither the Creed nor the Lord's Prayer.
4 But before we explain this advantage and necessity of the Creed, it is enough at first for the simpleminded to learn to comprehend and understand the Creed itself.
5 In the first place, the Creed has until now been divided into twelve articles. Yet, if all the doctrinal points that are written in the Scriptures and that belong to the Creed were to be distinctly set forth, there would be far more articles. They could not all be clearly ex-
6 pressed in so few words. But to make the Creed most easily and clearly understood as it is to be taught to children, we shall briefly sum up the entire Creed in three chief articles, according to the three persons in the Godhead (Colossians 2:9). Everything that we believe is related to these three persons. So the First Article, about God the Father, explains creation. The Second Article, about the Son, explains redemption. And the Third, about the Holy Spirit, explains sanctification.
7 We present them as though the Creed were briefly summarized in so many words: I believe in God the Father, who has created me; I believe in God the Son, who has redeemed me; I believe in the Holy Spirit, who sanctifies me. One God and one faith, but three persons. Therefore, three articles or confes-
8 sions. Let us go over the words briefly.

## ARTICLE I

Through His Word God calls forth the words we speak back to Him. In this way, Luther says, the entire Creed is a response to the First Commandment. Since God is the maker of heaven and earth, we realize that all we are, all we will ever become, and all we pos-

sess depends entirely on our Creator. All He does for us, all He daily provides—indeed His warding off of dangers of every description—are merely part of His many blessings. For this reason, we are duty bound to love, praise, thank, and devote to Him all the works set forth in the Ten Commandments. Luther laments how few people actually believe what the Creed teaches about our utter dependence on God. However, daily study of this article leads us to recognize God's fatherly and loving heart. We confess His greatest treasure for us in the Second and Third Articles of the Creed.

---

I believe in God the Father Almighty,   9
maker of heaven and earth.

This shows and sets forth most briefly   10
what is God the Father's essence, will, activity, and work. The Ten Commandments have taught that we are to have not more than one God (Deuteronomy 6:4). So it might be asked, "What kind of a person is God? What does He do? How can we praise, or show and describe Him, that He may be known?" Now, that is taught in this and in the following article. So the Creed is nothing other than the answer and confession of Christians arranged with respect to the First Commandment. It is as if you were to ask a   11 little child, "My dear, what sort of a God do you have? What do you know about Him?" The child could say, "This is my God: first, the Father, who has created heaven and earth. Besides this One only, I regard nothing else as God. For there is no one else who could create heaven and earth."

But for the learned and those who are   12 somewhat advanced, these three articles may all be expanded and divided into as many parts as there are words. But now for young scholars let it suffice to make the most necessary points, as we have said, that this article refers to the Creation. We emphasize the words "Creator of heaven and earth." But what is the force of this, or what do you mean by these words, "I believe in God the Father Almighty, maker of heaven and earth?" Answer: "This is what I mean and believe, that I am God's creature (2 Corinthians 5:17). I mean that He has given and constantly preserves (Psalm 36:6) for me my body, soul, and life, my members great and small, all my senses, reason, and understanding, and so on. He gives me food and drink, clothing and support, wife and children, domestic servants, house and home, and more. Besides, He causes all created things to serve for the uses and necessities of life. These include the sun, moon, and stars in the heavens, day and night, air, fire, water, earth, and whatever it bears and produces. They include birds and fish, beasts, grain, and all kinds of produce (Psalm 104). They also include whatever else there is for bodily and temporal goods, like good government, peace, and security." So we learn from this article that none of us owns for himself, nor can preserve, his life nor anything that is here listed or can be listed. This is true no matter how small and unimportant a thing it might be. For all is included in the word *Creator*.

Further, we also confess that God the Father has not only given us all that we have and see before our eyes, but He daily preserves and defends us against all evil and misfortune (Psalm 5:11). He directs all sorts of danger and disaster away from us. We confess that He does all this out of pure love and goodness, without our merit, as a kind Father. He cares for us so that no evil falls upon us. But to speak more about this belongs in the other two parts of this article, where we say, "Father Almighty."

Now, all that we have, and whatever else is in heaven and upon the earth, is daily given, preserved, and kept for us by God. Therefore, it is clearly suggested and concluded that it is our duty to love, praise, and thank Him for these things without ceasing (1 Thessalonians 5:17–18). In short, we should serve Him with all these things, as He demands and has taught in the Ten Commandments.

We could say much here, if we were to wander, about how few people believe this article. For we all pass over it, hear it, and say it. Yet we do not see or consider what the words teach us. For if we believed this teaching with the heart, we would also act according to it (James 2:14). We would not strut about proudly, act defiantly, and boast as though we had life, riches, power, honor, and such, of ourselves (James 4:13–16). We would not act as though others must fear and serve us, as is the practice of the wretched, perverse world. The world is drowned in blindness and abuses all the good things and God's gifts only for its own pride, greed, lust, and luxury. It never once thinks about God, so as to thank Him or acknowledge Him as Lord and Creator.

This article ought to humble and terrify us all, if we believed it. For we sin daily (Hebrews 3:12–13) with eyes, ears, hands, body and soul, money and possessions, and with everything we have. This is especially true of those who fight against God's Word. Yet Christians have this advantage: they acknowledge that they are duty bound to serve God for all these things and to be obedient to Him.

We ought, therefore, daily to recite this article. We ought to impress it upon our mind and remember it by all that meets our eyes and by all good that falls to us. Wherever we escape from disaster or danger, we ought to remember that it is God who gives and does all these things. In these escapes we sense and see His fatherly heart and His surpassing love toward us (Exodus 34:6). In this way the heart would be warmed and kindled to be thankful, and to use all such good things to honor and praise God.

24    We have most briefly presented the meaning of this article. This is how much is necessary at first for the most simple to learn about what we have, what we receive from God, and what we owe in return. This is a most excellent knowledge but a far greater treasure. For here we see how the Father has given Himself to us, together with all creatures, and has most richly provided for us in this life. We see that He has overwhelmed us with unspeakable, eternal treasures by His Son and the Holy Spirit, as we shall hear (Colossians 2:2).

## ARTICLE II

God withholds nothing from us, but gives all that we need for our life on earth. Even more, He gives us all that we need for eternal life with Him in heaven. Luther focuses on the one phrase he believes is the very essence of this article: "in Jesus Christ, . . . our Lord." Providing a sweeping description of Creation and the fall, Luther notes that the word *we* includes every single person in the horrible drama of the Garden of Eden. In that sin we all fell away from God and were doomed to everlasting damnation. Yet Christ, our Lord, came and snatched us from the jaws of hell. This description of Christ's victory over Satan would have been very familiar to the people who first read the Large Catechism. Many paintings from that era depict hell with horrifying detail, showing men and women being led into the gaping mouth of a dragonlike creature. Luther uses the biblical motif of Christ as Victor to describe His work of salvation for us. Jesus offered His own precious blood as satisfaction for our sins. This article

of the Creed is essential for proper understanding and confession of the Gospel.

————————

And in Jesus Christ, His only Son, our    25
Lord, who was conceived by the Holy Spirit, born of the virgin Mary, suffered under Pontius Pilate, was crucified, died and was buried. He descended into hell. The third day He rose again from the dead. He ascended into heaven and sits at the right hand of God the Father Almighty. From thence He will come to judge the living and the dead.

Here we learn to know the Second Person    26
of the Godhead. We see what we have from God over and above the temporal goods mentioned before. We see how He has completely poured forth Himself (Matthew 26:28) and withheld nothing from us (2 Corinthians 8:9). Now, this article is very rich and broad. But in order to explain it briefly also and in a childlike way, we shall take up one phrase and sum up the entire article. As we have said, we may learn from this article how we have been redeemed. We shall base this on these words, "In Jesus Christ, our Lord."

Now, if you are asked, "What do you be-    27
lieve in the Second Article about Jesus Christ?" answer briefly,

"I believe that Jesus Christ, God's true Son, has become my Lord."

"But what does it mean to become Lord?"

"It is this. He has redeemed me from sin, from the devil, from death, and from all evil. For before I did not have a Lord or King, but was captive under the devil's power, condemned to death, stuck in sin and blindness" (see Ephesians 2:1–3).

For when we had been created by God the    28
Father and had received from Him all kinds

of good, the devil came and led us into disobedience, sin, death, and all evil (Genesis 3). So we fell under God's wrath and displeasure and were doomed to eternal damnation, just 29 as we had merited and deserved. There was no counsel, help, or comfort until this only and eternal Son of God—in His immeasurable goodness—had compassion upon our misery and wretchedness. He came from 30 heaven to help us (John 1:9). So those tyrants and jailers are all expelled now. In their place has come Jesus Christ, Lord of life, righteousness, every blessing, and salvation. He has delivered us poor, lost people from hell's jaws, has won us, has made us free (Romans 8:1–2), and has brought us again into the Father's favor and grace. He has taken us as His own property under His shelter and protection (Psalm 61:3–4) so that He may govern us by His righteousness, wisdom, power, life, and blessedness.

31    Let this, then, be the sum of this article: the little word *Lord* means simply the same as *redeemer*. It means the One who has brought us from Satan to God, from death to life, from sin to righteousness, and who preserves us in the same. But all the points that follow in this article serve no other purpose than to explain and express this redemption. They explain how and by whom it was accomplished. They explain how much it cost Him and what He spent and risked so that He might win us and bring us under His dominion. It explains that He became man (John 1:14), was conceived and born without sin (Hebrews 4:15), from the Holy Spirit and from the virgin Mary (Luke 1:35), so that He might overcome sin. Further, it explains that He suffered, died, and was buried so that He might make satisfaction for me and pay what I owe (1 Corinthians 15:3–4), not with silver or gold, but with His own precious blood (1 Peter 1:18–19). And He did all this in order

to become my Lord. He did none of these things for Himself, nor did He have any need for redemption. After that He rose again from the dead, swallowed up and devoured death (1 Corinthians 15:54), and finally ascended into heaven and assumed the government at the Father's right hand (1 Peter 3:22). He did these things so that the devil and all powers must be subject to Him and lie at His feet (Hebrews 10:12–13) until finally, at the Last Day, He will completely divide and separate us from the wicked world, the devil, death, sin, and such (Matthew 25:31–46; 13:24–30, 47–50).

To explain all these individual points 32 does not belong to brief sermons for children. That belongs to fuller sermons that extend throughout the entire year, especially at those times that are appointed for the purpose of treating each article at length—for Christ's birth, sufferings, resurrection, ascension, and so on.

Yes, the entire Gospel that we preach is 33 based on this point, that we properly understand this article as that upon which our salvation and all our happiness rests. It is so rich and complete that we can never learn it fully.

## ARTICLE III

The salvation Christ won on the cross has truly come to pass (objective reality). But unless the Holy Spirit applies that salvation to us personally and individually (subjectively), it will remain hidden from us. *Sanctification* is often understood to refer to our good works. Here Luther uses it, as the Bible often does, to describe the entire work of the Holy Spirit bringing us salvation, including justification. Luther drives home the point that "Church" is, first and foremost, the people the Holy Spirit is gathering together through the preaching of the Gospel. It is not primarily a building or an institution.

Luther suggests it is best to understand the "communion of saints" as a "community of saints" or a "holy community." It is not holy because of their works, but because of the Holy Spirit's work in their midst. Within the Church the Holy Spirit, through preaching and through "signs" (that is, the sacraments), forgives us and keeps us in the faith. Therefore, in this sense, it is right to say that outside the Church there is no salvation. This is *not* because of an infallible papacy, but because of what is going on by the Spirit's power. He works the forgiveness of sins and continues that work to the very end of time. (See AC VII/VIII; SA III XII.)

---

34   I believe in the Holy Spirit, the holy Christian Church, the communion of saints, the forgiveness of sins, the resurrection of the body, and the life everlasting. Amen.

35   I cannot connect this article (as I have said) to anything better than Sanctification. Through this article the Holy Spirit, with His office, is declared and shown: He makes people holy (1 Corinthians 6:11). Therefore, we must take our stand upon the term *Holy Spirit*, because it is so precise and complete that 36 we cannot find another. For there are many kinds of spirits mentioned in the Holy Scriptures, such as the spirit of man (1 Corinthians 2:11), heavenly spirits (Hebrews 12:23), and evil spirits (Luke 7:21). But God's Spirit alone is called the Holy Spirit, that is, He who has sanctified and still sanctifies us. For just as the Father is called "Creator" and the Son is called "Redeemer," so the Holy Spirit, from His work, must be called "Sanctifier," or "One who makes holy."

37   "But how is such sanctifying done?"

Answer, "The Son receives dominion, by which He wins us, through His birth, death, resurrection, and so on. In a similar way, the Holy Spirit causes our sanctification by the following: the communion of saints or the Christian Church, the forgiveness of sins, the resurrection of the body, and the life everlasting. That means He leads us first into His holy congregation and places us in the bosom of the Church. Through the Church He preaches to us and brings us to Christ."

38   Neither you nor I could ever know anything about Christ, or believe on Him, and have Him for our Lord, unless it were offered to us and granted to our hearts by the Holy Spirit through the preaching of the Gospel (1 Corinthians 12:3; Galatians 4:6). The work of redemption is done and accomplished (John 19:30). Christ has acquired and gained the treasure for us by His suffering, death, resurrection, and so on (Colossians 2:3). But if the work remained concealed so that no one knew about it, then it would be useless and lost. So that this treasure might not stay buried, but be received and enjoyed, God has caused the Word to go forth and be proclaimed. In the Word He has the Holy Spirit bring this treasure home and make it our 39 own. Therefore, sanctifying is just bringing us to Christ so we receive this good, which we could not get ourselves (1 Peter 3:18).

40   Learn, then, to understand this article most clearly. You may be asked, "What do you mean by the words *I believe in the Holy Spirit?*"

You can then answer, "I believe that the Holy Spirit makes me holy, as His name implies."

41   "But how does He accomplish this, or what are His method and means to this end?"

Answer, "By the Christian Church, the forgiveness of sins, the resurrection of the body, and the life everlasting. For in the first 42 place, the Spirit has His own congregation in the world, which is the mother that conceives and bears every Christian through God's Word (Galatians 4:26). Through the Word He reveals and preaches, He illumines and enkindles hearts, so that they understand, accept, cling to, and persevere in the Word" (1 Corinthians 2:12).

43    Where the Spirit does not cause the Word to be preached and roused in the heart so that it is understood, it is lost (Matthew 13:19). This was the case under the papacy, where faith was entirely put under the bench. No one recognized Christ as his Lord or the Holy Spirit as his Sanctifier. That is, no one believed that Christ is our Lord in the sense that He has gained this treasure for us, without our works and merit (Romans 4:6), and

44   made us acceptable to the Father. What, then, was lacking? This: the Holy Spirit was not there to reveal it and cause it to be preached. But men and evil spirits were there. They taught us to obtain grace and be saved by our

45   works. There is no Christian Church in that. For where Christ is not preached, there is no Holy Spirit who creates, calls, and gathers the Christian Church, without which no one can come to Christ the Lord.

46    Let this be enough about the sum of this article. But since the parts that are numbered here are not quite clear to the simple, we shall go over them also.

47    The Creed calls the "holy Christian Church" a "communion of saints." Both expressions, taken together, are identical. But in the past the expression "communion of saints" was not there. This phrase has been poorly and unwisely translated into the German as a *communion* of saints. If it is to be rendered plainly, it must be expressed quite differently in a German way. In the same way, the word *ecclesia* properly means in German

48   "a gathering." But we are used to seeing it translated as the word *Church,* by which the simple do not understand a gathered multi-

tude but the consecrated house or building. This is true even though the house ought not to be called a Church, just because the multitude gathers there. For we who gather there make and choose for ourselves a particular place and give a name to the house according to the gathering.

So the word *Church* really means nothing other than a common gathering, and is not really German, but Greek (as is also the word *ecclesia*). For in their own language the Greeks call it *kyria,* as in Latin it is called *curia.* Therefore, in real German, in our mother tongue, it ought to be called "a Christian congregation or gathering" or, best of all and most clearly, "holy Christendom."

49    So also the word *communio,* which is added, ought not to be translated "communion," but "congregation." It is nothing else than an interpretation or explanation by which someone meant to show what the Christian Church is. Our people understood neither Latin nor German. They have translated this word "communion of saints," although no German dialect says this or understands it this way. But to speak correct German, it ought to be "a congregation of saints"; that is, a congregation made up purely of saints, or, to speak yet more plainly,

50   "a holy congregation." I say this in order that the words "communion of saints" may be understood. The expression has become so established by custom that it cannot be cast aside easily, and it is treated almost as heresy if someone attempts to change a word.

51    But this is the meaning and substance of this addition: I believe that there is upon earth a little holy group and congregation of pure saints, under one head, even Christ (Ephesians 1:22). This group is called together by the Holy Spirit in one faith, one mind, and understanding, with many different gifts, yet agreeing in love, without sects or schisms

52  (Ephesians 4:5–8, 11). I am also a part and member of this same group, a sharer and joint owner of all the goods it possesses (Romans 8:17). I am brought to it and incorporated into it by the Holy Spirit through having heard and continuing to hear God's Word (Galatians 3:1–2), which is the beginning of entering it. In the past, before we had attained to this, we were altogether of the devil, knowing nothing about God and about

53  Christ (Romans 3:10–12). So, until the Last Day, the Holy Spirit abides with the holy congregation or Christendom (John 14:17). Through this congregation He brings us to Christ and He teaches and preaches to us the Word (John 14:26). By the Word He works and promotes sanctification, causing this congregation daily to grow and to become strong in the faith and its fruit, which He produces (Galatians 5).

54  We further believe that in this Christian Church we have forgiveness of sin, which is wrought through the holy Sacraments and Absolution (Matthew 26:28; Mark 1:4; John 20:23) and through all kinds of comforting promises from the entire Gospel. Therefore, whatever ought to be preached about the Sacraments belongs here. In short, the whole Gospel and all the offices of Christianity belong here, which also must be preached and taught without ceasing. God's grace is secured through Christ (John 1:17), and sanctification is wrought by the Holy Spirit through God's Word in the unity of the Christian Church. Yet because of our flesh, which we bear about with us, we are never without sin (Romans 7:23–24).

55  Everything, therefore, in the Christian Church is ordered toward this goal: we shall daily receive in the Church nothing but the forgiveness of sin through the Word and signs, to comfort and encourage our consciences as long as we live here. So even though we have sins, the grace of the Holy Spirit does not allow them to harm us. For we are in the Christian Church, where there is nothing but continuous, uninterrupted forgiveness of sin. This is because God forgives us and because we forgive, bear with, and help one another (Galatians 6:1–2).

56  But outside of this Christian Church, where the Gospel is not found, there is no forgiveness, as also there can be no holiness. Therefore, all who seek and wish to earn holiness not through the Gospel and forgiveness of sin, but by their works, have expelled and severed themselves from this Church (Galatians 5:4).

57  However, while sanctification has begun and is growing daily (2 Thessalonians 1:3), we expect that our flesh will be destroyed and buried with all its uncleanness (Romans 6:4–11). Then we will come forth gloriously and arise in a new, eternal life of entire and perfect holiness. For now we are only half

58  pure and holy. So the Holy Spirit always has some reason to continue His work in us through the Word. He must daily administer forgiveness until we reach the life to come. At that time there will be no more forgiveness, but only perfectly pure and holy people (1 Corinthians 13:10). We will be full of godliness and righteousness, removed and free from sin, death, and all evil, in a new, immortal, and glorified body (1 Corinthians 15:43, 53).

59  You see, all this is the Holy Spirit's office and work. He begins and daily increases holiness upon earth through these two things: the Christian Church and the forgiveness of sin. But in our death He will accomplish it altogether in an instant (1 Corinthians 15:52) and will forever preserve us therein by the last two parts [of the Creed].

60  But the term "resurrection of the flesh" used here does not agree with good German

wording. For when we Germans hear the word *flesh*, we think of nothing more than a butcher block. But in good German wording we would say "resurrection of the body." However, it is not a big issue, as long as we understand the words right.

61     Now this is the article of the Creed that must always be and remain in use. For we have already received creation. Redemption, too, is finished. But the Holy Spirit carries on His work without ceasing to the Last Day. For that purpose He has appointed a congregation upon earth by which He speaks and does

62     everything. For He has not yet brought together all His Christian Church (John 10:16) or granted all forgiveness. Therefore, we believe in Him who daily brings us into the fellowship of this Christian Church through the Word. Through the same Word and the forgiveness of sins He bestows, increases, and strengthens faith. So when He has done it all, and we abide in this and die to the world and to all evil, He may finally make us perfectly and forever holy. Even now we expect this in faith through the Word.

63     See, here you have the entire divine essence, will, and work shown most completely in quite short and yet rich words. In these words all our wisdom stands, which surpasses and exceeds the wisdom, mind, and reason of all people (1 Corinthians 1:18–25). The whole world with all diligence has struggled to figure out what God is, what He has in mind and does. Yet the world has never been able to grasp the knowledge and understanding of any of these things. But here we have

64     everything in richest measure. For here in all three articles God has revealed Himself and opened the deepest abyss of His fatherly heart and His pure, inexpressible love (Ephesians 3:18–19). He has created us for this very reason, that He might redeem and sanctify us. In addition to giving and imparting to

us everything in heaven and upon earth, He has even given to us His Son and the Holy Spirit, who brings us to Himself (Romans 8:14, 32). For (as explained above) we could 65 never grasp the knowledge of the Father's grace and favor except through the Lord Christ. Jesus is a mirror of the fatherly heart (John 14:9; Colossians 1:15; Hebrews 1:3), outside of whom we see nothing but an angry and terrible Judge. But we couldn't know anything about Christ either, unless it had been revealed by the Holy Spirit (1 Corinthians 2:12).

These articles of the Creed, therefore, di- 66 vide and separate us Christians from all other people on earth. Even if we were to concede that everyone outside Christianity—whether heathen, Turks, Jews, or false Christians and hypocrites—believe in and worship only one true God, it would still be true that they do not know what His mind toward them is and cannot expect any love or blessing from Him. Therefore, they abide in eternal wrath and damnation. For they do not have the Lord Christ, and, besides, are not illumined and favored by any gifts of the Holy Spirit (1 Corinthians 2:9–16; Hebrews 6:4–6).

From this you see that the Creed is a doc- 67 trine quite different from the Ten Commandments. For the Commandments teach what we ought to do. But the Creed tells what God does for us and gives to us. Furthermore, apart from this, the Ten Commandments are written in all people's hearts (Romans 2:15). However, no human wisdom can understand the Creed. It must be taught by the Holy Spirit alone (1 Corinthians 2:12). The teaching of the Commandments, there- 68 fore, makes no Christian. For God's wrath and displeasure abide upon us still, because we cannot keep what God demands of us. But the Creed brings pure grace and makes us godly and acceptable to God. For by this 69

Christ Teaches His Disciples to Pray;
from 1530 Large Catechism

knowledge we have love and delight in all God's commandments (Romans 7:22). Here we see that God gives Himself to us completely. He gives all that He has and is able to do in order to aid and direct us in keeping the Ten Commandments. The Father gives all creatures. The Son gives His entire work. And the Holy Spirit bestows all His gifts.

70    Let this be enough about the Creed to lay a foundation for the simple, so that they may not be burdened. Then, if they understand the substance of it, they themselves may afterward strive to gain more, refer to these parts whatever they learn in the Scriptures, and may ever grow and increase in richer understanding (Ephesians 4:14–15; 2 Peter 3:14). For as long as we live here, we shall daily have enough to do to preach and to learn this.

# PART 3

## Prayer

### THE LORD'S PRAYER

As Christians, prayer is a constant in our life, for we are always in need of God's mercy. Christ gave us the Lord's Prayer so that we will both know *how* to pray and for *what* to pray. Prayer is a habit for the Christian, but experience teaches that it is a habit easily broken. While mindless and unthinking repetition presents a problem, repeating the same prayer throughout one's life does not. In his Small Catechism, Luther advises the use of set forms and patterns of prayer and recommends devoting times throughout each day to pray the Lord's Prayer. Because the prayer Jesus taught us is God's Word, we know He loves to hear it. True prayer is never offered to earn or merit God's favor, but rather flows from a heart that is justified through faith. Luther urges the development of good prayer habits that begin in childhood. Prayer is the Christian's weapon against the devil's many temptations.

----

We have now heard what we must do and 1 believe, in what things the best and happiest life consists. Now follows the third part, how we ought to pray. For we are in a situation 2 where no person can perfectly keep the Ten Commandments, even though he has begun to believe. The devil with all his power, together with the world and our own flesh, resists our efforts. Therefore, nothing is more necessary than that we should continually turn towards God's ear, call upon Him, and pray to Him. We must pray that He would give, preserve, and increase faith in us and the fulfillment of the Ten Commandments (2 Thessalonians 1:3). We pray that He would remove everything that is in our way and that opposes us in these matters. So that we might 3 know what and how to pray, our Lord Christ has Himself taught us both the way and the words (Luke 11:1–4), as we shall see.

But before we explain the Lord's Prayer 4 part by part, it is most necessary first to encourage and stir people to prayer, as Christ and the apostles also have done (Matthew 6:5–15). And the first thing to know is that it 5 is our duty to pray because of God's commandment. For that's what we heard in the Second Commandment, "You shall not take the name of the LORD your God in vain" (Exodus 20:7). We are required to praise that holy name and call upon it in every need, or to pray. To call upon God's name is nothing other than to pray (e.g., 1 Kings 18:24). Prayer is just as strictly and seriously commanded 6 as all other commandments: to have no other God, not to kill, not to steal, and so on. Let no one think that it makes no difference whether he prays or not. Common people think this, who grope in such delusion and ask, "Why should I pray? Who knows whether God heeds or will hear my prayer? If I do not pray, someone else will." And so they fall into the habit of never praying. They build a false argument, as though we taught that there is no duty or need for prayer, because we reject false and hypocritical prayers (Matthew 6:5).

7   But it is certainly true that the prayers that have been offered up till now, when men were babbling and bawling in the churches (Matthew 6:7), were not prayers. Such outward matters of prayer, when they are properly done, may be a good exercise for young children, scholars, and simple persons. They may be called singing or reading, but not re-

8   ally praying. But praying, as the Second Commandment teaches, is to call upon God in every need. He requires this of us and has not left it to our choice. But it is our duty and obligation to pray, if we would be Christians, just as it is our duty and obligation to obey our parents and the government. For by calling upon God's name and praying, His name is honored and used well. This you must note above all things, so that you may silence and reject thoughts that would keep

9   and deter us from prayer. It would be useless for a son to say to his father, "What good does my obedience do me? I will go and do what I can. It makes no difference." But there stands the commandment, "You shall and must obey." So here prayer is not left to my will to do it or leave it undone, but it shall and must be offered at the risk of God's wrath and displeasure.

This point is to be understood and noted

10   before everything else. Then by this point we may silence and cast away the thoughts that would keep and deter us from praying, as though it does not matter if we do not pray,

or as though prayer was commanded for those who are holier and in better favor with God than we are. Indeed, the human heart is by nature so hopeless that it always flees from God and imagines that He does not wish or desire our prayer, because we are sinners and have earned nothing but wrath (Romans 4:15). Against such thoughts (I say), we   11 should remember this commandment and turn to God, so that we may not stir up His anger more by such disobedience. For by this commandment God lets us plainly understand that He will not cast us away from Him or chase us away (Romans 11:1). This is true even though we are sinners. But instead He draws us to Himself (John 6:44), so that we might humble ourselves before Him (1 Peter 5:6), bewail this misery and plight of ours, and pray for grace and help (Psalm 69:13). Therefore, we read in the Scriptures that He is also angry with those who were punished for their sin, because they did not return to Him and by their prayers turn away His wrath and seek His grace (Isaiah 55:7).

Now, from the fact that prayer is so   12 solemnly commanded, you are to conclude and think that no one should in any way despise his prayer. Instead, he should count on prayer. He should always turn to an illustra-   13 tion from the other commandments. A child should in no way despise his obedience to father and mother, but should always think, "This work is a work of obedience. What I do I do for no other reason than that I may walk in the obedience and commandment of God. On this obedience I can settle and stand firm, and I can value it as a great thing, not because of my worthiness, but because of the commandment." So here also, we should think about the words we pray and the things we pray for as things demanded by God and done in obedience to Him. We should think, "On my account this prayer would amount to nothing. But it shall succeed, because God has commanded it." Therefore, everybody—no matter what he has to say in prayer—should always come before God in obedience to this commandment.

14 We pray, therefore, and encourage everyone most diligently to take this counsel to heart and by no means to despise our prayer. For up to now it has been taught in the devil's name that no one should think about these things. People thought it was enough to have done the act of praying, whether God would hear it or not. But that is staking prayer on a risk and murmuring it at a venture; there-

15 fore, it is a lost prayer. For we let thoughts like these lead us astray and stop us: "I am not holy or worthy enough. If I were as godly and holy as St. Peter or St. Paul, then I would pray." But put such thoughts far away. For the same commandment that applied to St. Paul applies also to me. The Second Commandment is given as much on my account as on his account, so that Paul can boast about no better or holier commandment.

16 You should say, "My prayer is as precious, holy, and pleasing to God as that of St. Paul or of the most holy saints. This is the reason: I will gladly grant that Paul is personally more holy, but that's not because of the commandment. God does not consider prayer because of the person, but because of His Word and obedience to it. For I rest my prayer on the same commandment on which all the saints rest their prayer. Furthermore, I pray for the same thing that they all pray for and always have prayed. Besides, I have just as great a need of what I pray for as those great saints; no, even a greater one than they."

17 Let this be the first and most important point, that all our prayers must be based and rest upon obedience to God, regardless of who we are, whether we are sinners

18 or saints, worthy or unworthy. We must

know that God will not have our prayer treated as a joke. But He will be angry and punish all who do not pray, just as surely as He punishes all other disobedience. Furthermore, He will not allow our prayers to be in vain or lost. For if He did not intend to answer your prayer, He would not ask you to pray and add such a severe commandment to it.

19 In the second place, we should be more encouraged and moved to pray because God has also added a promise and declared that it shall surely be done for us as we pray. He says in Psalm 50:15, "Call upon Me in the day of trouble; I will deliver you." And Christ says in the Gospel of St. Matthew, "Ask, and it will be given to you; . . . for everyone who asks re-

20 ceives" (7:7–8). Such promises certainly ought to encourage and kindle our hearts to pray with pleasure and delight. For He testifies with His own Word that our prayer is heartily pleasing to Him. Furthermore, it shall certainly be heard and granted, in order that we may not despise it or think lightly of it and pray based on chance.

21 You can raise this point with Him and say, "Here I come, dear Father, and pray, not because of my own purpose or because of my own worthiness. But I pray because of Your commandment and promise, which cannot fail or deceive me." Whoever, therefore, does not believe this promise must note again that he outrages God like a person who thoroughly dishonors Him and accuses Him of falsehood.

22 Besides this, we should be moved and drawn to prayer. For in addition to this commandment and promise, God expects us and He Himself arranges the words and form of prayer for us. He places them on our lips for how and what we should pray (Psalm 51:15), so that we may see how heartily He pities us in our distress (Psalm 4:1), and we may never doubt that such prayer is pleasing to Him

23 and shall certainly be answered. This (the Lord's Prayer) is a great advantage indeed over all other prayers that we might compose ourselves. For in our own prayers the conscience would ever be in doubt and say, "I have prayed, but who knows if it pleases Him or whether I have hit upon the right proportions and form?" Therefore, there is no nobler prayer to be found upon earth than the Lord's Prayer. We pray it daily (Matthew 6:11), because it has this excellent testimony, that God loves to hear it. We ought not to surrender this for all the riches of the world.

24 The Lord's Prayer has also been prescribed so that we should see and consider the distress that ought to drive and compel us to pray without ceasing (1 Thessalonians 5:17). For whoever would pray must have something to present, state, and name, which he desires. If he does not, it cannot be called a prayer.

25 We have rightly rejected the prayers of monks and priests, who howl and growl day and night like fiends. But none of them think of praying for a hair's breadth of anything. If we would assemble all the churches, together with all churchmen, they would be bound to confess that they have never from the heart prayed for even a drop of wine. For none of them has ever intended to pray from obedience to God and faith in His promise. No one has thought about any need. But when they had done their best they thought no further than this: To do a good work, by which they might repay God. They were unwilling to take anything from Him, but wished only to give Him something.

26 But where there is to be a true prayer, there must be seriousness. People must feel their distress, and such distress presses them and compels them to call and cry out. Then prayer will be made willingly, as it ought to be. People will need no teaching about how to prepare for it and to reach the proper devotion. But the distress that ought to concern 27 us most (both for ourselves and everyone), you will find abundantly set forth in the Lord's Prayer. Therefore, this prayer also serves as a reminder, so that we meditate on it and lay it to heart and do not fail to pray. For we all have enough things that we lack. The great problem is that we do not feel or recognize this. Therefore, God also requires that you weep and ask for such needs and wants, not because He does not know about them (Matthew 6:8), but so that you may kindle your heart to stronger and greater desires and make wide and open your cloak to receive much (Psalm 10:17).

28 Every one of us should form the daily habit from his youth of praying for all his needs. He should pray whenever he notices anything affecting his interests or that of other people among whom he may live. He should pray for preachers, the government, neighbors, household servants, and always (as we have said) to hold up to God His commandment and promise, knowing that He will not have them disregarded. This I say be- 29 cause I would like to see these things brought home again to the people so that they might learn to pray truly and not go about coldly and indifferently. They become daily more unfit for prayer because of indifference. That is just what the devil desires, and for which he works with all his powers. He is well aware what damage and harm it does him when prayer is done properly.

30 We need to know this: all our shelter and protection rest in prayer alone. For we are far too weak to deal with the devil and all his power and followers who set themselves against us. They might easily crush us under their feet. Therefore, we must consider and take up those weapons with which Christians must be armed in order to stand against the

devil (2 Corinthians 10:4; Ephesians 6:11).
31 For what do you imagine has done such great things up till now? What has stopped or quelled the counsels, purposes, murder, and riot of our enemies, by which the devil thought he would crush us, together with the Gospel? It was the prayer of a few godly people standing in the middle like an iron wall for our side. Otherwise they would have witnessed a far different tragedy. They would have seen how the devil would have destroyed all Germany in its own blood. But now our enemies may confidently ridicule prayer and make a mockery of it. However, we shall still be a match both for them and the devil by prayer alone, if we only persevere
32 diligently and do not become slack. For whenever a godly Christian prays, "Dear Father, let Your will be done" (see Matthew 6:10), God speaks from on high and says, "Yes, dear child, it shall be so, in spite of the devil and all the world."

33 Let this be said as encouragement, so that people may learn, first of all, to value prayer as something great and precious and to make a proper distinction between babbling and praying for something. For we by no means reject prayer. We reject the bare, useless howling and murmuring, as Christ Himself also rejects and prohibits long idle talk
34 (Matthew 6:7). Now we shall most briefly and clearly explain the Lord's Prayer. Here there is included in seven successive articles, or petitions, every need that never ceases to apply to us. Each is so great that it ought to drive us to keep praying the Lord's Prayer all our lives.

## THE FIRST PETITION

We pray using the name given us in our Baptism, by which God makes us a part of Himself. God's name is holy among us when we believe, teach, and live according to His Word. In the worst possible way God's name is profaned among us when men preach and teach contrary to God's Word and when people live an openly evil life. Luther's highest concern is that God's name be kept holy through genuine biblical teaching, in contrast to all the false teaching in the world. Luther's hymn "Lord, Keep Us Steadfast in Your Word" is a powerful application of these truths.

---

Hallowed be Thy name.   35

This is, indeed, somewhat difficult, and   36 not expressed in good German. For in our mother tongue we would say, "Heavenly Father, help us in every way so that Your name may be holy."

"But what does it mean to pray that His   37 name may be holy? Is it not holy already?"

Answer, "Yes, it is always holy in its nature, but in our use it is not holy." For God's name was given to us when we became Christians and were baptized (Matthew 28:19). So we are called God's children and have the Sacraments, by which He connects us with Himself so that everything that belongs to God must serve for our use (Romans 8:16–17).

Now, here is a great need that we ought   38 to be most concerned about. This name should have its proper honor; it should be valued holy and grand as the greatest treasure and sanctuary that we have. As godly children we should pray that God's name, which is already holy in heaven, may also be and remain holy with us upon earth and in all the world.

"But how does it become holy among   39 us?"

Answer, as plainly as it can be said: "When both our doctrine and life are godly and Christian." Since we call God our Father in this prayer, it is our duty always to act and behave ourselves as godly children, that He may not receive shame, but honor and praise from us.

40 Now, God's name is profaned by us either through our words or in our works. (For whatever we do upon the earth must be ei-

41 ther words or works, speech or act.) In the first place, then, God's name is profaned when people preach, teach, and say in God's name what is false and misleading. They use His name like an ornament and attract a market for falsehood. That is, indeed, the greatest way to profane and dishonor the di-

42 vine name. Furthermore, men, by swearing, cursing, conjuring, and other such actions, grossly abuse the holy name as a cloak for

43 their shame (1 Peter 2:16). In the second place, God's name is profaned by an openly wicked life and works, when those who are called Christians and God's people are adulterers, drunkards, misers, enviers, and slanderers (1 Corinthians 5:11). Here again God's name must come to shame and be profaned

44 because of us. It is a shame and disgrace for a flesh-and-blood father to have a bad, perverse child that opposes him in words and deeds. Because of that child the father suffers contempt and reproach. In the same way also, it brings dishonor upon God if we are called by His name and have all kinds of goods from Him, yet we teach, speak, and live in any other way than as godly and heavenly children. People would say about us that we must not be God's children, but the devil's children (1 John 2:29).

45 So you see that in this petition we pray for exactly what God demands in the Second Commandment. We pray that His name not be taken in vain to swear, curse, lie, deceive, and so on, but be used well for God's praise and honor. For whoever uses God's name for any sort of wrong profanes and desecrates this holy name. This is how it used to be when a Church was considered desecrated, when a murder or any other crime had been committed in it. Or a pyx or relic was desecrated—as though they were holy in themselves—when they became unholy by misuse.

46 So this point is easy and clear if only the language is understood: to hallow means the same as to praise, magnify, and honor both in word and deed.

47 Here, now, learn what great need there is for such prayer. Because we see how full the world is of sects and false teachers, who all wear the holy name as a cover and sham for their doctrines of devils (1 Timothy 4:1), we should by all means pray without ceasing (1 Thessalonians 5:17) and cry out and call upon God against all people who preach and believe falsely. We should pray against whatever opposes and persecutes our Gospel and pure doctrine and would suppress it, as do the bishops, tyrants, enthusiasts, and such (2 Thessalonians 2:3–4). Likewise, we should pray for ourselves who have God's Word but are not thankful for it, nor live like we ought ac-

48 cording to the Word. If you pray for this with your heart, you can be sure that it pleases God. For He will not hear anything more dear to Him than that His honor and praise is exalted above everything else and that His Word is taught in its purity and is considered precious and dear.

## THE SECOND PETITION

In this petition we are praying to God that the kingdom of Christ will come and remain among us, both in this life and finally on the Last Day. We ask God that we will remain faithful and daily grow in His grace, so that many more will come to Christ's kingdom. This petition shows that God wants us to ask not only for small cares and needs of life, but also for great things from Him. If God invites us to pray for such great and wonderful things as His kingdom of grace, surely He will provide also for our daily needs.

---

Thy kingdom come.

49    In the First Petition we prayed about God's honor and name. We prayed that He would prevent the world from adorning its lies and wickedness with God's name, but that He would cause His name to be valued as great and holy both in doctrine and life, so that He may be praised and magnified in us. Here we pray that His kingdom also may 50    come. But just as God's name is holy in itself, and we still pray that it be holy among us, so also His kingdom comes of itself, without our prayer. Yet we still pray that it may come to us, that is, triumph among us and with us, so that we may be a part of those people among whom His name is hallowed and His kingdom prospers.

51    "But what is God's kingdom?"

Answer, "Nothing other than what we learned in the Creed: God sent His Son, Jesus Christ, our Lord, into the world to redeem and deliver us from the devil's power (1 John 3:8). He sent Him to bring us to Himself and to govern us as a King of righteousness, life, and salvation against sin, death, and an evil conscience. For this reason He has also given His Holy Spirit, who is to bring these things home to us by His holy Word and to illumine and strengthen us in the faith by His power."

52    We pray here in the first place that this may happen with us. We pray that His name may be so praised through God's holy Word and a Christian life that we who have accepted it may abide and daily grow in it, and that it may gain approval and acceptance among other people. We pray that it may go forth with power throughout the world (2 Thessalonians 3:1). We pray that many may find entrance into the kingdom of grace (John 3:5), be made partakers of redemption (Colossians 1:12–14), and be led to it by the Holy Spirit (Romans 8:14), so that we may all together remain forever in the one kingdom now begun.

For the coming of God's kingdom to us 53 happens in two ways: (a) here in time through the Word and faith (Matthew 13); and (b) in eternity forever through revelation (Luke 19:11; 1 Peter 1:4–5). Now we pray for both these things. We pray that the kingdom may come to those who are not yet in it, and, by daily growth that it may come to us who have received it, both now and hereafter in eternal life. All this is nothing other than 54 saying, "Dear Father, we pray, give us first Your Word, so that the Gospel may be preached properly throughout the world. Second, may the Gospel be received in faith and work and live in us, so that through the Word and the Holy Spirit's power (Romans 15:18–19), Your kingdom may triumph among us. And we pray that the devil's kingdom be put down (Luke 11:17–20), so that he may have no right or power over us (Luke 10:17–19; Colossians 1), until at last his power may be utterly destroyed. So sin, death, and hell shall be exterminated (Revelation 20:13–14). Then we may live forever in perfect righteousness and blessedness" (Ephesians 4:12–13).

From this you see that we do not pray 55 here for a crust of bread or a temporal, perishable good. Instead, we pray for an eternal inestimable treasure and everything that God Himself possesses. This is far too great for any human heart to think about desiring, if God had not Himself commanded us to pray for the same. But because He is God, 56 He also claims the honor of giving much more and more abundantly than anyone can understand (Ephesians 3:20). He is like an eternal, unfailing fountain. The more it pours forth and overflows, the more it continues to give. God desires nothing more seriously from us than that we ask Him for much and great things. In fact, He is angry if we do not ask and pray confidently (Hebrews 4:16).

57

It's like a time when the richest and most mighty emperor would tell a poor beggar to ask whatever he might desire. The emperor was ready to give great royal presents. But the fool would only beg for a dish of gruel. That man would rightly be considered a rogue and a scoundrel, who treated the command of his Imperial Majesty like a joke and a game and was not worthy of coming into his presence. In the same way, it is a great shame and dishonor to God if we—to whom He offers and pledges so many inexpressible treasures—despise the treasures or do not have the confidence to receive them, but hardly dare to pray for a piece of bread.

58

All this is the fault of shameful unbelief that does not even look to God for enough decent food to satisfy the stomach. How much less does such unbelief expect to receive eternal treasures from God without doubt? Therefore, we must strengthen ourselves against such doubt and let this be our first prayer. Then, indeed, we shall have everything else in abundance, as Christ teaches, "Seek first the kingdom of God and His righteousness, and all these things will be added to you" (Matthew 6:33). For how could He allow us to suffer lack and to be desperate for temporal things when He promises to give us what is eternal and never perishes (1 Peter 1:4)?

## THE THIRD PETITION

By faith we cling to God's holy name and His holy kingdom. But evil opposes us and tries to snatch God's kingdom from us. Luther says

we pray that God will work His will among us and protect and keep us safe from our old sinful flesh and from all the evil in the world. The devil will spare no effort to make us fall away from God's kingdom. We Christians bear a holy cross: temptations, dangers, and intense struggle throughout our life. It is foolish for us to think that a Christian's life is easy. Therefore, we ask God to work His gracious will for us and to provide us with the strength we need.

---

Thy will be done on earth as it is in heaven.

59

So far we have prayed that God's name be honored by us and that His kingdom triumph among us. In these two points is summed up all that deals with God's honor and our salvation. We receive God as our own and all His riches. But now arises a need that is just as great: we must firmly keep God's honor and our salvation, and not allow ourselves to be torn from them. In a good government it is not only necessary that there be those who build and govern well. It is also necessary to have those who defend, offer protection, and maintain it firmly. So in God's kingdom, although we have prayed for the greatest need—for the Gospel, faith, and the Holy Spirit, that He may govern us and redeem us from the devil's power—we must also pray that God's will be done. For there will be strange events if we are to abide in God's will. We shall have to suffer many thrusts and blows on that account from everything that seeks to oppose and prevent the fulfillment of the first two petitions.

60

61

No one can believe how the devil opposes and resists these prayers. He cannot allow anyone to teach or to believe rightly. It hurts him beyond measure to have his lies and abominations exposed, which have been

62

honored under the most fancy, sham uses of the divine name. It hurts him when he himself is disgraced, is driven out of the heart, and has to let a breach be made in his kingdom. Therefore, he chafes and rages as a fierce enemy with all his power and might. He marshals all his subjects and, in addition, enlists the world and our own flesh as his

63 allies. For our flesh is in itself lazy and inclined to evil (Romans 7:18), even though we have accepted and believe God's Word. The world, however, is perverse and wicked. So he provokes the world against us, fans and stirs the fire, so that he may hinder and drive us back, cause us to fall, and again bring us under his power (2 Corinthians

64 2:11; 1 Timothy 3:6–7). Such is all his will, mind, and thought. He strives for this day and night and never rests a moment. He uses all arts, wiles, ways, and means that he can invent.

65    If we would be Christians, therefore, we must surely expect and count on having the devil with all his angels and the world as our enemies (Matthew 25:41; Revelation 12:9). They will bring every possible misfortune and grief upon us. For where God's Word is preached, accepted, or believed and produces fruit, there the holy cross cannot be missing (Acts 14:22). And let no one think that he shall have peace (Matthew 10:34). He must risk whatever he has upon earth—possessions, honor, house and estate, wife and chil-

66 dren, body and life. Now, this hurts our flesh and the old Adam (Ephesians 4:22). The test is to be steadfast and to suffer with patience (James 5:7–8) in whatever way we are assaulted, and to let go whatever is taken from us (1 Peter 2:20–21).

67    So there is just as great a need, as in all the other petitions, that we pray without ceasing, "Dear Father, Your will be done, not the devil's will or our enemies' or anything that would persecute and suppress Your holy Word or hinder Your kingdom. Grant that we may bear with patience and overcome whatever is to be endured because of Your Word and kingdom, so that our poor flesh may not yield or fall away because of weakness or sluggishness."

68    Look, we have in these three petitions, in the simplest way, the needs that relate to God Himself. Yet they are all for our sakes. Whatever we pray concerns us alone. As we have said before, we pray that what must be done without us anyway may also be done in us. As His name must be hallowed and His kingdom come whether we pray or not, so also His will must be done and succeed. This is true even though the devil with all his followers raise a great riot, are angry and rage against it, and try to exterminate the Gospel completely. But for our own sakes we must pray that, even against their fury, His will be done without hindrance among us also. We pray so that they may not be able to accomplish anything and that we may remain firm against all violence and persecution and submit to God's will.

69    Such prayer, then, is to be our protection and defense now. It is to repel and put down all that the devil, pope, bishops, tyrants, and heretics can do against our Gospel. Let them all rage and attempt their utmost and deliberate and resolve how they may suppress and exterminate us, so that their will and counsel may prevail. Over and against this one or two Christians with this petition alone shall be our wall (Ezekiel 22:30), against which they shall run and dash themselves to pieces. We

70 have this comfort and confidence: the devil's will and purpose and all our enemies shall and must fail and come to nothing, no matter how proud, secure, and powerful they know themselves to be. For if their will were not broken and hindered, God's kingdom

could not remain on earth nor His name be hallowed.

## THE FOURTH PETITION

"Daily Bread" encompasses everything we need for our life here on earth. Luther explains in this petition that our greatest need is good governing authorities. Through them God provides us with what we need for this body and life. Nothing in this life will be "good" unless we live in peace and security; history readily proves Luther's point. The devil is intent on thwarting good government and causing unrest and turmoil. Yet God gives daily necessities even to the wicked. God wants us to pray for them too, so that we recognize that He gives us all good things as a gracious gift.

———————

71 Give us this day our daily bread.

72 Here, now, we consider the poor bread-basket, the necessaries of our body and of the temporal life. It is a brief and simple word, but it has a very wide scope. For when you mention and pray for daily bread, you pray for everything that is necessary in order to have and enjoy daily bread. On the other hand, you also pray against everything that interferes with it. Therefore, you must open wide and extend your thoughts not only to the oven or the flour bin, but also to the distant field and the entire land, which bears and brings to us daily bread and every sort of nourishment. For if God did not cause food to grow and He did not bless and preserve it in the field, we could never take bread from the oven or have any to set upon the table.

73 To sum things up, this petition includes everything that belongs to our entire life in the world, for we need daily bread because of life alone. It is not only necessary for our life that our body have food and clothes and other necessaries. It is also necessary that we spend our days in peace and quiet among the people with whom we live and have dealings in daily business and conversation and all sorts of doings (1 Thessalonians 4:11; 2 Thessalonians 3:12; 1 Timothy 2:2). In short, this petition applies both to the household and also to the neighborly or civil relationship and government. Where these two things are hindered so that they do not prosper as they should, the necessaries of life also are hindered. Ultimately, life cannot be maintained. There is, indeed, the greatest 74 need to pray for earthly authority and government. By them, most of all, God preserves for us our daily bread and all the comforts of this life. Though we have received from God all good things in abundance, we are not able to keep any of them or use them in security and happiness if He did not give us a permanent and peaceful government. For where there are dissension, strife, and war, there the daily bread is already taken away or is at least hindered.

It would be very proper to place on the 75 coat of arms of every pious prince a loaf of bread or a wreath of herbs instead of a lion. Or one could impress it on money. This would remind both princes and their subjects that by their office we have protection and peace. Without them, we could not eat and keep our daily bread. Therefore, princes are also worthy of all honor. We should give to them for their office what we ought and can, as to people through whom we enjoy what we have in peace and quietness. Otherwise we would not keep a farthing. In addition, we should also pray for them (1 Timothy 2:1–2) that through them God may bestow on us more blessings and goods.

Let this be a very brief explanation and 76 sketch, showing how far this petition extends through all conditions on earth. On this topic anyone might indeed make a long prayer. With many words one could list all the things that are included, like when we ask God to give us food and drink, clothing, house and home, and health of body. Or when we ask that He cause the grain and fruit of the field to grow and mature well. Furthermore, we ask that He help us at home with good housekeeping and that He give and preserve for us a godly wife, children, and servants. We ask that He cause our work, trade, or whatever we are engaged in to prosper and succeed, favor us with faithful neighbors and good friends, and other

77 such things. Likewise, we ask that He give wisdom, strength, and success to emperors, kings, and all estates, and especially to the rulers of our country and to all counselors, magistrates, and officers. Then they may govern well and vanquish the Turks and all enemies. We ask that He give to subjects and the common people obedience, peace, and

78 harmony in their life with one another. On the other hand, we ask that He would preserve us from all sorts of disaster to body and livelihood, like lightning, hail, fire, flood, poison, plague, cattle disease, war and bloodshed, famine, destructive beasts,

79 wicked men, and so forth. It is well to impress all this upon the common people (Deuteronomy 6:7): these things come from God and must be prayed for by us.

80 But this petition is especially directed also against our chief enemy, the devil. For all his thought and desire is to deprive us of all that we have from God or to hinder it. He is not satisfied to obstruct and destroy spiritual government by leading souls astray with his lies and bringing them under his power. He also prevents and hinders the stability of all government and honorable, peaceable relations on earth. There he causes so much contention, murder, treason,

and war. He also causes lightning and hail to destroy grain and cattle, to poison the air,
81 and so on. In short, he is sorry if anyone has a morsel of bread from God and eats it in peace. If it were in his power and our prayer (next to God) did not prevent him, we would not keep a straw in the field, a farthing in the house, yes, not even our life for an hour. This is especially true of those who have God's Word and would like to be Christians.

82 You see, in this way, God wishes to show us how He cares for us in all our need and faithfully provides also for our earthly sup-
83 port. He abundantly grants and preserves these things, even for the wicked and rogues (Matthew 5:45). Yet, He wishes that we pray for these goods in order that we may recognize that we receive them from His hand and may feel His fatherly goodness toward us in them (Psalm 104:28; 145:16). For when He withdraws His hand, nothing can prosper or be maintained in the end. Indeed, we daily
84 see this and experience it. How much trouble there is now in the world only on account of bad coins, daily oppression, raising of prices in common trade, and bargaining and labor by those who greedily oppress the poor and deprive them of their daily bread! This we must suffer indeed. But let such people take care so that they do not lose the benefits of common intercession. Let them beware lest this petition in the Lord's Prayer speak against them.

## THE FIFTH PETITION

God forgives our sins, even if we do not realize it. In this petition we pray for forgiveness so that we recognize and accept this gift from God. We need this petition so that our conscience will be strengthened in the struggle against sin. The phrase "as we forgive those who sin against us" is added so that we will extend God's gracious forgiveness to others who sin against us. By doing so we exhibit God's forgiveness to us.

---

85    And forgive us our trespasses as we forgive those who trespass against us.

86    This part now applies to our poor miserable life. Although we have and believe God's Word, do and submit to His will, and are supported by His gifts and blessings, our life is still not sinless. We still stumble daily and transgress because we live in the world among people. They do us much harm and give us reasons for impatience, anger, re-

87    venge, and such. Besides, we have the devil at our back. He attacks us from every side and fights—as we have heard—against all the previous petitions. So it is not possible to stand firm at all times in such a constant conflict.

88    There is here again great need for us to call upon God and to pray, "Dear Father, forgive us our trespasses." It is not as though He did not forgive sin without and even before our prayer. (He has given us the Gospel, in which is pure forgiveness before we prayed or ever thought about it [Romans 5:8].) But the purpose of this prayer is that we may recog-

89    nize and receive such forgiveness. The flesh in which we daily live is of such a nature that it neither trusts nor believes God (Romans 7:14–18). It is ever active in evil lusts and devices, so that we sin daily in word and deed (Genesis 6:5), by what we do and fail to do (James 2:15–16). By this the conscience is thrown into unrest, so that it is afraid of God's wrath and displeasure. So it loses the comfort and confidence derived from the Gospel. Therefore, it is always necessary that we run here and receive consolation to comfort the conscience again.

90    But this should serve God's purpose of breaking our pride and keeping us humble.

God has reserved this right for Himself: if anyone wants to boast of his godliness and despise others, that person is to think about himself and place this prayer before his eyes. He will find that he is no better than others (Romans 12:3) and that in God's presence all must tuck their tails and be glad that they can gain forgiveness. Let no one think that as    91 long as he lives here he can reach such a position that he will not need such forgiveness (1 John 1:8). In short, if God does not forgive without stopping, we are lost.

It is, therefore, the intent of this petition    92 that God would not regard our sins and hold up to us what we daily deserve. But we pray that He would deal graciously with us and forgive, as He has promised, and so grant us a joyful and confident conscience to stand before Him in prayer (Hebrews 10:22). For where the heart is not in a right relationship with God, or cannot take such confidence, it will not dare to pray anymore. Such a confident and joyful heart can spring from nothing else than the certain knowledge of the forgiveness of sin (Psalm 32:1–2; Romans 4:7–8).

There is here attached a necessary, yet    93 comforting addition: "As we forgive." He has promised that we shall be sure that everything is forgiven and pardoned, in the way that we also forgive our neighbor. Just as we    94 daily sin much against God, and yet He forgives everything through grace, so we, too, must ever forgive our neighbor who does us injury, violence, and wrong, shows malice toward us, and so on. If, therefore, you do not    95 forgive, then do not think that God forgives you (Matthew 18:23–25). But if you forgive, you have this comfort and assurance, that you are forgiven in heaven. This is not be-    96 cause of your forgiving. For God forgives freely and without condition, out of pure grace, because He has so promised, as the

Gospel teaches. But God says this in order that He may establish forgiveness as our confirmation and assurance, as a sign alongside of the promise, which agrees with this prayer in Luke 6:37, "Forgive, and you will be forgiven." Therefore, Christ also repeats it soon after the Lord's Prayer, and says in Matthew 6:14, "For if you forgive others their trespasses, your heavenly Father will also forgive you," and so on.

97    This sign is therefore attached to this petition. When we pray, we remember the promise and think, "Dear Father, for this reason I come and pray for You to forgive me, not so that I can make satisfaction or can merit anything by my works. I pray because You have promised and attached the seal to this prayer that I should be as sure about it as though I had Absolution pronounced by You Yourself." For Baptism and 98    the Lord's Supper—appointed as outward signs—work as seals (Ephesians 1:13). In the same way also, this sign can serve to confirm our consciences and cause them to rejoice. It is especially given for this purpose, so that we may use and practice forgiveness every hour, as a thing that we have with us at all times.

### THE SIXTH PETITION

In this petition Luther sets forth the three-fold source of temptation: our sinful human flesh, the world around us, and the devil. Luther identifies our sinful human nature as the "old Adam," a biblical metaphor for our sinful flesh, as opposed to the "new man," which we have been given by the new Adam, Christ. Luther distinguishes between feeling temptation to sin and giving in to sin. We all are tempted in various ways, according to our age and situation in life. We pray in this petition that the Lord will provide a way out of temptation and graciously help us so that we do not sin.

And lead us not into temptation.    99

We have now heard enough about what    100 toil and labor is needed to keep all that we pray for and to persevere. This, however, is not done without weakness and stumbling. Although we have received forgiveness and a good conscience and are entirely acquitted, yet our life is of such a nature that we stand today, and tomorrow we fall (Isaiah 40:6–8). Therefore, even though we are godly now and stand before God with a good conscience, we must pray again that He would not allow us to fall again and yield to trials and temptations.

Temptation, however, or (as our Saxons    101 in olden times used to call it) *Bekörunge*, is of three kinds: of the flesh, of the world, and of the devil. For we dwell in the flesh and    102 carry the old Adam about our neck. He exerts himself and encourages us daily to unchastity, laziness, gluttony and drunkenness, greed and deception, to defraud our neighbor and to overcharge him (Galatians 5:19–21; Colossians 3:5–8). In short, the old Adam encourages us to have all kinds of evil lusts, which cling to us by nature and to which we are moved by the society, the example, and what we hear and see of other people. They often wound and inflame even an innocent heart.

Next comes the world, which offends us    103 in word and deed. It drives us to anger and impatience. In short, there is nothing but hatred and envy, hostility, violence and wrong, unfaithfulness, vengeance, cursing, railing, slander, pride and haughtiness, with useless finery, honor, fame, and power. No one is willing to be the least. Everyone desires to sit at the head of the group and to be seen before all (Luke 14:7–11).

Then comes the devil, pushing and pro-    104 voking in all directions. But he especially agitates matters that concern the conscience and spiritual affairs. He leads us to despise and disregard both God's Word and works. He tears us away from faith, hope, and love (1 Corinthians 13:13), and he brings us into misbelief, false security, and stubbornness. Or, on the other hand, he leads us to despair, denial of God, blasphemy, and innumerable other shocking things. These are snares and nets (2 Timothy 2:26), indeed, real fiery darts that are shot like poison into the heart, not by flesh and blood, but by the devil (Ephesians 6:12, 16).

05  Great and grievous, indeed, are these dangers and temptations, which every Christian must bear. We bear them even though each one were alone by himself. So every hour that we are in this vile life, we are attacked on all sides (2 Corinthians 4:8), chased and hunted down. We are moved to cry out and to pray that God would not allow us to become weary and faint (Isaiah 40:31; Hebrews 12:3) and to fall again into sin, shame, and unbelief. For otherwise it is impossible to overcome even the least temptation.

06  This, then, is what "lead us not into temptation" means. It refers to times when God gives us power and strength to resist the temptation (1 Corinthians 10:13). However, the temptation is not taken away or removed. While we live in the flesh and have the devil around us, no one can escape his temptation and lures. It can only mean that we must endure trials—indeed, be engulfed in them (2 Timothy 2:3). But we say this prayer so that we may not fall and be drowned in them.

07  To feel temptation is, therefore, a far different thing from consenting or yielding to it. We must all feel it, although not all in the same way. Some feel it in a greater degree and more severely than others. For example, the young suffer especially from the flesh. Afterward, when they reach middle life and old age, they feel it from the world. But others who are occupied with spiritual matters, that is, strong Christians, feel it from the devil. Such feeling, as long as it is against our will 108 and we would rather be rid of it, can harm no one. For if we did not feel it, it could not be called a temptation. But we consent to it when we give it the reins and do not resist or pray against it.

Therefore, we Christians must be armed 109 (Ephesians 6:10–18) and daily expect to be constantly attacked. No one may go on in security and carelessly, as though the devil were far from us. At all times we must expect and block his blows. Though I am now chaste, patient, kind, and in firm faith, the devil will this very hour send such an arrow into my heart that I can scarcely stand. For he is an enemy that never stops or becomes tired. So when one temptation stops, there always arise others and fresh ones.

So there is no help or comfort except to 110 run here, take hold of the Lord's Prayer, and speak to God from the heart like this: "Dear Father, You have asked me to pray. Don't let me fall because of temptations." Then you will see that the temptations must stop and finally confess themselves conquered. If you 111 try to help yourself by your own thoughts and counsel, you will only make the matter worse and give the devil more space. For he has a serpent's head (Revelation 12:9). If it finds an opening into which it can slip, the whole body will follow without stopping. But prayer can prevent him and drive him back.

## THE SEVENTH AND LAST PETITION

Luther rightly notes that the original Greek says, "Deliver us from the evil one." The devil is the sum of all evil. In this petition we pray that God will rescue us from any and all forms of the devil's tricks and plots to make us sin and fall away from God. Luther had a very vivid and realistic view of the devil's active presence and power in this world. The Bible speaks of the devil prowling around like a roaring lion, seeking people to devour. We should note that Luther does not offer an explanation for the common conclusion to the Lord's Prayer familiar to most Protestant Christians: "For Thine is the kingdom . . ." (1 Chronicles 29:11–13). These words are not necessarily part of the original text of the Lord's Prayer and may have been inserted into later copies of the Gospel (perhaps in the second century). Nevertheless, they are fine and appropriate words. But the Lord's Prayer, as prayed in Luther's time and still often among Roman Catholics today, concludes simply with this Seventh Petition. *Amen* is a hearty "Yes! May it be so!" that we say in faith, believing that God will hear and answer our prayer in and through Christ.

---

112    But deliver us from evil. Amen.

113    In the Greek text this petition reads, "Deliver or preserve us from the evil one," or "the hateful one." It looks like Jesus was speaking about the devil, like He would summarize every petition in one. So the entire substance of all our prayer is directed against our chief enemy. For it is he who hinders among us everything that we pray for: God's name or honor, God's kingdom and will, our daily bread, a cheerful good conscience, and so forth.

114    Therefore, we finally sum it all up and say, "Dear Father, grant that we be rid of all these

115    disasters." But there is also included in this petition whatever evil may happen to us under the devil's kingdom: poverty, shame, death, and, in short, all the agonizing misery and heartache of which there is such an unnumbered multitude on the earth. Since the devil is not only a liar, but also a murderer

(John 8:44), he constantly seeks our life. He wreaks his vengeance whenever he can afflict our bodies with misfortune and harm. Therefore, it happens that he often breaks men's necks or drives them to insanity, drowns some, and moves many to commit suicide and to many other terrible disasters (e.g., Mark 9:17–22). So there is nothing for    116 us to do upon earth but to pray against this archenemy without stopping. For unless God preserved us, we would not be safe from this enemy even for an hour.

You see again how God wishes for us to    117 pray to Him also for all the things that affect our bodily interests, so that we seek and expect help nowhere else except in Him. But    118 He has put this matter last. For if we are to be preserved and delivered from all evil, God's name must first be hallowed in us, His kingdom must be with us, and His will must be done. After that He will finally preserve us from sin and shame, and, besides, from everything that may hurt or harm us.

So God has briefly placed before us all the    119 distress that may ever come upon us, so that we might have no excuse whatever for not praying. But all depends upon this, that we learn also to say "Amen." This means that we do not doubt that our prayer is surely heard and that what we pray shall be done (2 Corinthians 1:20). This is nothing else than    120 the word of undoubting faith, which does not pray on a dare but knows that God does not lie to him (Titus 1:2). For He has promised to grant it. Therefore, where there is no such faith, there cannot be true prayer either.

It is, therefore, an evil deception on those    121 who pray as though they could not dare from the heart to say "Yes!" and positively conclude that God hears them. Instead, they remain in doubt and say, "How can I be so bold as to boast that God hears my prayer? For I am but a poor sinner," and other such things.

122    The reason for this is, they do not respect God's promise, but they rely on their own work and worthiness, by which they despise God and accuse Him of lying. 123 Therefore, they receive nothing. As St. James says, "But let him ask in faith, with no doubting, for the one who doubts is like a wave of the sea that is driven and tossed by the wind. For that person must not suppose that he will receive anything from the Lord" 124 (1:6–7). Behold, God attaches such importance to this fact that we can be sure we do not pray in vain, so that we do not despise our prayer in any way.

# PART 4

## Baptism

Baptism is not our work, but God's work. It is a priceless treasure God gives and faith receives or grasps. God's Word of Gospel-promise makes Baptism what it is. Baptism gives us great comfort and strength when our sins accuse us, when we realize how we stand guilty before God. Then, says Luther, the Christian is to say, "But I am baptized!" Luther comments about infant Baptism since, in his time as today, some Christians deny infants this precious Sacrament. Luther's defense of infant Baptism is interesting. He says simply that if God did nothing through Baptism, how do baptized children believe in Him? For Luther, the fact that the gift of the Holy Spirit is given even to very small children is proof enough that God works in and through Baptism. Luther also explains how Baptism encompasses what was known as "penance." So for Luther, Confession and Absolution are subsumed under Baptism and the proclamation of the Gospel. True repentance is daily returning to Baptism. Baptism is our daily garment, by which we suppress the old Adam and grow up in the new Adam, being clothed with the righteousness of Christ. (See AC IX; SA III V.)

1    We have now finished the three chief parts of common Christian doctrine. Besides these we have yet to speak of our two Sacraments instituted by Christ. Every Christian also ought to have at least an ordinary, brief instruction about the Sacraments, because without them he cannot be a Christian. Unfortunately, up to now, no instruction about them has been given. But, in the first place, 2 we take up Baptism, by which we are first received into the Christian Church (John 3:5). However, in order that Baptism may be easily understood, we will present it in an orderly manner. We present only what is necessary for us to know. We will leave to the learned the topic of how Baptism is to be maintained and defended against heretics and sects.

In the first place, we must above all things 3 know well the words on which Baptism is founded. Everything refers to these words that must be said on the subject. The Lord Christ says in Matthew 28:19:

> Go therefore and make disciples of all 4 nations, baptizing them in the name of the Father and of the Son and of the Holy Spirit.

Likewise in St. Mark 16:16:

> Whoever believes and is baptized will 5 be saved, but whoever does not believe will be condemned.

In the first place, you must note in these 6 words that here stand God's commandment and institution. Let us not doubt that Baptism is divine. It is not made up or invented by people. For as surely as I can say, "No one has spun the Ten Commandments, the Creed, and the Lord's Prayer out of his head; they are revealed and given by God Himself."

So also I can boast that Baptism is no human plaything, but it is instituted by God Himself. Furthermore, Baptism is most solemnly and strictly commanded so that we must be baptized or we cannot be saved. I note this lest anyone regard Baptism as a silly matter, like

7 putting on a new red coat. For it is of the greatest importance that we value Baptism as excellent, glorious, and exalted. We contend and fight for Baptism chiefly because the world is now so full of sects arguing that Baptism is an outward thing and that outward

8 things are of no benefit. But let Baptism be a thoroughly outward thing. Here stand God's Word and command, which institute, establish, and confirm Baptism. What God institutes and commands cannot be an empty thing. It must be a most precious thing, even though it looked like it had less value than a

9 straw. Up to now people could consider something great when the pope with his letters and bulls gave away indulgences and confirmed altars and churches, solely because of the letters and seals. So we ought to value Baptism much more highly and more precious, because God has commanded it. Besides, it is done in His name. For these are the words, "Go, baptize." However, do not baptize in your name, but in God's name.

10 To be baptized in God's name is to be baptized not by men, but by God Himself. Therefore, although it is performed by human hands, it is still truly God's own work. From this fact everyone may readily conclude that Baptism is a far higher work than any work performed by a man or a saint. For what work can we do that is greater than God's work?

11 But here the devil is busy to fool us with false appearances and lead us away from God's work to our own works. For there is a much more splendid show when a Carthusian does many great and difficult works. We

all think much more of the things that we do and merit ourselves. But the Scriptures teach 12 this: Even though we collect in one pile the works of all the monks, however splendidly they may shine, they would not be as noble and good as if God should pick up a single straw. Why? Because the person is nobler and better. Here, then, we must not judge the person according to the works, but the works according to the person (Matthew 7:16–20), from whom they must get their nobility. But 13 insane reason will not consider this. Because Baptism does not shine like the works that we do, it is valued as nothing.

From this now learn a proper under- 14 standing of the subject and how to answer the question of what Baptism is. It is not mere ordinary water, but water comprehended in God's Word and command and sanctified by them (Ephesians 5:26–27). So it is nothing other than a divine water. Not that the water in itself is nobler than other water, but that God's Word and command are added to it.

It is pure wickedness and blasphemy of 15 the devil when our "new spirits" mock at Baptism, leaving God's Word and institution out of it. They look on Baptism in no other way than as water that is taken from the well. Then they blather and say, "How does a handful of water help the soul?" Yes, my 16 friend, who does not know that water is water? (If tearing things apart is what we are after.) But how dare you interfere with God's order? How dare you tear away the most precious treasure with which God has connected and enclosed Baptism, and that He will not allow to be separated? For the kernel in the water is God's Word or command and God's name. His name is a treasure greater and nobler than heaven and earth.

Understand the difference, then. Baptism 17 is quite a different thing from all other water.

This is not because of its natural quality but because something more noble is added here. God Himself stakes His honor, His power, and His might on it. Therefore, Baptism is not only natural water, but a divine, heavenly, holy, and blessed water, and whatever other terms we can find to praise it. This is all because of the Word, which is a heavenly, holy Word, which no one can praise enough. For it has, and is able to do, all that God is

18 and can do (Isaiah 55:10–11). In this way it also gets its essence as a Sacrament, as St. Augustine also taught, "When the Word is joined to the element or natural substance, it becomes a Sacrament," that is, a holy and divine matter and sign.

19    We always teach that the Sacraments and all outward things that God ordains and institutes should not be considered according to the coarse, outward mask, the way we look at a nutshell. But we respect them because

20 God's Word is included in them. For we also speak of the parental estate and of civil government in this way. If we intend only to recognize that they have noses, eyes, skin, and hair, flesh and bones, they look like Turks and heathen. Someone might start up and say, "Why should I value them more than others?" Because this commandment is added, "Honor your father and your mother" (Exodus 20:12). I see a different person, adorned and clothed with God's majesty and glory. The commandment, I say, is the gold chain about his neck. Yes, that is the crown upon his head, which shows me how and why one must honor this flesh and blood.

21    So, and even much more, you must honor Baptism and consider it glorious because of the Word. For God Himself has honored it both by words and deeds. Furthermore, He confirmed it with miracles from heaven. Do you think it was a joke that, when Christ was baptized, the heavens were opened and the Holy Spirit descended visibly, and everything was divine glory and majesty (Luke 3:21–22)?

22    I encourage again that these two—the water and the Word—by no means be separated from each other and parted. For if the Word is separated from it, the water is the same as the water that the servant cooks with. It may indeed be called a bathkeeper's baptism. But when the Word is added, as God has ordained, it is a Sacrament. It is called Christ's Baptism. Let this be the first part about the holy Sacrament's essence and dignity.

23    In the second place, since we know now what Baptism is and how it is to be regarded, we must also learn why and for what purpose it is instituted. We must learn what it profits, gives, and works. For this also we cannot find a better resource than Christ's words quoted above, "Whoever believes and is baptized will be saved" (Mark 16:16). Therefore, state it

24 most simply in this way: the power, work, profit, fruit, and purpose of Baptism is this— to save (1 Peter 3:21). For no one is baptized in order that he may become a prince, but, as the words say, that he "be saved." We know

25 that to be saved is nothing other than to be delivered from sin, death, and the devil (Colossians 1:13–14). It means to enter into Christ's kingdom (John 3:5), and to live with Him forever.

26    Here you see again how highly and preciously we should value Baptism, because in it we receive such an unspeakable treasure. This also proves that it cannot be ordinary, mere water. For mere water could not do such a thing. But the Word does it and, as I said above, so does the fact that God's name is included in Baptism. Where God's name is,

27 there must also be life and salvation (Psalm 54:1). So Baptism may certainly be called a divine, blessed, fruitful, and gracious water. Such power is given to Baptism by the Word

that it is a washing of new birth, as St. Paul also calls it in Titus 3:5.

28    Our would-be wise, "new spirits" assert that faith alone saves, and that works and outward things do nothing. We answer, "It is true, indeed, that nothing in us is of any use 29  but faith, as we shall hear still further." But these blind guides are unwilling to see this: faith must have something that it believes, that is, of which it takes hold (2 Timothy 1:13; Titus 1:9) and upon which it stands and rests (1 Corinthians 2:5). So faith clings to the water and believes that in Baptism, there is pure salvation and life. This is not through the water (as we have stated well enough), but through the fact that it is embodied in God's Word and institution, and that God's name abides in it. Now, if I believe this, what else is it than believing in God as the One who has given and planted His Word (Mark 4:14) into this ordinance and offers to us this outward thing by which we may gain such a treasure?

30    Now, these "new spirits" are so crazy that they separate faith and the object to which faith clings and is bound, even if it is something outward. Yes, it shall and must be something outward, so that it may be grasped by our senses and understood, and by them be brought into the heart. For indeed, the entire Gospel is an outward, verbal preaching (Romans 10:17; 1 Corinthians 1:21). In short, what God does and works in us He intends to work through such outward ordinances. Therefore, wherever He speaks—indeed, no matter what direction or by whatever means He speaks—faith must look 31  there. It must hold to that object. Now here we have the words "Whoever believes and is baptized will be saved" (Mark 16:16). What else can these words refer to but Baptism, that is, to the water included in God's ordinance? Therefore, it makes sense that whoev-er rejects Baptism rejects God's Word, faith, and Christ, who directs us to Baptism and binds us to Baptism.

In the third place, since we have learned   32 Baptism's great benefit and power, let us see further who is the person that receives what 33 Baptism gives and profits. This is again most beautifully and clearly expressed in the words "Whoever believes and is baptized will be saved" (Mark 16:16). That is, faith alone makes the person worthy to receive profitably the saving, divine water. Since these blessings are presented here and promised through the words in and with the water, they cannot be received in any other way than by believing them with the heart (Romans 10:9). Without   34 faith it profits nothing, even though Baptism is in itself a divine overwhelming treasure. Therefore, this single phrase, "Whoever believes," does so much. It excludes and repels all the works that we can do, when we suppose that we gain and merit salvation by our works. For it is determined that whatever is not faith does nothing or receives nothing (Hebrews 11:6).

But if the "new spirits" say, as they are ac-   35 customed, "Still Baptism is itself a work, and you say works are of no use for salvation. What, then, becomes of faith?" Answer, "Yes, our works, indeed, do nothing for salvation. Baptism, however, is not our work, but God's." For, as was stated, you must completely distinguish Christ's Baptism from a bathkeeper's baptism. God's works are saving and necessary for salvation. They do not exclude, but demand, faith. For without faith they could not be grasped. By allowing the   36 water to be poured upon you, you have not yet received Baptism in a way that benefits you at all. But it becomes beneficial to you if you have yourself baptized with this thought: this is according to God's command and ordinance, and besides, it is done in God's name. In this way you may receive the promised salvation in the water. Now, your fist cannot do this, nor your body; but the heart must believe it (Ezekiel 36:25–26; Hebrews 10:22).

37 So you see plainly that there is no work done here by us, but a treasure, which God gives us and faith grasps (Ephesians 2:8–9). It is like the benefit of the Lord Jesus Christ upon the cross, which is not a work, but a treasure included in the Word. It is offered to us and received by faith. Therefore, the "new spirits" violate us by shouting against us as though we preach against faith. For we alone insist upon it as being so necessary that without it nothing can be received or enjoyed.

38 So we have these three parts, which must be known about this Sacrament, especially that God's ordinance is to be held in all honor. The Sacrament alone would be enough, even though it is an entirely outward thing. It is like the commandment "Honor your father and your mother," which refers to bodily flesh and blood. In these words we do not think about the flesh and blood, but God's commandment in which flesh and blood are included, and on account of which the flesh is called father and mother. So even if we had only these words, "Go and baptize," or such, it would be necessary for us to accept

39 them and do them as God's ordinance. Now there is not only God's commandment and injunction here, but also the promise. Because of this, Baptism is still far more glorious than whatever else God has commanded and ordained. It is, in short, so full of consolation and grace that heaven and earth can-

40 not understand it. But it requires skill to believe this, for the treasure is not lacking, but this is lacking: people who grasp it and hold it firmly.

41 Therefore, every Christian has enough in Baptism to learn and to do all his life. For he has always enough to do by believing firmly what Baptism promises and brings: victory over death and the devil (Romans 6:3–6), forgiveness of sin (Acts 2:38), God's grace (Titus 3:5–6), the entire Christ, and the Holy Spirit with His gifts (1 Corinthians 6:11). In

42 short, Baptism is so far beyond us that if timid nature could realize this, it might well doubt whether it could be true. Think about

43 it. Imagine there was a doctor somewhere who understood the art of saving people from death or, even though they died, could restore them quickly to life so that they would afterward live forever. Oh, how the world would pour in money like snow and rain. No one could find access to him because of the throng of the rich! But here in Baptism there is freely brought to everyone's door such a treasure and medicine that it utterly destroys death and preserves all people alive.

44 We must think this way about Baptism and make it profitable for ourselves. So when our sins and conscience oppress us, we strengthen ourselves and take comfort and say, "Nevertheless, I am baptized. And if I am baptized, it is promised to me that I shall be saved and have eternal life, both in soul and

45 body." For that is the reason why these two things are done in Baptism: the body— which can grasp nothing but the water—is sprinkled and, in addition, the Word is spo-

46 ken for the soul to grasp. Now, since both, the water and the Word, make one Baptism, therefore, body and soul must be saved and live forever (1 Corinthians 15:53). The soul lives through the Word, which it believes, but the body lives because it is united with the soul and also holds on through Baptism as it is able to grasp it. We have, therefore, no greater jewel in body and soul. For by Baptism we are made holy and are saved (1 Corinthians 6:11). No other kind of life, no work upon earth, can do this.

Let this be enough about Baptism's nature, blessing, and use, for it fulfills the present purpose.

## INFANT BAPTISM

47    Here a question arises by which the devil, through his sects, confuses the world: *Infant Baptism.* Do children also believe? Are they

48    rightly baptized? Briefly we say about this, let the simple dismiss this question from their minds. Refer it to the learned. But if you wish to answer, answer as follows:

49    The Baptism of infants is pleasing to Christ, as is proved well enough from His own work. For God sanctifies many of those who have been baptized as infants and has given them the Holy Spirit. There are still many people even today in whom we perceive that they have the Holy Spirit both because of their doctrine and life. It is also given to us by God's grace that we can explain the Scriptures and come to the knowledge of Christ, which is impossible without the Holy

50    Spirit (1 Corinthians 12:3). But if God did not accept the Baptism of infants, He would not give the Holy Spirit nor any of His gifts to any of them. In short, during the long time up to this day, no person on earth could have been a Christian. Now, God confirms Baptism by the gifts of His Holy Spirit, as is plainly seen in some of the Church Fathers, like St. Bernard, Gerson, John Hus, and others. These people were baptized in infancy, and since the holy Christian Church cannot perish until the end of the world, the sects must acknowledge that such infant Baptism is pleasing to God. For God can never be opposed to Himself or support falsehood and wickedness, or for its promotion impart His

51    grace and Spirit. This is indeed the best and strongest proof for the simpleminded and unlearned. For the sects shall not take from us or overthrow this article: "I believe in . . . the holy Christian Church, the communion of saints."

52    Further, we say that we are not very concerned to know whether the person baptized believes or not. For Baptism does not

53    become invalid on that account. But everything depends on God's Word and command. Now this point is perhaps somewhat difficult. But it rests entirely on what I have said, that Baptism is nothing other than water and God's Word in and with each other (Ephesians 5:26). That is, when the Word is added to the water, Baptism is valid, even though faith is lacking. For my faith does not make Baptism, but receives it. Now, Baptism does not become invalid even though it is wrongly received or used. As stated above, it is not bound to our faith, but to the Word.

54    Suppose a Jewish person should come dishonestly today and with evil intent, and we should baptize him in all good faith. We must say that his Baptism is still genuine. For here is the water together with God's Word, even though the person does not receive it as he should. It is like those who go to the Sacrament unworthily yet still receive the true Sacrament, even though they do not believe (1 Corinthians 11:27).

55    So you see that the objection of the sectarians is empty. As we have said, even though infants did not believe (which, however, is not the case), still their Baptism would be valid. We have now shown this. No one should rebaptize infants. Nothing is taken away from the Sacrament even though someone approaches it with evil purpose. So he could not be allowed to take it a second time the self-same hour on account of his abuse, as though he had not received the true Sacrament at first. That would blaspheme and profane the Sacrament in the worst way. How dare we think that God's Word and or-

dinance should be wrong and invalid because we make a wrong use of it?

56 I say, if you did not believe then, believe now and say this: The Baptism certainly was right. But I, unfortunately, did not receive it aright. I myself also, and all who are baptized, must say this before God, "I come here in my faith and in that of others. Yet I cannot rest in this, that I believe, and that many people pray for me. But in this I rest, that Baptism is Your Word and command. It is just like when I go to the Sacrament trusting not in my faith, but in Christ's Word. Whether I am strong or weak, I commit that to God. But I know this, that He asks me to go, to eat and to drink, and so on, and He gives me His body and blood (Matthew 26:26–28). That will not deceive me or prove false to me."

57 So we do likewise in infant Baptism. We bring the child in the conviction and hope that it believes, and we pray that God may grant it faith (Luke 17:2; Ephesians 2:8). But we do not baptize it for that reason, but solely because of God's command. Why? Because we know that God does not lie (Titus 1:2). I and my neighbor and, in short, all people, may err and deceive. But God's Word cannot err.

58 They are arrogant, clumsy minds that draw together such ideas and conclusions as these, "Where there is not the true faith, there also cannot be true Baptism." That's as if I would conclude, "If I do not believe, then Christ is nothing." Or "If I am not obedient, then father, mother, and government are nothing." Is that a correct conclusion, that whenever anyone does not do what he ought, the work that he ought to do shall be

59 come nothing and of no value? My dear, just invert the argument and rather draw this conclusion: For this very reason Baptism *is* something and *is* right, because it has been wrongly received. For if Baptism was not

right and true in itself, it could not be misused or sinned against. The saying is, "Abuse does not destroy the essence, but confirms it." For gold is not the less gold even though a harlot wears it in sin and shame.

60 Therefore, let it be decided that Baptism always remains true and retains its full essence. This is true even though a single person should be baptized, and he, in addition, should not truly believe. For God's ordinance and Word cannot be made inconsistent or be 61 changed by people. But these people, the fanatics, are so blind that they do not see God's Word and command. They think about Baptism and those who administer it just like they think about water in the brook or in pots, or like any common person. Because they do not see faith or obedience in infants, they conclude that infant Baptisms are to be considered invalid. Here lurks a concealed re- 62 bellious devil, who would like to tear the crown from authority's head and then trample it underfoot (Matthew 7:6). And in addition, he would like to pervert and reduce to nothing all God's works and ordinances. Therefore, we must be watchful and well 63 armed (2 Corinthians 10:4). We must not allow ourselves to be directed or turned away from the Word, in order that we may not think of Baptism as a mere empty sign, like the fanatic's dream (Jeremiah 23:25).

64 Lastly, we must also know what Baptism signifies and why God has ordained just this outward sign and ceremony for the Sacrament by which we are first received into the Christian Church. The act or ceremony is 65 this: we are sunk under the water, which passes over us, and afterward are drawn out again. These two parts, (a) to be sunk under the water and (b) drawn out again, signify Baptism's power and work. It is nothing other than putting to death the old Adam and affecting the new man's resurrection

after that (Romans 6:4–6). Both of these things must take place in us all our lives. So a truly Christian life is nothing other than a daily Baptism, once begun and ever to be continued. For this must be done without ceasing, that we always keep purging away whatever belongs to the old Adam. Then what belongs to the new man may come 66 forth. But what is the old man? It is what is born in human beings from Adam: anger, hate, envy, unchastity, stinginess, laziness, arrogance—yes, unbelief. The old man is infected with all vices and has by nature noth-67 ing good in him (Romans 7:18). Now, when we have come into Christ's kingdom (John 3:5), these things must daily decrease. The longer we live the more we become gentle, patient, meek, and ever turn away from unbelief, greed, hatred, envy, and arrogance.

68    This is Baptism's true use among Christians, as signified by baptizing with water. Therefore, where this is not done, the old man is left unbridled. He continually becomes stronger. That is not using Baptism, 69 but working against Baptism. For those who are without Christ cannot help but become worse daily, just as the proverb says, which expresses the truth "Worse and worse—the 70 longer a vice lasts, the worse it gets." If a year ago someone was proud and greedy, then he is more proud and greedy this year. So the vice grows and increases with him from his youth up. A young child has no special vice. But when it grows up, it becomes unchaste and impure. When it reaches maturity, real vices begin to triumph. The longer the child lives, the more vices.

71    Therefore, the old man goes unrestrained in his nature if he is not stopped and suppressed by Baptism's power. On the other hand, where people have become Christians, the old man daily decreases until he finally perishes. That is truly being buried in Bap-

tism and daily coming forth again. There-72 fore, the outward sign is appointed not only for a powerful effect, but also for an illustration. Therefore, where faith flourishes with 73 its fruit, there it has no empty meaning, but the work of mortifying the flesh goes with it (Romans 8:13). But where faith is lacking, it remains a mere unfruitful sign.

Here you see that Baptism, both in its 74 power and meaning, includes also the third Sacrament, which has been called repentance. It is really nothing other than Baptism. What else is repentance but a serious attack 75 on the old man, that his lusts be restrained, and an entering into a new life? Therefore, if you live in repentance, you walk in Baptism. For Baptism not only illustrates such a new life, but also produces, begins, and exercises it. For in Baptism are given grace, the Spirit, 76 and power to suppress the old man, so that the new man may come forth and become strong (Romans 6:3–6).

Our Baptism abides forever. Even though 77 someone should fall from Baptism and sin, still we always have access to it. So we may subdue the old man again. But we do not 78 need to be sprinkled with water again (Ezekiel 36:25–26; Hebrews 10:22). Even if we were put under the water a hundred times, it would still be only one Baptism, even though the work and sign continue and remain. Repentance, therefore, is nothing 79 other than a return and approach to Baptism. We repeat and do what we began before, but abandoned.

I say this lest we fall into the opinion in 80 which we were stuck for a long time. We were imagining that our Baptism is something past, which we can no longer use after we have fallen again into sin. The reason for this is that Baptism is regarded as only based on the outward act once performed and completed. This arose from the fact that St. 81

Jerome wrote that "repentance is the second plank by which we must swim forth and cross over the water after the ship is broken, on which we step and are carried across when 82 we come into the Christian Church." By this teaching Baptism's use has been abolished so that it can no longer profit us. Therefore, Jerome's statement is not correct, or at any rate is not rightly understood. For the ship of Baptism never breaks, because (as we have said) it is God's ordinance and not our work (1 Peter 3:20–22). But it does happen, indeed, that we slip and fall out of the ship. Yet if anyone falls out, let him see to it that he swims up and clings to the ship until he comes into it again and lives in it, as he had done before.

83    In this way one sees what a great, excellent thing Baptism is. It delivers us from the devil's jaws and makes us God's own. It suppresses and takes away sin and then daily strengthens the new man. It is working and always continues working until we pass from this estate of misery to eternal glory.

84    For this reason let everyone value his Baptism as a daily dress (Galatians 3:27) in which he is to walk constantly. Then he may ever be found in the faith and its fruit, so that he may suppress the old man and grow up in 85 the new. For if we would be Christians, we must do the work by which we are Chris- 86 tians. But if anyone falls away from the Christian life, let him again come into it. For just as Christ, the Mercy Seat (Romans 3:25), does not draw back from us or forbid us to come to Him again, even though we sin, so all His treasure and gifts also remain. Therefore, if we have received forgiveness of sin once in Baptism, it will remain every day, as long as we live. Baptism will remain as long as we carry the old man about our neck.

# PART 5

# The Sacrament of the Altar

In this Sacrament we cling to and trust God's Word alone. Jesus does not lie to us or deceive us. Therefore, when He tells us the bread and wine are His body and blood, they are what He says. The key to understanding the benefit of the Sacrament is Christ's words "for you." What we receive in this Sacrament is a great "treasure": the forgiveness of sins. The whole Gospel is comprehended in this Sacrament and is offered to us through the Word, which promises that in and under the bread and wine we receive the body and blood that was sacrificed on the cross for our salvation. Those who believe the Words of promise receive the forgiveness this Sacrament promises. Luther urges Christians to receive the Sacrament frequently. Those who realize the enormity of their sin, how many dangers abound, and how great Christ's gifts are that are given in the Sacrament will receive the Lord's Supper as often as possible. This is precisely why the early Lutheran congregations began to offer the Lord's Supper every Lord's Day and on other festival days to those wishing to receive it. (See AC X; SA III VI; FC Ep VII and SD VII.)

Just as we have heard about Holy Baptism, so we must also speak about the other Sacrament, in these same three points: What is it? What are its benefits? and Who is to receive it? And all these points are established through the words by which Christ has instituted this Sacrament. Everyone who desires 2 to be a Christian and go to this Sacrament should know them. For it is not our intention to let people come to the Sacrament and administer it to them if they do not know what they seek or why they come. The words, however, are these:

3    Our Lord Jesus Christ, on the night He was betrayed, took bread, and when He had given thanks, He broke it and gave it to the disciples and said, "Take, eat; this is My body, which is given for you. This do in remembrance of me."

In the same way also, He took the cup after supper, and when He had given thanks, He gave it to them, saying: "Drink of it, all of you; this is My blood of the new testament, which is shed for you for the forgiveness of sins. This do, as often as you drink it, in remembrance of Me."

4    Here also we do not wish to enter into controversy and fight with the defamers and blasphemers of this Sacrament, but to learn first (as we did with Baptism) what is of the greatest importance. The chief point is God's Word and ordinance or command. For the Sacrament has not been invented nor introduced by any man. Without anyone's counsel and deliberation it has been instituted by
5    Christ. The Ten Commandments, the Lord's Prayer, and the Creed keep their nature and worth, even if you never keep, pray, or believe them. So also this honorable Sacrament remains undisturbed. Nothing is withdrawn or taken from it, even though we use and ad-
6    minister it unworthily. Do you think God cares about what we do or believe, as though on that account He should allow His ordinance to be changed? Why, in all worldly matters everything stays the way God has created and ordered it, no matter how we
7    employ or use it. This point must always be taught, for by it the chatter of nearly all the fanatical spirits can be repelled. For they regard the Sacraments, unlike God's Word, as something that we do.

8    "Now, what is the Sacrament of the Altar?"

Answer, "It is the true body and blood of our Lord Jesus Christ, in and under the bread and wine, which we Christians are commanded by Christ's Word to eat and to drink." Just as we have said that Baptism is   9
not simple water, so here also we say that though the Sacrament is bread and wine, it is not mere bread and wine, such as are ordinarily served at the table (1 Corinthians 10:16–17). But this is bread and wine included in, and connected with, God's Word.

It is the Word, I say, that makes and sets   10
this Sacrament apart. So it is not mere bread and wine, but is, and is called, Christ's body and blood (1 Corinthians 11:23–27). For it is said, "When the Word is joined to the element or natural substance, it becomes a Sacrament." This saying of St. Augustine is so properly and so well put that he has scarcely said anything better. The Word must make a Sacrament out of the element, or else it remains a mere element. Now, it is not the   11
word or ordinance of a prince or emperor. But it is the Word of the grand Majesty, at whose feet all creatures should fall and affirm it is as He says, and accept it with all reverence, fear, and humility (Isaiah 45:23; Philippians 2:10).

With this Word you can strengthen your   12
conscience and say, "If a hundred thousand devils, together with all fanatics, should rush forward, crying, 'How can bread and wine be Christ's body and blood?' and such, I know that all spirits and scholars together are not as wise as is the Divine Majesty in His little finger" (see 1 Corinthians 1:25). Now here   13
stands Christ's Word, "Take, eat; this is My body. . . . Drink of it, all of you; this is My blood of the new testament," and so on. Here we stop to watch those who will call themselves His masters and make the matter different from what He has spoken. It is true, indeed, that if you take away the Word or

The Sacrament of the Altar;
from 1530 Large Catechism

14 regard the Sacrament without the words, you have nothing but mere bread and wine. But if the words remain with them, as they shall and must, then, by virtue of the words, it is truly Christ's body and blood. What Christ's lips say and speak, so it is. He can never lie or deceive (Titus 1:2).

15 It is easy to reply to all kinds of questions about which people are troubled at the present time, such as this one: "Can even a wicked priest serve at and administer the Sacrament?" And whatever other questions like this there may be. 16 For here we conclude and say, "Even though an imposter takes or distributes the Sacrament, a person still receives the true Sacrament, that is, Christ's true body and blood, just as truly as a person who receives or administers it in the most worthy way." For the Sacrament is not founded upon people's holiness, but upon God's Word. Just as no saint on earth, indeed, no angel in heaven, can make bread and wine be Christ's body and blood, so also no one can change or 17 alter it, even though it is misused. The Word by which it became a Sacrament and was instituted does not become false because of the person or his unbelief. For Christ does not say, "If you believe or are worthy, you receive My body and blood." No, He says, "Take, eat and drink; this is My body and blood." Likewise, He says, "Do this" (i.e., what I now do, 18 institute, give, and ask you, take). That is like saying, "No matter whether you are worthy or unworthy, you have here His body and blood by virtue of these words that are added 19 to the bread and wine." Note and remember this well. For upon these words rest all our foundation, protection, and defense against all errors and deception that have ever come or may yet come.

20 So we have, in a brief way, covered the first point that deals with this Sacrament's essence. Now examine further the effectiveness and benefits that really caused the Sacrament to be instituted. This is its most necessary part, so that we may know what we should seek and gain there. This is plain and 21 clear from the words just mentioned, "This is My body and blood, given and shed *for you* for the forgiveness of sins." Briefly, that is like 22 saying, "For this reason we go to the Sacrament: there we receive such a treasure by and in which we gain forgiveness of sins." "Why so?" "Because the words stand here and give us this. Therefore, Christ asks me to eat and drink, so that this treasure may be my own and may benefit me as a sure pledge and token. In fact, it is the very same treasure that is appointed for me against my sins, death, and every disaster."

23 On this account it is indeed called a food of souls, which nourishes and strengthens the new man. For by Baptism we are first born anew (John 3:5). But, as we said before, there still remains the old vicious nature of flesh and blood in mankind. There are so many hindrances and temptations of the devil and of the world that we often become weary and faint, and sometimes we also stumble (Hebrews 12:3).

24 Therefore, the Sacrament is given as a daily pasture and sustenance, that faith may refresh and strengthen itself (Psalm 23:1–3) so that it will not fall back in such a battle, but become ever stronger and stronger. 25 The new life must be guided so that it continually increases and progresses. 26 But it must suffer much opposition. For the devil is such a furious enemy. When he sees that we oppose him and attack the old man, and that he cannot topple us over by force, he prowls and moves about on all sides (1 Peter 5:8). He tries every trick and does not stop until he finally wears us out, so that we either renounce our faith or throw up our hands and put up our feet, becoming indifferent or impatient.

27 Now to this purpose the comfort of the Sacrament is given when the heart feels that the burden is becoming too heavy, so that it may gain here new power and refreshment.

28 But here our wise spirits twist themselves about with their great art and wisdom. They cry out and bawl, "How can bread and wine forgive sins or strengthen faith?" They hear and know that we do not say this about bread and wine. Because, in itself, bread is bread. But we speak about the bread and wine that is Christ's body and blood and has the words attached to it. That, we say, is truly the treasure—and nothing else—through which such 29 forgiveness is gained. Now the only way this treasure is passed along and made our very own is in the words "Given . . . and shed for you." For in the words you have both truths, that it is Christ's body and blood, and that it 30 is yours as a treasure and gift. Now Christ's body can never be an unfruitful, empty thing that does or profits nothing. Yet, no matter how great the treasure is in itself, it must be included in the Word and administered to us. Otherwise we would never be able to know or seek it.

31 Therefore also, it is useless talk when they say that Christ's body and blood are not given and shed for us in the Lord's Supper, so we could not have forgiveness of sins in the Sacrament. Although the work is done and the forgiveness of sins is secured by the cross (John 19:30), it cannot come to us in any other way than through the Word. How would we know about it otherwise, that such a thing was accomplished or was to be given to us, unless it were presented by preaching or the oral Word (Romans 10:17; 1 Corinthians 1:21)? How do they know about it? Or how can they receive and make the forgiveness their own, unless they lay hold of and 32 believe the Scriptures and the Gospel? But now the entire Gospel and the article of the Creed—I believe in . . . the holy Christian Church, . . . the forgiveness of sins, and so on—are embodied by the Word in this Sacrament and presented to us. Why, then, should we let this treasure be torn from the Sacrament when the fanatics must confess that these are the very words we hear everywhere in the Gospel? They cannot say that these words in the Sacrament are of no use, just as they dare not say that the entire Gospel or God's Word, apart from the Sacrament, is of no use.

33 So we have covered the entire Sacrament, both what it is in itself and what it brings and profits. Now we must also see who is the person that receives this power and benefit. That is answered briefly, as we said above about Baptism and often elsewhere: Whoever believes the words has what they declare and bring. For they are not spoken or proclaimed to stone and wood, but to those who hear them, to whom He says, "Take, eat," and so 34 on. Because He offers and promises forgiveness of sin, it cannot be received except by faith. This faith He Himself demands in the Word when He says, "Given . . . and shed for you, " as if He said, "For this reason I give it, and ask you to eat and drink it, that you may claim it as yours and enjoy it." Whoever now 35 accepts these words and believes that what they declare is true has forgiveness. But whoever does not believe it has nothing, since he allows it to be offered to him in vain and refuses to enjoy such a saving good. The treasure, indeed, is opened and placed at everyone's door, yes, upon his table. But it is necessary that you also claim it and confidently view it as the words tell you. This is the 36 entire Christian preparation for receiving this Sacrament worthily. Since this treasure is entirely presented in the words, it cannot be received and made ours in any other way than with the heart. Such a gift and eternal

37 treasure cannot be seized with the fist. Fasting, prayer, and other such things may indeed be outward preparations and discipline for children, so that the body may keep and bring itself modestly and reverently to receive Christ's body and blood. Yet the body cannot seize and make its own what is given in and with the Sacrament. This is done by the faith in the heart, which discerns this treasure and

38 desires it. This may be enough for what is necessary as a general instruction about this Sacrament. What may be said about it further belongs to another time.

39     In conclusion, since we now have the true understanding and doctrine of the Sacrament, there is also need for some admonition and encouragement. Then people may not let such a great treasure—daily administered and distributed among Christians—pass by unnoticed. So those who want to be Christians may prepare to receive this praiseworthy

40 Sacrament often. For we see that people seem weary and lazy about receiving the Sacrament. A great multitude hears the Gospel. Yet because the nonsense of the pope has been abolished and we are freed from his laws and coercion, they go one, two, three years, or even longer without the Sacrament. They act as though they were such strong

41 Christians that they have no need of it. Some allow themselves to be hindered and held up by the excuse that we have taught that no one should approach the Sacrament except those who feel hunger and thirst, which drive them to it. Some pretend that it is a matter of liberty and not necessary. They pretend that it is enough to believe without it. For the most part, they go so far astray that they become quite brutish and finally despise both the Sacrament and God's Word.

42     Now, it is true, as we have said, that no one should by any means be forced or compelled to go to the Sacrament, lest we institute a new murdering of souls. Nevertheless, it must be known that people who deprive themselves of and withdraw from the Sacrament for such a long time are not to be considered Christians. For Christ has not instituted it to be treated as a show. Instead, He has commanded His Christians to eat it, drink it, and remember Him by it.

43     Indeed, those who are true Christians and value the Sacrament precious and holy will drive and move themselves to go to it. We will present something on this point so that the simpleminded and the weak who also would like to be Christians may be more stirred up to consider the cause and need that ought to move them. In other matters

44 applying to faith, love, and patience, it is not enough to teach and instruct alone. There is also need for daily encouragement (Hebrews 10:24–25). So here also there is need for us to continue to preach so that people may not become weary and disgusted. For we know and feel how the devil always opposes this and every Christian exercise. He drives and deters people from them as much as he can.

45     We have, in the first place, the clear text in Christ's very words, "Do this in remembrance of Me" (Luke 22:19). These are inviting and commanding words by which all who would be Christians are told to partake of this Sacrament. Therefore, whoever wants to be Christ's disciple, with whom He here speaks, must also consider and keep this Sacrament. They should not act from compulsion, being forced by others, but in obedience to the Lord Jesus Christ, to please Him.

46 However, you may say, "But the words are added, 'As often as you drink it'; there He compels no one, but leaves it to our free

47 choice." I answer, "That is true, yet it is not written so that we should never do so. Yes, since He speaks the words 'As often as you

drink it,' it is still implied that we should do it often. This is added because He wants to have the Sacrament free. He does not limit it to special times, like the Jewish Passover, which they were obliged to eat only once a year. They could only have it on the fourteenth day of the first full moon in the evening (Exodus 12:6, 18). They still must not change a day." It is as if He would say by these words, "I institute a Passover or Supper for you. You shall enjoy it not only once a year, just upon this evening, but often, when and where you will, according to everyone's opportunity and necessity, bound to no place or appointed

48  time." But the pope later perverted this and again made the Sacrament into a Jewish feast.

49  So you see, it is not left free in the sense that we may despise it. I call that despising the Sacrament if one allows a long time to elapse—with nothing to hinder him—yet never feels a desire for it. If you want such freedom, you may just as well have the freedom to not be a Christian and not have to believe or pray. One is just as much commanded by Christ as the other. But if you want to be a Christian, you must from time to time fulfill and obey this commandment.

50  For this commandment ought always to move you to examine yourself (1 Corinthians 11:28; 2 Corinthians 13:5) and to think, "See, what sort of a Christian I am! If I were one, I would certainly have some small longing for what my Lord has commanded me to do."

51  Since we act like strangers toward the Sacrament, it is easy to see what sort of Christians we were under the papacy. We went to the Sacrament from mere compulsion and fear of human commandments, without natural longing and without love, and never thought about Christ's command-

52  ment. But we neither force nor compel anyone. Nor does anyone have to do it to serve or please us. This should lead and constrain you

by itself, that the Lord desires it and that it is pleasing to Him. You must not let people force you to faith or any good work. We are doing no more than talking about and encouraging you about what you ought to do—not for our sake, but for your own sake. The Lord invites and allures you. If you despise it, you must answer for that yourself (2 Corinthians 5:10).

53  Now, this is to be the first point, especially for those who are cold and indifferent. Then they may reflect upon it and rouse themselves. For this is certainly true, as I have found in my own experience, and as everyone will find in his own case: if a person withdraws like this from the Sacrament, he will daily become more and more callous and cold, and will at last disregard the Sacrament

54  completely. To avoid this, we must examine our heart and conscience (1 Corinthians 11:28; 2 Corinthians 13:5), and we must act like people who desire to be right with God (Psalm 78:37). The more this is done, the more the heart will be warmed and enkindled, so it may not become entirely cold.

55  But if you say, "How can I come if I feel that I am not prepared?" Answer, "That is also my cause for hesitation, especially because of the old way under the pope." At that time we tortured ourselves to be so perfectly pure that God could not find the least blemish in us. For this reason we became so timid that we were all instantly thrown into fear and said to ourselves, "Alas! we are unwor-

56  thy!" Then nature and reason begin to add up our unworthiness in comparison with the great and precious good. Then our good looks like a dark lantern in contrast with the bright sun, or like filth in comparison with precious stones. Because nature and reason see this, they refuse to approach and wait until they are prepared. They wait so long that one week trails into another, and half the

57  year into the other  If you consider how good and pure you are and labor to have no hesitations, you would never approach.

58  Therefore, we must make a distinction here between people. Those who are lewd and morally loose must be told to stay away (1 Corinthians 5:9–13). They are not prepared to receive forgiveness of sin, since they do not desire it and do not wish to be godly.

59  But the others, who are not such callous and wicked people, and who desire to be godly, must not absent themselves. This is true even though otherwise they are feeble and full of infirmities. For St. Hilary also has said, "If anyone has not committed sin for which he can rightly be put out of the congregation and be considered no Christian, he ought not stay away from the Sacrament, lest he should

60  deprive himself of life." No one will live so well that he will not have many daily weaknesses in flesh and blood.

61  Such people must learn that it is the highest art to know that our Sacrament does not depend upon our worthiness. We are not baptized because we are worthy and holy. Nor do we go to Confession because we are pure and without sin. On the contrary, we go because we are poor, miserable people. We go exactly because we are unworthy. This is true unless we are talking about someone who desires no grace and Absolution nor intends to change.

62  But whoever would gladly receive grace and comfort should drive himself and allow no one to frighten him away. Say, "I, indeed, would like to be worthy. But I come, not upon any worthiness, but upon Your Word, because You have commanded it. I come as one who would gladly be Your disciple, no matter what becomes of my worthiness."

63  This is difficult. We always have this obstacle and hindrance to encounter: we look more upon ourselves than upon Christ's Word and lips. For human nature desires to act in such a way that it can stand and rest firmly on itself. Otherwise, it refuses to approach. Let this be enough about the first point.

64  In the second place, there is besides this command also a promise, as we heard above. This ought most strongly to stir us up and encourage us. For here stand the kind and precious words, "This is My body, which is given for you. . . . This is My blood . . . shed for you for the forgiveness of sins." These

65  words, I have said, are not preached to wood and stone, but to me and you. Otherwise, Christ might just as well be silent and not institute a Sacrament. Therefore consider, and read yourself into this word *you,* so that He may not speak to you in vain.

66  Here He offers to us the entire treasure that He has brought for us from heaven. With the greatest kindness He invites us to receive it also in other places, like when He says in St. Matthew 11:28, "Come to Me, all who labor and are heavy laden, and I will give you rest." It is surely a sin and a shame that He so cor-

67  dially and faithfully summons and encourages us to receive our highest and greatest good, yet we act so distantly toward it. We permit so long a time to pass without partaking of the Sacrament that we grow quite cold and hardened, so that we have no longing or love for it. We must never think of the Sacra-

68  ment as something harmful from which we had better flee, but as a pure, wholesome, comforting remedy that grants salvation and comfort. It will cure you and give you life both in soul and body. For where the soul has recovered, the body also is relieved. Why, then, do we act as if the Sacrament were a poison, the eating of which would bring death?

69  To be sure, it is true that those who despise the Sacrament and live in an unchristian way receive it to their hurt and damna-

tion (1 Corinthians 11:29–30). Nothing shall be good or wholesome for them. It is just like a sick person who on a whim eats and drinks 70 what is forbidden to him by the doctor. But those who are mindful of their weakness desire to be rid of it and long for help. They should regard and use the Sacrament just like a precious antidote against the poison that they have in them. Here in the Sacrament you are to receive from the lips of Christ forgiveness of sin. It contains and brings with it God's grace and the Spirit with all His gifts, protection, shelter, and power against death and the devil and all misfortune.

71    So you have, from God, both the command and the promise of the Lord Jesus Christ. Besides this, from yourself, you have your own distress, which is around your neck. Because of your distress this command, invitation, and promise are given. This ought to move you. For Christ Himself says, "Those who are well have no need of a physician, but those who are sick" (Matthew 9:12). In other words, He means those who are weary and heavy-laden with their sins, with the fear of death, temptations of the flesh, and of the 72 devil. If, therefore, you are heavy laden and feel your weakness, then go joyfully to this Sacrament and receive refreshment, comfort, 73 and strength (Matthew 11:28). If you wait until you are rid of such burdens, so that you might come to the Sacrament pure and wor- 74 thy, you must stay away forever. In that case Christ pronounces sentence and says, "If you are pure and godly, you have no need of Me, and I, in turn, no need of you." Therefore, the only people who are called unworthy are those who neither feel their weaknesses nor wish to be considered sinners.

75    But if you say, "What, then, shall I do if I cannot feel such distress or experience hunger and thirst for the Sacrament?" Answer, "For those who are of such a mind that they do not realize their condition I know no better counsel than that they put their hand into their shirt to check whether they have flesh and blood. And if you find that you do, then go, for your good, to St. Paul's Epistle to the Galatians. Hear what sort of a fruit your flesh is:

> Now the works of the flesh are evident: sexual immorality, impurity, sensuality, idolatry, sorcery, enmity, strife, jealousy, fits of anger, rivalries, dissensions, divisions, envy, drunkenness, orgies and things like these. (Galatians 5:19–21)

Therefore, if you cannot discern this, at 76 least believe the Scriptures. They will not lie to you, and they know your flesh better than you yourself. Yes, St. Paul further concludes in Romans 7:18, "I know that nothing good dwells in me, that is, in my flesh." If St. Paul may speak this way about his flesh, we cannot assume to be better or more holy than him. But the fact that we do not feel our weakness 77 just makes things worse. It is a sign that there is a leprous flesh in us that can't feel anything. And yet, the leprosy rages and keeps spreading. As we have said, if you are quite 78 dead to all sensibility, still believe the Scriptures, which pronounce sentence upon you. In short, the less you feel your sins and infirmities, the more reason you have to go to the Sacrament to seek help and a remedy.

In the second place, look around you. See 79 whether you are also in the world, or if you do not know it, ask your neighbors about it. If you are in the world, do not think that there will be lack of sins and misery. Just begin to act as though you would be godly and cling to the Gospel. See whether no one will become your enemy, and, furthermore, do you harm, wrong, and violence, and likewise give you cause for sin and vice. If you have not experienced this, then let the Scriptures tell you about it, which everywhere give this praise and testimony about the world.

80    Besides this, you will also have the devil about you. You will not entirely tread him under foot (Luke 10:19), because our Lord Christ Himself could not entirely avoid him.
81 Now, what is the devil? Nothing other than what the Scriptures call him, a liar and a murderer (John 8:44). He is a liar, to lead the heart astray from God's Word and to blind it, so that you cannot feel your distress or come to Christ. He is a murderer, who cannot bear
82 to see you live one single hour. If you could see how many knives, darts, and arrows are every moment aimed at you (Ephesians 6:16), you would be glad to come to the Sacrament as often as possible. But there is no reason why we walk about so securely and carelessly, except that we neither think nor believe that we are in the flesh and in this wicked world or in the devil's kingdom.
83    Therefore, try this and practice it well. Be sure to examine yourself (1 Corinthians 11:28), or look about you a little, and just keep to the Scriptures. If even then you still feel nothing, you have even more misery to regret both to God and to your brother. Then take this advice and have others pray for you. Do not stop until the stone is removed from
84 your heart (Ezekiel 36:25–26). Then, indeed, the distress will not fail to become clear, and you will find that you have sunk twice as deep as any other poor sinner. You are much more in need of the Sacrament against the misery which, unfortunately, you do not see. With God's grace, you may feel your misery more and become hungrier for the Sacrament, especially since the devil doubles his force against you. He lies in wait for you without resting so that he can seize and destroy you, soul and body. You are not safe from him for one hour. How soon he can have you brought suddenly into misery and distress when you least expect it!

Let this, then, be said for encouragement, 85 not only for those of us who are old and grown, but also for the young people, who ought to be brought up in Christian doctrine and understanding. Then the Ten Commandments, the Creed, and the Lord's Prayer might be taught to our youth more easily. Then they would receive them with pleasure and seriousness, and so they would use them from their youth and get used to them. For 86 the old are now nearly past this opportunity. So these goals and others cannot be reached unless we train the people who are to come after us and succeed us in our office and work. We should do this in order that they also may bring up their children successfully, so that God's Word and the Christian Church may be preserved. Therefore, let every father 87 of a family know that it is his duty, by God's order and command, to teach these things to his children, or to have the children learn what they ought to know (Ephesians 6:4). Since the children are baptized and received into the Christian Church, they should also enjoy this communion of the Sacrament, in order that they may serve us and be useful to us. They must all certainly help us to believe, love, pray, and fight against the devil.

# An Exhortation to Confession

Luther was very concerned to purge false notions about private Confession, but he never intended the practice itself to fall into disuse. He laments that since it is no longer mandatory among Lutherans, people neglect it. In addition to private Confession to a pastor, there are two additional kinds of confession. One is confession to God alone; this is practiced throughout one's life. There is also the confession of sins one Christian makes to another. Christians are to confess their sins to one another and forgive one another openly and publicly without hesitation. Christians absolve one another of sins because of the gift of Absolution Christ has given to the Church, commanding us to absolve one another. In his exhortation Luther admonishes Christians to privately confess their sins so that they will hear the Lord's absolving Word from the lips of another human being. God's Word applied in this very personal way is another great treasure, which is so great and precious we should be willing to run more than a hundred miles to receive it. (See AC XI, XII and XXV; SA III III and VIII.) (The following text is adapted from *Luther's Large Catechsim: A Contemporary Translation with Study Questions*, tr. F. Samuel Janzow [St. Louis: CPH, 1978]; pp. 122–27.)

Here now follows an exhortation to Confession.

1   We have always urged that Confession should be voluntary and that the pope's tyranny should cease. As a result we are now rid of his coercion and set free from the intolerable load and burden that he laid upon Christendom. As we all know from experience, there had been no rule so burdensome as the one that forced everyone to go to Confession on pain of committing the most serious of mortal sins. That law also placed on consciences the heavy burden and torture of having to list all kinds of sin, so that no one was ever able to confess perfectly enough.

3   The worst was that no one taught or even knew what Confession might be or what help and comfort it could give. Instead, it was turned into sheer terror and a hellish torture that one had to go through even if one detested Confession more than anything.

4   These three oppressive things have now been lifted, and we have been granted the right to go to Confession freely, under no pressure of coercion or fear; also, we are released from the torture of needing to list all sins in detail; besides this we have the advantage of knowing how to make a beneficial use of Confession for the comfort and strengthening of our consciences.

5   Everyone is now aware of this. But unfortunately people have learned it only too well. They do as they please and apply their freedom wrongfully as if it meant that they ought not or must not go to Confession. For we readily understand whatever is to our advantage, and we find it especially easy to take in whatever is mild and gentle in the Gospel. But, as I have said, such pigs should not be allowed near the Gospel nor have any part of it. They should stay under the pope and let themselves continue to be driven and pestered to confess, to fast, and so on. For whoever does not want to believe the Gospel, live according to it, and do what a Christian ought to be doing, should not enjoy any of its benefits either. Imagine their wanting to 6 enjoy only the benefits without accepting any of the responsibilities or investing anything of themselves—what sort of thing is that! We do not want to make preaching available for that sort nor to grant permission that our freedom and its enjoyment be opened up to them. Instead, we will let the pope and the likes of him take over and force them to his will, genuine tyrant that he is. The rabble that will not obey the Gospel (2 Thessalonians 1:8) deserves nothing else than the kind of jailer who is God's devil and hangman. But 7 to others who gladly hear the Gospel we must keep on preaching, admonishing, encouraging, and coaxing them not to forget the precious and comforting treasure offered in the Gospel. Therefore, we here intend to say also a few words about Confession in order to instruct and admonish the uninformed.

8 In the first place, I have said that besides the Confession here being considered there are two other kinds, which may even more properly be called the Christians' common confession. They are (a) the confession and plea for forgiveness made to God alone and (b) the confession that is made to the neighbor alone. These two kinds of confession are included in the Lord's Prayer, in which we pray, "Forgive us our trespasses as we forgive those who trespass against us" (Matthew 6:12), and so on. In fact, the entire Lord's

9 Prayer is nothing else than such a confession. For what are our petitions other than a confession that we neither have nor do what we ought, as well as a plea for grace and a cheerful conscience? Confession of this sort should and must continue without letup as long as we live. For the Christian way essentially consists in acknowledging ourselves to be sinners and in praying for grace.

10 Similarly, the other of the two confessions, the one that every Christian makes to his neighbor, is also included in the Lord's Prayer. For here we mutually confess our guilt and our desire for forgiveness to one another (James 5:16) before coming before God and begging for His forgiveness (Matthew 5:23–24). Now, all of us are guilty of sinning against one another; therefore, we may and should publicly confess this before everyone without shrinking in one another's

11 presence. For what the proverb says is true, "If anyone is perfect, than all are." There is no one at all who fulfills his obligations toward God and his neighbor (Romans 3:10–12). Besides such universal guilt, there is also the particular guilt of the person who has provoked another to rightful anger and

12 needs to ask his pardon. So we have in the Lord's Prayer a double absolution: there we are forgiven both our offenses against God and those against our neighbor, and there we

forgive our neighbor and become reconciled to him.

13 Besides this public, daily, and necessary confession, there is also the confidential confession that is only made before a single brother. If something particular weighs upon us or troubles us, something with which we keep torturing ourselves and can find no rest, and we do not find our faith to be strong enough to cope with it, then this private form of confession gives us the opportunity of laying the matter before some brother. We may receive counsel, comfort, and strength when and however often we wish. That we should

14 do this is not included in any divine command, as are the other two kinds of confession. Rather, it is offered to everyone who may need it, as an opportunity to be used by him as his need requires. The origin and establishment of private Confession lies in the fact that Christ Himself placed His Absolution into the hands of His Christian people with the command that they should absolve one another of their sins (Ephesians 4:32). So any heart that feels its sinfulness and desires consolation has here a sure refuge when he hears God's Word and makes the discovery that God through a human being looses and absolves him from his sins.

15 So notice then, that Confession, as I have often said, consists of two parts. The first is my own work and action, when I lament my sins and desire comfort and refreshment for my soul. The other part is a work that God does when He declares me free of my sin through His Word placed in the mouth of a man. It is this splendid, noble, thing that

16 makes Confession so lovely, so comforting. It used to be that we emphasized it only as our work; all that we were then concerned about was whether our act of confession was pure and perfect in every detail. We paid no attention to the second and most necessary part of

Confession, nor did we proclaim it. We acted just as if Confession were nothing but a good work by which payment was to be made to God, so that if the confession was inadequate and not exactly correct in every detail, then the Absolution would not be valid and the sin

17 unforgiven. By this the people were driven to the point where everyone had to despair of making so pure a Confession (an obvious impossibility) and where no one could feel at ease in his conscience or have confidence in his Absolution. So they not only rendered the precious Confession useless to us but also made it a bitter burden (Matthew 23:4) causing noticeable spiritual harm and ruin.

18    In our view of Confession, therefore, we should sharply separate its two parts far from each other. We should place slight value on our part in it. But we should hold in high and great esteem God's Word in the Absolution part of Confession. We should not proceed as if we intended to perform and offer Him a splendid work, but simply to accept and receive something from Him. You dare not come saying how good or how bad you are.

19 If you are a Christian, I in any case, know well enough that you are. If you are not, I know that even better. But what you must see to is that you lament your problem and that you let yourself be helped to acquire a cheerful heart and conscience.

20    Moreover, no one may now pressure you with commandments. Rather, what we say is this: Whoever is a Christian or would like to be one is here faithfully advised to go and get the precious treasure. If you are no Christian and do not desire such comfort, we shall leave it to another to use force on

21 you. By eliminating all need for the pope's tyranny, command, and coercion, we cancel them with a single sweep. As I have said, we teach that whoever does not go to Confession willingly and for the sake of obtaining

the Absolution, he may as well forget about it. Yes, and whoever goes around relying on the purity of his act of making confession, let him stay away.  Nevertheless, we strongly 22 urge you by all means to make confession of your need, not with the intention of doing a worthy work by confessing but in order to hear what God has arranged for you to be told. What I am saying is that you are to concentrate on the Word, on the Absolution, to regard it as a great and precious and magnificently splendid treasure, and to accept it with all praise and thanksgiving to God.

If this were explained in detail and if the 23 need that ought to move and lead us to make confession were pointed out, then one would need little urging or coercion. For everyone's own conscience would so drive and disturb him that he would be glad to do what a poor and miserable beggar does when he hears that a rich gift of money or clothing is being handed out at a certain place. So as not to miss it, he would run there as fast as he can and would need no bailiff to beat and drive him on. Now, suppose that in place of the in- 24 vitation one were to substitute a command to the effect that all beggars should run to that place but would not say why nor mention what they should look for and receive there. What else would the beggar do but make the trip with distaste, without thinking of going to get a gift but simply of letting people see what a poor, miserable beggar he is? This would bring him little joy and comfort but only greater resentment against the command that was issued.

In just this way the pope's preachers kept 25 silent in the past about the splendid gift and inexpressible treasure to be had through Confession. All they did was to drive people in crowds to Confession, with no further aim than to let them see what impure, dirty people they were. Who could go willingly to Confession under such circumstances? We, however, do not say that people should look at you to see how filthy you are, using you as a mirror to preen themselves. Rather, we give this counsel: If you are poor and miserable, then go to Confession and make use of its healing medicine. He who feels his misery and need will no doubt develop such a longing for it that he will run toward it with joy. But those who pay no attention to it and do not come of their own accord, we let them go their way. Let them be sure of this, however, that we do not regard them as Christians.

So we teach what a splendid, precious, and comforting thing Confession is. Furthermore, we strongly urge people not to despise a blessing that in view of our great need is so priceless. Now, if you are a Christian, then you do not need either my pressuring or the pope's orders, but you will undoubtedly compel yourself to come to Confession and will beg me for a share in it. However, if you want to despise it and proudly continue without Confession, then we must draw the conclusion that you are no Christian and should not enjoy the Sacrament either. For you despise what no Christian should despise. In that way you make it so that you cannot have forgiveness of your sins. This is a sure sign that you also despise the Gospel.

To sum it up, we want to have nothing to do with coercion. However, if someone does not listen to or follow our preaching and its warning, we will have nothing to do with him (1 Corinthians 5:11), nor may he have any share in the Gospel. If you were a Christian, then you ought to be happy to run more than a hundred miles to Confession and not let yourself be urged to come. You should rather come and compel us to give you the opportunity. For in this matter the compulsion must be the other way around: we must act under orders, you must come into freedom. We pressure no one, but we let ourselves be pressured, just as we let people compel us to preach to administer the Sacrament.

When I urge you to go to Confession, I am doing nothing else than urging you to be a Christian. If I have brought you to the point of being a Christian, I have thereby also brought you to Confession. For those who really desire to be true Christians, to be rid of their sins, and to have a cheerful conscience already possess the true hunger and thirst. They reach for the bread, just as Psalm 42:1 says of a hunted deer, burning in the heat with thirst, "As a deer pants for flowing streams, so pants my soul for You, O God." In other words, as a deer with anxious and trembling eagerness strains toward a fresh, flowing stream, so I yearn anxiously and tremblingly for God's Word, Absolution, the Sacrament, and so forth. See, that would be teaching right about Confession, and people could be given such a desire and love for it that they would come and run after us for it, more than we would like. Let the papists plague and torment themselves and others who pass up the treasure and exclude themselves from it. Let us, however, lift our hands in praise and thanksgiving to God (1 Timothy 2:8) for having graciously brought us to this our understanding of Confession.

# THE FORMULA OF CONCORD

## FIRST PART

Summary Content (Epitome)

of the
Articles in Controversy
among the theologians of the Augsburg Confession, set
forth and reconciled in a Christian way, according to the
direction of God's Word, in the following summary.

Christ on the Cross with Angels

Albrecht Dürer dramatically shows that the blood Christ shed on the cross and its saving benefits are given to us in the Sacrament of the Altar. Without the shedding of blood, there is no forgiveness of sins.

# INTRODUCTION TO THE FORMULA OF CONCORD

*I will rather lose my head and suffer Wittenberg to be battered down than submit to a demand that violates my conscience.*

—Elector John Frederick the Magnanimous

Following Luther's death in 1546, it seemed that the shining light of the Gospel would be snuffed out. Threats from without, and controversies within, endangered the Lutheran Church. The survival of Lutheranism was a result of God's gracious work through brave laypeople and pastors who refused to compromise the teachings of God's Word. The story from 1546 until 1580 (when the Book of Concord was published) is one of courage and cowardice, weakness and strength. All Christians and, most important, all who bear the name *Lutheran,* need to learn about this struggle for the truth.

The controversy that raged for thirty-five years concluded with thousands of lay leaders, pastors, and theologians agreeing to live in harmony with one another on the basis of a common confession of the faith, the Lutheran Confessions, as contained in the Book of Concord of 1580.

Only four months after Luther's death (February 18, 1546), the pope and the Holy Roman Emperor, Charles V, entered into a secret agreement to crush the Reformation and force the Lutherans back under the pope's authority (June 26, 1546). Their agreement stated:

> In the name of God and with the help and assistance of his Papal Holiness, his Imperial Majesty should prepare himself for war, and equip himself with soldiers and everything pertaining to warfare against those who objected to the Council, against the Smalcald League, and against all who were addicted to the false belief and error in Germany, and that he do so with all his power and might, in order to bring them back to the old faith and to the obedience of the Holy See. (Bente, p. 219)

The Emperor tried to keep the situation secret, but the pope issued a public decree on July 4, 1546. It stated:

> It has always been our concern how to root out the weeds of godless doctrines which the heretics have sowed throughout Germany. . . . Now it has come to pass that, by the inspiration of the Holy Ghost, our dearest son in Christ, Charles, the Roman Emperor, has decided to employ the sword against these enemies of God. And for the protection of religion we intend to promote this pious enterprise with all our own and the Roman Church's possessions. Accordingly, we admonish all Christians to assist in this war with their prayers to God and their alms, in order that the godless heresy may be rooted out and the dissension removed . . . To each and all who do these things we grant the most complete indulgence and remission of all their sins. (Bente, 219)

John Frederick the Magnanimous (1503–54)

The scar from the wound that John Frederick suffered in the Battle of Mühlberg (1547) is dramatically visible in this period woodcut. He was captured and lost his title and holdings. He was repeatedly threatened with death if he would not recant his Lutheran confession. He steadfastly refused to recant.

The fate of the Gospel hung in the balance. Powerful forces were moving to crush the Lutherans. Shortly after the emperor and the pope had reached an agreement on how best to deal with the Lutheran problem, the Smalcaldic War broke out in Germany. The military power of the emperor and pope proved too much for the Lutheran princes. The threat of war caused some who had previously confessed their allegiance to the Augsburg Confession to remain neutral or, even worse, to betray their fellow Lutherans. Maurice, Duke of Saxony, actually joined the emperor. On April 24, 1547, the armies of the Smalcaldic League were crushed at the battle of Mühlberg.

The elector of Saxony, John Frederick the Magnanimous, was taken prisoner and sentenced to death. He received the news of his death sentence while playing a game of chess with his fellow prisoner, Duke Ernest of Lüneburg. John Frederick took the news with remarkable courage and peace. He did not believe the emperor would execute him, but responded by saying that if he was to be killed he wanted time to put his affairs in order and send a final message to his wife and children. Then he looked at Ernest and said, "Let us continue the game; it is your move."

One Lutheran territory after another fell to the Emperor. Torgau was taken and the imperial armies marched on Wittenberg. It surrendered without a fight on May 19, 1547. Emperor Charles himself entered the Castle Church in Wittenberg, where Martin Luther was buried. As he stood at Luther's grave, his soldiers urged him to exhume the remains of the heretic Luther and burn them. Charles said simply, "I make war on the living, not on the dead." This was truly a remarkable reaction, considering how long Charles had been struggling with the Lutheran Reformation. In 1521 he had heard Luther utter the famous words "I cannot and will not recant." Twenty-six years later Charles's military defeat of Lutheran territories was complete.

## The Augsburg Interim

Though Charles had won a military victory, he realized that only the mass slaughter of hundreds of thousands of people could eliminate Lutheranism. He chose instead to pursue political and ecclesiastical compromises. Some Lutherans were willing to go along with his plan. The emperor issued a series of commands on May 15, 1548, that became known as the Augsburg Interim. He ordered all Lutheran rulers and ministers to obey his orders and do nothing to oppose them. They were not to teach, preach, or write against the Augsburg Interim in any way. It was called an "Interim" because the document was intended to govern Church matters until all things could be settled formally at a general Church council.

The Interim allowed the Lutheran clergy to marry and to celebrate the Lord's Supper by giving the people both the consecrated bread and wine, but it demanded that they immediately restore a number of specifically Roman ceremonies and customs. It demanded that they acknowledge the pope to be the head of the Church by divine right and to receive again the authority of the Roman bishops. It insisted that they again receive Roman doctrines and practices, such as transubstantiation and the seven sacraments. It denied or omitted the doctrine of justification by grace through faith alone. Ironically, the pope was not satisfied even with this. He demanded total rejection of everything Lutheran, which made many Lutheran rulers and ministers realize that they had nothing to expect but total persecution if they submitted to the Augsburg Interim.

Tragically, Philip Melanchthon was willing to compromise with Rome for the sake of peace. His courage failed him and he soon became the leader of a group of Lutherans known as Philippists, who looked for ways to compromise with Rome. They were willing to surrender a number of key points of biblical teaching so that they might save themselves. It was clear, though, that the future held nothing but further compromise. It looked as though all was lost and Rome would eventually demand that all Lutherans renounce their faith and return again to the false and damning doctrine of Rome. Melanchthon and his followers were even willing to accept the Augsburg Interim's compromise of the doctrine of justification, allowing it to state that we are not saved by grace through faith alone, but that justification is in part based on a person's renewal and life. This teaching was a total denial of everything Martin Luther had struggled and worked so hard for!

Throughout Germany, Charles and his Italian and Spanish troops enforced the Augsburg Interim brutally. Cities that did not accept it were deprived of their liberties. Constance fell after a courageous defense and was annexed to Austria. Magdeburg resisted the armies of Charles the longest and was outlawed three times. It was never conquered. Its citizens sent their response to Charles: "We are saved neither by an Interim nor by an Exterim, but by the Word of God alone" (Bente, p. 222). Pastors who refused to follow the regulations of the Augsburg Interim were removed from office and banished; some were imprisoned and some were even executed. In Swabia and along the Rhine River, some four hundred pastors went to prison rather than agree to the Interim. They were exiled, and some of their families were killed or died as a result. Jacob Sturm of Augsburg presented a list of grievances to the local Roman bishop, who responded, "If necessary, one might proceed against heretics also with fire." Sturm responded, "Indeed, you may kill people by fire, but even in this way you cannot force their faith" (Bente, p. 222–23). Some preachers left for England. But even still, the Interim was not accepted as widely as the emperor and pope had hoped.

In Northern Germany, the stronghold of Lutheranism, territories such as Saxony fiercely opposed the Interim. Many cities rejected it entirely. Elector Joachim of Brandenburg gathered three hundred pastors to sign the Augsburg Interim. One old pastor, named Leutinger, standing in front of the author of the Interim, Agricola, said, "I love Agricola, and more than him I love my Elector; but my Lord Jesus Christ I love most" (Bente, 223). Then he took the Augsburg Interim document that he had been told to sign and threw it into flames of the fireplace. A layman, Margrave Hans of Küstrin, threw the pen away that he was handed for the purpose of signing the Interim, saying, "I shall never adopt this poisonous concoction, nor submit to any council. Rather sword than pen; blood rather than ink!" (Bente, 223). In the region of Mansfeld, Luther's home territory, the leaders there told the emperor that if he

## Emperor Charles V, 1547

In 1547, Charles defeated the Lutheran Smalcaldic League. The pope urged him to punish Lutherans harshly wherever he found them, even to the point of killing them. Charles knew there was such widespread support he would not be able to carry out the pope's wishes entirely. Instead, Charles opted for diplomatic efforts to turn Lutheranism toward Roman Catholicism. This strategy failed after a number of years of bitter controversy. Charles ended his years a broken man, abdicating his throne and going to live in a monastery in Spain. Ironically, when Charles entered Wittenberg with his conquering army, he was urged to exhume the remains of Martin Luther, buried in the Castle Church. It is reported that he said, "I make war on the living, not on the dead," and refused to allow Luther's remains to be disturbed.

tried to force them to adopt the Augsburg Interim, the preachers would all leave and the people would revolt and kill their leaders.

One of the greatest heroes of this time was the ruler of Saxony, Elector John Frederick the Magnanimous. In spite of the great pressure on him, he refused to compromise his faith. He quietly, but firmly, refused to accept the Interim for his land. The emperor offered to lift the sentence of death on John Frederick, but again he refused. The Elector said, "I will rather lose my head and suffer Wittenberg to be battered down than submit to a demand that violates my conscience" (Bente, 224). Charles V realized the precarious political situation he was in. He may have defeated the armies of the Lutheran princes on the battlefield, but he could not force the people or the princes to renounce their faith. He realized he could not simply kill entire populations.

Charles kept Elector John Frederick of Saxony in prison, trying to pressure him to change his mind. Repeatedly Charles threatened and appealed to John Frederick. Finally, John Frederick wrote Charles:

> I cannot refrain from informing Your Majesty that since the days of my youth I have been instructed and taught by the servants of God's Word. By diligently searching the prophetic and apostolic Scriptures I have also learned to know, and (this I testify as in the sight of God) unswervingly to adhere in my con-

## Tilemann Hesshusius (1527–88)

A pugnacious advocate and defender of genuine Lutheranism after Luther's death. He opposed the Crypto-Calvinists in Wittenberg and elsewhere, suffered exile, and relentlessly defended the biblical doctrine of Christ's bodily presence in the Lord's Supper. For example, when he was ordered to serve Holy Communion with a Calvinist minister in Heidelberg, Hesshusius refused and tried to wrestle the chalice away from the man. In Magdeburg he was deposed (1562) for criticizing false doctrine. Elector Augustus I exiled him from Jena (1573) for tirelessly attacking the false doctrine of the Crypto-Calvinists at Wittenberg University. (This was before Augustus I realized the deception by the Wittenberg faculty.) Ironically, after all his efforts, Hesshusius refused to sign the Formula of Concord and deterred the people of the territory of Brunswick from signing it because he wanted false teachers mentioned by name. He also criticized Gnesio-Lutherans, such as Flacius, for their error concerning original sin.

## Sibylla (1512–54)

The courageous and faithful wife of John Frederick the Magnanimous. After her husband's defeat (1547), she was instrumental in organizing the defense of Wittenberg. Charles V exiled Sibylla and her sons (the Lords Regent of Electoral Saxony) in Weimar, where John Frederick was imprisoned. They were not permitted to stay with him, and at various times they were deprived of any contact with him. Charles V pressured Sibylla by threatening her husband's life and the lives of her sons, attempting to force her to support the Interim and compromise her Lutheran confession. Sibylla encouraged her sons to be true to Lutheranism. She chose separation from her home and husband, rather than compromise her faith.

science to this, that the articles composing the Augsburg Confession, and whatever is connected therewith, are the correct, true, Christian, pure doctrine, confirmed by, and founded in, the writings of the holy prophets and apostles, and of the teachers who followed in their footsteps, in such a manner that no substantial objection can be raised against it. . . . Since now in my conscience I am firmly persuaded of this, I owe this gratefulness and obedience to God, who has shown me such unspeakable grace, that, as I desire to obtain eternal salvation and escape eternal damnation, I do not fall away from the truth of His almighty will which His Word has revealed to me, and which I know to be the truth. For such is the comforting and also the terrible word of God: "Whosoever therefore shall confess Me before men, him will I confess also before My Father which is in heaven. But whosoever shall deny Me before men, him will I also deny before My Father which is in heaven" [Matthew 10:32–33]. If I should acknowledge and adopt the Interim as Christian and godly, I would have to condemn and deny against my own conscience, knowingly and maliciously, the Augsburg Confession, and whatever I have heretofore held and believed concerning the Gospel of Christ and approve with my mouth what I regard in my heart and conscience as altogether contrary to the holy and divine Scriptures. This, O my God in heaven, would indeed be misusing and cruelly blaspheming Thy holy name, . . . for which I would have to pay all too dearly with my soul. For this is truly the sin against the Holy Ghost concerning which Christ says that it shall never be forgiven, neither in this nor in the world to come, *i.e.*, in eternity. (Bente, 224–25)

In response to this letter, Charles ordered that they remove the Bible and Luther's writings from John Frederick's room. John Frederick responded that they were able indeed to deprive him of his books, but could never tear out of his heart what he had learned from them. When the faithful Lutheran pastors of Augsburg were banished because they refused to use the Augsburg Interim, Elector John Frederick told them, "Though the Emperor has banished you from the realm, he has not banished you from heaven. Surely, God will find some other country where you may preach His Word" (Bente, 225).

## Melanchthon's Failure and the Leipzig Interim

In a tragic irony of history, just at the moment when strong leadership was needed most from Philip Melanchthon, he failed to provide it. Lutherans throughout Germany looked to Melanchthon to renounce the Augsburg Interim boldly and publicly, but he did not. Instead, he and others worked on a compromise document, which became known as the Leipzig Interim. (Flacius called it an "Interim" to identify it with the Augsburg Interim.)

The purpose of the Leipzig Interim was to craft a document that would allow Lutherans to avoid the demands of the Augsburg Interim and, supposedly, retain the doctrine of justification by grace, through faith alone, while yielding in other matters. Melanchthon was willing to receive back a number of Roman rituals and practices, thinking that it would be possible to compromise on things external to the Gospel. However, the Leipzig Interim was a document that sacrificed Lutheran doctrine, both in content and in practice. There was a purposeful ambiguity about the Leipzig Interim, designed to let Lutherans and Romanists interpret matters in their own way. The doctrine of justification through faith alone was nowhere mentioned in the Leipzig Interim. The Roman idea that a person is saved by an infusion of grace was allowed. Faith was said to require works for salvation. The pope was spoken of no longer as antichrist. Pastors who still sang Luther's hymn "Lord, Keep Us Steadfast in Your Word" were banished in some territories. (The original words to that hymn include a prayer that God would curb murderous Turks and Papists.)

As a result of the Leipzig Interim there arose great opposition from Lutherans known as "Gnesio-Lutherans." (*Gnesio* means "genuine.") They opposed the Leipzig Interim and were forced openly to oppose Philip Melanchthon, who championed it.

Magdeburg became the center of Gnesio-Lutheranism and was in a state of theological warfare with Melanchthon and the Wittenberg theologians. Even the Reformed theologian John Calvin wrote Melanchthon, on June 18, 1550, about "externals" (adiaphora). He pleaded for Melanchthon to recognize that "externals" did matter. Calvin said,

> You extend the adiaphora [principle of indifferent things] too far. Some of them plainly conflict with the Word of God. . . . By yielding but a little, you alone have caused more lamentations and complaints than a hundred ordinary men by open apostasy. (Bente, 234)

There began an extended period of controversy and turmoil across the Lutheran territories in Germany. From 1548 until 1574 there was high tension. Wittenberg became a hotbed and seat of Philippist theology and practice, but was eventually overtaken by Calvinists. Through very careful strategy they had persuaded Elector Augustus I that they were the rightful heirs of Luther and Melanchthon. After Melanchthon's death in 1560, the controversy continued. Pastors who wanted to remain faithful to Luther's vision for the Church suffered banishment and untold hardship.

## Maurice and the Religious Peace of Augsburg

Eventually the Leipzig Interim proved to be even a political failure. Elector Maurice, who had prevailed upon Melanchthon and his allies to draft the Leipzig Interim, soon recognized that it had not resulted in peace. Instead, it caused even more controversy and division throughout Germany. People viewed Elector Maurice as a "Judas" and betrayer of faithful leaders like Elector John Frederick. Maurice realized that it was politically more expedient for him to be viewed as a champion of Lutheranism than as a traitor. And so he made secret plans to drive the emperor and his troops out of Augsburg. This is precisely what happened on April 5, 1552. Emperor Charles V was forced to flee from Augsburg, and even the Roman theologians meeting at Trent were so afraid, they interrupted their meetings and fled to their homes.

As a result of Maurice's victory over Charles, the treaties of Passau (August 2, 1552) and Augsburg (1555) were signed. These treaties guaranteed religious liberty to the Lutherans and other Protestants. It placed Lutherans and Roman Catholics on an equal footing in the empire and set in place this principle: He who rules, his the religion (*Cuius regio, eius religio*). In other words, every prince had the right to control religion in his particular territory. Those who chose not to conform would be permitted to leave peacefully for a friendlier territory. This political compromise ended the open warfare and conflict among rulers, but did not end the theological

Duke Maurice of Saxony (1521–53)

Maurice joined forces with Charles V and betrayed his cousin, John Frederick, resulting in his defeat and capture at the battle of Mühlberg in 1547. In return, Charles V stripped John Frederick of his position as Elector and gave it to Maurice, who attempted to impose the Augsburg Interim on his territories. When that didn't work, Maurice forced through the preparation of another document, which was called the "Leipzig Interim" by the genuine Lutherans. This led to the Adiaphoristic Controversy, which was resolved by Article X of the Formula of Concord. Maurice later turned on Charles V and defeated his forces in 1552, resulting, ironically, in an agreement that gave relative freedom of religion in many parts of Germany. After Maurice was killed in battle (1553), Augustus I of Saxony became Elector. Augustus largely funded the publication of the Book of Concord in 1580.

controversies that developed as a result of the compromises of the Augsburg and Leipzig Interims. The Church was not unified in doctrine. (See "Controversies and the Formula of Concord," p. 521.)

The Philippist theologians of Electoral Saxony, once the stronghold of Luther's reforms, took the lead in propagating this compromising and vacillating theology. They were located at the Universities of Wittenberg and Leipzig. The Gnesio-Lutherans were centered in Ducal Saxony. They included Amsdorf, Flacius, Wigand, Gallus, Judex, Mörlin and Tilemann Hesshusius, Timan, and Westphal. Although later some of them would fall into error in their zeal to defend the truth, they stood steadfast against the compromising theology of the Philippists. The Universities of Magdeburg and Jena were their strongholds. (The sons of John Frederick had founded the University of Jena in 1547.) From Jena the leader of the Gnesio-Lutherans—Matthias Flacius—conducted a long and hard fight to preserve genuine Lutheranism.

## The Development of the Formula of Concord

Between the Philippists on the one side and the Gnesio-Lutherans on the other, there soon arose a third group who, although not involved in the heavy controversies during this time, came to play a key role in working to resolve the controversies. They would eventually prepare the Formula of Concord. Through their efforts, true peace was restored throughout the Lutheran churches in Germany. Prominent leaders among them were Brentz, Andreae, Selnecker, Chytraeus, and chiefly Martin Chemnitz (1522–86). Chemnitz's work and leadership led him to be called "the second Martin." So important was Martin Chemnitz's role in retaining authentic Lutheranism that there soon was coined the expression "If the second Martin had not come, the first Martin would not have stood."

Chemnitz and his colleagues built on the theological strengths of Gnesio-Lutheranism, clearly rejecting the theological agenda of the Philippists. But they also worked hard to move the theological discussions away from personality conflicts. They focused on the issues involved. They identified where arguing for the sake of arguing was going on and avoided falling into extreme positions, one way or the other. They identified where theological errors had been made both by Philippists and Gnesio-Lutherans. They clearly rejected any form of compromise of the truth, doctrinal indifference, and union of truth with error.

The first step toward the Formula of Concord was taken in 1573 by Jacob Andreae, who published six sermons that provided a careful analysis of the issues in controversy at the time. Andreae was the chancellor of the University of Tübingen. He proposed biblical solutions to the controversies. The popularity of his sermons helped convince a number of other Lutheran theologians that it was time to resolve the controversies wracking the Church. Andreae was encouraged to take six of his sermons and format them into a more formal confession of faith. The result of his work was the Swabian Concord of 1574.

Nicholas von Amsdorf (1483–1565)

Nicholas von Amsdorf was Luther's lifelong friend and ally. At the request of Elector John Frederick, Luther consecrated Amsdorf as the first Lutheran bishop in the Naumburg region. Amsdorf warned Luther that after his death, Melanchthon could not be counted on to remain strong. His warning tragically proved true. Amsdorf provided decisive leadership by opposing the Interim after Luther's death. He mentored and supported Matthias Flacius. At an important gathering called by the sons of John Frederick to consider how they would respond to the Interim while their father was in captivity, Amsdorf stood up and said, "We Lutherans remain with our teaching and faith forever. This I know for certain because the Word of the Lord endures forever! To Rome, Trier, Cologne, I say, here you will find only defiance. Go ahead, play your pipes, we will dance" (Oliver K. Olson, *Matthias Flacius and the Survival of Luther's Reform* [Wiesbaden: Harrassowitz Verlag, 2002], 94). He also said, "I will persevere in the Augsburg Confession, and putting everything else behind, look forward alone to being able to participate in eternal joy after this wretched, sorry, and troubled life." He lived to the unusually old age of 82. He was buried in the chancel of St. George Church, Eisenach, in the shadow of the Wartburg Castle.

## Engraving of Rulers Signing the Book of Concord

The 1703 printing of the Book of Concord was one of the first to include historical and theological introductions. Leipzig master engraver C. F. Boetius prepared this intricate engraving. Top left: Elector Augustus I of Saxony, the man responsible for publishing the Book of Concord in 1580. Top right: Christian II of Saxony, who ruled 1591–1611; he was ruler when the Book of Concord was reprinted in 1602. Center: The Saxon electors' coat of arms. Above is the Lutheran motto, "The Word of the Lord endures forever" (Latin). Two figures hold the banner. The one holding arrows symbolizes government's duty to wage war when necessary. The other figure holds a dove's feather, symbolizing the peace government is to protect. God's Hebrew name *YHWH* appears in a shining triangle, symbolizing the Holy Trinity. Right background: Martin Chemnitz (right) and Jacob Andreae (left) watch Elector Augustus I sign the Book of Concord. Foreground: Heinrich of Albertine Saxony (who ruled 1539–41) subscribing to the Confessions. To his left stands John the Steadfast of Ernestine Saxony, who ruled 1525–32. (The Albertine line of rulers took over the Ernestine territory in Wittenberg in 1547.) John the Steadfast is holding a book that says, "The Augsburg Confession, June 25, 1530, Taught Alone." At right, an angel holds a cross with the words "through faith alone" (German). Martin Luther stands on the right watching. He holds the New Testament and points to an open book with Bible references: 2 Chronicles 29:1–5, 10–11, 30 speaks about faithful King Hezekiah, the service of faithful priests, and Hezekiah's order that priests must praise and worship Yahweh alone; also 2 Chronicles 31:1–2, 20–21, to which Luther is pointing, describes Israel destroying idols and reinstituting true worship of God and good king Hezekiah, who did what was right. Front of desk: The various writings contained in the Book of Concord. The Formula of Concord is open to the words "Augustus, Elector of Saxony, authorized printing." It rests on Luther's Small Catechism. The three books to the right of the Formula are the Ecumenical Creeds, the Apology, and the Augsburg Confession. On the shelf below are Luther's Large Catechism, the Saxon Visitation Articles, and the Smalcald Articles. An altar in the right foreground has an open Bible ("The Entire Holy Scripture"), a chalice, a paten holding communion hosts, and a burning candle next to a crucifix. This engraving is typical of the illustrations used at that time, rich with meaning and true confession.

Martin Chemnitz was one of the most important figures in the development of the Formula of Concord. He worked tirelessly to achieve doctrinal harmony among as many laypeople, pastors, and theologians as possible. He was not given to a brusque and abrasive personality, as were certain leaders among the Gnesio-Lutherans. He was more diplomatic. As a young man he attended the aging Martin Luther's lectures on Genesis in Wittenberg. Melanchthon was also one of his beloved teachers. Chemnitz carefully studied Holy Scripture. He read virtually every book available written by the Early Church Fathers. He eventually became the leading pastor in the territory of Brunswick. His title was "superintendent" of the ministerial consistory of the territory. He was passionate about carefully teaching the pastors in his territory how to be good pastoral theologians. Chemnitz was appointed by his sovereign, Duke Julius of Brunswick, to help revise and rewrite Andreae's Swabian Concord. The new document was known as the Swabian-Saxon Concord of 1575. In the following years several theologians from Southern Germany, including Lucas Osiander and Balthasar Bidenbach, prepared their own document, proposing resolutions to the various theological controversies. It was known as the Maulbronn Formula.

In May of 1576 six theologians from various regions in Germany were called together by Elector Augustus for a theological convention. They were Jacob Andreae, Nicholas Selnecker, Andrew Musculus, Christopher Cornerus, David Chytraeus, and Martin Chemnitz. (See the Preface to the Book of Concord, pp. 29–38.) They met in the city of Torgau at the Hartenfels Castle. They worked to combine the Swabian-Saxon Concord and the Maulbronn Formula into a single document, which was known as the Torgau Book. Elector Augustus asked Jacob Andreae to provide a short summary of this document, which became known as the Epitome of the Formula of

Bergen Abby

Bergen Cloister at Magdeburg as it appeared in 1577;
site of the final drafting of the Formula of Concord

Martin Chemnitz (1522–86)

Jacob Andreae (1528–90)

David Chytraeus (1531–1600)

Concord. They circulated their document to a number of theologians throughout various Lutheran territories. Chemnitz, Selnecker, and Andreae came together at a former monastery, a cloister in the city of Bergen near the town of Magdeburg. Here they considered carefully the suggestions and comments received from reviewers. On May 28, 1577, they were joined by their other three colleagues and they signed the final version of the Formula of Concord. It was submitted to Elector Augustus, who accepted it. From 1577 to 1580 Andreae, and particularly Martin Chemnitz, worked very hard through patient persuasion and conversation to convince many laypeople, pastors, and theologians to accept the Formula of Concord. They prepared an introduction to the Formula of Concord and gathered together other key Lutheran statements of faith. Chemnitz worked tirelessly to advance the cause of concord— harmony and peace— in the Church, based on common confession of the truth of God's Word.

## Publication and Circulation of the Book of Concord

Work on the first printing of the official German edition of the Book of Concord began with Jacob Andreae in 1578. But the official publication date was not until June 25, 1580, in Dresden, fifty years to the day that the Augsburg Confession had been read to Charles V. Nicholas Selnecker was responsible for the publication of a Latin edition of the Book of Concord in 1580. This text was revised at a convention in Qüdlinburg (December, 1582; Martin Chemnitz was involved in this effort). The revised edition of the Book of Concord in Latin was published at Leipzig in 1584.

June 25, 1580, therefore, is as important a day for Lutherans as is October 31, 1517, the date Luther posted the Ninety-five Theses. As a result of the hard work of Chemnitz and others, over eight thousand laypeople, pastors, and theologians had signed their names to the Book of Concord. Throughout Germany, and eventually in lands throughout the world, the Book of Concord united people around the true teachings of God's Holy Word.

## A Most Useful Book

The Lutheran Reformation was compromised when Philip Melanchthon—one of Luther's closest allies—refuted key truths of the Scriptures for the sake of outward peace with Rome and the Reformed theologians. The work of the second-generation Lutherans, led by Martin Chemnitz, returned the Lutheran Church to the solid biblical foundation of Luther's important teachings. Their efforts blocked the spread of the Roman Catholic Counter-Reformation (1545–1648) and rescued Protestant congregations throughout Europe from extermination. Following the publication of the Book of Concord in 1580, the Lutheran Church was blessed with a period of remarkable growth and development and a full flowering of uniquely Lutheran schools and culture (c. 1580–1730). In fact, until 1832, all ministers in the territory of Saxony were required to subscribe to the Book of Concord as well as the Saxon Visitation Articles of 1592 (pp. 676–79). The peace and stability brought by the Book of Concord allowed Lutherans to begin mission work in North America, Ethiopia, India, and other places.

Hans Sachs (1494–1576)

Hans Sachs was a poet, musician, and playwright who lived and worked in Nürnberg. He was also a shoemaker and guild master. He wrote more than four thousand songs and over two thousand fables, morality plays, comedies, and ballads. He was an ardent Lutheran, and wrote the poem "The Nightingale of Wittenberg" in Luther's honor. A number of his tunes were used for Lutheran hymns. He is an example of the faithful laity who supported and spread Lutheranism in the sixteenth century.

## TIMELINE

| | |
|---|---|
| 1545 | Council of Trent's first session begins |
| 1546 | Luther dies at Eisleben, February 18 Pope Paul III and Charles V conspire to end Reformation by force, June 26 |
| 1547 | Battle of Mühlberg, Smalcaldic League defeated, April 24 |
| 1548 | Augsburg Interim proclaimed, May 15 |
| 1552 | Maurice attacks, drives Charles V out of Augsburg, April 5 Luther's wife, Katharina von Bora, dies, December 20 |
| 1555 | Peace of Augsburg allows territorial rulers to decide religion for their subjects |
| 1560 | Philip Melanchthon dies, April 19 |
| 1563 | Council of Trent ends, settling Roman doctrine and establishing Roman Catholic Church |
| 1572 | St. Bartholomew's Day Massacre of Protestant Huguenots in France, August 24–26 |
| 1573 | Jacob Andreae preaches (and then publishes) six sermons on controversies |
| 1574 | The Swabian Concord |
| 1576 | The Torgau Book published; Formula of Concord's "Epitome" summarized |
| 1577 | Formula of Concord's "Solid Declaration" completed |
| 1580 | Book of Concord first published in Dresden on the fiftieth anniversary of the presentation of the Augsburg Confession, June 25; signing begins Latin edition prepared by Selnecker |
| 1584 | Leipzig edition of the Book of Concord published (revised Latin) |
| 1592 | Saxon Visitation Articles |

## OUTLINE

Generally, the articles include the following elements: (a) status of the controversy; (b) affirmative statements of biblical teaching; and (c) negative statements against false teaching.

---

The Summary Content, Rule, and Norm

I. Original Sin

II. Free Will, or Human Powers

III. The Righteousness of Faith before God

IV. Good Works

V. The Law and the Gospel

VI. The Third Use of God's Law

VII. The Holy Supper of Christ

VIII. The Person of Christ

IX. The Descent of Christ to Hell

X. Church Practices

XI. God's Eternal Foreknowledge and Election

XII. Other Factions and Sects

# THE SUMMARY CONTENT, RULE, AND NORM

## ACCORDING TO WHICH ALL TEACHINGS SHOULD BE JUDGED AND THE ERRONEOUS TEACHINGS THAT HAVE OCCURRED SHOULD BE DECIDED AND EXPLAINED IN A CHRISTIAN WAY

What is the sole source of doctrine in the Church? The Bible, and the Bible alone. God's Word is the pure fountain and source of God's truth. Church creeds and confessions, however, function as witnesses to that truth. As such, they are accepted standards by which we can discern between true and false teaching. Churches can, do, and should insist that called pastors and other Church workers pledge themselves unconditionally to the Church's confession. In this way, the Church's confession safeguards the pure teaching of God's Word. Does this contradict the statement that the Bible alone is the source and norm of doctrine? No. Confessions are not the *source* of doctrine, but are a *standard* or *norm* by which preaching and teaching are evaluated, because they are based on God's Word. This may be a fine nuance, but it is an important one. Today, in authentically Lutheran churches, pastors and other church workers pledge to faithfully teach and practice according to the Scriptures and the Lutheran Confessions, just as they have done for nearly five hundred years.

---

1    1. We believe, teach, and confess that the only rule and norm according to which all teachings, together with all teachers, should be evaluated and judged (2 Timothy 3:15–17) are the prophetic and apostolic Scriptures of the Old and New Testament alone. For it is written in Psalm 119:105, "Your word is a lamp to my feet and a light to my path." St. Paul has written, "even if we or an angel from heaven should preach to you a gospel contrary to the one we preached to you, let him be accursed" (Galatians 1:8).

However, other writings by ancient or   2 modern teachers—no matter whose name they bear—must not be regarded as equal to the Holy Scriptures. All of them are subject to the Scriptures (1 Corinthians 14:32). Other writings should not be received in any other way or as anything more than witnesses that testify about how this pure doctrine of the prophets and apostles was preserved after the time of the apostles, and at what places.

2. Right after the time of the apostles, and   3 even while they were still living, false teachers and heretics arose (Titus 3:9–10). Therefore, *symbols* (i.e., brief, concise confessions) were written against the heretics in the Early Church. These symbols were regarded as the unanimous, universal Christian faith and confession of the orthodox and true Church. They are *the Apostles' Creed, the Nicene Creed*, and *the Athanasian Creed*. We pledge ourselves to these symbols, and in this way we reject all heresies and teachings that have been introduced into God's Church against them.

3. However, schisms in matters of faith   4 have also happened in our time. Therefore, we regard as the unanimous consensus and declaration of our Christian faith and confession—especially against the papacy and its false worship, idolatry, superstition, and

against other sects—the first, *unaltered Augsburg Confession*. It is the symbol of our time, and it was delivered to the Emperor, Charles V, at Augsburg in the year 1530 in the great Diet. We hold to this confession along with its *Apology* and the *Articles* composed at *Smalcald* in the year 1537, which the chief theologians signed at that time.

5 Such matters also concern the laity and the salvation of their souls. Therefore, we also confess Dr. Luther's *Small* and *Large Catechisms* as they are included in Luther's works. They are "the layman's Bible" because everything necessary for a Christian to know for salvation is included in them, which is handled more extensively in the Holy Scriptures.

6 As announced above, all teachings are to be conformed in this way. What is contrary to these confessions is to be rejected and condemned, as opposed to the unanimous declaration of our faith.

7 In this way the distinction between the Holy Scriptures of the Old and of the New Testament and all other writings is preserved. The Holy Scriptures alone remain the judge, rule, and norm. According to them—as the only touchstone—all teachings shall and must be discerned and judged to see whether they are good or evil (1 Thessalonians 5:21–22), right or wrong.

8 The other symbols and writings mentioned above are not judges like the Holy Scriptures. They are only a testimony and declaration of the faith. They show how the Holy Scriptures have been understood and explained in regard to controversial articles in God's Church by those living at that time. Also, they show how the opposite teaching was rejected and condemned.

# I. ORIGINAL SIN

Is sin part of mankind's very essence? No, for if it were, God could be accused of creating sin. However, sin is a very deep and thorough corruption of our human nature—a horrible and terrible corruption. No one except Christ Jesus, our Lord, can overcome this corruption for us and save us from it. Because of this sin, spiritually we are utterly and completely dead. But there is hope! As Christ raised Lazarus from the dead, so today He brings us to life again through His Gospel in Word and Sacraments. The biblical position on this issue is explained in Articles I and II. (See also AC II; Ap II; SA III I; FC SD I.)

---

# STATUS OF THE CONTROVERSY
## THE CHIEF QUESTIONS IN THIS CONTROVERSY

1 Is *original sin* really, without any distinction, a person's corrupt nature, substance, and essence? Is it the chief and greater part of his essence (i.e., the rational soul itself in its highest state and powers)? Or even after the fall, is there a distinction between original sin and a person's substance, nature, essence, body, and soul, so that the nature itself is one thing and original sin is another, which belongs to the corrupt nature and corrupts the nature?

### AFFIRMATIVE STATEMENTS

**The Pure Teaching, Faith, and Confession according to the Standard and Summary Declaration Mentioned Before**

2 1. We believe, teach, and confess that there is a distinction between man's nature and original sin. This applied not only when he was originally created by God pure and holy and without sin (Genesis 1:31), but it

also applies to the way we have that nature now after the fall. In other words, we distinguish between the nature itself (which even after the fall is and remains God's creature) and original sin. This distinction is as great as the distinction between God's work and the devil's work.

3    2. We believe, teach, and confess that this distinction should be maintained with the greatest care. For this doctrine (that no distinction is to be made between our corrupt human nature and original sin) conflicts with the chief articles of our Christian faith about creation, redemption, sanctification, and the resurrection of our body. It cannot stand with them.

4    God created the body and soul of Adam and Eve before the fall. But He also created our bodies and souls after the fall. Even though they are corrupt, God still acknowledges them as His work, as it is written in Job 10:8, "Your hands fashioned and made me." (See also Deuteronomy 32:18; Isaiah 45:9–10; 54:5; 64:8; Acts 17:28; Psalm 100:3; 139:14; Ecclesiastes 12:1.)

5    Furthermore, God's Son has received this human nature (John 1:14), but without sin. Therefore, He did not receive a foreign nature, but our own flesh in the unity of His person. In this way He has become our true Brother. Hebrews 2:14 says, "Since therefore the children share in flesh and blood, He Himself likewise partook of the same things." Again, "For surely it is not angels that He helps, but He helps the offspring of Abraham. Therefore He had to be made like His brothers in every respect, . . . yet without sin" 

6    (2:16; 4:15). In the same way, Christ redeemed human nature as His work, sanctifies it, raises it from the dead, and gloriously adorns it as His work. But original sin He has not created, received, redeemed, or sanctified. He will not raise it, adorn it, or save it in the elect. In the blessed resurrection original sin will be entirely destroyed (1 Corinthians 5:51–57).

7    The distinction can easily be discerned between (a) the corrupt nature, (b) the corruption, which infects the nature, and (c) the corruption by which the nature became corrupt.

8    3. On the other hand, we believe, teach, and confess that original sin is not a minor corruption. It is so deep a corruption of human nature that nothing healthy or uncorrupt remains in man's body or soul, in his inward or outward powers (Romans 3:10–12). As the Church sings:

Through Adam's fall is all corrupt,
Nature and essence human.

9    This damage cannot be fully described (Psalm 19:12). It cannot be understood by reason, but only from God's Word. We affirm 10 that no one but God alone can separate human nature and this corruption of human nature from each other. This will fully come to pass through death, in the blessed resurrection. At that time our nature, which we now bear, will rise and live eternally without original sin and be separated and divided from it. As it is written in Job 19:26–27, "After my skin has been thus destroyed, yet in my flesh I shall see God, whom I shall see for myself, and my eyes shall behold."

## NEGATIVE STATEMENTS

### Rejection of the False, Opposite Teachings

11    1. We reject and condemn the teaching that original sin is only a debt based on what has been committed by another person without any corruption of our nature.

12    2. We reject and condemn the teaching that evil lusts are not sin, but are created, essential properties of human nature. This is taught as though the above-mentioned defect and damage were not truly sin, because

of which a person would be a child of wrath without Christ.

13     3. We likewise reject the Pelagian error. It alleged that human nature even after the fall is not corrupt, and especially in spiritual things human nature has remained entirely good and pure in its natural powers.

14     4. We reject the teaching that original sin is only a slight, insignificant spot on the outside, smeared on human nature, or a blemish that has been blown upon it, beneath which the nature has kept its good powers even in spiritual things.

15     5. We reject the teaching that original sin is only an outward obstacle to the good spiritual powers and not a spoiling or lack of the powers. It is not like when a magnet is smeared with garlic juice, and its natural power is not removed, but only blocked; or when a stain can be easily wiped away, like a spot from the face or paint from a wall.

16     6. We reject the teaching that in a person the human nature and essence are not entirely corrupt, but a person still has something good in him, even in spiritual things (e.g., capacity, skill, aptitude, or ability in spiritual things to begin, to work, or to help working for something good).

17     7. On the other hand, we also reject the false teaching of the Manichaeans, who taught that original sin, like something essential and self-sustaining, has been infused by Satan into human nature and intermingled with it, like when poison and wine are mixed.

18     8. We reject the teaching that the natural man does not sin, but something else sins apart from man and, on account of this, human nature is not accused but only original sin in the nature.

19     9. We also reject and condemn as a Manichaean error the teaching that original sin is properly and without any distinction the substance, nature, and essence itself of the corrupt person. This teaching states that a distinction between the corrupt nature (as such) after the fall and original sin should not even be conceived of, nor that they could be distinguished from each other even in thought.

20     10. Now, original sin is called by Dr. Luther "nature sin," "person sin," and "essential sin." This is not because the nature, person, or essence of man is itself—without any distinction—original sin. He uses such words in order to show the distinction between original sin, which belongs to human nature, and other sins, which are called actual sins.

21     11. Original sin is not an actual sin that is committed. It is inherent to the nature, substance, and essence of humanity. So even if no wicked thought should ever arise in the heart of a corrupt person, no idle word should be spoken, no wicked deed should be done, human nature is still corrupted through original sin. Original sin is born in us because of the sinful seed and is a source of all other actual sins, such as wicked thoughts, words, and works, as it is written in Matthew 15:19, "out of the heart come evil thoughts." Also Genesis 8:21 says, "The intention of man's heart is evil from his youth." (See also Genesis 6:5.)

22     12. There is also to be noted well the different uses of the word *nature*, by which the Manichaeans hide their error and lead astray many simple people. For sometimes this word means the essence of mankind, as when it is said, "God created human nature." At other times it means the attitude and the base quality of a thing, which belongs to its nature or essence, as when it is said, "The nature of the serpent is to bite, and the nature and way of man is to sin, and is sin." Here the word *nature* does not mean the substance of

mankind, but something that belongs to the nature or substance.

23 13. Now, consider the Latin terms *substantia* (substance) and *accidens* (a nonessential quality). They are not words of Holy Scripture and, besides, are unknown to the ordinary person. So they should not be used in sermons before ordinary, uninstructed people. Simple people should be spared them.

24 But in the schools, among the learned, these words are rightly kept in disputes about original sin. For they are well known and used without any misunderstanding to distinguish exactly between the essence of a thing and what attaches to it in an accidental way.

25 The distinction between God's work and that of the devil is made in the clearest way by these terms. For the devil can create no substance, but can only, in an accidental way—with God's consent—corrupt the substance created by God.

## II. FREE WILL

Since the fall into sin, the will of mankind is so blind and corrupt that we can chose only to do evil. We are spiritually dead by nature, enemies of God and naturally hostile toward Him. While we are free to choose in earthly matters, we have no power, ability, or free will in spiritual matters. Before conversion we are entirely incapable—in any way—of responding to or cooperating with God's grace. After conversion and because of Christ, the new man in us does in fact respond to and cooperate with God the Holy Spirit. In addition to discussing free will, this article emphasizes the care we are to take when explaining biblical truths. We should stick to the pattern of sound doctrine and refrain from introducing novel ways of speaking about Bible teachings. We should use the

very words and phrases used in the Lutheran Confessions to explain the Bible. It is very unwise to take time-tested words explaining one thing and use them to explain another. This only leads to confusion and error. (See also AC XVIII; Ap XVIII; FC SD II.)

---

# STATUS OF THE CONTROVERSY

## THE CHIEF QUESTIONS IN THIS CONTROVERSY

1 The will of mankind is found in four different states: (a) before the fall; (b) since the fall; (c) after regeneration; and (d) after the resurrection of the body. The chief question in this article is only about the will and ability of mankind in the second state. That is, what powers in spiritual matters does a person have after the fall of our first parents and before regeneration? Can a person by his own powers—prior to and before his regeneration by God's Spirit—get ready and prepare himself for God's grace? Can a person accept or reject the grace offered through the Holy Spirit in the Word and holy Sacraments?

## AFFIRMATIVE STATEMENTS

**The Pure Teaching about This Article, according to God's Word**

2 1. This is our teaching, faith, and confession on this subject: in spiritual matters the understanding and reason of mankind are completely blind and by their own powers understand nothing, as it is written in 1 Corinthians 2:14, "The natural person does not accept the things of the Spirit of God, for they are folly to him, and he is not able to understand them because they are spiritually discerned."

3 2. Likewise, we believe, teach, and confess

that the unregenerate will of mankind is not only turned away from God, but also has become God's enemy. So it only has an inclination and desire for that which is evil and contrary to God, as it is written in Genesis 8:21, "the intention of man's heart is evil from his youth." Romans 8:7 says, "The mind that is set on the flesh is hostile to God, for it does not submit to God's law; indeed, it cannot." Just as a dead body cannot raise itself to bodily, earthly life, so a person who by sin is spiritually dead cannot raise himself to spiritual life. For it is written in Ephesians 2:5, "even when we were dead in our trespasses, [He] made us alive together with Christ." And 2 Corinthians 3:5 says, "Not that we are sufficient in ourselves to claim anything as coming from us, but our sufficiency is from God."

4    3. God the Holy Spirit, however, does not bring about conversion without means. For this purpose He uses the preaching and hearing of God's Word, as it is written in Romans 1:16, the Gospel "is the power of God for salvation to everyone who believes." Also Romans 10:17 says, "Faith comes from hearing, and hearing through the word of Christ." It is God's will that His Word should be heard and that a person's ears should not be closed (Psalm 95:8). With this Word the Holy Spirit is present and opens hearts, so that people (like Lydia in Acts 16:14) pay attention to it and are converted only through the Holy Spirit's grace and power, who alone does the work of converting a person. For without His grace, and if He does not grant the increase, our willing and running, our planting, sowing, and watering (1 Corinthians 3:5–7)—are all nothing. As Christ says in John 15:5, "apart from Me you can do nothing." With these brief words the Spirit denies free will its powers and ascribes everything to God's grace, in order that no one may boast before God (1 Corinthians 1:29; 2 Corinthians 12:5; Jeremiah 9:23).

## NEGATIVE STATEMENTS

### Contrary False Teaching

So we reject and condemn all the following errors as contrary to the standard of God's Word:    7

1. The insane ideas of the philosophers who are called Stoics. We reject also the ideas of the Manichaeans, who taught that everything that happens must so happen and cannot happen otherwise; everything that a person does, even in outward things, he does by compulsion; he is forced to do evil works and deeds, such as inchastity, robbery, murder, theft, and the like.    8

2. We also reject the error of the Pelagians. They taught that a person by his own powers, without the Holy Spirit's grace, can turn himself to God, believe the Gospel, be obedient from the heart to God's Law, and so merit the forgiveness of sins and eternal life.    9

3. We also reject the error of the Semi-Pelagians. They teach that a person by his own powers can begin his conversion, but cannot complete it without the Holy Spirit's grace.    10

4. Some have acknowledged that a person is too weak to begin his conversion by his free will before regeneration, and that he cannot turn himself to God by his own powers and be obedient to God from the heart. Yet, they still assert that if the Holy Spirit has made a beginning by the preaching of the Word and has offered His grace in the Word, then a person's will, from its own natural powers, can add something. A person's will, though little and feebly, can help and cooperate, qualify and prepare itself for grace, and so embrace and accept the Word, and believe the Gospel.    11

5. Some have taught that a person—after he has been born again—can perfectly observe and completely fulfill God's Law, and    12

that this fulfilling is our righteousness before God, by which we merit eternal life.

13    6. We also reject and condemn the error of the Enthusiasts. They imagine that God without means, without the hearing of God's Word, and also without the use of the holy Sacraments, draws people to Himself and enlightens, justifies, and saves them. (We call people *enthusiasts* who expect the heavenly illumination of the Spirit without the preaching of God's Word.)

14    7. Some teach that in conversion and regeneration God entirely exterminates the substance and essence of the old Adam, and especially the rational soul. They say that in conversion and regeneration He creates a new essence of the soul out of nothing.

15    8. We reject cases where the following expressions are used without explanation: a person's will before, in, and after conversion resists the Holy Spirit, and the Holy Spirit is given to those who resist Him intentionally and persistently. For, as Augustine says, in conversion "God makes willing persons out of the unwilling and dwells in the willing."

16    We reject cases where the expressions of ancient and modern teachers of the Church are used without explanation, when it is said, "God draws, but He draws the willing." Likewise, some say, "In conversion a person's will is not idle, but also does something." We maintain that, because these expressions have been introduced for confirming the false opinion about the powers of the natural free will in a person's conversion, against the doctrine of God's grace, they do not conform to sound doctrine. Therefore, when we speak of conversion to God, these sayings should be avoided.

17    On the other hand, it is correctly said that in conversion God—through the drawing of the Holy Spirit—makes willing people out of stubborn and unwilling ones. And after such conversion, in the daily exercise of repentance, the regenerate will of a person is not idle, but cooperates in all the works of the Holy Spirit, which He performs through us.

9. Dr. Luther has written that a person's   18 will in his conversion is *purely passive*, that is, that it does nothing at all. This is to be understood with respect to divine grace in the kindling of the new movements, that is, when God's Spirit, through the heard Word or the use of the holy Sacraments, lays hold of a person's will and works in him the new birth and conversion. When the Holy Spirit has worked and accomplished this, and a person's will has been changed and renewed by His divine power and working alone, then the new will of that person is an instrument and organ of God the Holy Spirit. So that person not only accepts grace, but he also cooperates with the Holy Spirit in the works that follow.

There are only two efficient causes for a   19 person's conversion: (1) the Holy Spirit and (2) God's Word, as the instrument of the Holy Spirit, by which He works conversion. A person must hear this Word. However, it is not by that person's own powers, but only through the grace and working of the Holy Spirit that he trusts the Word and receives it.

## III. THE RIGHTEOUSNESS OF FAITH BEFORE GOD

This article repeats the very heart of the Gospel. We are justified by God's grace alone, through faith alone, which receives the righteousness of Christ. This article addresses precisely how this happens. The entire Christ, God and man, is our righteousness. Our righteousness before God consists in forgiveness in Christ, without our works, and God's application of Christ's righteousness to us. Faith is the *means*, or instrument, by which we receive Christ's righteousness, not the *cause* of our righteousness in Christ. The Holy Spirit, working through the means of grace, bestows the gift of faith. We are saved by God's grace in Christ through faith alone, but that does not mean that faith is ever alone. Good works are the fruit of justifying faith. Those who willfully, knowingly, and continually choose to commit sins show they no longer possess saving faith. For such people the Law must drive them to despair over their dire circumstances and the sure prospect of hell, and the Gospel must cleanse, pardon, and renew them through faith in Christ. King David's repentance of adultery and murder, and the prophet Nathan's comforting absolution, is used to illustrate this truth. (See also AC IV; Ap IV; SA II I; SA III XIII; FC SD III.)

# STATUS
# OF THE CONTROVERSY

## THE CHIEF QUESTION IN THIS CONTROVERSY

1     It is unanimously confessed in our churches, in accordance with God's Word and the meaning of the Augsburg Confession, that we poor sinners are justified before God and saved alone through faith in Christ. Christ alone is our Righteousness, who is true God and man, because in Him the divine and human natures are personally united with each other (Jeremiah 23:6; 1 Corinthians 1:30; 2 Corinthians 5:21). The question has arisen: "According to which nature is Christ our Righteousness?" From this, two opposing errors have arisen in some churches.

2     One side has held that Christ, according to His divinity alone, is our Righteousness, if He dwells in us through faith. Contrasted with this divinity, dwelling in us through faith, the sins of all people must be regarded as a drop of water compared to a great ocean. Others, on the contrary, have held that Christ is our Righteousness before God according to His human nature alone.

## AFFIRMATIVE STATEMENTS

### The Pure Teaching of the Christian Churches against Both Errors Just Mentioned

1. Against both the errors just mentioned, we unanimously believe, teach, and confess that Christ is our Righteousness (1 Corinthians 1:30) neither according to His divine nature alone nor according to His human nature alone. But it is the entire Christ who is our Righteousness according to both natures. In His obedience alone, which as God and man He offered to the Father even to His death (Philippians 2:8), He merited for us the forgiveness of sins and eternal life. For it is written, "For as by the one man's disobedience the many were made sinners, so by the one man's obedience the many will be made righteous" (Romans 5:19).   3

2. We believe, teach, and confess what our righteousness before God is this: God forgives our sins out of pure grace, without any work, merit, or worthiness of ours preceding, present, or following. He presents and credits to us the righteousness of Christ's obedience (Romans 5:17–19). Because of this righteousness, we are received into grace by God and regarded as righteous.   4

3. We believe, teach, and confess that faith alone is the means and instrument through which we lay hold of Christ. So in Christ we lay hold of that righteousness that benefits us before God, for whose sake this faith is credited to us for righteousness (Romans 4:5).   5

4. We believe, teach, and confess that this faith is not a bare knowledge of Christ's history, but it is God's gift (Ephesians 2:8). By this gift we come to the right knowledge of   6

Christ as our Redeemer in the Word of the Gospel. And we trust in Him that for the sake of His obedience alone we have—by grace—the forgiveness of sins and are regarded as holy and righteous before God the Father and are eternally saved.

7   5. We believe, teach, and confess that according to the usage of Holy Scripture the word *justify* means, in this article, "to absolve, that is, to declare free from sins." Proverbs 17:15 says, "He who justifies the wicked and he who condemns the righteous are both alike an abomination to the LORD." Also Romans 8:33 says, "Who shall bring any charge against God's elect? It is God who justifies."

8   At times the words *regeneration* and *renewal of life* (*regeneratio* and *vivificatio*) are used in place of *justify*, as in the Apology. This is done with the same meaning. But, in other places, the renewal of a person is understood by these terms and is distinguished from justification through faith.

9   6. We believe, teach, and confess that many weaknesses and defects cling to the true believers and truly regenerate, even up to the day they are buried (1 John 1:8). Still, they must not on that account doubt either their righteousness, which has been credited to them through faith, or the salvation of their souls. They must regard it as certain that for Christ's sake, according to the promise and immovable Word of the Holy Gospel, they have a gracious God.

10   7. We believe, teach, and confess that it is necessary to teach with special diligence the *particulae exclusivae* for the preservation of the pure doctrine about the righteousness of faith before God. We mean the *exclusive particles*, that is, the following words of the holy apostle Paul, by which Christ's merit is entirely separated from our works and the honor is given to Christ alone. For the holy apostle Paul writes, "Of grace," "without merit," "without Law," "without works," "not of works." All these words together mean that we are justified and saved through faith alone in Christ (Ephesians 2:8; Romans 1:17; 3:24; 4:3–25; Galatians 3:11; Hebrews 11).

8. We believe, teach, and confess that the   11 contrition that comes before justification, and the good works that follow it, do not belong to the article of justification before God. Yet one is not to imagine a kind of faith that can exist and abide with, and alongside of, a wicked intention to sin and to act against the conscience. But after man has been justified through faith, then a true living faith works by love (Galatians 5:6). Good works always follow justifying faith and are surely found with it—if it is true and living faith (James 2:26). Faith is never alone, but always has love and hope with it (1 Corinthians 13:13).

## ANTITHESES OR NEGATIVE STATEMENTS

**Contrary Teaching Rejected**

We reject and condemn all the following   12 errors:

1. Christ is our Righteousness according   13 to His divine nature alone.

2. Christ is our Righteousness according   14 to His human nature alone.

3. Where the righteousness of faith is   15 spoken of in the sayings of the prophets and apostles, the words *justify* and *to be justified* are not to mean "declaring or being declared free from sins," and "obtaining the forgiveness of sins." But they actually mean "being made righteous before God, because of love infused by the Holy Spirit, virtues, and the works following them."

4. Faith not only looks to Christ's obedi-   16 ence, but also to His divine nature, since it dwells and works in us, and by this indwelling our sins are covered.

5. Faith is the sort of trust in Christ's obe-   17

dience that can exist and remain in a person even when he has no genuine repentance, in whom also no love follows, but who persists in sins against his conscience.

18     6. Not God Himself, but only God's gifts dwell in believers.

19     7. Faith saves on this account: because the renewal by faith is begun in us, which dwells in love for God and one's neighbor.

20     8. Faith has the first place in justification, yet renewal and love also belong to our righteousness before God in a particular way. Although renewal and love are not the chief cause of our righteousness, nevertheless our righteousness before God is not entire or perfect without such love and renewal.

21     9. Believers are justified before God and saved jointly by Christ's righteousness credited to them and by the new obedience begun in them. Or, believers are justified in part by the credit of Christ's righteousness, but in part also by the new obedience begun in them.

22     10. The promise of grace is made our own through faith in the heart, by the confession made with the mouth, and by other virtues.

23     11. Faith does not justify without good works, so that good works are necessarily required for righteousness, and without their presence a person cannot be justified.

## IV. GOOD WORKS

It is wrong to say that good works are necessary for salvation. It is also wrong to say that they are harmful for salvation. Just as wrong, however, is to demand avoiding the discussion of good works altogether. Perhaps the best analogy of good works—and a biblical one at that—is to think of them as fruit on a tree (Matthew 7:17). A living tree bears fruit. A dead tree bears no fruit. A person who is alive through faith in Christ will do good works. On the other hand, a person who is spiritually dead, that is, without faith in Christ, may perform certain outward actions, but they are not good works. While good works play no role in our salvation, they are very much part of our lives as God's children. Good works in the Christian life do not result from our fearing God's punishment. Rather, they result from God loving us. God's perfect love in Christ drives out all fear and replaces it with a heart, soul, and mind that love Him and serve our neighbor. (See also AC VI; AC XX; Ap V; Ap XX; SA III XIII; FC SD IV.)

# STATUS
# OF THE CONTROVERSY

### THE CHIEF QUESTION
### IN THE CONTROVERSY
### ABOUT GOOD WORKS

Concerning the doctrine of good works 1 two divisions have arisen in some churches:

1. First, some theologians have become 2 divided because of the following expressions. One side wrote, "Good works are necessary for salvation. It is impossible to be saved without good works." They also wrote, "No one has ever been saved without good works." But the other side, on the contrary, wrote, "Good works are harmful to salvation."

2. Afterward, a schism arose between 3 some theologians because of the two words *necessary* and *free*. The one side argued that the word *necessary* should not be used about the new obedience, which, they say, does not flow from necessity and coercion, but from a voluntary spirit. The other side insisted on the word *necessary*. They say obedience is not our option, but regenerate people are obliged to render this obedience.

From this dispute about the terms, a con- 4 troversy arose afterward about the subject itself. For the one side contended that among Christians the Law should not be presented at all, but people should be encouraged to do good works from the Holy Gospel alone. The other side contradicted this.

## AFFIRMATIVE STATEMENTS

### The Pure Teaching of the Christian Churches about This Controversy

5     For the thorough statement and decision of this controversy, our doctrine, faith, and confession is as follows:

6     1. Good works certainly and without doubt follow true faith—if it is not a dead, but a living faith—just as fruit grows on a good tree (Matthew 7:17).

7     2. We believe, teach, and confess that good works should be entirely excluded from the question about salvation, just as they are excluded from the article of justification before God. The apostle testifies with clear words when he writes as follows, "Just as David also speaks of the blessing of the one to whom God counts righteousness apart from works: . . . 'Blessed is the man against whom the Lord will not count his sin'" (Romans 4:6–8). And again, "For by grace you have been saved through faith. And this is not your own doing; it is the gift of God, not a result of works, so that no one may boast" (Ephesians 2:8–9).

8     3. We also believe, teach, and confess that all people, but especially those who are born again and renewed by the Holy Spirit, are obligated to do good works (Ephesians 2:10).

9     4. In this sense the words *necessary*, *shall*, and *must* are used correctly and in a Christian way to describe the regenerate, and are in no way contrary to the form of sound words and speech.

10     5. Nevertheless, if the words mentioned (i.e., *necessity* and *necessary*) are used when talking about regenerate people, then only due obedience—not coercion—is to be understood. For the truly believing, so far as they are regenerate, do not offer obedience from coercion or the driving of the Law, but from a voluntary spirit. For they are no more under the Law, but under grace (Romans 6:14; 7:6; 8:14).

11     6. We also believe, teach, and confess that when it is said, "The regenerate do good works from a free spirit," this is not to be understood as though it were an option for the regenerate person to do or not to do good when he wants, as though a person can still retain faith if he intentionally perseveres in sins (1 John 2:5–9).

12     7. This is not to be understood in any other way than as the Lord Christ and His apostles themselves declare. In other words, the free spirit does not obey from fear of punishment, like a servant, but from love of righteousness, like children (Romans 8:15).

13     8. However, this willingness in God's elect children is not perfect. It is burdened with great weakness, as St. Paul complains about himself in Romans 7:14–25 and Galatians 5:17.

14     9. Nevertheless, for the sake of the Lord Christ, the Lord does not charge this weakness to His elect, as it is written, "There is therefore now no condemnation for those who are in Christ Jesus" (Romans 8:1).

15     10. We believe, teach, and confess also that works do not maintain faith and salvation in us, but God's Spirit alone does this, through faith. Good works are evidences of His presence and indwelling (Romans 8:5, 14).

## NEGATIVE STATEMENTS

### False Contrary Doctrine

16     1. We reject and condemn the following ways of speaking when they are taught and written: "Good works are necessary to salvation." Also, "No one ever has been saved without good works." Also, "It is impossible to be saved without good works."

17    2. We reject and condemn as offensive and detrimental to Christian discipline the bare expression "Good works are harmful to salvation."

18    In these last times it is certainly no less needful to encourage people to Christian discipline and to do good works. We need to remind them of how necessary it is that they exercise themselves in good works as a declaration of their faith (Matthew 5:16) and gratitude to God (Hebrews 13:15–16). But works should not be mingled in the article of justification. For people may be just as damned by an Epicurean delusion about faith as they are by papistic and Pharisaic confidence in their own works and merits.

19    3. We also reject and condemn the teaching that faith and the indwelling of the Holy Spirit are not lost by willful sin, but that the saints and elect retain the Holy Spirit even though they fall into adultery and other sins and persist in them.

# V. THE LAW AND THE GOSPEL

How one defines *Law* and *Gospel* is key to keeping both teachings properly distinguished. This article provides a careful definition of these two terms, both in a narrow sense and in a wide sense. Strictly speaking, the Gospel is entirely and only about the good news of our salvation in Christ: what He has done for us through His life, death, and resurrection. When Law and Gospel are properly distinguished, it is the narrow definition of each that is being discussed. A person who claims, therefore, that the Gospel is about what we are to do, confuses both Law and Gospel. (See also SA III II and IV; FC SD V.)

---

# STATUS OF THE CONTROVERSY

## THE CHIEF QUESTION IN THIS CONTROVERSY

1    Is the preaching of the Holy Gospel properly not just a preaching of grace (which announces the forgiveness of sins) but also a preaching of repentance and reproof (rebuking unbelief, which some people say is not rebuked in the Law but only through the Gospel)?

## AFFIRMATIVE STATEMENTS

### The Pure Doctrine of God's Word

2    1. We believe, teach, and confess that the distinction between the Law and the Gospel is to be kept in the Church with great diligence as a particularly brilliant light. By this distinction, according to the admonition of St. Paul, God's Word is rightly divided (2 Timothy 2:15).

3    2. We believe, teach, and confess that the Law is properly a divine doctrine (Romans 7:12). It teaches what is right and pleasing to God, and it rebukes everything that is sin and contrary to God's will.

4    3. For this reason, then, everything that rebukes sin is, and belongs to, the preaching of the Law.

5    4. But the Gospel is properly the kind of teaching that shows what a person who has not kept the Law (and therefore is condemned by it) is to believe. It teaches that Christ has paid for and made satisfaction for all sins (Romans 5:9). Christ has gained and acquired for an individual—without any of his own merit—forgiveness of sins, righteousness that avails before God, and eternal life (Romans 5:10).

6    5. The term *Gospel* is not used in one and the same sense in the Holy Scriptures. That's why this disagreement originally arose.

Therefore, we believe, teach, and confess that if the term *Gospel* is understood to mean Christ's entire teaching that He proposed in His ministry, as His apostles did also (this is how it is used in Mark 1:15; Acts 20:21), then it is correctly said and written that the Gospel is a preaching of repentance and of the forgiveness of sins.

7      6. The Law and the Gospel are also contrasted with each other. Likewise also, Moses himself as a teacher of the Law and Christ as a preacher of the Gospel are contrasted with each other (John 1:17). In these cases we believe, teach, and confess that the Gospel is not a preaching of repentance or rebuke. But it is properly nothing other than a preaching of consolation and a joyful message that does not rebuke or terrify. The Gospel comforts consciences against the terrors of the Law, points only to Christ's merit, and raises them up again by the lovely preaching of God's grace and favor, gained through Christ's merit.

8      7. Concerning the revelation of sin, Moses' veil hangs (2 Corinthians 3:12–16) before the eyes of all people as long as they hear the bare preaching of the Law, and nothing about Christ. Therefore, they do not learn from the Law to see their sins correctly. They either become bold hypocrites (who swell with the opinion of their own righteousness) like the Pharisees (Matthew 23), or they despair like Judas (Matthew 27:3–5). Therefore, Christ takes the Law into His hands and explains it spiritually (Matthew 5:21–48; Romans 7:14). In this way God's wrath is revealed from heaven against all sinners (Romans 1:18), so that they see how great it is. In this way they are directed back to the Law, and then they first learn from it to know their sins correctly—a knowledge that Moses never could have forced out of them.

9      According to this, the preaching of the suffering and death of Christ, the Son of God, is a serious and terrifying proclamation and declaration of God's wrath. By such preaching people are first led into the Law correctly—after Moses' veil has been removed from them. Then they understand correctly for the first time what great things God requires of us in His Law, none of which we can keep. Therefore, they know we are to seek all our righteousness in Christ.

8. Yet as long as all this (namely, Christ's   10 suffering and death) proclaims God's wrath and terrifies a person, it is still not properly the preaching of the Gospel. It remains the preaching of Moses and the Law, and it is, therefore, an alien work of Christ. Passing through this teaching, Christ arrives at His proper office, that is, to preach grace, console, and give life, which is properly the preaching of the Gospel.

## NEGATIVE STATEMENTS

### Contrary Doctrine That Is Rejected

We reject and regard as incorrect and   11 harmful the teaching that the Gospel, strictly speaking, is a preaching of repentance or rebuke and not just a preaching of grace. For by this misuse the Gospel is converted into a teaching of the Law. Christ's merit and Holy Scripture are hidden, Christians are robbed of true consolation, and the door is opened again to the papacy.

# VI. THE THIRD USE OF GOD'S LAW

God uses His Law in three ways: to maintain external discipline in society, to lead us to recognize our sin, and to guide Christians so that they will know what is pleasing to Him. These three functions, or uses, of the Law are often described as a curb, mirror, and a rule. Because the old sinful flesh clings to us until we die, we Christians need the Law as a guide for works that are pleasing to God and are appointed by God for us to do. Otherwise, we would simply dream up or imagine things pleasing to God. There are not three Laws, but one Law with three functions. God uses His Law among us in three distinct ways to accomplish His will. (See also SC, Morning Prayer and The Table of Duties; FC SD VI.)

# STATUS
# OF THE CONTROVERSY

## THE CHIEF QUESTION IN THIS CONTROVERSY

1  The Law was given to people for three reasons: (1) that by the Law outward discipline might be maintained against wild, disobedient people; (2) that people may be led to the knowledge of their sins by the Law; and (3) that after they are regenerate and the flesh still cleaves to them, they might on this account have a fixed rule according to which they are to regulate and direct their whole life. A dissension has arisen between a few theologians about the third use of the Law, namely, whether it is to be taught to regenerate Christians. The one side has said Yes; the other, No.

## AFFIRMATIVE STATEMENTS

### The True Christian Teaching about This Controversy

2  1. We believe, teach, and confess that, even though people who are truly believing in Christ and truly converted to God have been freed and exempted from the curse and coercion of the Law, they are still not without the Law on this account. They have been redeemed by God's Son in order that they may exercise themselves in the Law day and night (Psalm 1:2; Psalm 119). Even our first parents before the fall did not live without Law. They had God's Law written into their hearts, because they were created in God's image (Genesis 1:26–27; 2:16–17; 3:3).

3  2. We believe, teach, and confess that the preaching of the Law is to be encouraged diligently. This applies not only for the unbelieving and impenitent, but also for true believers, who are truly converted, regenerate, and justified through faith.

4  3. Although believers are regenerate and renewed in the spirit of their mind, in the present life this regeneration and renewal is not complete. It is only begun. Believers are, by the spirit of their mind, in a constant struggle against the flesh. They struggle constantly against the corrupt nature and character, which cleaves to us until death. This old Adam still dwells in the understanding, the will, and all the powers of humanity. It is necessary that the Law of the Lord always shine before them, so that they may not start evil and self-created forms of worship from human devotion. The Law of the Lord is also necessary so that the old Adam (Romans 6:6) may not use his own will, but may be subdued against his will. This happens not only by the warning and threatening of the Law, but also by punishments and blows, so that a person may follow and surrender himself as a captive to the Spirit. (See 1 Corinthians 9:27; Romans 6:12, Galatians 6:14; Psalm 119; Hebrews 13:21; 12:1.)

5  4. Now, consider the distinction between the works of the Law (Galatians 2:16) and the fruit of the Spirit (Galatians 5:22–23). We believe, teach, and confess that the works of the Law are those that are done according to the Law. They are called works of the Law as long as they are only forced out of a person by teaching the punishment and threatening of God's wrath.

6  5. Fruit of the Spirit, however, are the

works wrought by God's Spirit, who dwells in believers. The Spirit works through the regenerate. These works are done by believers because they are regenerate. They act as though they knew of no command, threat, or reward. In this way God's children live in the Law and walk according to God's Law. St. Paul calls this the "law of Christ" and the "Law of my mind" in his letters. (See Romans 7:23–25; 8:7; 8:2; Galatians 6:2.)

7    6. The Law is and remains—both to the penitent and impenitent, both to regenerate and unregenerate people—one and the same Law. It is God's unchangeable will. The difference, as far as obedience is concerned, is only in the person. For one who is not yet regenerate follows the Law out of constraint and unwillingly does what it requires of him (as also the regenerate do according to the flesh). But the believer, so far as he is regenerate, acts without constraint and with a willing spirit to do what no threat of the Law (however severe) could ever force him to do.

### NEGATIVE STATEMENTS

**False Contrary Doctrine**

8    We reject the teaching that the Law must not be applied to Christians and true believers (in the way and degree mentioned above) but only to unbelievers, non-Christians, and the unrepentant. Such a teaching would be erroneous, which harms and conflicts with Christian discipline and true godliness.

# VII. THE HOLY SUPPER OF CHRIST

On the basis of the Word and promise of Christ, Lutherans believe that the true body and true blood of Jesus are actually present (under the bread and wine), distributed, and orally received in Holy Communion. All who commune receive Christ's body and blood:

worthy or unworthy, believing or unbelieving, godly or godless. Reformed Christians, deriving their theology from the teachings of Ulrich Zwingli and John Calvin, deny that Christ is truly present in, with, and under the bread and wine. They speak of His spiritual or symbolic presence. This article also rejects many false views held by the Roman Catholic Church. When it comes to the Lord's Supper, the clear Word of God must take captive our human reason. This applies to all matters of Christian doctrine and is a comment that echoes Martin Luther's famous words in 1521 at the Diet of Worms. When he was ordered to recant his teachings Luther said, "My conscience is captive to the Word of God." (See also AC X; AC XXII; Ap X; Ap XXII; SA III VI; SC VI; LC V; FC SD VII.)

---

The Zwinglian teachers are not to be    1 counted among the theologians who receive the Augsburg Confession. They separated from our theologians at the very time when this Confession was presented. Yet they are advancing themselves and are attempting—under the name of this Christian Confession—to spread their error. Therefore, we also intend to make a necessary statement about this controversy.

# STATUS OF THE CONTROVERSY

### CHIEF CONTROVERSY BETWEEN OUR TEACHING AND THAT OF THE SACRAMENTARIANS REGARDING THIS ARTICLE

Question: In the Holy Supper, are the    2 true body and blood of our Lord Jesus Christ (a) truly and essentially present, (b) distributed with the bread and wine, and (c) received with the mouth by all those who use this Sacrament—whether they are worthy or unworthy, godly or ungodly, believing or unbelieving? Are they received by the believing for consolation and life, but by the unbelieving for judgment? The Sacramentarians say No. We say Yes.

3    To explain this controversy, it must be noted in the beginning that there are two kinds of Sacramentarians. Some are openly crass Sacramentarians. They declare in plain, clear words what they believe in their hearts, that in the Holy Supper nothing but bread and wine is present, distributed, and 4 received with the mouth. Others, however, are crafty Sacramentarians. They are the most harmful of all. In part, they talk very fancy, using our own words. They pretend that they also believe a true presence of the true, essential, living body and blood of Christ in the Holy Supper. However, they say that this happens *spiritually* through faith. 5 Nevertheless, under these fancy words they hold precisely the former crass opinion, namely, that in the Holy Supper nothing is present and received with the mouth except bread and wine. For with them the word *spiritually* means nothing other than the Spirit of Christ or the power of Christ's absent body and His merit that is present. But for them Christ's body is in no mode or way present, except above in the highest heaven. They say we should elevate ourselves into heaven by the thoughts of our faith. And there—not at all in the bread and wine of the Holy Supper—we should seek Christ's body and blood.

## AFFIRMATIVE STATEMENTS

### Confession of the Pure Teaching about the Holy Supper against the Sacramentarians

6    1. We believe, teach, and confess that in the Holy Supper Christ's body and blood are truly and essentially present, and that they are truly distributed and received with the bread and wine.

2. We believe, teach, and confess that the 7 words of Christ's testament are not to be understood in any other way than the way they read, according to the letter. So the bread does not signify Christ's absent body and the wine His absent blood. But, because of the sacramental union, the bread and wine are truly Christ's body and blood.

3. Now, about the consecration, we be- 8 lieve, teach, and confess that no work of man or recitation of the minister produces this presence of Christ's body and blood in the Holy Supper. Instead, this presence is to be credited only and alone to the almighty power of our Lord Jesus Christ.

4. At the same time we also believe, 9 teach, and confess unanimously that in the use of the Holy Supper the words of Christ's institution should in no way be left out. Instead, they should be publicly recited, as it is written in 1 Corinthians 10:16, "The cup of blessing that we bless" and so forth. This blessing occurs through the reciting of Christ's words.

5. In this matter the ground on which we 10 stand against the Sacramentarians is what Dr. Luther has laid down in his *Confession concerning Christ's Supper.*

The first point is this article of our Chris- 11 tian faith: Jesus Christ is true, essential, natural, perfect God and man in one person, undivided and inseparable.

The second: God's "right hand" is every- 12 where. Christ is placed there in deed and in truth according to His human nature. He is present, rules, and has in His hands, and beneath His feet, everything that is in heaven and on earth (as Scripture says in Ephesians 1:22), where no other man or angel, but only Mary's Son is placed. Therefore, He can do this.

13    The third: God's Word is not false or deceitful (Titus 1:1–3).

14    The fourth: God has and knows of various ways to be in any place, and not only one way, which philosophers call *local* (*localis*).

15    6. We believe, teach, and confess that Christ's body and blood are received with the bread and wine, not only spiritually through faith, but also orally. Yet not in a "Capernaitic" way, but in a supernatural, heavenly way, because of the sacramental union. Christ's words clearly show this, when Christ gives direction to take, eat, and drink, as was also done by the apostles. For it is written in Mark 14:23, "And they all drank of it." St. Paul likewise says in 1 Corinthians 10:16, "The bread that we break, is it not a participation in the body of Christ?" That is to say: He who eats this bread eats Christ's body, which also the chief ancient teachers of the Church—Chrysostom, Cyprian, Leo I, Gregory, Ambrose, Augustine—unanimously testify.

16    7. We believe, teach, and confess that not only the true believers in Christ and the worthy, but also the unworthy and unbelievers receive Christ's true body and blood. However, they do not receive them for life and consolation, but for judgment and condemnation, if they are not converted and do not repent (1 Corinthians 11:27–29).

17    Although they thrust Christ as a Savior away from themselves, yet they must receive Him, even against their will, as a strict Judge. They must admit that He is just as present to exercise and render judgment on unrepentant guests as He is present to work life and consolation in the hearts of the true believers and worthy guests.

18    8. We believe, teach, and confess also that there is only one kind of unworthy guests: those who do not believe. About these guests it is written in John 3:18, "Whoever does not believe is condemned already." And this judgment becomes greater and more grievous, being aggravated by the unworthy use of the Holy Supper (1 Corinthians 11:29).

19    9. We believe, teach, and confess that no true believer—as long as he has living faith, however weak he may be—receives the Holy Supper to his judgment. For the Supper was instituted especially for Christians weak in faith, yet repentant. It was instituted for their consolation and to strengthen their weak faith (Matthew 9:12; 11:5, 28).

20    10. We believe, teach, and confess that all the worthiness of guests of this heavenly feast is and is founded on Christ's most holy obedience and perfect merit alone. We receive these for ourselves by true faith, and by the Sacrament we are assured of them. Our worthiness is not at all in our virtues or inward and outward preparations.

## NEGATIVE STATEMENTS

### Contrary, Condemned Teachings of the Sacramentarians

21    On the other hand, we unanimously reject and condemn all the following erroneous articles. They are opposed and contrary to the teaching presented above, the simple faith, and the confession about the Lord's Supper.

22    1. The papistic transubstantiation. It is taught in the papacy that during the Holy Supper the bread and wine lose their substance and natural essence, and that they are annihilated. They say they are changed into Christ's body, and only the outward form remains.

23    2. The papistic sacrifice of the Mass for the sins of the living and the dead.

24    3. For laypeople only one form of the Sacrament is given. Contrary to the plain words of Christ's testament, the cup is withheld from them. They are robbed of His blood.

25    4. The teaching that the words of Christ's testament must not be understood or believed simply as they read, but that His words are difficult expressions, whose meaning must be sought first in other passages of Scripture.

26    5. In the Holy Supper Christ's body is not received orally with the bread. But with the mouth only bread and wine are received. Christ's body, however, is only received spiritually through faith.

27    6. The bread and wine in the Holy Supper are nothing more than tokens by which Christians recognize one another.

28    7. The bread and wine are only figures, points of comparison, and representations of Christ's far absent body and blood.

29    8. The bread and wine are no more than a memorial, seal, and pledge. We are assured through them that when faith elevates itself to heaven, it becomes a partaker of Christ's body and blood there. This happens as surely as we eat bread and drink wine in the Supper.

30    9. In the Holy Supper the assurance and confirmation of our faith concerning salvation happen through the external signs of bread and wine alone. They do not happen through Christ's truly present body and blood.

31    10. In the Holy Supper only the power, effect, and merit of Christ's absent body and blood are distributed.

32    11. Christ's body is so enclosed in heaven that there is no way it can be at once and at one time in many or all places on earth where His Holy Supper is celebrated.

33    12. Christ has not promised and could not have caused the essential presence of His body and blood in the Holy Supper. For the nature and the property of the human nature He received cannot allow this presence or permit it.

34    13. God, by all His power, is not able (which is dreadful to hear) to cause His body to be essentially present in more than one place at one time.

35    14. Not the all-powerful words of Christ's testament, but faith, produces and makes Christ's body and blood present in the Holy Supper.

36    15. Believers must not seek Christ's body in the bread and wine of the Holy Supper. They must raise their eyes from the bread to heaven and there seek Christ's body.

37    16. Unbelieving, unrepentant Christians do not receive Christ's true body and blood in the Holy Supper, but only bread and wine.

38    17. At this heavenly meal the worthiness of the guests comes not only from true faith in Christ, but also from people's outward preparation.

39    18. Even the true believers, who have and hold a true, living, pure faith in Christ, can receive this Sacrament to their judgment. For they are still imperfect in their outward life.

40    19. The external visible elements of the bread and wine should be adored in the Holy Sacrament.

41    20. Likewise, we also hand over all proud, frivolous, blasphemous questions (which decency forbids us to mention), and other expressions to God's just judgment. Most blasphemously and with great offense to the Church such things are proposed by the Sacramentarians in a crass, carnal, Capernaitic way about the supernatural, heavenly mysteries of this Sacrament.

42    21. We utterly condemn the Capernaitic eating of Christ's body, as though His flesh were torn with the teeth and digested like other food. The Sacramentarians—against the testimony of their conscience, after all our frequent protests—willfully label us with this view. In this way they make our teaching hateful to their hearers. On the other hand, we hold and believe, according to the simple words of

Christ's testament, the true, yet supernatural eating of Christ's body and also the drinking of His blood. Human senses and reason do not comprehend. But, as in all other articles of faith, our reason is brought into captivity to the obedience of Christ (2 Corinthians 10:5). This mystery is not grasped in any other way than through faith alone, and it is revealed in the Word alone.

# VIII. THE PERSON OF CHRIST

Many objections to the Lutheran doctrine of the Lord's Supper are based on faulty understandings. These misunderstandings concern the relationship of Christ's divine and human natures. The issue confronting the writers of the Formula of Concord was this: Does the human nature of Christ share in the divine attributes so that Christ, according to both natures, is present everywhere, even under the bread and wine of the Lord's Supper? The biblical position, explained in this article, is clearly Yes. The doctrine of the incarnation—Christ the Son of God taking on human flesh—is a powerful comfort and treasure for Christians, and Article VIII explains why. Many ancient heresies about Christ are rejected by this article, and along with them the Christological errors of Reformed theology. Appended to many editions of the Book of Concord was a listing of various quotations from Scripture and Early Church Fathers demonstrating that the Lutheran doctrine concerning Christ's two natures is the same as that of the Early Church. A translation of this document, *The Catalog of Testimonies*, is included with this edition (pp. 651–75). (See also Apostles' Creed; Nicene Creed; Athanasian Creed; AC III; Ap III; SA I; SA II I; SC II; LC II; FC SD VIII.)

From the controversy about the Holy 1 Supper a disagreement has arisen between the pure theologians of the Augsburg Confession and the Calvinists. The Calvinists have also confused some other theologians about the person of Christ and the two natures in Christ and their properties.

# STATUS OF THE CONTROVERSY

## THE CHIEF QUESTIONS IN THIS CONTROVERSY

The chief question, however, has been 2 this: Because of the personal union, do the divine and human natures, and also their properties, really have communion with each other? In other words (in deed and truth), do the divine and human natures commune with each other in the person of Christ, and how far does this communion extend?

The Sacramentarians have asserted that 3 the divine and human natures in Christ are united personally in such a way that neither one has real communion. This means (in deed and truth) that they do not share with the other nature what is unique to either nature. They share nothing more than the name alone. For they plainly say, "The personal union does nothing more than make the names common." In other words, God is called man, and man is called God. Yet this happens in such a way that the divine has no real communion (that is, in deed and truth) with humanity. And humanity has nothing in common with divinity, its majesty, and properties. Dr. Luther and those who agreed with him have contended against the Sacramentarians for the contrary teaching.

## AFFIRMATIVE STATEMENTS

### The Pure Teaching of the Christian Church about the Person of Christ

4   To explain this controversy and settle it according to the guidance of our Christian faith, our doctrine, faith, and confession is as follows:

5   1. The divine and human natures in Christ are personally united. So there are not two Christs, one the Son of God and the other the Son of Man. But one and the same person is the Son of God and Son of Man (Luke 1:35; Romans 9:5).

6   2. We believe, teach, and confess that the divine and human natures are not mingled into one substance, nor is one changed into the other. Each keeps its own essential properties, which can never become the properties of the other nature.

7   3. The properties of the divine nature are these: to be almighty, eternal, infinite, and to be everywhere present (according to the property of its nature and its natural essence, of itself), to know everything, and so on. These never become properties of the human nature.

8   4. The properties of the human nature are to be a bodily creature, to be flesh and blood, to be finite and physically limited, to suffer, to die, to ascend and descend, to move from one place to another, to suffer hunger, thirst, cold, heat, and the like. These never become properties of the divine nature.

9   5. The two natures are united personally (i.e., in one person). Therefore, we believe, teach, and confess that this union is not the kind of joining together and connection that prevents either nature from having anything in common with the other personally (i.e., because of the personal union). It is not like when two boards are glued together, where neither gives anything to the other or takes anything from the other. But here is described the highest communion that God truly has with the man. From this personal union, the highest and indescribable communion results. There flows everything human that is said and believed about God, and everything divine that is said and believed about the man Christ. The ancient teachers of the Church explained this union and communion of the natures by the illustration of iron glowing with fire, and also by the union of body and soul in man.

6. We believe, teach, and confess that God   10 is man and man is God. This could not be true if the divine and human natures had (in deed and truth) absolutely no communion with each other.

For how could the man, the Son of Mary,   11 in truth be called or be God, or the Son of God the Most High, if His humanity were not personally united with the Son of God? How could He have no real communion (that is, in deed and truth) with the Most High, but only share God's name?

7. So we believe, teach, and confess that   12 Mary conceived and bore not merely a man and no more, but God's true Son. Therefore, she also is rightly called and truly is "the mother of God."

8. We also believe, teach, and confess that   13 it was not a mere man who suffered, died, was buried, descended to hell, rose from the dead, ascended into heaven, and was raised to God's majesty and almighty power for us. But it was a man whose human nature has such a profound (close), indescribable union and communion with God's Son that it is one person with Him.

9. God's Son truly suffered for us. How-   14 ever, He did so according to the attributes of the human nature, which He received into the unity of His divine person and made His

own. He did this so that He might be able to suffer and be our High Priest for our reconciliation with God, as it is written in 1 Corinthians 2:8, "They would not have crucified the Lord of glory." And Acts 20:28 says, "Which He obtained with His own blood."

15    10. We believe, teach, and confess that the Son of Man really is exalted. He is (in deed and truth) exalted according to His human nature to the right hand of God's almighty majesty and power. For He was received into God when He was conceived of the Holy Spirit in His mother's womb, and His human nature was personally united with the Son of the Highest.

16    11. Christ always had this majesty according to the personal union. Yet He abstained from using it in the state of His humiliation, and because of this He truly increased in all wisdom and favor with God and men. Therefore, He did not always use this majesty, but only when it pleased Him. Then, after His resurrection, He entirely laid aside the form of a servant, but not the human nature, and was established in the full use, manifestation, and declaration of the divine majesty. In this way He entered into His glory (Philippians 2:6–11). So now not just as God, but also as man He knows all things and can do all things. He is present with all creatures, and has under His feet and in His hands everything that is in heaven and on earth and under the earth, as He Himself testifies in Matthew 28:18, "All authority in heaven and on earth has been given to Me" (see also John 13:3). And St. Paul says in Ephesians 4:10, "He . . . ascended far above all the heavens, that He might fill all things." Because He is present, He can exercise His power everywhere. To Him everything is possible and everything is known.

17    12. Christ may give His true body and blood in the Holy Supper, as one who is pres-

ent—and it is very easy for Him to do so. He does not do this according to the mode or ability of the human nature, but according to the mode and ability of God's right hand. Dr. Luther says this in accordance with our Christian faith [as we teach it to] children: this presence of Christ in the Holy Supper is not physical or earthly, nor Capernaitic; yet it is true and substantial, as the words of His testament read, "This is, is, *is* My body," and so on.

18    Our doctrine, faith, and confession about the person of Christ is not divided, as it was by Nestorius. He denied the true communion of the properties of both natures in Christ (*communicatio idiomatum*). So he divided the person, as Luther has explained in his book *Concerning Councils* (LW 41:95–106). The natures, together with their properties, are not mixed with each other into one essence (as Eutyches erred). The human nature in the person of Christ is not denied or annihilated. Nor is either nature changed into the other. Christ is and remains to all eternity God and man in one undivided person. Next to the Holy Trinity, this is the highest mystery, upon which our only consolation, life, and salvation depends, as the apostle testifies in 1 Timothy 3:16.

## NEGATIVE STATEMENTS

**Contrary False Doctrine about the Person of Christ**

19    We reject and condemn as contrary to God's Word and our simple Christian faith all the following erroneous articles, if they are taught:

20    1. God and man in Christ are not one person. But the Son of God is one, and the Son of Man another, as Nestorius raved.

21    2. The divine and human natures have been mingled with each other into one essence, and the human nature has been

changed into the Deity, as Eutyches fanatically asserted.

22    3. Christ is not true, natural, and eternal God, as Arius held.

23    4. Christ did not have a true human nature consisting of body and soul, as Marcion imagined.

24    5. The personal union only makes the names and titles common to both natures.

25    6. To say, "God is man, man is God" is only "a phrase and mode of speaking." For Divinity, they say (in deed and truth), has nothing in common with the humanity, nor the humanity with the Deity.

26    7. It is nothing but words (*communicatio verbalis*) when it is said, "the Son of God died for the sins of the world" or "the Son of Man has become almighty."

27    8. The human nature in Christ has become an infinite essence in the same way as the Divinity. It is present everywhere in the same way as the divine nature because of this essential power and property, communicated to, and poured out into, the human nature and separated from God.

28    9. The human nature has become equal to and like the divine nature in its substance and essence, or in its essential properties.

29    10. Christ's human nature is locally extended to all places of heaven and earth, which should not even be said about the divine nature.

30    11. Because of the character of the human nature, it is impossible for Christ to be in more than one place at the same time, much less everywhere, with His body.

31    12. Only the mere humanity has suffered for us and redeemed us, and God's Son in the suffering had actually no communion with the humanity, as though it did not concern Him.

32    13. Christ is present with us on earth in the Word, the Sacraments, and in all our troubles, only according to His divinity. This presence does not at all apply to His human nature. They also say that after having redeemed us by His suffering and death, Christ has nothing to do with us any longer on earth.

14. God's Son assumed the human na-   33 ture. After He laid aside the form of a servant, He does not perform all the works of His omnipotence in, through, and with His human nature. He only performs some, and only in the place where His human nature is located.

15. According to His human nature He is   34 not at all capable of almighty power and other attributes of the divine nature, which goes against Christ's clear declaration in Matthew 28:18, "All authority in heaven and on earth has been given to Me," and of St. Paul in Colossians 2:9, "For in Him the whole fullness of deity dwells bodily."

16. Greater and more power is given to   35 Christ than to all angels and other creatures; but He has no communion with God's almighty power, nor has this been given to Him. Therefore, they make up a "middle power," a power between God's almighty power and the power of other creatures, given to Christ according to His humanity by the exaltation. This would be less than God's almighty power and greater than that of other creatures.

17. Christ, according to His human   36 mind, has a certain limit as to how much He is to know. He knows only what is fitting and needful for Him to know for His office as Judge.

18. Christ does not yet have a perfect   37 knowledge of God and all His works. Yet it is written about Him in Colossians 2:3, "In whom are hidden all the treasures of wisdom and knowledge."

19. It is impossible for Christ, according   38

to His human mind, to know what has been from eternity, what at present is occurring everywhere, and what will be in eternity.

39      20. Matthew 28:18, "All authority in heaven and on earth has been given to Me," is wrongly taught, as are other such verses. This passage is interpreted and blasphemously perverted to say that all power in heaven and on earth was restored (i.e., delivered again to Christ according to the divine nature) at the resurrection and His ascension to heaven. This argues as though Christ had also (according to His divinity) laid this power aside and abandoned it in His state of humiliation. Not only the words of Christ's testament are perverted by this teaching, but also the way is prepared for the accursed Arian heresy. Ultimately, Christ's eternal deity is denied. And so Christ, and with Him our salvation, are entirely lost if this false doctrine is not firmly opposed from the permanent foundation of the divine Word and our simple Christian faith.

# IX. THE DESCENT OF CHRIST TO HELL

This article attests that Christ descended into hell to proclaim and announce His victory over sin, death, and the devil; not as part of His atonement for the sins of the world. It put an end to the squabbling that had arisen among Lutherans over the meaning of Christ's descent to hell, and it based its conclusions on one of Luther's sermons discussing this issue. (See also Apostles' Creed; Nicene Creed; Athanasian Creed; SA I; SC II; LC II; FC SD IX.)

# STATUS OF THE CONTROVERSY

## THE CHIEF CONTROVERSY ABOUT THIS ARTICLE

1   This article has also been disputed among some theologians who have subscribed to the Augsburg Confession: When and in what manner did the Lord Christ, according to our simple Christian faith, descend to hell? Was this done before or after His death? Did this happen only to His soul, only to the divinity, or with body and soul, spiritually or bodily? Does this article belong to Christ's passion or to His glorious victory and triumph?

2   This article, like the preceding article, cannot be grasped by the senses or by our reason. It must be grasped through faith alone. Therefore, it is our unanimous opinion that there should be no dispute over it. It should be believed and taught only in the simplest way. Teach it like Dr. Luther, of blessed memory, in 3 his sermon at Torgau in the year 1533 [WA 37:62–67]. He has explained this article in a completely Christian way. He separated all useless, unnecessary questions from it, and encouraged all godly Christians to believe with Christian simplicity.

4   It is enough if we know that Christ descended into hell, destroyed hell for all believers, and delivered them from the power of death and of the devil, from eternal condemnation and the jaws of hell. We will save our questions about how this happened until the other world. Then not only this mystery, but others also will be revealed that we simply believe here and cannot grasp with our blind reason.

# X. CHURCH PRACTICES

## WHICH ARE CALLED ADIAPHORA OR MATTERS OF INDIFFERENCE

This article addresses matters that Scripture neither commands nor forbids. *Adiaphora* is a Greek word. It does not mean that something makes no difference or doesn't matter. In certain situations, keeping practices, or omitting them, can be a grave obstacle and offense to the Gospel and may even lead to its contradiction and denial. This article contains a key insight that agreement in doctrine and *all its articles* is necessary for Church fellowship, not complete unity in external practices. This is no "bare minimum" approach to Church teaching or fellowship. It explains and interprets Article VII of the Augsburg Confession, which refers to the Gospel rightly and unanimously preached according to the pure understanding of it. This article has in view territorial churches, not simply individual congregations, when it talks about making changes in the Church's ceremonies. Therefore, Article X is not used properly if it is used to justify significant diversity in the worship practices of the congregations in the same church, or area. At the time the Formula of Concord was written there were groupings of pastors and congregations known as consistories. The consistory would agree on a particular order of worship, rites, ceremonies, and other practices. The superintendent of the consistory, among his other duties, would be responsible for assuring that pastors and congregations were using the agreed-upon church order. (Martin Chemnitz, for example, was the superintendent of the Consistory of Braunschweig.)

(See also AC XIV; AC XXIV; AC XXVI; AC XXVIII; Ap XIV; Ap XV; Ap XXIV; Ap XXVIII; SA III XV; FC SD X.)

A disagreement has also arisen among the theologians of the Augsburg Confession about ceremonies or Church rites that are neither commanded nor forbidden in God's Word, but have been introduced into the Church for the sake of good order and fitting use. 1

# STATUS OF THE CONTROVERSY

## THE CHIEF CONTROVERSY ABOUT THIS ARTICLE

The chief question has been about a time of persecution and a matter of confession, even when the enemies of the Gospel have not reached an agreement with us in doctrine. Can some abolished ceremonies (which in themselves are matters of indifference and are neither commanded nor forbidden by God) be re-established by the pressure and demand of the adversaries without harming our conscience? May we compromise with them in such ceremonies and adiaphora? To this question one side has said Yes; the other, No. 2

### AFFIRMATIVE STATEMENTS

**The Correct and True Teaching and Confession about This Article**

1. For settling this controversy, we unanimously believe, teach, and confess that some ceremonies or Church practices are neither commanded nor forbidden in God's Word, but have been introduced only for the sake of fitting and good order. Such rites are not in and of themselves divine worship. They are not even a part of it. Matthew 15:9 says, "In vain do they worship Me, teaching as doctrines the commandments of men." 3

2. We believe, teach, and confess that the community of God [Latin: the churches of God] (in every place [Latin: in every land] 4

and at every time according to its circumstances) has the power to change such worship ceremonies in a way that may be most useful and edifying to the community of God [Latin: the churches of God].

5   3. Nevertheless, all frivolity and offense should be avoided in this matter. Special care should be taken to exercise patience toward the weak in faith (1 Corinthians 8:9; Romans 14:13).

6   4. We believe, teach, and confess that during a time of persecution, when a plain confession is required of us, we should not yield to the enemies in such matters of adiaphora. For the apostle has written in Galatians 5:1, "For freedom Christ has set us free; stand firm therefore, and do not submit again to a yoke of slavery." He also writes in 2 Corinthians 6:14, "Do not be unequally yoked with unbelievers. For what partnership has righteousness with lawlessness? Or what fellowship has light with darkness?" Also note Galatians 2:5, "To them we did not yield in submission even for a moment, so that the truth of the gospel might be preserved for you." For in such a case it is no longer a question about adiaphora. But it concerns the truth of the Gospel, Christian liberty, and sanctioning open idolatry. It also concerns the prevention of offense to the weak in the faith. In such a case we have nothing to concede. We should plainly confess and endure what God sends because of that confession, and whatever He allows the enemies of His Word to inflict on us.

7   5. We believe, teach, and confess also that no church should condemn another because one has less or more outward ceremonies than the other, for those are not commanded by God. This is true as long as they have unity with one another in the doctrine and all its articles and in the right use of the holy Sacraments. This practice follows the well-known saying "Disagreement in fasting does not destroy agreement in faith."

## NEGATIVE STATEMENTS

### False Teaching about This Article

We reject and condemn as wrong and 8 contrary to God's Word when the following are taught:

1. Human ordinances and institutions in 9 the Church should be regarded as a divine worship in themselves or part of it.

2. When such ceremonies, ordinances, 10 and institutions are violently forced on the community of God [Latin: the churches of God] as necessary, contrary to its Christian freedom, which it has in outward things.

3. In a time of persecution and public 11 confession, we may yield to the enemies of the Gospel in such adiaphora and ceremonies or compromise with them (which damages the truth).

4. When these outward ceremonies and 12 adiaphora are abolished as though the community of God [Latin: the churches of God] were not free to use one or more ceremonies in Christian freedom, according to its circumstances, as may be most useful at any time for the Church.

# XI. GOD'S ETERNAL FOREKNOWLEDGE AND ELECTION

Although this article was not written in response to a specific controversy among Lutherans, it was wisely included. John Calvin and his followers had developed a teaching commonly known as "double predestination." This crass and horrible teaching states that God has foreordained and predestined some people to go to hell, no matter what, while others He has foreordained and predestined to go to heaven. Article XI clearly dismantles this dreadful and nonbiblical teaching and exposes it as a great error. The Bible's teachings about election are meant only for Christians. The doctrine of election is meant to comfort Christians during hard and difficult trials. Our salvation in Christ is so sure and certain that our relationship with God was known by Him before the foundation of the world. Only those who believe in Christ trouble themselves about their election. Those who truly are unbelievers, or who have fallen away from the Christian faith, are not concerned about such things. When we are tempted in this life, this article points us to God's gracious Gospel promise, which is delivered and sealed to us in the Word and Sacraments. (See also SC II; FC SD XI.)

---

1 No public disagreement has arisen among the theologians of the Augsburg Confession about this article. But since election is a comforting article—if treated properly— and to prevent offensive disputes about it in the future, it is also explained in this writing.

## AFFIRMATIVE STATEMENTS

**The Pure and True Teaching about This Article**

2 1. To begin with, the distinction between God's foreknowledge and His eternal predestination ought to be kept accurately.

3 2. God's foreknowledge is nothing else than this: God knows all things before they happen, as it is written in Daniel 2:28, "But there is a God in heaven who reveals mysteries, and He has made known to King Nebuchadnezzar what will be in the latter days."

4 3. This foreknowledge extends over the godly and the wicked alike. But it is not the cause of evil or of sin. In other words, it is not what causes people to do wrong (which originally arises from the devil and mankind's wicked, perverse will). Nor does it cause their

ruin, for which they themselves are responsible. But foreknowledge only regulates this and fixes a limit on their ruin, how long it should last. All this happens to serve His elect for their salvation, even though such ruin is evil in itself.

5 4. Predestination, or God's eternal election, covers only the godly, beloved children of God. It is a cause of their salvation, which He also provides. He plans what belongs to it as well. Our salvation is founded so firmly on it that the gates of hell cannot overcome it (John 10:28; Matthew 16:18).

6 5. It is not to be investigated in God's secret counsel. It is to be sought in God's Word, where it is revealed.

7 6. God's Word leads us to Christ, who is the Book of Life, in whom all are written and elected who are to be saved in eternity. For it is written in Ephesians 1:4, "Even as He chose us in Him [Christ] before the foundation of the world."

8 7. Christ calls all sinners to Himself and promises them rest. He is eager that all people should come to Him and allow themselves to be helped. He offers them Himself in His Word and wants them to hear it and not to plug their ears or despise the Word. Furthermore, He promises the power and working of the Holy Spirit and divine assistance for perseverance and eternal salvation so that we may remain steadfast in the faith and gain eternal salvation.

9 8. We should not reach conclusions about our election to eternal life based on reason or God's Law. That would lead us either into a reckless, loose, Epicurean life or into despair. It would stir up destructive thoughts in people's hearts. For they cannot, as long as they follow their reason, successfully keep themselves from thinking, "If God has elected me to salvation, I cannot be condemned, no matter what I do." And again, "If I am not

elected to eternal life, it doesn't matter what good I do; it is in vain anyway."

10  9. The true judgment about predestination must be learned alone from the Holy Gospel about Christ, in which it is clearly testified, "For God has consigned all to disobedience, that He may have mercy on all (Romans 11:32); not wishing that any should perish, but that all should reach repentance" (2 Peter 3:9), and believe in the Lord Christ. (See also Ezekiel 18:23; 33:11, 18; 1 John 2:2.)

11  10. Now, let whoever is concerned about God's revealed will act on the order that St. Paul has described in the Epistle to the Romans. Paul first directs people to repentance (Romans 1–2), to knowledge of sins (Romans 3:1–20), to faith in Christ (Romans 3:21–5:21), to divine obedience (Romans 6–8). Then he speaks of the mystery of God's eternal election (Romans 9–11). This doctrine is useful and consolatory to the person who proceeds in this way.

12  11. However, "many are called, but few are chosen" (Matthew 22:14). This does not mean that God is unwilling to save everybody. But the reason some are not saved is as follows: They do not listen to God's Word at all, but willfully despise it, plug their ears, and harden their hearts. In this way they block the ordinary way (Luke 16:29–31) for the Holy Spirit so He cannot perform His work in them. Or, when they have heard God's Word, they make light of it again and ignore it. But their wickedness is responsible for this, not God or His election (2 Peter 2:1–3; Luke 11:49–52; Hebrews 12:25–26).

13  12. A Christian should concern himself with the article about God's eternal election only as far as it has been revealed in God's Word. His Word presents Christ to us as the Book of Life, which He opens and reveals to us by the preaching of the Holy Gospel, as it is written in Romans 8:30, "And those whom He predestined He also called." In Him we are to seek the eternal election of the Father, who has determined in His eternal divine counsel (Ephesians 1:11–12) that He would save no one except those who know His Son Christ and truly believe in Him. Other thoughts are to be banished. For they do not come from God, but from the suggestion of the evil foe. With such thoughts he attempts to weaken or entirely remove us from the glorious comfort we have in this helpful doctrine. In other words, we know that out of pure grace, without any merit of our own, we have been elected in Christ to eternal life. No one can pluck us out of His hand (John 10:29). He has not only promised this gracious election with mere words, but has also certified it with an oath and sealed it with the holy Sacraments. We can call these to mind in our most severe temptations and take comfort in them, and with them we can quench the fiery darts of the devil (Ephesians 6:16).

14  13. Besides, we should act with the greatest diligence, to live according to God's will. As St. Peter encourages in 2 Peter 1:10, "make your calling and election sure." We should especially cling to the revealed Word, which cannot and will not fail us.

15  14. By this brief explanation of God's eternal election, glory is entirely and fully given to God. Out of pure mercy alone, without any of our merit, He saves us according to the purpose of His will. No reason is given to anyone for despair or a vulgar, wild life.

## ANTITHESES OR NEGATIVE STATEMENTS

### False Teachings about This Article

16  We believe and hold this: When anyone teaches the doctrine about God's gracious election to eternal life in such a way that troubled Christians cannot comfort them-

selves with this teaching, but are led to despondency or despair, or when the unrepentant are strengthened in their wild living, then the doctrine of election is not treated according to God's Word and will. Instead, this doctrine is being taught according to reason and by the encouragement of cursed Satan. It is as the apostle testifies in Romans 15:4: "Whatever was written in former days was written for our instruction, that through endurance and through the encouragement of the Scriptures we might have hope." Therefore, we reject the following errors:

17    1. God is unwilling that all people repent and believe the Gospel.

18    2. When God calls us to Himself, He is not eager that all people should come to Him.

19    3. God is unwilling that everyone should be saved. But some—without regard to their sins, from God's mere counsel, purpose, and will—are chosen for condemnation so that they cannot be saved.

20    4. Something in us causes God's election—not just God's mercy and Christ's most holy merit—because of which God has elected us to everlasting life.

21    All these are blasphemous and dreadful erroneous doctrines. By them all the comfort that Christians have in the Holy Gospel and the use of the holy Sacraments is taken away from them. Therefore, these doctrines should not be tolerated in God's Church.

22    This is the brief and simple explanation of the disputed articles. For a time, they have been debated and taught controversially among the theologians of the Augsburg Confession. Therefore, every simple Christian—according to the guidance of God's Word and his simple catechism—can see what is right or wrong. For not only the pure doctrine has been stated, but also the erroneous, contrary doctrine has been repudiated and rejected.

So the offensive divisions that have happened are thoroughly settled.

23    May Almighty God and the Father of our Lord Jesus grant the grace of His Holy Spirit so that we may all be one in Him and constantly abide in this Christian unity, which is well pleasing to Him! Amen.

# XII. OTHER FACTIONS AND SECTS

## THAT NEVER EMBRACED THE AUGSBURG CONFESSION

This article lists and condemns a host of false teachings, and the groups promoting them, as potentially damning. Review the points made here by the writers of the Formula of Concord and compare them to the teachings of religions today. Through such comparisons, one may agree that "there is nothing new under the sun" (Ecclesiastes 1:9). Modern errors, false teachings, and heresies are merely recycled from the past, repackaged with attractive gimmicks, and sold to new, unsuspecting "customers." (See also FC SD XII.)

---

1    In order that heresies and sects may not be pinned on us silently (for in the preceding explanation, we have made no mention of them), we intend at the end of this writing simply to make a list. The list will show the articles in which the heretics err and teach contrary to our Christian faith and confession (to which we have often referred).

## ERRONEOUS ARTICLES OF THE ANABAPTISTS

2    The Anabaptists are divided among themselves into many factions, because one fights for more errors, another for less. However, they all in common profess the sort of doctrine that cannot be tolerated or allowed

in the Church, in the commonwealth and secular government, or in home life.

**Articles That Cannot Be Tolerated in the Church**

3    1. Christ did not receive His body and blood from the Virgin Mary, but brought them with Him from heaven.

4    2. Christ is not true God, but is only superior to other saints, because He has more gifts of the Holy Spirit than any other holy man.

5    3. Our righteousness before God stands not on the sole merit of Christ alone, but in renewal, and therefore in our own godliness in which we walk. This is based in great part on one's own special, self-chosen spirituality. In fact, it is nothing other than a new kind of monasticism.

6    4. Children who are not baptized are not sinners before God, but righteous and innocent. In their innocence, because they have not yet gained the use of their reason, children are saved without Baptism. According to their assertion, children do not need Baptism. Therefore, they reject the entire teaching about original sin and what belongs to it.

7    5. Children are not to be baptized until they have gained the use of their reason and can confess their faith themselves.

8    6. The children of Christians, because they have been born of Christian and believing parents, are holy and children of God even without and before Baptism. And for this reason they do not attach much importance to the Baptism of children or encourage it, contrary to the clear words of God's promise, which applies only to those who keep His covenant and do not despise it (see Genesis 17:7–14; also Acts 2:38–39 and Colossians 2:11–15).

9    7. There is no true Christian congregation in which sinners are still found.

10    8. No sermon is to be heard or attended in those churches where formerly papal Masses have been celebrated and said.

11    9. A godly person must not have anything to do with the ministers of the Church who preach the Gospel according to the Augsburg Confession and rebuke the sermons and errors of the Anabaptists. Also, a person must not serve or in any way work for them, but must flee from them and shun them as perverters of God's Word.

**Articles That Cannot Be Tolerated in the Government**

12    1. Under the New Testament, public office is not a calling that pleases God.

13    2. A Christian cannot with a good, clear conscience hold or fulfill public office.

14    3. In cases that require action, a Christian cannot use the office of the magistracy against the wicked without harming his conscience. For protection and defense, citizens may invoke the power that the magistrates possess and have received from God.

15    4. A Christian cannot take an oath with a good conscience. Nor can a Christian promise loyalty with an oath to the hereditary prince of his country or sovereign.

16    5. Under the New Testament public officials cannot, without injury to conscience, impose capital punishment on evildoers.

**Articles That Cannot Be Tolerated in Domestic Life**

17    1. A Christian cannot with a good conscience hold or possess property, but is in duty bound to devote his property to the common treasury.

18    2. A Christian cannot with a good conscience be an innkeeper, merchant, or maker of weapons.

19    3. Married people may be divorced on account of differences in faith. One may abandon the other and be married to another person who shares his faith.

## ERRONEOUS ARTICLES
## OF THE SCHWENKFELDIANS

20    1. All those who regard Christ as a creature according to the flesh have no true knowledge of Christ as the reigning King of heaven.

21    2. By exaltation, Christ's flesh has assumed all divine properties with this result: Christ as man is in might, power, majesty, and glory altogether (as regards degree and position) of equal essence to the Father and to the Word. So now there is only one essence, property, will, and glory of both natures in Christ. And now Christ's flesh belongs to the essence of the holy Trinity.

22    3. The ministry of the Church—the Word preached and heard—is not the means God the Holy Spirit uses to teach people and work in them the saving knowledge of Christ, conversion, repentance, faith, and new obedience.

23    4. The water of Baptism is not how God the Lord seals the adoption of sons and works regeneration.

24    5. Bread and wine in the Holy Supper are not means through and by which Christ gives us His body and blood.

25    6. A Christian who is truly regenerated by God's Spirit can perfectly keep and fulfill God's Law in this life.

26    7. A congregation that does not excommunicate or regularly ban people is not truly Christian.

27    8. A minister of the Church who is not truly renewed, regenerate, righteous, and godly cannot helpfully teach other people or distribute genuine, true Sacraments.

## ERROR OF THE NEW ARIANS

28    Christ is not true, essential, natural God, of one eternal, divine essence with God the Father and the Holy Spirit. He is only adorned with divine majesty inferior to and alongside of God the Father.

## ERROR OF THE ANTI-TRINITARIANS

29    This is an entirely new sect, not heard of before in Christendom. They believe, teach, and confess that there is not only one, eternal, divine essence of the Father, Son, and Holy Spirit. But [they teach that] God the Father, Son, and Holy Spirit are three distinct persons. Each person has its essence distinct and separate from the other persons of the Godhead. Some in this sect think that all three persons are of equal power, wisdom, majesty, and glory (just as otherwise three people are distinct and separate from one another in their essence). Others think that these three persons and essences are unequal with one another in essence and properties, so that the Father alone is properly and truly God.

30    These and similar articles, one and all, with whatever other errors depend on and follow from them, we reject and condemn as wrong, false, and heretical. They are contrary to God's Word, the three Creeds, the Augsburg Confession and Apology, the Smalcald Articles, and Luther's Catechisms. All godly Christians of both high and low estate should be on their guard to the extent that they hold dear their soul's welfare and their salvation.

31    This is the doctrine, faith, and confession of us all. We will give an account of it on the Last Day before the just judge, our Lord Jesus Christ. We will not speak or write anything against this doctrine, either secretly or publicly. By God's grace we intend to persevere in it. After mature deliberation we have testified, in the true fear of God and invocation of His name, by signing this Epitome with our own hands.

⚭

# CONTROVERSIES AND THE FORMULA OF CONCORD

To understand the Formula of Concord, you need to understand the controversies that it settled. What follows is a summary of the various controversies, listed in the order in which they arose and referenced to the articles in the Formula that discuss them.

## The Antinomian Controversy (1527–56; Articles V and VI)

In 1527, John Agricola argued with Martin Luther about repentance (contrition), saying that it is not worked in us by the Law, but by the Gospel. This was a view that, in a modified form, was later defended also by Wittenberg Philippists. Some eventually rejected the so-called third use of the Law.

The Gospel is the good news that God has provided salvation for all humanity because of, for the sake of, and through Christ and Christ alone. This is the central and most important teaching of the Bible and, consequently, the very heart of what Lutheranism is all about. Taking that central truth, some Lutherans went too far and said that God's Law simply no longer applies to Christians. They said that the Gospel is the only valid Word of God for Christians. They rejected any place for God's Law in the life of the Christian, denying that it provided a guide for Christian behavior. Those who held anti-Law views were called "Antinomians," *nomos* being the Greek word for *law*.

Article V of the Formula describes the key distinction in Christian theology, without which there can be no proper understanding of the Bible and no pure and clear teaching and preaching of God's Word. The proper distinction between Law and Gospel is essential.

The Formula of Concord carefully explains how the word *Gospel* is used in different ways. It explains that the Bible itself has a variety of uses for that word. The Formula of Concord discusses Law and Gospel in terms of their content and their functions. When *Gospel* is used in the phrase "Law and Gospel" it is used very specifically and narrowly to refer to salvation in Christ. The functions of God's Law cannot be transferred to the Gospel. Both Law and Gospel must be proclaimed. The Holy Spirit works through both Law and Gospel. The chief function of the Law is to accuse us of sin. The Law is always accusing us of sin, precisely so that we will be led by the Gospel to cling to Christ, the Savior. The Law, therefore, is used by the Holy Spirit to lead us to repent. The Gospel is how the Holy Spirit gives us faith and keeps us in faith, that is, to trust in Christ, and Christ alone, for our salvation. Without the Law, the Gospel cannot be comprehended. Without the Gospel, the Law either drives people to despair or makes them self-righteous hypocrites.

The crucifixion of Jesus Christ is the best example of how one historical event can be used to preach both Law and Gospel. His death shows the severity of the penalty for our sins. This is the preaching of the Law. Through it we become aware of the seriousness of our sin and sinful condition. But when the crucifixion is preached to show that sins are no longer counted against us, then the Gospel is being preached. Historical events are in themselves neither Law nor Gospel, but they can be preached for the sake of Law or Gospel. The categories of Law and Gospel are categories through which the entire biblical account is to be interpreted so that people may first acknowledge and repent of sin and then turn in God-given faith to Christ, believing that for His sake God regards them as righteous and innocent.

Article VI is a continuation of Article V. It asserts that the Law has a unique place for Christians. Lutheranism summarizes three functions of God's Law by referring to the Law as (a) a curb, to contain great outbreaks of sin in the world; as (b) a mirror, its chief use, by which the Holy Spirit reveals our sin to us; and as (c) a rule, or guide, by which we know what pleases God. This threefold distinction is thoroughly biblical and, therefore, thoroughly Lutheran.

The third use of the Law is a function the Law has in the life of a believer. From the standpoint of forgiveness and justification in Christ, believers can encounter God's Law, yet not regard it as a threat. Instead, under the renewing of the Holy Spirit they recognize in God's unchangeable will the way they freely and spontaneously want to live.

It is not possible for a person to deny the third use of the Law and be regarded as genuinely Lutheran.

## The Controversy over Christ's Descent into Hell (1544; Article IX)

A Lutheran pastor in Hamburg, John Aepinus, taught that Christ's descent to hell was part of His suffering and humiliation. Aepinus's colleagues opposed him, arguing that Christ descended into hell in glory. Thankfully, this controversy was quickly resolved.

In the Ancient Church there was no unanimous opinion about the meaning of Christ's visit to hell, which is described in 1 Peter 3:18–22. Some thought it meant that Christ went to hell to release the Old Testament saints from a special place reserved for them so that they could finally reach heaven. A very popular view was that Christ's descent into hell was a "victory tour" whereby Christ proclaimed His triumph over Satan and all the forces of evil.

Aepinus speculated that from the time between Christ's death on Friday until Sunday, when He appeared to the women, Christ's body remained in the tomb and His spirit descended to hell as part of the atonement. Others resisted this view and simply pointed to Jesus' words on the cross, when He said, "It is finished" (John 19:30). They said, "Finished means finished."

The Formula of Concord asserts that Christ descended to proclaim victory and that this must be accepted through faith and not speculated on. It comforts Christians to know that Christ has been everywhere and seen everything—even hell. Satan holds no ground or refuge from God's judgment.

# The Controversy about Adiaphora
# (1548–55; Article X)

The Church has always had practices that are not expressly commanded or forbidden by God's Word (e.g., the hour at which worship services are held). *Adiaphora* is a Greek word that describes these practices. It means "things morally indifferent" or "nonessentials in faith or conduct." Of course, the Church would not need a doctrinal article on things that "do not really matter." But, in fact, adiaphora *do* matter (as anyone can tell you, who has missed worship due to changes in service times). Adiaphora are matters left to Christian judgment and done in Christian freedom. It was precisely a controversy over such things that caused the first recognizable split among Lutherans after Luther's death.

After the Lutheran princes were defeated by Charles V on the battlefield at Mühlberg in 1547, the Augsburg Interim and then the Leipzig Interim were forced on the Lutherans. These statements were intended as compromise documents to stabilize matters until a general council of the Roman Church met to resolve matters once and for all (the Council of Trent, 1545–63). The Wittenberg and Leipzig theologians (Melanchthon, Eber, Pfeffinger, and others.) defended them, which forced the use of Roman ceremonies in the Lutheran Church. The controversy erupted when Philip Melanchthon and his followers were willing to give in to Roman demands that they reintroduce certain customs and practices in the Church. The pope and emperor required and demanded the changes and would not make them matters of free choice.

Champions of a consistent and determined Lutheranism opposed these abuses. They taught, "Nothing is an adiaphoron in cases of confession and offense." If a human ordinance is given the status of a divine command or is viewed as necessary for salvation, it must be resisted without any compromise.

To insist on something that is not expressly commanded, or forbidden, by Holy Scripture is a violation of Gospel freedom and adds to the Gospel. Therefore, the "genuine" or *Gnesio Lutherans*, led most notably by Matthias Flacius, were forced to resist the practices and even to oppose Philip Melanchthon, their former teacher. Melanchthon and his supporters (known as "Philippists") argued for the compromises with Rome. They claimed that it was the only way to preserve Lutheranism, since they were under the thumb of the Holy Roman Emperor Charles V.

## Adiaphora Today

Confessional Lutheranism, unlike many other Christian churches, does not have any set requirements for how the Church is governed and structured. We do not require, like Rome, a hierarchy flowing from a pope through bishops. Unlike many Reformed churches, we do not believe there is a divine mandate for classes of clergy, such as elders.

So also in worship, because there is no divinely mandated order of worship set forth in the New Testament, we do not insist on a precise form by way of divine command. The Lutheran concern is always for what best supports the pure teaching of the Gospel and the proper administration of the Sacraments. We ask ourselves, "What order and pattern of worship best supports and reflects Lutheranism's biblical doctrine?" That is the real issue.

From the very early days of the Reformation Luther and his colleagues developed precise orders of worship, keeping as much of the historic liturgy as they could without compromising the Gospel. Here in America, confessional Lutheran leaders such as C. F. W. Walther taught that because the Lutheran Church is always surrounded by Reformed theology and practice, it is always in a state of confession. Therefore, Lutherans should rejoice to use the historic liturgy, art, crucifixes, vestments and all that is part of our Lutheran heritage, not allowing it to be viewed as wrong or as an impediment to the Gospel.

As changes are considered in the worship service, remember that no human ceremony is required for proper worship of God. It is wrong to suggest that there is a precisely defined way of worshiping God. Lutheran leaders such as Martin Chemnitz worked very hard to develop well-regulated worship services and liturgical practices. Changes were only permitted after careful consultation of all the clergy in a particular area, in order to preserve the Church's unity in doctrine, as reflected by unity in worship practices. The thought that a pastor would, from Sunday to Sunday, write a new liturgy was quite unimaginable to Lutherans in those years, for they cherished the good, ancient liturgy and worship traditions and the unity and peace that com-

### Andreas Osiander (1498–1552)

Osiander was largely responsible for one of the most important controversies after Luther's death: Are we justified because of the Christ who dwells in us, or the work of Christ for us, outside of us? Though he opposed the Augsburg Interim, he fell into grave error on the doctrine of justification. Article III rejected Osiander's errors.

mon worship practices brought to the Church. Such practices made it possible for the consistent, solid teaching and preaching of God's Word.

The message of Article X on Adiaphora is that no human ordinance can be demanded as being a command from God and necessary for salvation; nor can anyone demand that Lutherans stop using the good, ancient Church customs or suggest that to use these customs is Roman Catholic and, thus, wrong and inappropriate for today. Most important, at a time of persecution, clear and faithful confession is required, and therefore nothing can be compromised, given up, changed, or added that would compromise pure doctrine by giving the impression of unity where in fact there is not unity in doctrine.

## The Controversy about Christ's Righteousness (1549–66; Article III)

The errors that required this topic to be dealt with in the Formula of Concord are somewhat unique in Church history. Andreas Osiander taught that a person is declared righteous by God, justified, because the divine nature of Christ takes up residence within his or her heart, and for that reason, God declares that person righteous. Eastern Orthodoxy is probably most close to this error, with its heavy emphasis on the indwelling grace of Christ as key to a person's salvation. Francesco Stancaro, an Italian professor at Königsberg, Germany, came to a similar conclusion, but said that it was Christ's human nature residing within a person that causes God to justify him or her.

George Major (1502–74)

Major was a strong supporter and advocate of the Leipzig Interim. He advocated the view that good works are necessary for salvation, saying later they are necessary to retain faith. Article IV repudiated Major's errors.

There are serious doctrinal problems for both of these false views. Both views begin by wrongly dividing Christ's divine and human natures, something that is never permitted by Scripture. The two natures in the one person of Christ were most precisely confessed by the Council of Chalcedon, a council affirmed strongly by genuine confessional Lutheranism. (See the Nicene Creed, p. 42.)

Even more serious an error in this controversy was how justification was defined as the indwelling of Christ in the believer. The Bible bases our justification not on the indwelling of Christ but on the work of Christ saving us through His perfect life of obedience to God's Law and His perfect self-sacrifice on the cross. Christ's work occurs outside of us. Our justification is entirely a consequence of Christ's work for us, on our behalf, but not in us. Because of Christ's life and death, God declares us righteous, just as a judge declares a guilty person not guilty because someone has taken his place and taken the guilty person's punishment on himself.

The Bible does teach that a blessing of salvation is the dwelling of the Trinity within a believer. It teaches that mankind is sanctified (that is, made holy) by the indwelling of God as a gift and result of justification. The danger of saying that justification is something happening inside of a human being is that people will be looking always within themselves, instead of looking to Christ's objective work. The Latin phrase *extra nos*, literally "outside us," is a handy way of describing the biblical and, therefore, Lutheran teaching about justification.

When Osiander and Stancaro attempted to base justification on what is going on inside of a person, instead of Christ's external, objective work and God's gift, they were in fact reverting back to the errors of the Roman view of justification. The Roman theologians taught justification as an ongoing process that is only completed by what happens within a person. This turns the Gospel into a Law and throws out certainty in Christ by replacing it with dependence on a person's internal response, reactions, and attitudes about Christ.

## The Controversy over Good Works
## (1551–62; Article IV)

Luther insisted on the Bible's teaching that salvation is truly by grace alone, through faith alone. This led immediately to the accusation by Rome that Lutheranism was opposed to good works, or worse yet, didn't believe there was now any binding Law from God.

One of the longest articles in the Augsburg Confession is Article XX on Good Works. It demonstrates clearly the Lutheran sensitivity to these concerns and provides a response to the false accusation that Lutheranism is not concerned about good works. The Formula of Concord had to take up this issue again.

When the Leipzig Interim document was prepared, Melanchthon permitted the phrase "good works are necessary for salvation" to be included. Even though he attempted to explain this statement in a correct sense, it led to great offense and controversy. The Interim favorably quoted from certain phrases in Melanchthon's writings. One of his followers, George Major, was absolutely blunt about it. Major taught that good works are necessary for salvation and that without good works nobody can be saved. Nicholas von Amsdorf rejected Major's teaching, but introduced a new error on the opposite side. Amsdorf insisted that good works are harmful and detrimental to salvation. The Formula of Concord settled this controversy by insisting that good works are necessary for Christians, but that the words "for salvation" should be left out of this statement.

When it comes to our salvation, there is only one good work that saves us—Christ's sacrificial life and death on our behalf! There is only One who is good—Christ Jesus, our Lord. His good work alone is what saves people from eternal damnation. The trust that God creates and gives as a gift of grace is a living and active faith, not a dead, static, intellectual assent. Faith does not have the option of refusing to perform good works. By God's grace, this faith is lived out in service to others—a life of good works. But it is not the works of believers that save them, it is God's grace through Christ, our Lord.

## The Controversy about Synergism (1555–60; Article II)

*Synergism* comes from two Greek words that mean "to work with." Synergism describes any teaching that implies a person has the ability to "work with" God to achieve salvation. Melanchthon and many of his followers held that people cooperate in their conversion by their own natural powers. Melanchthon had written that the three reasons people are saved are (a) the Holy Spirit, (b) God's Word, and (c) a person's nonresisting will. The last cause is synergistic, because it suggests that a person in fact contributes something to his or her salvation, namely, "nonresistance." Other Reformers strongly opposed this teaching (Amsdorf, Flacius, and others). As Flacius stated, "God alone converts a person . . . He does not exclude the human will, but all efficaciousness and work of the will."

The Formula of Concord formally adopted Martin Luther's position on free will as he explained it in his great treatise *The Bondage of the Will.* Luther directed this work against the great humanist scholar Erasmus and his book *The Freedom of the Will.*

Luther based his views on Holy Scripture, which taught that because of the fall into sin, a human being is by nature dead in sin. The human will is incapable of beginning conversion or of cooperating with God's grace before conversion. The Holy Spirit, working through the Gospel, gives to a person the gift of trust in Christ. Therefore, faith is entirely God's doing, not a matter of human choice or deciding or cooperating with God. All matters of faith are gifts of God. This issue is critical to maintaining the absolute supremacy of God's grace, for if anything is attributed to the powers of the human will, it may be possible to speak of salvation by grace, but not by grace alone.

This article in the Lutheran Confessions clearly sets Lutheranism apart from Roman Catholicism on the one hand, and much of Protestant and so-called Evangelical Christianity on the other. Both of these traditions hold that there is within a human being some ability to cooperate with God's grace. This explains the Roman doctrine of "infused grace," that is, the teaching that God infuses, or permeates, grace into a person so that the person may respond and merit salvation. This also explains why many Protestant Christians emphasize "making a decision" for Jesus, believing that there is within human beings the ability to respond to grace and thus "choose to follow" Jesus.

# The Crypto-Calvinist Controversy
## (1560–74; Articles VII and VIII)

To understand this controversy, one must go back to the Marburg Colloquy (1529). At this conference, the father of Reformed theology, Ulrich Zwingli, insisted that the Lutherans and the Reformed agreed on doctrinal matters. However, Luther and his colleagues said that they did not agree, pointing to Zwingli's symbolic interpretation of the Lord's Supper as the chief example of differences between them.

Years later, after Zwingli and Luther died, John Calvin became the leading figure among the Reformed and Philip Melanchthon became the leading figure among the Lutherans. Melanchthon was responsible for funneling many of Calvin's teachings into the Lutheran Church. He developed a close relationship with Calvin. In fact, Calvin came to regard Melanchthon as one of his most important fathers in the faith.

Calvin wanted to distance himself from the purely "symbolic" interpretation of the Lord's Words of Institution, which Zwingli had defended. (Yet, in *The Consensus Tigurinus*, Calvin wrote that it is an impious superstition to believe that Christ's body and blood are actually present under the bread and wine in the Lord's Supper.) To accommodate his Reformed friends, Melanchthon revised the Augsburg Confession in 1540. He changed it so that it would be possible for Calvin and others like him to agree with the Confession. In fact, Calvin signed this version of the Augsburg Confession! This altered version of the Augsburg Confession, called the *Variata*, confused a number of Lutheran lay leaders. (See Preface to the Book of Concord, pp. 29–38.)

The Calvinists began to infiltrate key Lutheran cities, including Wittenberg. By using deceptive and vague terms, they made it seem as though they were Lutheran, when in fact they were not. False doctrine is often disguised with carefully chosen words and phrases intended to make people think one thing, when in fact another is intended. Because of these deceptions, the movement became known as "Crypto-Calvinism" (*crypto* means "hidden").

Tragically, the center of Crypto-Calvinistic heresy was none other than Wittenberg, the place of Luther's lifework. Elector Maurice of Saxony was the descendant of Luther's first protector, Frederick the Wise. Maurice welcomed Crypto-Calvinist professors into his territory. He even persecuted and drove out genuine Lutherans who spoke out against the infiltrating Calvinists.

Maurice's brother, Augustus, became Elector of Saxony in 1553. Genuine Lutheran theologians finally persuaded Augustus that there were major problems with the Wittenberg faculty. Augustus carefully questioned the professors. They replied with quotes from Luther, but added many ambiguous quotes from Melanchthon. They fiercely attacked Matthias Flacius and other key Lutheran theologians who had questioned their teaching. They persuaded Augustus that, in fact, they were right and that the genuine Lutherans were wrong. Augustus began removing the last remaining genuine Lutherans from his faculty and territory.

Then a remarkable turn of events opened Augustus's eyes to what was really going on. Casper Peucer (Melanchthon's son-in-law) sent a letter to a court preacher who was part of the Calvinist conspiracy. The letter urged the preacher to influence Elector Augustus by giving the elector's wife a Calvinist prayer book. By mistake, Peucer's letter was delivered to an orthodox Lutheran court preacher, who showed it to Elector Augustus. Augustus was outraged. After careful investigation, he dismissed the Calvinistic Wittenberg faculty and brought in genuine Lutheran professors from Magdeburg and Jena. Augustus became an ardent supporter of genuine Lutheranism and was instrumental in the production of the Formula of Concord in 1577 and the publication of the Book of Concord in 1580.

## The Response of the Formula of Concord

The articles on Christ and His Supper were written with the Crypto-Calvinist situation in view. In several respects, these two articles are the most important in the Formula of Concord. In Article VII Luther's writings and the other confessional documents are generously quoted. Four arguments from Luther's *Confession concerning Christ's Supper* (1528) are taken over into the Formula: (a) Jesus is inseparably God and man, (b) Jesus is at God's right hand and is therefore everywhere and capable of doing all things, (c) God's Word does not lie, and (d) God is not limited to one place at one time. Lutherans see the Lord's Supper as a union between the earthly elements

PROMPTE   ET SINCERE ·

### John Calvin (1509–64)

After Zwingli's death (1531), John Calvin eventually become a leader of the Reformation in Switzerland and elsewhere. He is, for all practical purposes, the chief founder of the Reformed churches. From Geneva, Reformed theology, or "Calvinism," branched out into many parts of Europe, giving rise to the Hugenots in France, the Dutch Reformed, and the Scottish Presbyterians. It heavily influenced Anglicanism in England, which in turn gave rise to the Puritans, and eventually also the Baptists and Methodists. Most non-Lutheran Protestant theology stems from Calvinism. Articles VII, VIII, and XI are directed in large part against Reformed errors.

of bread and wine and the actual body and blood of Jesus Christ. The Lutheran Confessions coined a term to describe this, *sacramental union*. The strongest attacks in these articles are directed against the "Sacramentarian" (Reformed) views that deny Christ's actual presence under the bread and wine. Sixteen different views are rejected and condemned.

However, what must be made perfectly clear is that Lutheranism does not assert the biblical teaching of Christ's presence in His Supper on the basis of philosophical arguments, or on the basis of the doctrine of the two natures in Christ. These points, though true and valid, are all marshaled to defend the chief and foremost foundation of the reality of the Lord's presence in His Supper: the words of Christ Himself. When the Reformed or others deny that the Lord means *is* when He says, "This is My body," Lutherans point first to Jesus' words. In fact, this is what Luther meant at the Marburg Colloquy when he said, "It is written."

## Calvinism Today

Many Reformed theologians, then and now, try to justify their interpretation of Christ's words by appealing to philosophy or Christology. Modern attempts to combine Lutheranism and Reformed theology are similar to the compromising and deceptive way Calvinizing Lutherans tried to move away from Luther's biblical confession of the Lord's Supper. There is, however, an even more dangerous influence on Lutheran and Reformed ecumenical compromises today—the rise of "higher criticism." This school of thought regards the Bible less as God's Word and more as human opinion. Due to "higher critical" views of the Bible, liberal Lutherans and Calvinists no longer regard the Gospel records of Jesus' words as historically reliable. Therefore, they have agreed that one cannot be sure about what Jesus actually said. Sadly, they conclude that one certainly cannot be "dogmatic" about a particular understanding or interpretation of Jesus' words, "This *is* My body."

## The Controversy about Original Sin
## (1560–75; Article I)

There are tragic ironies in the history of the development of the Formula of Concord. Greatest among these is the fact that Philip Melanchthon was most responsible for nearly destroying Lutheranism after the death of Luther. Melanchthon tended to compromise and embrace what clearly was contrary to the Lutheran Reformation. Nearly as ironic is the fact that the greatest of all the Gnesio-Lutherans, Matthias Flacius, also fell into error when trying to defend the doctrine of original sin. Flacius struggled for many years to oppose Melanchthon's compromises. He was largely responsible for preserving Luther's life and legacy. To the credit of the men responsible for the Formula of Concord, they rejected the errors of both these prominent figures. They insisted on a proper biblical teaching on original sin.

This controversy has a lot to do with the use of philosophical terms, which Luther always warned against using, particularly as one preached and taught Christian laity. Such terms provided great potential for needless offense, confusion, and misunderstanding. This controversy certainly justified Luther's concern. Because controversy and error were being espoused, it was necessary for the Formula of Concord to deal with these philosophical terms.

Matthias Flacius maintained that original sin is not an *accident*, but the very *substance* of fallen humanity. The Lutherans (including the Philippists) were practically unanimous in opposing this error. *Accident* refers to something that "just happens to be there." It is a characteristic that is not essential to a person or a thing. For example, if a person wears a hat, that would be called an "accident." He would still be a human being whether he had the hat on or not. However, certain human characteristics are *essential*. For example, a human being is either a man or a woman. Gender is an essential human characteristic.

In the Augsburg Confession, Lutheranism insisted that original sin is so deep a corruption of human nature that it prevents a person from contributing anything to his or her own salvation. After Luther's death Melanchthon suggested that a person can, and in fact does, cooperate with God's grace in salvation. Flacius responded with the best of intentions. But by claiming that sin was of the very essence or substance of humanity, he went too far.

After the fall into sin, mankind was plunged into a condition by which we are sinful from the moment of conception. But this sinful condition is not a part of our essence as human beings. To say that sin is essential to a human would require us to teach that God created sin and created mankind sinful. This is not so. Therefore, original sin is not of the very essence or substance of humanity, but is accidental to it.

If taken to its logical conclusion, Flacius's position would require us to believe that God Himself is the creator and cause of sin. Flacius stubbornly clung to his error and would not heed the pleas of his friends and colleagues. He would not recognize where his zealous defense of truth was leading him—into more error.

Article I of the Formula of Concord, therefore, had to make clear what the Bible teaches. Since the fall, human nature is not sin itself, but it is sinful. The Formula wisely points out that to suggest God created sin would mean that God's Son assumed sin itself into divinity in the incarnation. What is more, if sin is part of a person's very substance, then it too will be resurrected on the Last Day to spend eternity in heaven, an absurd idea, in view of Scripture.

The incident with Flacius is a good warning to those who are zealous to defend truth. They must not go so far in defending truth that they end up in error through overstatement or overreaction.

# THE FORMULA OF CONCORD

## SECOND PART
A Thorough, Pure, Correct, and Final
### REPETITION AND DECLARATION

of Some Articles of the Augsburg Confession
about Which, for Some Time, There Has Been Controversy
among Some Theologians Who Subscribe to Them,
Decided and Settled according to the Analogy of God's Word
and the Summary Contents of Our Christian Doctrine.

## OUTLINE

When Jacob Andreae prepared articles in the Epitome of the Formula of Concord, he consistently presented (a) the status of the controversy, (b) affirmative statements of doctrine, and (c) negative statements against false doctrine. The Solid Declaration does not follow this same consistent presentation and is much longer. Therefore, the editors have provided subheads for the sake of easier reading and reference. These subheads are included in the following outline.

---

For historical introductions to the Solid Declaration, see pp. 473–89 and 521–31.

# THE FORMULA OF CONCORD

1   By the Almighty's special grace and mercy, the teaching about the chief articles of our Christian religion (which under the papacy had been horribly clouded by human teachings and ordinances) had been explained and purified again from God's Word by Dr. Luther, of blessed and holy memory. The papistic errors, abuses, and idolatries 2 had been rebuked by him. Nevertheless, this pure reformation was regarded by its opponents as a new teaching. It was violently (though without foundation) charged with being entirely against God's Word and the Christian ordinances. In addition, the Reformation was burdened by unsupportable 3 slanders and accusations. The Christian electors, princes, and estates of the Empire at that time had embraced the pure doctrine of the Holy Gospel. They also had their churches reformed in a Christian manner according to God's Word. At the great Diet of Augsburg in the year 1530 they had a Christian Confession prepared from God's Word and delivered to Emperor Charles V. In this way they clearly and plainly made their Christian Confession about what was being held and taught in the Christian evangelical churches on the chief articles. They focused especially on the articles in controversy between themselves and the papists. Although this Confession was received with disfavor by their opponents, still, thank God, it remains unrefuted and undefeated to this day.

4   To this Christian Augsburg Confession, so thoroughly grounded in God's Word, we here pledge ourselves again from our inmost hearts. We abide by its simple, clear, and unadulterated meaning as the words convey it. We regard this Confession as a pure Christian symbol. At the present time, this Confession ought to be found alongside God's Word among true Christians. They should act just as in former times when certain great controversies had arisen in God's Church. Symbols and Confessions were proposed, to which the pure teachers and hearers at that time pledged themselves with heart and mouth. We intend also, by the Almighty's 5 grace, to abide faithfully by this Christian Confession (mentioned several times before) until our death just as it was delivered in the year 1530 to Emperor Charles V. Whether in this writing or in any other, it is our plan not to withdraw in the least from that oft-cited Confession, nor to propose another or new Confession.

The Christian doctrine of this Confes- 6 sion has for the most part remained unchallenged, except for what has been challenged by the papists. Yet it cannot be denied that some theologians have departed from some great and important articles of this Confession. Either they have not understood the true meaning of the other articles, or they have not continued steadfastly in them. Occasionally some even tried to attach a foreign meaning to this Confession. At the same time they wanted to be regarded as followers of the Augsburg Confession (and to help themselves and make their boast about it). Serious 7 and harmful divisions have arisen in the pure evangelical churches from this. The same thing happened during the lives of the holy apostles among those who wanted to be called Christians and boasted of Christ's doctrine—horrible errors likewise arose. Some sought to be justified and saved by the works of the Law (Acts 15:1–29). Others denied the resurrection of the dead (1 Corinthians 15:12). Still others did not believe that Christ was true and eternal God. The holy apostles had to attack these teachings forcefully in their sermons and writings (Galatians 1:8). They did this although such fundamental errors and severe controversies could not happen at that time without offense both to unbelievers and to those weak in the faith. In a similar way our opponents today, the papists, rejoice over the divisions that have arisen among us. They rejoice in the unchristian and vain hope that these disagreements might finally cause the downfall of the pure doctrine. Meanwhile, those who are weak in faith are greatly offended and disturbed. Some of them doubt whether, amid such disagreements, the pure doctrine is with us. Still others do not know with whom to side regarding the articles in controversy. For the controversies that have happened are not (as some would regard them) mere misunderstandings or disputes about words, with one side failing to grasp the meaning of the other well enough and the difficulty lying in a few words that are not of great importance. The controversial subjects are important and great. They are of such a nature that the opinion of the party in error cannot be tolerated in God's Church, much less be excused or defended.

10    Necessity requires us to explain these disputed articles according to God's Word and approved writings. Everyone who has Christian understanding can notice which opinion about the controversial matters agrees with God's Word and the Christian Augsburg Confession, and which does not. Then sincere Christians who have the truth at heart may guard and protect themselves against the errors and corruptions that have arisen.

# THE COMPREHENSIVE SUMMARY, FOUNDATION, RULE, AND NORM

By Which All Dogmas Should
Be Judged according to God's Word,
and the Controversies That Have Arisen
Should Be Explained and Decided
in a Christian Way

For thorough, permanent unity in the Church, it is necessary, above all things, that we have a comprehensive, unanimously approved summary and form of teaching. The common doctrine must be brought together from God's Word and reduced to a small circle of teaching, which the churches that are of the true Christian religion must confess. They must do this just as the Ancient Church always had its fixed symbols for this use. Furthermore, this should not be based on private writings, but on the kind of books that have been composed, approved, and received in the name of the churches that pledge themselves to one doctrine and religion. Therefore, we have declared to one another with heart and mouth that we will not make or receive a separate or new confession of our faith. Instead, we will confess the public common writings, which always and everywhere were held and used as such symbols or common confessions in all the churches of the Augsburg Confession before the disagreements arose among those who accept the Augsburg Confession. We will confess them as long as there are on all sides, in all articles, a unanimous agreement with the pure doctrine of the divine Word, as the sainted Dr. Luther explained it.

1. First, then, are the prophetic and apostolic Scriptures of *the Old and New Testaments* as the pure, clear fountain of Israel. They are the only true standard or norm by which all teachers and doctrines are to be judged.

The Resurrection of Christ

Christ risen from the dead is the hope and joy of Christians.
We shall see Him face-to-face in heaven.

4      2. In ancient times the true Christian doctrine, in a pure, sound sense, was collected from God's Word into brief articles or chapters against the corruption of heretics. Therefore, we confess, in the second place, *the three Ecumenical Creeds: the Apostles', the Nicene, and the Athanasian*. They are glorious confessions of the faith, brief, devout, and founded on God's Word. All the heresies that had at that time arisen in the Christian Church are clearly and irrefutably answered by these creeds.

5      3. In the third place, in these last times, by special grace, God has brought the truth of His Word to light again from the darkness of the papacy through the faithful service of the precious man of God, Dr. Luther. According to the Word of God, this doctrine has been collected from it into the articles and chapters of the Augsburg Confession against the corruptions of the papacy and other sects. Therefore, we also confess *the first, unaltered Augsburg Confession* as our symbol for this time. This is not because it was written by our theologians. We confess it because it has been taken from God's Word and well founded firmly in the Word of God. We confess it precisely in the form in which it was committed to writing, in the year 1530, and presented to Emperor Charles V at Augsburg by some Christian electors, princes, and estates of the Roman Empire as a common Confession of the reformed churches. By this Confession, our reformed churches are distinguished from (a) the papists and (b) other rejected and condemned sects and heresies. This follows the custom and usage of the early Church, just as later councils, Christian bishops, and teachers appealed to the Nicene Creed, and confessed it.

6      4. In the fourth place, an extensive *Apology* was composed, published, and printed in 1531 regarding the proper and true sense of the oft-quoted Augsburg Confession. This was done after the Confession's presentation, so that we might explain ourselves at greater length and guard against the papists. This was also done so that condemned errors might not sneak into God's Church under the Augsburg Confession's name or dare to seek cover under it. We unanimously confess this Apology also. Not only is the Augsburg Confession explained by the Apology (as much as is necessary and guarded), but it is also proven by clear, irrefutable testimonies of Holy Scripture.

7      5. In the fifth place, we also confess *the Articles* composed, approved, and received *at Smalcald,* in the great assembly of theologians, in the year 1537. We confess them as they were first framed and printed in order to be delivered in the Council at Mantua (or wherever it would be held) in the name of the estates, electors, and princes. They confessed it as an explanation of the above-mentioned Augsburg Confession, in which, by God's grace, they were resolved to abide. In the Smalcald Articles the Augsburg Confession's doctrine is repeated and some articles are explained at greater length from God's Word. Besides this, the cause and reasons are indicated, as far as necessary, why we have abandoned the papistic errors and idolatries and can have no fellowship with them. They also explain why we do not know, and cannot think of, a way for coming to any agreement with the pope on these points.

8      6. In the sixth place, these highly important matters also concern the common people and laymen. Because they are Christians, they must distinguish between pure and false doctrine for their salvation. Therefore, we also confess *the Small* and *the Large Catechisms of Dr. Luther,* as they were written by him and included in his works. They have been unanimously approved and received by

all churches holding to the Augsburg Confession and have been publicly used in churches, schools, and in homes. Furthermore, the Christian doctrine from God's Word is put together in them in the most correct and simple way and explained, as far as is necessary for simple laypeople.

9    In the pure churches and schools these public, common writings have always been respected as the sum and model of the doctrine that Dr. Luther (of blessed memory) has admirably pulled together from God's Word and firmly established against the papacy and other sects. We want to appeal to his full explanations in his doctrinal and polemical writings. We do so in the same way and as far as Dr. Luther himself has given necessary and Christian encouragement about his writings in the Latin preface to his published works. He has clearly drawn up this distinction: God's Word alone should be and remain the only standard and rule of doctrine, to which the writings of no man should be regarded as equal. Everything should be subjected to God's Word.

10    Other good, useful, pure books, expositions of the Holy Scriptures, refutations of errors, and explanations of doctrinal articles are not rejected by this point. As long as they are consistent with the above-mentioned type of doctrine, these works are considered useful expositions and explanations. They can be helpful. What has been said so far about the summary of our Christian doctrine is only intended to mean this: we should have a unanimously accepted, definite, common form of doctrine. All our evangelical churches should confess it together and in common. Because this Confession has been derived from God's Word, all other writings should be judged and adjusted to it to determine the extent to which they are to be approved and accepted.

11    For this purpose we brought together the above-mentioned writings: *the Augsburg Confession, Apology, Smalcald Articles, Luther's Large* and *Small Catechisms* as the frequently mentioned summary of our Christian doctrine. This was done because these have always and everywhere been regarded as the common, unanimously accepted meaning of our churches. Furthermore, they have been signed at that time by the chief and most enlightened theologians, and they have held sway in all evangelical churches and schools. Also, as mentioned before, 12 they were all written and sent out before the divisions among the theologians of the Augsburg Confession arose. Therefore, they are held to be impartial, and neither can nor should be rejected by either side of those who have entered into controversy. No one who is a follower of the Augsburg Confession without guile will complain about these writings. They will cheerfully accept and tolerate them as witnesses of the truth. No one can think ill about us because we get an explanation and decision about the articles in controversy from these writings. As we lay down 13 God's Word—the eternal truth—as the foundation, we also introduce and quote these writings as a witness of the truth and as the unanimously received, correct understanding of our predecessors who have steadfastly held to the pure doctrine.

## ANTITHESIS OR FALSE DOCTRINE IN THE DISPUTED ARTICLES

It is not only necessary that the pure, 14 wholesome doctrine be rightly presented for the preservation of pure doctrine and for thorough, permanent, godly unity in the Church, but it is also necessary that the opponents who teach otherwise be reproved (1 Timothy 3; 2 Timothy 3:16; Titus 1:9). Faithful shepherds, as Luther says, should do both things: (a) feed or nourish the lambs and (b) resist the wolves. Then the sheep may flee from strange voices (John 10:5–12) and may separate the precious from the worthless (Jeremiah 15:19).

15 Regarding these matters, we have thoroughly and clearly told one another the following: a distinction should and must by all means be kept between (a) unnecessary and useless wrangling (the Church should not allow itself to be disturbed by this, since it destroys more than it builds up) and (b) when the kind of controversy arises that involves the articles of faith or the chief points of Christian doctrine. Then the false, opposite doctrine must be reproved for the defense of the truth.

16 The aforesaid writings offer the Christian reader—who delights in and has a love for the divine truth—clear and correct information about each and every disputed article of our Christian religion. They show what he should regard and receive as right and true according to God's Word of the prophetic and apostolic Scriptures. They also show what he should reject, shun, and avoid as false and wrong. The truth must be preserved distinctly and clearly and distinguished from all errors. Nothing must be hidden and concealed under common words. Therefore, we have clearly and directly declared ourselves to one another on the chief and most important articles taken one by one. At the present time these articles have come into controversy so that there might be a public, definite testimony, not only for those now living, but also for our descendants. We make known what is and should remain the unanimous understanding and judgment of our churches in reference to the articles in controversy:

17 1. First, we reject and condemn all heresies and errors that were rejected and condemned in the primitive, ancient, orthodox Church, on the true, firm ground of the holy, divine Scriptures.

2. Second, as just mentioned, we reject 18 and condemn all sects and heresies that are rejected in the writings of the comprehensive summary of the Confession of our churches.

3. Third, within thirty years divisions 19 arose among some theologians of the Augsburg Confession because of the *Interim* and for other reasons. Therefore, it has been our purpose to state and to declare plainly, purely, and clearly in thesis and antithesis our faith and confession about each and every one of these divisions. This means we state the true doctrine and the opposite doctrine, in order that the foundation of divine truth might be clear in all articles. In this way all unlawful, doubtful, suspicious, and condemned doctrines might be exposed (wherever and in whatever books they may be found, and whoever may have written them, or who even now may be ready to defend them). So everyone may be faithfully warned against the errors, which are spread here and there in some theologians' writings. No one should be misled in this matter by the reputation of any person. From this declaration 20 the Christian reader will inform himself in every emergency. He will compare it with the writings listed above, and he will find out exactly what was confessed in the beginning about each article in the comprehensive summary of our religion and faith. He will note what was later restated at different times and is repeated by us in this document. He will see that it is in no way contradictory, but is the simple, unchangeable, permanent truth. Therefore, we do not change from one doctrine to another, as our adversaries falsely assert. We eagerly desire to be found loyal to the once-delivered Augsburg Confession and its unanimously accepted Christian meaning. Through God's grace we desire to

abide firmly and constantly by the Augsburg Confession in opposition to all corruptions that have entered.

# I. ORIGINAL SIN

For an annotation on this article, see p. 492. (See also AC II; Ap II; SA III III; FC Ep I.)

___

## STATUS OF THE CONTROVERSY

1  A controversy about original sin has arisen among some theologians of the Augsburg Confession. What is it precisely? One side argued this: through Adam's fall, mankind's nature, substance, and essence are corrupt. Since the fall, the nature, substance, and essence of a human being (or, the chief, highest part of his essence, i.e., the rational soul in its highest state or chief powers) is original sin itself. This has been called "nature-sin" or "person-sin" because it is not a thought, word, or work, but the nature itself. From original sin, as from a root, spring all other sins. So since the fall, there is now no difference whatever between the nature and essence of mankind and original sin because the nature is corrupt through sin.

2  The other side taught, in opposition, that original sin is not truly the nature, substance, or essence of mankind (i.e., a person's body or soul, which even now, since the fall, are and remain God's creation and creatures in us). But original sin is something *in* mankind's nature, body, and soul, and *in* all a person's powers. It is a horrible, deep, inexpressible corruption of mankind's nature

The Fall

and powers. So mankind lacks the righteousness in which he was originally created. In spiritual things he is dead to good and perverted to all evil. Because of this corruption and inborn sin, which dwells in man's nature, all actual sins flow forth from the heart. Therefore, a distinction must be maintained between the nature and essence of the corrupt person and his body and soul, which are God's creation and creatures in us even since the fall. These are distinct from original sin, which is the devil's work, by which the nature has become corrupt.

3    This controversy about original sin is not unnecessary wrangling. If this doctrine is rightly presented from, and according to, God's Word, and separated from all Pelagian and Manichaean errors, then the benefits of the Lord Christ and His precious merit, also the gracious work of the Holy Spirit, are better known and praised even more (as the Apology says). Furthermore, due honor is rendered to God if His work and creation in mankind is rightly distinguished from the devil's work, by which 4 human nature has been corrupted. Therefore, to explain this controversy in the Christian way and according to God's Word, and to maintain the correct, pure doctrine of original sin, we will collect from the above-mentioned writings the thesis and antithesis into brief chapters, that is, the correct doctrine and its opposite.

## AFFIRMATIVE STATEMENTS

5    1. First, it is true that Christians should regard and recognize the actual transgression of God's commandments as sin; but sin is also that horrible, dreadful hereditary sickness by which the entire human nature is corrupted. This should above all things be regarded and recognized as sin indeed. Yes, it is the chief sin, which is a root and foun-

tainhead of all actual sins. By Dr. Luther it is  6 called a "nature sin" or "person sin." He says this to show that, even if a person would not think, speak, or do anything evil (which, however, is impossible in this life, since the fall of our first parents), his nature and person are nevertheless sinful. Before God they are thoroughly and utterly infected and corrupted by original sin, as by a spiritual leprosy. Because of this corruption and because of the fall of the first man, the human nature or person is accused or condemned by God's Law. So we are by nature the children of wrath, death, and damnation, unless we are delivered from them by Christ's merit.

2. Second, the following is also clear and  7 true, as Article XIX of the Augsburg Confession teaches: God is not a creator, author, or cause of sin. By the instigation of the devil through one man, sin (which is the devil's work) has entered the world (Romans 5:12; 1 John 3:7). Even today, in this corruption, God does not create and make sin in us. Original sin is multiplied from sinful seed, through fleshly conception and birth from father and mother (Psalm 51:5). God at the present day still creates and makes the human nature in people.

3. Third, reason doesn't know and un-  8 derstand what this hereditary evil is (Psalm 19:12). As the Smalcald Articles say, it must be learned and believed from the revelation of Scripture. The Apology briefly summarized this under the following main points:

a. Because of the disobedience of Adam  9 and Eve, hereditary evil is the guilt by which we are all in God's displeasure and are, by nature, children of wrath, as the apostle shows (Romans 5:12–14; Ephesians 2:3).

b. Second, original sin is a complete ab-  10 sence or lack of the created state of hereditary righteousness in Paradise, or of God's image, according to which man was originally created in truth, holiness, and righteousness. At the same time, original sin is an inability and unfitness for all the things of God. Or, as the Latin words read, "The definition of original sin takes away from the unrenewed nature the gifts, the power, and all activity for beginning and accomplishing anything in spiritual things."

11 c. Original sin (in human nature) is not just this entire absence of all good in spiritual, divine things. Original sin is more than the lost image of God in mankind; it is at the same time also a deep, wicked, horrible, fathomless, mysterious, and unspeakable corruption of the entire human nature and all its powers. It is especially a corruption of the soul's highest, chief powers in the understanding, heart, and will. So now, since the fall, a person inherits an inborn wicked disposition and inward impurity of heart, an evil lust and tendency. We all by disposition and nature inherit from Adam a heart, feeling, and thought that are, according to their highest powers and the light of reason, naturally inclined and disposed directly against God and His chief commandments (Matthew 22:36–40). Yes, they are hostile toward God, especially in divine and spiritual things (Romans 8:7). For in other respects, regarding natural, outward things that are subject to reason, a person still has power, ability, and to a certain degree understanding—although very much weakened. All of this, however, has been so infected and contaminated by original sin that it is of no use before God (Romans 8:8).

13 d. The punishment and penalty of original sin, which God has imposed upon Adam's children and upon original sin, are death, eternal damnation (Romans 3:23), and also other bodily, spiritual, temporal, eternal miseries. These include the devil's tyranny and dominion. So human nature is subject to the devil's kingdom (Colossians 1:13) and has been surrendered to his power. It is held captive under his sway, who stupefies and leads astray many a great, learned person in the world through dreadful error, heresy, and other blindness, and otherwise rushes people into all sorts of crime.

14 e. Fifth, this hereditary evil is so great and horrible that, only for the sake of the Lord Christ, can it be covered and forgiven before God in those baptized and believing. Furthermore, human nature, which is perverted and corrupted by original sin, must and can be healed only by the regeneration and renewal of the Holy Spirit (Titus 3:5). However, this healing is only begun in this life. It will not be perfect until the life to come (Ephesians 4:12–13).

15 These points, which have been quoted here only in a summary way, are set forth more fully in the above-mentioned writings of the common confession of our Christian doctrine.

## PELAGIAN AND MANICHAEAN ERRORS

16 This doctrine must be kept and guarded so that it may not turn either to the Pelagian or the Manichaean side. For this reason the contrary doctrine about this article, which is condemned and rejected in our churches, should also be briefly stated.

17 1. First, in opposition to the old and the new Pelagians, the following false opinions and dogmas are condemned and rejected: original sin is only guilt, because of what has been committed by another person, without any corruption of our nature.

18 2. Sinful, evil lusts are not sins, but states or created and essential characteristics of the nature.

19 3. Or the teaching that the above-men-

tioned defect and evil are not properly and truly sin before God, because of which a person without Christ must be a child of wrath and damnation, also in the dominion and under Satan's power (unless he is grafted into Christ and is delivered through Him).

20    4. The following and similar Pelagian errors are also condemned and rejected: nature, even since the fall, is said to be uncorrupt and that especially in spiritual things it is entirely good and pure. In its natural powers it is said to be perfect.

21    5. Original sin is only outward—a slight, insignificant spot sprinkled or a stain dashed on the nature of mankind. Or it is a corruption only in some outward things. Under and with original sin, human nature still possesses and retains its integrity and power even in spiritual things.

22    6. Original sin is not a spoiling or a lack, but only an outward difficulty for these spiritual good powers. It is like when a magnet is smeared with garlic juice. Its natural power is not removed by the juice, but only hindered. Nor can this stain of original sin be washed away easily, like a spot from the face, or paint from the wall.

23    7. Those who teach that human nature has been greatly weakened and corrupted through the fall, but that it still has not entirely lost all good in divine, spiritual things are also rebuked and rejected. They teach that what is sung in our churches, "Through Adam's fall is all corrupt, Nature and essence human," is not true, but from natural birth human nature still has something good in it, even though it is small, little, and slight. They suggest human nature has a capacity, skill, aptness, or ability to begin, to effect, or to help

24 effect something in spiritual things. About outward, temporal, worldly things and transactions, which are subject to reason, there will be an explanation in the following article.

These and similar contrary doctrines are 25 condemned and rejected because God's Word teaches that the corrupt human nature, of and by itself, has no power for anything good in spiritual, divine things, not even for the smallest things, such as good thoughts. Not only is this true, but the corrupt nature can do nothing in God's sight of and by itself. It can only sin (Genesis 6:5; 8:21).

In the same way this doctrine must also 26 be guarded on the other side against Manichaean errors. So the following erroneous doctrines are rejected and so are similar doctrines: in the beginning, human nature was created pure and good, but after the fall original sin is infused and mixed with the nature from outside itself by Satan (as something essential). It is like when poison is mingled with wine.

Human nature was originally created 27 pure, good, and holy in Adam and Eve. Sin did not enter their nature through the fall in the way enthusiastically taught by the Manichaeans, as though Satan had created or made some evil substance and mixed it with their nature. By Satan's seduction through the fall, Adam lost his created state of hereditary righteousness according to God's judgment and sentence. Human nature is perverted and corrupted as a punishment, by this deprivation or deficiency, want, and injury, that was caused by Satan. So now human nature is passed down (together with this defect and corruption) to all people, who are conceived and born in a natural way from father and mother. Since the 28 fall, human nature is not created pure and good at first, but only afterward corrupted by original sin. In the first moment of our conception the seed from which a person is formed is sinful and corrupt (Psalm 51:5). Furthermore, original sin is not something by itself, existing independently in, or apart from, the nature of the corrupt person. It is neither the real essence, body, or soul of the corrupt person or the person himself. Original sin and human nature (corrupted by original sin) cannot and should not be distinguished as though the nature were pure, good, holy, and uncorrupted before God, while original sin alone (which dwells in human nature) is evil.

30    Augustine writes that the Manichaeans teach that it is not the corrupt person who sins because of inborn original sin, but something different and foreign in a person. And so, God does not accuse and condemn by the Law human nature as corrupt by sin, but only original sin in it. For, as stated above in the thesis (i.e., in the explanation of the pure doctrine about original sin), the person's entire nature, which is born in the natural way from father and mother, is entirely and to the farthest extent corrupted and perverted by original sin. Human nature is corrupt in body and soul, in all its powers, as regards and concerns the goodness, truth, holiness, and righteousness created with it in Paradise. Nevertheless, human nature is not entirely exterminated or changed into another substance, which could be called unlike our nature according to its essence and, therefore, cannot be of one essence with us.

31    Because of this corruption, a person's entire corrupt nature is accused and condemned by the Law unless the sin is forgiven for Christ's sake (Galatians 3:10–11).

32    The Law accuses and condemns our nature, not because we have been created human by God, but because we are sinful and wicked. Since the fall, human nature is condemned, not because its essence is God's work and creation in us, but because and so far as it has been poisoned and corrupted by sin.

## THE CORRUPT NATURE

33    Original sin is like a spiritual poison and leprosy, as Luther says. It has poisoned and corrupted the whole human nature. So we cannot show and point out to the eye, human nature by itself or original sin by itself. Nevertheless, there is the corrupt nature, or essence of the corrupt person (body and soul—the person himself) whom God has created. (Original sin dwells in a person. It also corrupts the nature and essence of the entire person.) And there is *original* sin, which dwells in human nature or essence and corrupts it. They are not one and the same thing. For example, in outward leprosy the body that is leprous and the leprosy on or in the body are not one thing, properly speaking. But a distinction must also be maintained between our nature as created and preserved by God (in which sin is indwelling) and original sin (which dwells in the nature). These two things can, and must, be considered, taught, and believed separately according to Holy Scripture.

34    Furthermore, the chief articles of our Christian faith drive and compel us to preserve this distinction. For instance, in the article of creation, Scripture testifies that God has created human nature not only before the fall, but that it is God's creature and work also since the fall. (See Deuteronomy 32:6; Isaiah 45:11; 54:5; 64:8; Acts 17:25; Revelation 4:11.)

35    Job says:

Your hands fashioned and made me, and now You have destroyed me altogether. Remember that You have made me like clay; and will You return me to the dust? Did You not pour me out like milk and curdle me like cheese? You clothed me with skin and flesh, and knit me together with bones and sinews. You have granted me life and steadfast love, and Your

36   David says:

> I praise You for I am fearfully and wonderfully made. Wonderful are Your works; my soul knows it very well. My frame was not hidden from You, when I was being made in secret, intricately woven in the depths of the earth. Your eyes saw my unformed substance; in Your book were written, every one of them, the days that were formed for me, when as yet there were none of them. (Psalm 139:14–16)

care has preserved my spirit. (Job 10:8–12)

37   In the Ecclesiastes of Solomon it is written, "And the dust returns to the earth as it was, and the spirit returns to God who gave it" (Ecclesiastes 12:7).

38   These passages clearly testify that God, even since the fall, is the creator of mankind. He creates his body and soul. Therefore, corrupt mankind cannot, without any distinction, be sin itself. Otherwise, God would be a creator of sin. Our Small Catechism also confesses this in the explanation of the First Article, where it is written:

> I believe that God has made me and all creatures. He has given me my body and soul, eyes, ears, and all my members, my reason, and all my senses, and still preserves them.

Likewise, in the Large Catechism it is written:

> This is what I mean and believe, that I am God's creature. I mean that He has given and constantly preserves for me my body, soul, and life, my members great and small, all my senses, reason, and understanding.

Nevertheless, this same creature and work of God is sadly corrupted by sin. For the material from which God now forms and makes man was corrupted and perverted in Adam and is thus passed along by inheritance to us.

39   Here pious Christian hearts justly ought to consider God's unspeakable goodness. God does not immediately cast from Himself this corrupt, perverted, sinful material into hellfire. No, He forms and makes the present human nature from it (which is sadly corrupted by sin) in order that He may cleanse it from all sin, sanctify, and save it by His dear Son.

40   From this article, the distinction is now clearly and indisputably found. Original sin does not come from God. God is not sin's creator or author. Nor is original sin God's creature or work, but it is the devil's work.

41   If there was no difference at all between the nature or essence of our body and soul (which is corrupted by original sin) and original sin (by which the nature is corrupted) one of the following would be true: because God is the creator of our nature, He also created and made original sin, which would also be His work and creature. Or, because sin is the devil's work, Satan would be the creator of our nature, of our body and soul. They would also have to be Satan's work or creation if, without any distinction, our corrupt nature was thought to be sin itself. Both of these teachings are contrary to the article of our Christian faith.

42   Therefore, in order that God's creation and work in mankind may be distinguished from the devil's work, we say that it is God's creation that a person has body and soul. Also, it is God's work that a person can think, speak, do, and work anything. For "in Him we live and move and have our being" (Acts 17:28). But human nature is corrupt. Its thoughts, words, and works are wicked. This is originally Satan's work, who has corrupted God's work in Adam through sin. From Adam, sin is passed down to us by inheritance (Romans 5:12).

43   Second, in the article of Redemption the Scriptures testify forcefully that God's Son received our human nature without sin. So He was in all ways—sin excluded—made like us, His brethren (Hebrews 2:14–17). Therefore, all the old orthodox teachers have maintained that Christ, according to His received humanity, is of one essence with us, His brothers. For He has received His human nature, which in all respects (sin alone excluded) is like our human nature in its essence and all essential attributes. They have condemned the contrary doctrine as obvious heresy.

44   If there were no distinction between the nature or essence of corrupt mankind and original sin, one of the following must be true: Christ did not receive our nature, because He did not receive sin. Or because Christ received our nature, He also received sin. Both of these ideas are contrary to the Scriptures. God's Son received our nature, and not original sin. Therefore, it is clear from this fact that human nature (even since the fall) and original sin are not one and the same thing. They must be distinguished.

45   Third, in the article of Sanctification Scripture testifies that God cleanses, washes, and sanctifies mankind from sin (1 Corinthians 6:11; 1 John 1:7) and that Christ saves His people from their sins (Matthew 1:21). Sin, therefore, cannot be a person himself. For God receives a person into grace for Christ's sake. But God remains hostile to sin eternally. Therefore, it is unchristian and horrible to hear that original sin is baptized in the name of the Holy Trinity, sanctified and saved, and other similar expressions found in the writings of the recent Manichaeans. We will not offend simpleminded people with further examples.

46   Fourth, in the article of the Resurrection Scripture testifies that precisely the substance of our flesh, but without sin, will rise again (1 Corinthians 15:42, 54–57). In eternal life we shall have and keep precisely this soul, but without sin.

47   If there was no difference at all between our corrupt body and soul and original sin, one of the following would be true (contrary to this article of the Christian faith): our flesh will not rise again at the Last Day, and in eternal life we shall not have the present essence of our body and soul, but another substance (or another soul), because then we shall be without sin. Or at the Last Day sin will also rise again and will be and remain in the elect in eternal life.

48   It is clear that this teaching (with all that depends on it and follows from it) must be rejected. For it is asserted and taught that original sin is the nature, substance, essence, body, or soul itself of corrupt mankind. It is taught that between our corrupt nature, substance, and essence and original sin there is no distinction whatever. For the chief articles of our Christian faith forcefully and emphatically testify why a distinction should and must be maintained between mankind's nature or substance (which is corrupted by sin) and the sin (with which and by which mankind is corrupted). A simple statement of the doctrine and the contrary teaching (in theses and antitheses) in this controversy is enough in this place for the chief issue itself. The subject is not argued at length, but only the principal points are treated, article by article.

## TERMS AND EXPRESSIONS

50   For terms and expressions, it is best and safest to use and retain the form of sound words used about this article in the Holy Scriptures and the above-mentioned books.

51   To avoid argument about words and expressions, which are applied and used in var-

ious senses, they should be carefully and distinctly explained. For example, it is said that God creates the nature of people. By the term *nature* the essence, body, and soul of people are understood. But often the character or disposition of a thing is called its nature. For example, it is said that it is the nature of the serpent to bite and poison. In a similar way, Luther says that sin and sinning are the character and nature of corrupt mankind.

52     *Original sin* properly means the deep corruption of our nature, as it is described in the Smalcald Articles. But sometimes the concrete person or the subject (i.e., a person himself with body and soul, in which sin is and dwells) is also included under this term, because a person is corrupted by sin, poisoned, and sinful. For example, Luther says, "Your birth, your nature, and your entire essence is sin," that is, sinful and unclean.

53     Luther himself explains that by "nature-sin," "person-sin," and "essential sin" he means that not only the words, thoughts, and works are sin, but that the entire nature, person, and essence of a person are altogether corrupted from the root by original sin.

54     A congregation of ordinary people ought to be spared the Latin words *substantia* and *accidens* in public sermons, for they are unknown to ordinary people. But learned people among themselves, or with others to whom these words are not unknown, may use such terms in discussing this subject, as Eusebius, Ambrose, and especially Augustine, and also still other eminent Church teachers have done. For these terms were necessary to explain this doctrine in opposition to the heretics. The terms assume a division that has no middle ground. So everything that exists must be either *substantia* (i.e., a self-existent essence) or *accidens* (i.e., an outward thing that does not exist by itself essentially, but is in another self-existent essence and can

be distinguished from it). Cyril and Basil also use this distinction.

Among others, the following is a sure, indisputable axiom in theology: every *substantia* or self-existing essence (so long as it is a substance) is either God Himself or God's work and creation. In many writings against the Manichaeans, in common with all true teachers, Augustine has condemned and rejected the following statement after due consideration and with seriousness: original sin is man's nature or substance. Like Augustine, all the learned and intelligent have also always maintained: when something does not exist by itself—it is not a part of another self-existing essence, but exists, subject to change, in another thing—it is not a *substantia*. That is, it is not something self-existing. Instead, it is an *accidens*. That is, it is something accidental. So Augustine is accustomed to speak in this way constantly: original sin is not human nature itself, but an accidental defect and damage in human nature. Before this controversy, people spoke in this way, also in our schools and churches, according to the rules of logic, freely and without being suspected of heresy. They were never condemned on this account either by Dr. Luther or any orthodox teacher of our pure, evangelical churches.

It is the indisputable truth that everything that is, is either a substance or an accident (i.e., either a self-existing essence or something accidental in it). This has just been shown and proven by testimonies of the Church teachers. No truly intelligent person has ever had any doubts about this. Therefore, necessity constrains here, and no one can avoid it. If the question is asked whether original sin is a substance (that is, something existing by itself and not in something else) or whether it is a nonessential quality, that is, something not existing by itself but in another, one must confess directly and firmly that original sin is no substance, but an accident (nonessential quality).

58 For this reason, too, God's Church will never be able to have permanent peace in this controversy, but instead the dissension will grow stronger and continue if the church's ministers remain in doubt about whether original sin is a substance or an *accident*, and whether it is rightly and properly named so.

59 If the churches and schools are to be thoroughly relieved of this scandalous and very mischievous controversy, it is necessary that everyone be properly instructed about this matter.

60 But if it is further asked what kind of an accident (nonessential quality) original sin is, that is another question. No philosopher, no papist, no sophist, indeed, no human reason, however sharp it may be, can give the right explanation to this. All understanding and every explanation of it must be derived solely from the Holy Scriptures. They testify that original sin is an unspeakable evil and such an entire corruption of human nature that in it and all its inward and outward powers, nothing pure or good remains. Everything is entirely corrupt, so that because of original sin a person is truly spiritually dead in God's sight (Ephesians 2:5). All a person's powers are dead to what is good.

61 In this way, then, original sin is not weakened by the word *accident* (nonessential quality). It is explained according to God's Word, the way Dr. Luther has written with great seriousness against the weakening of original sin in his Latin exposition of Genesis 3. *Accident* (a nonessential quality) serves only to show the distinction between God's work (which our nature is, even though it is corrupt) and the devil's work (the sin that dwells in God's work and is the most profound and indescribable corruption of it).

62 Luther, in his treatment of this subject, has used the term *accident*, and also the term *quality*, and has not rejected them. But at the same time he has, with special seriousness and great zeal, taken the greatest pains to explain and to impress upon every single reader what a horrible *quality* and *accident* it is. For by it human nature is not merely polluted, but is so deeply corrupted that nothing pure or incorrupt has remained in it. His words on Psalm 90 show this:

> Whether we call original sin a *quality* or a *disease*, it is indeed the utmost evil, that we are not only to suffer God's eternal wrath and eternal death, but that we do not even understand what we suffer.

And again, on Genesis 3 he writes: "We are infected with the poison of original sin from the bottom of the foot to the top of the head, because this happened to us in a still perfect nature."

Cain kills Abel

## II. FREE WILL, OR HUMAN POWERS

For an annotation on this article, see p. 495.
(See also AC XVIII; Ap XVIII; FC Ep II.)

### STATUS OF THE CONTROVERSY

1    A division about free will has arisen not only between the papists and us, but also among some theologians of the Augsburg Confession themselves. Therefore, we will, first of all, show exactly the points in controversy.

2    Mankind's free will is found and can be considered in four unique conditions. The question now is not what the condition of mankind was *before the fall*, or what he is able to do in *outward things* (which apply to this earthly life) *since the fall* and before his conversion. Also, the question is not what sort of a free will he will have in spiritual things after he has been regenerated and is controlled by God's Spirit, or when he rises *from the dead*. The chief question is only this and this alone: What is the intellect and will of the *unregenerate* person able to do *in his conversion* and *regeneration* from his *own powers remaining* after the fall? Is he able, when God's Word is preached and God's grace is offered, to prepare himself for grace, accept the same, and agree with it? This is the question about which there has been a controversy among some theologians in the churches of the Augsburg Confession for quite a number of years now.

3    One side has held and taught that a person cannot from his own powers fulfill God's command or truly trust in God, or fear and

love Him, without the Holy Spirit's grace. Nevertheless, a person still has enough of his natural powers left before regeneration that he is able to prepare himself to a certain extent for grace and to agree (although weakly). However, he cannot accomplish anything by these powers, but must give up in the struggle if the Holy Spirit's grace is not added.

4 Both the ancient and modern enthusiasts have taught that God converts people and leads them to the saving knowledge of Christ through His Spirit, without any created means and instrument; in other words, without the outward preaching and hearing of God's Word.

## AFFIRMATIVE STATEMENTS

5 Against both these parties the pure teachers of the Augsburg Confession have taught and argued the following: by the fall of our first parents mankind was so corrupted that in divine things having to do with our conversion and the salvation of our souls we are by nature blind (Ephesians 4:18). When God's Word is preached, a person does not and cannot understand God's Word, but regards it as foolishness (1 Corinthians 2:14). Also, he does not draw near to God on his own. He is and remains God's enemy until he is converted, becomes a believer, and is regenerated and renewed (Romans 5:10). This happens by the Holy Spirit's power through the Word when it is preached and heard, out of pure grace, without any cooperation of his own (Titus 3:4–7).

6 In order to explain this controversy in a Christian way, according to the guidance of God's Word, and to decide it by His grace, our doctrine, faith, and confession are as follows:

7 In spiritual and divine things the unregenerate person's intellect, heart, and will are utterly unable, by his natural powers, to understand, believe, accept, think, will, begin, effect, do, work, or concur in working anything. They are entirely dead to what is good (Ephesians 2:5). They are corrupt. So in mankind's nature since the fall, before regeneration, there is not the least spark of spiritual power remaining or present. No person can prepare himself for God's grace or accept the grace God offers. A person is not capable of grace for and of himself. He cannot apply or accommodate himself to it. By his own powers he is not able to aid, do, work, or agree in working anything toward his conversion. He cannot do this fully, halfway, or even in part—not even in the smallest or most trivial part. He is sin's servant (John 8:34) and the devil's captive, by whom he is moved (Ephesians 2:2; 2 Timothy 2:26). Therefore, the natural free will according to its perverted disposition and nature is strong and active only to do what is displeasing and contrary to God (Genesis 6:5).

8 This declaration and general reply to the chief question and statement of the controversy presented in the introduction to this article is confirmed and substantiated by the following arguments from God's Word. Although these arguments are contrary to proud reason and philosophy, we know that the wisdom of this perverted world is only foolishness before God (1 Corinthians 1:19–20). Articles of faith must be judged only from God's Word.

9 First, mankind's reason or natural intellect does still have a dim spark of the knowledge that there is a God. It also knows about the doctrine of the Law (Romans 1:19–21, 24, 32). Yet it is so ignorant, blind, and perverted that even when the most ingenious and learned people on earth read or hear the Gospel of God's Son and the promise of eternal salvation, they cannot by their own pow-

ers perceive, apprehend, understand, or believe and regard it as true. They want to understand these spiritual things with their reason. But the more diligently and seriously they try, the less they understand or believe. Before they become enlightened and are taught by the Holy Spirit, they regard all this only as foolishness or fictions.

10    The natural person does not accept the things of the Spirit of God, for they are folly to him. (1 Corinthians 2:14)

> For since, in the wisdom of God, the world did not know God through wisdom, it pleased God through the folly of what we preach to save those who believe. (1 Corinthians 1:21)

> Now this I say and testify in the Lord, that you must no longer walk as the Gentiles [that is, those not born again of God's Spirit] do, in the futility of their minds. They are darkened in their understanding, alienated from the life of God because of the ignorance that is in them, due to their hardness of heart. (Ephesians 4:17–18)

> To you it has been given to know the secrets of the kingdom of heaven, but to them it has not been given. . . . This is why I speak to them in parables, because seeing they do not see, and hearing they do not hear, nor do they understand. (Matthew 13:11–13; see also Luke 8:18)

> No one understands; no one seeks for God. All have turned aside; together they have become worthless; no one does good, not even one. (Romans 3:11–12)

The Scriptures flatly call natural man in spiritual and divine things *darkness* (Ephesians 5:8; Acts 26:18). John 1:5 says, "The light shines in the darkness" (that is, in the dark, blind world, which does not know or regard God), "and the darkness has not overcome it." Likewise, the Scriptures teach that a sinful person is not only weak and sick, but also finished and entirely dead (Ephesians 2:1–5; Colossians 2:13).

11    Now, a person who is physically dead cannot from his own powers prepare or make himself come back to life again. So the person who is spiritually dead in sins cannot by his own strength make or apply himself to acquire spiritual and heavenly righteousness and life. This is true unless he is delivered and brought to life by God's Son from the death of sin.

12    The Scriptures deny to the intellect, heart, and will of the natural man all readiness, skill, capacity, and ability to think, to understand, to be able to do, to begin, to will, to undertake, to act, to work, or to agree to work anything good and right in spiritual things from himself.

> Not that we are sufficient in ourselves to claim anything as coming from us, but our sufficiency is from God. (2 Corinthians 3:5)

> Together they have become worthless. (Romans 3:12)

> My word finds no place in you. (John 8:37)

> The darkness has not overcome it [the light]. (John 1:5)

"The natural person does not accept [or, as the Greek word properly signifies, grasps not, comprehends not, accepts not] the things of the Spirit of God" (1 Corinthians 2:14). This means he is not capable of spiritual things. For they are foolishness to him; neither can he know them. Much less will he 13 truly believe the Gospel or agree with it and regard it as truth.

For the mind that is set on the flesh [or the mind of the natural man] is hostile to God, for it does not submit to God's law; indeed, it cannot. (Romans 8:7)

14    In a word, what God's Son says remains eternally true, "For apart from Me you can do nothing" (John 15:5).

Paul says, "For it is God who works in you, both to will and to work for His good pleasure" (Philippians 2:13).

To all godly Christians who feel and experience in their hearts a small spark or longing for divine grace and eternal salvation this precious passage is very comforting. For they know that God has kindled in their hearts this beginning of true godliness. He will further strengthen and help them in their great weakness to persevere in true faith unto the end (1 Peter 5:10).

15    Here belong also all the prayers of the saints in which they ask that they may be taught, enlightened, and sanctified by God. By this very act they declare that they cannot get those things that they ask of God from their own natural powers. For example, in Psalm 119 alone, David prays more than ten times that God would give him understanding, that he might rightly comprehend and learn the divine teaching. Similar prayers are in Paul's writings (Ephesians 1:17; Colossians 1:9; Philippians 1:9). These prayers and passages about our ignorance and inability have been written for us. They are not written to make us idle and remiss in reading, hearing, and meditating on God's Word, but that we should first thank God from the heart that by His Son He has delivered us from the darkness of ignorance and the captivity of sin and death (Ephesians 4:8). Through Baptism and the Holy Spirit He has regenerated and illumined us.

After God (through the Holy Spirit in Baptism) has kindled and caused a beginning of the true knowledge of God and faith, we should pray to Him without ceasing (1 Thessalonians 5:17). We should ask that through the same Spirit and His grace, by means of the daily exercise of reading and doing God's Word, He would preserve in us faith and His heavenly gifts, strengthen us from day to day, and keep us to the end. For unless God Himself is our schoolmaster, we can study and learn nothing that is acceptable to Him and helpful to ourselves and others.    16

Second, God's Word testifies that the intellect, heart, and will of the natural, unregenerate person in divine things are not only turned entirely away from God, but also are turned and perverted against God to every evil. Also, a person is not only weak, incapable, unfit, and dead to good, but is also sadly perverted, infected, and corrupted by original sin so that he is entirely evil, perverse, and hostile to God by his disposition and nature. He is very strong, alive, and active in everything that is displeasing and contrary to God.    17

> For the intention of man's heart is evil from his youth. (Genesis 8:21)

> The heart is deceitful above all things, and desperately sick; who can understand it? (Jeremiah 17:9)

St. Paul explains this passage for Jeremiah, writing,

> For the mind that is set on the flesh is hostile to God. (Romans 8:7)

> For the desires of the flesh are against the Spirit, and the desires of the Spirit are against the flesh, for these are opposed to each other. (Galatians 5:17)

> For we know that the law is spiritual,

but I am of the flesh, sold under sin. (Romans 7:14)

For I know that nothing good dwells in me, that is, in my flesh. (Romans 7:18)

For I delight in the law of God, in my inner being, but I see in my members another law waging war against the law of my mind and making me captive to the law of sin that dwells in my members. (Romans 7:22–23)

18 The natural or fleshly free will in St. Paul and in other regenerate people strives against God's Law, even after regeneration. Was it not much more stubborn and hostile to God's Law and will before regeneration? Therefore, this is clear (as it is further declared in the article about original sin, to which we now refer for the sake of brevity): (a) the free will, from its own natural powers, cannot work or agree to work anything for its own conversion, righteousness, and salvation, nor follow, believe, or agree with the Holy Spirit, who through the Gospel offers a person grace and salvation; (b) from its inborn, wicked, rebellious nature it resists God and His will with hostility, unless it is enlightened and controlled by God's Spirit.

19 Because of this the Holy Scriptures compare the heart of the unregenerate person to a hard stone (Ezekiel 36:26). It does not yield to the one who touches it, but resists. It is like a rough block and a wild, unmanageable beast (Jeremiah 2:23–24). This does not mean that since the fall a person is no longer a rational creature, or is converted to God without hearing and meditating on the divine Word. It does not mean a person fails to understand outward, worldly things, or of his free will do, or abstain from doing, anything good or evil.

As Dr. Luther says about Psalm 90[91]: 20 In worldly and outward affairs, which apply to the livelihood and maintenance of the body, a person is cunning, intelligent, and quite active. But in spiritual and divine things, which apply to the salvation of the soul, a person is like a pillar of salt, like Lot's wife (Genesis 19:26), indeed, like a log and a stone. He is like a lifeless statue, which uses neither eyes nor mouth, neither sense nor heart. For a 21 person neither sees nor perceives God's terrible and fierce wrath resulting from sin and death. He always continues in his security, even knowingly and willingly. In this way he falls into a thousand dangers, and finally into eternal death and damnation. No prayers, no supplications, no warnings, indeed, also no threats, no chiding, are of any help. Indeed, all teaching and preaching is lost on him until he is enlightened, converted, and regenerated by the Holy Spirit. For only mankind, not stone or 22 block, was created for renewal by the Holy Spirit. According to God's just, strict sentence, He has utterly cast away the fallen evil spirits forever. Nevertheless, out of special, pure mercy, He has willed that poor fallen human nature might again become and be capable of and be a participant in conversion, God's grace and eternal life. This comes not from its own natural, active skill, ability, or capacity (for a person's nature is stubbornly hostile against God). It comes only from pure grace, through the gracious effective working of the Holy Spirit.

Dr. Luther calls this *capacity* (not active, but 23 passive), which he explains as follows:

When the Fathers defend free will, they are speaking of this: it is capable of freedom in this sense, that by God's grace it can be converted to good and become truly free, for which it was created in the beginning. (WA 2:647)

Augustine has also written in a similar way (*Against Julian*, Book 2). See Dr. Luther on Hosea 6. Also see the *Church Postil* on the Epistle for Christmas and on the Gospel for the third Sunday after Epiphany.

24   Before a person is enlightened, converted, regenerated, renewed, and drawn by the Holy Spirit, he can by himself and by his own natural powers begin, work, or agree to work in spiritual things and in his own conversion or regeneration as little as a stone, a block, or a lump of clay. He can control the outward members of his body and hear the Gospel. To a certain extent he can meditate on it and discuss it, as is to be seen in the Pharisees and hypocrites (Matthew 23:25–28). Nevertheless, he regards it as foolishness and cannot believe it. In this respect he acts even worse than a block. For he is rebellious and hostile to God's will, unless the Holy Spirit is effective on him and kindles and works in him faith and other abilities pleasing to God, and obedience.

25   Third, in this way, too, the Holy Scriptures do not credit the human powers of the natural free will with conversion, faith in Christ, regeneration, renewal, and all that belongs to their effective beginning and end. They do not credit free will the whole way, half way, or in any way, even in the smallest or most trivial way. They credit conversion solely and completely to the Holy Spirit's divine work, as also the Apology teaches.

26   Reason and free will are able to live an outwardly decent life to a certain extent. But only the Holy Spirit causes a person to be born anew (John 3:5) and to have inwardly another heart, mind, and natural desire. He opens the mind and heart to understand the Scriptures and to listen to the Word, as it is written in Luke 24:45, "Then He opened their minds to understand the Scriptures."

One who heard us was a woman named Lydia, from the city of Thyatira, a seller of purple goods, who was a worshiper of God. The Lord opened her heart to pay attention to what was said by Paul. (Acts 16:14)

For it is God who works in you, both to will and to work for His good pleasure. (Philippians 2:13)

God exalted Him at His right hand as Leader and Savior, to give repentance to Israel and forgiveness of sins. (Acts 5:31)

God may perhaps grant them repentance leading to a knowledge of the truth. (2 Timothy 2:25)

For it has been granted to you that for the sake of Christ you should not only believe in Him but also suffer for His sake. (Philippians 1:29)

For by grace you have been saved through faith. And this is not your own doing; it is the gift of God. (Ephesians 2:8)

Jesus answered them, "This is the work of God, that you believe in Him whom He has sent." (John 6:29)

But to this day the LORD has not given you a heart to understand or eyes to see or ears to hear. (Deuteronomy 29:4; see also Matthew 13:15)

He saved us, not because of works done by us in righteousness, but according to His own mercy, by the washing of regeneration and renewal of the Holy Spirit, whom He poured out on us richly through Jesus Christ our Savior. (Titus 3:5–6)

And I will give them one heart, and a new spirit I will put within them. I will remove the heart of stone from their flesh and give them a heart of flesh, that they may walk in My statutes and keep My rules and obey them. (Ezekiel 11:19–20; see also Deuteronomy 30:6; Psalm 51:10)

For we are His workmanship, created in Christ Jesus for good works, which God prepared beforehand, that we should walk in them. (Ephesians 2:10)

Therefore, if anyone is in Christ, he is a new creation. The old has passed away; behold, the new has come. (2 Corinthians 5:17; see also Galatians 6:15)

Every good gift and every perfect gift is from above. (James 1:17)

No one can come to Me unless the Father who sent Me draws him. (John 6:44)

No one knows the Father except the Son and anyone to whom the Son chooses to reveal Him. (Matthew 11:27)

No one can say "Jesus is Lord" except in the Holy Spirit. (1 Corinthians 12:3)

For apart from Me you can do nothing. (John 15:5)

Not that we are sufficient in ourselves to claim anything as coming from us, but our sufficiency is from God. (2 Corinthians 3:5)

What do you have that you did not receive? If then you received it, why do you boast as if you did not receive it? (1 Corinthians 4:7)

27 St. Augustine writes about this passage in particular. By it he was convinced that he must lay aside his former wrong opinion, when he had believed the following in his treatise *On Predestination*, chapter 3: "I erred in this matter. I believed that God's grace consists only of this: God reveals His will in the preaching of the truth. But our faith in the preached Gospel is our own work and is within our own powers." Likewise, St. Augustine writes further, "[I erred when] I said that it is within our own power to believe the Gospel and to will. But it is God's work to give the power to do something to those who believe and will."

28 This teaching is founded on God's Word and conforms to the Augsburg Confession and other writings mentioned above, as the following testimonies prove.

29 In Article XX (29–32) the Augsburg Confession says as follows:

> The Holy Spirit is received through faith, hearts are renewed and given new affections, and then they are able to bring forth good works. . . . Without the Holy Spirit people are full of ungodly desires. They are too weak to do works that are good in God's sight (John 15:5). Besides, they are in the power of the devil, who pushes human beings into various sins, ungodly opinions, and open crimes.

And a little afterward (XX 36):

> For without faith human nature cannot, in any way, do the works of the First or Second Commandment.

30 These passages clearly testify that the Augsburg Confession does not at all recognize the human will in spiritual things as free. But it says that a person is the devil's captive. How, then, is a person able to turn

himself to the Gospel or Christ by his own powers?

31 The Apology (Article XVIII 70–73) teaches this about free will:

> We do not deny freedom to the human will. The human will has freedom in the choice of works and things that reason understands by itself. . . . For without the Holy Spirit, human hearts lack the fear of God. Without trust toward God, they do not believe that they are heard, forgiven, helped, and preserved by God.
> 32 Therefore, they are godless. For "a diseased tree [cannot] bear good fruit" (Matthew 7:18). And "without faith it is impossible to please [God]" (Hebrews 11:6). Although we admit that free will has the freedom and power to perform the extreme works of the Law, we do not assign spiritual matters to free will.

Here it is clearly seen that the Apology credits no ability to the human will, either for beginning good or for working by itself.

33 In the Smalcald Articles (Sin; III I 5) the following errors about the free will are also rejected, "A person has a free will to do good and not to do evil," and so on. And shortly afterward (III I 10) it is also rejected as an error when people teach, "Scripture does not teach that the Holy Spirit with His grace is necessary for a good work."

34 Furthermore, we read the following in the Smalcald Articles (Repentance; III III 40):

> In Christians, this repentance continues until death. For through one's entire life, repentance contends with the sin remaining in the flesh. Paul testifies that he wars with the law in his members (Romans 7:14–25) not by his own powers, but by the gift of the Holy Spirit that follows the forgiveness of sins (Romans 8:1–17). This gift daily cleanses and sweeps out the remaining sins and works to make a person truly pure and holy.

35 These words say nothing at all about our will, or that even in regenerate people our will does anything by itself. But they credit this work to the gift of the Holy Spirit, who cleanses a person and makes him daily more godly and holy (1 Corinthians 6:11). Our own powers are entirely excluded from this work.

36 In Dr. Luther's Large Catechism (II 52–53), this is written:

> I am also a part and member of this same group, a sharer and joint owner of all the goods it possesses (Romans 8:1–17). I am brought to it and incorporated into it by the Holy Spirit through having heard and continuing to hear God's Word (Galatians 3:1–2), which is the beginning of entering it.
> 37 In the past, before we had attained to this, we were altogether of the devil, knowing nothing about God and about Christ (Romans 3:10–12). So, until the Last Day, the Holy Spirit abides with the holy congregation or Christendom (John 14:17). Through this congregation He brings us to Christ and He teaches and preaches to us the Word (John 14:26). By the Word He works and promotes sanctification, causing this congregation daily to grow and to become strong in the faith and its fruit, which He produces (Galatians 5).

38 In this passage the Catechism does not mention with a single word our free will or cooperation. It credits everything to the Holy Spirit who, through the preaching office, brings us into the Christian Church, sanctifies us in the Church, and causes us to grow daily in faith and good works.

39 Even in this life the regenerate advance to the point that they want to do what is good and love it, and even do good and grow in it. Still, this (as stated above) is not of our will and ability, but of the Holy Spirit. Paul himself speaks about this, saying that the Spirit works such *willing and doing* (Philippians 2:13). Also in Ephesians 2:10 he credits this work to God alone, when he says, "For we are His workmanship, created in Christ Jesus for good works, which God prepared beforehand, that we should walk in them."

40 In Dr. Luther's Small Catechism, it is written:

> I believe that I cannot by my own reason or strength believe in Jesus Christ, my Lord, or come to Him. But the Holy Spirit has called me by the Gospel, enlightened me with His gifts, sanctified and kept me in the true faith. In the same way He calls, gathers, enlightens, and sanctifies the whole Christian Church on earth and keeps it with Jesus Christ in the one true faith.

41 In the explanation of the Second Petition of the Lord's Prayer the following words occur, "How is this done? When our heavenly Father gives us His Holy Spirit, so that by His grace we believe His holy Word and lead a godly life here in time and there in eternity."

42 These testimonies state that by our own powers we cannot come to Christ. God must give us His Holy Spirit, by whom we are enlightened, sanctified, and thus brought to Christ through faith and kept with Him. No mention is made either of our will or cooperation.

43 To this we will add a passage in which Dr. Luther later declared personally, with a solemn protest that he intended to persevere in this teaching unto the end. In his *Confession concerning Christ's Supper,* he says:

I herewith reject and condemn as sheer error all doctrines that glorify our free will, as diametrically contrary to the help and grace of our Savior Jesus Christ. Outside of Christ death and sin are our masters and the devil is our god and lord, and there is no power or ability, no cleverness or reason, with which we can prepare ourselves for righteousness and life or seek after it. On the contrary, we must remain the dupes and captives of sin and the property of the devil to do and to think what pleases them and what is contrary to God and His commandments. (LW 37:362–63)

44 In these words Dr. Luther, of blessed and holy memory, credits our free will with no power at all to qualify itself for righteousness or strive after it. But he says that a person is blinded and held captive to do only the devil's will, and to do what is contrary to God the Lord. Therefore, there is no cooperation of our will in a person's conversion. A person must be drawn and born anew by God (John 6:44). Otherwise, there is no thought in our hearts that of itself could turn to the Holy Gospel for the purpose of accepting it. Dr. Luther also wrote this way in his book *The Bondage of the Will* (1525), in opposition to Erasmus. Luther clarified and supported this position well and thoroughly. Afterward he repeated and explained it in his glorious commentary on the Book of Genesis, especially on Genesis 26. Luther's meaning and understanding (about some other peculiar disputed points introduced here and there by Erasmus, as of absolute necessity, and such) have been firmly stated by him in the best and most careful way against all misunderstanding and perversion. We also appeal to this book and refer others to it.

45 This is teaching incorrectly: to assert that

an unregenerate person still has so much power that he can desire to receive the Gospel and to be comforted by it, and that the natural human will cooperates somehow in conversion. For such an erroneous opinion is contrary to the holy, divine Scripture, the Christian Augsburg Confession, its Apology, the Smalcald Articles, the Large and the Small Catechisms of Luther, and other writings of this excellent, highly enlightened theologian.

46 This doctrine about the inability and wickedness of our natural free will and about our conversion and regeneration (that it is God's work alone and not from our powers) is abused in an unchristian way by both enthusiasts and the Epicureans. As a result of their speeches, many people have become disorderly and dissolute. They have grown idle and lazy in all Christian exercises of prayer, reading, and devout meditation. They say that, since they are unable by their own natural powers to convert themselves to God, they will always strive against God with all their might, or will wait until God converts them by force, against their will. Or since they can do nothing in these spiritual things, and since everything is the work of God the Holy Spirit alone, they will regard, hear, or read neither the Word nor the Sacrament. But they will wait until God, without means, instills into them His gifts from heaven, so that they can truly feel and see in themselves that God has converted them.

47 Other discouraged hearts might perhaps fall into difficult thoughts and doubts about whether God has chosen them and will work His gifts also in them through the Holy Spirit. They do this especially when they are aware of no strong, intense faith and sincere obedience in themselves, but only of weakness, fear, and misery.

## CONVERSION

48 For this reason we will now explain further from God's Word how (a) a person is converted to God; (b) how and through what means (namely, through the oral Word and the holy Sacraments) the Holy Spirit wants to be effective in us, to work and bestow in our hearts true repentance, faith, and new spiritual power and the ability to do good; and (c) how we should respond to these means and use them.

49 It is not God's will that anyone should be damned, but that all people should be converted to Him and be saved eternally (2 Peter 3:9).

> Say to them, As I live, declares the Lord God, I have no pleasure in the death of the wicked, but that the wicked turn from his way and live. (Ezekiel 33:11)

> For God so loved the world, that He gave His only Son, that whoever believes in Him should not perish but have eternal life. (John 3:16)

50 Out of His immense goodness and mercy, God provides for the public preaching of His divine eternal Law and His wonderful plan for our redemption, that of the holy, only saving Gospel of His eternal Son, our only Savior and Redeemer, Jesus Christ. By this preaching He gathers an eternal Church for Himself from the human race and works in people's hearts true repentance, knowledge of sins, and true faith in God's Son, Jesus Christ. By this means, and in no other way (i.e., through His holy Word, when people hear it preached or read it, and through the holy Sacraments when they are used according to His Word), God desires to call people to eternal salvation. He desires to draw them to Himself and convert, regenerate, and sanctify them.

51 For since, in the wisdom of God, the world did not know God through wisdom, it pleased God through the folly of what we preach to save those who believe. (1 Corinthians 1:21)

[Peter] will tell you what you must do. (Acts 10:6)

So faith comes from hearing, and hearing through the word of Christ. (Romans 10:17)

Sanctify them in the truth; Your word is truth.... I do not ask for these only, but also for those who will believe in Me through their word. (John 17:17–20)

The eternal Father calls down from heaven about His dear Son and about all who preach repentance and forgiveness of sins in His name, "Listen to Him" (Matthew 17:5).

52 All who want to be saved ought to listen to this preaching. For the preaching and hearing of God's Word are the Holy Spirit's instruments. By, with, and through these instruments the Spirit desires to work effectively, to convert people to God, and to work in them both to will and to do (Philippians 2:13).

53 A person can hear and read this Word outwardly, even though he is not yet converted to God and regenerate. As said above, a person even since the fall has a free will to a certain extent in these outward things. So he can go to church and listen or not listen to the sermon.

54 God works through this means (i.e., the preaching and hearing of His Word). He breaks our hearts (Jeremiah 4:3–4) and draws us to Him (John 6:44). Through the preaching of the Law, a person comes to know his sins and God's wrath. He experiences in his heart true terrors, contrition, and sorrow. Through the preaching of, and reflection on, the Holy Gospel about the gracious forgiveness of sins in Christ, a spark of faith is kindled in him. This faith accepts the forgiveness of sins for Christ's sake and comforts itself with the Gospel promise. So the Holy Spirit (who does all this) is sent into the heart (Galatians 4:6).

55 The preacher's planting and watering and the hearer's running and hearing would both be in vain and no conversion would follow it if the power and effectiveness of the Holy Spirit were not added (1 Corinthians 3:6–7). The Spirit enlightens and converts hearts through the Word preached and heard. So people believe this Word and agree with it. Neither preacher nor hearer is to doubt this grace and effectiveness of the Holy Spirit. They should be certain that when God's Word is preached purely and truly, according to God's command and will, and people listen attentively and seriously and meditate on it, God is certainly present with His grace. He grants, as has been said, what otherwise a person can neither accept nor give by his own powers.

56 For we should not and cannot always judge from feeling about the presence, work, and gifts of the Holy Spirit, as to how and when they are experienced in the heart. They are often covered and happen in great weakness. Therefore, we should be certain about and agree with the promise that God's Word preached and heard is truly an office and work of the Holy Spirit. He is certainly effective and works in our hearts by them (2 Corinthians 2:14–17; 3:5–6).

57 If a person will not listen to preaching or read God's Word, but despises God's Word and congregation, and so dies and perishes in his sins, he cannot comfort himself with God's eternal election or receive His mercy. For Christ, in whom we are chosen, offers to all people His grace in the Word and holy Sacraments. He sincerely wants it to be

heard. He has promised that where two or three are gathered together in His name and have His holy Word, He will be in their midst (Matthew 18:20).

58    When such a person despises the instrument of the Holy Spirit and will not listen, no injustice is done to him if the Holy Spirit does not enlighten him but allows him to remain in the darkness of his unbelief and to perish. For it is written about this matter, "How often would I have gathered your children together as a hen gathers her brood under her wings, and you would not!" (Matthew 23:37).

59    In this respect it may well be said that a person is not a stone or block. For a stone or block does not resist the person who moves it. It does not understand and doesn't care what is being done with it. But a person with his will resists God the Lord until he is converted. It is true that a person before his conversion is still a rational creature, having an understanding and will. However, he does not understand divine things. He does not have the will to desire something good and helpful. He can do nothing at all about his conversion (as has also been said above frequently), and is in this way much worse than a stone and block. For he resists God's Word and will, until God awakens him from the death of sin, enlightens, and renews him.

60    God does not force a person to become godly. (Those who always resist the Holy Spirit and persistently oppose the known truth are not converted, as Stephen says about the hardened Jewish people [Acts 7:51].) Yet God the Lord draws the person whom He wants to convert (John 6:44). He draws him in such a way that his darkened understanding is turned into an enlightened one and his perverse will into an obedient one. This is what the Scriptures call creating a clean heart (Psalm 51:10).

For this reason it is not correct to say that    61 a person can do something good and helpful in divine things before his conversion. Because a person is "dead in [his] trespasses" (Ephesians 2:5) before his conversion, there can be no power to work anything good in divine things in him. Therefore, he has no way of doing something good and helpful in divine things. When we talk about how God    62 works in a person, it is true that God has one way of working in him, as in a rational creature. He has another way of working in some other irrational creature, or in a stone or block. Yet, before a man's conversion, nothing at all can be credited to him for doing good in spiritual matters.

When a person has been converted, and    63 is thus enlightened, and his will is renewed, then a person wants to do what is good (so far as he is regenerate or a new man). Then that person will "delight in the law of God, in [his] inner being" (Romans 7:22) and from that time forward does good to such an extent and as long as he is moved by God's Spirit, as Paul says in Romans 8:14, "For all who are led by the Spirit of God are sons of God." This moving by the Holy Spirit is not a    64 coercion. The converted person does good spontaneously, as David says in Psalm 110:3, "Your people will offer themselves freely on the day of your power." Nevertheless, the conflict between the flesh and spirit remains in the regenerate. St. Paul wrote about this in Romans 7:21–23:

So I find it to be a law that when I want to do right, evil lies close at hand. For I delight in the law of God, in my inner being, but I see in my members another law waging war against the law of my mind and making me captive to the law of sin that dwells in my members.

So then, I myself serve the law of God with my mind, but with my flesh I serve the law of sin. (Romans 7:25)

For the desires of the flesh are against the Spirit, and the desires of the Spirit are against the flesh, for these are opposed to each other, to keep you from doing the things you want to do. (Galatians 5:17)

65 From this evidence the following is certain: as soon as the Holy Spirit has begun His work of regeneration and renewal in us through the Word and holy Sacraments, we can and should cooperate through His power, although still in great weakness. This cooperation does not come from our fleshly natural powers, but from the new powers and gifts that the Holy Spirit has begun in 66 us in conversion. St. Paul clearly and eagerly encourages that "working together with Him, then, we appeal to you not to receive the grace of God in vain" (2 Corinthians 6:1). But this is to be understood in no other way than the following: the converted person does good to such an extent and as long as God by His Holy Spirit rules, guides, and leads him. As soon as God would withdraw His gracious hand from that person, he could not for a moment keep obeying God. But if anyone would take St. Paul's words in this sense—the converted person cooperates with the Holy Spirit the way two horses draw a wagon together—this could not be allowed in any way without damaging the divine truth.

Working together with him, then, we appeal to you not to receive the grace of God in vain. (2 Corinthians 6:1)

For we are God's fellow workers. You are God's field, God's building.(1 Corinthians 3:9)

But by the grace of God I am what I am, and His grace toward me was not in vain. On the contrary, I worked harder than any of them, though it was not I, but the grace of God that is with me. (1 Corinthians 15:10)

What agreement has the temple of God with idols? For we are the temple of the living God; as God said, "I will make My dwelling among them and walk among them, and I will be their God, and they shall be My people." (2 Corinthians 6:16)

67 There is a great difference between baptized and unbaptized people. According to the teaching of St. Paul in Galatians 3:27, "For as many of you as were baptized into Christ have put on Christ," and are made truly regenerate. They now have a freed will. As Christ says, they have been made free again (John 8:36). Therefore, they are able not only to hear the Word, but also to agree with it and accept it, although in great weakness.

68 We receive in this life only the firstfruit of the Spirit (Romans 8:23). The new birth is not complete, but only begun in us. The combat and struggle of the flesh against the spirit remains even in the elect and truly regenerate people (Galatians 5:17). For a great difference can be seen among Christians. Not only is it true that one is weak and another strong in the spirit, but each Christian also experiences differences in himself. At one time he is joyful in spirit, and at another fearful and alarmed. At one time he is intense in love, strong in faith and hope, and at another time he is cold and weak.

69 When the baptized act against their conscience, allowing sin to rule in them, they grieve the Holy Spirit in them and lose Him (Ephesians 4:30). They do not need to be re-

baptized. But they must be converted again, as has been said well enough before.

70     This is certainly true: in genuine conversion a change, new emotion, and movement in the intellect, will, and heart must take place. The heart must perceive sin, dread God's wrath, turn from sin, see and accept the promise of grace in Christ, have good spiritual thoughts, have a Christian purpose and diligence, and fight against the flesh. Where none of these happen or are present,

71 there is no true conversion. But the question is about the effective cause. Who works this in us? How does a person have this? How does he get it? Therefore, this teaching informs us that, since the natural powers of mankind cannot do anything or help toward it (1 Corinthians 2:14; 2 Corinthians 3:5), God, out of His infinite goodness and mercy, comes first to us. He causes His Holy Gospel to be preached. The Holy Spirit desires to work and accomplish this conversion and renewal in us. Through preaching and meditation on His Word God kindles faith and other godly virtues in us. They are the Holy

72 Spirit's gifts and works alone. Therefore, this teaching directs us to the means that the Holy Spirit desires to begin and do this. It also teaches us about how those gifts are preserved, strengthened, and increased. It warns us that we should not let God's grace be bestowed on us in vain, but diligently use it and ponder how great a sin it is to hinder and resist such works of the Holy Spirit (Acts 7:51).

73     From this thorough explanation of the entire teaching about free will, we can now judge, at last, the questions about which, for quite a number of years, there has been controversy in the churches of the Augsburg Confession:

> Does a person before, in, or after his conversion resist the Holy Spirit? Does he do nothing whatsoever, but only allow what God works in him? In conversion does a person act like— and is he—a block? Is the Holy Spirit given to those who resist Him? Does conversion happen by coercion, so that God makes people convert by force against their wills?

Now we can see, expose, censure, and reject the following opposite dogmas and errors:

## NEGATIVE STATEMENTS

74     1. First, the folly of the Stoics and Manichaeans, who asserted that everything that happens must happen in this way, that a person does everything from coercion. And even in outward works a person's will has no freedom or ability to perform (to a certain extent) outward righteousness and respectable behavior. A person cannot avoid outward sins and vices. A person's will is coerced to do outward wicked deeds, unchastity, robbery, murder, and such.

75     2. Second, the error of the gross Pelagians, that the free will, from its own natural powers, without the Holy Spirit, can turn to God and believe the Gospel. People can be obedient to God's Law from the heart, and by this voluntary obedience the heart can merit the forgiveness of sins and eternal life.

76     3. Third, the error of the papists and scholastics, who have acted in a somewhat more crafty way. They have taught that a person from his own natural powers can begin to do good and to convert himself. Then, because a person is too weak to bring it to completion, the Holy Spirit comes to the aid of the good begun from a person's own natural powers.

77     4. Fourth, the teaching of the Synergists, who pretend that a person is not absolutely dead to good in spiritual things, but is badly wounded and half dead. The free will is too weak to make a beginning and to convert it-

self to God by its own powers. It can't be obedient to God's Law from the heart. Nevertheless, when the Holy Spirit makes a beginning, calls us through the Gospel, and offers His grace, the forgiveness of sins, and eternal salvation, then the free will, from its own natural powers, can meet God. To a certain extent, although feebly, the will can do something toward salvation; it can help and cooperate in it and can qualify itself for it. The will can apply itself to grace, can grasp and accept it, and can believe the Gospel. It can also cooperate, by its own powers, with the Holy Spirit, in the continuation and maintenance of this work.

78 Against this teaching, it has been shown at length above that the power known to qualify one's self for grace naturally does not come from our own natural powers, but only from the Holy Spirit's work.

79 5. Likewise, we reject the following teaching of the popes and monks: after regeneration a person can completely fulfill God's Law in this life, and through this fulfillment of the Law he is righteous before God and merits eternal life.

80 6. On the other hand, the enthusiasts should be rebuked with great seriousness and zeal. They should not be tolerated in any way in God's Church. They imagine that God, without any means, without the hearing of the divine Word, and without the use of the holy Sacraments, draws people to Himself, enlightens, justifies, and saves them.

81 7. We should also rebuke those who imagine that in conversion and regeneration God creates a new heart and new person in such a way that the substance and essence of the old Adam, and especially the rational soul, are completely destroyed, and a new essence of the soul is created out of nothing. St. Augustine clearly rebukes this error in his comments on Psalm 25, where he quotes the passage from Paul in Ephesians 4:22, "Put off your old self . . ." Augustine explains this in the following words:

> Lest anyone might think that the substance or essence of a person is to be laid aside, he himself explains what it is to lay aside the old man, and to put on the new, when he says in the following words: "Putting away lying, speak the truth." Behold, that is to put off the old man and to put on the new.

82 8. Likewise, the following expressions should not be used without being explained: the human will before, in, and after conversion resists the Holy Spirit, and the Holy Spirit is given to those who resist Him.

83 The preceding explanation makes this matter clear. Where (a) no change at all in intellect, will, and heart happens through the Holy Spirit to what is good, and (b) a person does not at all believe the promise (and is not made fit by God for grace, but entirely resists the Word), there no conversion takes place or can exist. For conversion is the kind of change through the Holy Spirit's work in a person's intellect, will, and heart that by the Holy Spirit's work a person can receive the offered grace. Indeed, all those who stubbornly and persistently resist the Holy Spirit's works and movements—which take place through the Word—do not receive, but grieve and lose the Holy Spirit.

## TERMS AND EXPRESSIONS

84 There still remains also in the regenerate a rebelliousness of which the Scriptures speak: "the desires of the flesh are against the Spirit" (Galatians 5:17). Also of "the passions of the flesh, which wage war against your soul" (1 Peter 2:11). And, "in my members another law wages war against the law of my mind" (Romans 7:23).

85 The person who is not regenerate resists

God altogether and is entirely a servant of sin (John 8:34; Romans 6:16). The regenerate person, however, delights in God's Law after the inward man, but nevertheless sees in the members of his body the law of sin, which wars against the law of the mind. So he serves God's Law with his mind, but the law of sin with the flesh (Romans 7:25). In this way the correct opinion can and should be thoroughly, clearly, and definitively explained and taught.

86   Chrysostom and Basil have said, "God draws, but He draws the willing"; "Only be willing, and God will anticipate you." Likewise, the Scholastics (and papists) have said, "In conversion the will of man is not idle, but effects something." (These expressions have been raised to confirm the natural free will in a person's conversion, against the teaching about God's grace.) It is clear from the explanation presented earlier that they are not in harmony with the form of sound doctrine, but are contrary to it. Therefore, they ought to be avoided when we speak about conversion to God.

87   The conversion of our corrupt will, which is nothing other than restoring it back to life from spiritual death, is only and solely God's work (just as the restoration of life in the resurrection of the body must also be credited to God alone). This has been fully set forth above and proved by clear testimonies of Holy Scripture.

88   In conversion God changes stubborn and unwilling people into willing people through the drawing of the Holy Spirit. After such conversion, in the daily exercise of repentance, a person's regenerate will is not idle, but also cooperates in all the Holy Spirit's works that He does through us. How this happens has already been explained well enough above.

89   Luther says about conversion that a person is purely passive. This means a person does nothing at all toward conversion, but only undergoes what God works in him. Luther does not mean that conversion takes place without the preaching and hearing of God's Word. Nor does he mean that in conversion no new emotion whatever is awakened in us by the Holy Spirit and no spiritual operation begun. But he means that a person by himself, or from his natural powers, cannot do anything or help toward his conversion. Conversion is not only in part, but totally an act, gift, present, and work of the Holy Spirit alone. He accomplishes and does it by His power and might, through the Word, in a person's intellect, will, and heart, "while the person does or works nothing, but only undergoes it." It is not like a figure cut into stone or a seal impressed into wax, which knows nothing about it, which neither sees or wills it. Rather, it happens the way that has just been described and explained.

90   The young people in the schools have also been greatly confused about "the doctrine of the three efficient causes of the conversion of an unregenerate person to God." They are confused about the way the three causes (i.e., God's Word preached and heard, the Holy Spirit, and the human will) come together. It is again clear from the explanation presented above that conversion to God is a work of God the Holy Spirit alone. He is the true Master who alone works this in us. For this He uses the preaching and hearing of His Holy Word as His ordinary means and instrument. The intellect and will of an unregenerate person are nothing other than "what needs to be converted," for they are the intellect and will of a spiritually dead person, in whom the Holy Spirit works conversion and renewal. A person's will that is to be converted does nothing toward this work, but undergoes God's work alone in him, until he

is regenerate. Then that person works with the Holy Spirit to do what is pleasing to God in other good works that follow, in the way and to the extent fully set forth above.

# III. THE RIGHTEOUSNESS OF FAITH BEFORE GOD

For an annotation on this article, see pp. 497–98. (See also AC IV; Ap IV; SA II I; SA III XIII; FC Ep III.)

## THE STATUS OF THE CONTROVERSY

1    The third controversy that has arisen among some theologians of the Augsburg Confession is about the righteousness of Christ or of faith, which God credits by grace, through faith, to poor sinners for righteousness.

2    One side has contended that the righteousness of faith, which the apostle calls God's righteousness, is God's essential righteousness. They say this is Christ Himself as God's true, natural, and essential Son, who dwells in the elect by faith and moves them to do right. And so He is their righteousness. Compared with this great ocean of righteousness, the sins of all people are like a drop of water.

3    Against this, others have held and taught that Christ is our righteousness according to His human nature alone.

4    In opposition to both these groups it has been unanimously taught by the other teachers of the Augsburg Confession that Christ is our righteousness not according to His divine nature alone, nor according to His human nature alone, but according to both natures. For He has redeemed, justified, and saved us from our sins as God and man, through His complete obedience. Therefore, the righteousness of faith is the forgiveness of sins, reconciliation with God, and our adoption as God's children only on account of Christ's obedience. Christ's obedience alone —out of pure grace—is credited for righteousness through faith alone to all true believers. They are absolved from all their unrighteousness by this obedience.

5    Besides this controversy, other disputes have been caused and stirred up because of the Interim. Other disputes about the article of justification will be explained in antitheses, that is, listing the errors that are contrary to the pure teaching in this article.

## JUSTIFICATION BY FAITH

6    This article about justification by faith (as the Apology says) is the chief article in all Christian doctrine. Without this teaching no poor conscience can have any firm consolation or truly know the riches of Christ's grace. Dr. Luther also has written about this:

> If this one teaching stands in its purity, then Christendom will also remain pure and good, undivided and unseparated; for this alone, and nothing else, makes and maintains Christendom. . . . Where this falls, it is impossible to ward off any error or sectarian spirit. (LW 14:37)

7    Paul says especially about this article, "a little leaven leavens the whole lump" (1 Corinthians 5:6). Therefore, in this article he zealously and seriously urges the exclusive parts of speech. This means the words by which people's works are excluded from justification (i.e., "apart from works of the law," "apart from works," "by grace" [Romans 3:28; 4:6; Ephesians 2:8–9]). These show how highly necessary it is that in this article, along with the pure doctrine, the antithesis (i.e., all contrary doctrine) be stated separately, exposed, and rejected by this method.

8    We want to explain this controversy in a

St. Paul

Christian way by means of God's Word, and settle it by His grace. Therefore, this is our doctrine, faith, and confession:

9    We unanimously believe, teach, and confess the following about the righteousness of faith before God, in accordance with the comprehensive summary of our faith and confession presented above. A poor sinful person is justified before God, that is, absolved and declared free and exempt from all his sins and from the sentence of well-deserved condemnation, and is adopted into sonship and inheritance of eternal life, without any merit or worth of his own. This happens without any preceding, present, or subsequent works, out of pure grace, because of the sole merit, complete obedience, bitter suffering, death, and resurrection of our Lord Christ alone. His obedience is credited to us for righteousness.

10    These treasures are brought to us by the Holy Spirit in the promise of the Holy Gospel. Faith alone is the only means through which we lay hold on, accept, apply,
11    and take them for ourselves. This faith is God's gift (Ephesians 2:8–9), by which we truly learn to know Christ, our Redeemer, in the Word of the Gospel and trust in Him. We trust that for the sake of His obedience alone we have the forgiveness of sins by grace, are regarded as godly and righteous by God the Father, and are eternally saved.
12    Therefore, it is considered and understood to be the same thing when Paul says (a) we are "justified by faith" (Romans 3:28) or (b) "faith is counted as righteousness" (Romans 4:5) and when he says (c) "by the one man's obedience the many will be made righteous" (Romans 5:19) or (d) "so one act of righteousness leads to justification and life
13    for all men" (Romans 5:18). Faith justifies not because it is such a good work or because it is so beautiful a virtue. It justifies

because it lays hold of and accepts Christ's merit in the promise of the Holy Gospel. For this merit must be applied and become ours through faith, if we are to be justified by it. Therefore, the righteousness that is    14    credited to faith or to the believer out of pure grace is Christ's obedience, suffering, and resurrection, since He has made satisfaction for us to the Law and paid for our sins. Christ is not man alone, but God and    15    man in one undivided person. Therefore, He was hardly subject to the Law (because He is the Lord of the Law), just as He didn't have to suffer and die for His own sake. For this reason, then, His obedience (not only in His suffering and dying, but also because He was voluntarily made under the Law in our place and fulfilled the Law by this obedience) is credited to us for righteousness. So, because of this complete obedience, which He rendered to His heavenly Father for us by doing and suffering and in living and dying, God forgives our sins. He regards us as godly and righteous, and He eternally saves us. This righteousness is brought to us    16    by the Holy Spirit through the Gospel and in the Sacraments. It is applied, taken, and received through faith. Therefore, believers have reconciliation with God, forgiveness of sins, God's grace, sonship, and are heirs of eternal life.

The word *justify* here means to declare    17    righteous and free from sins and to absolve a person from eternal punishment for the sake of Christ's righteousness, which is credited by God to faith (Philippians 3:9). This use and understanding of this word is common in the Holy Scriptures of the Old and the New Testament.

He who justifies the wicked and he who condemns the righteous are both alike an abomination to the LORD. (Proverbs 17:15)

[Woe to those] who acquit the guilty for a bribe, and deprive the innocent of his right! (Isaiah 5:23)

Who shall bring any charge against God's elect? It is God who justifies [that is, absolves from sins and acquits]. (Romans 8:33)

## THE TERM *REGENERATION*

18  The word *regeneration* is sometimes used for the word *justification*. Therefore, it is necessary that this word be properly explained, in order that the renewal that follows justification by faith may not be confused with the actual justification by faith, but that they may be properly distinguished from each other.

19  In the first place, the word *regeneration* (*regeneratio*) is used to mean both the forgiveness of sins for Christ's sake alone and, at the same time, the succeeding renewal that the Holy Spirit works in those who are justified by faith. Then again, it is sometimes used to mean only the forgiveness of sins and that we are adopted as God's sons. It is in this latter sense that the word is used much of the time in the Apology, where it is written that justification before God is regeneration. St. Paul, too, has used these words as distinct from each other:

He saved us . . . by the washing of regeneration and renewal of the Holy Spirit. (Titus 3:5)

20  The words "making alive" have sometimes been used in a similar sense. For when a person is justified through faith (which the Holy Spirit alone does), this is truly a regeneration. In this he becomes a child of God instead of a child of wrath (Ephesians 2:3). So he is transferred from death to life, as it is written, "When we were dead in our trespasses, [God] made us alive together with Christ" (Ephesians 2:5). Likewise, "The righteous shall live by faith" (Romans 1:17; see also Habakkuk 2:4). This is how the word is usually used in the Apology.

21  Again, it is often used for sanctification and renewal, which follows the righteousness of faith. Dr. Luther has used it this way in his book about the Church and the Councils, and elsewhere.

22  We teach that through the Holy Spirit's work we are born anew and justified. But the sense is not that after regeneration no unrighteousness clings anymore to the justified and regenerate in their being and life. It means that Christ covers all their sins (which in this life still dwell in nature) with His complete obedience. But despite this they are declared and regarded godly and righteous by faith and for the sake of Christ's obedience (which Christ rendered to the Father for us from His birth to His most humiliating death on the cross [Philippians 2:8]). Still, because of their corrupt nature, they are and will remain sinners to the grave. Nor, on the other hand, is this the meaning: without repentance, conversion, and renewal we can or should yield to sins and remain and continue in them.

23  True contrition must come first. Out of pure grace, for the sake of the only Mediator, Christ (1 Timothy 2:5), without any works and merit, people are righteous before God in the way stated above (i.e., they are received into grace). The Holy Spirit is also given to them. He renews and sanctifies them and works in them love for God and for their neighbor. But the beginning of renewal is imperfect in this life. Sin still dwells in the flesh, even in the regenerate. Therefore, the righteousness of faith before God comes from the free crediting of Christ's righteousness, without the addition of our works. So our sins are forgiven us and covered and are not charged against us (Romans 4:6–8).

24    If the article of justification is to remain pure, the greatest attention must be given with special diligence. Otherwise, what comes before faith, and what follows after it, will be mixed together or inserted into the article of justification as necessary and belonging to it. For it is not one and the same thing to talk about conversion and to talk about justification.

25    Not everything that belongs to conversion also belongs to the article of justification. Only God's grace, Christ's merit, and faith belong and are necessary to the article of justification. Faith receives these blessings in the promise of the Gospel, by which Christ's righteousness is credited to us. From this we receive and have forgiveness of sins, reconciliation with God, sonship, and are made heirs of eternal life.

26    True, saving faith is not in people who lack contrition and sorrow and who have a wicked plan to remain and continue in sins. But true contrition comes first, and genuine faith is in or with true repentance.

27    Love is a fruit that surely and necessarily also follows true faith. The fact that a person does not love is a sure sign that he is not justified. He is still in death or has lost the righteousness of faith again, as John says (1 John 3:14). But Paul says in Romans 3:28, "For we hold that one is justified by faith apart from works of the law." He shows that neither the contrition that comes first, nor the works that follow, belong in the article or action of justification by faith. Good works do not come before justification, but follow it. A person must first be justified before he can do good works.

28    In the same way, renewal and sanctification also do not belong in the article or matter of justification before God, even though it is a benefit of the Mediator, Christ, and a work of the Holy Spirit. Sanctification follows justification since, on account of our corrupt flesh, sanctification is not entirely perfect and complete in this life. Dr. Luther writes well about this in his beautiful and large commentary on the Epistle to the Galatians, in which he says the following:

29    We concede that good works and love must also be taught; but this must be in its proper time and place, that is, when the question has to do with works, apart from this chief doctrine. But here the point at issue is how we are justified and attain eternal life. To this we answer with Paul: We are pronounced righteous solely by faith in Christ, not by the works of the Law or

Christ Heals the Paralyzed Man

by love. This is not because we reject works or love, as our adversaries accuse us of doing, but because we refuse to let ourselves be distracted from the principal point at issue here, as Satan is trying to do. So since we are now dealing with the topic of justification, we reject and condemn works; for this topic will not allow of any discussion of good works. On this issue, therefore, we simply cut off all laws and all works of the Law. (LW 26:137)

That's what Luther says.

30   Troubled hearts should have a firm, sure consolation. Also, due honor should be given to Christ's merit and God's grace. Therefore, the Scriptures teach that the righteousness of faith before God stands only in the gracious reconciliation or the forgiveness of sins, which is presented to us out of pure grace, only for the sake of the merit of the Mediator, Christ. This is received through faith alone in the Gospel promise. In the same way also, in justification before God, faith relies neither on contrition nor on love or other virtues. Faith relies on Christ alone and on His complete obedience by which He has fulfilled the Law for us. This obedience is credited to believers for righteousness.

31   Furthermore, neither contrition nor love nor any other virtue, but faith alone is the only means and instrument by which, and through which, we can receive and accept God's grace, Christ's merit, and the forgiveness of sins, which are brought to us in the Gospel promise.

32   It is also correct to say that believers who have been justified through faith in Christ first have the righteousness of faith credited to them in this life. Then, they also have the initial righteousness of the new obedience or of good works. But these two types of righteousness must not be mixed with each other or both be injected into the article of justification by faith before God. For this initial righteousness or renewal in us is incomplete and impure in this life because of the flesh. A person cannot stand with and on the ground of this righteousness before God's court. Before God's court only the righteousness of Christ's obedience, suffering, and death—which is credited to faith—can stand. So only for the sake of this obedience is the person pleasing and acceptable to God and received into adoption and made an heir of eternal life. (This is true even after his renewal, when he has already many good works and lives the best life.)

33   Here belongs also what St. Paul writes in Romans 4:3. Abraham was justified before God through faith alone, for the sake of the Mediator, without the cooperation of his works. This was true not only when Abraham was first converted from idolatry and had no good works, but also afterward, when he had been renewed by the Holy Spirit and adorned with many excellent good works (Genesis 15:6; Hebrews 11:8). Paul asks the following question in Romans 4:1–3: At that time, on what did Abraham's righteousness before God rest for everlasting life, by which he had a gracious God and was pleasing and acceptable to Him?

34   He answers:

> To the one who does not work but trusts Him who justifies the ungodly, his faith is counted as righteousness, just as David also [Psalm 32:1] speaks of the blessing of the one to whom God counts righteousness apart from works. (Romans 4:5–6)

35   Therefore, even though people who are converted and believe in Christ have the beginning of renewal, sanctification, love, virtue,

and good works, these cannot and should not be drawn into, or mixed with, the article of justification before God. This is so the honor due to Christ may remain with Christ the Redeemer and tempted consciences may have a sure consolation, since our new obedience is incomplete and impure.

## THE EXCLUSIVE TERMS

36    This is what the apostle Paul means when he urges so diligently and zealously the exclusive terms in this article of faith (i.e., the words by which works are excluded from the article of justification: *by grace, without merit, without works, not of works.*) These exclusives are all summed up in this expression: *Through faith alone in Christ we are justified before God and saved* (Romans 3:28). For thereby works are excluded. This does not mean that a true faith can exist without contrition, or that good works should, must, and dare not follow true faith as sure and undoubtable fruit. It does not mean that believers dare not or must not do anything good. But good works are excluded from the article of justification before God because they must not be drawn into, woven into, or mixed with the act of justifying poor sinners before God. They are not necessary. They do not belong to this act. The true sense of the exclusive terms in the article of justification comes from the following, which should also be taught in this article with all diligence and seriousness:

37    1. Through these terms all our own works, merit, worthiness, glory, and confidence in all our works are entirely excluded from the article of justification. So our works shall not stand or be regarded as the cause or the merit of justification—not entirely, not half, not in the least part—upon which God could or ought to look. We cannot rely on our works in this article and action.

2. This remains the office and property of faith alone. It alone, and nothing else, is the means or instrument with and through which God's grace and Christ's merit in the Gospel promise are received, apprehended, accepted, applied to us, and appropriated. Love and all other virtues or works are excluded from this office and property of such application or appropriation.     38

3. Neither renewal, sanctification, virtues, nor good works are at all a form, part, or cause of justification, that is, our righteousness before God. They are not to stand or be set up as a part or cause of our righteousness. They are not to be mixed into the article of justification under any pretext, title, or name whatever, as though they are necessary and belong to justification. The righteousness of faith stands alone in the forgiveness of sins out of pure grace, for the sake of Christ's merit alone. These blessings are brought to us in the Gospel promise and are received, accepted, applied, and appropriated through faith alone.     39

In the same way the order between faith and good works must remain and be maintained, just as the order between justification and renewal (or sanctification) must be maintained.     40

Good works do not come before faith, neither does sanctification come before justification. First, in conversion faith is kindled in us by the Holy Spirit from the hearing of the Gospel. Faith lays hold of God's grace in Christ, by which the person is justified. Then, when the person is justified, he is also renewed and sanctified by the Holy Spirit. From this renewal and sanctification the fruit of good works then follow. This should not be understood as though justification and renewal were separated from one another in such a way that a genuine faith sometimes could exist and continue for a time together with evil inten-     41 tion. Only the order of causes and effects, of antecedents and consequents is indicated, how one comes first or follows the other. What Luther has correctly said remains true:

> Faith and good works well agree and fit together; but it is faith alone, without works, that lays hold of the blessing. Yet it is never, ever, alone.

This has been set forth above.

42    Many disputes are usefully explained well by this true distinction. The Apology shows this in reference to James 2:20, 24. For when we speak of faith and how it justifies, we refer to the doctrine of St. Paul: that faith alone, without works, justifies (Romans 3:28). This is because faith alone applies and makes Christ's merit our own, as has been said. But if the question is about where and how a Christian can see and distinguish, either in himself or in others, a true living faith from a false and dead faith, that is a different matter. Many useless, secure Christians dream up a delusion for themselves in place of faith, even though they have no true faith. The Apology gives this answer: "James calls that a *dead faith* where good works and fruit of the Spirit of every kind do not follow." And to this effect the Latin edition of the Apology says, "St. James teaches correctly when he denies that we are justified by a faith that lacks works, which is dead faith."

43    James speaks, as the Apology says, about the works of those who have already been justified through Christ, reconciled with God, and received forgiveness of sins through Christ. If the question is about how faith has this result and what belongs to faith so that it justifies and saves, it is false and incorrect to say that faith cannot justify without works. Or, faith justifies or makes righteous if it has love with it, for the sake of which love justification is ascribed to faith. Or, the presence of works with faith is necessary if a person is to be justified by faith before God. Or, the presence of good works in the article of justification, or for justification, is needful, so that good works are a cause without which a person cannot be justified, and that they are not really excluded from the article of justification by the exclusive terms: *without works,* and such (i.e., when St. Paul says, *absque operibus*). For faith makes righteous only because, as a means and instrument, it lays hold of, and accepts, God's grace and Christ's merit in the Gospel promise.

## NEGATIVE STATEMENTS

44    Let this be enough, according to the plan of this document, as a summary explanation of the doctrine of justification by faith. For this is described at length in the above-mentioned writings. From these, the antitheses (i.e., the false contrary doctrines) also are clear. In other words, in addition to the errors listed above, the following and similar errors must be rebuked, exposed, and rejected, since they conflict with the explanation now published, as when it is taught:

45    1. Our love or good works are a merit or cause of justification before God, either entirely or at least in part.

46    2. Or by good works a person must make himself worthy and fit so that Christ's merit may be given to him.

47    3. Our real righteousness before God is the love or renewal the Holy Spirit works in us and which is in us.

48    4. Or two things or parts belong to the righteousness of faith before God: (a) the gracious forgiveness of sins, and then, (b) renewal or sanctification.

49    5. Faith justifies only initially, either in part or primarily, and that our newness or love justifies even before God, either completely or secondarily.

50    6. Believers are justified before God, or are righteous before God, both by credit and by beginning to act righteous at the same time, or partly by the credit of Christ's righteousness and partly by the beginning of new obedience.

51    7. The application of the promise of grace happens both by faith of the heart and confession of the mouth, and also by other virtues. This means that faith makes righteous for this reason alone, that righteousness is begun in us by faith, or (in this way) that faith takes the first step in justification. Nevertheless, renewal and love also belong to our righteousness before God. However, love belongs in such a way that it is not the chief cause of our righteousness. But our righteousness before God is not entire and complete without such love and renewal. Likewise, believers are justified and righteous before God at the same time by the righteousness given by Christ and the initial, new obedience, or in part by the crediting of Christ's righteousness and in part by beginning new obedience. Likewise, the promise of grace is gained for us by faith in the heart and confession made with the mouth, and by other virtues.

52    This is incorrect—a person must be saved in some other way or through something other than justification before God. So we are indeed justified before God through faith alone, without works. But it is impossible to be saved without works or obtain salvation without works.

53    This is false because it is directly opposed to the declaration of Paul, "[Blessed is] the one to whom God counts righteousness apart from works" (Romans 4:6). Paul's reason is that we receive both salvation and righteousness in one and the same way. In fact, when we are justified through faith, we receive adoption at the same time and are made heirs of eternal life and salvation. For this reason Paul uses and emphasizes the exclusive terms, that is, those words by which works and our own merits are entirely excluded. He uses "by grace," "apart from works," as forcibly in the article about salvation as in the article about righteousness.

## OUR RIGHTEOUSNESS

54    The dispute about God's essential righteousness dwelling in us must also be correctly explained. In the elect (who are justified by Christ and reconciled with God), God the Father, Son, and Holy Spirit (who is the eternal and essential righteousness) dwells by faith. (For all Christians are temples of God [1 Corinthians 3:16–17] the Father, Son, and Holy Spirit, who also moves them to do right.) Yet this indwelling of God is not the righteousness of faith St. Paul describes and that he calls God's righteousness for the sake of which we are declared righteous before God. But it comes after the righteousness of faith, which is nothing else than the forgiveness of sins and the gracious adoption of the poor sinner for the sake of Christ's obedience and merit alone.

55    In our churches it is acknowledged among the theologians of the Augsburg Confession that all our righteousness is to be sought outside the merits, works, virtues, and worthiness of ourselves and of all people. Our righteousness rests alone on Christ the Lord. Therefore, how Christ is called our Righteousness in this matter of justification must be carefully considered. I mean, that our righteousness rests not on one or the other nature in Christ, but on Christ's entire person, who as God and man is our Righteousness in His only, entire, and complete obedience.

56    Even if Christ had been conceived and born without sin by the Holy Spirit and had

fulfilled all righteousness in His human nature alone, and yet had not been true and eternal God, this obedience and suffering of His human nature could not be credited to us for righteousness. Also, if God's Son had not become man, the divine nature alone could not be our righteousness. Therefore, we believe, teach, and confess that the entire obedience of Christ's entire person (which He has offered to the Father for us, even to His most humiliating death on the cross) is credited to us for righteousness. For the human nature alone, without the divine, could not by obedience or suffering make satisfaction to eternal, almighty God for the sins of all the world. However, the divinity alone, without the humanity, could not mediate between God and us.

57 As mentioned above, the obedience not only of one nature, but of the entire person, is a complete satisfaction and atonement for the human race. By this obedience God's eternal, unchangeable righteousness, revealed in the Law, has been satisfied. So our righteousness benefits us before God and is revealed in the Gospel. Faith relies on this before God, which God credits to faith, as it is written in Romans 5:19:

> For as by the one man's disobedience the many were made sinners, so by the one man's obedience the many will be made righteous.

> The blood of Jesus His Son cleanses us from all sin. (1 John 1:7)

> The righteous shall live by his faith. (Habakkuk 2:4; see also Romans 1:17)

58 Neither Christ's divine nor human nature by itself is credited to us for righteousness, but only the obedience of the person who is at the same time God and man. And faith thus values Christ's person because it was made under the Law (Galatians 4:4) for

us and bore our sins, and, in His going to the Father, He offered to His heavenly Father for us poor sinners His entire, complete obedience. This extends from His holy birth even unto death. In this way, He has covered all our disobedience, which dwells in our nature, and its thoughts, words, and works. So disobedience is not charged against us for condemnation. It is pardoned and forgiven out of pure grace alone, for Christ's sake.

## OTHER NEGATIVE STATEMENTS

59 We unanimously reject and condemn (besides the above-mentioned) the following and all similar errors, as contrary to God's Word, the doctrine of the prophets and apostles, and our Christian faith:

60 1. When it is taught that Christ is our righteousness before God according to His divine nature alone.

61 2. Christ is our righteousness according to His human nature alone.

62 3. In the passages from the prophets and apostles, when the righteousness of faith is spoken of, the words *justify* and *to be justified* do not mean to declare free from sins and to receive the forgiveness of sins. But they mean actual and real righteousness because of love infused by the Holy Spirit, virtues, and the works following from it.

63 4. Faith looks not only to Christ's obedience, but also to His divine nature as it dwells and works in us. By this indwelling our sins are covered before God.

64 5. Faith is the kind of trust in Christ's obedience that can be and remain in a person even though he has no genuine repentance, even though no love follows, but he continues in sins against his conscience.

65 6. God does not dwell in believers, only God's gifts dwell in them.

66 These and similar errors, one and all, we unanimously reject as contrary to God's

clear Word. By God's grace we abide firmly and constantly in the doctrine of the righteousness of faith before God, as it is embodied, expounded, and proved from God's Word in the Augsburg Confession, and the Apology issued after it.

67 Concerning what is needed further for the proper explanation of this profound and chief article of justification before God—upon which depends the salvation of our souls—we direct readers to another document. For the sake of brevity we refer everyone to Dr. Luther's beautiful and glorious commentary on the Epistle of St. Paul to the Galatians.

# IV. GOOD WORKS

For an annotation on this article, see p. 500. (See also AC VI; AC XX; Ap V; Ap XX; SA III XIII; FC Ep IV.)

## STATUS OF THE CONTROVERSY

1 A disagreement about good works has arisen among the theologians of the Augsburg Confession. One side uses the following words and way of speaking: "Good works are necessary for salvation; it is impossible to be saved without good works." Likewise, "No one has been saved without good works." They say good works are required of true believers as the fruit of faith, and faith without love is dead, although such love is no cause of salvation.

2 The other side argued that good works are indeed necessary—however, not for salvation, but for other reasons. The expressions mentioned above are not to be tolerated in the Church. (They are not in accord with the form of sound doctrine and with the Word, and have always been and still are used by the papists to oppose the doctrine of our Christian faith, in which we confess that *faith alone justifies and saves.*) This is argued in order that the merit of Christ, our Savior, may not be diminished, and the promise of salvation may be and remain firm and certain to believers.

3 In this controversy the following disputed proposition, or expression, was also used by a few people, "Good works are harmful to salvation." Some have also argued that good works are not *necessary*, but are *voluntary*. They are not forced by fear and the penalty of the Law, but are to be done from a voluntary spirit and a joyful heart. Over against this the other side argued *that good works are necessary.*

4 This latter controversy was originally caused by the words *necessary* and *free*, because the word *necessary* means not only the eternal, unchangeable order according to which all people are obliged and duty bound to obey God, but sometimes also refers to a coercion, by which the Law forces people to do good works.

5 Later there was a dispute in which not only the words, but the doctrine itself was attacked in the most violent manner. It was argued that the new obedience in the regenerate is not necessary because of the above-mentioned divine order.

## AFFIRMATIVE STATEMENTS

6 In order to explain this disagreement in a Christian way and according to the guidance of God's Word, and by His grace to settle it completely, our doctrine, faith, and confession are as follows:

7 First, there is no controversy among our theologians about the following points in this article: it is God's will, order, and command that believers should walk in good works. Truly good works are not those that everyone does himself from a good intention, or which are done according to human

The Fiery Furnace

traditions, but those that God Himself has prescribed and commanded in His Word. Also, truly good works are done not by our own natural powers, but in this way: when a person is reconciled with God through faith and renewed by the Holy Spirit. Or, as Paul says, a person is "created in Christ Jesus for good works" (Ephesians 2:10).

8    Nor is there a controversy about how and why the good works of believers are pleasing and acceptable to God (although in this flesh they are impure and incomplete). They are acceptable for the sake of the Lord Christ, through faith, because the person is acceptable to God. There are works that apply to maintaining of external discipline. These are also done by, and required of, the unbelieving and unconverted. These works are com-

mendable before the world and rewarded by God in this world with temporal blessings. Nevertheless, they do not come from true faith. Therefore, in God's sight they are sins, that is, stained with sin, and are regarded by God as sins and impure because of the corrupt nature and because the person is not reconciled with God. "A healthy tree cannot bear bad fruit, nor can a diseased tree bear good fruit" (Matthew 7:18), as it is also written, "for whatever does not proceed from faith is sin" (Romans 14:23). A person must first be accepted by God, for the sake of Christ alone, if that person's works are to please Him.

Faith must be the mother and source of   9 works that are truly good and well pleasing to God, which God will reward in this world and in the world to come. This is why St. Paul calls them true *fruit of faith*, also *fruit of the Spirit* (Galatians 5:22–23). For, as Dr. Luther writes in the Preface to St. Paul's Epistle to the Romans:

10

> Faith, however, is a divine work in us that changes us and makes us to be born anew of God, John 1[:12–13]. It kills the old Adam and makes us altogether different men, in heart and spirit and mind and powers; it brings with it the Holy Spirit. O, it is a living, busy, active, mighty thing, this faith. It is impossible for it not to be doing good works incessantly. It does not ask whether good works are to be done, but before the question is asked, it has already done them, and is constantly doing them. Whoever does not do such works, however, is an unbeliever. He gropes and looks around for faith and good works, but knows neither what faith is nor what good works are. Yet he talks and talks, with many words, about faith and good works.

11

12

> Faith is a living, daring confidence in God's grace, so sure and certain that the believer would stake his life on it a thousand times. This knowledge of and confidence in God's grace makes men glad and bold and happy in dealing with God and all creatures. And this is the work that the Holy Spirit performs in faith. Because of it, without compulsion, a person is ready and glad to do good to everyone, to serve everyone, to suffer everything, out of love and praise to God, who has shown him this grace. Thus it is impossible to separate works from faith, quite as impossible as to separate heat and light from fire. (LW 35:370–71)

Since there is no controversy on these points among our theologians, we will not treat them here at length. We will only explain ourselves, part against part, in a simple and plain manner about the controversial points.

13

## CLARIFICATION OF TERMS

First, regarding the necessity or voluntary nature of good works, it is clear that in the Augsburg Confession and its Apology these expressions are often used and repeated— good works are necessary. Likewise, they say it is necessary to do good works, which necessarily follow faith and reconciliation. Likewise, we necessarily are to do, and must do, the kind of good works God has commanded. In the Holy Scriptures themselves the words *necessity*, *needful*, and *necessary*, as well as *ought* and *must*, are used to describe what we are bound to do because of God's ordinance, command, and will. (See Romans 13:5; 1 Corinthians 9:9; Acts 5:29; John 15:12; 1 John 4:21).

14

It is for this reason that the sayings and propositions just mentioned (in this Christian and proper understanding) are unfairly condemned and rejected by some people. These sayings should rightly be employed and used to reject the secure, Epicurean delusion. For many create for themselves a dead faith or delusion that lacks repentance and good works. They act as though there could be true faith in a heart at the same time as the wicked intention to persevere and continue in sin (Romans 6:1–2). This is impossible. Or, they act as though a person could have and keep true faith, righteousness, and salvation even though he is and remains a corrupt and unfruitful tree, from which no good fruit comes at all. In fact, they say this even though a person persists in sins against conscience or purposely engages again in these sins. All of this is incorrect and false.

15

16    In this matter the following distinction must be noted. The meaning of these expressions must be a necessity based on Christ's ordinance, command, and will and based on our obligation, but not a necessity based on coercion. In other words, when the word *necessary* is used, it should be understood not as force, but only as the order of God's un-

17 changing will, whose debtors we are. His commandment points out that the creature should be obedient to its Creator. In other places (2 Corinthians 9:7; Philemon 14; and 1 Peter 5:2) something is said to be *of necessity* that is wrung from a person against his will, by force or otherwise, so that he acts outwardly for the sake of appearance, but without and against his will. God does not want such hypocritical works. The people of the New Testament are to be a willing people (Psalm 110:3) and sacrifice freely (Psalm 54:6), "not reluctantly or under compulsion" (2 Corinthians 9:7). They are to be "obedient from the heart" (Romans 6:17), "for God

18 loves a cheerful giver" (2 Corinthians 9:7). In this understanding, and in this sense, it is correctly said and taught that truly good works should be done willingly, or from a voluntary spirit, by those whom God's Son has made free. The dispute about the voluntary nature of good works was engaged in by some people specifically to make this point.

19    Here, again, it is well to note the distinction that St. Paul makes in Romans 7:22–23:

> For I delight in the law of God, in my inner being, but I see in my members another law [that is not only unwilling or disinclined, but also] waging war against the law of my mind.

Regarding the unwilling and rebellious flesh, Paul says, "I discipline my body and keep it under control" (1 Corinthians 9:27) and "those who belong to Christ Jesus have cru-

cified [slain] the flesh with its passions and desires" (Galatians 5:24). (See also Romans 8:13.) When it is asserted and taught that 20 good works are free to believers in the sense that they are optional for them to do or not to do, this is false, and must be rejected. It is false to say that believers might or could act against God's Law and still have faith and God's favor and grace.

## NEGATIVE STATEMENTS

Second, when it is taught that good 21 works are necessary, it must also be explained why they are necessary. These reasons are listed in the Augsburg Confession and Apology.

We must be on our guard well to make 22 sure that works are not brought in and mixed into the article of justification and salvation. Therefore, the following propositions are justly rejected: *good works are necessary for believers to be saved; therefore, it is impossible to be saved without good works*. This is directly contrary to the doctrine about the exclusive terms in the article of justification and salvation. In other words, these positions conflict with the words St. Paul uses to exclude entirely our works and merits from the article of justification and salvation and to credit everything to God's grace and Christ's merit alone, as explained in the preceding article. These propositions take the comfort of 23 the Gospel away from afflicted, troubled consciences. They give reason to doubt, and are dangerous in many ways. They strengthen assumptions about one's own righteousness and increase confidence in one's own works. Besides, they are accepted by the papists, and are used in their interest against the pure doctrine of the alone-saving faith. Further- 24 more, they are contrary to the form of sound words. For it is written, "David also speaks of the blessing of the one to whom God counts righteousness apart from works" (Romans 4:6). Likewise, in Article VI (3) of the Augsburg Confession it is written that we are saved "without works, through faith alone." So Dr. Luther, too, rejected and condemned these propositions when they were used

25    1. by the false prophets among the Galatians;

26    2. by the papists, in very many places;

27    3. by the Anabaptists, when they present this interpretation: We should not rest faith on the merit of works, but we must still have works as necessary for salvation;

28    4. and also by some of Luther's own followers, who wanted to interpret this proposition as follows: Although we require works as necessary to salvation, we do not teach people to trust in works. (See Luther's Commentary on Genesis 22.)

29    For these reasons, it is right for this matter to remain settled in our churches. The ways of speaking just mentioned should not be taught, defended, or excused. Instead, they should be thrown out of our churches and rejected as false and incorrect. These are expressions that were renewed because of the Interim. They originated from it and were again drawn into discussion in times of persecution. This happened when there was special need for a clear, correct confession against all sorts of corruptions and adulterations of the article of justification.

## PRESERVATION IN THE FAITH

30    Third, whether good works preserve salvation, or whether they are necessary for preserving faith, righteousness, and salvation is another issue in dispute. This again is of high and great importance, for "the one who endures to the end will be saved" (Matthew 24:13). Also, "For we share in Christ, if indeed we hold our original confidence firm to the end" (Hebrews 3:14). We must also explain well and precisely how righteousness and salvation are preserved in us, lest salvation be lost again.

31    Above all, this false Epicurean delusion is to be seriously rebuked and rejected: some imagine that faith, and the righteousness and salvation that they have received, cannot be lost through sins or wicked deeds, not even through willful and intentional ones. They imagine that a Christian retains faith, God's grace, righteousness, and salvation even though he indulges his wicked lusts without fear and shame, resists the Holy Spirit, and purposely engages in sins against conscience.

32    Against this deadly delusion the following true, unchangeable, divine threats and severe punishments and warnings should be repeated often and impressed upon Christians who are justified through faith:

> Do not be deceived: neither the sexually immoral, nor idolaters, nor adulterers . . . will inherit the kingdom of God. (1 Corinthians 6:9–10)

> Those who do such things will not inherit the kingdom of God. (Galatians 5:21; see also Ephesians 5:5)

> If you live according to the flesh you will die. (Romans 8:13)

> On account of these the wrath of God is coming [upon the children of disobedience]. (Colossians 3:6)

33    The Apology provides an excellent model that shows how and when exhortations to good works can be made without darkening the doctrine of faith and of the article of justification. In Article XX (90), on the passage 2 Peter 1:10, "Be all the more diligent to make your calling and election sure," it says:

> Peter speaks of works following the forgiveness of sins and teaches why

they should be done. They should be done so that the calling may be sure, that is, should they fall from their calling if they sin again. Do good works in order that you may persevere in your calling, in order that you do not lose the gifts of your calling. They were given to you before, and not because of works that follow, and which now are kept through faith. Faith does not remain in those who lose the Holy Spirit and reject repentance.

34 On the other hand, this does not mean that faith lays hold of righteousness and salvation only in the beginning and then resigns its office to works as though they had to sustain faith, the righteousness received, and salvation. It means that the promise, not only of receiving, but also of retaining righteousness and salvation, is firm and sure to us. St. Paul (Romans 5:2) ascribes to faith not only the entrance to grace, but says that we stand in grace and boast of the future glory. In other words, he credits the beginning, middle, and end *to faith alone.*

> They were broken off because of their unbelief, but you stand fast through faith. (Romans 11:20)

> [He will] present you holy and blameless and above reproach before Him, if indeed you continue in the faith. (Colossians 1:22–23)

> By God's power [you] are being guarded through faith for a salvation. (1 Peter 1:5)

> Obtaining the outcome of your faith, the salvation of your souls. (1 Peter 1:9)

35 It is clear from God's Word that faith is the proper and only means through which righteousness and salvation are not only re-

ceived, but also preserved by God. Therefore, it is right to reject the Council of Trent's decree, and whatever elsewhere is set forth with the same meaning. For they say our good works preserve salvation, or the righteousness of faith that has been received, or even faith itself. They say it is either entirely or in part kept and preserved by our works.

36 Before this controversy quite a few pure teachers used similar expressions to explain the Holy Scriptures. However, they in no way intended to confirm the above-mentioned errors of the papists. Still, a controversy arose over such expressions, from which all sorts of offensive distractions followed. Therefore, according to St Paul's admonition (2 Timothy 1:13) it is safe to hold fast both to "the pattern of the sound words" and to the pure doctrine itself. In this way, much unnecessary wrangling may be cut off and the Church preserved from many scandals.

## COMMENTS ON PHILIPPIANS 3:7–8

37 Fourth, regarding the idea that good works are harmful to salvation, we explain ourselves clearly as follows: If anyone wants to drag good works into the article of justification, rest his righteousness or trust for salvation on them, and merit God's grace and be saved by them, St. Paul himself answers, not us. He says and repeats it three times (Philippians 3:7–8)—such a person's works are not only useless and a hindrance, but are also *harmful.* This is not the fault of the good works themselves, but of the false confidence placed in the works, contrary to God's clear Word.

38 However, it by no means follows that we are to say simply and flatly: *Good works are harmful to believers' salvation.* In believers good works are signs of salvation when they are done from true causes and for true ends. That is, in the sense in which God requires

them of the regenerate (Philippians 1:20). It is God's will and clear command that believers should do good works. The Holy Spirit works this in believers, and God is pleased with good works for Christ's sake. He promises a glorious reward for good works in this life and the life to come.

39 For this reason, too, this idea is rebuked and rejected in our churches. As a flat statement it is false and offensive. Discipline and decency might be impaired by it, and a barbarous, loose, secure, Epicurean life be introduced and strengthened. A person should avoid what is harmful to his salvation with the greatest diligence.

40 Christians should not be frightened away from good works, but should be admonished and urged to do them most diligently. Therefore, this bare proposition cannot and must not be tolerated, used, or defended in the Church.

# V. THE LAW AND THE GOSPEL

For an annotation on this article, see p. 502. (See also SA III II and IV; FC Ep V.)

---

## STATEMENT OF THE CONTROVERSY

1 The distinction between the Law and the Gospel is a particularly brilliant light. It serves the purpose of rightly dividing God's Word (2 Timothy 2:15) and properly explaining and understanding the Scriptures of the holy prophets and apostles. We must guard this distinction with special care, so that these two doctrines may not be mixed with each other, or a law be made out of the Gospel. When that happens, Christ's merit is hidden and troubled consciences are robbed of comfort, which they otherwise have in the Holy Gospel when it is preached genuinely

and purely. For by the Gospel they can support themselves in their most difficult trials against the Law's terrors.

2 In this matter a disagreement has occurred among some theologians of the Augsburg Confession. One side asserted that the Gospel is properly not only a preaching of grace, but is, at the same time, also a preaching of repentance, which rebukes the greatest sin: unbelief. The other side held and argued that the Gospel is not properly a preaching of repentance or rebuke. That properly belongs to God's Law, which reproves all sins, including unbelief. The Gospel is properly a preaching of God's grace and favor for Christ's sake. Through the Gospel the unbelief of the converted, which previously dwelt in them, and which God's Law reproved, is pardoned and forgiven.

## CLARIFICATION OF TERMS

3 When we see this disagreement clearly, we note that it has been caused chiefly by this: the term *Gospel* is not always used and understood in one and the same sense. It is used in two ways in the Holy Scriptures and also by ancient and modern Church teachers. 4 Sometimes it is used to mean the entire doctrine of Christ, our Lord, which He proclaimed in His ministry on earth and commanded to be proclaimed in the New Testament. Therefore, this includes the explanation of the Law and the proclamation of the favor and grace of God His heavenly Father. For it is written, "The beginning of the gospel of Jesus Christ, the Son of God" (Mark 1:1). And shortly afterward the chief points are stated: *Repentance and forgiveness of sins.* So when Christ after His resurrection commanded the apostles to "proclaim the gospel to the whole creation" (Mark 16:15), He compressed the sum of this doctrine into a few words. He also said, "Thus it is written,

God Speaking to Moses

Fall and Judgment

that the Christ should suffer and on the third day rise from the dead, and that repentance and forgiveness of sins should be proclaimed in His name to all nations" (Luke 24:46–47). Paul, too, calls his entire doctrine the Gospel (Acts 20:21). He summarizes this doctrine under two points: *Repentance toward God*

5 *and faith toward our Lord Jesus Christ*. In this sense the general definition of the word *Gospel*, when used in a wide sense and without the proper distinction between the Law and the Gospel, is correctly said to be a preaching of repentance and the forgiveness of sins. For John, Christ, and the apostles began their preaching with repentance and explained and taught not only the gracious promise of the forgiveness of sins, but also

6 God's Law. Furthermore, the term *Gospel* is used in another way. In its proper sense, *Gospel* does not mean the preaching of repentance, but only the preaching of God's grace. This follows directly after the preaching of repentance, as Christ says, "Repent and believe in the gospel" (Mark 1:15).

7    Likewise, the term *repentance* is not used in the Holy Scriptures in one and the same sense. In some passages of Holy Scripture it is used and taken to mean a person's entire conversion. For example, "Unless you repent, you will all likewise perish" (Luke 13:5). And, "There will be more joy in heaven over one sinner who repents" (Luke

8 15:7). But in this passage (Mark 1:15) and elsewhere, when repentance and faith in Christ (Acts 20:21), or repentance and forgiveness of sins (Luke 24:46–47), are mentioned as distinct, *to repent* means nothing other than to truly acknowledge sins, to be heartily sorry for them, and to stop doing

9 them. This knowledge comes from the Law. It is not enough for saving conversion to God if faith in Christ is not added. The comforting preaching of the Holy Gospel

offers His merits to all penitent sinners who are terrified by the preaching of the Law. The Gospel proclaims the forgiveness of sins, not to coarse and self-secure hearts, but to the bruised or penitent (Luke 4:18). The preaching of the Gospel must be added so that the repentance may lead to salvation and not to the Law's contrition or terrors (2 Corinthians 7:10).

Merely preaching the Law, without   10 Christ, either makes proud people, who imagine that they can fulfill the Law by outward works, or forces them utterly to despair. Therefore, Christ takes the Law into His hands and explains it spiritually (Matthew 5:21–48; Romans 7:14; 1:18). He reveals His wrath from heaven on all sinners and shows how great it is. In this teaching sinners are directed to the Law, and from it they first learn to know their sins correctly—a confession that Moses could never wrestle out of them. For as the apostle testifies (2 Corinthians 3:14–15), even though Moses is read, the veil he put over his face is never lifted. So they cannot understand the Law spiritually, and what great things it requires of us, and how severely it curses and condemns us because we cannot keep or fulfill it. "But when one turns to the Lord, the veil is removed" (2 Corinthians 3:16).

Christ's Spirit must not only comfort, but   11 also through the office of the Law "convict the world concerning sin" (John 16:8). In the New Testament, as the prophet says, He must do the work of another (reprove), in order that He may afterward do His own work, which is to comfort and to preach grace (Isaiah 28:21). To this end the Spirit was obtained for us through Christ and sent. For this reason He is also called the Comforter, as Dr. Luther has explained in his comments on the Gospel for the Fifth Sunday after Trinity, in the following words:

12 Anything that preaches about our sins and God's wrath (let it be done however or whenever it will), that is all a preaching of the Law. Again, the Gospel is such a preaching as shows and gives nothing else than grace and forgiveness in Christ. Yet it is true and right that the apostles and preachers of the Gospel (as Christ Himself also did) confirm the preaching of the Law. They begin the Law with those who do not yet acknowledge their sins nor are terrified at God's wrath; as Jesus says, "When [the Holy Spirit] comes, he will convict the world concerning sin . . . because they do not believe in Me" (John 16:8–9). Yes, what more forceful, more terrible declaration and preaching of God's wrath against sin is there than the suffering and death of Christ, His Son? But as long as all this preaches God's wrath and terrifies people, it is not yet the preaching of the Gospel nor Christ's own preaching, but that of Moses and the Law against the impenitent. For the Gospel and Christ were never ordained and given for the purpose of terrifying and condemning, but for comforting and cheering those who are terrified and timid. (WA 22:87, 3–18)

13 And again, Luther wrote:

Christ says, "[The Holy Spirit] will convict the world concerning sin" (John 16:8), which cannot be done except through the explanation of the Law. (WA 15:228, 15–17)

14 So, too, the Smalcald Articles say:

The New Testament keeps and urges the office of the Law, as St. Paul does when he says, "The wrath of God is revealed from heaven against all ungodliness and unrighteousness of men" (Romans 1:18) . . . But to this office of the Law, the New Testament immediately adds the consoling promise of grace through the Gospel. (SA III III 1–4)

The Apology says: "In the preaching of 15 repentance, it is not enough to preach the Law, or the Word that convicts of sin. . . . The Gospel must be added (Ap V 136). Therefore, the two doctrines belong together and should also be taught next to each other, but in a definite order and with a proper distinction. The Antinomians, or assailants of the Law, are justly condemned. They abolish the preaching of the Law from the Church and want sins to be rebuked, and repentance and sorrow to be taught, not from the Law, but from the Gospel.

### AFFIRMATIVE STATEMENTS

In order that everyone may see that we 16 conceal nothing in the disagreement we are describing, we present the matter to the eyes of the Christian reader plainly and clearly:

We unanimously believe, teach, and con- 17 fess that the Law is properly a divine doctrine in which God's righteous, unchangeable will is revealed. It shows what the quality of a person should be in his nature, thoughts, words, and works, in order that he may be pleasing and acceptable to God. It also threatens its transgressors with God's wrath and temporal and eternal punishments. For as Luther writes against the lawstormers (Antinomians):

Everything that reproves sin is and belongs to the Law. Its peculiar office is to rebuke sin and to lead to the knowledge of sins (Romans 3:20; 7:7).

Because unbelief is the root and wellspring of all sins that must be rebuked and reproved, the Law rebukes unbelief also.

18   It is true that the Law with its doctrine is illustrated and explained by the Gospel. Nevertheless, it remains the Law's peculiar office to rebuke sins and teach about good works.

19   The Law rebukes unbelief, that is, when people do not believe God's Word. Now the Gospel is God's Word, and it alone properly teaches and commands people to believe in Christ. The Holy Spirit, through the Law's office, also rebukes unbelief, that is, when people do not believe in Christ.

20   Yet it is properly the Gospel alone that teaches about saving faith in Christ. Now, a person has not kept God's Law, but has transgressed it when his corrupt nature, thoughts, words, and works fight against it. Therefore, he is under God's wrath, death, all temporal calamities, and the punishment of hellfire. The Gospel is properly a doctrine that teaches what a person should believe, so that he receives forgiveness of sins with God. In other words, it teaches that God's Son, our Lord Christ, has taken upon Himself and borne the Law's curse and has atoned and paid for all our sins. Through Him alone we again enter into favor with God, receive forgiveness of sins through faith and are delivered from death and all the punishments of sins, and are eternally saved.

21   Everything that comforts, that offers God's favor and grace to transgressors of the Law, is, and is properly called, the Gospel. It is a good and joyful message that God will not punish sins, but will forgive them for Christ's sake.

22   Every penitent sinner ought to believe (i.e., place his confidence) in the Lord Christ alone. For Christ "was delivered up for our trespasses and raised for our justification" (Romans 4:25). "He made Him to be sin who knew no sin, so that in Him we might become the righteousness of God" (2 Corinthians 5:21), "whom God made our wisdom and our righteousness and sanctification and redemption" (1 Corinthians 1:30). His obedience is credited to us for righteousness before God's strict court, so that the Law, as set forth above, is a ministry that kills through the letter and preaches condemnation (2 Corinthians 3:7). The Gospel "is the power of God for salvation to everyone who believes" (Romans 1:16), which preaches righteousness and gives the Spirit (1 Corinthians 1:18; Galatians 3:2). Dr. Luther taught this distinction with special diligence in nearly all his writings and has properly shown that the knowledge of God from the Gospel is far different from that which is taught and learned from the Law. Even the pagans, to a certain extent, had a knowledge of God from the natural law. But they neither knew Him nor glorified Him correctly (Romans 1:19–32).

## USING LAW AND GOSPEL

23   From the beginning of the world these two proclamations have always been taught alongside each other in God's Church, with a proper distinction. The descendants of the well-respected patriarchs, and the patriarchs themselves, called to mind constantly how in the beginning a person had been created righteous and holy by God. They know that through the fraud of the Serpent, Adam transgressed God's command, became a sinner, and corrupted and cast himself with all his descendants into death and eternal condemnation. They encouraged and comforted themselves again by the preaching about the woman's seed, who would bruise the Serpent's head (Genesis 3:15); Abraham's seed, in whom "all the nations of the earth [will] be blessed" (Genesis 22:18); David's Son, who should "bring back the preserved of Israel" and be "a light for the nations" (Isaiah 49:6; see also Psalm 110:1; Luke 2:32), and

who "was wounded for our transgressions; He was crushed for our iniquities . . . and with His stripes we are healed" (Isaiah 53:5).

24 These two doctrines, we believe and confess, should always be diligently taught in God's Church forever, even to the end of the world. They must be taught with the proper distinction of which we have heard: (a) through the preaching of the Law and its threats in the ministry of the New Testament the hearts of impenitent people may be terrified, and (b) they may be brought to a knowledge of their sins and to repentance. This must not be done in such a way that they lose heart and despair in this process. "So then, the law was our guardian until Christ came, in order that we might be justified by faith" (Galatians 3:24); so the Law points and leads us not from Christ, but to Christ, who "is the end of the law" (Romans 10:4).

25 People must be comforted and strengthened again by the preaching of the Holy Gospel about Christ, our Lord. In other words, to those who believe the Gospel, God forgives all their sins through Christ, adopts them as children for His sake, and out of pure grace—without any merit on their part—justifies and saves them. However, He does not do this in such a way that they may abuse God's grace and may sin hoping for grace (Romans 6:1).

26 Paul thoroughly and forcefully shows this in the distinction between the Law and the Gospel (2 Corinthians 3:6–9).

27 The doctrines of the Law and the Gospel may not be mixed and confused with each other. What belongs to the one may not be applied to the other. When that happens Christ's merit and benefits are easily hidden and the Gospel is again turned into a doctrine of the Law, as happened in the papacy. For then Christians are deprived of the true comfort they have in the Gospel against the Law's terrors, and the door is again opened in God's Church to the papacy. Therefore, the true and proper distinction between the Law and the Gospel must be taught and preserved with all diligence. Whatever causes confusion between the Law and the Gospel should be diligently prevented (i.e., by which the two doctrines, Law and Gospel, may be confused and mixed into one doctrine). It is, therefore, dangerous and wrong to convert the Gospel (properly so called, as distinguished from the Law) into a preaching of repentance or rebuke. Otherwise, if understood in a general sense of the entire doctrine, the Apology says also several times that the Gospel is a preaching of repentance and the forgiveness of sins. Meanwhile, the Apology also shows that the Gospel is properly the promise of the forgiveness of sins and of justification through Christ, and the Law is a doctrine that reproves sins and condemns.

# VI. THE THIRD USE OF GOD'S LAW

For an annotation on this article, see pp. 503–4. (See also SC, Morning Prayer and Table of Duties; FC Ep VI.)

### STATUS OF THE CONTROVERSY

1 God's Law is useful (a) because external discipline and decency are maintained by it against wild, disobedient people; (b) likewise, through the Law people are brought to a knowledge of their sins; and also, (c) when people have been born anew by God's Spirit, converted to the Lord, and Moses's veil has been lifted from them (2 Corinthians 3:13–16), they live and walk in the Law (Psalm 119:1). A disagreement has arisen between a few theologians about this third and final use of the Law. One side taught and 2

maintained that the regenerate do not learn the new obedience (in what good works they ought to walk) from the Law. They argued that this teaching about good works is not to be encouraged from the Law. They say the regenerate have been made free by God's Son, have become the temples of His Spirit, and therefore do freely of themselves what God requires of them. They act by the prompting and impulse of the Holy Spirit, just as the sun by itself (without any foreign impulse) com-

3  pletes its ordinary course in the sky. Against this the other side taught the following: The truly believing are certainly moved by God's Spirit. According to the inner man, they do God's will from a free spirit. Yet the Holy Spirit uses the written Law for instruction with them. By this the truly believing also learn to serve God, not according to their own thoughts, but according to His written Law and Word. This is a sure rule and standard of a godly life and walk. The Law shows how to order a life in accordance with God's eternal and unchangeable will.

## AFFIRMATIVE STATEMENTS

4      For the explanation and final settlement of this disagreement we unanimously believe, teach, and confess that people who truly believe and are truly converted to God, justified Christians, are liberated and made free from the *curse of the Law* (Galatians 3:10). Yet they should daily exercise themselves in the Law of the Lord, as it is written, "Blessed is the man . . . [whose] delight is in the law of the LORD, and on His law he meditates day and night" (Psalm 1:1–2; see also 119:1). The Law is a mirror in which God's will and what pleases Him are exactly portrayed. This mirror should be constantly held up to the believers and be diligently encouraged for them without ceasing.

5      "The law is not laid down for the just" as the apostle testifies (1 Timothy 1:9), but for the unrighteous. Yet this is not to be understood in a simplistic way, as though the justified are to live without Law. God's Law has been written in their heart (Romans 2:15). Also a law was given to the first man immediately after his creation (Genesis 2:15–17): He was to conduct himself according to this law. What St. Paul means is that the curse of the Law cannot burden those who have been reconciled to God through Christ. Nor must the Law confuse the regenerate with its coercion, for they have pleasure in God's Law in the inner man (Romans 7:22).

If God's believing and elect children were  6 completely renewed in this life by the indwelling Spirit, so that in their nature and all its powers they were entirely free from sin, they would not need any law. They would need no one to motivate them, either. They would do by themselves, and completely voluntarily, without any instruction, admonition, urging or driving of the Law, what they are in duty bound to do according to God's will. They would act just like the sun, the moon, and all heavenly constellations, which have their regular course by themselves. They would act unobstructed, without admonition, urging, driving, force, or compulsion, according to God's order, which He once appointed for them. Indeed, they would act just like the holy angels, who offer an entirely voluntary obedience.

However, believers are not renewed in  7 this life perfectly or completely. Their sin is covered by Christ's perfect obedience, so that it is not charged against believers for condemnation. Also, the putting to death of the old Adam (Romans 6:6) and the renewal in the spirit of their mind (Ephesians 4:23) is begun through the Holy Spirit. Nevertheless, the old Adam still clings to them in their nature and all its inward and outward powers.

8   The apostle has written about this:

> For I know that nothing good dwells in me, that is, in my flesh. (Romans 7:18)

> I do not understand my own actions. For I do not do what I want, but I do the very thing I hate. (Romans 7:15)

> But I see in my members another law waging war against the law of my mind and making me captive to the law of sin that dwells in my members. (Romans 7:23)

> For the desires of the flesh are against the Spirit, and the desires of the Spirit are against the flesh, for these are opposed to each other, to keep you from doing the things you want to do. (Galatians 5:17)

9   Because of these fleshly lusts, God's truly believing, elect, and regenerate children need the daily instruction and admonition, warning, and threatening of the Law in this life. But they also need frequent punishments. So they will be roused, the old man driven out of them, and they will follow God's Spirit, as it is written:

> It is good for me that I was afflicted, that I might learn Your statutes. (Psalm 119:71)

> But I discipline my body and keep it under control, lest after preaching to others I myself should be disqualified. (1 Corinthians 9:27)

> If you are left without discipline, in which all have participated, then you are illegitimate children and not sons. (Hebrews 12:8)

Dr. Luther has fully explained this at greater length in the Summer Part of the Church Postil, on the Epistle for the Nineteenth Sunday after Trinity.

10   We must also explain clearly what the Gospel does, produces, and works toward the new obedience of believers. We must also explain the Law's office in this matter, regarding believers' good works.

11   The Law indeed says it is God's will and command that we should walk in a new life (Romans 6:4). But it does not give the power and ability to begin and to do it. The Holy Spirit renews the heart. He is given and received, not through the Law, but through the preaching of the Gospel (Galatians 3:14). 12   Thereafter, the Holy Spirit uses the Law in order to teach the regenerate from it and to point out and show them in the Ten Commandments what is the "will of God, what is good and acceptable and perfect" (Romans 12:2) in what "good works, which God prepared beforehand, that we should walk" (Ephesians 2:10). He encourages them to this. When they are idle, negligent, and rebellious in this matter because of the flesh, He rebukes them through the Law. So the Spirit carries out both offices together: He slays and makes alive (Deuteronomy 32:39). He leads into hell and brings up again. For His office is not only to comfort, but also to rebuke. For it is written, "when [the Holy Spirit] comes, He will convict the world [which includes also the old Adam] concerning sin and righteousness and judgment" (John 16:8). Sin is every- 13   thing that is contrary to God's Law. St. Paul 14   says, "All Scripture is breathed out by God and profitable for teaching, for reproof" (2 Timothy 3:16), and to rebuke is the Law's special office. Therefore, as often as believers stumble, they are rebuked by the Holy Spirit from the Law. By the same Spirit they are raised up and comforted again with the preaching of the Holy Gospel.

15   As far as possible, all misunderstanding should be prevented, and the distinction between the Law's works and the Spirit's works should be properly taught and preserved.

Therefore, this is to be noted with special diligence: when we speak of good works that agree with God's Law (for otherwise they are not good works), then the word *Law* has only one sense. It means God's unchangeable will, according to which people are to guide themselves in their lives.

16   The difference, however, is in the works, because there is a difference in the people who strive to live according to this Law and will of God. For as long a person is not regenerate and guides himself according to the Law, he does the works because they are commanded. So from fear of punishment or desire for reward, he is still under the Law. His works are properly called by St. Paul "works of the Law" (e.g., Romans 3:20), for they are extorted by the Law, like the works of slaves. These are "saints" after the order of Cain (Jude 11).

17   When a person is born anew by God's Spirit, liberated from the Law (i.e., freed from this driver), and led by Christ's Spirit, he lives according to God's unchangeable will revealed in the Law. Since he is born anew, he does everything from a free, cheerful spirit. These works are not properly called "works of the Law," but works and "fruit of the Spirit" (Galatians 5:22). Or as St. Paul names it, "the law of [the] mind" (Romans 7:23) and the "law of Christ" (1 Corinthians 9:21). For such people are no longer under the Law, but under grace, as St. Paul says in Romans 8:2.

18   Believers are not completely renewed in this world. The old Adam clings to them right up to the grave. Therefore, the struggle between the spirit and the flesh remains in them. They delight in God's Law according to the inner man (Romans 7:22), but the law in their members struggles against the law in their mind. Therefore, they are never without the Law. Nevertheless, they are not under (Romans 6:14), but in the Law. They live and

walk in the Law of the Lord, and yet do nothing in the Law because of force.

As far as the old Adam is concerned, 19 which still clings to them, he must be driven not only by the Law, but also by punishments. Nevertheless, he does everything against his will and under coercion, no less than the godless are driven and held in obedience by the Law's threats (1 Corinthians 9:27; Romans 7:18–19).

This doctrine of the Law is needed by be- 20 lievers in order that they may not make up a holiness and devotion of their own. Using God's Spirit as an excuse, they must not set up a self-chosen worship, without God's Word and command. For it is written:

> "You shall not do according to . . . whatever is right in [your] own eyes," but "be careful to obey all these words that I command you," "you shall not add to it or take from it." (Deuteronomy 12:8, 28, 32)

The doctrine of the Law is also necessary 21 in and with the use of believers' good works. Otherwise, a person can easily imagine that his work and life are entirely pure and perfect. But God's Law prescribes good works to believers in this way: it shows and indicates at the same time, as in a mirror, that in this life works are still imperfect and impure in us. So we must say with the beloved Paul, "I am not aware of anything against myself, but I am not thereby acquitted" (1 Corinthians 4:4). So Paul, when encouraging the regenerate to do good works, clearly presents to them the Ten Commandments (Romans 13:9). He recognizes from the Law that his good works are imperfect and impure (Romans 7:7–13). And David declares:

> I will run in the way of Your commandments. (Psalm 119:32)

> [But] enter not into judgment with

Your servant, for no one living is righteous before You. (Psalm 143:2)

22    Although in this life the good works of believers are imperfect and impure because of sin in the flesh, nevertheless they are acceptable and well pleasing to God. This is not taught by the Law, which requires a completely perfect, pure obedience if it is to please God. But the Gospel teaches how and why our spiritual offerings are acceptable to God through faith for Christ's sake (1 Peter 2:5; Hebrews 11:4; 13:5). In this way Christians are not under the Law, but under grace (Romans 6:14). For by faith in Christ the persons are freed from the Law's curse and condemnation. Their good works, although they are still imperfect and impure, are acceptable to God through Christ. Because, in so far as they have been born anew according to the inner man, they do what is pleasing to God. They act not by coercion of the Law, but by the renewing of the Holy Spirit, voluntarily and spontaneously from their hearts. However, they still have a constant struggle against the old Adam.

24    The old Adam, like an unruly, stubborn ass, is still a part of them. It must be forced to obey Christ. It not only requires the teaching, admonition, force, and threatening of the Law, but it also often needs the club of punishments and troubles. This goes on until the body of sin is entirely put off (Romans 6:6) and a person is perfectly renewed in the resurrection. Then he will need neither the preaching of the Law nor its threats and punishments, just as he will no longer need the Gospel. These belong to this imperfect life.

25    Just as people will see God face-to-face, so they will—through the power of God's indwelling Spirit—do the will of God with unmingled joy, voluntarily, unconstrained, without any hindrance, and with entire purity and perfection. They will rejoice in it eternally.

## NEGATIVE STATEMENT

We reject and condemn the teaching that    26 the Law, in the above-mentioned way and degree, should not be urged on Christians and the true believers, but only on the unbelieving, unchristians, and impenitent. This is a deadly error and harmful to Christian discipline, and also to true godliness.

# VII. THE HOLY SUPPER

For an annotation on this article, see p. 505. (See also AC X; AC XXII; Ap X; Ap XXII; SA III VI; SC VI; LC V; FC Ep VII.)

———

In the opinion of some people, the com-    1 ments in this article should perhaps not be included in this document. We intend to explain the articles that have been drawn into controversy among the theologians of the Augsburg Confession. (When the Confession was first written and presented to the Emperor at Augsburg in 1530, the Sacramentarians soon withdrew entirely and separated. They presented their own Confession.) Still, some theologians and others who boast about the Augsburg Confession have agreed in this article with the Sacramentarians during the last few years. They no longer speak secretly, but partly public. They have labored against their own conscience to force and to pervert the Augsburg Confession to make it entirely in harmony with the Sacramentarian teaching in this article. We neither can nor should leave out our testimony by our confession of the divine truth in this document. We must repeat the true sense and proper understanding of Christ's words and of the Augsburg Confession on this article. We recognize this to be our duty. So far as we are able, by God's help, we shall preserve this pure doctrine also for posterity. We will faithfully warn our hearers, together with other godly Christians, against this deadly error, which is entirely contrary to the divine Word and the Augsburg Confession, and has been frequently condemned.

## STATUS
## OF THE CONTROVERSY

### The Chief Controversy between Our Teaching and That of the Sacramentarians in This Article

2     Some Sacramentarians strive to use words that come as close as possible to the Augsburg Confession and the form and way of speech in our churches. They confess that in the Holy Supper Christ's body is truly received by believers. Still, when we insist that they state their meaning precisely, sincerely,

and clearly, they all say this in unison: Christ's true essential body and blood is absent from the consecrated bread and wine in the Holy Supper as far as the highest heaven is from the earth. For their own words state this, "We say that Christ's body and blood are as far from the signs as the earth is distant from the highest heaven." Therefore, they understand this presence of Christ's body not as a presence here on earth, but only with respect to faith. In other words, our faith is reminded and excited by the visible signs, just as it is by the Word preached. It elevates itself and ascends above all heavens. It receives and enjoys Christ's body, which is present there in heaven. Yes, they say they receive Christ Himself, together with all His benefits, in a true and essential way, but

3

Manna from Heaven in the Wilderness

nevertheless only in a spiritual way. For they hold that as the bread and wine are here on earth and not in heaven, so Christ's body is now in heaven and not on earth. So nothing else is received by the mouth in the Holy Supper than bread and wine.

4　　Originally, they asserted that the Lord's Supper is only an outward sign, by which Christians are known. They held that nothing else is offered in the Supper than mere bread and wine (which are bare signs of Christ's absent body). When this fiction would not stand the test, they confessed that the Lord Christ is truly present in His Supper. They said He is present *by the communication of attributes*, that is, according to His divine nature alone, but not with His body and blood.

5　　Afterward, when they were forced by Christ's words to confess that Christ's body is present in the Supper, they still understood and declared only a spiritual presence. They declared it was a partaking through faith of His power through faith, efficacy, and benefits. For they say Christ's Spirit is everywhere and dwells here on earth. Therefore, through the Spirit our bodies are united with Christ's body, which is in heaven.

6　　The result was that many noble people were deceived by these fine, praise-worthy words when they asserted and boasted that they were of no other opinion than that the Lord Christ is present in His Supper truly, essentially, and as a living person. They understand this according to His divine nature alone, and not of His body and blood. They say His body and blood are now in heaven, and nowhere else. He gives us His true body and blood with the bread and wine to eat, to partake of them spiritually through faith, but not bodily with the mouth.

7　　They understand the words of the Supper, "Eat; this is My body," not properly, as they read, according to the letter, but as figurative expressions. So eating Christ's body means nothing other than believing. *Body* means a symbol, that is, a sign or figure of Christ's body. The body is not in the Supper on earth, but only in heaven. The word *is* they interpret sacramentally, or in a symbolic way. They do this so that no one may think that Christ's flesh is joined with the signs and is now present on earth in an invisible way, beyond our understanding. In other words, 8 Christ's body is united with the bread sacramentally, or symbolically. So believing, godly Christians do partake spiritually of Christ's body (which is above, in heaven) just as they eat the bread with the mouth. But they are used to cursing and condemning the following as a horrible blasphemy: Christ's body is essentially present here on earth in the Supper, although invisibly and in a way beyond understanding. It is received orally, with the consecrated bread, even by hypocrites or those who only appear to be Christians.

## WHAT THE AUGSBURG CONFESSION MEANS

Against the Sacramentarians' opinion, this 9 is what is taught in the Augsburg Confession from God's Word about the Lord's Supper: "That the body and blood of Christ are truly present and distributed to those who eat the Lord's Supper" (AC X 1). The contrary doctrine is rejected (namely, that of the Sacramentarians, who presented their own confession at the same time at Augsburg. They said that the body of Christ, because He has ascended to heaven, is not truly and essentially present here on earth in the Sacrament).

This opinion is clearly expressed in 10 Luther's Small Catechism in the following words:

*What is the Sacrament of the Altar?*
Answer: It is the true body and blood

of our Lord Jesus Christ, under the bread and wine, for us Christians to eat and to drink, instituted by Christ Himself. (SC VI 1–2)

11 In the Apology this is not only explained still more clearly, but is also established by the passage from Paul (1 Corinthians 10:16) and by the testimony of Cyril, in the following words:

> Article X has been approved, in which we confess the following: We believe that in the Lord's Supper Christ's body and blood are truly and substantially present and are truly administered with those things that are seen (bread and wine) to those who receive the Sacrament. . . . Since Paul says, "The bread that we break, is it not a participation in the body of Christ?" (1 Corinthians 10:16), it would follow, that if the Lord's body were not truly present, the bread is not a communion of the body, but only of Christ's spirit. We have determined that not only the Roman Church affirms Christ's bodily presence. The Greek Church also now believes, and formerly believed, the same. (Ap X 54–55)

Testimony is produced from Cyril that Christ dwells also bodily in us in the Holy Supper by the communication of His flesh.

12 Afterward, the people at Augsburg who delivered their own Confession about this article seemed to be willing to approve the Confession of our churches. Then the following *Formula Concordiae* (i.e., articles of Christian agreement) between the Saxon theologians and those of Upper Germany was composed and signed at Wittenberg in 1536 by Dr. Martin Luther and other theologians on both sides:

13 We have heard how Mr. Martin Bucer explained his own opinion and the opinion of the other preachers who came with him from the cities. About the Holy Sacrament of the body and blood of Christ, they taught the following:

14 They confess, according to the words of Irenaeus, that in this Sacrament there are two things, a heavenly and an earthly. So they hold and teach that with the bread and wine the body and blood of Christ are truly and essentially present, offered, and received. They do not believe in transubstantiation (i.e., an essential transformation of the bread and wine into the body and blood of Christ). Nor do they hold that the body and blood of Christ are included in the bread locally (i.e., otherwise permanently united with the bread and wine even after the use of the Sacrament). Yet they concede that through the sacramental union the bread is the body of Christ, and such. For apart from the use, 15 when the bread is laid aside and preserved in the sacramental vessel (the pyx), or is carried about in the procession and exhibited, as is done in popery, they do not hold that the body of Christ is present.

16 Second, they hold that the institution of this Sacrament made by Christ is effective in Christendom, and that it does not depend on the worthiness or unworthiness of the minister who offers the Sacrament, or of the one who receives it. Since St. Paul says even the unworthy partake of the Sacrament, they hold that the body and blood of Christ are also truly offered to the unworthy, and the unworthy truly receive them. This happens if the institution and command of the Lord

Christ are observed. But such persons receive them to condemnation, as St. Paul says. For they misuse the holy Sacrament, because they receive it without true repentance and without faith. For it was instituted for this purpose, that it might testify that the grace and benefits of Christ are here applied to those who truly repent and comfort themselves by faith in Christ. They are incorporated into Christ and are washed by His blood.

17  In the following year, the chief theologians of the Augsburg Confession assembled from all Germany at Smalcald and deliberated about what to present in the Council about this doctrine of the Church. By common consent the Smalcald Articles were composed by Dr. Luther and signed by all the theologians, jointly and severally. In these articles the proper and true meaning is clearly expressed in short, plain words. They agree most accurately with Christ's words. Every device and loophole is barred 18  to the Sacramentarians. (They had interpreted the *Formula Concordiae*—the above-mentioned articles of union, framed the preceding year—to their advantage. They perverted them to say that Christ's body is offered with the bread in no other way than as it is offered, together with all His benefits, by the Word of the Gospel. And by the "sacramental union" only the spiritual presence of the Lord Christ by faith is meant). 19  Here is what the Smalcald Articles [III VI 1] declare:

> The bread and wine in the Supper are Christ's true body and blood. These are given and received not only by the godly but also by wicked Christians. (1 Corinthians 11:29–30)

20    Dr. Luther has also more fully expounded and confirmed this opinion from God's Word in the Large Catechism [V 8], where it is written:

> "Now, what is the Sacrament of the Altar?" Answer, "It is the true body and blood of our Lord Jesus Christ, in and under the bread and wine, which we Christians are commanded by Christ's Word to eat and to drink."

And shortly after [LC V 10]:    21

> It is the Word, I say, that makes and sets this Sacrament apart. So it is not mere bread and wine, but is, and is called, Christ's body and blood (1 Corinthians 11:23–27).

Again [V 12–19]:    22

> With this Word you can strengthen your conscience and say, "If a hundred thousand devils, together with all fanatics, should rush forward, crying, 'How can bread and wine be Christ's body and blood?' and such, I know that all spirits and scholars together are not as wise as is the Divine Majesty in His little finger" (see 1 Corinthians 1:25). Now here stands Christ's Word, "Take, eat; this is My body.... Drink of it, all of you; this is My blood of the new testament," and so on. Here we stop to watch those who will call themselves His masters and make the matter different from what He has spoken. It is true, indeed, that if you    23 take away the Word or regard the Sacrament without the words, you have nothing but mere bread and wine. But if the words remain with them, as they shall and must, then, by virtue of the words, it is truly Christ's body and blood. What Christ's lips say and speak, so it is. He can never lie or deceive (Titus 1:2).

> It is easy to reply to all kinds of questions about which people are troubled    24

at the present time, such as this one: "Can even a wicked priest serve at and administer the Sacrament?" And whatever other questions like this there may be. For here we conclude and say, "Even though an imposter takes or distributes the Sacrament, a person still receives the true Sacrament, that is, Christ's true body and blood, just as truly as a person who receives or administers it in the most worthy way." For the Sacrament is not founded upon people's holiness, but upon God's Word. Just as no saint on earth, indeed, no angel in heaven, can make bread and wine be Christ's body and blood, so also no one can change or alter it, even though it is misused.

25 The Word by which it became a Sacrament and was instituted does not become false because of the person or his unbelief. For Christ does not say, "If you believe or are worthy, you receive My body and blood." No, He says, "Take, eat and drink; this is

26 My body and blood." Likewise, He says, "Do this" (i.e., what I now do, institute, give, and ask you, take). That is like saying, "No matter whether you are worthy or unworthy, you have here His body and blood by virtue of these words that are added to the bread and wine." Note and remember this well. For upon these words rest all our foundation, protection, and defense against all errors and deception that have ever come or may yet come.

27 This is what the Large Catechism says, in which the true presence of Christ's body and blood in the Holy Supper is established from God's Word. This presence is understood to be received not only by the believing and worthy, but also by the unbelieving and unworthy.

28 Dr. Luther foresaw in the Spirit that after his death some would try to make it seem that he had backed away from the above-mentioned doctrine and other Christian articles. Therefore, he has added the following protest to his *Confession concerning Christ's Supper:*

29 I see that schisms and errors are increasing proportionately with the passage of time, and that there is no end to the rage and fury of Satan. Hence lest any persons during my lifetime or after my death appeal to me or misuse my writings to confirm their error, as the sacramentarian and baptist fanatics are already beginning to do, I desire with this treatise to confess my faith before God and all the world, point by point. I am determined to abide by it until my death and (so help me God!) in this faith to depart from this world and to appear before the judgment seat of our Lord Jesus Christ. Hence if any one shall

30 say after my death, "If Luther were living now, he would teach and hold this or that article differently, for he did not consider it sufficiently," etc., let me say once and for all that by the grace of God I have most diligently traced all these articles through the Scriptures, have examined them again and again in the light thereof, and have wanted to defend all of them as certainly as I have now defended the sacrament of the altar. I am not drunk

31 or irresponsible. I know what I am saying, and I well realize what this will mean for me before the Last Judgment at the coming of the Lord Jesus Christ. Let no one make this out to be a joke or idle talk; I am in dead earnest, since by the grace of God I have learned to know a great deal

Martin Luther and John Hus Serving the Sacrament
of the Altar to the Dukes of Saxony

From left to right, foreground: John the Steadfast (1468–1532), Martin Luther, John
Hus, Frederick the Wise (1463–1525); background: Luther hearing the confession
of John Frederick I (1503–54). The three sons of John Frederick are in the background, from left to right, John Frederick III, John William, and John Frederick II.
Sibylla, wife of John Frederick I is shown next to her husband. The blood from the
five wounds of Christ is pouring into a fountain resting on the altar, a symbol for the
distribution of Christ's blood in the Sacrament of the Altar.

about Satan. If he can twist and pervert the Word of God and the Scriptures, what will he not be able to do with my or someone else's words? (LW 37:360–61)

32 After this protest, Dr. Luther, of blessed memory, presents, among other articles, this as well:

In the same way I also say and confess that in the sacrament of the altar the true body and blood of Christ are orally eaten and drunk in the bread and wine, even if the priests who distribute them or those who receive them do not believe or otherwise misuse the sacrament. It does not rest on man's belief or unbelief but on the Word and ordinance of God—unless they first change God's Word and ordinance and misinterpret them, as the enemies of the sacrament do at the present time. They, indeed, have only bread and wine, for they do not also have the words and instituted ordinance of God but have perverted and changed it according to their own imagination. (LW 37:367)

33 Dr. Luther, above others, certainly understood the true and proper meaning of the Augsburg Confession. He constantly remained steadfast in that Confession till the end of his life, and he defended it shortly before his death. He repeated his faith about this article with great zeal in his last Confession, where he writes:

I regard them all as being cut from the same piece of cloth, as indeed they are. For they do not want to believe that the Lord's bread in the Supper is His true, natural body which the godless person or Judas receives orally just as well as St. Peter and all the saints. Whoever (I say) does not want

to believe that, let him not trouble me with letters, writings, or words and let him not expect to have fellowship with me. This is final. (*Brief Confession concerning the Holy Sacrament* [1544]; LW 38:304)

34 From these explanations, and especially from that of Dr. Luther as the leading teacher of the Augsburg Confession, any intelligent person who loves truth and peace can undoubtedly see what has always been the proper meaning and understanding of the Augsburg Confession on this article.

35 In addition to Christ's and St. Paul's expressions (the bread in the Supper *is the body of Christ* or *the communion of the body of Christ*), the following forms are also used: *under the bread, with the bread, in the bread.* With these words the papistic transubstantiation may be rejected and the sacramental union of the bread's unchanged essence and Christ's body may be shown. In the same 36 way, the expression "the Word became flesh" (John 1:14) is repeated and explained by the equivalent expressions "the Word . . . dwelt among us" (John 1:14); likewise, "in Him the whole fullness of deity dwells bodily" (Colossians 2:9); likewise, "God was with Him" (Acts 10:38); likewise, "in Christ God was" (2 Corinthians 5:19), and the like. These show that the divine essence is not changed into the human nature. But the two natures, unchanged, are personally united. Many eminent ancient teachers, such as 37 Justin, Cyprian, Augustine, Leo, Gelasius, Chrysostom, and others, use this comparison about the words of Christ's testament, "This is My body." Just as in Christ two distinct, unchanged natures are inseparably united, so in the Holy Supper the two substances—the natural bread and Christ's true natural body—are present together here on earth in the appointed administration of

38 the Sacrament. This union of Christ's body and blood with the bread and wine is not a personal union (as that of the two natures in Christ). But Dr. Luther and our theologians, in the frequently mentioned Articles of Agreement (*Formula Concordiae*) in the year 1536 and in other places, call it a *sacramental union*. By this they wish to show that, although they use these distinct modes of speech: *in the bread, under the bread, with the bread*, yet they have received Christ's words properly. They read, and have understood the proposition that the words of Christ's testament ("This is My body") are not a figurative, allegorical expression or comment, but are a unique expression.

39 Justin says:

> This we receive not as common bread and common drink. We receive them as Jesus Christ, our Savior, who through the Word of God became flesh. For the sake of our salvation He also had flesh and blood. So we believe that the food blessed by Him through the Word and prayer is the body and blood of our Lord Jesus Christ.

40 Likewise, Dr. Luther also in his Large Catechism, especially in his last Confession, about the Lord's Supper, with great seriousness and zeal defends the very form of expression that Christ used at the first Supper.

41 Dr. Luther is to be regarded as the most distinguished teacher of the churches that confess the Augsburg Confession. His entire doctrine in sum and substance is embraced in the articles of the frequently mentioned Augsburg Confession, which was presented to Emperor Charles V. Therefore, the proper meaning and sense of the oft-mentioned Augsburg Confession can and should be derived from no other source more properly and correctly than from the doctrinal and polemical writings of Dr. Luther.

## THE WORDS OF INSTITUTION

42 This very opinion, just stated, is founded on the only firm, immovable, and undoubtable rock of truth. It comes from the words of institution, in the holy, divine Word. This was how it was understood, taught, and spread by the holy evangelists and apostles and their disciples and hearers.

43 Concerning our Lord and Savior Jesus Christ, as our only Teacher, this solemn command has been given from heaven to all people, "listen to Him" (Matthew 17:5). He is not a mere man or angel, neither is He just true, wise, and mighty, but He is the eternal Truth and Wisdom itself and Almighty God. He knows very well what and how He is to speak. He can also powerfully effect and do everything that He says and promises. He says, "Heaven and earth will pass away, but My words will not pass away" (Luke 21:33); "All authority in heaven and on earth has been given to Me" (Matthew 28:18).

44 Consider this true, almighty Lord, our Creator and Redeemer, Jesus Christ, after the Last Supper. He is just beginning His bitter suffering and death for our sins. In those sad last moments, with great consideration and solemnity, He institutes this most venerable Sacrament. It was to be used until the end of the world with great reverence and obedience. It was to be an abiding memorial of His bitter suffering and death and all His benefits. It was a sealing of the New Testament, a consolation of all distressed hearts, and a firm bond of unity for Christians with Christ, their Head, and with one another. In ordaining and instituting the Holy Supper He spoke these words about the bread, which He blessed and gave: "Take, eat; this is My body, which is given for you," and about the

cup, or wine: "This is My blood of the new testament, which is shed for you for the forgiveness of sins."

45 We are certainly duty-bound not to interpret and explain these words in a different way. For these are the words of the eternal, true, and almighty Son of God, our Lord, Creator, and Redeemer, Jesus Christ. We cannot interpret them as allegorical, figurative, turns of phrases, in a way that seems agreeable to our reason. With simple faith and due obedience we receive the words as they read, in their proper and plain sense. We do not allow ourselves to be diverted from Christ's words by any objections or human contradictions spun from human reason, however appealing they may appear to reason.

46 When Abraham heard God's Word about offering his son (Genesis 22), he had reason enough to debate whether the words should be understood literally or with a tolerable or mild interpretation. They conflicted openly not only with all reason and with the divine and natural law, but also with the chief article of faith about the promised Seed, Christ, who was to be born of Isaac. Nevertheless, when the promise of the blessed Seed from Isaac was given to him, Abraham honored God's truthfulness. He confidently concluded and believed that what God promised He could also do, although it appeared impossible to his reason (Hebrews 11:17–19). So also about Isaac's sacrifice he understood and believed God's Word and command plainly and simply, as they read according to the letter. He committed the matter to God's almighty power and wisdom, which, he knew, has many more modes and ways to fulfill the promise of the Seed from Isaac than he could comprehend with his blind reason.

47 We, too, are simply to believe with all humility and obedience our Creator and Redeemer's plain, firm, clear, solemn words and command, without any doubt and dispute about how it agrees with our reason or is possible. For these words were spoken by that Lord who is infinite Wisdom and Truth itself. He can do and accomplish everything He promises.

48 All the circumstances of the Holy Supper's institution testify that these words of our Lord and Savior, Jesus Christ (which in themselves are simple, plain, clear, firm, and beyond doubt), cannot and must not be understood other than in their usual, proper, and common meaning. For Christ gives this command at the table and at supper. There is certainly no doubt that He speaks of real, natural bread and of natural wine. Also, He speaks of oral eating and drinking, so there can be no metaphor (i.e., a change of meaning) in the word *bread*, as though Christ's body were a spiritual bread or a spiritual food of souls. Christ is careful not to use 49 metonymy either. In other words, there is no change of meaning in the word *body*. He does not speak about a sign for His body, or about a symbol or figurative body, or about the power of His body and the benefits that He has earned by the sacrifice of His body for us. Instead, He speaks about His true, essential body (which He delivered into death for us) and about His true, essential blood (which He shed for us on the tree of the cross for the forgiveness of sins).

50 Surely there is no interpreter of Jesus Christ's words as faithful and sure as the Lord Christ Himself. He understands best His words and His heart and opinion. He is the wisest and most knowledgeable for explaining them. He does not use allegory to make His last will and testament and His everabiding covenant and union. He does not use allegory elsewhere in presenting and confirming all articles of faith, and in the institution of all other signs of the covenant and of

grace or Sacraments (e.g., circumcision, the various offerings in the Old Testament, and Holy Baptism). He does not use allegorical words, but entirely proper, simple, believable, and clear words. In order that no misunderstanding can take place, He explains them more clearly with the words "Given for you," 51 "shed for you." He also lets His disciples rest in the simple, proper sense, and commands them that they should teach all nations to keep what He had commanded them, the apostles.

52    All three evangelists (Matthew 26:26–28; Mark 14:22–24; Luke 22:19–20) and St. Paul, after Christ's ascension, received the same institution of the Lord's Supper (1 Corinthians 11:23–26). Unanimously and with the same words and syllables they repeat these distinct, clear, firm, and true words of Christ about the consecrated and distributed bread, "This is My body." They all repeat these words in one way, without any interpretation, turn of phrase, figure, and change. Therefore, there is 53 no doubt about the other part of the Sacrament. The words of Luke and Paul, "This cup is the new covenant in My blood," can have no other meaning than what St. Matthew and St. Mark give: "This [namely, what you orally drink out of the cup] is My blood of the covenant," whereby I establish, seal, and confirm with you men this: My testament and new covenant (i.e., the forgiveness of sins).

54    St. Paul repeats, confirms, and explains Christ's words where he writes as follows, "The cup of blessing that we bless, is it not a participation in the blood of Christ? The bread that we break, is it not a participation in the body of Christ?" (1 Corinthians 10:16). This is to be considered with all diligence and seriousness. It is an especially clear testimony of the true, essential presence and distribution of the body and blood of Christ in the Supper. From this we clearly learn that not only the cup that Christ blessed at the first Supper, and not only the bread that Christ broke and distributed, but also the bread we break and the cup we bless, is the communion of Christ's body and blood. So all who eat this bread and drink of this cup truly receive, and are partakers of, Christ's true body and blood. Imagine that Christ's 55 body was present and partaken of—not truly and essentially—but only according to its power and efficacy. Then the bread would have to be called not a communion of the body, but of the Spirit, power, and benefits of Christ, as the Apology argues and concludes. Now imagine that Paul were speaking only of 56 the spiritual communion of Christ's body through faith (as the Sacramentarians pervert this passage). Then Paul would not say that the bread, but that the spirit or faith, was the communion of Christ's body. But he says that the bread is the communion of Christ's body and that all who partake of the consecrated bread also become partakers of Christ's body. Therefore, he must indeed be speaking not of a spiritual but of a sacramental or oral participation of Christ's body, which is common to godly Christians and those who are Christians only in name.

    This is shown also by the causes and cir- 57 cumstances of this entire exposition of St. Paul. For he frightens and warns those who ate of offerings to idols and had fellowship with heathen devil-worship, and nevertheless went also to the Lord's table and became partakers of Christ's body and blood. He warns them so that they do not receive Christ's body and blood for judgment and condemnation to themselves. For all those who become partakers of the consecrated and broken bread in the Supper have communion also with Christ's body. Therefore, St. Paul cannot be speaking of spiritual communion with Christ, which no person can abuse, and against which also no one is to be warned.

58 Our dear fathers and predecessors, like Luther and other pure teachers of the Augsburg Confession, explain this statement of Paul in such a way that it agrees completely with Christ's words. They write that the bread we break is the distributed body of *Christ*, or the common (communicated) body of *Christ*, distributed to those who receive the broken bread.

## TWO TYPES OF EATING

59 We unanimously abide by this simple, well-founded explanation of this glorious testimony (1 Corinthians 10). We are truly shocked that some are now so bold that they venture to quote the passage below. Previously, even they attributed this to the Sacramentarians, as a foundation for their error. Now they say that in the Supper Christ's body is only partaken of spiritually.

> The bread is the communion of Christ's body. In other words, it is that by which we have fellowship with Christ's body, which is the Church. Or it is the means by which we believers are united with Christ, just as the Word of the Gospel, received by faith, is a means through which we are spiritually united to Christ and built into Christ's body, which is the Church.

60 It is not only godly, pious, and believing Christians who orally receive Christ's true body and blood in the Sacrament. So do unworthy, godless hypocrites, like Judas and his ilk, who have no spiritual communion with Christ, and who go to the Lord's Table without true repentance and conversion to God. St. Paul teaches clearly that by their unworthy eating and drinking they grievously sin against Christ's body and blood. For he says:

> Whoever, therefore, eats the bread or drinks the cup of the Lord in an unworthy manner [sins not merely against the bread and wine, not merely against the signs or symbols and emblems of the body and blood, but] will be guilty of profaning the body and blood of the Lord. (1 Corinthians 11:27)

Such a person dishonors, abuses, and disgraces the body and blood, like the Jewish people, who by their actions violated Christ's body and killed Him. The Ancient Christian Fathers and Church teachers have unanimously understood and explained this passage in this way.

61 There is a two-fold eating of Christ's flesh. One is spiritual, which Christ describes especially in John 6:54. This "eating" happens in no other way than with the Spirit and faith, in preaching and meditation on the Gospel, as well as in the Lord's Supper. By itself this is useful and helpful, and necessary for all Christians, at all times, for salvation. Without this spiritual participation the sacramental or oral eating in the Supper is not only not helpful, but is even harmful and damning.

62 This spiritual eating is nothing other than *faith*. It means to hear God's Word (in which Christ, true God and man, is presented to us, together with all benefits that He has purchased for us by His flesh given into death for us, and by His blood shed for us, namely, God's grace, the forgiveness of sins, righteousness, and eternal life). It means to receive it with faith and keep it for ourselves. It means that in all troubles and temptations we firmly rely—with sure confidence and trust—and abide in this consolation: we have a gracious God and eternal salvation because of the Lord Jesus Christ.

63 The other eating of Christ's body is *oral* or *sacramental*, when Christ's true, essential

body and blood are orally received and partaken of in the Holy Supper by all who eat and drink the consecrated bread and wine in the Supper. This is done by the believing as a certain pledge and assurance that their sins are surely forgiven them and that Christ dwells in them and is at work in them. This supper is received by the unbelieving for 64 their judgment and condemnation. The words of the institution by Christ clearly declare this. At the table and during the Supper He offers His disciples natural bread and natural wine, which He calls His true body and true blood. At the same time He says, "Eat" and "drink." In view of the circumstances, this command clearly cannot be understood as anything other than oral eating and drinking. However, this is not in a crude, carnal, Capernaitic way, but in a supernatu- 65 ral way, beyond understanding. Afterward, the other command adds still another spiritual eating, when the Lord Christ says further, "This do in remembrance of Me." He requires *faith*.

66    All the ancient Christian teachers teach clearly and in full agreement with the entire holy Christian Church. According to these words of Christ's institution and the explanation of St. Paul, Christ's body is not only received spiritually through faith (which occurs also outside of the Sacrament) but also orally (not only by believing and godly people, but also by unworthy, unbelieving, false, and wicked Christians). Since it is too long to be listed here, we would, for the sake of brevity, have the Christian reader referred to the exhaustive writings of our theologians.

67    It is clear how unjustly and wickedly the Sacramentarian fanatics (Theodore Beza) ridicule the Lord Christ, St. Paul, and the entire Church. For they call this oral partaking, and that of the unworthy, "two horses' hairs and a device of which the devil is ashamed."

They also call the doctrine about Christ's majesty "Satan's excrement, by which the devil deceives and tricks other people." In other words, they speak so horribly of it that a godly Christian person should be ashamed to translate it.

It must also be carefully explained who 68 the unworthy guests of this Supper are. They are those who go to this Sacrament without true repentance and sorrow for their sins, without true faith and the good intention of amending their lives. By their unworthy oral eating of Christ's body, they load themselves with damnation (i.e., with temporal and eternal punishments) and become guilty of profaning Christ's body and blood.

Some Christians have a weak faith and 69 are shy, troubled, and heartily terrified because of the great number of their sins. They think that in their great impurity they are not worthy of this precious treasure and Christ's benefits. They feel their weakness of faith and lament it, and from their hearts desire that they may serve God with stronger, more joyful faith and pure obedience. These are the truly worthy guests for whom this highly venerable Sacrament has been especially instituted and appointed. For Christ says:                                   70

> Come to Me, all who labor and are heavy laden, and I will give you rest. (Matthew 11:28)

> Those who are well have no need of a physician, but those who are sick. (Matthew 9:12)

> [God's] power is made perfect in weakness. (2 Corinthians 12:9)

> As for the one who is weak in faith, welcome him; . . . for God has welcomed him. (Romans 14:1–3)

> Whoever believes in [the Son of God, be it with a strong or with a weak

faith,] may have eternal life. (John 3:15)

71 Worthiness does not depend on the greatness or smallness, the weakness or strength of faith. Instead, it depends on Christ's merit, which the distressed father of little faith (Mark 9:24) enjoyed as well as Abraham, Paul, and others who have a joyful and strong faith.

72 Let the foregoing be said of the true presence and twofold partaking of Christ's body and blood. These happen either through faith, spiritually, or also orally, both by the worthy and the unworthy.

## CONSECRATION AND ADMINISTRATION

73 A misunderstanding and disagreement among some teachers of the Augsburg Confession has also happened about consecration and the common rule. Some say that "nothing is a sacrament without the appoint-
74 ed use." We have reached a brotherly and unanimous agreement with one another about this matter, declaring it in the following way. The word or work of any man does not produce the true presence of Christ's body and blood in the Supper. This is true whether we consider the merit or recitation of the minister or the eating, drinking, or faith of the communicants. Christ's presence should be credited only to Almighty God's power and our Lord Jesus Christ's word, institution, and ordination.

75 Jesus Christ's true and almighty words, which He spoke at the first institution, were effective not only at the first Supper. They endure, are valid, operate, and are still effective. So in all places where the Supper is celebrated according to Christ's institution and His words are used, Christ's body and blood are truly present, distributed, and received, because of the power and effectiveness of the words that Christ spoke at the first Supper. Where His institution is observed and His words are spoken over the bread and cup, and the consecrated bread and cup are distributed, Christ Himself, through the spoken words, is still effective *by virtue of the first institution*, which He wants to be repeated there through His word. As Chrysostom says 76 in his *Sermon about the Passion:*

Christ Himself prepared this table and blesses it. For no man makes the bread and wine set before us into Christ's body and blood, only Christ Himself, who was crucified for us. The words are spoken by the mouth of the priest. But by God's power and grace, by the word, where Christ says: "This is My body," the elements presented are consecrated in the Supper. The declaration "Be fruitful and multiply and fill the earth" (Genesis 1:28) was spoken only once. But it is ever effective in nature, so that it is fruitful and multiplies. So also this declaration, "This is My body; this is My blood," was spoken once. But even to this day and up to His second coming it is effective and works so that in the Supper of the Church His true body and blood are present.

Luther also writes: 77

This command and institution of His have the power to accomplish this, that we do not present and receive not simply bread and wine but His body and blood, as His words indicate: "This is My body, this is My blood." So it is not our work or speaking but the command and ordinance of Christ which make the bread the body and the wine the blood, beginning with the first Lord's Supper and continuing to the end of the world, and it is administered daily through our ministry or office. (LW 38:199)

78 Also:

Here, too, if I were to say over all the bread there is, "This is the body of Christ," nothing would happen, but when we follow His institution and command in the Supper and say, "This is My body," then it is His body, not because of our speaking or our declarative word, but because of His command in which He has told us so to speak and to do and has attached His own command and deed to our speaking. (LW 37:184)

79 In the administration of the Holy Supper the words of institution are to be publicly spoken or sung before the congregation distinctly and clearly. They should in no way be
80 left out. Obedience should be rendered to
81 Christ's command, "This do." The hearers' faith about the nature and fruit of this Sacrament should be aroused, strengthened, and confirmed by Christ's Word (about the presence of Christ's body and blood, about the forgiveness of sins, and about all the benefits that have been purchased by the death and shedding of Christ's blood that are bestowed
82 on us in Christ's testament). And third, the elements of bread and wine should be consecrated or blessed for this holy use, so that Christ's body and blood may be administered to us to be eaten and to be drunk, as Paul declares, "the cup of blessing that we bless" (1 Corinthians 10:16). This indeed happens in no other way than through the repetition and recitation of the words of institution.

83 However, this blessing, or the recitation of the words of Christ's institution alone, does not make a Sacrament if the entire action of the Supper, as it was instituted by Christ, is not kept. (For example, it is not kept when the consecrated bread is not distributed, received, and partaken of, but is enclosed, sacrificed, or carried about.) Christ's command "This do" must be observed unseparated and inviolate. (This embraces the 84 entire action or administration in this Sacrament. In an assembly of Christians bread and wine are taken, consecrated, distributed, received, eaten, drunk, and the Lord's death is shown forth at the same time.) St. Paul also places before our eyes this entire action of the breaking of bread or of distribution and reception (1 Corinthians 10:16).

To preserve this true Christian doctrine 85 about the Holy Supper, and to avoid and abolish many idolatrous abuses and perversions of this testament, the following useful rule and standard has been derived from the words of institution: Nothing has the nature of a Sacrament apart from the use instituted by Christ or apart from the action divinely instituted. This means, if Christ's institution is not kept as He appointed it, then there is no Sacrament. This is by no means to be rejected, but can and should be encouraged and maintained with benefit in God's Church. The use or action here does not 86 mean chiefly faith. Nor does it mean the oral participation alone. It means the entire external, visible action of the Lord's Supper instituted by Christ: the *consecration*, or words of institution, the *distribution* and *reception*, or oral partaking of the consecrated bread and wine, of Christ's body and blood. Apart 87 from this use, it is to be regarded as no Sacrament, like when the bread is not distributed in the papistic Mass but is offered up as a sacrifice or enclosed, carried around, and exhibited for adoration. Likewise, the water of Baptism, when used to consecrate bells or to cure leprosy, or otherwise exhibited for worship, is no Sacrament or Baptism. This rule has been established at the beginning against these papistic abuses and has been explained by Dr. Luther himself (see Martin Luther's *Second Letter to Simon Wolferinus* [July 20, 1543], Luther's Works, Latin, Jena Edition 4:585; also in WA Br. 10:348–49).

88    Meanwhile, we must call attention to the fact that the Sacramentarians artfully and wickedly pervert this useful and necessary rule. They do this to deny the true, essential presence and oral partaking of Christ's body, which happens here on earth by both the worthy and the unworthy. They interpret this rule as referring to the spiritual and inner use of faith. They speak as though it were no Sacrament to the unworthy, and the partaking of the body happened only spiritually, through faith. Or they speak as though faith made Christ's body present in the Holy Supper, and therefore unworthy, unbelieving hypocrites do not receive Christ's body as being present.

89    It is not our faith that makes the Sacrament, but only the true Word and institution of our almighty God and Savior, Jesus Christ. His Word always is and remains effective in the Christian Church. It is not invalidated or rendered ineffective by the worthiness or unworthiness of the minister, nor by the unbelief of the one who receives it. This is just like the Gospel. Even though godless hearers do not believe it, the Gospel is and remains nonetheless the true Gospel, only it does not work for salvation in the unbelieving. So whether those who receive the Sacrament believe or do not believe, Christ remains nonetheless true in His words when He says, "Take, eat; this is My body." He makes Himself present not by our faith, but by His almighty power.

90    It is a deadly, shameless error that some people cunningly pervert this familiar rule to say that faith makes Christ's body present and partakes of it, rather than the almighty power of our Lord and Savior, Jesus Christ.

## CHRIST'S BODY AND THE SACRAMENT

91    Let us consider the Sacramentarians' various imaginary reasons and futile counter-arguments about the human body's essential and natural attributes, about Christ's ascension, about His departure from this world, and the like. These have one and all been refuted thoroughly and in detail, from God's Word, by Dr. Luther in his polemical writings: *Against the Heavenly Prophets, That These Words, "This Is My Body," Still Stand Firm*. Likewise, he refutes them in his *Large* and *Brief Confession concerning the Holy Supper* (LW 37:151–372; 38:279–319), and in his other writings. Since his death, nothing new has been advanced by the factious spirits. Therefore, for the sake of brevity we would direct the Christian reader to these writings and refer to them.

92    We neither will, nor can, nor should allow ourselves to be led away by thoughts of human wisdom. No matter what outward appearance or authority they may have, they cannot lead us away from the simple, distinct, and clear sense of Christ's Word and testament to a strange opinion, other than what the words read. According to what is stated above, we understand and believe the words simply. Our reasons are those that Dr. Luther himself presented. Upon them we have rested in this matter ever since the controversy about this article arose. In the very beginning, these reasons were presented 93 against the Sacramentarians in the following words (Dr. Luther in his *Confession concerning Christ's Supper*):

My grounds, on which I rest in this matter, are as follows:

94   The first is this article of our faith, that Jesus Christ is essential, natural, true, complete God and man in one person, undivided and inseparable.

95   The second, that the right hand of God is everywhere.

96   The third, that the Word of God is not false or deceitful.

97   The fourth, that God has and knows various ways to be present at a certain place, not only the single one of which the fanatics prattle, which the philosophers call "local." (LW 37:214)

98   Luther also says:

Thus the one body of Christ has a threefold existence, or all three modes

99   of being at a given place. First, the circumscribed corporeal mode of presence, as when He walked bodily on earth, when He occupied and yielded space according to His size. He can still employ this mode of presence when He wills to do so, as He did after His resurrection and as He will do on the Last Day, as Paul says in I Timothy [6:15], "Whom the blessed God will reveal," and Colossians 3[:4], "When Christ your life reveals Himself." He is not in God or with the Father or in heaven according to this mode, as this mad spirit dreams, for God is not a corporeal space or place. The passages which the spiritualists adduce concerning Christ's leaving the world and going to the Father speak of this mode of presence.

100   Secondly, the uncircumscribed, spiritual mode of presence according to which He neither occupies nor yields space but passes through everything created as He wills. To use some crude illustrations, my vision passes through and exists in air, light, or water and does not occupy or yield any space; a sound or tone passes through and exists in air or water or a board and a wall and neither occupies nor yields space; likewise light and heat go through and exist in air, water, glass, or crystals and the like, but without occupying or yielding space, and many more like these. He employed this mode of presence when He left the closed grave and came through closed doors, in the bread and wine in the Supper, and, as people believe, when He was born in His mother.

101   Thirdly, since He is one person with God, the divine, heavenly mode, according to which all created things are indeed much more permeable and present to Him than they are according to the second mode. For if according to the second mode He can be present in and with created things in such a way that they do not feel, touch, measure, or circumscribe him, how much more marvelously will He be present in all created things according to this exalted third mode, where they cannot measure or circumscribe Him but where they are present to Him so that He measures and circumscribes them. You must place this existence of Christ, which constitutes Him one person with God, far, far beyond things created, as far as God transcends them; and on the other hand, place it as deep in and as near to all created things as God is in them. For He is one indivisible person with God, and wherever God is, He must be also, otherwise our faith is false.

102   But who can explain or even conceive how this occurs? We know indeed

that it is so, that He is in God beyond all created things, and is one person with God. But how this happens, we do not know; it transcends nature and reason, even the comprehension of all the angels in heaven, and is known only to God. Since this is true, even though unknown to us, we should not give the lie to His words until we know how to prove certainly that the body of Christ cannot in any circumstances be where God is and that this mode of being is a fiction. Let the fanatics prove it! They will give it up.

103    I do not wish to have denied by the foregoing that God may have and know still other modes whereby Christ's body can be in a given place. My only purpose was to show what crass fools our fanatics are when they concede only the first, circumscribed mode of presence to the body of Christ although they are unable to prove that even this mode is contrary to our view. For I do not want to deny in any way that God's power is able to make a body be simultaneously in many places, even in a corporeal and circumscribed manner. For who wants to try to prove that God is unable to do that? Who has seen the limits of His power? The fanatics may indeed think that God is unable to do it, but who will believe their speculations? How will they establish the truth of that kind of speculation? (LW 37:222–24)

Thus far Luther.

104    From these words of Dr. Luther, it is clear in what sense the word *spiritual* is used in our churches in this matter. For the Sacramentarians think this word *spiritual* means nothing other than the spiritual communion, when true believers are incorporated into Christ the Lord in the Spirit and become true spiritual members of His body.

When Dr. Luther or we use the word *spiritual* in this matter, we understand this: the spiritual, supernatural, heavenly way that Christ is present in the Holy Supper. He works not only consolation and life in the believing, but also condemnation in the unbelieving. By this use, we reject the Capernaitic thoughts of the crude and fleshly presence that is attributed to and forced on our churches by the Sacramentarians against our many public protests. This is also how we want the word *spiritually* to be understood when we say that in the Holy Supper Christ's body and blood are spiritually received, eaten, and drunk. Even though this participation happens with the mouth, the way it happens is spiritual.    105

Our faith in this article about the true presence of Christ's body and blood in the Holy Supper is based on the *truth and omnipotence* of the true, almighty God, our Lord and Savior Jesus Christ. This foundation is strong and firm enough to strengthen and establish our faith in all temptations about this article. They overthrow and refute all the Sacramentarians' counterarguments and objections, however agreeable and plausible they may be to our reason. A Christian heart can rest securely and rely firmly on these truths.    106

## NEGATIVE STATEMENTS

With heart and mouth we reject and condemn as false, erroneous, and misleading all errors that do not agree with but contradict and oppose the doctrine mentioned above and founded on God's Word, such as these:    107

1. The papistic transubstantiation. It is taught that the consecrated or blessed bread and wine in the Holy Supper entirely lose their substance and essence. They are    108

changed into the substance of Christ's body and blood in such a way that only the mere form of bread and wine is left, or the accidents without the object. The bread is no longer bread. According to their assertion it has lost its natural essence. Christ's body is present under the form of the bread even apart from the administration of the Holy Supper (e.g., when the bread is enclosed in the pyx or is carried about for display and adoration). For nothing can be a Sacrament without God's command and the appointed use for which it is instituted in God's Word, as was shown above.

109  2. We likewise reject and condemn all other papistic abuses of this Sacrament, like the abomination of the sacrifice of the Mass for the living and dead.

110  3. Also, contrary to Christ's public command and institution only one form of the Sacrament is administered to the laity. These papistic abuses have been thoroughly refuted by means of God's Word and the testimonies of the Ancient Church, in the common Confession and the Apology of our churches, the Smalcald Articles, and our theologians' other writings.

111  However, in this document we have tried to present only our confession and explanation about the true presence of Christ's body and blood especially against the Sacramentarians. Some of them shamelessly sneak into our churches under the name of the Augsburg Confession. Therefore, we will also state and list here especially the Sacramentarians' errors, in order to warn our hearers to guard against and look out for them.

112  With heart and mouth we reject and condemn as false, erroneous, and misleading all Sacramentarian opinions and teachings. These do not agree with, but contradict and oppose, the doctrine presented above, founded on God's Word:

113  1. They assert that the words of institution are not to be understood simply in their proper meaning, as they read, about the true, essential presence of Christ's body and blood in the Supper. Instead, they are to be twisted, by turns of phrases or figurative interpretations, to a new, strange sense. We reject all such Sacramentarian opinions and self-contradictory notions (some of which even conflict with one another!), however many and various they may be.

114  2. The oral partaking of Christ's body and blood in the Supper is denied by the Sacramentarians. On the contrary, it is taught that Christ's body in the Supper is partaken of only spiritually through faith. So in the Supper our mouth receives only bread and wine.

115  3. It is taught that bread and wine in the Supper should be regarded as nothing more than tokens by which Christians are to recognize one another.

4. Or, they are only figures, comparisons, and representations of Christ's far-absent body. Just as bread and wine are the outward food of our body, so also Christ's absent body, with His merit, is our souls' spiritual food.

116  5. Or, they are no more than tokens or memorials of Christ's absent body. By these signs, as an external pledge, we should be assured that faith turns from the Supper and ascends beyond all heavens. There above a person truly partakes of Christ's body and blood as he truly receives the outward signs with the mouth in the Supper. So the assurance and confirmation of our faith happen in the Supper only through the outward signs and not through Christ's true, present body and blood offered to us.

117  6. Or, in the Supper the power, effectiveness, and merit of Christ's far-absent body are distributed only to those who have faith.

We become partakers of His absent body. In this way just mentioned, the sacramental union is to be understood with respect to the analogy of the sign and what is signified. This means the bread and wine have a resemblance to Christ's body and blood.

118    7. Or, Christ's body and blood can only be received and partaken of spiritually, through faith.

119    8. It is taught that because of His ascension into heaven, Christ is enclosed and restricted by His body in a definite place in heaven. He cannot or will not be truly present with us in the Supper, which is celebrated according to Christ's institution on earth. But He is as far and remote from it as heaven and earth are from each other. Some Sacramentarians have willfully and wickedly falsified the text "Christ must occupy heaven" (see Acts 3:21) for the confirmation of their error. Instead of this translation they have rendered it "Christ must be received or be restricted and enclosed by heaven or in heaven," so that in His human nature He can or will in no way be with us on earth.

120    9. Christ has not promised the true, essential presence of His body and blood in His Supper. He cannot and will not give it, because the nature and property of His received human nature could not allow or permit it.

121    10. It is taught that not only Christ's Word and omnipotence, but also faith makes Christ's body present in the Supper. For this reason the words of institution in the administration of the Supper are omitted by some. The papistic consecration is rightly rebuked and rejected, in which the power to produce a Sacrament is credited to the speaking as the priest's work. Yet the words of institution can or should in no way be left out of the administration of the Supper, as is shown in the preceding declaration.

122    11. Believers are not to seek, by reason of the words of Christ's institution, Christ's body with the bread and wine of the Supper. Instead, they are directed with their faith away from the bread of the Supper to heaven, to the place where the Lord Christ is with His body, that they should become partakers of it there.

12. We reject the teaching about unbelieving and impenitent, wicked Christians who bear Christ in name only, but do not have the right, true, living, and saving faith. Some teach that they do not receive Christ's body and blood in the Supper, but only bread and wine. And since there are only two kinds of guests found at this heavenly meal, the worthy and the unworthy, we reject the distinction made among the unworthy. Some assert that when using the Holy Supper the godless Epicureans and scoffers at God's Word (who are in the Church's outward fellowship) do not receive Christ's body and blood for condemnation, but they only receive bread and wine.    123

13. We reject the teaching that worthiness comes not only from true faith, but also from a person's own preparation.    124

14. We reject this teaching: even true believers, who have and keep a right, true, living faith, and yet lack the so-called sufficient preparation of their own, could receive this Sacrament to condemnation, just like the unworthy guests.    125

15. It is taught that the elements or the visible species or forms of the consecrated bread and wine must be adored. However, no one—unless he is an Arian heretic—can and will deny that Christ Himself, true God and man, is truly and essentially present in the Supper. Christ should be adored in spirit and in truth in the true use of the Sacrament, as He is in all other places, especially where His congregation is assembled.    126

16. We reject and condemn also all dar-    127

ing, frivolous, blasphemous questions and expressions that are presented in a crude, fleshly, Capernaitic way about the supernatural, heavenly mysteries of this Supper.

128    Other additional *antitheses*, or rejected contrary doctrines, have been rebuked and rejected in the preceding explanation. For the sake of brevity, we will not repeat them here. Whatever other condemnable or erroneous opinions there may still be, over and above those just stated, can be easily gathered and named from the preceding explanation. We reject and condemn everything that is not in agreement with, but contrary and opposed to, the teaching recorded above and thoroughly grounded in God's Word.

# VIII. THE PERSON OF CHRIST

For an annotation on this article, see p. 509. (See also Apostles' Creed; Nicene Creed; Athanasian Creed; AC III; Ap III; SA I; SA II I; SC II; LC II; FC Ep VIII.)

## STATUS OF THE CONTROVERSY

1    A controversy has also arisen among the theologians of the Augsburg Confession about the person of Christ. This did not arise among them first but sprang originally from the Sacramentarians.

2    In opposition to the Sacramentarians, Dr. Luther maintained the true, essential presence of Christ's body and blood in the Supper with solid arguments from the words of institution. The objection was raised against him by the Zwinglians that, if Christ's body were present at the same time in heaven and on earth in the Holy Supper, it could be no real, true human body. For such majesty was said to be peculiar to God alone. They said Christ's body was not capable of it.

3    Dr. Luther contradicted and effectively refuted this, as his doctrinal and polemical writings about the Holy Supper show. We publicly confess these writings, as well as his doctrinal writings. After Luther's death, some 4 theologians of the Augsburg Confession sought—though still unwilling to do so publicly and clearly—to confess that they were in agreement with the Sacramentarians about the Lord's Supper. Nevertheless, they introduced and used precisely the same false arguments about Christ's person by which the Sacramentarians dared to remove the true, essential presence of Christ's body and blood from His Supper. They said that nothing should be credited to the human nature in the person of Christ that is above or contrary to its natural, essential property. On account of this they have accused Dr. Luther's doctrine (and all those who follow it because it conforms with God's Word) of almost all the ancient monstrous heresies.

## AFFIRMATIVE STATEMENTS

5    We want to explain this controversy in a Christian way, in conformity with God's Word, according to the guidance of our simple Christian faith. By God's grace we want to entirely settle this. Therefore, our unanimous doctrine, faith, and confession are as follows:

6    We believe, teach, and confess that God's Son from eternity has been a particular, distinct, entire, divine person. Yet He is true, essential, perfect God with the Father and the Holy Spirit. In the fullness of time He received also the human nature into the unity of His person. He did not do this in such a way that there are now two persons or two Christs. Christ Jesus is now in one person at the same time true, eternal God, born of the Father from eternity, and a true man, born of the most blessed Virgin Mary. This is written in Romans 9:5, "from their race, according to

the flesh, is the Christ who is God over all, blessed forever."

7   We believe, teach, and confess that now, in this one undivided person of Christ, there are two distinct natures: the divine, which is from eternity, and the human, which in time was received into the unity of the person of God's Son. These two natures in the person of Christ are never either separated from or mingled with each other. Nor are they changed into each other. Each one abides in its nature and essence in the person of Christ to all eternity.

8   We believe, teach, and confess also that both natures mentioned remain unmingled and undestroyed in their nature and essence. Each keeps its natural, essential properties to all eternity and does not lay them aside. Neither do the essential properties of the one nature ever become the essential properties of the other nature.

9   We believe, teach, and confess that it is natural to be almighty, eternal, infinite, everywhere present at the same time, and all-knowing. In other words, it agrees with the properties of [the divine] nature and its natural essence. These are essential attributes of the divine nature. Never in eternity do they become essential properties of the human nature.

Christ Carries the Cross

10     On the other hand, these are properties of the human nature: being a bodily creation or creature, flesh and blood, finite and located in one place; it suffers, dies, ascends, and descends; it moves from one place to another, suffers hunger, thirst, cold, heat, and the like. These properties never become properties of the divine nature.

11     We believe, teach, and confess that now, since the incarnation, each nature in Christ does not exist by itself so that each is, or makes up, a separate person. These two natures are so united that they make up one single person, in which the divine and the received human nature are and exist at the same time. So now, since the incarnation, there belongs to the entire person of Christ personally not only His divine nature, but also His received human nature. So without His divinity, and also without His humanity, the person of Christ or the incarnate Son of God is not complete. We mean the Son of God who has received flesh and become man (John 1:14). Therefore, Christ is not two distinct persons, but one single person, even though two distinct natures are found in Him, unconfused in their natural essence and properties.

12     We also believe, teach, and confess that the received human nature in Christ has and retains its natural, essential properties. But over and above these, through the personal union with the Deity, and afterward through glorification, Christ's human nature has been exalted to the right hand of majesty, power, and might, over everything that can be named, not only in this world, but also in that which is to come (Ephesians 1:21).

13     Consider this majesty, to which Christ has been exalted according to His humanity. He did not first receive it when He rose from the dead and ascended into heaven. He received it when He was conceived in His mother's womb and became man, and the divine and human natures were personally united with each other. However, this personal union is not to be understood (as some 14 incorrectly explain it) as though the two natures, the divine and the human, were united with each other, like two boards are glued together. Some say that (in deed and truth) they have no communion whatsoever with each other. This was the error and heresy of 15 Nestorius and Samosatenus. As Suidas and Theodore, presbyter of Raithu, testify, they taught and held that the two natures have no communion whatsoever with each other. In this way, the natures are separated from each other, and the two Christs are constituted. So Christ is one, and God the Word (who dwells in Christ) is another.

This is what Theodore the Presbyter 16 writes:

At that time the heretic Manes lived, and also one by the name of Paul. Though born in Samosata, he was a bishop at Antioch in Syria. He wickedly taught that the Lord Christ was nothing other than a mere man in whom God the Word dwelt, just as in every prophet. Therefore, he also held that the divine and human natures are apart from each other and separate. In Christ they have no communion whatever with each other, just as though Christ were one, and God the Word, who dwells in Him, the other.

Against this condemned heresy the Chris- 17 tian Church has always simply believed and held that the divine and the human nature in the person of Christ are so united that they have a true communion with each other. The natures are not mingled in one essence. But, as Dr. Luther writes, they come together in one person. So, on account of this personal 18 union and communion, the ancient teachers of the Church, before and after the Council of Chalcedon, frequently used the word *mixture*, in a good sense and with true discrimination. To prove this, many testimonies of the Fathers, if necessary, could be quoted. These are to be found frequently also in the writings of our divines, and they explain the personal union and communion using the illustration of the soul and body, and of glow-

19   ing iron. For the body and soul, as also fire and iron, have communion with each other. This is not by a phrase or mode of speaking, or in mere words, that is, so that it is merely a form of speech or mere words. But the communion is true and real. Nevertheless, there is no mixing or equalizing of the natures introduced like when mead is made from honey and water, which is no longer pure water or pure honey, but a mixed drink. It is far different in the union of the divine and the human nature in the person of Christ. It is a far different, more grand, and altogether indescribable communion and union between the divine and the human nature in the person of Christ. Because this union and communion, God is man and man is God. Neither the natures nor their properties are intermingled, but each nature keeps its essence and properties.

20   This personal union does not exist nor can be thought of without such a true communion of the natures. Not just the mere human nature—whose property it is to suffer and die—has suffered for the sins of the world, but the Son of God Himself truly suffered. However, He suffered according to the received human nature. In accordance with our simple Christian faith, He truly died, although the divine nature can neither

21   suffer nor die. Dr. Luther has fully explained this in his *Confession concerning Christ's Supper* in opposition to the blasphemous *alloeosis,* or interchange, of Zwingli, who

taught that one nature should be taken and understood for the other. Dr. Luther has committed that teaching, as a devil's mask, to the abyss of hell.

22   For this reason, the ancient teachers of the Church combined both words, *communion* and *union*, in the explanation of this mystery and have explained the one word by the other. (See Irenaeus, Book 4, chap. 37; Athanasius, in the *Letter to Epictetus*; Hilary, *Concerning the Trinity*, Book 9; Basil and Gregory of Nyssa, in Theodoret; Damascus, Book 3, chap. 19.)

23   On account of this personal union and communion of the divine and the human nature in Christ we believe, teach, and confess what is said about the majesty of Christ according to His humanity, according to our simple Christian faith: He sits at the right hand of the almighty power of God. We also confess what follows from that. All of this would mean nothing and could not stand if this personal union and communion of the natures in the person of Christ did not exist (in deed and truth).

24   On account of this personal union and communion of the natures, Mary, the most blessed Virgin, did not bear a mere man. But, as the angel (Gabriel) testifies, she bore a man who is truly the Son of the most high God (Luke 1:35). He showed His divine majesty even in His mother's womb, because He was born of a virgin, without violating her virginity. Therefore, she is truly the mother of God and yet has remained a virgin.

25   He did all His miracles by the power of this personal union. He showed His divine majesty, according to His pleasure, when and as He willed. He did this not just after His resurrection and ascension, but also in His state of humiliation. For example:
(a) At the wedding at Cana of Galilee (John 2:1–11)

The Ascension of Christ

(b) When He was twelve years old, among the learned (Luke 2:42–50)

(c) In the garden, when with a word He cast His enemies to the ground (John 18:6)

(d) In death, when He died not simply as any other man, but in and with His death conquered sin, death, devil, hell, and eternal damnation (Colossians 2:13–15)

The human nature alone would not have been able to do these miracles if it had not been personally united and had communion with the divine nature.

26 The human nature, after the resurrection from the dead, is exalted above all creatures in heaven and on earth. This is nothing other than that He entirely laid aside the form of a servant (Philippians 2:7–11). He did not lay aside His human nature, but retains it to eternity. He has the full possession and use of the divine majesty according to His received human nature. However, He had this majesty immediately at His conception, even in His mother's womb. As the apostle testifies (Philippians 2:7), He laid it aside. As Dr. Luther explains, He kept it concealed in the state of His humiliation and did not always use it, but only when He wanted to use it.

27 Now He has ascended to heaven, not merely as any other saint, but as the apostle testifies (Ephesians 4:10), above all heavens. He also truly fills all things, being present everywhere, not only as God, but also as man. He rules from sea to sea and to the ends of the earth, as the prophets predict (Psalm 8:1, 6; 93:1–4; Zechariah 9:10) and the apostles testify (Mark 16:20). He did this everywhere with them and confirmed their word

28 with signs. This did not happen in an earthly way. As Dr. Luther explains, this happened according to the way things are done at God's right hand. "God's right hand" is no set place in heaven, as the Sacramentarians assert without any ground in the Holy Scriptures. It is nothing other than God's almighty power, which fills heaven and earth. Christ is installed according to His humanity (in deed and truth), without confusing or equalizing the two natures in their essence and essential properties. By this communicated divine 29 power, according to the words of His testament, He can be and is truly present with His body and blood in the Holy Supper. He has pointed this out for us by His Word. This is possible for no other man, because no man is united with the divine nature the way Jesus, the Son of Mary, is. No man is installed in such divine almighty majesty and power through and in the personal union of the two natures in Christ. For in Him the divine and 30 the human nature are personally united with each other. So in Christ "the whole fullness of deity dwells bodily" (Colossians 2:9). In this personal union the two natures have such a grand, intimate, indescribable communion that even the angels are astonished by it. As St. Peter testifies, they have their delight and joy in looking into it (1 Peter 1:12). All of this will soon be explained in order and somewhat more fully.

This personal union, as it has been stated 31 and explained above, is the basis of a further teaching. Another doctrine flows from the way in which the divine and the human nature in the person of Christ are united with each other. The two natures not only have the names in common, but they also have communion with each other (in deed and truth) without commingling or equalizing their essences. From this point flows teaching about the true communion of the properties of the natures. More will be said about this below.

This is certainly true: properties do not 32 leave their subjects. In other words, each nature keeps its essential properties. These are not separated from the nature and poured into the other nature, as water from one vessel into another. So there could not be any communion of properties if the personal union or communion of the natures in the person of Christ were not true. Next to the article of the Holy Trinity this is the greatest mystery in heaven and on earth. Paul says, "Great indeed, we confess, is the mystery of godliness: He was manifested in the flesh" (1 Timothy 3:16). The apostle Peter testifies in clear words (2 Peter 1:4) that we also, in whom Christ dwells only by grace, on account of that great mystery, are "partakers of the divine nature" in Christ. Therefore, what kind of communion of the divine nature must that be of which the apostle says, "in [Christ] the whole fullness of deity dwells bodily" so that God and man are one person?

35  It is highly important that this doctrine about the communion of the properties of both natures be treated and explained with proper discrimination. There are many ways and modes of speaking about the person of Christ and of its natures and properties. When these are used without proper distinction, the doctrine becomes confused and the simple reader is easily led astray. Therefore, the following explanation should be carefully noted. For the purpose of making it plainer and simpler, it may be organized under three headings:

36      1. In Christ two distinct natures exist and remain unchanged and unconfused in their natural essence and properties. Yet there is only one person consisting of both natures. Therefore, that which is an attribute of only one nature is attributed not to that nature alone, as separate. It is attributed to the entire person, who is at the same time God and man (whether the person is called God or man).

37      In this way of speaking, it does not make sense that what is attributed to the person is at the same time a property of both natures.

But its nature is distinctively explained by what is ascribed to the person. So "His Son . . . was descended from David according to the flesh" (Romans 1:3). Also: Christ was "put to death in the flesh" (1 Peter 3:18) and "suffered in the flesh" (1 Peter 4:1).

38  However, beneath the words—when it is said that what is peculiar to one nature is attributed to the entire person—secret and open Sacramentarians conceal their deadly error. They do this by naming the entire person, but meaning only the one nature, and entirely excluding the other nature. They speak as though the mere human nature had suffered for us, as Dr. Luther in his *Confession concerning Christ's Supper* has written about the *alloeosis* of Zwingli. We will present here Luther's own words, in order that God's Church may be guarded in the best way against this error:

39      [Zwingli] calls it alloeosis when something is said about the divinity of Christ which after all belongs to His humanity, or vice versa—for example, in Luke 24[:26], "Was it not necessary that the Christ should suffer these things and so enter into His glory?" Here he [Zwingli] performs a sleight-of-hand trick and substitutes the human nature for Christ. Beware, beware, I say, of this alloeosis, for it is the devil's mask since it will finally construct a kind of Christ after whom I would not want to be a Christian, that is, a Christ who is and does no more in His passion and His life than any other ordinary saint. For if I believe that only the human nature suffered for me, then Christ would be a poor Savior for me, in fact, He Himself would need a Savior. In short, it is indescribable what the devil attempts with this alloeosis! (LW 37:209–10)

40

41    And shortly afterward:

> Now if the old witch, Lady Reason, alloeosis' grandmother, should say that the Deity surely cannot suffer and die, then you must answer and say: That is true, but since the divinity and humanity are one person in Christ, the Scriptures ascribe to the divinity, because of this personal union, all that happens to humanity, and vice versa.

42    

> And in reality it is so. Indeed, you must say that the person (pointing to Christ) suffers, and dies. But this person is truly God, and therefore it is correct to say: the Son of God suffers. Although, so to speak, the one part (namely, the divinity) does not suffer, nevertheless the person, who is God, suffers in the other part (namely, in the humanity). (LW 37:210)

> For the Son of God truly is crucified for us, i.e., this person who is God. For that is what He is—this person, I say, is crucified according to His humanity. (LW 37:211)

43    And again, shortly afterward:

> If Zwingli's alloeosis stands, then Christ will have to be two persons, one a divine and the other a human person, since Zwingli applies all the texts concerning the passion only to the human nature and completely excludes them from the divine nature. But if the works are divided and separated, the person will also have to be separated, since all the doing and suffering are not ascribed to natures but to persons. It is the person who does and suffers everything, the one thing according to this nature and the other thing according to the other nature, all of which scholars know perfectly well. Therefore we regard our Lord

Christ as God and man in one person, "neither confusing the natures nor dividing the person." (LW 37:212–13)

44    Dr. Luther also says in his book *On the Councils and the Church* (1539):

> We Christians should know that if God is not in the scale to give it weight, we, on our side, sink to the ground. I mean it this way: if it cannot be said that God died for us, but only a man, we are lost; but if God's death and a dead God lie in the balance, His side goes down and ours goes up like a light and empty scale. Yet He can also readily go up again, or leap out of the scale! But He could not sit on the scale unless He become a man like us, so that it could be called God's dying, God's martyrdom, God's blood, and God's death. For God in His own nature cannot die; but now that God and man are united in one person, it is called God's death when the man dies who is one substance or one person with God. (LW 41:103–4)

Thus far Luther.

45    It is clear that it is incorrect to say or write that the above-mentioned expressions ("God suffered, God died") are only verbal assertions, that is, mere words, and that it is not so in fact. For our simple Christian faith proves that God's Son, who became man, suffered for us, died for us and redeemed us with His blood.

46    2. In fulfilling Christ's office, the person does not act and work in, with, through, or according to only one nature. It works in, according to, with, and through both natures. As the Council of Chalcedon expresses it, one nature works in communion with the other what is a property of each. Therefore, Christ 47 is our Mediator, Redeemer, King, High Priest, Head, Shepherd, and so on, not according to

one nature only (whether it be the divine or the human), but according to both natures. This teaching has been treated more fully in other places.

48    3. However, it is a much different thing when the question, declaration, or discussion is about whether the natures in the personal union in Christ have nothing else or nothing more than only their natural, essential properties. It has been mentioned above that they have and keep these.

49    Regarding the divine nature in Christ, in God there is no change (James 1:17). His divine nature, in its essence and properties, suffered no subtraction or addition by the incarnation. It was not, in or by itself, either diminished or increased by it.

50    Regarding the received human nature in the person of Christ, some have wished to argue that even in the personal union with divinity it has nothing else and nothing more than only its natural, essential properties according to which it is in all things like its brethren (Hebrews 2:17). On this account, they argue that nothing should or could be attributed to the human nature in Christ that is beyond, or contrary to, its natural properties, even though the testimony of Scripture

51    speaks that way. This opinion is false and incorrect. This is so clear from God's Word that even their own associates rebuke and reject this error. For the Holy Scriptures and the Ancient Fathers from the Scriptures forcefully testify: The human nature has been personally united with the divine nature in Christ. It was glorified and exalted to the right hand of God's majesty and power. After the form of a servant and humiliation had been laid aside, the human nature did receive—apart from, and over and above its natural, essential, permanent properties—special, high, great, supernatural, mysterious, indescribable, heavenly privileges and excel-lences in majesty, glory, power, and might above everything that can be named. It has them not only in this world, but also in that which is to come (Ephesians 1:21). So we conclude about the work of Christ's office: the human nature in Christ is equally used [at the same time] in its measure and mode. It also has its power and efficacy. This is true not only from, and according to, its natural, essential attributes, or only so far as their ability extends, but chiefly from, and according to, the majesty, glory, power, and might that it has received through the personal union, glorification, and exaltation. Today, 52 even the adversaries can or dare scarcely deny this. Except they still dispute and contend that those are only created gifts or finite qualities, as in the saints, with which the human nature in Christ is endowed and adorned. According to their thoughts or from their own argumentations or proofs, they want to measure and calculate what the human nature in Christ could or should be capable of or incapable of without becoming annihilated.

The best, most certain, and surest way in 53 this controversy is this: according to His received human nature through the personal union, Christ has glorification, or exaltation. What His received human nature is capable of beyond the natural properties, without becoming annihilated, no one can know better or more thoroughly than the Lord Christ Himself. He has revealed this in His Word, as much as is needful for us to know about it in this life. We must simply believe everything for which we have clear, certain testimonies in the Scriptures in this matter. We should in no way argue against it, as though the human nature in Christ could not be capable of the same.

What has been said about the created 54 gifts that have been given and imparted to the human nature in Christ is indeed correct and true. The nature possesses them in or of itself. But these do not reach the majesty that the Scriptures, and the Ancient Fathers from Scripture, attribute to the received human nature in Christ.

55    To make alive, to have all judgment and all power in heaven and on earth, to have all things in His hands, to have all things subject beneath His feet, to cleanse from sin, and so on, are not created gifts. These are divine, infinite properties. Yet, according to the declaration of Scripture, these have been given and communicated to the man Christ. (See John 5:27; 6:39; Matthew 28:18; Daniel 7:14; John 3:35; 13:3; Matthew 11:27; Ephesians 1:22; Hebrews 2:8; 1 Corinthians 15:27; John 1:3.)

56    This communication is not to be understood as a phrase or way of speaking, or just words about the person according to the divine nature alone, but according to the received human nature. The following three strong, irrefutable arguments and reasons show this:

57    1. First, here is a unanimously received rule of the entire ancient orthodox Church. Holy Scripture testifies that what Christ received in time He did not receive according to the divine nature. (According to this nature He has everything from eternity.) But the person of Christ has received attributes in time by reason of and with respect to the received human nature.

58    2. Second, the Scriptures testify clearly (John 5:21, 27; 6:39–40) that the power to give life and to execute judgment has been given to Christ because He is the Son of Man and since He has flesh and blood.

59    3. Third, the Scriptures speak not merely in general of the Son of Man, but also indicate clearly His received human nature, "the blood of Jesus His Son cleanses us from all sin" (1 John 1:7). This is true not only according to the merit of Christ's blood that was once attained on the cross. But in this place John means that in the work or act of justification, not only the divine nature in Christ but also His blood actually cleanses us from all sins (1 John 1:7). So in John 6:48–58 Christ's flesh is a life-giving food. The Council of Ephesus also concluded from this statement that Christ's flesh has power to give life. Many other glorious testimonies of the ancient orthodox Church about this article are cited elsewhere.

60    Now Christ, according to His human nature, has received this. It has been given and communicated to the received human nature in Christ. We shall and must believe this according to the Scriptures. But, as said above, the two natures in Christ are united in such a way that they are not mingled with each other or changed one into the other. Each retains its natural, essential property, so that the properties of one nature never become properties of the other nature. Therefore, this doctrine must be rightly explained and diligently guarded against all heresies.

61    We, then, invent nothing new by ourselves, but receive and repeat the explanations that the ancient orthodox Church has given about this from the good foundation of Holy Scripture. This divine power, life, might, majesty, and glory was given to the received human nature in Christ. This did not happen the way the Father from eternity has communicated to the Son (according to the divine nature) His essence and all divine attributes, by which He is of one essence with the Father and is equal to God. (For Christ is equal to the Father only according to the divine nature. According to the received human nature, He is beneath God. From this it is clear that we make no confusion, equalization, or abolition of natures in Christ.) So the power to give life is not the same in Christ's flesh as it is in His divine nature, where it is an essential property.

62    Furthermore, this communication or impartation has not happened through an essential or natural infusion of the properties of the divine nature into the human. In other words, Christ's humanity would not have these by itself and apart from the divine essence. Nor has the human nature in Christ entirely laid aside its natural, essential properties. It is not transformed into divinity. In and by itself, it does not become equal to divinity with these communicated properties. Nor does it mean that there should now be identical or equal natural, essential properties and operations for both natures. For these and similar erroneous doctrines were rightly rejected and condemned in the ancient approved councils on the basis of Holy Scripture. *For in no way is conversion, confusion, or equalization of the natures in Christ or of their essential properties to be made or allowed.*

63    We have never understood that the impartation or communion that happens (in deed and truth) applies to any physical communication or essential transfusion. In other words, we have never talked about an essential, natural communion or effusion, by which the natures would be commingled in their essence and their essential properties. Some have craftily and wickedly, against their own conscience, perverted these words and phrases in order to make the pure doctrine suspected. But we have only contrasted these words with verbal communication. We have applied them to this doctrine when such persons assert that it is only a phrase and way of speaking; that is, nothing more than mere words, titles, and names. They have laid so much stress on this that they would know of no other communion. Therefore, for the true explanation of Christ's majesty, we have used such terms of real communion. We wanted to show by them that this communion has happened (in deed and truth) without any confusion of natures and their essential properties.

This is what we hold and teach, in con-   64 formity with the ancient orthodox Church, as it has explained this teaching from the Scriptures: the human nature in Christ has received this majesty through the personal union. This happened because the entire fullness of the divinity dwells in Christ (Colossians 2:9), not as in other holy men or angels, but bodily, as *in its own body*. The divinity shines forth with all its majesty, power, glory, and effectiveness in the received human nature. It does this voluntarily when and as Christ wills. In, with, and through the human nature, Christ shows, uses, and acts on His divine power, glory, and efficacy, as the soul does in the body and fire in glowing iron. (By means of these illustrations, as was also mentioned above, the entire Ancient Church has explained this doctrine.) This power was concealed and   65 withheld at the time of the humiliation. But now, after the form of a servant has been laid aside, it is fully, powerfully, and publicly exercised before all saints, in heaven and on earth. In the life to come we shall also behold His glory face-to-face (John 17:24).

There is and remains in Christ only one   66 divine omnipotence, power, majesty, and glory, which is peculiar to the divine nature alone. But it shines, manifests, and exercises itself fully—yet voluntarily—in, with, and through the received, exalted human nature in Christ. In glowing iron there are not two kinds of power to shine and burn. But the power to shine and to burn is a property of the fire. Since the fire is united with the iron, it manifests and exercises this power to shine and to burn in, with, and through the glowing iron. From this union also the glowing iron has the power to shine and to burn without changing the essence and the natural properties of fire and iron.

67    This guides how we understand the testimonies of Scripture that speak of the majesty to which the human nature in Christ is exalted. We do not understand them to mean that the divine majesty, which is peculiar to the divine nature of God's Son, is in the person of the Son of Man to be ascribed to Christ simply and purely according to His divine nature. Nor do we understand them to mean that this majesty is to be in Christ's human nature in such a way that His human nature would only have the title and name by a phrase and manner of speaking (i.e., only in words, but [in deed and truth] doesn't have

68    any communion whatever with it). For in that way it might also be said truthfully that all the fullness of the Godhead dwells bodily in all the creatures in whom God dwells (especially believers and saints). (God is a spiritual, undivided essence. Therefore, He is present everywhere and in all creatures. Wherever He is dwelling—but especially in believers and saints—there He has His majesty with Him.) We could say that all treasures of wisdom and knowledge are hid, and all power in heaven and earth is given, because the Holy Spirit, who has all power, is

69    given to believers. In this way, then, no distinction would be made between Christ, according to His human nature, and other holy men! So Christ would be deprived of His majesty, which He has received above all creatures, as a man or according to His

70    human nature. For no other creature—neither man nor angel—can or shall say, "All authority in heaven and on earth has been given to Me" (Matthew 28:18). For although God is in the saints with all the fullness of His Godhead that He has everywhere with Himself, He does not dwell in them bodily. Nor is He personally united with them as in

Christ. For from such personal union it follows that Christ says, even according to His human nature, "All authority in heaven and on earth has been given to Me" (Matthew 28:18). Also John 13:3 says, "Jesus, knowing that the Father had given all things into His hands." Also Colossians 2:9 says, "For in Him the whole fullness of deity dwells bodily." Also Scripture says, "You have crowned Him with glory and honor, putting everything in subjection under His feet. Now in putting everything in subjection to Him, He left nothing outside His control" (Hebrews 2:7–8; see also Psalm 8:6). "He is excepted who put all things in subjection under Him" (1 Corinthians 15:27).

71    By no means, however, do we believe, teach, and confess an infusion of God's majesty and of all its properties into Christ's human nature by which the divine nature is weakened, or anything that belongs to it is surrendered to another nature that it does not keep for itself. Nor do we say that the human nature in its substance and essence should have received equal majesty, separate or distinct from the nature and essence of God's Son, like when water, wine, or oil is poured from one vessel into another. For the human nature, and no other creature in heaven or on earth, is capable of receiving God's omnipotence in such a way that it would become in itself an almighty essence, or have in and by itself almighty properties. Then the human nature in Christ would be denied and would be entirely converted into the divinity. Such teaching is contrary to our Christian faith and also to the teaching of all the prophets and apostles.

72    We believe, teach, and confess that God the Father has given His Spirit to Christ, His beloved Son, according to the received humanity. (Because of this He is called also *Messiah*; i.e., the Anointed.) He has not re-

ceived His gifts with limits as other saints. For on Christ the Lord, according to His received human nature, rests "the Spirit of wisdom and understanding, the Spirit of counsel and might, the Spirit of knowledge and the fear of the LORD" (Isaiah 11:2; see also Colossians 2:3; Isaiah 61:1). (According to His divinity, He is of one essence with the Holy Spirit.) This not in such a way that, as a man, He knew and could do only some things, like other saints know and can do things by God's Spirit, who works in them only created gifts. According to His divinity, Christ is the Second Person in the Holy Trinity. And from Him, as also from the Father, the Holy Spirit proceeds (John 15:26). So the Spirit is and remains Christ's (1 Peter 1:11) and the Father's own Spirit to all eternity, not separated from God's Son. Therefore, as the Church Fathers say, the entire fullness of the Spirit has been communicated by the personal union to Christ according to the flesh, which is personally united with God's Son. This voluntarily manifests and shows itself with all its power in, with, and through Christ's human nature. So Christ (according to His human nature) not only knows some things and is ignorant of others (Matthew 24:36), but He also can do some things and is unable to do others. Yet even now (according to the *received* human nature), He knows and can do all things. For on Him the Father poured the Spirit of wisdom and power without measure. So as man, Christ has received all knowledge and all power (in deed and truth) through this personal union. And so all the treasures of wisdom are hidden in Him. All power is given to Him. He is seated at the right hand of God's majesty and power. From history it can be learned that at the time of the Emperor Valens there was among the Arians a peculiar sect that was called the Agnoetae. They had this name be-

73

74

75

cause they imagined that the Son, the Father's Word, knew all things, but that His received human nature is ignorant of many things. Gregory the Great wrote against them.

The divine and the human nature have this personal union with each other in the person of Christ and have the communion resulting from it (in deed and truth). For this reason, there is attributed to Christ (according to the flesh) what His flesh, according to its nature and essence, cannot be by itself. Apart from this union, His flesh cannot have these attributes: His flesh is a truly life-giving food and His blood a truly life-giving drink (John 6:55). The two hundred Fathers of the Council of Ephesus have testified that Christ's flesh is a life-giving flesh. Therefore, this man only, and no man besides, either in heaven or on earth, can say with truth, "Where two or three are gathered in My name, there am I among them" (Matthew 18:20). Also, "And behold, I am with you always, to the end of the age" (Matthew 28:20).

We do not understand these testimonies to mean that only Christ's divinity is present with us in the Christian Church and congregation, and that such presence does not apply to Christ according to His humanity in no way whatever. For in that way Peter, Paul, and all the saints in heaven—since divinity, which is everywhere present, dwells in them—would also be with us on earth. However, the Holy Scriptures say this only about Christ, and no other man. We hold that by these words the majesty of the man Christ is declared. Christ has received this majesty, according to His humanity, at the right hand of God's majesty and power. So also, according to His received human nature and with the same, He can be, and also is, present where He wants to be. He is present especially in His Church and congregation on earth as Mediator, Head, King, and High Priest. This

76

77

78

presence is not a part, or only one half of Him. Christ's entire person is present, to which both natures belong, the divine and the human—not only according to His divinity, but also according to, and with, His received human nature. He is our Brother (Hebrews 2:17), and we are flesh of His flesh and

79  bone of His bone (Genesis 2:23). He has instituted His Holy Supper for the certain assurance and confirmation of this, so that He will be with us, and dwell, work, and be effective in us also according to that nature from which He has flesh and blood.

80  Upon this firm foundation Dr. Luther, of blessed memory, has also written about Christ's majesty according to His human nature.

81  In the *Confession concerning Christ's Supper* he writes this about the person of Christ:

> Now, since He [Christ] is a man who is supernaturally one person with God, and apart from this man there is no God, it must follow that according to the third supernatural mode, He is and can be wherever God is and that everything is full of Christ through and through, even according to His humanity—not according to the first, corporeal, circumscribed mode, but according to the supernatural, divine
>
> 82  mode. Here you must take your stand and say that wherever Christ is according to His divinity, He is there as a natural, divine person and He is also naturally and personally there, as His conception in His mother's womb proves conclusively. For if He was the Son of God, He had to be in His mother's womb naturally and personally and become man. But if He is present naturally and personally wherever He is, then He must be man there, too, since He is not two separate persons but a single person. Wherever this person is, it is the single, indivisible person, and if you can say, "Here is God," then you must also say, "Christ the man is present too."
>
> And if you could show me one place where God is and not the man, then the person is already divided and I could at once say truthfully, "Here is God who is not man and has never become man." But no God like that 83 for me! For it would follow from this that space and place had separated the two natures from one another and thus had divided the person, even though death and all the devils had been unable to separate and tear them apart. This would leave me a poor sort 84 of Christ, if He were present only at one single place, as a divine and human person, and if at all other places He had to be nothing more than a mere isolated God and a divine person without the humanity. No, comrade, wherever you place God for me, you must also place the humanity for me. They simply will not let themselves be separated and divided from each other. He has become one person and does not separate the humanity from Himself. (LW 37:218–19)

85  In his *Treatise on the Last Words of David*, which Dr. Luther wrote shortly before his death, he says the following:

> According to the second, the temporal, human birth Christ was also given the eternal dominion of God, yet temporarily and not from eternity. For the human nature of Christ was not from eternity as His divine nature was. It is computed that Jesus, Mary's Son, is 1543 years old this year. But from the moment when deity and humanity

were united in one Person, the Man, Mary's Son, is and is called almighty, eternal God, who has eternal dominion, who has created all things and preserves them "through the communication of attributes" . . . , because He is one Person with the Godhead and is also very God. Christ refers to this in Matthew 11:27: "All things have been delivered to Me by My Father," and in Matthew 28:18: "All authority in heaven and on earth has been given to Me." To which "Me"? "To Me, Jesus of Nazareth, Mary's incarnate Son. I had this from My Father from eternity, before I became man, but when I became man, it was imparted to Me in time according to My human nature, and I kept it concealed until My resurrection and ascent into heaven, when it was to be manifested and glorified. Thus St. Paul declares in Romans 1:4, He was glorified, or "designated Son of God in power." John speaks of this as being "glorified" in chapter 7:39. (LW 15:293–94)

86    Similar testimonies are found in Dr. Luther's writings, but especially in the book *That These Words Still Stand Firm*, and in the *Confession concerning Christ's Supper*. To these writings, as well-grounded explanations of Christ's majesty at God's right hand, and of His testament, we have referred for the sake of brevity. We have referred to them in this article, as well as in the Holy Supper, as has been mentioned before.

87    When such majesty is denied to Christ according to His humanity, we regard it as a deadly error. For by this the very great consolation mentioned above is taken from Christians, which they have in the promise about the presence and dwelling with them of their Head, King, and High Priest. He has promised them that not only His mere divinity would be with them (which to us poor sinners is like a consuming fire on dry stubble). But Christ promised that He—He, the man who has spoken with them, who has experienced all tribulations in His received human nature, and who can therefore have sympathy with us, as with men and His brethren—He will be with us in all our troubles also according to the nature by which He is our brother and we are flesh of His flesh.

## NEGATIVE STATEMENTS

88    We unanimously reject and condemn, with mouth and heart, all errors not in accordance with the teaching presented. These are contrary to the prophetic and apostolic Scriptures, the pure symbols, and our Christian Augsburg Confession:

89    1. When it is believed or taught by anyone that on account of the personal union the human nature is mingled with the divine or is changed into it.

90    2. The human nature in Christ is everywhere present in the same way as the divinity, as an infinite essence, by essential power and property of its nature.

91    3. The human nature in Christ has become equal to and like the divine nature in its substance and essence or in its essential properties.

92    4. Christ's humanity is locally extended in all places of heaven and earth. This should not be attributed even to the divinity. But Christ—by His divine omnipotence—wherever He will, can be present with His body, which He has placed at the right hand of God's majesty and power. This is especially the case where He has, in His Word, promised His presence (as in the Holy Supper). His omnipotence and wisdom can well accomplish this without change or abolition of His true human nature.

93     5. Christ's mere human nature has suffered for us and redeemed us, with which God's Son is said to have had no communion whatever in suffering.

94     6. Christ is present with us on earth in the Word preached and in the right use of the holy Sacraments only according to His divinity. This presence of Christ does not in any way apply to His received human nature.

95     7. The received human nature in Christ has (in deed and truth) no communion whatever with the divine power, might, wisdom, majesty, and glory, but has in common only the mere title and name.

96     These errors, and all that are contrary and opposed to the doctrine presented above, we reject and condemn as contrary to God's pure Word, the Scriptures of the holy prophets and apostles, and our Christian faith and confession. Since in the Holy Scriptures Christ is called a mystery upon which all heretics dash their heads, we admonish all Christians not to arrogantly indulge their reason in crafty investigations about such mysteries. With the beloved apostles, they should simply believe. They should close the eyes of their reason and bring their understanding into captivity to the obedience of Christ (2 Corinthians 10:5), and rejoice without ceasing in the fact that our flesh and blood is placed so high at the right hand of God's majesty and almighty power. In this way we will certainly find constant consolation in every difficulty and remain well guarded against deadly error.

# IX. THE DESCENT OF CHRIST TO HELL

For an annotation on this article, see p. 513. (See also Apostles' Creed; Nicene Creed; Athanasian Creed; SA I; SC II; LC II; FC Ep IX.)

Even in the Ancient Christian teachers of the Church, as well as among some of our teachers, different explanations of the article about Christ's descent to hell are found. Therefore, we abide in the simplicity of our Christian faith. Dr. Luther has pointed us to this in a sermon about Christ's descent to hell, which he delivered in the castle at Torgau in the year 1533. In the Creed we confess, "I believe . . . in Jesus Christ, His only Son, our Lord, who . . . was crucified, died and was buried. He descended into hell." In this Confession Christ's burial and descent to hell are distinguished as different articles. We simply 1 believe that the entire person (God and man) descended into hell after the burial, conquered the devil, destroyed hell's power, and took from the devil all his might. We should 2 not, however, trouble ourselves with high and difficult thoughts about how this happened. With our reason and our five senses this article can be understood as little as the preceding one about how Christ is placed at the right hand of God's almighty power and majesty. We are simply to believe it and cling to the Word. So we hold to the substance and consolation that neither hell nor the devil can take captive or injure us and all who believe in Christ.

# X. CHURCH PRACTICES

Called *Adiaphora*, or Indifferent Things

For an annotation on this article, see p. 514. (See also AC XIV; AC XXIV; AC XXVI; AC XXVIII; Ap XIV; Ap XV; Ap XXIV; Ap XXVIII; SA III XV; FC Ep X.)

## STATUS OF THE CONTROVERSY

1] Some ceremonies and Church practices are neither commanded nor forbidden in God's Word, but are introduced into the

Church with good intention, for the sake of good order and proper custom, or otherwise to maintain Christian discipline. A dispute has arisen among some theologians of the Augsburg Confession about these practices.

2 One side holds that even during persecution and in a matter of confession, when the enemies of the Gospel are not in agreement with us in doctrine, some ceremonies (that are adiaphora in themselves, and are neither commanded nor forbidden by God) may be reestablished in compliance with the adversaries' pressure and demand without damage to our conscience. So in such adiaphora (or matters of indifference), we may compromise with our adversaries.

3 The other side contended that during persecution, in a matter of confession, especially when it is the adversaries' goal by force and compulsion, or in a sly manner, to suppress the pure doctrine, and gradually to reintroduce their false doctrine into our churches, this can in no way be allowed even in adiaphora without damage to conscience and harm to the divine truth.

4 To explain this controversy, and by God's grace finally to settle it, we present to the Christian reader this simple statement about the matter:

## AFFIRMATIVE STATEMENTS

5 Under the title and excuse of outward adiaphora, things are proposed that are in principle contrary to God's Word, although painted another color. These ceremonies are not to be regarded as adiaphora, in which one is free to do as he wants. They must be avoided as things prohibited by God. In a similar way in such a situation ceremonies should not be regarded as genuine free adiaphora, or matters of indifference. This is because they make a show or pretend that our religion and that of the papists are not far apart in order to avoid persecution, or they pretend that the papist's ceremonies are not at least highly offensive to us. When ceremonies are intended for this purpose, and are required and received (as though through them contrary religions are reconciled and became one body), we cannot regard them as adiaphora. When returning to the papacy and departing from the Gospel's pure doctrine and true religion should happen or gradually follow from such ceremonies, we cannot regard them as adiaphora.

6 For in this case what Paul writes shall and must win out:

> Do not be unequally yoked with unbelievers. For what partnership has righteousness with lawlessness? Or what fellowship has light with darkness? . . . Therefore go out from their midst, and be separate from them. (2 Corinthians 6:14–17)

7 Likewise, when there are useless, foolish displays that are not profitable for good order, Christian discipline, or evangelical practice in the Church, these also are not genuine adiaphora, or matters of indifference.

8 Regarding genuine adiaphora, or matters of indifference (as explained before), we believe, teach, and confess the following: such ceremonies, in and of themselves, are not worship of God, nor any part of it. They must be properly distinguished from ceremonies that are. As it is written, "in vain do they worship Me, teaching as doctrines the commandments of men"(Matthew 15:9).

9 We believe, teach, and confess that the community of God in every place and every time has, according to its circumstances, the good right, power, and authority to change and decrease or increase ceremonies that are truly adiaphora. They should do this thoughtfully and without giving offense, in an orderly and appropriate way, whenever it

is considered most profitable, most beneficial, and best for good order, Christian discipline, and the Church's edification. Furthermore, we can yield and give in with a good conscience to the weak in faith in such outward adiaphora. Paul teaches this in Romans 14 and proves it by his example (see Acts 16:3; 21:26; 1 Corinthians 9:19).

10    We also believe, teach, and confess that at a time of confession, when the enemies of God's Word want to suppress the pure doctrine of the Holy Gospel, God's entire church, indeed, every single Christian, but especially the ministers of the Word, as the directors of the community of God [Latin: God's church], is bound by God's Word to confess the doctrine freely and openly. They are bound to confess every aspect of pure religion, not only in words, but also in works and actions. In this case, even in adiaphora, they must not yield to the adversaries or permit these adiaphora to be forced on them by their enemies, whether by violence or cunning, to the detriment of the true worship of God and the introduction and sanction of idolatry. For it is written:

11

> For freedom Christ has set us free; stand firm therefore, and do not submit again to a yoke of slavery. (Galatians 5:1)

> Yet because of false brothers secretly brought in—who slipped in to spy out our freedom that we have in Christ Jesus, so that they might bring us into slavery—to them we did not yield in submission even for a moment, so that the truth of the gospel might be preserved for you. (Galatians 2:4–5)

12    In this place Paul speaks about circumcision, which at that time had become an adiaphoron (1 Corinthians 7:18–19). At other times circumcision was observed by Paul (in Christian and spiritual freedom, Acts 16:3). The false apostles pushed circumcision (Acts 15:1) in order to establish their false doctrine that the works of the Law were necessary for righteousness and salvation (2 Corinthians 11:13). They misused circumcision to confirm their error in people's minds. Therefore, Paul says that he would not yield even for an hour, in order that the truth of the Gospel might continue unimpaired (Galatians 2:5).

Paul yields and gives way to the weak    13
concerning food and the observance of times or days (Romans 14:6). But to the false apostles, who wanted to impose these on the conscience as *necessary things*, he will not yield even in matters that are adiaphora. "Therefore let no one pass judgment on you in questions of food and drink, or with regard to a festival or a new moon or a Sabbath" (Colossians 2:16). When Peter and Barnabas yielded somewhat in such an emergency, Paul openly rebukes them according to the truth of the Gospel as people who were not acting right in this matter (Galatians 2:11–14).

This case is no longer a question about    14
outward matters of indifference, which in their nature and essence are free. They cannot produce a command or prohibition that they must or must not be used. The case presented by Paul is a question, in the first place, about the outstanding article of our Christian faith. For the apostle testifies, "so that the truth of the gospel might be preserved for you" (Galatians 2:5). The Gospel is obscured and perverted by such compulsion or command, because such adiaphora are publicly required for the approval of false doctrine, superstition, and idolatry, and for the suppression of pure doctrine and Christian liberty, or at least are abused for this purpose by the adversaries and are viewed this way.

15    The article about Christian freedom is at stake here. The Holy Spirit, through the holy apostle's mouth, sincerely told His Church to preserve this article, as we have just heard. As soon as Christian freedom is weakened and human traditions are forced on the Church with coercion, as though it were wrong and a sin to omit them, the way is already prepared for idolatry. In this way, human traditions are multiplied and regarded as a divine worship, not only equal to God's ordinances, but even placed above them.

16    Furthermore, idolaters are confirmed in their idolatry by such yielding and conforming in outward things, where there has not previously been Christian unity in doctrine. On the other hand, true believers are grieved, offended, and weakened in their faith. Every Christian, for the sake of his soul's welfare and salvation, is bound to avoid both of these, as it is written:

Woe to the world for temptations to sin!" (Matthew 18:7)

The Call of Isaiah

But whoever causes one of these little ones who believe in Me to sin, it would be better for him to have a great millstone fastened around his neck and to be drowned in the depth of the sea. (Matthew 18:6)

17    But what Christ says is to be especially remembered:

So everyone who acknowledges Me before men, I also will acknowledge before My Father who is in heaven. (Matthew 10:32)

18    However, this has always and everywhere been the faith and confession about such matters, by the chief teachers of the Augsburg Confession. We are following in their footsteps and we intend to persevere in their confession by God's grace. Their confession is shown by the following testimonies drawn from the Smalcald Articles, which were composed and signed in the year 1537:

### From the Smalcald Articles (1537)

19    The Smalcald Articles (On the Church) speak about this as follows:

We do not agree with them [the papal bishops] that they are the Church. They are not the Church. Nor will we listen to those things that, under the name of Church, they command or forbid. Thank God, today a seven-year-old child knows what the Church is, namely, the holy believers and lambs who hear the voice of their Shepherd (John 10:11–16). (SA III XII 1–2)

And shortly before this ("Ordination and the Call"):

If the bishops would be true bishops and would devote themselves to the Church and the Gospel, we might grant them to ordain and confirm us and our preachers. This would be for the sake of love and unity, but not because it was necessary. However, they would have to give up all comedies and spectacular display of unchristian parade and pomp. But they do not even want to be true bishops, but worldly lords and princes, who will neither preach, nor teach, nor baptize, nor administer the Lord's Supper, nor perform any work or office of the Church. Furthermore, they persecute and condemn those who do discharge these functions, having been called to do so. So the Church should not be deprived of ministers because of the bishops. (SA III X 1–2)

20    In the article "The Papacy," the Smalcald Articles say

Therefore, just as we cannot worship the devil himself as Lord and God, so we cannot endure his apostle—the pope or Antichrist—in his rule as head or lord. For what his papal government really consists of . . . is to lie and kill and destroy body and soul eternally. (SA II IV 14)

21    In the Treatise on the Power and Primacy of the Pope, which is appended to the Smalcald Articles and was also signed by the theologians present with their own hands, are these words:

Do not let them burden the Church with traditions. Do not let the authority of anyone prevail more than God's Word. (Tr 11)

22    And shortly afterward:

This being the case, all Christians should beware of participating in the godless doctrine, blasphemies, and unjust cruelty of the pope. They should desert and condemn the pope with his followers as the kingdom of

Antichrist, just as Christ has commanded, "Beware of false prophets" (Matthew 7:15). Paul commands that godless teachers should be avoided and condemned as cursed (Galatians 1:8; Titus 3:10). And he says, "Do not be unequally yoked with unbelievers. . . . What fellowship has light with darkness?" (2 Corinthians 6:14). (Tr 41)

23 To want to separate one's self from so many lands and nations and to profess a separate doctrine is a serious matter. But here stands God's command that everyone should beware and not agree with those who hold false doctrine or who think of supporting it through cruelty.

24 Dr. Luther, too, has fully instructed God's Church in a special treatise about what should be thought of ceremonies in general, and especially of adiaphora (*A Report to a Good Friend on Both Kinds in the Sacrament, in Regard to the Mandate of the Bishop of Meissen* [1528] [WA 26:560–618]). This was also done in 1530, and can be seen in several of his letters.

25 From this explanation everyone can understand what every Christian church and every Christian person are to do or to leave undone, without injury to conscience, with respect to adiaphora. This applies most of all to preachers. In this way God may not be angered, love may not be injured, the enemies of God's Word may not be strengthened, nor the weak in faith offended.

### NEGATIVE STATEMENTS

26 1. We reject and condemn as wrong when human rules in themselves are regarded as a service or part of God's service.

27 2. We also reject and condemn as wrong cases when these rules are forced on God's Church as necessary by coercion.

28 3. We also reject and condemn as wrong

the opinion of those who hold that during persecution we may comply with the enemies of the Holy Gospel (which leads to the detriment of the truth) by restoring such adiaphora, or come to an agreement with them.

29 4. We likewise regard it as a sin that deserves to be rebuked when during persecution anything is done that is contrary and opposed to the Christian confession. This includes indifferent matters or doctrine and what otherwise applies to religion, for the sake of the enemies of the Gospel, in word and act.

30 5. We also reject and condemn abolishing these adiaphora as though the community of God [Latin: the churches of God] at any time and place in any land was not free to use one or more ceremonies in Christian liberty, according to its circumstances, as may be most useful to the Church.

31 So the churches will not condemn one another because of differences in ceremonies when, in Christian liberty, one has less or more of them. This applies as long as they are otherwise agreed with one another in the doctrine and all its articles, and also in the right use of the holy Sacraments. This fits the well-known saying, "Disagreement in fasting does not destroy agreement in the faith."

# XI. GOD'S ETERNAL FOREKNOWLEDGE AND ELECTION

For an annotation on this article, see pp. 515–16. (See also SC II; FC Ep XI.)

### PREVENTING DISAGREEMENT

1 Among the theologians of the Augsburg Confession there has not yet arisen any public dispute at all about the eternal election of God's children that has caused offense and

has become widespread. Yet this article has been brought into very painful controversy in other places. Even among our theologians there has been some agitation about it. Furthermore, the theologians did not always use the same expressions. By the help of divine grace, we want to prevent disagreement and separation in the future among our successors on account of this teaching. Therefore, as much as in us lies, we want to present an explanation of this teaching here. Then everyone may know what our unanimous doctrine, faith, and confession is also on this

2 article. For the teaching about this article— if taught from, and according to, the pattern of the divine Word—neither can nor should be regarded as useless or unnecessary, much less as offensive or harmful. For the Holy Scriptures not just in one place or randomly, but in many places, thoroughly discuss

3 and explain this teaching. Furthermore, we should not neglect or reject the teaching of the divine Word because of abuse or misunderstanding. But for that very reason, the true meaning should and must be explained from the foundation of the Scriptures in order to turn away all abuse and misunderstanding. The plain summary and substance of this article are presented in the following points:

## AFFIRMATIVE STATEMENTS

4      First, the distinction between *God's eternal foreknowledge* and the *eternal election of His children to eternal salvation* is to be made carefully. Foreknowledge or prevision means that God sees and knows everything before it happens. This is called *God's foreknowledge*, which extends over all creatures, good and bad. In other words, He foresees and foreknows everything that is or will be, that is happening or will happen, whether it is good or bad. For all things, whether they are past or future, are clear and present before God. This is written in Matthew 10:29:

> Are not two sparrows sold for a penny? And not one of them will fall to the ground apart from your Father.

> Your eyes saw my unformed substance; in Your book were written, every one of them, the days that were formed for me, when as yet there were none of them. (Psalm 139:16)

> I know your sitting down and your going out and coming in, and your raging against Me. (Isaiah 37:28)

*God's eternal election*, or *predestination*, 5 means God's preordaining to salvation. It does not include both the godly and the wicked, but only God's children, who were elected and ordained to eternal life before the world's foundation was laid. As Paul says in Ephesians 1:4–5, "He chose us in Him. . . . He predestined us for adoption through Jesus Christ."

*God's foreknowledge* foresees and foreknows 6 what is evil, yet not in the sense that it is God's gracious will that evil should happen. Everything that the perverse, wicked will of the devil and of people wants and desires to try and do, God sees and knows before it happens. His foreknowledge sees its order also in wicked acts or works, since a limit and measure is fixed by God for the evil that God does not will. He limits how far it should go, how long it should last, and when and how He will hinder and punish it. God the Lord rules over all (Psalm 103:19) of this so that it must flow to the glory of the divine name and to the salvation of His elect, and for that reason the godless must be astonished (1 Corinthians 2:7–8).

The beginning and cause of evil is not 7 God's foreknowledge. (For God does not create and do evil, neither does He help or promote it.) The cause of this evil is the wicked, perverse will of the devil and of people, as it is written in Hosea 13:9, "He destroys you, O Israel, for you are against Me, against your helper." Also, "For You are not a God who delights in wickedness" (Psalm 5:4).

8  God's eternal election does not just foresee and foreknow the salvation of the elect. From God's gracious will and pleasure in Christ Jesus, election is a cause that gains, works, helps, and promotes our salvation and what belongs to it. Our salvation is so founded on it that "the gates of hell shall not prevail against it" (Matthew 16:18), as is written in John 10:28, "no one will snatch [My sheep] out of My hand." And again, "and as many as were appointed to eternal life believed" (Acts 13:48).

This eternal election or ordination of  9  God to eternal life must not be considered in God's secret, mysterious counsel in a simpleminded way. It is not as though election included nothing further, or nothing more belonged to it, or nothing more were to be considered in it, than that God foresaw who and how many were to be saved and who and how many were to be damned. Nor should we think that He only held a sort of military muster, such as, "This one shall be saved, that one shall be damned; this one shall remain steadfast in faith to the end, that one shall not remain steadfast."

From this notion many get and imagine  10  strange, dangerous, and deadly thoughts. These cause and strengthen either self-confidence and lack of repentance or hopelessness and despair. So people fall into troublesome

Joseph Sold into Slavery

thoughts, and say, "Before the foundation of the world was laid" (Ephesians 1:4), God has foreknown His elect to salvation. And God's foreknowledge cannot fail or be hindered or changed by anyone (Isaiah 14:27; Romans 9:19). In view of this, if I am elected to salvation, nothing can hurt me, even if I perform all sorts of shameful sins without repentance, have no regard for the Word and Sacraments, concern myself neither with repentance, faith, prayer, or godliness. I will and must still be saved, because God's foreknowledge must come to pass. If, however, I am not foreknown, nothing helps me anyway, even though I busy myself with the Word, repent, believe, and so on. For I cannot hinder or change God's foreknowledge."

11 In fact, even when godly hearts have repentance, faith, and good intentions to live by God's grace in a godly way, thoughts like these arise: "If you are not foreknown from eternity to salvation, your every effort and entire labor is no help." This happens especially when they see their weakness and the examples of those who have not persevered, but have fallen away again.

12 Against this false delusion and thought we should set up the following clear argument, which is sure and cannot fail: All Scripture is inspired by God. It is not for self-confidence and lack of repentance, but "for reproof, for correction, and for training in righteousness" (2 Timothy 3:16). Also, everything in God's Word has been written for us, not so that we should be driven to despair by it, but so that "through the encouragement of the Scriptures we might have hope" (Romans 15:4). Therefore, there is no question that lack of repentance or despair should not in any way be caused or strengthened by the sound sense or right use of this teaching about God's eternal foreknowledge. The Scrip-

tures teach this doctrine only to direct us to the Word (Ephesians 1:13; 1 Corinthians 1:7), to encourage repentance (2 Timothy 3:16) and godliness (Ephesians 1:14; John 15:3), and to strengthen faith and assure us of our salvation (Ephesians 1:13; John 10:27–30; 2 Thessalonians 2:13–14).

13 If we want to think or speak correctly and usefully about eternal election, or the predestination or preordination of God's children to eternal life, we should make it our custom to avoid speculating about God's bare, secret, concealed, mysterious foreknowledge. Instead, we should think or speak about how God's counsel, purpose, and ordination in Christ Jesus—who is the true Book of Life—is revealed to us through the Word. In other 14 words, the entire teaching about God's purpose, counsel, will, and ordination belongs to our redemption, call, justification, and salvation. They should be treated together the way Paul treats them and has explained this article (Romans 8:29–30; Ephesians 1:4–10) and as Christ treated it in the parable of Matthew 22:1–14; namely, that God in His purpose and counsel ordained the following:

15 1. The human race is truly redeemed and reconciled with God through Christ. By His faultless obedience, suffering, and death, Christ merited for us the righteousness that helps us before God and also merits eternal life.

16 2. Such merit and benefits of Christ are presented, offered, and distributed to us through His Word and Sacraments.

17 3. By His Holy Spirit, through the Word, when it is preached, heard, and pondered, Christ will be effective and active in us, will convert hearts to true repentance and preserve them in the true faith.

18 4. The Spirit will justify all those who in true repentance receive Christ by a true faith. He will receive them into grace, the adoption

of sons, and the inheritance of eternal life (Galatians 3:19).

19    5. He will also sanctify in love those who are justified, as St. Paul says (Ephesians 1:4).

20    6. He also will protect them in their great weakness against the devil, the world, and the flesh. He will rule and lead them in His ways (Deuteronomy 8:6), raise them again when they stumble (Proverbs 4:11–12), comfort them under the cross and in temptation (2 Corinthians 1:3–5), and preserve them for life eternal (John 12:25).

21    7. He will also strengthen, increase, and support to the end the good work that He has begun in them (Philippians 1:6), if they cling to God's Word, pray diligently, abide in God's goodness, and faithfully use the gifts they received (Matthew 25:14–30).

22    8. Finally, He will eternally save and glorify in life eternal those whom He has elected, called, and justified.

23    God has prepared salvation not only in general in this counsel, purpose, and ordination. In grace He has considered and chosen to salvation each and every one of the elect who are to be saved through Christ. He has also ordained that in the way just mentioned He will, by His grace, gifts, and efficacy, bring them to salvation. He will aid, promote, strengthen, and preserve them.

24    All this, according to the Scriptures, is included in the teaching about God's eternal election to adoption and eternal salvation, and is to be understood by it. It must never be excluded or omitted when we speak about God's purpose, predestination, election, and ordination to salvation. When our thoughts about this article are formed according to the Scriptures in this way, we can simply adapt ourselves to it by God's grace.

25    The following issue also belongs to the further explanation and saving use of the teaching about God's predestination to salvation: Only the elect, whose names are written in the book of life (Revelation 21:27), are saved. Therefore, how can we know, or why and how can we perceive who the elect are and who can and should receive this teaching for comfort?

26    In this matter we should not judge according to our reason, or according to the Law or from any outward appearance. Neither should we attempt to investigate the secret, concealed depth of divine predestination. Instead, we should listen to God's revealed will. For He has made "known to us the mystery of His will" (Ephesians 1:9) and made it clear through Christ so that it might be preached (2 Timothy 1:9).

27    This is revealed to us in the way Paul says "those whom He predestined [elected and foreordained] He also called" (Romans 8:30). God does not call without means, but through the Word. For He has commanded "that repentance and forgiveness of sins should be proclaimed in His name" (Luke 24:47). St. Paul also testifies in a similar way when he writes, "Therefore, we are ambassadors for Christ, God making His appeal through us. We implore you on behalf of Christ, be reconciled to God" (2 Corinthians 5:20). The King calls the guests that He wants to have at His Son's wedding through the ministers He sends out (Matthew 22:2–14). He sends some at the first and some at the second, third, sixth, ninth, and even at the eleventh hour (Matthew 20:3–6).

28    If we want to think about our eternal election to salvation helpfully, we must in every way hold strongly and firmly to this truth: just as the preaching of repentance is universal, so also the promise of the Gospel is universal, that is, it belongs to all people. For this reason Christ has given these commands:

Repentance and forgiveness of sins should be proclaimed in His name to all nations. (Luke 24:47)

For God so loved the world, that He gave His only Son. (John 3:16)

Behold, the Lamb of God, who takes away the sin of the world! (John 1:29)

The bread that I will give for the life of the world is My flesh. (John 6:51)

The blood of Jesus His Son cleanses us from all sin. (1 John 1:7)

[Jesus] is the propitiation for our sins, and not for ours only but also for the sins of the whole world. (1 John 2:2)

Come to Me, all who labor and are heavy laden, and I will give you rest. (Matthew 11:28)

For God has consigned all to disobedience, that He may have mercy on all. (Romans 11:32)

Not wishing that any should perish, but that all should reach repentance. (2 Peter 3:9)

The same Lord is Lord of all, bestowing His riches on all who call on Him. (Romans 10:12)

The righteousness of God through faith in Jesus Christ [is] for all who believe. (Romans 3:22)

For this is the will of My Father, that everyone who looks on the Son and believes in Him should have eternal life. (John 6:40)

It is Christ's command that this promise of the Gospel also should be offered to everyone in common to whom repentance is preached (Luke 24:47; Mark 16:15).

29   We should not think of this call of God, which is made through the preaching of the Word, as a juggler's act. But we should know that God reveals His will by this call. He will work through the Word in the people He calls, so that they may be enlightened, converted, and saved. For the Word, by which we are called, is a ministry of the Spirit, which gives the Spirit, or by which the Spirit is given (2 Corinthians 3:8). It is God's power unto salvation (Romans 1:16). The Holy Spirit wants to be effective through the Word, and to strengthen and give power and ability. It is God's will that we should receive the Word, believe it, and obey it.

30   For this reason the elect are described as follows: "My sheep hear My voice, and I know them, and they follow Me. I give them eternal life" (John 10:27–28). "In Him we have obtained an inheritance, having been predestined according to the purpose of Him who works all things according to the counsel of His will" (Ephesians 1:11). They hear the Gospel, believe in Christ, pray and give thanks, are sanctified in love, have hope, patience, and comfort under the cross. (See Ephesians 1:13; Romans 8:25.) Although all this is very weak in them, they hunger and thirst for righteousness (Matthew 5:6).

31   "The Spirit Himself bears witness with our spirit that we are children of God. . . . The Spirit helps us in our weakness. For we do not know what to pray for as we ought, but the Spirit Himself intercedes for us with groanings too deep for words" (Romans 8:16–26).

32   Holy Scripture also testifies that God, who has called us, is faithful. So when He has begun the good work in us, He will also preserve it to the end and perfect it, if we ourselves do not turn from Him, but firmly hold on to the work begun to the end. He has promised His grace for this very purpose. (See 1 Corinthians 1:9; Philippians 1:6; 1 Peter 5:10; 2 Peter 3:9; Hebrews 3:2.)

33    We should concern ourselves with this revealed will of God. We should follow and diligently think about it. Through the Word, by which He calls us, the Holy Spirit bestows grace, power, and ability for this purpose. We should not sound the depths of God's hidden predestination, as it is written in Luke 13:23–24, where one asks, "Lord, will those who are saved be few?" and Christ answers, "Strive to enter through the narrow door." So Luther says:

> But you had better follow the order of this epistle [of Romans]. Worry first about Christ and the gospel, that you may recognize your sin and His grace. Then fight your sin, as the first eight chapters here have taught. Then, when you have reached the eighth chapter, and are under the cross and suffering, this will teach you correctly of predestination in chapters 9, 10, and 11, and how comforting it is. (*Preface to the Epistle of St. Paul to the Romans* [1546]; LW 35:378)

34    "Many are called, but few are chosen" (Matthew 22:14). This does not stem from the fact that God's call, which is made through the Word, has the following meaning. It is not as though God said: "Outwardly, through the Word, I indeed call all of you to My kingdom, everyone to whom I give My Word. However, in My heart I do not mean this for everyone, but only for a few. For it is My will that most of those whom I call through the Word shall not be enlightened or converted. Instead, they shall be and remain damned, even though I explain Myself differently to them through the Word, in the call."

35    For this would be to assign contradictory wills to God. In this way it would be taught that God, who surely is Eternal Truth, contradicts Himself, when, in fact, God punishes such wickedness in people, when a person states one purpose and thinks and means another in the heart (Psalm 5:9; 12:2–4). By this notion the necessary basis of comfort is made completely uncertain and void. For we are daily reminded and encouraged that we are to learn and conclude what His will toward us is only from God's Word, through which He works with us and calls us. We should believe and not doubt what it affirms to us and promises.

36    For this reason Christ causes the promise of the Gospel not only to be offered in general, but He also seals it through the Sacraments. He attaches them like seals of the promise, and by them He confirms the Gospel to every believer in particular.

37    On this account, as the Augsburg Confession in Article XI says, we also keep private Absolution. We teach that it is God's command that we believe such Absolution. We should regard it as sure that, when we believe the word of Absolution, we are as truly reconciled to God as though we had heard a voice from heaven (John 12:28–30), as the Apology also explains this article. This consolation would be entirely taken from us if we did not understand God's will toward us from the call that is made through the Word and through the Sacraments.

38    The Holy Spirit certainly wants to be present with the Word preached, heard, and considered, and He wants to be effective and work through it. Yet this foundation would be overthrown and taken from us if we misunderstand election. Therefore, the meaning is not at all like the one referred to above, that the elect are to be the sort of people who despise God's Word, thrust it from them, blaspheme and persecute it (Matthew 22:5–6; Acts 13:46); or, when they hear it, harden their hearts (Hebrews 4:2, 7), resist the Holy Spirit (Acts 7:51), persevere in sins without repentance (Luke 14:18–20), do not truly be-

lieve in Christ (Mark 16:16), only make an outward show (Matthew 7:22; 22:12), or seek other ways to righteousness and salvation outside of Christ (Romans 9:31). Further-40 more, God has ordained in His counsel that the Holy Spirit should call, enlighten, and convert the elect through the Word (Romans 10:17). He will justify and save all those who by true faith receive Christ. In the same way, He also determined in His counsel that He will harden (Romans 9:18), reprobate, and condemn those who are called through the Word if they reject the Word and resist the Holy Spirit (Acts 7:51). This is true even though the Spirit wants to be effective and work in them through the Word and perse-vere through the Word. In this way "many are called, but few are chosen" (Matthew 22:14).

41    Few receive the Word and follow it. Most despise the Word and will not come to the wedding (Matthew 22:3–6). The cause for this contempt for the Word is not God's fore-knowledge, but the perverse human will. The human will rejects or perverts the means and instrument of the Holy Spirit, which God of-fers it through the call. It resists the Holy Spirit, who wants to be effective, and who works through the Word, as Christ says: "How often would I have gathered your chil-dren together as a hen gathers her brood under her wings, and you would not!" (Matthew 23:37).

42    Many "hear the word, receive it with joy. But these have no root; they believe for a while, and in time of testing fall away" (Luke 8:13). The reason is not that God was un-willing to grant grace for perseverance to those in whom He "began a good work," for that is contrary to St. Paul (Philippians 1:6). The reason is that they willfully turn away again from the holy commandment, grieve and embitter the Holy Spirit, involve them-selves again in the world's filth, and redeco-rate their hearts as homes for the devil. For them their last situation is worse than the first. (See 2 Peter 2:10–20; Ephesians 4:30; Hebrews 10:26; Luke 11:24–26.)

This is how much of the mystery of pre-43 destination is revealed to us in God's Word. If we abide by this teaching and cling to it, it is a very useful, saving, consoling teaching. It establishes very effectively the article that we are justified and saved without any works and merits of ours, purely out of grace alone, for Christ's sake. Before the time of the world, before we existed, yes, even before the foundation of the world was laid— when, of course, we could do nothing good—we were chosen by grace in Christ to salvation, according to God's purpose (Ro-mans 9:11; 2 Timothy 1:9). Furthermore, all 44 opinions and erroneous teachings about the powers of our natural will are overthrown by this. God in His counsel, before the time of the world, decided and ordained that He Himself would produce and work in us by His Holy Spirit's power. Through the Word, He would do everything that belongs to our conversion.

This doctrine also provides the excellent, 45 glorious consolation that God was greatly concerned about the conversion, righteous-ness, and salvation of every Christian. He so faithfully provided for it that even before the foundation of the world was laid, He consid-ered it, and in His purpose ordained how He would bring me to salvation and preserve me in salvation. He wanted to secure my salva-46 tion so well and so certainly, since through the weakness and wickedness of our flesh sal-vation could easily be lost from our hands, or through the devil's and the world's craft and might it could be snatched and taken from us. Therefore, He ordained in His eternal purpose what cannot fail or be overthrown. He placed salvation for safekeeping in the almighty hand of our Savior, Jesus Christ, from which no one can snatch us (John 10:28). Therefore, Paul asks in Romans, because we "are called according to His purpose" (8:28), who "will be able to separate us from the love of God in Christ Jesus our Lord"? (8:39).

47

48    Furthermore, this doctrine provides glorious consolation under the cross and amid temptations. In other words, God in His counsel, before the time of the world, determined and decreed that He would assist us in all distresses. He determined to grant patience, give consolation, nourish and encourage hope, and produce an outcome for us

49    that would contribute to our salvation. Also, Paul teaches this in a very consoling way. He explains that God in His purpose has ordained before the time of the world by what crosses and sufferings He would conform every one of His elect to the image of His Son. His cross shall and must work together for good for everyone, because they are called according to God's purpose. Therefore, Paul has concluded that it is certain and beyond doubt that neither "tribulation, or distress," neither "death nor life," or other such things "will be able to separate us from the love of God in Christ Jesus our Lord." (See Romans 8:28, 29, 35, 38, 39.)

50    This article provides a glorious testimony that God's Church will exist and abide in opposition to all the gates of hell (Matthew 16:18). Likewise, it teaches what God's true Church is, so that we may not be offended by the great authority of the false church (Romans 9:24–25).

51    Powerful rebukes and warnings are taken from this article, such as these:

> [They] rejected the purpose of God for themselves. (Luke 7:30)
>
> For I tell you, none of those men who were invited shall taste my banquet. (Luke 14:24)
>
> Many are called, but few are chosen. (Matthew 20:14)
>
> He who has ears to hear, let him hear. (Luke 8:8)
>
> Take care then how you hear. (Luke 8:18)

So the teaching about this article can be used for our benefit, comfort, and salvation.

52    But a distinction must be made with special care between what is clearly revealed about election in God's Word and what is not revealed. For, in addition to what has been revealed in Christ about this (which we have spoken about up to this point), God has kept secret and concealed much about this mystery. He reserved it for His wisdom and knowledge alone. We should not investigate this, indulge our thoughts in this matter, draw conclusions, or inquire curiously. Instead, we should cling to the revealed Word. This warning is most urgently needed.

53    Our curiosity always has greater pleasure in giving itself to these matters than with what God has revealed to us about this matter in His Word. We cannot harmonize God's revelation with our reason, which we have not been commanded to do anyway.

54    There is no doubt that God foresaw before the time of the world, and still knows, exactly, which people who are called will believe and which will not believe. He also knows which of the converted will persevere and which will not persevere. He knows which will return after a fall and which will fall into stubbornness. He also knows the number of how many there are of these on either side. Beyond all doubt this is perfectly known to God. However, God has reserved

55    this mystery for His wisdom. He has revealed nothing to us about it in His Word,

much less commanded us to investigate it with our thoughts. Instead, He has seriously discouraged us from that (Romans 11:33–35). Therefore, we should not reason in our thoughts, draw conclusions, or inquire curiously into these matters, but we should cling to His revealed Word, to which He points us.

56    Without any doubt God also knows and has determined for everyone the time and hour of his call and conversion. But this time has not been revealed to us. Therefore, we have the command always to keep proclaiming the Word, entrusting the time and hour of conversion to God (Acts 1:7).

57    We see that God gives His Word at one place, but not at another. He removes it from one place and allows it to remain at another. Also, one person is hardened, blinded, given over to a depraved mind, while another, who is indeed in the same guilt, is converted again, and so on. In these and similar questions Paul (Romans 11:22–24) fixes a certain

58    limit to show us how far we should go. In part, we should recognize God's judgment. They are well-deserved penalties for sins when God punishes a land or nation for despising His Word so that the punishment extends also to their descendants, as is seen

59    among the Jewish people (Exodus 20:5). By these punishments, in some lands and persons, God shows His severity to those who are His in order to point out what we all would have well deserved and would be worthy and worth. For we act wickedly in opposition to God's Word. We often grieve the Holy Spirit terribly (Ephesians 4:30). God shows His punishment in order that we may live in fear of Him and acknowledge and praise His goodness, to the exclusion of, and contrary to, our merit in and with us. He gives His Word to us and leaves it, and He does not harden and reject us.

Because our nature has been corrupted    60 by sin, and is worthy of and subject to God's wrath and condemnation, God does not owe us the Word, the Spirit, or grace. When He graciously bestows these gifts, we often thrust them from us and make ourselves unworthy of everlasting life (Acts 13:46). Therefore, He displays His righteous, well-deserved judgment in some countries, nations, and persons. And when we are placed alongside of them and compared with them, we may learn to recognize and praise God's pure, unmerited grace in the vessels of mercy (Romans 9:23) more diligently.

No injustice is done to those who are    61 punished and receive the wages of their sins. But to the rest—to those whom God gives and preserves His Word, by which people are enlightened, converted, and preserved—God commends His pure grace and mercy, without their merit.

When we get this far in this article, we remain    62 on the right way, as it is written in Hosea 13:9, "He destroys you, O Israel, for you are against Me, against your helper."

Regarding the things in this dispute that    63 would soar too high and beyond these limits, we should, with Paul, place a finger on our lips, and remember and say, "Who are you, O man, to answer back to God?" (Romans 9:20).

We neither can nor should investigate    64 and fathom everything in this article, the great apostle Paul declares. After having argued much about this article from God's revealed Word, as soon as he comes to the point where he shows what God has reserved for His hidden wisdom about this mystery, he suppresses and cuts it off with the following words, "Oh, the depth of the riches and wisdom and knowledge of God! How unsearchable are His judgments and how inscrutable His ways! For who has known the mind of the Lord?" (Romans 11:33–34). In other words, we cannot know about matters outside of and beyond what God has revealed to us in His Word.

65    This eternal election of God is to be considered in Christ, and not outside of or without Christ. For "in Christ," the apostle Paul testifies, "He chose us in Him before the foundation of the world," as it is written, "He has blessed us in the Beloved" (Ephesians 1:4, 6). However, this election is revealed from heaven through the preaching of His Word, when the Father says, "This is My beloved Son, with whom I am well pleased; listen to Him" (Matthew 17:5). Christ says, "Come to Me, all who labor and are heavy laden, and I will give you rest" (Matthew 11:28). Concerning the Holy Spirit Christ says, "He will glorify Me, for He will take what is mine and declare it to you" (John 16:14). So the entire Holy Trinity—God the Father, Son, and Holy Spirit—directs all people to Christ, as to the Book of Life, in whom they should seek the Father's eternal election. For this has been decided by the Father from eternity: whom He would save He would save through Christ. Christ Himself says, "No one comes to the Father except through Me" (John 14:6). And again, "I am the door. If anyone enters by Me, he will be saved" (John 10:9).

67    However, Christ, as God's only-begotten Son, who is in the bosom of the Father (John 1:18), has announced the Father's will to us. In this way He has also announced our eternal election to eternal life. He says, "The kingdom of God is at hand; repent and believe in the gospel" (Mark 1:15). Likewise He says, "For this is the will of My Father, that everyone who looks on the Son and believes in Him should have eternal life" (John 6:40). And again, "For God so loved the world, that He gave His only Son, that whoever believes in Him should not perish but have eternal life" (John 3:16).

68    The Father wants all people to hear this proclamation and desires that they come to Christ. Christ does not drive these people from Him, as it is written, "whoever comes to Me I will never cast out" (John 6:37).

69    In order that we may come to Christ, the Holy Spirit works true faith through the hearing of the Word. The apostle testifies about this when he says, "faith comes from hearing, and hearing through the word of Christ" (Romans 10:17), that is, when it is preached in its truth and purity.

70    Whoever would be saved should not trouble or torment himself with thoughts about God's secret counsel, about whether he also is elected and ordained to eternal life. Miserable Satan usually attacks with these thoughts and afflicts godly hearts. But they should hear Christ, who is the Book of Life, and hear about God's eternal election to eternal life for all of His children. Christ testifies to all people without distinction that it is God's will that all people should come to Him "who labor and are heavy laden" with sin, in order that He may give them rest and save them (Matthew 11:28).

71    According to Christ's teaching they should abstain from their sins, repent, believe His promise, and entirely trust in Him. Since we cannot do this by ourselves, by our own powers, the Holy Spirit desires to work these things—repentance and faith—in us through the Word and Sacraments. In order 72 that we may receive this, persevere in it, and remain steadfast, we should beg God for His grace, which He has promised us in Holy Baptism. No doubt He will give it to us according to His promise, as He has said,

> What father among you, if his son asks [him for bread, will give him a stone; or if he asks] for a fish, will in-

stead of a fish give him a serpent; or if he asks for an egg, will give him a scorpion? If you then, who are evil, know how to give good gifts to your children, how much more will the heavenly Father give the Holy Spirit to those who ask Him! (Luke 11:11–13)

73    The Holy Spirit dwells in the elect, who have become believers, as in His temple (1 Corinthians 6:19). He is not idle in them, but moves God's children to obey God's commands. Therefore, believers, too, should not be idle, much less resist the work of God's Spirit. They should practice all Christian virtues, in all godliness, modesty, temperance, patience, and brotherly love; and they should give all diligence to make their calling and election sure (2 Peter 1:10). They should do this so that the more they find the Spirit's power and strength within them,

74    they may doubt their election less. For the Spirit bears witness to the elect that they are God's children (Romans 8:16). Sometimes they fall into temptation so terribly that they imagine they can no longer perceive the power of God's indwelling Spirit, and so they say with David, "I had said in my alarm, 'I am cut off from Your sight'" (Psalm 31:22). Yet they should, without regard to what they experience in themselves, again say with David the words immediately following (as is written in the same place), "But You heard the voice of my pleas for mercy when I cried to You for help."

75    Our election to eternal life is founded not on our godliness or virtue, but on Christ's merit alone and His Father's gracious will. He cannot deny Himself (2 Timothy 2:13), because He is unchangeable in will and essence (Hebrews 6:17–18). Therefore, when His children depart from obedience and stumble, He has called them to repentance

again through the Word, and the Holy Spirit wants by the Word to be effective in them for conversion. When they turn to Him (Jeremiah 31:18–19) again in true repentance by a right faith, He will always show His old paternal heart to all who tremble at His Word and from their heart turn again to Him, as it is written:

> If a man divorces his wife and she goes from him and becomes another man's wife, will he return to her? Would not that land be greatly polluted? You have played the whore with many lovers; [yet return again to Me,] declares the Lord. (Jeremiah 3:1)

Furthermore, the declaration in John 6:44    76 is right and true, "No one can come to Me unless the Father who sent Me draws him." However, the Father will not do this without means, but has ordained His Word and Sacraments for this purpose as ordinary means and instruments. It is not the will of the Father or of the Son that a person should not hear or should despise the preaching of His Word and wait for the drawing of the Father without the Word and Sacraments. For the Father draws indeed by the power of His Holy Spirit. However, He works according to His usual way. He works by the hearing of His holy, divine Word, as with a net (Matthew 13:47–48), by which the elect are plucked from the devil's jaws. Every poor sin-    77 ner should therefore attend to the Word, hear it attentively, and not doubt the Father's drawing. For the Holy Spirit will be with His Word in His power, and will work by it. That is the Father's drawing.

The reason why not all who hear the    78 Word believe, and some are therefore deeply condemned, is not because God had begrudged them their salvation. It is their own fault. They have heard the Word in such a way as not to learn, but only to despise, blaspheme, and disgrace it. They have resisted the Holy Spirit, who through the Word wanted to work in them, as was the case at the time of Christ with the Pharisees and their followers. Therefore, the apostle distinguishes with special care the work of God (who alone makes vessels of honor) and the work of the devil and of people. By the instigation of the devil, not God, a person has made himself a vessel of dishonor. For it is written, "[God] endured with much patience vessels of wrath prepared for destruction, in order to make known the riches of His glory for vessels of mercy, which He has prepared beforehand for glory" (Romans 9:22–23).

80    Here, then, the apostle clearly says that God *endured* with much long-suffering the vessels of wrath. But He does not say that He *made* them vessels of wrath. If that had been His will, He would not have required any great long-suffering for it. The reason that they are fitted for destruction belongs to the devil and to people themselves, and not to God.

81    All preparation for condemnation is by the devil and a person, through sin. In no way does it come from God, who does not want any person to be damned. How, then, should He Himself prepare any person for condemnation? God is not a cause of sins. He is also not the cause of punishment or damnation. The only cause of damnation is sin. "For the wages of sin is death" (Romans 6:23). Just as God does not will sin and has no pleasure in sin, so He does not desire "the death of the wicked" (Ezekiel 33:11), nor has He pleasure in his condemnation. He is not willing "that any should perish, but that all should reach repentance" (2 Peter 3:9). So, too, it is written in Ezekiel 33:11, "As I live, declares the Lord GOD, I have no pleasure in the death of the wicked, but that the wicked

turn from his way and live." (See also Ezekiel 18:23.) St. Paul testifies in clear words that    82 from vessels of dishonor, vessels of honor may be made by God's power and working. He writes, "Therefore, if anyone cleanses himself from what is dishonorable, he will be a vessel for honorable use, set apart as holy, useful to the master of the house, ready for every good work" (2 Timothy 2:20–21). A person who should cleanse himself must first have been unclean and a vessel of dishonor. He says clearly about the vessels of mercy that the Lord Himself has prepared them for glory. He does not say this about the damned. They themselves, and not God, have prepared themselves as vessels of damnation.

Furthermore, remember that God pun-    83 ishes sin with sins. This means that because of their self-confidence, lack of repentance, and willful sins, He later punishes with hardheartedness and blindness those who had been converted (Hebrews 6:4–6). This punishment should not be interpreted to mean that it never had been God's good pleasure that such persons should come to the knowledge of the truth and be saved. For both these facts are God's revealed will:

1. God will receive into grace all who repent and believe in Christ.

2. He also will punish those who willfully turn away from the holy commandment and again entangle themselves in the world's filth (2 Peter 2:20–21), decorate their hearts for Satan (Luke 11:24–26), and despise God's Spirit (Hebrews 10:29). They will be hardened, blinded, and eternally condemned if they persist in such things.

Even Pharaoh perished in this way. (Of    84 whom it is written in Exodus 9:16; Romans 9:17, "But for this purpose I have raised you up, to show you My power, so that My name may be proclaimed in all the earth.") This was not because God had begrudged him salvation or because it had been His good pleasure that Pharaoh should be damned and lost. For God is not willing that any should perish (2 Peter 3:9); "[He also has] no pleasure in the death of the wicked, but that the wicked turn from his way and live" (Ezekiel 33:11).

85    God did harden Pharaoh's heart. In other words, Pharaoh always sinned again and again and became more hardened the more he was warned. That was a punishment of his earlier sin and horrible tyranny that in many and various ways he acted inhumanly toward the children of Israel against his heart's accusations. God caused His Word to be preached and His will to be proclaimed to Pharaoh. Nevertheless, Pharaoh willfully stood up immediately against all rebukes and warnings. Therefore, God withdrew His hand from him, Pharaoh's heart became hardened and stubborn, and God executed His judgment on him. For he was guilty of nothing other

86    than hellfire. So the holy apostle also introduces the example of Pharaoh for no other reason than to prove God's justice by it, which He exercises toward the unrepentant despisers of His Word. By no means, however, has the apostle intended or understood this to mean that God begrudged salvation to him or any person. He doesn't mean God had ordained Pharaoh to eternal damnation in His secret counsel so that Pharaoh should not be able, or that it should not be possible for him, to be saved.

87    This doctrine and explanation of the eternal and saving choice of God's elect children entirely gives God all the glory. In Christ He saves us out of pure mercy, without any merits or good works of ours. He does this according to the purpose of His will, as it is written, "He predestined us for adoption through Jesus Christ, according to the purpose of His will, to the praise of His glorious grace, with which He has blessed us

in the Beloved" (Ephesians 1:5–6). Therefore, 88 it is false and wrong when it is taught that not only God's mercy and Christ's most holy merit, but also something in us is a cause of God's election, on account of which God has chosen us to eternal life. Before we had done anything good, also before we were born, yes, even before the foundations of the world were laid, He elected us in Christ. And "in order that God's purpose of election might continue, not because of works but because of His call—she was told, 'The older will serve the younger.' As it is written, 'Jacob I loved, but Esau I hated'" (Romans 9:11–13; see also Genesis 25:23; Malachi 1:2–3).

Furthermore, this teaching gives no one a 89 cause either for despair or for a shameless, loose life. By this teaching, people are taught that they must seek eternal election in Christ and His Holy Gospel, as in the Book of Life. This excludes no penitent sinner, but beckons and calls all poor, heavy-laden, and troubled sinners to repentance and the knowledge of their sins. It calls them to faith in Christ and promises the Holy Spirit for purification and renewal. It gives the most en- 90 during consolation to all troubled, afflicted people, so that they know their salvation is not placed in their own hands. Otherwise they would lose their salvation much more easily than was the case with Adam and Eve in Paradise, yes, every hour and moment. But salvation is in God's gracious election, which He has revealed to us in Christ, out of whose hand no person shall snatch us (John 10:28; 2 Timothy 2:19).

If anyone presents the teaching about 91 God's gracious election in such a way that troubled Christians cannot get comfort out of it, but are pushed to despair; or if anyone teaches it so that the impenitent are confirmed in their sinfulness, then it is undoubtedly sure and true that such a doctrine is not taught according to God's Word and will. It is taught according to human reason and the instigation of the devil.

92   For, as the apostle testifies:

Whatever was written in former days was written for our instruction, that through endurance and through the encouragement of the Scriptures we might have hope. (Romans 15:4)

But when this consolation and hope are weakened or entirely removed by Scripture, it is certain that it is understood and explained contrary to the Holy Spirit's will and meaning.

93   This simple, correct, useful explanation has a firm and good foundation in God's revealed will. We abide by it. We flee from, and shun, all lofty, difficult questions and disputes. We reject and condemn whatever is contrary to these simple, useful explanations.

## CONCLUSION
## OF THE CONTROVERSIAL ARTICLES

94   So much for the controversial articles that have been discussed for many years among the theologians of the Augsburg Confession. Some have erred and severe controversies, that is, religious disputes, have arisen in these articles.

95   From our explanation, friends and enemies and, therefore, everyone, may clearly see that we have no intention of yielding any part of God's eternal, immutable truth for the sake of temporal peace, tranquility, and unity (which is not in our power to do anyway). Such peace and unity would have no permanence, since it is devised against the truth and for its suppression. We are even less willing to adorn and conceal a corruption of the pure doctrine and clear, condemned errors. We do yearn with heartfelt pleasure and

96   love for unity. On our part, we are sincerely willing and anxious to advance that unity (according to our utmost power) by which

God's glory remains unharmed. We willingly advance unity where nothing of the divine truth of the Holy Gospel is surrendered, no room is given to the least error, and poor sinners are brought to true, genuine repentance, raised up by faith, confirmed in new obedience, and justified and eternally saved alone through the sole merit of Christ.

# XII. OTHER FACTIONS AND SECTS

### That Never Confessed the Augsburg Confession

For an annotation on this article, see p. 518. (See also FC Ep XII.)

---

## INTRODUCTION

The sects and factions that have never   1 confessed the Augsburg Confession, and that have not been directly mentioned in our explanation, are groups such as the Anabaptists, Schwenckfeldians, New Arians, and Anti-Trinitarians. Their errors have been   2 unanimously condemned by all churches of the Augsburg Confession. We have not wanted to make particular and special mention of them in this explanation because at the present time this explanation has been our only aim.

Our opponents have shameless mouths   3 that have shouted allegations throughout the whole world against our churches and teachers. They claimed that you cannot find two preachers who agree about each and every article of the Augsburg Confession, but that they are torn apart and separated from one another to such an extent that they themselves no longer know what the Augsburg Confession is and what its proper meaning is. Therefore, we did not present this com-   4 mon Confession briefly or merely by signing our names, but we wanted to make a pure, clear, distinct declaration about all the disputed articles that have been discussed and argued among the theologians of the Augsburg Confession. 5 We did this so that everyone may see we do not want to hide or cover up all this in a cunning way, or to come to 6 an agreement only in appearance. We want to remedy the matter thoroughly, and wanted to set forth our opinion on these matters in such a way that even our adversaries themselves must confess that in all this we abide by the true, simple, natural, and proper sense of the Augsburg Confession. We desire, by God's grace, to persevere constantly in this confession until our end. And as long as it depends on our ministry, we will not overlook error or be silent, lest anything contrary to the genuine sense of the Augsburg Confession is introduced into our churches and schools, in which the almighty God and Father of our Lord Jesus Christ has appointed us teachers [Latin: doctors] and pastors.

7   However, we do not want the condemned errors of the factions and sects we just mentioned 8 to be silently ascribed to us. For the most part these groups, as is the nature of such spirits, secretly stole in at certain places. They did this especially at a time when no place or room was given to the pure Word of the Holy Gospel, when all its sincere teachers and confessors were persecuted, and the deep darkness of the papacy still prevailed. Poor, simple people, in their simplicity (who could not help but feel the clear idolatry and false faith of the papacy), embraced whatever was called the Gospel and was not papistic. We cannot avoid testifying against these groups publicly, before all Christendom. We have no part or fellowship with their errors, be they many or few. We reject and condemn them one and all. They are wrong and heretical, and are contrary to the Scriptures of the prophets and apostles and to our Christian Augsburg Confession, which is well grounded in God's Word.

## ERRONEOUS ARTICLES
## OF THE ANABAPTISTS

9   For instance, the erroneous, heretical doctrines of the Anabaptists are not to be tolerated and allowed in the Church or in the commonwealth or in domestic life. For they teach the following:

10   1. Our righteousness before God includes not only Christ's sole obedience and merit, but also our renewal and our own piety in which we walk before God. For the most part, they base this on their own peculiar ordinances and self-chosen spirituality, as a new sort of monasticism.

11   2. Children who are not baptized are not sinners before God, but are righteous and innocent, and are saved by their innocence without Baptism. They do not need Baptism. So they deny and reject the entire teaching about original sin and what belongs to it.

12   3. Children are not to be baptized until they have gained the use of reason and can confess their faith themselves.

13   4. The children of Christians, since they have been born of Christian and believing parents, are holy and God's children even before and without Baptism. For this reason they do not consider the Baptism of children to be important or encourage it. They do this contrary to the clear words of the promise (Acts 2:38–39), which extends only to those who keep God's covenant and do not despise it (Genesis 17:9; Colossians 2:11–15).

14   5. A congregation in which sinners are still found is no true Christian assembly.

15   6. No sermon should be heard or attended in those churches in which the papal Masses have previously been said.

16 7. No one should have anything to do with those ministers of the Church who preach the Holy Gospel according to the Augsburg Confession and rebuke the errors of Anabaptists. Also, they say that no one should serve or work for them in any way, but should run away from them and shun them as perverters of God's Word.

17 8. Under the New Testament a governmental office is not a godly estate.

18 9. A Christian cannot with a good, inviolate conscience hold a governmental office.

19 10. A Christian cannot without injury to conscience use a government office against the wicked in matters that may occur; neither can the government's subjects appeal to its power.

20 11. A Christian cannot with a good conscience take an oath before a court or do homage to his prince or hereditary sovereign with an oath.

21 12. Officials cannot without injury to conscience take the life of evildoers.

22 13. A Christian cannot with a good conscience hold or possess any property, but is duty bound to devote it to the common treasury.

23 14. A Christian cannot with a good conscience be an innkeeper, merchant, or a weapon maker.

24 15. Married persons may be divorced because of differences in faith. The one may abandon the other and be married to another of his own faith.

25 16. Christ did not receive His flesh and blood from the Virgin Mary, but brought them with Him from heaven.

26 17. Christ is not true, essential God either, but only has more and higher gifts and glory than other men.

27 And still more articles of this kind, for they are divided among themselves into many sects. One has more and another fewer errors, and so their entire sect is in reality nothing but a new kind of monasticism.

## ERRONEOUS ARTICLES OF THE SCHWENCKFELDIANS

28 In a similar way, the Schwenckfeldians assert the following:

29 1. First, all people have no knowledge of heaven's reigning King, Christ, if they regard Christ according to the flesh, or His received humanity, as a created being. Christ's flesh has by exaltation so assumed all divine properties that in might, power, majesty, and glory He is in every respect, in degree and position of essence, equal to the Father and the eternal Word. So they say there is the same essence, properties, will, and glory of both natures in Christ, and that Christ's flesh belongs to the essence of the Holy Trinity.

30 2. The ministry of the Church—the Word preached and heard—is not a means by which God the Holy Spirit teaches people and works in them saving knowledge of Christ, conversion, repentance, faith, and new obedience.

31 3. The water of Baptism is not a means by which God the Lord seals adoption and works regeneration.

32 4. Bread and wine in the Holy Supper are not means by which Christ distributes His body and blood.

33 5. A Christian who is truly regenerated by God's Spirit can in this life keep and fulfill God's Law perfectly.

34 6. A congregation in which no public excommunication or regular process of the ban is observed is not a true Christian congregation.

35 7. The Church minister who is not truly renewed, righteous, and godly cannot teach other people with profit or administer real, true Sacraments.

## ERRONEOUS ARTICLES
## OF THE NEW ARIANS

36    The New Arians teach that Christ is not true, essential, natural God, of one eternal divine essence with God the Father. They say He is only adorned with divine majesty inferior to, and beside, God the Father.

## ERRONEOUS ARTICLES
## OF THE NEW ANTI-TRINITARIANS

37    1. Some Anti-Trinitarians reject and condemn the ancient, approved Nicene and Athanasian Creeds. They condemn both their sense and words. These people teach that there is not just one eternal divine essence of the Father, Son, and Holy Spirit. They teach that, just as there are three distinct persons (God the Father, Son, and Holy Spirit), so each person has also its essence distinct and separate from the other persons. They say that all three are either like three men—distinct and separate in their essence, of the same power, wisdom, majesty, and glory—or are unequal in essence and properties.

38    2. The Father alone is true God.

## CONCLUSION

These and similar articles, one and all, with what belongs to them and follows from them, we reject and condemn as wrong, false, heretical, and contrary to God's Word, the three Creeds, the Augsburg Confession and Apology, the Smalcald Articles, and Luther's Catechisms. All godly Christians should beware of these articles to the extent that the welfare and salvation of their souls is dear to them.    39

In the sight of God and of all Christendom, we want to testify to those now living and those who will come after us. This declaration presented here about all the controverted articles mentioned and explained above—and no other—is our faith, doctrine, and confession. By God's grace, with intrepid hearts, we are willing to appear before the judgment seat of Christ with this Confession and give an account of it (1 Peter 4:5). We will not speak or write anything contrary to this Confession, either publicly or privately. By the strength of God's grace we intend to abide by it. Therefore, after mature deliberation, we have, in the fear of God and by calling on His name, attached our signatures with our own hands.    40

1. Nicholaus Selnecker  2. Christopher Cornerus  3. Andrew Musculus
4. Martin Chemnitz  5. David Chytraeus  6. Jacob Andreae

# ACKNOWLEDGEMENTS

The editors gratefully acknowledge the helpful assistance and support of the following individuals and institutions. We thank Concordia Seminary—St. Louis and Prof. David Berger, Director of Library Services, for the use of various rare books. We thank Rev. Dr. Ken Schurb and Rev. Dr. Karl Barth for their many valuable observations and suggestions throughout the project. We thank Rev. Dr. James Kellerman for his translation of the indulgence that appears at the end of the Augsburg Confession. We appreciate the help of Dr. M. Patrick Graham, the Margaret A. Pitts Professor of Theological Bibliography and Director of the Pitts Theological Library, who provided invaluable assistance in the identification of period woodcuts from the Pitts Theological Library Digital Archive, particularly those for the Small Catechism. Rev. Matthew Harrison graciously provided free access to his collection of copies of sixteenth-century woodcuts, engravings, and period art. We thank the museum of the Wartburg Castle in Eisenach, Germany, for their assistance in providing access to the painting of Philip of Hesse. Our gratitude is also extended to the Toledo Art Institute for their courtesy in providing the painting of John Frederick the Magnanimous with various key Lutheran figures. Thanks to the congregation of St. Peter and St. Paul in Weimar, Germany, for the excellent, detailed description of their Cranach altar painting. We thank Mrs. Karen Pauls for her diligent attention to the design and layout of this complex volume. Special thanks to Mrs. Caryn Hill for her diligent attention to a myriad of details in the editorial work on this project, including the complex task of indexing. Mrs. Debb Andrus devoted countless hours copyediting much of this edition and we thank her for her meticulous care and concern. We especially thank the Board of Directors of Concordia Publishing House, Mr. Robert Knox, Chairman, for their enthusiastic support of this new edition of the Book of Concord and their encouragement along the way. And finally, we thank and praise our gracious God for the entire staff of Concordia Publishing House, each of whom, in many and various ways, contributed to the production and distribution of this volume.

*Ↄↄ*

# APPENDIXES

---

## APPENDIX A:
## CATALOG OF TESTIMONIES

From Scripture and the orthodox Ancient Church that show what
Scripture and the Early Church taught about the person of Christ
and the Divine Majesty of His human nature, who is exalted
to God's omnipotent right hand. They also show what forms
of speech are used by Scripture and the orthodox Early Church.

### Editorial Introduction

The Catalog of Testimonies was appended to several early editions of the Book of
Concord to show that Lutheran teaching about the two natures of Christ is thoroughly in line with the historic and universal faith of the Christian Church. The doctrine of
the two natures in Christ, known as *Christology*, is the foundation for the Bible's
teaching about justification. Justification without biblical Christology becomes a
philosophical abstraction. Christology makes justification what it is: a powerful, present, joyful reality through Word and Sacrament by means of which the God-man,
Jesus Christ, is present with us, and for us, according to both His divine and human
nature, giving us forgiveness, life, and salvation. Reformed theologians denied that
Christ's human nature is present under the bread and wine of the Lord's Supper and
accused Lutherans of making up new understandings about the two natures in Christ.
Therefore, it was necessary for Lutherans to refute these claims and show that their
doctrine is, in fact, thoroughly in keeping with Scripture and the Ancient Church Fathers, who taught the same things.

Note: In these quotations the divine nature of Christ is often referred to as "the Word,"
a reference to John 1, in which the Son of God is referred to as "the Word." References are given as to where the quotes may be found. Some of these (e.g., those to

---

Migne) are in the original language. Where available, references are provided to English translations (e.g., *The Nicene and Post-Nicene Fathers of the Church*). Here is a key to the reference sources:

*ANF* = *Ante-Nicene Fathers.* Ed. Alexander Roberts and James Donaldson. Edinburgh: T&T Clark.

*CSEL* = *Corpus Scriptorum Ecclesiasticorum Latinorum*

Denzinger = *Enchiridion symbolorum definitionum et declarationum de rebus fidei et morum.* Ed. Heinrich Denzinger and Peter Huennermann. Freiburg: Herder, 1991.

*Epistolae* = *Epistolae Romanorum Pontificum Genuinae et quae ad eos Scriptae Sunt.* Ed. Andreas Thiel. Braunsberg: Peter, 1868.

Ferrar = *The Proof of the Gospel: Being the Demonstratio Evangelical of Eusebius of Caesarea.* Ed. W. J. Ferrar. New York: Macmillan, 1920.

*Library* = *Library of the Fathers of the Holy Catholic Church.* Trans. E. B. Pusey, et al. Oxford: Parker, 1836–85.

*MPG* = *Patrologiae cursus completus: Series Graece.* Ed. Jacques-Paul Migne. 161 vols. Paris and Turnhout, 1857–66.

*MPL* = *Patrologiae cursus completus: Series Latina.* Ed. Jacques-Paul Migne. 221 vols. Paris, 1844–80.

*NPNF* = *Nicene and Post-Nicene Fathers.* Ed. Philip Schaff. New York: Christian Literature Publishing, 1892.

Robinson = *Nag Hammadi and Manichaean Studies.* Ed. J. M. Robinson and H. J. Klimkeit. Leiden: Brill, 1994.

Theophylact = *The Explanation by Blessed Theophylact of the Holy Gospel according to St. Matthew.* House Springs, MO: Chrysostom Press, 1992.

# To the Christian Reader

Some people claim that the Book of Concord deviates from the phrases and ways of speaking used by the pure, Ancient Church and Church Fathers, particularly in those articles concerning the person of Christ. They say that new, strange, made-up, unusual, and unheard-of expressions have been introduced. The Book of Concord appeals to the Ancient Church and Church Fathers, but many quotations from the Church Fathers were too long to include in the Book of Concord itself. Excerpts were carefully prepared and delivered to several electors and princes. They are printed here as an appendix at the end of the Book of Concord, in regard to particular points, for the purpose of providing the reader a thorough and correct accounting.

A person will easily recognize that when these doctrines are taught in the Book of Concord nothing new has been introduced, either in the doctrinal issues themselves, or in phrases and ways of speaking. We have spoken and taught about these mysteries, first of all, just as Holy Scripture does, and also as the ancient, pure Church did. Therefore, when the Book of Concord teaches about the unity of the person of

Christ, the distinction of the two natures in Christ, and their essential properties, it is doing so just as the Fathers and councils of the ancient, pure Church have. They all taught that there are not two persons, but one Christ. In this person there are two distinct natures, the divine and human nature, which are not separated or intermingled or transformed into each other. Each nature has and retains its essential attributes, to all eternity, never laying them aside. The essential attributes of the one nature, which are truly and properly ascribed to the entire Person, never become attributes of the other nature. This is proven by the following testimonies from the ancient pure councils.

### The Council of Ephesus

Canon 4:

> If anyone divides the words of Scripture that speak about the two persons, or hypostases, of Christ and apply some of them to Him as a man in such a way that the Word is separated from God, or without the Word of the Father, or takes other statements from Scripture and says they apply only to Him as God, that is the Word from God the Father, let him be anathema.

Canon 5:

> If anyone dares to say that Christ was a God-bearing man and not truly God by nature and that thus: If anyone dares to say that the man *Christ* is the Bearer of God, and instead of saying that He is God, truly the Son of God by nature, the "Word made flesh," who was made a partaker of flesh and blood precisely like us, let him be anathema.

Canon 6:

> If anyone does not confess that Christ is, at the same time, God and man, because the Word was made flesh, let him be accursed.

Canon 12:

> If anyone does not confess that the Word of God suffered in the flesh, was crucified in the flesh, and tasted death in the flesh, becoming the firstborn from the dead, although as God He is life and gives life, let him be accursed. (Denzinger, 255–57, 263)

### The Council of Chalcedon (AD 451)

As cited by Evagrius, book 2, chapter 4:

> Following the holy Fathers, we confess one and the same Son, our Lord Jesus Christ. With one voice we confess that He is perfect in deity and perfect in humanity. He is the truly God and truly man, consisting of a rational soul and body. He is consubstantial with the Father in regard to His deity and is consubstantial with us according to His humanity. He is like us in every way, except He is without sin. He was begotten before the world out of the Father according to His divinity. The same person was, in the last days, born for us and for our salvation from the Virgin Mary, the Mother of God, according to His

humanity. We confess that one and the same Jesus Christ, the Son, the Lord, the only-begotten, is known in two natures, without commingling, without changing, without division and without separation. The difference between the two natures is in no way abolished because of the Personal Union. The unique aspects of each nature are preserved. They are not run together into one person and substance, neither divided or torn into two persons. There is one and the same only-begotten Son, God the Word and the Lord Jesus Christ. We acknowledge one single Lord Christ who is at one and the same time the only-begotten Son, the Word of the Father and also true man. The prophets of old and the Christ Himself have taught us these things concerning Him, as well as the symbol that the Fathers have handed down to us. (*MPG,* 86:2507/8C–2509/10A)

## Tenth Synodical Letter of Leo to Flavianus Used by the Council of Chalcedon

Tenth Synodical Epistle of Leo to Flavianus (chapter 3, folio 92):

The Personal Union has taken place in this way. The distinct aspects of each nature are unimpaired. The two natures remain unmingled and unchanged. Each nature comes together into one person. Therefore, Divine Majesty assumes human lowliness. Divine Power assumes human weakness. The Eternal Divine Being assumes the mortality of human nature. For the purpose of paying the debt of our condition, the immortal nature that cannot suffer has been united to the human nature that can suffer. This happened so that the same Mediator could die according to one nature, and could not die according to the other nature in order that our single Mediator, who could not die according to the Divine Nature, might die for us according to the human nature.

Likewise (chapter 4, folio 93):

He who is truly God is also truly man, since both the humility of the man and the loftiness of God exist in one person. Just as God did not change when He took pity on us and assumed the human nature, so man was not consumed by divine dignity and glory. For each nature does what is unique to it, in communion with the other. The Word does what belongs to the Word, the Son of God, and the flesh carries out what belongs to the flesh. One of these natures flashes forth in the miracles, the other sinks beneath injuries. Yes, there is still one single Mediator, God and man. He is God because in the beginning was the Word and the Word was God, by whom all things were made. He is man because the Word was made flesh, and because He was born of woman. We read that the Son of Man descended from heaven when the Son of God assumed flesh of the Virgin Mary, thus indicating the unity of the Person with two natures.

And again (chapter 5, folio 93):

It is said that the Son of God was crucified and buried. He suffered these things not in His very divinity, by which He is consubstantial with the Father, but in the infirmity of His assumed human nature. (Denzinger, 293–95)

So far the words of the Council of Ephesus and of Chalcedon. These councils agree with all the other holy Fathers. This is precisely what the learned men in our schools want to indicate when they speak of these matters in the abstract and the concrete. The Book of Concord refers to this fact when it says of these issues, "All of which the learned know well." These words must be retained in their true sense in the schools. Concrete terms are words that refer to the entire person in Christ, such as *God* and *man*. Abstract terms are words used to talk about the two natures in Christ, such as *divinity* and *humanity*. Therefore, according to this distinction, it is correct to say, speaking concretely [*in concreto*], "God is man and man is God." On the other hand it is incorrect to say, speaking abstractly [*in abstracto*], "Divinity is humanity and humanity is divinity." The same rule applies also to the essential attributes of each nature in Christ. This means that the attributes of one nature cannot be predicated of the other nature in the abstract, as though they were attributes of the other nature. Therefore, the following expressions would be false and incorrect. It would be wrong for a person to say, "The human nature is Omnipotence and is from eternity." Thus, again, since the attributes of one nature in Christ cannot be predicated of the other, one could not say, "Mortality is immortality and immortality is mortality." If one were to speak this way, the distinction between the two natures in Christ and their attributes would be abolished. They would be confounded with each other, changed into the other, and thus made equal and alike.

We must not only know, but also firmly believe, that the human nature that Christ received into His person has, and retains to all eternity, its essence and the naturally essential attributes. This is very important and the greatest consolation for Christians. We must also know from the revelation of Holy Scripture, and not doubt, the majesty to which the human nature has truly and actually been elevated by the Personal Union. The human nature has become a personal participant in the divine majesty.

These truths have been extensively explained in the Book of Concord, which has not introduced new, strange, made-up, unheard-of paradoxes and expressions into the Church of God. To show this to everyone, the following Catalog of Testimonies, first from the Holy Scriptures, then also from the ancient, pure teachers of the Church, especially from leaders in the first four ecumenical councils, will show how they have spoken about the person of Christ and the two natures in Christ. These quotations have been arranged under several distinct topics, so that the Christian reader will find it easier to work his way through them.

# I.

The majesty of the divine nature is communicated to the human nature. When the Holy Scriptures, and also the Fathers, speak of the majesty that the human nature of Christ has received through the personal union, they use the words *communica-*

*tion, communion, sharing, bestowed* and *given.*

Behold, with the clouds of heaven there came one like a son of man, and He came to the Ancient of Days and was presented before Him. And to Him was given dominion and glory and a kingdom, that all peoples, nations, and languages should serve Him; His dominion is an everlasting dominion, which shall not pass away, and His kingdom one that shall not be destroyed. (Daniel 7:13–14)

Jesus, knowing that the Father had given all things into His hands. (John 13:3)

All things have been handed over to Me by My Father. (Matthew 11:27)

All authority in heaven and on earth has been given to Me. (Matthew 28:18)

Therefore God has highly exalted Him and bestowed on Him the name that is above every name, so that at the name of Jesus every knee should bow, in heaven and on earth and under the earth. (Philippians 2:9–10)

And He put all things under His feet. (Ephesians 1:22; see also Psalm 8:6; 1 Corinthians 15:27; Hebrews 2:8)

EUSEBIUS, Evangelical *Demonstration*, book 4, chapter 13:

The Word of the Father has of Himself *communicated* what was His to the received man. He has communicated divine power to the received mortal nature, but has not received for Himself anything out of the mortal nature. (*MPG*, 22:288A/B; Ferrar, 1:188)

And again, chapter 14:

The Word, making this human being worthy of eternal life as he has always been, and putting him in communion in His deity and blessedness. (*MPG*, 22:289A; Ferrar, 1:190–91)

ATHANASIUS, *Letter to Epictetus*, quoted also by Epiphanius against the Dimoeritae (*Heresies*, 77):

The Word did not become flesh in order to add to divinity. In order that flesh might rise up, He came forth from Mary, not that the Word might become better. There was a great addition to the human body from communion and union with the Word. (*MPG*, 42:656C, 26:1065A/B; *NPNF*, ser. 2, 4:573)

EPIPHANIUS, *Heresies*, 69:

It is clear that the flesh from Mary and that came from our race was transformed into glory in the Transfiguration, having acquired the glory of the Godhead, heavenly honor and perfection and glory which the flesh did not have from the beginning, but received in the union with God the Word. (*MPG*, 42:332D; Robinson, 26: *The Panarion of Epiphanius of Salamis*, Books 2 and 3, 398–99)

CYRIL, *Dialogue*, book 5:

How, then, does the flesh of Christ make alive? Because of the union with the living Word, which is accustomed to communicate the endowments of His nature to His own body. (*MPG,* 75:962B–963C)

THEODORET, *Interpretation of the Epistle to the Ephesians*:

That the nature received from us is a *participant* in the same honor of Him who received it and that no difference in worship appears, but the divinity which is not seen is worshiped through the nature which is seen—this surpasses every miracle. (*MPG,* 82:517A)

DAMASCENE, in Book 3, *Of the Orthodox Faith*, chapters 7, 15:

The Divine Nature *communicates* or *imparts* its own excellent qualities to the flesh, while remaining incapable of suffering. It does not share in the sufferings of the flesh. (*MPG,* 94:1012C, 1058C; *NPNF,* ser. 2, 9[pt. 2]:52)

Also, in chapter 19:

The flesh has communion with the divine operations of the Word, because the divine operations are carried out through the body. He that works both in a divine and human fashion is one. It is necessary to know that just as His holy mind carries out natural human functions, so also it participates in the divinity of the Word. The Word works, arranges, governs, perceives, knows and determines everything in the entire universe, not simply as the mind of a man, but as being made one in person with God, as being constituted with the mind of God. (*MPG,* 94:1080B/C; *NPNF,* ser. 2, 9[pt. 2]:68)

# II.

Christ received divine majesty here in time, not according to His divine nature, but according to the human nature that He received, that is, according to the flesh, as man, or the Son of Man.

Testimony from the Holy Scriptures:

After making purification for sins, He sat down at the right hand of the Majesty on high. (Hebrews 1:3)

At present, we do not yet see everything in subjection to Him. But we see Him who for a little while was made lower than the angels, namely Jesus, crowned with glory and honor because of the suffering of death. (Hebrews 2:8–9)

But from now on the Son of Man shall be seated at the right hand of the power of God. (Luke 22:69)

And the Lord God will give to Him the throne of His father David, and He will reign over the house of Jacob forever, and of His kingdom there will be no end. (Luke 1:32–33)

He has granted the Son also to have life in Himself. And He has given Him authority to execute judgment, because He is the Son of Man. (John 5:26–27)

Testimonies from the Church Fathers:

ATHANASIUS, quoted by Theodoret, Dialogue 2, page 330:

Whenever Scripture says that the Word received glory in time, it is speaking about His humanity, not His divinity. (*MPG*, 83:181A)

ATHANASIUS, in the *Oration against the Arians*, 2 and 4 (f. 347. 490 f. 492, ed. Colon., 1686):

Scripture does not mean that the substance of the Word has been exalted. It is talking about His humanity. He is said to be exalted according to the flesh. Since it is His body, it is proper to say that as man He was exalted and received something, with respect to His body, according to His humanity. His body receives those things that the Word always possessed according to His deity and perfection from the Father. As a man, He says that He received the power that as God He always has. He who glorifies others, says, "Glorify me," in order to show that He had flesh that lacked such things. When the flesh of His humanity receives glorification, He speaks as if He Himself had received it. Therefore we must always keep in mind when reading the Holy Scriptures that none of those things that He says He received in time, He received as though He did not already have them. For, being God and the Word, naturally He always had those things. But He says that He received them according to His humanity so that, even as He received them in Himself, in the flesh, He might in the future hand them over to us, from the same flesh, to be firmly possessed. (*MPG*, 26:95C, 98–99, 406B/C, 410A/B; *NPNF*, ser. 2, 4:330, 415)

ATHANASIUS, *On the Assumed Humanity*, against Apollinarius (pp. 603 and 611, ed. Colon., 1686):

When Peter says that Jesus was God, both Lord and Christ, He is not talking about His divinity, but about His humanity. The Word was always Lord. He did not become Lord only after the cross. Rather, His divinity made the humanity both Lord and Christ. (*MPG*, 26:1022A/B)

And:

Whatever the Scriptures say that the Son has received, this is said in respect to receiving in His body. This body is the firstfruits of the Church. Accordingly, God raised up and exalted first His own body, but afterward members of His body. (*MPG*, 26:1003B)

With these words Athanasius explained what the whole Church said later.

BASIL THE GREAT, *Against Eunomius*, book 4 (p. 769, ed. Paris):

When the Lord is celebrated, and receives a name (Philippians 2:9) that is above every name, and when He says, "All authority in heaven and on earth has been given to Me" (Matthew 28:18) and "I live because of the Father" (John 6:57) and "Glorify Me … with the glory that I had with You before the world existed" (John 17:5) these things must be understood of the incarnation, not of His Deity. (*MPG*, 29:694C, 597C, 701A/B)

AMBROSE:

You have learned that He can subject all things to Himself according to the operation of Deity. Learn now that He receives, according to His flesh, all things in subjection to Him, as it is written in Ephesians 1. According to the flesh, therefore, all things are delivered to Him as His subjects. (*MPL*, 19:714B; *NPNF*, ser. 2, 10:307; *MPL*, numbers this chapter "15")

AMBROSE, book 5, chapter 2 (p. 99):

God does give the apostles a participation in His seat, but to Christ, according to His humanity, He gives a common participation in the divine seat. (*MPL*, 16:691B; *NPNF*, ser. 2, 10:294)

And in chapter 6 (p. 108):

In Christ our common human nature has, according to the flesh, obtained the prerogative of the heavenly seat. (*MPL*, 16:713B; *NPNF*, ser. 1, 14:307; *MPL* numbers this chapter "4")

CHRYSOSTOM, Heb. 1, Serm. 3, p. 117 (tom. 4: *Homilies*, 3, p. 1493):

In regard to the flesh, the Father has commanded the angels to worship Him. (*MPG*, 63:28; *NPNF*, ser. 1, 14:375)

THEOPHYLACT, on John 3 (p. 235; ed. Paris, 1631, f. 605):

He gave all things into His Son's hand, according to humanity. (*MPG*, 123:1225A)

OECUMENIUS from Chrysostom, Heb. 1 (t. 2, op. p. 324, ed. 1631):

As the Son of God, He has an eternal throne. "Thy throne," says God, "is forever and ever." After the cross and passion He was deemed worthy of honor, not as God, but as man, and He received what He had as God." And a little after: "Therefore, as man, He hears, 'Sit at My Right hand,'" for as God He has eternal power. (*MPG*, 119:289A/B.)

CYRIL, book 9, *Thesauri*, chapter 3 (tom. 2, p. 110):

As man, He ascended to ruling power. (*MPG*, 75:363C)

The same, book 2, chapter 17:

As man He sought glory that He always had as God. He doesn't say these things as though He had ever been destitute of His own glory, but because He wanted to bring His own temple [His body] into the glory that He always has as God. (*MPG*, 75:439/40A, a passage that expresses the idea of this citation, though not in its precise words)

The same, book 2, *Ad Reginas:*

That He received glory, power, and rule over all things must be referred to the conditions [properties] of *humanity*. (*MPG*, 76:1359C, a passage that expresses the idea of this citation, though not in its precise words)

THEODORET, on Psalm 2 (t. 1, p. 242):

Though Christ, as God, is by nature Lord, He receives universal power also as a man. (*MPG*, 80:880A)

On Psalm 110 (t. 1, p. 242):

"Sit at My right hand"—this was said *according to the human nature.* As God, He has eternal dominion. *As man,* He has received what He had as God. *As man,* therefore, He hears what is said to Him, "Sit at My right hand." For as God, He has eternal dominion. (*MPG,* 80:1768B)

On Hebrews 1 (t. 2, p. 154) Theodoret says:

Christ always received worship and adoration from the angels, for He always was God. Now they are adoring Him also as man. (*MPG,* 82:686C)

LEO, Epist. 23 (folio 99; Ep. [23 and 83] 46 and 97, ff. 261 and 317, ed. Lugd., 1700), treating of Eph. 1, says:

Let the enemies of the truth openly explain when, and according to which nature, the almighty Father raised His Son above all things, and similarly, according to what nature He subjected all things. All things have always been subject to His divine nature, as Creator. If power was added to the divine nature, or His sublime divine nature was exalted, then that means it was inferior to Him who did the exalting. It would mean that the divine nature of Christ actually was in need of something to be added to it and that it depended on another divine nature. Arius welcomes those who hold such views into his fellowship. (*MPL,* 54:869; *NPNF,* ser. 2, 12:59)

LEO, Epist. 83 (folio 134):

We understand that "exaltation" and "a name above every name" have to do with the human nature, which was enriched by a great increase in glorification, although there is absolutely one and the same person, divine and human. In the incarnation nothing was taken away from the Word that had to be returned to it by means of a gift from the Father. The "form of a servant" is the human nature's humility, which now has been exalted to the glory of divine power. So, divine things were never done without man, human things [never] done without God. (*MPL,* 54:1066; *NPNF,* ser. 2, 12:94)

Whatever Christ has received in time He has received as man. Things are conferred on man, which he did not have; however, according to the Word, the Son also has all things, in no way different from what the Father has. (*MPL,* 54:1066–67; *NPNF,* ser. 2, 12:94)

VIGILIUS, book 5, *Against Eutyches* (Ep. 66 sq., ed. Divion., 1664. 4):

The divine nature does not need to be elevated to honor, or to be increased by advancing its dignity. The divine nature does not need to merit all power on heaven and earth through obedience. Therefore, according to the fleshly nature, He [Christ] acquired these things. According to the nature of the Word he never lacked them. Did the Creator have to obtain these things as a gift in these last times because He had no power and dominion over his creature? (*MPL,* 62:141A/D, 142B)

NICEPHORUS, book 1, chapter 36 (folio 86):

His disciples saw Him on the mount of Transfiguration, where He affirmed that the highest power in heaven and earth had been given to Him, according to His humanity. (*MPG*, 145:742B)

# III.

The Holy Scriptures, likewise the holy Fathers of the ancient, pure Church, speak about this mystery in abstract terms, making it very clear that the human nature, by means of the personal union, truly and actually receives and uses the majesty of the divine nature.

Whoever feeds on My flesh and drinks My blood has eternal life.... For My flesh is true food, and My blood is true drink. (John 6:54–55)

The blood of Jesus His Son cleanses us from all sin. (1 John 1:7)

How much more will the blood of Christ, who through the eternal Spirit offered Himself without blemish to God, purify our conscience from dead works to serve the living God. (Hebrews 9:14)

Take, eat; this is My body . . . Drink of it, all of you, for this is My blood of the covenant (Matthew 26:26–28)

EUSTACHIUS, quoted by Theodoret, Dialogue 2 (p. 40):

He prophesied that He, that is, Christ the man, the human nature of Christ, would sit on a holy throne and share it with the Divine Spirit, thus showing that God dwells in Him without separation. (*MPG*, 83:176B)

The same, quoted in Gelasius:

The man Christ, who increased in wisdom, age and favor, received dominion over all things. (*Epistolae*, 1:544)

And:

Christ, in His very body, came to His apostles and said, "All power in heaven and on earth has been given to me." It was the external temple that received this power, not God, that is, not according to His divinity, which built the external temple of extraordinary beauty. (*Epistolae*, 1:554)

ATHANASIUS, *On the Arian and the Catholic Confession* (t. 2, op. p. 579, ed. Colon.):

God was not changed into human flesh or substance, but in Himself glorified the nature that He received, so that the human, weak, mortal flesh and nature received divine glory in order to have all power in heaven and on earth, which it did not have before it was received by the Word. (This work was traditionally assigned to Athanasius in the Middle Ages but was in fact composed by Vigilius of Thapsus; *MPL*, 62:305B)

The same author (*l.c.*, pp. 597 and 603), *On the Assumed Humanity*, against Apollinarius (p. 530):

In Philippians 2, Paul talks about His body as a temple. His flesh is exalted, not He who is the Most Exalted One. To His flesh He gave the name above every name, that at the name of Jesus every knee should bow and every tongue confess that Jesus Christ is the Lord, to the glory of the Father.

ATHANASIUS adds a general rule:

When Scripture talks about the glorification of Christ, it is talking about the flesh, which has received glory. Whatever Scripture says that the Son has received, it is saying this according to His humanity, not His divinity. So, when the Apostles say that all the fullness of the Godhead dwells bodily in Christ, we must understand that this fullness dwells in the flesh of Christ. (*MPG*, 26:987–90)

The same author, quoted by Theodoret, Dialogue 2 (t. 3, p. 286):

"Sit on My right hand," has been said to the Lord's body.

Also:

Therefore, it is the body to which He says, "Sit on My right hand." (*MPG*, 83:180B)

ATHANASIUS, *On the Incarnation*, as quoted in Cyril in his *Defense of the Eighth Anathema*, and in his book *On the True Faith to the Queens*:

The holy catholic Church condemns anyone who says that the human flesh of our Lord is not to be worshiped and adored as the flesh of the Lord and God. (*MPG*, 76:350C, 1211)

The same, *On Humanity Assumed* (p. 603, ed. Colon.):

Whatever Scripture says that the Son has received, it understands as having been received *according to His body*. His body is the firstfruits of the Church; therefore, the Lord first raised and exalted His body, and afterward also the members of His body. (*MPG*, 26:1003B)

HILARY, book 9 (p. 136):

Since the Word received human flesh, the flesh was united to the glory of the Word and possesses the glory of the Word. Thus, the man Jesus remained in the glory of God the Father. (*MPL*, 10:326–27; *NPNF*, ser. 2, 9:167)

EUSEBIUS OF EMISSA, in his homily on the Sixth Holiday after Easter (*Feria 6, paschatos in homiliis, patrum*, p. 297):

He who, according to His divinity, always had power over all things with the Father and the Holy Spirit, now also according to His humanity has received power over all things. This man who suffered not long ago rules over heaven and earth and in fact does here and there whatever He wants to do. (*MPG*, 86:486–88)

GREGORY OF NYSSA, quoted by Gelasius and Theodoret, Dialogue 2 (t. 2, p. 333):

Acts 2:33 says that Christ was exalted to the right hand of God. Who was exalted? The lowly one or the highest one? What is lowly, except the human nature? Who else besides the divine is the highest? God, being the Highest, does not need to be exalted. The apostle says that the human nature was exalted by becoming Lord and Christ. Therefore, when the apostle says that God exalted Him, this does not mean that the Lord was, before the world, existing in some lower estate. What it means is that what was lowly, His human nature, was exalted to the right hand of God. . . . The right hand of God the Creator, the Lord, the one by whom all things were made and without whom nothing that exists was made, has itself, through the union, raised up to its own height the man who was united with it. (*MPG*, 83:193, 195; see also *Epistolae*, 1:549)

BASIL THE GREAT, *Against Eunomius*, book 2 (p. 661, ed. Paris):

In Acts 2, when Peter says, "God has made the same Jesus whom you crucified both Lord and Christ," he is using the words "the same" to refer almost entirely to the human nature, seen by all. . . . When he says, "God has made Him both Lord and Christ," he is saying that power and dominion over all things was entrusted to His humanity by the Father. (*MPG*, 29:577A/B)

EPIPHANIUS, *Against the Ariomanites* (p. 327, t. 1; folio 728, ed. Paris, 1638):

When Peter adds, "this same Jesus whom you crucified" it is obvious that he is talking about the *incarnation* of the Lord, that is, His flesh, so that the incarnate flesh might not be left behind by the uncreated Word that cannot suffer, but might be united above to the uncreated Word. This is why God made that which was conceived by Mary and united to deity, both Lord and Christ. (*MPG*, 42:268B/C; Robinson, 360)

AMBROSE, book 3, chapter 12, *Of the Holy Ghost* (t. 2, p. 157 [folio 765, ed. Colon.]):

Angels do not adore only the divinity of Christ, but also His footstool. . . . The prophet says that the earth the Lord took upon Himself when He assumed flesh is to be adored. Therefore, we understand "footstool" to mean the earth, that is, the flesh of Christ, which we today also adore in the Sacraments, and which the apostles adored in the Lord Jesus. (*MPL*, 16:827A, 828B–829A; *NPNF*, ser. 2, 10:145–46; *MPL* numbers this chapter "11")

AUGUSTINE, *Of the Words of the Lord*, Discourse 58 (t. 10, p. 217):

If Christ is not, by nature, God, but a creature, He is not to be worshiped or adored as God. They may reply and say, "But why do you adore His flesh if you admit that it is a creature? Why are you as devoted to His flesh as you are to His divinity?" (*MPL*, 39:2200)

AUGUSTINE answers:

It says, "Worship His footstool" (Psalm 99:5). His footstool is the earth. Christ took upon Himself earth of earth, because flesh is of the earth. He received His flesh from the flesh of Mary. Because He walked here in this same flesh, He gave us this very flesh to eat for salvation. No one who eats this flesh does not first worship it. Therefore, this is why the footstool of the Lord is worshiped. We not only not sin by worshiping it, we sin if we do not worship it. (*MPL*, 37:1264; *NPNF*, ser. 1, 8:485)

CHRYSOSTOM, on Hebrews 2 (p. 125):

It is great and wonderful and awe-inspiring that our flesh is seated above and worshiped by angels and archangels, by seraphim and cherubim. When I reflect on this, I am entranced and seem to be outside of myself. (*MPG*, 63:47; *NPNF*, ser. 1, 14:388)

The same, on 1 Corinthians 10 (p. 174, t. 6, p. 740, and t. 5, p. 261, ed. Frankf.):

This body, even when it is lying in a manger, is worshiped by the Magi. They took a long trip, and when they arrived, they worshiped with a lot of fear and trembling. (*MPG*, 61:202; *NPNF*, ser. 1, 12:143)

The same, in Epist. 65 to Leo:

Let us learn to know to which nature the Father said, "Share My seat." It is the same nature to which had been said, "You are dust and to dust you shall return."

THEOPHYLACT, from Chrysostom, on Matthew 28 (p. 311 [ed. Lutet., 8, 1631, fols. 184. 605]):

Since the human nature, which is united with the Word and only shortly before been condemned, is now seated in heaven, it is appropriate for Him to have said, "All power is given to Me in heaven." For the human nature, only recently having served, is now, in Christ, ruling over all things. (*MPG*, 123:484D; *Theophylact*, 257–58)

The same, on John 3:

He has given all things into the Son's hand, according to His humanity. (*MPG*, 123:1225A)

CYRIL, *On the Incarnation*, chapter 11 (t. 4, p. 241; t. 5, p. 695):

The Word introduced Himself into that which He was not, in order that man's nature might also become what it was not, being made resplendent with the grandeur of divine majesty, raised beyond nature, not that it has put the unchanging God beneath its nature. (*MPG*, 75:1383A; *Library*, 44:198)

Council of Ephesus (Cyril, t. 4, p. 140 [*Apologet, adv. Orient.*, t. 6, folio 196]), in Canon 11:

If anyone does not confess that the flesh of the Lord makes alive, because it was made the Word's own flesh, who makes everything alive, let him be anathema. (*MPG*, 76:311)

Cyril also (*ibid.*, p. 140; t. 4, p. 85), in his explanation of this anathematization, says that Nestorius was unwilling to ascribe the ability to make alive to the *flesh* of Christ, but explained the passages in John 6 as referring to the divinity alone. (*MPG*, 76:311; *NPNF*, ser. 2, 14:217)

THEODORET, Dialogue 2:

The body of the Lord was deemed worthy to be seated at the right hand of

God. It is worshiped by every creature and is called the body of the Lord of Nature, the body of God. (*MPG*, 83:168C)

The same author, on Psalm 8:

The human nature of Christ has received from God the honor of having dominion over the universe. (*MPG*, 80:920B)

LEO (folio 94 [Ep. 25, folio 246]), Epist. 11:

It is a promotion of that which is received, the human nature, not of God, when it is said that God has exalted Him and has given Him a name above every name, the name of Jesus, at which every knee should bow, and every tongue confess that Jesus Christ is Lord to the glory of God the Father. (*MPL*, 54:807; *NPNF*, ser. 2, 12:49)

DAMASCENE, book 3, chapter 18 (p. 251):

"Christ's divine will was eternal and omnipotent. His human will began in time and underwent its own natural and expected emotions. It was not omnipotent according to its own nature, but, because it truly and by nature became the will of God, it is also omnipotent." This means, as explained by a commentator: "The divine will has, by its own nature, the power to do all things that it wants to do, but Christ's human will does not have power to do everything it could do, by its nature, but it is united to God the Word. (*MPG*, 94:1076–77; *NPNF*, ser. 2, 9[pt. 2]:66)

The same, chapter 19:

The flesh of Christ is in fellowship with the operating divinity of the Word. Divine actions are accomplished by means of the body because He who is working through the divinity and humanity is one. It is necessary to know that His holy mind works according to its natural functions and therefore shares in understanding, knowing, and managing all things in the entire universe, not as the mere mind of a man, but as personally united with God; it is the mind of God. (*MPG*, 94:1080B/C; *NPNF*, ser. 2, 9[pt. 2]:68)

The same, in the same book, chapter 21:

The human nature does not, in and of itself, have knowledge of the future; but the Lord's soul, because of its personal identity and union with the Word Himself, apart from other divine criteria, was also rich in knowledge about the future.... We say that this Master and Lord of all creation, the one Christ, who is at the same time God and man, knows all things. For in Him are hidden all the treasures of wisdom and knowledge. (*MPG*, 94:1085A/C; *NPNF*, ser. 2, 9[pt. 2]:69)

NICEPHORUS, book 18, chapter 36:

When Christ was seen by His disciples on the mount in Galilee, He asserted that the highest power in heaven and on earth has been given to Him by the Father, that is, according to His human nature. (*MPG*, 145:742B)

# IV.

The Holy Scriptures, and the Fathers, understood that the majesty that Christ received in time included not only created gifts with their limited qualities, but also the glory and majesty of divinity that belongs to God, to which His human nature, in the person of the Son of God, had been exalted, and thus, the human nature received the power and efficacy of the divine nature that are peculiar to the Deity.

> And now, Father, glorify Me in Your own presence with the glory that I had with You before the world existed. (John 17:5)

> For in Him the whole fullness of deity dwells bodily. (Colossians 2:9)

HILARY, *On the Trinity*, book 3 (p. 28):

> The Word made flesh prayed that that which was from time, that is, has a beginning in time, might receive the glory of that brightness, which is without time. (*MPL*, 10:85B; *NPNF*, ser. 2, 9[pt. I]:66)

GREGORY OF NYSSA, quoted by Gelasius and Theodoret, Dialogue 2, concerning the saying of Peter, Acts 2:

> Being exalted by the right hand of God, etc. (t. 2, p. 333 [al. 330]): "This (right hand of God), through the union, raised to its own height the Man united to it. (*MPG*, 83:196; *Epistolae*, 1:549)

The same, *Concerning the Soul*:

> God, the Word, is never changed by the communion that He has with the body and soul, neither does He partake of their imperfection; rather, He transmits to them the power of His divinity and remains the same that He was even before the union.

BASIL THE GREAT, *On the Holy Nativity of Christ* (p. 231):

> How is Deity in the flesh? Just as fire is in iron, not by turning into iron, but by imparting itself into the iron. For fire does not run out to the iron, but remaining in its place, imparts its own specific power, which is not diminished when it is imparted. It fills the entire mass and becomes partaker of it. (Pseudo-Basil, *MPG*, 31:1460C)

EPIPHANIUS, in Ancoratus (folio 504 [folio 86, ed. Colon.]):

> Strengthening an earthly body with divinity, He united it into one power, brought it into one Divinity, being one Lord and one Christ, not two Christs nor two Gods, and so forth. (*MPG*, 43:168C/D)

CYRIL, on John, book 4, chapter 23:

> You are not entirely unwise when you deny that the flesh is able to make something alive. For if you are talking about the flesh alone, no, it cannot make anything alive at all. It is in need of something to make it alive. But when you are finished examining very carefully the mystery of the incarnation, having learned to know the life that dwells in the flesh, you will believe that although the flesh is not able to do anything by itself, it has nevertheless

become life-giving, because it has been united to the life-giving Word. It has been joined to the Word and so now it has been made capable of giving life. The flesh of Christ did not drag the Word of God down to its corruptible nature; rather, the flesh was elevated to the power of the better nature. Therefore, although the nature of the flesh, insofar as it is flesh, cannot make anything alive; nevertheless, it is able to do this because it has received the entire operation of the Word. The flesh of Paul or Peter or others cannot do this, but that of Life itself in which the fullness of the Godhead dwells bodily, can do this. Therefore, the flesh of all others can do nothing, only the flesh of Christ can make alive, because in it dwells the only-begotten Son of God. (*MPG*, 73:602C; *Library*, 43:435)

AUGUSTINE, *Against Felicianus the Arian*, chapter 11:

I cannot agree that it is true to say that the Deity experienced the violence done to His body in the same way that we know the flesh was glorified by the majesty of the Deity. (*MPL*, 42:1165)

THEODORET, chapter *Of Antichrist* (t. 2, p. 411):

The Word that became man did not confer a partial grace on the received [human] nature; rather, it pleased God that the whole fullness of Deity dwelt in it. (*MPG*, 83:530–31)

The same, on Psalm 21 (t. 1, p. 110):

If the received nature has been joined with the Divinity that received it, it participates and associates with the same glory and honor of the Divinity. (*MPG*, 80:1023C)

The same, on Hebrews 1:

The human nature itself, after the resurrection, attained divine glory. (*MPG*, 82:683B)

DAMASCENE, book 3, capp. 7. 15:

The divine nature imparts to the flesh its own excellences, while it remains impassible and does not participate in the passions of the flesh. (*MPG*, 94:1012C, 1058C; *NPNF*, ser. 2, 9[pt. 2]:52)

# V.

Christ, as God, has divine majesty essentially in one way. It is His possession, part of His very essence, in and of Himself. As man He has it another way, as a result of the personal union, not in and of His very essence as a man.

I am the way, and the truth, and the life. (John 14:6)

He has granted the Son also to have life in Himself. . . . because He is the Son of Man. (John 5:26–27)

CYRIL, book 12, *Thesauri*, chapter 15 (t. 2, p. 167 [t. 5, ed. Paris, 1638]):

There is one condition and quality pertaining to the creature and another to the Creator. Our nature, received by the Son of God, has exceeded its measure and by grace has been transferred into the condition of the One receiving it. (*MPG*, 75:535, 538)

The same, on John, book 2, chapter 144 (t. 1, p. 134 [t. 4, ed. Paris, 1638]):

Christ added the reason why He said that life and the power of judgment had been given Him by the Father. He said that it is because He is the Son of Man so that we would understand that all things were given to Him as man. However, the only-begotten Son is not a partaker of life, but is life by nature. (*MPG*, 73:383A/B; *Library*, 43:272)

The same, book 3, chapter 37 (t. 1, p. 181):

The body of Christ makes alive because it is the body of Life itself, retaining the power of the Word, now incarnate. It is full of the power of Him by whom all things exist and continue to live. (*MPG*, 73:519D–522A; *Library*, 43:376)

The same, book 4, chapter 14 (p. 201):

Because the Savior's flesh was joined to the Word of God, who is by nature Life, it was made life-giving. (*MPG*, 73:566D; *Library*, 43:410)

And chapter 18 (p. 204):

I filled My body with life. I received mortal flesh, but since I am by nature Life, I dwell in the flesh. I completely transformed it according to My life. (*MPG*, 73:586C; *Library*, 43:424)

Chapter 24 (p. 210):

The flesh, by its very nature, cannot on its own make anything alive. But in Christ it is not alone. It is united to the Son of God, who is in very essence Life. Therefore, when Christ says that His flesh gives life, He is not ascribing the power to make alive in the same way as He Himself, or His own Spirit, is able to make alive. For the Spirit makes alive by Himself. The flesh rises to this power by the personal union. We cannot understand with our minds or express with our tongue how this happens. We receive in silence and firm faith. (*MPG*, 73:603C/D; *Library*, 43:437)

The same, book 10, chapter 13 (p. 501):

The flesh of life, having been made the flesh of the Only-Begotten, has been brought to the power of life. (*MPG*, 74:343A/B)

The same, book 11, chapter 21 (p. 552):

Christ's flesh is not holy in and of itself. It is transformed by union with the Word into the power of the Word. It is the cause of salvation and sanctification to those who partake of it. Therefore, we say that that divinity works effectively through the flesh, not because of the flesh, but because of the Word. (*MPG*, 74:519A)

Book 6, Dialogue (t. 5, op. ed. cit.):

Christ is glorified by the Father, not because He is God, but because He was man. It was not a result of His own nature that He was divinely effective. He received it by the union and ineffable concurrence that God the Word is understood to have with humanity. (*MPG,* 75:1026A)

From the same author, *On the True Faith, to Theodosius* (p. 278):

He introduced His life into the received human body by virtue of the union. (*MPG,* 76:1190A/B)

In the same place (p. 279):

The Word is life-giving because of the inexpressible birth from the living Father. Yet, we should recognize where the effectiveness of divine glory is ascribed also to His own flesh. Also: We confess that the earthly flesh is incapable of giving life, so far as its own nature is concerned. (*MPG,* 76:1190A/B)

EPIPHANIUS, *Against the Ariomanites,* p. 337 (*Haeres.,* 69; p. 789, ed. Colon.):

His human nature was not something living apart, by itself; neither did He ever speak with the Divinity separated from the human nature, existing apart from it, as though they were two different persons, but always with the human nature united with the divine nature (there being one consecration), and even now the human nature knows the most perfect things because it is united in God and joined to the one Deity. (*MPG,* 42:305C/D; Robinson, 383)

AUGUSTINE, *Of the Words of the Lord,* Discourse 58 (t. 10, pp. 217–18):

I certainly do adore the Lord's flesh, yes, the perfect humanity in Christ, because it has been received by the divinity and united to Deity. I confess that there are not two different persons, but that one and same Son of God is God and man. In a word, if you separate man from God, I never believe or serve Him. (*MPL,* 39:220)

Also:

If anyone is disdainful about worshiping humanity, not a bare humanity by itself, but united to divinity, that is, the one Son of God, who is true God and true man, he will die eternally. (*MPL,* 39:220)

The same, *De Civitate,* book 10, chapter 24:

The flesh of Christ, by itself, does not cleanse believers, but through the Word, by which it has been received. (*MPL,* 41:301; *CSEL,* 40:486, 11; *NPNF,* ser. 1, 2:195)

COUNCIL OF EPHESUS, Canon 11 (in Cyril, t. 6, p. 196):

If anyone does not confess that the Lord's flesh is life-giving, for the reason that it was appropriated to the Word that gives life to all things, let him be anathema. (Denzinger, 262)

THEOPHYLACT, on John 3 (pp. 605, 184, ed. cit.):

He has given all things into His Son's hand, according to humanity. But if also according to divinity, what do we mean by this? The Father has given all things to the Son by reason of nature, not of grace. (*MPG,* 123:1225A)

The same, on Matthew 28:

> If you want to understand the statement, "All power is given to Me in heaven and on earth," as something God said about the Word, then understand that this means that everyone, both the willing and unwilling, acknowledge Me as God. But when this is said of the human nature, then understand it this way: I, previously the condemned nature, am now truly God according to the unconfused union with the Son of God, and I have received power over all things. (*MPG*, 123:484–85; *Theophylact*, 258)

DAMASCENE (book 3, chapter 17):

> He did divine things not according to the capabilities of the flesh, but because the Word, united to His flesh, displayed its own capabilities. For glowing iron does not burn because of some natural power it has, but only because it is united with fire. Therefore, in itself the flesh is mortal, but because of its personal union to the Word, it is able to give life. (*MPG*, 94:1069B/C; *NPNF*, ser. 2, 9[pt. 2]:66)

The same author (chapter 18):

> Christ's divine will was both eternal and omnipotent, etc. But His human will not only began in time, but also endured natural human qualities. It was not omnipotent, but because it truly has, by nature, become the will also of God the Word, it is also omnipotent. (*MPG*, 94:1076–77; *NPNF*, ser. 2, 9[pt. 2]:66)

> This is, as explained by a commentator:

> The divine will has, by its own nature, the power to do all things that it wants to do, but Christ's human will does not have power to do everything by nature, but only because it is united to God the Word.

The same author, in the same book, chapter 21:

> The human nature does not possess essential knowledge of the future; but the soul of the Lord, because of its union with the Word and the personal identity with it, was rich in the knowledge of the future, in addition to other divine attributes. (And at the end of the chapter:) We say that the one Christ, Master, and Lord of all creation, at the same time God and man, knows also all things. For in Him are hid all the treasures of wisdom and knowledge. (*MPG*, 94:1085A/C; *NPNF*, ser. 2, 9[pt. 2]:69)

From the same author (Book 2, chapter 22):

> Although the soul of the Lord by nature did not know the future, because it was personally united to the Word it had knowledge of all things, not by grace, but because of the personal union. (Shortly afterward:) Since the natures in our Lord Jesus Christ are distinct, the natural wills, that is, the powers of will, are also distinct. (*MPG*, 94:948A/B; *NPNF*, ser. 2, 9[pt 2]:69)

# VI.

The divine nature powerfully demonstrates and actually exerts its majesty, power, and efficacy (which is unique to the divine nature and always remains so) in, with, and through the human nature that is personally united to it. The human nature has such majesty because the entire fullness of the Godhead dwells personally in the received human flesh and blood of Christ.

Whom God put forward as a propitiation by His blood. (Romans 3:25)

Since, therefore, we have now been justified by His blood. (Romans 5:9)

And through Him to reconcile to Himself all things, whether on earth or in heaven, making peace by the blood of His cross. (Colossians 1:20)

ATHANASIUS, Oration 4, *Against the Arians* (*Epist. ad Adelph* c. *Arian*, t. 1, p. 161, ed. Colon.):

Why should the Lord's body not be worshiped when the Word, by stretching out His bodily hand, healed the person who was sick with a fever, and by speaking with a human voice raised Lazarus, and by extending His hands on the cross overthrew the prince of the air? (*MPG*, 26:1082B; *NPNF*, ser. 2, 4:577)

The same author, in Dialog 5, *Of the Trinity* (t. 2, op, f. 257):

God the Word, who was united to a man, does not perform miracles apart from the human nature. It has pleased him to work divine miracles through it, and in it, and with it. (And shortly afterward:) According to His good pleasure He made the humanity perfect above its own nature and did not prevent it from being a rational living being, a creature, a true human nature. (*MPG*, 28:1280–81)

CYRIL, *De Recta Fide ad Theodosium* (t. 5, op.):

The soul, having obtained union with the Word, descended into hell; but, using its divine power and efficacy, it said to the ones in bondage, "Go forth!"(*MPG*, 76:1166A)

The same author, book 1, *Ad Reginas*:

Christ, as God, gives life through His own flesh. (*MPG*, 76:1282B)

# VII.

The communication of divine majesty occurs also in glory, without mingling, annihilation, or denial of the human nature.

For the Son of Man is going to come with His angels in the glory of His Father. (Matthew 16:27)

[He] will come in the same way as you saw Him go into heaven. (Acts 1:11)

ATHANASIUS, Dialog 5, *Of the Trinity* (t. 2, f. 257, ed. Colon.):

According to His good pleasure He made the humanity perfect above its own nature and did not prevent it from being a rational living being, a creature, a true human nature. (*MPG*, 28:1280–81)

THEOPHYLACT, from Chrysostom, on Matthew 28 (p. 184):

> I, previously the condemned nature, being God, according to the unconfused union with the Son of God, have received power over all things. (*MPG*, 123:485A; *Theophylact*, 258)

CYRIL, book 4, chapter 24 (t. 4, p. 377, and 3, f. 783):

> He has shown that His entire body is full of the life-giving energy of the Spirit, not because it has lost the nature of flesh and has been turned into Spirit, but because it is united with Spirit, it has acquired the entire power to make alive. (*MPG*, 73:603B; *Library*, 43:437)

The same author, *Of the Incarnation*, chapter 8:

> By way of illustration, think of how fire adheres to a burning coal of wood, so also God the Word, united to humanity, has transformed the received nature into its glory and efficacy. God has been united to humanity in a way that we cannot fully understand, but has conferred on it even the operation of His [divine] nature. (*MPG*, 75:1379; *Library*, 44:194)

THEODORET, Dialogue 2 (t. 4, f. 82 and 112):

> The body of the Lord arose, glorified with divine glory and therefore incapable of decay and suffering. It arose immortal and is worshiped by human powers; nevertheless, it is still a body, having the former circumscription. (*MPG*, 83:163A)

The same author, in Dialogue 3, approves this sentence of Apollinarius:

> If the nature of iron is not changed when it is mingled with fire to such an extent that the iron is able to do things that pertain to the fire, neither therefore is the union of God with a body a change of the body, although it gives the body the ability to do divine things. (*MPG*, 83:215B)

DAMASCENE, book 3, chapter 17:

> The Lord's flesh was enriched with divine operations because of its complete personal union with the Word, but in no way did it experience any loss of those things that belong naturally to it. (*MPG*, 94:1069B; *NPNF*, ser. 2, 9[pt. 2]:66)

The same, book 2, chapter 22:

> Although the Lord's soul by nature did not know the future, nevertheless, because it was personally united to God the Word, it had knowledge of all things, not by grace, but because of the personal union.

And shortly afterward:

> Since the natures in Christ are distinct, the natural wills, that is, the powers of will, are also distinct. (*MPG*, 94:948A/B; *NPNF*, ser. 2, 9[pt. 2]:37)

# VIII.

According to its own nature, and because of the personal union, the human nature is a participant in, and capable of, the divine majesty that belongs to God.

For in Him the whole fullness of deity dwells bodily. (Colossians 2:9)

In whom are hidden all the treasures of wisdom and knowledge. (Colossians 2:3)

JUSTIN, in *Expositio Fidei*, p. 182 (f. 389, ed. Colon., 1686]:

Christ is not in others as He is in the Father, not because He is not in them, but because they are not capable of receiving the Divine as He has.

Also:

A defiled body does not receive rays of divinity. (*MPG*, 6:1237–39)

And shortly afterwards:

The Sun of Righteousness is, in substance, present equally to all things, since He is God. We, however, are weak and our eyes are dim because of the filth of sin. We are incapable of receiving the light. His own temple, His own pure eye, is capable of receiving the splendor of all the light, since it has been formed by the Holy Spirit and is altogether separated from sin. (*MPG*, 6:1240)

ORIGEN, *De Principiis*, book 2, chapter 6 (t. 1, op. f. 698 and 749, ed. Basil):

The entire soul of Christ receives the entire Word. It is received into His light and splendor. (*MPG*, 11:211C; *ANF*, 4:282)

Book 4:

The soul of Christ, united to the Word of God, is made fully capable of receiving the Son of God. (*MPG*, 11:405D; *ANF*, 4:378)

AUGUSTINE, Ep. 57:

Although God is entirely present to all creatures and dwells especially in believers, they do not entirely receive Him. According to differences in their ability to receive Him, some possess and receive more of Him, and others less. But when it comes to Christ, our Head, the Apostle says, "In Him dwells all the fullness of Deity bodily" (Colossians 2:9). (*MPL*, 33:837, 383, 847; *CSEL*, 52:113, 115–16; *Library*, 30:252)

# IX.

It is well known and undeniable that the Godhead, with its divine majesty, is not locally circumscribed [limited] by the flesh as though it were shut up in a container. Athanasius, Origen, Gregory of Nyssa and others correctly state this, and so does the Book of Concord, which expressly rejects it as an error to teach that the humanity of Christ has been locally expanded into all places, or that, by the personal union, the human nature of Christ has been transformed into an infinite essence. Nevertheless, since the divine and human nature in Christ are personally and inseparably united in Christ, the Holy Scriptures and holy Fathers testify that wherever Christ is, He is not there with only half His person, or with only a part of His person, for instance, the divinity alone, separate and bare, minus and without His assumed humanity, or that He is somehow personally united to it or separated from it, outside of the personal union with the humanity. His entire person, as God and man, according to the mode of the personal union with the humanity, which is an inscrutable mystery, is everywhere present in a way and in a measure that is known to God.

> He who descended is the one who also ascended far above all the heavens, that He might fill all things. (Ephesians 4:10)

OECUMENIUS explains it this way:

> Long ago He filled all things with His bare divinity. In order to fill all things with His flesh He became incarnate, both descending and ascending. (*MPG*, 118:1217/1220)

THEOPHYLACT, on the same passage (*Comment. in Eph.*, p. 535, ed. Lond., 1636):

> He fills all things with His dominion and working in the flesh, since even before He had filled all things with His divinity. These things oppose Paul of Samosata and Nestorius. (*MPG*, 124:1083D)

LEO, Epist. 10 (Ep. 24, chapter 5, p. 245, and in Serm., f. 121, ed. cit.):

> The Church catholic lives and advances in this faith, that in Christ Jesus we do not believe in the humanity without the true divinity, nor in the divinity without the true humanity. (*MPL*, 54:777; *NPNF*, ser. 2, 12[pt. 1]:42–43)

The same, in Discourse 3, *On the Passion:*

> The catholic faith teaches and requires that we know that in our Redeemer two natures have united and that while their unique properties remain, a union of both substances has taken place since the time that the Word became flesh in the womb of the Blessed Virgin. Therefore, we are not to think of God without thinking that He is man. Nor are we to think of the man, without thinking that He is God. (*MPL*, 54:319B; *NPNF*, ser. 2, 12[pt. 1]:165)

# X.

Since the article of Christology is especially intended to direct us to where we should seek and apprehend the entire person of the Mediator, God and man, the Book of Concord, as also all other holy Fathers, directs us not to wood, or stone, or anything else, but to that which Christ has pointed and directed us in His Word.

CYRIL, book 2, on John, chapter 32 (t. 3, p. 1063, ed. cit.):

> Christ's garments were divided into four parts, but His mantle alone remained undivided. This is a sign of a mystery. The four corners of the earth have been brought to salvation. They share the garment of the Word, that is, His flesh, among themselves in such a way that it is not divided. For the Only-Begotten, passing into each, so to be shared by each, sanctifies their soul and body by His flesh. He is all in all indivisibly and entirely. Because He is one,

He is everywhere, but in no way divided. (*MPG*, 74:659B/C)

THEOPHYLACT, on John 19 (f. 825, ed. cit.):

The holy body of Christ is indivisible even while it is "divided" and distributed to the four corners of the earth. It is distributed among them individually and sanctifies the soul of each one with the body. The Only-Begotten is by His own flesh in all, entirely and indivisibly because He is everywhere. He has in no way been divided, even as Paul exclaims [Ephesians 4:12]. (*MPG*, 124:278A/B)

CHRYSOSTOM (t. 4, p. 1773, ed. Basil. and t. 6, f. 846, ed. Frankf.), Homil. 17, *Ad Ebr.*, p. 16 (and AMBROSE, chapter 10, *Ad Hebraicos*):

Since He is offered up in many places, are there many Christs? Not at all. The one Christ is everywhere, being completely here and completely there, one body. For as He who is offered in many places is one body, and not many bodies, so is He also one sacrifice. He is that High Priest of ours who has offered the sacrifice that cleanses us. We also now offer that which, having been offered then, was not consumed. This is done in remembrance of that which was done then. "This do," says He, "in remembrance of Me." For we do not make another sacrifice, as the high priest, but always the same. We rather bring about a remembrance of the sacrifice. (Note: This quote is against the propitiatory sacrifice of the papist Mass). (*MPG*, 63:131; *NPNF*, ser. 1, 14:449)

# Conclusion

Christian reader, these testimonies of the ancient teachers of the Church have been provided here not to suggest that our Christian faith is founded on the authority of men. The true saving faith is not founded on any church teacher, old or new, but only and alone on God's Word, as contained in the Scriptures of the holy prophets and apostles, an unquestionable witness of divine truth. With his special and uncanny crafts, Satan has caused fanatics to lead men from the Holy Scriptures—which, thank God! even a common layman can now read with benefit—to the writings of the Ancient Church, which are like a broad ocean. A person who has not read the Fathers carefully cannot know precisely whether or not these new teachers are quoting their words correctly and thus they leave a person in grievous doubt. This is why we have been compelled to declare, with this Catalog, and to show everyone that this new false doctrine has as little foundation in the ancient, pure teachers of the Church as in the Holy Scriptures. It is, in fact, diametrically opposed to it. They quote the Church Fathers in such a way as to give them a false meaning, contrary to the Fathers' will. They do this just as they wantonly pervert the simple, plain, and clear words of Christ's testament and the pure testimonies of the Holy Scriptures. Because of this, the Book of Concord directs everyone to the Holy Scriptures and the simple Catechism. The person who clings to this basic form with true, simple faith provides what is best for his soul and conscience, since it is built on a firm and immovable Rock (Matthew 7; 17; Galatians 1; Psalm 119).

# APPENDIX B:
# CHRISTIAN VISITATION ARTICLES
# 1592

### ARTICLE I
## The Holy Supper

The pure and true doctrine of our churches concerning the Holy Supper:

I. The words of Christ, "Take, eat, this is My body; drink, this is My blood" are to be understood simply and according to the letter, as they read.

II. In the Sacrament there are two things that are given and received with each other: one earthly, which is bread and wine; and one heavenly, which is the body and blood of Christ.

III. This giving and receiving occurs here on earth, and not above in heaven.

IV. It is the true natural body of Christ that hung on the cross, and the true natural blood that flowed from the side of Christ.

V. The body and blood of Christ are received not only by faith spiritually, which can also occur outside of the Supper, but here with the bread and wine orally. Yet this happens in an unexplainable and supernatural way, as a pledge and assurance of the resurrection of our bodies from the dead.

VI. The oral partaking of the body and blood of Christ is done not only by the worthy, but also by the unworthy, who approach without repentance and true faith. Nevertheless, this leads to a different result: by the worthy for salvation, by the unworthy for judgment.

### ARTICLE II
## The Person of Christ

The pure and true doctrine of our churches on this article concerning the person of Christ:

I. In Christ there are two distinct natures, the divine and the human. These remain to eternity unconfused and unseparated.

II. These two natures are personally so united with each other that there is only one Christ, and one person.

III. Because of this personal union, it is rightly said (and it is true also in deed and truth) that God is man, and man, God. Also, Mary bore the Son of God, and God redeemed us with His own blood.

IV. Through this personal union and the exaltation that followed it, Christ, according to His flesh, has been placed at God's right hand. He has received all power in heaven and on earth, and has become partaker of all divine majesty, honor, power, and glory.

## ARTICLE III
# Holy Baptism

The pure and true doctrine of our churches concerning this article of Holy Baptism:

I. There is but *one* Baptism and *one* washing—not the kind that removes the filth of the body, but one that washes us from sins.

II. Through Baptism, as the washing of regeneration and renewing of the Holy Spirit, God saves us. He works in us such righteousness and cleansing from sins that the person who perseveres in this covenant and confidence unto the end is not lost, but has eternal life.

III. All who are baptized into Christ Jesus are baptized into His death. Through Baptism they are buried with Him into His death and have put on Christ.

IV. Baptism is the washing of regeneration because in Baptism we are born anew. We are sealed with and graciously given the Spirit of adoption.

V. Unless a person is born of water and the Spirit, he cannot enter into the kingdom of God (John 3:5). However, this does not refer to a case of necessity.

VI. That which is born of the flesh is flesh (John 3:6). By nature we all are the children of God's wrath, for we are begotten of sinful seed and are all conceived in sins.

## ARTICLE IV
# Predestination and the Eternal Providence of God

The pure and true doctrine of our churches concerning this article:

I. Christ has died for all people and, as the Lamb of God, has borne the sins of the whole world.

II. God created no one for condemnation, but wants all people to be saved, and to come to the knowledge of the truth. Therefore, He commands all to hear His Son Christ in the Gospel. By the Gospel He promises the power and working of the Holy Spirit for conversion and salvation.

III. Many people are condemned by their own guilt who are either unwilling to hear the Gospel of Christ or later fall from grace. This happens either by error against the foundation of grace or by sins against conscience.

IV. All sinners who repent are received into grace, and no one is excluded, even though his sins were as scarlet. For God's mercy is much greater than the sins of all the world, and God has compassion on all His works.

FALSE AND ERRONEOUS DOCTRINE OF THE CALVINISTS

# Concerning the Holy Supper:

I. [Calvinists teach] that the words of Christ cited above are to be understood in a figurative way, and not as they read.

II. In the Supper there are only bare signs; the body of Christ, however, being as far away from the bread as the highest heaven is from the earth.

III. Christ is present in the bread and wine only by His power and working, and not with His body, just as the sun is present and effective here below on earth by its brilliancy and working, while the sun itself is above in the sky.

IV. The bread is a figurative body (*typicum corpus*), which is only signified and prefigured.

V. Christ's body is received by faith alone, which soars into heaven. His body is not received orally.

VI. Only the worthy receive Christ's body and blood. However, the unworthy who do not have faith that can ascend into heaven receive nothing but bread and wine.

FALSE AND ERRONEOUS DOCTRINE OF THE CALVINISTS

# Concerning the Person of Christ,

WHICH CONFLICTS ESPECIALLY WITH THE THIRD AND FOURTH ARTICLES OF THE PURE DOCTRINE:

I. In the first place, Calvinists teach that the expression "God is man" and "Man is God" is figurative.

II. The human nature has communion with the divine not in deed and truth, but only in name and words.

III. It is impossible for God, with all His omnipotence, to cause the natural body of Christ to be at the same time in more than one place.

IV. By His exaltation Christ, according to His human nature, has received only created gifts and finite power, and neither knows nor can do all things.

V. Christ, according to His human nature, rules absently, just as the King of Spain rules the new islands.

VI. It is damnable idolatry if the confidence and faith of the heart is placed in Christ not only according to His divine, but also according to His human nature, and the honor of adoration is directed to both natures.

FALSE AND ERRONEOUS DOCTRINE OF THE CALVINISTS

# Concerning Holy Baptism:

I. Calvinists teach that Baptism is an outward washing of water, whereby an inner washing from sins is only signified.

II. Baptism neither works nor confers regeneration, faith, the grace of God, and salvation, but only signifies and seals these.

III. Not all who are baptized with water, but only the elect, receive from Baptism the grace of Christ or the gift of faith.

IV. Regeneration occurs not in and at Baptism, but only afterward in adult years, and in some people not until old age.

V. Salvation does not depend on Baptism. So emergency Baptism should not be permitted in the Church. If the service of the Church cannot be obtained, the child should be allowed to die without Baptism.

VI. Children of Christians are holy before Baptism and from their mothers' wombs. Indeed, while still in their mothers' wombs, they are in the covenant of eternal life. Otherwise, holy Baptism could not be administered to them.

### FALSE AND ERRONEOUS DOCTRINE OF THE CALVINISTS

## Concerning Predestination and the Providence of God:

I. Christ died, not for all people, but only for the elect.

II. God created most people for eternal condemnation and is unwilling that they be converted and saved.

III. The elect and regenerate cannot lose faith and the Holy Spirit and be condemned, even though they commit great sins and crimes of every kind.

IV. Those who are not elect must be condemned, and cannot attain salvation, even though they are baptized a thousand times, daily go to the Lord's Supper, and also live as holy and blameless as ever possible.

# APPENDIX C:
## ABOUT THIS EDITION

Our text for the Book of Concord is not a new translation from the original German and Latin texts. This reader's edition is an updated version of the translation originally prepared by William H. T. Dau and G. Friedrich Bente for the *Concordia Triglotta*, published in 1921.

For years, readers have appreciated the *Triglotta* translation. But over time it has become less and less readable for a variety of reasons. When Dau and Bente prepared their text, high school and college Latin courses were common. The audience for their English translation was more accustomed to seeing Latin-based terms and the complex sentences preferred in Latin composition. In the past eighty years, Latin instruction has virtually disappeared and English grammatical style has trended toward more simple and direct sentences. In view of these changes, we updated Dau and Bente's fine translation for modern use.

For example, their translation, closely following Latin and German style, often piled up subordinate clauses in complex sentences. Some of these sentences made up full paragraphs or covered an entire page. We have often simplified these passages by changing the subordinate clauses into independent sentences. Then we started the main clause with *therefore*, to show the relationship between the sentences. When we could not see a clear method for updating Dau and Bente's translation, we referred to the German and Latin texts for help in providing a simpler, clearer text.

Where Dau and Bente often used Latin-based words, we have used more common English words, often updating with contemporary meanings in mind. For example, the word *remission* now means something quite different to the English reader than it did a few generations ago. Today, this term makes us think of cancer and medical treatment instead of God's mercy. Therefore, throughout the manuscript, we have changed *remission* to the more familiar word *forgiveness*.

When the German and Latin texts differed from each other or included unique passages, Dau and Bente inserted the different reading in brackets. We deleted this bracketed material in most cases and focused on providing an English version for either the Latin or the German. (See Bente's preface on p. 681 for information on the base text of each document.)

# APPENDIX D:
## PREFACE TO THE *CONCORDIA TRIGLOTTA*

Memorialized by the Faculty of Concordia Seminary, St. Louis, Missouri, the Evangelical Lutheran Synod of Missouri, Ohio, and Other States, assembled as Fifteenth Delegate Synod from June 20 to 29, 1917, at Milwaukee, Wisconsin, unanimously passed the very appropriate resolution to publish as a memorial of the Quadricentennial of the Glorious Reformation a German-Latin-English edition of the Book of Concord containing the Symbols of the Evangelical Lutheran Church.

The work on *Concordia Triglotta* was begun immediately. Chiefly owing to the economic conditions created by the World War, however, the completion of the large undertaking was delayed much longer than anticipated. And the fact that we are now in a position to write the preface to the finished book, together with its detailed indexes and extensive historical introductions, we regard and gratefully acknowledge as a special favor of God, whom alone also we credit with whatever merit anyone may anywhere justly ascribe to this work, or any part of it.

As for the German and Latin texts embodied in *Concordia Triglotta,* the former was compared with the original German edition, published 1580 at Dresden. Obsolete forms as *Gezeugnis, Oberkeit, gebeutet,* and, as a rule, also such forms as *nimmet, gehet, stehet,* and so on, were replaced with *Zeugnis, obrigkeit, gebeitet, nimmt, geht, steht,* and so forth. The Latin text was revised according to the first authentic Latin edition, published 1584 in Leipzig, and quite a number of misprints still found in Mueller's eleventh edition of 1912 were corrected.

While I, the undersigned, alone am responsible for the Latin and German text, the English translation of the *Triglot* is throughout the joint effort of Prof. W. H. T. Dau and myself. It is based on the original German and Latin texts, respectively, and on the existing English translations, chiefly those incorporated in Jacobs's *Book of Concord.*

The preface to the *Christian Book of Concord,* the *Augsburg Confession,* the *Apology of the Augsburg Confession,* and the treatise *Of the Power and Primacy of the Pope* are translated from the Latin; the *Smalcald Articles,* the two *Catechisms* of Luther, the *Formula of Concord,* and the *Visitation Articles,* from the German. In the *Catalog of Testimonies,* the translation of the introduction, the ten theses, and the conclusion are based on the German text, while the passages quoted from *Orthodox Antiquity* are translated from the original Greek and Latin, respectively.

The Lutheran Church differs from all other churches in being essentially the Church of the pure Word and unadulterated Sacraments. Not the great number of her adherents, not her organizations, not her charitable and other institutions, not her beautiful customs and liturgical forms, and so forth, but the precious truths confessed by her symbols in perfect agreement with the Holy Scriptures constitute the true beauty and rich treasures of our Church, as well as the never-failing source of her vitality and power.

Wherever the Lutheran Church ignored her symbols or rejected all or some of them, there she always fell an easy prey to her enemies. But wherever she held fast to her God-given crown, esteemed and studied her Confessions, and actually made them a norm and standard of her entire life and practice, there the Lutheran Church flourished and confounded all her enemies.

Accordingly, if Lutherans truly love their Church, and desire and seek her welfare, they must be faithful to her Confessions and constantly be on their guard lest anyone rob her of her treasure. To strengthen this loyalty and to further facilitate the study of our "Golden Concordia,"—such is the object also of this Jubilee Edition— the *Triglot Concordia*.

May God be pleased, as in the past, so also in the future, to bless our Church, and graciously keep her in the true and only saving Christian faith as set forth and confessed in the Lutheran symbols, whose paramount object is to maintain the gem of Luther's Reformation, the blessed doctrine of salvation by grace only, which most wonderfully magnifies the great glory of our God, and alone is able to impart solid comfort to poor sinners.

F. Bente
Concordia Seminary, St. Louis, Missouri
July 4, 1921

# INDEXES

## ABBREVIATIONS

| | |
|---|---|
| AC | Augsburg Confession |
| Ap | Apology of the Augsburg Confession |
| Ep | Epitome of the Formula of Concord |
| FC | Formula of Concord |
| LC | Large Catechism |
| LW | Luther's Works, American Edition |
| SA | Smalcald Articles |
| SC | Small Catechism |
| SD | Solid Declaration of the Formula of Concord |
| Tr | Treatise on the Power and Primacy of the Pope |
| WA | Weimar Edition of Luther's Works |

## Citation Examples

AC XX 4 (Augsburg Confession, Article XX, paragraph 4)

Ap IV 229 (Apology of the AC, Article IV, paragraph 229)

FC SD X 24 (Solid Declaration of the Formula of Concord, Article X, paragraph 24)

FC Ep V 8 (Epitome of the Formula of Concord, Article V, paragraph 8)

LC V 32, 37 (Large Catechism, Part 5, paragraphs 32 and 37)

SA III I 6 (Smalcald Articles, Part III, Article I, paragraph 6)

SC III 5 (Small Catechism, Part III, paragraph 5)

Tr 5 (Treatise, paragraph 5)

# GLOSSARY

**Absolve.** To set free from sin. By virtue of his office and in the name and stead of Christ, a pastor absolves those who have confessed their sins, affirmed their faith in Christ, and promise to amend their lives (Matthew 16:19; 18:18; John 20:19–23). The Lutheran Church retained private Confession and Absolution as "the very voice of the Gospel," declaring that it would be impious to abolish it (AC XI; Ap XI 2; SA III VIII; SC V). Absolution may be called a Sacrament (Ap XIII 4).

**Accident.** (Latin: *accidens.*) That which does not exist by itself essentially but subsists in another self-existent essence (FC Ep I 23; FC SD I 54; see also *Substance*).

**Adiaphora.** (singular = *adiaphoron.*) From the Greek, meaning "indifferent things." Church rites neither commanded nor forbidden by God (e.g., making the sign of the cross; bowing during the Gloria Patri). Church rites cease being indifferent when by their use or disuse they compromise the confession of faith (FC Ep X; FC SD X).

**Administer. Administration.** To faithfully deliver God's Word and Sacraments to the intended recipients.

**Allegory.** Understanding Scripture in symbolic terms. In this view, the "heavenly" meaning behind a biblical person or event should be the focus of scriptural interpretation. Rejected by Luther and other reformers in favor of literal Bible interpretation, unless context directs otherwise.

**Alloeosis.** A figure of speech used by Zwingli to teach that the Scripture spoke figuratively when it ascribed the human attributes of Christ to His whole person, as when Christ appeared bodily after the resurrection (e.g., for Zwingli, Luke 24:26 could only describe Christ's human nature).

**Alms. Almsgiving.** (Greek: *eleemosyne*, "mercy, pity.") *Alms* means gifts to the poor, but in some sectors of the Early Church alms were divided into four parts: for the bishops, for other clergy, for the poor, and for the repair of churches. Idea imported from the Apocrypha that giving alms was meritorious; Luther restored almsgiving to its New Testament status as a work of the new life of faith.

**Anathema.** In the New Testament and in Church terminology a solemn curse, pronounced in God's name on heretics and the ungodly (Galatians 1:8–9; 1 Corinthians 16:22). Designates eternal separation from God (Romans 9:3); also used as a formula for sinful cursing (1 Corinthians 12:3; Acts 23:14).

**Apology.** (Greek: *apologia*, "defense.") A public defense or clarification of stated belief.

**Apostle.** (Greek: *apostolos*, "sent one.") One of the Twelve, or St. Paul, who was chosen by Jesus to guide the mission of the Early Church.

**Article.** Sections of a document or other piece of writing indicated by specific numbers or letters.

**Atonement.** (Greek: *katallage* [Romans 5:11]; often otherwise "reconciliation" [Romans 5:10; 2 Corinthians 5:19]). Look at the word, *at-one-ment.* It properly reflects a mutual exchange, or a drawing together of parties previously separated. God's action in Christ to forgive sin in order to restore the relationship between Himself and His fallen creatures.

**Attrition.** Term used by Roman theologians: hatred of sin arising from love of the offended God is called "perfect *contrition*," while other motives such as fear of hell and of punishment, or realization of the heinousness of sin, is called *attrition*. The Roman Church teaches that attrition alone does not justify, but that it prepares the penitent to receive grace, and that if people properly receive the Sacrament of Penance, they are justified.

**Benefit.** Mercy or kindness resulting in spiritual or temporal blessings.

**Bishop.** (Greek: *episkospos,* "overseer.") Used in the New Testament for those who governed and directed the Christian communities. The New Testament does not distinguish between bishops and presbyters (Acts 14:23; 20:17, 28). The Lutheran Symbols recognized the rank of bishops and described their true function as preaching the Gospel, administering the Sacraments, and using the Keys (AC XXVIII; Ap XXVIII; Tr 60–82; SA II IV 9; III 10).

**Call. Calling.** A person's occupation or duties before God. Every baptized Christian has been called to at least one area of service with specific responsibilities, whether as mother or father, son or daughter, engineer, teacher, citizen, employee, and so on. Through the Church, God calls men into service as pastors. Also referred to as *vocation.*

**Canon.** (Greek: *kanon,* "rule" or "standard.") May refer to (a) particular dogmatic formulations approved by Church councils; (b) the authoritative list of the books of the Bible; or (c) the unchanging high point of the Mass containing the Words of Institution and certain prayers.

**Capernaitic.** Term derived from a misinterpretation of Jesus' discourse at Capernaum on the bread of life (John 6:26–58). Instead of a "spiritual" eating and drinking of the true body and true blood of Christ in the Eucharist, capernaitic eating refers to a coarse "rending" of His flesh by the mouth.

**Catechism.** (Greek: *katechein,* "to teach.") Primarily a manual of religious instruction often published in question-and-answer format. *See* pp. 335–37.

**Catechumen.** (See *Catechism.*) A person receiving instruction and examination in the basics of the Christian faith and life, leading either to Baptism and/or confirmation.

**Catholic.** (Greek: *katholikos,* "universal," or "general.") A term first applied to the Christian Church as a whole in a letter of Ignatius (ca. AD 110): "Where Christ is, there is the catholic Church." In Lutheran theology (as in early Christendom) the word is often used of the one, holy, catholic ("Christian"), and apostolic Church united to Christ by faith, and transcending time, space, and all other barriers.

**Christendom.** Properly, Christianity as exemplified by its distinct teachings concerning Jesus of Nazareth; secondarily, areas where such teachings corporately or institutionally appear .

**Clementines.** Writings ascribed to Clement of Rome, of which only Clement's first letter to the Corinthians is considered authentic.

**Cloister.** (Middle Latin: *claustrum,* "room in a monastery.") 1. A monastery or convent. 2. A covered passage on the side of a court with one side walled and the other open, usually connecting buildings around an open court.

**Collection.** Money or other goods gathered to support the Church, clergy, or poor.

**Concordia.** (Latin: "with the same heart.") Harmony and union based on agreement in doctrine.

**Concupiscence.** The material element of original sin (AC II 4), which seeks and loves carnal things (not only sinful lusts of the body, but also carnal wisdom and righteousness), ignores and despises God, lacks fear and trust in Him, hates His judgment and flees it, is angry at Him, despairs of His mercy, and trusts in temporal things (Romans 7:7, 23; 1 Corinthians 2:14; Ap II). The Roman Church regards concupiscence as the tendency to, but not actual, sin.

**Condign merit.** See *Meritum condigni.*

**Confess.** 1. To profess or openly acknowledge one's faith in anyone or anything, especially in Christ and His Gospel (Matthew 10:32; Luke 12:8; 1 John 2:23; 4:15). 2. To express agreement with that which is confessed: creed, confession, or symbol. 3. To acknowledge, admit, or disclose one's own sins, either publicly or privately.

**Confessor.** 1. One who avows faith. 2. A martyr in the early Church. 3. One who is known for a holy life, especially under persecution. 4. A pastor who hears private Confession and pronounces Absolution.

**Confirmation.** A Church rite associated with post-baptismal instruction in the basics of the Christian faith.

**Congruent merit.** *See* Meritum congrui.

**Contrition.** Movement of the heart prior to conversion, namely, "that the heart perceive sin, [and] dread God's wrath" (FC SD II 70). Scripture teaches two truths about contrition: (1) Contrition always precedes genuine conversion (FC SD II 70). Fear of God's wrath and damnation always precedes faith (Joel 2:12; Mark 1:15; Luke 15:18; 18:13; 24:47; Acts 2:37: 16:29; FC SD II 54, 70). True contrition is not active, that is, fabricated remorse, but passive, that is, true sorrow of the heart, suffering, and pain of death (SA III III 2). It should not be concluded from this that contrition is a cause of forgiveness (Romans 3:28). (2) Contrition in no way brings about, implements, or occasions justification through faith (FC SD II, 30–31).

**Corporeal.** (Latin: *corpus*, "body.") Having not simply a spiritual substance, but also a material substance, or a body.

**Covenant.** A formal, binding agreement between two or more parties promising the fulfillment of some act. In the Bible, covenants with God are generally associated with God's initiation of the covenant, His promise of some action associated with the covenant, and the shedding of blood. By virtue of His cross, the Lord's Supper is the "New Covenant" for the forgiveness of sins (Matthew 26:26–28; Mark 14:22–24; Luke 22:19–20; 1 Corinthians 11:23–26).

**Covet.** The desire to gain at the expense of another.

**Curia.** In Roman Church usage, the departments and officials used by the pope to administer the affairs of the church, although in a broader sense the term includes all dignitaries and officials forming the immediate entourage of the pope.

**Decalogue.** (Greek: *deka logoi*, the "ten words.") The fundamental moral Law given by God to Moses at Sinai: The Ten Commandments (Exodus 19; Deuteronomy 5).

**Decretals.** Compilations of Roman Church laws and regulations, especially authoritative papal decisions on certain matters. Some, such as the Pseudo-Isidorian Decretals, were a combination of both genuine and spurious documents.

**Diet.** The deliberative assembly of the Holy Roman Empire composed of lay and clerical leaders.

**Diocese.** (Greek: *dioikesis*, "housekeeping," or "administration.") Territory administered by a bishop normally assisted by lesser clergy, and divided into parishes. Term derived from civil designation of territories beyond the empire.

**Dispensation.** Relaxation of an ecclesiastical law (vows, oaths, Church practices such as fasting, etc.) in a special case. The Council of Trent limited this power to the pope.

**Doctrine.** (Latin: *docere*, "to teach.") The teachings, principles, or tenets held and spread by a group.

**Dogma.** (Greek: *dokein*, "to seem.") A doctrine or doctrines (usually of the Church) considered authoritative on their own merits.

**Ecclesiastical.** (Greek: *ekklesia*, "assembly.") Having to do with the Church, its leadership, ritual, or members.

**Ecumenical.** (Greek: *oikoumene*, "the inhabited world.") Worldwide, or universal in nature and scope (see *Catholic*).

**Elder.** Term derived from the Old (Exodus 3:16) and New Testaments (Luke 7:3). The Greek word *presbyteros*, "elder," is a synonym for *episkopos* "bishop" (Acts 20:17, 28), "ruler" (1 Timothy 5:17), and "pastor" (1 Peter 5:1–4).

Large congregations had a number of presbyters or elders (James 5:14; Acts 15:4, 6, 23; 20:17, 28; 21:18). At least some elders preached and taught (1 Timothy 5:17).

**Enchiridion.** (Greek: *encheiridion*, "handbook.") A manual or handbook of Christian teaching. A name for the catechism.

**Enthusiasm. Enthusiasts.** Belief that Christians should expect special revelations or experiences from the Holy Spirit. Enthusiasts expect God to draw, enlighten, justify, and save them without the means of grace (Word and Sacraments).

**Ethics.** 1. A discipline with such concepts as good, bad, duty, and obligation. 2. A set of moral principles or values. 3. The philosophical study of behavior and principles of conduct.

**Eucharist.** (Greek: *eucharistesas*, "when He had given thanks," [1 Corinthians 11:24].) The Breaking of Bread (Matthew 26:26; 1 Corinthians 10:16), Holy Communion (1 Corinthians 10:16–17), the Lord's Table (1 Corinthians 10:21), the Lord's Supper (1 Corinthians 11:20), the Mass.

**Evangelical.** (Greek: *euangelion*, "good news.") Term meaning "loyal to the Gospel of Jesus Christ." The Lutheran Reformation was evangelical in that it emphasized the doctrine of Christ's atonement for sin.

*Ex opere operato.* (Latin: "for the sake of the work performed.") In the Roman Church, Sacraments, simply based on their technical performance, confer grace so long as the recipient does not put an obstacle (usually mortal sin) in the way. According to this view, faith in the heart of the recipient is not required.

**Faith.** 1. The body of truth found in creeds (objective). 2. The human response to divine activity (subjective); the personal appropriation of divine truth (itself a "gift," not a "work" [Ephesians 2:8–9]).

**Foreordained.** Predestined; selected, determined, or planned in advance.

**Gospel.** 1. The Gospel of Jesus Christ, in its proper and narrow sense, is the glad tidings of forgiveness, peace, life, and joy, the eternal divine counsel of redemption, of which Christ Himself ever was, is, and will be the living center, the very heart and soul. The Gospel (a) imparts the forgiveness of sin; (b) produces true joy and the zeal to do good works; and (c) destroys sin both outwardly and inwardly.

2. In the broad sense, the term *Gospel* may also refer to the sum of Christian teaching, including both Law and Gospel.

3. The word *Gospel* also designates a particular account of Jesus written by one of the four evangelists.

**Grace.** God's good will and favor in Christ toward sinners who can plead no merit. Grace implies mercy or compassion for one who has by every right forfeited his or her claim to love. God's grace to the sinner is "free" because it is not grounded in any worthiness of mankind (Romans 11:6). In the Roman Church, grace is more of a power given by God to do good works ("infused grace") so as to earn righteousness.

**Heresy.** (Greek: *hairesis*, "act of choosing," then "chosen opinion.") Stubborn error in an article of faith in opposition to Scripture.

**Holy.** Without sin, perfect in goodness or righteousness, or set apart for a divine purpose.

**Image of God.** The knowledge of God and holiness of the will, which was present in man before the fall (Colossians 3:10; Ephesians 4:24). This image is to be restored fully in believers only at Christ's Second Coming.

**Indulgences.** Roots of the Roman doctrine of indulgences reach back to the ancient practice of penitential discipline. As the penitential system changed its character and the Roman sacrament of penance evolved, penance was no longer regarded as a mere expression of sorrow for sin or even as the discharge of church penalties, but as pleasing to God, meritorious, and compensatory for sin. It was held to remove, according to the degree of its merit, a portion of that temporal punishment of sin (chiefly purgatory) that could not be removed by Absolution. Commutations of penance, or indulgences, became commutations of divine punishment and were gained by giving money to churches and monasteries, by pilgrimages, and sometimes by direct payment to the priest. *Contrition*, or at least *attrition*, was in theory necessary to gain indulgence. *See* pp. 90–91.

**Institute.** To set up, establish, or begin.

**Interim.** The provisional agreement in religious matters until the next Church council.

**Jubilee.** Also called "holy years." Often, popes offer plenary indulgences (removal of the temporal punishment of sins) to the faithful who participate in certain activities during jubilee years.

**Jurisdiction.** Ecclesial power, authority, or responsibility granted to pastors and/or bishops either by divine or human right (Tr 60–82).

**Justification.** Judicial act of God consisting in the charging of our sin to Christ and the crediting of Christ's righteousness to us. This justification is received through the gift of faith. The Lutheran Confessions call the doctrine of justification the most important teaching of divine revelation (Ap IV 2, 3; FC SD III 6). Justification is both objective (won by Christ for all people) and subjective (applied personally through the means of grace).

**Keys.** The peculiar, special, unique spiritual power given by Christ to the whole Church (Matthew 16:19; 18:15–20; John 20:22–23; Revelation 1:18). It includes all spiritual rights, duties, and privileges necessary for the welfare of the Church on earth, and conveys God's grace through preaching, absolving, administering Baptism and the Lord's Supper, and through mutual conversation and consolation. In particular, the Office of the Keys (administered by pastors [AC V]) gives power to forgive and retain sins (loosing and binding), not merely to announce and declare to people the forgiveness or retention of sins, but actually to give forgiveness to penitent sinners and to deny forgiveness to impenitent sinners (John 20:23; 2 Corinthians 2:10).

**Kyria.** (Greek for "curia.") *See* Curia.

**Law.** God's will, which shows people how they should live in order to please God (e.g., the Ten Commandments), condemns their failure to fulfill His will (sin), and threatens God's wrath because of sin. The preaching of the Law is the cause of contrition. Although the ceremonial laws of the Old Testament have been abolished (Colossians 2:16–17), the Moral Law (*see* Decalogue) is in force until the end of time (Matthew 5:18).

**Levitical.** Having to do with the Levites, the biblical Book of Leviticus, or (in general) Jewish ceremonial laws.

**Liturgy.** (Greek: *leitourgia*, "public service.") In a narrow sense, *liturgy* means the order of service for the celebration of Holy Communion. In a wider sense, the term means the whole system of formal worship.

**Mass.** (From Latin: *missa*, perhaps from the concluding words of public worship, *Ite, missa est*, "Go; it is the dismissal.") An older name for the Lord's Supper, which in the Middle Ages became the most common name for the service in the Western Church. Lutherans kept the Mass, although purified from certain abuses (AC XXIV 1, 40; Ap XXIV 1).

**Material.** Having to do with matter or physical substance; not spiritual.

***Meritum condigni.*** (Latin: "condign merit.") According to Roman Church teaching, the reward people gain for themselves by grace. God rewards the actions of believers out of a sense of justice, as holding a debt, for the work performed. The Confessions reject the distinctions of condignity and congruity as screens for Pelagianism (Ap IV 19) robbing Christ of His honor, giving it to people (Ap V 195–197), and leading eventually to doubt and despair (Ap V 200).

***Meritum congrui.*** (Latin: "congruent merit.") According to Roman Church teaching, the reward people gain for themselves by their own power. God rewards the actions of believers on the basis of His own liberality. *See* Meritum condigni.

**Metonymy.** A figure of speech whereby one word, possessing characteristics or associations with another word, is used as its substitute. Example: "I am the *Vine*; you are the *branches*" (John 15:5).

**Nature.** The essence or inherent attributes of a thing.

**Office.** 1. A particular position or area of responsibility having certain prescribed duties; 2. Any number of religious services (i.e., a "choir office").

**Office of the Keys.** *See* Keys.

**Omnipotence.** (Greek: "all-power.") An attribute of God by reason of which He can and does perform whatever He pleases (Psalm 115:3).

*Omnis utriusque sexus.* (Latin: "All of both sexes.") The twenty-first canon of the Fourth Lateran Council (1215), which commanded every Christian having reached the age of discretion to confess all sins to a priest and to receive Holy Communion, at least annually during Easter. Failure to do so could result in excommunication.

**Oracles.** In Greek and Roman religions, revelation given through divine means; often refers to the person through whom a god speaks.

**Orthodox.** (Greek: "right teaching," or "right praise.") Implies conformity to a certain standard; used especially in a religious sense of correct doctrine and worship.

**Pagan.** (Latin: *paganus*, "of the country.") A religious, or non-religious person, opposed to Christianity. Since Christianity first came to cities of the Roman empire, those who lived in the country adhered longer to non-Christian religions; hence the association of the word *pagan* with the concept of unbelief.

**Papacy. Papal.** The office of the Roman pope. Having to do with the pope, his authority, or the Roman Church in general.

**Parish.** Territory of a congregation in which it exercises its usual functions; part of a diocese.

**Passover.** A major Jewish festival recalling the Exodus of the Hebrew people from Egypt (Exodus 12:21–51).

**Pastor.** (Latin: "shepherd.") Christ continues His prophetic and priestly work through the work of the ministry; those who are called by Christian congregations or groups of congregations are Christ's undershepherds, Christ Himself being the one Lord and Master (Matthew 23:8; 1 Peter 5:4). The means of grace were given to the Church by God, who calls certain men through her to administer them to the congregation. Also referred to as bishops (or overseers), presbyters (or elders), teachers, and ministers (*see* Acts 20:28; 1 Corinthians 4:1; 12:29; Ephesians 4:11–12; 1 Timothy 3:1–13; Titus 1:5).

**Petition.** A formal request; refers also to sections of the Lord's Prayer or specific prayers made during the Prayer of the Church.

**Piety.** Devout; conforming to a certain belief or standard of conduct, especially in religious matters.

**Polemical.** (Greek: *polemos*, "battle.") Controversial discussions or arguments involving attack and/or refutation.

**Postil.** (Latin: *postilla*, probably from *post ilia*, "after those words of the text.") Explanation of a biblical text; originally perhaps a gloss, later a homily, then a collection of homilies.

**Power of the Keys.** *See* Keys.

*Praescientia.* (Latin: "foreknowledge.") The attribute of God whereby He knows in advance all future events.

**Predestination.** The doctrine that God, before the foundation of the world, chose us in His Son, Jesus Christ, out of the mass of sinful mankind unto faith, the adoption of sons, and everlasting life (Ephesians 1:4; 3:11; 2 Thessalonians 2:13; 2 Timothy 1:9). This election is not based on any good quality or act of the elect (those predestined), nor was it made in view of those who eventually would come to faith. Rather, our predestination in Christ is based solely on God's grace, the good pleasure of His will in Christ Jesus. While the Bible does teach the predestination of the elect, it does not (contra Calvin) teach the predestination of the damned, nor does it solve the problem of the human intellect seeking to understand universal grace and predestination (*see* FC Ep XI, 5–7; FC SD XI 14–23).

**Presbyter.** *See* Elder.

**Promise.** (Latin: "to send forth.") A binding pronouncement granting the right to expect fulfillment of that which is specified. An early Lutheran term for the Gospel.

**Propitiate. Propitiation.** (Greek: *hilasterion.*) Atonement. Hebrews 9:5 translates this word as "mercy seat"; the Hebrew equivalent (*kapporeth* [Exodus 25:17]) means the cover or lid of the ark of the covenant on which the High Priest, once a year, would sprinkle blood to propitiate, or make atonement for, the sins of the people. This was a type of the propitiatory sacrifice of Christ on the cross. *See also* Atonement.

**Providence.** The activity of God whereby He uninterruptedly upholds, preserves, governs, and directs lifeless creation, plant life, animal life, the world of people, and all that concerns people, heaven, hell—indeed everything (see Job 9:5–6; Psalm 104:13–14; 145:15; 139:13; 31:15; Luke 12:6–7; Hebrews 1:1–3).

**Purgatory.** In Roman Church teaching, all who have not been thoroughly perfected in this life will be "purged" by fire in an intermediate state of existence between earth and heaven. Masses, prayers, and good works by the living aid those suffering in purgatory and reduce its sentence. Those who die with mortal sin unconfessed and unabsolved do not enter purgatory, but hell.

**Pyx.** (Latin: "box.") Container, frequently made of metal, for holding the consecrated host, or Communion bread. Used with chalice and paten in distribution of Holy Communion, although during the Medieval era it became associated with devotion to the reserved bread outside of the Eucharist.

**Recant.** To formally renounce a belief, statement, or writing previously disseminated.

**Recapitulation.** A summary of the chief parts of a document or thesis.

**Reconciliation.** Synonymous with atonement (*see* Atonement; Propitiation) in the sense of the act of reconciling and so restoring friendly relations.

**Redeem.** (Latin: "buy back.") Recovery from sin and death by the obedience and sacrifice of Christ, who is therefore called the Redeemer ( Job 19:25; Isaiah 59:20; Matthew 20:28; Romans 3:24). The subject is sinful mankind, under guilt and the curse of the Law and the power and dominion of the devil, servants of sin, liable to death and eternal punishment. Redemption applies to all, but is not free; the ransom paid was divinely sealed by the resurrection (1 Corinthians 15:3–20).

**Regenerate.** (Latin: "reborn.") The act of divine grace by which the sinner is delivered from the power of darkness and transferred into the kingdom of Christ (Colossians 1:13).

**Repentance.** In a wide sense, change from a rebellious state to one of harmony with God's will, from trusting in human merit to trusting in Christ's merit. Embraces contrition and justifying faith; sometimes the fruit of repentance are included (Ap XII 28). In the narrow sense, faith and fruit are not included. The means to repentance is God's Word (see Jeremiah 31:18; Acts 5:31). Sometimes taken as an equivalent to penance and penitence.

**Requiem.** (Latin: first word of the first antiphon in the Roman Church rite, which begins, "*Grant* them eternal rest, O Lord.") A mass for the dead.

**Righteousness.** God's righteousness is the essential perfection of His nature. The term *righteousness* is applied to Christ not only in view of His essential righteousness, but also in view of the righteousness that He gained for mankind (Jeremiah 23:6, *see also* Justification). The righteousness of the Law is the obedience that the Law requires (*see* Law; Gospel). The righteousness of the Christian is the righteousness of faith (*see* Conversion; Faith; Justification).

**Rite. Ritual.** Prescribed ceremonial practice, or a specific action as part of a formal worship service.

**Rosary.** In the Roman Church, a string of prayer beads and the devotion for which it is used. There are 150 smaller beads divided into fifteen groups, called decades, by insertion of fifteen larger beads. The devotion is begun and ended in various ways. As the beads are fingered, an Ave Maria (the *Hail Mary*) is said for each small one and a Lord's Prayer for each larger one. Indulgences are traditionally connected with reciting the rosary.

**Sabbath.** Day of rest corresponding to the day of rest after creation (Genesis 2:3; Exodus 20:8, 11; 31:17). The Old Testament laws concerning the seventh-day Sabbath have been abrogated by Christ, who is Himself our "Sabbath rest" (Hebrews 4:9–11).

**Sacrament.** (Latin: *sacramentum,* "something to be kept sacred.") In Church usage, the term has various meanings: (1) a secret; (2) the Gospel revelation; (3) a mystery; (4) a Church rite (e.g., Baptism and Holy Communion); (5) the Office of the Holy Ministry. According to Luther, the chief Sacrament is Christ Himself (WA 6, 97).

In the Lutheran Church, a Sacrament is a sacred act that (1) was instituted by God; (2) has a visible element; and (3) offers the forgiveness of sins earned by Christ. The Sacraments include Baptism, the Lord's Supper, and also Absolution (if one counts the pastor as the visible element; *see* Ap XII 41; Ap XIII 3–5; LC IV, 74).

**Saint.** The word *saint* has been used by the Church in several ways. In Scripture it refers to believers on earth (Acts 9:32; Romans 1:7) and in heaven (Matthew 27:52). Throughout Church history, it has been used to designate one set apart (canonized) as especially holy (e.g., St. Paul, St. Francis of Assisi).

In Lutheran usage, the title of "saint" is not used for anyone except those who were canonized before the Reformation.

**Sanctification.** In a wide sense, sanctification includes all effects of God's Word (Acts 26:18; Ephesians 5:26; 2 Thessalonians 2:13; Hebrews 10:14; 1 Peter 1:2). *See also* Conversion. In a narrow sense, sanctification is the spiritual growth (1 Corinthians 3:9; 9:24; Ephesians 4:15; Philippians 3:12) that follows justification (Matthew 7:16–18; John 3:6; Ephesians 2:10). By God's grace (Galatians 5:22–23; Philippians 2:13), a Christian cooperates in this work (2 Corinthians 6:1; 7:1; Philippians 2:12; 1 Timothy 4:14, FC SD II 65–66.) Through the Holy Spirit's work, faith is increased daily, love strengthened, and the image of God renewed but not perfected in this life.

**Satisfaction.** According to Roman Church teaching, temporal punishments (justly due because of sin) can be paid through penance.

**Schism. Schismatics.** (Greek: *schizein,* "to divide, tear, cleave asunder, open, cut apart.") Used of divergent opinions (John 7:43: Acts 14:4). The Church uses the term in the sense of dissension, division, or discord (1 Corinthians 1:10; 11:18; 12:25). Schismatics disrupt Church harmony and unity.

**See.** The seat (center of power and authority) of a bishop; the jurisdiction of a bishop.

**Sin.** The breaking of God's Law (Romans 4:15; 1 John 3:4). Sin may be divided into original sin (the inherited tendency to sin and God's resultant condemnation) and actual sin. Actual sin (every thought, emotion, word, or act conflicting with God's Law) may be involuntary or may be done ignorantly (Acts 17:30) and includes sins of commission (Matthew 15:19; James 1:15) and sins of omission (James 4:17). Sin arouses God's righteous wrath and deserves His punishment. Willful sin sears the conscience; repeated, it hardens the heart and may lead to, but is not identical with, the unpardonable sin against the Holy Spirit.

**Sophistry.** Subtle reasoning or argumentation designed to deceive.

**Substance.** (Latin: *substantia*). The essential nature of a thing; that which exists by itself essentially, such as created human nature (FC Ep I 23; FC SD I 21, 54; *see also* Accident).

**Supererogation.** In Roman Church teaching, the works done over and above those that are required for salvation, especially by members of holy orders. These may be credited to those who fall short of requirements (*see* Indulgences).

**Synecdoche.** A figure of speech, in which a part substitutes for the whole or the whole for a part. Example: "*Tickling the ivories*" for "playing the piano."

**Synods.** Ecclesiastical assemblies convened for discussion and settlement of questions affecting the faith and discipline of the Church. In Lutheran teaching, the theological basis for synods is found in Acts 15. In synods, congregations converse with one another and express unity in doctrine, order, and life. The authority of synods derives from the activity of the Holy Spirit.

**Testament.** A covenant between God and human beings. A will or expression of someone's desire as to the disposal of their property at their death.

**Theologian.** A student or practitioner of theology.

**Tonsure.** (Latin: *tondere*, "to shear.") Clipping or shaving part or all or the top of the head as a sacred rite. In Roman Church practice, the ceremony admitting a layman to the clerical state.

**Transubstantiation.** (Latin: "the change of one substance to another.") In Roman Church teaching, the material substance or basic reality of the bread and wine in the Eucharist are changed by the action of the priest into the body and blood of Jesus Christ. Meanwhile, their outward appearances, colorations, tastes, dimensions, and so on, are not affected by this change.

**Treasury of merits.** In the Roman Church the alleged treasury of merits (filled by the merits of Christ and superabundant works of saints) is that from which the Church grants indulgences (*see* Indulgences; Supererogation).

**Union.** (Latin: *unus*, "one.") The bringing together of two or more things.

**Venial.** The Lutheran Confessions speak of sin that is mortal or deadly, that is, irreconcilable with faith (Ap IV 48, 64, 109, 115). When believers fall into open sin, faith has departed (SA III III 43–44). One who obeys lust does not retain faith (Ap IV 144). Venial sins, while still under condemnation, do not deprive one of the grace of the Holy Spirit and of faith.

**Vicar.** One who substitutes for or represents another. Anciently, a secular cleric who officiated in a church owned by a religious order.

**Visitor.** One selected by the German Lutheran princes in the 1520s to organize the churches, establish schools, and ascertain the fitness of Lutheran clergy. On later visits, progress was checked and further recommendations were made.

**Worship.** The broadest definition of *worship* is the response of the creature to the Creator. Christian worship can only be defined accurately, however, by further defining "Creator" as "He who revealed Himself in Jesus Christ and makes Himself known through the Holy Spirit." In common usage, *worship* properly designates the reception of the means of grace—Baptism, Absolution, Word, and Holy Communion. However, worship also describes mankind's response to God in prayer, praise, confession of faith, and thanksgiving. This is not limited to the worship service itself, but encompasses anywhere and everywhere all that a Christian says and does by faith in Jesus Christ (Romans 12:1).

# A VISUAL OVERVIEW OF THE REFORMATION

Use these explanations of the color paintings for an overview of the Reformation.

1. *Praying Hands*, 1508, drawing by Albrecht Dürer (1471–1528). This is a most popular piece of Renaissance art, known to Christians worldwide. Many Renaissance artists welcomed the Reformation. Credit: Graphische Sammlung Albertina, Vienna, Austria. Art Resource, New York.

2. *The Landauer Altarpiece*, 1511, by Albrecht Dürer. With Hans Holbein, Albrecht Dürer was one of the greatest Northern European Renaissance painters. This painting depicts leaders of the Church, on the lower left, and earthly princes, on the lower right, joining the saints and angels in worship of the Holy Trinity. God the Father is seen holding His Son, Christ crucified, with the Holy Spirit depicted as a dove above Them both. Dürer was influenced by Luther's early writings. When Luther was "kidnapped" and taken to the Wartburg for protection, Dürer, believing him to be dead, wrote in his diary, "O God, if Luther is dead, who will henceforth explain to us the Gospel?" Credit: Kunsthistorisches Museum, Vienna, Austria. The Bridgeman Art Library, New York.

3. *The Ten Commandments*, 1516, by Lucas Cranach the Elder (1472–1553). Painted for display in the Council Room in the Wittenberg City Hall. Credit: Lutherhalle, Wittenberg, Germany. The Bridgeman Art Library, New York.

4. *The Dead Christ*, 1521, by Hans Holbein the Younger (1497–1543). The theme of the dead Christ was a popular form of devotion in the Medieval Church, and still is to this day in many parts of the world. The various plagues that raged throughout Medieval Europe contributed to this morbid fascination with death. The Reformation restored proper balance between meditation on the suffering and dead Christ and praise and thanksgiving for the risen, victorious, ever-living Christ. Credit: Kunstmuseum, Basel. Giraudon/ Art Resource, New York.

5. *Portrait of Martin Luther*, c. 1523, age 40, by Lucas Cranach the Elder. Here Luther is seen without his tonsure, the special haircut worn by monks in the Middle Ages, but he is still wearing an Augustinian monk's cowl, or cloak with a hood. His hand rests on his most cherished personal possession, a red leather-bound copy of the Psalms in Latin. Luther committed the Psalms and many other major portions of the Vulgate to memory through constant reading and meditation. Luther appeared in public for the first time without his monk's cowl in October of 1524. This is the last portrait Cranach painted of Luther dressed as a monk. See p. 719. Credit: German National Museum, Nürnberg. Art Resource, New York.

6. *Martin Luther's Seal.* The most enduring symbol of the Lutheran Reformation is the seal that Luther himself designed to represent his theology. By the early 1520s, this seal begins to appear on the title page of Luther's works. Luther explained that the red heart with a black cross at the center should remind us that the righteous live by faith in the Crucified One. The heart rests in a white rose, to show that faith gives joy, comfort, and peace. The rose is white, not red, because white is the color of the heavenly spirits and angels. The white rose stands in a field of blue, the color of heaven, to show that joy in the spirit and in faith in this life is only the beginning of future heavenly joy. Surrounding the sky-blue field is a gold ring, to show that happiness and joy in heaven has no end, but lasts forever, just as gold is the highest, most noble and precious metal.

7. *Portrait of Elector Frederick the Wise,* c. 1523, by Lucas Cranach the Elder. Frederick the Wise (1486–1525) was Luther's protector in the early days of the Reformation, when Luther's enemies were many and his friends were few. See p. 712. Credit: Deutsches Historisches Museum, Berlin, Germany. Art Resource, New York.

8. *Allegory of the Old and New Testaments* by Hans Holbein the Younger. Holbein was under the influence of Reformation theology when he went to England in 1526 with a letter of introduction from Erasmus for Henry VIII. From left to right, the painting shows a skeleton in a coffin, depicting *Mors* (death). Above it stand Adam and Eve sinning by eating the forbidden fruit, showing *Peccatum* (sin). On the mountain above them is Moses receiving the *Lex* (Law). Underneath Moses is seen the serpent in the wilderness, prefiguring the *Mysterium Justificationis* (the mystery of Justification). In the far background is Moses throwing down the Commandments at the site of the rebellious children of Israel worshiping the golden calf. Dominating the painting is a picture of *Homo* (man) with *Esayas Propheta* (Isaiah the Prophet), whose prophecy underneath, translated, is, "Behold, the virgin shall conceive and bear a son" (Isaiah 7:14). Man is sitting on a stone with a Bible verse from Romans 7 on it, "Wretched man that I am! Who will deliver me from this body of death?" On his right is *Ioannes Baptista* (John the Baptist), pointing man to Christ, and underneath are John's words, "Behold, the Lamb of God, who takes away the sin of the world" (John 1:29). To the immediate right of John the Baptist is the victorious resurrected Christ, stepping out of the tomb, trampling death and the devil underfoot, with the words *Victoria Nostra* (Our Victory) next to the open tomb. In the middle left background is Christ with the Apostles, with the words *Agnus Dei* (Lamb of God). He is heading toward the Cross, over which are the words *Iustificatio Nostra* (Our Justification). To the left of the cross is seen the shepherds in the field at night hearing the angels' message of good news of a Savior. On top of the mountain on the right side is the Blessed Virgin Mary receiving the annunciation, the news that she will be the Mother of our Lord; the word *Gratia* (grace) is seen with the cherub holding the cross. Credit: National Gallery of Scotland, Edinburgh, Scotland. The Bridgeman Art Library, New York.

9. *Portrait of Martin Luther,* 1529, by Lucas Cranach the Elder. "In silence and hope is your strength," say the Latin words at the top of the painting, taken from Isaiah 30:15. Notice that in this painting Luther is wearing academic garb and a doctoral beret. This is one of the more well-known portraits of Martin Luther. See p. 719. Credit: Museo Poldi Pezzoli, Milan, Italy. Scala/Art Resource, New York.

10. *The Presentation of the Augsburg Confession,* 1617, German school, artist unknown. This massive painting hangs in the chancel of St. George Church in Eisenach, Germany. It was commissioned for the one-hundredth anniversary of the Lutheran Reformation, 1617, and modeled on earlier woodcuts. Seated on his throne is Charles V, and kneeling before him are electors and princes of Germany, including John the Steadfast, who is holding a Bible open to the verse, "We hold that one is justified by faith apart from works of the law" (Romans 3:28). Scenes from Lutheran church life are also portrayed, including, from far right to left, a Lutheran service of preaching and Holy Communion, a Baptism of an infant, a wedding, lectures, and Church musicians. Notice the statues, crucifixes, vestments, and other church ornamentation that were common to Lutheranism, which, unlike the Reformed Church, retained all the good traditions of the historic Church. Later, in the eighteenth century, Pietism legalistically deprived many Lutheran congregations of their traditional art and practices. The painting is not precisely accurate, however. The kneeling man on the left holds in his hands the Augsburg Confession. Credit: Georgenkirche, Eisenach,

Germany. The Bridgeman Art Library, New York.

11. *Paradise*, 1530, by Lucas Cranach the Elder. The creation of Adam and Eve and the fall into sin are presented. God creates Eve in the upper right. In the center, God is commanding Adam and Eve not to eat of the tree of the knowledge of good and evil. Just above God's pointing hand is a picture of the creation of Adam. The far left of the painting shows the fall into sin and the expulsion from the Garden. God confronts Adam and Eve with their sin on the left. Credit: Staatliche Kunstsammlungen, Dresden.

12. *Portrait of Philip Melanchthon*, 1532, by Lucas Cranach the Elder. This portrait was painted two years after Philip Melanchthon (1497–1560) wrote the Augsburg Confession and the Apology of the Augsburg Confession. After Luther's death, Melanchthon sought compromise with Roman Catholicism and Calvinism as a way of preserving Lutheranism, one of the most sad and ironic chapters in the Reformation. See p. 723. Credit: AKG-Images. London.

13. *Babylon Burning, the Apocalypse of St. John* (Revelation 18), from an early edition of Luther's translation of the New Testament. Credit: Art Resource, New York.

14. *Portrait of Philip of Hesse, the Magnanimous*, 1534, by Hans Krell (1490–1565). Philip (1504–67) was one of the most energetic Lutheran leaders of the Reformation era. He was an early supporter and advocate for Luther's reforms, embracing Lutheranism at the age of twenty. He soon became a firm ally of the Electors of Saxony, even emblazoning their motto, "The Word of the Lord endures forever," on his army's cannons. His wife was the daughter of Duke George of Saxony, one of Luther's most bitter opponents. Philip was taken captive in the Battle of Mühlberg (1547) along with John Frederick the Magnanimous. He signed a compromise with Charles V in order to be released

from prison. His remarkable energy and zeal was a strong factor in the success of Martin Luther's work. See p. 727. Credit: The Wartburg Castle, Eisenach, Germany.

15. *The Harvest at the End of Time* (Revelation 14:14), colored woodcut from the Luther Bible of 1534, by the Lucas Cranach workshop. The complete translation of the Luther Bible in 1534 contained numerous woodcuts prepared by the Lucas Cranach workshop. (These were hand-colored at the printer, Hans Lufft, in Wittenberg, Germany.) The Reformed Church and the more radical wing of the Reformation opposed the use of such images and paintings, statues, and crucifixes. In *Against the Heavenly Prophets in Matters of Images and Sacrament*, Luther makes very plain why paintings and images are not sinful, but are quite helpful: "My image breakers must also let me keep, wear, and look at a crucifix or a Madonna. . . . Images for memorial and witness, such as crucifixes and images of saints, are to be tolerated. This is shown above to be the case even in the Mosaic Law. And they are not only to be tolerated, but for the sake of the memorial and the witness, they are praiseworthy and honorable, as the witness stones of Joshua [Joshua 24:26] and of Samuel [1 Samuel 7:12]" (LW 40:88, 91). Credit: Bible Society, London, UK. The Bridgeman Art Library, New York.

16. *The Creation*, woodcut from the Luther Bible of 1534, by the Lucas Cranach workshop. Credit: Bible Society, London, UK. The Bridgeman Art Library, New York.

17. *The Fall of the Beast* (Revelation 19:19–21), from the Luther Bible of 1534, by the Lucas Cranach workshop; hand colored by the Cranach workshop. This image was copied from the Zerbster Prunkbibel, printed by Hans Lufft in 1541. Credit: Zerbst Stadtarchiv AKG, London.

18. *Portrait of John the Steadfast*, 1535, by Lucas Cranach the Elder. John the Steadfast

(1468–1532) was the brother of Frederick the Wise. During his reign as ruler of Saxony, he played a key leadership role at the Diet of Augsburg, encouraging and insisting on bold confession on the part of the Lutheran princes before Emperor Charles V. See p. 717. Credit: Hamburg Kunsthalle, Hamburg, Germany. Bridgeman Art Library, New York.

19. *Portrait of John Bugenhagen*, 1537, by Lucas Cranach the Elder. John Bugenhagen (1485–1558), was ordained a priest in 1509 and became a lecturer on the Bible and the Church Fathers in 1517. At first he was opposed to Martin Luther, but then he became convinced Luther was correct after reading Luther's *Babylonian Captivity of the Church* in 1520. He became the head pastor of St. Mary's Church in Wittenberg in 1523, a position he held until his death in 1558. He was a key organizer of the Reformation in Germany, Denmark, and Scandinavia. He helped draft a foundational document for the Augsburg Confession in Torgau, with Luther, Melanchthon, and others. His work on Church orders was adopted in many places. Bugenhagen came under the influence of Melanchthon after Luther's death and did not oppose the Augsburg Interim. He then helped Melanchthon draft the Leipzig Interim. Thus, when the Imperial forces of Charles V captured Wittenberg in 1547, Bugenhagen was treated with great courtesy and respect by Charles V. But Bugenhagen returned to faithful Lutheranism in 1550 with his *Commentary on Jonah*, in which he protested Roman Catholic errors. Before he retired from active duty in 1557, he carefully warned Lutheran pastors against theological compromise. See p. 705. Credit: Lutherhalle, Wittenberg, Germany. Photo by Constantin Beyer, Artothek.

20. *Jesus Blesses the Little Children*, 1538, by Lucas Cranach the Elder. This is one of several versions of this scene painted by Lucas Cranach. Notice the infant who is holding Christ's shoulder and the mother grasping at Christ's cloak to have Him bless her child. The apostles look on with little enthusiasm. This was a painting and theme used by Lutherans to help teach the power and blessing of infant Baptism. Credit: Staatliche Kunstsammlungen, Dresden.

21. *Portrait of John Frederick the Magnanimous of Saxony and Wittenberg Reformers*, 1543, by Lucas Cranach the Elder. John Frederick the Magnanimous is surrounded by key Lutheran leaders who had helped him and guided him. From left to right are Martin Luther, George Spalatin, Chancellor Gregory Brück, and Philip Melanchthon. See p. 716. Credit: Toledo, Ohio, Museum of Art. Gift of Edward Drummond Libbey.

22. *Double Portrait of Martin Luther and Philip Melanchthon*, 1543, by Lucas Cranach the Elder. The stress and strain of the Lutheran Reformation are seen on the face of Martin Luther, shown here at age 60, three years before his death. Melanchthon is 46. Credit: Galleria degli Uffizi. AKG-Images. London.

23. *Elijah and the Priests of Baal*, 1545, by Lucas Cranach the Elder. This painting is 4 feet by 8 feet and, like the painting of Paradise (no. 11), contains a wealth of detail. Cranach graphically shows Elijah's offering consumed by fire, while the priests of Baal seek their gods' blessing in vain. In the upper left is the gory result of their idolatry, a scene that also portrays the brutality of the hand-to-hand warfare that was common in the sixteenth century.

24. *Wittenberg Altar Painting*, 1547, by Lucas Cranach the Elder. This massive painting dominates the interior of St. Mary Church in Wittenberg, Germany. The painting was completed and installed in 1547, the same year that Emperor Charles V captured Wittenberg. Cranach portrays the Sacraments of Baptism, Communion, and Absolution. (Curiously, Melanchthon is shown administering Baptism, though there is no record that Melanchthon ever baptized anyone.) Cranach's son Lucas is shown handing a cup

to Martin Luther, posed as one of the Apostles in the center panel. On the right, Pastor Bugenhagen, Luther's pastor, is absolving a man with the loosing key and withholding forgiveness with the binding key, sending away a man with his hands bound. (Private Confession and Absolution was practiced in the sixteenth and seventeenth centuries and fell out of common use as a result of Pietism in the eighteenth century. The windowed structures behind the altar are confessional booths.) When Charles V captured Wittenberg, one of his soldiers thrust his sword through the painting of Luther preaching, piercing his neck and body, shouting out, "Even in death, this beast rages on." Credit: Church of St. Mary, Wittenberg, Germany. The Bridgeman Art Library, New York.

25. *Detail from the Cranach Altar in St. Mary Church, Wittenberg.* Luther preaching. Luther is pointing to Christ crucified, the essential substance of all faithful Lutheran preaching. Seen in the crowd on the left is Lucas Cranach, the bearded man on the upper left. Luther's wife, Katie, is seated in the front, with Luther's son Hans at her knee. One of Luther's daughters is looking directly out of the painting. Credit: Church of St. Mary, Wittenberg, Germany. The Bridgeman Art Library, New York.

26. *Portrait of John Frederick the Magnanimous, Elector of Saxony,* 1547, by Titian (c. 1485–1576). This unique portrait was commissioned by Emperor Charles V and painted soon after the Battle of Mühlberg (1547), in which John Frederick (1503–54) was defeated and taken captive. As the painting indicates, he suffered a severe cut on his face, resulting in a significant loss of blood and permanent disfigurement. Titian captures a look that bespeaks sadness, resignation, and yet quiet determination. In spite of the fact that he was taken in battle, wounded, stripped of his titles and possessions, and sent into exile, John Frederick refused to renounce his Lutheran convictions. See p. 716. Credit: Museo del Prado, Madrid, Spain.

Erich Lessing/Art Resource, New York.

27. *Lucas Cranach at Age 77,* 1550, self-portrait. Lucas Cranach the Elder was truly one of the most remarkable laymen of the Reformation era. He came to Wittenberg in 1504 and built up multiple businesses: a painting studio and workshop, a pharmacy, and a publishing and printing workshop. He eventually lived in one of the largest private homes in Wittenberg, facing the city hall on the town square. He became a convinced follower of Martin Luther, and his paintings showed the influence of the Reformation—moving from paintings of Madonnas and saints, to pictures of Christ and various biblical scenes and themes. Due largely to Lucas Cranach, we have many paintings of the various Lutheran rulers, Martin Luther, Philip Melanchthon, and other key figures in the Lutheran Reformation. See p. 708. Credit: Galleria degli Uffizi Firenze, Scala. Art Resource, New York.

28. *Unfinished Portrait of Elector Augustus I of Saxony,* c. 1553, by Lucas Cranach the Younger. Augustus (1526–86) was initially deceived by hidden Calvinists at the University of Wittenberg, but when their plots and schemes were fully brought to light in 1574, Augustus exiled many from his lands and supported the efforts to unify Lutherans throughout Germany. He gave 80,000 Taulers to publish the Book of Concord in 1580. See p. 703. Credit: Muse Saint-Denis, Regime, France. The Bridgeman Art Library, New York.

29. *Engraving of Matthias Flacius,* date and artist unknown. Matthias Flacius (1520–75) is the Latinized name of Matia Vlacich. Flacius was one of the first persons to raise the alarm when he saw the theology and teachings of Luther being compromised by Philip Melanchthon. Flacius struggled to preserve genuine Lutheranism for the rest of his life. He was known as a pugnacious and irascible man. While rejecting Flacius's errors on original sin, for the most part the Formula

of Concord came down on the side of Flacius and his associates known as the Gnesio-Lutherans, or "Genuine Lutherans," and rejected the compromising tendencies and theological errors of Philip Melanchthon and his supporters, known as the "Philippists." See p. 712. Credit: Herzog August Bibliothek, Wolfenbüttel, Germany.

30. *Painting of Martin Chemnitz*, date and artist unknown. At the age of 14, while at school in Wittenberg, Chemnitz (1522–86) had a brief opportunity to hear Martin Luther preach. He studied under Melanchthon and substituted for Melanchthon in some of his classes. He was ordained in 1554 by John Bugenhagen. Chemnitz tried to bring peace to the Lutheran Church after attending bitter and hostile conferences between the Philippists and Gnesio-Lutherans. He worked closely with other "second generation" Lutherans, such as Jacob Andreae and Nicholas Selnecker. Chemnitz was the driving force behind the theological precision of the Formula of Concord. His comprehensive refutation, *The Examination of the Council of Trent,* earned him the title "the most villainous Lutheran" from his Roman Catholic adversaries. Lutherans attached another phrase to Chemnitz, "If Martin [Chemnitz] had not come, Martin [Luther] would not have stood." After Martin Luther, there was no more productive or influential theologian in the Lutheran Church than Martin Chemnitz. See p. 707. Credit: From the J. A. O. Preus collection in the Archives of The Lutheran Church—Missouri Synod, Concordia Historical Institute, St. Louis, Missouri.

31. *The Weimar Altarpiece,* 1555, by Lucas Cranach the Elder; completed by Lucas Cranach the Younger. This richly detailed painting was paid for and provided to the church by John Frederick the Magnanimous. Cranach was unable to complete it before his death in 1553, but his son Lucas finished it. In addition to being a rich presentation of biblical truth, it is also a strong personal con-

fession of faith by Lucas Cranach. He put himself squarely between John the Baptist and Martin Luther, looking out of the painting straight into the viewer's eyes. The blood of Christ is pouring directly onto Cranach's head, a powerful confession of the fact that our forgiveness, life, and salvation is given by God as a gift through the shed blood of Jesus Christ. Martin Luther's finger is pointing to three verses in an open Bible: 1 John 1:7 ("The blood of Jesus His Son cleanses us from all sin"); Hebrews 4:16 ("Let us then with confidence draw near to the throne of grace, that we may receive mercy and find grace to help in time of need"); and John 3:14 ("As Moses lifted up the serpent in the wilderness, so must the Son of Man be lifted up"). The painting shows the giving of the Law to Moses, the angel announcing Christ's birth to the shepherds in the fields, the bronze snake in the wilderness, and a picture of death and Satan driving a sinner into hell. The predominant image is of Jesus Christ crucified in the center, with the risen Christ destroying death and the devil, trampling them underfoot. Beneath the cross a lamb holds a banner with the words "The Lamb of God that takes away the sin of the world." This painting forms the center panel of a three-piece altar painting. The panel to the left has a portrait of John Frederick the Magnanimous and his wife kneeling in adoration. Above them is a banner with the first letters of the motto of the Reformation, "The Word of the Lord endures forever." The panel on the right shows their three sons kneeling. Credit: Altar der Peter und Paulkirche in Weimar. Mitteltafel: Christus am Kreuz. Weimar, Stadtpfarrkirche. Photo by Constantin Beyer, Artothek.

32. Title page from a 1580 edition of the Book of Concord. The volume from which this page was copied belonged to C. F. W. Walther, who signed his name in pencil. Credit: Pritzlaff Memorial Library Rare Book Collection, Concordia Seminary, St. Louis, Missouri.

# ART CREDITS FOR WOODCUTS AND ENGRAVINGS

The Richard C. Kessler Reformation Collection; Pitts Theology Library, Candler School of Theology, Emory University

94, 101, 111, 119, 123, 127, 137, 151, 160, 165, 173, 178, 180 (top), 183, 206 (bottom), 222, 226, 230, 249, 261, 269, 274, 316, 342, 343, 344, 345, 346, 347, 348, 349, 350, 351, 352, 353, 354, 355, 356, 357, 358, 359, 360, 361, 362, 363, 364, 365, 366, 367, 369, 370, 371, 541, 550, 567, 570, 577, 583, 592, 612, 615, 629, 633

Rev. Matthew C. Harrison Private Collection
49, 50, 56, 62, 63, 81, 96, 130, 180 (bottom), 186, 206 (top), 280, 286, 289, 325, 478, 481, 483, 487, 524, 525, 529

Rev. Paul T. McCain Private Collection
484

*The Complete Woodcuts of Albrecht Dürer*, edited by Willi Kurth (New York: Arden Book Company, 1936)
40, 46, 472, 537

Pritzlaff Memorial Library Rare Book Collection; Concordia Seminary Library, St. Louis, Missouri
334, 378, 381, 433, 459, 486

The Smithey Collection of Reformation Works, Pritzlaff Memorial Library Rare Book Collection; Concordia Seminary Library, St. Louis, Missouri
55, 192, 215, 264, 303, 474, 477, 478, 489, 597

# INDEX OF PERSONS AND GROUPS

**Abel.** (ancient history) Son of Adam and Eve, a shepherd. Killed by his jealous brother Cain. Abel was a righteous prophet (Matthew 23:35), a man of faith (Hebrews 11:4), and the first example of martyrdom, whose blood cried out against injustice.

**Abelard, Peter.** (1079–1142) Scholastic theologian, lectured at Paris. Contributed to flowering of Scholasticism by using logical analysis to arrive at religious realities; emphasized exemplary love manifested in Christ's death. In *Sic et Non*, Abelard shows the Fathers to be contradictory, ambiguous, or both, arousing a critical attitude.

**Abraham.** (d. c. 1991 BC) The first patriarch of Israel (Genesis 11:26–25:18). He received God's promises and blessings by faith (Genesis 12) before the covenant of circumcision or the Law of Moses was given (Galatians 3). In St. Paul and the Lutheran Confessions, Abraham is a shining example of faith.

**Adam.** (ancient history) The first human being, husband of Eve (Genesis 1:26–5:5). Adam bore responsibility for the fall into sin, which cursed all humankind. Christ is called the "Second Adam" because He takes away the sin of all humankind (Romans 5:12–19). The Lutheran Confessions often refer to the "old Adam," our sinful nature that resulted from Adam's fall into sin.

**Adam [Krafft] of Fulda.** (1493–1558) Preacher in Hesse. Humanist; taught at Erfurt; became Lutheran; court preacher of Philip of Hesse; superintendent of Marburg (1526); professor of theology at Marburg (1527). Signed SA (1537). Corvinus signed the AC and Ap on his behalf.

**Adrian VI.** (1459–1523) From Utrecht; theologian, tutor of Charles V. Pope from 1522–23; sought to reform the Roman Curia and stop the spread of the Reformation.

**Aepinus, John.** (1499–1553) Student of Luther. Persecuted in Brandenburg; banished for teaching Lutheran theology. Rector in Stalsund.Pastor in Hamburg (1532); then superintendent and cathedral pastor. Signed SA. Raised controversy in Hamburg by teaching that Christ's descent into hell was part of His suffering (1544), a view rejected by the FC Ep IX and FC SD IX. Opposed Augsburg Interim, prepared Confession against it (1548). Strong opponent of the Philippists. Aepinus documented teaching of "faith alone" in writings of the Early Church Fathers.

**Aerius.** (fourth century) Priest in Pontus (Asia Minor). Known for his view that there is no distinction between bishops and priests in terms of their function. Believed observance of Easter was a Jewish superstition and that it was wrong for the Church to prescribe fasts. Condemned by the Church in his day for saying that prayers and giving alms for the dead was useless. Roman polemicists, such as Bellarmine, called Lutherans "Aerians" for teaching that prayers for the dead, and to the dead, are useless.

**Aeschines.** (c. 389–c. 314 BC) Athenian orator. Cited in the Lutheran Confessions to assert that key issues in a debate must be dealt with instead of wandering into side issues.

**Agnoetae.** From Greek, "to be ignorant." 1. Fourth-century sect that denied God could know all things. 2. Sixth-century sect that taught Christ did not know all things.

**Agricola, John.** (c. 1494–1566) Educated in Leipzig and Wittenberg. Kept minutes at Leipzig Debate (1519). Sent by Luther to help reform Frankfurt am Main (1525). Taught at Eisleben from 1525 and Wittenberg from 1536. Brandenburg court preacher from 1540. Helped to write Augsburg Interim (1547). Agricola emphasized that Christians are under the Gospel rather than under Law. Argued with Melanchthon about role of Commandments in Christian life (1527). Luther called Agricola's position *antinomianism*, that is, denial of any role for the Law in Christian living. By 1540, Luther considered Agricola an enemy of the Gospel. After Luther's death, Agricola sided strongly with the Philippist movement. FC rejected Agricola's view on the Law (FC Ep V and FC SD V).

**Agricola, Stephen.** (c. 1491–1547) Imprisoned for Lutheran preaching (1522–24). Pastor at St. Anna, Augsburg, from 1525. Preacher in Hof, Bavaria from 1531, Sulzbach from 1543, and Eisleben from 1545. At Marburg Colloquy (1529), attended Smalcald meeting (1537), and signed the SA.

**Albert of Brandenburg.** (1490–1545) Archbishop of Magdeburg (1513). Also archbishop and Elector of Mainz (1514), by special favor of Pope Leo X. Cardinal (1518). Leo granted Albert the right to sell indulgences in Saxony and Brandenburg to raise money for St. Peter's Cathedral, Rome. Albert hired John Tetzel for this purpose. These indulgences caused Luther to write the Ninety-five Theses, sparking the Reformation. Albert was open to the Reformation at first, but supported Rome from 1525 onward.

**Albert, Duke of Prussia.** (1490–1568) Last grand master of monastic order, the Teutonic Knights (chosen, 1511). Won for Lutheranism by Andreas Osiander the Elder (1522). In 1523, Luther advised Albert to dissolve the monastic order and to marry. First Hohenzollern Duke of Prussia from 1525. Founded University of Königsberg (1544).

**Alexander of Hales.** (c. 1170 or 1185–1245) Called "Doctor beyond reproach"; "Teacher of teachers"; "King of theology." Franciscan (1236). Scholastic theologian and philosopher. Studied and taught in Paris. His handbook of theology teaches that the Sacraments place a permanent spiritual mark on those who receive them (indelible charac-

ter); also, the saints' extra good works can be used for indulgences, which forgive people's sins (treasury of merits).

**Alexander the Great.** (356–323 BC) Educated by Aristotle. Conqueror from Greece to India, including the Jewish people.

**Ambrose.** (340–397) Noted leader in Early Church. Studied for a legal career. After the bishop of Milan died, Ambrose (as government official) maintained order during dispute between the Nicenes and Arians. The people suddenly called for him to be bishop. Since he was still a catechumen, he was baptized at once. Eight days later, he was consecrated as bishop (374). Noted defender of the Nicene Creed. Ambrose rebuked Emperor Theodosius I for a massacre in Thessalonica and took the unprecedented step of excommunicating a Christian emperor. His example encouraged the idea that the State should support and further the Church's work and the Church should support and further the State's work. Encouraged celibacy, voluntary poverty, martyrdom. Baptized Augustine of Hippo. Helped develop liturgical music.

**Ambrosiaster.** (Pseudo-Ambrose) Name first given by Erasmus to the author of fourth-century Latin commentaries on St. Paul's thirteen epistles. The Reformers often quote these commentaries because of their teaching on justification and faith.

**Amsdorf, Nicholas.** (1483–1565) Studied at Wittenberg; lectured there on theology and philosophy. Canon and rector. Friend of Luther, under whose influence he turned from Aristotle's philosophy to study Augustine. With Luther at Leipzig Debate (1519) and Diet of Worms (1521). Called to Magdeburg (1524); reformed the city with Creutziger the Elder. Carried the Gospel to many cities. Extensive correspondence with Luther. John Frederick appointed him as the first evangelical bishop of Naumburg-Zeitz (1542) because he was gifted, learned, a noble, and unmarried. Expelled from Naumburg as a result of battle of

Mühlberg (1547). Moved to Weimar; helped found university at Jena and took charge of the Jena edition of Luther's Works. Fled to Magdeburg, where he joined opposition to Leipzig Interim.

**Anabaptists.** From Greek word for "rebaptize." 1. Fourth-century term for groups that rebaptized (a) people baptized by heretics, and (b) people baptized by clergy who later fell from faith during persecution.

2. During Reformation, name of reproach applied to groups insisting on rebaptism of people baptized as infants. Anabaptists were most influential from Switzerland down the Rhine River to Holland. Modern groups include Mennonites, Amish, Swiss Brethren, and others.

**Andreae, Jacob.** (1528–90) At 18, preacher at Stuttgart. Chancellor of Tubingen. Active reformer in Southern Germany. Explained teaching of the Reformation to King Anthony of Navarre at Paris and Patriarch Jeremias II of Constantinople. Failed to unite Gnesio-Lutherans and Philippists at Zerbst (1570). Preached and published sermons on controversial points, leading to his work on FC.

**Anhalt, Wolfgang von.** (1492–1566) Prince; met Luther at Worms (1521) and favored Reformation. Signed AC (1530). Joined Smalcaldic League. Exiled by emperor. Present at Luther's death. Opposed Interim.

**Anna.** Name given by tradition to the mother of the Virgin Mary.

**Anthony.** (c. 251–c. 356) Egyptian hermit known as father of Christian monasticism. Organized communities of hermits who lived separately but gathered for worship.

**Antichrist.** Term used in the New Testament (a) of all false teachers (1 John 2:18; 4:3), and (b) of one outstanding adversary of Christ (1 John 2:18). Characteristics of Antichrist are taken from Daniel 7; 8; 11:31–38; Revelation 11; 13; 17; 18; writings of John; and especially 2 Thessalonians 2:3–12. The Apology shows that the papacy has marks of Antichrist as depicted by Daniel (Ap VII–VIII 24; Ap XV 19; Ap XXIII 25; Ap XXIV 51) and by Paul (Ap VII–VIII 4). It speaks of papacy as part of the kingdom of Antichrist (XV 18). The Smalcald Articles hold that the pope, by his doctrine and practice, has clearly shown his office as Antichrist since it exceeds even the Turks and Tartars in keeping people from their Savior. The Formula of Concord quotes the Smalcald Articles on Antichrist.

**Antinomians.** From Greek for "against the law." Group teaching that a Christian is free from all moral law. *See* p. 521.

**Antitrinitarians.** See Socinus.

**Apollinarius of Laodicea.** (c. 310–c. 390) Bishop in Syria who opposed Arians. Close friend of Athanasius. Erred by teaching that Christ did not have a human soul. Condemned at Council of Constantinople (381).

**Apollonia.** (d. c. 248) An early Christian martyr who had her teeth knocked out. Invoked for dental problems.

**Apollos.** (first century) Christian teacher from Alexandria (Acts 18:24–28).

**Aquinas, Thomas.** See Thomas Aquinas.

**Arians.** See Arius.

**Aristippus.** (c. 435–c. 356 BC) Greek philosopher of hedonism; disciple of Socrates.

**Aristophanes.** (c. 448–c. 380 BC) Greek playwright. Caricatured (probably playfully) in *The Clouds* as petty, bourgeois, antidemocratic.

**Aristotle.** (384–322 BC) A great and versatile philosopher. Pupil of Plato for twenty years. Tutor of Alexander the Great. Founded a school of philosophy near Athens (335). Often called the father of logic and of the empirical system. Emphasized inductive reasoning. Through Scholasticism, his influence on the Church peaked in the twelfth and thirteenth centuries. As a young professor, Luther lectured on Aristotle's texts but later regarded him as the source for many Roman heresies.

**Arius.** (d. c. 336) Priest in a suburb of Alexandria, Egypt; arch-heretic in Early Church. Taught that Jesus was divine but not equal to God the Father. The Council of Nicaea (325) refuted and rejected the heresy of Arius and his followers in the famous Nicene Creed, but the aftermath of the controversy troubled Christendom for almost two centuries.

**Athanasius.** (c. 293–c. 373) Called the "Father of Orthodoxy," his life shows great heroism, fortitude, and faith. As deacon he accompanied his bishop, Alexander, to the Council of Nicaea (325). He became bishop of Alexandria three years later. Known for defense of Nicene Creed against the heresy of Arius. Suffered exile numerous times. Brought together the Greek theologians of the East (who emphasized that the Godhead is made up of three Persons) with the theologians of the West (who insisted that God is One). Led to present form of the Nicene Creed at the Council of Constantinople (381). He did not write the Athanasian Creed, but it is based on his teaching. *See* pp. 43–44.

**Audians.** (fourth century) Christian sect founded by Audius. They were Quartodecimans, and increasingly heretical. As a layperson, Audius criticized worldly ways of clergymen. Ordained bishop illicitly. Banned to Scythia. In old age he worked as missionary to the Gothic tribes.

**Augustine.** (354–430) Renowned North African Christian teacher and philosopher. Had a pagan father, Christian mother (Monica). Joined Manichean sect. Under influence of Ambrose at Milan, converted during study of the Book of Romans (386). Baptized the following year. Returned to North Africa, sold family inheritance, and founded a monastery with a clerical school. Bishop of Hippo Regius (396). Vigorously fought heresies of Pelagius, Donatists, and others. His writings were the basis of Western theology until overshadowed by Scholasticism. Augustine taught justification by grace, but only for the elect. Luther joined the Augustinian Hermits and studied Augustine's writings. Luther broke with Augustine's theology to emphasize Scripture alone. Augustine's views on predestination greatly influenced John Calvin and Reformed theology.

**Augustus I.** (1526–86) Elector of Saxony who succeeded his brother Maurice (1553). Staunch Lutheran. When fooled by the Crypto-Calvinists, Augustus deposed the true Lutherans, who rejected the Calvinizing Wittenberg Catechism and the Dresden Consensus. However, when J. Cureus published *Exegesis perspicua* in c. 1574, which actually attacked the Lutheran doctrine of the Lord's Supper, Augustus imprisoned the deceivers and spent 80,000 Taler to help bring into being the Book of Concord of 1580. *See also* pp. 528–29.

**Aurifaber, John.** (1519–75) Zealous Lutheran; collector and publisher of Reformation documents. Studied at Wittenberg (1537). Tutor of young counts of Mansfeld (1540–45). Luther's *famulus* or attendant at Wittenberg (1545). At Luther's death: "I took care of his bodily needs, and I closed his eyes." Defended Luther's teaching in later doctrinal controversies. Editor for Jena edition of Luther's Works (1556). Published Luther's *Table Talk* (1566).

**Baal.** The Canaanite storm god, often worshiped by ancient Israelites (see 1 Kings 18). The Lutheran Confessions refer to this history in describing the evil worship practices of the papacy.

**Bacchanals.** Devotees of Bacchus, the Greek god of wine and intoxication.

**Barbara.** (date and history uncertain) According to tradition, daughter of a pagan in Nicomedia (Asia Minor). Martyred by her father after she converted to Christianity.

**Basil.** (c. 330–c. 379) Called "The Great." Bishop of Caesarea after Eusebius. Opposed Arianism and other heresies. A Greek liturgy is attributed to him.

**Bede.** (673–735) Called "the Venerable" and "the Teacher of the Middle Ages." Wrote scientific and theological treatises, including commentaries on the Bible and hymns. Preserved teaching of earlier Church Fathers. His greatest work is a history of the Church in England.

**Benedict of Nursia.** (c. 480–c. 543) Established a monastery at Monte Cassino (Italy; c. 529). Using earlier writings of Basil, Cassian, and others, he created the Benedictine Rule, almost universally adopted by Western monasteries in the Middle Ages.

**Benedictines.** *See* Benedict of Nursia.

**Bernard of Clairvaux.** (1091–1153) Called "Teacher of flowing honey." Influential abbot because of his deep piety and eloquence. Joined the Cistercians (1115) and founded a cloister at Clairvaux, France. Wore himself out in severe self-discipline. A pious and humble Christian who diligently read his Bible and loved his Savior. Worked up enthusiasm for the Crusades, though he frowned on using force against heretics. Luther deeply valued Bernard's sermons. His poetry inspired Paul Gerhardt's unforgettable hymn, "O Sacred Head, Now Wounded."

**Beyer, Christian.** (c. 1482–1535) German lawyer. Taught at Wittenberg from 1507. Mayor of Wittenberg from 1513. Saxon chancellor from 1528. He read the Augsburg Confession before the emperor at the Diet of Augsburg (1530).

**Beza, Theodore.** (1519–1605) French humanist and Reformed theologian. Professor of Greek at Lausanne. Professor and pastor at Geneva. Defended burning of heretic Servetus. Suceeded Calvin as leader of Reformed theology. Strongly opposed Lutheran doctrines on the Lord's Supper and person of Christ.

**Bidenbach, Balthasar.** (1533–78) Provost at Stuttgart. Attended Maulbronn Colloquy (1564). With L. Osiander the Elder, wrote the Maulbronn Formula (1576), antecedent of the Formula of Concord. Successor of J. Brentz. Wrote homiletic works on 1 Kings and Romans. Hymnist.

**Biel, Gabriel.** (c. 1420–95) German Scholastic philosopher. Nominalist. Supported semi-Pelagianism, mechanical theory of Sacraments, "mighty dignity" of priests, and immaculate conception of Mary. Wrote commentary on Sentences of Peter Lombard. His writings were among the first theological works read by Luther.

**Blaurock, George.** (d. 1529) Monk; later leader of Swiss Anabaptists; burned in persecution at Innsbruck.

**Bonaventure.** (1221–74) Called "Seriphic (Angelic) Teacher." Italian philosopher, cardinal, Scholastic theologian, poet, mystic. Taught at Paris. Minister General of Franciscans (1257). Tried to prove that Christian doctrine agrees with reason. Denied the doctrine of the immaculate conception of Mary.

**Boniface VIII.** (c. 1235–1303) Italian. Pope from 1294. Issued decrees (papal laws). His bull *Unum Sanctam* defended the doctrine of papal authority over all creatures.

**Bora, Katharina von.** (1499–1552) From impoverished family of the lower nobility. At age 6 she was put into a nunnery. In April 1523, she and eight others escaped from the institution and went to Wittenberg. Katharina was taken into the home of Reichenbach, a minor town official. After a number of unsuccessful attempts to get Katharina happily married, Luther decided to wed her himself. The historic marriage took place on June 13, 1525, in the home of Pastor Bugenhagen. Katharina bore six children. Katharina was a faithful, thrifty wife, and Luther freely commented on his appreciation for her. After his death (1546), Katharina lived through six rather troubled years. She was to receive various pensions and grants, but these arrived irregularly or not at all. When an epidemic broke out in Wittenberg (1552), she fled the town in a wagon. But the horses got out of control, and, while jumping from the vehicle, she was drenched with ice-cold water and mud. She died days later, trusting in the Savior, whom her husband had glorified.

1. Praying Hands (1508) by Albrecht Dürer
For a Visual Overview of the Reformation, turn to pp. 693–98.

2. The Landauer Altarpiece (1511) by Albrecht Dürer

3. The Ten Commandments (1516) by Lucas Cranach the Elder

4. The Dead Christ (1521) by Hans Holbein the Younger

5. Martin Luther (c. 1523; age 40) by Lucas Cranach the Elder

6. Martin Luther's Seal

7. Elector Frederick the Wise (c. 1523) by Lucas Cranach the Elder

8. Allegory of the Old and New Testaments
by Hans Holbein the Younger

IN SILENCIO ET SPE ERIT · M · L · FORTITVDO VESTRA

9. Martin Luther (1529) by Lucas Cranach the Elder

10. The Presentation of the Augsburg Confession
German School (1617), artist unknown

11. Paradise (1530) by Lucas Cranach the Elder

12. Philip Melanchthon, Age 35, (1532) by Lucas Cranach the Elder

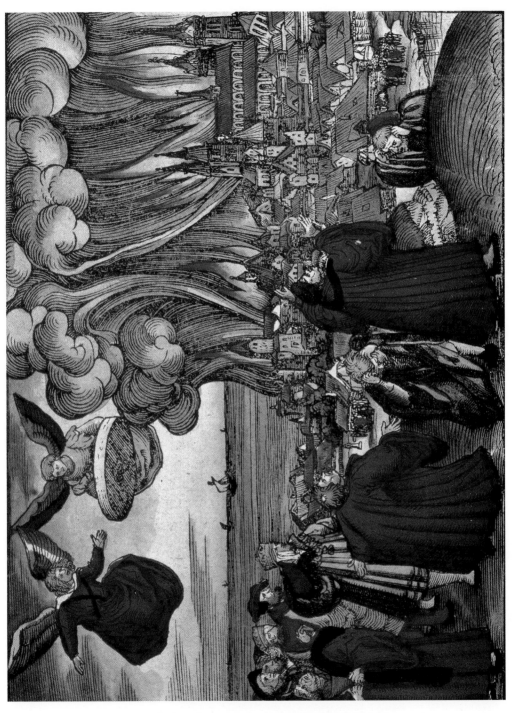

13. Babylon Burning, the Apocalypse of St. John
(Luther New Testament)

14. Philip of Hesse, the Magnanimous (1534)
by Hans Krell

15. The Harvest at the End of Time (1534 Luther Bible)
by the Lucas Cranach workshop

16. The Creation (1534 Luther Bible)
by the Lucas Cranach workshop

17. The Fall of the Beast (1534 Luther Bible)
by the Lucas Cranach workshop

18. John the Steadfast (1535) by Lucas Cranach the Elder

EFFIGIES IOH BVGENHAGII POMERANI·
LVCA CRONACHIO PICTORE·
·M·D·XXXVII·

19. John Bugenhagen (1537) by Lucas Cranach the Elder

20. Jesus Blesses the Little Children (1538)
by Lucas Cranach the Elder

21. John Frederick the Magnanimous of Saxony and Wittenberg Reformers (1543) by Lucas Cranach the Elder

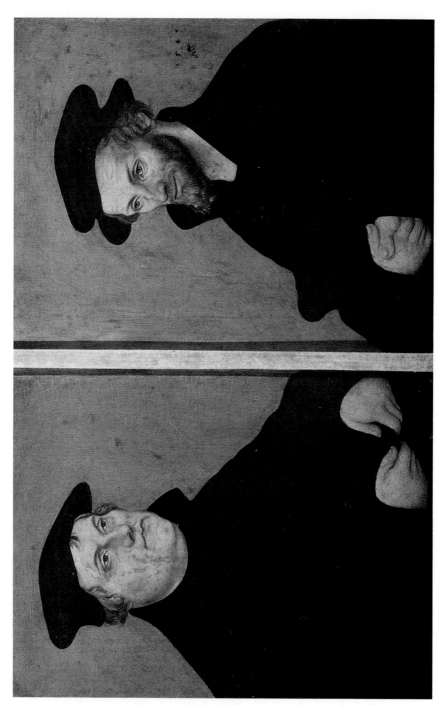

22. Double Portrait of Martin Luther and Philip Melanchthon
(1543) by Lucas Cranach the Elder

23. Elijah and the Priests of Baal (1545)
by Lucas Cranach the Elder

24. Wittenberg Altar Painting (1547) by Lucas Cranach the Elder

25. Detail from the Cranach Altar in St. Mary Church, Wittenberg

26. John Frederick the Magnanimous, Elector of Saxony (1547) by Titian

27. Lucas Cranach at Age 77 (1550), self-portrait

28. Unfinished Portrait of Elector Augustus I of Saxony (c. 1553)
by Lucas Cranach the Younger

29. Engraving of Matthias Flacius

30. Martin Chemnitz

31. The Weimar Altarpiece (1555) by Lucas Cranach the Elder
and Lucas Cranach the Younger

CONCORDIA

יהוה

# Christliche,

## Widerholete einmütige Bekentnüs

nachbenanter Churfürsten/ Fürsten vnd Stende
Augspurgischer Confession/ vnd derselben
Theologen Lere vnd glaubens:

Mit angeheffter/ in Gottes wort/ als der einigen Richt-
schnur/ wolgegründter erklerung etlicher Artickel/ bey
welchen nach D. Martin Luthers seligen absterben/
Disputation vnd streit vorgefallen.

## Aus einhelliger vergleichung vnd

beuehl obgedachter Churfürsten/ Fürsten vñ Stenden/
derselben Landen/ Kirchen/ Schulen vnd Nachkommen/
zum vnderricht vnd warnung in Druck
vorfertiget.

Mit Churf. G. zu Sachsen befreihung.

## Dreßden. M. D. LXXX.

32. Title page from a 1580 edition of the Book of Concord

**Brentz, John.** (1499–1570) Met Luther at Heidelberg Disputation (1518). Forced to flee for preaching Lutheran doctrine (1522). Settled at Hall, Swabia. Tried to help peasants after their defeat in Peasants' War (1525). Wrote large and small catechisms (1528). Consistently supported Luther in Communion Controversy. Attended Marburg Colloquy (1529). Supported Augsburg Confession (1530) against Bucer and Zwingli. Introduced numerous Lutheran church orders. Chief reformer of Württemberg. Reformed the University of Tübingen (1537). Attended meeting at Smalcald (1537). Work in Hall interrupted by Smalcaldic War (1546–47) and Interim (1548). Forced to flee by Charles V, narrowly escaped arrest. He prepared the Württemburg Confession, which he took to the Council of Trent (March 1552) but was not allowed to read it to the Council. Brentz was Luther's most reliable friend in Southern Germany. Declined many calls so he could help safeguard confessional Lutheranism in Württemberg. Deep piety, with pastoral concern for all Christians, but without compromise.

**Brück, Gregory.** (1485–1557) Counselor of Elector Frederick "the Wise." Later served as chancellor. Presented the German and Latin texts of the AC to Emperor Charles V on June 25, 1530.

**Bucer, Martin.** (1491–1551) German Protestant reformer. Dominican. Erasmus inclined him towards Protestantism; views influenced by Luther at Heidelberg Disputation (1518). Introduced Reformation at Strasbourg (1523). His views of the Lord's Supper, approaching those of Zwingli, exposed him to Luther's criticism. At Augsburg (1530) he generally agreed with Lutheran views but would not subscribe to the AC. Helped draw up Tetrapolitan Confession. At Diet of Regensburg he tried to unite Protestants and Romanists. Refusing to sign Interim, he accepted an invitation by Cranmer to teach theology at Cambridge and to further the Reformation in England.

**Bugenhagen, John.** (Pomeranus; 1485–1558) Called "pastor of the Reformation." Luther's *Babylonian Captivity* won him permanently for the Reformation. Came to Wittenberg (1521) and lectured on the Psalms. Pastor of St. Mary's Church from 1522. Assisted Luther in translation of the Bible. Celebrated its publication every year with a little festival in his home. His sermons were warm and direct. Motto: "If you know Christ well, it is enough, though you know nothing else; if you know not Christ, what else you learn does not matter."

**Bullinger, John Henry.** (1504–75) Swiss Reformer from 1522. Succeeded Zwingli as chief pastor of Zurich and leader of Reformation among German Swiss (1531). Helped draw up First and Second Helvetic Confessions. Wrote with Calvin the *Consensus Tigurinus*.

**Cain.** (ancient history) Son of Adam and Eve, a tiller of the soil (Genesis 4). God did not accept Cain's sacrifice and warned him about sin. Cain killed his brother Abel and was cursed by God. In the Lutheran Confessions he is an example of hypocrisy.

**Cajetan, Thomas de Vio.** (1469–1534) Italian cardinal and defender of papal supremacy. Admirer of Thomas Aquinas. General of the Dominican order (1517). Made cardinal (1517). Papal legate to the Diet of Augsburg (1518), with task of moving Luther to recant. Confounded and embarrassed by Luther's superior knowledge of Scripture, Cajetan began to study the Bible himself. His commentaries grew more and more critical of Roman doctrine. However, he continued to follow Rome, to serve the papacy, and to oppose Lutheranism.

**Calvin, John.** (1509–64) Studied for priesthood. Transferred to law. Influenced by humanism and Reformation. Had joined Reformation by 1533. Roused by the persecution of French Protestants, he issued a treatise in their behalf, addressed to Francis I, *Institutes of the Christian Religion* (1536), the classic exposition of Calvin's theology (early editions show a close dependence on Luther). Lucid, systematic, and exhaustive writer. Under Bucer's influence, his doctrinal views on predestination and Church order came to maturity. In 1541, married a widow, Idelette de Bure. (She died in 1549, leaving two stepchildren. Calvin's natural austerity was heightened by domestic troubles.) Called to Geneva, he insisted on complete authority. In 1553, at Calvin's insistence, Servetus was executed on charges of heresy. Though subject to chronic illness, Calvin lectured and preached several times a week and wrote many works. Founded Academy of Geneva (1559). Calvin had a formal and legalistic approach to Christianity in contrast to Luther's warm and evangelical spirit. God's sovereignty, honor, and glory are paramount in Calvin's system. He understood Christ's presence in the Lord's Supper in only a spiritual sense. He taught that God chose some people for heaven but others for hell (double predestination).

**Calvinists.** *See* Calvin.

**Campeggius, Lorenzo.** (1474–1539) Papal nuncio and cardinal; sent to Germany to enforce Edict of Worms. Archbishop of Bologna. Leader at Regensburg (1524). At Augsburg (1530) with Charles V, where he tried to bribe Melanchthon.

**Carlstadt, Andreas.** (c. 1480–1541) Revolutionist of the Reformation; Professor at Wittenberg; supported Luther's Ninety-five Theses; tangled with J. Eck at the Leipzig Debate (1519); introduced Reformation at Wittenberg by force (1521); preacher at Orlamünde (1523/24); rejected Baptism and the Lord's Supper as Sacraments and abolished ceremonies in undue haste; expelled by Saxon authorities (1524); wandered from place to place; associated with Zwingli at Zurich, and finally with Bullinger at Basel. During Luther's Wartburg retreat, vanity and impulsiveness got the better of Carlstadt, and he rushed reform with ill-advised haste. Even the extreme radicalism of Thomas Münzer found favor in his eyes. Luther returned to Wittenberg and quieted the storm successfully, while Carlstadt went back to teaching. Carlstadt finally withdrew to a little farm, dressed and lived like a peasant, and wanted to be known as "neighbor Andrew." But his temperament could not endure this either. He returned to the ministry at Orlamünde.

**Carthusians.** Monastic order noted for uncommon severity in its practices. Disheartened by degeneracy in the Church, Bruno of Cologne formed a colony of hermits (1084) and founded La Grand Chartreuse (hence the name Carthusians). It boasts that it is the only monastic order that never required reforms. Its rule prescribes practical isolation, even from brother monks. The smallest details of life are regulated.

**Cassiodorus, Flavius Magnus Aurelius.** (c. 485–c. 583) Statesman, author, and educator. Retired to a monastery he founded c. 540 on the Gulf of Squillace. Set up a curriculum on which the quadrivium and trivium of Medieval schools and today's modern liberal-arts education are based. Wrote many works.

**Castor and Pollux.** Twin deities in Greek and Roman mythology. Patrons of distressed sailors.

**Celsus.** (second century) Platonist philosopher; opponent of Christianity; known through Origen's reply *Against Celsus*.

**Cephas.** Simon Peter, the apostle.

**Charlemagne.** (742–814) Charles I, the first Holy Roman Emperor, crowned by Pope Leo III. Conquered and Christianized the Saxons. Through Alcuin, implemented Church and educational reforms.

**Charles V.** (1500–58) Holy Roman Emperor; elected 1519, crowned 1530. King (Charles I) of Spain (1516–66). He suppressed or tolerated the Reformation based on his political and military needs in the struggle with the French and Turks.

**Chemnitz, Martin.** (1522–86) At Wittenberg and Königsberg became associated with Georg Sabinus, son-in-law of Melanchthon. Melanchthon impressed on Chemnitz the importance of the proper distinction between Law and Gospel. Studied Peter Lombard and Luther. Opposed Osiander in justification controversy. Member of Wittenberg faculty (January 1554); lectured on Melanchthon's *Loci Communes*. Struggles with Jesuits began (1562) when Chemnitz attacked Cologne Jesuits. Made wide use of patristic evidence. Issued theological opinion regarding Majoristic controversy (1568). With Chytraeus reworked Jacob Andreae's Swabian Concordia (1574–75) to produce Swabian-Saxon Concordia; participated in Torgau Conference (1576) and in Bergen Abbey Conference (1577) in which FC was produced. A popular adage runs: "If Martin [Chemnitz] had not come, Martin [Luther] would not have stood."

**Christopher.** (history uncertain) Patron saint of travelers, ferrymen, and so forth. According to tradition, a third-century martyr. Legend refers the name *Christopher* ("Christbearing") to his bearing of Christ, in the form of a child, across a river.

**Chrysippus.** (c. 280–207 BC) A Stoic; *see* Stoics.

**Chrysostom, John.** (c. 345–407) Patriarch of Constantinople from 398. His name means "goldenmouthed." Intended to follow law, but turned to the Bible instead, leading the life of a strict ascetic in the first years after his Baptism. Started reforms at Constantinople and laid the foundation for systematic charitable work. Deposed and banished to Asia Minor (403); died on the way. Fame rests chiefly on his sermons, in which he reached great heights of oratory.

**Church Fathers.** Recognized teachers of the Church from the close of the apostolic age to dates variously set between the seventh and ninth centuries.

**Chytraeus, David.** (1531–1600) Studied law, philology, philosophy, and theology at Tübingen (influenced by J. Camerarius, E. Schnepf, J. Heerbrand), theology at Wittenberg (under P. Melanchthon, M. Luther, P. Eber); taught languages at Heidelberg (1546); returned to Tübingen (1547); lectured on rhetoric, astronomy, and Melanchthon's *Loci Communes* at Wittenberg (1548); traveled abroad c. 1550; professor of religion (1551), theology (1553) at Rostock. Present at Diet of Augsburg (1555 and 1566), Consultation of Worms (1557); with other theologians at the 1561 Naumburg Diet he warned against "the acceptance of the later editions" of the AC; wrote reactions of Rostock University to Weimar Confutation (1567); helped prepare Church Order for Lower and Upper Austria (1569), Styria (1574); member of consistory of Rostock (1570); rewrote articles on free will (II) and Lord's Supper (VII) for Swabian-Saxon Concordia (1574); one of 17 who prepared Torgau Book (1576); produced the Bergen Book with Jacob Andreae, M. Chemnitz, N. Selnecker, A. Musculus, and C. Cornerus.

**Cicero, Marcus Tullius.** (106–43 BC) Roman statesman, orator. Slain under second triumvirate. Noted for his orations, eclectic treatment of philosophical and religious subjects.

**Clement of Rome.** (first century) One of the earliest bishops of Rome. Wrote to the Christians in Corinth.

**Cölius, Michael.** Court preacher in Mansfeld. Signed SA (1537). Also subscribed to AC and Ap. Witnessed and reported on Luther's death.

**Constance.** See Council of Constance.

**Constantine I.** (c. 280–337) "The Great." Roman emperor from 306. According to tradition, before the Battle of the Milvian Bridge (312), saw the sign of the cross in the sky with words "by this sign you shall conquer." Granted imperial toleration and favor to Christianity. Convened the Council of Nicaea (325). Moved the seat of government from Rome to Byzantium.

**Cornelius.** (d. 253) Bishop of Rome (251–53) exiled under Roman persecution.

**Cornerus, Christopher.** (1518–94) Professor at Frankfort on the Oder; general superintendent at Brandenburg; worked on FC at Torgau (1576), Bergen (1577). Works include commentaries on Scripture and the ecumenical creeds.

**Council(s).** Gathering(s) of Church leaders to settle issues of faith and practice, dating back to the Early Church (see Acts 15). The fifteenth century Conciliar Movement sought to guide the Church through councils rather than through the papacy. The Lutheran Confessions respect the decisions of councils but subordinate them to God's Word, since councils had erred in the past.

**Council of Constance.** (1414–18) A council intended to bring about a reformation of the Church. The papal schism that began in 1378 was settled, electing Martin V. Excommunicated John Wycliffe posthumously (1415), and had his bones burned (1427) and their ashes thrown into the Swift. John Hus (1415) and Jerome of Prague (1416) were also condemned by this council and burned at the stake. Reforms were urged by lower clergy, monks, doctors, and professors, but the would-be reformers disagreed among themselves and their agitation practically came to naught, largely because the abuses they attacked concerned such matters as papal procedure, administration and income of vacant benefices, simony, indulgences, and dispensations, from which the pope, cardinals, and other Roman Church officials received much of their income.

**Council of Trent.** (1545–47, 1551–52, and 1562–63) Regarded as the nineteenth ecumenical council by the Roman Church. Met in three assemblies. In the first assembly, accepted traditional canon of Scripture (including Apocrypha), authorized the Vulgate, and defined Scripture and tradition as the two sources of religious truth. Rejected Lutheran view of imputed, or forensic, righteousness in the doctrine of justification. In the second, canons were established on the Eucharist, Penance, and Extreme Unction. The last assembly reaffirmed episcopal residencies; agreements concerning the sacrifice of the Mass, orders, and the establishment of seminaries were also reached. Anathemas of Protestant doctrines and affirmations of Roman Church teachings, along with the success of reform decrees, mark the council as one of the most important factors of the Catholic, or Counter, Reformation. This council established the Roman Catholic Church in distinction from Medieval catholicism, which Lutherans regard as part of their heritage.

**Corvinus, Anthony.** (1501–53) Expelled from cloister because of his Lutheranism (1523). Preacher who advanced Reformation in Northeim, Hildesheim, and Calenberg-Göttingen. Opposed Augsburg Interim; imprisoned (1549–52).

**Cranach, Lucas,** the Elder (1472–1553) Court painter under Frederick the Wise (c. 1505) and under John the Steadfast and John Frederick. Painted portraits of Luther and practically all important Lutheran reformers. His art shows evangelical understanding of Scripture and Church. Sons Hans (d. 1537) and Lucas the Younger (1515–86) worked with their father and continued his style. Lucas took his name from Kronach in Upper Franconia, where he was born. He was influenced by Renaissance painters and humanist scholars while living and studying in Vienna around 1503. Until 1508, Cranach signed his works with the initials of his name. In that year the elector gave him the winged snake as a motto, and this motto or *Kleinod*, as it was called, superseded the initials on all his pictures after that date. He became a fast friend of Martin Luther and played an important role in arranging for Luther's marriage celebration. He was the baptismal sponsor for Luther's oldest son, Hans. He was a member of the Wittenberg town council and served for a while as mayor of Wittenberg. After the defeat of the Smalcaldic League's armies in 1547, he wrote to Albert of Brandenburg at Königsberg to tell him of the capture of John Frederick the Magnanimous: "I cannot conceal from your Grace that we have been robbed of our dear prince, who from his youth upwards has been a true prince to us, but God will help him out of prison, for the emperor is bold enough to revive the papacy, which God will certainly not allow." During the siege of Wittenberg, Charles V called for Cranach, whom he remembered from his childhood, and summoned him to his camp at Pistritz. Cranach came and reminded Charles of his early sittings for portraits by Cranach when he was a boy, and begged on his knees for kind treatment to the elector. John Frederick ordered Cranach to his side and Cranach left his prosperous businesses and spent time with his elector in his exile, returning home with him in 1552. Cranach died on October 16, 1553.

**Crell, Paul.** (1531–79) Taught at Wittenberg. With Eber, he rejected the ubiquity of Christ but taught the bodily presence of Christ in the Lord's Supper.

**Creutziger, Caspar, Sr.** (1504–48) "Stenographer of the Reformation," recorded many of Luther's sermons and lectures. Fast friend of Melanchthon. Introduced the Reformation in Leipzig, his native city, in 1539. Prominent in translation of the Bible under the leadership of Luther. Troubled over Smalcald War and the attempts at a religious settlement thereafter. Like Melanchthon, ready to yield and compromise.

**Curii.** The Roman Senate (Ap XXIII 2).

**Cusanus.** *See* Nicholas of Cusa.

**Cyprian.** (c. 200–58) Son of a Carthaginian senator. Taught rhetoric. Converted to Christianity (c. 245). Bishop of Carthage by popular acclaim (c. 248). Fled during Decian persecution; returned (251) under Gallus, successor of Decius; condemned and beheaded under Valerian. According to his view, bishops are successors of the apostles and, like them, specially endowed with the Holy Spirit. The episcopate is a unity, each bishop representing the whole office. From the unity of the episcopate springs the unity of the Church, outside of which there is no salvation. Although Cyprian considered the Bishop of Rome the successor of St. Peter, he addressed him as an equal.

**Cyprian of Antioch in Pisidia.** (third–fourth century) Converted magician. According to one account beheaded with Justina in Diocletian persecution.

**Cyril of Alexandria.** (c. 376–444) Influential spokesman of the Eastern Church. Strongly opposed Nestorian heresy about the person of Christ and was largely instrumental in having Nestorius himself deposed. A prolific writer, he helped in particular to clarify the Trinitarian and Christological controversies. Passionate and bitter in his polemics.

**Damascene.** See John of Damascus.

**Daniel.** (sixth century BC) Old Testament prophet most often mentioned in the Lutheran Confessions. The Confessions describe his preaching to Nebuchadnezzar, king of Babylon, which resulted in the king's conversion (Daniel 4). Daniel also prophesied about the coming of Antichrist (Daniel 11).

**David.** (d. c. 970 BC) King of Israel, prophet, and psalmist. The Lutheran Confessions describe David as an example of sincere repentance and faith.

**Deacons.** From Greek word for "servant." An office of early Christian ministry established by the apostles (Acts 6:1–6; Philippians 1:1; 1 Timothy 3:8–13). In the Early Church, deacons were ranked below bishops and presbyters. They distributed the Lord's Supper to those who couldn't attend church and assisted during the divine service. Lutherans retained the office of deacon as assistants to pastors.

**Demosthenes.** (384–322 BC) Greatest Athenian orator.

**Devil.** See Satan.

**Diana.** Ancient Roman goddess of women and childbirth.

**Didymus the Blind.** (c. 313–c. 398) Blind from age 4; leader of catechetical school in Alexandria.

**Dietrich of Bern.** (c. 454–526) Name used in Teutonic legends for Theodoric the Great, king of the Ostrogoths, who conquered Italy.

**Dietrich, Veit.** (1506–49) Luther's secretary (1527); with Luther at Marburg (1529) and at Coburg (1530). Served as private instructor; member of Wittenberg faculty. Pastor in Nürnberg (1535); attended Regensburg Conference (1546); involved in politics of Smalcaldic War; removed from office (1547); opposed Interim in Nürnberg.

**Diogenes Laertius.** (third century BC) Author of the lives and doctrines of ancient Greek philosophers.

**Dionysius the Areopagite.** 1. Converted by Paul at Athens (Acts 17:34); tradition regards him as the first bishop of Athens. 2. Unknown author (c. AD 500), long identified wrongly with Paul's convert. Works include many mystical treatises.

**Dionysius the Great** (c. 190–c. 264) Bishop of Alexandria. Pupil of Origen, led Catechetical School (233). Fled Decian persecution (250); captured, then escaped. An important theologian because of his strong leadership and decisions during third-century controversies.

**Dominic.** (1171–1221) Priest; founder of the Dominicans (see below).

**Dominicans.** "Order of Preachers" also called "Friars Preachers" founded by Dominic while engaged in efforts to convert the Albigenses of South France (1215). It adopted the Augustinian rule and was committed to poverty and dedicated to teaching, preaching, and scholarship. The rule of poverty was soon disregarded and eliminated altogether by 1477. Dominicans were to strengthen faith and combat heresy. Most Inquisitors were

**Dominicans.** John Tetzel and Thomas Aquinas were Dominicans.

**Donatists.** *See* Donatus.

**Donatus.** (fourth century) Possibly referring to one of two North African leaders by this name: Donatus of Casae Nigrae or Donatus of Carthage. Donatist sect formed after protests against consecration of Caecilian as bishop of Carthage (311). Donatists held that to be persecuted was a mark of the Church, Sacraments administered by a person deserving excommunication were invalid, and a church failing to excommunicate such leaders ceased to be the true Church and its Baptism was invalid. Donatists held that only they were the true Church.

**Draconites, John.** (1494–1566) Pastor and professor who supported Luther. Signed SA.

**Duns Scotus, John.** (c. 1265–c. 1308) Scottish Franciscan; Scholastic teacher at Oxford, Paris, and Cologne; opposed theological system of Thomas Aquinas. Followers called Scotists.

**Dürer, Albrecht.** (1471–1528) Painter and engraver for Maximillion I and Charles V. Made woodcuts to illustrate the Book of Revelation, as well as many other splendid works. *See* p. 693.

**Eber, Paul.** (1511–69) Professor of Latin (1541) and Hebrew (1557) at Wittenberg; poet; castle preacher, city preacher, and general superintendent of electorate (1558). Associate of Melanchthon; sided with Philippists after Luther's death.

**Eck, John.** (1486–1543) Clever dialectician. Professor at Ingolstadt from 1510. Obliged by his superiors to pass judgment on the Ninety-five Theses of Luther, with whom he had stood in friendly relation. The two clashed especially in the Leipzig Debate (June 27–July 16, 1519). In Rome, Eck was largely instrumental in getting Leo X to issue against Luther, on June 15, 1520, the bull *Exsurge, Domine.* Champion of Medieval Romanism and papal supremacy at the Diet of Augsburg (1530), and was active in this capacity in all later similar religious conventions. Eck never became a noted author but is generally regarded as Luther's ablest opponent.

**Enthusiast(s).** From Greek for "one possessed by a god." The Lutheran Confessions use this term to describe fanatics who believed that God spoke to them without the Holy Scriptures and would save them without the means of grace.

**Epicureans.** See Epicurus.

**Epicurus.** (c. 341–c. 270 BC) Greek philosopher; founded Epicurean school of thought. Founded school at Athens (c. 306). Lived with followers in a secluded and austere way. Developed philosophy of pleasure and contemplation.

**Epiphanius.** (c. 315–403) Greek Church Father; bishop of Salamis (Constantia); elected metropolitan bishop by the bishops of Cyprus (367). Highly esteemed for monastic asceticism, learning, piety, self-denying care for the poor, and zeal for orthodoxy. Wrote against heretics.

**Erasmus of Rotterdam, Desiderius.** (1469–1536) One of the most learned men of his age. Guardians forced him into a monastery; became a priest but never had a parish and never performed priestly functions. Edited an edition of the Greek New Testament, which was published in Basel (1516) and was later used by Luther in his Bible translation. Recognized the many ills of Christendom, but they moved him to laughter rather than to tears. He looked to a humanistic education for a gradual and peaceful reform of the Church. At first sympathetic to Luther's ambitions, he drew farther and farther away from the Reformation because of its positiveness, its emphasis on Scripture alone, and its refusal to submit to Rome. Wrote against Luther in defense of the free will of people, a point of Scholastic doctrine. Luther refuted him in his book *On the Bondage of the Will*. The controversy left Erasmus mistrusted by both Romanists and by Protestants.

**Ernest the Confessor.** (1497–1546) Duke of Brunswick-Lüneburg; nephew of Frederick the Wise. Introduced Lutheranism into duchy (1527); signed AC (1530).

**Esau.** (nineteenth century BC) Son of the Patriarch Isaac, brother of Jacob (Genesis 25–28, 32–33). Father of the Edomites.

**Eunomius** (Eunomians). (c. 335–c. 394) Arian heretic; Anomoean leader; bishop Cyzicus in Mysia (Asia Minor). Refuted by the Cappadocian Fathers.

**Eunuch.** A male servant whose testicles have been removed so that he might work among royal women.

**Euripides.** (d. c. 407 BC) Athenian tragic playwright.

**Eusebius of Caesarea.** (c. 260–c. 339) "The father of Church history." Bishop of Caesarea (c. 313); high in favor with Constantine I; convinced the Council of Nicaea (325) of his orthodoxy by submitting a creed, probably that which his church at Caesarea had been using. Wrote famous *Church History*.

**Eusebius of Emesa**, Syria. (c. 295–c. 359) Probably a disciple of Eusebius of Caesarea; sympathized with Semi-Arians.

**Eustathius of Antioch**, Syria. (d. c. 337 AD) Patriarch of Antioch, Syria; opposed school of Origen; opposed Arians at Nicaea (325); deposed at Arian synod of Antioch (c. 326/331) and exiled to Thrace. Eustathians in Antioch refused to recognize bishops of Arian consecration, thus causing the Eustathian, later Meletian, schism.

**Eutyches** (c. 378–454; Eutychianism) Asserted that there were two natures in Christ before, but only one after, the incarnation. In opposition to Nestorianism, Eutyches taught that the human nature in Christ was absorbed or swallowed up by the divine nature. Condemned at Council of Chalcedon.

**Evagrius Ponticus.** (c. 346–c. 399) Deacon and noted preacher at Constantinople; retired as monk to Nitrian desert.

**Evangelist.** (first century) Author of a New Testament Gospel (Matthew, Mark, Luke, and John).

**Eve.** (ancient history) The first woman, wife of Adam (Genesis 1–4).

**Faber, John.** (1478–1541) Called "Hammer of Heretics" after one of his works; vicar-general at Constance (1518); humanist friend of Erasmus; participated in disputations at Zurich (1523) and Baden (1526) against Zwingli; bishop of Vienna (c. 1530); wrote against Luther.

**Faber, Wendel.** (first half of sixteenth century) Teacher at Eisleben; by 1537, court preacher of Count Gebhard von Mansfeld at Seeburg; signed SA and Tr; opposed J. Agricola in Antinomian Controversy.

**Fagius, Paul.** (c. 1504–49) Pastor at Isny, Württemberg (1538). Established a Hebrew press; pastor Konstanz (c. 1543); pastor and professor of Old Testament at Strasbourg (1544); went to England (1549) as a result of Interim; professor Old Testament at Cambridge; friend of Bucer.

**Fathers.** *See* Church Fathers.

**Febris.** Roman goddess of fever, who needed to be appeased so she would remove sickness.

**Ferdinand I.** (1503–64) Brother of Charles V; born in Alcalá de Henares, Spain; king of Hungary and Bohemia (1526), Germany (1531); ruled Holy Roman Empire (1556–64).

**Figenbotz, Conrad.** (d. after 1540) Pastor of Halberstadt and Goslar, later Zerbst; represented Anhalt-Zerbst at Smalcald (1537); signed SA.

**Flacius, Matthias.** (1520–75) His relative, Baldo Lupetino, pointed him to Luther; went to Augsburg (1539), then Basel, where he began a three-year "soul struggle." Spent time at Tübingen as professor of Greek; came to Wittenberg and into close contact with Melanchthon and Luther (1541). Cured of "soul struggle" (c. 1543) in his own opinion by doctrine of justification. Professor of Hebrew at Wittenberg (1544). Criticized Augsburg and Leipzig Interims. Held that the Interim

introduced not only ceremonial but also doctrinal errors (*see* Adiaphoristic Controversy, p. 523). Left Wittenberg for Magdeburg (1549); wrote a history, *Magdeburg Centuries.* Active in Majoristic, Osiandrian, and Synergism controversies. While at Magdeburg he took part in attempts to reconcile warring parties within Lutheranism. Professor at Jena (1557). Opposed union formula with Reformed; insisted on disputation. Refused to sign Jacob Andreae's articles for proposed union of German churches. Gnesio-Lutherans (including T. Hesshusius and J. Wigand) and Andreae attacked Flacius's teaching on original sin. (Refuted in FC I.)

**Fortunatus** (c. 530–c. 610) Bishop of Poitiers (c. 600). Poet and hymn writer.

**Francis of Assisi.** (c. 1181–1226) *See* Franciscans.

**Franciscans.** Order founded in 1209 by Francis of Assisi. Their early years were marked by strict poverty, limited use of property, begging, humble service to all, and mission endeavors; but the order was wracked for more than a century by disputes about the question of poverty. Bonaventure, Duns Scotus, and William of Ockham were members of the order. In 1517, a split took place between the stricter faction (Friars Minor proper [Observant]) and the moderate faction (Friars Minor Conventual). The Friars Minor Capuchins were founded c. 1528 by an Observant priest; they became one of the most powerful agencies of the Counter Reformation. The Second Order (Poor Clares) was founded 1212. There is also a Third Order (Tertiaries).

**Franck, Sebastian.** (c. 1499–c. 1543) Bishop of Donauwörth. Free-thinker; priest; Protestant (1525); independent mystic (1528); opposed by Luther and Melanchthon.

**Frederick III, the Wise** (1463–1525) Elector of Saxony from 1486. Called "the Wise" because of his vision and astuteness, which raised little Saxony to the rank of the most influential power in Germany. At the death of Maximilian I (1519), Frederick was offered the Imperial crown, but he declined it. Frederick was largely a nationalist and worked toward strengthening his own government rather than that of the Empire and the Church. He was a devout son of the Church. In 1493, he went on a pilgrimage to the Holy Land and returned with a thumb of Anna, his favorite saint. This he added to the more than 5,000 relics he kept in the Castle Church at Wittenberg. In 1502, he had established Wittenberg University, to which Luther was called (1508). When Luther's reformatory activity began to attract public notice, Frederick protected Luther. He would have no one condemned unheard and unconvicted, nor would he have an offense that had been committed in his country tried at Rome. Frederick and Luther communicated through Spalatin, Frederick's secretary. Gradually the Gospel exerted its power on this devout Medieval man and Frederick became a Lutheran in faith—if not in public confession. He abolished the exhibition of his precious relics in 1523 and discontinued Masses in the Castle Church. Two years later, on his deathbed, he received Communion in the Lutheran and Scriptural form.

**Friars.** From Latin, *frater*, "brother." Members of a monastic order that lives on almsgiving (mendicant).

**Gabriel.** 1. Archangel. 2. *See* Biel, Gabriel.

**Gaius Caesar.** (first century) *See* Julius Caesar.

**Galatians.** (first century) Members of congregation(s) in Asia Minor to whom Paul wrote about justification and the use of Law and Gospel.

**Gallus, Nicholaus.** (real family name: Han, or Hahn; c. 1516–70) Pastor and Reformation leader in Regensburg; opposed Interim (1548); co-worker of M. Flacius in Magdeburg (1549); opposed adiaphorism of Wittenberg theologians and Reformed leanings of P. Melanchthon; gave Flacius refuge (1562–66). Works include *Disputation von Mitteldingen.*

**Gelasius I.** (d. 496) Pope 492–496. Asserted papal supremacy.

**Geltner, Peter.** (d. 1572) Preacher at Frankfort who signed SA, AC, and Ap.

**Gennadius of Marseilles.** (d. c. 500) Presbyter; historian; semi-Pelagian. Works include *On Illustrious Men* (continuation of a similar work by Jerome).

**George.** (d. c. 303) Patron saint of England and of the Order of the Garter; allegedly of noble Cappadocian descent; perhaps a Christian martyr; legend of his combat with a dragon to liberate a princess arose c. twelfth century, possibly founded on the myths of Perseus and Siegfried.

**George, Duke of Saxony.** (1471–1539) Head of Albertine Saxony from 1500 until his death. Interested in the welfare of his country and its people; saw the many evils in the Church and appreciated Luther's Ninety-five Theses. But a sermon of Luther that stressed faith alone (*sola fide*) shocked him, and this estrangement developed into intense antipathy, which was fanned by his secretaries, Jerome Emser and, after 1527, John Cochlaeus. George fought a losing battle against the Reformation both in his country and in his own heart. Emser's edition of the German Bible, authorized by him, was in part a capitulation. When he directed his dying son John to Christ alone, he showed that the Reformation had captured his heart.

**George Ernest.** (1511–83) Count of Henneberg-Schleusingen (1559–83); helped write Maulbronn Formula; instituted a Church order; signed Book of Concord (October 17, 1579).

**George the Pious.** (1484–1543) Margrave of Brandenburg-Ansbach. Helped his brother Albert of Prussia Lutheranize Prussia; aided the Reformation in Silesia and Ansbach; protested at Speyer (1529). Courageous Lutheran confessor at Diet of Augsburg (1530) and staunch ally of Elector John the Steadfast.

**Gerson, John.** (c. 1363–c. 1429) Chancellor at University of Paris (1395). Drawn to the problem of papal schism, Gerson influenced the Councils of Pisa and Constance. Hostility kept Gerson from returning to France. He spent time in Bavaria and Austria and concluded his life in pastoral and literary activities at Lyons, France. His chief concern was that the people, both educated and simple, would live truly pious lives. He has been spoken of as a pre-reformer, but he held that for salvation man must "do what is in him."

**Gnesio-Lutherans.** ("Genuine Lutherans") After the death of Luther, so-called genuine Lutheranism was represented by such men as Amsdorf, Flacius, Wigand, Gallus, Judex, Mörlin, Hesshusius, Timan, Westphal of Hamburg, Hunnius, Poach, and E. Sarcerius. Headquarters were at Jena beginning 1557. Their opponents were called Philippists.

**Gordius.** (eighth century BC) Father of King Midas of Phrygia. Tied the legendary "Gordian knot." The knot was like a complicated puzzle. Whoever solved it by untying the knot would rule Asia. Alexander the Great responded by hacking the knot apart with his sword.

**Gratian.** (d. c. 1159) Compiler of the *Decreta*, the basis of canon law. The *Decreta* contains almost 4,000 quotes from Early and Medieval Christianity, which were used to guide the Church.

**Grebel, Conrad.** (c. 1498–1526) Follower of Zwingli. Anabaptist Mennonites originated in Switzerland and the Netherlands; Grebel founded the Swiss group at Zurich (1525).

**Greeks.** 1. The ancient Greeks. 2. The Greek-speaking Christians of the East.

**Gregory I, the Great.** (c. 540–604) Bishop of Rome, "Doctor of the Church." His Pastoral Rule was a standard of pastoral care.

**Gregory of Nazianzus.** (329–89) Bishop of Nazianzus, Cappadocia; called "The Theologian"; was a great Christian orator and poet.

**Gregory of Nyssa.** (c. 331–c. 396) Bishop of Nyssa, Cappadocia. Younger brother of Basil of Caesarea. Famous for his catechetical sermons.

**Gustavus Adolfus II.** (1594–1632) "Lion of the North; Snow King." King of Sweden (1611–32); grandson of Gustavus I; father of Christina. Championed Protestant cause in Germany in Thirty Years' War. Landed in Pomerania (1630); conquered much of Germany; killed in the Battle of Lützen on November 16, 1632.

**Hausmann, Nicholas.** (c. 1478–1538) Close friend of Luther; reformer; preacher at Schneeberg (1519); succeeded J. W. Egranus at Zwickau (1521); opposed by Zwickau prophets; went to Dessau (1532). Died of a stroke while delivering his initial sermon on November 3, 1538. His death deeply moved Luther. "What we teach, he lives," the Reformer said of him.

**Heathen.** *See* Pagans.

**Helt, George.** (c. 1485–1545) Advisor of George III of Anhalt; present at the February 1537 meeting of the Smalcaldic League at Smalcald; signed SA and Tr.

**Henry VIII.** (1491–1547) Tudor king of England (1509–47); joined Holy League against France (1511); appointed Wolsey lord chancellor (1515); received title "Defender of the Faith" from pope (1521) for opposing Luther. In conflict with pope because the latter refused to grant him an annulment from Catherine of Aragon; secured from Parliament the Act of Supremacy (1534), creating a national church with king as head; closed monasteries and confiscated their property. In 1533, Thomas Cranmer, a prelate with Lutheran leanings, was consecrated Archbishop of Canterbury. There now followed a quasi reform in England by the dissolution of monasteries (1535–36), the promulgation of the Ten Articles (1539), the translation of the Bible with the royal sanction, and even an exploration of the possibility of a working agreement with the reformers on the Continent, especially Luther and his associates.

Luther was correct when he remarked that Henry wanted to kill the pope's body, that is, papal authority in England, but desired to keep the pope's soul, papal doctrine.

**Heracles.** (third century) Taught at Origen's Catechetical School; elected bishop of Alexandria by elders.

**Hermits.** From Greek *eremites*, "living in the desert." Religious orders whose members lead solitary lives.

**Herod the Great.** (47–4 BC) Governor and king of Galilee and Judea on behalf of the Roman Empire. He attempted to kill the baby Jesus (Matthew 2).

**Hesshusius, Tilemann.** (1527–88) Gnesio-Lutheran professor and pastor. Expelled from Rostock for opposing worldliness (1557). Deposed at Heidelberg (1559) for refusing to subscribe to the *Variata*. Deposed at Magdeburg (1562) for opposing edict forbidding polemics. Exiled (1573) by Elector Augustus of Saxony. Made bishop of Samland (peninsula of former East Prussia; 1573). Deposed (1577) on charges of false doctrine in Christology. Professor at Helmstedt (1577). Helped to deter Brunswick from accepting FC.

**Heyderich, Caspar.** (1516–86) As early as 1528 studied at Wittenberg. From 1540–41 he labored in Joachimstal as the successor of John Mathesius. Returning to Wittenberg, he received a master's degree (1541). Here he also became a frequent guest at Luther's table until he became the court preacher of Duchess Catherine of Saxony, the widow of Henry the Pious, at Freiberg (1543).

**Hilary of Arles.** (c. 401–49) Archbishop of Arles, France; leader of semi-Pelagians.

**Hilary of Poitiers.** (c. 315–67) "Athanasius of the West." Opposed Arianism; banished (356) to Phrygia, in Asia Minor, an Arian stronghold. Returned (c. 361); he purged Gaul of the Arian heresy, but was less successful in Italy; outstanding Latin theologian; hymnist.

**Hilten, John.** (c. 1425–c. 1500) Franciscan apocalyptic writer; said to have foretold the Reformation (Ap XXVII 1–4).

**Holbein, Hans, the Younger.** (c. 1497–1543) Painter and engraver. *See* p. 693.

**Homer.** (Dates have been assigned to him ranging from 1200 to 850 BC.) Greek poet of the Iliad (on Trojan War) and Odyssey (wanderings of Odysseus [Ulysses]). These two epic poems, sometimes called "the Bible of the Greeks," may be composite products of many poets.

**Horace.** (65–8 BC) Famous Roman poet.

**Hugh of St. Victor.** (c. 1096–1141) Spent most of adult life in abbey of St. Victor, Paris; combined mysticism and dialectics in treatment of theology.

**Hus, John.** (c. 1370–1415) Forerunner of the Reformation. Studied at University of Prague, became priest (1400) and rector of the university (1402). A follower of Wycliffe, he clearly recognized the need for reformation. He was put under the great ban of the Church of Rome (1412). Refusing to be silenced, he countered by writing his book *On the Church*. Hus taught the sole authority of Scripture and held that the Church is the body of the elect. Though he preached Christ as Savior, he confused Law and Gospel and mixed justification with sanctification. After three public hearings, the Council of Constance condemned him to be burned publicly as a heretic on July 6, 1415, because "no faith should be observed toward a heretic." His ashes were flung into the Rhine.

**Irenaeus.** (d. c. 200 AD) Greek Church Father; Bishop of Lyons (178); opposed Gnosticism and other heresies; worked zealously for the spread of Christianity and defense of its doctrines; developed a concept of recapitulation (restoration of all things); emphasized apostolic succession and tradition.

**Irenaeus.** (fourth century) Correspondent with Ambrose.

**Irenaeus, Christopher.** (c. 1522–c. 1595) Rector at Bernburg and Ascherleben (1545); pastor at Eisleben (1562); court preacher at Coburg and Weimar. He supported M. Flacius and opposed J. Andreae.

**Isaac.** (c. 2066–c. 1886 BC) Son of Abraham and Patriarch of Israel (Genesis 21–28), through whom God promised a Savior would be born.

**Isaiah.** (eighth century BC) Prophet in OT Judah. Cited often in the Lutheran Confessions.

**Israel.** The Hebrew people of the OT, named for the Patriarch Jacob, whom God called "Israel" (Genesis 32:22–32). The Lutheran Confessions regard the good and bad events of Israel's history as examples for warning and teaching the Church.

**Jacob.** (c. 2006–c. 1859 BC) Son of Isaac and Patriarch of Israel. God gave him the name Israel (Genesis 32:22–32).

**Januarius.** (fifth century) Leading Donatist bishop in the region of Hippo, at Case Nigrae in Numidia.

**Jeremiah.** (d. c. 585 BC) Prophet in OT Judah.

**Jeroboam I.** (d. c. 909) The first king of the northern tribes of Israel, which broke away during the reign of Rehoboam of Judah (1 Kings 12). He reintroduced idolatry in ancient Israel (the golden calves).

**Jerome.** (b. c. 340s–d. c. 420) Church Father. Baptized at 19 in Rome, where he had gone to study rhetoric and philosophy; traveled, settling finally at Bethlehem. Turned from secular studies to the things of God during his first stay at Antioch; secretary to Bishop Damasus I of Rome. Works include revision of the Latin Bible (Vulgate) and commentaries on books of the Bible. However, he never seems to have clearly understood Christ's redemptive work.

**Jerome of Prague.** (c. 1360–1416) Friend of John Hus, copied *Dialogus* and *Trialogus* of John Wycliffe, whom he championed. Council of Constance condemned him to be publicly burned as a heretic (1416).

**Jesse.** (eleventh century BC) Israelite of the tribe of Judah, father of King David (1 Samuel 16).

**Jesus of Nazareth.** (eternal God, born of the virgin Mary c. 4 BC) The Christ and Savior of the world. Subject especially of AC III; Ap III; SA II I; FC Ep VIII and SD VIII.

**Jews.** Descendants of the Israelite tribe of Judah and other Israelites who followed the leadership of Judah. Mary and Jesus descended from this tribe. Because the Jewish leadership rejected Jesus as God, antagonism has long existed between Jewish people and Christians.

**Joachim, Elector(s) of Brandenburg.** 1. Joachim I Nestor (1484–1535). Elector (1499–1535); father of Joachim II; founded University of Frankfurt an der Oder (1506); opposed Luther; helped organize League of Dessau.

2. Joachim II Hektor (1505–71). Elector (1535–71); son of Joachim I; Protestant from 1539.

3. Joachim Friedrich (1546–1608). Elector (1598–1608); son of John George, Elector of Brandenburg; bishop of Havelberg (1553), Lebus (1555); first evangelical archbishop of Magdeburg (1566–98). Disbanded cloisters; removed Roman ceremonies; unwillingly yielded to requests of Magdeburg nobility to introduce FC; desired union between Lutherans and Reformed.

**Job.** (second millennium BC) OT figure known for his suffering and patience. The Lutheran Confessions commend him because He sought God's will more than escape from suffering.

**John Casimir.** (1564–1633) Son of John Frederick II; duke of Saxe-Coburg; established Gymnasium at Coburg; befriended J. Gerhard. His guardian signed BOC.

**John Frederick.** (1503–54) Elector and duke of Saxony; called "the Magnanimous" because of his spirit and bearing under misfortune. Son of John the Steadfast; educated by Spalatin; early supporter of Luther; went with his father to Diet of Augsburg (1530). Elector of Ernestine Saxony (1532–47). Impulsive; not a far-sighted politician. Unity of the Smalcaldic League suffered from disagreements between John Frederick and Philip of Hesse, leaders of the League (e.g., John Frederick took a strict Lutheran position; Philip favored union with other Protestants). He antagonized Maurice, duke of Saxony (1542) by unilaterally trying to introduce the Reformation into the city of Wurzen, whose see was under joint protection of electoral and ducal Saxony; war between the two Saxonies was averted only by efforts of Luther and Philip. He was suspicious of colloquies and rejected papal overtures for a council. Did not attend diets and similar meetings after Smalcald (1537). He had asked Luther for a position paper; result was the SA. When Charles V prepared to attack the Smalcaldic League, John Frederick was slow in taking counter measures. With the outbreak of the Smalcaldic War (July 1546), John Frederick left his realm with an army to engage the Imperial forces, but returned when Maurice, who had joined the cause of Charles V, invaded electoral Saxony. John Frederick reconquered most of his land, repelling Maurice, but was wounded, defeated, and captured by Imperial forces at Mühlberg on April 24, 1547. Condemned to death by Charles V; sentence commuted to life imprisonment when Wittenberg surrendered; released by Maurice (1552) but did not regain title. Reorganized the University of Wittenberg (1535–36); benefactor of University of Leipzig; laid the plans for the University of Jena (founded 1558). He loved and venerated Luther and consulted him even on matters of a secular and, at times, of a political nature. He was the moving spirit behind the publication of the first complete edition of Luther's Works, the Wittenberg edition, and laid the plans for another, the Jena edition, which was to contain only what the Reformer himself had written.

**John Frederick II.** (1529–95) Duke of Saxony; son of John Frederick the Magnanimous; father of John Casimir; allowed to rule small part of his father's land by Charles V after 1547; deposed (1566); imprisoned (1567).

**John George.** (1525–98) Elector and margrave of Brandenburg-Küstrin 1571–98; son of Joachim II Hektor; father of Joachim Friedrich.

**John of Damascus.** (d. c. 750) Greek theologian, called "Doctor of the Church." Monk near Jerusalem; priest; hymnist. Involved in iconoclastic controversy. His writings greatly influenced both Eastern and Western theologians.

**John the Steadfast.** (or "Constant"; 1468–1532) Brother of Frederick the Wise; father of John Frederick; received scholarly education; knight; elector of Saxony (1525); early supporter of Luther. After publication of Luther's New Testament (1522), John read the Bible daily. Luther preached at his court in Weimar (October 1522) and wrote a treatise for him (1523). John was tolerant toward Münzer and Carlstadt, did not interfere with abolition of the Corpus Christi procession, and permitted Protestant observance of the Lord's Supper. After becoming elector, he refused to make common cause against Lutherans with his cousin, George the Bearded. Issued a directive on August 16, 1525, making Ernestine Saxony evangelical. Signed treaty with Philip of Hesse (February 27, 1526) and led Lutheran party at 1526 Diet of Speyer; approved church visitations suggested by Hausmann; at 1529 Diet of Speyer he defended the evangelical interpretation of the recess of the 1526 diet and protested with others the resolution of the Roman majority; at the 1530 Augsburg Diet he took a heroic stand against Charles V; led Smalcaldic League (1531). His motto: The Word of the Lord endures forever. His servants displayed the motto on their uniforms.

**Jonas, Justus.** (1493–1555) One of Luther's dearest friends. Present at Luther's death; preached on 1 Thessalonians 4:13–14 at the first funeral service in honor of the departed Refomer. Jonas became professor and rector of the university at Erfurt at the age of 26, and a doctor of Holy Scripture in 1521. He was with Luther at Worms, Marburg, and elsewhere. Eloquent preacher and a noted linguist. He translated many of Luther's writings, notably *On the Bondage of the Will*. After the disastrous Smalcaldic War in 1547, he had to flee from Charles V. (Jonas had once suggested the insertion of Charles V into the Creed next to that of Pontius Pilate.) Jonas energetically opposed all doctrinal compromises and concessions. As his life's motto he had chosen Galatians 1:10.

**Jovinian.** (fl. 385–400) Called a heretic, known only from writings of his opponents, including Jerome. His views developed from his opposition to Eastern monasticism and included these: married people have equal merit with unmarried and widows; fasting not better than thankful feasting; Mary conceived, but did not bear Christ as a virgin, since childbearing ends virginity; the regenerate are essentially sinless. Excommunicated in 390.

**Judas Iscariot.** (first century) Disciple of Jesus who betrayed Him to the Jewish authorities (Matthew 26:14–56). In the Lutheran Confessions, Judas is an example of someone who lacked true contrition or repentance, ending his life in despair. Since Judas was a hypocrite, the pope and people who receive the Lord's Supper without faith are also called "Judas" in the Confessions.

**Judex, Mattaeus (Matthew).** (1528–64) Vice-principal of Gymnasium and deacon Magdeburg; professor of theology at Jena (1560); deposed and banned (1561); to Magdeburg, Wismar, and Rostock. Gnesio-Lutheran. Contributed to *Magdeburg Centuries*.

**Julian the Apostate.** (c. 331–363) Roman emperor (361–363). Although reared Christian, embraced paganism; developed strong anti-Christian policy.

**Julius.** (1528–89) Bishop of Wolfenbüttel, Germany; duke of Brunswick (1568–89); introduced the Reformation there.

**Julius III, Pope.** (1487–1555) Cardinal (1536); Council of Trent's first president and papal legate (1545); pope from 1550–55; confirmed Society of Jesus (1550) and increased its privileges; sent Pole to reunite England with Roman Church (1554); patron of Michelangelo.

**Julius Caesar.** (100–44 BC) Roman general and emperor; was betrayed and murdered at the Roman senate house.

**Juno.** One of the most important female goddesses of Rome, wife of Jupiter and queen of the gods. Famous for her jealousy.

**Jupiter.** Most important Roman deity, king of the gods, ruler of storms. Husband of Juno.

**Jurist.** A lawyer.

**Justin Martyr.** (c. 100–c. 165) From Samaria, of heathen parents; Platonist; converted to Christianity (c. 130); established Christian school at Rome. Wrote in defense of Christianity.

**Justinian I.** (483–565) "Justinian the Great." Eastern Roman emperor from 527–565; brilliant ruler; tried to restore the religious and political unity of the Empire, but failed to prevent increased estrangement between the Eastern and the Western Churches; efforts to codify Roman law resulted in Code of Justinian, a revision and updating of the Code of Theodosius II; it decreed the destruction of Hellenism. Closed the philosophical school at Athens (529); promoted Christian missions; restricted civil rights and religious affairs of Jews; made Niceno-Constantinopolitan Creed the sole symbol of the Church; accorded legal force to the canons of the first four ecumenical councils.

**Juvenal.** (c. 60–c. 140) Roman poet and satirist.

**Knights.** *See* p. 313

**Laity.** Laypeople. Division of church members into clergy and laity is valid if the words simply distinguish those who have been called into the ministry from those who have not been so called. But with the rise of the priestly system, which culminated in the papacy, the idea that the priesthood formed an intermediate class between God and people became prevalent, and the term *clergy* took on added, hierarchic meaning in that context. The doctrine of justification by faith alone abolished human mediation between people and God. Luther effectively proclaimed the priesthood of all believers (see 1 Peter 2:9). As a result, the laity recovered its proper position and lay representation again became possible.

**Lang, John.** (c. 1487–1548) Reformer of Erfurt. Augustinian monk (1506); priest (1508); friend of Luther; supported Luther at the 1519 Leipzig Debate. Introduced new order of service in Erfurt (1525). Signed SA (1537).

**Lawrence.** (third century) Deacon at Rome; martyr; Reformers cited him as an example of a saint who did not trust in his works.

**Leo I.** (c. 390–461) Pope (440–61); opposed Pelagianism, Manichaeism, and Priscillianists; pressed claims to jurisdiction in Spain, Gaul, and Africa; persuaded Attila to spare Rome (452). First bishop of Rome to achieve recognition of claim to supremacy as successor of Peter (hence regarded by many as the first pope in distinction from preceding bishops of Rome); held jurisdiction in the Western church; his definition of the person of Christ was adopted by the Council of Chalcedon.

**Leo X.** (1475–1521) Pope from 1513–21; used his influence in the interest of his family; misunderstood the importance of Luther (1519), excommunicated him (1521).

**Lombard, Peter.** *See* Peter Lombard.

**Lot.** (twenty-first century BC) The Patriarch Abraham's nephew, who moved his family into the evil city of Sodom (Genesis 13–14). His wife turned into a pillar of salt when she disobeyed the angel's warning about looking back toward Sodom (Genesis 19:26).

**Lucian of Samosata.** (c. 115–c. 200) Pagan satirist. Regarded Christians with contemptuous indifference and depicted them as kind but gullible.

**Lucina.** A pious woman in the early traditions of the Roman Church; she removed the bodies of Peter and Paul from the catacombs and placed them in her own tomb.

**Luke.** (first century) Physician and evangelist. Author of the Gospel according to St. Luke and the Acts of the Apostles. An associate of the apostle Paul (Luke 1:1–4; 2 Timothy 4:11).

**Lüneburg, Duke Ernest.** See Ernest the Confessor.

**Luther, Martin.** (November 10, 1483–February 18, 1546) Born and died in Eisleben, Germany. Luther probably first saw a Bible in Magdeburg, under instruction of the Brethren of the Common Life at the Cathedral School. Entered University of Erfurt (spring 1501). Father wanted him to be a lawyer. Entered Erfurt Law School (May 1505). Then, quite unexpectedly on July 17, 1505, entered the very strict Black Cloister of the local Augustinian Hermits (their black outer coat gave them their name). Later, he often spoke of a severe thunderstorm that terrified him and caused him to pray to St. Anne, promising to become a monk. Luther did not find peace of mind and soul in the monastery, but he determined to keep his vows. Ordained a priest (spring, 1507). Celebrated first mass on May 2, 1507, in the presence of his father, other relatives, and many friends. Continued studies (1507–12); became a doctor of theology in biblical studies, specifically the Old Testament. The more Luther studied Medieval theology and the more he became involved in the labyrinth of Scholasticism, the more concerned he grew. The main problem that disturbed him was how to find a gracious God.

Luther was sent to Wittenberg (1508) to teach moral philosophy. Returned to Erfurt (1509). In November 1510, Luther and another monk set out on foot for Rome to help settle some matters pertaining to the Augustinian Order. They reached Rome in January of 1511. Luther was shocked by the worldliness of some Italian clergy. While praying for his grandparents, he climbed the Holy Steps (*Scala Sancta*), said to be the steps Christ had climbed on Good Friday. Shortly after his return to Germany, he was sent back to the University of Wittenberg, where he was trained to succeed John Staupitz in the chair of Lecturer in the Bible as soon as he had earned the doctorate (awarded on October 18–19, 1512, in the Wittenberg Castle Church). While lecturing on Genesis, Psalms, Romans, Galatians, and Hebrews from 1512–18, Luther departed from Scholasticism to hold a thoroughly biblical theology. Probably in the fall of 1514, while lecturing on Psalm 71, he first began to realize that salvation is not based on works but on God's grace. He did not fully understand all its implications but said later that he had found, as he called it, the "Gate to Paradise" (WA 54: 186). Eventually won the University faculty to his views. By 1517, the school had become a center of biblical studies. The "New Theology," which was Christ-centered and stressed Scripture alone, was too dynamic to leave the Medieval Church unaffected.

Conflict with traditional Scholastic theology began over the sale of indulgences. Luther posted notice of a debate on the school bulletin board (the north door of the Castle Church) on October 31, 1517, listing ninety-five theses for discussion. The theses rapidly spread through Germany. Many people agreed with Luther. Financial returns from indulgence sales in Germany were greatly reduced, bringing immediate reaction from John Tetzel (indulgence salesman in Luther's territory), from Tetzel's fellow Dominicans, and from Albert of Brandenburg. (Albert was hoping to pay the "fee" for his appointment as Archbishop of Mainz, which made him holder of three church positions simultaneously [contrary to church law].)

The uproar pressured Pope Leo X to silence Luther. He instructed the Augustinian Order to discipline its recalcitrant member. At the Heidelberg Disputation (April 1518) Luther won new friends. Instead of reprimanding him, the Order asked him to write an elaboration of his original Ninety-five Theses. Under influence of the Saxon Dominican provincial, the fiscal procurator of Rome opened Luther's case, charging "suspicion of heresy." September 1518, Luther was summoned to appear at Augsburg before papal legate Cajetan. Luther was willing to be convinced on the basis of Scripture that indulgences were biblical. But the differences could not be reconciled. Staupitz released Luther from the vow of obedience to the Augustinian order (mid-October 1518). Cajetan recommended to Frederick III that Luther be either banished or surrendered to Rome.

On Luther's initiative, Wittenberg University faculty sent a letter (November 22, 1518) to Frederick III, expressing complete agreement with Luther's views. With this statement of Luther's case and the advice of his court, Frederick III refused to surrender Luther to Rome unless an unbiased tribunal proved Luther was a heretic. Luther hoped for a solution by a general Church council. Roman Church leaders on the case include Karl von Milititz and John Eck, the latter known especially from the Leipzig Debate (1519). First hopeful of cleansing the Church of error, Luther began to realize that no reformation of the existing body, permeated with error in head and members, was possible.

After the election of Charles V (1519) as Holy Roman Emperor, Rome again focused on Luther. Universities of Louvain and Cologne issued condemnations of Luther's theology (1519). Pope Leo wrote the bull *Exsurge, Domine* ("Arise, O Lord"; June 15, 1520), giving Luther sixty days to recant. It also required all his writings to be burned. At Wittenberg, Luther responded by burning the Canon Law and the bull. Rome's reply was the bull of excommunication (January 3, 1521).

Charles was pressured to condemn Luther, so he summoned Luther to appear at the Diet of Worms (1521). There, Luther resisted all efforts to persuade him to recant. Privately and publicly he said he could not recant unless convinced of error by Scripture. Lacking the necessary support of German princes to secure Luther's condemnation, Charles waited until the Diet had been dismissed. Then, in a special session, Charles declared Luther a heretic and outlaw, who could be killed on sight. Luther's prince, who left the Diet earlier because of illness, anticipated the outcome and arranged to have Luther placed in "protective custody" at the Wartburg.

At the Wartburg Luther reexamined his position and resolved to remain steadfast in the pure doctrine of the Scriptures. He spent his time at the Wartburg working, especially on a German New Testament.

Luther returned to Wittenberg (March 1522) to quiet the confused situation created by the ill-considered leadership of Andreas Carlstadt and Gabriel Zwilling. Luther preached a series of eight sermons on love and restored order. Hymn singing was introduced and the liturgy revised slowly and conservatively, providing greater participation by the congregation.

The political situation after the Diet of Worms was confused. The Edict of Worms could not be enforced. New economic forces brought on other disturbances culminating in the Knights' Revolt and the Peasants' War (1520s). In both cases, Luther's writings were misunderstood. When he called on forces of law and order to quell the revolt, he was accused by his enemies of turning against the peasants.

The Diet of Speyer (1529) nullified an earlier pronouncement permitting a prince to control religious affairs in his realm. Followers of the pope and of Luther prepared for violence. A rift developed among Luther's followers and Zwingli's followers. This divided Protestantism. An attempt to resolve their differences at the Marburg Colloquy (1529) ended in agreement on all points except the bodily presence of Christ in the Lord's Supper. Attempts to reconcile Romanists and Protestants included the 1530 Diet of Augsburg.

Luther's teaching from the Ninety-five Theses (1517) to the Small and Large Catechisms (1529) reveals how much Luther grew in his understanding of Scripture and its application. He grew dramatically in the 1520s during the theological struggles with Rome, the Anabaptists, and the Reformed. He changed from an excitable young monk—who did not realize how people would twist his words—to a steady churchman.

He married Katharina von Bora (June 13, 1525) and started a family. Eventually they had six children, two of whom died young. In 1527, plague devastated Wittenberg. The Luthers turned their home into a hospital, ministering to the spiritual and physical needs of numerous people. They refused to flee from the plague when so many neighbors were in need.

Historians and theologians must keep these events and Luther's growth in mind as they read his earliest writings and sermons. They should compare them with his later texts—especially Luther's texts in the Book of Concord—to gain the clearest understanding of what Luther taught.

Luther led an amazingly active and productive life. Works include the Large and Small Catechisms; sermon studies providing materials for the "emergency preachers" who filled pulpits made vacant by conversion of many congregations from Medieval Romanism to Lutheranism; a complete German Bible (1534); many tracts, letters, and treatises.

In 1535, Luther began his monumental lectures on Genesis, which embody his mature views on numerous topics and took him ten years to produce. During the Smalcald Conference (1537), Luther nearly died from an illness and had to leave matters in Melanchthon's hands. Luther wrote the Smalcald Articles in preparation for a Church council that was to meet in Mantua that year. The pope later cancelled the council. In 1539, Luther issued *On Councils and the Church*, a work of profound historical and theological scholarship, written to overthrow the claims of the papacy and define the Church.

Luther's many duties and years of rigorous monastic life took their toll. He suffered from numerous physical problems. Late in 1545, he was asked to arbitrate a family quarrel among the princes of Mansfeld. Though old, ill, and loath to undertake a winter journey of about eighty miles from Wittenberg, Luther went to Eisleben. Judging the family quarrel proved hard. While there, Luther also preached four times and helped conduct several services. The quarrel was settled February 17, 1546. That evening Luther felt severe chest pains. Despite treatment, he died early the following morning in the presence of sons Martin and Paul, two doctors, and others.

Testimony of the love and esteem with which he was regarded by the people was the homage given his mortal remains as the funeral cortege returned to Wittenberg, where his body was laid to rest.

**Lydia.** (first century) A woman of Thyatira who heard the Gospel from St. Paul and believed (Acts 16:13–15).

**Magdeburg, Joachim.** (c. 1525–after c. 1587) Brother of Johann Magdeburg; banished for refusing to comply with Interim; worked with M. Flacius on *Magdeburg Centuries*; hymnist; composer.

**Major, George.** (1502–74) Lutheran theologian; friend of Luther; preacher and professor. His involvement in Leipzig Interim incurred the wrath of Flacius, Amsdorf, Gallus, and others, who accused him of denying the Lutheran doctrine of justification. He denied the charge but taught that good works are necessary for salvation, later that they are necessary to retain faith; his phrases are repudiated by FC IV.

**Mani.** (c. 216–c. 277) Founded Manichaeism. Allegedly received divine revelations; claimed to be the last and highest prophet; traveled probably to India and perhaps China; became acquainted with Buddhism; returned to Persia; successfully opposed by Magi; perhaps suffered a cruel death in prison. *See* Manichaeans.

**Manichaeans.** 1. Religion founded by Mani. 2. Dualistic philosophy of nature, including Gnostic, Zoroastrian, and Christian elements. Held that the kingdom of light and kingdom of darkness were in conflict from eternity. Manichaeism spread over the Roman Empire and was a menace to the Church. Augustine of Hippo was Manichaean in his youth. Manichaeans and Manichaeism are referred to in AC I 5; Ap XVIII 1; FC Ep I 17, 19, 22; II 8; FC SD I 26, 27, 30, 45.

**Marcion.** (second century) Heretic from Sinope in Pontas. Moved to Rome, developed and organized his own version of Christianity. Rejected the Old Testament as the work of an inferior god (Demiurge). Rejected all the Law and taught that the Christian message was a message of pure love from the supreme god. Taught that only the Gospel of Luke and the Epistles of Paul were authoritive Scripture. He edited them for use among his followers. This caused Christian leaders to carefully consider and publish which books should be read in church and consulted as genuine and authoritive for Christian teaching (canonical).

**Mark.** (first century) Evangelist, author of the Gospel according to St. Mark. An associate of the apostles Peter and Paul (2 Timothy 4:11).

**Mary.** (first century) The virgin mother of Jesus. In the Lutheran Confessions her name appears most often in quotations of the creeds. She is often called "blessed." Jesus received His flesh from Mary.

**Matthew.** (first century) Apostle chosen by Jesus (Matthew 9:9–13). Evangelist, author of the Gospel according to St. Matthew. His Gospel was the most widely used among early Christian teachers.

**Maurice of Saxony.** (1521–53) Duke of Saxony (1541–53); in return for guarantee of territory (protectorate of the bishoprics of Magdeburg and Halberstadt) and the title of elector, he helped Charles V crush John Frederick, Maurice's cousin; tried to find common ground between Charles V and the Protestant states in the Leipzig Interim; feared growing power of Charles V; angered at harsh treatment of his father-in-law, Philip of Hesse; turned against Charles V, defeated him at Innsbruck, Austria, and forced him to agree to the terms of the convention of Passau; died at Sievershausen in battle against Albert, Margrave of Brandenburg-Kulmbach.

**Melanchthon, Philip.** (February 16, 1497–April 19, 1560) Born in Bretten, Lower Palatinate (Baden), Germany; educated at Heidelberg and Tübingen; educated in classics and served as corrector in the print shop of Thomas Anshelm at Tübingen (1514); gained praise of Erasmus for style (1515); became known as a humanist; published a Greek grammar (1518); recommended by Reuchlin for University of Wittenberg and arrived there on August 25, 1518. Won by Martin Luther for the study of theology. He abandoned plans to issue an edition of Aristotle; studied and taught theology and other subjects; Melanchthon's lectures were attended by hundreds and sometimes outstripped Luther's in popularity. On November 25, 1520, Melanchthon married Katharina, the daughter of a mayor of Wittenberg, Hans Krapp. They had four children; enjoyed 37 years of marriage.

The movement of the Zwickau Prophets and the Peasants' War in the 1520s emphasized the need for an education program to implement the Lutheran Reformation. Melanchthon devised methods and planned an education process using classic languages and philosophy, as the basis for specialized vocational studies. Princes were patrons of the organized program of instruction. Melanchthon was also prominent in the preparation of the Articles for Visitors. (Every parish in electoral Saxony was surveyed and religious and moral life supervised.)

Melanchthon's fame spread, and he declined repeated calls, such as those to Tübingen, to France, and to England. He more or less fathered the universities of Marbug, Königsberg, and Jena, while helping to reorganize Leipzig. He set in place widespread education reforms throughout Germany. Therefore he is often called *Praeceptor Germaniae*, "the teacher of Germany."

In 1521, Melanchthon issued *Loci Communes*, the first Lutheran work on dogmatics. It was reprinted more than eighty times during his lifetime. Luther himself was greatly impressed by the 1521 edition; he said it should be made part of the canon of the Bible.

During Luther's absence at Wartburg, Melanchthon revealed some of his weaknesses. He was a thoughtful leader but was also timid and hesitant. His philosophical tendencies made him overcautious and indecisive. Melanchthon strongly opposed Zwingli's doctrine of the Lord's Supper at Marburg (1529). But his weaknesses caused difficulties at Augsburg in 1530, where Melanchthon was theological spokesman for the Reformation. Guided by Luther, Melanchthon prepared the Augsburg Confession (1530) and the Apology (1531).

The 1535 and later editions of *Loci Communes* increasingly reflected Melanchthon's synergism. Melanchthon had a prominent role in the Wittenberg Concord (1536), signed by some Swiss Reformed. The Colloquy of Worms (1540) revealed Melanchthon's tendency to make concession. He began his rather arbitrary alterations of the Augsburg Confession (called "Variata"). These were rooted in certain doctrinal differences that he began to reveal. Those who espoused these alterations were later called "Philippists." His most harmful compromise was the approval of the Leipzig Interim (1548). Though Melanchthon served the Lutheran Reformation heroically—especially during Luther's lifetime—his weaknesses also brought much grief and division. This made it necessary for the next generation to prepare The Book of Concord, which rescued the Lutheran Reformation.

**Menius, Justus.** (c. 1499–1558) Reformer of Thuringia; early follower of Luther; superintendent at Eisenach (1529); took part in church visitations, the 1529 Colloquy of Marburg, the February 1537 meeting of the Smalcaldic League, and the 1540 Hagenau Colloquy; signed the 1536 Wittenberg Concord and had F. Myconius sign the SA for him; wrote extensively against Anabaptists, his treatment becoming standard for Lutheran polemics; defended G. Major and taught that beginning of new life in believers is necessary for salvation.

**Mercury.** Messenger of the Roman gods, known for his speed.

**Monks.** Male members of a monastic order or one who lives in solitary retirement from the world to practice asceticism. Many monks followed Luther, but most opposed the Reformation because it attacked their self-righteousness.

**Moses.** (fifteenth century BC) Hebrew prophet from the tribe of Levi who led Israel out of Egypt (the Book of Exodus) and author of the first five books of the Bible (Genesis–Deuteronomy). After Moses received the Law from God, his face shone with divine light (Exodus 34:29–35); Jerome translated this as "horns of light," hence many artists depicted Moses with horns. The Lutheran Confessions sometimes use the name *Moses* to mean the Law.

**Mörlin, Joachim.** (1514–71) Deacon at Wittenberg and Luther's chaplain (1539); superintendent at Arnstadt (1540–43); deposed (1543/44); superintendent at Göttingen (1544–50); opposed Interim; dismissed; pastor and inspector at Königsberg (1550–53);

involved in Osiandrian controversy; resigned as superintendent at Brunswick (1553/54– 1567); bishop of Samland at Königsberg (1567).

**Münzer, Thomas.** (c. 1489–1525) Radical enthusiast and fanatic. In 1520, he became preacher at Zwickau. Always emotionally excitable and disturbed, he felt the urge to become a reformer and on occasion would sign himself "Martin's competitor for the affection of the Lord." Münzer taught that God speaks directly to the soul, without the "dead letter of the Word." This "inner light" persuaded the fanatic to attempt the destruction of all the "ungodly," the overthrow of government, and the establishment of a society along communistic lines. Dismissed from Zwickau, he went to Allstedt and from there to Mühlhausen. After a nightmare regime in this community he and his duped hordes were defeated at Frankenhausen (May 1525). Münzer was executed.

**Muslims.** Followers of Islam and the prophet Muhammad. Referred to as Turks. Turks attacked Eastern Europe throughout the Reformation period. Fear of Turkish invasion helped keep the Christian rulers of Europe from war with one another. This gave the Reformation time to develop and spread. Luther wrote the hymn "Lord, Keep Us Steadfast in Your Word" as a prayer against the Turks and the papacy. He researched Islam to prepare a defense against their religion in case the Turks successfully invaded Germany.

**Musculus, Andrew.** (1514–81) Professor at Frankfurt an der Oder; wrote against the Interim, Osiander the Elder, Stancaro, Melanchthon, Calvin; general superintendant at Brandenburg after J. Agricola (d. 1566); present at Torgau (1576), Bergen (1577). Works include *Thesaurus* (compilation of excerpts from writings of Luther).

**Myconius, Frederick.** (1490–1546) Reformed theologian. Taught in Basel and Zurich; coworker of Zwingli. Helped write first Basel Confession and the first Helvetic Confession.

**Nathan.** (eleventh century BC) Hebrew Prophet and counselor to King David (2 Samuel 12) who led David to repentance.

**Nazarites.** Israelites who took special vows, separating themselves in service to the Lord (Number 6).

**Nazianzus.** See Gregory of Nazianzus.

**Nebuchadnezzer.** (sixth century BC) Ruler of Babylonian empire, which defeated the kingdom of Judah.

**Nestorius.** (d. c. 451) Nestorianism. Studied at Antioch; monk; patriarch Constantinople (428); condemned by 431 Council of Ephesus for false teaching in Christology and deposed; sent back to monastery at Antioch; banished to Upper Egypt (436).

**Nicephorus** (c. 750/758–c. 828) Represented Leo IV at Second Council of Nicaea; patriarch Constantinople (806); founded monastery on the Propontis; defended veneration of images; deposed (815).

**Nicholas, Bishop of Myra.** (fl. first half of fourth century). Bishop of Myra, in Lycia, Asia Minor; patron saint of Russians, sailors, and children; according to legend, provided dowries for three maidens; stories of his secret gifts to children on his feast (December 6) came to be connected with Christmas, and his name was corrupted into Santa Claus.

**Nicholas of Cusa.** (1401–64) Member council of Basel; supported first the conciliar, then the papal party; cardinal (1448); bishop and reformer Brixen (Bressanone), Italy. Doubted Scholastic proofs of theological truths; extolled "learned ignorance"; held that God is the coincidence of opposites; tried to give intuition cognitive meaning in mathematical terms; anticipated Copernicus with a theory of the rotation of the earth on its axis; proposed calendar reform; said the world would end in 1734.

**Nicholas of Lyra.** (c. 1270–1340) Franciscan teacher at Paris. Knew Hebrew and read rabbinic commentaries on the Bible. Sought to interpret the Bible literally. Most famous work is his Postilla, written between 1322 and 1330, though not published until after his death. Luther thought highly of Lyra.

**Ninevites.** (eighth century BC) Citizens of ancient Nineveh, the capital of the Assyrian empire. They repented through the preaching of Jonah (Jonah 3).

**Novatians.** Group led by Novatian (third century), a strict Roman presbyter. The Novatians opposed the lenient policies of the bishops toward those who fell away during persecution but wanted to return to the Church after persecution ended.

**Nuns.** Women belonging to a religious order who live in contemplation and mortification.

**Oecolampadius, John.** (1482–1531) *See* p. 62.

**Öniken, Gerhard.** (c. 1485–1562) Spokesman for Lutheranism in the Rhine-Westphalia-Lippe territory; pastor Söst (1532), Lemgo (1533–35); superintendent of Minden (1535–40); present at the February 1537 meeting of the Smalcaldic League and signed the SA.

**Origen.** (c. 185–c. 254) Greek Church Father; taught school and instructed catechumens in Alexandria (202); mystic and ascetic; mutilated himself from misunderstanding of Matthew 19:12. His ordination in Palestine (230) was not regarded as valid in Alexandria; exiled; taught school at Caesarea in Palestine (231–233); suffered in persecution under Decius. Doctrines held by, or attributed to, him are called Origenism. His commentaries are marred by his highly fanciful and allegorical interpretations. The Fifth Ecumenical Council of Constantinople condemned him as a heretic in 553.

**Osiander, Andreas.** (1498–1552) *See* p. 524.

**Osiander, Lukas.** (the Elder; 1534–1604) Superintendant at Blaubeuren and Stuttgart; court preacher and consistorial councillor; abbot Adelberg (1596); deposed and banished but permitted to return to Stuttgart; hymnist. With B. Bidenbach, wrote the Maulbronn Formula.

**Ötinger, Conrad.** (d. 1540) Court preacher of Philip of Hesse and of Ulrich of Württemberg (1534); signed SA.

**Otto, Anton.** (b. 1505) Studied under Luther at Wittenberg; as pastor preached against third use of the Law as a source of Majorism and synergism (1565).

**Ovid.** (43 BC–AD 17) Latin poet most responsible for recording classical mythology.

**Pagans.** From Latin *paganus*, "of the country." A religious or nonreligious person opposed to Christianity. Since Christianity first came to cities of the Roman empire, those who lived in the country adhered longer to non-Christian religions; hence the association of the word *pagan* with the concept of unbelief.

Related to *heathen*, meaning "one living on the heath, the uncultivated land," that is, a savage or unbeliever.

**Panormitanus.** (1386–1445) Benedictine. Teacher, abbot, and canon lawyer who wrote commentaries on Gratian's Decretals and other canon law.

**Papists.** A derogatory title for followers of the pope.

**Patriarchs.** Abraham, Isaac, and Jacob.

**Paul III.** (1468–1549) Pope during writing of SA.

**Paul of Samosata.** (third century AD). Bishop of Antioch (260–272); dynamic monarchian; followers called Paulianists, Samosatenes, and Samosatenians.

**Peasants.** *See* p. 313.

**Pelagians.** *See* Pelagius.

**Pelagius.** (c. 354/360–c. 418/420) British or Irish monk. Visited Rome (c. 400), Carthage (c. 410/411), and Palestine. Pelagian Controversy. Expelled c. 418. Disappeared from history. Wrote commentaries on 13 Epistles of Paul; a book on faith; treatises on Christian life, virginity, and the divine Law; letters. Pelagius and his followers held that a person's nature is not corrupt since the fall but is still in its original state of moral indifference and depends on the individual will to develop the moral germ of his nature and be saved. Ac-

cording to Pelagius, grace and salvation from Christ are not necessary.

**Pertinax, Publius Helvius.** (126–193) Roman Emperor (January–March, 193). Son of a freed slave. Rose through military and senate to become emperor. Enforced unpopular economic policies. Killed by a small group of soldiers.

**Peter Lombard.** (c. 1100–c. 1160/64) "Master of the Sentences"; Scholastic; taught at Paris (c. 1139); bishop of Paris (1159); helped blend mysticism and Scholasticism. Works include *The Sentences*, a collection of doctrinal statements of the Fathers, with contradictions resolved dialectically. This book is the first dogmatic of the Western Church. The Lateran Council of 1215 made it the theological textbook of the Church. It became the foundation of Scholastic theology. Luther lectured on the Sentences at the beginning of his career. But he soon came to see that Peter, for all his logical keenness, "never got into the Bible" and that in many respects his doctrinal position was unscriptural.

**Petilian.** (fl. c. 400) Donatist bishop of Certa who wrote about Baptism. Augustine corresponded with him and wrote against his views.

**Peucer, Caspar.** (1525–1602) Son-in-law of Melanchthon; professor at Wittenberg (1554); general superintendent of Latin schools; physician to elector Augustus of Saxony; furthered Crypto-Calvinism; arrested (1574); imprisoned; released (1586); physician and councillor Dessau.

**Pfeffinger, John.** (1493–1573) Priest; preacher Passau (1521), where he heard of Luther; fled when threatened with arrest; studied at Wittenberg (1524); pastor Sonnenwalde (1527), Eicha (1530), Belgern (1532); pastor and first Lutheran superintendent Leipzig (1540/41); helped introduce Reformation in Schönburg; professor at Leipzig (1544); connected with developments that led to the Leipzig Interim; Philippist. Works include moral, ascetic, and polemic writings. *See* Synergism Controversy, p. 527.

**Phalaris.** (c. 570–c. 549 BC) A tyrant in Sicily, known for his cruelty.

**Pharaoh.** The ruler of ancient Egypt. In Exodus 1–14, the Pharaoh opposed God and His prophet, Moses.

**Pharisees.** (from second century BC) 1. A Jewish group known for strict observance of the Law. The Pharisees often argued with Jesus, who rebuked them for self-righteousness (Matthew 23). Later Jewish rabbis continued their teachings and practices. 2. In the Lutheran Confessions, those who trust in good works for their salvation are called Pharisees.

**Philip of Hesse.** (1509–67) Favorably impressed by Luther at Worms (1521); began to study the New Testament and the Reformer's writings. After the Protest at Speyer (1529), he tried to unite all friends of the Gospel and persuaded Luther, Zwingli, and others to discuss doctrinal differences at Marburg. In the following year he, signed AC. When the Smalcaldic League was formed (1531), he became its moving spirit and even sought the participation of England, France, and Denmark in the protective alliance. After the unfortunate Smalcaldic War, Philip was a prisoner in the Netherlands for five years. He was a man of great ambitions and strong passions.

**Phocas.** The name appears in various connections in the mingled stream of ancient legend and tradition. He is said to have been a gardener at Sinope in Pontus, bishop of Sinope, martyr in Trajan or Diocletian persecution, a martyr of unspecified time at Antioch. There probably were two or more men named Phocas. In the East, the patron saint of mariners is called Phocas.

**Pindar.** (522–443 BC) Great Greek poet who celebrated the winners of the Greek festival games and recorded Greek myths.

**Pius II.** (1405–64) Pope from 1458–64; before he became pope he supported the conciliar movement, but in 1460 he condemned it in his bull *Execrabilis*.

**Platina, Bartholomeo.** (1421–81) Italian humanist. Wrote *Lives of the Popes*.

**Plato.** (c. 428/427–347 BC) Greek philosopher. Founded the Academy (c. 386 BC), which became the first endowed university. Influenced by Socrates. Plato held that the material sensible world is merely a temporary copy of permanent unchanging Forms, which are the object of all real knowledge. The link between such a dualistic universe is the immortal soul, which has had contact with the Forms before being born in a body and which, during its human existence, relearns as best possible its prebirth knowledge by recollection. The best government is possible only when philosophers (the rational element of the state) attain adequate concept of the perfect Forms and become rulers. Plato's influence on other philosophers and Early Church Fathers (especially Augustine of Hippo and Origen) is inestimable.

**Poach, Andrew.** (1516–1585) Loyal Lutheran theologian who worked in the spirit and with the zeal of Luther, whom he ardently admired. In 1541, he was sent to Halle with Justus Jonas in the interest of the Reformation. But the disastrous outcome of the Smalcaldic War drove him from Halle to Nordhausen. Accepted a call to Erfurt (1550). Here he labored for almost a quarter century, becoming noted as a preacher and a staunch defender of strict Lutheranism. In 1559, Poach published an edition of Luther's *House Postil*, which was prepared from notes by George Rörer of the sermons Luther had delivered in his home (1530–34). His continued refusal to have anything to do with what might look like a condoning of, or a concession to, the Church of Rome involved him in controversies. Finally lost his position and accepted a pastorate at Mühlhausen, then at Weimar, and then near Jena, where he died.

**Pollux.** See Castor.

**Polyphemus.** In Homer's *Odyssey*, the Cyclops (one-eyed giant) who trapped Odysseus's men.

**Pomeranus.** See Bugenhagen, John.

**Pompey the Great.** (106–48 BC) A great Roman general.

**Pontius Pilate.** (first century) The Roman governor who ordered Jesus to be crucified (Matthew 27:11–26).

**Pope.** From Greek and Latin, "father." The title was first used for any bishop. In 1073, Gregory VII concluded that the term could only be used for a bishop of Rome.

**Porphyry.** (c. 232/233–c. 304) Neoplatonist philosopher. Studied under Plotinus. Works include *Against the Christians.*

**Princes.** *See* p. 313.

**Prosper of Aquitaine.** (c. 390–c. 455/463) Follower of Augustine of Hippo; associate with Leo I. Wrote against semi-Pelagians, in defense of Augustine, and against the thirteenth *collatio* of J. Cassianus.

**Ramiro.** (twelfth century) King who left monastic life to rule Aragon, Spain.

**Rechabites.** A group in ancient Israel that abstained from wine, did not farm, and lived in tents (Jeremiah 35:6–8).

**Rhegius, Urban.** (1489–1541) Preacher at Augsburg. Sided with Luther against Rome and Zwingli. Preacher at Celle (1530). Superintendent at Lüneburg (1531). Signed Wittenberg Concord (1536) and SA (1537).

**Rochio, St.** (c. 1295–c. 1327 or c. 1350–c. 1378/79?). Shadowy legendary figure; said to have been born in Montpellier, France; allegedly made a pilgrimage to Rome, curing many sick on the way.

**Romans.** 1. Pagans of pre-Christian Rome. 2. Recipients of Paul's letter to the Roman Church (first century). 3. Supporters of the bishop of Rome (the pope).

**Rufinus, Tyrannius** (c. 345–c. 410) Latin theologian; lived as monk in Egypt, on the Mount of Olives, where he founded a monastery with Melania the Elder, and at Aquileia; friend of Jerome, but bitterly opposed him over doctrines of Origen. Translated Greek

Christian writers into Latin.

**Sabinus.** (third century) Bishop chosen by Christians in Spain after their bishops had offered pagan sacrifices during the Decian persecution. The election of Sabinus was confirmed through ordination administered by neighboring bishops.

**Sachs, Hans.** (1494–1576) *See* p. 489.

**Sacramentarian.** Luther's name for Zwingli, Oecolampadius, and other Reformed theologians who held that in Communion the bread and wine are Christ's body and blood only in a "sacramental" (i.e., symbolic) sense.

**Samosatenes.** *See* Paul of Samosata.

**Sarah.** (twenty-first century BC) The wife of the Patriarch Abraham, the mother of the Israelite nation. Sarah showed exemplary devotion to her husband.

**Sardanapalus.** (seventh century BC) King of Assyria. Remembered for his love of pleasure.

**Satan.** "Accuser" (1 Peter 5:8). Originator of all wickedness (Ephesians 2:2), an opponent of God's kingdom. He is the tempter of the faithful (1 Peter 5:8–9); led Eve into sin and so became the originator and king of death (Hebrews 2:14). Originally created good, Satan and the evil spirits fell through their own fault (2 Peter 2:4). Everlasting punishment was prepared for the devil and his angels (Matthew 25:41).

**Saul.** (eleventh century BC) The first king of Israel, from the tribe of Benjamin (1 Samuel 8–10). In the Lutheran Confessions, Saul is an example of despair and unrepentance.

**Saxons.** The residents of Saxony, Germany.

**Schlaginhaufen, John.** (d. c. 1560) Recorded Luther's table talk (1531/32); for many years he all but lived in Luther's house. This intimacy continued after he had accepted a parish at Zahna (1532), close to Wittenberg; later superintendent at Köthen; signed SA. In his earlier years he was sickly and inclined to depression and melancholy. Luther often gave him comfort. In later years he showed decisiveness and energy of action, which made him a valued supporter of the Reformation.

**Schneeweiss, Simon.** (sixteenth century) Court preacher of George of Brandenburg-Ansbach; pastor Crailsheim, North Württemberg, Germany (1534); took part in Hagenau Colloquy, Colloquy of Worms, and Regensburg Conference (1540–41); signed SA.

**Schnepf, Erhard.** (1495–1558) Helped reform Nassau and Württemberg; signed SA; professor at Tübingen (1544); forced to leave (1548) for opposing Interim; professor at Jena (1549); opposed Philippists at Consultation of Worms (1557).

**Scholastics.** From Greek for "school." Philosophical movement dominant in the later Middle Ages. Concerned with dogmatics. Accepted the body of doctrine then current as complete. Used dialectics and speculation in discussing and trying to comprehend, harmonize, and prove doctrines through reason. Reasoning patterned largely on Aristotle.

**Schwenckfeld, Caspar.** (c. 1489/90–1561) Protestant mystic. Studied at Cologne and Frankfurt an der Oder. Not ordained. Supported the Reformation from c. 1518, helped introduce it in Silesia, but was soon estranged from it. Rejected justification, Scripture as the only source and norm of faith, efficacy of Sacraments as means of grace, infant Baptism, and the Augsburg Confession. Fled persecution from place to place. Followers called Schwenkfeldians.

**Schwenkfeldians.** *See* Schwenckfeld, Caspar.

**Scotus, John Duns.** *See* Duns Scotus, John.

**Sebastian, St.** (third century) Born perhaps Milan, Italy. According to tradition, a martyr, pierced by arrows, perhaps then beaten to death under Diocletian (probably near the end of the third century); said to have been an army officer.

**Sectarians.** Members of a sectarian group, usually defined as exclusive or narrow-minded adherence to a sect, denomination, party, or

school of thought. In the Confessions this term describes the Anabaptists.

**Selnecker, Nicholas.** (c. 1528/30–1592) Organist at Nürnberg at c. age 12; studied in Wittenberg from c. 1549 under Melanchthon; lectured on philology, philosophy, and theology; court preacher Dresden c. 1558; professor of theology Jena (1565); professor and pastor Leipzig (1568); court preacher Wolfenbüttel (1570); later active at Halle, Magdeburg, and Hildesheim, changing theological circumstances largely determining his movements. Helped develop Thomas Choir, Leipzig. Helped prepare and promote FC and a defense of the Book of Concord (1582).

**Semi-Pelagians.** Theologians who accepted Pelagius's teaching that the human will could cooperate with divine grace in salvation. Held that the reason some are saved, others not, lies in an inner condition and receptivity in people, some making proper use of the will, others not. Free will is only partially impaired but needs the help of divine grace; salvation is dependent on grace and the right use of natural powers. J. Cassianus of Massilia was an early leader of semi-Pelagians, who were first called Massilians. *See* Pelagius.

**Seneca, Lucius Annaeus.** (c. 4 BC–65 AD) Roman rhetorician, eclectic Stoic philosopher, statesman, poet; tutor of young Nero; later councillor of Nero, who turned against him; suicide by Nero's order. Held ethical goal to be life in harmony with nature; life is preparation for death. Seneca's apocryphal correspondence with the apostle Paul was known to Jerome.

**Sibylla.** (1512–54) Wife of John Frederick the Magnanimous. *See* p. 478.

**Socinus.** Name of two Italian anti-Trinitarians connected with the beginnings of Socinianism. 1. Lelio Francesco Maria Sozini (1525–62). Uncle of F. P. Sozzini (*see* 2); studied theology; came to doubt the Trinity and other doctrines repugnant to reason; traveled widely in Reformation lands and became acquainted with Melanchthon and

Calvin. 2. Fausto Paolo Sozzini (1539–1604). Nephew of L. F. M. Sozini (*see* 1); studied theology; became firmly established in anti-Trinitarianism; held court positions at Florence, Italy (1562–74); lived at Basel, Switzerland (1574–78); to Transylvania (1578), but theological turmoil and outbreak of the plague caused him to leave; to Poland (1579), where he freed scattered anti-Trinitarians from Anabaptists and chiliastic groups and organized them; lived mainly in Krakow, under abuse and opposition, till driven out of the city (1598).

**Socrates.** (c. 470–399 BC) Greek philosopher. Twice defied government ruling he regarded as unjust. Critical of poor government and popular theology of his day. Convicted on charges of corrupting the youth and of being unfaithful to the religion and gods of the state. Chose death by poison hemlock. Socrates developed a method of inquiry and instruction by questions and answers (known as the Socratic method); it led to the notion that virtue is teachable, evil is the result of ignorance, and the virtues are one.

**Socrates Scholasticus.** (c. 380–after 440) Greek Church historian. Wrote a history covering the period 306–439, continuing the *Church History* of Eusebius of Caesarea.

**Solomon.** (tenth century BC) The third king of Israel, the son of David. He wrote and compiled Proverbs, Ecclesiastes, Song of Songs, and some psalms. Israel reached the height of its power under Solomon's wise leadership.

**Sophists.** (c. fifth century BC) Traveling professors in ancient Greece. Socrates condemned them as deceivers who used false logic. Their name became associated with poor logic.

**Spalatin, George.** (1484–1545) Priest 1508; tutored John Frederick; served Frederick the Wise in several capacities. He became a firm and faithful friend of Luther, who wrote over 400 letters to him. Moved to Altenburg (1525), where he had received a canonry (1511); took part in 1526 Diet of Speyer; active in church visitations; attended the 1530 Diet of Augsburg and wrote an account of it; took sick Luther home from Smalcald (1537); helped reform Albertine Saxony under Henry the Pious; helped install Amsdorf as Bishop of Naumburg-Zeitz (1542). Never robust, he aged quickly because of his restless activity. One of Luther's bosom friends, Spalatin is no doubt one of the most deserving and influential characters on the crowded stage of the Reformation period.

**Stancaro, Francesco.** (c. 1501–74) Monk trained in Scholastic theology; opposed Osiander the Elder at Königsberg; held that Christ is a mediator with God only in his human nature. (Refuted in FC III.)

**Staupitz, John** (c. 1469–1524) Descendant of an ancient noble family of Meissen, Saxony. Became an Augustinian monk and studied theology at Tübingen, receiving the doctor's degree in that subject. In 1502, he helped Frederick the Wise found the university at Wittenberg and became dean of its theological faculty; in 1503, he was made vicar general of Augustinians for the province of Germany. Through Staupitz's influence, Luther was called to Wittenberg (1508) to teach dialectics and ethics, was induced to ascend the pulpit, and became a doctor of theology (1512). From the first, Scripture, rather than Scholasticism, had attracted Staupitz. He himself directed Luther to study the Bible and was, therefore, at first sympathetic to the Reformation. But his disposition was quiet, sensitive, and contemplative. Therefore, he gradually withdrew from the movement, joined the Benedictine order of monks (1519), became abbot of a convent at Salzburg (1522), and died there (1524). His motto is said to have been "Jesus, I am Thine; save me." Just how clearly he recognized the *sola fide* of Scripture and the Reformation is unknown, but both Luther and the Reformation owe him a debt of gratitude.

**Stoics.** From Greek *stoa*, a porch where Zeno of Citium taught in Athens. Greco-Roman school of philosophy founded c. 300 BC by

Zeno; divided philosophy into logic, physics (including religion), and ethics. Earlier Stoics stressed logic, later Stoics stressed ethics. Stoicism is a form of materialistic monism. It is deterministic, regarding God as the all-pervading energy (spirit, *pneuma*), law, and reason *(logos)* that gives order and beauty to the world. In ethics, people must recognize that they cannot change the predetermined course of events. Absolutely self-sufficient, Stoics can practice the virtues: practical wisdom, bravery, justice, self-control. They are not bound to things or life itself.

**Sturm, Jakob.** (1489–1553) Reformer, statesman, educator; aided Protestants at Diets of Speyer (1526 and 1529) and Augsburg (1530). Helped draw up Tetrapolitan Confession; helped found a gymnasium at Strasbourg, which became a pattern for many similar schools.

*Suidas.* (perhaps late tenth century) Byzantine encyclopedic work; includes comments on early Christian writings. *Suidas* was regarded (perhaps erroneously) as the author's name.

**Summists.** Commentators on the theological works of Thomas Aquinas and other medieval Scholastic theologians.

**Synergists.** From Greek *synergeo*, "to work with." The concept of people cooperating with God in their own conversion. The synergistic view rests on such arguments as these: (1) if people can do nothing in their conversion, they will become careless and fatalistic; (2) the call to repent implies power to repent; (3) if people are entirely passive, conversion is mechanical; (4) God makes conversion possible, people make it real; (5) since people can hinder conversion, they can also cooperate in it; (6) ability to resist implies ability to cease resisting. Scripture teaches that people are saved by God's grace, not by works (Ephesians 2:8–10). *See* Synergism Controversy, p. 527.

**Tartars.** People spread from Eastern Europe to the Sea of Japan, remembered for their tempers and surprising strength in battle. Euro-

peans associated their name with *Tartarus*, a name for hell.

**Tertullian.** (c. 155/160–c. 220/230) Schooled in rhetoric and jurisprudence; Christian (from c. 190/195); catechist (or presbyter) Carthage. Held that the end of the world, preceded by troubles and apostasy, was near, and that only the empire held off impending doom. Espoused Montanism in later life.

**Theodore of Raithu.** (fl. c. 550) Monk at monastery of Raithu, Gulf of Suez. Wrote against the ancient Christological heresies and defended Chalcedonian orthodoxy.

**Theodoret of Cyrrhus.** (c. 386/393–before 466) Church historian and bishop of Cyrrhus, Syria (423); influenced by Theodore of Mopsuestia; deposed (449) by "Robber Synod" of Ephesus, reinstated by Council of Chalcedon (451).

**Theologians.** 1. People who study theology. 2. In the Lutheran Confessions, a name for the Medieval Scholastics.

**Theophylact.** (c. 1050–c. 1108) Also called Vulgarius. Archbishop of Ochrida and metropolitan of Bulgaria (c. 1078 or 1090). Works include commentaries on some OT books and on the NT, except Revelation.

**Thomas Aquinas.** (1225–74) Called "Angelic Teacher." Leading Scholastic theologian, most influential in Roman theology even today. Dominican (1244). Taught at Cologne and Paris (1253). Doctor of theology (1257), called to teach at various places in Italy. His most noted work is *Summa theologiae* (three volumes), left incomplete at his death. Defended the papal hierarchy and the primacy of the pope, teaching the infallibility of the pope and the supreme temporal power of the papacy. Taught that God saves us by infusing sanctifying grace. Dominated largely by the philosophy of Aristotle, yet holding that reason is subservient to theology.

**Timan, John.** (before 1500–57) Lutheran theologian. Educated at Wittenberg; pastor and reformed at Bremen; opposed Anabaptists; attended 1537 meeting of the Smalcaldic League and the Colloquy of Worms and Regensburg Conference (1540/41); opposed Interim. Signed SA and Tr as John of Amsterdam.

**Turks.** *See* Muslims.

**Ulrich, Duke of Württemberg.** (1487–1550) Duke in 1498 (assumed personal control in 1503); introduced Reformation into Württemberg; member of Smalcaldic League.

**Ulysses.** The legendary Greek hero and main character in Homer's *Odyssey*.

**Valens.** (364–78) Roman Emperor. Baptized as an Arian. Killed along with two-thirds of his army in a battle with Goths at Adrianople.

**Valentine.** (d. 269) Priest or bishop martyred at Rome (there are two different accounts) under the Emperor Claudius. Commemorated on February 14, a time associated with a pagan festival about love.

**Valentinians.** (second century) A sect of Gnosticism led by Valentinus; an ancient heresy that mingled Jewish, Christian, and Greek philosophical ideas into a new religious system.

**Venus.** The Roman goddess of love.

**Vigilantius.** (fl. c. 400) A presbyter of Aquitaine. He visited Jerome at Bethlehem, but they argued. Vigilantius attacked Jerome as a follower of Origen. Jerome accused Vigilantius of rejecting the cult of saints and martyrs, vigils, celibacy, and monasticism.

**Virgins.** 1. The young women of Jesus' parable in Matthew 25. 2. People practicing celibacy.

**Vulgarius.** See Theophylact.

**Westphal, Joachim.** (1510–74) Pupil of Luther and Melanchthon; teacher at the Hamburg Johanneum; lectured at Wittenberg; pastor (1541), superintendent (1571) Hamburg. Held with Höck that Christ's descent into hell was an expression of His complete humiliation and vicarious suffering; sided with Flacius in Adiaphoristic Controversy; opposed Melanchthon and Major; defended Luther's doctrine of the Lord's Supper against Calvin and Bullinger.

**Wigand, John.** (1523–87) Taught in Nürnberg (1541–44); preacher Mansfeld (1546); superintendent and pastor Magdeburg (1553); professor at Jena (1560); deposed (1561); superintendent Wismar (1562); returned to Jena (1568); deposed again (1573); professor Königsberg; bishop of Pomerania (1575), Samland (1577). Staunch Lutheran in various controversies. Co-author *Magdeburg Centuries. See* The Adiaphora Controversy, p. 523 , and Synergism Controversy, p. 527.

**William of Paris.** (c. 1180/90–1248/49) William of Auvergne. Theologian and philosopher. Taught theology at Paris; bishop of Paris (1228). Works significant for the development of Scholasticism. Called William Peraldus.

**Wycliffe, John.** (1320–84) "Evangelical Teacher." Connected with Oxford University as student or teacher most of his life; parish priest, last at Lutterworth, a small market town near Birmingham. Wycliffe's repeated opposition to the pope's meddling in English affairs of State and Church and his other anti-Roman activities caused his citation before ecclesiastical tribunals. This failed to silence him. He trained and sent out itinerant preachers. With Nicholas of Hereford, he translated Bible from Latin Vulgate and issued complete English Bible. His attack on transubstantiation aroused bitter controversy with mendicant friars. At times he seemed to teach the Lutheran doctrine of the Lord's Supper, and then again spoke of the bread and wine as being "Christ's body and blood figuratively and spiritually." Ascribed a certain degree of merit to the good works of a Christian. Upheld separation of Church and State and taught that the Church is the congregation of the elect. Considered enforced celibacy immoral and apparently also thought it unscriptural. Maintained that Christ is only Head of Church and that pope is Antichrist, yet never left the Roman Church. Excommunicated (1415) by the Council of

Constance; bones burned and ashes thrown into the Swift (1428).

**Wycliffites.** *See* Wycliffe, John.

**Zeno of Citium** (c. 336–264 BC) Greek philosopher; founder of Stoicism.

**Zephaniah.** (seventh century BC) Judean prophet, author of Book of Zephaniah.

**Zwilling, Gabriel.** (Didymus; c. 1487–1558) Educated at Wittenberg and Erfurt; left Augustinian order (1521); active in iconoclastic movement; yielded to Luther; preacher at Altenburg (1522); preacher (1523); pastor (1525); superintendent at Torgau (1529); deposed because of his opposition to Interim (1549). Signed SA.

**Zwingli, Ulrich.** (1484–1531) Founder of the Swiss Reformed Church. Received a humanistic education and became a parish priest. Always interested in public and political affairs, he was for a while field chaplain of the Swiss forces. Served as priest at Glarus, Einsiedeln, and Zurich. Testified against some abuses of Rome. Stimulated to active reformatory work by the writings of Luther (1520). But the principle of rationalism, which was strong in the humanistic Swiss, led him to interpret Scripture to the satisfaction of his reason. In consequence, he denied the real presence of Christ's body and blood in the Sacrament, as appeared publicly in the Marburg Colloquy (1529) with the Lutheran theologians. In the following year he published his *Ratio fidei*, his statement or norm of faith. This shows an approach and a spirit that are clearly different from those of Luther. Zwingli took an active part in far-reaching politico-religious plans for the reformation of Switzerland but fell at the battle of Cappel (1531). He had been secretly married (1522).

**Zwinglians.** *See* Zwingli, Ulrich.

# Teaching and Preaching Illustrations

# BIBLE REFERENCE INDEX

# SUBJECT INDEX

# C

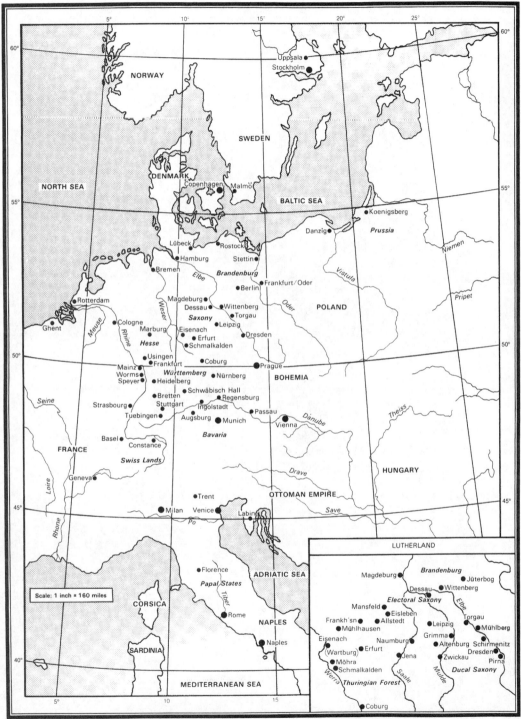

**Map by Erwin Weber**

REFERENCE MAP OF CENTRAL EUROPE IN THE TIME OF THE REFORMATION

Scale: 1 inch = 160 miles